D0576260

ScottForesman

LITERATURE

AND INTEGRATED STUDIES

Annotated Teacher's Edition
Volume One

World Literature

ScottForesman

Editorial Offices: Glenview, Illinois
Regional Offices: San Jose, California • Tucker, Georgia
Glenview, Illinois • Oakland, New Jersey • Dallas, Texas

acknowledgments

Cover (detail): *The Afterglow in Egypt* by William Holman Hunt, 1834. Southampton City Art Gallery. **T5(l)** © Tony Freeman/Photo Edit **T5(r)** © David Young-Wolff/Photo Edit **T20(t)** © Karen Holsinger Mullen/ Unicorn Stock Photos **T20(c)** © David Young-Wolff/Photo Edit **T20(b)** © Robert Brenner/Photo Edit **T22(t)** © Steve Bourgeois/Unicorn Stock Photos **T22(b)** © Michael Newman/Photo Edit **T23** © Richard Hutchings/Photo Edit **T24(b)** © David Young-Wolff/PhotoEdit **T24(t)** © Dana White/PhotoEdit **T26(t)** © Superstock, Inc. **T27(b)** © Michael Newman/Photo Edit **T28** © Jeff Greenberg/Photo Edit **T29** © Superstock, Inc. **T30(b)** © Martin R. Joni/Unicorn Stock Photos **T31(t)** © Superstock, Inc. **T31(c)** © Superstock, Inc. **T31(b)** © Jeff Greenberg/Photo Edit **T32(c)** © Mary Kate Denny/PhotoEdit **T32(b)** © Billy E. Barnes/PhotoEdit **T32(t)** © David Young-Wolff/ PhotoEdit **T34(t)** © Aneal Vohra/Unicorn Stock Photos **T34(b)** © Michael Newman/Photo Edit **T35** © David Young-Wolff/Photo Edit **T36(l)** © David Young-Wolff/PhotoEdit **T36(r)** Alinari/Art Resource **T38(t)** © Tony Freeman/Photo Edit **T38(b)** © Michael Newman/ Photo Edit **T39** © Superstock, Inc. **118e(t)** Hiroyuki Matsumoto/Tony Stone Images **181f(t)** Larry Ulrich/Tony Stone Images

ISBN: 0-673-29462-5

1.800.554.4411
http://www.scottforesman.com

1 2 3 4 5 6 7 8 9 10 DR 03 02 01 00 99 98 97 96

contents

Forms of Literature

World Literature

American Literature

English Literature

a step ahead

ScottForesman Literature and Integrated Studies is a multi-dimensional program that is a step ahead of other literature series . . . from in-depth multicultural explorations to integration that includes interdisciplinary study to a strong new focus on media and visual literacy.

A step ahead . . .

- **In Literary Content** that combines thematic organization with an innovative blend of classic and modern literature.
- **In Integration** that blends outstanding literature with rich, structured writing assignments and solid skills instruction.
- **In Interdisciplinary Studies** that capture students' attention, command their interest, and explore the natural links between literature and other subject areas.
- **In Skills Focus** that introduces reading, vocabulary, literary, writing, and language skills in context plus special attention on the media and visual literacy skills students need in today's world.
- **In Achieving Success for All Students** with strong support for reading comprehension; extensive help for students with limited English proficiency; mini-lessons on vocabulary, spelling, grammar and mechanics, and strategic reading; suggestions for both at-risk and gifted students—plus a Teacher's Resource File with more than 1500 pages of additional materials.
- **In Useful, User-Friendly Technology** at every level and for every purpose . . . beginning with test generators and journal-writing software . . . moving on to 3 exciting new CD-ROM programs on custom publishing, Shakespeare, and in-depth research on more than 40 major authors . . . and,
- **In Unparalleled Support for Novels** with 36 literature kits for major literary works taught across the curriculum.

A Pupil Book with Authentic Integration

- Integration begins with thematic groups of literature.
- Literature lessons incorporate reading, critical thinking, literary, and vocabulary skills.
- Interdisciplinary studies move beyond the language arts into other content areas.
- Scaffolded writing workshops present assignments based on the literature.
- Language skills are embedded in the writing workshops at point of use.

Innovative Materials to Support Student Lessons

- 2-volume Annotated Teacher's Editions provide traditional and non-traditional lesson support, a rich variety of mini-lessons, and abundant help for students who are less-proficient in English.
- Teacher's Resource Files are filled with a wealth of skill-building and enrichment materials that allow each teacher to adjust the program to meet class needs and teaching styles.

Useful, User-Friendly Technology and Supplemental Materials

- Software programs include discs for assessment, writing, and journal keeping.
- AuthorWorks™, a 7-disc CD-ROM research database with Project books, provides a wealth of author information.
- The ScottForesman Custom Literature Database CD-ROM holds over 1400 additional selections with lessons and correlations to student anthology.
- The top-rated BBC Shakespeare CD-ROM series presents 5 of the bard's best-loved plays.
- NovelWorks™ kits supply in-depth teaching materials for 36 popularly taught novels.
- Points of Departure—a supplemental literature series—includes 7 titles with focused coverage of specialized literary genres.

goals

To bring teachers and students these unique materials, ScottForesman sought the guidance and direction of America's premier educators in order to forge an exciting new pedagogy, ambitious and flexible enough to move easily into the next millennium. Two program goals guided the creation of these materials:

To assist students in becoming lifelong readers and critical thinkers

To help teachers renew the excitement of teaching and to revitalize their role as important professionals in today's society

literature-based integration

AN AUTHENTIC BLEND

Authentic integration occurs when the language arts — including literature, reading, vocabulary, writing, and language skills — are carefully woven together so that one flows naturally into another and students acquire **new information at point of use** rather than in isolation.

ScottForesman Literature and Integrated Studies provides a **tightly-crafted integration** of lessons in the pupil books as is illustrated by abbreviated tables of contents such as the one shown. These literature organizers appear at the beginning of each integrated grouping.

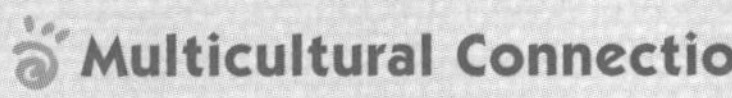

Multicultural Connection
Authentic multicultural themes begin here and are woven throughout each unit.

Literature
Thematic groupings of classic and contemporary selections make literature relevant for students.

Interdisciplinary Study
Theme-related studies in other disciplines are part of a fresh approach to integration.

Writing Workshop
Writing process assignments include revising and editing lessons.

Part One

Romantic Truths and Terrors

The Romantic movement of the early 1800s optimistically proclaimed that any determined individual could better society. Yet, there was an ominous side to Romanticism as well—a fascination with death and an interest in the unknown, unpredictable parts of the human psyche.

Multicultural Connection **Individuality** may mean either accepting or rejecting cultural norms or group standards. How do the narrators and characters in the following selections express their individuality?

220 UNIT THREE: AMERICAN CLASSIC

In 1845 Thoreau built a cabin in the woods by Walden Pond and lived there for two years. He wanted to simplify his life to the point where he could learn what the true essentials in life were. While there, he planned to write and study nature. Thoreau began his book, Walden, *after he left the pond, and finished it in 1854. Modern photographer Elliot Porter, who took the photo on the right, has found inspiration for his work in Thoreau's writings.*

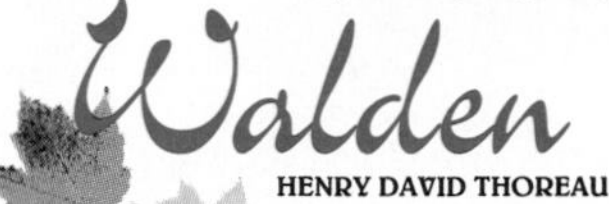

Walden

HENRY DAVID THOREAU

When first I took up my abode in the woods, that is, began to spend my nights as well as days there, which, by accident, was on Independence Day, or the fourth of July, 1845, my house was not finished for winter, but was merely a defense against the rain, without plastering or chimney, the walls being of rough weather-stained boards, with wide chinks, which made it cool at night. The upright white hewn studs and freshly planed door and window casings gave it a clean and airy look, especially in the morning, when its timbers were saturated with dew, so that I fancied that by noon some sweet gum would exude from them. To my imagination it retained throughout the day more or less of this auroral character, reminding me of a certain house on a mountain which I had visited the year before. This was an airy and unplastered cabin, fit to entertain a traveling god, and where a goddess might trail her garments. The winds which passed over my dwelling were such as sweep over the ridges of mountains, bearing the broken strains, or celestial parts only, of terrestrial music. The morning wind forever blows, the poem of creation is uninterrupted; but few are the ears that hear it. Olympus[1] is but the outside of the earth every where. . . .

I was seated by the shore of a small pond, about a mile and a half south of the village of Concord and somewhat higher than it, in the midst of an extensive wood between that town and Lincoln, and about two miles south of that our only field known to fame, Concord Battle Ground; but I was so low in the woods that the opposite shore, half a mile off, like the rest, covered with wood, was my most distant horizon. For the first week, whenever I looked out on the pond it impressed me like a tarn high up on the side of a mountain, its bottom far above the surface of other lakes, and, as the sun arose, I saw it throwing off its nightly clothing of mist, and here and there, by degrees, its soft ripples or its smooth reflecting surface was revealed, while the mists, like ghosts, were stealthily[2] withdrawing in every direction into the woods, as at the breaking up of some nocturnal conventicle.

1. **Olympus** (ō lim′pəs), mountain home of the gods in Greek mythology.
2. stealthily (stelth′ə lē), *adv.* secretly; slyly.

226 UNIT THREE: AMERICAN CLASSIC

On-page vocabulary

Vocabulary study words are underlined and defined on the page where they appear.

The very dew seemed to hang upon the trees later into the day than usual, as on the sides of mountains. . . .

I went to the woods because I wished to live deliberately, to front only the essential facts of life, and see if I could not learn what it had to teach, and not, when I came to die, discover that I had not lived. I did not wish to live what was not life, living is so dear; nor did I wish to practice resignation, unless it was quite necessary. I wanted to live deep and suck out all the marrow of life, to live so sturdily and Spartanlike[3] as to put to rout all that was not life, to cut a broad swath and shave close, to drive life into a corner, and reduce it to its lowest terms, and, if it proved to be mean, why then to get the whole and genuine meanness of it, and publish its meanness to the world; or if it were sublime, to know it by experience, and be able to give a true account of it in my next excursion. For most men, it appears to me, are in a strange uncertainty about it, whether it is of the devil or of God, and have *somewhat hastily* concluded that it is the chief end of man here to "glorify God and enjoy him forever."

CLARIFY: What kind of life does Thoreau want to live?

Still we live meanly,[4] like ants; though the fable tells us that we were long ago changed into men; like pygmies we fight with cranes; it is error upon error, and clout upon clout, and our best virtue has for its occasion a superfluous[5] and evitable wretchedness. Our life is frittered away by detail. An honest man has hardly need to count more than his ten fingers, or in extreme cases he may add his ten toes, and lump the rest. Simplicity, simplicity, simplicity! I say, let your affairs be as two or three, and not a hundred or a thousand; instead of a million count half a dozen, and keep your accounts on your thumb nail. In the midst of this chopping sea of civilized life, such are the clouds and storms and quicksands and thousand-and-one items to be allowed for, that a man has to live, if he would not founder and go to the bottom and not make his port at all, by dead reckoning, and he must be a great calculator indeed who succeeds. Simplify, simplify. Instead of three meals a day, if it be necessary eat but one; instead of a hundred dishes, five; and reduce other things in proportion. Our life is like a German Confederacy, made up of petty states, with its boundary forever fluctuating, so that even a German cannot tell you how it is bounded at any moment. The nation itself, with all its so called internal improvements, which, by the way, are all external and superficial, is just such an unwieldy and overgrown establishment, cluttered with furniture and tripped up by its own traps, ruined by luxury and heedless expense, by want of calculation and a worthy aim, as the million households in the land; and the only cure for it as for them is in a rigid economy, a stern and more than Spartan simplicity of life and elevation of purpose. It lives too fast. Men think that it is essential that the *Nation* have commerce, and export ice, and talk through a telegraph, and ride thirty miles an hour, without a doubt, whether *they* do or not; but whether we should live like baboons or like men, is a little uncertain. If we do not get out sleepers, and forge rails, and devote days and nights to the work, but go to tinkering upon our *lives* to improve *them*, who will build railroads? And if railroads are not built, how shall we get to heaven in season? But if we stay at home and mind our business, who will want railroads? We do not ride on the railroad; it rides upon us. . . .

I left the woods for as good a reason as I went there. Perhaps it seemed to me that I had several more lives to live, and could not spare any more time for that one. It is remarkable how easily and

3. **Spartanlike,** *adj.* simply; without frills. In ancient Greece, the inhabitants of the city of Sparta were known for their simple and severe manner of living.
4. meanly (mēn′lē), *adv.* of a small-minded nature.
5. superfluous (sú pėr′flü əs), *adj.* more than is needed.

228 UNIT THREE: AMERICAN CLASSIC

Reading help

Interlinear questions are used to guide students through more difficult selections.

Informational art captions

Quality fine-art pieces are enhanced with provocative questions that often extend the multicultural focus.

How does the composition of this painting, *Men Are Square* (1919) by Gerrit A. Beneker, reflect the cultural values of **individuality** and self-reliance?

Self-Reliance

RALPH WALDO EMERSON

To believe your own thought, to believe that what is true for you in your private heart is true for all men,—that is genius. Speak your latent conviction, and it shall be the universal sense; for the inmost in due time becomes the outmost, and our first thought is rendered[1] back to us by the trumpets of the Last Judgment. Familiar as the voice of the mind is to each, the highest merit we ascribe to Moses, Plato and Milton is that they set at naught books and traditions, and spoke not what men, but what *they* thought. A man should learn to detect and watch that gleam of light which flashes across his mind from within, more than the lustre of the firmament[2] of bards and sages. Yet he dismisses without notice his thought, because it is his. In every work of genius we recognize our own rejected thoughts; they come back to us with a certain alienated majesty. . . .

1. render (ren′dər), *v.* give in return.
2. **firmament** (fėr′mə mənt), *n.* arch of the heavens; sky.

222 UNIT THREE: AMERICAN CLASSIC

in total integration of all skills and disciplines

interdisciplinary studies

A NEW DIMENSION

For the first time in any series, integration moves beyond the language arts to include **other content areas.** *ScottForesman Literature and Integrated Studies* presents highly motivating, visually appealing interdisciplinary sections that generate student excitement, provide **informational reading** opportunities, and **connect literature to the real world.**

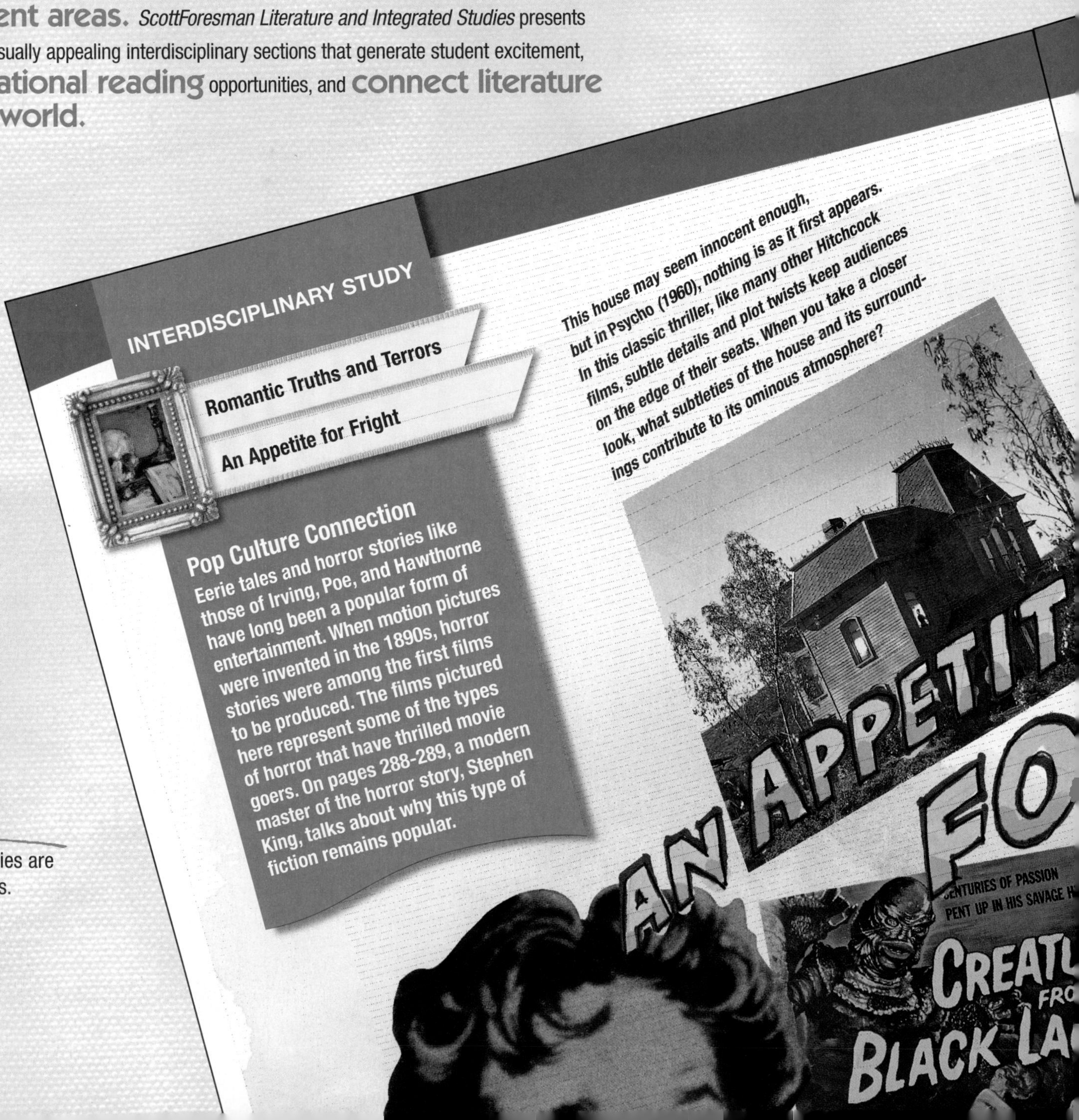

INTERDISCIPLINARY STUDY

Romantic Truths and Terrors

An Appetite for Fright

Pop Culture Connection
Eerie tales and horror stories like those of Irving, Poe, and Hawthorne have long been a popular form of entertainment. When motion pictures were invented in the 1890s, horror stories were among the first films to be produced. The films pictured here represent some of the types of horror that have thrilled movie goers. On pages 288-289, a modern master of the horror story, Stephen King, talks about why this type of fiction remains popular.

This house may seem innocent enough, but in Psycho (1960), nothing is as it first appears. In this classic thriller, like many other Hitchcock films, subtle details and plot twists keep audiences on the edge of their seats. When you take a closer look, what subtleties of the house and its surroundings contribute to its ominous atmosphere?

AN APPETIT

FO

CENTURIES OF PASSION PENT UP IN HIS SAVAGE H

CREAT

FRO

BLACK LA

Literary links

Interdisciplinary studies are based on unit themes.

a step ahead

in blending cross-curricular content with language arts

Making connections

Studies in history, sociology, psychology, science, math, geography, careers, and pop culture make literature come alive for students.

What's on the Other Side of the Door?

from **Danse Macabre**
STEPHEN KING

I want to say something about imagination purely as a tool in the art and science of scaring people. The idea isn't original with me; I heard it expressed by William F. Nolan at the 1979 World Fantasy Convention. Nothing is so frightening as what's behind the closed door, Nolan said. You approach the door in the old, deserted house, and you hear something scratching at it. The audience holds its breath along with the protagonist as she or he (more often she) approaches that door. The protagonist throws it open, and there is a ten-foot-tall bug. The audience screams, but this particular scream has an oddly relieved sound to it. "A bug ten feet tall is pretty horrible," the audience thinks, "but I can deal with a ten-foot-tall bug. I was afraid it might be a *hundred* feet tall." . . .

Bill Nolan was speaking as a screenwriter when he offered the example of the big bug behind the door, but the point applies to all media. What's behind the door or lurking at the top of the stairs is never as frightening as the door or the staircase itself. And because of this, comes the paradox: the artistic work of horror is almost always a disappointment. It is the classic no-win situation. You can scare people with the unknown for a long, long time (the classic example, as Bill Nolan also pointed out, is the Jacques Tourneur film with Dana Andrews, *Curse of the Demon*), but sooner or later, as in poker, you have to turn your down cards up. You have to open the door and show the audience what's behind it. And if what happens to be behind it is a bug, not ten but a hundred feet tall, the audience heaves a sigh of relief (or utters a scream of relief) and thinks, "A bug a hundred feet tall is pretty horrible, but I can deal with that. I was afraid it might be a *thousand* feet tall." . . .

The *danse macabre* is a waltz with death. This is a truth we cannot afford to shy away from. Like the rides in the amusement park which mimic violent death, the tale of horror is a chance to examine what's going on behind doors which we usually keep double-locked. Yet the human imagination is not content with locked doors. Somewhere there is another dancing partner, the imagination whispers in the night—a partner in a rotting ball gown, a partner with empty eye sockets, green mold growing on her elbow-length gloves, maggots squirming in the thin remains of her hair. To hold such a creature in our arms? Who, you ask me, would be so mad? Well . . . ?

"You will not want to open this door," Bluebeard tells his wife in the most horrible of all horror stories, "because your husband has forbidden it." But this, of course, only makes her all the more curious . . . and at last, her curiosity is satisfied.

"You may go anywhere you wish in the castle," Count Dracula tells Jonathan Harker, "except where the doors are locked, where of course you will not wish to go." But Harker goes soon enough.

And so do we all. Perhaps we go to the forbidden door or window willingly because we understand that a time comes when we must go whether we want to or not . . . and not just to look but to be pushed through. Forever.

The theme of horror is not limited to books and films—it also shows up in fine art, such as this painting,* That Which I Should Have Done I Did Not Do *(1931-41) by American artist Ivan Albright. What techniques does Albright use to create a feeling of dread?

Responding

1. How is reading a scary book different from watching a scary movie? Which do you prefer?
2. Which of the selections you read would translate best into a horror movie? Why?
3. Do you agree with King's explanation of the continuing appeal of horror in films and literature?

288 UNIT THREE: AMERICAN CLASSIC

289

STEVEN McQUEEN
CORSEAUT · ROWE
JACK H. HARRIS · IRVIN S. YEAWORTH, JR. · THEODORE SIMONSON
FRIGHT
Released in 1986, Friday the 13th Part VI was one in a long series of Friday the 13th movies that started in 1980. These extremely violent slasher films ushered in, along with others, what critics have called a "depressing trend in American films." How is the horror portrayed in these movies different from earlier films?
JASON LIVES
FRIDAY THE 13TH PART VI

INTERDISCIPLINARY STUDY

Health Connection

Horror has a reputation of being somehow less than respectable. Yet some health experts believe that horror, in moderate doses, might actually be good for you! Read the following article, and decide whether you agree.

The Thrill of Chills

by Ellen Blum Barish

Does the idea of riding a roller coaster at an amusement park excite you or terrify you? How about watching Freddy Krueger in *Nightmare on Elm Street* in a dark theater? Do you ever pick up a Stephen King novel, or do you stick with drama and romance?

Lots of teens say there is nothing like a good scare from the thrill of an amusement park ride or a tense moment from a horror story. In fact, there are so many who think so, that the "chill industry" is doing very well, thank you.

According to a recent survey of young people age 10 to 13, 89 percent had seen at least one movie in the *Friday the 13th* or *Nightmare on Elm Street* series; 62 percent had seen at least four of them. *Friday the 13th* grossed a total of $200 million dollars. Horror fans have made horror writer Stephen King a millionaire many times over.

In spite of the evidence showing that the chill industry is anything but frozen, there are people who would rather stay far away from scary rides and hold-your-breath movies. But, is one approach better than the other? Is seeking chills a healthy pursuit for teens?

Experts say yes . . . and no. For example, going to a horror movie is experiencing a safe and sometimes much-needed escape, says horror critic Douglas E. Winter. "We love to see something so grotesque and unexpected that it makes us scream or laugh . . . secure in the knowledge that in the fun house of fear, such behavior is not only accepted but encouraged," Winter wrote in 1985, the year he published a book of interviews with horror writers called *The Faces of Fear.*

"Every horror story," Winter writes, "has a happy ending. We have a simple escape—we can just wake up and say it was all a dream."

The "dream" can also be a way of preparing for life, according to Dr. Lenore Terr, a San Francisco child psychologist. Dr. Terr says that going to a horror movie or riding a roller coaster can help us feel in control. "It is a way for us to confront our fears," Dr. Terr says, "and gain mastery over our feelings."

There is a feeling of reassurance, notes Dr. Terr, "when you come out (of the movie) alive." . . .

But there is a downside to too much chill seeking. Long-term viewing of the creep shows and horror flicks may lead to violent or aggressive behavior in some young people, says a 1990 American Academy of Pediatrics statement.

Other experts point out that too much horror movie watching or roller coaster riding is like too much of anything—unhealthy—and can keep a teen from experiencing a variety of other activities. . . . Chill seekers should keep in mind that the chill seeking is a temporary, fun, thrill-like experience. . . .

Almost everyone is afraid of something, even if it isn't ghostly. You may steer clear of roller coasters but enjoy in-line skating because it's fast. Or you may change the TV channel if a horror movie comes on but not fear jumping from the high diving board at the pool.

It's healthy to try new things every once in a while—like taking a well-thought-out risk. It's worth finding out what you like, what you dislike, and what you want to avoid. A good scare now and then can help you sort out those feelings.

Responding

1. Do you agree that reading or viewing horror stories can, in moderation, be healthy for you? Explain your answer.

290

Interdisciplinary

integrated writing

A SCAFFOLDED APPROACH

Students write about ideas, themes, and characters from the literature—often connecting these ideas to their own lives. To help each student experience **success in writing**, workshops are carefully **scaffolded** to provide support for writers who need it and flexibility for writers who are ready to try new strategies and techniques. Each workshop begins with a **Writer's Blueprint** that lists guidelines for creating a successful paper. In addition, the workshop includes Revising and Editing **(Grammar)** lessons integrated at point of use.

in providing students with a blueprint for writing success

Writing in Style

Assignment After reading stories by Poe and Hawthorne, you know that each author has his own distinctive style. Now see if you can imitate one of these author's styles.

WRITER'S BLUEPRINT

Product	A scene from a story
Purpose	To explore the ominous side of American Romanticism through the styles of Poe and Hawthorne
Audience	People who are familiar with Poe and Hawthorne
Specs	As the writer of a successful paper, you should:

- ❑ Analyze the style of "The Pit and the Pendulum" and "Dr. Heidegger's Experiment." Imitate the style of one of these authors in a scene from a story of your own. Set your scene in modern times with your own original plot and characters.
- ❑ Take care not to copy anything directly, but to imitate your author's style so skillfully that your audience will recognize your source.
- ❑ Use the technique of contrast to help develop mood.
- ❑ Follow the rules of grammar, usage, mechanics, and spelling. Take special care to avoid spelling mistakes in which you use too few letters.

PREWRITING

style (stīl), *n.* characteristic way in which a writer uses language.

Analyze style. To imitate Poe or Hawthorne, you'll first need to examine their work closely. To get started, look at the Literary Source.

292 UNIT THREE: AMERICAN CLASSIC

Clear guidelines

The Writer's Blueprint tells students exactly what to do to achieve a well-written paper.

Strategies

Literary and student models, plus a wide array of options and organizers, offer help to every student.

Notice how Poe uses a semicolon to combine sentences—he does this often. These and other observations about Poe's style are noted in the chart below. You'll find that they hold true for Poe's other stories as well.

Poe—"The Pit and the Pendulum"

Elements of Style	Observations	Examples
Sentence structure (length, variety)	—uses semicolons to combine sentences —likes exclamations	"My eyes followed its outward . . . unspeakable!"
Vocabulary	—lots of long, physical modifiers	—spasmodically,
Imagery	—shows people in the grip of terror	—"Still I quivered in every nerve . . ."
Figurative language		

LITERARY SOURCE

"My eyes followed its outward or upward whirls with the eagerness of the most unmeaning despair; they closed themselves spasmodically at the descent, although death would have been a relief, oh! how unspeakable! Still I quivered in every nerve . . ."

from "The Pit and the Pendulum" by Edgar Allan Poe

Use a chart like this one to analyze the Poe and Hawthorne selections. Then decide which author's style you'd rather work with.

OR . . .

Look through more stories by these authors. Check to see that your observations hold true for them as well, and add new observations to your chart.

Brainstorm scene ideas. With a group of people who've chosen the same author as you, discuss ideas for a scene. Remember that your scene will be set in today's world, and that the plot and characters will be your own original creations.

Plan your scene by making notes on the setting, characters, action, dialogue, and mood. For tips on creating a strong mood, see the Revising Strategy on page 294.

STEP 2 DRAFTING

Before you draft, review the Writer's Blueprint, your style chart, and writing plan.

As you draft, here are some things to keep in mind.

- Remember that you're imitating the author's style only. The plot and characters must be your own original creations.
- Use vivid verbs to make the action come alive for the reader.

STEP 3 REVISING

Ask a partner for comments on your draft before you revise it.

✔ Have I imitated the author's style successfully?

✔ Have I developed a strong mood?

LITERARY SOURCE

"Age, with its miserable train of cares and sorrows and diseases, was remembered only as the trouble of a dream, from which they had joyously awoke. The fresh gloss of the soul, so early lost . . . again threw its enchantment over all their prospects."

from "Dr. Heidegger's Experiment" by Nathaniel Hawthorne

Revising Strategy

Using Contrast to Develop Mood

Contrast is one technique that writers use to develop a mood. In the Literary Model, notice how Hawthorne contrasts images of old age with images of youth to create a mood of miraculous joy and exhilaration. In the Student Model below, notice how the writer used contrast to help develop a mood of doom. Can you tell which author this writer is imitating?

STUDENT MODEL

Was this then to be my ironical fate? Was I, a fisherman, to be put to death in the depths of the very ocean from which I had made my living? My wrists wriggled and squirmed in the padlocked chains like nightcrawlers on a hook; in two parallel columns, bubbles from my nostrils, life! rose from the [black and murky] depths to which I had plummeted, escaping ever upward toward the [brilliant sunlit] surface of the sea.

STEP 4 EDITING

Ask a partner to review your revised draft before you edit. When you edit, look for errors in grammar, usage, spelling, and mechanics. In addition, check for spelling errors that come from leaving certain letters out of words.

Editing Strategy

Using Too Few Letters

If you don't hear certain letters when you pronounce a word, you may misspell it. Practice saying each word below carefully, being sure to pronounce the underlined part. Look for mistakes with words like these when you edit your work.

prob<u>ab</u>ly	fav<u>o</u>rite	desp<u>er</u>ate	diff<u>er</u>ent
asp<u>i</u>rin	rem<u>em</u>bered	temp<u>er</u>ature	sep<u>a</u>rate

STEP 5 PRESENTING

Here are some suggestions for presenting your narrative.

- Have a Poe/Hawthorne imitator contest. Appoint a panel of judges to decide who did the best job, and present the winners with certificates.
- Turn your scene into a radio play with music and sound effects.

STEP 6 LOOKING BACK

Self-evaluate. What grade would *you* give your paper? Look back at the Writer's Blueprint and give yourself a score for each point, from 6 (superior) down to 1 (inadequate).

Reflect. What have you learned about the ominous side of American Romanticism and about the writer's craft from doing this assignment? Write responses to these questions.

✔ From looking at the styles, characters, and plots of Poe and Hawthorne, what sorts of conclusions could you draw about the society in which they lived?

✔ In the future, when people look back on literature, movies, and television shows of the 1990s, what are some conclusions you think they will draw about our society?

For Your Working Portfolio Add your narrative and your reflection responses to your working portfolio.

Grammar

Editing strategy lessons are an important part of every workshop.

The last step

Each workshop ends with suggestions for self-evaluation and reflection.

annotated teacher's edition

Along with objectives, annotations, and lesson support, the two-volume Teacher's Edition includes three important features.

A focus on **mini-lessons** at the bottom of most left-hand pages. Mini-lesson subjects include grammar, study skills, spelling, vocabulary, visual literacy, technology, literary language, and speaking/listening.

Support for students of **all abilities and learning styles,** especially those who are less proficient in English. Specific teaching tips for these students have been provided by professional educators and can be found at the bottom of most right-hand pages.

Point-of-use cross-references to support materials and technology.

in a user-friendly, 2-volume teacher's edition with strategies for helping all students

A multitude of minis

Mini-lessons on a wide variety of skills are located at the bottom of most left pages.

During Reading

Selection Objectives

- To reflect on the consequences of conformity and nonconformity
- To identify examples of figurative language
- To analyze main and supporting ideas
- To recognize verb forms

Unit 3 Resource Book
Graphic Organizer, p. 1
Study Guide, p. 2

Theme Link

The theme of Romanticism and a search for truth is reflected in Emerson's uncompromising dedication to the value of an individual's convictions. He and many Romantics held an optimistic view of the world, unlike pessimistic Romantic writers, such as Nathaniel Hawthorne and Herman Melville.

Vocabulary Preview

render, give in return
bestow, give as a gift
hinder, get in the way; make difficult
importune, ask urgently or repeatedly
capitulate, surrender

Students can add the words and definitions to their word lists in the Writer's Notebook.

Art Study

Response to Caption Question
The man is depicted in a confident, self-contained pose.

Gerrit A. Beneker (1882–1934) painted portraits of industrial workers and people who worked at sea, such as fishermen.

222

How does the composition of this painting, *Men Are Square* (1919) by Gerrit A. Beneker, reflect the cultural values of **individuality** and self-reliance? ➤

Self-Reliance

RALPH WALDO EMERSON

To believe your own thought, to believe that what is true for you in your private heart is true for all men,—that is genius. Speak your latent conviction, and it shall be the universal sense; for the inmost in due time becomes the outmost, and our first thought is rendered[1] back to us by the trumpets of the Last Judgment. Familiar as the voice of the mind is to each, the highest merit we ascribe to Moses, Plato and Milton is that they set at naught books and traditions, and spoke not what men, but what *they* thought. A man should learn to detect and watch that gleam of light which flashes across his mind from within, more than the lustre of the firmament[2] of bards and sages. Yet he dismisses without notice his thought, because it is his. In every work of genius we recognize our own rejected thoughts; they come back to us with a certain alienated majesty. . . .

1. render (ren′dər), *v.* give in return.
2. **firmament** (fėr′mə mənt), *n.* arch of the heavens; sky.

222 Unit Three: American Classic

MINI-LESSON: GRAMMAR

Verb Forms

Teach Verbs such as *becomes, replied,* and *(have) done* illustrate **present, past,** and **past participle** forms. Another verb form, or part, is **present participle** (example: *betraying*). Review the forms of these and other verbs in "Self-Reliance," pointing out uses of past participles, such as passive voice *(is rendered)* and perfect tenses *(has tried).*

Activity Ideas

- Students can find verbs in present and future tense and in imperatives that use the present form. Examples include *speak* and *dismiss* (p. 222) and *can come* and *will live* (p. 223).
- Students can identify past participles, such *(has) tried* and *(is) given* (p. 223).

Unit 3 Resource Book
Grammar, p. 4

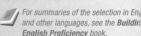

For summaries of the selection in En[glish] and other languages, see the ***Buildin[g] English Proficiency*** *book.*

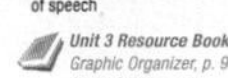

During Reading

Selection Objectives

- To explore Romantic themes concerning what is important in life
- To analyze an argument
- To recognize allusions and their communicative value
- To understand affixes and parts of speech

Unit 3 Resource Book
Graphic Organizer, p. 9
Study Guide, p. 10

Theme Link

Love of nature was part of Romanticism, and no one better expressed that love than Thoreau at Walden. This interlude and his act of civil disobedience exemplified his convictions about personal freedom.

Vocabulary Preview

stealthily, secretly, slyly
meanly, in a small-minded way
superfluous, more than is needed
enterprise, undertaking or project
garret, a space or room in a house just below a sloping roof
dissipation, a scattering in different directions
obsequious, polite or obedient, from hope of gain
abolitionist, person who advocates doing away with an institution or custom, such as slavery
hindrance, person or thing that hinders; an obstacle
abet, urge or assist, especially in doing wrong

Students can add the words and definitions to their word lists in the Writer's Notebook.

In 1845 Thoreau built a cabin in the woods by Walden Pond and lived there for two years. He wanted to simplify his life to the point where he could learn what the true essentials in life were. While there, he planned to write and study nature. Thoreau began his book, Walden, *after he left the pond, and finished it in 1854. Modern photographer Elliot Porter, who took the photo on the right, has found inspiration for his work in Thoreau's writings.*

Walden

HENRY DAVID THOREAU

When first I took up my abode in the woods, that is, began to spend my nights as well as days there, which, by accident, was on Independence Day, or the fourth of July, 1845, my house was not finished for winter, but was merely a defense against the rain, without plastering or chimney, the walls being of rough weather-stained boards, with wide chinks, which made it cool at night. The upright white hewn studs and freshly planed door and window casings gave it a clean and airy look, especially in the morning, when its timbers were saturated with dew, so that I fancied that by noon some sweet gum would exude from them. To my imagination it retained throughout the day more or less of this auroral character, reminding me of a certain house on a mountain which I had visited the year before. This was an airy and unplastered cabin, fit to entertain a traveling god, and where a goddess might trail her garments. The winds which passed over my dwelling were such as sweep over the ridges of mountains, bearing the broken strains, or celestial parts only, of terrestrial music. The morning wind forever blows, the poem of creation is
1 uninterrupted; but few are the ears that hear it. Olympus[1] is but the outside of the earth every where. . . .

I was seated by the shore of a small pond, about a mile and a half south of the village of Concord and somewhat higher than it, in the midst of an extensive wood between that town and Lincoln, and about two miles south of that our only field known to fame, Concord Battle Ground; but I was so low in the woods that the opposite shore, half a mile off, like the rest, covered with wood, was my most distant horizon. For the first week, whenever I looked out on the pond it impressed me like a tarn high up on the side of a mountain, its bottom far above the surface
2 of other lakes, and, as the sun arose, I saw it throwing off its nightly clothing of mist, and here and there, by degrees, its soft ripples or its smooth reflecting surface was revealed, while the mists, like ghosts, were stealthily[2] withdrawing in every direction into the woods, as at the breaking up of some nocturnal conventicle.

1. **Olympus** (ō lim′pəs), mountain home of the gods in Greek mythology.
2. stealthily (stelth′ə lē), *adv.* secretly; slyly.

1 Literary Focus
Allusion

Olympus also is known as Mount Olympus.

Question What does Thoreau suggest about the whole outdoors by calling it Olympus? *(Possible response: that any outdoor place is a worthy residence for gods)*

2 Literary Element
Figurative Language

Questions What does Thoreau say Walden Pond "throws off" each morning? *(its nightly mists)*

To what human action does he compare this morning change? *(to taking off night clothes)*

SELECTION SUMMARY
Walden, Civil Disobedience

Walden The selection from *Walden* gives Thoreau's account of life at Walden Pond, beginning in lyrical terms with a description of his cabin and its beautiful natural surroundings. Thoreau details his reasons for living at the pond; contrasts his simple life there with the complex and artificial life in society; and records philosophical reflections on solitude and the nature of human existence.

Civil Disobedience The passionate excerpt from "Civil Disobedience" focuses on the relationship between individuals and government, particularly on individual responsibility for actions taken by government in the name of its citizens. He recounts his short jail stay when he withheld tax payments to resist what he saw as immoral government actions.

For summaries in other languages, see the ***Building English Proficiency*** *book.*

BUILDING ENGLISH PROFICIENCY
ESL LEP ELD SAE LD

Building Vocabulary with Antonyms

Students can use Thoreau's descriptive language to increase their vocabularies. They can make a T-chart, like the one shown.

- List words from the selection, such as the ones from page 226, as shown.
- Explain that antonyms are words with opposite meanings. Provide examples of antonyms, such as *hot, cold, true,* and *false.*
- Have students write antonyms or words with contrasting meanings for the words in the left column of the chart, or other words chosen from the selection.

first	(last)
began	(ended, stopped)
rough	(smooth)
stealthily	(open)

Art Study

Photographer Eliot Porter, renowned for his images of New England, Appalachia, Baja California, Antarctica, Egypt, and other places, also is an expert on birds. His book *In Wilderness Is the Preservation of the World: From Henry David Thoreau* has been reprinted by the Sierra Club (1988, 1989).

There is a time in every man's education when he arrives at the conviction that envy is ignorance; that imitation is suicide; that he must take himself for better for worse as his portion; that though the wide universe is full of good, no kernel of nourishing corn can come
1 to him but through his toil bestowed[3] on that plot of ground which is given to him to till. The power which resides in him is new in nature, and none but he knows what that is which he can do, nor does he know until he has tried. . . .

Trust thyself: every heart vibrates to that iron string. Accept the place the divine providence has found for you, the society of your contemporaries, the connection of events. Great men have always done so, and confided themselves childlike to the genius of their age, betraying their perception that the absolutely trustworthy was seated at their heart, working through their hands, predominating in all their being. . . .

Whoso would be a man, must be a nonconformist.[4] He who would gather immortal palms must not be hindered[5] by the name of goodness, but must explore if it be goodness. Nothing is at last sacred but the integrity of your own mind. Absolve you to yourself, and you shall have the suffrage of the world. I remember an answer which when quite young I was prompted to make to a valued adviser who was wont to importune[6] me with the dear old doctrines of the church. On my saying, "What have I to do with the sacredness of traditions, if I live wholly from within?" my friend suggested,—"But these impulses may be from below, not from above." I replied, "They do not seem to me to be such; but if I am the Devil's child, I will live then from the Devil." No law can be sacred to me but that of my nature. Good and bad are but names very readily transferable to that or this; the only right is what is after my constitution; the only wrong what is against it. A man is to carry himself in the presence of all opposition as if every thing were titular[7] and ephemeral[8] but he. I am ashamed to think how easily we
capitulate[9] to badges and names, to large societies and dead institutions. . . . 2

The other terror that scares us from self-trust is our consistency; a reverence for our past act or word because the eyes of others have no other data for computing our orbit than our past acts, and we are loath to disappoint them. . . .

A foolish consistency is the hobgoblin of little minds, adored by little statesmen and philosophers and divines. With consistency a great soul has simply nothing to do. He may as well concern himself with his shadow on the wall. Speak what you think now in hard words and tomorrow speak what tomorrow thinks in hard words again, though it contradict every thing you said today.—"Ah, so you shall be sure to be misunderstood."—Is it so bad then to be misunderstood? Pythagoras was misunderstood, and Socrates, and Jesus, and Luther, and Copernicus, and Galileo, and Newton, and every pure and wise spirit that ever took flesh. To be great is to be misunderstood. . . .

Insist on yourself; never imitate. Your own gift you can present every moment with the cumulative force of a whole life's cultivation; but of the adopted talent of another you have only an extemporaneous half possession. . . .

A political victory, a rise of rents, the recovery of your sick or the return of your absent friend, or some other favorable event raises your spirits, and you think good days are preparing for you. Do not believe it. Nothing can bring you peace but yourself. Nothing can bring you peace but the triumph of principles.

3. bestow (bi stō′), *v.* give as a gift.
4. **nonconformist** (non′kən fôr′mist), *n.* person who refuses to be bound by established customs.
5. hinder (hin′dər), *v.* get in the way; make difficult.
6. importune (im′pôr tün′), *v.* ask urgently or repeatedly.
7. **titular** (tich′ə lər), *adj.* in title or name only.
8. **ephemeral** (i fem′ər əl), *adj.* lasting only for a very short time.
9. capitulate (kə pich′ə lāt), *v.* surrender.

1 Literary Focus
Figurative Language

Emerson uses an extended metaphor, comparing a person's intellectual and spiritual life to a farmer's cultivation of a plot of ground.

Questions How can someone till (farm) his or her plot of ground, or mind? *(Possible response: by carefully attending to one's experience and thoughts)*

What "corn" can be harvested from it? *(Possible response: understanding and insight)*

2 Reader's Response
Personal Connections

Question What "badges," names, societies, and institutions affect people today?

Check Test

1. According to Emerson, what do geniuses accept about themselves? *(their own thoughts or convictions)*
2. Does Emerson think it is better to be a conformist or a nonconformist? *(nonconformist)*
3. What does he think of being consistent in what a person says and thinks? *(Possible response: Consistency is not necessary; it's better to be true to what you believe at any time.)*
4. Why are great people often misunderstood? *(because they think differently from others or don't worry what others think)*
5. Whose principles are key in deciding how to live, according to this essay? *(Each person must live by her or his own principles.)*

Unit 3 Resource Book
Alternate Check Test, p. 5

BUILDING ENGLISH PROFICIENCY
ESL LEP ELD SAE LD

Making Personal Connections

To help students understand Emerson's philosophy, consider either of these talking or writing activities.

- Discuss whether Emerson's ideas are applicable only to adults. Ask whether—or to what extent—teenagers could follow his advice, if they should want to.
- Ask students in pairs to devise and write their own "rules for life" or "rules for thinking." These may be similar in format to Emerson's sentences. They may draw on proverbs and cultural ideas known to the students. The class might create a collage of the ideas.

Building English Proficiency
Activities, p. 183

Easy on the eyes

Large type, as shown above, makes teacher notes easy to read.

Other Teacher's Edition Features

- Unit Planning Pages
- Selection Summaries
- Art Study Notes and Questions
- Historical Notes
- Suggestions for both At-Risk and Gifted students
- Check Tests
- Multicultural Notes
- Cross-Curricular Connections
- Writing Workshop Assessment Criteria

Building student success

Most right-hand pages contain special help for students who are less-proficient in English.

teacher's resource file

Flexibility and options are built into the Teacher's Resource File which contains **over 1500 pages of copy masters and transparencies** plus software and audio cassettes to support your teaching style and address each student's needs.

For ease of use, all copy masters that relate to an individual selection are located together in Unit Resource Books—one Resource Book for each unit in the student anthology.

Unit Resource Books

Selection materials

Graphic Organizers
Study Guides
Vocabulary Worksheets
Grammar, Usage, and Mechanics Worksheets
Selection and Vocabulary Check Tests
Selection Tests

Unit materials

Interdisciplinary Worksheets
Writing Workshop Support Pages
Unit Test

The Resource File Also Includes

- Program Overview
- Resources for Building English Proficiency
- Reading, Writing & Grammar SkillBook
- Transparency Collection
- The World of Work: Investigations and Activities
- Assessment Handbook
- Test Generator
- Writing Software
- Audio Cassettes (15-20 cassettes per grade)

in providing an abundance of quality enrichment materials

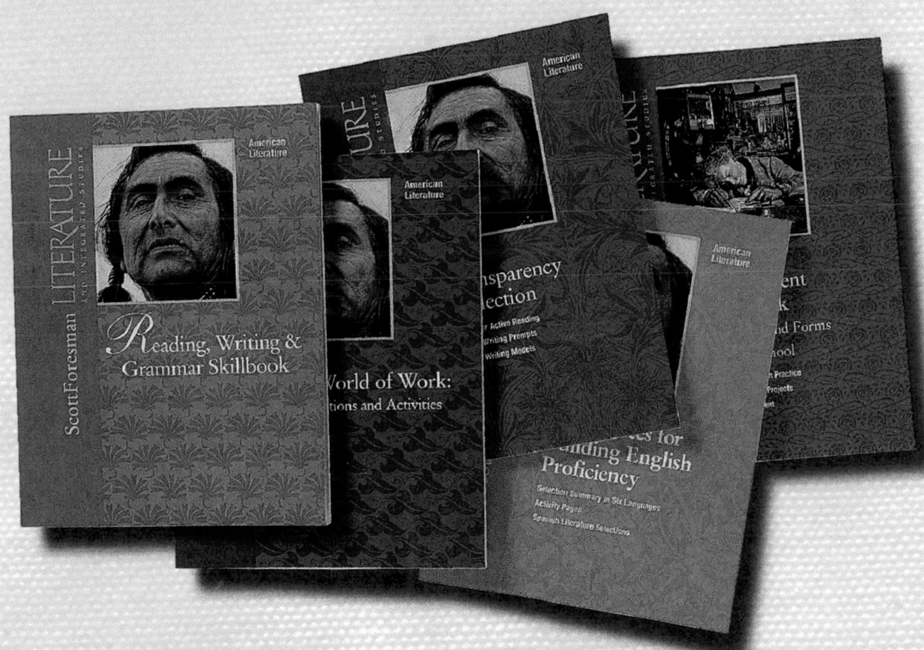

user friendly technology

CD-ROMS

AuthorWorks™ CD-Rom Series

A 7-disc CD-ROM series produced in cooperation with the Library of Congress offers fascinating, in-depth studies of a broad range of well-known authors. Writers' lives are accessed through a rich database of information about their personal lives, their writings, and their times. Material is presented through various media including slideshows, oral readings, movies, music, interviews, historical documents, maps, text screens, and so forth. Extensive project books for each grade level direct student research, which can be captured and transported into multimedia reports.

AuthorWorks™ Authors

Chinua Achebe
Isabel Allende
Jane Austen
William Blake
Emily & Charlotte Brontë
Gwendolyn Brooks
Albert Camus
Willa Cather
Anton Chekhov
Joseph Conrad
Robert Cormier
Stephen Crane
E. E. Cummings
Charles Dickens
Emily Dickinson
Rita Dove
F. Scott Fitzgerald
Robert Frost
Nadine Gordimer
Lorraine Hansberry
Thomas Hardy
Nathaniel Hawthorne
Ernest Hemingway
Langston Hughes
Zora Neale Hurston
Henrik Ibsen
D.H. Lawrence
Ursula Le Guin
Doris Lessing
Jack London
Guy de Maupassant
Arthur Miller
Flannery O'Connor
George Orwell
Alan Paton
Edgar Allan Poe
Cynthia Rylant
Bernard Shaw
Mary Shelley
Gary Soto
John Steinbeck
Henry David Thoreau
Leo Tolstoy
Mark Twain
Yoshiko Uchida
Derek Walcott
Walt Whitman
Elie Wiesel
William Wordsworth
Richard Wright
W.B. Yeats
Laurence Yep
Paul Zindel

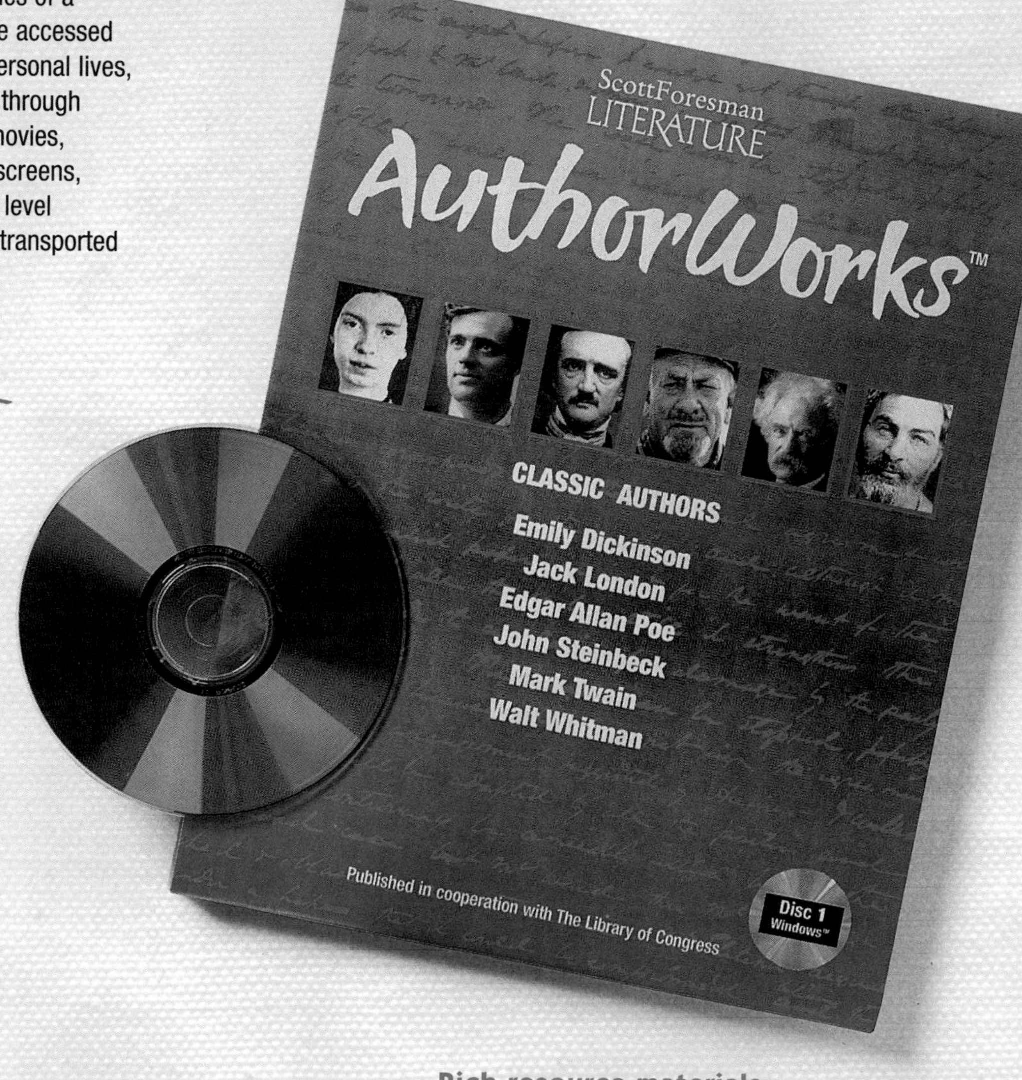

ScottForesman
LITERATURE
AuthorWorks™
CLASSIC AUTHORS
Emily Dickinson
Jack London
Edgar Allan Poe
John Steinbeck
Mark Twain
Walt Whitman
Published in cooperation with The Library of Congress
Disc 1
Windows™

Rich resource materials

Published in cooperation with the Library of Congress.

More Software

Test Generator allows teachers to customize assessment.

Writer's Resource supports pupil book assignments and provides grammar lessons and research paper instruction.

Writer's Notebook includes selection-based prompts; allows students to keep a personal journal on computer; provides opportunities for dialectical journal writing.

BBC Shakespeare CD-ROM Series

Bring favorite plays to life with this top-rated series produced by the BBC. Each disc includes the complete play script, scenes from professional productions, interviews with well-known drama and literary figures, plus extensive background on Shakespeare and the Globe Theater.

in making technology that works for you and your students

ScottForesman Custom Literature Database CD-ROM

Personalize your literature teaching with an additional 1400 contemporary and classic literary works. Selections are easily accessed through genre, author, title, ethnicity, literary themes, or grade level indexes and produce high quality reproducible prints. Special selections are keyed directly to the themes in the ScottForesman pupil anthologies and are accompanied by custom teaching materials.

novel works

NovelWorks™ is ScottForesman's answer to teaching novels and other longer works. Quality collections of resource materials in a convenient kit are available for 36 popular middle school and high school titles.

NovelWorks™ Titles

To Kill a Mockingbird
Johnny Tremain
The Call of the Wild
The Pearl
The Diary of Anne Frank
The Adventures of Tom Sawyer
Where the Red Fern Grows
The Clay Marble
The Outsiders
Hatchet
Eyes of Darkness
Roll of Thunder, Hear My Cry
Nilda
Their Eyes Were Watching God
Farewell to Manzanar
The Odyssey
Things Fall Apart
The Adventures of Huckleberry Finn
Great Expectations
Lord of the Flies
The Joy Luck Club
A Separate Peace
Like Water for Chocolate
The Great Gatsby
Black Boy
Lord Jim
The Scarlet Letter
Wuthering Heights
Jane Eyre
Animal Farm
The Mayor of Casterbridge
A Raisin in the Sun
Bless Me, Ultima
Cry, the Beloved Country
Cyrano de Bergerac
The Grapes of Wrath

Each Kit Contains

Teacher's Resource Book Over 80 pages of teaching support offers background, vocabulary, chapter-by-chapter support, literary themes and elements, maps, time lines, media resources, fine art studies, and assessment options.

Writing Options Book 4 complete writing lessons—one in each major mode—with grammar and punctuation mini-lessons and assessment rubrics.

Thematic Connections Book Additional literary selections further explore the work's major themes.

Audio Cassette 60-minute audio cassette offers dramatic readings, essential for students needing extra language support.

a step ahead

in support for teaching novels

Points of Departure

A low-cost, high-interest series of supplemental literature texts to accent the main anthology.

Titles include

- Crossroads (young adult literature)
- Multicultural Voices
- Reflections on a Gift of Watermelon Pickle (poetry)
- World Writers Today
- American Studies Album
- An Introduction to the Humanities
- The Bible as/in Literature

Activity Cards 4 cards, each with 8 activities, explore themes and develop cross-curricular connections.

Research Cards 4 cards with 4–5 suggested ideas per card focus on and develop research projects.

Fine Art Transparencies Full-color reproductions of fine art introduce and explore major themes.

BookTalk Reproducible newsletter engages students' interest and introduces them to the literary work and author. 60-minute audio cassette offers dramatic readings, essential for students needing extra language support.

Documents 5 historical items help build background and context for the work and provide unique bulletin board material.

Literature and Integration

Statement of Philosophy: ScottForesman Literature and Integrated Studies

by Alan C. Purves

Director of the Center for Writing and Literacy

State University of New York at Albany
Albany, New York

This collection of books, computer disks, CD-ROM's and other materials has the following purpose: to present literature of quality from around the world to a variety of students and to encourage them to become thoughtful readers, writers, and users of a variety of media.

In assembling these materials, the consultants, writers, and editors have a philosophy they would like to share. The philosophy involves beliefs about reading and responding to literature, about the role of the classroom and the teacher, and about the nature of learning in English.

Reading

For most people reading begins with looking. When we read, we use our eyes (or if we know Braille, our fingertips), and we see the shapes of letters, words, paragraphs, poems, stories, plays, and other kinds of text materials on the page or on the screen. As we look at these collections of marks in relation to the white space we begin to make sense of them, to connect them with ideas, arguments, events, feelings, and questions of one sort or another. When we do this we are responding to what we have read and understood.

We can't avoid having a response to our reading. Perhaps we stop reading, turn the page, scratch our head, nod, yawn, get ideas, make mental pictures, cry, laugh, or decide to do something as a result of our reading. Reading is reading in and between the lines and it is responding to what we see. Studies have shown that most people see similar things in a given text and that their responses are quite similar.

Our responses are generated partly by what we are reading now and partly by what we have read, seen, heard, or done in the past. When we read a story we tend to meet it halfway. We have ideas, images, and meanings of words in our head. They are often activated by what we read. We may identify with a particular character because she reminds us of what we were like at a particular time or because she seems like a person we know. These responses result from our past and present images and associations as they meet the words, images, characters, places, and ideas in the literature we read.

If our responses result from past experiences, why are they often so similar to one another when each of us has had quite distinct experiences? In part it is because all of us are sharing the same words, sentences, images, and events in the story. In part it is because we share attitudes and understandings concerning people, places, and events. We all tend to be sad when the villain menaces the girl or when the favorite dog dies. We all know the hero wears a white hat and doesn't smoke. We all tend to laugh at the same jokes. These are common emotions caused by years of association of the emotion to the event. A lot of what we read or watch uses these common scenes, images, and people. Literary people call them conventions, stereotypes, motifs, or archetypes. They work because they are consistent and expected. Where people's responses mainly differ lies in what they say or do about their responses. These differences depend on how each individual has learned to express his or her response. In school, teachers want students to think about what they have read and how they respond to what they have read. We want to push their responses into new dimensions.

Literature

As students go through school reading literature, talking and writing about it, and taking tests on it, they pick up ideas of what makes a good response. These ideas then become habits of reading, talking, and writing. Although scholars and critics of literature argue the fine points of criticism and theory, they generally agree that all of them are based on three broad sets of questions about a work of literature.

1. **How can we understand the work in light of the place and time in which it was written?**

2. **How can we understand the work in terms of our own time?**
3. **What are the implications of the work?**

These three broad questions are the heart of this series and its instructional program. We have placed them after the selections to shape students' responses to the literature in this anthology. The essential first step in this shaping is to ask students to describe what happened to them upon reading the selection, and we suggest a variety of means to get them to begin to shape their first responses. Then we build on this first step by moving to broader questions, which will help students become thoughtful readers and responders. Dealing with these questions will also help them see literature in terms of the author and the author's culture, explore themes in a cultural and historical context, see the relationship between the literature and other art forms, and relate the literature to their on-going lives as students and as creative, thoughtful people. In the classroom we can help students explore these questions.

In exploring the first broad question about understanding a literary work in its time, students need to deal with the big ideas, the major events, and the everyday concerns of the past or of countries or cultures. Students then come to see that the words on the page did not come there by magic; they were put there by someone who had a purpose, something to say, some desire to give readers pleasure, to excite them, to make them think.

In exploring the second question, students come to understand how the interpretation and judgment of a work of literature today can be different from what it might have been in the past. We read and look at things in terms of our contemporary concerns, and in doing so we make even ancient works come alive for us. The story of Macbeth is not just the story of some people in Scotland nearly a thousand years ago; nor is it a story geared only to the concerns of playgoers in Shakespeare's England; *Macbeth* deals with themes and issues that can be found on the nightly news—stories about political intrigue and domestic violence. How do people deal with these passions today? Are they like Macbeth?

The third question is equally important. In asking it we move beyond the work to look at the larger issues and concerns that reading and understanding the work bring to mind. Some students may see how the work can suggest other kinds of expression, a video, a set of poems, an animation, a dramatic reading. Others may be inspired to do further reading. Still others may be led to explore a variety of presentations of the work (film versions, for example), or another treatment of the themes and issues (in a history course). Some students may want to create a hypermedia production around the text and their response to it. The shaping of these extensions takes place in the classroom, and it is in the shaping that we help students explore new dimensions of themselves and the literature. An important outcome will be that the literature remains alive in the students' minds.

Although the order of these three questions may vary depending on which seems the most immediate or relevant to you and your students, they invite students to explore historical background, genre and literary form, authors and related arts, themes and major issues of past and current concern, and the nature of the creative process itself.

Integration

In creating this program, we do not see literature separate from writing or the study of language. Literature is made up of language which has a structure, a history. The structure and history of the language helped shape the way in which the selections were written and help shape the way your students write and make their attempts to become authors themselves.

Reading and writing are the two dimensions of literacy. In a literature program we begin by looking at the writing of others and turn to the writing of our students. The compositions that emerge from our students should receive as careful attention from us as we ask students to give to the works in the books we assign. In reading we ask the students to seek to know the author; in writing we ask them to seek to know their audience. The two activities are closely related. They are related to speaking and listening as well; after all, much literature was and still is performed orally, and talk and discussion are among the most valuable aspects of a classroom.

Ours is a world in which literature is not confined to words on a page.

Nor do we see the literature that is printed and bound in books or the writing of your students as separate from literature that is presented on the screen, on audio or video disks, or in one of the new multimedia or hypermedia versions. Ours is a world in which literature is not confined to words on a page. Just as your students are aware of the variety of media as an audience, so they should explore those media as creators and shapers. Many of the activities we suggest ask students to explore dimensions of composition beyond writing on the page. We hope they will have a chance to explore hypertext and hypermedia, drama, video, simulation gaming, theater, and many of the other ways by which people express and communicate their ideas and understandings. Learning in English goes far beyond reading and writing. It is indeed a way by which each student can master a variety of media and gain a further degree of independence as a user of all the power of language and literature.

Writing and Thinking Critically

Fostering Critical Thinking and Writing Through Writing Workshop

by Carol Booth Olson
University of California, Irvine
Irvine, California

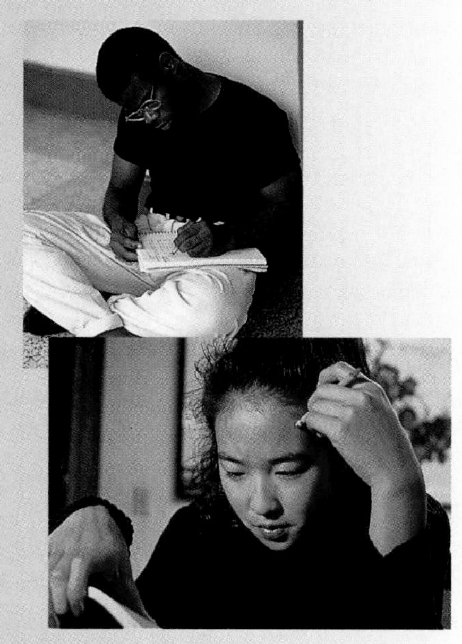

The lessons in the Writing Workshop section that concludes each group of literary selections blend learning theory, composing process research, and the practical strategies of the National Writing Project. They are designed to help students cope with the cognitive demands of two questions they juggle simultaneously: *What do I want to say?* and *How do I transform what I want to say into a written product?*

Underlying the way the lessons have been developed are a number of fundamental premises about thinking that inform the teaching of writing.

Writing is a mode of thinking. In order to produce a composition, writers must generate ideas, plan for both the process of writing and for the written product itself, translate thought into print, revise what they have articulated, and evaluate the effectiveness of their efforts. In short, in moving from conception to completion, writers tap all of the levels of Bloom's taxonomy of the cognitive domain (201–207).

Thinking is progressive. As Piaget observed, the mind is better able to make cognitive leaps when learning moves from the concrete to the abstract. Individual thinking/writing tasks should begin by focusing on something tangible and/or concrete. For example, students who observe a seashell are encouraged to think analogically by creating similes about the seashell. An overall writing curriculum should also *move progressively.* Such a *progression* might take the form of sequencing the domains of writing from descriptive to narrative to expository, or it might involve moving from known to unknown audiences.

Thinking is cumulative and recursive. All thinking experiences build upon one another. However, the pathway to more complex thought is not a linear one. Researchers have noted that writing, in particular, is a recursive process. Writers often go back in their thinking in order to move forward with their writing. Therefore, teachers who use a stage process model of composition which moves from prewriting to writing to revising and editing should continually invite students to think about their thinking and their writing by revisiting what they have written. So too, a writing curriculum should be scaffolded in such a way that students must go back to prior learning in order to move forward to the next task.

> **...students must go back to prior learning in order to move forward to the next task.**

Thinking is not taught but fostered. Thinking is an innate capacity which can be enhanced through the act of writing. Hilda Taba concludes that "how people think may depend largely on the kinds of 'thinking experience' they have had" (12). The teacher, then, plays a crucial role by providing students with thinking experiences that facilitate cognitive growth. Writing is one of the most complex and challenging thinking experiences the teacher can provide.

The key to independent thinking and writing is practice. Teachers must provide students with the guided practice in a range of thinking and writing tasks that will enable them to develop and internalize a repertoire of problem-solving strategies that they can apply with confidence to future thinking/writing challenges.

With these premises in mind, the designers of the Writing Workshop lessons selected a type of writing that was compatible with the themes and issues of the literary works (for example, a descriptive poem, an autobiographical incident, an interpretive essay, a persuasive letter, a reflective essay, and so forth) and then did a task analysis to determine how best to "scaffold" the lesson activities in a way that would give students practice in the key thinking and writing skills called for in the assignment.

> **...the ultimate goal of instructional scaffolding is to gradually withdraw the teacher-guided practice ...**

In a scaffolded approach, the teacher analyzes the language task to be carried out by the students, determines the difficulties that task is likely to pose, and then selects and provides guided practice in strategies that enable students to approach and complete the task successfully. Just as a real scaffold is a temporary structure that holds workers and materials while a building is under construction, the ultimate goal of instructional scaffolding is to gradually withdraw the teacher-guided practice when students demonstrate that they have internalized the strategies and can apply them independently.

The Writing Workshop lesson scaffolds provide a framework of thinking and writing activities to help students move from conception to completion. While there is no one description of the writing process, the format below uses a stage process model of composition to guide students from the prewriting or *generating* phase of writing to the *planning* phase, from drafting to revising, and then to editing and evaluation.

Writing Workshop Lesson Format:

Title of Lesson—Identifies the writing task students will focus on.

Assignment—Provides a brief abstract of the writing task.

Writer's Blueprint:

- **Product**—Identifies the type of writing called for in the assignment.
- **Audience**—Specifies the audience for whom the writing is intended.
- **Specs**—Lists the specific features of a successful written product.

Prewriting—Provides a sequence of activities that help the writer connect the writing task to the literary selections and generate ideas about what to write. Activities may include clustering, quick writes, drawing, mapping, role-playing, and so forth.

Plan your Product—Helps students focus on how to get their ideas down in written form. Students formulate a writing plan using charts, microtheme forms, outlines, time lines, storyboards, and so forth.

Drafting—Gives tips for how to get started, how to make the writing focused and/or lively, important elements of the writing task to highlight, and so forth.

Revising—Presents students with a mini-lesson on specific strategies to work on to enhance the written product—for example, how to show and not just tell or how to use the active rather than the passive voice.

Editing—Focuses on an element of correctness that is relevant to the writing task. For instance, a task that requires dialogue may focus on the rules for writing a dialogue.

Presenting—Gives students ideas regarding how to publish or disseminate their work via displays, read-arounds, creating class books, presenting their papers to another class, and so forth.

Looking Back—Invites students to reflect upon what they have written and the lessons learned—both about the craft of writing and about life.

Ultimately, the goal of the Writing Workshop lessons is to provide students with a range of options for writing about literature and life, to introduce them to specific writing types or products, and to help them to develop a repertoire of strategies they can internalize and apply as autonomous learners to future thinking and writing challenges.

References

Bloom, Benjamin, ed. *Taxonomy of Educational Objectives–Handbook I: Cognitive Domain.* New York: David McKay Company, Inc., 1956.

Taba, Hilda. *Thinking in Elementary School Children.* Washington, D.C.: U.S. Dept. of Health, Education and Welfare, Cooperative Research Project No. 1574, 1964.

Interdisciplinary Studies

Making Connections: An Interdisciplinary Approach

by Catherine Porter Small
American Studies Teacher and Social Studies Coordinator
Nicolet High School
Glendale, Wisconsin

"The Winslow Homer film is in my room for the week. Sign up if you want it. Can we all go to West Bend together for that exhibit before it leaves?"
—Rick (English)

"Let's rename that course 'Gender in literature, history and art.' It reflects the curriculum of that elective more accurately."
—Julie (History and English)

"The symphony's fall performance for students is about the American Dream. There's even a selection from that opera about Malcolm X. Shall we do a field trip?"
—Lon (English)

"When do you want me to do the architecture slide lecture for your students? Next week will work for me."
—Kathy (History)

"Public television is running a special on American jazz this week. I'll tape it for our teamed class if you want."
—John (History)

"Has anyone got a tape on the Salem witch trials I can use? It's Crucible *time again."*
—Jan (English)

"Aren't you going to the NCSS? Please look in on the session on making connections between history and science. I've got a live one interested in the science department."
—Dennis (History)

The Interdisciplinary Inoculation for Teachers

Burn-out is a professional disease among teachers. Stressed out and overworked, veterans of the school wars are susceptible to digging in, doing it the old way, and preserving energy. After years of the paper burden, it may be that English teachers are most susceptible to the dreaded disease, with history teachers close behind. Yet the memos above are just a sampling of those I received from colleagues during the first quarter this year. One teacher has taught sixteen years and the rest between twenty and thirty. I teach American History and American Literature and taught my first classes in 1974, but I'm still fired up and so are they. We've received the interdisciplinary inoculation against burn-out. Our intellectual health has improved along with our students'.

However, when we began interdisciplinary courses at the freshman and junior years seven years ago, not all of these teachers initially embraced it with equal fervor.

"Is this just one more swing in the educational pendulum?"

"Will I lose coverage in a course that already contains too much material and too few days?"

"I don't know enough to teach this way! What do I know about the other disciplines?"

To make the connections necessary to establish a new curriculum of this kind, we had to begin to rely on the expertise of others in our school and community. History teachers wrote simple time lines of major events to jog the memory of the English teachers. English teachers reviewed the plots of novels read long ago by history teachers. We all invited each other to classes. Regular meetings revolved around ways to make linkages, sharing discoveries. We threw lesson plans and hand-outs in each others' mailboxes. Nobody minded much the extra time they were taking because they saw the possibilities of teaching in an expanded way from a wider understanding with a safety net of their fellows. Ultimately, we saved time as we worked with one another, and collegiality replaced the lonely, closed classroom.

The unexpected benefit of establishing, developing, and maintaining interdisciplinary connections has been in the professional growth of the faculty. We've attended workshops, institutes, concerts, and art exhibitions together, and we call upon one another's expertise on a regular basis.

Cooperative learning takes place at the faculty level. I suspect the interdisciplinary approach has been the inoculation that has prevented that dreaded burn-out that assaults too many veteran teachers. I've seen colleagues who were tired get reinspired, including myself. Perhaps it's not the inoculation as much as the mental exercise that produces the teaching fitness.

The Advantages for Students

I ran into Tanya at a restaurant a few years ago. She was in my history class before we used an interdisciplinary approach. She said, "I'm embarrassed that I only got a D in your class. But you'll be glad to know that I took History of American Art last year. I learned so much! Now I get it. I even read historical novels all the time." I should have offered the apology. She was a visual learner, and I was a print teacher. She brought interest and capability to class that I had not tapped. Now she would use the images of Paul Revere and Jacob Lawrence and George Caleb Bingham as text too. Now she would read Black Boy while studying the Great Migration. Now she would "get it."

The advantages for the students are clear. Interdisciplinary study provides a context for learning, a background for the figures of literature. When we learn anything in context, comprehension improves. When comprehension improves, interest increases. When interest increases and learning occurs in context, students retain what they learn better than they do when they learn subjects in isolation. Each of us has had the experience of making connections sloppily, and sadly too late. If only we'd taken that American history class at the same time we'd taken the American literature course, the literature would have made sense. If only we'd taken Western Civilization while we took Art Appreciation, or perhaps Philosophy, we would have understood.

Marshal McLuhan, the media guru of the sixties, warned us that we would be teaching a new breed of young people not as enamored with print media as their parents because they learned in an electronic environment of television, radio, and movies. They would be visual and aural learners in print-dominant schools. Our first attempt to meet this challenge was to expand technology and resources: audiotapes and videotapes flooded the classrooms. Newer technologies have followed, especially those linked to computers. What we frequently missed, however, was that the way we learn outside the classroom has less to do with technology and more to do with the way the world works: separating the disciplines is in itself artificial. Writers don't write isolated from their culture. They are informed by the intellectual ferment of their history and times. All literature has time and setting. Poets respond to their times. History is written from perspectives shaped by the artistic response to events. Visual artists create works of art that have symbolic content, real or imaginary, in styles shaped by the milieu of the American experience. To study these subjects separately is as limiting to students as studying from the printed page alone. Providing linkage provides real insight. And insight leads to wisdom.

In a meaningful way, an interdisciplinary approach can put to a consistent use the educational buzzwords and concepts that keep reemerging: cultural literacy, upper-level thinking skills, writing across the curriculum, multiple intelligences, authentic assessment, cooperative learning, and so on. These are the natural tools of such a curriculum. The insights students gain are audible: "Aha! Now I get it."

Guidelines for Developing a Program

The following guidelines may assist you in starting or expanding a program:

1. If you make it a goal to look for connections, you will find them, either thematically or chronologically, or, best of all, both.
2. If your state has a humanities council, apply for a grant for workshop time.
3. Your goal is to give the students entry-level knowledge in disciplines that do not fall under the course headings. You don't have to be an expert.
4. Discover the strengths of your faculty. Much of what you want to include in your curriculum can be taught to you or your students by other teachers with expertise developed either inside or outside classrooms.
5. Document your linkages so they can be duplicated by other teachers or even next year.
6. Challenge the students to look for and articulate connections. Popular music lyrics sometimes contain strong references to arts and letters.
7. Teach new, test new. If you take twenty minutes to allow students to "read" Winslow Homer's painting, "Prisoners at the Front," while studying the Civil War, questions about it had better show on the next test.
8. Use your textbooks in new ways. Help students discover the assumptions their text was based on. Use the illustrations for developing context. Have the students look for connections in their other texts.

A Final Word

Thirty years ago, I entered college as an English major and met the New Criticism. As I understood it, each work should stand alone and be judged on its own merits. The author's life, the times he (of course) lived in, the "conversation" he was having with other artists who used other media of expression were to be ignored. How sterile. How threadbare. What unfortunate training for so many of us. For the future English majors in our classes, that old New Criticism might work. For the rest, and especially for the Tanyas in our classes, they deserve as rich a fabric as we can weave.

Professional Commentary
Multiculturalism

Developing Multicultural Understanding

by Carlos E. Cortés
Professor Emeritus of History
University of California, Riverside
Riverside, California

According to the futurist Alvin Toffler, "All education springs from some image of the future. If the image of the future held by a society is grossly inaccurate, its educational system will betray its youth."

This integrated language arts series is based upon an image of the future—that schools must strive to help young people prepare for life in our increasingly multicultural society and the rapidly shrinking globe. This means helping students develop better interpersonal and intergroup understanding—a sense of their own place on the map of humanity, a deeper insight into the similarities and differences that link them to others with whom they share our nation and planet, an ability to understand the roots of their own points of view and the perspectives of others, a capacity for making informed, considered choices in multicultural situations, and a facility for communicating effectively with those who may come from both similar backgrounds and significantly different cultural heritages.

In addressing the topic of multicultural understanding, each grade-level book includes a wide range of selections written by women and men of different ethnic, racial, religious, and (in most of the books) national backgrounds. These selections provide windows for examining varieties of human experience—varieties that often emerge from different cultures, traditions, and group experiences, as examined by both insiders (those who belong to those groups) and outsiders (external observers).

Some selections examine specific cultures, the manner in which they have established traditions, the ways they have changed, and the processes by which they have influenced and been influenced by individuals who are a part of those cultures. Other selections examine cultures as they operate within a large context, such as racial, ethnic, or religious groups within a nation. Still other selections examine multicultural interactions, whether between nations, among groups within nations, or among individuals of different racial, ethnic, cultural, religious, or gender identities.

But this series goes well beyond merely including different perspectives; it also encourages students to examine the basic relationship of commonality and diversity—similarities and differences—within the human experience, to engage a continuing set of fundamental multicultural themes, and to consider the implications of these themes for their own lives.

Underlying the entire multicultural approach are the three basic questions. What human similarities link people of all backgrounds? What group differences contribute to the uniqueness of each individual? What are the implications of those similarities and differences for successful and constructive living in a multicultural world that is shrinking by the day because of advances in communication and transportation?

Multicultural Themes

To explore these three increasingly critical questions, this series continuously addresses seven fundamental, inevitably overlapping and interacting multicultural themes—**Groups, Individuality, Perspective, Interactions, Change, Choice,** and **Communication**. While there are many themes that could be addressed when examining the topic of diversity, we have decided that these seven themes are so essential to multicultural understanding that all students will benefit from examining them.

1. GROUPS—the process by which groups come into existence and develop, including the ways by which groups of peoples—ranging from family units to globe-spanning cultures—have created group norms, values, codes, and behavioral guidelines (such as rules and laws), have developed internal diversity, and have interacted with, influenced, and been influenced by those who belong to those groups.

2. INDIVIDUALITY—the process by which an individual develops her or his own personal uniqueness, including relating to the multiple groups to which she or he belongs, by accepting and drawing upon group norms, values, and heritage; by challenging group or community expectations or pressures; and by dealing with the consequences of those decisions and actions.

3. PERSPECTIVE—the process by which individuals and groups, including cultures and nations, develop patterns of viewing and reacting to the world around them.

4. INTERACTIONS—the process by which people respond to each other, including the various types of interactions that occur when individuals or groups of people of different backgrounds come together, such as through cooperation, conflict, and efforts to build understanding and discover common ground.

5. CHANGE—the process by which groups and individuals undergo and respond to change over time.

6. CHOICE—the process by which individuals and sometimes groups make critical choices, such as when confronted with crises, significant changes, intergroup contact, or collisions between group expectations and individual desires.

7. COMMUNICATION—the process through which individuals and groups have managed or failed to communicate, as well as the process by which different cultures have developed their own languages, literatures, and other forms of expression.

Some of these themes are highlighted explicitly in individual selections; some are used to connect the discussion of various selections; all are used as basic themes for each book. Whether or not these themes are stated explicitly in connection with specific selections in either the student or teacher edition, all can be drawn upon whenever teachers or students find them appropriate and enriching. While each book explores the seven themes in different ways, the following suggested exploratory questions may be useful at any grade level.

(1) GROUPS—*How does group experience and culture emerge and develop?* This theme is examined within the frameworks of a variety of groups–for example, ethnic, racial, gender, age, and religious groups. How does a particular group's experience create common, uniting group bonds, traditions, worldviews, and shared connections—what we often call culture? In what respects have different groups' experiences led to internal diversity—comparing the experiences and cultures of different groups?

2. INDIVIDUALITY—*What are the relationships between an individual and the multiple groups to which she or he is connected?* How is an individual influenced by different types of group connections—for example, by his or her gender, or by coming from one or more ethnic, racial, religious or national heritages? What group pressures, norms, rules, expectations, or restrictions are sometimes imposed by groups on their members in an effort to create conformity or unity? How have some people accepted and embraced group norms and responsibilities, while others have challenged and struggled against group expectations and pressures? Why have some individuals attained special prominence within group cultural contexts? Why have some people become role models who transcend group boundaries?

> **How have history, heritage, culture, and experience influenced the varying ways that different individuals and groups have viewed the same events?**

3. PERSPECTIVE—*How have different individuals and groups perceived various events and how have those perceptions influenced their actions?* How and why have group perspectives or worldviews emerged? How have history, heritage, culture, and experience influenced the varying ways that different individuals and groups have viewed the same events? How have differing, sometimes competing, perspectives divided people and caused conflict? How have some people learned to look beyond their own perspectives to understand the perspectives of others?

4. INTERACTIONS—*What happens when different groups or individuals of different group backgrounds come into contact?* How have different groups perceived each other? How have understanding or animosity developed? How have people erected, maintained, or destroyed barriers that separate or restrict groups or individuals? How have people built bridges to connect groups or individuals so that intergroup cooperation, harmony, equality, and justice can be created?

5. CHANGE—*How do individuals and groups react to change?* What happens as people grow older or move into new cultural situations? How have groups responded to change, such as by modifying their cultures or struggling to preserve traditions?

6. CHOICE—*How do individuals and groups exercise choice in varying cultural or intercultural situations?* How does culture influence choice—for example, by encouraging or restricting certain choices? How do individuals exercise options despite cultural pressures or restraints?

7. COMMUNICATION—*What roles does communication play in intercultural living?* How have cultural experience, heritage, identity, and perceptions influenced communication, both in expression and reception? What opportunities, obstacles, and complications in communication have developed when individuals or groups of different backgrounds come into contact?

It is our hope that this series, in addition to providing students with a rich, diverse selection of literature, will further their understanding of the multicultural dimensions of the current world and the future in which they will live. We believe that our multicultural approach will both enrich their examination of the selections and help prepare them to become better and more constructive societal and global contributors.

Professional Commentary

Building English Proficiency

The Importance of Background Knowledge in Second-Language Learning

by Lily Wong Fillmore
University of California, Berkeley
Berkeley, California

Just as readers must apply their linguistic knowledge to the interpretation of the texts they read, so too must they make use of their knowledge of the world and their prior experiences in reading. Writers have in mind an "ideal reader," as Charles Fillmore (1982) has described it, when they construct any text. The "ideal reader" for the texts they are writing is one with just the language skills and background knowledge required to arrive at complete understandings of the texts the writers intended them to understand. However, no text contains every bit of information needed to understand it fully. Writers generally assume a level of prior knowledge and cultural and real world experience when they write, depending on the age and background of the intended readers of their texts. If they believe that the intended readers are unlikely to be familiar with certain words or concepts used in the text, they will define or discuss them in the text itself. Otherwise, they can simply presuppose that the readers will be able to apply their knowledge of language and of how it works to assist in the reading and interpretation of the text, and that they will draw on their knowledge of the world and on their experiences to fill in the gaps in the text. The ideal reader then is one who has the cultural background, experience and linguistic knowledge to do just what the writer hopes the intended readers of the text will be able to do when they read it.

That fact presents a special problem to educators who are concerned with finding or preparing appropriate instructional materials and texts for children from diverse cultural and linguistic backgrounds. Writers of educational materials in the U.S. generally assume that the readers of their materials will be English speakers with a mainstream, American cultural background, with the cognitive and linguistic development that is typical for students at whatever grade-level the materials are intended. But will such materials work for children from cultural and linguistic backgrounds that are different from those assumed by their writers? Is it necessary to provide materials that are specifically designed and prepared for them, or can these children be given the same materials that are available to other students? These are questions that are raised especially where English language learners are concerned. How, the question goes, can children deal with texts that are as complex as those used for mainstream students? How can they possibly comprehend materials that presuppose cultural background, knowledge and experiences that they don't already have? Shouldn't they be given materials that are culturally familiar, that deal with the world as they know and have experienced it?

> **It is by reading that children, particularly English learners, build up their store of cultural and background knowledge.**

I will argue that the education of children irrespective of their background would be greatly diminished if educators were to choose materials for them that were in any way narrowed or lowered in level because of putative deficiencies in the children's backgrounds. Such decisions must take into account the role authentic and challenging materials play in building children's background and in supporting language development. Children also gain the very kind of background that they need to have to deal with materials they read in school from the literature and textbooks they have already read. This argument might seem rather circular at first glance. How do children get the background they needed in the first place?

If with each story they read, children were to encounter a few new thoughts, words, experiences, glimpses of other worlds, understandings of someone else's perspective, it would not take long for them to have the rich and varied experiences and background that are needed to deal with any piece of text they are likely to get in school. It is by reading that children, particularly English learners, build up their store of cultural and background knowledge. Perhaps that is how most English language learners eventually come to master not only English, but to have the kind of cultural background and schemata (Bartlett, l932; Rumelhart, l980) that the text writers assume readers have and can apply to the interpretation of the materials they are writing.

The Teacher's Role in Making Written Texts Work as English Input

I believe that written texts are perhaps the most reliable and consistent source of academic English input children can have. This is not to suggest that teachers do not have a role to play in providing help and access to this kind of English for children who are learning it as a second language. Even a short text can offer to children the grammar and vocabulary of written English. However, texts do not by themselves reveal how the language in them works, nor do they provide many clues as to what the words that appear in them mean or how they are used. Granted, when readers are quite proficient in the language used in the text, they are usually able to figure out the meaning of some of the words they don't know based on the contexts in which the unfamiliar words are used (Sternberg & Powell, l983). But there is a limit on how many words in a text can be unfamiliar or new to a reader—perhaps 8 to 10 percent. When the percentage is that high, the reader will have much greater difficulty using context to figure out what new words mean. Until language learners are relatively proficient in English, there will be much that is new to them in any text. They will find it hard to use texts as input for language learning without help. This is especially true if the learners are insecure in their knowledge of the role played by the grammatical forms such as "from," "should," and "before" in indicating relationships and meanings in sentences and texts. Any text is pretty uninformative by itself, where language learners are concerned. To serve as input for language learning, not only does it have to be a well-formed text—which is to say, it must be coherent and cohesive, well constructed and interesting. It goes without saying that it must be a good example of grammatical English for it to work as English input. But the content has to be engaging, too—it has got to hold the attention of language learners, and be a great enough challenge to them to be worth the effort they have to make to read a text they can't easily understand. The best instances of such texts can be found in children's literature.

The question is, what role do teachers play in helping children make use of the written materials, especially authentic children's literature, as input for language learning? Such materials work as input —1) when teachers provide the support learners need for making sense of the text; 2) when they call attention to the way language is used in the text; 3) when they discuss the meaning and interpretation of sentences and phrases within the text with the learners; 4) when they help the learners notice that words they find in a text may have been encountered or used in other places; and 5) when they help them discover the grammatical cues that indicate relationships such as cause and effect, antecedent and consequence, comparison and contrast, and so on in the text.

In short, teachers help written texts become usable input—not only by helping children make sense of the text—but by drawing their attention, focusing it, in fact, on how language is used in the materials they read. Done consistently enough, the learners themselves will soon come to notice the way language is used in the materials they read. When they can do that, everything they read will be input for learning.

References

Bartlett, F. (1931) *Remembering.* Cambridge: Cambridge University Press.

Fillmore, C.J. (1982) Ideal readers and real readers. In D. Tannen (Ed.) *Analyzing Discourse: Text and Talk. Georgetown Round Table on Language and Linguistics l981.* Georgetown University Press, 248-270.

Rumelhart, D.E. (1980) Schemata: The building blocks of cognition. In R.J. Spiro, B.C. Bruce & W.J. Brewer (Eds.) *Theoretical Issues in Reading Comprehension.* Hillsdale NJ: Erlbaum.

Sternberg, R.J. & Powell, J,S, (1983) Comprehending verbal comprehension. *American Psychologist,* 8, 878-893.

Building English Proficiency

Building English Proficiency among ESL Students: Theory and Practice

by Dr. Jim Cummins
Professor Modern Language Centre and Curriculum Department
Ontario Institute for Studies in Education
Ontario, Canada

In many urban centers across North America, the numbers of students who are learning English as a second language (ESL) have increased dramatically in recent years. These students face a formidable challenge in meeting the standards of academic English required to graduate from high school. Considerable research has shown that, although conversational fluency in English often is acquired fairly rapidly (within about two years), it normally takes between five and ten years for ESL students to catch up to grade expectations in academic aspects of the language. There are two reasons for this:

- Academic language is much more complex than conversational language in terms of vocabulary and syntax.
- ESL students must catch up with a moving target insofar as speakers of English as a first language (L1) continue to grow every year in academic language abilities, such as reading and writing skills, range of vocabulary, and command of complex syntax.

In order to promote academic language development among ESL students, it is important to provide abundant opportunities for students to develop their thinking abilities, to encourage them to read and write extensively, and, above all, to let them feel your support in the personal journeys they are taking into a new language and culture.

Keep up the Cognitive Challenge!

The flip side of this is "don't dumb down the content!" ESL students are as intellectually bright as the other students in your class; they just don't have full command of the language at this point in time. They need cognitive challenge to maintain their interest and motivation just as much as any other student.

Provide Contextual Support!

In order for ESL students to be able to participate in cognitively challenging activities, they usually will require more contextual support than English L1 students. This contextual support is provided in two basic ways:

- Activating students prior knowledge and sparking their interest and motivation to invest academic effort. Activating prior knowledge mobilizes relevant concepts and information that students already possess, thereby making the learning process more efficient.
- Present content through visual or graphic displays (maps, Venn diagrams, semantic webs, outlines of chronological or causal sequences, etc.) that allow concepts to be taught in concrete ways that all students can figure out.

Brain Power in Action!

Both of these approaches increase students' brain power by activating and/or building their conceptual knowledge. The more students already know, the more they can comprehend, and the more they comprehend, the more they learn. These approaches also free up brain power. Because students have grasped the concept, they have more brain power to focus on the language itself and extend their understanding of vocabulary and syntax.

Extending Personal Horizons Through Reading and Writing

The importance of providing ample opportunities and encouragement for students to read and write volumes (literally!) cannot be overstated. Academic language, the language of text, is found only in books. You don't find it in the playground or on the street, or on popular television. If ESL students are not reading a lot, and reading in a variety of genres, they are not getting access to the language they need for graduation.

Technology

The CD-ROM Research Environment

by Mary Cron
Rymel Multimedia
Rolling Hills Estates, California

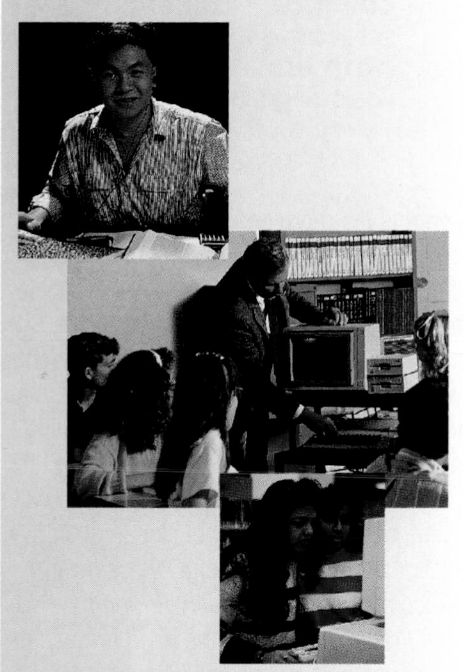

In the early 1980s, I was sitting with a group of teachers at one of the early educational technology conferences. With feet up in comfortable overstuffed lobby chairs, we fantasized about the future—*way* into the future—to a day when educational computer programs might be in color, present more than drill and practice options, have music and realistic sound effects instead of annoying beeps, and contain *much* more content. Conversation ended in laughter. Not in our lifetimes.

The Vision

Even in those early days, we were beginning to frame a vision of a multi-sensory on-line learning environment engaging to students of various learning styles and interests. We didn't just want students to be drilled and tested. In this information-rich, on-line world we envisioned, students could explore, hypothesize, gather information, analyze—in other words, use and develop their critical thinking skills. Happily, the future arrived much faster than any of the armchair visionaries anticipated. The CD-ROM format and accompanying developments in sound compression, video, and hardware capabilities have made it possible to include thousands of colorful images and pages of text.

Multimedia Research

A multimedia research environment presents information on a topic or set of related topics. Students can explore this information dynamically through a variety of inviting graphic navigational screens and sorting techniques.

In this CD-ROM environment students have more enthusiasm for research and spend more time working on their investigations than they do using print only.

The CD-ROM research environment also teaches important skills in media literacy that will prepare students for the learning tools they will use in higher education and in the workplace. These tools include mosaic thinking; analytical investigation of text, visual, and audio content; and the use of multimedia tools to create and present their own knowledge effectively.

Thinking Mosaically

One of the most difficult adjustments those of us from the print world have had to make when producing and using CD-ROM applications is to give up thinking only in linear terms. CD-ROM, with its quick sorting capabilities, is an amazing door opener to this mosaic world. In the CD-ROM research environment, students are able to make their own investigative choices connecting topics and ideas in a variety of ways. They can search for key words, type of media, topics, themes, and projects. Because the environment is highly interactive, their choices quickly activate new research paths.

Critical Analysis

Because the media is varied, the CD-ROM research environment requires students to go further than just analyzing text. They have photographs, audio, video, fine art, and illustrations both contemporary and archival to examine as potential sources of information. They have to weigh the viability, point of view, and usefulness of that information. They learn to observe and listen carefully and to question what they see and hear in any media. These are important critical-thinking skills in a media-driven society.

Using Multimedia Tools to Present Knowledge

Finally, in a multimedia research environment, student investigation results in the communication of new knowledge to others. Production tools are provided that enable students to enter their ideas, collect evidence of different media to support opinions, and prepare a sequenced presentation. The use of a multimedia bibliography and credits throughout the presentation discourages student plagiarism and reinforces the importance of accurate research to support hypotheses.

Ways of Learning

Learning Modalities and the Successful Teacher

by Dr. Jerry Hay
Director of Middle and High School Programs
Spalding University
Louisville, Kentucky

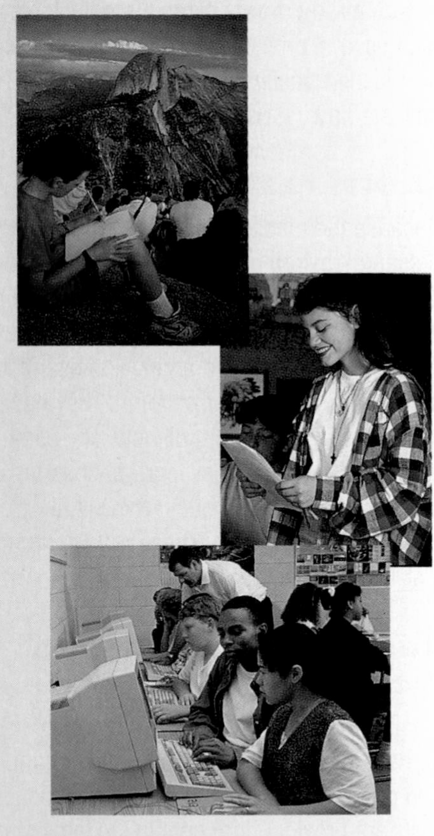

Imagine a conversation between two people of different cultures. The cultures need not be the cultures of different countries, but could even be the cultures of different socio-economic classes. During conversation, the speaker uses a word that the other does not understand. When the speaker recognizes the look of confusion on the other's face, the speaker begins to use all of the other words known to mean about the same thing. When these new words also fail to communicate, the speaker employs metaphors, similes, and analogies to help with the transfer of meaning. The speaker may eventually resort to a combination of grunts, facial expressions, body movements, and wild gestures to communicate. We have all experienced the frustration of failed communication from both ends of a conversation. This experience is in itself a rationale for using learning style theory in the teaching of literature.

Like the two conversationalists of different cultures, communication occurs only when meaning is transferred in a mode mutually understood. In a conversation, the speakers use a variety of words and gestures as needed only when stimulated by a lack of understanding. If one person in a conversation knew ahead of time that the other person best understood a particular language, vocabulary, or jargon, it would be possible to plan for the most effective and efficient conversation by taking that communication strength into account. Teachers face the same dilemma; they must communicate daily with a large group of students who may each have a particular communication or learning strength. Knowing about the learning strengths of students facilitates effective teaching.

How People Learn

A variety of theories deal with the differences in learning modalities. While each theory is unique, all contribute to an understanding of how people learn. These theories range from genetic to developmental and from broad to the very specific. One general theory considers the differences in function between the right and left lobes of the brain. This right brain–left brain theory, discussed in Betty Edward's' book, *Drawing on the Right Side of the Brain*, contends that the left side of the brain controls logical, linear thought while the right side of the brain controls the more general, global thought processes. Edwards also contends that teaching students to think or learn in only one lobe of the brain limits their perceptions of content. She advocates that teachers best serve students when they combine teaching strategies that incorporate both linear and global learning opportunities. Literature students benefit from not only the study of plot and character development, but also the study of global relationships. Walter Barbe and Raymond Swassing, in *Teaching Through Modality Strengths: Concepts and Practices*, support the need for teachers to recognize and address a variety of learning strengths in students. Learning modalities relate to strengths. It is logical for teachers to address these learning strengths and thus increase the rate or extent of learning by providing information through the most efficient channel for each student.

> **...teachers best serve students when they combine teaching strategies that incorporate both linear and global learning strategies.**

Recognizing the four learning modalities, teachers can arrange learning experiences for students that increase the rate of individual success by emphasizing the appropriate learning modality for each student. Teachers can also take the approach of systematically including all the learning strengths to ensure the greatest rate of student success. Students with a visual learning modality learn by seeing or watching demonstrations, think in pictures, and respond best to visual arts. Auditory-modality students learn through verbal instruction, think in sounds, and favor the musical arts. Kinesthetic learners learn by doing and by being physically involved, think with a physical memory, and react to all art in expressions of movement, touch, and physical involvement. Social learners respond best to learning situations within groups, think in terms of relationships within groups, and react to art as a social relationship.

Related to the realization that people can have different thought modalities, other researchers advance the belief that individuals have multiple intelligences or learning styles. Howard Gardner, in *Frames of Mind: The Theory of Multiple Intelligences*, contends that individuals have at least seven varieties of intelligences. He also feels students learn successfully when taught by teachers who incorporate learning opportunities that cater to the various intelligences. David Lazear, in *Seven Ways of Knowing: Teaching for Multiple Intelligences*, extends Gardner's approach by suggesting that teachers not only can incorporate learning based on the various intelligences but also can expand and develop their own multiple intelligences through a systematic program of intellectual exercises. These seven intelligences can easily be related to learning modality theory. Of the seven intelligences, verbal/linguistic is comparable to the auditory learning modality; visual/spatial intelligence is the visual learning modality; inter- and intra-personal intelligences relate directly to the social learning modality and rhythmic/musical and body/kinesthetic intelligences parallel the kinesthetic learning modality. The logical/mathematical intelligence can be equated either to visual or auditory learning modalities.

Effective Teaching

How do any or all of these different theories about how people learn affect the teaching of literature or any other content? These theories, which recognize that all people learn with different modalities or strengths, should influence how all content is taught. Literature students with any one of the four learning modalities will flourish in a classroom providing a combination of learning experiences that include opportunities for visual, auditory, kinesthetic, and social learning. To be effective, each lesson need not include all four learning modalities on any given day; but attention should be given to all four within a given unit of study. It is true that many teachers maintain excellent learning climates that, over the course of a term, may contain more than one of the learning modalities. There is a difference, however, between the accidental utilization of this approach, and deliberately planned teaching that recognizes and takes advantage of the learning modalities. The difference between the accidental and the planned utilization of learning modalities can be the difference between the occasionally successful and the consistently successful classroom. Without consistent application, theory is just speculation about possibilities.

Consider students in the 12–18 year age range. This age group presents the richest assortment of likes, dislikes, personalities, strengths, weaknesses, and learning preferences. These factors change on an almost daily basis and could change on an hourly basis for middle-school students. Flexibility and adaptability are the prerequisites for dealing with this age group. The use of modality learning theory to design, deliver, and assess instruction is one path to a consistent flexibility in meeting student needs.

Students benefit from instruction consistent with learning modality theory because this classroom will provide for the development and support of authentic self-esteem. Student success is the most effective source of student self-esteem. Too often, the activities planned for the development and support of student self-esteem are artificial, with little or no relationship to the content of the class. The self-esteem resulting from these "add-on" activities will usually last only for the duration of the activity. Teach to a student's learning strength and the positive feelings about education will last well beyond the moment. In addition to improved self-esteem developed through authentic learning success, the student should actually learn more in a classroom based on learning modalities. This is the most important outcome of the application of learning modalities in teaching. As teachers, we may actually be more successful, particularly with those students overlooked in the past because they did not learn as well in the dominant learning modality of our instruction.

Increased success in student learning, in addition to the boost any teacher would enjoy from this phenomenon, also carries the added bonus of better classroom management. That the successful, involved student is not a disruptive student is a universally held belief among experienced teachers. Ignore a student's learning strength and that student will be involved in activities other than those planned by the teacher. Students who experience success, and who come to expect to experience continued success, will likely be assets to the teacher and to the class.

Each of the theories regarding differentiated learning, or learning modalities, illustrates the basic concept that humans are different in many ways, including the way in which they most effectively learn. Many of our differences are superficial and easily identified; learning strengths are not as easily recognized. The interrelatedness of Edward's right brain–left brain theory, Gardner's seven intelligences, and Barbe's modality strengths all support a classroom that recognizes the differing learning strengths of the students. The successful teacher uses those learning differences to create a learning climate supportive of all students. The recognition of learning strengths will lead to a more successful student and a more successful teacher.

Professional Commentary

Media Literacy

Beyond Print: Media and Visual Literacy

by Dr. Harold M. Foster
Professor of English Education
The University of Akron
Akron, Ohio

The future is here and it is both an opportunity and a threat. The future offers unlimited information and entertainment. It offers an endless stream of choices and enticements. But it will take all your time if you let it.

The future is on your televisions and on your movie screens. Never before has television and film offered as many choices or technological advances. Every aspect of life may be affected by these media.

These media are neither good nor bad. They are powerful. Used with judgment and restraint, the media are an incredibly positive force. Used thoughtlessly and capriciously, the media can be dangerously manipulative. The key to productive engagement with the complex array of communication systems is education. And that is exactly the purpose of the *Beyond Print* feature of this text series. By engaging reflection and perception about the media, this section educates the young people who use this text.

These media are neither good nor bad. They are powerful.

Television

Television is the most pervasive of all the media. It is ubiquitous like central heating. Many televisions sets are on whenever anybody is home, whether someone is actively watching or not. Most of the time television is a low-engagement medium. Viewers watch it with the lights on. Much of the time television is what people use to fall asleep. Thus, the images and values of television seep into the lives of people without their complete awareness.

However, there are moments of great intensity on television like the finish of an excitingly close sports event or the reporting of a devastating hurricane. During the moments of intensity, television becomes a national cathedral—as when John F. Kennedy was assassinated—or a global village square where everyone goes to hear the news or to dwell on the most earth shattering events. Think about the power of a medium which can engage the attention of almost the entire world at the same time. The Olympics do that in some ways. The election of a president certainly has most of the U.S. mesmerized. The Tienanmen Square uprising and the collapse of the Berlin Wall captured the attention of much of the world. The few voices that bring people all this information are amazingly powerful.

Television is good news for those intelligent enough to form their own opinions, who can see through the endless stream of commercials and fantasy lifestyles television portrays. Television is good news for those who turn TV off and read. Television is good news for those people who see television as a tool to enhance their lives, but also realize that television is not life. These are the citizens who use television wisely and understand the medium and the role it plays.

But there is the other scenario. What about the people who have television on all the time, who watch it but seldom think about what they see? What about those that watch anything? How about people who seldom talk to their families, and never read, and hardly ever engage with people unless they have to? What about people who unwittingly take on the ethos of television: money is everything; how you look is who you are; problems are solved in an hour; sex is easy and without emotional consequences; if you don't get your way, hit or shoot the guy; buy, buy, buy; if you are bored, change the channel?

Are there viewers out there like this—viewers who see their own lives through the distorted prism of TV? Most people who study television think so; most members of our government think so; most responsible mothers, fathers, and guardians of children think so; even many of the people who bring us television think so.

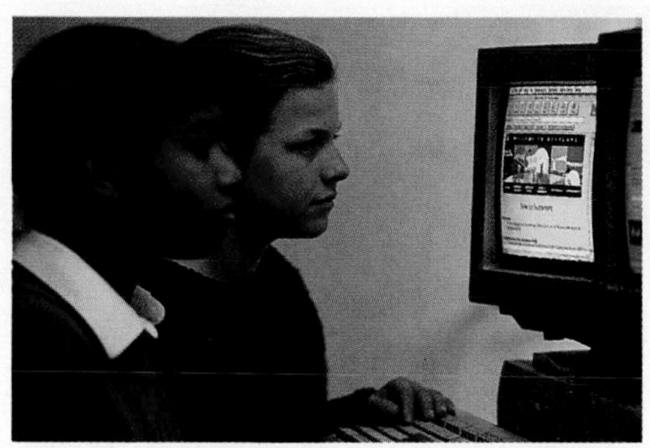

So in a free society what do you do about this? You educate and through education not only do you hope to eliminate the negative impact of television, you hope to help make television a wonderful part of the lives of young people. Television is a blessing. Let us use it wisely.

Movies

The *Beyond Print* feature in this anthology also concerns film. Film is different from television. It is a more intense medium. Film works by having light pass through a translucent celluloid cell and projecting a sharp image of the picture from the cell onto a screen. The sense of movement is created by flicking the cells past this bright, projected light at a rate of 24 pictures per second. This flicking creates an illusion of movement akin to the illusion found in children's toys where you flick cards or pages of a series of pictures and it appears that the objects are moving.

When you view a film these pictures on a screen have great emotional impact. Even though the technology is old, nothing yet comes close to the quality of a motion picture. A lighted room ruins the image so you watch films in the dark, eyes riveted to the screen. Your attention seldom wanders. Films are meant to be viewed without distraction, as if someone else was creating a dream for the viewer. These dreamlike qualities of movies make them potentially very powerful.

Most people love movies. They are a wonderful form of entertainment and escape, and truly great movies are so much more, a world-class art as lofty and sublime as any other art form. These qualities are why films need to be studied. The more a person knows about film, the more likely it is that the person will appreciate the best that film has to offer and will have critical viewing standards for all films.

Seeing, Speaking, and Listening

Beyond Print also deals with seeing, speaking, and listening—skills which are even more important now with modern communication technology. Both film and television require people to be perceptive about seeing. Film in particular can be like a moving painting where the more trained you are to see the better viewer you will be. *Beyond Print* broadens the scope of its young readers through activities which educate them to appreciate fine painting and photography.

Speaking and listening are ageless skills made even more important by a culture which rewards those who can move an audience. *Beyond Print* provides many opportunities to use oral skills to argue and persuade.

Perhaps even more important than speaking for a truly sensitive, caring culture are people with the ability to listen to each other. *Beyond Print* offers the opportunity to engage in active listening exercises. These exercises require careful and precise listening, a skill so often ignored in this society to its detriment.

Reading and Writing

Beyond Print provides student-friendly activities to promote reading and writing. All of the activities in *Beyond Print* come at the end of units or unit parts in the series. But, the ultimate goal of these texts is as it should be, to create good readers. Reading is still at the heart of society. Those who read well will write the television and movies which sadly keep so many others in the population barely literate. That is why so many of the *Beyond Print* activities involve reading and writing. Also, learning about the media creates more selective viewers who may have some time left over for reading. So *Beyond Print* not only promotes an understanding of the new literacies, but also promotes through that understanding a heightened awareness of the importance of reading and writing.

Goals

These are the educational goals of *Beyond Print*:

1. To transform students into discriminating TV and film viewers who can distinguish good from bad, exploitation from communication.
2. To sensitize students so they perceive how television and film are designed to influence and manipulate them.
3. To educate students to understand television and film visually and thematically so they can analyze and critique the media they watch.
4. To develop critical awareness so students will pass up at least the very worst of the electronic media and have time to read and study.
5. To develop in students an aesthetic appreciation for the finest the electronic media have to offer.
6. To educate students to see with perception and understanding all visual media including photography and painting.
7. To help students speak and listen with power and intelligence to prepare for a culture which rewards those who are effective public speakers and cherish those who listen with compassion and deep understanding to others.

(Adapted from Harold M. Foster's *Crossing Over: Whole Language for Secondary English Teachers*, Harcourt Brace, Fort Worth, Texas, 1994, p. 197.)

Professional Commentary

Visual Literacy

Art in the Literature Classroom

by Neil Anstead

Coordinator of the Humanitas Program

Cleveland Humanities Magnet School

Reseda, California

Students as visual learners

Many years ago when I started teaching literature, my goal was to hook kids with ideas. But it didn't take long for me to find out that many of my students didn't learn easily from words alone, and when they had to struggle with the language, they gave up before arriving at concepts. After a lot of struggle and failure, I started looking for other meaningful ways to supplement the use of words in order to gain understanding. My initial efforts were with music, lyrics, and even opera; these helped, but not enough. Next, I turned to the visual arts; the results were not a cure-all, but they were much better than before. In using art in the literature classroom, one can either begin with the literature or begin with the art.

Moving from the literature to the art

When studying *Macbeth*, I wanted my students to understand that individualism was a dominant force in the Renaissance, and that when carried to extreme, it could be very dangerous. Macbeth's career is a good example.

To introduce the concept of individualism, we first studied a well-known art work, Michelangelo's *Pietà*. If it had been sculpted in the Middle Ages, we might never have known the name of its creator. At that time, signing one's name to any creative effort was considered a sin of pride. God was the creator and the individual was simply his vehicle. But by the time of the Renaissance, artists were egotistical about their efforts, and when Michelangelo overheard his recently finished sculpture attributed to another artist, he boldly put his name across the Madonna's sash. He, not God, was the creator.

Next, we looked at the Florence Baptistery Doors, the so-called *Doors of Paradise*. Had they been made in the Middle Ages, artists would have worked cooperatively as they had on the great cathedrals. Not so in the Renaissance. The church held a competition for a single artist to create these magnificent portals. Students can identify with these concrete images of self-centeredness; indeed, it is one of the legacies of the Renaissance in their lives. These art works, together with others, became the background for the study of Shakespeare's *Macbeth*, and the experience proved helpful.

Another benefit of using art in conjunction with literature emerged as we worked together with images. It seemed to promote a holistic habit of mind. If *Macbeth*, the *Pietà*, and the *Doors of Paradise* reflect the spirit of individualism, and if individualism is a fundamental concept that pervades Renaissance culture, then we speculated that we would find this same characteristic elsewhere. And sure enough, we found it in Machiavelli, in the competition between city states, and in the development of mercantile capitalism.

Moving from the art to the literature

I started by saying that many of my students are finding it increasingly difficult to learn from words alone. At this point the reader might ask, "Then why not use art as a starting point and work toward literature?" My response is, "Indeed, why not?" Another example might prove instructive.

Although many of today's high school students were born after the Vietnam War, the war is still affecting their lives. Because it influenced all aspects of American society—economics, political philosophy, attitudes about war, the visual arts, film, literature, and more—it is best treated as an interdisciplinary topic. If starting with literary works proves difficult, try using the Vietnam War Memorial.

Students will be interested to know that Maya Lin designed the Memorial as a school project, and that even though it won in the design competition for a veterans' memorial, many politicians never dreamed it would be constructed. It was controversial from the very beginning. Memorials are normally imposing white marble monuments, not black granite walls sunk into the ground. Compare it to the Washington Monument that stands nearby. What does its color and location suggest? And why does it have a polished surface? When we see ourselves as we peruse the names of the dead, do we question our own part in the war? Was that the intent? And aren't the names on most war memorials arranged according to rank? On the Maya Lin memorial, they are listed according to date of death. Is it really an art work? and if so, are there any antecedents? Finally, why have two traditional monuments been added to it?

Experience has taught me that students will be engaged if there is controversy. Furthermore, I think they will identify with Maya Lin, a young Asian student who did her homework to the best of her ability, struggled, and eventually won out over powerful opponents.

> **Ours is a world in which literature is not confined to words on a page.**

A transitional activity might be to read some short first-person narratives of Vietnam soldiers. Such accounts have frequently become the raw material for good literature. The actual books or stories you end up using depend on many things, the reading ability of your students, the time allotted, and the availability of textbooks to mention a few.

Students probably learn as much from pictures as they do from the printed words. I wish I had a dollar for every student who told me that he or she learned more history by studying art history than from a history textbook. Lovers of words may feel uncomfortable with this, but I think it's true. Therefore, I encourage you to use the images that have been carefully selected for this book. They do more than beautify the pages, they provide a point of entry. And in the process, students might end up appreciating art, which is a bonus.

Guidelines in evaluating art

The following are a few points to consider when you evaluate art for possible use in the literature classroom:

- *Will the artwork engage your students?* Some works—Dali's *Persistence of Memory* is a good example—immediately intrigue kids; others can be made interesting through a teacher's scholarship and enthusiasm.
- *Are the interdisciplinary links between the artwork and the literature clear and natural?* If students can grasp these connections easily, it will enhance both their cultural understanding and enthusiasm for learning.
- *Does the artwork, in conjunction with literature, serve as a springboard for interesting writing assignments and other projects?* The full value of art in the classroom is not realized unless students work with it creatively—in writing, in discussion, and in a broad range of creative projects.
- *Is there good, accessible critical literature about this artwork?* Don't make your preparation more difficult by focusing on obscure works that will be difficult to research. Museum curatorial and education staffs can be useful resources.

Professional Commentary

Assessing Student Learning

The Dimensions of Assessment

by Alan C. Purves

Director of the Center for Writing and Literacy

State University of New York at Albany

Albany, New York

We all know that what is important in any class is what is on the test. Although we provide a lot of questions and assignments which could be considered "The Test," we think they should be used in another way, one that will help students become more mature, self-confident, and independent learners. That is why there is an assessment strand—one that is as important as the instructional strand.

You are surrounded by assessment. You are asked "How am I doing?" by students, "How is my child doing?" by parents or caretakers, "How are they doing?" by administrators at the building, district, state, and national level. You are told by administrators that there are local, state, or national examinations that your students must take; you are asked by parents to help their students prepare for college entrance or scholarship examinations, and you may even be asked to take teaching examinations yourself. How do you work through that maze of demands?

Many people think that tests are the same as assessment, but tests are only a small part of today's whole assessment activity. When students ask, "How am I doing?" they may not be satisfied with a test score. One student may want to know if something about what she's reading is worth anything to you and to the class. Another may want to know if his class participation is valued and how and for what. A third might be concerned with your rating of her capacity to work with others. A fourth may be concerned with his progress towards a goal. Students usually want to know how well they are doing as part of their on-going work; for them assessment is a part of learning. Assessment therefore should be an integral part of your teaching.

Teaching literature and the language arts encourages a great variety of activities, including individual and collaborative projects, reading logs, writing about literature and its relation to other subjects, working on computers, taking quizzes, taking part in classroom discussion, creating and participating in drama, working on art projects, and much more. This variety does not lend itself to a single test. All these facets of what it means to learn English and literature need to be thought of as part of the assessment of your students' work and of your class. A comprehensive assessment package needs to match a complex subject matter, and assessment has many audiences, many questions, and many things to attend to. The audiences include you as the teacher, other teachers, the students, parents, and the school and community.

Assessment is not just an examination at the end of the quarter or the year. It begins before the first day of class.

Course Objectives

Assessment is not just an examination at the end of the quarter or the year. It begins before the first day of class. You need to look at your syllabus, the anthology, and other materials you are using. Start by defining your course objectives:

- What do you want students to know at the end of the quarter or the end of the year?
- What do you want students to do that they couldn't do before taking this course? To put it another way, what skills do you want them to develop?

- What habits of reading and writing do you want them to acquire? Knowledge, practice, and habits are the core of any curriculum and plan of instruction. As you look at the materials, the selections, and the activities you are going to use, it helps to keep these questions in mind. What sorts of products will tell you whether the students have gained in their knowledge, their skills, and their habits? These will form the evidence for the assessment of their learning. The list of products can be large:

  final tests and examinations
  unit tests
  quizzes
  short papers
  on-going records
  reading logs
  tapes of discussions
  projects
  art works
  musical performances or compositions
  research papers
  computer programs
  dramatic presentations
  videotapes
  photographs
  out-of-class publications
  contest materials
  cross-subject papers or projects

Some of these may be individual student work, some may be collaborative projects with one or more partners, and some may be whole class projects. You should plan which of these you are going to require and which you are going to suggest.

Developing a Sense of Independence

One of the ways you can develop a sense of independence in students' learning involves giving students responsibility for their own work by setting broad goals for their learning and then inviting them to set their own specific goals. By setting and monitoring their own progress, students take command of their own learning. For some students a goal might be to read a novel by Toni Morrison; for another student it might be to finish a chapter of a book. Both are worthy goals; each is right for a particular student at a particular time.

By setting and monitoring their own progress, students take command of their own learning.

A second way to make students' learning more independent is to provide students with opportunities to do projects that are complex and involve bringing together a number of sources of information and a number of skills. Many of these projects may be group projects such as the creation of a diorama, the presentation of a play, a debate, a video production of a class interpretation, or the like.

We have found that central to the setting and reaching of goals in literature and writing is the portfolio. During the course of the year students

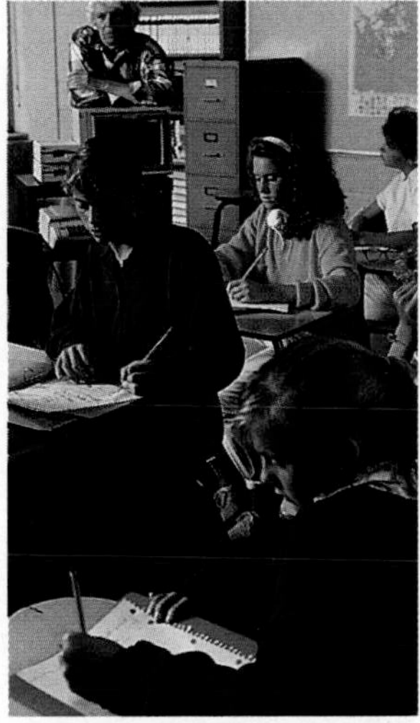

keep a working portfolio of their reading logs, their drafts and papers, their projects and tapes. As they go through this portfolio periodically they look for signs of their growth in the ways in which they have met or exceeded their goals. At the end of the year, they prepare a presentation portfolio, a formal presentation of themselves as readers and writers. This is an important testimony to the worth of each student's efforts. Accomplishing a successful portfolio is a sign that students have gained maturity as readers and writers.

Teachers in all sorts of classrooms report that students do better when they become partners in their assessment rather than simply taking assigned tests. When they know what is expected of them and how they are going to be judged, students become more responsible and serious about their work. If this approach works in the world of business, sports, and the professions, there is no reason why it can't work in school as well. After all, school and life should not be separated.

Program Skill Development

Scope and Sequence

Literature — Grades	6	7	8	9	10	11	12
Literature Appreciation							
Appreciate literary selections representing various genres	X	X	X	X	X	X	X
Understand characteristics of major literary genres	X	X	X	X	X	X	X
Recognize universal themes in literature	X	X	X	X	X	X	X
Recognize the relationship of literary structure and/or devices to meaning	X	X	X	X	X	X	X
Appreciate literature representing a variety of cultures and traditions	X	X	X	X			
Appreciate selections from world literature					X		
Appreciate selections from the American literary heritage						X	
Appreciate selections from the British literary heritage							X
Recognize topics characteristic of major writers of the period						X	X
Value literature from various periods in history	X	X	X	X	X	X	X
Understand that literature selections reflect a cultural context	X	X	X	X	X	X	X
Understand that literature selections reflect a social context	X	X	X	X	X	X	X
Understand that literature selections may reflect a political context						X	X
Choose to read independently	X	X	X				

Literature — Grades	6	7	8	9	10	11	12
Genres							
Biography/Autobiography	X	X	X	X	X	X	X
Drama/Play (including Comedy, Tragedy)	X	X	X	X	X	X	X
Essay	X	X	X	X	X	X	X
Expository nonfiction	X	X		X	X		
Fable	X	X	X	X	X	X	X
Folk tale	X	X	X	X	X	X	X
Historical document		X	X		X	X	X
Legend	X	X	X	X	X	X	X
Literary criticism							X
Genres cont.							
Myth	X	X	X	X	X	X	X
Narrative nonfiction	X	X	X	X	X		
Parable							X
Novel	X	X	X	X	X	X	X
Poetry (include lyric, narrative, ballad, epic)	X	X	X	X	X	X	X
Short Story	X	X	X	X	X	X	X

Literature — Grades	6	7	8	9	10	11	12
Literary Terms and Techniques							
Allegory							X
Alliteration	X	X	X	X	X	X	X
Allusion						X	X
Archetype							X
Characterization	X	X	X	X	X	X	X
Denotative and connotative language						X	X
Dialect	X	X	X	X	X	X	X
Dialogue	X	X	X	X	X	X	X
Diction	X	X	X	X	X	X	X
Figurative language	X	X	X	X	X	X	X
Flashback		X	X	X			
Foreshadowing			X	X	X	X	X
Hyperbole	X	X	X	X	X	X	X
Idiom	X	X	X	X	X	X	X
Imagery	X	X	X	X	X	X	X
Irony (dramatic; situational)		X	X	X	X	X	X
Metaphor	X	X	X	X	X	X	X
Meter				X	X	X	X
Mood	X	X	X	X	X	X	X
Multiple narration							X
Onomatopoeia	X	X	X	X	X	X	X
Personification	X	X	X	X	X	X	X
Plot	X	X	X	X	X	X	X

Literature

Literary Terms and Techniques cont.

	Grades 6	7	8	9	10	11	12
Point of view	X	X	X	X	X	X	X
Pun				X	X	X	X
Repetition	X	X	X	X	X	X	X
Rhythm	X	X	X	X	X	X	X
Rhyme	X	X	X	X	X	X	X
Satire						X	X
Setting	X	X	X	X	X	X	X
Simile	X	X	X	X	X	X	X
Sound devices	X	X	X	X	X	X	X
Stream of consciousness						X	X
Style	X	X	X	X	X	X	X
Symbolism	X	X	X	X	X	X	X
Theme	X	X	X	X	X	X	X
Tone	X	X	X	X	X	X	X

Writing

Use the Writing Process

	Grades 6	7	8	9	10	11	12
Prewrite							
Choose writing tools and/or equipment	X	X	X	X	X	X	X
Use technology	X	X	X	X	X	X	X
Choose topics of interest to self and others	X	X	X	X	X	X	X
Narrow topics	X	X	X	X	X	X	X
Set schedule and intermediate goals	X	X	X	X	X	X	X
Consider audience and purpose	X	X	X	X	X	X	X
Use sources such as personal experience and literature	X	X	X	X	X	X	X
Use strategies to generate ideas	X	X	X	X	X	X	X
Use aural and visual stimuli to generate ideas	X	X	X	X	X	X	X
Gather information and technical data	X	X	X	X	X	X	X
Organize ideas; outline	X	X	X	X	X	X	X

Writing

Use the Writing Process cont.

	Grades 6	7	8	9	10	11	12
Develop Draft							
Establish a thesis				X	X	X	X
Write supporting ideas	X	X	X	X	X	X	X
Include related paragraphs in longer papers				X	X	X	X
Provide examples, reasons, evidence	X	X	X	X	X	X	X
Provide incidents and anecdotes	X	X	X	X	X	X	X
Include information (facts, statistics) from variety of sources	X	X	X	X	X	X	X
Use sensory details	X	X	X	X	X	X	X
Use figurative language		X	X				
Use tone, point of view and style appropriate to topic and purpose	X	X	X				
Order ideas: time, importance, cause and effect, compare and contrast, spatial order	X	X	X	X	X	X	X
Use literary devices				X	X	X	X
Use introduction, middle, conclusion	X	X	X	X	X	X	X
Develop a personal voice/style				X	X	X	X
Revise							
Improve content by adding, deleting, reorganizing information	X	X	X	X	X	X	X
Alter mood, plot, characterization, or voice	X	X	X	X	X	X	X
Generalize from specific information	X	X	X	X	X	X	X
Analyze writing for reasoning				X	X	X	X
Examine word choice (vivid/specific nouns, active/concrete verbs)	X	X	X	X	X	X	X
Maintain consistent voice	X	X	X	X	X	X	X
Check appropriateness of formality/informality			X	X	X	X	X
Achieve precision in meaning				X	X	X	X
Choose vocabulary appropriate to intent	X	X	X	X	X	X	X
Combine sentences	X	X	X	X	X	X	X
Expand sentences	X	X	X	X	X	X	X

Scope and Sequence

Writing	Grades 6	7	8	9	10	11	12
Use the Writing Process cont.							
Improve sentences using parallel structure, details, a variety of sentence structures, and effective transitions	✗	✗	✗	✗	✗	✗	✗
Proofread/Edit							
Interact with peers in editing	✗	✗	✗	✗	✗	✗	✗
Use conferences in editing	✗	✗	✗				
Develop analytic criteria for responding				✗	✗	✗	✗
Check for legibility	✗	✗	✗	✗	✗	✗	✗
Edit for sentence fragments			✗				
Edit for run-on sentences			✗				
Use conventions of standard English	✗	✗	✗	✗	✗	✗	✗
Cite sources appropriately						✗	✗
Present							
Use visuals, graphics	✗	✗	✗	✗	✗	✗	✗
Produce oral discourse/composition	✗	✗	✗	✗	✗	✗	✗
Keep portfolio	✗	✗	✗	✗	✗	✗	✗
Share written discourse orally	✗	✗	✗	✗	✗	✗	✗
Write in a Variety of Modes							
Narrative	✗	✗	✗	✗	✗	✗	✗
Descriptive	✗	✗	✗	✗	✗	✗	✗
Expository/Informative	✗	✗	✗	✗	✗	✗	✗
Persuasive/Argumentative	✗	✗	✗	✗	✗	✗	✗
Personal Expression	✗	✗	✗	✗	✗	✗	✗
Expressive/Creative/Imaginative	✗	✗	✗	✗	✗	✗	✗
Use a Variety of Forms and Techniques							
Advertisement	✗	✗	✗	✗	✗	✗	✗
Analysis/speculation about effects (CA)	✗	✗	✗	✗	✗	✗	✗
Answers to essay questions					✗	✗	✗
Autobiographical incident (CA)	✗	✗	✗	✗	✗	✗	✗

Writing	Grades 6	7	8	9	10	11	12
Use a Variety of Forms and Techniques cont.							
Bibliography			✗	✗	✗	✗	✗
Biographical sketch	✗	✗	✗	✗	✗	✗	✗
Business letter	✗	✗	✗	✗	✗	✗	✗
Cause/effect	✗	✗	✗	✗	✗	✗	✗
Character sketch/description/study	✗	✗	✗	✗	✗	✗	✗
Cite information from primary and secondary sources				✗	✗	✗	✗
Clarification	✗	✗	✗	✗	✗	✗	✗
Comparison/contrast	✗	✗	✗	✗	✗	✗	✗
Controversial issue/position paper (CA)				✗	✗	✗	✗
Critique/review (book, play, movie, TV)	✗	✗	✗	✗	✗	✗	✗
Definition/explanation	✗	✗	✗	✗	✗	✗	✗
Develop criteria to evaluate research project							✗
Develop visuals for oral presentation	✗	✗	✗	✗	✗	✗	✗
Dialogue	✗	✗	✗	✗	✗	✗	✗
Diary/journal/ log entry	✗	✗	✗	✗	✗	✗	✗
Editorial/statement of opinion	✗	✗	✗	✗	✗	✗	✗
Essay	✗	✗	✗	✗	✗	✗	✗
Evaluation/evaluative writing (CA)	✗	✗	✗	✗	✗	✗	✗
Friendly letter; thank you notes; invitations	✗	✗	✗	✗	✗	✗	✗
I-Search paper	✗	✗	✗	✗	✗	✗	✗
Imaginative writing	✗	✗	✗	✗	✗	✗	✗
Interpretation (CA)	✗	✗	✗	✗	✗	✗	✗
Letter of application (job, college, scholarship)						✗	✗
Letter of complaint						✗	✗
Memoir	✗	✗	✗			✗	✗
News article;/feature story	✗	✗	✗				
Observational writing/reflection (CA)	✗	✗	✗	✗	✗	✗	✗
Personal narrative	✗	✗	✗	✗	✗	✗	✗
Poem	✗	✗	✗	✗	✗	✗	✗
Problem/solution	✗	✗	✗	✗	✗	✗	✗

Writing

Use a Variety of Forms and Techniques cont. — Grades	6	7	8	9	10	11	12
Proposal				X	X	X	X
Questionnaire; interview; survey	X	X	X	X	X	X	X
Reflective Essay (CA)	X	X	X	X	X	X	X
Report based on conclusions from direct observation	X	X	X	X	X	X	X
Research paper that interprets and/or theorizes							X
Research report/ report of information (CA)	X	X	X	X	X	X	X
Resumé							X
Science fiction/fantasy					X	X	
Script or play	X	X	X	X	X	X	
Speculation about causes and effects (CA)				X	X	X	X
Speech/oral presentation		X	X	X	X	X	X
Story (include myth, tall tale, fable, etc.)	X	X	X	X	X	X	X
Summary	X	X	X	X	X	X	X
Support or refute a formal proposition							X
Synthesize information from several sources	X	X	X	X	X	X	X
Technical report in nontechnical language							X
Use documentation for sources					X	X	X
Use technical and statistical data				X	X	X	X
Writing about literature	X	X	X	X	X	X	X

Grammar

Grammar, Usage, Mechanics, Spelling — Grades	6	7	8	9	10	11	12
Understand sentence structure (syntax)	X	X	X	X	X	X	X
Analyze grammatical structures						X	X
Recognize the functions of all the parts of speech in sentences		X	X	X	X	X	X
Understand the origins and development of the English language							X
Recognize sentence fragments	X	X	X	X	X	X	X

Grammar

Grammar, Usage, Mechanics, Spelling cont. — Grades	6	7	8	9	10	11	12
Recognize run-on sentences	X	X	X	X	X	X	X
Produce simple, compound, and complex sentences	X	X	X	X	X	X	X
Produce compound-complex sentences				X	X	X	X
Apply knowledge of subordinate and coordinate clauses					X	X	X
Use the parts of speech effectively in sentences	X	X	X	X	X	X	X
Use parallel construction				X	X	X	X
Use affixes to change a word from one part of speech to another					X	X	
Apply standard usage in writing							
Noun and pronoun forms	X	X	X	X	X	X	X
Singular and plural nouns	X	X	X	X	X	X	X
Possessive nouns	X	X	X	X	X	X	X
Indefinite pronouns	X	X	X	X	X	X	X
Pronoun-antecedent agreement	X	X	X	X	X	X	X
Subject-verb agreement	X	X	X	X	X	X	X
Verb forms	X	X	X	X	X	X	X
Consistent verb tense	X	X	X	X	X	X	X
Recognize colloquialisms, slang, idioms, and jargon				X	X	X	X
Recognize American dialects						X	
Apply conventions of standard written English in writing							
Capitalization	X	X	X	X	X	X	X
Quotation marks and dialogue	X	X	X	X	X	X	X
Sentence punctuation	X	X	X	X	X	X	X
Comma	X	X	X	X	X	X	X
Semicolon			X	X	X	X	X
Colon	X	X	X	X	X	X	X
Hyphen			X	X	X	X	X
Apostrophe	X	X	X	X	X	X	X
Paragraph indention	X	X	X	X	X	X	X

Scope and Sequence

Grammar	Grades 6	7	8	9	10	11	12
Grammar, Usage, Mechanics, Spelling cont.							
Word choice	X	X	X	X	X	X	X
Manuscript form	X	X	X	X	X	X	X
Apply the rules of spelling in writing	X	X	X	X	X	X	X
Avoid commonly misspelled words	X	X	X				
Adding endings	X	X	X				
Write legibly	X	X	X	X	X	X	X

Reading/Thinking	Grades 6	7	8	9	10	11	12
Strategies							
Use prereading strategies	X	X	X	X	X	X	X
Predict outcomes	X	X	X	X	X	X	X
Set purposes for reading	X	X	X	X	X	X	X
Use prior knowledge	X	X	X	X	X	X	X
Preview	X	X	X	X	X	X	X
Set intermediate goals for reading						X	X
Comprehend	X	X	X	X	X	X	X
Recall details and facts	X	X	X	X	X		
Order events	X	X	X	X			
Understand sequence	X	X	X	X	X	X	X
Recognize cause and effect	X	X	X	X	X	X	X
Classify	X	X	X	X	X	X	X
Compare and contrast	X	X	X	X	X	X	X
Make judgments	X	X	X	X	X	X	X
Recognize main idea, supporting details	X	X	X	X	X	X	X
Generalize; draw conclusions	X	X	X	X	X	X	X
Visualize	X	X	X				
Distinguish between fact and nonfact, opinion	X	X	X	X	X	X	X
Connect ideas/see relationships	X	X	X				

Reading/Thinking	Grades 6	7	8	9	10	11	12
Strategies cont.							
Respond critically to literature							
Question	X	X	X	X	X	X	X
Predict	X	X	X	X	X	X	X
Clarify (or Interpret)	X	X	X	X	X	X	X
Infer				X	X	X	X
Analyze				X	X	X	X
Evaluate	X	X	X	X	X	X	X
Connect	X	X	X	X	X	X	X
Summarize				X	X	X	X
Synthesize	X	X	X	X	X	X	X
Relate literature to personal experience	X	X	X	X	X	X	X
Relate literature to human concerns; recognize values	X	X	X	X	X	X	X
Respond creatively to literature in written, oral, dramatic, and graphic ways	X	X	X	X	X	X	X
Evaluate author's viewpoint; detect bias	X	X	X	X	X	X	X
Identify author's purpose	X	X	X	X	X	X	X
Identify author's qualification						X	X
Recognize the use of persuasion	X	X	X	X	X	X	X
Recognize propaganda	X	X	X	X	X	X	X
Recognize assumptions and implications						X	X
Use problem-solving techniques	X	X	X	X	X	X	X
Detect fallacies in reasoning						X	X
Understand that a literary selection may have more than one level of meaning					X	X	X
Adjust reading rate	X	X	X	X	X	X	X
Adapt reading strategies to different purposes (skim, scan)	X	X	X	X	X	X	X
Use fix-it strategies (reviewing, questioning)	X	X	X	X	X	X	X
Use self-questioning	X	X	X				
Apply reading strategies to content area material	X	X	X				
Apply the fundamentals of logic			X				

Speaking

Speaking, Listening, Media and Visual Literacy	6	7	8	9	10	11	12
Formal and informal situations							
Whole group discussion	X	X	X	X	X	X	X
Collaborative group discussion	X	X	X	X	X	X	X
Partner discussion	X	X	X				
Debate	X	X	X	X	X	X	X
Dramatization	X	X	X				
Speech/talk	X	X	X	X	X	X	X
Choral reading	X	X	X				
Interview	X	X	X	X	X	X	X
Interpretive reading	X	X	X	X	X	X	X
Readers theater	X						
Personal experience	X	X	X				
Parliamentary procedure	X	X	X				
Oral report	X	X	X	X	X	X	X
Use appropriate speaking behavior for a variety of purposes	X	X	X	X	X	X	X
To inform	X	X	X	X	X	X	X
To entertain	X	X	X	X	X	X	X
To persuade	X	X	X	X	X	X	X
To respond	X	X	X	X	X	X	X
To summarize	X	X	X	X	X	X	X
To give directions	X	X	X	X	X	X	X
To conduct a meeting	X	X	X	X	X	X	X
Social occasions	X	X	X	X	X	X	X
Use topic, vocabulary, tone, and style appropriate to audience, purpose, time, time limits, and place	X	X	X	X	X	X	X
Demonstrate poise and confidence	X	X	X	X	X	X	X
Communicate clearly and effectively							
Phrasing	X	X	X	X	X	X	X
Rate	X	X	X	X	X	X	X
Pitch, modulation, volume, inflection	X	X	X	X	X	X	X
Enunciation/pronunciation	X	X	X	X	X	X	X

Speaking

Speaking, Listening, Media and Visual Literacy cont.	6	7	8	9	10	11	12
Plan a speech/talk	X	X	X	X	X	X	X
Focus and limit topic	X	X	X	X	X	X	X
Gather and organize information	X	X	X	X	X	X	X
Outline	X	X	X	X	X	X	X
Draft the speech	X	X	X	X	X	X	X
Present a speech	X	X	X	X	X	X	X
Monitor audience reaction	X	X	X	X	X	X	X
Respond to audience questions	X	X	X	X	X	X	X
Be open to constructive criticism	X	X	X	X	X	X	X
Use multi-media or technology as appropriate	X	X	X	X	X	X	X
Understand nonverbal cues							
Eye contact	X	X	X	X	X	X	X
Gestures	X	X	X	X	X	X	X
Facial expression	X	X	X	X	X	X	X
Movement	X	X	X	X	X	X	X
Monitor audience reaction	X	X	X	X	X	X	X
Respond to audience questions	X	X	X	X	X	X	X
Use multimedia or technology as appropriate	X	X	X	X	X	X	X
Understand strategies used in discussion (contribute ideas; support contributions)	X	X	X	X	X	X	X

Listening

Formal and informal situations	6	7	8	9	10	11	12
Advertising/commercials			X	X	X	X	X
Discussion	X	X	X	X	X	X	X
Debate	X	X	X	X	X	X	X
Dramatization	X	X	X				
Speech/talk/oral report	X	X	X	X	X	X	X
News item	X	X	X	X	X	X	X
Interview	X	X	X	X	X	X	X
Interpretive (dramatic) reading	X	X	X	X	X	X	X

Scope and Sequence

Speaking	Grades 6	7	8	9	10	11	12
Listening cont.							
Listen for a variety of purposes, including information, entertainment, appreciation of literature and language, directions, understanding of cultural differences	X	X	X	X	X	X	X
Listening skills/responses/behaviors							
Realize purpose of speaker	X	X	X	X	X	X	X
Set purpose for listening	X	X	X				
Suspend judgment	X	X	X				
Detect transitional words	X						
Understand verbal and nonverbal cues	X	X	X				
Identify relevant information	X	X	X				
Take notes			X				
Focus attention				X	X	X	X
Identify patterns of organization	X	X	X			X	X
Recognize different speaking styles used for different purposes	X	X	X			X	X
Identify criteria for evaluating a speech	X	X	X	X	X	X	X
Identify a central theme or thesis			X			X	X
Monitor understanding	X	X	X	X	X	X	X
Detect bias and propaganda techniques	X	X	X	X	X	X	X
Recall/retell	X	X	X				
Elaborate	X	X	X				
Ask questions	X	X	X	X	X	X	X
Identify inferences	X	X	X	X	X	X	X
Analyze			X			X	X
Evaluate	X	X	X	X	X	X	X
Summarize/synthesize	X	X	X	X	X	X	X
Follow directions	X	X	X				
Write responsively	X	X	X				
Distinguish fact from opinion	X	X	X	X	X	X	X
Provide constructive criticism			X				
Respond to speakers in a variety of ways	X	X	X				
Express opinions	X	X	X	X	X	X	X

Speaking	Grades 6	7	8	9	10	11	12
Media and Visual Literacy							
Interact with non-print media (drama, film, TV, computers) for a variety of purposes	X	X	X	X	X	X	X
Use media for learning	X	X	X	X	X	X	X
Use technology and other media as a means of expression	X	X	X	X	X	X	X
Recognize different purposes of media							
Entertainment	X	X	X	X	X	X	X
Information	X	X	X	X	X	X	X
Communication	X	X	X	X	X	X	X
Compare and contrast print and non-print media	X	X	X	X	X	X	X
Respond critically to nonprint media (criticize, evaluate, analyze)	X	X	X	X	X	X	X
Recognize the effectiveness of nonverbal modes of communication	X	X	X	X	X	X	X
Recognize bias	X	X	X	X	X	X	X
Recognize propaganda	X	X	X	X	X	X	X
Distinguish between fact and opinion	X	X	X	X	X	X	X
Understand and evaluate impact of mass media					X		
Compare and contrast print and non-print media	X	X	X	X	X	X	X
Describe characteristics of the arts	X	X	X				
Identify processes and tools used to produce art	X	X	X				
Demonstrate skills in creating art	X	X	X				
Work with design, drawing, painting, printmaking, sculpture, and fiber arts		X	X				
Identify and appreciate significant works of art from major historical periods	X	X	X	X	X	X	X
Analyze how major works of art reflect societies, cultures, and civilizations	X	X	X	X	X	X	X
Draw conclusions about/evaluate art	X	X	X	X	X	X	X
Relate art to personal experience	X	X	X	X	X	X	X
Express experiences in visual form	X	X	X	X	X	X	X

Vocabulary

Vocabulary and Study Skills	6	7	8	9	10	11	12
Expand reading vocabulary	X	X	X	X	X	X	X
Use context clues for word meaning	X	X	X	X	X	X	X
Use dictionaries for word meaning	X	X	X	X	X	X	X
Use appropriate grade-level vocabulary	X	X	X	X	X	X	X
Read uncommon low-frequency words	X	X	X	X			
Recognize multimeaning words	X	X	X	X			
Expand vocabulary using structural analysis	X	X	X	X	X	X	X
Understand content area vocabulary	X	X	X	X	X	X	X
Recognize ambiguities and shades of meaning				X	X	X	
Understand antonyms, synonyms	X	X	X				
Understand homonyms	X	X	X				
Use etymologies/word origins		X	X	X	X	X	X
Understand connotations, denotations				X	X	X	X
Understand analogies					X	X	X
Recognize colloquialisms				X	X	X	X
Recognize idioms	X	X	X	X	X	X	X
Recognize dialect			X	X	X	X	X
Recognize root words	X	X	X				
Use affixes	X	X	X				
Recognize slang				X	X		
Recognize jargon				X	X		
Locate, use, and evaluate reference sources							
Almanac	X	X	X	X	X		
Bibliography	X	X	X	X	X	X	X
Card catalog; electronic retrieval system	X	X	X	X	X	X	X
Database	X	X	X	X	X	X	X
Dictionary/Glossary	X	X	X	X	X	X	X
Electronic Media	X	X	X	X	X	X	X
Encyclopedia	X	X	X	X	X	X	X
Handbook, style manual	X	X	X	X	X	X	X
Newspapers/periodicals	X	X	X	X			

Vocabulary

Vocabulary and Study Skills cont.	6	7	8	9	10	11	12
Reader's Guide	X	X	X	X			
Software	X	X	X	X	X	X	X
Telephone directory	X	X	X	X	X	X	X
Thesaurus	X	X	X	X	X	X	X
Interpret graphic sources	X	X	X	X	X	X	X
Charts/tables	X	X	X	X			
Graphs	X	X	X	X			
Schedules	X	X	X	X			
Diagrams	X	X		X			
Maps/atlases	X			X	X		
Apply reading strategies to content area reading	X	X	X	X	X	X	X
Create and use graphic organizers	X	X	X	X	X	X	X
Follow directions	X	X	X	X	X	X	X
Outline	X	X	X	X	X	X	X
Take notes	X	X	X	X	X	X	X
Use the parts of a book (footnotes, text features, appendices, etc.)	X	X	X	X	X	X	X
Use both primary and secondary sources			X			X	X
Use test taking stratiegies	X	X	X	X	X	X	X
Use text features	X						

Multicultural

Multicultural Awareness and Appreciation	6	7	8	9	10	11	12
Recognize, respect, and appreciate the similarities and differences in the literature and languages of diverse cultures	X	X	X	X	X	X	X
Learn about and appreciate the past and present contributions of diverse groups and individuals	X	X	X	X	X	X	X
Explore how people of diverse groups express similar values and goals	X	X	X	X	X	X	X
Respect, value, and appreciate diverse opinions	X	X	X	X	X	X	X

Scope and Sequence

Multicultural	Grades 6	7	8	9	10	11	12
Multicultural Awareness and Appreciation cont.							
Develop sensitivity to discriminatory practices	X	X	X	X	X	X	X
Develop positive self-image based on one's own culture	X	X	X	X	X	X	X
Develop cultural awareness to aid in solving conflicts in school and community	X	X	X	X	X	X	X

Habits	Grades 6	7	8	9	10	11	12
Habits and Attitude							
Integrate reading and writing into school, home, and leisure-time activities	X	X	X	X	X	X	X
Pursue ongoing personal reading and writing interests	X	X	X	X	X	X	X
Schedule reading and writing time	X	X	X				
Challenge self to expand reading and writing horizons	X	X	X	X	X	X	X
Read for enjoyment	X	X	X	X	X	X	X
Read to gather and clarify information	X	X	X	X	X	X	X
Read and write for purpose of discovery	X	X	X	X	X	X	X
Communicate with diverse audiences	X	X	X	X	X	X	X
Read in order to discover interrelationships of concepts/disciplines	X	X	X	X	X	X	X
Read and write to clarify personal thinking and understanding	X	X	X	X	X	X	X
Use reading and writing in decision-making and negotiating	X	X	X	X	X	X	X
Assess the suitability of materials	X	X	X	X	X	X	X
Work cooperatively with others toward a common goal	X	X	X	X	X	X	X
Work with others to discover meaning in literary selections	X	X	X	X	X	X	X
Work with others to develop and publish a piece of writing	X	X	X	X	X	X	X
Work cooperatively to solve problems	X	X	X	X	X	X	X

Life Skills	Grades 6	7	8	9	10	11	12
Life Skills							
Change	X	X	X	X	X	X	X
Self-image/awareness/acceptance	X	X	X	X	X	X	X
Communications (conflict resolution)	X	X	X	X	X	X	X
Personal management (planning, energy, stress, etc.)	X	X	X	X	X	X	X
Team management	X	X	X	X	X	X	X
Service	X	X	X	X	X	X	X
Life cycles	X	X	X	X	X	X	X
Consumer and Job-Related Skills							
Read product labels for information	X	X	X	X	X		
Find information in a warranty, policy, or contract	X	X	X	X	X	X	X
Job application	X	X	X	X	X	X	X
Multi-paragraph letter to apply for a job	X	X	X	X	X	X	X
Interviews	X	X	X	X	X	X	X
Resumé				X	X	X	X

Assessment Skills	Grades 6	7	8	9	10	11	12
Performance-based Assessment							
Student portfolios	X	X	X	X	X	X	X
Teacher observation	X	X	X	X	X	X	X
Peer assessment	X	X	X	X	X	X	X
Self-assessment	X	X	X	X	X	X	X
Integration of writing, literature, and comprehension	X	X	X	X	X	X	X
Activities	X	X	X	X	X	X	X

ScottForesman

LITERATURE

AND INTEGRATED STUDIES

Middle School: Grade Six

Middle School: Grade Seven

Middle School: Grade Eight

Forms in Literature

World Literature

American Literature

English Literature

The cover features a detail of William Holman Hunt's *The Afterglow in Egypt,* which appears in full on this page. He began this study of a peasant woman during a visit to Egypt in 1854, complaining of "the difficulty of getting the model day by day and the horrible trials of dust and wind." Hunt's title refers to the period after sunset in which a brilliant light sometimes lingers in the western sky. *Southampton City Art Gallery*

ScottForesman
LITERATURE
AND INTEGRATED STUDIES

World Literature

Senior Consultants

Alan C. Purves
State University of New York at Albany

Carol Booth Olson
University of California, Irvine

Carlos E. Cortés
University of California, Riverside (Emeritus)

ScottForesman

Editorial Offices: Glenview, Illinois
Regional Offices: San Jose, California • Tucker, Georgia • Glenview, Illinois • Oakland, New Jersey • Dallas, Texas

Visit ScottForesman's Home Page at http://www.scottforesman.com

Acknowledgments

Texts

6 "Through The Tunnel" from *The Habit of Loving* by Doris Lessing. Copyright © 1955 by Doris Lessing. Originally appeared in *The New Yorker.* Copyright renewed. Reprinted by permission of HarperCollins Publishers, Inc. and Jonathan Clowes Ltd.

19 "Two Kinds" from *The Joy Luck Club* by Amy Tan. Copyright © 1989 by Amy Tan. Reprinted by permission of G. P. Putnam's Sons.

30 "The Censors" by Luisa Valenzuela. Reprinted by permission of Rosario Santos Literary Agent.

36 "The Voter" by Chinua Achebe. Reprinted by permission of the author.

45 "The Other Wife" from *The Other Woman* by Colette, translated from the French by Margaret Crosland. Copyright © 1971, 1972 by Peter Owen, Ltd. Reprinted by permission of Simon & Schuster, Inc. and Peter Owen Ltd. Publishers.

52 From *Mozart: A Life* by Maynard Solomon. Copyright © 1995 by Maynard Solomon. Reprinted by permission of HarperCollins Publishers, Inc.

66 "The Monkey's Paw" from *The Lady of the Barge* by W. W. Jacobs. Reprinted by permission of The Society of Authors.

79 "The Demon Lover" from *Collected Stories* by Elizabeth Bowen. Copyright 1946 and renewed © 1974 by Elizabeth Bowen. Reprinted by permission of Alfred A. Knopf, Inc.

87 "An Astrologer's Day" from *Malagudi Days* by R. K. Narayan. Published by Viking Press. Copyright © R. K. Narayan. Reprinted by permission of the Wallace Literary Agency, Inc.

104 "The Rain Came" by Grace A. Ogot from *Land Without Thunder.* Reprinted by permission of East African Educational Publishers Ltd.

continued on page 852

ISBN: 0-673-29448-X

1.800.554.4411
http://www.scottforesman.com

1 2 3 4 5 6 7 8 9 10 DR 03 02 01 00 99 98 97 96

Senior Consultants

Alan C. Purves

Professor of Education and Humanities, State University of New York at Albany; Director of the Center for Writing and Literacy. Dr. Purves developed the concept and philosophy of the literature lessons for the series, consulted with editors, reviewed tables of contents and lesson manuscript, wrote the Assessment Handbooks, and oversaw the development and writing of the series testing strand.

Carol Booth Olson

Director, California Writing Project, Department of Education, University of California, Irvine. Dr. Olson conceptualized and developed the integrated writing strand of the program, consulted with editors, led a team of teachers in creating literature-based Writing Workshops, and reviewed final manuscript.

Carlos E. Cortés

Professor Emeritus, History, University of California, Riverside. Dr. Cortés designed and developed the multicultural strand embedded in each unit of the series and consulted with grade-level editors to implement the concepts.

Series Consultants

Visual and Media Literacy/Speaking and Listening/Critical Thinking

Harold M. Foster. Professor of English Education and Secondary Education, The University of Akron, Akron. Dr. Foster developed and wrote the Beyond Print features for all levels of the series.

ESL and LEP Strategies

James Cummins. Professor, Modern Language Centre and Curriculum Department, Ontario Institute for Studies in Education, Toronto.

Lily Wong Fillmore. Professor, Graduate School of Education, University of California at Berkeley.

Drs. Cummins and Fillmore advised on the needs of ESL and LEP students, helped develop the Building English Proficiency model for the program, and reviewed strategies and manuscript for this strand of the program.

Fine Arts/Humanities

Neil Anstead. Coordinator of the Humanitas Program, Cleveland Humanities Magnet School, Reseda California. Mr. Anstead consulted on the fine art used in the program.

Reviewers and Contributors

Pupil and Teacher Edition

Jay Amberg, Glenbrook South High School, Glenview, Illinois **Edison Barber,** St. Anne Community High School, St. Anne, Illinois **Lois Barliant,** Albert G. Lane Technical High School, Chicago, Illinois **James Beasley,** Plant City Senior High School, Plant City, Florida **Linda Belpedio,** Oak Park/River Forest High School, Oak Park, Illinois **Richard Bruns,** Burges High School, El Paso, Texas **Kay Parks Bushman,** Ottawa High School, Ottawa, Kansas **Jesús Cardona,** John F. Kennedy High School, San Antonio, Texas **Marlene Carter,** Dorsey High School, Los Angeles, California **Patrick Cates,** Lubbock High School, Lubbock, Texas **Timothy Dohrer,** New Trier Township High School, Winnetka, Illinois **Margaret Doria,** Our Lady of Perpetual Help High School, Brooklyn, New York **Lucila Dypiangco,** Bell Senior High School, Bell, California **Judith Edminster,** Plant City High School, Plant City, Florida **Mary Alice Fite,** Columbus School for Girls, Columbus, Ohio **Montserrat Fontes,** Marshall High School, Los Angeles, California **Diane Fragos,** Turkey Creek Middle School, Plant City, Florida **Joan Greenwood,** Thornton Township High School, Harvey, Illinois **William Irvin,** Pittsfield Public Schools, Pittsfield, Massachusetts **Carleton Jordan,** Montclair High School, Montclair, New Jersey **Mark Kautz,** Chapel Hill High School, Chapel Hill, North Carolina **Elaine Kay,** Bartow High School, Bartow, Florida **Roslyn Kettering,** West Lafayette Junior/Senior High School, West Lafayette, Indiana **Kristina Kostopoulos,** Lincoln Park High School, Chicago, Illinois **Julia Lloyd,** Harwood Junior High School, Bedford, Texas **John Lord,** Ocean Township High School, Oakhurst, New Jersey **Dolores Mathews,** Bloomingdale High School, Valrico, Florida **Jim McCallum,** Milford High School, Milford, Massachusetts **Monette Mehalko,** Plant City Senior High School, Plant City, Florida **Lucia Podraza,** DuSable High School, Chicago, Illinois **Frank Pool,** Anderson High School, Austin, Texas **Alice Price,** Latin School, Chicago, Illinois **Anna J. Roseboro,** The Bishop's School, La Jolla, California **Peter Sebastian,** Granite Hills High School, El Cajon, California **Rob Slater,** East Forsyth High School, Winston Salem, North Carolina **Catherine Small,** Nicolet High School, Glendale, Wisconsin **Dennis Symkowiak,** Mundelein High School, Mundelein, Illinois **Rosetta Tetteh,** Senn High School, Chicago, Illinois **Pamela Vetters,** Harlandale High School, San Antonio, Texas **Polly Walwark,** Oak Park High School, Oak Park, Illinois **Karen Wrobleski,** San Diego High School, San Diego, California **Dru Zimmerman,** Chapel Hill High School, Chapel Hill, North Carolina

Multicultural Review Board

Duane BigEagle, writer and teacher, Tomales, California **Maria Campanario,** Raphael Hernandez School, Stoughton, Massachusetts **Pat Canty,** Beverly Woods Middle School, Charlotte, North Carolina **Jesús Cardona,** John F. Kennedy High School, San Antonio, Texas **Diego Davalos,** Chula Vista High School, Chula Vista, California **Sandra Dickerson,** Milwaukee Public Schools, Milwaukee, Wisconsin **Lucila Dypiangco,** Bell Senior High School, Bell, California **Marion Fleming,** Roselle Junior/Senior High School, Roselle, New York **Gloria Garcia,** Madero Middle School, Chicago, Illinois **Thelma Hernandez,** Edison Junior High School, San Antonio, Texas **Yvonne Hutchinson,** Markham Intermediate School, Los Angeles, California **Narva Jackson,** Roselle Junior/Senior High School, Roselle, New York **May Lee,** Baldwin Senior High School, Baldwin, New York **Dolores Mathews,** Bloomingdale High School, Valrico, Florida **Jack Matsumoto,** Edison Regional Gifted Center, Chicago, Illinois **James Masao Mitsui,** Hazen High School, Renton, Washington **Ed Ramirez,** Wang School, Derry, New Hampshire **Harolene Steele,** Hill Middle School, Winston-Salem, North Carolina **Suthinee Suktrakul,** North Cross High School, North Cross, Georgia **Jerry Tagami,** New Harbor High School, Newport Beach, California **Barbara Wheeler,** Harford County Public Schools, Bel Air, Maryland **Raymond Zamarippa,** Bowie Junior High School, Irving, Texas

English Language Development (ESL/LEP)

Kate Alvidrez, Newton High School, Newton, Iowa **Judy Bebelaar,** International Studies Academy, San Francisco, California **Rebecca Benjamin,** University of New Mexico, Albuquerque, New Mexico **Ioana Cummins,** Toronto, Ontario **Nancy Duke S. Lay,** City College of New York, New York, New York **Doti Foster,** Lubbock Independent School District, Lubbock, Texas **Bridget Hawthorne,** Oliver Hazard Perry Middle School, Providence, Rhode Island **Sandra Huezo,** Gompers Secondary School, San Diego, California **Nancy Hykel,** Harlandale High School, San Antonio, Texas **Mary Ann Jentel,** Madonna High School for Girls, Chicago, Illinois **Jose Lebron,** Julia De Burgos Middle School, Philadelphia, Pennsylvania **Mary Linnstaedter,** Nimitz High School, Houston, Texas **Mayra Menendez,** School Board of Broward County, Fort Lauderdale, Florida **Sharese Tisby,** Waukegan High School, Waukegan, Illinois **Sylvia Velazquez,** Braddock Senior High School, Miami, Florida **Greta Vollmer,** International Studies Academy, San Francisco, California **Shirley Wright,** Longview Independent School District, Longview, Texas **Suzanne Zweig,** Norwood Park School, Chicago, Illinois

Writer's Workshop Prompt Writers

Bill Burns, Sonora High School, LaHabra, California **Patricia Clark,** Century High School, Santa Ana, California **Glenn Patchell,** Irvine High School, Irvine, California **Maureen Rippee,** Woodrow Wilson High School, Long Beach, California **Julie Simpson,** Sunny Hills High School, Fullerton, California

Student Model Writers

Julia Besterfeldt Susan Biebel Chelsea Brown Lisa Cason Elizabeth Ratliff Sheila Chalegua Brandi Cleaver Christian DeVos Lynn DeWitt William Eckmann Maggie Gorecki David Hardy Melanie Jetter Louis Kholodovsky Charly Kittay Michael J Kurcz Samantha Anne La'o Courtney Ann Lambke William McKelphin Karen Miramontes Hollie Nygaard Chinyera Osuji Adam Peterson Elizabeth Ratliff Jeremy A. Redburn Kimyona Roberts Brendon Rose Morgan Russell-Dempsey Rebecca Ryan Mark Sarna Melissa Villalon C. M. Wiggins

Student Active Reading Panel

Nina Grigsby Isaac Saposnik Mika Uehara

Contents

vii

▶ EXPLORING A THEME THROUGH SEVERAL GENRES

Part Three: Dealing with Consequences

viii

Unit 2 Making Judgments

Part One: On Trial

▶ EXPLORING A THEME THROUGH SEVERAL GENRES

Part Two: Beneath the Surface

x

Unit 3 Answering the Call

Part One: Arthurian Legends

▶ EXPLORING A THEME THROUGH SEVERAL GENRES

Part Two: Many Kinds of Heroes

Unit 4 What Really Matters?

xiii

▶ EXPLORING A THEME THROUGH SEVERAL GENRES

Part Two: Something of Value

xiv

Unit 5 A Place in the World

xv

Part Two: Reflections

xvi

▶ EXPLORING A THEME THROUGH SEVERAL GENRES

Part Three: Culture Crossroads

xvii

Unit 6 Power Plays

xviii

Glossaries, Handbooks, and Indexes

Genre Overview

Short Stories

Poetry

xix

Plays

Nonfiction

Legends

Feature Overview

Genre Overviews

Interdisciplinary Studies

Reading Mini-Lessons

Writing Workshops

Beyond Print

xxi

Before Reading

MODEL FOR ACTIVE READING

Introduce

Introduce students to the active readers identified on the page. You may want to point out the icons that are associated with each reader so that students will be able to follow their comments as they read.

Model for Active Reading

Good readers read actively. They become involved in what they read, relating the characters and situations to people and events in their own lives. They question, clarify, predict, and in other ways think about the story or article they are reading. These three students agreed to let us in on their thoughts as they read "The False Gems." You might have different ideas and questions than they did about this story. However, their ways of responding will give you ideas for how you can get actively engaged as you read literature.

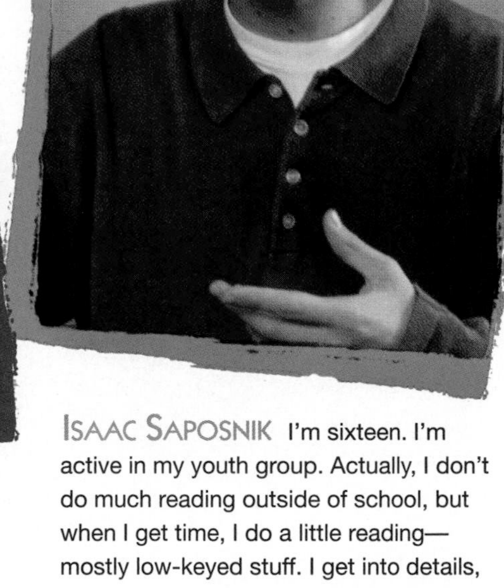

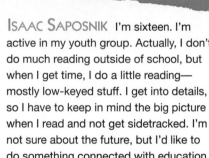

NINA GRIGSBY Well, I'm sixteen. I like ballet, singing—I sing in the choir, CDs. I read a lot, sometimes two books a week. The books I really like are romances. I guess you could say I read two ways: kind of casually for the romances; more deliberately for school stuff that I know I'll be tested on. I want to be a writer.

ISAAC SAPOSNIK I'm sixteen. I'm active in my youth group. Actually, I don't do much reading outside of school, but when I get time, I do a little reading—mostly low-keyed stuff. I get into details, so I have to keep in mind the big picture when I read and not get sidetracked. I'm not sure about the future, but I'd like to do something connected with education.

MIKA UEHARA Well, I'm into sports. I'm captain of the girls volleyball team. What else? I like to hang out and talk lots on the phone. Like Isaac, I don't read that much, but I do like magazines. I'd like to be a psychologist or something in the medical field.

Six Reading Strategies

Following are some of the techniques that good readers use, often without being aware of them.

Question Ask questions that arise as you read.

Example: Is Madame Lantin happy with her life? Would she be so dependent on others for her support if she lived today?

Clarify Clear up confusion and answer questions.

Example: Oh, I see what's going on. M. Lantin wasn't suspicious because he thought the gems were false.

Summarize Review what has happened so far.

Example: The Lantins seemed to have had a happy married life. After she dies, he doesn't wait long to remarry, but this time he chooses a very different woman.

Predict Use what has happened so far to make reasonable guesses about what might happen next.

Example: M. Lantin doesn't seem like the kind of person who spends money wisely. I bet he uses up his fortune quickly.

Evaluate Use your common sense and evidence in the selection to arrive at sound opinions and valid conclusions.

Example: Madame Lantin, who wanted both marital security and wealth, worked out a clever scheme to have it both ways.

Connect Compare the text with something in your own experience, with another text, or with ideas within the text.

Example: Based on stories I've read and movies or TV programs I've seen, I'd say that instant wealth usually makes people unhappy.

Six Reading Terms Explained

Review with students the techniques used by good readers. Ask them to demonstrate examples of *question, predict, clarify, summarize, evaluate,* and *connect.*

During Reading

THE FALSE GEMS

Option 1

Read the story aloud in class, asking volunteers to play the role of the readers by reading their comments. Other students may want to make their own comments as the reading proceeds.

Option 2

Assign students to read the story silently in class or for homework. Suggest that they write down their own questions and comments as they read, in preparation for a class discussion of the story.

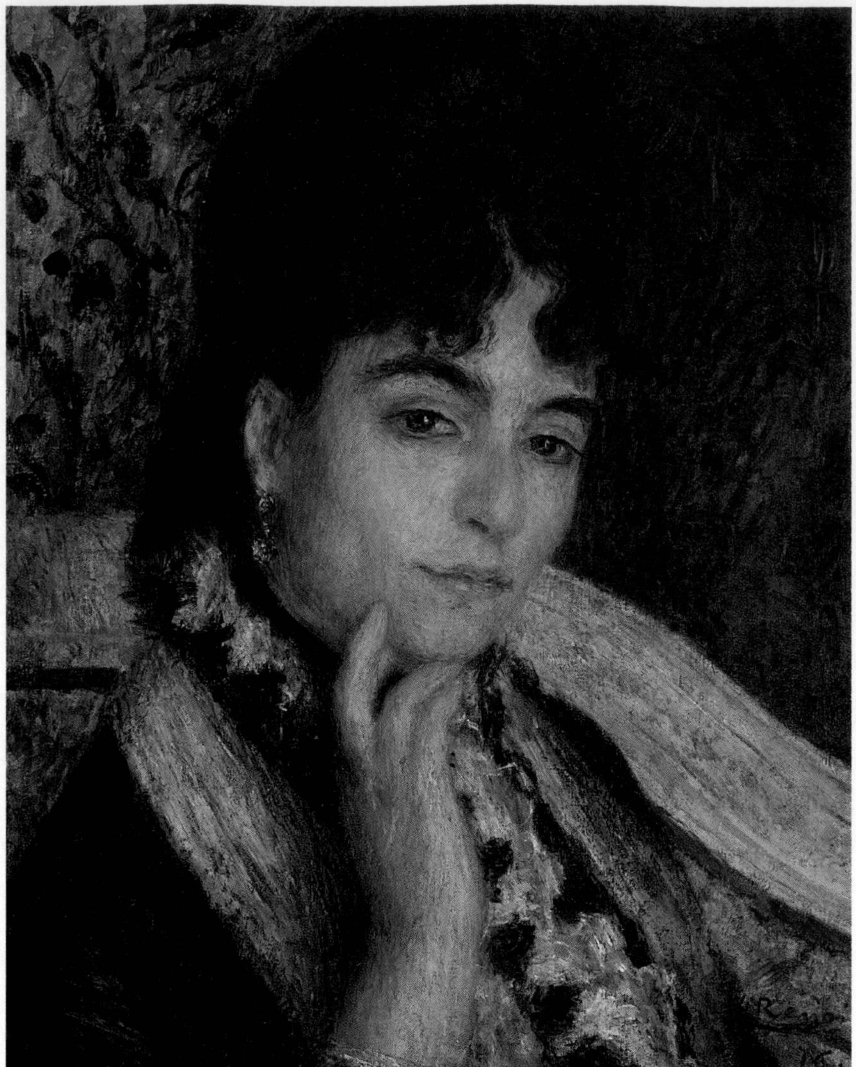

The False Gems

GUY DE MAUPASSANT

M. Lantin had met the young woman at a *soirée,* at the home of the assistant chief of his bureau, and at first sight had fallen madly in love with her.

She was the daughter of a country physician who had died some months previously. She had come to live in Paris, with her mother, who visited much among her acquaintances, in the hope of making a favorable marriage for her daughter. They were poor and honest, quiet and unaffected.

The young girl was a perfect type of the virtuous woman whom every sensible young man dreams of one day winning for life. Her simple beauty had the charm of angelic modesty, and the imperceptible smile which constantly hovered about her lips seemed to be the reflection of a pure and lovely soul. Her praises resounded on every side. People never tired of saying: "Happy the man who wins her love! He could not find a better wife."

Now M. Lantin enjoyed a snug little income of $700, and, thinking he could safely assume the responsibilities of matrimony, proposed to this model young girl and was accepted.

He was unspeakably happy with her; she governed his household so cleverly and economically that they seemed to live in luxury. She lavished the most delicate attentions on her husband, coaxed and fondled him, and the charm of her presence was so great that six years after their marriage M. Lantin discovered that he loved his wife even more than during the first days of their honeymoon.

He only felt inclined to blame her for two things: her love of the theater, and a taste for false jewelry. Her friends (she was acquainted with some officers' wives) frequently procured for her a box at the theater, often for the first representations of the new plays; and her husband was obliged to accompany her, whether he willed or not, to these amusements, though they bored him excessively after a day's labor at the office.

After a time, M. Lantin begged his wife to get some lady of her acquaintance to accompany her. She was at first opposed to such an arrangement; but, after much persuasion on his part, she finally consented—to the infinite delight of her husband.

Now, with her love for the theater came also the desire to adorn her person. True, her costumes remained as before, simple, and in the most correct taste; but she soon began to ornament her ears with huge rhinestones which glittered and sparkled like real diamonds. Around her neck she wore strings of false pearls, and on her arms bracelets of imitation gold.

◄ *Madame Alphonse Daudet* by Pierre Auguste Renoir (1841–1919) illustrates the artist's interest in the human figure and in rich colors and glowing light. Do you think an oil portrait like this can reveal as much about a person as a photograph would?

MIKA I remember this author from French class. (connect)

ISAAC De Maupassant has a thing about gems. In "The Necklace," the gems were false, but she thought they were real. (connect)

MIKA Interesting contrasts: She's rich in beauty and charm, and poor financially. (evaluate)

NINA I noticed adjectives like *honest, quiet, unaffected, perfect, angelic, pure, lovely.* Is she too good to be true? (question)

NINA There's a change of tone here. Maybe things aren't so perfect. (evaluate)

ISAAC *false jewelry*—It seems odd that such a pure and simple woman would be so fond of fake jewels. (evaluate)

ISAAC *infinite*—This is a strange word here. I wonder why he uses it. (question)

ISAAC *false pearls, imitation gold*—It makes them sound tacky. (evaluate)

XXV

Her husband frequently remonstrated with her, saying:

"My dear, as you cannot afford to buy real diamonds, you ought to appear adorned with your beauty and modesty alone, which are the rarest ornaments of your sex."

But she would smile sweetly, and say:

"What can I do? I am so fond of jewelry. It is my only weakness. We cannot change our natures."

Then she would roll the pearl necklaces around her fingers, and hold up the bright gems for her husband's admiration, gently coaxing him:

"Look! are they not lovely? One would swear they were real."

M. Lantin would then answer, smilingly:

"You have Bohemian tastes, my dear."

Often of an evening, when they were enjoying a tête-à-tête by the fireside, she would place on the tea table the leather box containing the "trash," as M. Lantin called it. She would examine the false gems with a passionate attention as though they were in some way connected with a deep and secret joy, and she often insisted on passing a necklace around her husband's neck, and laughing heartily would exclaim: "How droll you look!" Then she would throw herself into his arms and kiss him affectionately.

One evening in the winter she attended the opera, and on her return was chilled through and through. The next morning she coughed, and eight days later she died of inflammation of the lungs.

M. Lantin's despair was so great that his hair became white in one month. He wept unceasingly; his heart was torn with grief, and his mind was haunted by the remembrance, the smile, the voice—by every charm of his beautiful, dead wife.

Time, the healer, did not assuage his grief. Often during office hours, while his colleagues were discussing the topics of the day, his eyes would suddenly fill with tears, and he would give vent to his grief in heartrending sobs. Everything in his wife's room remained as before her decease; and here he was wont to seclude himself daily and think of her who had been his treasure—the joy of his existence.

But life soon became a struggle. His income, which in the hands of his wife had covered all household expenses, was now no longer sufficient for his own immediate wants; and he wondered how she could have managed to buy such excellent wines, and such rare delicacies, things which he could no longer procure with his modest resources.

He incurred some debts and was soon reduced to absolute

ISAAC *remonstrated*—I'm not sure about meaning. Oh, judging from what follows, it must mean "disagreed." (clarify)

ISAAC "It is my only weakness." We've been told that she's modest, but this doesn't sound very modest. (evaluate)

MIKA The "deep and secret joy" seems to foreshadow something. I wonder why these false gems mean so much to her? (question)

NINA This seems so sudden and unexpected. Only one paragraph on her death makes it sound unimportant. (evaluate)

NINA The words *torn, haunted, heartrending* seem so dramatic. So does his white hair. (evaluate)

NINA *Assuage* must mean "heal." (clarify)

MIKA I agree that time is a healer. (connect)

NINA The word *treasure* here is interesting. It suggests that she was like a gem. Gems were her treasure; she was his treasure. (connect)

MIKA Life does become a struggle when you lose a loved one. (connect)

poverty. One morning, finding himself without a cent in his pocket, he resolved to sell something, and, immediately, the thought occurred to him of disposing of his wife's paste jewels. He cherished in his heart a sort of rancor against the false gems. They had always irritated him in the past, and the very sight of them spoiled somewhat the memory of his lost darling.

To the last days of her life, she had continued to make purchases, bringing home new gems almost every evening. He decided to sell the heavy necklace which she seemed to prefer, and which, he thought, ought to be worth about six or seven francs; for although paste it was, nevertheless, of very fine workmanship.

He put it in his pocket and started out in search of a jeweler's shop. He entered the first one he saw, feeling a little ashamed to expose his misery, and also to offer such a worthless article for sale.

"Sir," said he to the merchant, "I would like to know what this is worth."

The man took the necklace, examined it, called his clerk and made some remarks in an undertone; then he put the ornament back on the counter, and looked at it from a distance to judge of the effect.

M. Lantin was annoyed by all this detail and was on the point of saying: "Oh! I know well enough it is not worth anything," when the jeweler said: "Sir, that necklace is worth from twelve to fifteen thousand francs; but I could not buy it unless you tell me now whence it comes."

The widower opened his eyes wide and remained gaping, not comprehending the merchant's meaning. Finally he stammered: "You say—are you sure?" The other replied dryly: "You can search elsewhere and see if anyone will offer you more. I consider it worth fifteen thousand at the most. Come back here if you cannot do better."

M. Lantin, beside himself with astonishment, took up the necklace and left the store. He wished time for reflection.

Once outside, he felt inclined to laugh, and said to himself: "The fool! Had I only taken him at his word! That jeweler cannot distinguish real diamonds from paste."

A few minutes after, he entered another store in the Rue de la Paix. As soon as the proprietor glanced at the necklace, he cried out:

"Ah, *parbleu!* I know it well; it was bought here."

M. Lantin was disturbed, and asked:

"How much is it worth?"

ISAAC *paste jewels*—This sounds like an arts and crafts project (evaluate)

ISAAC *Rue de la Paix*—Street of Peace. I wonder if this name is significant. Will he find peace of mind? (question)

"Well, I sold it for twenty thousand francs. I am willing to take it back for eighteen thousand when you inform me, according to our legal formality, how it came to be in your possession."

This time M. Lantin was dumbfounded. He replied:

"But—but—examine it well. Until this moment I was under the impression that it was paste."

Said the jeweler:

"What is your name, sir?"

"Lantin—I am in the employ of the Minister of the Interior. I live at No. 16 Rue des Martyrs."

The merchant looked through his books, found the entry, and said: "That necklace was sent to Mme. Lantin's address, 16 Rue des Martyrs, July 20, 1876."

The two men looked into each other's eyes—the widower speechless with astonishment, the jeweler scenting a thief. The latter broke the silence by saying:

"Will you leave this necklace here for twenty-four hours? I will give you a receipt."

"Certainly," answered M. Lantin, hastily. Then, putting the ticket in his pocket, he left the store.

He wandered aimlessly through the streets, his mind in a state of dreadful confusion. He tried to reason, to understand. His wife could not afford to purchase such a costly ornament. Certainly not. But, then, it must have been a present!—a present!—a present from whom? Why was it given her?

He stopped and remained standing in the middle of the street. A horrible doubt entered his mind—she? Then all the other gems must have been presents, too! The earth seemed to tremble beneath him—the tree before him was falling—throwing up his arms, he fell to the ground, unconscious. He recovered his senses in a pharmacy into which the passers-by had taken him, and was then taken to his home. When he arrived he shut himself up in his room and wept until nightfall. Finally, overcome with fatigue, he threw himself on the bed, where he passed an uneasy, restless night.

The following morning he arose and prepared to go to the office. It was hard to work after such a shock. He sent a letter to his employer requesting to be excused. Then he remembered that he had to return to the jeweler's. He did not like the idea; but he could not leave the necklace with that man. So he dressed and went out.

It was a lovely day; a clear blue sky smiled on the busy city below, and men of leisure were strolling about with their hands in their pockets.

Observing them, M. Lantin said to himself: "The rich, indeed, are happy. With money it is possible to forget even the deepest

ISAAC Why is it so important where the jewels have come from? Could the jeweler have made a mistake about their worth? (question). Or maybe he thinks this guy's a thief.

NINA *Rue des Martyrs* is a street mentioned in "The Necklace." (connect)

ISAAC I wonder if the word *Martyrs* is significant. Is someone being offered up? (connect)

MIKA How did she get the gems? from whom? (question) Everything flashes before his eyes. He is having a moment of revelation. He's very upset. (summarize)

ISAAC "The earth seemed to tremble beneath him"—Something awful occurs to him. Could she have been having an affair? (question)

ISAAC *lovely, smiled, leisure, strolling*—This sure seems like an entirely different mood. (evaluate)

NINA M. Lantin's observation here is ironic. I don't think that he'll be happy if he's rich. (predict)

sorrow. One can go where one pleases, and in travel find that distraction which is the surest cure for grief. Oh! if I were only rich!"

He began to feel hungry, but his pocket was empty. He again remembered the necklace. Eighteen thousand francs! Eighteen thousand francs! What a sum!

He soon arrived in the Rue de la Paix, opposite the jeweler's. Eighteen thousand francs! Twenty times he resolved to go in, but shame kept him back. He was hungry, however—very hungry, and had not a cent in his pocket. He decided quickly, ran across the street in order not to have time for reflection, and entered the store.

The proprietor immediately came forward and politely offered him a chair; the clerks glanced at him knowingly.

"I have made inquiries, M. Lantin," said the jeweler, "and if you are still resolved to dispose of the gems, I am ready to pay you the price I offered."

"Certainly, sir" stammered M. Lantin.

Whereupon the proprietor took from a drawer eighteen large bills, counted and handed them to M. Lantin, who signed a receipt and with a trembling hand put the money into his pocket.

As he was about to leave the store, he turned toward the merchant, who still wore the same knowing smile, and lowering his eyes, said:

"I have—I have other gems which I have received from the same source. Will you buy them also?"

The merchant bowed: "Certainly, sir."

M. Lantin said gravely: "I will bring them to you." An hour later he returned with the gems.

The large diamond earrings were worth twenty thousand francs; the bracelets thirty-five thousand; the rings, sixteen thousand; a set of emeralds and sapphires, fourteen thousand; a gold chain with solitaire pendant, forty thousand—making the sum of one hundred and forty-three thousand francs.

The jeweler remarked, jokingly:

"There was a person who invested all her earnings in precious stones."

M. Lantin replied, seriously:

"It is only another way of investing one's money."

That day he lunched at Voisin's and drank wine worth twenty francs a bottle. Then he hired a carriage and made a tour of the Bois, and as he scanned the various turn-outs with a contemptuous air he could hardly refrain from crying out to the occupants:

"I, too am rich!—I am worth two hundred thousand francs."

MIKA I think that getting rid of these gems would mean the loss of his memories of past happiness with Madame Lantin. (evaluate)

MIKA He reacts to money like most people do. I remember his wife's observation. "We cannot change our natures." (connect)

NINA I'll bet they look at him *knowingly* because they know that his wife was cheating on him. (clarify)

ISAAC He's going to be rich. I bet he'll end up spending all the money. (predict)

NINA Now that we know the gems are real, they're described in a more dignified way—as "large diamond earrings," "a set of emeralds and sapphires," "a gold chain with solitaire pendant." When they were false they sounded gaudy: *huge rhinestones, false, imitation, worthless, paste, glittered.* (evaluate)

MIKA He's already assuming the "contemptuous" air of a rich person. He'll probably become a snob. (predict)

Suddenly he thought of his employer. He drove up to the office, and entered gaily, saying:

"Sir, I have come to resign my position. I have just inherited three hundred thousand francs."

He shook hands with his former colleagues and confided to them some of his projects for the future; then he went off to dine at the Café Anglais.

He seated himself beside a gentleman of aristocratic bearing, and during the meal informed the latter confidentially that he had just inherited a fortune of four hundred thousand francs.

For the first time in his life he was not bored at the theater, and spent the remainder of the night in a gay frolic.

Six months afterward he married again. His second wife was a very virtuous woman, with a violent temper. She caused him much sorrow.

MIKA The way he exaggerates the gems' worth and mentions his inheritance suggests now that he's wealthy he has an inflated idea of himself. (evaluate)

ISAAC *Violent* and *virtuous* don't seem to mix. Rather abrupt ending. (evaluate)

Discussion After Reading

General Comments

ISAAC Is there supposed to be a moral here? Maybe "Money brings sorrow." But the wife seemed pretty happy when she had the jewels, so this moral doesn't apply. (evaluate)

After thinking about the story, I see lots of lines are ironic that I didn't think were when I first read them. Like when Madame Lantin says jewels were her only weakness. This isn't true. I think she was really good and virtuous before she met him, but her desire for money corrupted her. That's how I'd sum up the point of the story: Money corrupts. (evaluate)

ISAAC It's interesting that he goes from happy (with first wife) to sad (when she dies) to happy (when he first is rich) to sad (when he remarries.) Well, at least his new wife doesn't sound like she'll be false. (summarize)

NINA This ending seems ironic. His new wife is "virtuous" but causes him much sorrow. His first wife, who was described as "virtuous" but really wasn't, made him happy. (evaluate)

MIKA Now I get the title. She is the false gem. She's put on a false front. (clarify)

ISAAC I finally understand why he didn't originally suspect her of being unfaithful. He thought the gems were false! He would have suspected her if he had known that they were real. (clarify)

NINA This final paragraph is so compact, it reminds me of the paragraph where Madame Lantin dies. (connect)

MIKA The story is full of contrasts. The final one is his two very different wives—one who is really virtuous though violent, the other who only appears to be virtuous but is gentle and gracious. Maybe the author is saying you can't have it both ways. (summarize)

Is it sometimes difficult for you to talk about literature once you've read it? Take some cues from active readers, who reflect and respond in a variety of ways. After reading "The False Gems," these three students reveal their personal reactions (Shaping Your Response) and literary responses (Analyzing the Story), along with the connections they have made to their own experiences (Extending the Ideas). These are the types of questions you will find in this book.

Shaping Your Response

Rate Madame Lantin as a wife from 1–10 with 10 being the ideal wife.

ISAAC I'd give her a 5. I think she really loves her husband—she gives him lots of attention and she runs the house well. She's probably a good person but wanted gems and would do anything for them.

MIKA Maybe a 4 but not very high. After all, she's unfaithful.

NINA Originally I wanted to give her a 10, but once I figured out what was going on, I'd say a 1 or 2. I think that the second wife will be much better, even though she has a bad temper.

Analyzing the Story

What examples of irony can you find in the story?

MIKA First of all, there's the title. She has "false" gems that we find out are real. She's a false gem, although he thought she was true.

NINA Just about everything seems ironic when you reread the story: ". . . she governed his household so cleverly and economically that they seemed to live in luxury." Here, she's getting all this money on the side; no wonder it appears they live in luxury. All those words like *virtuous, pure,* and *perfect* are really ironic. How about "It is my only weakness"?

Extending the Ideas

What other stories, movies, TV programs, or real-life situations does this story remind you of?

ISAAC "The Necklace," also by de Maupassant. We just read *One Hundred Years of Solitude* by García Márquez, and the situations seem very similar. People will do anything for money. In the novel, Aureliano takes up with Petra so their animals will mate and they can make money.

MIKA This reminds me of the movie *Indecent Proposal.* It's also like a news story about someone winning the lottery. I wonder if instant millionaires are miserable in the end.

The False Gems xxxi

After Reading

DISCUSSION AFTER READING

Shaping Your Response

This question encourages students to respond personally to the story as they experienced it. Encourage as many students as possible to share their reactions. Ask them which of the readers most closely reflects their own responses.

Analyzing the Story

This question directs students back to the story to look for details that will help them understand the author's purpose in writing. You may want to explain literary terms and techniques as they apply to the story.

Extending the Ideas

This question asks students to make connections to their own experiences and to look at other works of art (books, movies, television programs, and so on) in comparison to the story. Are students familiar with the works mentioned by the readers? What other suggestions do they have?

Transparency Collection
Models for Active Reading
Short Story, 1A–1G
Nonfiction, 2A–2D
Poetry, 3A–3B

Part One: Pushing Toward the Top

Planning Unit 1: Meeting the Challenge

Literature	Integrated Language Arts			
	Literary	**Writing/Grammar, Usage and Mechanics**	**Reading, Thinking, Listening, Speaking**	**Vocabulary/Spelling**
Through the Tunnel *by Doris Lessing* Short Story *(average)* p.6	Theme Setting, simile Characterization Plot	Comparison Explanation Advice column Clarity Subject-verb agreement	Recognize values Predict outcomes	Word webs Use dictionary for foreign words
Two Kinds *by Amy Tan* Short Story *(average)* p.18	Characterization Theme, conflict Similes, foreshadowing Plot, symbol	Explanation Dialogue Letter Writing simple sentences	Compare and contrast	Use specialized dictionaries
The Censors *by Luisa Valenzuela* Short Story *(average)* p.30	Satire	Brief explanation Satirical description Letter Apostrophes	Recognize propaganda techniques	
The Voter *by Chinua Achebe* Short Story *(average)* p.36	Proverbs Character	Dilemma and its resolution Write an advertisement based on a proverb Dashes		Folk etymology
The Other Wife *by Colette* Short Story *(average)* p.44	Point of view Characterization	Rewrite Before Reading notes using different techniques Monologue Journal Use the pronouns *Who* and *Whom*	Identify assumptions/detect bias Compare and contrast	Synonyms

Meeting Individual Needs

Multi-modal Activities	Mini-Lessons
Creating a travel brochure Drawing a color picture Art talk Expanding vocabulary Visualizing the setting Exploring theme Making science connections	Clarity Using dictionary for foreign words Subject-verb agreement
Creating a portrait gallery Report Making real-life connections Making personal connections Comparing characters Expressing emotions	Writing simple sentences Using specialized dictionaries Draw conclusions Informal speech
Writing a code Designing stamps Exploring a topic	Apostrophes
Creating a scroll picture Poster Research and report Making geographical connections Exploring satire	Dashes Folk etymology
Talk show Oral report Performing story as a play Comparing characters Expanding vocabulary through prefixes	Using the pronouns *Who* and *Whom*

Interdisciplinary Studies
So Young, So Talented

Format	Content Area	Highlights	Skill
Collage: **Early Starters**	Multicultural	Comparison of fictional characters and people that developed talent at a young age.	Recognize values
Article: **Mozart: The Music Magician** *by Maynard Solomon*	Humanities	Description of a young Mozart and of audience reactions to his performances.	Demonstrate poise and confidence
Article: **Measuring Up**	Science	General information on IQ testing.	Follow directions

Writing Workshop

Mode	Writing Format	Writing Focus	Proofreading Skills
Expository writing	An interpretive essay	Writing focused paragraphs	Punctuating quotations from literature

Program Support Materials

For Every Selection

Unit Resource Book
Graphic Organizer
Study Guide
Vocabulary Worksheet
Grammar Worksheet
Spelling, Speaking and Listening, or Literary Language Worksheet
Alternate Check Test
Vocabulary Test
Selection Test

For Every Writing Workshop

Unit Resource Book
Prewriting Worksheet
Revising Strategy Worksheet
Editing Strategy Worksheet
Presentation Worksheet
Writing Rubric
Transparency Collection
Fine Art Transparency
Student Writing Model Transparencies

For Every Interdisciplinary Study

Unit Resource Book
Study Guide
Mini-Lesson Skill Worksheet

Assessment

Unit Resource Book
TE Check Tests
Alternate Check Test (blackline master)
Vocabulary Test (blackline master)
Selection Test (blackline master)
Test Generator Software
Assessment Handbook

anning Unit 1: Meeting the Challenge

Literature	Integrated Language Arts: Literary	Writing/Grammar, Usage and Mechanics	Reading, Thinking, Listening, Speaking	Vocabulary/Spelling
The Monkey's Paw *by W. W. Jacobs* Short Story *(average)* p. 66	Plot Setting, conflict Imagery, mood Climax	Journal entry Rewrite ending Letter Quotation marks	Recognize values Identify assumptions Visualize Cause and effect Synthesize information Inference	Etymology
The Demon Lover *by Elizabeth Bowen* Short Story *(average)* p. 79	Flashback Mood, imagery Characterization Figurative language	List Write a review Semicolons	Analogy Recognize values Synthesize	Etymology
An Astrologer's Day *by R. K. Narayan* Short Story *(average)* p.87	Dialogue Setting	Paragraph Classified advertisement Science article Summarize a Greek myth Compound-complex sentences	Draw conclusions Predict outcomes Analogy	Antonyms Shades of meaning
The Masque of the Red Death *by Edgar Allan Poe* Short Story *(challenging)* p. 95	Mood Tone, imagery Setting, style	Description Describe a nightmare Director's notes Adjectives and adverbs	Generalize Visualize Understand sequence	Words in context
The Rain Came *by Grace Ogot* Short Story *(average)* p. 104	Setting Characterization Irony, imagery Theme	Compare ideas Extend ending Write lyrics Noun and pronoun forms	Recognize values Compare and contrast Make judgments Generalize	Determine correct word usage Use reference sources

Meeting Individual Needs

Multi-modal Activities	Mini-Lessons
Trial Art talk Exploring key concepts Exploring adjectives Tracking story details Exploring emotions	Etymology Quotation marks Compare and contrast Plot
Director's notes Oral report Analyzing flashbacks Exploring mood	Semicolons Etymology
Making a mobile Comparing and discussing various astrological charts Analyzing character Sequencing story events	Shades of meaning Compound-complex sentences
Designing a brochure Creating a floor plan Drawing the setting Exploring Gothic horror	Words in context Adjectives and adverbs Mood
Making a picture book Making a banner Making a portfolio Analyzing characters' choices Exploring figurative language Tracking changes in setting Interpreting a story's ending	Noun and pronoun forms Using reference sources Setting

Interdisciplinary Studies
Random, Rigged, or Rational?

Format	Content Area	Highlights	Skill
Article: **On Display: The Quiz Show That Was Rigged**	Media	This article explores the extent of randomness, rationality and/or rigging in quiz shows.	Finding information
Worksheet: **Playing the Numbers**	Math	These pages explore statistics and the concept of odds.	Bar graphs and probability
Short Stories: **Hedging Your Bets**	Math	This page addresses rationalization and reasoning skills.	Reading aloud

Writing Workshop

Mode	Writing Format	Writing Focus	Proofreading Skills
Persuasive writing	A group proposal for a TV show	Creating a business-like tone	Using commas correctly

Program Support Materials

For Every Selection

Unit Resource Book
Graphic Organizer
Study Guide
Vocabulary Worksheet
Grammar Worksheet
Spelling, Speaking and Listening, or Literary Language Worksheet
Alternate Check Test
Vocabulary Test
Selection Test

For Every Writing Workshop

Unit Resource Book
Prewriting Worksheet
Revising Strategy Worksheet
Editing Strategy Worksheet
Presentation Worksheet
Writing Rubric
Transparency Collection
Fine Art Transparency
Student Writing Model Transparencies

For Every Interdisciplinary Study

Unit Resource Book
Study Guide
Mini-Lesson Skill Worksheet

Assessment

Unit Resource Book
TE Check Tests
Alternate Check Test (blackline master)
Vocabulary Test (blackline master)
Selection Test (blackline master)
Test Generator Software
Assessment Handbook

anning Unit 1: Meeting the Challenge

Literature	Integrated Language Arts			
	Literary	**Writing/Grammar, Usage and Mechanics**	**Reading, Thinking, Listening, Speaking**	**Vocabulary/Spelling**
The Interlopers *by Saki* Short Story *(average)* p. 128	Irony Foreshadowing Dynamic characters Point of view	Journal entry Write an obituary New ending Pronoun-antecedent agreement	Compare and contrast Problem solving Summarize	Solve riddles
The Boar Hunt *by José Vasconcelos* Short Story *(average)* p. 136	Moral Irony Foreshadowing Personification and metaphor	Complete an observation Advertisement Brief dialogue Compound sentences	Make judgments Compare and contrast	Synonyms
from Red Azalea *by Anchee Min* Autobiography *(challenging)* p. 145	Conflict Setting, symbolism Metaphor Characterization Fable	Compare challenges Comparison of ages in different times Draft eight questions Poem Verbals	Analogies Compare and contrast Discussion, evaluate Generalization Recognize values	Negative connotations
He-y, Come on Ou-t! *by Shinichi Hoshi* Short Story *(easy)* p. 156	Inference Dialogue Plot	List Newspaper editorial Story and headline Futuristic fantasy Indefinite pronouns	Recognize assumptions Make judgments	Word analogies
Flash Cards *by Rita Dove* Poem *(average)* P.164 **In Memory of Richi** *by Carmen Tafolla* Poem *(average)* p.165 **The Rabbit** *by Edna St. Vincent Millay* Poem *(average)* p. 166	Sound devices (rhyme, alliteration, and onomatopoeia) Sonnet form	Poetry web Write a rap Write a poem Conjunctions	Figurative language Recognize values	Opposites

Meeting Individual Needs

Multi-modal Activities	Mini-Lessons
Planning a radio play Movie poster Applying geographical information Understanding characters	Irony Pronoun-antecedent agreement
Radio talk program Drawing a cartoon Exploring key concepts Exploring mood	Compound sentences Moral
Making a time line Co-anchor a special news report Understanding historical background Analyzing characterization Evaluating an argument Understanding causes and effects	Conflict Verbals Negative connotations Detecting bias
Sales pitch—infomercial Comic book rewrite Informative infomercial Relating theme and dialogue Speculating about the future	Indefinite pronouns
Research and presentation Chalk talk Making personal connections Exploring poetic language	Conjunctions

Interdisciplinary Studies
Lessons Through the Ages

Format	Content Area	Highlights	Skill
Article: **Traditional Wisdom**	Multicultural	This selection contains an assortment of fables and proverbs.	Interpretive reading Create and use graphic organizers

Writing Workshop

Mode	Writing Format	Writing Focus	Proofreading Skills
Expository writing	An interpretive essay	Clarifying cause-effect relationships	Clarifying pronoun references

Program Support Materials

For Every Selection

Unit Resource Book
Graphic Organizer
Study Guide
Vocabulary Worksheet
Grammar Worksheet
Spelling, Speaking and Listening, or Literary Language Worksheet
Alternate Check Test
Vocabulary Test
Selection Test

For Every Writing Workshop

Unit Resource Book
Prewriting Worksheet
Revising Strategy Worksheet
Editing Strategy Worksheet
Presentation Worksheet
Writing Rubric
Transparency Collection
Fine Art Transparency
Student Writing Model Transparencies

For Every Interdisciplinary Study

Unit Resource Book
Study Guide
Mini-Lesson Skill Worksheet

Assessment

Unit Resource Book
TE Check Tests
Alternate Check Test (blackline master)
Vocabulary Test (blackline master)
Selection Test (blackline master)
Test Generator Software
Assessment Handbook

Unit 1 Supplemental Resources

Media and Technology

Part One Selections

Through the Tunnel

Audiotape The author reads her work in *Doris Lessing Reads Her Short Stories,* Jeffrey Norton Publishers.

Community Resources Students might be interested in hearing the experiences of someone whose work involves administering first to those who are sick or injured. Such people might include police personnel, firefighters, paramedics, lifeguards, doctors, nurses, and so on.

Two Kinds

Videotape *The Joy Luck Club*, 139 minutes, Hollywood Pictures Home Video, 1994, is based on Amy Tan's novel.

Home Connection Ask a student to invite a family member who is a musician to visit the class and discuss: How important is musical culture in the home in the development of ability in music? What kind of employment opportunities are available for musicians?

The Censors

Videotape *The Day They Came to Arrest the Book*, 47 minutes, Filmfair, 1988, based on a novel by Nat Hentoff, deals with censorship.

The Voter

Audiotape Listen to the author reading in *Chinua Achebe Reads*, 88 minutes, American Audio Prose Library.

Videotape Bill Moyers interviews the author in *Chinua Achebe: A World of Ideas*, 30 minutes, PBS Video.

Home Connection Students might ask a relative who has served as a poll-watcher or has officiated at a local election to visit the class and discuss the voting process in their community.

The Other Wife

Videotape *Colette,* 13 minutes, Coronet/MTI, explores the life and works of the author.

Part Two Selections

The Monkey's Paw

Videotape *Monkey's Paw*, 28 minutes, Learning Corp. of America, 1983, is based on Jacobs's short story.

Home Connection For an at-home activity, students might poll family members on questions relating to luck: What is luck? Are there people who are consistently lucky or unlucky? Can a person do anything to insure good luck or ward off bad luck? If an individual were given three wishes, what should this lucky person wish for?

The Demon Lover

Community Resources In her story "The Demon Lover," Elizabeth Bowen took an uncanny narrative motif from an old ballad and gave it a contemporary setting. Students might be interested in using community resources such as local libraries or historical museums to research a strange episode from the community's early history that might be serve as the basis of a short story or play.

An Astrologer's Day

Community Resources Astrology is regarded very seriously in traditional Indian culture, and people's horoscopes affect many important decisions in their lives, such as who they marry. Students might be interested in using community

Connections to
Custom Literature Database

For Part One "Pushing Toward the Top" Selections with Lessons

- "The Loreley" by Heinrich Heine
- The American Standard by Booker T. Washington

Additional theme-related selections can be accessed on the ScottForesman database.

Connections to
Custom Literature Database

For Part Two "Trying to Beat the Odds" Selections with Lessons

- "The Cop and the Anthem" by O. Henry
- "The Man with the Twisted Lip" by Sir Arthur Conan Doyle

Additional theme-based selections can be accessed on the ScottForesman database.

resources such as local libraries or cultural centers to do research on Indian beliefs and customs regarding astrology.

The Masque of the Red Death

Audiotape "The Masque of the Red Death" is included in the unabridged collection, *Edgar Allan Poe Short Stories,* 1 hour 41 minutes, Listening Library, 1994.

Videotape *Edgar Allan Poe: Architect of Dreams*, 40 minutes, Monterey Home Video, 1995, looks at the author and his work.

Computer Software Students will enjoy a multimedia presentation of Poe and his work in the CD-ROM, *Poe's Tales of Terror*, Macintosh, Queue.

Community Resources You might invite local health officials to visit the school and talk with students about what the community would do in the event of an epidemic.

The Rain Came

Home Connection With growing populations placing greater and greater demands on available resources of fresh water, water conservation is going to be a fact of life in the future for many communities. Students might investigate use of water in their homes, and then, working with other family members, create a plan for water conservation in the event of a drought.

Part Three Selections

The Interlopers

Videotape *The Interlopers,* 24 minutes, Barr Films, 1979, is a film version of Saki's story.

Home Connection A student might ask a family member who is a professional involved in settling disputes to visit the class and discuss arbitration techniques. Such people might include lawyers, family counselors, and others.

The Boar Hunt

Community Resources You might set up a forum in the classroom on the environmental impact of hunting, inviting a representative from a group such as the National Rifle Association to present the pro-hunting position, and a representative from a group opposed to hunting, such as Friends of Wildlife. to present the opposing view.

Red Azalea

Computer Software *China: Home of the Dragon*, CD-ROM for Macintosh and MPC, Orange Cherry, covers 4,000 years of history and culture.

Home Connection The background of "Red Azalea" is the Chinese Cultural Revolution, a period of social unrest in the late 1960s and early 1970s. The U.S. was going through a period of political turmoil at about the same time. Have students ask family members who lived through the era of civil rights and anti-war demonstrations to discuss their memories of the period.

He–y, Come on Ou–t

Community Resources Recycling programs have been successfully implemented in many communities. Students might be interested in hearing from several people involved in different stages of such a program, for example sanitation officials and dealers in recycled materials.

Flash Cards/In Memory of Richi/The Rabbit

Audiotape Students will enjoy listening to Rita Dove reading from "Thomas & Beulah" and being interviewed in *Rita Dove*, 29 minutes, New Letters. Carmen Tafolla reads her work in *Carmen Tafolla*, 29 minutes, New Letters, 1991.

Videotape Consider showing *Edna St. Vincent Millay*, 60 minutes, Films for the Humanities & Sciences, 1994.

Home Connection Ask a student who comes from a bilingual home to invite a family member to class and discuss the experiences of moving from one language culture to another.

Connections to
Custom Literature Database

For Part Three "Dealing with Consequences" Selections with Lessons

- "A New England Nun" by Mary E. Wilkins Freeman
- "The Ballad of Reading Gaol" by Oscar Wilde

Additional theme-related selections can be accessed on the ScottForesman database.

Connections to
AuthorWorks

Information about the life and times of Doris Lessing, Chinua Achebe, Edgar Allan Poe, and Rita Dove is available on ScottForesman's AuthorWorks CD-ROM.

Unit 1

Meeting the Challenge

Art Study

The Bicycle Race was painted in 1938 by Mexican artist Antonio Ruiz (1897–1964). As a young man Ruiz painted film sets for Universal Studios in Hollywood, California. He eventually returned to Mexico where he worked as a teacher and later founded his own art school.

Many of Ruiz's best paintings are scenes of everyday life rendered in a clear, dry style. Ruiz's later paintings were very often surreal and characterized by fantastic and distorted images.

Question What have you learned about Mexican culture from the painting? *(Students may mention the colors of the Mexican flag; how the people are dressed; that the race may have political implications as well as being a competition.)*

Question Some of the branches in the upper left corner look like feet. Do you think the artist intended for the branches to look this way? Why? *(Students may think that the feet suggest that someone who is unseen by others is looking at the race.)*

UNIT 1

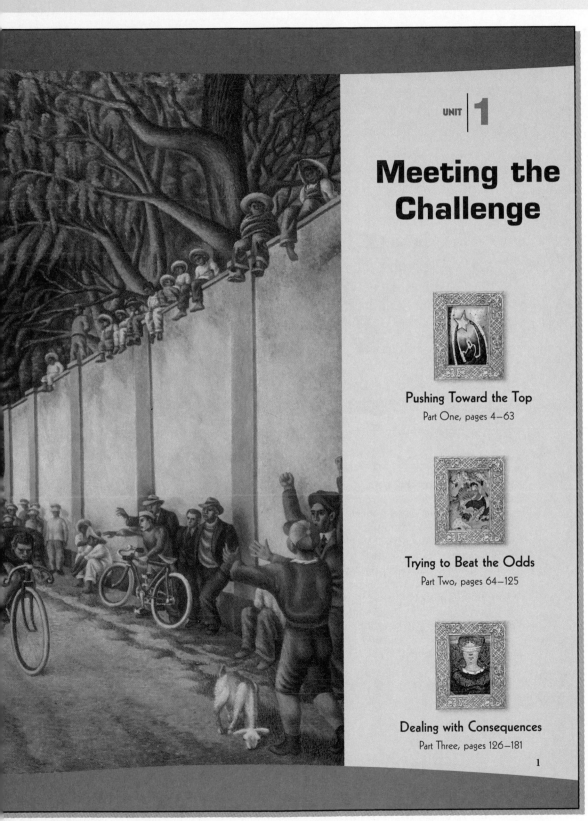

Meeting the Challenge

1

THEMATIC CONNECTION

As people strive to reach personal goals, they define and evaluate their standards of excellence.

Part One
Pushing Toward the Top

Part One features literature that explores how characters meet challenges posed by nature, family, society, and their own values.

Ideas to Explore

- Why do some people strive to excel?
- What makes a goal worth achieving?

Part Two
Trying to Beat the Odds

The literature explores struggles against forces beyond human control.

Idea to Explore

How much control do people have over the future?

Part Three
Dealing with Consequences

This literature focuses on how people face the consequences of their actions.

Idea to Explore

What does it mean to take responsibility for your actions?

Art Study

The first picture of a man holding a star was painted by Normand Cosineau. A hunting party appears in the painting, *Akbar Hunting a Tiger Near Gwalior.* A woman in a blindfold appears on a tarot card used to tell fortunes.

Genre Overview: Short Story

EXPLORING CONCEPTS

- The basic elements of a short story are plot, character, setting, point of view, and theme.
- The plot is a pattern of events that usually revolve around a conflict, which eventually reaches a climax and resolution.
- The thoughts, words, and actions of characters reveal their motives and goals.
- Setting can create mood, affect plot, influence characters, and even convey theme.
- A fictional narrator may be someone inside or outside the story.
- A story may convey different themes to different readers.

Question Which of the five highlighted quotations from stories in this unit most makes you want to read that story? Why? *(Students might cite the adventure suggested by the Lessing quotation, the suspense of the Ogot quotation, or the profound personal feeling of the Tan quotation.)*

Research Activity Students might use the library catalog to list collections of stories and identify the many ways in which stories are organized and anthologized—for example: by nationality, time period, author's gender, length, setting, or theme.

Genre Overview

Reading

When you read a short story, you get to know fictional characters and become involved in the situations and dilemmas they face. This involvement doesn't just happen by chance. Because they have to pack a lot into a few pages, short story writers must quickly engage readers, using the elements described here. At the end of this unit, you will find not only short stories, but poems and nonfiction that explore a common theme. With such a mixture, you can discover which elements are unique to short stories, and which can be found in other types of literature.

A young woman... must die so that the country may have rain.

—*Grace Ogot, "The Rain Came"*

PLOT

First comes the **plot**—the pattern of events that is the framework of a narrative. As you read, note what sets these events in motion and how one event leads to the next. The basic ingredient that energizes a plot is **conflict.** Sometimes the conflict is a struggle between the main character or characters and an adverse character, group, or outside force. At other times, the conflict is within a character. A story's conflict intensifies until it reaches a **climax,** a turning point at which the conflict is confronted head-on. The end of the conflict is called the **resolution.**

...her eyes, and her wavy golden hair, disguised her as a fragile and soulful blond.

—*Colette, "The Other Wife"*

CHARACTERS

Also central to a short story are the **characters**—the personalities that pop from the page. We get to know some fictional characters more intimately than real people because we can share their innermost thoughts. Authors have several ways of acquainting us with characters. They may depict them directly by stating the character's appearance and thoughts. At times, however, writers choose to suggest certain character traits, requiring that the reader make inferences based on what is done or said by other characters.

a Short Story

...our caravan descended the Andean slopes, leading to the endless green ocean.

—José Vasconcelos, "The Boar Hunt"

After seeing my mother's disappointed face once again, something inside me began to die.

—Amy Tan, "Two Kinds"

POINT OF VIEW

Just as important as the people and places in a story is the person who is telling it—the narrator who filters what is being told and seen. An author's choice of narrator dictates the **point of view.** If the narrator is a character in the story, then this first-person point of view presents a very personal and limited picture of what you learn. "Two Kinds" has a first-person narrator. But frequently, the narrator is someone outside the story—a third-person narrator, as in "Through the Tunnel" and "The Censors." In this third-person point of view, a narrator can be limited like the first-person narrator, or can be omniscient—knowing everything about the characters and their thoughts.

SETTING

Stories take readers places. The **setting** of a story—the time and place in which events occur—serves as a backdrop for characters and events. The when and where of stories in this unit range from a medieval castle to a polling booth in Nigeria and a school in Maoist China. A setting may help create the atmosphere, or **mood,** in a story. For example, an empty house during wartime London in "The Demon Lover," establishes a mood of tension and terror. Setting can also be vital to understanding characters, customs, and events, as it is in "The Rain Came."

He would do it if it killed him....

—Doris Lessing, "Through the Tunnel"

THEME

During and after reading, you will find yourself reflecting on ideas common to these stories, as well as links between the fictional characters and situations and those in the real world. These links form the theme of the story. For instance, in "Through the Tunnel," Jerry's changing relationship with his mother and his need to prove himself indicate a universal journey toward maturity. Different readers may find different themes in a story, and a single story can have several themes.

3

MATERIALS OF INTEREST

Books

- *Short Story Writers and Their Work: A Guide to the Best, Second Edition* by Brad Hooper (American Library Association, 1992)
- *The Collected Stories of Colette* edited by Robert Phelps (Farrar, Straus, 1983)
- *Stories* by Doris Lessing (Knopf, 1978)
- *What's Your Story? A Young Person's Guide to Writing Fiction* by Marion Dane Bauer (Clarion Books, 1992)
- *Mozart: His Life and Times* by Peggy Woodford (Midas Books, 1977)
- *Teleliteracy: Taking Television Seriously* by David Bianculli (Continuum, 1992)

Multimedia

- *The American Short Story Collection* (videocassettes, color, each less than 60 minutes) by Learning in Focus, Inc. Distributed by Monterey Home Video. Includes such classic stories as Katherine Anne Porter's "The Jilting of Granny Weatherall," Sherwood Anderson's "I'm a Fool," and F. Scott Fitzgerald's "Bernice Bobs Her Hair."
- *The Joy Luck Club* (videocassette, color, 139 minutes). Hollywood Pictures Home Video, 1993. Screenplay by Amy Tan, directed by Wayne Wang. Rated R.
- *Encarta Multimedia Encyclopedia*, article on "Short Story" (Microsoft, 1995)

Preview

Pushing Toward the Top

FOR ALL STUDENTS

Do you agree with the statement "Winning is everything?" Why or why not?

Explain to students that the selections they will be reading demonstrate ways of facing personal challenges and meeting standards.

To further explore the theme, use the Fine Art Transparency referred to below.

Transparency Collection
Fine Art Writing Prompt 1

For At-Risk Students

- Have students identify contemporary athletes, musicians, actors, and so on, who have overcome great odds to become successful.
- Discuss what qualities enabled these people to succeed.

For Students Who Need Challenge

Have each student nominate a person to receive the award for "The Most Extraordinary Achievement of the Decade" and give the reason for the nomination.

For Visual Learners

Preview the illustrations in this group of selections and have students discuss what the images suggest about the stories.

MULTICULTURAL CONNECTION

Individuals combine their cultural background and their own personal values to establish standards of excellence. Have students explore different ways that their culture measures success, and how they would measure their own success for the same activity, such as playing a sport or doing schoolwork.

Part One

Pushing Toward the Top

You are about to meet some characters who are determined to succeed—to be the best. But although they are willing to go to great lengths to excel, not all these people come out winners in their push to the top.

Multicultural Connection **Individuality** may involve asserting oneself against group culture. As you read the following selections, decide how the pursuits of individual goals are influenced by a larger cultural context.

IDEAS THAT WORK

Comparing Characters

So many of our students have personal stories to share about trying to reach a seemingly unattainable goal. I use quickwrites to stimulate ideas for classroom discussions.

Once we have discussed the individual stories, I often have the students use graphic organizers and Venn diagrams to compare and contrast the values and motivations of the characters in all of the stories. Another more dramatic way to study characters is to encourage students to take on the personas of different characters. They can even come in costume! Then the rest of the class can ask questions of the "characters." It is important for students to realize that some of the characters are more noble than others in their quest to reach the top.

Karen Wroblewski
Spring Valley, California

Before Reading

Through the Tunnel

by Doris Lessing Zimbabwe/Great Britain

Doris Lessing
born 1919

The mission of the writer is to provide the world with a "small personal voice," according to Doris Lessing. Growing up in Southern Rhodesia (now Zimbabwe but then part of the British Empire), Lessing quit school at fourteen, began writing novels, and left the family's farm to work in the city. In 1949, after writing her first book, she moved to England where she still lives. She has written essays, short stories, a science fiction series, and many novels, including *The Golden Notebook,* a classic of feminist literature. Lessing's concerns include politics, the changing role of women in society, and the effects of technology.

Building Background

An Explosion of Light "He felt he was dying. He was no longer quite conscious. He struggled on in the darkness between lapses into unconsciousness. An immense, swelling pain filled his head, and then the darkness cracked with an explosion of green light. His hands, groping forward, met nothing." Imagine finding yourself in a situation like that described above. Where are you? How did you come to be here? What will you do to get out of this situation? Explain to a partner what you imagine. You may want to illustrate the situation. Now speculate on how this quoted description might be related to a story titled "Through the Tunnel."

Literary Focus

Theme You will often link the stories you read or movies you see with your own experiences. Jerry's experience in "Through the Tunnel" may remind you of a time you responded to a dare or of a cartoon superhero who lived up to her reputation. You might call these common links something like "improving yourself," "struggling to succeed," or "initiation." Such links are called **themes**. Not everyone finds the same theme in a work or gives it the same label, and stories may have more than one theme.

Writer's Notebook

Risky Business Before reading "Through the Tunnel," think about times in your life when you have taken risks. Were they foolish risks, or did they pay off? Zero in on a particular risk and record how you felt before, during, and after taking it. Speculate on whether or not you would do things differently now.

Before Reading

Building Background

Explain to students what is meant by the term *cliffhanger,* and through discussion elicit examples of how cliffhangers are used in television shows and movies to create suspense.

Literary Focus

You might lead a discussion on contemporary **themes** in popular media. Examples of such themes are "violence begets violence," "the triumph of the underdog," and "struggle and transformation."

Writer's Notebook

Offer examples of positive and negative risks and let students suggest others.

Positive Risks	Negative Risks
taking tougher classes	*driving too fast*
telling someone you that love him or her	*staying out late*
helping a drowning person	*stealing or borrowing money*

Connections to **AuthorWorks**

Doris Lessing is a featured author in the AuthorWorks CD-ROM series.

SUPPORT MATERIALS OVERVIEW

Unit 1 Resource Book
- Graphic Organizer, p. 1
- Study Guide, p. 2
- Vocabulary, p. 3
- Grammar, p. 4
- Alternate Check Test, p. 5
- Vocabulary Test, p. 6
- Selection Test, pp. 7–8

Building English Proficiency
- Literature Summaries
- Activities, p. 167

Reading, Writing & Grammar SkillBook
- Vocabulary, pp. 20–21
- Writing, pp. 113–114
- Grammar, pp. 215–216

The World of Work
- Deep Sea Diver, p. 1
- Create a Budget, p. 2

Technology
- Personal Journal Software
- Custom Literature Database: For a story of another boy's challenges, see *David Copperfield* by Charles Dickens on the database.
- Test Generator Software

During Reading

Selection Objectives

- to explore the theme of meeting a challenge
- to discuss the concept of theme
- to predict the outcome of a story
- to practice subject-verb agreement in writing

Unit 1 Resource Book
Graphic Organizer, p. 1
Study Guide, p. 2

Theme Link

The theme of "Pushing Toward the Top" is developed when Jerry pushes himself to meet the self-imposed challenge of matching the physical prowess of older boys.

Vocabulary Preview

contrition, guilt
promontory, high point of land extending from the coast
luminous, full of light; shining
supplication, a humble and earnest prayer
beseeching, asking earnestly; begging
myriad, a great number
incredulous, doubting; skeptical

Students can add the words and definitions to their Writer's Notebook.

1 Literary Element
Setting

Question What are the elements of the setting? *(a wild and rocky bay, a path overlooking the bay, a crowded beach)*

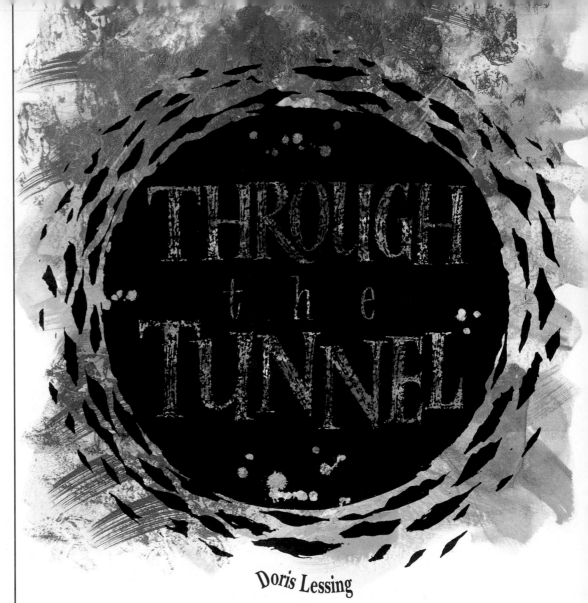

THROUGH the TUNNEL

Doris Lessing

1 Going to the shore on the first morning of the vacation, the young English boy stopped at a turning of the path and looked down at a wild and rocky bay, and then over to the crowded beach he knew so well from other years. His mother walked on in front of him, carrying a bright striped bag in one hand. Her other arm, swinging loose, was very white in the sun. The boy watched that white, naked arm, and turned his eyes, which had a frown behind them,

SELECTION SUMMARY

Through the Tunnel

Jerry, an eleven-year-old English boy on vacation with his mother at a seaside resort, encounters a group of older boys while swimming. He watches in fascination and fear as all the boys dive into the bay and swim underwater through a hidden tunnel in a rock barrier. Knowing that he can't attempt the feat, he tries to keep their acceptance by showing off. They reject him. Later, Jerry discovers the tunnel for himself. Over many days, he persists in disciplining himself to hold his breath long enough to survive the long and dangerous swim through the tunnel. At last he attempts the ordeal and succeeds.

*For summaries in other languages, see the **Building English Proficiency** book.*

toward the bay and back again to his mother. When she felt he was not with her, she swung around. "Oh, there you are, Jerry!" she said. She looked impatient, then smiled. "Why, darling, would you rather not come with me? Would you rather—" She frowned, conscientiously worrying over what amusements he might secretly be longing for, which she had been too busy or too careless to imagine. He was very familiar with that anxious, apologetic smile. Contrition[1] sent him running after her. And yet, as he ran, he looked back over his shoulder at the wild bay; and all morning, as he played on the safe beach, he was thinking of it.

He was very familiar with that anxious, apologetic smile. Contrition sent him running after her.

Next morning, when it was time for the routine of swimming and sunbathing, his mother said, "Are you tired of the usual beach, Jerry? Would you like to go somewhere else?"

"Oh, no!" he said quickly, smiling at her out of that unfailing impulse of contrition—a sort of chivalry. Yet, walking down the path with her, he blurted out, "I'd like to go and have a look at those rocks down there."

She gave the idea her attention. It was a wild-looking place, and there was no one there; but she said, "Of course, Jerry. When you've had enough, come to the big beach. Or just go straight back to the villa, if you like." She walked away, that bare arm, now slightly reddened from yesterday's sun, swinging. And he almost ran after her again, feeling it unbearable that she could go by herself, but he did not.

She was thinking. Of course he's old enough to be safe without me. Have I been keeping him too close? He mustn't feel he ought to be with me. I must be careful.

He was an only child, eleven years old. She was a widow. She was determined to be neither possessive nor lacking in devotion. She went worrying off to her beach.

As for Jerry, once he saw that his mother had gained her beach, he began the steep descent to the bay. **2** From where he was, high up among red-brown rocks, it was a scoop of moving bluish green fringed with white. As he went lower, he saw that it spread among small promontories[2] and inlets of rough, sharp rock, and the crisping, lapping surface showed stains of purple and darker blue. Finally, as he ran sliding and scraping down the last few yards, he saw an edge of white surf and the shallow, luminous[3] movement of water over white sand, and beyond that, a solid, heavy blue.

He ran straight into the water and began swimming. He was a good swimmer. He went out fast over the gleaming sand, over a middle region where rocks lay like discolored monsters under the **3** surface, and then he was in the real sea—a warm sea where irregular cold currents from the deep water shocked his limbs.

When he was so far out that he could look back not only on the little bay but past the promontory that was between it and the big beach, he floated on the buoyant surface and looked for his mother. There she was, a speck of yellow under an umbrella that looked like a slice of orange peel. He swam back to shore, relieved at being sure she was there, but all at **4** once very lonely.

On the edge of a small cape that marked the side of the bay away from the promontory was a loose scatter of rocks. Above them, some boys

1. **contrition** (kən trish′ən), *n.* guilt.
2. **promontory** (prom′ən tôr′ē), *n.* high point of land extending from the coast.
3. **luminous** (lü′mə nəs) *adj.* full of light; shining.

2 Geographical Note

Where Sea Meets Shore

This story takes place on the beaches and rocky coast of a seaside resort. A bay is a wide inlet of water—not as large as a gulf—that indents a shoreline among promontories, which are extensions of the land that often serve as rocky bases for fishing, swimming, and diving.

3 Literary Element

Simile

Questions

- What simile does the author use to describe the rocks? *(The rocks are like the bodies of "discolored monsters" lying in wait under the water.)*
- What feeling does this simile give you about swimming in this place? *(Possible responses: fear, anxiety, caution, or recklessness)*

4 Reader's Response

Making Personal Connections

Questions How would you describe Jerry's mixture of feelings at this point? Do his emotions sound authentic to you? Why or why not? *(Possible response: He seems to be both daring and anxious. Like most adolescents, he wants to be independent and separate, yet he also is unsure of being completely on his own.)*

BUILDING ENGLISH PROFICIENCY

Expanding Vocabulary

Keeping a vocabulary notebook will help students increase their knowledge and use of English vocabulary. Encourage them to jot down unfamiliar or unusual words and phrases as they read.

1. Work with students to determine the words that describe feelings (*conscientiously, anxious, apologetic, contrition*) and give examples of when or why people might have such feelings.
2. Students can use the words orally and show, by facial expressions or acting, the feelings associated with the words.
3. Invite students to write original sentences with each word.

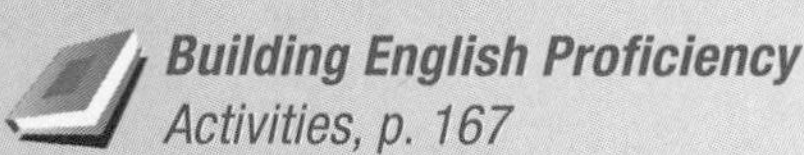
Building English Proficiency
Activities, p. 167

5 Literary Focus

Theme

Question What is Jerry's "craving"? *(Possible responses: a desire to be accepted by peers, a desire to enter the world of older teenagers, a longing to break away from his mother)*

Question What do you think is the most difficult challenge facing someone who wants to join a new group? *(Possible responses: lack of self-confidence, a feeling of isolation, ignorance of the group's rules, possible rejection)*

6 Reading/Thinking Skills

Recognize Values

Questions

- At first the boys seem to accept Jerry; later they seem to reject him. What is their judgment of him? *(Possible response: The other boys judge Jerry as a good swimmer, but too childish.)*
- What are other values that kids use when they decide whether or not to allow someone into their group? *(Possible responses: age, language, behavior, race)*

were stripping off their clothes. They came running, naked, down to the rocks. The English boy swam toward them, but kept his distance at a stone's throw. They were of that coast; all of them were burned smooth dark brown and speaking a language he did not understand. To
5 be with them, of them, was a craving that filled his whole body. He swam a little closer; they turned and watched him with narrowed, alert dark eyes. Then one smiled and waved. It was enough. In a minute, he had swum in and was on the rocks beside them, smiling with a desperate, nervous supplication.[4] They shouted cheerful greetings at him; and then, as he preserved his nervous, uncomprehending smile, they understood that he was a foreigner strayed from his own beach, and they proceeded to forget him. But he was happy. He was with them.

"Look at me! Look!" and he began splashing and kicking in the water like a foolish dog.

They began diving again and again from a high point into a well of blue sea between rough, pointed rocks. After they had dived and come up, they swam around, hauled themselves up, and waited their turn to dive again. They were big boys—men, to Jerry. He dived, and they watched him; and when he swam around to take his place, they made way for him. He felt he was accepted and he dived again, carefully, proud of himself.

Soon the biggest of the boys poised himself, shot down into the water, and did not come up. The others stood about, watching. Jerry, after waiting for the sleek brown head to appear, let out a yell of warning; they looked at him idly and turned their eyes back toward the water. After a long time, the boy came up on the other side of a big dark rock, letting the air out of his lungs in a sputtering gasp and a shout of triumph. Immediately the rest of them dived in. One moment, the morning seemed full of chattering boys; the next, the air and the surface of the water were empty. But through the heavy blue, dark shapes could be seen moving and groping.

Jerry dived, shot past the school of underwater swimmers, saw a black wall of rock looming at him, touched it, and bobbed up at once to the surface, where the wall was a low barrier he could see across. There was no one visible; under him, in the water, the dim shapes of the swimmers had disappeared. Then one, and then another of the boys came up on the far side of the barrier of rock, and he understood that they had swum through some gap or hole in it. He plunged down again. He could see nothing through the stinging salt water but the blank rock. When he came up the boys were all on the diving rock, preparing to attempt the feat again. And now, in a panic of failure, he yelled up, in English, "Look at me! Look!" and he began splashing and kicking in the water like a foolish dog.

They looked down gravely, frowning. He knew 6
the frown. At moments of failure, when he clowned to claim his mother's attention, it was with just this grave, embarrassed inspection that she rewarded him. Through his hot shame, feeling the pleading grin on his face like a scar that he could never remove, he looked up at the group of big brown boys on the rock and shouted, "*Bonjour! Merci! Au revoir! Monsieur, monsieur!*"[5]

4. supplication (sup′lə kā′shən), *n.* a humble and earnest prayer.

5. ***"Bonjour!*** (bô zhür′) ***Merci!*** (mer sē′) ***Au revoir!*** (ō rə vwär′) ***Monsieur . . ."*** (mə syər′), French terms meaning "good morning," "thank you," "good-by," and "mister" or "sir."

MINI-LESSON: GRAMMAR

Clarity

Teach Lessing uses strong verbs and simple declarative sentences to describe action. She provides the reader with clear images of the character's actions through such basic declarative sentence structures as "the boy watched," "he ran," "he floated," and "he swam."

Activity Idea Encourage students to identify simple declarative sentences throughout the story that propel the action. Have students find five sentences in the story that describe physical actions. Then ask students to write a paragraph about an adventure they have had, using strong, vivid verbs to convey the action.

while he hooked his fingers round his ears and waggled them.

Water surged into his mouth; he choked, sank, came up. The rock, lately weighted with boys, seemed to rear up out of the water as their weight was removed. They were flying down past him, now, into the water; the air was full of falling bodies. Then the rock was empty in the hot sunlight. He counted one, two, three. . . .

At fifty, he was terrified. They must all be drowning beneath him, in the watery caves of the rock! At a hundred, he stared around him at the empty hillside, wondering if he should yell for help. He counted faster, faster, to hurry them up, to bring them to the surface quickly, to drown them quickly—anything rather than the terror of counting on and on into the blue emptiness of the morning. And then, at a hundred and sixty, the water beyond the rock was full of boys blowing like brown whales. They swam back to the shore without a look at him.

He climbed back to the diving rock and sat down, feeling the hot roughness of it under his thighs. The boys were gathering up their bits of clothing and running off along the shore to another promontory. They were leaving to get away from him. He cried openly, fists in his eyes. There was no one to see him, and he cried himself out.

It seemed to him that a long time had passed, and he swam out to where he could see his mother. Yes, she was still there, a yellow spot under an orange umbrella. He swam back to the big rock, climbed up, and dived into the blue pool among the fanged and angry boulders. Down he went, until he touched the wall of rock again. But the salt was so painful in his eyes that he could not see.

He came to the surface, swam to shore, and went back to the villa to wait for his mother. Soon she walked slowly up the path, swinging her striped bag, the flushed, naked arm dangling beside her. "I want some swimming goggles," he panted, defiant and beseeching.[6]

She gave him a patient inquisitive look as she said casually, "Well, of course, darling."

But now, now, now! He must have them this minute, and no other time. He nagged and pestered until she went with him to a shop. As soon as she had bought the goggles, he grabbed them from her hand as if she were going to claim them for herself, and was off, running down the steep path to the bay. **7**

Jerry swam out to the big barrier rock, adjusted the goggles, and dived. The impact of the water broke the rubber-enclosed vacuum, and the goggles came loose. He understood that he must swim down to the base of the rock from the surface of the water. He fixed the goggles tight and firm, filled his lungs, and floated, face down, on the water. Now, he could see. It was as if he had eyes of a different kind—fish eyes that showed everything clear and delicate and wavering in the bright water.

Under him, six or seven feet down, was a floor of perfectly clean, shining white sand, rippled firm and hard by the tides. Two grayish shapes steered there, like long, rounded pieces of wood or slate. They were fish. He saw them nose toward each other, poise motionless, make a dart forward, swerve off, and come around again. It was like a water dance. A few inches above them the water sparkled as if sequins were dropping through it. Fish again—myriads[7] of minute fish, the length of his fingernail, were drifting through the water, and in a moment he could feel the innumerable tiny touches of them against his limbs. It was like swimming in flaked silver. The great rock the big boys had swum through rose sheer out of the white sand—black, tufted lightly with greenish weed. He could see no gap in it. He swam down to its base. **8**

6. **beseeching** (bē sēch′ing), *adj.* asking earnestly; begging.

7. **myriad** (mir′ē əd), *n.* a great number.

7 Literary Element
Characterization

Question Do you think Jerry's nagging about the swimming goggles reveals something positive or negative about him? Explain your response. *(Possible responses: Students may feel that Jerry's insistence shows that he is determined to reach his goal, or they may feel that the word choice of the author —"this minute," "nagged," "pestered"—suggests that Jerry is acting more like a spoiled child.)*

The World of Work
Deep Sea Diver

For the real-life experiences of a deep sea diver, use–

The World of Work
pp. 1–2

8 Literary Element
Similes

Questions What simile does the author use to describe the movement of the fish *("like a water dance")* and the touch of the fish *("like swimming in flaked silver")*?

What do you think these similes suggest about how Jerry feels now about being in the sea? *(They suggest that Jerry is discovering that the sea is a beautiful, magical place where animals and wood seem alike, where fish seem to dance, and where a human being can float through an atmosphere that sparkles like silver.)*

BUILDING ENGLISH PROFICIENCY

Visualizing the Setting

Having a clear idea of the setting is a key to understanding this story.

1. Ask students to imagine the setting as you read the following sentences aloud.
   - "They began diving again and again from a high point into a well of blue sea between rough, pointed rocks."
   - "Then one, and then another of the boys came up on the far side of the barrier of rock, and he understood that they had swum through some gap or hole in it."
2. Invite two volunteers to draw their ideas of the setting on the chalkboard. Have students discuss and suggest changes until the setting is accurate.
3. You might have a volunteer show the path of the boys' dive into the water and through the tunnel.

MINI-LESSON: VOCABULARY

Using Dictionaries for Foreign Words

Teach Point out to students that English-speakers often use French words without realizing that they are doing so. Examples of such words may include *bon appetit* (which appears in the story) and *ambiance.*

Activity Idea Students can find examples in a dictionary of other French words beginning with *bon: bon bon, bon jour, bon mot, bon soir, bon voyage.* Ask students to:

- list each word with its definition on a sheet of paper
- write a sentence demonstrating correct usage of each word

David Wojnarowicz used spray paint to construct *The Untidiness of the Ocean* in 1982. What is the most forceful image in the first panel of the painting? How does the second panel show a different balance of power?

Responses to Caption Questions
Possible responses: In the first panel, the swimmer is the forceful image, shown in control, as if the ocean were a room that he has put in order (made tidy). In the second panel, the swimmer is overpowered by nature and drowns. Meanwhile the flying fish proceed unaffected by this human disaster.

Wojnarowicz uses a most unusual word to describe the ocean in his title—*untidiness.* The painting suggests untidiness in its depiction of a story of human inability to maintain order in this vast environment. Nature's order in this painting pays no attention to individual human intentions. The painter may be showing that the ocean is not orderly, but in constant change.

Visual Literacy Repetition is a fundamental visual concept that often suggests order, control, and reliable patterns or cycles.

Question What elements in the painting show repetition? *(Response: the rows of flying fish, the lines and dots in the water, the swimmer's strokes)*

BUILDING ENGLISH PROFICIENCY

ESL LEP ELD SAE LD

Exploring Theme

Exploring Jerry's desire for independence and the obstacles to his independence will lead students to understand theme of this story.

Activity Ideas

- Suggest that students make a personal connection by recalling how they felt at Jerry's age. Have them talk about the kind of independence they wanted and the obstacles they faced.
- Show their responses in the form of a chart or web with these headings: **Need for independence, Fears.** Refer to the chart when discussing the theme.

9 Literary Focus
Theme

Question What qualities does Jerry show he possesses that may enable him to meet the challenge of the tunnel? *(Possible response: persistence, courage, curiosity)*

10 Reader's Response
Making Personal Connections

Question Have you ever felt that there was something you had to do, had to achieve, or had to possess? What made you feel that way? Possible responses are shown in the chart.

Had to do, achieve, or possess	What made you feel that way
attend a party	*wanting to be popular*
pass a test	*meeting a personal goal*

11 Literary Focus
Theme

You might tie the concept of *control* to rites of passage. Engage students in a discussion of the relationship between self-control and becoming an adult. Lessing has Jerry move from being out of control when he is yelling the French words to controlling his breathing to controlling his panic in the face of death in the tunnel.

9 Again and again he rose, took a big chestful of air, and went down. Again and again he
10 groped over the surface of the rock, feeling it, almost hugging it in the desperate need to find the entrance. And then, once, while he was clinging to the black wall, his knees came up and he shot his feet out forward and they met no obstacle. He had found the hole.

He gained the surface, clambered about the stones that littered the barrier rock until he found a big one, and, with this in his arms, let himself down over the side of the rock. He dropped, with the weight, straight to the sandy floor. Clinging tight to the anchor of stone, he lay on his side and looked in under the dark shelf at the place where his feet had gone. He could see the hole. It was an irregular, dark gap; but he could not see deep into it. He let go of his anchor, clung with his hands to the edges of the hole, and tried to push himself in.

He got his head in, found his shoulders jammed, moved them in sidewise, and was inside as far as his waist. He could see nothing ahead. Something soft and clammy touched his mouth; he saw a dark frond moving against the grayish rock and panic filled him. He thought of octopuses, of clinging weed. He pushed himself out backward and caught a glimpse, as he retreated, of a harmless tentacle of seaweed drifting in the mouth of the tunnel. But it was enough. He reached the sunlight, swam to shore, and lay on the diving rock. He looked down into the blue well of water. He knew he must find his way through that cave, or hole, or tunnel, and out the other side.

11 First, he thought, he must learn to control his breathing. He let himself down into the water with another big stone in his arms, so that he could lie effortlessly on the bottom of the sea. He counted. One, two, three. He counted steadily. He could hear the movement of blood in his chest. Fifty-one, fifty-two . . . His chest was hurting. He let go of the rock and went up into the air. He saw that the sun was low. He rushed to the villa and found his mother at her supper. She said only "Did you enjoy yourself?" and he said "Yes."

All night the boy dreamed of the water-filled cave in the rock, and as soon as breakfast was over he went to the bay.

That night, his nose bled badly. For hours he had been underwater, learning to hold his breath, and now he felt weak and dizzy. His mother said, "I shouldn't overdo things, darling, if I were you."

> ...Jerry exercised his lungs as if everything, the whole of his life ... depended upon it.

That day and the next, Jerry exercised his lungs as if everything, the whole of his life, all that he would become, depended upon it. Again his nose bled at night, and his mother insisted on his coming with her the next day. It was a torment to him to waste a day of his careful self-training, but he stayed with her on the other beach, which now seemed a place for small children, a place where his mother might lie safe in the sun. It was not his beach.

He did not ask for permission, on the following day, to go to his beach. He went, before his mother could consider the complicated rights and wrongs of the matter. A day's rest, he discovered, had improved his count by ten. The big boys had made the passage while he counted a hundred and sixty. He had been counting fast, in his fright. Probably now, if he tried, he could get through that long tunnel, but he was not going to try yet. A curious, most unchildlike persistence, a controlled impatience, made him wait. In the meantime, he lay underwater on the white sand, littered now by stones he had brought down from the upper air,

MINI-LESSON: GRAMMAR
Subject-Verb Agreement

Teach Remind students that singular subjects and plural subjects may occur within the same sentence and that each verb must agree with its subject. Use this example:

"When he came up the boys (was, <u>were</u>) all on the diving rock, preparing to attempt the feat again."

Activity Idea For practice, students can write a description of Jerry using these criteria:

- from the point of view of one of the older boys
- using present tense
- using both singular and plural subjects
- showing correct subject-verb agreement

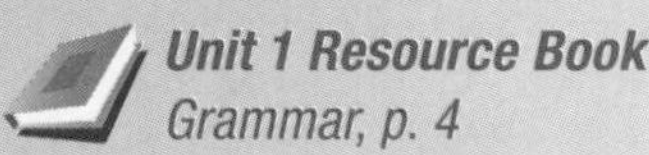
Unit 1 Resource Book
Grammar, p. 4

and studied the entrance to the tunnel. He knew every jut and corner of it, as far as it was possible to see. It was as if he already felt its sharpness about his shoulders.

He sat by the clock in the villa, when his mother was not near, and checked his time. He was incredulous[8] and then proud to find he could hold his breath without strain for two minutes. The words "two minutes," authorized by the clock, brought close the adventure that was so necessary to him.

In another four days, his mother said casually one morning, they must go home. On the day before they left, he would do it. He would do it if it killed him, he said defiantly to himself. But two days before they were to leave—a day of triumph when he increased his count by fifteen—his nose bled so badly that he turned dizzy and had to lie limply over the big rock like a bit of seaweed, watching the thick red blood flow on the rock and trickle slowly down to the sea. He was frightened. Supposing he turned dizzy in the tunnel? Supposing he died there, trapped? Supposing—his head went around, in the hot sun, and he almost gave up. He thought he would return to the house and lie down, and next summer, perhaps, when he had another year's growth in him—*then* he would go through the hole.

But even after he had made the decision, or thought he had, he found himself sitting up on the rock and looking down into the water; and he knew that now, this moment, when his nose had only just stopped bleeding, when his head was still sore and throbbing—this was the moment when he would try. If he did not do it now, he never would. He was trembling with fear that he would not go; and he was trembling with horror at that long, long tunnel under the rock, under the sea. Even in the open sunlight, the barrier rock seemed very wide and very heavy; tons of rock pressed down on where he would go. If he died there, he would lie until one day—perhaps not before next year—those big boys would swim into it and find it blocked.

He put on his goggles, fitted them tight, tested the vacuum. His hands were shaking. Then he chose the biggest stone he could carry and slipped over the edge of the rock until half of him was in the cool, enclosing water and half in the hot sun. He looked up once at the empty sky, filled his lungs once, twice, and then sank fast to the bottom with the stone. He let it go and began to count. He took the edges of the hole in his hands and drew himself into it, wriggling his shoulders in sidewise as he remembered he must, kicking himself along with his feet. 12

Soon he was clear inside. He was in a small rock-bound hole filled with yellowish-gray water. The water was pushing him up against the roof. The roof was sharp and pained his back. He pulled himself along with his hands—fast, fast—and used his legs as levers. His head knocked against something; a sharp pain dizzied him. Fifty, fifty-one, fifty-two . . . He was without light, and the water seemed to press upon him with the weight of rock. Seventy-one, seventy-two. . . There was no strain on his lungs. He felt like an inflated balloon, his lungs were so light and easy, but his head was pulsing. 13

He was being continually pressed against the sharp roof, which felt slimy as well as sharp. Again he thought of octopuses, and wondered if the tunnel might be filled with weed that could tangle him. He gave himself a panicky, convulsive kick forward, ducked his head, and swam. His feet and hands moved freely, as if in open water. The hole must have widened out. He thought he must be swimming fast, and he was frightened of banging his head if the tunnel narrowed.

A hundred, a hundred and one . . . The water paled. Victory filled him. His lungs were beginning to hurt. A few more strokes and he would be out. He was counting wildly; he said a hundred and fifteen, and then, a long time later, a hundred and fifteen again. The water was a

8. **incredulous** (in krej′ə ləs), *adj.* doubting; skeptical.

12 Reading/Thinking Skills
Predict Outcomes

Questions At this point in the story, now that Jerry has entered the tunnel, what do you think will happen to him? What makes you think this? *(Possible responses: He will succeed in swimming all the way through the tunnel because he has shown all the qualities for success; he will not quite make it because he is too young, or he will drown in the tunnel because he has attempted something too foolish and risky.)*

13 Literary Element
Plot

Remind students that plot refers to the action of a story as it is organized around a conflict. Discuss with students how Lessing uses suspense to develop the plot. For example, point out that suspense is created by the repetition of the numbers that Jerry is counting in his head. Elicit from students why this technique is effective. *(Possible response: because the reader knows Jerry's limit for holding his breath is about two minutes, whereas he had counted to 160 when timing the older boys)*

BUILDING ENGLISH PROFICIENCY

Making Science Connections

Use a stopwatch to help students understand the training that Jerry has taken upon himself.

1. Set the stopwatch, asking students to hold their breaths as long as they can. Count aloud while they do so. List various times on the chalkboard as students run out of breath.

2. Read aloud (or have a volunteer read aloud) the passage that describes Jerry's swim through the tunnel while students hold their breaths and the stopwatch runs. (Most or all students will have to breathe before Jerry would have been able to do so.)

3. Allow students to discuss their reactions. Ask: Just how much of a challenge was this? Allow students to discuss personal experiences relating to swimming and the sea.

14 Literary Focus
Theme

Questions Discuss what Jerry has achieved by going through the tunnel.

Possible responses:

- Jerry acquired self-knowledge about his physical capabilities, intelligence, courage, and determination.
- He gained confidence that he could be on his own because he accomplished the feat alone.

Encourage students to generalize about what anyone might achieve by meeting a challenge.

The Author Speaks

Lessing on the role of the writer: "I think a writer's job is to provoke questions. I like to think that if someone's read a book of mine, they've had—I don't know what—the literary equivalent of a shower. Something that would start them thinking in a slightly different way perhaps. That's what I think writers are for."

Check Test

1. Where does this story take place? *(on the rocky shore of a bay, near a crowded beach)*

2. What does the tunnel go through? *(an underwater wall of rock)*

3. How do the other boys react to Jerry when they first watch him swim and dive? *(They accept him.)*

4. Why does Jerry decide to swim the tunnel several days before he planned to? *(He felt that "if he did not do it now, he never would.")*

5. After Jerry emerges from the tunnel, what is the only thing he wants to do? *(go home and lie down)*

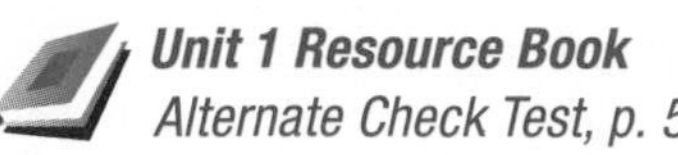

Unit 1 Resource Book
Alternate Check Test, p. 5

clear jewel-green all around him. Then he saw, above his head, a crack running up through the rock. Sunlight was falling through it, showing the clean, dark rock of the tunnel, a single mussel shell, and darkness ahead.

He was at the end of what he could do. He looked up at the crack as if it were filled with air and not water, as if he could put his mouth to it to draw in air. A hundred and fifteen, he heard himself say inside his head—but he had said that long ago. He must go on into the blackness ahead, or he would drown. His head was swelling, his lungs cracking. A hundred and fifteen, a hundred and fifteen pounded through his head, and he feebly clutched at rocks in the dark, pulling himself forward, leaving the brief space of sunlit water behind. He felt he was dying. He was no longer quite conscious. He struggled on in the darkness between lapses into unconsciousness. An immense, swelling pain filled his head, and then the darkness cracked with an explosion of green light. His hands, groping forward, met nothing; and his feet, kicking back, propelled him out into the open sea.

He drifted to the surface, his face turned up to the air. He was gasping like a fish. He felt he would sink now and drown; he could not swim the few feet back to the rock. Then he was clutching it and pulling himself up onto it. He lay face down, gasping. He could see nothing but a red-veined, clotted dark. His eyes must have burst, he thought; they were full of blood. He tore off his goggles and a gout of blood went into the sea. His nose was bleeding and the blood had filled the goggles.

He scooped up handfuls of water from the cool, salty sea, to splash on his face, and did not know whether it was blood or salt water he tasted. After a time, his heart quieted, his eyes cleared, and he sat up. He could see the local
boys diving and playing half a mile away. He did 14
not want them. He wanted nothing but to get back home and lie down.

In a short while, Jerry swam to shore and climbed slowly up the path to the villa. He flung himself on his bed and slept, waking at the sound of feet on the path outside. His mother was coming back. He rushed to the bathroom, thinking she must not see his face with bloodstains, or tearstains, on it. He came out of the bathroom and met her as she walked into the villa, smiling, his eyes lighting up.

"Have a nice morning?" she asked, laying her hand on his warm brown shoulder a moment.

"Oh, yes, thank you," he said.

"You look a bit pale." And then, sharp and anxious, "How did you bang your head?"

"Oh, just banged it," he told her.

She looked at him closely. He was strained; his eyes were glazed looking. She was worried. And then she said to herself, Oh, don't fuss! Nothing can happen. He can swim like a fish.

They sat down to lunch together.

"Mummy," he said, "I can stay underwater for two minutes—three minutes, at least." It came bursting out of him.

"Can you, darling?" she said. "Well, I shouldn't overdo it. I don't think you ought to swim anymore today."

She was ready for a battle of wills, but he gave in at once. It was no longer of the least importance to go to the bay.

After Reading

Making Connections

Shaping Your Response

1. Draw in your notebook the spectrum below and place an **X** to show how brave or foolish you think Jerry is. Be prepared to discuss your response.

   foolish ⟵————⟶ brave

2. Why do you think Jerry chooses to swim through the tunnel despite his doubts?
3. If this were a video game, what could be the level before swimming through the tunnel or the next level afterwards?

Analyzing the Story

4. Describe the changing relationship between Jerry and his mother during the story. Do you think these changes reflect Jerry's growing maturity or something else? Explain.
5. Describe Jerry's external and internal **conflicts** while accomplishing his goal.
6. How does the older boys' attitude toward Jerry change during the time he is with them?
7. After swimming through the tunnel, Jerry no longer considers the bay important. In your opinion, what does this change in attitude reflect about Jerry?

Extending the Ideas

8. Would you say that Jerry's acts are motivated by group pressure or by **individual** standards? Explain.
9. Provide examples from your experience, books, TV, or movies of both adults and children who are trying to prove themselves.

Literary Focus: Theme

One way to arrive at a **theme**, or underlying main idea, of "Through the Tunnel" is to think about why Jerry behaves as he does. Examine the following three examples. Then choose the statement you think comes closest to what you consider the theme of the story, or add your own theme statement. Explain why you chose it.

1. A young boy puts himself through strict training to swim successfully through a perilously long underwater tunnel.
2. To be treated like an adult, act like one!
3. The accomplishment of a difficult task through one's own will and effort can be an important step in growing up.

After Reading

MAKING CONNECTIONS

1. Students may suggest that Jerry is more brave than foolish.

2. Students may respond that Jerry needs to perform something daring to break away from being a child and from being tied to his mother.

3. Responses for the previous video level (less hazardous) may include swimming along the shore or diving among the rocks. Responses for the next level (more hazardous) may include swimming through the tunnel and fighting an octopus or getting entangled in seaweed along the way.

4. He goes from being dependent and seeking assurance, to needing the company of his mother and the other boys, to finally being independent and looking within himself for approval.

5. Jerry's external conflict is with nature: the danger of the tunnel and the limitations of his body. His internal conflict is a battle to master his fears and assert his will power.

6. At first, they accept him. Later, after he acts childishly, they ignore him.

7. Jerry needs to prove himself. Having done so, he no longer needs to demonstrate his abilities—to himself or to anyone else.

8. Individual standards seem uppermost in Jerry's story; however, the power of the group of older boys is ever-present even though they do not speak to Jerry.

9. Possible responses may include such experiences as needing to stay home alone without a baby-sitter, learning to drive a car, saving someone's life, or winning an athletic competition.

LITERARY FOCUS: THEME

Many students often confuse theme with plot. Remind them that a theme is an idea about human nature or the human condition the author tries to convey and that a theme is not usually stated as a single sentence in a story.

- Remind students who choose the first statement that a theme doesn't usually mention a specific character or a particular plot event.
- This injunction does not fully reflect Jerry's motivations in the story.
- This statement accurately reflects at least one of the main themes of the story, although some students may state other meaningful themes.

VOCABULARY STUDY

Possible words for each word web include:

incredulous—skeptical, unbelieving, doubting

beseeching—asking, begging, imploring

contrition—remorse, sorrow, penitence

luminous—shining, bright, glowing

myriad—thousands, multitude, numerous

promontory—headland, cape

supplication—request, prayer, entreaty

More Practice Students can choose additional words and make webs for them. Consulting a thesaurus might help them as they build the webs.

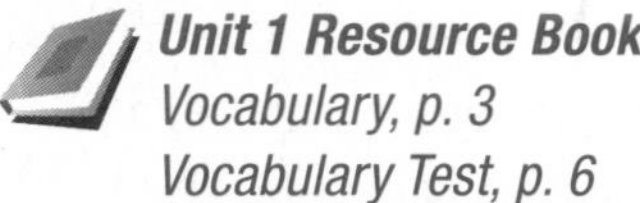

Unit 1 Resource Book
Vocabulary, p. 3
Vocabulary Test, p. 6

WRITING CHOICES

Writer's Notebook Update

Suggest that students review the details of "Through the Tunnel" in order to pinpoint the similarities and differences between Jerry's risk and their own. Some students may benefit from a list of categories for comparison, such as:

- the persons involved
- the setting or environment
- the motivation
- the obstacles or dangers
- the reward or prize
- the personal satisfaction

Selection Test

Unit 1 Resource Book
pp. 7–8

Vocabulary Study

beseeching
contrition
luminous
myriad
promontory
supplication

Make a word web to illustrate meanings for two of the listed words. An example has been done for you.

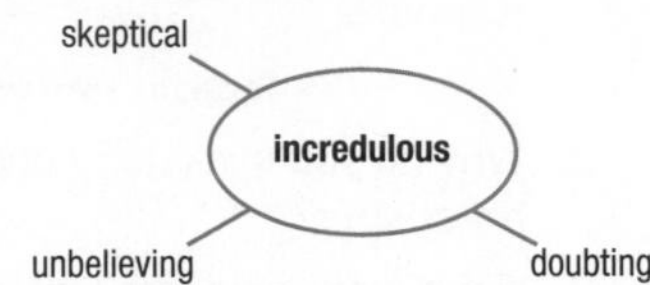

Expressing Your Ideas

Writing Choices

Writer's Notebook Update Before you read "Through the Tunnel," you wrote about a risk that you have taken and the emotions associated with it. In a paragraph, write a comparison between the risk Jerry takes and your own. How are they alike? How are they different?

On the Other Hand Just before he decides to attempt the tunnel, Jerry considers the possibility of becoming stuck in the tunnel and drowning. The prospect nearly makes him put off the swim until the following year, "when he had another year's growth in him." Write an **explanation** telling how the theme of the story would be different had Jerry delayed.

Dear Abby Worried that she is being overly protective, Jerry's mother asks an advice columnist how much freedom she should give her son during their seaside vacation. Respond to Jerry's mother as if you were writing an **advice column** that might be published in a newspaper.

Other Options

Club Med? Use the details about setting in the story plus your imagination to create a **travel brochure** describing the setting of "Through the Tunnel" as the perfect vacation place. Mention sports and activities vacationers could enjoy here, along with qualities of the landscape and water that make this an ideal spot. Remember that you are creating a persuasive piece to appeal to a wide audience.

Get the Picture After skimming the story again and checking the Glossary at the back of the book for the meaning of such words as *promontory* or *luminous,* draw a **color picture** of the setting. Decide which element of the land- or seascape should be the central focus and which should be background. Alternately, you could create a three-dimensional model of the same setting.

Brush Up Working with a partner, examine the picture on pages 10-11 and reread the caption. How does this picture make you feel? What do you think the use of color adds to the overall effect? What other details about the art do you find noteworthy? Then explain in an **art talk** whether or not you think this picture is an appropriate way to launch the theme "Pushing Toward the Top."

16 UNIT ONE: MEETING THE CHALLENGE

OTHER OPTIONS

Club Med?

Suggest that students read some actual travel brochures or magazine advertisements before planning their own brochure. Also, they can analyze the ages, geographical locations, and budgets of their intended audience.

Before Reading

Two Kinds

by Amy Tan USA

Amy Tan
born 1952

Amy Tan, whose Chinese name, An-mei, means "blessing from America," wrote her first novel, *The Joy Luck Club*, in order to understand her cultural heritage and the conflicts between her mother and herself. Tan was born in California, shortly after her parents emigrated from China and more than one hundred years after the first wave of Chinese immigrants came to America. Although her parents had hoped she would become a neurosurgeon, Tan majored in English in college and became a free-lance business writer before she began writing novels. For recreation, she reads, plays jazz piano, and shoots pool.

Building Background

The Need to Succeed Do you feel that young people are often pushed too hard by parents, teachers, coaches, or family members to accomplish and excel? Think about the difference between encouragement and pressure in preparation for reading "Two Kinds."

Literary Focus

Characterization Plot and setting are important, of course, but what really makes fiction come alive is people! From the moment the mother in "Two Kinds" says, "You can be best anything," readers know that she will be a **"character"** in every sense of the word. As you read this story, think about the two major characters, a mother and her daughter. Ask yourself, "What kind of people are they? Why do they act and feel as they do?"

Writer's Notebook

When Push Comes to Shove In this story, a mother is so eager for her daughter to excel that she pushes and pushes until the daughter defiantly pushes back. Jot down several motives that a parent, guardian, teacher, or coach might have for wanting a child to excel.

Before Reading

Building Background

Encourage students to consider various types of young people who have faced extraordinary pressures. Some are:

- athletes (tennis, skating, gymnastics)
- child actors and actresses
- gifted students

Literary Focus

Remind students that complex **characters** often have complex motivations. Making a chart like the one below may help students analyze characters' behaviors.

Specific Action	Possible Motivation
taking daughter for Shirley Temple haircut	*financial success; family pride; envy*

Writer's Notebook

Remind students that every writer's own real-world experiences are great assets. As they make their lists of motives, encourage them to consider what they know about themselves, people they have known, and people they have read about.

Connections to **NovelWorks**

NovelWorks: *The Joy Luck Club* offers a rich variety of unique materials for teaching the novel.

SUPPORT MATERIALS OVERVIEW

Unit 1 Resource Book
- Graphic Organizer, p. 9
- Study Guide, p. 10
- Vocabulary, p. 11
- Grammar, p. 12
- Alternate Check Test, p. 13
- Vocabulary Test, p. 14
- Selection Test, pp. 15–16

Building English Proficiency
- Literature Summaries
- Activities, p. 168

Reading, Writing & Grammar SkillBook
- Reading, pp. 65–66
- Writing, pp. 111–112
- Grammar, pp. 138–139

Technology
- Audiotape 1, Side B
- Personal Journal Software
- Custom Literature Database: For a short story about a father and son, see "Discovery of a Father" by Sherwood Anderson.
- Test Generator Software

Art Study

Responses to Caption Questions
Students may suggest:

- age
- the loneliness of having to practice by herself
- an ambiguous attitude toward the music

The French painter Henri Matisse (1869–1954) was one of the greatest of modern masters. Matisse rebelled against the wishes of his family (not unlike Jing-mei in Tan's story) and gave up a career as a lawyer. He worked as a part-time decorator and endured great poverty in order to study painting. Deeply influenced by the painter he idolized, Paul Cézanne (1839–1906), Matisse experimented for years with color and form. Finally, after the turn of the century, he began to exhibit and sell his paintings. Late in his life, he applied his brilliance as a colorist and his sense of rhythmic composition to a new medium—paper cutouts—which manifest the purity and simplicity of expression he always sought.

Visual Literacy The *mood,* or atmosphere, of a painting results from many factors. Ask students to identify how each of the following factors contributes to the mood of the painting:

- colors (dark or bright)
- balance (orderly or chaotic)
- setting (comfortable or threatening)
- subject (formal or informal)

SELECTION SUMMARY

Two Kinds

Jing-Mei looks back on scenes of her childhood when she rebelled against her mother's efforts to make her a prodigy. Her mother, who had lost her family and possessions in China, sees America as a potential paradise. She works to make Jing-mei into a prodigy by directing her to imitate the feats of other famous children. Finally, the mother is convinced her daughter will be a famous pianist. The girl submits to lessons given by a local teacher who is enthusiastic but deaf. The mother brags that her daughter is as brilliant as a neighbor's child who has won chess tournaments. At a formal recital, the girl plays badly, shaming herself and her family. After the recital, she accuses her mother of trying to make her into something that she is not. She says that she wishes she were dead, like her mother's previous children—and the lessons stop. Years later, after her mother's death, Jing-mei plays the piano.

*For summaries in other languages, see the **Building English Proficiency** book.*

Two Kinds

Amy Tan

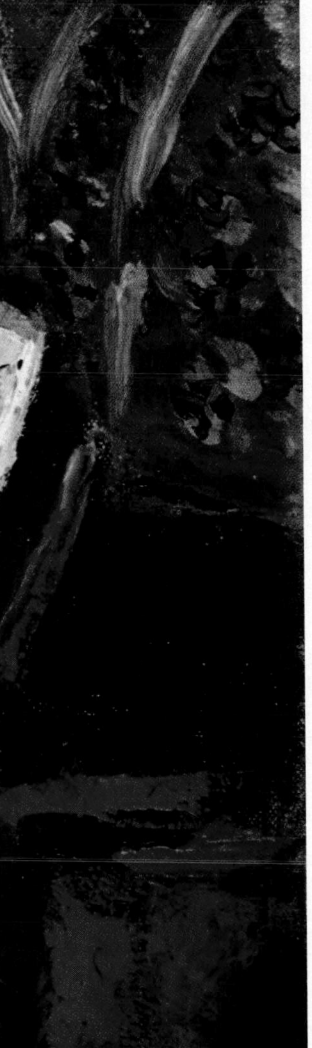

My mother believed you could be anything you wanted to be in America. You could open a restaurant. You could work for the government and get good retirement. You could buy a house with almost no money down. You could become rich. You could become instantly famous. 1

"Of course you can be prodigy,[1] too," my mother told me when I was nine. "You can be best anything. What does Auntie Lindo know? Her daughter, she is only best tricky."

America was where all my mother's hopes lay. She had come here in 1949 after losing everything in China: her mother and father, her family home, her first husband, and two daughters, twin baby girls. But she never looked back with regret. There were so many ways for things to get better.

We didn't immediately pick the right kind of prodigy. At first my mother thought I could be a Chinese Shirley Temple.[2] We'd watch Shirley's old movies on TV as though they were training films. My mother would poke my arm and say, *"Ni kan"*—You watch. And I would see Shirley tapping her feet, or singing a sailor song, or pursing her lips into a very round O while saying, "Oh my goodness."

"Ni kan," said my mother as Shirley's eyes flooded with tears. "You already know how. Don't need talent for crying!"

Soon after my mother got this idea about Shirley Temple, she took me to a beauty training school in the Mission district[3] and put me in the hands of a student who could barely hold the scissors without shaking. Instead of getting big fat curls, I emerged with an

1. **prodigy** (prod′ə jē), *n.* person endowed with amazing brilliance or talent, especially a remarkably talented child.
2. **Shirley Temple,** popular child movie star of the 1930s and 1940s.
3. **Mission district,** a section of the city of San Francisco.

Henri Matisse made the mood more important than details in this 1924 oil painting, called *La Petite Pianiste.* What does the girl in this painting seem to have in common with Jing-mei in the story?

During Reading

Selection Objectives

- to explore the theme of attaining standards set by oneself
- to analyze characterization
- to write simple sentences

Unit 1 Resource Book
Graphic Organizer, p. 9
Study Guide, p. 10

Theme Link

The theme of "Pushing Toward the Top" is developed as the daughter copes with her mother's attempts to push her to excel.

Vocabulary Preview

prodigy, person endowed with amazing brilliance or talent, especially a remarkably talented child
reproach, blame or disapproval
listlessly, seemingly too tired to care about anything
entranced, delighted; charmed
frenzied, greatly excited; frantic
mesmerizing, hypnotic
arpeggio, the sounding of the individual notes of a chord
reverie, dreamy thoughts, especially of pleasant things
discordant, not in harmony
dawdle, waste time, loiter
devastate, make desolate, destroy
fiasco, a complete or ridiculous failure, humiliating breakdown

Students can add the words and definitions to their Writer's Notebooks.

BUILDING ENGLISH PROFICIENCY

ESL LEP ELD SAE LD

Making Real-Life Connections

The first sentence of "Two Kinds" establishes the character of Jing-mei's mother—but it also provides a springboard for thinking about careers.

1. Create a web on the chalkboard. Ask students to volunteer careers such as the examples on the following illustration.

2. Students may discuss their own and their families' expectations of career opportunities in this country.

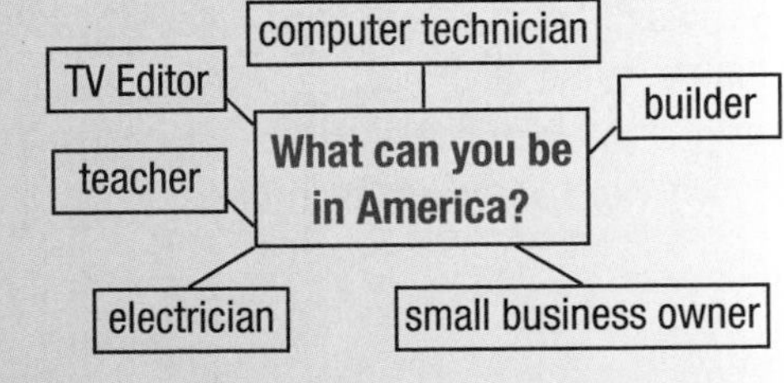

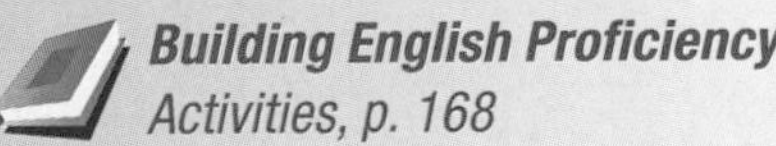

Building English Proficiency
Activities, p. 168

1 Literary Element
Theme

Question What basic idea is established in the opening sentence of the story? *(Possible response: The opening sentence introduces the conflict that will drive the entire story—the mother will impose upon the daughter her belief in unlimited potential achievement.)*

2 Literary Focus
Characterization

Questions What does the narrator imagine will be the results of being "perfect"? What does each result suggest about her character?

- *Her mother and father would adore her, suggesting that she craves their love.*
- *She would be beyond reproach, so she won't be blamed for anything.*

3 Reader's Response
Making Personal Connections

Questions Do you think the narrator's reaction upon looking in the mirror is a common one among teenagers? Why or why not? *(Possible responses: Yes, adolescence is a common time for being dissatisfied with oneself.)*

4 Literary Focus
Characterization

Questions

- What does the narrator discover about herself by looking closely at her reflection in the mirror? *(Possible response: her strength of will)*
- In what ways do you think her self-discovery is likely to make her life more difficult? *(Possible response: Her self-discovery will probably now cause conflict in circumstances which she previously would have accepted.)*

uneven mass of crinkly black fuzz. My mother dragged me off to the bathroom and tried to wet down my hair.

"You look like Negro Chinese," she lamented, as if I had done this on purpose.

The instructor of the beauty training school had to lop off these soggy clumps to make my hair even again. "Peter Pan is very popular these days," the instructor assured my mother. I now had hair the length of a boy's, with straight-across bangs that hung at a slant two inches above my eyebrows. I liked the haircut and it made me actually look forward to my future fame.

In fact, in the beginning, I was just as excited as my mother, maybe even more so. I pictured this prodigy part of me as many different images, trying each one on for size. I was a dainty ballerina girl standing by the curtains, waiting to hear the right music that would send me floating on my tiptoes. I was like the Christ child lifted out of the straw manger, crying with holy indignity. I was Cinderella stepping from her pumpkin carriage with sparkly cartoon music filling the air.

2 In all of my imaginings, I was filled with a sense that I would soon become *perfect.* My mother and father would adore me. I would be beyond reproach.[4] I would never feel the need to sulk for anything.

But sometimes the prodigy in me became impatient. "If you don't hurry up and get me out of here, I'm disappearing for good," it warned. "And then you'll always be nothing."

Every night after dinner, my mother and I would sit at the Formica kitchen table. She would present new tests, taking her examples from stories of amazing children she had read in *Ripley's Believe It or Not,* or *Good Housekeeping, Reader's Digest,* and a dozen other magazines she kept in a pile in our bathroom. My mother got these magazines from people whose houses she cleaned. And since she cleaned many houses each week, we had a great assortment. She would look through them all, searching for stories about remarkable children.

The first night she brought out a story about a three-year-old boy who knew the capitals of all the states and even most of the European countries. A teacher was quoted as saying the little boy could also pronounce the names of the foreign cities correctly.

"What's the capital of Finland?" my mother asked me, looking at the magazine story.

All I knew was the capital of California, because Sacramento was the name of the street we lived on in Chinatown. "Nairobi!" I guessed, saying the most foreign word I could think of. She checked to see if that was possibly one way to pronounce "Helsinki" before showing me the answer.

The tests got harder—multiplying numbers in my head, finding the queen of hearts in a deck of cards, trying to stand on my head without using my hands, predicting the daily temperatures in Los Angeles, New York, and London.

One night I had to look at a page from the Bible for three minutes and then report everything I could remember. "Now Jehoshaphat had riches and honor in abundance and . . . that's all I remember, Ma," I said.

And after seeing my mother's disappointed face once again, something inside of me began to die. I hated the tests, the raised hopes and failed expectations. Before going to bed that night, I looked in the mirror above the bathroom sink and when I saw only my face staring back—and that it would always be this ordinary face—I began to cry. Such a sad, ugly girl! I made high-pitched noises like a crazed animal, trying to scratch out the face in the mirror. 3

And then I saw what seemed to be the prodigy side of me—because I had never seen that face before. I looked at my reflection, blinking so I could see more clearly. The girl staring back at me was angry, powerful. This girl and I were the same. I had new thoughts, willful thoughts, or rather thoughts filled with lots of 4

4. reproach (ri prōch′), *n.* blame or disapproval.

MINI-LESSON: GRAMMAR
Writing Simple Sentences

Teach Remind students that a simple sentence has only one main clause and no subordinate clauses. Point out that an author does not always need to write compound and complex sentences to express ideas forcefully. Point out Tan's use of simple sentences, including the following sentences on p. 20:

- "My mother and father would adore me."
- "I hated the tests, the raised hopes and failed expectations."
- "This girl and I were the same."

Activity Ideas

For practice, each student can:

- identify several more simple sentences in the story
- write a simple sentence describing each of the characters in the story
- write a simple sentence summarizing each of the major events in the story

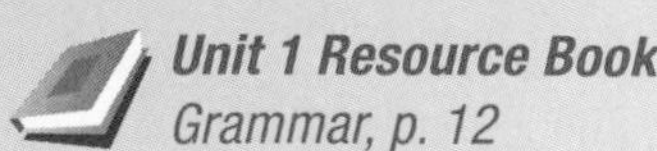

Unit 1 Resource Book
Grammar, p. 12

won'ts. I won't let her change me, I promised myself. I won't be what I'm not.

So now on nights when my mother presented her tests, I performed listlessly,[5] my head propped on one arm. I pretended to be bored. And I was. I got so bored I started counting the bellows of the foghorns out on the bay while my mother drilled me in other areas. The sound was comforting and reminded me of the cow jumping over the moon. And the next day, I played a game with myself, seeing if my mother would give up on me before eight bellows. After a while I usually counted only one, maybe two bellows at most. At last she was beginning to give up hope.

Two or three months had gone by without any mention of my being a prodigy again. And then one day my mother was watching *The Ed Sullivan Show*[6] on TV. The TV was old and the sound kept shorting out. Every time my mother got halfway up from the sofa to adjust the set, the sound would go back on and Ed would be talking. As soon as she sat down, Ed would go silent again. She got up, the TV broke into loud piano music. She sat down. Silence. Up and down, back and forth, quiet and loud. It was like a stiff embraceless dance between her and the TV set. Finally she stood by the set with her hand on the sound dial.

She seemed entranced[7] by the music, a little frenzied[8] piano piece with this mesmerizing[9] quality, sort of quick passages and then teasing lilting ones before it returned to the quick playful parts.

"Ni kan," my mother said, calling me over with hurried hand gestures. "Look here."

I could see why my mother was fascinated by the music. It was being pounded out by a little Chinese girl, about nine years old, with a Peter Pan haircut. The girl had the sauciness of a Shirley Temple. She was proudly modest like a proper Chinese child. And she also did this fancy sweep of a curtsy, so that the fluffy skirt of her white dress cascaded slowly to the floor like the petals of a large carnation.

In spite of these warning signs, I wasn't worried. Our family had no piano and we couldn't afford to buy one, let alone reams of sheet music and piano lessons. So I could be generous in my comments when my mother bad-mouthed the little girl on TV.

"Play note right, but doesn't sound good! No singing sound," complained my mother.

"What are you picking on her for?" I said carelessly. "She's pretty good. Maybe she's not the best, but she's trying hard." I knew almost immediately I would be sorry I said that.

"Just like you," she said. "Not the best. Because you not trying." She gave a little huff as she let go of the sound dial and sat down on the sofa.

The little Chinese girl sat down also to play an encore of "Anitra's Dance" by Grieg. I **5**
remember the song, because later on I had to learn how to play it.

Three days after watching *The Ed Sullivan Show,* my mother told me what my schedule would be for piano lessons and piano practice. She had talked to Mr. Chong, who lived on the first floor of our apartment building. Mr. Chong was a retired piano teacher and my mother had traded housecleaning services for weekly lessons and a piano for me to practice on every day, two hours a day, from four until six.

When my mother told me this, I felt as though I had been sent to hell. I whined and then kicked my foot a little when I couldn't stand it anymore.

"Why don't you like me the way I am? I'm *not* **6**
a genius! I can't play the piano. And even if I could, I wouldn't go on TV if you paid me a million dollars!" I cried.

My mother slapped me. "Who ask you be

---

5. **listlessly** (list′lis lē), *adv.* seemingly too tired to care about anything.
6. ***The Ed Sullivan Show,*** a weekly television variety show of the 1950s and 1960s.
7. **entranced** (en transd′), *adj.* delighted; charmed.
8. **frenzied** (fren′zēd), *adj.* greatly excited; frantic.
9. **mesmerizing** (mez′mə rī′zing), *adj.* hypnotic.

5 Historical Note
Classical Music

Tan refers to several classical composers and compositions in "Two Kinds." Each has special relevance to the characters or theme of the story.

- Edvard Grieg (1843–1907), Norwegian composer who blended Romantic and folk elements (p. 21). "Anitra's Dance" is a selection from *Peer Gynt* (1875) in which Anitra is a spirited and independent girl.
- Ludwig van Beethoven (1770–1827), German Romantic composer who broke the bonds of the classical period (p. 22). He became deaf in the later years of his life.
- Robert Schumann (1810–1856), German Romantic composer (p. 23). "Pleading Child" (p. 23) and "Perfectly Contented" (p. 26) are selections from *Kinderscenen* (*Scenes from Childhood,* 1838), a cycle of short piano pieces.
- *Madame Butterfly* (p. 24), an opera (1904) by Italian composer Giacomo Puccini (1858–1924). Butterfly, is a Japanese woman who kills herself because she is trapped in a traditional role.

6 Literary Element
Conflict

Question Of what does Jing-mei accuse her mother? Do you think the accusation is justified? *(Possible responses: She accuses her mother of not liking her for herself, but for what she might become. The mother is wrong to change her, or she is trying to help her child.)*

BUILDING ENGLISH PROFICIENCY

Making Personal Connections

Ask students why "I won't be what I'm not" and "Why don't you like me the way I am?" (page 21) might be considered key sentences in the story. *(They tell the reader how Jing-mei feels about herself.)*

1. Suggest that pairs or small groups of students create two descriptions by listing traits. One lists describes what Jing-mei thinks of herself; the other describes what the mother thinks of Jing-mei.

2. Have students share and discuss their descriptions. Encourage them to use their own experiences about how they see themselves and others as a comparison.

7 Literary Element
Similes

Remind students that a simile is a comparison using the words *like* or *as.*

Question What vivid similes does Tan use on page 22? Possible responses:

- "She had this peculiar smell like a baby that had done something in its pants."
- "And her fingers felt like a dead person's, like an old peach I once found in the back of the refrigerator."
- ". . . I just played some nonsense that sounded like a cat running up and down on top of garbage cans."
- "He marched stiffly to show me how to make each finger dance up and down, staccato like an obedient little soldier."

8 Reading/Thinking Skills
Compare and Contrast

Jing-mei calls her practicing "dutiful," yet she admits that she is learning poorly in order to be true to herself. At this point, you can open a discussion of the differences and similarities between this character and Jerry in "Through the Tunnel." Guide them to discuss motivation, ability, and traits of the two characters as they trained themselves.

genius?" she shouted. "Only ask you be your best. For you sake. You think I want you be genius? Hnnh! What for! Who ask you!"

"So ungrateful," I heard her mutter in Chinese. "If she had as much talent as she has temper, she would be famous now."

Mr. Chong, whom I secretly nicknamed Old Chong, was very strange, always tapping his fingers to the silent music of an invisible orchestra. He looked ancient in my eyes. He had lost most of the hair on top of his head and he wore thick glasses and had eyes that always looked tired and sleepy. But he must have been younger than I thought, since he lived with his mother and was not yet married.

I met Old Lady Chong once and that was enough. She had this peculiar smell like a baby that had done something in its pants. And her fingers felt like a dead person's, like an old peach I once found in the back of the refrigerator; the skin just slid off the meat when I picked it up.

> . . . I just played some nonsense that sounded like a cat running up and down on top of garbage cans.

I soon found out why Old Chong had retired from teaching piano. He was deaf. "Like Beethoven!" he shouted to me. "We're both listening only in our head!" And he would start to conduct his frantic silent sonatas.

7 Our lessons went like this. He would open the book and point to different things, explaining their purpose: "Key! Treble! Bass! No sharps or flats! So this is C major! Listen now and play after me!"

And then he would play the C scale a few times, a simple chord, and then, as if inspired by an old, unreachable itch, he gradually added more notes and running trills and a pounding bass until the music was really something quite grand.

I would play after him, the simple scale, the simple chord, and then I just played some nonsense that sounded like a cat running up and down on top of garbage cans. Old Chong smiled and applauded and then said, "Very good! But now you must learn to keep time!"

So that's how I discovered that Old Chong's eyes were too slow to keep up with the wrong notes I was playing. He went through the motions in half-time. To help me keep rhythm, he stood behind me, pushing down on my right shoulder for every beat. He balanced pennies on top of my wrists so I would keep them still as I slowly played scales and arpeggios.[10] He had me curve my hand around an apple and keep that shape when playing chords. He marched stiffly to show me how to make each finger dance up and down, staccato like an obedient little soldier.

He taught me all these things, and that was how I also learned I could be lazy and get away with mistakes, lots of mistakes. If I hit the wrong notes because I hadn't practiced enough, I never corrected myself. I just kept playing in rhythm. And Old Chong kept conducting his own private reverie.[11]

So maybe I never really gave myself a fair chance. I did pick up the basics pretty quickly, and I might have become a good pianist at that young age. But I was so determined not to try, not to be anybody different that I learned to play only the most ear-splitting preludes, the most discordant[12] hymns.

Over the next year, I practiced like this, dutifully in my own way. And then one day I heard my mother and her friend Lindo Jong both talk- 8

10. arpeggio (är pej′ē ō), *n.* the sounding of the individual notes of a chord.
11. reverie (rev′ər ē), *n.* dreamy thoughts, especially of pleasant things.
12. discordant (dis kôrd′nt), *adj.* not in harmony.

MINI-LESSON: VOCABULARY
Using Specialized Dictionaries

Teach Students may find their research work easier by learning that libraries usually include in their collections of reference books many dictionaries devoted to specialized fields. Such dictionaries—in fields ranging throughout the arts and sciences—define terms and provide examples of concepts. Usually these dictionaries are written by specialists and experts in each particular field.

Activity Ideas Have students:

- list the music-related words (such as *scale, sonata, prelude*) in this short story
- locate a specialized music dictionary in the library, such as *The Harvard Dictionary of Music* or *The New Grove Dictionary of Music and Musicians,* and find the definitions of the words on their lists
- list the names of some of the other specialized dictionaries they find in the library and identify the specialized field to which each dictionary is devoted

ing in a loud bragging tone of voice so others could hear. It was after church, and I was leaning against the brick wall wearing a dress with stiff white petticoats. Auntie Lindo's daughter, Waverly, who was about my age, was standing farther down the wall about five feet away. We had grown up together and shared all the closeness of two sisters squabbling over crayons and dolls. In other words, for the most part, we hated each other. I thought she was snotty. Waverly Jong had gained a certain amount of fame as "Chinatown's Littlest Chinese Chess Champion."

"She bring home too many trophy," lamented Auntie Lindo that Sunday. "All day she play chess. All day I have no time to do nothing but dust off her winnings." She threw a scolding look at Waverly, who pretended not to see her.

"You lucky you don't have this problem," said Auntie Lindo with a sigh to my mother.

And my mother squared her shoulders and bragged: "Our problem worser than yours. If we ask Jing-mei wash dish, she hear nothing but music. It's like you can't stop this natural talent."

And right then, I was determined to put a stop to her foolish pride.

A few weeks later, Old Chong and my mother conspired to have me play in a talent show which would be held in the church hall. By then, my parents had saved up enough to buy me a secondhand piano, a black Wurlitzer spinet with a scarred bench. It was the showpiece of our living room.

For the talent show, I was to play a piece called "Pleading Child" from Schumann's *Scenes from Childhood.* It was a simple, moody piece that sounded more difficult than it was. I was supposed to memorize the whole thing, playing the repeat parts twice to make the piece sound longer. But I dawdled[13] over it, playing a few bars and then cheating, looking up to see what notes followed. I never really listened to what I
9 was playing. I daydreamed about being somewhere else, about being someone else.

The part I liked to practice best was the fancy curtsy: right foot out, touch the rose on the carpet with a pointed foot, sweep to the side, left leg bends, look up and smile.

My parents invited all the couples from the Joy Luck Club to witness my debut. Auntie Lindo and Uncle Tin were there. Waverly and her two older brothers had also come. The first two rows were filled with children both younger and older than I was. The littlest ones got to go first. They recited simple nursery rhymes, squawked out tunes on miniature violins, twirled Hula Hoops, pranced in pink ballet tutus, and when they bowed or curtsied, the audience would sigh in unison, "Awww," and then clap enthusiastically.

When my turn came, I was very confident. I remember my childish excitement. It was as if I knew, without a doubt, that the prodigy side of me really did exist. I had no fear whatsoever, no nervousness. I remember thinking to myself, This is it! This is it! I looked out over the audience, at my mother's blank face, my father's yawn, Auntie Lindo's stiff-lipped smile, Waverly's sulky expression. I had on a white dress layered with sheets of lace, and a pink bow in my Peter Pan haircut. As I sat down I envisioned people jumping to their feet and Ed Sullivan rushing up to introduce me to everyone on TV.

And I started to play. It was so beautiful. I was so caught up in how lovely I looked that at first I didn't worry how I would sound. So it was a surprise to me when I hit the first wrong note and I realized something didn't sound quite right. And then I hit another and another followed that. A chill started at the top of my head and began to trickle down. Yet I couldn't stop playing, as though my hands were bewitched. I kept thinking my fingers would adjust themselves back, like a train switching to the right
track. I played this strange jumble through two  10

13. **dawdle** (dô′dl), *v.* waste time; loiter.

9 Literary Element
Foreshadowing

Questions How does the author foreshadow Jing-mei's disastrous performance? *(Jing-mei's attitude and behavior signal that she'll play poorly: her daydreams of being somewhere else and someone else; her poor practicing; her thinking that she could be on TV; her lack of nervousness and interest in the music, her focus on her appearance.)*

10 Reader's Response
Making Personal Connections

Questions Do Jing-mei's reactions to this embarrassing incident sound authentic? How do you feel now about embarrassing incidents from your past? *(Possible response: Students will probably agree that Jing-mei's trembling and shame sound realistic; they may say they still feel shame about their own embarrassing moments, or they may now laugh about them or have learned from them.)*

BUILDING ENGLISH PROFICIENCY

Comparing Characters

Help students understand the indirect bragging that Jing-mei's and Waverly's mothers engage in. Write or repeat the mothers' statements. Then ask students to state in their own words what the mothers really mean.

Auntie Lindo: "She bring home too many trophy. . . ." *(Waverly is amazingly talented and she has the trophies to prove it.)*

Jing-mei's mother: "Our problem worse than yours. . . . " *(Jing-mei has an amazing musical talent.)*

Continue the discussion by asking whether students feel embarrassed when parents praise or criticize them to others. Ask volunteers to share their experiences.

11 Literary Focus

Characterization

Questions After all her own personal humiliation, what truly devastates Jing-mei? What does she believe that her mother is feeling? What does her reaction suggest about her character?

Possible responses:

- *Jing-mei tells us she is devastated by her mother's blank expression.*
- *She believes her mother feels a sense of total loss.*
- *Her reaction suggests she possesses a deep love and sympathy for her mother.*

12 Multicultural Note

China—Perspective on Obedience

The moral philosopher Confucius (551–479 B.C.) had an enormous impact on cultural norms in China. The mother's point of view in Tan's story reflects the traditional Chinese and Confucian ideal of a child-parent relationship. In *China: A Cultural History,* historian Arthur Cotterell expresses the concept this way:

"[Confucius] said that in accordance with the rules of *li* [propriety] affection and respect should be expressed during the lifetime of one's parents through obedience and after their death by proper burial and the bringing of offerings to their tombs. Filial piety *(xiao)* involved the continuation of deference to parents into full adulthood; it was never the simply natural attitude of children."

repeats, the sour notes staying with me all the way to the end.

When I stood up, I discovered my legs were shaking. Maybe I had just been nervous and the audience, like Old Chong, had seen me go through the right motions and had not heard anything wrong at all. I swept my right foot out, went down on my knee, looked up and smiled. The room was quiet, except for Old Chong, who was beaming and shouting, "Bravo! Bravo! Well done!" But then I saw my mother's face, her stricken face. The audience clapped weakly, and as I walked back to my chair, with my whole face quivering as I tried not to cry, I heard a little boy whisper loudly to his mother, "That was awful," and the mother whispered back, "Well, she certainly tried."

And now I realized how many people were in the audience, the whole world it seemed. I was aware of eyes burning into my back. I felt the shame of my mother and father as they sat stiffly throughout the rest of the show.

We could have escaped during intermission. Pride and some strange sense of honor must have anchored my parents to their chairs. And so we watched it all: the eighteen-year-old boy with a fake mustache who did a magic show and juggled flaming hoops while riding a unicycle. The breasted girl with white makeup who sang from *Madame Butterfly* and got honorable mention. And the eleven-year-old boy who won first prize playing a tricky violin song that sounded like a busy bee.

After the show, the Hsus, the Jongs, and the St. Clairs from the Joy Luck Club came up to my mother and father.

"Lots of talented kids," Auntie Lindo said vaguely, smiling broadly.

"That was somethin' else," said my father, and I wondered if he was referring to me in a humorous way, or whether he even remembered what I had done.

Waverly looked at me and shrugged her shoulders. "You aren't a genius like me," she said matter-of-factly. And if I hadn't felt so bad, I would have pulled her braids and punched her stomach.

But my mother's expression was what devastated[14] me: a quiet, blank look that said she had lost everything. I felt the same way, and it seemed as if everybody were now coming up, like gawkers at the scene of an accident, to see what parts were actually missing. When we got on the bus to go home, my father was humming the busy-bee tune and my mother was silent. I kept thinking she wanted to wait until we got home before shouting at me. But when my father unlocked the door to our apartment, my mother walked in and then went to the back, into the bedroom. No accusations. No blame. And in a way, I felt disappointed. I had been waiting for her to start shouting, so I could shout back and cry and blame her for all my misery. 11

I assumed my talent-show fiasco[15] meant I never had to play the piano again. But two days later, after school, my mother came out of the kitchen and saw me watching TV.

"Four clock," she reminded me as if it were any other day. I was stunned, as though she were asking me to go through the talent-show torture again. I wedged myself more tightly in front of the TV.

"Turn off TV," she called from the kitchen five minutes later.

I didn't budge. And then I decided. I didn't have to do what my mother said anymore. I wasn't her slave. This wasn't China. I had listened to her before and look what happened. She was the stupid one. 12

She came out from the kitchen and stood in the arched entryway of the living room. "Four clock," she said once again, louder.

"I'm not going to play anymore," I said nonchalantly. "Why should I? I'm not a genius."

---

14. **devastate** (dev′ə stāt′), *v.* make desolate; destroy.
15. **fiasco** (fē as′kō), *n.* a complete or ridiculous failure; humiliating breakdown.

MINI-LESSON: READING/THINKING SKILLS

Draw Conclusions

Teach Unlike the conclusion about Mr. Chong that Jing-mei draws on page 22, here she draws an incorrect conclusion that her mother would let her stop playing piano.

Questions

- What observation does Jing-mei make before concluding that her mother will end the piano lessons? *(She observes the look on her mother's face and misinterprets it as a look of defeat.)*
- What does she not interpret correctly? *(She underestimates her mother's stubbornness and will to succeed.)*

Activity Idea Ask students to write a paragraph in which they draw a conclusion about what Jing-mei would do if she were offered a chance to take dance lessons. Have students:

- observe Jing-mei's previous responses
- interpret Jing-mei's responses
- conclude what her reaction would be

She walked over and stood in front of the TV. I saw her chest was heaving up and down in an angry way.

"No!" I said, and I now felt stronger, as if my true self had finally emerged. So this was what had been inside me all along.

"No! I won't!" I screamed.

She yanked me by the arm, pulled me off the floor, snapped off the TV. She was frighteningly strong, half pulling, half carrying me toward the piano as I kicked the throw rugs under my feet. She lifted me up and onto the hard bench. I was sobbing by now, looking at her bitterly. Her chest was heaving even more and her mouth was open, smiling crazily as if she were pleased I was crying.

"You want me to be someone that I'm not!" I sobbed. "I'll never be the kind of daughter you want me to be!"

"Only two kinds of daughters," she shouted in Chinese. "Those who are obedient and those who follow their own mind! Only one kind of daughter can live in this house. Obedient daughter!"

"Then I wish I wasn't your daughter. I wish you weren't my mother," I shouted. As I said these things I got scared. It felt like worms and toads and slimy things crawling out of my chest, but it also felt good, as if this awful side of me had surfaced, at last.

This papercut image from the Shanxi Province of China provides two views of a girl—a profile and a view of her full face. What similarities and differences can you find between this piece of art and the Matisse painting on page 18?

"Too late change this," said my mother shrilly.

And I could sense her anger rising to its breaking point. I wanted to see it spill over. And that's when I remembered the babies she had lost in China, the ones we never talked about. "Then I wish I'd never been born!" I shouted. "I wish I were dead! Like them." 13

It was as if I had said the magic words. Alakazam!—and her face went blank, her mouth closed, her arms went slack, and she backed out of the room, stunned, as if she were blowing away like a small brown leaf, thin, brittle, lifeless.

It was not the only disappointment my mother felt in me. In the years that followed, I failed her so many times, each time asserting my own will, my right to fall short of expectations. I didn't get straight A's. I didn't become class president. I didn't get into Stanford. I dropped out of college.

For unlike my mother, I did not believe I could be anything I wanted to be. I could only be me.

And for all those years, we never talked about the disaster at the recital or my terrible accusations afterward at the piano bench. All that remained unchecked, like a betrayal that was now unspeakable. So I never found a way to ask her why she had hoped for something so large that failure was inevitable.

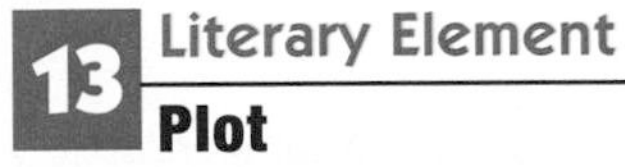

Art Study

Responses to Caption Questions
Students may suggest:

- both works depict a young girl or woman alone
- in both works the girl appears to be in a contemplative mood
- the Matisse painting provides many more details of setting
- the papercut suggests character with a few simple outlines, while the painting fleshes out the figure

13 Literary Element
Plot

Remind students that the climax, or turning point, of a plot is the point at which the action reaches its most intense pitch and a decisive event occurs.

Questions What is the decisive event that occurs at the climax in the story? *(Possible response: Jing-mei asserts her desire to be dead rather than obey her mother.)*

Use this opportunity to discuss the four main types of conflict:

- person against another person
- person against nature
- person against society
- a conflict within a person

Allow students to take positions on whether the main conflict is between Jing-mei and her mother or between Jing-mei and herself. *(Jing-mei and her mother are in conflict. While their beliefs bring them pain and disappointment, they do not doubt themselves.)*

BUILDING ENGLISH PROFICIENCY

Expressing Emotions

Ask a volunteer to read the sentence on page 25 that describes Jing-mei's anger. ("It felt like worms and toads. . . .") Explain that there are many ways to express emotion dramatically.

Activity Ideas

- Ask students to think of other ways to express Jing-mei's anger. Encourage them to pantomime, give a dramatic reading, draw, and so on. Allow students to respond in first languages other than English.
- Have students explore how to express other emotions. Quickly brainstorm and list other feelings—for example, joy, surprise, jealousy, embarrassment, irritation, or fear. Encourage students to use various techniques to show one of the listed emotions.

14 Literary Focus
Characterization

At this point, when the differences between Jing-mei her mother seem greatest, you may wish to use a Venn diagram to discuss their traits. *Possible responses: **Jing-mei:** childish, immature, governed by American standards; **her mother:** practical, driven, insensitive, governed by Chinese standards; **both:** willful, vain)*

15 Literary Element
Symbol

Remind students that a symbol is something that stands for something else.

Question What do the two songs symbolize to Jing-mei at the end of the story? *(Possible responses: the double-sided, love-hate relationship Jing-mei has with her mother; her past and present feelings toward her mother)*

Check Test

1. What does Jing-mei's mother want her to be? *(a prodigy, a success, the best she can be)*
2. Why is Mr. Chong an ineffective teacher? *(He is deaf and doesn't correct Jing-mei's errors.)*
3. What happens at the talent show? *(Jing-mei plays badly, humiliating herself and her mother.)*
4. What does Jing-mei say that finally stops her mother from making her play the piano? *("I wish I were dead! Like them," referring to her mother's previous children.)*
5. What does Jing-mei do with the piano after her mother's death? *(She has it tuned and plays the old songs on it.)*

Unit 1 Resource Book
Alternate Check Test, p. 13

And even worse, I never asked her what frightened me the most: Why had she given up hope?

For after our struggle at the piano, she never mentioned my playing again. The lessons
14 stopped. The lid to the piano was closed, shutting out the dust, my misery, and her dreams.

So she surprised me. A few years ago, she offered to give me the piano, for my thirtieth birthday. I had not played in all those years. I saw the offer as a sign of forgiveness, a tremendous burden removed.

"Are you sure?" I asked shyly. "I mean, won't you and Dad miss it?"

"No, this your piano," she said firmly. "Always your piano. You only one can play."

"Well, I probably can't play anymore," I said. "It's been years."

"You pick up fast," said my mother, as if she knew this was certain. "You have natural talent. You could been genius if you want to."

"No I couldn't."

"You just not trying," said my mother. And she was neither angry nor sad. She said it as if to announce a fact that could never be disproved. "Take it," she said.

But I didn't at first. It was enough that she had offered it to me. And after that, every time I saw it in my parents' living room, standing in front of the bay windows, it made me feel proud, as if it were a shiny trophy I had won back.

Last week I sent a tuner over to my parents' apartment and had the piano reconditioned, for purely sentimental reasons. My mother had died a few months before and I had been getting things in order for my father, a little bit at a time. I put the jewelry in special silk pouches. The sweaters she had knitted in yellow, pink, bright orange—all the colors I hated—I put those in moth-proof boxes. I found some old Chinese silk dresses, the kind with little slits up the sides. I rubbed the old silk against my skin, then wrapped them in tissue and decided to take them home with me.

After I had the piano tuned, I opened the lid and touched the keys. It sounded even richer than I remembered. Really, it was a very good piano. Inside the bench were the same exercise notes with handwritten scales, the same secondhand music books with their covers held together with yellow tape.

I opened up the Schumann book to the dark little piece I had played at the recital. It was on the left-hand side of the page, "Pleading Child." It looked more difficult than I remembered. I played a few bars, surprised at how easily the notes came back to me.

And for the first time, or so it seemed, I noticed the piece on the right-hand side. It was called "Perfectly Contented." I tried to play this one as well. It had a lighter melody but the same flowing rhythm and turned out to be quite easy. "Pleading Child" was shorter but slower; "Perfectly Contented" was longer, but faster. 15
And after I played them both a few times, I realized they were two halves of the same song.

MINI-LESSON: SPEAKING AND LISTENING
Informal Speech

Teach Many students find it challenging to try to explain why they like something, yet this is one of the most common questions asked of them. Provide them with the following tips:

- Tell how the item affects you personally.
- Tell how it affects people you know.
- Tell how it compares with other such items.

Activity Idea Have students each give a one-minute informal speech explaining why they like a particular song. Suggest that they: identify a song and write down a few thoughts as they think about what they will say. Remind them that they do not need to memorize informal speeches. You can evaluate short informal speeches on clarity of thought and economy of expression.

After Reading

Making Connections

Shaping Your Response

1. Rate Jing-mei and her mother on a scale from 1-10 with 10 being what you consider an ideal mother or daughter. Be ready to explain your ratings.

Character	Rating
Jing-mei	
Mother	

2. For which **character** do you feel more sympathy—the mother or Jing-mei? Why?

Analyzing the Story

3. Do you think the mother's plan for her daughter to become a prodigy is unrealistic? Why or why not?
4. Reread the final paragraph of the story. What do you think Jing-mei has learned?
5. Why might Tan have titled her story "Two Kinds"? To what do you think this phrase refers?

Extending the Ideas

6. Do you think that Jing-mei's mother is more concerned with group norms than with letting her daughter develop as an **individual**? Explain.
7. In your opinion, could the mother's background in China have influenced her to push Jing-mei? Why or why not?
8. In your opinion, is proving herself as an **individual** as important to Jing-mei as it is to Jerry in "Through the Tunnel"? Explain.
9. Think of people who have demonstrated notable talent or genius. To what extent do you think such people are born with these gifts? To what extent are outside influences and support responsible?

Literary Focus: Characterization

One of a fiction writer's greatest challenges involves the creation of believable **characters**. Sometimes characters seem realistic and complex (or three-dimensional); sometimes they may seem unrealistic and one-dimensional. To make characters come alive, writers may describe their physical appearance and situation; reveal their thoughts and words; show the reactions of other characters to them.

- Find an example of each method of characterization in the story.

LITERARY FOCUS: CHARACTERIZATION

Remind students that the three basic methods of characterization described on page 27 may be expressed this way:

- the writer's words about the character
- the character's own words
- the responses of other characters

Students can create a characterization chart like the one illustrated here.

Jing-mei's words as a young girl	"Why don't you like me the way I am?"
Jing-mei's words as an adult	"I did not believe I could be anything I wanted to be."
Response of other characters	"Only ask you be your best. For you sake."

After Reading

MAKING CONNECTIONS

1. Responses will vary, although most students will probably rate Jing-mei highly because of her independent spirit, honesty, and common adolescent problems. Possibly the mother has good intentions but pushes her daughter too hard.

2. Most students will likely sympathize with Jing-mei and identify with her struggles. Some students may sympathize with the mother because of her tragic losses and her desires for her family.

3. Possible responses: prodigies are born with great talent; the mother is unrealistic in expecting her daughter to perform brilliantly where she has shown little talent.

4. Possible responses: Jing-mei realizes she was the "pleading" child and now, as an adult, she is "perfectly contented." The conflict has not been resolved—Jing-mei knows that she and her mother were two kinds of people.

5. Possible responses: two kinds of people in the mother and daughter; two images of Jing-mei, the rebellious daughter and the satisfied adult; two approaches to bringing up children, American and Chinese.

6. Responses will vary, but students are likely to see the mother's actions as driven by her own beliefs and those of her friends and that she doesn't believe that a child's individuality is important.

7. In drawing conclusions, students should contrast the mother's experience in China—the lack of economic opportunity and the loss of her family and possessions—with the possibilities for Jing-mei in the United States.

8. Both Jing-mei and Jerry have a desire to become the persons they believe they want to become. Jerry shows this by overcoming a physical obstacle, Jing-mei by resisting the authority of her mother.

9. Encourage students to consider local as well as widely renowned achievers. Responses will vary, though students should realize that even the greatest natural talents have to be nurtured, developed, and disciplined.

VOCABULARY STUDY

Vocabulary words, as used in context, should reflect correct meanings and connotations.

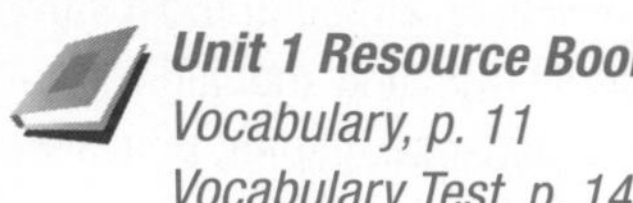

Unit 1 Resource Book
Vocabulary, p. 11
Vocabulary Test, p. 14

WRITING CHOICES

Writer's Notebook Update

Students' review of the details of the story, should help them realize that complex characters usually have complex motivations. As students attempt to explain the mother's behavior, no single detail, such as the mother's background in China, may provide full support for a motivation. Encourage students to be open to a variety of explanations.

Rebel with a Cause

Students may find it useful to identify a specific topic as the basis of the dialogue before they begin writing. You may also want to remind students that a dialogue about goals need not assume that the parent and child are in conflict, nor need it be a shouting match. A dialogue, after all, includes listening to another person as well as speaking your own mind.

Selection Test

Unit 1 Resource Book
pp. 15–16

Vocabulary Study

arpeggio
dawdle
devastate
discordant
entranced
fiasco
frenzied
listlessly
mesmerizing
prodigy
reproach
reverie

Use eight of the vocabulary words to write about one of the following.

- a plot summary of "Two Kinds"
- a description of a frenzied prodigy
- an ad for a new miracle product

Expressing Your Ideas

Writing Choices

Writer's Notebook Update Reread the list of motives you wrote down before reading "Two Kinds." Do any of these help explain why the mother acts as she does? Write an explanation of why you think Jing-mei's mother pushes her. Cite evidence from the story to support your ideas.

Rebel with a Cause Create your own version of a Jing-mei and her mother. Write a **dialogue** between a parent and a child that reflects their different goals. Put the characters in a specific situation—for example, a shopping mall, an athletic event, a family reunion. Begin in the middle of an argument, and fill in background details. You might use vocabulary words such as *fiasco, discordant,* and *reproach* to create a mood of conflict.

Dear Jong Jing-mei's mother regularly corresponds with an older brother who lives in China, telling him about her family. Write a **letter** the mother might have written after either the talent show or the angry conversation with her daughter that made her appear "stunned, as if she were blowing away like a small brown leaf, thin, brittle, lifeless."

Other Options

Portrait Gallery Create a portrait gallery of young people who have displayed notable talent in a particular field. You may include celebrities or people you know who have not achieved fame. Draw **pictures** or use **photographs**, and write a caption beneath each one. Then find an interesting way to display your work in the classroom. You might look at the Interdisciplinary Study on pages 50–54 for inspiration.

Talent Shows Several movies of the 1990s deal with child prodigies. In *Little Man Tate,* director and star Jodie Foster—herself a prodigy—creates a realistic portrait of a youthful genius. *Searching for Bobby Fischer* and *Hoop Dreams* depict talented chess and basketball players, respectively. You might give a **report** on one of these movies or, if your teacher agrees, bring it to class for viewing. Then lead a discussion on the advantages and drawbacks that come with exceptional talent, as well as the best way to nurture such talent.

OTHER OPTIONS

Talent Shows

You may want to suggest that students:

- ask a librarian to help them find books on exceptional young people
- report on "gifted and talented" programs in your school district
- research and report on tests and organizations that identify a person's aptitude for a particular occupation

Before Reading

The Censors

by Luisa Valenzuela Argentina

Luisa Valenzuela
born 1938

One of Argentina's most famous authors, Luisa Valenzuela (lü ē′sə val′ən-zwā′lə) "plays with words, turns them inside out, weaves them into sensuous webs." Born in Buenos Aires in 1938, the daughter of a physician and a well-respected writer, Valenzuela wrote and published her first story at eighteen. Many of her works deal with the harsh military rule of Argentina after the brief return of Juan Perón to the presidency in 1973. Valenzuela currently divides her time between Buenos Aires and New York City, where she teaches creative writing.

Building Background

Strange to Say Cryptographers, professional decoders of secret messages, have been asked to crack a code. The security of their nation depends on their success! What do you know about their methods? Have you ever decoded or created a secret language — something more complicated than Pig Latin? Working in small groups, try to decipher the following code: *2-5 1-12-5-18-20-5-4! BSNT XJMM BSSJWF PO BJS GPSDF POF GSJEBZ.*

In the story you are about to read, Juan, the main character, becomes so inventive at detecting messages in letters that he can find in a simple phrase a plot to overthrow the government.

Literary Focus

Satire The art of criticizing a subject by mocking it and evoking toward it an attitude of amusement, contempt, or scorn is called **satire**. The purpose of much satire is to bring about a change. What is being satirized in this cartoon?

THIS STRUCTURE WILL BE TORN DOWN AND REPLACED BY A NEW 44-STORY COOKIE

Writer's Notebook

Big Brother Is Watching You People living under a dictatorship are constantly aware that their every action is watched closely. For even the slightest offense, they might be picked up for questioning or punished. Jot down a list of ways your life would be different if you lived under this kind of government.

Before Reading

Building Background

In the first part of the message, the numbers are the positions of letters in the alphabet. In the second part, replace each letter by the letter that precedes it in the alphabet. The message reads: *Be alerted! Arms will arrive on Air Force One Friday.*

Literary Focus

The cartoon **satirizes** the way society destroys good things as it rushes toward progress.

Writer's Notebook

As an alternative assignment, students can write about going to a school where the rules are harsh and the punishment for breaking them severe. Suggest that they put their ideas in the form of a diary or journal.

More About Luisa Valenzuela

One of Valenzuela's favorite themes is the use of language by people in power to repress and dominate the weak.

Valenzuela is concerned with women's identity and women's rights. The narrator of each short story is a woman in her collection *Other Weapons*, Ediciones del Norte (1982) and Ediciones del Norte/Persea Books (1986), English translation.

SUPPORT MATERIALS OVERVIEW

Unit 1 Resource Book
- Graphic Organizer, p. 17
- Study Guide, p. 18
- Vocabulary, p. 19
- Grammar, p. 20
- Alternate Check Test, p. 21
- Vocabulary Test, p. 22
- Selection Test, pp. 23–24

Building English Proficiency
- Literature Summaries
- "The Censors" in Spanish
- Activities, p. 169

Reading, Writing & Grammar SkillBook
- Reading, pp. 74–75
- Writing, pp. 115–116
- Grammar, pp. 180–181

Technology
- Audiotape 2, Side A
- Personal Journal Software
- Custom Literature Database: For another short story about an obsession, see "Punch, Brothers, Punch" by Mark Twain on the database.
- Test Generator Software

During Reading

Selection Objectives

- to explore the theme of becoming self-destructive in pursuit of a goal
- to identify characteristics of satire
- to recognize propaganda techniques
- to practice using apostrophes correctly

Unit 1 Resource Book
Graphic Organizer, p. 17
Study Guide, p. 18

Theme Link

Juan "pushes toward the top" within a destructive system. As he achieves his goals, he brings about his own defeat.

Vocabulary Preview

irreproachable, free from blame, faultless
ulterior, beyond what is seen or expressed, hidden
staidness, the condition of having a settled, quiet character
sheer, unmixed with anything else, complete
albeit, even though, although
elapse, slip away, pass
conniving, giving aid to wrongdoing by not telling of it or by helping it secretly
subversive, tending to overthrow, causing ruin
zeal, eager desire or effort, earnest enthusiasm
distraction, disturbance of thought

Students can add the words and definitions to their Writer's Notebooks.

THE ~~POOR JUAN! ONE~~ CENSORS

Luisa Valenzuela

Poor Juan! One day they caught him with his guard down before he could even realize that what he had taken as a stroke of luck was really one of fate's dirty tricks. These things happen the minute you're careless and you let down your guard, as one often does. Juancito let happiness—a feeling you can't trust—get the better of him when he received from a confidential source Mariana's new address in Paris and he knew that she hadn't forgotten him. Without thinking twice, he sat down at his table and wrote her a letter. *The* letter that keeps his mind off his job during the day and won't let him sleep at night (what had he scrawled, what had he put on that sheet of paper he sent to Mariana?).

Juan knows there won't be a problem with the letter's contents, that it's irreproachable,[1] harmless. But what about the rest? He knows
1 that they examine, sniff, feel, and read between the lines of each and every letter, and check its tiniest comma and most accidental stain. He knows that all letters pass from hand to hand and go through all sorts of tests in the huge censorship offices and that, in the end, very few continue on their way. Usually it takes months, even years, if there aren't any snags; all this time the freedom, maybe even the life, of both sender and receiver is in jeopardy. And that's why Juan's so down in the dumps; thinking that something might happen to Mariana because of his letters. Of all people, Mariana, who must finally feel safe there where she always dreamed she'd live. But he knows that the *Censor's Secret Command* operates all over the world and cashes in on the discount in air rates; there's nothing to stop them from going as far as that hidden Paris neighborhood, kidnapping Mariana, and returning to their cozy homes, certain of having fulfilled their noble mission.

Well, you've got to beat them to the punch, do what everyone tries to do: sabotage the machinery, throw sand in its gears, get to the bottom of the problem so as to stop it.

This was Juan's sound plan when he, like many others, applied for a censor's job—not because he had a calling or needed a job: no, he applied simply to intercept his own letter, a consoling but unoriginal idea. He was hired immediately, for each day more and more censors are needed and no one would bother to check on his references.

Ulterior[2] motives couldn't be overlooked by the *Censorship Division,* but they needn't be too strict with those who applied. They knew how hard it would be for those poor guys to find the letter they wanted and even if they did, what's a letter or two when the new censor would snap up so many others? That's how Juan managed to join the *Post Office's Censorship Division,* with a certain goal in mind.

---

1. irreproachable (ir′i prō′chə bəl), *adj.* free from blame; faultless.
2. ulterior (ul tir′ē ər), *adj.* beyond what is seen or expressed; hidden.

1 Literary Focus
Satire

A technique often used in satire might be called "excess with a straight face." Invite students to call attention to examples of situations that are described in all seriousness but are clearly irrational: sniffing commas and trying to read meaning into accidental stains; Juan spending his whole life searching for one letter; a censor complaining of unhealthy work, and so on.

SELECTION SUMMARY

The Censors

Juan, who lives in an unnamed totalitarian state, writes a letter to his girlfriend Mariana who has fled to Paris. He grows frantic that censors will detect subversion in his harmless letter. He takes a job as a censor in order to intercept his own letter. Once in the Censorship Division, he rises in the organization after turning in a fellow employee who is organizing a strike. Soon he becomes devoted to the very system he set out to subvert. He congratulates himself on having discovered "his true mission" in life. In the end, he finds and censors his own letter, thus informing on himself and bringing about his own execution.

*For summaries in other languages, see the **Building English Proficiency** book.*

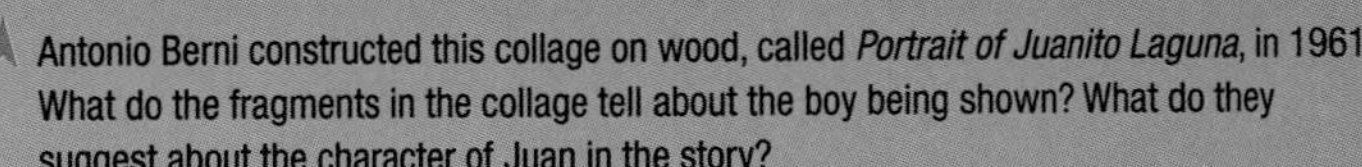

Antonio Berni constructed this collage on wood, called *Portrait of Juanito Laguna*, in 1961. What do the fragments in the collage tell about the boy being shown? What do they suggest about the character of Juan in the story?

Art Study

Responses to Caption Questions

- Students may suggest that the fragments convey that Juanito is tormented, torn, and haunted.
- Possible responses are that Juan is torn between love and duty. He is also haunted by his obsession.

The Argentinean painter Antonio Berni (1905-1981) expressed his social and political beliefs through his art. He produced two narrative series of large-scale works which combine painting with collage. One features Juanito Laguna, a boy of the Buenos Aires slums; in the other, the protagonist is the prostitute Ramona Montiel. In these works, Berni used old wood, empty bottles, iron, cardboard boxes—the very materials the slum inhabitants used to construct their shacks.

Question What reaction do you have when you realize that in this painting things from a garbage heap are used to illustrate a child? *(possible responses: shock, sadness, anger)*

Question Do you think an oil painting or pastel could produce the same effect? *(Students may suggest a variety of materials, but the effectiveness depends on the ability of the artist.)*

BUILDING ENGLISH PROFICIENCY

ESL LEP ELD SAE LD

Exploring a Topic

Considering the ways that dictatorships maintain control will help students better understand the irony of "The Censors."

Activity Ideas

- Suggest that pairs or small groups of students compose a chart with the headings *Story Clues* and *Speculations*. Have students list phrases and sentences from the story that tell what government officials do to be sure that no one rebels. Challenge them also to list additional ways that a dictatorial government might maintain control—through schools, the media, the job market, and so on.
- Encourage students to discuss their own experiences under the laws of a government—either liberal or oppressive.

Building English Proficiency
Activities, p. 169
"The Censors" in Spanish

2 Reading/Thinking Skills

Recognize Propaganda Techniques

Question What anti-government message is the author conveying by saying Juan is "shocked" by what he reads? *(Possible response: the author is showing how censorship and repression can destroy the good judgment of even the best people.)*

3 Reader's Response

Making Personal Connections

Juan's personality is changed by his job; further, his life becomes defined and determined by his job.

Question What are some positive and negative effects of jobs and careers? *Possible response:*

Positive Effects	Negative Effects
develop talents	*repress talent*
benefit society	*stifle creativity*

Question What do you think are the advantages and disadvantages of having a "true mission" in life? *(Possible responses: Advantages—the mission provides a sense of contributing to a larger cause. Disadvantages—the mission becomes an obsession, or blinds one to humanity.)*

Check Test

1. What does Juan do that causes him great anxiety? *(writes Mariana a letter)*
2. What does Juan fear? *(The censors will discover subversion in his letter and Mariana will be harmed.)*
3. What is Juan's plan? *(to become a censor and intercept his own letter)*
4. What does Juan do to his own letter? *(censors it, accusing himself of treason)*
5. What happens to Juan at the end? *(He is executed.)*

Unit 1 Resource Book
Alternate Check Test, p. 21

The building had a festive air on the outside which contrasted with its inner staidness.[3] Little by little, Juan was absorbed by his job and he felt at peace since he was doing everything he could to get his letter for Mariana. He didn't even worry when, in his first month, he was sent to *Section K* where envelopes are very carefully screened for explosives.

It's true that on the third day, a fellow worker had his right hand blown off by a letter, but the division chief claimed it was sheer[4] negligence on the victim's part. Juan and the other employees were allowed to go back to their work, albeit[5] feeling less secure. After work, one of them tried to organize a strike to demand higher wages for unhealthy work, but Juan didn't join in; after thinking it over, he reported him to his superiors and thus got promoted.

You don't form a habit by doing something once, he told himself as he left his boss's office. And when he was transferred to *Section J,* where letters are carefully checked for poison dust, he felt he had climbed a rung in the ladder.

By working hard, he quickly reached *Section E* where the work was more interesting, for he could now read and analyze the letters' contents. Here he could even hope to get hold of his letter which, judging by the time that had elapsed,[6] had gone through the other sections and was probably floating around in this one.

Soon his work became so absorbing that his noble mission blurred in his mind. Day after day he crossed out whole paragraphs in red ink, pitilessly chucking many letters into the censored basket. These were horrible days when he was
2 shocked by the subtle and conniving[7] ways employed by people to pass on subversive[8] messages; his instincts were so sharp that he found behind a simple "the weather's unsettled" or "prices continue to soar" the wavering hand of someone secretly scheming to overthrow the Government.

His zeal[9] brought him swift promotion. We don't know if this made him happy. Very few letters reached him in *Section B*—only a handful passed the other hurdles—so he read them over and over again, passed them under a magnifying glass, searched for microprint with an electronic microscope, and tuned his sense of smell so that he was beat by the time he made it home. He'd barely manage to warm up his soup, eat some fruit, and fall into bed, satisfied with having done his duty. Only his darling mother worried, but she couldn't get him back on the right road. She'd say, though it wasn't always true: Lola called, she's at the bar with the girls, they miss you, they're waiting for you. Or else she'd leave a bottle of red wine on the table. But Juan wouldn't overdo it: any distraction[10] could make him lose his edge and the perfect censor had to
be alert, keen, attentive, and sharp to nab 3
cheats. He had a truly patriotic task, both self-denying and uplifting.

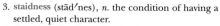

His basket for censored letters became the best fed as well as the most cunning basket in the whole *Censorship Division.* He was about to congratulate himself for having finally discovered his true mission, when his letter to Mariana reached his hands. Naturally, he censored it without regret. And just as naturally, he couldn't stop them from executing him the following morning, another victim of his devotion to his work.

3. **staidness** (stād′nes), *n.* the condition of having a settled, quiet character.
4. **sheer** (shir), *adj.* unmixed with anything else; complete.
5. **albeit** (ôl bē′it), *conj.* even though; although.
6. **elapse** (i laps′), *v.* slip away; pass.
7. **conniving** (kə nī′ving), *adj.* giving aid to wrongdoing by not telling of it or by helping it secretly.
8. **subversive** (səb vėr′siv), *adj.* tending to overthrow; causing ruin.
9. **zeal** (zēl), *n.* eager desire or effort; earnest enthusiasm.
10. **distraction** (dis trak′shən), *n.* disturbance of thought.

MINI-LESSON: GRAMMAR

Apostrophes

Teach Remind students of the correct use of apostrophes for possessives and contractions.

Activity Ideas

For practice, each student can:

- make a similar chart and add more examples from the story
- expand the chart by choosing other singular and plural nouns in the story and writing the correct possessives

Singular nouns	*fate's, Mariana's*
Noun ending in *-s*	*boss's*
Plural noun	*letters'*
Contractions	*you're, won't, aren't*

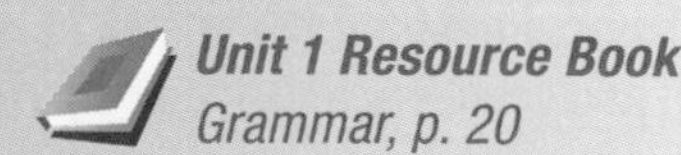

Unit 1 Resource Book
Grammar, p. 20

After Reading

Making Connections

Shaping Your Response

1. In your notebook, write three words that you think describe this story. Share your words with your classmates.
2. What advice would you have for people like Juan who get carried away with a job or goal?
3. If you had watched a film version of this story, what is the first thing you would say to a friend when it was over?

Analyzing the Story

4. What characteristics does Juan exhibit at the beginning of the story? at the end?
5. What do you think brings about the changes in Juan's **character**?
6. What does the story seem to be saying about the effect of a dictatorship on the individual?

Extending the Ideas

7. What **theme** might link this story to the first two in this group?
8. Some U.S. government employees (for example, those in security jobs) agree to sign away their right of free speech. Do you believe that a group should be able to make such demands on **individuals**? Why or why not?
9. Can you think of other forms of censorship that are practiced in your country? Do you think they are necessary? Explain.

Literary Focus: Satire

The purpose of **satire** is sometimes simply to entertain, but more frequently it is to bring about a change.

- What do you think is Valenzuela's purpose in this story?
- Do you think she is satirizing Juan's character, the political situation, or both? Explain.

Vocabulary Study

albeit
conniving
distraction
elapse
irreproachable
sheer
staidness
subversive
ulterior
zeal

Write the letter of the word that best completes each sentence.

1. The ____ with which Juan did his work pleased his boss.
   a. staidness **b.** zeal **c.** albeit **d.** distraction
2. Over four months would ____ before Juan found his letter.
   a. elapse **b.** albeit **c.** zeal **d.** sheer
3. No one suspected that Juan concealed a(n) ____ motive for wanting to become a censor.
   a. irreproachable **b.** sheer **c.** elapse **d.** ulterior

LITERARY FOCUS: SATIRE

- Valenzuela's purpose goes beyond entertainment. She wants to make readers aware of the consequences of repression and to convince people to force a change in government policy.
- Possible response: Valenzuela is satirizing Juan's character as an example of how human nature is corrupted by oppression. She is also satirizing the political situation by showing the government as inhumane and ever-present, and its deceit and cynicism.

After Reading

MAKING CONNECTIONS

1. Possible responses: *satiric, ironic, funny, futuristic, shocking*

2. Possible responses: make sure the goal doesn't conflict with your beliefs; consider how achieving your goal will affect others; do things in moderation.

3. Students might say the film was shocking or surprising, question whether or not Juan deserved to die, or speculate whether their own government could become repressive.

4. At the beginning, Juan is happy about Mariana; he is terrified by the government. By the end, he is obsessed with his job; he loses all individuality and concern for others, is absorbed into the system, and becomes its victim.

5. Juan begins changing when he turns in a colleague to advance himself. Soon he forgets about his original goal to save Mariana and gradually adopts the beliefs of his oppressors.

6. Possible response: a dictatorship—or any form of repression—robs individuals of the power to make their own informed decisions.

7. Possible themes include the value of setting your own goals, the force of ambition, and the sometimes harmful effects of the drive for achievement.

8. Students may respond that such demands are unreasonable and disruptive of private lives; that most groups make demands on individuals in order to make the group function properly; and that waiving free speech for some may protect the whole.

9. Possible responses: censoring song lyrics, refusing to broadcast certain television programs, banning certain books, and restricting the operations of some businesses. Issues raised may include protection, quality of life, repression, and freedom.

VOCABULARY STUDY

1. b
2. a
3. d
4. b
5. a

More Practice Students can use each of the ten vocabulary words in sentences about a present-day political situation.

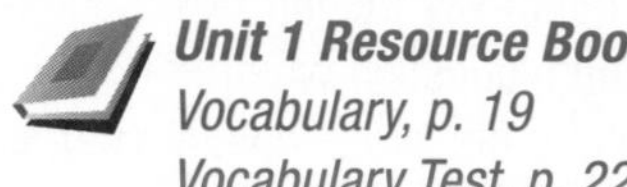
Unit 1 Resource Book
Vocabulary, p. 19
Vocabulary Test, p. 22

WRITING CHOICES

Writer's Notebook Update

Encourage students to imagine how living under such conditions would change their relationships to the people involved in their daily lives. Suggest that they consider their relationships to their parents, teachers, neighbors, and friends.

Some students coming to America from other countries may have painful memories of life under a dictatorship. They may or may not wish to share such memories. Allow these students to make up their own minds about the topics they address in their Writer's Notebooks.

Selection Test

Unit 1 Resource Book
pp. 23–24

4. After an explosion, workers went back to their jobs ____ some were frightened.

a. zeal **b.** albeit **c.** staidness **d.** conniving

5. Even though Juan was executed, no one could truly say it was because of any ____ political activities.

a. subversive **b.** elapse **c.** albeit **d.** zeal

Expressing Your Ideas

Writing Choices

Writer's Notebook Update Review the notes you made in your notebook before reading "The Censors." Compare your list of the ways your life might change under a dictatorship with the reality of Juan's life. Then write a brief explanation of how something in your daily routine (listening to TV or getting to school, for example) would change under a dictatorship.

Your Censor Is Showing Are you aware that censorship—the act of changing or suppressing speech, writing, art, or any expression that is considered damaging or subversive—exists worldwide? Consider, for example, school dress codes. Now imagine that every student could dress as he or she wanted for school, without interference. Write a **satirical description** of the scene as you walk through the halls for your first class.

Dear Mariana Draft the **letter** Juan writes to Mariana that results in his death. Be imaginative. Then take the role of censor, listing the words or phrases from the letter that seal Juan's doom and explaining why they are censored.

Other Options

XSJUF B DPEF Work with a small group to write a **message in code.** You might write a message in which only the fifth word or letter is significant, one with numbers instead of letters, or one in which each letter has been replaced by the letter that directly follows it in the alphabet (like the title above and the message in italics under Strange to Say, page 29). Exchange codes with another group and try to solve.

Stamp of Approval The Post Office in Juan's country has hired you, the country's greatest artist, to produce designs for new stamps that will represent the country's new flag or its symbolic animal. What the Post Office doesn't know is that you are planning to flee. Your stamps will satirize, not celebrate, these subjects. Draw the **stamps** so that your opinion of the regime is clear.

OTHER OPTIONS

XSJUF B DPEF (WRITE A CODE)

Students may find it helpful and even entertaining to use the library to research:

- the history of codes
- famous spies and code breakers
- how computers use codes
- cryptogram puzzlers

Before Reading

The Voter

by Chinua Achebe   Nigeria

Chinua Achebe
born 1930

Chinua Achebe (chin′wä′ ä chā′bā) grew up knowing two very different cultures: those of Christian Europe and traditional Africa. He was born in 1930 in Ogidi, a village of the Ibo people in Eastern Nigeria. He has been a writer, teacher, editor, and lecturer, as well as a political activist during his country's civil strife. His works describe the effects of European culture and Christianity on a vigorous, traditional African culture. In addition to his best-known novel, *Things Fall Apart,* he has written other novels, poetry, a children's book, and collections of essays and stories.

Building Background

About Nigeria "The Voter" takes place in Nigeria, a country in west Africa. You might do class research to complete the Fact Sheet on Nigeria.

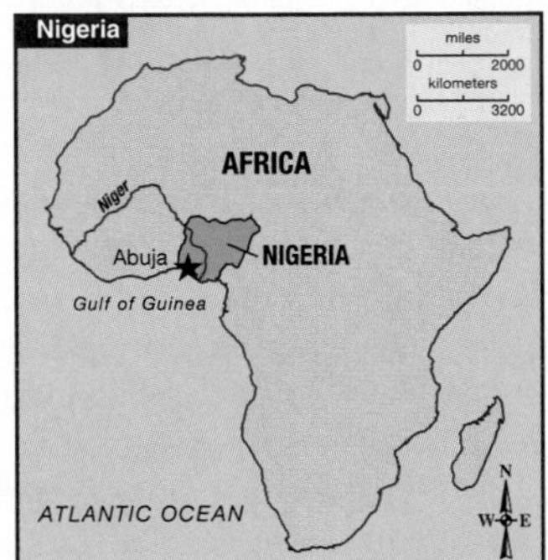

Fact Sheet

Population: about 105,000,000
Capital: Abuja
Area: 356,669 square miles
Major Ethnic Groups: Hausa, Yoruba, Ibo
Money: basic unit: Naira
Chief Products: ____________________
Elevation: ____________________
Government: ____________________

Literary Focus

Proverbs Brief traditional sayings containing popular wisdom are called **proverbs.** These sayings are an important component of all cultures. Be on the alert for common sayings such as "A bird in the hand is worth two in the bush" or "Early to bed, early to rise, makes a man healthy, wealthy, and wise" in conversations and writing. In west African culture, proverbs are especially important in daily speech. As you read "The Voter," note proverbs and the insights they provide into the characters and incidents.

Writer's Notebook

Look Before You Leap Think of a time that your agreed to do something and later realized you couldn't or didn't want to do it. What made you agree to do it in the first place? Why did you regret it later? Write a few sentences about your dilemma.

Before Reading

Building Background

Chief products of Nigeria include millet, sorghum, palm oil, cassava, yams, beef, cacao, corn, cotton, peanuts, rice, rubber, cement, and textiles. Elevation: highest—Dimlang Peak, 6,699 ft. above sea level; lowest—sea level. Government: 30 states divided into hundreds of local areas with councils; President heads the national government and commands the armed forces.

Literary Focus

Ask students to share **proverbs** that they know. Encourage students to speculate about where proverbs come from, what makes them last through time, and why people invent and remember them.

Writer's Notebook

If prompts are needed, suggest the following situations: doing a favor for someone, fulfilling a social commitment such as attending a party, taking a dare.

Connections to **AuthorWorks**

Chinua Achebe is a featured author in the AuthorWorks CD-ROM series.

Connections to **NovelWorks**

NovelWorks: *Things Fall Apart* offers a rich variety of unique materials for teaching the novel.

SUPPORT MATERIALS OVERVIEW

Unit 1 Resource Book
- Graphic Organizer, p. 25
- Study Guide, p. 26
- Vocabulary, p. 27
- Grammar, p. 28
- Alternate Check Test, p. 29
- Vocabulary Test, p. 30
- Selection Test, pp. 31–32

Building English Proficiency
- Literature Summaries
- Activities, p. 170

Reading, Writing & Grammar SkillBook
- Reading, pp. 22–23
- Writing, pp. 101–102
- Grammar, pp. 274–275

Technology
- Audiotape 2, Side A
- Personal Journal Software
- Custom Literature Database: For more proverbs, see "African Proverbs" on the database.
- Test Generator Software

Selection Objectives

- to explore the theme of conflicting claims on individual loyalty
- to recognize and use proverbs
- to analyze problem-solving techniques
- to use dashes correctly in writing

Unit 1 Resource Book
Graphic Organizer, p. 25
Study Guide, p. 26

Theme Link

In the process of "pushing toward the top," Rufus faces the challenge of conflicting commitments: his political ties, his desire for wealth, and his ancient tribal beliefs.

Vocabulary Preview

en masse, in a group; all together

proverbial, relating to proverbs; commonly spoken of

nonentity, a person or thing of little or no importance

electorate, the persons having the right to vote in an election

imminent, about to occur

stalwart, person who is strong, brave, and firm

rebuke, express disapproval of

deign, agree to; stoop or lower oneself to do something

decorum, proper behavior; good taste in conduct, speech, or dress

Students can add the words and definitions to their Writer's Notebooks.

1 Literary Focus
Proverbs

Achebe does not give the actual wording of an obviously well-known African proverb.

Questions What do you think might be the actual proverb about the fly and a dunghill? What do you think the proverb means? *(Possible response: "A fly may push a dunghill, but he won't budge it." The proverb is meant to suggest a futile effort.)*

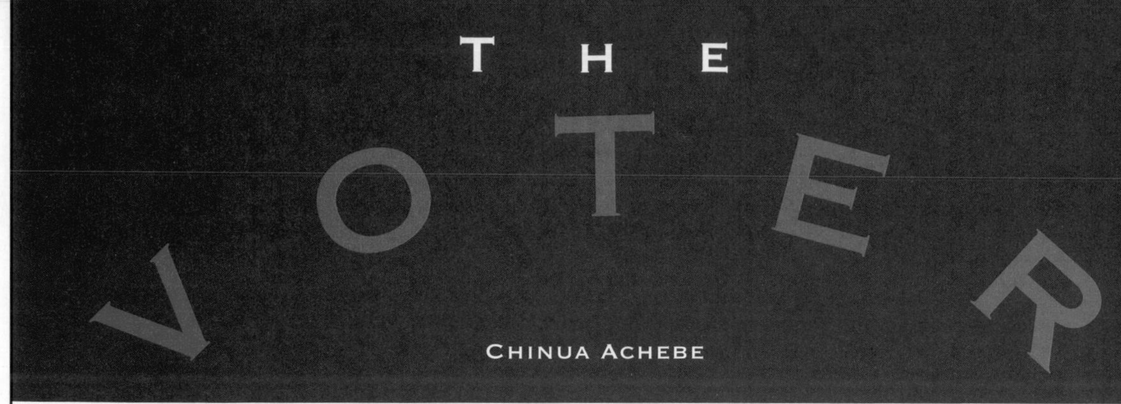

The Voter

Chinua Achebe

Rufus Okeke—Roof, for short—was a very popular man in his village. Although the villagers did not explain it in so many words Roof's popularity was a measure of their gratitude to an energetic young man who, unlike most of his fellows nowadays, had not abandoned the village in order to seek work—any work—in the towns. And Roof was not a village lout either. Everyone knew how he had spent two years as a bicycle repairer's apprentice in Port Harcourt[1] and had given up of his own free will a bright future to return to his people and guide them in these political times. Not that Umuofia needed a lot of guidance. The village already belonged *en masse*[2] to the People's Alliance Party, and its most illustrious son—Chief the Honorable Marcus Ibe—was Minister of Culture in the outgoing government (which was pretty certain to be the incoming one as well). Nobody doubted that the Honorable Minister would be re-elected in his constituency. Opposition to him was like the
1 proverbial[3] fly trying to move a dunghill. It would have been ridiculous enough without coming, as it did now, from a complete nonentity.[4]

As was to be expected Roof was in the service of the Honorable Minister for the coming elections. He had become a real expert in election campaigning at all levels—village, local government or national. He could tell the mood and temper of the electorate[5] at any given time. For instance he had warned the Minister months ago about the radical change that had come into the thinking of Umuofia since the last national election.

The villagers had had five years in which to see how quickly and plentifully politics brought wealth, chieftaincy titles, doctorate degrees and other honors, some of which like the last had still to be explained satisfactorily to them; for they expected a doctor to heal the sick. Anyhow, these honors had come so readily to the man they had given their votes to free of charge five years ago that they were now ready to think again.

Their point was that only the other day Marcus Ibe was a not too successful Mission-school teacher. Then politics had come to their village and he had wisely joined up, some say just in time to avoid imminent[6] dismissal arising from a female teacher's pregnancy. Today he was Chief the Honorable; he had two long cars and had just built himself the biggest house any-

1. **Port Harcourt,** a port city on the southern coast of Nigeria.
2. *en masse* (en mas′), in a group; all together. *[French]*
3. **proverbial** (prə vėr′bē əl), *adj.* relating to proverbs; commonly spoken of.
4. **nonentity** (non en′tə tē), *n.* a person or thing of little or no importance.
5. **electorate** (i lek′tər it), *n.* the persons having the right to vote in an election.
6. **imminent** (im′ə nənt), *adj.* about to occur.

Selection Summary

The Voter

Rufus Okeke is a popular and politically savvy young man in an African village just before a big national election. Rufus works to get out the vote for the People's Alliance Party and the village's own favorite son, Chief the Honorable Marcus Ibe, Minister of Culture, a clever politician who has become wealthy and distant from his people. Rufus "campaigns" among the village elders by offering them two shillings in exchange for their votes. The elders hold out for two more shillings before promising to vote for Ibe. Later, a member of the opposition party—the Progressive Organization Party—offers Rufus five pounds, a substantial sum, to secretly cast his ballot for Ibe's opponent. After being assured of complete confidentiality, Rufus agrees and is forced to swear on a fetish object that he will vote against Ibe. On voting day, he decides at the last moment to tear his voting slip in half and split his vote.

For summaries in other languages, see the ***Building English Proficiency*** *book.*

one had seen in those parts. But let it be said that none of these successes had gone to Marcus's head—as they well might. He remained a man of the people. Whenever he could he left the good things of the capital and returned to his village which had neither running water nor electricity. He knew the source of his good fortune, unlike the little bird who ate and drank and went out to challenge his personal spirit.[7] Marcus had christened his new house "Umuofia Mansions" in honor of his village and slaughtered five bulls and countless goats to entertain the people on the day it was opened by the Archbishop.

2 **EVALUATE: In your opinion, has Marcus Ibe remained "a man of the people"?**

3 Everyone was full of praise for him. One old man said: "Our son is a good man; he is not like the mortar which as soon as food comes its way turns its back on the ground." But when the feasting was over the villagers told themselves that they had underrated the power of the ballot paper before and should not do so again. Chief the Honorable Marcus Ibe was not unprepared. He had drawn five months' salary in advance, changed a few hundred pounds into shining shillings and armed his campaign boys with eloquent little jute bags. In the day he made his speeches; at night his stalwarts[8] conducted their whispering campaign. Roof was the most trusted of these campaigners.

7. **personal spirit.** In Ibo tradition, each person has a personal spirit to guide him or her through life.
8. **stalwart** (stôl′wərt), *n.* person who is strong, brave, and firm.

The Nigerian painter known as Middle Art painted an enamel self-portrait on his shop door titled *The Manager in Charge* in the 1970s. Does this manager appear to be "a man of the people," like Marcus?

2 Active Reading
Evaluate

Response Available evidence indicates that Ibe has not remained "a man of the people." He now lives in the city, owns a large house and two big cars, and only occasionally visits his home village, which still waits for running water and electricity.

3 Literary Focus
Proverbs

Students may need to discuss the role of the mortar in village life to understand this proverb. The mortar, or mixing bowl, is regularly used to prepare food. When not in use, it is stored facedown. The proverb is used here to compare the mortar to a greedy person who turns his back on his friends to fill himself with riches.

Responses to Caption Questions
The manager appears to be no more "a man of the people" than does Ibe. He is impeccably dressed in a modern Western-style business suit and his title asserts his authority over ordinary people. The painter may be making an ironic gesture by using his own face in this self-portrait and by using the image as his own shop door.

BUILDING ENGLISH PROFICIENCY

ESL LEP ELD SAE LD

Making Geographical Connections

Help students to a clearer understanding of how different government systems work. Let them work in pairs or small groups to construct simple Venn diagrams (such as the one shown) that compare and contrast the United States government with another country's. If possible, provide students with access to almanacs and other reference sources. Encourage students to share their observations of how elections are conducted in countries where they've lived.

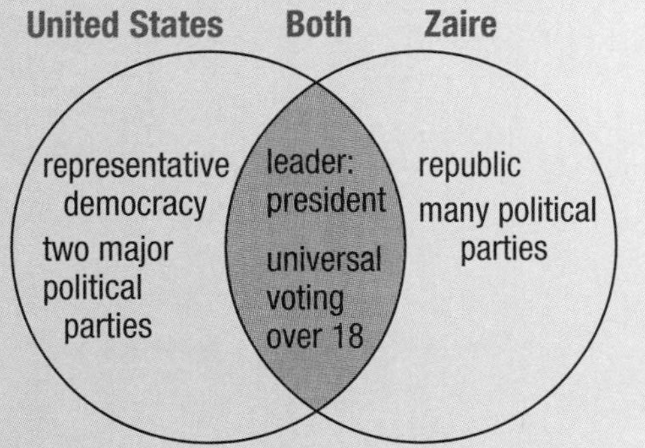

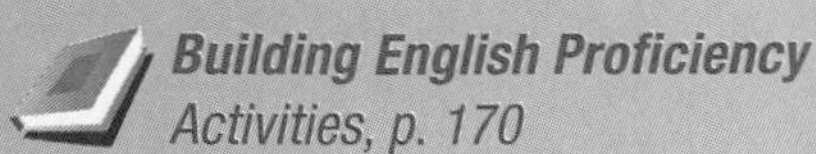
Building English Proficiency Activities, p. 170

4 Literary Element
Character

You might lead a discussion here on Rufus's pragmatism. For example, he applies the firewood proverb directly to himself and has no problem understanding the elders' point of view. This characteristic will continue to be important when he solves his problem at the end of the story.

5 Multicultural Note
Language and Politics in Nigeria

The characters in the story speak both English and Ibo, and their bilingualism is a direct result of Nigerian colonial history. The British took control of Nigeria in the late nineteenth and early twentieth centuries. Nigeria gained its independence in 1960.

The population of the Federal Republic of Nigeria consists of more than 250 different ethnic groups, which differ from one another in language as well as in customs and traditions. The three largest ethnic groups are the Hausa, the Yoruba, and the Igbo (also spelled Ibo). The Ibo form the majority of the population in southeastern Nigeria.

English is the official language of Nigeria and is commonly taught in the nation's schools; it is not the most commonly spoken language, however. Each of the 250 ethnic groups maintains its own distinct language, and thus the most widely spoken tongues are those of the Hausa, the Yoruba, and the Ibo.

"We have a Minister from our village, one of our own sons," he said to a group of elders in the house of Ogbuefi Ezenwa, a man of high traditional title. "What greater honor can a village have? Do you ever stop to ask yourselves why we should be singled out for this honor? I will tell you: it is because we are favored by the leaders of PAP. Whether we cast our paper for Marcus or not PAP will continue to rule. Think of the pipe-borne water they have promised us . . ."

Besides Roof and his assistant there were five elders in the room. An old hurricane lamp with a cracked, sooty, glass chimney gave out yellowish light in their midst. The elders sat on very low stools. On the floor, directly in front of each of them, lay two shilling pieces. Outside the moon kept a straight face.

"We believe every word you say to be true," said Ezenwa. "We shall every one of us drop his paper for Marcus. Who would leave an *ozo* feast and go to a poor ritual meal? Tell Marcus he has our papers, and our wives' papers too. But what we do say is that two shillings is shameful." He brought the lamp close and tilted it at the money before him as if to make sure he had not mistaken its value. "Yes, two shillings; it is too shameful. If Marcus were a poor man—which our ancestors forbid—I should be the first to give him my paper free, as I did before. But today Marcus is a great man and does his things like a great man. We did not ask him for money yesterday; we shall
4 not ask him tomorrow. But today is our day; we have climbed the *iroko* tree today and would be foolish not to take down all the fire-wood we need."

Roof had to agree. He had lately been taking down a lot of fire-wood himself. Only yesterday he had asked Marcus for one of his many rich robes—and had got it. Last Sunday Marcus's wife (the teacher that nearly got him in trouble) had objected (like the woman she was) when Roof pulled out his fifth bottle of beer from the kerosene refrigerator, and was roundly and publicly rebuked[9] by her husband. To cap it all Roof had won a land case recently because, among other things, he had been chauffeur-driven to the disputed site. So he understood the elders about the fire-wood.

"All right," he said in English and then reverted to Ibo. "Let us not quarrel about small things." He stood up and adjusted his robes. 5
Then he bent down like a priest distributing the host and gave one shilling more to every man: only he did not put it into their palms but on the floor in front of them. The men, who had so far not deigned[10] to touch the things, looked at the floor and shook their heads. Roof got up again and gave each man another shilling.

"I am through," he said with a defiance that was no less effective for being transparently faked. The elders too knew how far to go without losing decorum.[11] So when Roof added: "Go cast your paper for the enemy if you like!" they quickly calmed him down with a suitable speech

> THIS IYI COMES FROM MBANTA. YOU KNOW WHAT THAT MEANS. SWEAR THAT YOU WILL VOTE FOR MADUKA.

9. **rebuke** (ri byük′), *v.* express disapproval of.
10. **deign** (dān), *v.* agree to; stoop or lower oneself to do something.
11. **decorum** (di kôr′əm), *n.* proper behavior; good taste in conduct, speech, or dress.

MINI-LESSON: GRAMMAR
Dashes

Teach Remind students of the appropriate uses of dashes: to indicate an interruption or parenthetical comment, to signal a long appositive, and to emphasize additional information.

Question What functions do the dashes perform on page 38 of this story? *(The dashes indicate parenthetical comments and emphasize additional information.)*

Activity Ideas

For practice, each student can:
- identify the uses of other dashes in the story
- write sentences, based on the events of the story, using dashes correctly

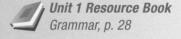

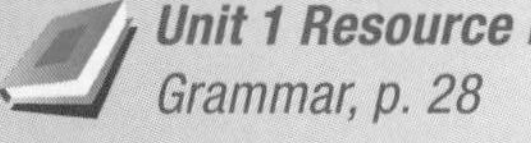
Unit 1 Resource Book
Grammar, p. 28

from each of them. By the time the last man had spoken it was possible—without great loss of dignity—to pick up the things from the floor.

The enemy Roof had referred to was the Progressive Organization Party (POP) which had been formed by the tribes down the coast to save themselves—as the founders of the party proclaimed—from "total political, cultural, social and religious annihilation." Although it was clear the party had no chance here it had plunged—with typical foolishness—into a straight fight with PAP, providing cars and loudspeakers to a few local rascals and thugs to go around and make a lot of noise. No one knew for certain how much money POP had let loose in Umuofia but it was said to be very considerable. Their local campaigners would end up very rich, no doubt.

Up to last night everything had been "moving according to plan"—as Roof would have put it. Then he had received a strange visit from the leader of the POP campaign team. Although he and Roof were well known to each other and might even be called friends his visit was cold and business-like. No words were wasted. He placed five pounds on the floor before Roof and said, "We want your vote." Roof got up from his chair, went to the outside door, closed it carefully and returned to his chair. The brief exercise gave him enough time to weigh the proposition. As he spoke his eyes never left the red notes on the floor.

"You know I work for Marcus," he said feebly. "It will be very bad . . ."

"Marcus will not be there when you put in your paper. We have plenty of work to do tonight; are you taking this or not?"

"It will not be heard outside this room?" asked Roof.

"We are after votes not gossip."

"All right," said Roof in English.

The man nudged his companion and he brought forward an object covered with red cloth and proceeded to remove the cover. It was a fearsome little affair contained in a clay pot with feathers stuck into it.

"This *iyi* comes from Mbanta. You know what that means. Swear that you will vote for Maduka. If you fail to do so, this *iyi* is to note."

Roof's heart had nearly flown out of his mouth when he saw the *iyi;* and indeed he knew the fame of Mbanta in these things. But he was a man of quick decision. What could a single vote cast in secret for Maduka take away from Marcus's certain victory? Nothing. 6

"I will cast my paper for Maduka; if not, this *iyi* take note."

"Das all," said the man as he rose with his companion, who had covered up the object again and was taking it back to their car.

"You know he has no chance against Marcus," said Roof at the door.

"It is enough that he gets a few votes now; next time he will get more. People will hear that he gives out pounds, not shillings, and they will listen."

Election morning. The great day every five years when the people exercised power—or thought they did. Weather-beaten posters on walls of houses, tree trunks and telegraph poles. The few that were still whole called out their message to those who could read. Vote for the People's Alliance Party! Vote for the Progressive Organisation Party! Vote for PAP! Vote for POP! The posters that were torn called out as much of the message as they could.

As usual Chief the Honorable Marcus Ibe was doing things in grand style. He had hired a highlife band from Umuru and stationed it at such a distance from the voting booths as just managed to be lawful. Many villagers danced to the music, their ballot papers held aloft, before proceeding to the booths. Chief the Honorable Marcus Ibe sat in the "owner's corner"[12] of his enormous green car and smiled and nodded.

12. **owner's corner,** the seat diagonally behind the driver, reserved for the owner of the car as a mark of respect.

6 Reader's Response

Making Personal Connections

Roof justifies his decision to himself using a common method: He tells himself that his vote won't matter.

Questions Do you think that Roof is making the right decision at this point in the story? Why or why not? *(Possible responses: Roof is planning to deceive his friends and calm his conscience with an excuse; Roof is shrewdly arranging to get the best of both worlds—he will appear to support Ibe and take the five pounds.)*

The Author Speaks

In a book of essays, *Hopes and Impediments* (1988), Achebe wrote about goals:

"Setting goals is a matter of intelligence and judgment. Faced with a confusing welter of problems all clamoring for solution at once, man's most rational strategy is to stay as cool as possible in the face of the confusion and attack the problems singly or in small manageable groups, one at a time. . . .

"But the problem with goals lies not only in the area of priorities and practicalities. There are appropriate and inappropriate goals, even wrong and unworthy goals. There are goals which place an intolerable strain on the pursuer. . . . [A] nation might set itself a goal that puts its very soul at risk."

BUILDING ENGLISH PROFICIENCY

Exploring Satire

Achebe uses satire to make fun of everyone in the story. To help students learn to recognize political satire, bring in political cartoons and discuss them. Then students can draw their own cartoon about "The Voter." To prepare:

1. Have them read aloud the paragraph on pages 39–40 that begins, "As usual . . . Ibe was doing things in a grand style." Discuss descriptive phrases that the author uses to let the reader know that he is ridiculing Ibe. Encourage volunteers to act the part of Ibe, as well as of the "enlightened" who approach.

2. Have students volunteer words that describe Ibe's and other characters' faults. *(greedy, crafty, vain, uninformed, gullible, unprincipled, superstitious)*

3. Students can choose one character or group and satirize him or her in a cartoon.

7 Reading/Thinking Skills
Solve Problems

Faced with a problem that seemingly has no solution, Roof uses "divergent thinking" and comes up with an imaginative answer.

Questions What problem-solving method does Roof use to find a way out of his dilemma? Do you think he has genuinely solved his problem? Why or why not? *(Roof's method is to stop seeing the problem as an either/or situation. His solution enables him to say he voted for Maduka and to say he voted for Ibe. Students may doubt that Roof has genuinely solved his problem, because he has violated his political principles for money.)*

8 Active Reading
Evaluate

Possible Response He has betrayed Ibe by not supporting him fully. Students may also discuss how corrupt leaders invite betrayals on the part of their followers.

Check Test

1. Who is Marcus Ibe? *(Minister of Culture, running for re-election)*
2. What does Ibe do to persuade people to vote for him? *(gives speeches and distributes money)*
3. What does the village elder Ezenwa tell Rufus about voting for Ibe? *(that Ibe is rich and should pay them more for their votes)*
4. What does Rufus do with the *iyi*? *(swears on it that he will fulfill his promise to vote for Maduka)*
5. What does Rufus do in the voting booth? *(tears his voting paper in half and puts one half in each box)*

Unit 1 Resource Book
Alternate Check Test, p. 29

One enlightened villager came up to the car, shook hands with the great man and said in advance: "Congrats!" This immediately set the pattern. Hundreds of admirers shook Marcus's hand and said "Corngrass!"

Roof and the other organizers were prancing up and down, giving last minute advice to the voters and pouring with sweat.

"Do not forget," he said again to a group of illiterate women who seemed ready to burst with enthusiasm and good humor, "our sign is the motor-car . . ."

"Like the one Marcus is sitting inside."

"Thank you, mother," said Roof. "It is the same car. The box with the car shown on its body is the box for you. Don't look at the other with the man's head: it is for those whose heads are not correct."

This was greeted with loud laughter. Roof cast a quick and busy-like glance towards the Minister and received a smile of appreciation.

"Vote for the car," he shouted, all the veins in his neck standing out. "Vote for the car and you will ride in it!"

"Or if we don't our children will," piped the same sharp old girl.

The band struck up a new number: "Why walk when you can ride?"

In spite of his apparent calm and confidence Chief the Honorable Marcus was a relentless stickler for detail. He knew he would win what the newspapers called "a landslide victory" but he did not wish even so to throw away a single vote. So as soon as the first rush of voters was over he promptly asked his campaign boys to go one at a time and put in their ballot papers.

"Roof, you had better go first," he said.

Roof's spirits fell; but he let no one see it. All morning he had masked his deep worry with a surface exertion which was unusual even for him. Now he dashed off in his springy fashion towards the booths. A policeman at the entrance searched him for illegal ballot papers and passed him. Then the electoral officer explained to him about the two boxes. By this time the spring had gone clean out of his walk. He sidled in and was confronted by the car and the head. He brought out his ballot paper from his pocket and looked at it. How could he betray Marcus even in secret? He resolved to go back to the other man and return his five pounds . . . FIVE POUNDS! He knew at once it was impossible. He had sworn on that *iyi*.

At this point he heard the muffled voice of the policeman asking the electoral officer what the man was doing inside. "Abi na pickin im de born?"[13]

Quick as lightning a thought leapt into Roof's mind. He folded the paper, tore it in two along the crease and put one half in each box. 7
He took the precaution of putting the first half into Maduka's box and confirming the action verbally: "I vote for Maduka."

EVALUATE: Do you think that Roof has betrayed Marcus Ibe? Why or why not? 8

They marked his thumb with indelible purple ink to prevent his return, and he went out of the booth as jauntily as he had gone in.

13. **Abi na pickin im de born?,** a question in pidgin English that is commonly asked in Nigeria and means literally, "Is he giving birth to a child in there?" It can be translated, "Why is he taking so long?"

MINI-LESSON: VOCABULARY
Folk Etymology

When someone says "Congrats" to Ibe, hundreds of other people repeat what they thought they heard and say "Corngrass." The invented word is formed by using familiar words or sounds to take the place of words or sounds which are unfamiliar. This process often takes place over a long period of time and gives birth to new and quite imaginative words. An example from American regional English is *sparrowgrass*, which, in parts of the southern United States, originated as *asparagus*.

Activity Idea Give students the opportunity to explore folk etymologies by:

- identifying words in their regional speech that seem to have folk origins
- researching in the library a book or article on folk etymologies
- finding and reporting on an appropriate entry in the *Dictionary of American Regional English*

After Reading

Making Connections

Shaping Your Response

1. Work with a partner to demonstrate for the class how you think Roof looks when he enters the voting booth and after he exits it. Have classmates guess the feelings you are trying to convey.
2. Why do you think Roof might have given up a "bright future" repairing bicycles?
3. In your opinion, does Roof have the qualities of an effective politician? Explain.

Analyzing the Story

4. What hints does Achebe provide that suggest Chief the Honorable Marcus Ibe may not be so honorable?
5. Achebe uses humor throughout "The Voter." Find examples and explain what, if anything, you think the use of humor adds to readers' feelings about Roof.
6. How would you describe Roof's **character?**

Extending the Ideas

7. Does the practice of buying votes occur nowadays? If so, where? How? What measures are taken to prevent voting abuse?

Literary Focus: Proverbs

Working in small groups, explain what these two **proverbs** from the story mean.

1. "Opposition to him was like the proverbial fly trying to move a dunghill."
2. "But today is our day; we have climbed the *iroko* tree today and would be foolish not to take down all the fire-wood we need."
3. How do the proverbs above illustrate the needs of the **individual** within the group?

Now see if you can explain what the following African proverbs mean. Are there English language equivalents for any of these?

- "One who is overcautious of his life is always killed by the fall of a dry leaf."
- "A hen cannot lay eggs and hatch them in the same day."
- "You do not give a hyena meat to look after."

After Reading

MAKING CONNECTIONS

1. Students will probably attempt to show anxiety and uncertainty when he enters the booth and relief and self-satisfaction when he exits.

2. Possible response: Roof could have earned good wages as a repairman, but politics offered more chances for wealth.

3. Possible response: He has the ability to compromise and persuade; his willingness to trade his loyalties for personal gain is a flaw some politicians exhibit.

4. Ibe abandoned his mission-school job, probably to avoid a scandal. Since his election, he lives in a big house, and owns two big cars, but has not managed to bring either running water or electricity into his village. He bribes people to vote for him.

5. Possible responses: calling the outgoing government "the incoming one as well" adds a humorous and satiric tone to Roof's activities. "Think of the pipe-borne water they have promised us" reveals with a touch of humor how Roof has been duped by the party. PAP and POP are humorous and satiric acronyms.

6. Possible responses: sly, clever, tricky, hypocritical, unprincipled, frightened, superstitious.

7. Students may point out that unscrupulous politicians exist in every country. Some officials dole out favors such as jobs; special interest groups give vacations and gifts to politicians in exchange for their votes. Individuals and organizations campaign for reform.

LITERARY FOCUS: PROVERBS

1. Sometimes it is futile for an individual to oppose an overwhelming force.

2. It would be foolish not to take advantage of an obvious opportunity.

3. Sometimes individuals feel helpless, forgetting that by working as a group they can be effective; when individuals see an opportunity for personal gain, they may forget the needs of the group.

- People who are too cautious let small impediments stop them from being happy. "Caution is the downfall of ambition."
- Patience is a necessary virtue. "You can't have your cake and eat it too."
- A person will always be true to his or her nature. Nature cannot be denied. "Don't put a fox in charge of a chicken coop."

VOCABULARY STUDY

1. c
2. b
3. d
4. a
5. c

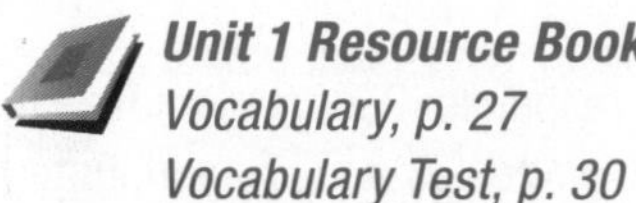

Unit 1 Resource Book
Vocabulary, p. 27
Vocabulary Test, p. 30

WRITING CHOICES

Writer's Notebook Update

Encourage students to make the situation clear for readers by indicating exactly the obstacle to be overcome or the decision to be made. Ask them to state both the facts and the feelings involved and to tell which weighed more in the final outcome.

A Stitch in Time

Some students may find it easier to begin with a proverb and then identify a business to attach to it. "Early to rise," for example, might be a good name for an alarm clock company. Students may find some good proverbs in a copy of Benjamin Franklin's *Poor Richard's Almanack.*

Selection Test

Unit 1 Resource Book
pp. 31–32

Vocabulary Study

Next to each number, write the letter of the word that best completes each sentence.

decorum
en masse
imminent
nonentity
proverbial

1. Something done *en masse* is done ____.
   a. well **b.** quickly **c.** together **d.** clumsily
2. *Proverbial* is most closely linked to the word ____.
   a. verb **b.** proverb **c.** prove **d.** rover
3. An *imminent* event is likely to happen ____.
   a. never **b.** often **c.** rarely **d.** soon
4. A *nonentity* is ____.
   a. unimportant **b.** thin **c.** loud **d.** greedy
5. *Decorum* refers to____.
   a. furniture **b.** nature **c.** behavior **d.** death

Expressing Your Ideas

Writing Choices

Writer's Notebook Update Look again at what you wrote in your notebook before reading "The Voter." Were you as resourceful as Roof in solving your problem? Build on your sentences to write a brief description of your dilemma and how you resolved it. You might want to use a vocabulary word or two.

A Stitch in Time Some proverbs have served as sources of inspiration for literary titles, musical compositions, group names, and so on. For example, "A rolling stone gathers no moss" has provided a name for songs, a musical group, and a magazine, among other things. Imagine you are starting your own business. Choose part of a proverb that would be a good name for your business and use your choice in a brief **ad**. For example, you might name your sewing service "A Stitch in Time."

Other Options

Scrollwork In ancient cultures, story pictures were sometimes drawn on long rolls, or scrolls, of papyrus or parchment. By slowly unrolling the scroll, one "read" the story, leisurely savoring each new scene and detail. Create a **scroll picture** that illustrates one of the proverbs appearing in Achebe's story, "The Voter," or another proverb of your choosing. Then reveal and explain your scroll to the class.

Pop Art Create a **poster** for PAP or POP, complete with the car or head logo, campaign slogans, and political promises that would be popular with the villagers.

More About Nigeria You might want to do additional research on Nigeria—its politics, resources, buildings, modes of transportation, and so on. **Report** your findings to the class.

OTHER OPTIONS

More About Nigeria

Suggest the following research tips:

- Read the entry on Nigeria in an encyclopedia to provide direction for further research.
- Narrow your research topic to a manageable idea.
- Read and report on Chinua Achebe himself, a writer actively involved in Nigerian politics.

Before Reading

The Other Wife

by Colette France

Colette
1873–1954

Thoroughly French in every respect, Colette (Sidonie Gabrielle Claudine Colette), was born in France's Burgundy region and died in Paris. When she was twenty, Colette married Henry Gauthier-Villars, a Paris journalist, music critic, and editor, who published her early work under his own pseudonym, Willy. Later, Colette become nationally recognized under her own name with such novels as *Chéri* (1920) and *Gigi* (1944). A touring actress and lecturer as well as a writer, Colette was the first woman in France given a state funeral. She is now regarded as one of the first modern writers to focus on relationships from the female point of view.

Building Background

Slice of Life The story goes that film director Alfred Hitchcock loved to get into an elevator with a friend and silently stand there until just before arriving at his floor. As the elevator doors opened and he moved into the corridor, Hitchcock would turn to his friend and say something like, "Well, I don't care what you say. I personally think that after she cut off his head—" And the doors would close, leaving behind a group of wide-eyed eavesdroppers to speculate on the possibilities. As a reader, you too will sometimes find yourself eavesdropping on a conversation and later having to fill in puzzle pieces and make inferences. Imagine yourself seated at a table in an exclusive French restaurant. A glamorous, well-dressed couple enters and sits at the table beside you. Eavesdrop a little, and decide if you would like to change places with "The Other Wife."

Literary Focus

Point of View The author's choice of narrator for a story determines the **point of view.** This choice affects the amount of information a reader will be given, as well as the angle from which this information will be presented. Some stories have a narrator who is a character in the story. In "The Other Wife," however, the narrator is not a character but an outsider.

Writer's Notebook

Excuse Me! Few people manage to get through life without enduring an awkward or embarrassing situation—at home, in class, or somewhere else. Before reading "The Other Wife," briefly describe such a situation, one you experienced or witnessed. Note when and where it took place, why it was awkward, and how it was resolved.

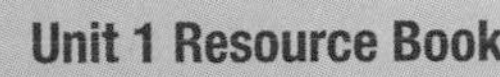

Before Reading

Building Background

Ask students to share overheard conversations that left them feeling curious, shocked, or mystified.

Literary Focus

A story told by an "outsider" is said to be told from the third-person **point of view.** This narrator is not part of the action. The third-person narrator's point of view may be:

- omniscient—able to see into the minds of all characters
- limited—confined to a single character's perceptions
- objective—describing only what can be seen

Writer's Notebook

Encourage students to freely jot down vivid concrete details of the experience including descriptions of their emotions. After they read, students will expand their personal accounts.

More About Colette

Gigi is Colette's most famous work, largely because it was turned into a popular musical by Alan Jay Lerner and Frederick Loewe. The 1958 film version, starring Leslie Caron and Maurice Chevalier, won nine Academy Awards.

SUPPORT MATERIALS OVERVIEW

Unit 1 Resource Book
- Graphic Organizer, p. 33
- Study Guide, p. 34
- Vocabulary, p. 35
- Grammar, p. 36
- Alternate Check Test, p. 37
- Vocabulary Test, p. 38
- Selection Test, pp. 39–40

Building English Proficiency
- Literature Summaries
- Activities, p. 171

Reading, Writing & Grammar SkillBook
- Vocabulary, pp. 15–17
- Reading, pp. 71–73
- Grammar, pp. 192–193

Technology
- Audiotape 2, Side B
- Personal Journal Software
- Custom Literature Database: For another short story about marriage, see "A New England Nun" by Mary E. Wilkins Freeman on the database.
- Test Generator Software

Art Study

Responses to Caption Questions

- The couple in the painting seems like Alice and Marc in that they are well-dressed and lunching in a fashionable restaurant. The woman seems to be staring intensely at the man, who is absorbed (or pretending to be absorbed) in the menu. He holds the rather straight-backed posture of Marc in the story.
- In the picture, the man seems cold and distant, unlike Marc. Students may also interpret the woman's expression as more challenging and aggressive than that of the grateful, happy Alice.

Visual Literacy Balance in a painting often conveys a large part of the artist's meaning. Point out to students that, although the man and woman are equally balanced on the two sides of the painting, the woman's hands intrude into the man's side.

Question What might the breaking of the balance created by the intrusion of the woman's hands into the man's side of the painting mean? *(Possible responses: a disruption of the quiet balance of the relationship of the characters; some kind of desire or request on the part of the woman)*

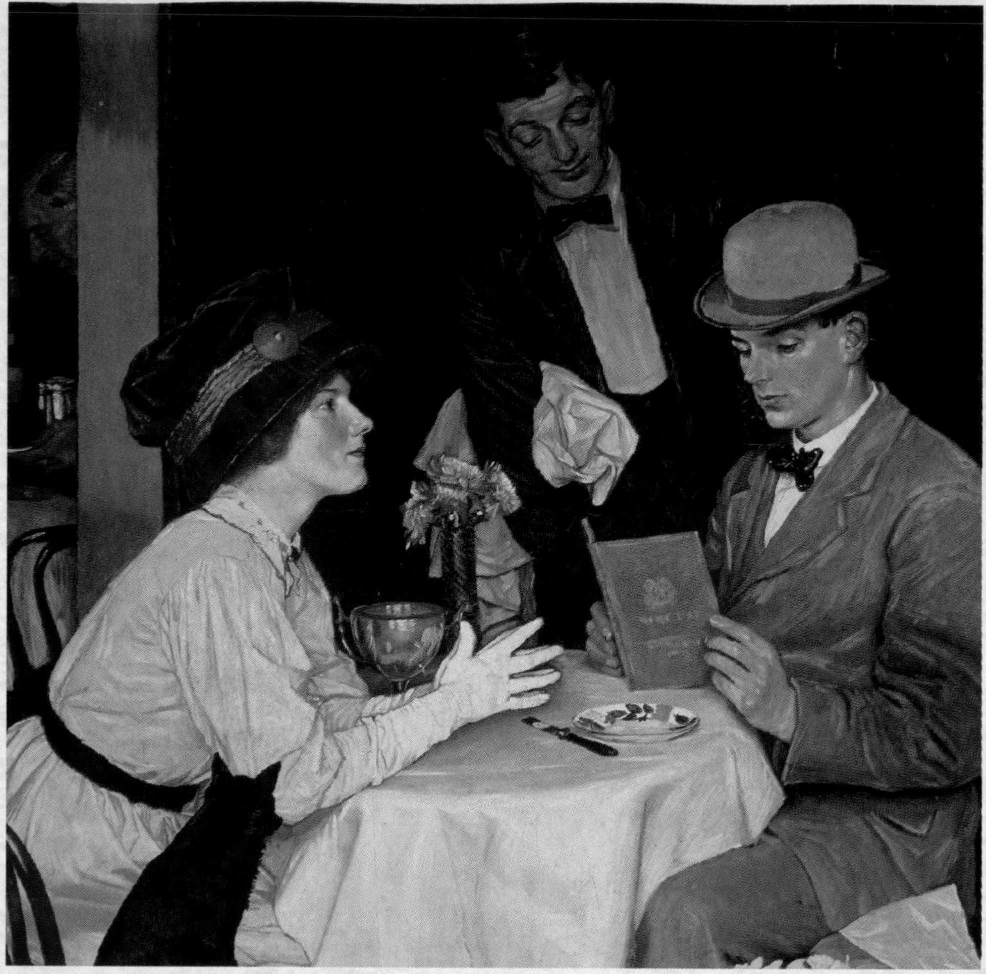

This 1912 work by Scottish painter William Strang shows a young couple on holiday. In what ways is the couple pictured both like and unlike your ideas of Alice and Marc in the story?

SELECTION SUMMARY

The Other Wife

Marc and Alice enter a fashionable restaurant and Marc firmly directs his wife to a seat away from the window. He tells Alice that he does not want to sit near his ex-wife, who is at a nearby table. Though they attempt to disguise it, both are conscious of the presence of the ex-wife. Alice is intrigued by the other woman's appearance and character. She notices that the woman has blue eyes, a fact her husband had never mentioned. Marc admits that he did not succeed in making her happy, but he asserts that he and Alice are happy. Suddenly, Alice feels dubious. She wonder what more the other wife could possibly have wanted.

For summaries in other languages, see the ***Building English Proficiency*** *book.*

The Other Wife

Colette

"For two? This way, *monsieur* and *madame*, there's still a table by the bay window, if *madame* and *monsieur* would like to enjoy the view."

Alice followed the *maître d'hôtel.*[1]

"Oh yes, come on, Marc, we'll feel we're having lunch on a boat at sea. . . ."

Her husband restrained her, passing his arm through hers.

"We'll be more comfortable there."

"There? In the middle of all those people? I'd much prefer . . ."

"Please, Alice."

He tightened his grip in so emphatic a way that she turned round.

"What's the matter with you?"

He said "shh" very quietly, looking at her intently, and drew her towards the table in the middle.

"What is it, Marc?"

"I'll tell you, darling. Let me order lunch. Would you like shrimps? Or eggs in aspic?"

"Whatever *you* like, as you know."

They smiled at each other, wasting the precious moments of an overworked, perspiring *maître d'hôtel* who stood near to them, suffering from a kind of St. Vitus' dance.[2]

"Shrimps," ordered Marc. "And then eggs and bacon. And cold chicken with cos lettuce salad. Cream cheese? *Spécialité de la maison?*[3] We'll settle for the *spécialité.* Two very strong coffees. Please give lunch to my chauffeur; we'll be leaving again at two o'clock. Cider? I don't trust it. . . . Dry champagne."

He sighed as though he had been moving a wardrobe, gazed at the pale noonday sea, the nearly white sky, then at his wife, finding her 1
pretty in her little Mercury-type hat[4] with its long hanging veil.

"You're looking well, darling. And all this sea-blue color gives you green eyes, just imagine! And you put on weight when you travel. . . . It's

---

1. ***maître d'hôtel*** (me′trə dō tel′), headwaiter. *[French]*
2. **St. Vitus' dance**, a nervous disease characterized by involuntary twitching of the muscles.
3. ***Spécialité de la maison*** (spā syal ē tā′ də lə-mā zōn′), specialty of the house. *[French]*
4. **Mercury-type hat.** The god Mercury is characteristically pictured wearing a rounded hat with small wings.

During Reading

Selection Objectives

- to explore the theme of reevaluating one's goals in light of new experiences
- to identify and analyze point of view
- to compare and contrast characters
- to practice correct use of *who* and *whom*

Unit 1 Resource Book
Graphic Organizer, p. 33
Study Guide, p. 34

Theme Link

Alice's encounter with her husband's ex-wife makes her question her own feeling of having reached the top through her marriage.

Vocabulary Preview

lustrous, shining; glossy
soulful, full of feeling; deeply emotional
incandescent, shining brightly; brilliant
furtive, done quickly and with stealth to avoid being noticed; sly
dubious, filled with or being in doubt; uncertain

Students can add the words and definitions to their Writer's Notebooks.

1 Literary Focus
Point of View

Third-person point of view enables a writer to include observations and comments that a character could not make. Here the third-person narrator uses a comparison to comment on Marc's character.

Question What do you think this comment means? *(Possible responses: Marc is weak, lazy, or easily bored.)*

BUILDING ENGLISH PROFICIENCY

ESL
LEP
ELD
SAE
LD

Comparing Characters

To learn more about the story's main characters, have pairs or small groups of students construct webs to illustrate what they know about a character.

1. Students can begin a web for Marc after reading page 45 and a web for Alice after reading page 46.

2. Ask students to add to the webs. They can discuss in what ways Marc and Alice are similar and what they would predict for the future of this couple.

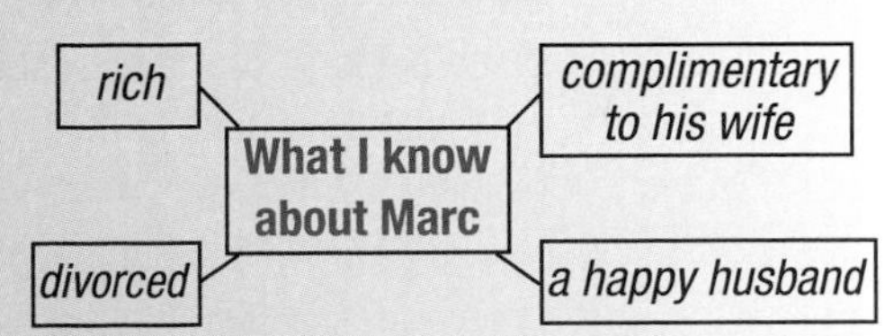

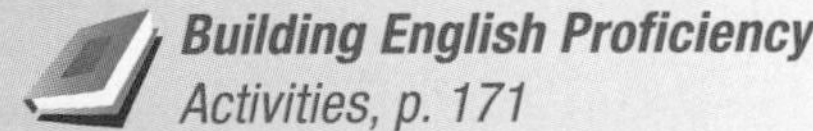

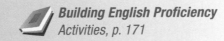

Building English Proficiency
Activities, p. 171

2 Reading/Thinking Skills
Identify Assumptions/ Detect Bias

Marc makes several revealing assumptions about his relationships with his wives.

Questions

- What does Marc assume when he says, "You were able to be happy with me."? *(He assumes Alice has found happiness and will never question it.)*
- What does Marc assume when he says, "There haven't been any guilty parties or victims."? What does this assumption reveal about him? *(Possible responses: He assumes his ex-wife feels neither guilt nor pain; it suggests he is unfeeling and shallow, having gone through a divorce without pain.)*

3 Literary Element
Characterization

The narrator suggests that Alice appears to be excessively grateful and conspicuously happy. Discuss with students the possible meanings of a character's overreactions.

Question What true feelings do you think overreactions can mask? *(Possible response: Students may feel that overreactions can mask doubt, guilt, or fear.)*

4 Literary Focus
Point of View

The third-person narrator reveals Alice and Marc's characters through their behavior; the narrator does not tell their unspoken thoughts. You may wish to refer to the three types of third-person point of view mentioned on p. 43 and allow students to discuss whether Colette has used an omniscient, limited, or objective third-person narrator. To this point "The Other Wife" is related from an objective third-person point of view, but at the end the narrator reveals Alice's thoughts. This point of view is the third-person limited.

nice, up to a point, but only up to a point!"

Her rounded bosom swelled proudly as she leaned over the table.

"Why did you stop me taking that place by the bay window?"

It did not occur to Marc Séguy to tell a lie.

"Because you'd have sat next to someone I know."

"And whom I don't know?"

"My ex-wife."

She could not find a word to say and opened her blue eyes wider.

"What of it, darling? It'll happen again. It's not important."

Alice found her tongue again and asked the inevitable questions in their logical sequence.

"Did she see you? Did she know that you'd seen her? Point her out to me."

"Don't turn round at once, I beg you; she must be looking at us. A lady with dark hair, without a hat; she must be staying at this hotel. . . . On her own, behind those children in red. . . ."

"Yes, I see."

Sheltered behind broad-brimmed seaside hats, Alice was able to look at the woman who fifteen months earlier had still been her husband's wife. "Incompatibility," Marc told her. "Oh, it was total incompatibility! We divorced like well-brought-up people, almost like friends, quietly and quickly. And I began 2 to love you, and you were able to be happy with me. How lucky we are that in our happiness there haven't been any guilty parties or victims!"

The woman in white, with her smooth, lustrous[5] hair over which the seaside light played in blue patches, was smoking a cigarette, her eyes half closed. Alice turned back to her husband, took some shrimps and butter, and ate composedly.

° ° °

Why didn't you ever tell me ... that she had blue eyes too?

° ° °

"Why didn't you ever tell me," she said after a moment's silence, "that she had blue eyes too?"

"But I'd never thought about it!"

He kissed the hand that she stretched out to the bread basket and she blushed with pleasure. Dark-skinned and plump, she might have seemed slightly earthy, but the changing blue of her eyes, and her wavy golden hair, disguised her as a fragile and soulful[6] blond. She showed overwhelming gratitude to her husband. She was immodest without knowing it and her entire person revealed overconspicuous signs of extreme happiness. 3

They ate and drank with good appetite and each thought that the other had forgotten the woman in white. However, Alice sometimes laughed too loudly and Marc was careful of his posture, putting his shoulders back and holding his head up. They waited some time for coffee, in silence. 4 An incandescent[7] stream, a narrow reflection of the high and invisible sun, moved slowly over the sea and shone with unbearable brilliance.

"She's still there, you know," Alice whispered suddenly.

"Does she embarrass you? Would you like to have coffee somewhere else?"

"Not at all! It's she who ought to be embarrassed! And she doesn't look as though she's having a madly gay time; if you could see her. . . ."

"It's not necessary. I know that look of hers."

"Oh, was she like that?"

He breathed smoke through his nostrils and wrinkled his brows.

5. **lustrous** (lus′trəs), *adj.* shining; glossy.
6. **soulful** (sōl′fəl), *adj.* full of feeling; deeply emotional.
7. **incandescent** (in′kən des′nt), *adj.* shining brightly; brilliant.

MINI-LESSON: GRAMMAR
Using the Pronouns who and whom

Teach Remind students that the pronoun *who* is used as the subject of a clause or sentence; *whom* is used as the direct or indirect object.

> Alice was able to look at the woman who fifteen months earlier had still been her husband's wife.

In this sentence, who is the subject of *had still been.*

> And whom I don't know?

W*hom* is the direct object of *don't know.*

Activity Ideas

For practice, students can insert either *who* or *whom* in the following sentences:

1. That is the woman ___ Alice disliked. *(whom)*
2. The other wife ___ had blue eyes was hard to please. *(who)*

Then they can write a dialogue between Alice and Marc as they return home, using the pronoun *who* and *whom* correctly.

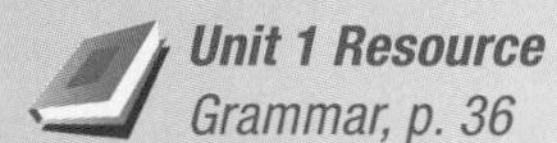

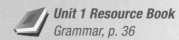

Unit 1 Resource Book
Grammar, p. 36

"Was she like that? No. To be frank, she wasn't happy with me."

"Well, my goodness!"

"You're delightfully generous, darling, madly generous. . . . You're an angel, you're . . . You love me. . . . I'm so proud, when I see that look in your eyes . . . yes, the look you have now. . . . She . . . No doubt I didn't succeed in making her happy. That's all there is to it, I didn't succeed."

"She's hard to please!"

Alice fanned herself irritably, and cast brief glances at the woman in white, her head lean-
5 ing against the back of the cane chair, her eyes closed with an expression of satisfied lassitude.

Marc shrugged his shoulders modestly.

"That's it," he admitted. "What can one do? We have to be sorry for people who are never happy. As for us, we're so happy. . . . Aren't we, darling?"

She didn't reply. She was looking with furtive[8] attention at her husband's face, with its good color and regular shape, at his thick hair, with its occasional thread of white silk, at his small, well-cared-for hands. She felt dubious[9] for
the first time, and asked herself: "What 6
more did she want, then?"

And until they left, while Marc was paying the bill, asking about the chauffeur and the route, she continued to watch, with envious curiosity, the lady in white, that discontented, hard-to-please, superior woman. . . .

---

8. **furtive** (fėr′tiv), *adj.* done quickly and with stealth to avoid being noticed; sly.

9. **dubious** (dü′bē əs), *adj.* filled with or being in doubt; uncertain.

5 Reading/Thinking Skills
Compare and Contrast

Questions

- What are Alice's actions and what feelings do they show? *(Possible response: Alice's irritable fanning of herself and glancing at the other woman are indications that she is angry at the woman, at her husband, or at her own inability to be as "superior.")*
- Can you imitate the ex-wife's expression of "satisfied lassitude"? *(Since* lassitude *means "weariness" or "indifference," students might act bored or relaxed with a slight smile.)*

6 Reader's Response
Making Personal Connections

Ask students if they agree that people periodically need to reevaluate their personal goals and definitions of happiness and success. Discuss with students how an important change or new perspective in life can trigger a need for this act of self-appraisal and goals.

Check Test

1. Why does Marc not want to sit near the window? *(because his ex-wife is seated there)*

2. What reason does Marc first give for the breakup with his wife? *(incompatibility)*

3. What physical detail does Alice mention that Marc had never told her? *(his ex-wife's blue eyes)*

4. What does Marc admit that he did not succeed in doing during his first marriage? *(making his wife happy)*

5. How does Alice reply when Marc asks her if they are happy? *(She does not reply.)*

Unit 1 Resource Book
Alternate Check Test, p. 37

BUILDING ENGLISH PROFICIENCY

Expanding Vocabulary Through Prefixes

Help students use this story to increase their knowledge of English word structure.

1. List on the board these words from the selection that begin with *in-* and *im-:*
- *incompatibility* [lack of harmony]
- *immodest* [bold and rude]
- *invisible* [not visible, not capable of being seen]

2. Have students find the words in the story and suggest what they mean. Clarify the meanings by explaining that the prefixes *in-* and *im-* mean *not* in these words. Write the meanings next to the words.

3. Invite volunteers to convey the meanings through gestures, while others use the words to describe the actions.

After Reading

MAKING CONNECTIONS

1. Responses will vary, but students may focus on feelings of doubt about her own happiness, confusion about her love, or anger and curiosity about Marc's ex-wife.

2. Possible responses: The marriage will last because Alice will not question herself any further or because both partners will grow in self-knowledge; the marriage will not last because of incompatibility or selfishness.

3. Possible response: Alice has begun to wonder if there is "something more" that she is missing. If Marc wasn't good enough for his first wife, maybe he isn't good enough for her.

4. Possible response: Marc married Alice precisely because she was so different from—and probably less demanding than—his first wife.

5. Possible responses: Not wearing a hat and smoking may suggest she is very independent. Leaning back with closed eyes may suggest world-weariness, calmness, or satisfaction.

6. The title is ambiguous. From each woman's perspective, the other woman is the "other wife."

7. In their responses students may point to problems of raising children, financial strains, and emotional pain. Friendly relationships may depend on a need to come to understanding for the sake of children or other family members, geographical proximity, and so on.

8. Possible responses: Contemporary women are less likely to rely upon marriage for self-definition.

After Reading

Making Connections

Shaping Your Response

1. Draw a head and a thought bubble extending from it. In the bubble, write what you think is going through Alice's mind as she leaves the restaurant.
2. Do you think this couple's marriage will last? Why or why not?

Analyzing the Story

3. At the end of the story, Alice "continued to watch, with envious curiosity, the lady in white, that discontented, hard-to-please superior woman. . . ." What do you think has happened during lunch to make her feel "dubious for the first time"?
4. Why might Marc have married Alice, who seems so different from his first wife?
5. Sometimes we can learn a great deal about a **character** who never says a word in a story. What do we learn about the first wife from the descriptions provided in the story?
6. To which of the two wives do you think the **title** of the story applies? Explain.

Extending the Ideas

7. What current social problems does the aftermath of a divorce produce for both spouses and children? Do you think it's possible for ex-husbands and ex-wives to maintain friendly relationships? Explain.
8. Alice, a character from several generations ago, finds the other woman threatening to her marriage and security. Do you think that contemporary women are more apt to be self-assured about their own **individuality** and worth outside of marriage?

Literary Focus: Point of View

Point of view refers to the perspective of the person telling a story. In this story, the narrator is not a character but an outsider, who sees events mainly through Alice's eyes. This point of view is said to be *third-person limited*. Examine the final two paragraphs of the story for insights the narrator provides about Alice.

- How do you think Alice would answer her own question, "What more did she want then"?
- Look back at another story you have read in this group. Decide if it is told by a character in the story (*first-person point of view*) or by an outside narrator (*third-person point of view*).

LITERARY FOCUS: POINT OF VIEW

- Help students to notice that, if it were not for the third-person narrator, we would not be aware that Alice is asking herself the question. Possible responses might focus on the former wife's need for more excitement in marriage, for more independence, or for more affection.
- "Through the Tunnel," "The Censors," and "The Voter" are told in the third-person point of view. "Two Kinds" is told in the first-person point of view.

Vocabulary Study

Colette chooses precise adjectives to convey her meaning. Provide one of the following synonyms for each italicized word below: sly, brilliant, uncertain, shining, deeply emotional.

dubious
furtive
incandescent
lustrous
soulful

1. "The woman in white, with her smooth, *lustrous* hair . . . was smoking a cigarette. . . ."
2. ". . . the changing blue of her eyes, and her wavy golden hair, disguised her as a fragile and *soulful* blonde."
3. "An *incandescent* stream . . . moved slowly over the sea and shone with unbearable brilliance."
4. "She was looking with *furtive* attention at her husband's face. . . ."
5. "She felt *dubious* for the first time. . . ."

Expressing Your Ideas

Writing Choices

Writer's Notebook Update Review the notes you recorded before reading "The Other Wife" about an awkward or embarrassing situation you witnessed or experienced. Now expand and rewrite your personal account using some techniques Colette uses—for example, a third-person narrator, dialogue, or powerful adjectives.

Speak Your Mind The silent first wife sitting by the bay window is well aware of the presence of her ex-husband and his new wife. Write a **monologue** that indicates what this ex-wife is thinking as she observes the pair. Limit your monologue to one of three time periods: the couple's entrance into the room, the period when they are eating lunch, or the settling of the bill and their exit from the room.

Alice's Journal Think about what Alice will write in her **journal** the evening of her encounter with Marc's first wife. Write a brief entry expressing the feelings she is experiencing.

Other Options

Face to Face Marc, Alice, and Marc's first wife meet on a **talk show** featuring ex-wives, present wives, and their husbands. In groups of four, brainstorm questions that a talk show host or hostess might ask these three characters, along with answers they might give. Then act out these four parts for the class.

What's for Lunch? Although the lunch this couple eats sounds romantic, it falls short of modern health standards. Champagne midday? Cholesterol-high foods such as eggs and bacon? Imagine the fat grams in cream cheese! In a small group, work with a health or science teacher or the school dietitian to find out the long-range effects frequent meals like this could have. Chart your findings and present them in an **oral report** to the class.

The Play's the Thing Perform "The Other Wife" as a **play** for radio, video, or the stage. If possible, incorporate music, sound effects, costumes, and simple props (stage "properties" such as glasses and plates).

VOCABULARY STUDY

1. **lustrous,** shining
2. **soulful,** deeply emotional
3. **incandescent,** brilliant
4. **furtive,** sly
5. **dubious,** uncertain

Unit 1 Resource Book
Vocabulary, p. 35
Vocabulary Test, p. 38

WRITING CHOICES

Writer's Notebook Update

Students should be sure to set up their situations clearly and completely so that readers understand why an event is awkward or embarrassing. Another narrative technique students can use is allowing a character's gestures to reveal their character.

Alice's Journal

Remind students that entries in a personal journal need not be neat paragraphs or even fully formed sentences. Questions, exclamations, fragments, images, isolated words—these may all come pouring out of Alice after her encounter.

Selection Test

Unit 1 Resource Book
pp. 39–40

Transparency Collection
Fine Art Writing Prompt 1

OTHER OPTIONS

Face to Face

Suggest the following preparation and performance tips:

- Write a description of your character or a list of his or her character traits.
- Imagine your character's background: age, place of birth, education, occupation, hobbies, etc.
- Do not use a canned speech. Listen carefully and respond to the other characters.

Interdisciplinary Study

Theme Link

People who achieve success at an early age must learn to deal with the consequences of that success. As students explore the Interdisciplinary Study, ask them to share contemporary examples of successful young people who grew in maturity and responsibility because of their success, as well as examples of those who did not.

Curricular Connection: Multicultural

Each culture creates its own definitions of success. Ask students to list three elements of their own definitions of "a successful human being."

Terms to Know

mosaic, a picture or design made by inlaying small bits of colored glass, stone, or tile in mortar

Hellenistic, referring to Greek history and culture after the death of Alexander the Great

sect, a religious denomination that is part of a larger group

prodigy, an extraordinarily talented person, especially a child

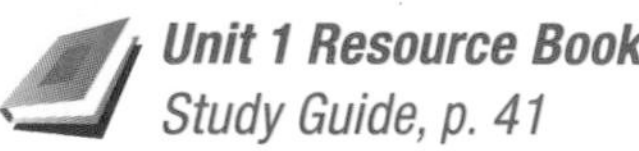

Unit 1 Resource Book
Study Guide, p. 41

INTERDISCIPLINARY STUDY

Pushing Toward the Top

So Young, So Talented

Multicultural Connection
Several of the stories in this group are about young people who feel pressure to excel. Compare these fictional characters with the people pictured on these pages, who displayed talent at an early age that directed their courses in later life.

Jodie Foster appeared in her first commercial at the age of three, made her first acclaimed motion picture at twelve, and entered Yale at seventeen. This award-winning actress now directs film as well.

EARLY

Alexander the Great (356-323 b.c.), who became King of Macedonia at twenty, conquered the stretch from Asia Minor to India. This mosaic copy of the Hellenistic painting, ***Battle of Issus,*** by Philoxenus captures him at the most dramatic moment of the battle.

This painting was created by Wang Yani at the age of five. Born in Gongcheng, China, she now exhibits her paintings of birds, flowers, monkeys, and trees in museums in Asia, Europe, and the United States.

MINI-LESSON: CRITICAL THINKING

Recognize Values

Teach Individual values affect decision-making, interpersonal relationships, and large group interactions. The values that direct human lives might be grouped into these four categories.

Material	money, possessions, health
Psychological	happiness, status
Intellectual	knowledge, aesthetic delight
Spiritual	religious beliefs, serenity

Activity Idea Have students imagine that they have been invited to participate in a "Guest Editorial" program on local television.

- Have each speaker present a two-minute commentary on one particular value.
- Each commentator may explore any aspect of a value that seems interesting—for example, why the value is common or uncommon, or why the value appeals to some people but not to others.

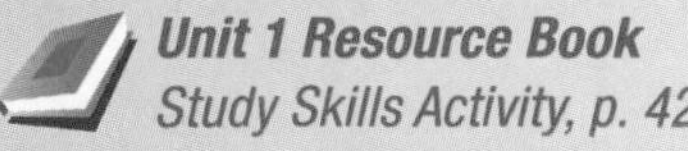

Unit 1 Resource Book
Study Skills Activity, p. 42

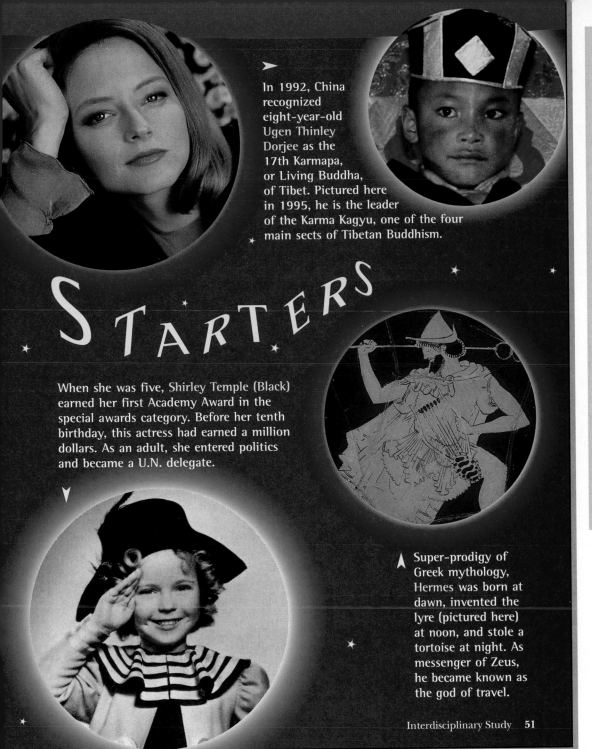

In 1992, China recognized eight-year-old Ugen Thinley Dorjee as the 17th Karmapa, or Living Buddha, of Tibet. Pictured here in 1995, he is the leader of the Karma Kagyu, one of the four main sects of Tibetan Buddhism.

STARTERS

When she was five, Shirley Temple (Black) earned her first Academy Award in the special awards category. Before her tenth birthday, this actress had earned a million dollars. As an adult, she entered politics and became a U.N. delegate.

Super-prodigy of Greek mythology, Hermes was born at dawn, invented the lyre (pictured here) at noon, and stole a tortoise at night. As messenger of Zeus, he became known as the god of travel.

Art Study

The images on these pages are all portraits. A portrait is a drawing, photograph, painting, mosaic, or sculpture of a person, especially of the person's face. Point out to students that portraits usually try to reveal the inner qualities—the character traits—of the subject.

Portraits can be formal or informal, and they can be used for a variety of purposes, such as

- to keep a memory of a loved one (as in a snapshot)
- to identify a person (as on a driver's license or passport)
- to glorify a political or military leader (as on a poster)
- to sell or endorse a product (as on a book jacket or cereal box)

Question What do you think the purposes of the portraits on pages 50–51 might be? *(Possible responses: to glorify a leader, to advertise a movie, to display a work of art, to exhibit the talent of the subject.)*

BUILDING ENGLISH PROFICIENCY

ESL
LEP
ELD
SAE
LD

Making Personal Connections

The young people on these pages all have reached many goals at early ages. Use one or both of the following activities to help students understand the phenomenon of the prodigy better.

Activity Ideas

- Ask students to choose one of the young people pictured. Have them brainstorm for questions that they would like to ask that person and then speculate about possible answers.
- Invite students to describe a talent they have that they think is preparing them for the future.

Terms to Know

quintessential, having the most pure and concentrated essence of something

fête, a festival, entertainment, or celebration

incarnation, embodiment; the perfect type of something

diverting, entertaining; amusing

clavier (klə vir′)**,** a stringed instrument with a keyboard, as an early piano or harpsichord

bereft, robbed; deprived

reciprocate, to give, do, or feel in return

Responding

1. Possible response Examples: athletes, particularly in sports that favor the very young, such as gymnastics and tennis; child actors and actresses; young computer geniuses; talent show and science-fair winners; class presidents

2. Possible response Some advantages are financial rewards, world travel, and avoiding dull daily routine. Some disadvantages are long, grueling hours of practice; a lonely, isolated childhood; and being perceived as a "freak."

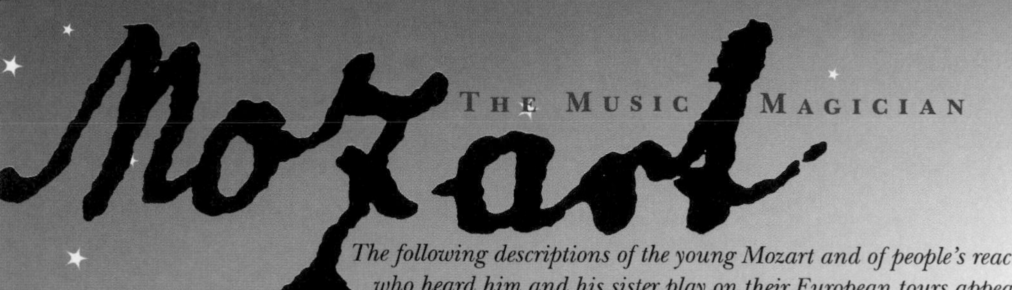

*The following descriptions of the young Mozart and of people's reactions who heard him and his sister play on their European tours appear in the biography **Mozart** by Maynard Solomon.*

The most famous musical prodigy in history, he was marked from the outset as the quintessential, perfect child. In an extraordinary series of triumphs, he was received, feted, and honored by the royal families of Europe—the king and queen of France, the empress of Austria and her son Emperor Joseph, the king and queen of England—and Pope Clement XIV himself. Mozart and his family were showered with money and expensive presents. He was kissed by empresses and petted by Marie Antoinette. And all because he was a gifted child, one who not only could perform wonders and miracles but was the very incarnation of a miracle, one whose small body exemplified the infinite perfectibility of the child and, by inference, of mankind....

Leopold Mozart [his father] did not exaggerate when he wrote home, "Everyone is amazed, especially at the boy, and everyone whom I have heard says that his genius is incomprehensible." Anecdotes of the visit to Schönbrunn confirm that the children put on a diverting entertainment: One of the ladies of the court assured the biographer Franz Niemetschek that both children made a "very great impression," recalling that "people could hardly believe their ears and eyes at the performance." It was said that the emperor teased the little "magician," as he was dubbed: "It is no great art to play with all your fingers; but if you could play with only one finger and on a covered keyboard, that would be something worthy of admiration." Naturally, Mozart was not fazed by this suggestion, which could not have been altogether unexpected, for he had brought along a bagful of keyboard tricks from Salzburg. He commenced "to play with one finger only, as precisely as possible; and then, he permitted the clavier keyboard to be covered and performed with marvelous dexterity, as though he had long been practicing this feat...."

But anyone who troubled to look could have perceived many early signs of Mozart's difficulty in sustaining his multiple burdens: he was quick to tears, stricken and often taken ill by the loss or absence of friends, bereft when his constant pleas to "love me" were not reciprocated. There was no indication that the child understood the extent to which he had been converted into an instrument of patriarchal ambition and subjected to the inevitable resentments that attach to a father's growing realization that he has become deeply dependent upon his little boy.

Responding

1. Who would you add to the picture gallery of talented young people? Explain your choices and provide captions.

2. Working with a partner, make a list of advantages and disadvantages to being a prodigy.

MINI-LESSON: SPEAKING AND LISTENING SKILLS

Demonstrate Poise and Confidence

Teach One of the qualities of prodigies that often astounds audiences is the poise and confidence that such young people project on stage. Point out to students that every speaker or performer—not only prodigies—can demonstrate such self-assurance.

For speakers, poise and confidence are matters of both mental and physical preparation and performance. Here are some tips for increasing poise and confidence.

- Talk about a subject you know well.
- Organize your thoughts in advance.
- Rehearse before a mirror.
- Stand straight and make eye contact with your audience.
- Don't hurry. Speak at a normal pace.

Activity Idea Have students give a two -to three-minute speech about a musical performer, actor, or actress they admire. Encourage students to

- choose a performer whose work is familiar to them
- prepare a simple, easy-to-remember outline of the speech
- express enthusiasm for someone they honestly admire

This portrait of Mozart and his father and sister is a watercolor by the French artist Louis de Carmontelle (1717-1806). What details from Solomon's biography present the young Mozart in a different light from that in the painting?

Art Study

The painting of Mozart with his father and sister is also a portrait. It is a watercolor by the French artist Louis de Carmontelle (1717–1806). De Carmontelle was also noted as a landscape architect who designed many parks.

Response to Caption Solomon mentions that the young Mozart was quick to burst out crying, that he was extremely affected by the loss or absence of friends, and that he felt he often had to ask for love and found that love was not given.

Interdisciplinary Activity Idea

Have students work in small groups to compare the life of Mozart to that of a well-known contemporary prodigy. They may choose a prodigy from pages 50–51 or someone else. Encourage them to do library or online research to find out more information about both prodigies. Direct students to categorize their comparisons under these headings: *Performances, School, Home Life.* Afterwards, engage students in a class discussion in which volunteers present their findings and draw conclusions based on their research.

BUILDING ENGLISH PROFICIENCY

Music Appreciation

The story of Mozart's life may amaze and amuse students. By appreciating some of his work, students can judge for themselves the ability Mozart possessed.

Activity Ideas

- Obtain some Mozart recordings and play them for the class. Have students discuss their feelings about the music. You also might invite students to draw while listening to music by Mozart.
- Invite a music teacher to class. Team-teach a study of Mozart's music and life.

Interdisciplinary Study

Theme Link

People try to measure human intelligence, although the will to succeed, a competitive spirit, and a practical sense of real-world problem-solving are usually greater factors in "success" than intelligence alone.

Curricular Connection: Science

Measuring intelligence has always been controversial, largely because of the assumptions and cultural biases of even the most well-intentioned test makers. Aptitude tests—tests that suggest the affinities of people for certain kinds of activities—may ultimately be more useful.

Responding

Possible Response Students might feel that questions on IQ tests do not reflect the abilities that people need to have in the everyday world. They might feel that high school graduates should know how to read, write, and perform basic mathematical operations.

Interdisciplinary Activity Idea

In anticipation of driving, have students devise questions that they think might be on the written portion of a driving test. The class can vote on the best questions to compile as a test for students to take as they complete driver education.

INTERDISCIPLINARY STUDY

Science Connection

Excellence can take many forms. One such form is intelligence. An intelligence test is one way to measure a person's ability to solve certain kinds of problems. But a high intelligence quotient (IQ) is no guarantee of achievement, and many talented, accomplished people have IQs considered normal or lower.

Measuring Up

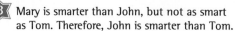

Although there is some connection between creativity and intelligence, a "creative" test taker may fare poorly on intelligence tests. Most intelligence tests involve questions dealing with memory, reasoning, factual recall, and ability with numbers. Such tests include few questions based on mechanical skills and do not measure creativity.

An intelligence quotient, or IQ, a number used to indicate a person's intelligence, is based on a comparison of his or her score on a particular test with the scores of others taking the same test.

Psychologists who design intelligence tests try to use material with which all test takers are familiar. Nevertheless, such tests are based on culture and experience to some degree. For example, someone who has always spoken English has an advantage over someone who learned English later in school. In an effort to be culture-fair, some tests attempt to use words, symbols, ideas, and pictures that are recognized by persons of different backgrounds.

What are the IQs of some famous people? The estimated IQ of the French writer Voltaire was reported to be 170, that of Italian painter Leonardo da Vinci was 135, and that of George Washington projected at 125.

Try answering the following questions, which are typical of those appearing on IQ tests. Answers are on this page.

1. If you rearrange the letters TRAACINCT, you will have the name of:
   a. a color
   b. an ocean
   c. a food
   d. an animal

2. What is the missing number? 4 6 10 ? 34 66
   a. 12
   b. 16
   c. 17
   d. 18
   e. 22

3. Mary is smarter than John, but not as smart as Tom. Therefore, John is smarter than Tom.
   a. True
   b. False
   c. Impossible to answer from the data given

4. Which is least like the others?
   a. iron
   b. oxygen
   c. gold
   d. salt
   e. nitrogen

5. Which one does not belong with the others?

a. b. c. d.

Responding

Do you consider questions on IQ tests too academic? What kinds of practical questions do you think people your age should be able to answer before graduating from high school? Work with a group to devise your own questions, based on real-life skills.

Answers: 1. b. Antarctic; 2. d. (Double each number and subtract 2.); 3. b; 4. d. (All the others are elements.); 5. c.

MINI-LESSON: STUDY SKILLS

Follow Directions

Teach Following directions is key to problem-solving and test-taking. Point out to students that, while most people pay attention to the nouns in directions, they should pay attention to verbs, adjectives, and prepositions as well. Note the key direction words in the chart at the right.

Activity Idea Have students write their own sets of directions for a task of their own or one of the following tasks.

- baking a cake
- installing a new computer game
- writing an essay

Then have students underline the key words in the set of directions.

Verbs	is/is not write analyze	compare belong interpret	contrast identify decide
Adjectives	better more	best worst	less least
Prepositions	before below opposite	after between under	above except without

Reading Mini-Lesson

Finding Main Idea and Supporting Details

The ability to find the main idea as you read is a useful skill, especially when reading nonfiction for information. For example, when you read an article in a reference book, it is the main idea that you need to remember. The main idea gives the most important point of the whole passage and can usually be summed up in one sentence. A writer includes details to support the main idea, to clarify it, or sometimes simply to add interesting information.

One strategy to help you identify the main idea in a passage is to look for key words as you read. You might organize these key words using a pie chart. For example, if you were reading an article on the construction of the Empire State Building, your pie chart might look like this:

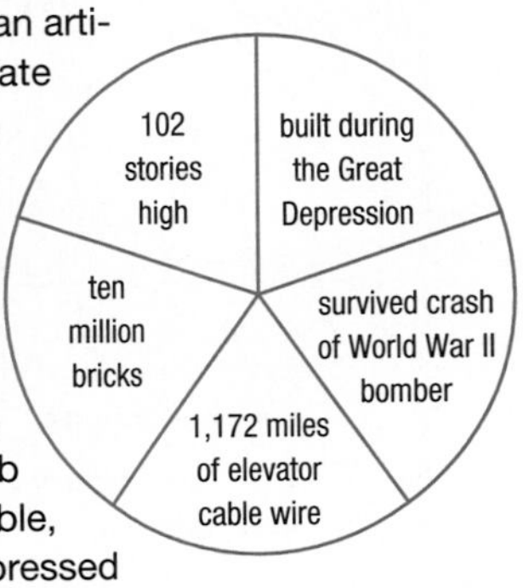

Looking at these key words and phrases, you might express the main idea of the article as "The construction of the Empire State Building was an extraordinary achievement." Remember not all details are equally important to the main idea. For example, King Kong's famous climb to the top of the building, however memorable, isn't really relevant to the main idea as expressed above.

Activity Options

1. Use a pie chart to diagram the main idea and supporting details in the passage from Maynard Solomon's biography of Mozart that appears on page 52.
2. Make a pie chart about a recent event in the news. Using the information in the chart, identify the main idea.
3. Research the careers of one of the prodigies pictured on pages 50–51. Write down at least three main ideas you discovered from your research, and list two or three supporting details for each main idea.

Reading Mini-Lesson

Teaching Objectives

- to practice identifying the main idea
- to practice identifying supporting details

Introduce

Bring in a current newspaper and ask a student to read the first several paragraphs of a current news story of interest to the class. Then elicit from students the main idea and two or three supporting details. Point out that details only add to or qualify the main idea.

Follow Up

After students have looked at the diagram, have them identify the main idea of an event they have experienced recently, such as a ball game at recess, a meal in the cafeteria, or a test in science class. Then have them add several supporting details that tell about the event.

Activity Options

Activity 1 Some students may want to start by identifying the main ideas of the individual paragraphs.

Activity 2 When students have finished their charts, they can compare their main ideas to the "news of the day" summary statements that appear in many newspapers.

Activity 3 Remind students to state main ideas in complete sentences.

CONTENT AREA READING

Using the Parts of a Book to Find the Main Idea

Students should be aware that many books, especially textbooks, will help them to identify main ideas and supporting details. Point out that writers do not usually try to hide or obscure the main idea; they make it as clear as possible.

- Part titles, chapter titles, and section headings often focus on a single topic and define the limits of the material covered in a particular section.
- In addition, some books include summaries, boxed features, and boldface names and terms that draw attention to some aspect of the main idea.

Writing Workshop

WRITER'S BLUEPRINT

Specs

The Specs in the Writer's Blueprint address these writing and thinking skills:

- summarizing
- generalizing
- supporting a position
- drawing conclusions
- writing focused paragraphs
- punctuating quotations

These Specs serve as your lesson objectives, and they form the basis for the **Assessment Criteria Specs** for a superior paper, which appear on the final TE page for this lesson. You might want to read them with students when you begin the lesson.

Linking Literature to Writing

Discuss how the characters in the literature handled their challenges. Have students make a list of strategies that worked and those that didn't work, to use when they write their conclusions.

Writing Workshop

Challenges: Up Close and Personal

Assignment You have read stories about characters meeting challenges, some more successfully than others. Now write an essay about handling challenges in everyday life.

WRITER'S BLUEPRINT

Product	An interpretive essay
Purpose	To explore the theme of meeting challenges
Audience	People who like to read but have never read these particular stories
Specs	As the writer of a successful essay, you should:

- ❑ Analyze how three characters from the stories respond to challenges. Then draw conclusions from your analysis.
- ❑ Begin by introducing your characters and briefly summarizing the challenges that each character faces. Give your readers enough background about the plot to be able to follow your train of thought. Remember, they haven't read these stories.
- ❑ Go on to deal with each character in detail, one at a time. First make a general statement that analyzes his or her responses to challenges. Then cite specific examples from the stories, including quotations, to support this general statement.
- ❑ In your conclusion, look back at your analyses and state the lessons that can be learned from them. State these lessons in terms of *do's* and *don't's* about how to meet challenges in everyday life.
- ❑ Write focused paragraphs that each develop a general idea with specific examples.
- ❑ Follow the conventions of standard written English. Punctuate quotations from the literature correctly.

The instructions that follow are designed to lead you to a successful essay.

WRITING WORKSHOP OVERVIEW

Product
Expository writing: An interpretive essay

Prewriting
Find challenges in the literature—Discuss your notes—Plan your essay
Unit 1 Resource Book
Prewriting Worksheets pp. 43–44

Drafting
Start writing
Transparency Collection
Student Models for Writing Workshop 1, 2

Revising
Ask a partner—Strategy: Writing Focused Paragraphs
Unit 1 Resource Book
Revising Worksheet p. 45

Editing
Ask a partner—Strategy: Punctuating Quotations from Literature
Unit 1 Resource Book
Grammar Worksheet p. 46
Grammar Check Test p. 47

Presenting
Read Aloud
Poster

Looking Back
Self-evaluate—Reflect—For Your Working Portfolio
Unit 1 Resource Book
Assessment Worksheet p. 48
Transparency Collection
Fine Art Writing Prompt 1

STEP 1 PREWRITING

Find challenges in the literature and make notes on the characters' responses. Organize your notes in a chart like this one:

Challenges	Responses	Specific Examples	Plan of Attack—
Jerry— "He knew he must find his way through . . . and out the other side."	—envies boys who can do it —is impatient to succeed —works to develop skills	—"a controlled impatience, made him wait" —devotes himself to "careful self-training"	always have a plan: define exactly what it is you need to do before you try to do it

LITERARY SOURCE

"He looked down into the blue well of water. He knew he must find his way through that cave, or hole, or tunnel, and out the other side." from "Through the Tunnel" by Doris Lessing

Discuss your notes with classmates and ask for comments. If you need to explain things that are unclear to a classmate, make additional notes on those explanations. Then look back at your additional notes and revise your plan accordingly.

OR . . .

You might also talk with people who haven't read the stories before. Explaining the plots to them may help you see things from different angles.

Plan your essay. Think about what you want to say in the introduction, body, and conclusion. Organize the information in your notes in a three-part outline that reflects the Specs in the Writer's Blueprint.

I. Introduction
- A. The three characters
- B. Their challenges

II. Body
- A. First character
  1. General statement
  2. Specific examples
- B. Second character
  1. General statement
  2. Specific examples
- C. Third character
  1. General statement
  2. Specific examples

III. Conclusion
- A. Lessons Learned
- B. *Do's*
- C. *Don't's*

OR . . .

Turn things around in the body of your essay. Give your specific examples first for each character and follow with the general statement.

BUILDING ENGLISH PROFICIENCY

Planning a Prewriting Strategy

To help students gain a concrete understanding of challenges, have them discuss challenges in their own lives.

1. Begin by presenting a challenge in your own life. Explain what it was and how you dealt with it.

2. Invite students to contribute examples of challenges from their own lives.

3. Then discuss any similarities between challenges students have faced and challenges facing the characters.

STEP 1 PREWRITING

Find challenges in the literature

This activity would work well as a whole-class or small-group activity. Start with a brief discussion of why we are presented with challenges and what we learn about ourselves as we handle them. For additional support, see the worksheet referenced below.

Unit 1 Resource Book
Prewriting Worksheet, p. 43

Discuss your notes

By this point, students should have an understanding of the importance of the challenges in the literature. Discussion and input from classmates should clarify any misunderstandings. Encourage students to add notes to their charts, as this will be helpful when they plan and draft.

Plan your essay

Remind students that planning is necessary to ensure that they meet the objectives specified in the blueprint. Planning will also make drafting easier. For additional support, see the worksheet referenced below.

Unit 1 Resource Book
Prewriting Worksheet, p. 44

Connections to **Writer's Notebook**

For selection-related prompts, refer to Writer's Notebook.

Connections to **Writer's Resource**

For additional writing prompts, refer to Writer's Resource.

STEP 2 DRAFTING

Start writing

Remind students that writing is a process, and the drafting part of the process allows them to develop content without having to stop and shift focus to correct mistakes. Encourage students to take advantage of the drafting tips if they have trouble getting started or moving from one part of the plan to the next.

The Student Models

The **transparencies** referenced below are authentic student models. Review them with the students before they draft. These questions will help:

1. For model 1, what specific examples did the writer use to make her point about unrealistic self-images?

2. What specific examples did the writer of model 2 use to make his point about suppression of impulse?

3. How could you improve model 1 in terms of sentence structure and technical correctness? Pay special attention to the opening sentence.

Transparency Collection
Student Models for Writing Workshop 1, 2

STEP 3 REVISING

Ask a partner (Peer assessment)

Encourage students to read their drafts aloud to each other. Remind them to listen carefully and take brief notes. If taking notes causes the listener to miss part of the reading, he or she should listen to the entire work and then do a brief free-writing immediately afterwards. Remind students that as listeners, they must keep their comments specific in order to be truly helpful.

STEP 2 DRAFTING

Start writing. Use your writing plan and Writer's Blueprint as guides. One of these drafting strategies might help.

- If you're drafting by hand, use a separate piece of paper for each paragraph. That way you'll have lots of room to revise.
- In the body, devote one paragraph to each character.
- For your conclusion, state each *do* and *don't* in a short, catchy sentence first. Then go on to explain it.

Here is part of one student's draft.

> "Through the Tunnel" tells the story of a young boy who meets his challenge by fighting his own impatience—and winning. Jerry's first impulse is to swim under, find the underwater tunnel, and quickly swim his way through—but his "most unchildlike persistence, a controlled impatience" makes him wait. Waiting is a good idea. If he had simply given in to his impulse and tried to swim the tunnel right away he would have probably drowned.

STUDENT MODEL

COMPUTER TIP
Try using the Cut and Paste functions to switch your body paragraphs around as you revise. See if the body of your essay reads better with a new order.

STEP 3 REVISING

Ask a partner to look over your draft and comment before you actually revise.

✔ Do my general statements really fit the character's responses?

✔ Do my specific examples really support my general statements?

✔ Have I written focused paragraphs?

MINI-LESSON: WRITING STYLE

Writing Focused Paragraphs

Teach Make a two-column chart headed "Main Idea" and "Supporting Details" on the board and have students fill it in with information from the student model paragraph on page 59. *(Main Idea—Juan's failure; Details—becomes obsessed, becomes censor, becomes own enemy)*

Activity Idea Have students fill in a chart for one or more of the paragraphs they wrote in their essays.

Apply Have students use their charts to help them revise their essays.

Revising Strategy

Writing Focused Paragraphs

In a focused paragraph, the writer:

- makes a definite point—a main idea
- develops this main idea with specific details
- stays focused on this main idea

In the paragraph at the right, the narrator states her mother's belief (in America you can be anything) and gives specific examples of "anything" (entrepreneur, civil servant, homeowner, celebrity). Every sentence focuses on the main idea. Notice how the writer of the draft below used a partner's comment to delete a sentence that doesn't focus on the main idea.

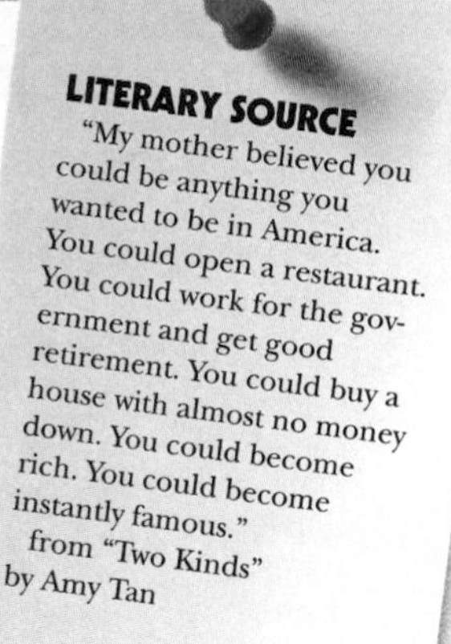

LITERARY SOURCE
"My mother believed you could be anything you wanted to be in America. You could open a restaurant. You could work for the government and get good retirement. You could buy a house with almost no money down. You could become rich. You could become instantly famous."
from "Two Kinds"
by Amy Tan

Juan, the protagonist of "The Censors," fails to meet his challenge when he becomes obsessed with it. His goal is to find letters from his beloved. Juan is saddened by the fact that he has not seen or heard of his love Marianna for quite some time. He has no doubt that the government censors are keeping her letters from getting through to him. Can he prevent the censoring of her letters if he himself becomes a censor? He fails because he actually becomes the enemy he sets out to defeat—the censor. ~~Jerry in "Through the Tunnel" also wants to find something, but Roof in "The Voter" doesn't.~~ *Does this sentence belong here?*

Revising Strategy: Writing Focused Paragraphs

Have students look over the student model and note the changes that were made. For additional support, see the mini-lesson at the bottom of page 58 and the worksheet referenced below.

Unit 1 Resource Book
Revising Worksheet, p. 45

Connections to **Writer's Resource**

Refer to the Grammar, Usage, and Mechanics Handbook on Writer's Resource.

BUILDING ENGLISH PROFICIENCY

Working with Partners

Writing partners can be useful in the prewriting, revising, and editing stages. Offer the following advice to help students work more effectively with writing partners.

1. Encourage partners to jot down notes as they listen and to speak from them.

2. Explain that partners always should feel free to offer ideas but should leave the final decisions about using those ideas up to the writer.

3. Suggest that partners practice giving positive feedback. Instead of saying, "I don't understand this," for example, students might try, "I'd like more information on this" or "I want to know why. . ."

STEP 4 EDITING

Ask a partner (Peer assessment)

You might want to have students work in editing groups, with each group member reading every paper for one specific technical area, such as spelling or complete sentences.

Editing Strategy: Punctuating Quotations from Literature

Remind students to use quotations in their essays to support their general statements. Have them look through their papers to make sure they have not left out any quotation marks. For additional support, see the mini-lesson at the bottom of this page and the worksheets referenced below.

Unit 1 Resource Book
Grammar Worksheet, p. 46
Grammar Check Test, p. 47

Connections to
Writer's Resource

Refer to the Grammar, Usage, and Mechanics Handbook on Writer's Resource.

STEP 4 EDITING

Ask a partner to review your revised draft before you actually edit it. Pay special attention to punctuating quotations from literature.

FOR REFERENCE. . .
More rules for punctuating quotations from literature are listed in the Language and Grammar Handbook at the back of this text.

Editing Strategy

Punctuating Quotations from Literature

When you edit an essay like this one, make sure you follow these rules for punctuating quotations from literature:

- Surround direct quotations with quotation marks.
- Use commas to set off words that precede or introduce a direct quotation.
- Place the end punctuation or the comma that ends the quotation inside the quotation marks.
- Begin a direct quotation that is a sentence with a capital letter.

Amy Tan writes, "My mother believed you could be anything you wanted to be in America."

Leaving out the quotation marks can lead to confusion. Notice how the writer of the draft below fixed mistakes in punctuating quotations from literature.

The whole system has been corrupted, and the device for this corruption is money. Rufus is in the position of bribing tribal elders for their very important votes in the election. They do not refuse him, for Rufus is a convincing speaker, but they do not accept without mild protest. One elder tells Rufus, "But what we do say is that two shillings is shameful," when Rufus offers him two shillings for his vote.

STUDENT MODEL

MINI-LESSON: GRAMMAR

Punctuating Quotations from Literature

Put these sentences on the board and ask students to determine whether the quotations have been correctly punctuated, and correct any errors.

John Lennon said, "Life is what happens to you while you're busy making other plans." *(correct)*

"Happiness is not being pained in body or troubled in mind according to Thomas Jefferson." *(comma and quotation marks after* mind, *not at end of sentence)*

"The pursuit of happiness is a most ridiculous phrase, said C. P. Snow. If you pursue it, you'll never find it." *(quotation marks after* phrase, *and before* If)

Unit 1 Resource Book
Grammar Worksheet, p. 46
Grammar Check Test, p. 47

STEP 5 PRESENTING

- Read your essay aloud to a partner and discuss your *do*'s and *don't*'s.
- Create a class poster of advice on meeting challenges. Include at least one *do* or *don't* from each person in class. Donate a copy to the school library.

STEP 6 LOOKING BACK

Self-evaluate. How well does your paper meet the Specs from the Writer's Blueprint? Evaluate yourself on each point, from 6 (superior) down to 1 (inadequate).

Reflect. Think about what you learned from writing this essay.

✔ Compare your rough draft with your finished copy. Jot down comments about the kinds of changes you made. What do they tell you about your strengths and weaknesses as a writer?

✔ How could you apply some of the *do*'s and *don't*'s to challenges facing you in your life right now?

For Your Working Portfolio Add your finished paper and reflection responses to your working portfolio.

STEP 5 PRESENTING

Read Aloud

You may want to have students work in small groups and discuss together.

Posters

Students could make more than one poster of advice on meeting challenges and include pictures or illustrations. The posters could be displayed in the library or taken to an elementary school and used for a bulletin board display.

STEP 6 LOOKING BACK

Self-evaluate

The *Assessment Criteria Specs* at the bottom of this page are for a superior paper. You might want to post these in the classroom. Students can then evaluate themselves based on these criteria. For a complete scoring rubric, use the *Assessment Worksheet* referenced below.

Unit 1 Resource Book
Assessment Worksheet, p. 48

Reflect

You may want to have students work in small groups first, discussing the two checked questions, before going off to write their answers individually. Encourage students to include these reflections in their portfolios.

To further explore the theme, use the Fine Art Transparency referenced below.

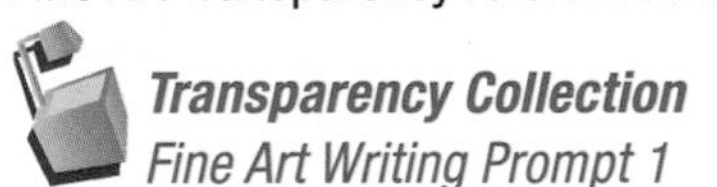
Transparency Collection
Fine Art Writing Prompt 1

ASSESSMENT CRITERIA SPECS

Here are the criteria for a superior paper. A full six-level rubric for this paper appears on the Assessment Worksheet referenced below.

6 Superior The writer of a 6 paper impressively meets these criteria:

- Insightfully analyzes how each of three characters responds to a challenge.
- Gives readers sufficient background to understand the analyses.
- Refers to specific images and examples from the text that solidly demonstrate each character's transformation.
- Quotes from the text accurately.
- Produces tightly-focused paragraphs that each develop a general idea with specific examples.
- Draws insightful conclusions as to how the lessons learned from these characters can be applied in everyday life.
- Uses correct paragraphing, punctuation, grammar, and spelling throughout. Punctuates quotations from literature correctly.

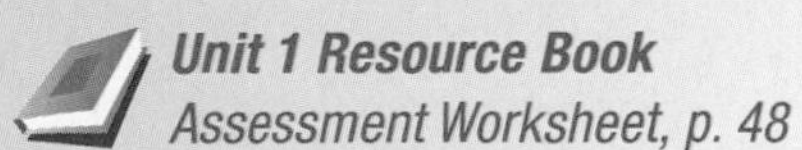
Unit 1 Resource Book
Assessment Worksheet, p. 48

Beyond Print

Teaching Objectives

- to recognize and understand camera terms
- to recognize how camera techniques influence viewers
- to transfer camera techniques to writing techniques

Curricular Connection: Visual Skills

You can use the popularity of movies and students' familiarity with movie-making to increase students' media literacy, as well as improve some of their writing skills.

Introduce

The degree to which America is becoming image-dependent is a matter of lively controversy. On the one hand, movies and television, not to mention computers, seem to have created an audience that prefers to extract information from pictures rather than from text. On the other hand, more books than ever are being published, people are writing more (thanks to computers), and storytelling and poetry readings are on the rise in popularity.

As a motivational activity, ask students to name a book they have read that has also been made into a movie. Which did they prefer? Why? What can books offer that movies cannot? What can movies offer that books cannot?

Beyond Print

Looking at Movies

Today America is a visual society that gets its information as much from images as from the printed word. Although a million people may buy a bestselling novel, many times that number could flock to see the film version. In order to become a more informed viewer of movies and TV, watch for ways (a lingering close-up, quick transitions between scenes, dissolves from one picture to the next) that the director or cameraperson tries to influence you. You might use similar techniques in your writing to appeal to your audience.

Transitions and editing Filmmakers may use special effects such as fade-outs and dissolves to represent relationships, indicate shifts in time or place, or establish contrasts. Scenes may be cut or rearranged to quicken the pace or present a flashback.

Camera angles A camera can pan a scene, linger, zoom in on important details, and make things appear important or insignificant. A camera can focus on a particular character's point of view, framing scenes according to a limited perspective.

Color Use of color can serve to develop character and mood. Note whether colors are muted or bright and whether black-and-white is used for effect. Observe how bright lighting produces a buoyant mood, while shadows can produce an ominous effect.

Music and sound effects Note whether music is used to create a mood, build tension, or signal an oncoming event.

Symbolic shots and gestures Sometimes an object or a gesture may be highlighted and invested with symbolic significance. For example, an overturned vase may suggest violence or upheaval.

Activity Options

1. Pick a scene from one of the stories in this group that lends itself to "filming." Brainstorm in groups ways that you could convert the written description into pictures, applying some of the camera techniques mentioned above. Present your ideas in the form of a few illustrated storyboards with written filming directions.

ANOTHER APPROACH

Sound Effects

Students who are more auditory than visual might prefer to learn more about the sounds of movies and try to convert some movie sound techniques to writing techniques.

- Have students research, list, and define movie terms that are connected with sound: for example, track, mixing, dubbing, score, fade, and motif.
- Have students list and define literary terms that are connected with sound: for example, onomatopoeia, alliteration, and rhyme.
- Have students write a passage of dialogue or description in which they reproduce in words a variety of sounds.
- They might also blend words and music by creating their own sound track.

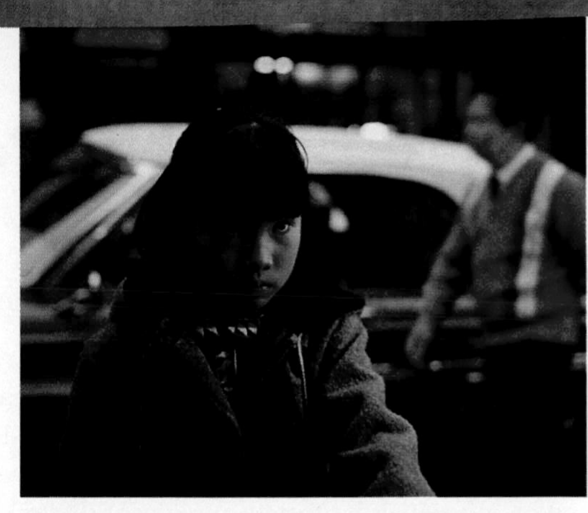

This still is from *The Joy Luck Club,* directed by Wayne Wang (Hollywood Pictures, 1993). ➤

2. Choose an item from your portfolio that could be rewritten using "camera techniques" such as close-ups, quick transitions, pans, or dissolves. You might use one of the following approaches.
   - Imagine that you are behind the camera as you edit your work. Focus on details and frame your images as a film director would.
   - Establish a clear point of view. Then shift your point of view at some place to lend emphasis or drama.

Camera Terms

close-up a shot taken at close range that focuses on one item or one aspect of a person and takes up almost the entire frame.

cut an immediate switch from one picture to another.

dissolve fade gradually from the screen while the succeeding picture or scene slowly appears.

fade-in/fade-out the gradual appearance or disappearance of a picture on a screen.

flashback a break in the continuous series of events to introduce some earlier event or scene.

frame a single picture or image.

pan move a camera from one side to another to take in a larger scene or to follow a moving object.

transition a change or passing from one condition, place, thing, activity, topic, etc., to another.

zoom move rapidly from one focus to another, as with a zoom lens.

Activity Options

Activity 1 Several dramatic scenes in this cluster of selections are likely candidates for filming, such as

- Jerry swimming underwater in "Through the Tunnel"
- Jing-mei confronting her mother after the piano recital in "Two Kinds"
- Roof swearing to vote for Maduka in "The Voter"

Encourage students to sketch out their ideas several times, considering alternative possibilities, before preparing their storyboards. Some students might use the library to find copies of printed screenplays to see how camera directions are expressed.

Activity 2 Encourage students to choose a portfolio item that contains some action, rather than all dialogue, description, or opinion. It may be helpful to discuss with students what framing an image involves: giving it a clearly defined shape and making it stand out from its background.

Art Study

Ask students to compare the expression on the face of the girl in the movie still with Jing-mei's feelings in the story "Two Kinds."

BUILDING ENGLISH PROFICIENCY

Interpreting Visual Information

Help students understand that images communicate ideas and emotions that can be analyzed just as words can.

Activity Ideas

- Write the following words on the chalkboard: *friendship, grief, love, anger, fear,* and *power.* Make sure that students understand each concept and can give verbal examples of it. Then invite students to either bring in nonverbal examples, such as photographs of these concepts, or to pantomime each concept.
- Invite a skilled professional or amateur videographer to demonstrate each of the camera terms defined on page 63. Discuss why a director might choose each kind of shot.

Preview

Trying to Beat the Odds

FOR ALL STUDENTS

- What does it mean to "trust to luck"?
- At what times should you rely on chance or luck? At what times should you try to control events in your life?

Read together the first paragraph on page 64. Tell students that this group of selections illustrates the degree to which chance, fate, and other forces determine a person's destiny.

To further explore the theme, use the Fine Art Transparency refered to below.

Transparency Collection
Fine Art Writing Prompt 2

For At-Risk Students

Ask students to

- think about their favorite horror movies or stories.
- discuss how most characters cannot escape the horror that threatens them.

Explain that "The Monkey's Paw" is a classic horror story in which ordinary people are faced with a powerful force that reveals their weaknesses.

For Students Who Need Challenge

The question of whether humans live by free will or are controlled by fate has long been debated. Encourage students to write their ideas, based on these questions.

- What do you think free will means?
- Do you think fate influences your life? Why?

MULTICULTURAL CONNECTION

In the following stories, an individual or outside force changes the lives of the group members. Discuss with students how an individual can influence a group in a good way.

Part Two

Trying to Beat the Odds

What are the odds you'll like the stories that follow? Take a chance and read them to find out. The characters you will meet here likewise take chances, many without success. But some of them do manage to succeed—through their wits or by sheer luck.

Multicultural Connection **Groups**, which supply a framework based on ethnicity, race, gender, age, religion, nationality, and other affinities, create a common thread, a unifying culture. Note the powerful influence exerted on individuals by groups in many of the following selections.

IDEAS THAT WORK

Elements of Suspense

At one time or another, we all try to beat the odds. When teaching "The Monkey's Paw," I ask the students about their own "good luck" objects and some of the times they received the luck they needed. These experiences can be used as a starting point for a journal entry or personal narrative.

All of the stories in this section contain an element of suspense. Have students explore the different elements of horror stories, mythology, or native folklore. Encourage them to try creating their own horror stories, myths, or folk tales.

"The Mask of the Red Death" lends itself to even more creativity. Have students make a mask and write the story of their masks. You may get some stories that would make Poe turn in his grave!

Richard Bruns
El Paso, Texas

Before Reading

The Monkey's Paw

by W. W. Jacobs Great Britain

W. W. Jacobs
1863–1943

W. W. (William Wymark) Jacobs was born in Wapping in the ship-docking section of London, England. There he got a taste of the waterfront that is reflected in many of his book titles, such as *Light Freights, The Lady of the Barge,* and *Deep Waters*, and in the plots of a number of his short stories. Jacobs worked as a civil servant until he was able to support himself by his writing. In addition to stories about life on the sea, Jacobs wrote bizarre tales and stories dealing with country life. A good example is his most famous story, "The Monkey's Paw," a classic horror tale of the supernatural.

Building Background

Your Wish Is My Command When the alarm clock sounded this morning, you may have stretched, rubbed the sleep from your eyes, and groggily mumbled, "I wish I never had to get up in the morning." Whoa! Be careful what you wish for. There might be disastrous consequences. Brainstorm with the class tales and stories you have heard where three wishes are part of the plot. What were the results of making these wishes?

Literary Focus

Plot Jacobs creates a mood of suspense that builds as the plot unfolds. **Plot** is a series of related events in a literary work. These events are organized around a *conflict* or problem, build to a *climax*, or point at which the conflict must be resolved, and finally result in a *resolution* of the conflict. As you read "The Monkey's Paw," note how each event leads to the next and how suspense mounts. The diagram below indicates plot elements.

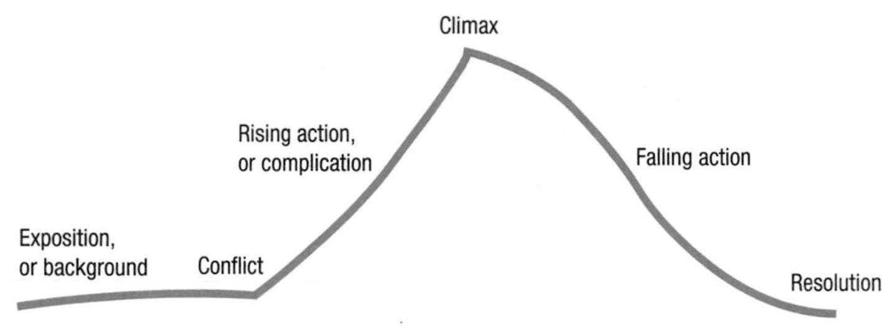

Writer's Notebook

Wishes Come in Threes Imagine you have found a magic lamp. You rub it to check its power, and WHOOSH—out comes a genie. Like most genies, this one offers you the chance to make three wishes that must be granted. What will you wish? In your notebook, write down three wishes you would want fulfilled, and explain your reasons for asking for each wish. Would you use all three wishes? Why or why not?

Before Reading

Building Background

Engage students in a discussion about the saying, "Be careful what you wish for—it might come true." Ask students if they have ever had a wish come true, only to be sorry later.

Literary Focus

Review with students the elements of **plot**—exposition, conflict, complication, climax, falling action, and resolution, and the characteristics that define each element. Encourage students to identify these elements as they read the selection.

Writer's Notebook

Students can brainstorm about what wishes they would make by considering these questions:

- What wishes might have lasting consequences, not only for yourself, but for the world?
- How can you phrase the wishes so they don't "backfire"?

More About W. W. Jacobs

Jacobs is known as "the O. Henry of the horror story." He also wrote humorous tales, many of which were set in the London docks area. He is the author of *Many Cargoes* (1896).

SUPPORT MATERIALS OVERVIEW

Unit 1 Resource Book
- Graphic Organizer, p. 49
- Study Guide, p. 50
- Vocabulary, p. 51
- Grammar, p. 52
- Alternate Check Test, p. 53
- Vocabulary Test, p. 54
- Selection Test, pp. 55–56

Building English Proficiency
- Selection Summaries
- Activities, p. 172

Reading, Writing & Grammar SkillBook
- Reading, pp. 45–46
- Grammar, Usage, and Mechanics, pp. 269–272

Technology
- Audiotape 3, Side A
- Personal Journal Software
- Custom Literature Database: For *The Monkey's Paw* adapted as a drama, see the database.
- Test Generator Software

During Reading

Selection Objectives

- to explore the theme of attempts to alter fate
- to identify and explore elements of plot
- to identify the origins and meanings of words
- to practice punctuation of quotations in a dialogue sequence

Unit 1 Resource Book
Graphic Organizer, p. 49
Study Guide, p. 50

Theme Link

The White family interferes with fate and faces the resulting challenge as they try to beat the odds.

Vocabulary Preview

rubicund, reddish; ruddy
grimace, a twisting of the face; ugly or funny smile
doggedly, not giving up; stubborn
talisman, stone, ring, etc., engraved with figures or characters supposed to have magic power; charm
maligned, spoken against; slandered
antimacassar, a small covering to protect the back or arms of a chair, sofa, etc., against soiling
avaricious, greedy for wealth
mutilated, cut, torn, or broken off a limb or other important part of; maimed
audible, that can be heard; loud enough to be heard
reverberate, echo back

Students can add the words and definitions to their Writer's Notebook.

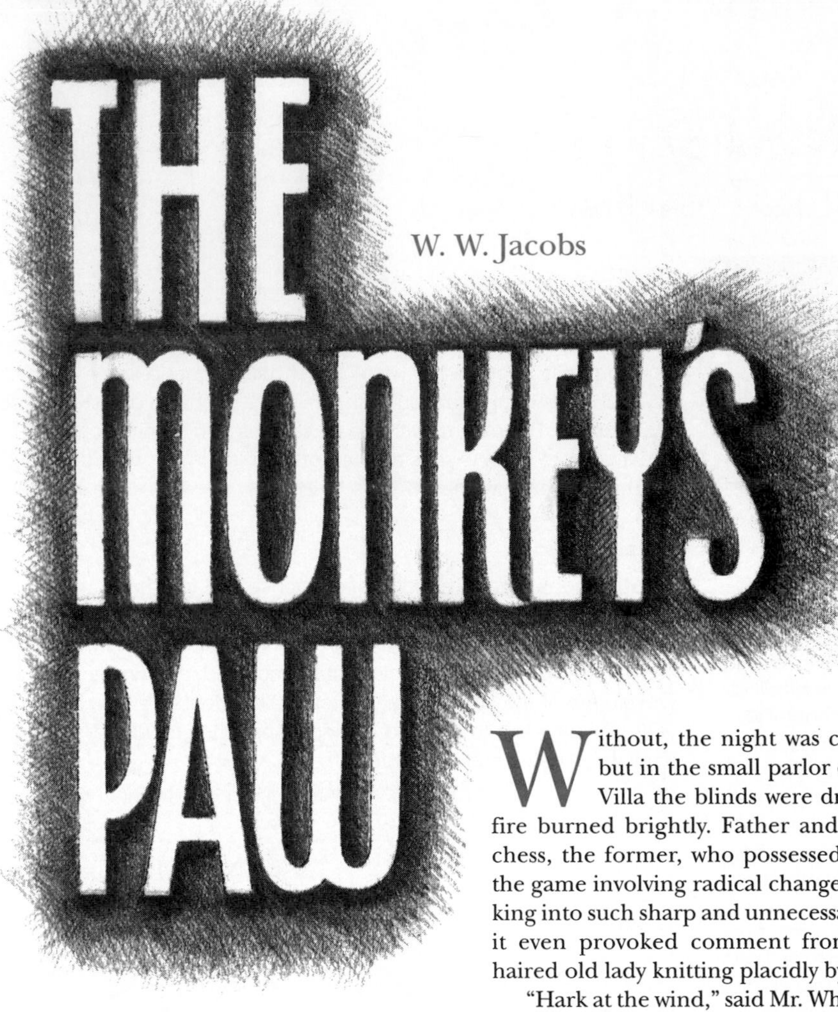

W. W. Jacobs

Without, the night was cold and wet, but in the small parlor of Laburnam Villa the blinds were drawn and the fire burned brightly. Father and son were at chess, the former, who possessed ideas about the game involving radical changes, putting his king into such sharp and unnecessary perils that it even provoked comment from the white-haired old lady knitting placidly by the fire.

"Hark at the wind," said Mr. White, who, having seen a fatal mistake after it was too late, was amiably desirous of preventing his son from seeing it.

"I'm listening," said the latter, grimly surveying the board as he stretched out his hand. "Check."[1] "I should hardly think that he'd come

1. **check,** a call made by a chess player to warn an opponent that the opponent's king piece is in danger and must be moved. When a chess player makes the winning move that will capture the opponent's king, he or she calls "Checkmate" or "Mate."

SELECTION SUMMARY

The Monkey's Paw

Mr. and Mrs. White and their son Herbert are visited by Sergeant-Major Morris, who has returned to England from India. He shows the family a monkey's paw and tells how it can grant a person three wishes. Though content with his life, Mr. White wishes for two hundred pounds to pay off the debt on their home. The next day the parents learn that Herbert has been caught in the machinery at his job and killed. The family receives two hundred pounds as compensation. Ten days later, Mr. White agrees to his wife's demand that he make the second wish—for Herbert to return. At night, they hear a knocking at the door. As Mrs. White struggles to unbolt the door, her husband makes the third wish. The knocking stops.

For summaries in other languages, see the ***Building English Proficiency*** *book.*

tonight," said his father, with his hand poised over the board.

"Mate," replied the son.

"That's the worst of living so far out," bawled Mr. White, with sudden and unlooked-for vio-
1 lence; "of all the beastly, slushy, out-of-the-way places to live in, this is the worst. Pathway's a bog, and the road's a torrent. I don't know what people are thinking about. I suppose because only two houses in the road are let, they think it doesn't matter."

"Never mind, dear," said his wife soothingly; "perhaps you'll win the next one."

Mr. White looked up sharply, just in time to intercept a knowing glance between mother and son. The words died away on his lips, and he hid a guilty grin in his thin gray beard.

"There he is," said Herbert White, as the gate banged to loudly and heavy footsteps came toward the door.

The old man rose with hospitable haste, and opening the door, was heard condoling with the new arrival. The new arrival also condoled with himself, so that Mrs. White said, "Tut, tut!" and coughed gently as her husband entered the room, followed by a tall burly man, beady of eye and rubicund[2] of visage.

"Sergeant-Major Morris," he said, introducing him.

The sergeant-major shook hands, and, taking the proffered seat by the fire, watched contentedly while his host got out whiskey and tumblers and stood a small copper kettle on the fire.

At the third glass his eyes got brighter, and he began to talk, the little family circle regarding with eager interest this visitor from distant parts, as he squared his broad shoulders in the chair and spoke of wild scenes and doughty deeds, of wars, and plagues and strange peoples.

"Twenty-one years of it," said Mr. White, nodding at his wife and son. "When he went away he was a slip of a youth in the warehouse. Now look at him."

"He don't look to have taken much harm," 2
said Mrs. White politely.

"I'd like to go to India myself," said the old 3
man, "just to look round a bit, you know."

"Better where you are," said the sergeant-major, shaking his head. He put down the empty glass and, sighing softly, shook it again.

"I should like to see those old temples and fakirs and jugglers," said the old man. "What was that you started telling me the other day about a monkey's paw or something, Morris?"

"Nothing," said the soldier hastily. "Leastways, nothing worth hearing."

"Monkey's paw?" said Mrs. White curiously.

"Well, it's just a bit of what you might call magic, perhaps," said the sergeant-major offhandedly.

His three listeners leaned forward eagerly. The visitor absent-mindedly put his empty glass to his lips and then set it down again. His host filled it for him.

"To look at," said the sergeant-major, fumbling in his pocket, "it's just an ordinary little paw, dried to a mummy."

He took something out of his pocket and prof-

2. **rubicund** (rü′bə kund), *adj.* reddish; ruddy.

1 Literary Element
Setting

Question What contrasts can you find in the setting? *(inside, a warm, bright country house; outside, cold, slushy, "beastly" place)*

2 Writing Style
Dialect

It might be noted to students that the author has Mrs. White use the nonstandard "He don't" instead of "He doesn't" to accurately reflect colloquial speech patterns of the time and place.

3 Historical Note
England and India

At the time this story takes place, India was part of the British Empire, and many British citizens pursued military or civil service careers in India. Beginning with the establishment of the British East India Company in 1600, England gradually gained administrative control as well as economic dominance over Indians—a situation which lasted until India won its independence in 1947.

BUILDING ENGLISH PROFICIENCY

ESL LEP ELD SAE LD

Exploring Key Concepts

The concept of fate is a key to understanding this classic story. Guide students in free-flowing discussion about fate. Track their responses in a web. A sample is shown.

1. Ask: What do you think about fate? What other stories do you know that deal with fate?

2. Extend the discussion by asking whether their ideas are based on experience, others' views, culture, or religion.

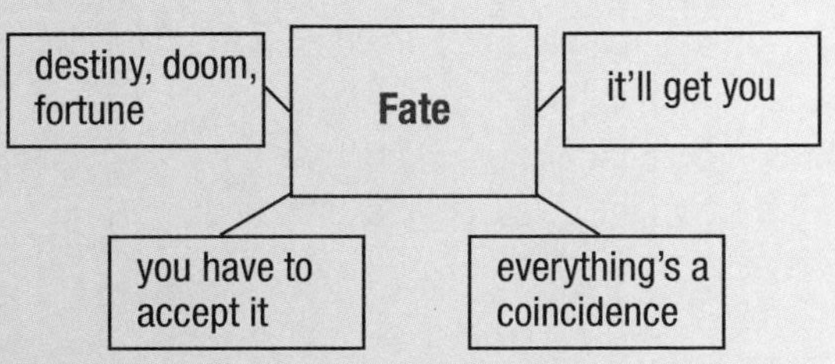

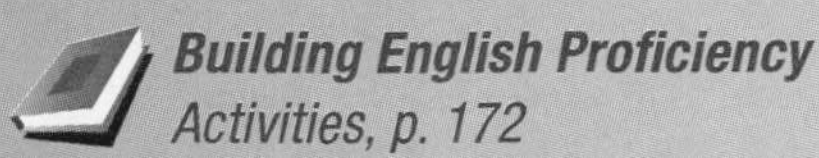
Building English Proficiency
Activities, p. 172

4 Reading/Thinking
Recognizing Values

Question What does the fakir think about the power that individuals have over their own lives? Do you agree? *(Possible responses: He considers fate to be a powerful and vengeful force that will always prevail. Students may say that individuals have power over their lives to various degrees.)*

Art Study

Response to Caption Question
Possible response: The man's serious expression and proper attire do not suggest that he is fascinated with anything magical. Yet students may say the sergeant-major, who has good reason to believe in magic, might resemble this portrait.

Sir William Schwenk Gilbert (1836–1911), painted here by Frank Holl, is best known for his verse collaborations with Sir Arthur Sullivan on comic operas such as *HMS Pinafore* and *The Mikado.* Explain whether or not this looks like a person who would believe in magic.

fered it. Mrs. White drew back with a grimace,[3] but her son, taking it, examined it curiously.

"And what is there special about it?" inquired Mr. White, as he took it from his son and, having examined it, placed it upon the table.

"It had a spell put on it by an old fakir," said the sergeant-major, "a very holy man. He
4 wanted to show that fate ruled people's lives, and that those who interfered with it did so to their sorrow. He put a spell on it so that three separate men could each have three wishes from it."

His manner was so impressive that his hearers were conscious that their light laughter jarred somewhat.

"Well, why don't you have three, sir?" said Herbert White cleverly.

The soldier regarded him in the way that

3. grimace (grə mās′, grim′is), *n.* a twisting of the face; ugly or funny smile.

MINI-LESSON: VOCABULARY

Etymology

Teach Exploring the origins of words can help students understand the words' modern meanings.

Activity Idea Divide the class into groups and assign one or more of these words from the selection to each group:

visage, fakir, wont, blotchy, presumptuous

Ask each group to:

- check a dictionary to see if each word is in its simplest form
- in the dictionary, find each word's etymology
- brainstorm the connection between the etymology and the word's modern meaning
- report the etymologies and meanings to the class

middle age is wont to regard presumptuous youth. "I have," he said quietly, and his blotchy face whitened.

"And did you really have the three wishes granted?" asked Mrs. White.

"I did," said the sergeant-major, and his glass tapped against his strong teeth.

"And has anybody else wished?" persisted the old lady.

"The first man had his three wishes, yes," was
5 the reply. "I don't know what the first two were, but the third was for death. That's how I got the paw."

His tones were so grave that a hush fell upon the group.

"If you've had your three wishes, it's no good to you now, then, Morris," said the old man at last. "What do you keep it for?"

The soldier shook his head. "Fancy, I suppose," he said slowly. "I did have some idea of selling it, but I don't think I will. It has caused enough mischief already. Besides, people won't buy. They think it's a fairy tale, some of them, and those who do think anything of it want to try it first and pay me afterward."

"If you could have another three wishes," said the old man, eyeing him keenly, "would you have them?"

"I don't know," said the other. "I don't know."

He took the paw, and dangling it between his forefinger and thumb, suddenly threw it upon the fire. White, with a slight cry, stooped down and snatched it off.

"Better let it burn," said the soldier solemnly.

"If you don't want it, Morris," said the other, "give it to me."

"I won't," said his friend doggedly.[4] "I threw it on the fire. If you keep it, don't blame me for what happens. Pitch it on the fire again, like a sensible man."

The other shook his head and examined his new possession closely. "How do you do it?" he inquired.

"Hold it up in your right hand and wish aloud," said the sergeant-major, "but I warn you of the consequences."

"Sounds like the *Arabian Nights*,"[5] said Mrs. White, as she rose and began to set the supper.

PITCH IT ON THE FIRE AGAIN, LIKE A SENSIBLE MAN.

"Don't you think you might wish for four pairs of hands for me?"

Her husband drew the talisman[6] from his pocket and then all three burst into laughter as the sergeant-major, with a look of alarm on his face, caught him by the arm.

"If you must wish," he said gruffly, "wish for something sensible."

Mr. White dropped it back into his pocket, and placing chairs, motioned his friend to the table. In the business of supper the talisman was partly forgotten, and afterward the three sat listening in an enthralled fashion to a second installment of the soldier's adventures in India.

"If the tale about the monkey's paw is not 6
more truthful than those he has been telling us," said Herbert, as the door closed behind their guest, just in time for him to catch the last train, "we shan't make much out of it."

"Did you give him anything for it, Father?" inquired Mrs. White, regarding her husband closely.

"A trifle," said he, coloring slightly. "He didn't want it, but I made him take it. And he pressed me again to throw it away."

"Likely," said Herbert, with pretended horror. "Why, we're going to be rich, and famous,

---

4. doggedly (dô′gid lē), *adv.* not giving up; stubborn.
5. ***Arabian Nights,*** a collection of old tales from Arabia, Persia, and India, dating from the 900s.
6. talisman (tal′i smən, tal′iz mən), *n.* stone, ring, etc., engraved with figures or characters supposed to have magic power; charm.

5 Reader's Response
Making Personal Connections

Questions

- Why might someone wish for death? *(The first two wishes brought such terrible tragedy or horror that death was better.)*
- Knowing this much of its history, would you want the monkey's paw? Explain. *(Possible responses: no, because it is a dangerous object, possibly causing death; yes, but I would be extremely careful about what I wished for)*

6 Reading/Thinking Skills
Identify Assumptions

Question Why does Herbert suspect that the tale about the monkey's paw is untrue? *(He finds the sergeant-major's stories unbelievable, so he thinks the tale of the paw may not be truthful either.)*

BUILDING ENGLISH PROFICIENCY

Exploring Adjectives

As developing English speakers, some students may find the placement of English adjectives a challenge.

1. Point out that, in many languages, adjectives often follow the nouns they describe. For example:

Spanish: año nuevo

English: new year

Ask volunteers for more examples.

2. Explain that in English, adjectives usually come before nouns.

This is my new coat.

Also, adjectives stand alone when they follow a form of the verb *to be.*

My coat is new.

3. Invite students to find examples of phrases that contain adjectives on pages 68–69. Let them experiment with letting the adjective precede and follow the noun. Some examples are: *a very holy man/the man is very holy; sensible man/who is sensible; blotchy face/the face was blotchy.*

7 Reader's Response
Draw Conclusions

Questions

- Judging from Mr. White's statement that he has all he wants, what is important to him? *(Response: his family's love and well-being, his home)*
- Then what makes him take the monkey's paw? *(Possible response: curiosity, remembering old hopes and dreams)*

8 Literary Focus
Plot

Take this opportunity to point out that the suspense begins to grow once the first wish is made.

Questions

- What does Mr. White say happens to the paw when he makes the wish? *(He says it twists in his hand.)*
- What is the Whites' reaction after making the wish? *(They are gloomy, which is unusual for them.)*

9 Literary Focus
Conflict

Question Contrast the scene at breakfast with the last scene from the night before. What conflict do these scenes illustrate? *(Mr. White's inner conflict between being happy with what he has—home and family—and a temptation to pursue his dreams—paying off his house)*

and happy. Wish to be an emperor, Father, to begin with; then you can't be henpecked."

He darted round the table, pursued by the maligned[7] Mrs. White armed with an antimacassar.[8]

Mr. White took the paw from his pocket and eyed it dubiously. "I don't know what to wish for, and that's a fact," he said slowly. "It seems to me
7 I've got all I want."

"If you only cleared the house,[9] you'd be quite happy, wouldn't you?" said Herbert, with his hand on his shoulder. "Well, wish for two hundred pounds,[10] then; that'll just do it."

His father, smiling shamefacedly at his own credulity, held up the talisman, as his son, with a solemn face somewhat marred by a wink at his mother, sat down at the piano and struck a few impressive chords.

"I wish for two hundred pounds," said the old man distinctly.

A fine crash from the piano greeted the words, interrupted by a shuddering cry from the old man. His wife and son ran toward him.

"It moved," he cried; with a glance of disgust at the object as it lay on the floor. "As I wished, it twisted in my hands like a snake."

"Well, I don't see the money," said his son, as he picked it up and placed it on the table, "and I bet I never shall."

"It must have been your fancy, Father," said his wife, regarding him anxiously.

He shook his head. "Never mind, though;
8 there's no harm done, but it gave me a shock all the same."

They sat down by the fire again while the two men finished their pipes. Outside, the wind was higher than ever, and the old man started nervously at the sound of a door banging upstairs. A silence unusual and depressing settled upon all three, which lasted until the old couple rose to retire for the night.

"I expect you'll find the cash tied up in a big bag in the middle of your bed," said Herbert, as he bade them good night, "and something horrible squatting up on top of the wardrobe watching you as you pocket your ill-gotten gains."

He sat alone in the darkness, gazing at the dying fire, and seeing faces in it. The last face was so horrible and so simian that he gazed at it in amazement. It got so vivid that, with a little uneasy laugh, he felt on the table for a glass containing a little water to throw over it. His hand grasped the monkey's paw, and with a little shiver he wiped his hand on his coat and went up to bed.

In the brightness of the wintry sun next 9
morning as it streamed over the breakfast table, Herbert laughed at his fears. There was an air of prosaic wholesomeness about the room which it had lacked on the previous night, and the dirty, shriveled little paw was pitched on the sideboard with a carelessness which betokened no great belief in its virtues.

"I suppose all old soldiers are the same," said Mrs. White. "The idea of our listening to such nonsense! How could wishes be granted in these days? And if they could, how could two hundred pounds hurt you, Father?"

"Might drop on his head from the sky," said the frivolous Herbert.

"Morris said the things happened so naturally," said his father, "that you might if you so wished attribute it to coincidence."

"Well, don't break into the money before I come back," said Herbert as he rose from the table. "I'm afraid it'll turn you into a mean, avaricious[11] man, and we shall have to disown you."

His mother laughed, and following him to

7. maligned (mā līnd′), *adj.* spoken against; slandered.
8. antimacassar (an′ti mə kas′ər), *n.* a small covering to protect the back or arms of a chair, sofa, etc., against soiling.
9. **cleared the house,** paid the debt that was still owed on the purchase of a house.
10. **two hundred pounds.** At the time of the story, this amount in British money was worth about one thousand American dollars.
11. avaricious (av′ə rish′əs), *adj.* greedy for wealth.

MINI-LESSON: GRAMMAR
Quotation Marks

Teach Point out to students that when a quotation is interrupted by explanatory words, such as *she said* or *he cried*, two sets of quotation marks are used. Each part of the quotation is separated from the interrupting phrase by commas or by a comma and a period. If the second part of the quotation is a complete sentence, it begins with a capital letter. Point out the use of quotations marks in these paragraphs on page 70.

"Well, I don't see the money," said his son, as he picked it up and placed it on the table, "and I bet I never shall."

"I suppose all old soldiers are the same," said Mrs. White. "The idea of our listening to such nonsense!"

Activity Idea For practice, each student can:

- write a dialogue that includes quotations for at least two characters
- use quotation marks effectively to identify the speaker in a passage

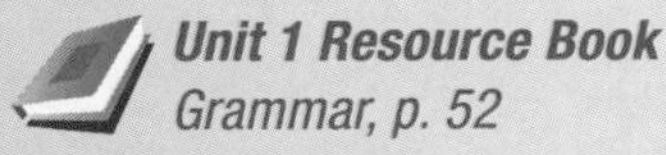
Unit 1 Resource Book
Grammar, p. 52

the door, watched him down the road, and returning to the breakfast table, was very happy at the expense of her husband's credulity. All of which did not prevent her from scurrying to the door at the postman's knock, nor prevent her from referring somewhat shortly to retired sergeant-majors of bibulous habits when she found that the post brought a tailor's bill.

"Herbert will have some more of his funny remarks, I expect, when he comes home," she said as they sat at dinner.

"I dare say," said Mr. White, pouring himself out some beer; "but for all that, the thing moved in my hand; that I'll swear to."

"You thought it did," said the old lady soothingly.

"I say it did," replied the other. "There was no thought about it; I had just—What's the matter?"

His wife made no reply. She was watching the mysterious movements of a man outside, who, peering in an undecided fashion at the house, appeared to be trying to make up his mind to enter. In mental connection with the two hundred pounds, she noticed that the
10 stranger was well dressed and wore a silk hat of glossy newness. Three times he paused at the gate and then walked on again. The fourth time he stood with his hand upon it, and then with sudden resolution flung it open and walked up the path. Mrs. White at the same moment placed her hands behind her and hurriedly unfastening the strings of her apron, put that useful article of apparel beneath the cushion of her chair.

She brought the stranger, who seemed ill at ease, into the room. He gazed at her furtively, and listened in a preoccupied fashion as the old lady apologized for the appearance of the room, and her husband's coat, a garment which he usually reserved for the garden. She then waited as patiently as her sex would permit for him to broach his business, but he was at first strangely silent.

11 "I—was asked to call," he said at last, and stooped and picked a piece of cotton from his trousers. "I come from Maw and Meggins."

The old lady started. "Is anything the matter?" she asked breathlessly. "Has anything happened to Herbert? What is it? What is it?"

Her husband interposed. "There, there, Mother," he said hastily. "Sit down, and don't jump to conclusions. You've not brought bad news, I'm sure, sir," and he eyed the other wistfully.

"I'm sorry—" began the visitor.

"Is he hurt?" demanded the mother wildly.

The visitor bowed in assent. "Badly hurt," he said quietly, "but he is not in any pain."

"Oh, thank God!" said the old woman, clasping her hands. "Thank God for that! Thank—"

She broke off suddenly as the sinister meaning of the assurance dawned upon her and she saw the awful confirmation of her fears in the other's averted face. She caught her breath, and turning to her slower-witted husband, laid her trembling old hand upon his. There was a long silence.

"He was caught in the machinery," said the visitor at length, in a low voice.

"Caught in the machinery," repeated Mr. White, in a dazed fashion, "yes."

He sat staring blankly out at the window, and taking his wife's hand between his own, pressed it as he had been wont to do in their old courting days nearly forty years before.

"He was the only one left to us," he said, turning gently to the visitor. "It is hard."

The other coughed, and rising, walked slowly to the window. "The firm wished me to convey their sincere sympathy with you in your great loss," he said, without looking round. "I beg that you will understand I am only their servant and merely obeying orders."

There was no reply; the old woman's face was white, her eyes staring, and her breath inaudible; on the husband's face was a look 12

10 Reading/Thinking Skills
Visualize

Encourage students to visualize the man who is walking near the White's gate. Invite them to remember what they have already learned about the appearance of the house, both inside and out.

11 Literary Focus
Plot

Question How does the stranger's entering the house add to the suspense of the story? *(The reader is forced to wonder why he seems so uneasy and is so slow to give his reason for coming.)*

12 Literary Element
Imagery

Questions

- Ask students to look for imagery that describes Mr. White when he realizes that Herbert has died. *(on his face was a "look such as his friend the sergeant might have carried into his first action")*
- What emotion does this image cause you to feel? *(Possible responses: pity for the old man; regret that Mr. White took the paw in the first place)*

BUILDING ENGLISH PROFICIENCY

ESL
LEP
ELD
SAE

LD

Tracking Story Details

Record students' comments in a chart as they talk about the three wishes and how each was fulfilled. Possible ideas are given in the chart shown.

When the chart has varied ideas, share this adage: "Be careful what you wish for—you just might get it." Ask: According to the chart, does the class agree? Why?

Wish	Result
1. *two hundred pounds*	*Herbert is killed*
2. *that Herbert returns*	*knocking at the door*
3. *that Herberts doesn't return*	*knocking stops*

13 Reading/Thinking Skills
Cause and Effect

Question Coincidence is the chance occurrence of two events at the same time or place. Could the amount of compensation, 200 pounds, be a coincidence? Why or why not? *(Possible response: The delivery of the exact amount of money is so closely tied to the wish that it seems like cause and effect.)*

14 Literary Focus
Plot

Point out to students that the conflict which sets the events of the plot into motion usually appears in one of two ways. In one, a character is dissatisfied with things as they are and tries to make changes and achieve his or her goal despite obstacles placed in his or her way. In the other, a character is content with the status quo until someone or something comes along and changes the situation; then the character tries to restore things to the way they were.

Question Which form of conflict occurs in "The Monkey's Paw"? Explain. *(the second form, because the Whites want life to be as it was before they made the wish)*

such as his friend the sergeant might have carried into his first action.

"I was to say that Maw and Meggins disclaim all responsibility," continued the other. "They admit no liability at all, but in consideration of your son's services they wish to present you with a certain sum as compensation."

Mr. White dropped his wife's hand, and rising to his feet, gazed with a look of horror at his visitor. His dry lips shaped the words, "How much?"

13 "Two hundred pounds," was the answer.

Unconscious of his wife's shriek, the old man smiled faintly, put out his hands like a sightless man, and dropped, a senseless heap, to the floor.

In the huge new cemetery, some two miles distant, the old people buried their dead, and came back to a house steeped in shadow and silence. It was all over so quickly that at first they could hardly realize it and remained in a state of expectation as though of something else to happen—something else which was to lighten this load, too heavy for old hearts to bear.

But the days passed, and expectation gave place to resignation—the hopeless resignation of the old, sometimes miscalled apathy. Sometimes they hardly exchanged a word, for now they had nothing to talk about, and their days were long to weariness.

It was about a week after that the old man, waking suddenly in the night, stretched out his hand and found himself alone. The room was in darkness, and the sound of subdued weeping came from the window. He raised himself in bed and listened.

"Come back," he said tenderly. "You will be cold."

"It is colder for my son," said the old woman and wept afresh.

The sound of her sobs died away on his ears. The bed was warm, and his eyes heavy with sleep. He dozed fitfully, and then slept until a sudden wild cry from his wife awoke him with a start.

"The paw!" she cried wildly. "The monkey's paw!"

He started up in alarm. "Where? Where is it? What's the matter?"

She came stumbling across the room toward him. "I want it," she said quietly. "You've not destroyed it?"

"It's in the parlor, on the bracket," he replied, marveling. "Why?"

She cried and laughed together, and bending over, kissed his cheek.

"I only just thought of it," she said hysterically. "Why didn't I think of it before? Why didn't *you* think of it?"

"Think of what?" he questioned.

"The other two wishes," she replied rapidly. "We've only had one."

"Was not that enough?" he demanded fiercely.

"No," she cried triumphantly; "we'll have one more. Go down and get it quickly, and wish our boy alive again."

The man sat up in bed and flung the bedclothes from his quaking limbs. "Good God! You are mad!" he cried, aghast. 14

"Get it," she panted; "get it quickly, and wish—Oh my boy, my boy!"

Her husband struck a match and lit the candle. "Get back to bed," he said unsteadily. "You don't know what you are saying."

"We had the first wish granted," said the old woman feverishly; "why not the second?"

"A coincidence," stammered the old man.

"Go and get it and wish," cried his wife, quivering with excitement.

The old man turned and regarded her, and his voice shook. "He has been dead ten days, and besides he—I would not tell you else, but—I could only recognize him by his clothing. If he was too terrible for you to see then, how now?"

"Bring him back," cried the old woman, and dragged him toward the door. "Do you think I fear the child I have nursed?"

He went down in the darkness, and felt his way to the parlor, and then to the mantelpiece. The talisman was in its place, and a horrible

MINI-LESSON: READING/THINKING

Compare and Contrast

Teach Invite students to consider how Mr. and Mrs. White have changed in their attitudes toward the monkey's paw.

Early in the story they were curious about the paw but did not take it seriously. Illustrate this view by pointing to the following passages on page 69.

> [Mr. White] shook his head and examined his new possession closely. "How do you do it?" he inquired.
>
> "Sounds like the *Arabian Nights*," said Mrs. White, as she rose and began to set the supper. "Don't you think you might wish for four pairs of hands for me?"

Have students compare and contrast the excerpts above with events on page 72.

Activity Idea Have students choose at least two quotes for each character that show how that character's views have changed. Invite students to share the quotations and decide which are the most revealing.

This illustration by Maurice Griffenhagen accompanied "The Monkey's Paw" when *Harper's* magazine published the story in 1902. What details in the illustration reinforce the mood in the story?

fear that the unspoken wish might bring his mutilated[12] son before him ere he could escape from the room seized upon him, and he caught his breath as he found that he had lost the direction of the door. His brow cold with sweat, he felt his way round the table, and groped along the wall until he found himself in the small passage with the unwholesome thing in his hand.

Even his wife's face seemed changed as he entered the room. It was white and expectant, and to his fears seemed to have an unnatural look upon it. He was afraid of her.

"Wish!" she cried, in a strong voice.

"It is foolish and wicked," he faltered. 15

"Wish!" repeated his wife.

He raised his hand, "I wish my son alive again."

The talisman fell to the floor, and he

12. mutilated (myü′tl ā′təd), *adj.* cut, torn, or broken off a limb or other important part of; maimed.

Art Study

Response to Caption Question The dominant position of the monkey's paw creates a magical atmosphere. The look of fascination on the man's face and the look of fear on the woman's face emphasize the horror.

15 Reading/Thinking Skills
Synthesize Information

Lead a discussion about each character's feelings about the monkey's paw. Point out that Mr. White is very reluctant to make the second wish. He is fearful to even pick up the monkey's paw. Invite students to compare the beliefs of Mr. White and Mrs. White with regard to the monkey's paw.

Questions

- What does Mr. White now believe about the talisman? *(He believes it is "foolish and wicked" to make a wish.)*
- Why might his wife refuse to listen and just want to make the wish? *(She is only thinking of having Herbert back again.)*
- Who has learned the fakir's lesson? *(Mr. White)*

BUILDING ENGLISH PROFICIENCY

Exploring Emotions

Discussing the emotion of grief will help students better understand the selection's climax and resolution.

1. Ask students what emotion both parents are feeling. *(grief, sadness, resignation)* Ask: Which parent is grieving more? What makes you think so? Have students find examples in the selection of the ways that each displays grief.

2. Ask students to think of other ways that people express grief. Encourage students to share traditions and views from their heritage and knowledge of their cultures.

3. Point out that a funeral is a ceremony that people often use to cope with death. Ask students for examples of other such ceremonies from other cultures, including their own.

16 Literary Element
Mood

Questions What images and descriptions intensify the mood? *(creaking stairs, a scurrying mouse, oppressive darkness, soft knock)*

17 Reading/Thinking Skills
Inference

Question What evidence is there that Mr. White knows what's behind the door? *(Possible responses: his fear that the paw would bring his son back in an inhuman form; his belief that wishing on the paw is wicked)*

18 Literary Focus
Climax

Challenge students to identify the story's climax—the decisive moment or turning point in a story or play when the action changes course or begins to resolve itself. The term *climax* may also mean the point of greatest interest or excitement. Readers can debate the exact point when the climax occurs.

Check Test

1. Who wins the chess game? *(Herbert)*
2. What is the tale about the monkey's paw? *(A fakir put a spell on it so that each of three men could be granted three wishes.)*
3. What does Mr. White wish for and how does the wish come true? *(He wishes for two hundred pounds, which he receives as compensation for his son Herbert's death.)*
4. What is Mr. White's second wish? *(He wishes for Herbert to be alive again.)*
5. When does Mr. White make his final wish? *(as Mrs. White is trying to open the door)*

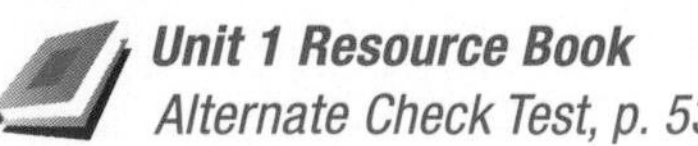
Unit 1 Resource Book
Alternate Check Test, p. 53

regarded it fearfully. Then he sank trembling into a chair as the old woman, with burning eyes, walked to the window and raised the blind.

He sat until he was chilled with the cold, glancing occasionally at the figure of the old woman peering through the window. The candle end, which had burned below the rim of the china candlestick, was throwing pulsating shadows on the ceiling and walls, until, with a flicker larger than the rest, it expired. The old man, with an unspeakable sense of relief at the failure of the talisman, crept back to his bed, and a minute or two afterward the old woman came silently and apathetically beside him.

Neither spoke, but both lay silently listening to the ticking of the clock. A stair creaked, and
16 a squeaky mouse scurried noisily through the wall. The darkness was oppressive, and after lying for some time screwing up his courage, he took the box of matches and striking one went downstairs for a candle.

At the foot of the stairs the match went out, and he paused to strike another, and at the same moment a knock, so quiet and stealthy as to be scarcely audible,[13] sounded on the front door.

The matches fell from his hand and spilled in the passage. He stood motionless, his breath suspended until the knock was repeated. Then
17 he turned and fled swiftly back to his room and closed the door behind him. A third knock sounded through the house.

"What's that?" cried the old woman, starting up.

"A rat," said the old man, in shaking tones—"a rat. It passed me on the stairs."

His wife sat up in bed listening. A loud knock resounded through the house.

"It's Herbert!" she screamed. "It's Herbert!"

She ran to the door, but her husband was before her, and catching her by the arm, held her tightly.

"What are you going to do?" he whispered hoarsely.

"It's my boy; it's Herbert!" she cried, struggling mechanically. "I forgot it was two miles away. What are you holding me for? Let go. I must open the door."

"For God's sake don't let it in," cried the old man, trembling. 18

"You're afraid of your own son," she cried, struggling. "Let me go. I'm coming, Herbert; I'm coming."

There was another knock, and another. The old woman with a sudden wrench broke free and ran from the room. Her husband followed to the landing, and called after her appealingly as she hurried downstairs. He heard the chain rattle back and the bottom bolt drawn slowly and stiffly from the socket. Then the old woman's voice, strained and panting.

"The bolt," she cried loudly. "Come down. I can't reach it."

But her husband was on his hands and knees groping wildly on the floor in search of the paw. If he could only find it before the thing outside got in. A perfect fusillade of knocks reverberated[14] through the house, and he heard the scraping of a chair as his wife put it down in the passage against the door. He heard the creaking of the bolt as it came slowly back, and at the same moment he found the monkey's paw and frantically breathed his third and last wish.

The knocking ceased suddenly, although the echoes of it were still in the house. He heard the chair drawn back and the door opened. A cold wind rushed up the staircase, and a long loud wail of disappointment and misery from his wife gave him courage to run down to her side, and then to the gate beyond. The street lamp flickering opposite shone on a quiet and deserted road.

---

13. **audible** (ô′də bəl), *adj.* that can be heard; loud enough to be heard.
14. **reverberate** (ri vėr′bər āt′), *v.* echo back.

MINI-LESSON: LITERARY FOCUS
Plot

Review the elements of plot discussed on page 65.

Activity Idea Students can work in pairs to draw a plot diagram like the one on page 65, and replace the terms with appropriate events from "The Monkey's Paw."

Possible responses:
- exposition—Morris's explanation of the three wishes
- conflict—the decision to take the paw
- complication—the death of Herbert
- climax—the knocking and the third wish
- falling action—the knocking stops
- resolution—no one is on the road

After Reading

Making Connections

Shaping Your Response

1. Would you recommend "The Monkey's Paw" to a friend to read? Why or why not?
2. What do you think is Mr. White's third wish? Why do you think he makes it?
3. To what degree, if any, do you think that the Whites are responsible for the tragedy that occurs? Explain.

Analyzing the Story

4. Contrast the **setting** outside the Whites' home with the scene in the living room before the sergeant-major's arrival.
5. What does Mr. White's way of playing chess show you about his **character**?
6. What do you think is more important in this story—**characterization** or **plot**?
7. What are some ways the author builds **suspense** in this story?

Extending the Ideas

8. What stories do you know that are built on the idea that fate, rather than free will determines the outcome of events? Would you prefer to believe that you control your own destiny or that fate controls your life? Explain.

Literary Focus: Plot

A series of related events that present and resolve a conflict is a story's **plot**. Conflicts that pit characters against each other, against nature, or against the forces of society are called *external conflicts*. Conflicts within the character such as struggles between duty and desire or between opposing emotions are called *internal conflicts*. Both internal and external conflicts occur in most stories.

- Identify two conflicts in the story.
- Draw an events chain to show four events that connect with those below.

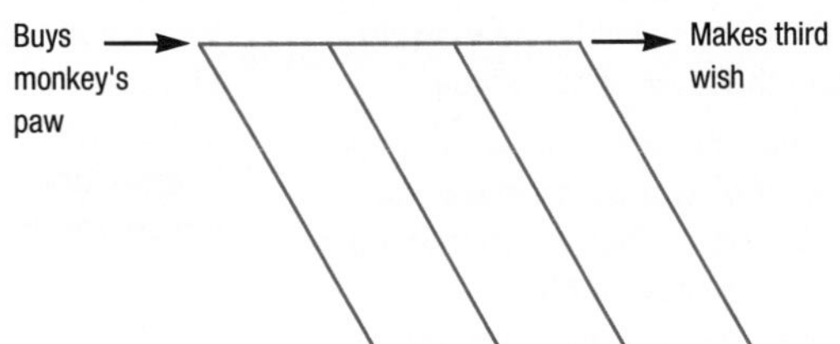

After Reading

MAKING CONNECTIONS

1. Possible response: Students who enjoy tales of horror and the supernatural would probably recommend this story.

2. He wishes for Herbert to be in his grave again, since he realizes Herbert has come back in an inhuman form.

3. Possible responses: The fakir would say they are responsible in that they tried to interfere with fate; students may say that they are not responsible because it was a coincidence.

4. It is wet and cold outside, but inside the family is cozy and happy by the brightly burning fire.

5. He is childlike, both temperamental and sweet.

6. Plot is more important because it creates the mood of suspense; the characters are not developed.

7. The author gives hints of ominous events to come through the chess game, the mood when characters talk about or use the monkey's paw, Herbert's saying he'll never see the money, the step-by-step actions at the end.

8. Possible responses: fairy tales such as "The Sleeping Beauty." Students may say they would prefer to control their own destinies so they can fulfill their own goals.

LITERARY FOCUS: PLOT

- Mr. White has an internal conflict when he wants to make the second wish but is afraid it is wicked to do so.
- Mr. and Mrs. White have an external conflict when he tries to prevent her from going downstairs and opening the door.
- An events chain may show: Mr. White makes the first wish; Herbert is killed; Mr. White makes the second wish; there is a knocking at the door.

VOCABULARY STUDY

1. d **6.** f
2. h **7.** g
3. i **8.** a
4. c **9.** b
5. j **10.** e

More Practice Students can practice using these vocabulary words by writing their own stories about a talisman that is completely different from the monkey's paw. Challenge students to include as many of the words as possible in their stories.

Unit 1 Resource Book
Vocabulary, p. 51
Vocabulary Test, p. 54

WRITING CHOICES

Writer's Notebook Update

If students decide it is better to make no wishes at all, they should explain their reasons.

Who's That Knocking on My Door?

If students write a new ending, they should try to maintain the author's writing style by continuing the same tone—the attitude of the author toward the characters and subject. For example, if Mrs. White opens the door to the sergeant-major, then Mr. White might act sheepish about having been afraid.

Selection Test

Unit 1 Resource Book
pp. 55–56

Vocabulary Study

On your paper, match each numbered word with the letter of its definition.

antimacassar
audible
avaricious
doggedly
grimace
maligned
mutilated
reverberate
rubicund
talisman

1.	rubicund	**a.**	loud enough to be heard
2.	antimacassar	**b.**	maimed
3.	avaricious	**c.**	echo back
4.	reverberate	**d.**	reddish
5.	doggedly	**e.**	a twisting of the face
6.	maligned	**f.**	spoken against
7.	talisman	**g.**	a charm
8.	audible	**h.**	covering for furniture
9.	mutilated	**i.**	greedy
10.	grimace	**j.**	stubbornly

Expressing Your Ideas

Writing Choices

Writer's Notebook Update Go back to your notebook and look at the wishes you wrote. Based on the outcome of the story, will you leave the wishes as written or rewrite them? Explain your thinking. Then rewrite any wishes that could be phrased in a "safer" way.

Who's That Knocking on My Door? Like other readers, you may have been disappointed not to find out who or what was outside the door. Think of a way to let the reader know these details without reducing the effectiveness of the story. Add a **new ending**, trying to maintain the level of suspense.

Fate and the Fakir The fakir who put the spell on the monkey's paw "wanted to show that fate ruled people's lives." Pretend that you are Mr. White and write a letter to Morris explaining whether the monkey's paw proved or disproved the fakir's belief.

Other Options

Put on Your Lawsuit The Whites have sued Sergeant-Major Morris for having given them the monkey's paw. Reenact a **trial** with one group representing the defense and another, the prosecution. Work up your respective cases, listing questions and anticipating questions that the other side might ask. One classmate can be Morris on trial, and another classmate can be the judge. After the case has been presented, let the rest of the class serve as jury to decide a verdict.

You As Art Critic With a partner, study the pictures that accompany this story. Ask yourselves questions about the mood and the images conveyed. Then present an **art talk** in which you describe the pictures and recommend whether or not you would keep the pictures that appear with this story or suggest new artwork.

OTHER OPTIONS

Put on Your Lawsuit

Encourage students to research court procedure or interview a trial lawyer for information that will make their trial of *Mr. and Mrs. White* v. *Sergeant-Major Morris* realistic and legally sound.

Students might also present a lawsuit in which the Whites sue Maw and Meggins for being responsible for Herbert's death.

You As Art Critic

Students can look for other works by the artists used in this selection to determine if their other paintings and illustrations display the same mood.

If they would like to replace the art in the story, students can do research to find illustrations they prefer.

Before Reading

The Demon Lover

by Elizabeth Bowen Ireland

Elizabeth Bowen
1899–1973

Elizabeth Bowen's fiction focuses on themes such as growing up, social pretensions, and coping in a war-torn society. Born in Dublin, Ireland, into an upper-class Anglo-Irish family, she began to write while a teenager. In 1923, she published her first collection of stories. As her reputation grew, she became a popular hostess of the London literary world, entertaining even during nightly air raids in World War II. Dedicated to the war effort, Bowen worked for the Ministry of Information and as an air-raid warden. In 1945, she published *The Demon Lover,* a collection of stories that started as a "diary" of her reactions to the war.

Building Background

War Nerves Life in London during World War II was anything but normal. Gas masks and wailing air-raid sirens were commonplace. Driving during the blackout at night was extremely hazardous because road signs had been removed to confuse potential invaders. People's nerves were frayed in anticipation of bombing or invasion. Elizabeth Bowen's stories set at this time penetrate the anxieties that resulted from these disturbing experiences. Use these details, along with the title and art in the story, to predict what "The Demon Lover" will be about.

Literary Focus

Flashback In a **flashback**, the action of a story is interrupted to show an episode that happened at an earlier time. A flashback can fill in years of chronological time. In "The Demon Lover," you will see how Elizabeth Bowen uses flashback to inform the reader of past events and to shed light on the main character. This information will help you evaluate Mrs. Drover and her behavior.

Writer's Notebook

What's Behind That Closed Door? Writer Stephen King observed that one of the scariest things in the world is what's behind the closed door. Do you agree that things you can't see are more frightening than those you can? Think about how details such as the slightly moving curtain, the small sound, and the empty room can convey a mood of terror and suspense. As you read "The Demon Lover," jot down words and phrases that you think contribute to a mood of horror.

Before Reading

Building Background

On the chalkboard, draw a three-column chart with headings **Clues, Predictions,** and **What Happens**. Encourage students to analyze clues and make predictions for this or their own chart, and to base their ideas on historical background, the title, art, and large quotes of the story. Have students compare their predictions to the story's outcome.

Literary Focus

Ask students to share examples of **flashbacks** from television shows and movies. Do students enjoy this technique?

Writer's Notebook

Would students include the word *demon* in their list? Discuss the word and whether it suggests horror. What other ideas come to mind, particularly in connection with the word *lover*?

More About Elizabeth Bowen

Bowen wrote primarily about people of the upper middle class, and is appreciated for her perceptive characterization. *Ivy Gripped the Steps* (1946), a collection of short fiction, and *The Heat of the Day* (1949), a spy novel, were based on her own war experiences.

SUPPORT MATERIALS OVERVIEW

Unit 1 Resource Book
- Graphic Organizer, p. 57
- Study Guide, p. 58
- Vocabulary, p. 59
- Grammar, p. 60
- Alternate Check Test, p. 61
- Vocabulary Test, p. 62
- Selection Test, pp. 63–64

Building English Proficiency
- Literature Summaries
- Activities, p. 173

Reading, Writing & Grammar SkillBook
- Reading, pp. 93–94
- Grammar, Usage, and Mechanics, pp. 148–149

Technology
- Audiotape 3, Side B
- Personal Journal Software
- Custom Literature Database: For a poem about lovers lost to war, see "Do not weep, maiden, for war is kind" by Stephen Crane on the database.
- Test Generator Software

During Reading

Selection Objectives

- to explore the theme of confronting life's mysterious forces
- to identify flashbacks
- to recognize dependent clauses

Unit 1 Resource Book
Graphic Organizer, p. 57
Study Guide, p. 58

Theme Link

Mrs. Drover "tries to beat the odds" as she faces the results of a mysterious love pact.

Vocabulary Preview

prosaic, ordinary; not exciting
refracted, bent (a ray of light, waves, etc.) from a straight course
precipitately, very hurriedly; suddenly
plight, promise solemnly; pledge (as in marriage)
desuetude, disuse
passé, old, stale *[French]*
emanate, come forth; spread out
aperture, an opening; hole

Students can add the words and definitions to their Writer's Notebooks.

Art Study

Responses to Caption Questions
Possible responses: dead air, traces of her former habit of life, rapidly heightening apprehension, dislocation, threat, desuetude, hollowness of the house, supernatural, suspension of her existence, passé air, the silence was so intense, remained for an eternity

SELECTION SUMMARY

The Demon Lover

World War II is taking place, and Mrs. Drover has returned to London from her family's temporary home in the country, a refuge from the bombings. Inside her locked and closed-up house, she finds a letter addressed to her from her fiancé of twenty-five years ago, a man who was lost in World War I. He writes that she must meet him that day as she had promised so long ago.

Shocked, Mrs. Drover recalls that the mysterious soldier had intimidated her and now she doesn't remember his face. Without gathering the belongings she came for, she leaves the house and takes off in a taxi. When the driver turns to look at her, she screams, but the taxi speeds away with her captive inside.

*For summaries in other languages, see the **Building English Proficiency** book.*

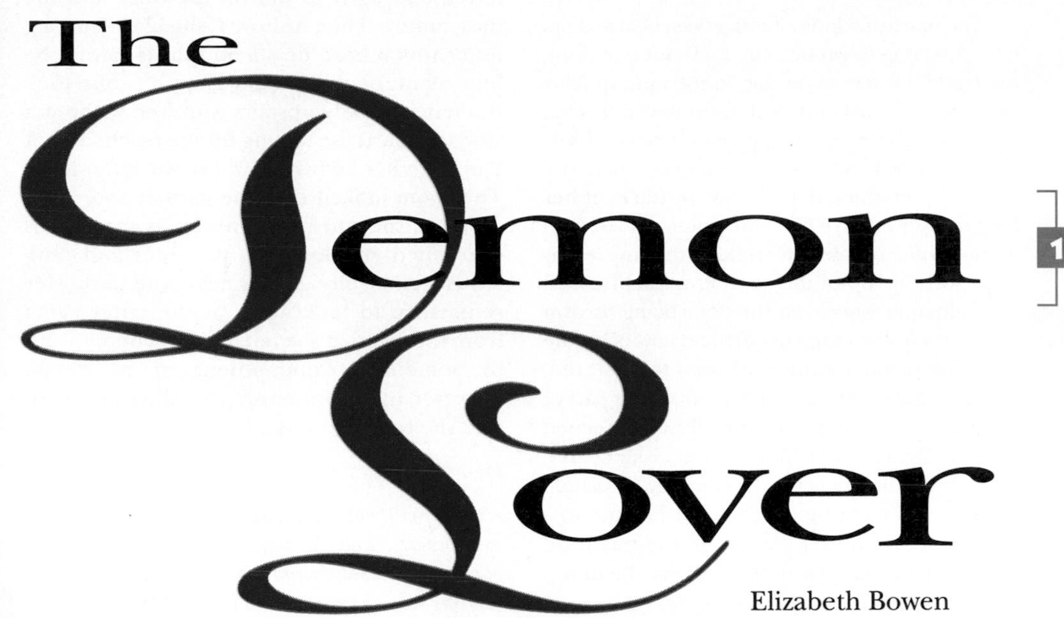

The Demon Lover

Elizabeth Bowen

Toward the end of her day in London Mrs. Drover went round to her shut-up house to look for several things she wanted to take away. Some belonged to herself, some to her family, who were by now used to their country life. It was late August; it had been a steamy, showery day; at the moment the trees down the pavement glittered in an escape of humid yellow afternoon sun. Against the next batch of clouds, already piling up ink-dark, broken chimneys and parapets stood out. In her once familiar street, as in any unused channel, an unfamiliar queerness had silted up; a cat wove itself in and out of railings but no human eye watched Mrs. Drover's return. Shifting some parcels under her arm, she slowly forced round her latchkey in an unwilling lock, then gave the door, which had warped, a push

◄ *Interior with a Seated Woman*, done by the Danish painter Vilhelm Hammershøi in 1908, is both realistic and eerie. Note the open doors, slivers of light, and unnatural stillness. What words and phrases in the story could you use to describe this picture?

1 Multicultural Note
Demons

"Demons" are spirits or semi-divine beings, often evil, that exist in many cultures. In ancient Greece, *daimon* referred to intermediaries between gods and humans. Latin sources refer to *daemon* as a spirit that might take possession of a human being. The *jinni* in Islamic folklore is a desert spirit that can be either malicious or benign. The *dibbuk* in Jewish tradition takes possession of people and speaks through them, causing them to behave wildly. Christians in medieval and early modern Europe believed demons were evil spirits.

2 Literary Element
Mood

Questions

- What is the mood of the opening paragraph? *(The mood is both eerie and mundane—as if something may be about to happen.)*
- How does the setting contribute to the mood? *(The street has an "unfamiliar queerness"; it is deserted except for a cat. Rain clouds are gathering.)*
- How do descriptive details add to the mood? *("broken chimneys and parapets stood out," denoting ruins; clouds are ominously "ink-dark"; the trees glitter in an "escape of humid yellow afternoon sun"; the door lock is "unwilling" to let her in)*

BUILDING ENGLISH PROFICIENCY

Using Description

A mood of mystery holds the reader's attention in this story. Help students see how adjectives help to establish mood.

1. Write the following phrases from page 79 on the chalkboard, without underlining the adjectives:

late August	unused channel
a steamy, showery day	unfamiliar queerness
humid yellow afternoon sun	no human eye
ink-dark, broken chimneys	unwilling lock

2. Have students identify the descriptive words, or adjectives, and explain through actions or drawings what they mean.

3. Point out that some words, such as *humid* do not suggest a particular mood, but that the combination of descriptions create a mood. Let students suggest words that create a mood of horror.

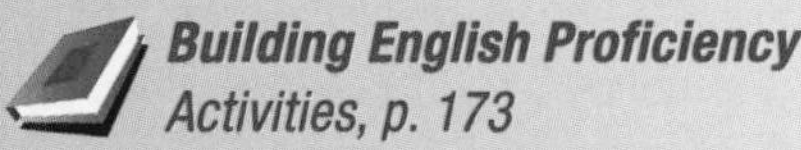
Building English Proficiency
Activities, p. 173

3 Literary Element
Imagery

Point out the description of what Mrs. Drover sees when she unshutters the window in the room. *(the smoke stain, the ring left by the vase, the bruise in the wallpaper left by the door handle, the claw marks of the piano's feet on the parquet)* Ask students what these ordinary household marks seem to mean to Mrs. Drover. *(Possible responses: They seem to be traces of her former life; she may feel she has lost her home because of the war.)*

4 Reader's Response
Making Personal Connections

Questions

- What sense do you have of the writer from the content of the letter? *(Possible response: cold, demanding, vain)*
- Why do you think the letter is signed "K"? (*Possible responses: It may have been the fiancé's initial; perhaps, because it is her initial, she is imagining the whole sequence.)*

with her knee. Dead air came out to meet her as she went in.

The staircase window having been boarded up, no light came down into the hall. But one door, she could just see, stood ajar, so she went quickly through into the room and unshuttered the big window in there. Now the prosaic[1] woman, looking about her, was more perplexed than she knew by everything that she saw, by traces of her long former habit of life—the yellow smoke stain up the white marble mantelpiece, the ring left by a vase on the top of the escritoire; the bruise in the wallpaper where, on the door being thrown open widely, the china handle had always hit the wall. The piano, having gone away to be stored, had left what looked like claw marks on its part of the parquet. Though not much dust had seeped in, each object wore a film of another kind; and, the only ventilation being the chimney, the whole drawing room smelled of the cold hearth. Mrs. Drover put down her parcels on the escritoire and left the room to proceed upstairs; the things she wanted were in a bedroom chest.

She had been anxious to see how the house was—the part-time caretaker she shared with some neighbors was away this week on his holiday, known to be not yet back. At the best of times he did not look in often, and she was never sure that she trusted him. There were some cracks in the structure, left by the last bombing,[2] on which she was anxious to keep an eye. Not that one could do anything—

A shaft of refracted[3] daylight now lay across the hall. She stopped dead and stared at the hall table—on this lay a letter addressed to her.

She thought first—then the caretaker *must* be back. All the same, who, seeing the house shuttered, would have dropped a letter in the box? It was not a circular, it was not a bill. And the post office redirected, to the address in the country, everything for her that came through the post. The caretaker (even if he *were* back) did not know she was due in London today—her call here had been planned to be a surprise—so his negligence in the manner of this letter, leaving it to wait in the dusk and the dust, annoyed her. Annoyed, she picked up the letter which bore no stamp. But it cannot be important, or they would know. . . . She took the letter rapidly upstairs with her, without a stop to look at the writing till she reached what had been her bedroom, where she let in light. The room looked over the garden and other gardens; the sun had gone in; as the clouds sharpened and lowered, the trees and rank lawns seemed already to smoke with dark. Her reluctance to look again at the letter came from the fact that she felt intruded upon—and by someone contemptuous of her ways. However, in the tenseness preceding the fall of rain she read it; it was a few lines.

Dear Kathleen,

You will not have forgotten that today is our anniversary, and the day we said. The years have gone by at once slowly and fast. In view of the fact that nothing has changed, I shall rely upon you to keep your promise. I was sorry to see you leave London, but was satisfied that you would be back in time. You may expect me, therefore, at the hour arranged.

Until then . . .
K.

Mrs. Drover looked for the date; it was today's. She dropped the letter onto the bedsprings, then picked it up to see the writing again—her lips, beneath the remains of lipstick, beginning to go white. She felt so much the change in her own face that she went to the mirror, polished a clear patch in it and looked at once urgently and stealthily in. She was confronted by a woman of forty-four, with

1. **prosaic** (prō zā′ik), *adj.* ordinary; not exciting.
2. **the last bombing**. The city of London was subjected to aerial bombardment many times during World War II, the time setting of the story.
3. **refracted** (ri frak′təd), *adj.* bent (a ray of light, waves, etc.) from a straight course.

MINI-LESSON: GRAMMAR
Recognize Dependent Clauses

Teach Point out that Elizabeth Bowen uses a style that is crisp, direct, and full of tension. Let students find sentences that are examples of these qualities.

Tell students that they can avoid writing wordy, rambling sentences and achieve a crisp style by combining sentences at the revising stage of their writing.

Activity Idea To recognize dependent clauses and practice combining sentences, have students do the following:

1. Understand that a dependent clause has a subject and verb, but can't stand alone as a sentence.

But as the rain began to come.

2. Combine the following by making some sentences dependent (subordinate) clauses and joining them with another sentence. Also, some sentences may be made joined.

She went to the chest. She unlocked it. She threw up the lid. She began to search. Where the things were. Who was a woman of forty-four.

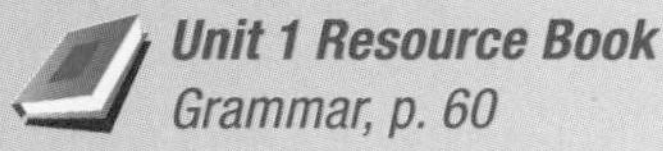

Unit 1 Resource Book
Grammar, p. 60

eyes staring out under a hat brim that had been rather carelessly pulled down. She had not put on any more powder since she left the shop where she ate her solitary tea. The pearls her husband had given her on their marriage hung loose round her now rather thinner throat, slipping into the V of the pink wool jumper her sister knitted last autumn as they sat round the fire. Mrs.
5 Drover's most normal expression was one of controlled worry, but of assent. Since the birth of the third of her little boys, attended by a quite serious illness, she had had an intermittent muscular flicker to the left of her mouth, but in spite of this she could always sustain a manner that was at once energetic and calm.

Turning from her own face as precipitately[4] as she had gone to meet it, she went to the chest where the things were, unlocked it, threw up the lid, and knelt to search. But as rain began to come crashing down she could not keep from looking over her shoulder at the stripped bed on which the letter lay. Behind the blanket of rain the clock of the church that still stood struck six—with rapidly heightening apprehension she counted each of the slow strokes, "The hour arranged . . . My God," she said, "*what* hour?
6 How should I . . . ? After twenty-five years, . . ."

The young girl talking to the soldier in the garden had not ever completely seen his face. It was dark; they were saying good-by under a tree. Now and then—for it felt, from not seeing him at this intense moment, as though she had never seen him at all—she verified his presence for these few moments longer by putting out a hand, which he each time pressed, without very much kindness, and painfully, onto one of the breast buttons of his uniform. That cut of the button on the palm of her hand was, principally, what she was to carry away. This was so near the end of a leave from France that she could only wish him already gone. It was August, 1916.[5] Being not kissed, being drawn away from and looked at intimidated Kathleen till she imagined spectral glitters in the place of his eyes. Turning away, and looking back up the lawn she saw, through branches of trees, the drawing-room window alight; she caught a breath for the moment when she could go running back there into the safe arms of her mother and sister, and cry: "What shall I do, what shall I do? He has gone."

Hearing her catch her breath, her fiancé said, without feeling, "Cold?"

"You're going away such a long way."

"Not so far as you think."

"I don't understand."

"You don't have to," he said. "You will. You know what we said."

"But that was—suppose you—I mean, suppose."

"I shall be with you," he said, "sooner or later. You won't forget that. You need do nothing but wait."

Only a little more than a minute later she was free to run up the silent lawn. Looking in through the window at her mother and sister, who did not for the moment perceive her, she already felt that unnatural
promise drive down between her and the rest of 7
all humankind. No other way of having given herself could have made her feel so apart, lost and foresworn. She could not have plighted[6] a more sinister troth.

Kathleen behaved well when, some months later, her fiancé was reported missing, presumed killed. Her family not only supported her but were able to praise her courage without stint because they could not regret, as a husband for her, the man they knew almost nothing about. They hoped she would, in a year or two, console herself—and had it been only a question of consolation things might have gone

4. **precipitately** (pri sip′ə tit′lē), *adv.* very hurriedly; suddenly.
5. **August, 1916,** a month during World War I, fought largely in Europe from 1914 to 1918.
6. **plight** (plīt), *v.* promise solemnly; pledge (as in marriage).

5 Literary Element
Characterization

Encourage students to analyze Mrs. Drover's character.

Question What does her expression of "controlled worry, but of assent" imply? *(Possible response: She worries about her family and the effects of the war, but goes along with what others demand.)*

6 Literary Focus
Flashback

Ask students to pick out signs that a flashback has begun. Point out that some flashbacks are announced in advance, while others flow naturally into the narrative. Some flashbacks may give details of a specific time in the past; others may explain all that happened from a time in the past up to the present moment. *(Mrs. Drover is thinking, "After twenty-five years," then the next paragraph begins with a young girl talking with a soldier. Further into the passage, it is revealed that the year is 1916.)*

7 Reader's Response
Making Personal Connections

Question *Foresworn* means "rejected" or "abandoned." What "unnatural," "sinister" promise might the young Kathleen have made? *(Possible response: to die with her lover, to give him her soul)*

BUILDING ENGLISH PROFICIENCY

ESL
LEP
ELD
SAE
LD

Analyzing Flashback

Help students understand the time periods in the story.

1. Read the text immediately before the passage that begins "The young girl." Explain that "After twenty-five years, . . ." and the ellipses (. . .) show the reader that the story's time has changed to the past.

2. With students, read the passage from "The young girl" to "nothing but wait."

3. Ask students to find words that signal time. List them and then let students talk about when events take place in the story. Students can add more words that denote time to the list as they read.

Words that Show Time
After twenty-five years
August, 1916
some months later
6:00 P.M.

8 Reading/Thinking Skills
Analogy

Questions

- What historical event is taking place in the flashback and again in the present? *(a world war)*
- Do you think it is a coincidence that the demon lover is present at these two periods? *(Possible response: The author may be suggesting that war is like a demon that controls your life, destroys, kills, and returns again.)*

9 Literary Element
Figurative Language

Question How does the author use figurative language to describe the crisis Mrs. Drover feels in her empty house? *(Possible response: The house has an air of being "a cracked cup" from which memory has leaked away. The hollowness of the house cancels "years on years of voices, habits, and steps.")*

10 Reading/Thinking Skills
Recognize Values

Question Why does Mrs. Drover feel she can't just run away? *(Possible response: She feels her dependability is important to her family, so she wants to collect the objects from their London home.)*

much straighter ahead. But her trouble, behind just a little grief, was a complete dislocation from everything. She did not reject other lovers, for these failed to appear; for years she failed to attract men—and with the approach of her thirties she became natural enough to share her family's anxiousness on this score. She began to put herself out, to wonder; and at thirty-two she was very greatly relieved to find herself being courted by William Drover. She married him, and the two of them settled down in this quiet, arboreal part of Kensington;[7] in this house the years piled up, her children were born and they all lived till
8 they were driven out by the bombs of the next war. Her movements as Mrs. Drover were circumscribed, and she dismissed any idea that they were still watched.

As things were—dead or living, the letter writer sent her only a threat. Unable, for some minutes, to go on kneeling with her back exposed to the empty room, Mrs. Drover rose from the chest to sit on an upright chair whose back was firmly against the wall. The desuetude[8] of her former bedroom, her married London home's whole air of being a cracked cup from which memory, with its reassuring
9 power, had either evaporated or leaked away, made a crisis—and at just this crisis the letter writer had, knowledgeably, struck. The hollowness of the house this evening canceled years on years of voices, habits, and steps. Through the shut windows she only heard rain fall on the roofs around. To rally herself, she said she was in a mood—and, for two or three seconds shutting her eyes, told herself that she had imagined the letter. But she opened them—there it lay on the bed.

On the supernatural side of the letter's entrance she was not permitting her mind to dwell. Who, in London, knew she meant to call at the house today? Evidently, however, this had

As things were — dead or living, the letter writer sent her only a threat.

been known. The caretaker, *had* he come back, had had no cause to expect her: he would have taken the letter in his pocket, to forward it, at his own time, through the post. There was no other sign that the caretaker had been in—but if not? Letters dropped in at doors of deserted houses do not fly or walk to tables in halls. They do not sit on the dust of empty tables with the air of certainty that they will be found. There is needed some human hand—but nobody but the caretaker had a key. Under circumstances she did not care to consider, a house can be entered without a key. It was possible that she was not alone now. She might be waited for, downstairs. Waited for—until when? Until "the hour arranged." At least that was not six o'clock; six had struck.

She rose from the chair and went over and locked the door.

The thing was, to get out. To fly? No, not 10
that: she had to catch her train. As a woman whose utter dependability was the keystone of her family life, she was not willing to return to the country, to her husband, her little boys and her sister, without the objects she had come to fetch.

Resuming work at the chest she set about making up a number of parcels in a rapid, fumbling-decisive way. These, with her shopping parcels, would be too much to carry; these meant a taxi—at the thought of the taxi her heart went up and her normal breathing resumed. I will ring up the taxi now; the taxi cannot come too soon: I shall hear the taxi out there running its engine, till I walk calmly down to it through the hall. I'll ring up—But no: the telephone is cut off. . . . She tugged at a knot she had tied wrong.

---

7. **Kensington,** a residential district in London.
8. **desuetude** (des′wə tüd), *n.* disuse.

MINI-LESSON: VOCABULARY
Etymology

Teach Elizabeth Bowen uses several words derived from the French language in "The Demon Lover," such as *parquet* and *escritoire.* Many commonly used English words come from French, and the French words had Latin origins.

Activity Idea Students can look in the story for words that may derive from the French, and check their choices by looking in the dictionary. Ask students to:

- identify the words and show their etymological origins before French, if applicable
- describe the connection between the words of French origin and their English meanings

The idea of flight . . . He was never kind to me, not really. I don't remember him kind at all. Mother said he never considered me. He was set on me, that was what it was—not love. Not love, not meaning a person well. What did he do, to make me promise like that? I can't remember—But she found that she could.

She remembered with such dreadful acuteness that the twenty-five years since then dissolved like smoke and she instinctively looked for the weal left by the button on the palm of her hand. She remembered not only all that he
11 said and did, but the complete suspension of *her* existence during that August week. I was not myself—they all told me so at the time. She remembered—but with one white burning blank as where acid has been dropped on a photograph; *under no conditions* could she remember his face.

So, wherever he may be waiting I shall not know him. You have no time to run from a face you do not expect.

The thing was to get to the taxi before any clock struck what could be the hour. She would slip down the street and round the side of the square to where the square gave on the main road. She would return in the taxi, safe, to her own door, and bring the solid driver into the house with her to pick up the parcels from room to room. The idea of the taxi driver made her decisive, bold; she unlocked the door, went to the top of the staircase, and listened down.

She heard nothing—but while she was hearing nothing the *passé*[9] air of the staircase was disturbed by a draft that traveled up to her face. It emanated[10] from the basement; down there a door or window was being opened by someone who chose this moment to leave the house.

The rain had stopped; the pavements steamily shone as Mrs. Drover let herself out by inches from her own front door into the empty street. The unoccupied houses opposite continued to meet her look with their damaged stare. Making toward the thoroughfare and the taxi, she tried not to keep looking behind. Indeed, the silence was so intense—one of those creeks of London silence exaggerated this summer by the damage of war—that no tread could have gained on hers unheard. Where her street debouched on the square where people went on living she grew conscious of and checked her unnatural pace. Across the open end of the square two buses impassively passed each other; women, a perambulator, cyclists, a man wheeling a barrow signalized, once again, the ordinary flow of life.

At the square's most populous corner should be—and was—the short taxi rank.[11] This evening, only one taxi—but this, although it presented its blank rump, appeared already to be alertly waiting for her. Indeed, without looking round the driver started his engine as she panted up from behind and put her hand on the door. As she did so, the clock struck seven. The taxi faced the main road; to make the trip back to her house it would have to turn—and she settled back on the seat and the taxi *had* turned before she, surprised by its knowing movement, recollected that she had not "said where." She leaned forward to scratch at the glass panel that divided the driver's seat from her own.

The driver braked to what was almost a stop, turned round, and slid the glass panel back; the jolt of this flung Mrs. Drover forward till her face was almost into the glass. Through the aperture[12] driver and passenger, not six inches between them, remained for an eternity eye to eye. Mrs. Drover's mouth hung open for some
seconds before she could issue her first scream. 12
After that she continued to scream freely and to beat with her gloved hands on the glass all round as the taxi, accelerating without mercy, made off with her into the hinterland of deserted streets.

---

9. *passé* (pa sā′), *adj.* old, stale. [*French*]
10. **emanate** (em′ə nāt′), *v.* come forth; spread out.
11. **taxi rank**, a place for taxis to line up.
12. **aperture** (ap′ər chər), *n.* an opening; hole.

11 Reading/Thinking Skills
Synthesize

Engage students in a discussion of what Mrs. Drover remembers about her former lover while she is packing her things. Challenge students to interpret the meaning of her "complete suspension" of her own existence during that week long ago, and why is it important to her that she cannot remember his face.

12 Literary Focus
Flashback

Invite students to imagine that the author has told the story's events in chronological order, without the use of flashback. Discuss the effect this would have on suspense, exposition, and development of the main character.

Check Test

1. Why is Mrs. Drover in London on this day? *(She has come to pick up some items from her boarded-up house.)*
2. How many years have passed since Mrs. Drover parted from the young man? *(twenty-five)*
3. What happened to her former fiancé? *(He was reported missing during World War I.)*
4. How does she decide to escape from the letter writer? *(She plans to take a taxi to the train station.)*
5. What causes Mrs. Drover to scream? *(seeing the taxi driver's face)*

Unit 1 Resource Book
Alternate Check Test, p. 61

BUILDING ENGLISH PROFICIENCY

ESL LEP ELD SAE LD

Exploring Mood

When Mrs. Drover's thoughts return to the present, the story's mood of suspense begins to increase dramatically. Let students identify events that build suspense by creating a graph. Supply the first event and let students work in pairs to add others. Possible responses are shown.

she locks the door		enters taxi at 7:00 P.M.		driver turns to face her	she screams

Some Suspense → **Great Suspense**

After Reading

MAKING CONNECTIONS

1. Possible response: She may have been distraught by the war and her closed-up house, and imagined events based on her past.
2. Students should refer to the predictions they made in the Building Background section on page 77.
3. Possible responses: This may be a story about the stresses of wartime living, or it may be a fantastic story about a demon lover of legend.
4. Possible responses: She may be taken away by the demon lover; she may have a nervous breakdown.
5. Her fiancé is reported missing; she feels dislocated for many years; she marries William Drover; she has a family; she is ill after her last son is born.
6. It is both ordinary and eerie, with an air of expectancy.
7. The empty street, the impending rain, the warped door.
8. When people live in a country that is being bombed, as England was, everyone is frightened and insecure, but they show these feelings in different ways.
9. The supernatural elements may be real, or they may be coincidence. However, each story is written in such a way that the supernatural seems the most logical.
10. Possible responses: They try to find reasons for evil, for events that happen that they can't control or understand.

After Reading

Making Connections

Shaping Your Response

1. Do you think that Mrs. Drover might have imagined any of the events or details in this story? Explain your answer.
2. Think about the prediction you made before reading. How were the ideas similar to or different from the story?
3. In your opinion, is this a story about love, about war, or about something else? Explain.
4. What do you think happens to Mrs. Drover after the story ends?

Analyzing the Story

5. Draw a time line like the one below and add at least five events in the story **plot** that occur between the wars.

6. How would you describe the **mood** in the first two paragraphs of the story?
7. What details in the **setting** contribute to this mood?

Extending the Ideas

8. How can war affect the behavior and perspective of a **group**? In answering, consider information provided on page 77.
9. What similarities do you find between this story and "The Monkey's Paw"?
10. Why do you think people are so intrigued with elements of the supernatural in movies and books?

Literary Focus: Flashback

A **flashback** interrupts the time order of a story to present past events that shed light on current ones.

- What details in the flashback to 1916 suggest that Mrs. Drover was uncomfortable in her relationship with the young soldier?
- What information about her fiancé provides insights about his character? How does this information seem in keeping with the final scene?

LITERARY FOCUS: FLASHBACK

- Responses: She is intimidated by his behavior at their parting; he presses her finger painfully onto his uniform button; she longs to be back with her mother and sister.
- Responses: He is not kind to her; he was set on her rather than seeming to love her; he exacts a sinister promise from her but will not explain what he means. The disappearance of Mrs. Drover at the end fits with her lover's certainty that she will be his.

Vocabulary Study

Use your Glossary, if necessary, to answer the following items.

aperture
emanate
passé
prosaic
refracted

1. The final syllable of *passé* rhymes with ____.
   a. see **b.** hay **c.** glass **d.** none of these
2. Which of the following could be *refracted*?
   a. food **b.** books **c.** light **d.** happiness
3. An *aperture* is a ____.
   a. lamp **b.** weather forecast **c.** hole **d.** bird
4. *Emanate* means to ____.
   a. spread out **b.** break **c.** lie **d.** ask
5. Someone who is *prosaic* is ____.
   a. thin **b.** odd **c.** forgetful **d.** ordinary

Expressing Your Ideas

Writing Choices

Writer's Notebook Update Compare the details you listed from the story with those of a classmate. Skim the story to find and list a few more details that establish the mood. You might use items from your list in the writing assignments that follow.

You, the Critic Do you think that this story should be interpreted in light of wartime stress and emptiness, or do you prefer to read it as simply a good ghost story that could have been set during any time period? Write a review for a literary magazine expressing your opinion.

Other Options

The Director's Chair Imagine that you are filming the end of this story. Reread the last three paragraphs. Then write **director's notes** to show how you would film this final scene (close-ups, distance shots, black/white or color), any special effects and sounds you would use, and what details you would emphasize (the clock, the street, Mrs. Drover's face, and so forth). You might want to review the article about critical viewing on pages 62–63 for ideas.

Eyewitness Reports As she enters the square near her house, Mrs. Drover notices buses, women, a baby carriage, cyclists, and a man pushing a wheelbarrow. You are a member of the police force looking into the disappearance of Mrs. Drover. Interview several people who saw her get into the taxi. In an **oral report**, identify these people, their whereabouts in the square, and any details they can provide.

Vocabulary Study

1. b
2. c
3. c
4. a
5. d

More Practice Students can make up sentences using the vocabulary words *precipitately, plight,* and *desuetude.*

Unit 2 Resource Book
Vocabulary, p. 59
Vocabulary Test, p. 62

WRITING CHOICE

Writer's Notebook Update

Students can look back at their Writer's Notebooks to see the list they made of things they found frightening. Then they can compare their ideas with details that establish the mood in the story.

Selection Test

Unit 1 Resource Book
pp. 63–64

OTHER OPTIONS

Eyewitness Reports

Students can act out the interview scene, taking different roles. Have students improvise, and answer the policemen according to whether they believe "The Demon Lover" is a horror story or a psychological thriller.

Before Reading

Building Background

To make predictions, the astrologer in this story relies on his observation and insights more than astrological signs. Ask students if they have made predictions about people or if others have made predictions about them. What skills or information did they use to make the predictions?

Literary Focus

The **dialogue** central to "An Astrologer's Day" presents an interplay between the astrologer and his customer. As is common in well-written dialogue, this exchange presents a give-and-take between the characters, not just a series of remarks made by alternating speakers.

Writer's Notebook

If students need prompts to get started on their lists, ask them how old they will be in ten years. Also mention categories of things that might affect their future such as health, the economy, the well-being of other members of the family, new technology, even wars in different parts of the world.

More About R.K. Narayan

Narayan's characters are tragi-comic, whimsical, and human, and his themes deal with the essentials of life.

Before Reading

An Astrologer's Day

by R. K. Narayan   India

R. K. Narayan
born 1906

R. K. Narayan (nä rī′yän), who once said, "Novels bore me but never people," eventually wrote his own novels that audiences have praised as anything but boring. Widely regarded as India's finest contemporary writer, Narayan often creates characters based on childhood memories of his grandmother's acquaintances, who dropped by to ask advice on subjects ranging from scorpion bites to marriage. Born in Madras, India, Narayan was an undistinguished student and taught briefly before becoming a writer. Many of his novels, which have been described as "concentrated miniatures of human experience," take place in the fictional town of Malgudi.

Building Background

What's in the Stars? Astrology is the study of how the stars, moon, sun, and planets influence life and events on earth. Some people believe that the heavenly bodies operate in patterns that reveal a person's character and future. Such people consult an astrologer, or a person who tells fortunes after studying the stars, before making important decisions. Astrologers learn about the influence of heavenly bodies by studying a horoscope, or birth chart, that shows the position of these bodies at the time of a person's birth.

Literary Focus

Dialogue A conversation that captures the exact words spoken between characters in a literary work is called **dialogue**. A writer often uses dialogue to give the reader information about the characters and to create mood. Dialogue can also help advance the plot and theme of a story. A great deal of background and information in "An Astrologer's Day" is related through dialogue.

Writer's Notebook

Our Stars or Ourselves?

> Men at some time are masters of their fates.
> The fault, dear Brutus, is not in our stars,
> But in ourselves, that we are underlings.

In these lines from Shakespeare's *Julius Caesar*, Cassius tells Brutus that people, not the stars, have the power to control their own lives. To what degree do you think you can control your destiny? To what degree do you think blind luck, fate, the stars, or other forces determine your destiny? Make a list of all the things that you think might determine what you'll be doing ten years from now. Circle those things over which you think you have some control.

SUPPORT MATERIALS OVERVIEW

Unit 1 Resource Book
- Graphic Organizer, p. 65
- Study Guide, p. 66
- Vocabulary, p. 67
- Grammar, p. 68
- Alternate Check Test, p. 69
- Vocabulary Test, p. 70
- Selection Test, pp. 71–72

Building English Proficiency
- Literature Summaries
- Activities, p. 174

Reading, Writing & Grammar SkillBook
- Reading, pp. 67–68
- Grammar, Usage, and Mechanics, pp. 157–158

Technology
- Audiotape 4, Side A
- Personal Journal Software
- Custom Literature Database: For another short story dealing with deceptive appearances, see "Hearts and Hands" by O. Henry on the database.
- Test Generator Software

An Astrologer's Day

1

R. K. Narayan

Punctually at midday he opened his bag and spread out his professional equipment, which consisted of a dozen cowrie shells, a square piece of cloth with obscure mystic charts on it, a notebook, and a bundle of palmyra writing. His forehead was resplendent[1] with sacred ash and vermilion, and his eyes sparkled with a sharp abnormal gleam which was really an outcome of a continual searching look for customers, but which his simple clients took to be a prophetic light and felt comforted. The power of his eyes was considerably enhanced[2] by their position—placed as they were between the painted forehead and the dark whiskers which streamed down his cheeks: even a half-wit's eyes would sparkle in such a setting. To crown the effect he wound a saffron-colored turban around his head. This color scheme never failed. People were attracted to him as bees are attracted to cosmos or

1. resplendent (ri splen′dənt), *adj.* very bright; splendid.
2. enhance (en hans′), *v.t.* add to; heighten.

During Reading

Selection Objectives

- to explore the theme of beating the odds
- to understand aspects of dialogue
- to identify compound-complex sentences

Unit 1 Resource Book
Graphic Organizer, p. 65
Study Guide, p. 66

Theme Link

A self-taught astrologer seems to have beaten the odds when he learns he is not guilty of murder.

Vocabulary Preview

resplendent, very bright; splendid
enhance, add to; heighten
vociferousness, noisiness; shouting
shrewd, clever; keen
impetuous, rushing with force and violence
paraphernalia, personal belongings
piqued, aroused; stirred up
jutka, a two-wheeled vehicle drawn by horse
haggling, disputing, especially about a price or the terms of a bargain
lorry, a long, flat, horse-drawn wagon without sides, set on four low wheels
jaggery, a coarse, dark sugar made from the sap of certain palm trees
pyol, a low bench, often outdoors

Students can add the words and definitions to their Writer's Notebooks.

SELECTION SUMMARY

An Astrologer's Day

An astrologer who works in a busy city had left his agrarian village abruptly years before. Although untrained as an astrologer, he succeeds because he is a good judge of human nature. In his dimly lit stall, he takes a client's challenge to predict the outcome of a search. The astrologer gives accurate details of the client's past, and describes how the man had been stabbed and left for dead. Eagerly, the wronged man asks if he will succeed in getting revenge, but the astrologer tells him that the attacker is dead. Happy that the attacker has met an early death, the client gives up his search and returns to his village. Later, the astrologer tells his wife that he is greatly relieved. He had fled his village because he thought he'd killed a man; now he knows that man is alive.

*For summaries in other languages, see the **Building English Proficiency** book.*

1 Historical Note

Astrology

The ancient Babylonians originated the practice of astrology. From Babylon it spread to China, India, and Europe. The earliest known horoscope using principles of astrology is dated at 409 B.C.

Art Study

Response to Caption Questions Possible response: Astrology was considered important in Indian culture.

The twelve signs of the zodiac coincided with the zodiacal constellations of 2,000 years ago. The movement of the stars over such a long period of time means that the signs of the zodiac no longer coincide with the constellations.

Visual Literacy Students can compare this rendering of the zodiac with the contemporary one on page 93. Invite students from a culture that considers astrology important to share their knowledge of astrology.

Questions What pictures and beings associated with the constellations and signs of the zodiac do you recognize in this drawing? *(Responses will include many of the images that represent the twelve signs of the zodiac.)*

MINI-LESSON: VOCABULARY

Shades of Meaning

Students can explore shades of meanings of words by referring to a thesaurus and a dictionary.

Teach Since a thesaurus usually provides several synonyms for a word, the exact meaning the writer wants may be hard to determine. To find the precise shade of meaning, the writer may need to look up the definitions of the synonyms in the dictionary.

Activity Idea Students can look in a thesaurus for synonyms of words presented in the text, then check a dictionary for the exact meaning they want to find.

- Suggest that students look for precise synonyms for these words from "An Astrologer's Day": *mystic, abnormal, sacred, flank, surge.*
- Encourage students to find other words in the story for which they can find synonyms. Then they can write sentences about the story using these new words.

dahlia stalks. He sat under the boughs of a spreading tamarind tree which flanked a path running through the Town Hall Park. It was a remarkable place in many ways: a surging crowd was always moving up and down this narrow road morning till night. A variety of trades and occupations was represented all along its way: medicine sellers, sellers of stolen hardware and junk, magicians, and above all, an auctioneer of cheap cloth, who created enough din all day to attract the whole town. Next to him in vociferousness[3] came a vendor of fried groundnut, who gave his ware a fancy name each day, calling it "Bombay Ice Cream" one day, and on the next "Delhi Almond," and on the third "Raja's Delicacy," and so on and so forth, and people flocked to him. A considerable portion of this
2 crowd dallied before the astrologer too. The astrologer transacted his business by the light of a flare which crackled and smoked up above the groundnut heap nearby. Half the enchantment of the place was due to the fact that it did not have the benefit of municipal lighting. The place was lit up by shop lights. One or two had hissing gaslights, some had naked flares stuck on poles, some were lit up by old cycle lamps, and one or two, like the astrologer's, managed without lights of their own. It was a bewildering crisscross of light rays and moving shadows. This suited the astrologer very well, for the simple reason that he had not in the least intended to be an astrologer when he began life; and he knew no more of what was going to happen to others than he knew what was going to happen to himself next minute. He was as much a stranger to the stars as were his innocent customers. Yet he said things which pleased and astonished everyone: that was more a matter of study, practice, and shrewd[4] guesswork. All the same, it was as much an honest man's labor as any other, and he deserved the wages he carried home at the end of the day. 3

He had left his village without any previous thought or plan. If he had continued there he would have carried on the work of his forefathers—namely, tilling the land, living, marrying, and ripening in his cornfield and ancestral home. But that was not to be. He had to leave home without telling anyone, and he could not rest till he left it behind a couple of hundred miles. To a villager it is a great deal, as if an ocean flowed between.

He had a working analysis of mankind's troubles: marriage, money, and the tangles of human ties. Long practice had sharpened his perception. Within five minutes he understood what was wrong. He charged three pice[5] per question, never opened his mouth till the other had spoken for at least ten minutes, which provided him enough stuff for a dozen answers and advices. 4 When he told the person before him, gazing at his palm, "In many ways you are not getting the fullest results for your efforts," nine out of ten were disposed to agree with him. Or he questioned: "Is there any woman in your family, maybe even a distant relative, who is not well disposed towards you?" Or he gave an analysis of character: "Most of your troubles are due to your nature. How can you be otherwise with Saturn where he is? You have an impetuous[6] nature and a rough exterior." This endeared him to their hearts immediately, for even the mildest of us loves to think that he has a forbidding exterior.

The nuts vendor blew out his flare and rose to go home. This was a signal for the astrologer to bundle up too, since it left him in darkness

◄ This zodiac drawing of the western and eastern hemispheres accompanied a horoscope commissioned by an Indian monarch in 1840. What can you infer from this information and the picture itself about the status of astrology in Indian culture?

3. **vociferousness** (vō sif′ər əs nəs), *n.* noisiness; shouting.
4. **shrewd** (shrüd), *adj.* clever; keen.
5. **pice** (pīs), *n.* an Indian coin of small value. Three pice would be equal to little more than half a U.S. cent.
6. **impetuous** (im pech′ü əs), *adj.* rushing with force and violence.

2 Literary Element
Setting

Question Why is the path in Town Hall Park a good place for the astrologer to do business? *(Possible responses: It is crowded with potential customers; the nearby groundnut vendor attracts a lot of people to the area; the poor lighting adds to the atmosphere around the astrologer.)*

3 Reader's Response
Making Personal Connections

Question Do you agree that "he deserved the wages he carried home at the end of the day"? *(Possible responses: He may deserve them because he pleased his customers through his study, practice, and shrewd guesswork.)*

4 Reading/Thinking Skills
Draw Conclusions

Lead students to discuss how the main character is able to tell fortunes.

Questions

- How does the astrologer obtain information from his customers. *(He lets them talk about themselves.)*
- What conclusion can you draw from this approach to telling fortunes? *(Possible response: Understanding human nature may be enough to make predictions about others.)*

BUILDING ENGLISH PROFICIENCY

ESL LEP ELD SAE LD

Analyzing Character

To help students understand why the astrologer is successful even though he knows little about astrology, guide them as they:

1. read or talk about parts of the story that show the astrologer knows that he cannot foretell the future
2. complete the chart with details from pages 87–89 to analyze how he succeeds
3. discuss people and businesses they know who use the same methods

Location	*busy market, dim lighting*
Action	*listens well, analyzes the customer*
Appearance	*yellow turban, painted forehead*

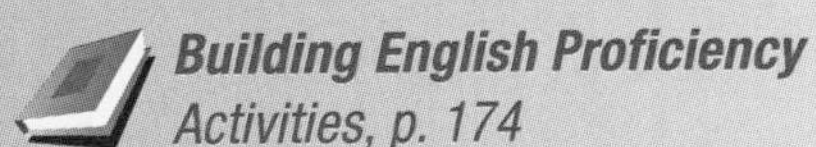
Building English Proficiency *Activities, p. 174*

5 Literary Focus
Dialogue

Discuss with students the functions a dialogue may serve in a story, such as to develop characterization, to create tension, to advance the plot, and to reflect the mood of the story.

Question At the beginning of the conversation between the astrologer and this client, what sense do you have of their personalities? *(Possible responses: client—irritable, argumentative; astrologer—persuasive, competitive)*

6 Reading/Thinking Skills
Predict Outcomes

Question Now that the astrologer has taken up the challenge, do you think he will make a sound prediction? *(Possible responses: No—the client is too smart; yes—his hesitation was a ruse.)*

7 Literary Focus
Dialogue

Question How does the relationship between the two men change once the astrologer begins to recount the client's history? *(Possible responses: It becomes friendlier. The client is pleased and even gives some information of his own; the astrologer has become willing to talk.)*

except for a little shaft of green light which strayed in from somewhere and touched the ground before him. He picked up his cowrie shells and paraphernalia[7] and was putting them back into his bag when the green shaft of light was blotted out; he looked up and saw a man standing before him. He sensed a possible client and said: "You look so careworn. It will do you good to sit down for a while and chat with me." The other grumbled some reply vaguely. The astrologer pressed his invitation, whereupon the other thrust his palm under his nose, saying: "You call yourself an astrologer?" The astrologer felt challenged and said, tilting the other's palm towards the green shaft of light. "Yours is a nature. . ." "Oh stop that," the other said. "Tell me something worthwhile. . . ."

5 Our friend felt piqued.[8] "I charge only three pice per question, and what you get ought to be good enough for your money. . . ." At this the other withdrew his arm, took out an anna,[9] and flung it out to him saying: "I have some questions to ask. If I prove you are bluffing, you must return that anna to me with interest."

"If you find my answers satisfactory, will you give me five rupees?"[10]

"No."

"Or will you give me eight annas?"

"All right, provided you give me twice as much if you are wrong," said the stranger. This pact was accepted after a little further argument. The astrologer sent up a prayer to heaven as the other lit a cheroot. The astrologer caught a glimpse of his face by the matchlight. There was a pause as cars hooted on the road, *jutka*[11] drivers swore at their horses, and the babble of the crowd agitated the semidarkness of the park. The other sat down, sucking his cheroot, puffing out, sat there ruthlessly. The astrologer felt very uncomfortable. "Here, take your anna back. I am not used to such challenges. It is late for me today. . . ." He made preparations to bundle up. The other held his wrist and said: "You can't get out of it now. You dragged me in while I was passing." The astrologer shivered in his grip; and his voice shook and became faint. "Leave me today. I will speak to you tomorrow." The other thrust his palm in his face and said: "Challenge is challenge. Go on." The astrologer proceeded with his throat drying up: "There is a woman. . . ."

"Stop," said the other. "I don't want all that. Shall I succeed in my present search or not? Answer this and go. Otherwise I will not let you go till you disgorge all your coins." The astrologer muttered a few incantations and replied: "All right. I will speak. But will you give 6 me a rupee if what I say is convincing? Otherwise I will not open my mouth, and you may do what you like." After a good deal of haggling[12] the other agreed. The astrologer said: "You were left for dead. Am I right?"

"Ah, tell me more."

"A knife has passed through you once?" said the astrologer.

"Good fellow!" He bared his chest to show the scar. "What else?"

"And then you were pushed into a well nearby in the field. You were left for dead."

"I should have been dead if some passer-by had not chanced to peep into the well," 7 exclaimed the other, overwhelmed by enthusiasm.

"When shall I get at him?" he asked, clenching his fist.

"In the next world," answered the astrologer. "He died four months ago in a far-off town. You will never see any more of him."

---

7. **paraphernalia** (par′ə fər nā′lyə), *n.* personal belongings.
8. piqued (pēkd), *adj.* aroused; stirred up.
9. **anna** (an′ə), *n.* an Indian coin equal to four pice. Sixteen annas make one rupee.
10. **rupee** (rü pē′), *n.* Officially worth about thirteen U.S. cents, the rupee actually had about the same buying power in India as the dollar has in the U.S.
11. ***jutka*** (jüt′kə), *n.* a two-wheeled vehicle drawn by horse.
12. **haggling** (hag′ling), *n.* disputing, especially about a price or the terms of a bargain.

MINI-LESSON: GRAMMAR
Compound-Complex Sentences

A compound-complex sentence has more than one main clause and at least one subordinate clause. A main clause has a subject and a predicate and can stand alone as a sentence. A subordinate clause has a subject and a predicate, but it cannot stand alone as a sentence.

Teach R.K. Narayan uses many kinds of sentences, including this compound-complex sentence.

(1) His forehead was resplendent with sacred ash and vermilion,

(2) and his eyes sparkled with a sharp abnormal gleam

(3) which was really an outcome of a continual searching look for customers,

(4) but which his simple clients took to be a prophetic light and felt comforted.

Here, 1 and 2 are main clauses and 3 and 4 are subordinate clauses.

Activity Idea To reinforce this skill, ask students to:

- look through the story to identify other compound-complex sentences
- write compound-complex sentences that describe a person and his or her actions or appearance

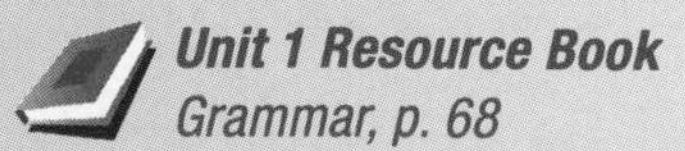
Unit 1 Resource Book
Grammar, p. 68

The other groaned on hearing it. The astrologer proceeded:

"Guru Nayak—"

"You know my name!" the other said, taken aback.

8 "As I know all other things. Guru Nayak, listen carefully to what I have to say. Your village is two days' journey due north of this town. Take the next train and be gone. I see once again great danger to your life if you go from home." He took out a pinch of sacred ash and held it to him. "Rub it on your forehead and go home. Never travel southward again, and you will live to be a hundred."

> And then you were pushed into a well nearby in the field. You were left for dead.

"Why should I leave home again?" the other said reflectively. "I was only going away now and then to look for him and to choke out his life if I met him." He shook his head regretfully. "He has escaped my hands. I hope at least he died as he deserved."

"Yes," said the astrologer. "He was crushed

9 under a lorry."[13] The other looked gratified to hear it.

The place was deserted by the time the astrologer picked up his articles and put them into his bag. The green shaft was also gone, leaving the place in darkness and silence. The stranger had gone off into the night, after giving the astrologer a handful of coins.

It was nearly midnight when the astrologer reached home. His wife was waiting for him at the door and demanded an explanation. He flung the coins at her and said: "Count them. One man gave all that."

"Twelve and a half annas," she said, counting. She was overjoyed. "I can buy some jaggery[14] and coconut tomorrow. The child has been asking for sweets for so many days now. I will prepare some nice stuff for her."

"The swine has cheated me! He promised me a rupee," said the astrologer. She looked up at him. "You look worried. What is wrong?"

"Nothing."

After dinner, sitting on the *pyol,*[15] he 10
told her: "Do you know a great load is gone from me today? I thought I had the blood of a man on my hands all these years. That was the reason why I ran away from home, settled here, and married you. He is alive."

She gasped. "You tried to kill!"

"Yes, in our village, when I was a silly youngster. We drank, gambled, and quarreled badly one day—why think of it now? Time to sleep," he said, yawning, and stretched himself on the *pyol.*

---

13. **lorry** (lôr′ē), *n.* a long, flat, horse-drawn wagon without sides, set on four low wheels.
14. **jaggery** (jag′ə rē), *n.* a coarse, dark sugar made from the sap of certain palm trees.
15. ***pyol*** (pī′ôl), *n.* a low bench, often outdoors.

8 Reader's Response
Challenging the Text

Question Do you as a reader believe that the astrologer knows all? *(Possible responses: No—the astrologer has always relied on his wits; yes—he suddenly has developed these powers.)*

9 Reading/Thinking Skills
Analogy

Let students compare the speakers of the dialogue to opponents vying in a sport by asking: Which sport does the dialogue remind you of? Who has scored? Who wins control of the dialogue?

10 Literary Focus
Dialogue

Discuss with students how the final dialogue resolves the story and explains any unanswered questions. Encourage students to find details that foreshadowed the ending, such as the astrologer's having to leave his village secretly.

Check Test

1. How does the astrologer dress to appear prophetic? *(He wears a saffron-colored turban, puts ash and vermilion on his forehead, and has dark whiskers on his face.)*
2. Why does he choose the park as his place of business? *(It is crowded; other vendors there attract customers.)*
3. What does the client want the astrologer to predict? *(whether or not he will succeed in his search)*
4. What does Guru Nayak want to do to the man who left him for dead? *(choke him to death)*
5. What new fact does the astrologer's wife learn about him? *(He tried to kill a man.)*

Unit 1 Resource Book
Alternate Check Test, p. 69

BUILDING ENGLISH PROFICIENCY

Sequencing Story Events

The story's resolution rests on an explanation of events that happened long before the story begins. Help students create a time line to understand the details of the past, especially the events that occurred between the astrologer and Guru Nayak.

The Astrologer's Life

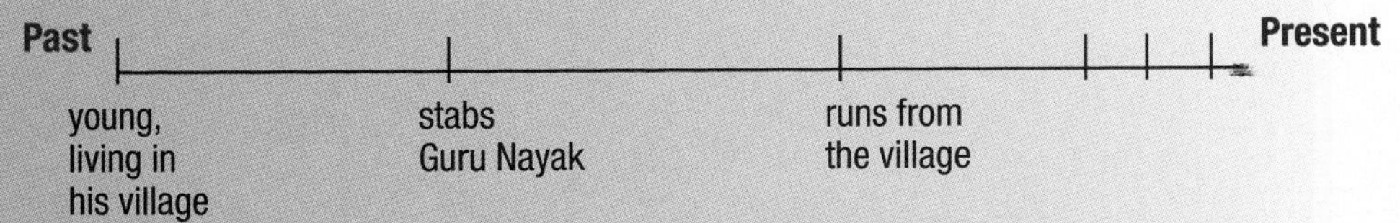

After Reading

MAKING CONNECTIONS

1. Possible responses: No, he does not seem honest; yes, he seems to understand people.

2. He is relieved that he did not kill the man.

3. It is entertaining, but it also reveals that most people who are living good lives may also have hidden guilt, flaws, and sorrows.

4. Some images are his forehead of ash and vermilion, his saffron-colored turban, his gleaming eyes, his whiskers, and his professional equipment.

5. The client doesn't recognize the astrologer because he can't see very much of his face. Also the client is not expecting him to be an astrologer; he knew him as a farmer.

6. Possible responses: Based on experience, what an astrologer says is true; there is no basis for believing such predictions.

7. Possible responses: medicine, psychology, many kinds of research, art; most professions

After Reading

Making Connections

Shaping Your Response

1. Would you like to have the astrologer for a friend? Why or why not?
2. How would you describe the astrologer's feelings at the end of the story?
3. Do you find this story instructive, merely entertaining, or something else? Explain.

Analyzing the Story

4. What **images** in the first paragraph help you picture the astrologer?
5. Can you **infer** why the client doesn't recognize the astrologer? Explain.

Extending the Ideas

6. How much faith would you put in an astrologer? Explain.
7. What other professions do you think require "study, practice, and shrewd guesswork"?

Literary Focus: Dialogue

The conversation between two or more people is called **dialogue**. Often dialogue in a story provides details that are crucial to the plot. Briefly recount previous events, revealed through dialogue, that enable the astrologer to give such an accurate "reading" to his client.

Vocabulary Study

On your paper, match the numbered word with the letter of its antonym.

enhance
piqued
resplendent
shrewd
vociferousness

1. resplendent	**a.** lessen
2. vociferousness	**b.** dark; dull
3. shrewd	**c.** stupid
4. enhance	**d.** calm
5. piqued	**e.** speechlessness

LITERARY FOCUS: DIALOGUE

The astrologer knew Guru Nayak had been stabbed and left for dead because he was the person responsible for the act. He knows how far away Guru Nayak's village is because he himself is from there.

Expressing Your Ideas

Writing Choices

Writer's Notebook Update Examine your list and the items you circled. Then use this information to write a paragraph titled "Fate and My Future."

Astrologer for Hire The astrologer is describing the services he provides in a **classified ad**. Write the ad, complete with a catchy headline and fees you think would be appropriate in American money.

Magic or Science? Many scientists around the world denounce astrology as a great hoax consisting of nothing more than magic and superstition. Is there a scientific foundation for the belief that the forces of the stars and planets at the time of our birth can shape our futures? Do some research on astrology. Then explain your findings by writing a **science article** for readers of *Science Today.*

Sky Talk Research one of the constellations and the Greek myth that tells its story. Write a **summary** of this myth. Then tell the myth to the class.

Other Options

Starmobile Work with a group to make a **mobile** of the twelve astrological signs. Present the mobile to the rest of the class, explaining each figure and its historical or mythological significance.

Culture Note Compare astrological charts from various cultures. Explain what these charts reveal about both universal themes and specific **group** experiences.

Asian lunar zodiac

VOCABULARY STUDY

1. b
2. e
3. c
4. a
5. d

More Practice Refer students to the words they located for the Vocabulary Mini-Lesson on page 88, and encourage them to find antonyms for those words.

Unit 1 Resource Book
Vocabulary, p. 67
Vocabulary Test, p. 70

WRITING CHOICES

Writer's Notebook Update

In this paragraph students can explain why some aspects of their lives may be affected by fate and why others are under their own control.

Astrologer for Hire

Remind students that they may want to make the ad's statements vague in the same way the astrologer used all-inclusive statements in his verbal advertisement.

Magic or Science?

Students may want to do historical research on astrology, using such sources as Daniel J. Boorstin's *The Discoverers* (1983).

Selection Test

Unit 1 Resource Book
pp. 71–72

OTHER OPTIONS

Starmobile

Encourage each group to use a different source as the basis for their astrological signs, so each mobile will be different.

Culture Note

Students may find that the way each culture interprets astrology reflects important aspects of that culture.

Before Reading

Building Background

Poe was striving to create an intense atmosphere in this story. Have students visualize the atmosphere in their community during a raging epidemic or plague and describe the scene. They might also recall their own memories of events that created widespread positive or negative emotions, such as a local team winning the World Series or a weather disaster.

Literary Focus

An author may create **mood** through setting and through the people or objects being described. Descriptive details and word connotations contribute to the mood.

The words in the web evoke feelings of fear and sadness and the idea of serious illness and death.

Writer's Notebook

From the quotations, students may note the idea that death is inevitable, unpredictable, and undiscriminating.

Connections to **AuthorWorks**

Edgar Allan Poe is a featured author in the AuthorWorks CD-ROM series.

Before Reading

The Masque of the Red Death

by Edgar Allan Poe USA

Edgar Allan Poe
1809–1849

Orphaned at three, Edgar Allan Poe was raised by the wealthy Allan family, who disowned him when he decided to pursue a literary career. By 1836, when he married his thirteen-year-old cousin, Virginia Clemm, Poe was a troubled young man. Her death in 1847 plunged him deeper into despair and alcoholism. Although he eventually enjoyed fame, Poe died in poverty after he was found battered and drunk on the streets of Baltimore. His contemporaries held widely different opinions of his artistry (one dismissed him as a "jingle man"). Nevertheless, today Poe's contributions to literature are universally acknowledged.

Building Background

It's Epidemic! A dreaded epidemic disease, plague had been reported in biblical accounts. In the mid 1330s, a plague known as **The Black Death** swept across Asia and Europe, killing an estimated 40 million by 1400 in Europe alone. Spread by bacteria that live in rats and other rodents and transmitted to humans by fleas, plague can kill a victim in under five days. Although now curable by early treatment with antibiotics, it still occurs occasionally, especially in developing regions of Asia, Africa, and South America. Modern viruses, such as Ebola, which erupted in Zaire in 1976 and again in 1995, are plaguelike in their swift, deadly outbreaks.

Literary Focus

Mood Edgar Allan Poe carefully chose his words and descriptions to set the mood of his stories. **Mood** is the overall atmosphere or prevailing feeling within a work of art. Examine the web of words and phrases from the first paragraph of "The Masque of the Red Death." What feelings do the words stir in you?

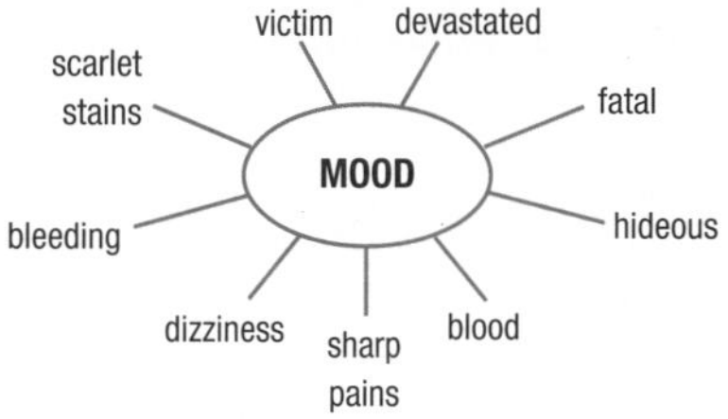

Writer's Notebook

Death Quotes Quickwrite your reactions to each of the following quotations about death.

"Death devours all lovely things. . . ." *Edna St. Vincent Millay*

"O! death's a great disguiser." *William Shakespeare*

"Pale Death kicks his way equally into the cottages of the poor and the castles of kings." *Horace*

SUPPORT MATERIALS OVERVIEW

Unit 1 Resource Book
- Graphic Organizer, p. 73
- Study Guide, p. 74
- Vocabulary, p. 75
- Grammar, p. 76
- Alternate Check Test, p. 77
- Vocabulary Test, p. 78
- Selection Test, pp. 79–80

Building English Proficiency
- Literature Summaries
- Activities, p. 175

Reading, Writing & Grammar SkillBook
- Vocabulary, pp. 1–2
- Reading, pp. 69–70
- Grammar, Usage, and Mechanics, pp. 230–231

Technology
- Audiotape 4, Side B
- Personal Journal Software
- Custom Literature Database: Additional selections by Edgar Allan Poe can be found on the database.
- Test Generator Software

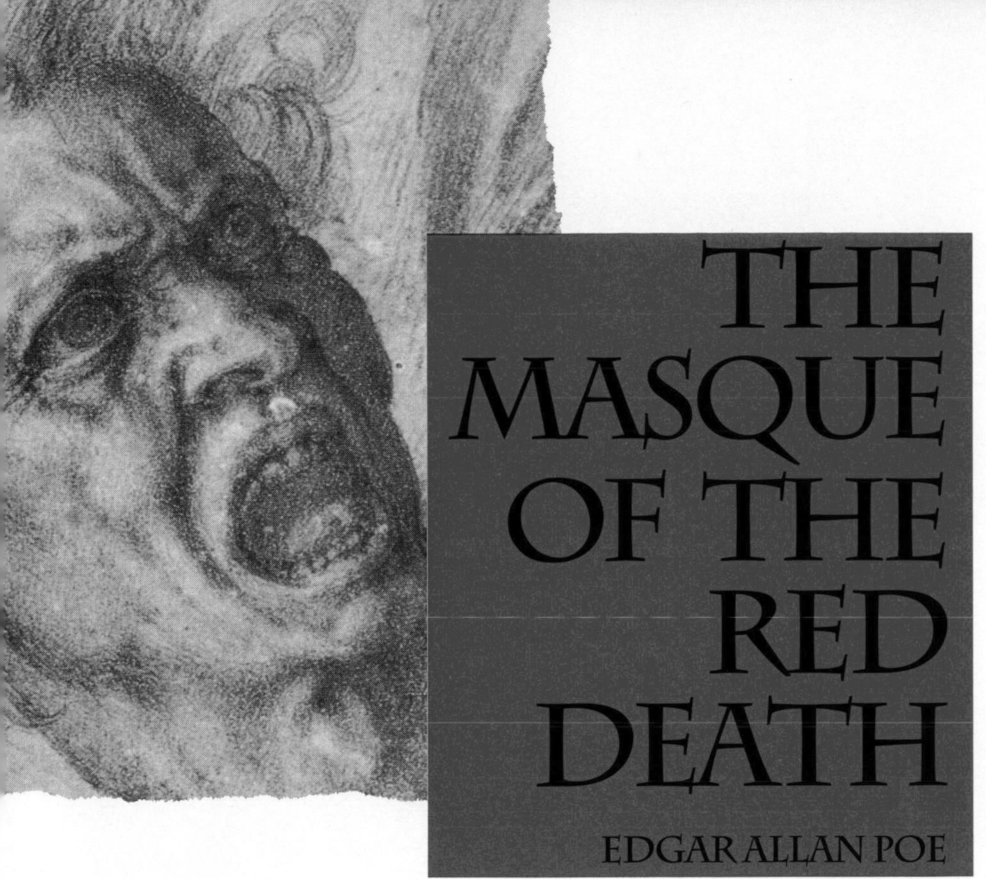

THE MASQUE OF THE RED DEATH

EDGAR ALLAN POE

The Red Death had long devastated the country. No pestilence had ever been so fatal, or so hideous. Blood was its Avatar[1] and its seal—the redness and the horror of blood. There were sharp pains, and sudden dizziness, and then profuse[2] bleeding at the pores, with dissolution. The scarlet stains upon the body and especially upon the face of the victim were the pest ban which shut him out from the aid and from the sympathy of his fellow men. And the whole seizure, progress, and termination of the disease were the incidents of half an hour.

But the Prince Prospero was happy and
1 dauntless and sagacious.[3] When his dominions
were half depopulated, he summoned to his presence a thousand hale and light-hearted friends from among the knights and dames of his court, and with these retired to the deep seclusion of one of his castellated[4] abbeys. This was an extensive and magnificent structure, the creation of the Prince's own eccentric yet august taste. A strong and lofty wall girdled it in. This wall had gates of iron. The courtiers, having entered, brought furnaces and massy hammers

1. **Avatar** (av′ə tär′), *n.* a sign or manifestation in bodily form; (in Hindu mythology) incarnation.
2. **profuse** (prə fyüs′), *adj.* very abundant.
3. **sagacious** (sə gā′shəs), *adj.* wise in a keen, practical way; shrewd.
4. **castellated** (kas′tl ā′tid), *adj.* built like a castle with turrets and battlements.

During Reading

Selection Objectives

- to explore the theme of trying to challenge fate
- to identify and explore the characteristics of mood
- to define words by examining context
- to differentiate between adjectives and adverbs

Unit 1 Resource Book
Graphic Organizer, p. 73
Study Guide, p. 74

Theme Link

Prince Prospero tries to improve his chances of surviving a plague, but the odds are against him.

Vocabulary Preview

profuse, very abundant
sagacious, wise in a keen, practical way; shrewd
castellated, built like a castle with turrets and battlements
voluptuous, giving pleasure to the senses
countenance, face
embellishment, decoration; adornment
piquancy, something stimulating to the mind
disapprobation, disapproval
blasphemous, speaking with abuse or contempt; profane
prostrate, lying flat with face downward

Students can add the words and definitions to their Writer's Notebooks.

SELECTION SUMMARY

The Masque of the Red Death

The Red Death—a horrible plague—has been devastating the country. Prince Prospero takes a thousand courtiers with him and retires to a walled abbey. In it he holds a magnificent masked ball in seven linked rooms, each of a different color. The seventh room is red and black and contains a gigantic clock that strikes at each hour. The Prince has also designed grotesque costumes for the revelers. As they dance, they avoid the ghastly seventh room and stop self-consciously each hour when the clock strikes. At midnight a stranger appears, dressed as the Red Death. The Prince runs at the stranger with a dagger, but falls to the floor, dead. Then the revelers attack the stranger, only to discover to their horror that it is the plague itself. They all die.

*For summaries in other languages, see the **Building English Proficiency** book.*

1 Literary Focus
Mood

Refer to the description of the mood shown on the web on page 94. Then ask students to describe the mood evoked by the description of Prince Prospero and his friends. *(Possible responses: light-hearted, healthy, powerful)*

Art Study

Responses to Caption Question
Possible responses: Tragedy can lead to a variety of reactions: hysteria, fear, depression, and denial. Life often presents joy and sorrow in the same moment.

Goya lived in Spain during a time of turmoil, experiencing the repressive Spanish monarchy and the brutal invasion of Spain by Napoleon's armies in 1808.

Despite his sympathy with liberal reform, he was much esteemed as a portrait painter in the royal court. One of his most famous works is *The Family of Charles IV,* which contrasts the beautifully painted costumes with the piercing revelation of the subjects' fatuity. His painting *The Third of May, 1808,* evokes the horror and cruelty of war in the stark image of Spaniards being shot by a French firing squad.

After the war Goya created a series of etchings based on proverbs and superstitions, *Los Proverbios* (1813–1818), which reveal a vision of subjectively experienced horror.

Question What contrasts of horror and festivity are shown in the painting? *(Possible responses: dancers with skeleton-like masks, others with doll-like happy masks; brutal masks, scenes of tender embraces)*

Like Poe's story, *The Burial of the Sardine* by Francisco Goya (1746–1826) mixes festive gaiety with gruesome horror. What effect do you think Poe and Goya intended by blending these opposing atmospheres? ➤

MINI-LESSON: VOCABULARY

Words in Context

Teach The context is the sentences or paragraphs in which a word appears. Students can often figure out the meaning of a new word by examining its context. Have students read this partial paragraph that refers to the abbey.

> A strong and lofty wall girdled it in. The wall had gates of iron. The courtiers, having entered, brought furnaces and massy hammers and welded the bolts. They resolved to leave means neither of ingress nor egress to the sudden impulses of despair or of frenzy from within. The abbey was amply provisioned. With such precautions the courtiers might bid defiance to contagion.

Activity Idea After reading the passage, students can work in pairs as they:

- choose words whose meanings are unclear *(Possible responses: girdled, massy, ingress, egress, provisioned, contagion)*
- try to determine the meaning of each word by examining its context
- check their ideas of the words' definitions in the dictionary

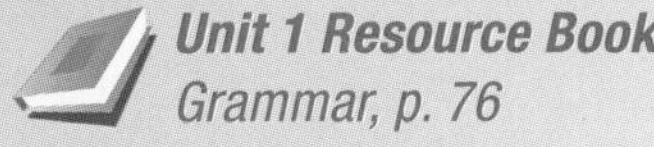

Unit 1 Resource Book
Grammar, p. 76

2 and welded the bolts. They resolved to leave means neither of ingress nor egress to the sudden impulses of despair or of frenzy from within. The abbey was amply provisioned. With such precautions the courtiers might bid defiance to contagion. The external world could take care of itself. In the meantime it was folly to grieve, or to think. The Prince had provided all the appliances of pleasure. There were buffoons, there were *improvisatori*,[5] there were ballet dancers, there were musicians, there was Beauty, there was wine. All these and security were within. Without was the Red Death. 3

It was toward the close of the fifth or sixth month of his seclusion, and while the pestilence raged most furiously abroad, that the Prince Prospero entertained his thousand friends at a masked ball of the most unusual magnificence.

It was a voluptuous[6] scene, that masquerade. But first let me tell of the rooms in which it was held. There were seven—an imperial suite. In many palaces, however, such suites form a long and straight vista, while the folding doors slide back nearly to the walls on either hand, so that the view of the whole extent is scarcely impeded. Here the case was very different, as might have been expected from the Prince's love of the bizarre. The apartments were so irregularly disposed that the vision embraced but little more than one at a time. There was a sharp turn at every twenty or thirty yards, and at each turn a novel effect. To the right and left, in the middle of each wall, a tall and narrow Gothic window looked out upon a closed corridor which pursued the windings of the suite. These windows were of stained glass whose color varied in accordance with the prevailing hue of the decorations of the chamber into which it opened. That at the eastern extremity was hung, for example, in blue—and vividly blue were its windows. The second chamber was purple in its ornaments and tapestries, and here the panes were purple. The third was green throughout, and so were the casements. The fourth was furnished and lighted with orange, the fifth with white, the sixth with violet. The seventh apartment was closely shrouded in black velvet tapestries that hung all over the ceiling and down the walls, falling in heavy folds upon a carpet of the same material and hue. But in this chamber only, the color of the windows failed to correspond with the decorations. The panes here were scarlet—a deep blood-color. Now in no one of the seven apartments was there any lamp or candelabrum, amid the profusion of golden ornaments that lay scattered to and fro or depended from the roof. There was no light of any kind emanating from lamp or candle within the suite of chambers. But in the corridors that followed the suite there stood, opposite to each window, a heavy tripod, bearing a brazier of fire, that projected its rays through the tinted glass and so glaringly illumined the room. And thus were produced a multitude of gaudy and fantastic appearances. But in the western or black chamber the effect of the firelight that streamed upon the dark hangings through the blood-tinted panes was ghastly in the extreme, and produced so wild a look upon the countenances[7] of those who entered that there were few of the company bold enough to set foot within its precincts at all.

CLARIFY: What do you know about the layout and lighting of these rooms? 4

It was in this apartment, also, that there stood against the western wall a gigantic clock of ebony. Its pendulum swung to and fro with a dull, heavy, monotonous clang; and when the

5. ***improvisatori*** (im′prō vē′zä tō′rē), *n. pl.* poets and singers of on-the-spot verses; performers who sing without rehearsal. [*Italian*]
6. **voluptuous** (və lup′chü əs), *adj.* giving pleasure to the senses.
7. countenance (koun′tə nəns), *n.* face.

2 Literary Element
Tone

Remind students that the tone is the author's attitude toward his subject. It should not be confused with mood.

Question What is the author's attitude toward Prince Prospero in this story? Look back at page 95 for clues. *(Poe is disdainful of the Prince, calling him "sagacious" while half his subjects have died; he mocks the Prince's taste and magnificence.)*

3 Reading/Thinking Skills
Generalize

Invite students to state contrasts they observed in the story. Then they should try to make a simple, general statement about the situation. Follow up with Poe's striking generalization in the first paragraph on page 97: "All these and security were within. Without was the Red Death."

4 Active Reading
Clarify

Response From east to west the seven rooms are blue, purple, green, orange, white, violet, and finally black and red. The rooms turn sharply every twenty or thirty yards. The only lighting comes from a brazier of fire outside each Gothic window. The light reflects against the stained glass that matches the color of the room.

BUILDING ENGLISH PROFICIENCY

ESL
LEP
ELD
SAE
LD

Drawing the Setting

Let groups of students choose one of their members to draw on the board the layout of the seven rooms in Prince Prospero's abbey. As they read and discuss details, the other members direct the "artist." Check the drawings to see if details such as the following are represented:

- a sharp turn every twenty or thirty yards
- tall, narrow Gothic windows of stained glass
- tripods with fires
- tapestries
- gigantic ebony clock
- order of the rooms' colors from east to west: blue, purple, green, orange, white, violet, black with scarlet windows

As students talk about their drawings, check for understanding of the following terms: *suites, prevailing hue, tapestries, candelabrum, apartments, tripod, brazier.*

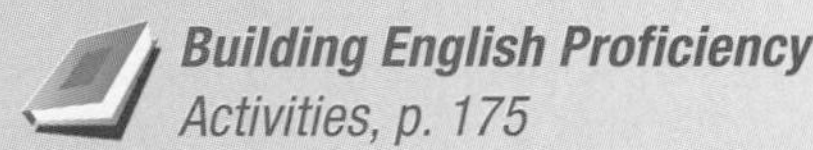

Building English Proficiency
Activities, p. 175

5 Literary Focus
Mood

Questions

- What sound does the giant ebony clock make, and what mood does it create when it chimes? *(Its sound is clear, loud, deep, and musical, but of a peculiar note. When it sounds each hour, it changes the party's mood from gaiety to fearfulness.)*
- Why do you think the clock's chimes cause people to turn pale? *(The chimes remind them that time is flying, and death will come.)*

6 Literary Element
Imagery

Discuss the lush imagery in the description of the masqueraders' costumes. Invite students to pick out words and phrases that they think are especially vivid. As students share their descriptions, ask others if they visualized the scene the same way.

7 Literary Element
Setting

Question How does the passage of time affect the westernmost room? *(Possible response: As the night passes, a deeper red light comes through the window. This combines with the black of the ceiling, walls, and floor to create an even eerier impression than it did earlier.)*

minute hand made the circuit of the face, and the hour was to be stricken, there came from the brazen lungs of the clock a sound which was clear and loud and deep and exceedingly musical, but of so peculiar a note and emphasis that, at each lapse of an hour, the musicians of the orchestra were constrained to pause, momentarily, in their performance, to hearken to the sound; and thus the waltzers perforce ceased their evolutions; and there was a brief disconcert of the whole gay company; and, while the chimes of the clock yet rang, it was observed that the giddiest grew pale, and the more aged and sedate passed their hands over their brows as if in confused revery or meditation. But when the echoes had fully ceased, a light laughter at once pervaded the assembly; the musicians looked at each other and smiled as if at their own nervousness and folly, and made whispering vows, each to the other, that the next chiming of the clock should produce in them no similar emotion; and then, after the lapse of sixty minutes (which embrace three thousand and six hundred seconds of the Time that flies) there came yet another chiming of the clock, and then were the same disconcert and tremulousness and meditation as before.

But, in spite of these things, it was a gay and magnificent revel. The tastes of the Prince were peculiar. He had a fine eye for colors and effects. He disregarded the *decora*[8] of mere fashion. His plans were bold and fiery, and his conceptions glowed with barbaric luster. There are some who would have thought him mad. His followers felt that he was not. It was necessary to hear and see and touch him to be *sure* that he was not.

He had directed, in great part, the movable embellishments[9] of the seven chambers, upon occasion of this great *fête;*[10] and it was his own guiding taste which had given character to the masqueraders. Be sure they were grotesque. There were much glare and glitter and piquancy[11] and phantasm—much of what has been since seen in *Hernani.*[12] There were arabesque figures with unsuited limbs and appointments. There were delirious fancies such as the madman fashions. There was much of the beautiful, much of the wanton, much of the bizarre, something of the terrible, and not a little of that which might have excited disgust. To and fro in the seven chambers there stalked, in fact, a multitude of dreams. And these—the dreams—writhed in and about, taking hue from the rooms, and causing the wild music of the orchestra to seem as the echo of their steps. And, anon, there strikes the ebony clock which stands in the hall of the velvet. And then, for a moment, all is still, and all is silent save the voice of the clock. The dreams are stiff frozen as they stand. But the echoes of the chime die away—they have endured but an instant—and a light, half-subdued laughter floats after them as they depart. And now again the music swells, and the dreams live, and writhe to and fro more merrily than ever, taking hue from the many tinted windows through which stream the rays from the tripods. But to the chamber which lies most westwardly of the seven, there are now none of the maskers who venture; for the night is waning away, and there flows a ruddier light through the blood-colored panes; and the blackness of the sable drapery appalls; and to him whose foot falls upon the sable carpet, there comes from the near clock of ebony a muffled peal more solemnly emphatic than any which reaches *their* ears who indulge in the more remote gaieties of the other apartments.

But these other apartments were densely crowded, and in them beat feverishly the heart

8. ***decora*** (dā kô′rā), *n.* plural of *decorum,* thing that is proper in behavior or tasteful in dress. *[Latin]*
9. **embellishment** (em bel′ish mənt), *n.* decoration; adornment.
10. ***fête*** (fet), *n.* feast or festival.
11. **piquancy** (pē′kən sē), *n.* something stimulating to the mind.
12. ***Hernani*** (er nä′nē), a romantic play by the French author Victor Hugo (1802–1885).

MINI-LESSON: GRAMMAR
Adjectives and Adverbs

Teach An adjective is a word that modifies a noun or pronoun by making its meaning more specific, as in "scarlet stains" or "profuse bleeding." *Scarlet* and *profuse* are adjectives modifying the nouns *stains* and *bleeding.*

An adverb is a word that modifies a verb, an adjective, or another adverb. In "the folding doors slide back nearly to the walls," *back* modifies the verb *slide* and *nearly* modifies the adverb *back.* In "there comes from the near clock of ebony a muffled peal more solemnly emphatic," *solemnly* modifies the adjective *emphatic* and *more* modifies the adverb *solemnly.*

Activity Idea Ask students to write four sentences with ample description from "Masque of the Red Death," and then:

- underline each adjective, and draw an arrow to the word or phrase it modifies
- circle each adverb, and draw an arrow to the word or phrase it modifies

If the sentences are missing one type of modifier, allow students to state that they found none. Then partners can check each other's work.

8 of life. And the revel went whirling on, until at length there commenced the sounding of midnight upon the clock. And then the music ceased, as I have told; and the evolutions of the waltzers were quieted; and there was an uneasy cessation of all things as before. But now there were twelve strokes to be sounded by the bell of the clock; and thus it happened, perhaps, that more of thought crept, with more of time, into the meditations of the thoughtful among those who reveled. And thus, too, it happened, perhaps, that before the last echoes of the last chime had utterly sunk into silence, there were many individuals in the crowd who had found leisure to become aware of the presence of a masked figure which had arrested the attention of no single individual before. And the rumor of this new presence having spread itself whisperingly around, there arose at length from the whole company a buzz, or murmur, expressive of disapprobation[13] and surprise—then, finally, of terror, of horror, and of disgust.

In an assembly of phantasms such as I have painted, it may well be supposed that no ordinary appearance could have excited such sensation. In truth the masquerade license of the night was nearly unlimited; but the figure in question had out-Heroded Herod,[14] and gone beyond the bounds of even the Prince's indefinite decorum. There are chords in the hearts of the most reckless which cannot be touched without emotion. Even with the utterly lost, to whom life and death are equally jests, there are matters of which no jest can be made. The whole company, indeed, seemed now deeply to feel that in the costume and bearing of the stranger neither wit nor propriety existed. The figure was tall and gaunt, and shrouded from head to foot in the habiliments of the grave. The mask which concealed the visage was made so nearly to resemble the countenance of a stiffened corpse that the closest scrutiny must have had difficulty in detecting the cheat. And yet all this might have been endured, if not approved, by the mad revelers around. But the mummer had gone so far as to assume the type of the Red Death. His vesture was dabbled in *blood*—and his broad brow, with all the features of the face, was besprinkled with the scarlet horror.

When the eyes of Prince Prospero fell upon this spectral image (which, with a slow and solemn movement, as if more fully to sustain its role, stalked to and fro among the waltzers) he was seen to be convulsed, in the first moment with a strong shudder either of terror or distaste; but, in the next, his brow reddened with rage.

"Who dares?" he demanded hoarsely of the courtiers who stood near him—"who dares insult us with this blasphemous[15] mockery? Seize him and unmask him—that we may know whom we have to hang at sunrise, from the battlements!"

CLARIFY: Why did the mummer's costume outrage Prince Prospero? 9

It was in the eastern or blue chamber in which stood the Prince Prospero as he uttered these words. They rang throughout the seven rooms loudly and clearly—for the Prince was a bold and robust man, and the music had become hushed at the waving of his hand.

It was in the blue room where stood the Prince, with a group of pale courtiers by his side. At first, as he spoke, there was a slight rushing movement of this group in the direction of the intruder, who at the moment was also near at hand, and now, with deliberate and stately 10

13. **disapprobation** (dis ap′prə bā′shən), *n.* disapproval.
14. **out-Heroded Herod** (her′əd), Herod was a tyrant depicted in medieval mystery plays. To "out-Herod" him would be to exceed him in outrageous extravagance.
15. **blasphemous** (blas′fəm əs), *adj.* speaking with abuse or contempt; profane.

8 Literary Element
Style

Have a volunteer read aloud the first paragraph on page 99 (beginning at the bottom of page 98). Point out to students how one sentence feeds into the next: from the whirling of the revelers, to the sounding of midnight, to the cessation of activity, to the company noticing the masked figure. The paragraph seems to move in a whirl like the dancers.

9 Active Reading
Clarify

Response The costume resembles a corpse that died of the Red Death. This is beyond even the Prince's "indefinite decorum." He is outraged that anyone would dare to dress like a plague victim, since he has gone to such extremes to keep out the Red Death.

10 Reading/Thinking Skills
Visualize

Encourage students to visualize the scene: the enraged Prince in the blue room and the silent masked figure slowly and solemnly walking—stalking—through the suite of rooms. Crowded in all but the last room are the wildly costumed revelers. Ask students what they think will happen. Will the courtiers seize and unmask the figure, as the Prince demands?

BUILDING ENGLISH PROFICIENCY

Exploring Gothic Horror

For students, the appearance of the masked figure may remind them of horror stories they have seen on TV or in movies. Help students explore the horror genre.

1. Have students locate and read aloud sentences that describe the masked figure. Ask them if they think that one quality of the figure is more frightening than another. For example, which is more frightening—the figure's height or its gauntness? Its costume or the dripping blood?

2. Have students name TV programs, movies, or other stories with a character similar to the one that Poe describes. Ask: How did these characters act? Was each more or less frightening than Poe's? Why or why not?

3. Encourage students to point out other similarities between Poe's vision of horror and more modern visions.

11 Reading/Thinking Skills
Understand Sequence

Involve students in tracking the sequence of the final events.

Question In what sequence do the events described in the next-to-last paragraph actually occur?

Response:

- The masked figure walks deliberately through the rooms and passes within a yard of the Prince. No one moves to stop him.
- The figure walks slowly to the black room; the Prince, ashamed of his own fear, dashes through the rooms with a drawn dagger.
- When he reaches the figure, the Prince drops the dagger and falls down dead.
- The others attack the masked figure, only to find it is an intangible thing.

Check Test

1. What happens to the victims of the Red Death? *(They have sharp pains, dizziness, bleeding—and are dead within half an hour.)*

2. When the country is "half depopulated" what does Prince Prospero do? *(He retires to an abbey with his courtiers to escape the Red Death.)*

3. Inside the abbey, what event does the Prince plan? *(a masked ball in a seven-room suite)*

4. What object is in the last room, and what does it do? *(a gigantic ebony clock; sounds the hours)*

5. Who is the masked figure that intrudes on the revelers? *(the Red Death)*

Unit 1 Resource Book
Alternate Check Test, p. 77

step, made closer approach to the speaker. But from a certain nameless awe with which the mad assumptions of the mummer had inspired the whole party, there were found none who put forth hand to seize him; so that, unimpeded, he passed within a yard of the Prince's person; and while the vast assembly, as if with one impulse, shrank from the centers of the rooms to the walls, he made his way uninterruptedly, but with the same solemn and measured step which had distinguished him from the first, through the blue chamber to the purple—through the purple to the green—through the green to the orange—through this again to the white—and even thence to the violet, ere a decided movement had been made to arrest him. It was then, however, that the Prince Prospero, maddening with rage and the shame of his own momentary cowardice, rushed hurriedly through the six chambers, while none followed him on account of a deadly terror that had seized upon all. He bore aloft a drawn dagger, and had approached, in rapid impetuosity, to within three or four feet of the retreating figure, when the latter, having attained the extremity of the velvet apartment, turned suddenly and confronted his pursuer. 11 There was a sharp cry—and the dagger dropped gleaming upon the sable carpet, upon which, instantly afterward, fell prostrate[16] in death the Prince Prospero. Then, summoning the wild courage of despair, a throng of the revelers at once threw themselves into the black apartment, and, seizing the mummer, whose tall figure stood erect and motionless within the shadow of the ebony clock, gasped in unutterable horror at finding the grave cerements and corpselike mask, which they handled with so violent a rudeness, untenanted by any tangible form.

> AND ONE BY ONE DROPPED THE REVELERS IN THE BLOOD-BEDEWED HALLS OF THEIR REVEL, AND DIED...

And now was acknowledged the presence of the Red Death. He had come like a thief in the night. And one by one dropped the revelers in the blood-bedewed halls of their revel, and died each in the despairing posture of his fall. And the life of the ebony clock went out with that of the last of the gay. And the flames of the tripods expired. And Darkness and Decay and the Red Death held illimitable dominion over all.

16. **prostrate** (pros′trāt), *adj.* lying flat with face downward.

MINI-LESSON: LITERARY FOCUS

Mood

Teach Remind students that the author can create the mood of the story through the setting, descriptive details, and word connotations.

Questions

- What people and things does Poe choose to describe? *(Possible responses: the cold-hearted Prince; the nature of the Red Death; the abbey)*
- How do these various elements help create the mood of horror in "The Masque of the Red Death"? *(Possible response: They make the reader feel like the victims—frightened and helpless.)*

Activity Idea Have students make a word web, like the one shown here or on page 94, for a mood such as horror, and use their ideas to write their own short story.

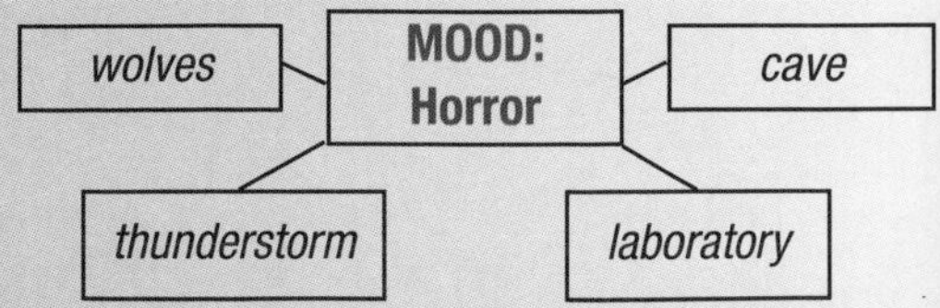

After Reading

Making Connections

Shaping Your Response

1. Stories by Poe frequently appear in high school literature anthologies. Judging from this story, can you see why? Explain.
2. What three words best describe your feelings at the end of this story? Write them in your notebook.
3. Do you think that Prince Prospero and his friends deserved their fate? Why or why not?

Analyzing the Story

4. What is **ironic** about the Prince's name? about the way he meets death?
5. What do you think the ebony clock **symbolizes**, or represents?
6. What would you say is the story's **conflict?**
7. Comment on Poe's use of color in this story. For example, do you think red and black were the best colors to assign to his final, fatal room?
8. Reread Poe's biography on page 94. How might his background have influenced his writing?

Extending the Ideas

9. Discuss "The Masque of the Red Death" as a moral fable about pursuing individual gratification over **group** welfare.

Literary Focus: Mood

Mood is the feeling an author conveys to the reader through the setting, imagery, details, and descriptions in a literary work.

- Find a passage that you think strongly conveys mood and read it aloud to the class.
- Then invite classmates to supply words that describe the mood of this passage.

After Reading

MAKING CONNECTIONS

1. Possible response: This is a classic example of a horror story; it's dramatic and has a thought-provoking message.

2. Possible responses: disgusted, frightened, validated, in awe of death.

3. Possible response: Yes, because they were indifferent to other victims, and they thought power and wealth could protect them.

4. His name connotes prosperity and being fortunate. He dies trying to kill the Red Death.

5. The clock symbolizes time passing, or the fact that death comes to everyone.

6. Possible responses: the Prince versus himself in that he denies that he can be killed by the Red Death; people against the forces of nature, which include death

7. In western cultures, red is the color of blood and black often represents death—colors suitable for the seventh room.

8. His difficult life may have influenced his writing. He lost his wife, and experienced despair and alcoholism.

9. Possible response: The revelers were paid in kind for trying to satisfy only themselves, and leaving the rest of the country to suffer.

LITERARY FOCUS: MOOD

- **Possible response** the paragraph that introduces the clock, starting at the bottom of page 97 through part of the first column of page 98
- **Possible responses** eerie, thought-provoking, nervousness, superficial gaiety, morbid

VOCABULARY STUDY

1. a
2. d
3. b
4. c
5. b

More Practice Describe a chilling scene, using the above vocabulary words as well as *profuse, voluptuous, piquancy, disapprobation,* and *blasphemous.*

Unit 1 Resource Book
Vocabulary, p. 75
Vocabulary Test, p. 78

WRITING CHOICES

Writer's Notebook Update

Students will choose the quotation they think best expresses the theme, and explain why.

'Twas a Very Bad Dream

Students might try to incorporate the emotions they have felt when they realized they were having a nightmare. Remind them to think of setting, characters, and action for their description.

Noteworthy

Let students work in groups to write a futuristic screenplay based on this story. Have them brainstorm:

- What will the setting be?
- Will the characters have dialogue?
- What kind of music should there be?

Selection Test

Unit 1 Resource Book
pp. 79–80

Vocabulary Study

Choose the letter of the word(s) that best completes or answers each item.

castellated
countenance
embellishment
prostrate
sagacious

1. If you were *prostrate*, you would be____.
   a. face down **b.** far away **c.** wealthy **d.** overweight
2. Which of the following is most likely to cover a *countenance*?
   a. a glove **b.** a shirt **c.** a tablecloth **d.** a mask
3. A *sagacious* person is ____.
   a. clumsy **b.** wise **c.** fearful **d.** cautious
4. Something without *embellishment* is ____.
   a. silent **b.** old fashioned **c.** plain **d.** rejected
5. Which of the following would most likely be *castellated*?
   a. an animal **b.** a building **c.** a dream **d.** flowers

Expressing Your Ideas

Writing Choices

Writer's Notebook Update Which of the quotations you wrote about in your notebook do you think best expresses the theme of "The Masque of the Red Death"? Write a description of how the quotation fits the story.

'Twas a Very Bad Dream Have you ever awakened with a jolt, only to realize you were having a nightmare? "The Masque of the Red Death" has a nightmarish quality in its bizarre setting, characters, and action. Describe a **nightmare** that is real or imaginary. Use clear images to portray bizarre elements.

Noteworthy Think about ideas for your own screenplay of "The Masque of the Red Death," designed for the 21st century. Jot down **director's notes** for items such as the following: contemporary setting; musical score; special effects; casting.

Other Options

Poe on Display The library will be displaying an exhibit as a special tribute to Edgar Allan Poe. You and a partner are commissioned to design a **brochure** advertising the exhibit. Research the author and his works—poems, detective stories, short stories—to learn more about his life and writing style. Use illustrations to make your brochure convey the mood created in Poe's stories.

Architectural Nightmare You are an architect commissioned to re-create a **floor plan** of the suite of rooms in which the masquerade took place. Reread the description of the seven rooms, noting the following questions: How are the rooms laid out? Where are the corridors located in relation to each room? How are windows arranged? Where is the only source of light? Where is the ebony clock? Now draw a detailed floor plan of the seven rooms, with a direction indicator and a color key.

OTHER OPTIONS

Poe on Display

Students will find in their research that Poe was a literary critic as well as a poet and fiction writer. His style was very important in both his poetry and prose. While their initial impression of him may be that of a horror story writer, students will realize that Poe was a meticulous technician.

Architectural Nightmare

After students have completed their floor plans, suggest that they build an architectural model of the suite of rooms.

Before Reading

The Rain Came

by Grace Ogot Kenya

Grace Ogot
born 1930

As a child growing up in Kenya, Grace Ogot listened to village storytellers recount native Luo folk tales and biblical stories. Years later, she recalled a story that made her cry as a child, and rewrote it as "The Rain Came." Ogot, whose works are distinguished by her Kenyan heritage, has said, "Stories of African traditional medicine and of the medicine man against the background of modern science and medicine fascinated me." Blending tradition with contemporary life, Ogot, whose bride price was twenty-five head of cattle, has worked in the Kenyan media and in politics, serving as a UN delegate and a member of parliament.

Building Background

Imagine This: The public address system in the classroom crackles with static as the principal's voice sounds: "May I have your attention please? In an effort to obtain more diverse grade distributions in this grading period, the students in each class must allot a D to three classmates and an F to two classmates—regardless of the grades earned by those students. All other students will retain the grades they have earned. Thank you, and have a nice day!"

Discuss as a class how you would choose the unlucky few to receive D's and F's. Now imagine that something more serious than grades were at stake. What if one person had to die to save an entire community? Keep this dilemma in mind as you read "The Rain Came."

Literary Focus

Setting The **setting** of a story is the time and place in which it occurs. "The Rain Came," which is based on an African folktale of the Luo tribe in Kenya, relies heavily on African traditions and surroundings. As you read this story, be aware of how the setting affects your understanding of the characters and events.

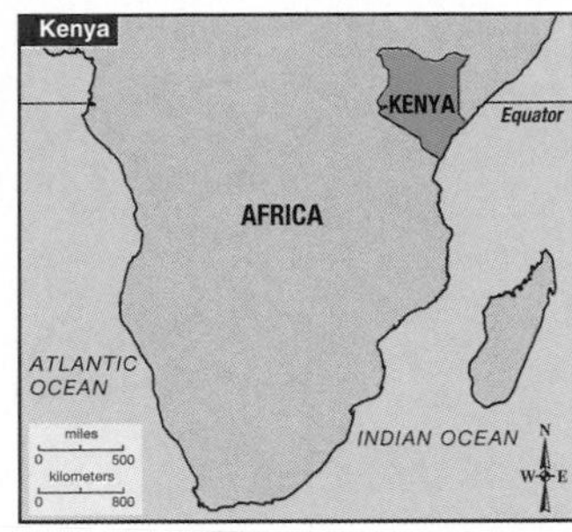

Writer's Notebook

Self-Sacrifice Throughout history people around the world have made sacrifices for the common good. Think about sacrifices that you would be willing to make on behalf of your family, friends, classmates, or community. Do you think that you have obligations to people you don't even know? Jot down your ideas on the subject.

Before Reading

Building Background

Allow students to discuss the concept of sacrifice. Begin by explaining that a sacrifice is an offering of an animal or human life, or of some material possession, to an object of worship or religious veneration. The purpose of sacrifice is to honor or appease the powerful presence.

Literary Focus

As they read, students should note details about the village and about the wilderness beyond the village. In this story the **setting** is integral, which means the events of the plot could not occur in the same way anywhere else.

Writer's Notebook

If students need further prompts, ask what obligations students feel to children of the future, to the environment, or to their heritage.

More About Grace Ogot

In addition to writing novels and short stories, Ogot has published books of Luo folklore in the Luo language. She uses her experience of both traditional life and the contemporary world in her fiction, as in this story. Other works include:

- *Land Without Thunder,* (1968)
- *The Other Woman,* (1976)

SUPPORT MATERIALS OVERVIEW

Unit 1 Resource Book
- Graphic Organizer, p. 81
- Study Guide, p. 82
- Vocabulary, p. 83
- Grammar, p. 84
- Alternate Check Test, p. 85
- Vocabulary Test, p. 86
- Selection Test, pp. 87–88

Building English Proficiency
- Literature Summaries
- Activities, p. 176

Reading, Writing & Grammar SkillBook
- Vocabulary, pp. 7–8
- Writing, pp. 103–104
- Grammar, Usage, and Mechanics, pp. 169–174, 179–185

The World of Work
- International Agency Worker, p. 3
- Make a Poster, p. 4

Technology
- Audiotape 5, Side A
- Personal Journal Software
- Custom Literature Database: For more tales and stories from Africa and other countries, see the database.
- Test Generator Software

During Reading

Selection Objectives

- to explore facing a challenge within society's traditions
- to identify and explore setting
- to practice using noun and pronoun forms effectively

Unit 1 Resource Book
Graphic Organizer, p. 81
Study Guide, p. 82

Theme Link

Labong'o, an African chief, knows that his village faces starvation because of drought. Though the odds are against him, he decides to sacrifice his only daughter to the lake monster so that rain will fall. His daughter beats all odds by escaping as the rain begins to fall.

Vocabulary Preview

consecrate, set apart as sacred; make holy

rebuke, express disapproval of

bereaved, deprived ruthlessly; robbed

rapt, so busy thinking of or enjoying one thing that you do not know what else is happening; distracted

calabash, a gourdlike fruit whose dried shell is used to make bottles, bowls, drums, pipes, and rattles

denizen, inhabitant or occupant of a place or region

saturated, soaked thoroughly

retaliation, paying back a wrong

Students can add the words and definitions to their Writer's Notebooks.

1 Literary Focus
Setting

Question What are some details about the setting? *(a village led by a chief, people live in huts and raise cattle, there is a drought)*

The Rain Came

Grace Ogot

The Chief was still far from the gate when his daughter Oganda saw him. She ran to meet him. Breathlessly she asked her father, "What is the news, great Chief? Everyone in the village is anxiously waiting to hear when it will rain." Labong'o held out his hands for his daughter but he did not say a word. Puzzled by her father's cold attitude Oganda ran back to the village to warn the others that the chief was back.

The atmosphere in the village was tense and confused. Everyone moved aimlessly and fussed in the yard without actually doing any work. A young woman whispered to her co-wife, "If they have not solved this rain business today, the chief will crack." They had watched him getting thinner and thinner as the people kept on pestering him. "Our cattle lie dying in the fields," they reported. "Soon it will be our children and then ourselves. Tell us what to do to save our lives, oh great Chief." So the chief had daily prayed with the Almighty through the ancestors to deliver them from their distress. **1**

Instead of calling the family together and giving them the news immediately, Labong'o went to his own hut, a sign that he was not to be disturbed. Having replaced the shutter, he sat in the dimly lit hut to contemplate.

SELECTION SUMMARY

The Rain Came

The Luo people face starvation because of a drought. Ndithi, the medicine man declares that, according to his vision, the ancestors will send rain if Chief Labong'o sacrifices his only daughter, Oganda, to the lake monster. Labong'o sorrowfully agrees, and Oganda learns that she will die. She is honored at a great feast where she searches for Osinda, whom she had hoped to marry, but he cannot be found. Then she sets off on the long path to the lake, knowing she must reach it by sunset. As she nears the lake, she begins to run into it, but Osinda suddenly appears and catches her. She faints. When she wakes, Osinda convinces her to escape with him along a differen path. He has made coats of twigs to protect them from the monster and the eyes of the ancestors. They flee and, just as the sun sets over the lake, rain falls in torrents.

For summaries in other languages, see the ***Building English Proficiency*** *book.*

2 It was no longer a question of being the chief of hunger-stricken people that weighed Labong'o's heart. It was the life of his only daughter that was at stake. At the time when Oganda came to meet him, he saw the glittering chain shining around her waist. The prophecy was complete. "It is Oganda, Oganda, my only daughter, who must die so young." Labong'o burst into tears before finishing the sentence. The chief must not weep. Society had declared him the bravest of men. But Labong'o did not care any more. He assumed the position of a simple father and wept bitterly. He loved his people, the Luo, but what were the Luo for him without Oganda? Her life had brought a new life in Labong'o's world and he ruled better than he could remember. How would the spirit of the village survive his beautiful daughter? "There are so many homes and so many parents who have daughters. Why choose this one? She is all I have." Labong'o spoke as if the ancestors were there in the hut and he could see them face to face. Perhaps they were there, warning him to remember his promise on the day he was enthroned when he said aloud, before the elders, "I will lay down my life, if necessary, and the life of my household, to save this tribe from the hands of the enemy." "Deny! Deny!" he could hear the voice of his forefathers mocking him.

3 When Labong'o was consecrated[1] chief he was only a young man. Unlike his father, he ruled for many years with only one wife. But people rebuked[2] him because his only wife did not bear him a daughter. He married a second, a third, and a fourth wife. But they all gave birth to male children. When Labong'o married a fifth wife she bore him a daughter. They called her Oganda, meaning "beans," because her skin was very fair. Out of Labong'o's twenty

1. **consecrate** (kon′sə krāt), *v.* set apart as sacred; make holy.
2. **rebuke** (ri byük′), *v.* express disapproval of.

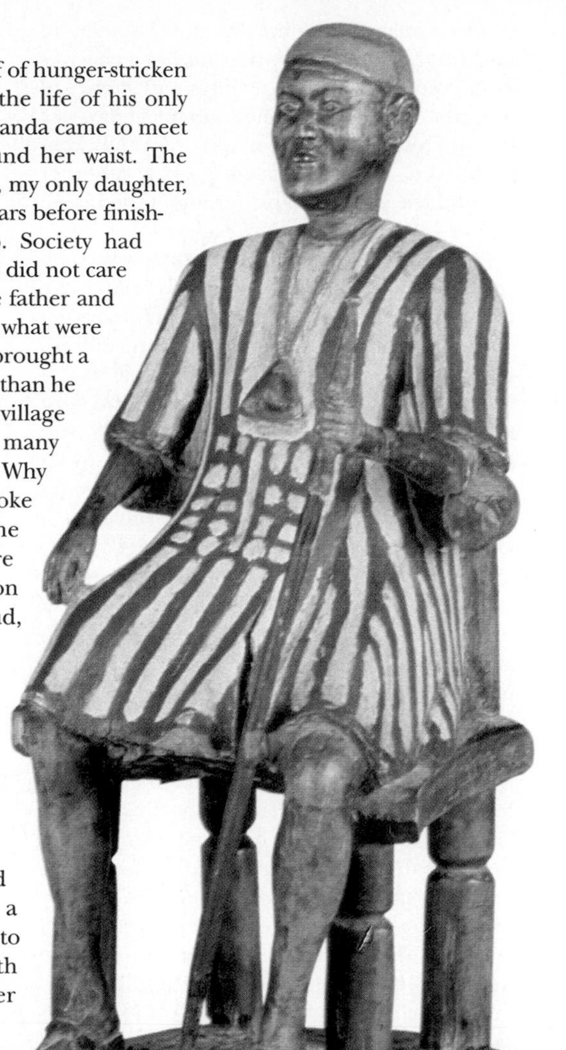

This painted wooden carving attributed to the Limba people of Sierra Leone presents a figure that appears both mythic and mortal. What character traits of Chief Labong'o does the carving reflect? ➤

2 Literary Element
Characterization

Question What conflicts does Labong'o face? *(conflicts between wanting his daughter alive and wanting his village to survive; between his personal desires and his promise to sacrifice everything for the good of the village)*

3 Reading/Thinking Skills
Recognize Values

Students may comment that the characters uphold traditions and customs that are very different from those in the United States. Some may seem shocking, such as the chief's having multiple wives and offering his daughter for sacrifice; others may seem enlightened, such as the close community spirit and the chief's efforts to father a female child.

Art Study

Responses to Caption Questions
Students may suggest that the sculpture shows Labong'o's traits of dignity, strength, and leadership.

Question Imagine that you are creating a sculpture that shows other traits of Labong'o. What would the sculpture look like? *(Possible responses: the chief with a child on his lap, showing his love for his daughter; or with his head in his hands, showing his self-doubt)*

BUILDING ENGLISH PROFICIENCY

ESL LEP ELD SAE LD

Analyzing Characters' Choices

Illustrate the characters' dilemmas by using a drawing.

- Write the word *choice* on the board and have students talk about ordinary choices they make, such as choices of foods and colors of clothing.
- Draw a simple outline of a man that represents the chief and write *Chief Labong'o's Choices* above it. Draw a vertical line through the figure. Point out that the characters in the story will have difficult choices.
- Have students talk about the conflicting choices the chief has *(to help his people survive, to sacrifice his daughter)* and put their responses on different sides of the chief's image.
- Use a similar drawing for Oganda at a later point in the story.

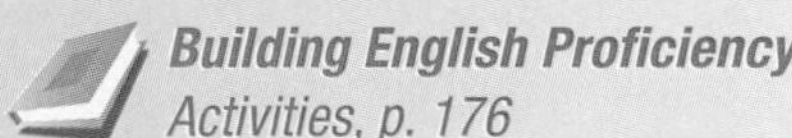

Building English Proficiency
Activities, p. 176

4 Multicultural Note
Religious Visions

According to the anthropologist Dr. Felicitas Goodman, the religious trance and its accompanying vision enable the participant to gain a different mode of perception. The medicine man, or *shaman*, uses the trance as a vehicle to reach an alternate reality. During the vision the participant sees the place and spirits that are expected within his or her culture. Thus, in "The Rain Came," Ndithi sees and hears the Luo ancestor, Podho, and sees the lake.

5 Reading/Thinking Skills
Compare and Contrast

Question What is the difference between the way Oganda's mother reacts to the word of the sacrifice and the way others in the household react? *(The mother is very sad; the others feel that Oganda is lucky to die to save her people; they are happy that rain may come.)*

6 Reading/Thinking Skills
Recognize Values

Elicit from students that in the Luo culture the needs of the group are more important than the needs of the individual. At this point you can ask students to contrast Western values about individuality with those of the Luo people.

children, Oganda was the only girl. Though she was the chief's favorite, her mother's co-wives swallowed their jealous feelings and showered her with love. After all, they said, Oganda was a female child whose days in the royal family were numbered. She would soon marry at a tender age and leave the enviable position to someone else.

Never in his life had he been faced with such an impossible decision. Refusing to yield to the rainmaker's request would mean sacrificing the whole tribe, putting the interests of the individual above those of the society. More than that. It would mean disobeying the ancestors, and most probably wiping the Luo people from the surface of the earth. On the other hand, to let Oganda die as a ransom for the people would permanently cripple Labong'o spiritually. He knew he would never be the same chief again.

4 The words of Ndithi, the medicine man, still echoed in his ears. "Podho, the ancestor of the Luo, appeared to me in a dream last night, and he asked me to speak to the chief and the people," Ndithi had said to the gathering of tribesmen. "A young woman who has not known a man must die so that the country may have rain. While Podho was still talking to me, I saw a young woman standing at the lakeside, her hands raised, above her head. Her skin was as fair as the skin of young deer in the wilderness. Her tall slender figure stood like a lonely reed at the river bank. Her sleepy eyes wore a sad look like that of a bereaved[3] mother. She wore a gold ring on her left ear, and a glittering brass chain around her waist. As I still marveled at the beauty of this young woman, Podho told me, 'Out of all the women in this land, we have chosen this one. Let her offer herself a sacrifice to the lake monster! And on that day, the rain will come down in torrents. Let everyone stay at home on that day, lest he be carried away by the floods.'"

Outside there was a strange stillness, except for the thirsty birds that sang lazily on the dying trees. The blinding mid-day heat had forced the people to retire to their huts. Not far away from the chief's hut, two guards were snoring away quietly. Labong'o removed his crown and the large eagle-head that hung loosely on his shoulders. He left the hut, and instead of asking Nyabog'o the messenger to beat the drum, he went straight and beat it himself. In no time the whole household had assembled under the siala tree where he usually addressed them. He told Oganda to wait a while in her grandmother's hut.

When Labong'o stood to address his household, his voice was hoarse and the tears choked him. He started to speak, but words refused to leave his lips. His wives and sons knew there was great danger. Perhaps their enemies had declared war on them. Labong'o's eyes were red, and they could see he had been weeping. At last he told them. "One whom we love and treasure must be taken away from us. Oganda is to die." Labong'o's voice was so faint, that he could not hear it himself. But he continued, "The ancestors have chosen her to be offered as a sacrifice to the lake monster in order that we may have rain."

They were completely stunned. As a confused murmur broke out, Oganda's mother fainted and was carried off to her own hut. But the other people rejoiced. They danced around singing and chanting. "Oganda is the lucky one to die for the people. If it is to save the people, let Oganda go." 5 6

In her grandmother's hut Oganda wondered what the whole family was discussing about her that she could not hear. Her grandmother's hut was well away from the chief's court and, much as she strained her ears, she could not hear what was said. "It must be marriage," she concluded. It was an accepted custom for the family to discuss their daughter's future marriage behind her back. A faint smile played on Oganda's lips as she thought of the

3. bereaved (bi rēvd′), *adj.* deprived ruthlessly; robbed.

MINI-LESSON: GRAMMAR
Noun and Pronoun Forms

Outside there was a strange stillness, except for the thirsty birds that sang lazily on the dying trees.

Teach Discuss with students that nouns and pronouns have a variety of forms. For example, in the lines above, *birds* and *trees* are concrete nouns, while *stillness* is an abstract noun.

He left the hut, and instead of asking Nyabog'o the messenger to beat the drum, he went straight and beat it himself.

In these lines, *He* and *it* are third-person singular pronouns. *Himself* is an intensive pronoun that adds emphasis to the pronoun *he.* Spend a few moments reviewing the identifying traits of each noun and pronoun form illustrated in the examples.

Activity Idea Students can:

- identify different forms of nouns and pronouns in the story
- identify to which character or characters each pronoun refers

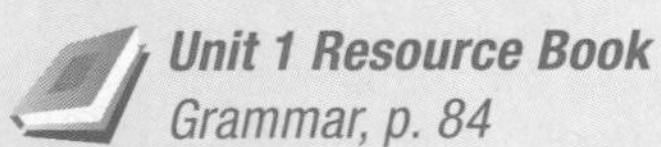
Unit 1 Resource Book
Grammar, p. 84

several young men who swallowed saliva at the mere mention of her name.

There was Kech, the son of a neighboring clan elder. Kech was very handsome. He had sweet, meek eyes and a roaring laughter. He would make a wonderful father, Oganda thought. But they would not be a good match. Kech was a bit too short to be her husband. It would humiliate her to have to look down at Kech each time she spoke to him. Then she thought of Dimo, the tall young man who had already distinguished himself as a brave warrior and an outstanding wrestler. Dimo adored Oganda, but Oganda thought he would make a cruel husband, always quarreling and ready to fight. No, she did not like him. Oganda fingered the glittering chain on her waist as she thought of Osinda. A long time ago when she was quite young Osinda had given her that chain, and instead of wearing it around her neck several times, she wore it round her waist where it could stay permanently. She heard her heart pounding so loudly as she thought of him. She whispered,
7 "Let it be you they are discussing, Osinda, the lovely one. Come now and take me away. . . ."

The lean figure in the doorway startled Oganda who was rapt[4] in thought about the man she loved. "You have frightened me, Grandma," said Oganda laughing. "Tell me, is it my marriage you were discussing? You can take it from me that I won't marry any of them." A smile played on her lips again. She was coaxing the old lady to tell her quickly, to tell her they were pleased with Osinda.

In the open space outside the excited relatives were dancing and singing. They were coming to the hut now, each carrying a gift to put at Oganda's feet. As their singing got nearer Oganda was able to hear what they were saying: "If it is to save the people, if it is to give us rain, let Oganda go. Let Oganda die for her people, and for her ancestors." Was she mad to think that they were singing about her? How could she die? She found the lean figure of her grandmother barring the door. She could not get out. The look on her grandmother's face warned her that there was danger around the corner. "Mother, it is not marriage then?" Oganda asked urgently. She suddenly felt panicky like a mouse cornered by a hungry cat. Forgetting that there was only one door in the hut Oganda fought desperately to find another exit. She must fight for her life. But there was none.

She closed her eyes, leapt like a wild tiger through the door, knocking her grandmother flat to the ground. There outside in mourning garments Labong'o stood motionless, his hands folded at the back. He held his daughter's hand and led her away from the excited crowd to the little red-painted hut where her mother was resting. Here he broke the news officially to his daughter.

For a long time the three souls who loved one another dearly sat in darkness. It was no good speaking. And even if they tried, the words could not have come out. In the past they had been like three cooking stones, sharing their burdens. Taking Oganda away from them would leave two useless stones which would not hold a cooking-pot. 8

News that the beautiful daughter of the chief was to be sacrificed to give the people rain spread across the country like wind. At sunset the chief's village was full of relatives and friends who had come to congratulate Oganda. Many more were on their way coming, carrying their gifts. They would dance till morning to keep her company. And in the morning they would prepare her a big farewell feast. All these relatives thought it a great honor to be selected by the spirits to die, in order that the society may live. "Oganda's name will always remain a living name among us," they boasted.

But was it maternal love that prevented

4. **rapt** (rapt), *adj.* so busy thinking of or enjoying one thing that one does not know what else is happening; distracted.

7 Literary Element
Irony

Dramatic irony refers to a situation in which the opposite of what is expected or hoped for happens to a character. These events are known in advance by other characters and by the reader.

Question What is ironic about Oganda's belief that the rest of the family is discussing her future marriage? *(They are actually discussing her death.)*

8 Literary Element
Imagery

Discuss the image of the three cooking stones—Oganda, her mother, and her father.

Questions

- How would the three stones be used? *(Possible response: They probably form a triangle around or in a campfire, and were used to hold a large pot.)*
- What happens when there are only two stones? *(The pot tips over.)*
- How is the setting necessary for this image to belong in the story? *(Cooking stones fit naturally in a setting of a traditional African village. The image would not make sense if the story took place in a different time or culture.)*

BUILDING ENGLISH PROFICIENCY

Exploring Figurative Language

Allow students to demonstrate and discuss the simile comparing "the three souls" to "three cooking stones, sharing their burdens" that describes the relationship between Oganda and her parents.

1. Bring in, or have students bring in, a cooking pot or pan and three stones that they think could be used as cooking stones.

2. Place the three rocks in various positions; balance the pot on each configuration.

3. Remove one rock and have students note what happens to the pot. (In most configurations, it tips over.)

4. Ask students to explain how the demonstration applies to Oganda and her parents. *(Possible response: All three people are needed to make a well-balanced family.)* Encourage them to use figurative language in their writing.

9 Literary Focus
Setting

Discuss the night setting. It is a cloudless sky, with a bright moon and stars. Again, the story's location in rural Africa is essential.

Questions

- How does the beauty of the night compare with the emotions of the celebrating people? *(They are rejoicing that rain will come; they are honoring Oganda. To these people, the night's beauty is appropriate.)*
- How does the night contrast with Oganda's emotions? *(The night is beautiful; she is miserable and misses Osinda.)*

10 Reading/Thinking Skills
Make Judgments

Allow students to speculate on the reasons for Osinda's absence. *(Possible reasons: He is acting cowardly; he is planning to save Oganda; he is working on a solution for the rain shortage.)*

Minya from rejoicing with the other women? Was it the memory of the agony and pain of childbirth that made her feel so sorrowful? Or was it the deep warmth and understanding that passes between a suckling babe and her mother that made Oganda part of her life, her flesh? Of course it was an honor, a great honor, for her daughter to be chosen to die for the country. But what could she gain once her only daughter was blown away by the wind? There were so many other women in the land, why choose her daughter, her only child! Had human life any meaning at all—other women had houses full of children while she, Minya, had to lose her only child!

Did her people really understand what it felt like to die young?

9 In the cloudless sky the moon shone brightly, and the numerous stars glittered with a bewitching beauty. The dancers of all age-groups assembled to dance before Oganda, who sat close to her mother, sobbing quietly. All these years she had been with her people she thought she understood them. But now she discovered that she was a stranger among them. If they loved her as they had always professed why were they not making any attempt to save her? Did her people really understand what it felt like to die young? Unable to restrain her emotions any longer, she sobbed loudly as her age-group got up to dance. They were young and beautiful and very soon they would marry and have their own children. They would have husbands to love and little huts for themselves. They would have reached maturity. Oganda touched the chain around her waist as she thought of Osinda. She wished Osinda were there too, among her friends. "Perhaps he is ill," she thought gravely. The chain comforted Oganda—she would die with it around her waist and wear it in the underground world.

In the morning a big feast was prepared for Oganda. The women prepared many different tasty dishes so that she could pick and choose. "People don't eat after death," they said. Delicious though the food looked, Oganda touched none of it. Let the happy people eat. She contented herself with sips of water from a little calabash.[5]

The time for her departure was drawing near, and each minute was precious. It was a day's journey to the lake. She was to walk all night, passing through the great forest. But nothing could touch her, not even the denizens[6] of the forest. She was already anointed with sacred oil. From the time Oganda received the sad news she had expected Osinda to appear any moment. But he was not there. A relative told her that Osinda was away on a private visit. Oganda realized that she would never see her beloved again. 10

In the afternoon the whole village stood at the gate to say goodbye and to see her for the last time. Her mother wept on her neck for a long time. The great chief in a mourning skin came to the gate barefooted, and mingled with the people—a simple father in grief. He took off his wrist bracelet and put it on his daughter's wrist saying, "You will always live among us. The spirit of our forefathers is with you."

Tongue-tied and unbelieving Oganda stood there before the people. She had nothing to say. She looked at her home once more. She could hear her heart beating so painfully within her. All her childhood plans were coming to an end. She felt like a flower nipped in the bud never to enjoy the morning

5. **calabash** (kal′ə bash), *n.* a gourdlike fruit whose dried shell is used to make bottles, bowls, drums, pipes, and rattles.
6. **denizen** (den′ə zən), *n.* inhabitant or occupant of a place or region.

MINI-LESSON: VOCABULARY
Using Reference Sources

Teach Explain that at times, students may need to use resources beyond a dictionary in order to learn more about a word. Read aloud the two sentences below, emphasizing the names of the plants.

In no time the whole household had assembled under the *siala tree* where he usually addressed them.

He then covered the whole of Oganda's body, except her eyes, with a leafy attire made from the twigs of *Bwombwe*.

There are names of plants in these two sentences—the *siala tree* and the *Bwombwe*. It is unlikely that students can find these words in a dictionary. They may need to look in reference books in a public library.

Activity Idea Students can:

- brainstorm where they might find information about these words (such as the encyclopedia or books on botany or Africa)
- visit the library to find plants native to their region
- incorporate these details in a story set in their locality

dew again. She looked at her weeping mother and whispered, "Whenever you want to see me, always look at the sunset. I will be there."

Oganda turned southwards to start her trek to the lake. Her parents, relatives, friends, and admirers stood at the gate and watched her go.

Her beautiful slender figure grew smaller and smaller till she mingled with the thin dry trees in the forest. As Oganda walked the lonely path that wound its way in the wilderness, she sang a song, and her own voice kept her company.

The ancestors have said Oganda must die.
The daughter of the chief must be sacrificed,
When the lake monster feeds on my flesh,
The people will have rain.
Yes, the rain will come down in torrents.
And the floods will wash away the sandy beaches
When the daughter of the chief dies in the lake.
My age-group has consented
My parents have consented
So have my friends and relatives.
Let Oganda die to give us rain.
My age-group are young and ripe,
Ripe for womanhood and motherhood.
But Oganda must die young,
Oganda must sleep with the ancestors.
Yes, rain will come down in torrents.

The red rays of the setting sun embraced Oganda, and she looked like a burning candle in the wilderness.

The people who came to hear her sad song were touched by her beauty. But they all said the same thing: "If it is to save the people, if it is to give us rain, then be not afraid. Your name will
11 forever live among us."

At midnight Oganda was tired and weary. She could walk no more. She sat under a big tree, and having sipped water from her calabash, she rested her head on the tree trunk and slept.

When Oganda woke up in the morning the sun was high in the sky. After walking for many
12 hours, she reached the *tong'*, a strip of land that separated the inhabited part of the country from the sacred place *(kar lamo)*. No layman could enter this place and come out alive— only those who had direct contact with the spirits and the Almighty were allowed to enter this holy of holies. But Oganda had to pass through this sacred land on her way to the lake, which she had to reach at sunset.

A large crowd gathered to see her for the last time. Her voice was now hoarse and painful, but there was no need to worry anymore. Soon she would not have to sing. The crowd looked at Oganda sympathetically, mumbling words she could not hear. But none of them pleaded for life. As Oganda opened the gate, a child, a young child, broke loose from the crowd, and ran towards her. The child took a small earring from her sweaty hands and gave it to Oganda saying, "When you reach the world of the dead, give this earring to my sister. She died last week. She forgot this ring." Oganda, taken aback by the strange request, took the little ring, and handed her precious water and food to the child. She did not need them now. Oganda did not know whether to laugh or cry. She had heard mourners sending their love to their sweethearts, long dead, but this idea of sending gifts was new to her.

Oganda held her breath as she crossed the barrier to enter the sacred land. She looked appealingly at the crowd, but there was no response. Their minds were too preoccupied with their own survival. Rain was the precious medicine they were longing for, and the sooner Oganda could get to her destination the better.

A strange feeling possessed Oganda as she picked her way in the sacred land. There were strange noises that often startled her, and her first reaction was to take to her heels. But she remembered that she had to fulfill the wish of her people. She was exhausted, but the path was still winding. Then suddenly the path ended on sandy land. The water had retreated miles away from the shore leaving a wide stretch of sand. Beyond this was the vast expanse of water.

Oganda felt afraid. She wanted to picture the

11 Reading/Thinking Skills
Generalize

Questions

- According to the villagers, what position in the society does Oganda now hold? *(She is the savior of her people; she will be remembered by the Luo forever.)*
- For herself, how does Oganda feel in relation to her people? *(Possible response: She feels cut off from the normal cycle of life.)*

12 Literary Focus
Setting

Invite students to draw the important places that make up the setting. Drawings should include the village, the wilderness outside of the village, the strip of land, the sacred place, and the lake.

Questions

- What route has Oganda taken so far? *(She has walked through the forest and come to the land that separates the inhabited land from the sacred place.)*
- Where does she go next? *(through the sacred place,* kar lamo, *and on to the lake)*
- How does the setting help to reveal Oganda's true beliefs? *(In this setting Oganda is free of the tribe's control. She can flee; instead, she decides to follow the traditional beliefs of her people, though it means her death.)*

BUILDING ENGLISH PROFICIENCY

Tracking Changes in Setting

Oganda leaves her village and travels southward to the place where she expects to die. Students can work in pairs as they draw maps that show Oganda's journey.

1. Prompt students to identify Oganda's starting point *(the village)* and her destination *(the lake).* As students read pages 108–111, have them talk about and jot down details that describe the land's geography, such as the forest, the strip of land that separates the village from the sacred land, and the sacred land.

2. When students finish their maps, call on volunteers to explain Oganda's travels.

3. Use the maps when you discuss the ending of the story.

Art Study

Responses to Caption Questions Students will recognize Mami Wata's human form and ordinary dress. Her mythic powers are shown by her power over the snake and her apparent strength. She is also shown as elevated and looking down on her surroundings.

Visual Literacy The principal function of art in traditional African society is to help influence the forces that affect people's lives. Unlike in Western societies, these forces are not viewed as being good or evil; instead, people may manipulate natural or supernatural powers through proper rituals to help themselves and their communities.

The World of Work

International Agency Worker

For the real-life experiences of an international agency worker, use—

The World of Work pp. 3–4

Like the carving on page 105, this Baule carving of the water spirit Mami Wata combines human and mythic elements. What details show Mami Wata's mythic traits? her humanity?

MINI-LESSON: LITERARY FOCUS

Setting

Teach In the integral setting of "The Rain Came," the events of the plot are dependent on the location. The setting is also integral to the characters, since the characters are influenced by the time and place in which they live.

While the village is not directly described, readers can infer its appearance through details mentioned in the story. For example, on page 104 we learn that the village has a gate and the chief has his own hut. Later it becomes clear that individuals or family members live in huts, that a household meets under a tree, and that there is open space enough to dance in.

The drought has a profound effect on the life of the village. The actions of all the people stem from this element of the setting.

Activity Idea Students can look in the story to find descriptions of the physical setting and how it affects the characters and events of the plot. Then have students:

- write a description of the village as they imagine it
- describe a modern setting; in it place a character who has a conflict of responsibilities

13 size and shape of the monster, but fear would not let her. The society did not talk about it, nor did the crying children who were silenced by the mention of its name. The sun was still up, but it was no longer hot. For a long time Oganda walked ankle-deep in the sand. She was exhausted and longed desperately for her calabash of water. As she moved on, she had a strange feeling that something was following her. Was it the monster? Her hair stood erect, and a cold paralyzing feeling ran along her spine. She looked behind, sideways and in front, but there was nothing except a cloud of dust.

Oganda pulled up and hurried but the feeling did not leave her, and her whole body became saturated[7] with perspiration.

The sun was going down fast and the lake shore seemed to move along with it.

Oganda started to run. She must be at the lake before sunset. As she ran she heard a noise coming from behind. She looked back sharply, and something resembling a moving bush was frantically running after her. It was about to catch up with her.

Oganda ran with all her strength. She was now determined to throw herself into the water even before sunset. She did not look back, but the creature was upon her. She made an effort to cry out, as in a nightmare, but she could not hear her own voice. The creature caught up with Oganda. In the utter confusion, as Oganda came face with the unidentified creature, a strong hand grabbed her. But she fell flat on the sand and fainted.

When the lake breeze brought her back to consciousness, a man was bending over her. "O . . .!" Oganda opened her mouth to speak, but she had lost her voice. She swallowed a mouthful of water poured into her mouth by the stranger.

"Osinda, Osinda! Please let me die. Let me run, the sun is going down. Let me die, let them have rain." Osinda fondled the glittering chain around Oganda's waist and wiped the tears from her face.

"We must escape quickly to the unknown land," Osinda said urgently. "We must run away from the wrath of the ancestors and the retaliation[8] of the monster."

"But the curse is upon me, Osinda, I am no good to you any more. And moreover the eyes of the ancestors will follow us everywhere and bad luck will befall us. Nor can we escape from the monster."

Oganda broke loose, afraid to escape, but Osinda grabbed her hands again.

"Listen to me, Oganda! Listen! Here are two coats!" He then covered the whole of Oganda's body, except her eyes, with a leafy attire made from the twigs of *Bwombwe.* "These will protect us from the eyes of the ancestors and the wrath of the monster. Now let us run out of here." He held Oganda's hand and they ran from the sacred land, avoiding the path that Oganda had followed.

The bush was thick, and the long grass entangled their feet as they ran. Halfway through the sacred land they stopped and looked back. The sun was almost touching the surface of the water. They were frightened. They continued to run, now faster, to avoid the sinking sun.

"Have faith, Oganda—that thing will not reach us."

When they reached the barrier and looked behind them trembling, only a tip of the sun could be seen above the water's surface.

"It is gone! It is gone!" Oganda wept, hiding her face in her hands.

"Weep not, daughter of the chief. Let us run, let us escape."

There was a bright lightning. They looked 14
up, frightened. Above them black furious clouds started to gather. They began to run. Then the thunder roared, and the rain came down in torrents.

7. **saturated** (sach′ə rā′tid), *adj.* soaked thoroughly.
8. **retaliation** (ri tal′ē ā′shən), *n.* paying back wrong.

13 Reader's Response
Making Personal Connections

Questions Do you remember any tales of a bogeyman that was supposed to frighten children into behaving? What did it look like, and what did it do? *(Allow students to share family, regional, or cultural tales of a bogeyman figure.)*

14 Literary Element
Theme

Question The author had several choices: to let Oganda live or die, and to let the rain fall or not. Why do you think the author had the rain come even though Oganda did not die? *(Possible responses: The author is saying that good intentions and bravery are enough to satisfy the ancestors; a person can be faithful to certain traditions without dying.)*

Check Test

1. What is the problem the Luo people face? *(a severe drought causing the cattle to die and threatening the people's survival)*

2. Who is Ndithi? *(the medicine man)*

3. Which young man does Oganda want to marry? *(Osinda)*

4. Why do the people have a feast? *(to honor Oganda)*

5. From what do the coats of twigs protect Osinda and Oganda? *(from the eyes of the ancestors and the wrath of the monster)*

Unit 1 Resource Book
Alternate Check Test, p. 85

BUILDING ENGLISH PROFICIENCY

Interpreting a Story's Ending

The final paragraph explains the story's title. However, it also may confuse students, because the relationship between the onset of the rains and the actions of Oganda and Osinda isn't clear.

Challenge students to offer their own interpretations of the tale's ending. Possible responses:

- Osinda and Oganda fooled the ancestors into thinking that she had thrown herself into the lake as a sacrifice.
- Since rain came without a sacrifice, the ancestors' power must be a myth.
- The ancestors decided to reward the courage of the young lovers by allowing Oganda to live and sending rain without a sacrifice.

After Reading

MAKING CONNECTIONS

1. Possible responses: yes, because I wanted Oganda to live; no, because I couldn't believe that rain would come without the sacrifice

2. Possible responses: accept the decision; flee; think of an alternative

3. Possible response: "I must do as the ancestors say, but I don't want to die!"

4. Possible response: because she will be remembered forever as the one who saved her people

5. Possible responses: She is accustomed to being the chief's favorite and to being loved by her friends and relatives. She loves her parents and is close to them. She follows her beliefs by agreeing to the sacrifice; later, she follows her own wishes and escapes.

6. Labong'o knows he is sworn to obey the ancestors, but he does not want to sacrifice his only daughter. He wants to save the people, yet he knows he will not rule as well when she is gone.

7. The chief tries to beat the odds that his people will starve by sacrificing his only daughter. His daughter beats all odds by escaping death and yet seeing that rain falls.

8. Possible responses: justified because she would have died, but Osinda, or fate, intervened; not justified because she should have followed her beliefs to the end

9. Possible responses: Christian stories of Jesus' crucifixion, evidence of the Celtic rituals of sacrifice, military personnel going on perilous missions

After Reading

Making Connections

Shaping Your Response

1. Were you satisfied with the ending of the story? Why or why not?
2. What would you do if you learned that you had been selected as the person your community would sacrifice during a crisis?
3. Draw a thought bubble and inside it write what you think are Oganda's feelings when she learns she is to be sacrificed.

Analyzing the Story

4. Why did the people think Oganda was lucky to be chosen?
5. Describe the **character** of Oganda, using details from the story.
6. What external and internal **conflict** does Labong'o undergo when he returns to the village at the beginning of the story?
7. How does this story reflect the **theme** "Trying to Beat the Odds"?

Extending the Ideas

8. Do you think that Oganda was justified in putting her personal interests above those of the **group**?
9. What other groups, cultures, and stories can you think of that include the tradition of sacrifice of one for the salvation of many?

Literary Focus: Setting

The **setting** is the time and place in which the action in a story occurs. The setting can also make the action and characters more believable.

- Given the setting and circumstances of the story, do you think Labong'o acted as a responsible father? Did Oganda act responsibly? Explain.
- Why is it important that this story is set in a tribal, agricultural society?

LITERARY FOCUS: SETTING

- Possible response: Labong'o acted as a responsible chief and father. As chief, he had sworn to lay down the life of his household if necessary. He was forced to sacrifice his daughter under the code by which he lived. Oganda acted responsibly when she went on her ritual journey. She may not have been responsible to her people when she ran away with Osinda, but the rain came nevertheless.
- In a tribal society the idea of community interest over the individual prevails, and an agricultural society depends on rain.

Vocabulary Study

Decide whether the italicized words are used correctly in the sentences below. Write *Correct* or *Incorrect*.

bereaved
calabash
denizen
rebuke
retaliation

1. Grace Ogot describes the reactions of a *bereaved* father who is expected to sacrifice his only daughter.
2. Any parent who loves his daughter as Labong'o does will *rebuke* her to show his affection.
3. All the co-wives of Labong'o live in the same *calabash*.
4. Each *denizen* of the village stands at the gate to say goodbye to Oganda.
5. Oganda fears the *retaliation* of the angry rain monster.

Expressing Your Ideas

Writing Choices

Writer's Notebook Update Glance at the notes you made before reading "The Rain Came." Compare your ideas on personal and social sacrifice to Oganda's. Write a paragraph that begins, "If I had been Oganda, I would have. . . ."

They Lived Happily Ever After Or did they? Extend the **ending** of the story to tell what happens to Oganda and Osinda after they escape the lake monster. You may want to describe the new setting where the couple lives.

Chant The sad song that Oganda sings as she walks the lonely path in the wilderness summarizes the story up to that point. With a partner, write new **lyrics** to describe the story events after she crosses the barrier to the sacred land. You might want to set your words to an existing melody or write your own music and perform your song for the class.

Other Options

Draw One for the Kids Rewrite and illustrate "The Rain Came" as a **picture book** for nursery school children. Pick out the main idea and details of the story. Sketch pictures to show each event. Summarize the text, writing no more than two simple sentences under each illustration. Work in a medium of your choice.

Raise Your Banner You are a member of the women's liberation movement in Kenya, marching in a parade to promote feminist literature. Do you think "The Rain Came" promotes feminism? Consider the following: Oganda's actions, her obedience to her father, her escape, her ideas of marriage, and her rescuer. Now make a **banner** either promoting this story or condemning it.

Marketing Gimmicks Imagine you work in the marketing department that is promoting the movie version of "The Rain Came." What products—games, drinking glasses, clothing, accessories, music—will you develop to promote the movie? Sketch out your ideas in a **portfolio** and present it to the class.

VOCABULARY STUDY

1. correct
2. incorrect
3. incorrect
4. correct
5. correct

MORE PRACTICE

Students can rewrite the sentences that had the incorrect words, replacing them with correct words.

Unit 1 Resource Book
Vocabulary, p. 83
Vocabulary Test, p. 86

WRITING CHOICES

They Lived Happily Ever After

Remind students that the couple "ran from the sacred land, avoiding the path that Oganda had followed." Students can think about the new path Oganda might follow—a path to new beliefs or to a combination of old and new beliefs and ways of life. Students may also want to address whether the couple suffered for angering the ancestors and the lake monster, and whether they found some way of obtaining forgiveness.

Chant

Play recordings of music from Kenya in order to give students an idea of how the tune might sound. Encourage students to try to find laments or journey songs to listen to.

OTHER OPTIONS

Draw One for the Kids

Students may want to use markers, crayons, or colored chalk to make the illustrations appealing to younger children.

Raise Your Banner

Students may want to consider that the story may reveal aspects of society that are harmful to women, in which case it may be considered a feminist statement.

Marketing Gimmicks

Students may suggest a calabash, gold chains, or coats made of twig.

Selection Test

Unit 1 Resource Book
pp. 87–88

Transparency Collection
Fine Art Writing Prompt 2

Interdisciplinary Study

Theme Link

People are often trying to beat the odds. They take risks and hope to be lucky. However, when people rig the odds instead of just trying to beat them, they cross the line into cheating.

Curricular Connection: Media

You can use the information in this interdisciplinary study to explore with students the ways television and other modern media have influenced people's views about what is just a coincidence or what is dishonest.

Terms to Know

random, occurring without definite reason or pattern

rigged, arranged in a dishonest way

scandal, someone or something that shocks people and causes shame and disgrace

fixing, getting the result wanted by trickery

Unit 1 Resource Book
Study Guide, p. 89

Trying to Beat the Odds

Random, Rigged, or Rational?

Media Connection

You might attribute the odd twists and outcomes of stories in this group to fortune, luck, or strange coincidence. This Interdisciplinary Study explores the sometimes fine line between things that are random, rigged, or rational.

On Display

The Quiz Show That Was Rigged

Is it cheating or is it just good fun when a television game show is rigged? That was one of the questions raised by the quiz show scandal of 1959 and the movie, *Quiz Show,* released in 1994.

Quiz shows were popular during the 1950s. Audiences like the family pictured on page 115 loved cheering their favorite contestants, shouting answers at the television set, and being amazed at what people knew. Charles Van Doren, who became reigning champion of the weekly quiz show, *Twenty-One,* was adopted as a hero by the American public. He was smart, handsome, and polite, and he came from a literary family. When Van Doren admitted to cheating on the show, many people felt betrayed. The fact that the producers had asked him to cheat only made the scandal worse.

Some people, especially the game show producers, claimed that rigging the game shows made them more exciting. Van Doren, who won more than $100,000.00, always claimed that he wanted only to promote knowledge and make learning popular. Others, however, were quick to point out that the audience expected—and identified with—real people solving real problems. They were cheated out of the real-life experience they expected. In short, they were handed a lie.

Would the game shows really have lacked drama and popular appeal if producers hadn't rigged them? No one knows for sure. We do know, however, that by "fixing" the games, the producers lost the trust and respect of their audience.

Ralph Fiennes plays a conflicted Charles Van Doren in the 1994 movie, Quiz Show.

MINI-LESSON: STUDY SKILLS

Finding Information

Teach Students may want to do research to develop the questions for their quiz show (see Interdisciplinary Activity Ideas, sidebar page 115). Each group will need to chose its broad subject first, such as history or music. Then the students may want to narrow the range, such as focusing on American history or popular music since 1990. To find the information, students may need several reference books from the library, though students may have their own books and other resources that they can use.

Activity Idea Students in each group can go to the library together. They can begin their research broadly and narrow their subject matter as they learn more.

- Students can read reference books, such as the encyclopedia or other books in the reference section.
- Students can look up their subject in the library's catalog, which may be a card catalog, bound volumes in alphabetical order, or on computer files.
- Students can ask the librarian for assistance in finding the different materials available.

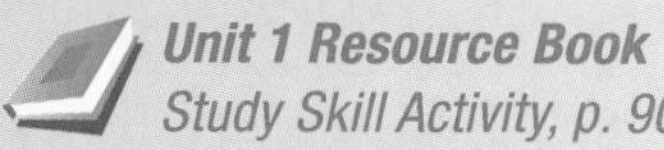

Unit 1 Resource Book
Study Skill Activity, p. 90

With his rise to fame as a human encyclopedia, Charles Van Doren became an American culture hero.

Responding

1. Do you think modern viewers would rather know the truth or merely be entertained? Explain.

2. Explain whether you think people should regard docudramas or reenactments on TV as fact or fiction.

Visual Literacy Encourage a class discussion on how the photography on these pages adds to the realism of the situation. On page 114, the picture is a still photograph from the movie about the quiz show scandal. The top picture on page 115 is a staged photograph of a family watching the real quiz show, "Twenty-One." The picture below is a still of the real Charles Van Doren on the television show.

Responding

1. Possible response Students may say that modern viewers would rather know the truth than "just" be entertained. Most people watch the news on television in order to keep informed. They probably watch shows or movies for entertainment.

2. Possible response Students may say that, while docudramas and reenactments can be interesting, they are not to be taken as the absolute truth.

Interdisciplinary Activity Idea

Students can work together to create a quiz show of their own. Have them work in groups to develop questions. Each group can choose a subject, such as history, music, or science, and make up questions pertaining to that subject. An announcer can ask two contestants the questions. The person who gets the most correct answers wins.

BUILDING ENGLISH PROFICIENCY

Exploring Key Concepts

The story of the quiz show scandal of 1959 evokes abstract ideas—greed, trust, and honesty. Invite students to consider these ideas in greater detail.

1. Discuss how students might feel if they found out that a game show or sporting event they like was rigged. Ask: How might this affect you, even if you didn't make or lose money as a result?

2. Ask students if they think that the rigging of quiz shows is cheating, and if so, how. Alternatively, have students record privately in their dialogue journals (in English or another first language) their feelings about cheating.

Interdisciplinary Study

Theme Link

Like the characters in the previous stories, people are exposed to issues of probability and statistics every day, often without being aware of them.

Curricular Connection: Math

You can use the information in this interdisciplinary study to explore with students the different uses of odds and statistics.

Terms to Know

statistics, the science of collecting and arranging number facts on a subject

phenomenally, unusually; remarkably

Solomon, a tenth century B.C. king of Israel, noted for his wisdom

countenance, the face

Azrael (az′rē əl), in Jewish and Islamic angelology, the angel who separates the soul from the body at death

boon, favor; request; benefit

infinitesimal, too small to be measured

INTERDISCIPLINARY STUDY

Math Connection

Try your luck answering these questions based on odds and statistics. Odds are that some of your guesses will be correct.

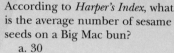

Playing the

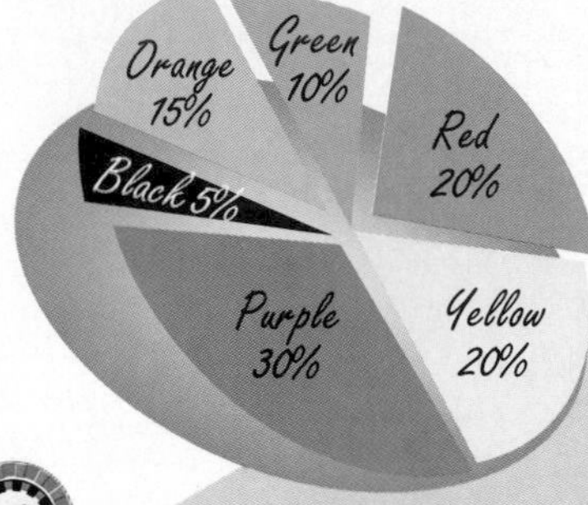

Use this pie chart to determine approximately how many purple spice drops you could expect to get in a handful of fifty.

a. 5
b. 10
c. 15

2

In being dealt five cards from a shuffled deck of 52 cards, what are your chances of getting two pair?

a. 1 in 21
b. 1 in 35
c. 1 in 50

3

According to *Harper's Index,* what is the average number of sesame seeds on a Big Mac bun?

a. 30
b. 60
c. 178

If you double a penny each day, how much will you get on the 30th day?

a. \$63,591.04
b. \$126,875.32
c. \$5,368,709.12

MINI-LESSON: VISUAL LITERACY

Bar Graphs and Probability

Teach Students can learn more about probability by trying an experiment and graphing it as a histogram. A histogram is a bar graph that shows the frequencies of events. For example, you can record the frequency of heads landing and the frequency of tails landing on a graph like the one below.

frequency: 6 – 4 – 2 –

heads tails

The more times you toss the coin, the more likely the landings will be equally heads and tails.

Activity Idea Students can work in groups to experiment with probability and make histograms.

- Roll one die ten times.
- Make a bar graph showing how many times each number on the die landed facing up.
- Now roll forty more times and graph the results. Are the numbers of heads and tails becoming more equal?

Numbers

Former Shenandoah Park Ranger Roy C. Sullivan had phenomenally bad luck with lightning. Guess how many times he was hit over a 24-year period.

a. 3
b. 7
c. 21

Are the odds of having a summer day with at least 0.01 inch of rain greater in Juneau, Alaska, or in Los Angeles, California?

A man named Marty Timmons had a lucky ticket that won two prizes in the New Jersey lottery: first $10,000 and then, an hour later, a million. What are the odds of anyone hitting both the jackpot and a consolation prize with one ticket in such a state lottery?

a. 334 million to 1
b. 334 billion to 1
c. 334 trillion to 1

Although the odds are unlikely, one assassinated U.S. President had a grandfather of the same name who also was assassinated. (The two also had sons with the same name and wives with the same name.) Who was he?

a. John F. Kennedy
b. Abraham Lincoln
c. James Garfield

You have tossed a coin 10 times and it has landed on heads every time. What are your chances of getting tails on the eleventh try?

a. 1 in 2
b. 1 in 10
c. 1 in 27

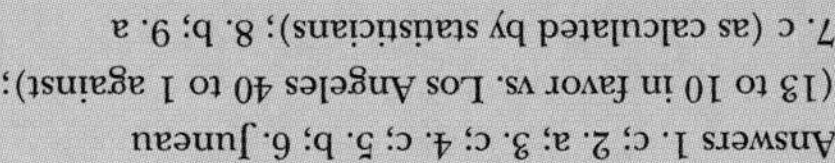

Answers 1. c; 2. a; 3. c; 4. c; 5. b; 6. Juneau (13 to 10 in favor vs. Los Angeles 40 to 1 against); 7. c (as calculated by statisticians); 8. b; 9. a

Research Topics

- Other graphs and charts that show statistics
- Statistics on school activities, such as what percentage of the students in your school play at least one sport
- Statistics on your community, such as what percentage of the land is used as public space or parks
- Means of testing the probability of a simple action, such as how many students will raise their left hand and how many will raise their right hand in response to a question

Interdisciplinary Activity Ideas

- Students can do an experiment with a deck of cards to see how many times they actually get two pair. Students should compare their findings with the actual answer.
- After students have answered questions 1–9 and determined how many they got right, have the class create a graph or chart that shows the number of correct answers for each question. Students should note that the writer of the article bet that everyone in the class would get more than one correct answer. Have students use the chart to determine if the writer was correct.

BUILDING ENGLISH PROFICIENCY

The problems on these pages are based on probability. You may wish to preface this feature by offering the following activity.

1. Have students take part in a drawing.

2. Give out numbered tickets and draw from a container with the same numbered tickets. Repeat the process several times and have students make observations about the results. To make the drawing even more interesting, you might offer several expensive prizes to the students whose numbers match the ones drawn.

3. Help students draw conclusions about the probability of their number being chosen.

If possible, work with a mathematics teacher to team-teach this activity.

Additional Background

Rumi (Jalal al-Din al-Rumi) was a Persian mystic and poet who lived from 1207 to 1273. The *Mathnavi*, his second collection of poetical works, is a long poem consisting of fables and anecdotes that describe the soul's quest for union with God.

Plutarch was a famous Greek biographer who lived from A.D. 46–120.

Responding

1. Possible response Students may say that the man's bomb wouldn't change anything because he would not set off his bomb. The probability of a bomb being on his plane remains the same.

2. Possible response Both the horse and the astrologer are not the source of the answers but are able to reflect the clients' own knowledge.

Hedging Your Bets

"It is no great wonder if, in the long process of time, while fortune takes her course hither and thither, numerous coincidences should spontaneously occur."

—*Plutarch*

One forenoon a freeborn nobleman arrived and ran into Solomon's hall of justice, his countenance pale with anguish and both lips blue. Then Solomon said, "Good sir, what is the matter?"

He replied, "Azrael [the Angel of Death] cast on me such a look, so full of wrath and hate."

"Come," said the king, "what boon do you desire now? Ask!"

"O protector of my life," said he, "command the wind to bear me from here to India. Maybe, when thy slave is come thither he will save his life."

Solomon commanded the wind to bear him quickly over the water to the uttermost part of India. Next day, at the time of conference and meeting, Solomon said to Azrael: "Didst thou look with anger on that Moslem in order that he might wander as an exile far from his home?"

Azrael said, "When did I look on him angrily? I saw him as I passed by, and looked at him in astonishment, for God had commanded me, saying, 'Hark, today do thou take his spirit in India.' From wonder I said to myself, 'Even if he has a hundred wings, 'tis a far journey for him to be in India today.'"

—*The Man Who Fled from Azrael*
Rumi from ***the Mathnavi***

A man who travels a lot was concerned about the possibility of a bomb on board his plane. He determined the probability of this, found it to be low but not low enough for him, so now he always travels with a bomb in his suitcase. He reasons that the probability of two bombs being on board would be infinitessimal.

—from *Innumeracy* by *John Allen Paulos*

During individual sessions astrologers pick up on clues about clients' personalities from their facial expressions, mannerisms, body language, etc. Consider the famous case of Clever Hans, the horse who seemed to be able to count. His trainer would roll a die and ask him what number appeared on the die's face. Hans would slowly paw the ground the appropriate number of times and then stop, much to the amazement of onlookers. What was not so noticeable, however, was that the trainer stood stone-still until the horse pawed the correct number of times, and then, consciously or not, stirred slightly, which caused Hans to stop. The horse was not the source of the answers but merely a reflection of the trainer's knowledge of the answer. People often unwittingly play the role of trainer to astrologers who, like Hans, reflect their clients' needs.

—from *Innumeracy* by *John Allen Paulos*

Responding

1. What is the fallacy of the reasoning of the man with the bomb?

2. Relate the story of Clever Hans to the astrologer in "An Astrologer's Day." How do both the astrologer and the horse "reflect their clients' needs"?

MINI-LESSON: SPEAKING & LISTENING

Reading Aloud

Teach Many students may benefit from listening to the anecdotes and sayings as they are read aloud by their classmates. Before assigning passages from page 118 to students to read, first allow them to practice reading aloud a passage of their own choosing.

Activity Idea Have students select a favorite passage to read aloud.

- Encourage students to practice at home.
- Students should read expressively those parts that they find most interesting and want to emphasize.
- After students read their favorite passages aloud in class, allow volunteers to practice with the excerpts from page 118 before presenting them to the class.

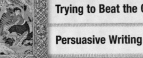

Writing Workshop

Selling an Idea

Assignment Imagine that a producer of a TV suspense series called *Beating the Odds* has asked you to submit a proposal for a show. Working in teams of three to five, create a proposal for a half-hour TV show based on one of the stories you read in this part of the unit.

WRITER'S BLUEPRINT

Product	A group proposal for a TV show
Purpose	To sell an idea
Audience	A TV producer
Specs	As the creators of an effective proposal, your group should:

- ❑ Agree on a story from this part as the basis for your proposal. Make a cover page naming the story and its author and listing team members.
- ❑ Describe the main characters and settings and summarize the plot. Suggest who ought to play each part and why. Explain how the settings and plot will be suspenseful. Use a no-nonsense, businesslike tone throughout.
- ❑ Present one crucial scene from the plot in script or storyboard form.
- ❑ Close by urging the producer to accept your proposal.
- ❑ Follow the rules of grammar, usage, spelling, and mechanics, including using commas correctly.

Writing Workshop

WRITER'S BLUEPRINT

Specs

The Specs in the Writer's Blueprint address these writing and thinking skills:

- describing
- summarizing
- using appropriate tone
- narrating
- persuading
- using commas correctly

These Specs serve as your lesson objectives, and they form the basis for the **Assessment Criteria Specs** for a superior paper, which appear on the final TE page for this lesson. You might want to read them with students when you begin the lesson.

Linking Literature to Writing

As you go over the blueprint, review with students how the setting and character descriptions enhance the mood of suspense in the literature selections. Discuss the moods of the selections. Have students create a web diagram to connect the various elements of mood to the different selections. Students can use the information in their webs during prewriting.

WRITING WORKSHOP OVERVIEW

Product
Persuasive writing: A group proposal for a TV show

Prewriting
Brainstorm ideas—Describe the main characters—Set the stage—Chart the plot-Choose a crucial scene—Brainstorm reasons—Plan the proposal—Do a live presentation
Unit 1 Resource Book
Prewriting Worksheets, pp. 91-92

Drafting
Before you draft—As you draft
Transparency Collection
Student Models for Writing Workshop 3, 4

Revising
Ask another group—Strategy: Creating a Businesslike Tone
Unit 1 Resource Book
Revising Worksheet, p. 93

Editing
Ask another group—Strategy: Using Commas Correctly
Unit 1 Resource Book
Grammar Worksheet, p. 94
Grammar Check Test, p. 95

Presenting
Scripted Scene
Radio Play

Looking Back
Self-evaluate—Reflect—For Your Working Portfolio
Unit 1 Resource Book
Assessment Worksheet, p. 96
Transparency Collection
Fine Art Writing Prompt 2

STEP 1 PREWRITING

Brainstorm Ideas

Use the activities in "Linking Literature to Writing" to begin the literature review. Have students continue in small groups, adding to their web diagrams and writing additional notes about each story. As a group, they will choose one story to use for their TV show proposal.

Describe the Main Characters

Have students work in groups to discuss the characters in the story they chose. Encourage them to look back in the literature and talk about what they remember about individual characters and how they pictured the characters as they read the selection. For additional support, see the worksheet referenced below.

Unit 1 Resource Book
Prewriting Worksheet, p. 91

Set the Stage

Talk briefly about what elements create a mood of suspense and why the mood is important to the setting. Have students make suggestions for elements that they can include in their setting to enhance the mood. Drawings or models of the setting will help students visualize and communicate their ideas. For additional support, see the worksheet referenced below.

Unit 1 Resource Book
Prewriting Worksheet, p. 92

Chart the Plot

Discuss why the climax is crucial to a story. Ask a question such as: *At what point in the story did you decide you had to finish reading it because you had to find out what happened?*

Brainstorm ideas. In your group, review the stories from this part. Jot down ideas about how you might adapt each story into a half-hour TV suspense show. Discuss which one would make the best TV show and make your choice.

Describe the main characters for your proposed show. Work with your group and use a chart like the one that follows to organize your ideas.

Main Characters	Actors to Play Them	Appearance	Personality	Motivations (wishes, dreams, needs)	Goals
Prince Prospero in "The Masque of the Red Death"	Sean Connery	"Had a fine eye for colors and effects . . . there were some who would have thought him mad."	—ignorantly, stubbornly fearless —knowing —eccentric	—to ward off death —to be happy —to indulge himself	escaping the Red Death

OR . . .
Make drawings or build a model of the settings. Consider backgrounds, furniture, colors, and light.

Set the stage. The setting—landscape, weather, light, architecture, furnishings, colors—should reflect the mood of the story. With your group, look back at the story and describe the suspenseful settings for your show.

Chart the plot. Fill in this chart of plot elements for your TV show by answering the questions.

Conflict	Key Scenes	Climax	Resolution
What problems do the characters face?	What events or complications move the plot along?	What is the most exciting part of the story?	How does the climax tie together the loose ends of the story?

MINI-LESSON: PREWRITING

Defining Suspense

Help students become aware of what creates suspense in a visual/auditory medium. Videotape a suspenseful television show for replay in the classroom. When replaying for critical viewing, use fast-forward, rewind, and pause controls to underscore elements of successful suspense, such as foreshadowing, music, and actors' actions and words. Pause to have students verbalize what it is they are seeing and hearing that creates suspense.

Choose a crucial scene, perhaps the climax. Sketch key moments from this scene on pieces of paper or poster board. On the back of each sketch make notes about the suspenseful settings and action and some lines of dialogue you might want to use.

Brainstorm reasons for accepting your proposal. Look back at your notes on character, setting, and plot. How are they suspenseful? Why will a TV audience want to watch your show? Choose the five best reasons from your list and arrange them in the order you plan to present them.

OR . . . Quickwrite for ten minutes or so about why the producer should accept your proposal. Have everyone in the group contribute, with one person doing the actual writing.

Plan the proposal. Look over the information your group has gathered as you make your writing plan. Use these categories to organize your ideas:

- Cover page
- Characters and actors to play them
- Settings and how they create suspense
- Key scenes in plot and how they create suspense
- Key moments from crucial scene
- Five persuasive reasons why producer should accept proposal

Do a live presentation of your plan. Assemble your materials on a table and go over them with another group. Try to make your plan sound as attractive as possible. When you finish, have the other group comment, and revise your plan in line with their comments.

STEP 2 DRAFTING

Before you draft, review the Writer's Blueprint, your writing plan, and your prewriting notes. Assign each group member a section of the proposal to draft.

As you draft, remember:

- You're writing this proposal as a group, so ask the other group members when you need advice or ideas.
- You're writing a business proposal, so use a businesslike tone when you address the producer. See the Revising Strategy in Step 3 of this lesson.

Choose a Crucial Scene

Students might sketch a couple of scenes they believe to be crucial and then choose their scene from these.

Brainstorm Reasons

If students get stuck finding reasons, suggest a quickwrite to help generate ideas.

Plan the Proposal

Explain to students that making a good plan ensures that they have included all the necessary elements for a successful proposal.

Do a Live Presentation

Remind students that this is an opportunity to get much-needed feedback on their ideas before they put them into action.

Connections to **Writer's Notebook**

For selection-related prompts, refer to Writer's Notebook.

Connections to **Writer's Resource**

For additional writing prompts, refer to Writer's Resource.

STEP 2 DRAFTING

Before You Draft

Encourage group members to cooperate and to ask for and give advice.

As You Draft

Direct students to look over the Revising Strategy on page 122 to help them incorporate a businesslike tone from the start.

BUILDING ENGLISH PROFICIENCY

Planning a Presentation Strategy

Offer the following activities to help students present their plans.

1. Suggest that students first rehearse their presentations by themselves. Encourage them to proceed without stopping, pausing only to jot down their reactions. Then they can discuss their comments, revise, and rehearse again.

2. When another group hears the presentation, remind group members to let it continue without interruption. Listeners can jot down questions and comments to discuss later.

The Student Models

The **transparencies** referenced below are authentic student models. Review them with students before they draft. These questions will help:

1. How do the writers establish a businesslike tone? Point out some examples of words and phrases that help establish this tone.

2. Which model seems more persuasive? Why?

3. Which writer creates a more suspenseful mood? What are some especially suspenseful details this writer supplies?

Transparency Collection
Student Models for Writing Workshop 3, 4

STEP 3 REVISING

Ask Another Group (Peer assessment)

After groups exchange drafts, have one member of each group read the draft aloud, with each of the other members listening for one specific element: characterization, setting, plot, mood, dialogue, and so on. Each listener should make comments on that element only. In this way, listeners won't be distracted by trying to listen for too many details at once.

Revising Strategy: Creating a Businesslike Tone

Have volunteers read the student model aloud without the revising changes first, then with the changes, and compare the tone of each version. For additional support, see the mini-lesson at the bottom of this page and the worksheet referenced below.

Unit 1 Resource Book
Revising Worksheet, p. 93

Connections to **Writer's Resource**

Refer to the Grammar, Usage, and Mechanics Handbook on Writer's Resource.

STEP 3 REVISING

Ask another group for comments on the draft before you revise it. Ask questions such as these.

✔ Have we explained how the settings and plots are suspenseful?

✔ Have we used a businesslike tone in making our proposal?

Revising Strategy

Creating a Businesslike Tone

Tone reflects the writer's attitude toward the audience. A textbook, like this one, has a somewhat formal tone, but friendly too, since the writers want you, the student, to enjoy learning.

In writing a business proposal like this one, in which you want to persuade your audience to buy your idea, you should:

- Come straight to the point—your audience does not have time to waste.
- Let the facts speak for themselves—don't tell people what to think.
- Keep a respectful distance—don't gush or use slang.

The writer of this student model used a partner's comment to help make the tone more businesslike.

STUDENT MODEL

The tension in "An Astrologer's Day" results from the imposing figure of the customer and the sudden new-found "abilities" of the astrologer. ~~The plot of this story is so tense. You'll be on the edge of your seat as the astrologer reveals all these really weird things he can do to the customer.~~ *At first* ~~Before that~~ it's the customer *who is* ~~who's really~~ mysterious. *The audience* ~~Everyone will~~ wonder*s* *who he is and what he wants* ~~who this guy is and what he's after~~.

Isn't this a little casual?

MINI-LESSON: WRITING STYLE

Creating a Businesslike Tone

Teach Tell students that word choice, choice of details, and sentence structure work together to create tone. A businesslike tone inclines the audience to take the writer's ideas seriously. Remind students that a formal tone often uses third-person point of view and formal language.

Activity Idea The introduction of an essay usually establishes the tone. Read opening sentences or introductory paragraphs from a variety of sources. Have students decide the tone; then have them change the tone by changing word choice, details, and sentence structure.

Apply Have students reread the introductions to their proposals and underline the details that establish a businesslike tone. Tell students to revise as needed to make the tone more businesslike.

STEP 4 EDITING

Ask another group to review your revised draft before you edit. When you edit, look for errors in grammar, usage, spelling, and mechanics. Pay special attention to errors in comma usage.

Editing Strategy

Using Commas Correctly

When you edit, be sure you use commas correctly. Here are some basic rules to guide you.

- In a series of three or more words, phrases, or clauses, use a comma to separate the items, and use a comma before the conjunction (*and, but, or, nor*).

  Edgar Allan Poe uses *somber, morbid, and grotesque* images to set the moods of his stories.

- When a descriptive phrase renames or explains the noun or pronoun it follows by adding extra information, set it off with commas.

  Prince Prospero, *a character in "The Masque of the Red Death,"* tries to avoid the plague by sealing himself in his castle.

- When the explanation in a descriptive phrase is vital to the meaning of the sentence, no comma is used.

  I meant the prince *in the story* instead of the real prince.

FOR REFERENCE
For more information on correct comma usage, see the Language and Grammar Handbook at the back of this text.

STEP 5 PRESENTING

Here are two ideas for presenting your proposal.

- Stage your scripted scene for the class with costumes and scenery. If you have access to a video recorder, you might videotape your production.
- Record your show as a radio play, with suspenseful sound effects and music.

MINI-LESSON: GRAMMAR

Using Commas Correctly

Display the following sentences. Ask students to tell where commas should be added, and why. Commas are correctly placed in these sentences, but omit them when displaying sentences for students.

1. Riding through the dark, silent forest was frightening. (separate two adjectives)

2. Prince Prospero planned his party, invited the guests, and tried to outwit the Red Death. (separate phrases in a series)

3. The wealthy people laughed, danced, ate, and grew very tired of one another. (separate a series of verbs)

4. Poe's story of the Red Death, according to one source, was about Europe during the Black Plague. (to enclose a phrase that interrupts the flow of the sentence)

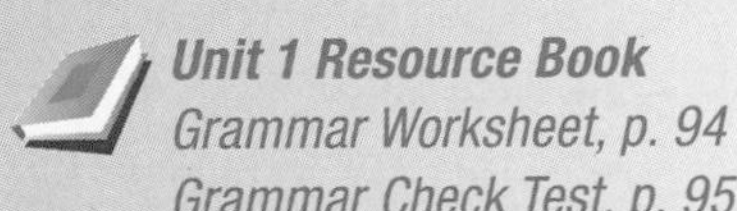

STEP 4 EDITING

Ask Another Group (Peer assessment)

Each group member might read the revised draft twice: once for a specific technical area, such as grammar, spelling, or comma usage; and again for an overall edit. Ask each group member to use a different-colored pencil so questions about corrections can be directed appropriately.

Editing Strategy: Using Commas Correctly

Have students review the rules presented in the Editing Strategy and check their papers for correct comma usage. For additional support, see the mini-lesson at the bottom of this page and the worksheets referenced below.

Unit 1 Resource Book
Grammar Worksheet, p. 94
Grammar Check Test, p. 95

Connections to
Writer's Resource

Refer to the Grammar, Usage, and Mechanics Handbook on Writer's Resource.

STEP 5 PRESENTING

Scripted Scenes

Encourage students to videotape their sample scenes. The tapes could be played for another literature class to introduce the cluster. The tapes could also be put in the school library to encourage reluctant readers to investigate literature.

Radio Play

Students could record their scenes on audio tape and present them as radio plays. Help students use distinctive character voices and imaginative sound effects.

STEP 6 LOOKING BACK

Self-evaluate

The *Assessment Criteria Specs* at the bottom of this page are for a superior paper. You might want to post these in the classroom. Students can then evaluate themselves based on these criteria. For a complete scoring rubric, use the *Assessment Worksheet* referenced below.

Unit 1 Resource Book
Assessment Worksheet, p. 96

Reflect

Before answering the first question, students might begin their reflection by defining their role and explaining their participation in the group process.

To further explore the theme, use the Fine Art Transparency referenced below.

Transparency Collection
Fine Art Writing Prompt 2

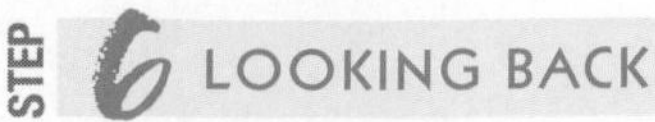

STEP 6 LOOKING BACK

Self-evaluate. Work with your group to decide on a grade for the proposal. Look back at the Writer's Blueprint and give your group's product a score on each point, from 6 (superior) down to 1 (inadequate). Discuss the results and try to agree on one grade for the whole group.

Reflect. Individually, think about what you have learned from this group writing process and write answers to these questions.

- What aspect of collaborating on this project was most interesting to you? Is working with a group ultimately more or less satisfying than working alone?
- What would you change or add to your proposal if you could revise it again? Explain.

For Your Working Portfolio Add a copy of the finished proposal and your reflection responses to your working portfolio.

ASSESSMENT CRITERIA SPECS

Here are the criteria for a superior paper. A full six-level rubric for this paper appears on the Assessment Worksheet referenced below.

6 Superior The writer of a 6 paper impressively meets these criteria:

- Creates a proposal that includes vivid descriptive details of the main characters, plot, and setting.
- Creates an interesting setting that clearly portrays a mood of suspense.
- Writes perceptive descriptions of character traits.
- Thoroughly outlines the plot.
- Does an in-depth portrayal of characterization and action of a crucial scene.
- Includes a cover page that names the story, its author, and group members.
- Uses a persuasive, businesslike tone to present facts and to come straight to the point.
- Uses correct punctuation, grammar, and spelling. Uses commas correctly.

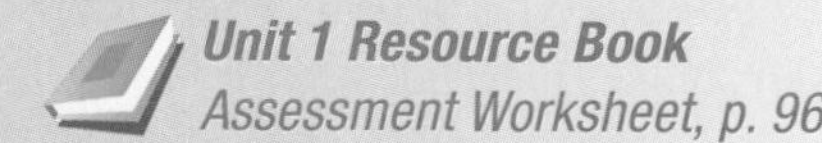

Unit 1 Resource Book
Assessment Worksheet, p. 96

Beyond Print

Computer Talk

If you think a server is a waitress and a hard drive is a traffic jam, read on and learn a few of the important terms in a new language.

Application A particular computer program or piece of software.

CD-ROM Compact Disc Read Only Memory. A CD-ROM is used to store information such as text, sound, pictures, and movies. While CD-ROMs look like audio CDs, they are readable only with a computer.

Database An organized collection of information.

Desktop The area on a computer screen that contains icons, menus, and windows.

Download To copy a file from a server or network.

Electronic Mail Messages sent over the Internet from one user to another.

Hard Drive A storage device usually found inside your computer.

Internet A series of servers connected across the country and world.

Log On The procedure for gaining access to a computer or network.

Menu A pull-down list of items at the top of the computer screen.

Modem A device that uses a phone line to connect your computer with a variety of online services or other computers.

Network Two or more computers connected together by cables, allowing them to communicate with each other.

Online Information available to a user through a network or telephone connection.

RAM Random Access Memory.

Server A computer that operates a network.

Activity Options

1. Create a dialogue between two people in "computerspeak." How many of these terms can you use and still make sense?
2. Create a glossary of your own with other technology terms, and add new terms as you come across them.

Beyond Print

Teaching Objectives

- to recognize and understand computer terms
- to recognize and understand network and Internet terms

Curricular Connection: Technology Skills

You can use this material to help students become more familiar with computer terms and with how a network and the Internet relate to an individual computer user.

Introduce

Before having students read this page, begin a class discussion on terms used in computer technology. Where do some of the words come from? What do they mean? How can you tell if a term is a noun or a verb? As students talk, mention some of the terms in the list. Students may tap into prior knowledge, and many will learn something new.

Activity Options

Activity 1 If students have access to computers, it may be easier for them to think of dialogue while they are actually working on the machines.

Activity 2 You may wish to have students add their terms to a list that remains posted in the library or a computer lab.

ANOTHER APPROACH

Presentations

Some—or many—of your students may be very knowledgeable about computers and the Internet. Encourage them to give informational presentations to the class. They may want to include pictures or diagrams that illustrate the terms. For example, they might show a model of a network or how a modem connects the computer to the Internet.

If your school has a computer network or access to the Internet, organize a class visit with the computer teacher. If possible, give students the opportunity to go online.

Preview

Dealing with Consequences

FOR ALL STUDENTS

Read together the first paragraph on this page and then have students discuss the following questions.

- Why do people often act without considering the consequences to themselves and others?
- Should people always be held responsible for the consequences of their actions? Why?

To further explore the theme, use the transparency referred to below.

Transparency Collection
Fine Art Writing Prompt 3

For At-Risk Students

Ask students to recall TV or movie characters who, because of irresponsible actions, caused serious consequences.

For Students Who Need Challenge

Have students research the legal concept of negligence.

- What is negligence?
- Describe a case in which a party was sued for negligence. What was the outcome?

For Social Learners

Have students describe a situation in which they had to deal with the consequences of someone else's behavior. How did they respond to it?

MULTICULTURAL CONNECTION

Discuss with the class what some of these "cultural situations and settings" may be. Some examples are school, home, movie theater, and so on.

Ask students if they've ever rejected rules in these setttings because their personal choices were in direct conflict.

Part Three

Dealing with Consequences

A hunting adventure in the jungles of Peru, a confrontation in China, a post-typhoon discovery in Japan—incidents in the selections you are about to read illustrate that people worldwide often act without considering the consequences.

Multicultural Connection **Choice** may be influenced by cultural situations and settings. In the following selections, do individuals choose to respect or reject such settings, and what are the results of their decisions?

Literature

IDEAS THAT WORK

Learning Lessons from the Characters

After students have read "The Interlopers," "The Boar Hunt," and "The Rabbit," encourage them to discuss how human nature and animal instinct contribute to the outcomes in these selections.

After students have completed the literature, direct half of them to write letters asking for advice on how get along with others to a character in this section. Each of the other students should randomly select a letter and write a response by assuming the role of the character to whom the letter is addressed. Encourage students to discuss and compare the responses of different characters.

Marlene Carter
Los Angeles, California

Before Reading

The Interlopers

by Saki Great Britain

Saki
1870–1916

H. H. Munro, who adopted the pen name Saki, is best known for stories that blend humor and horror. Munro was born in Akyab, Burma, where his father was a colonel in the Bengal Staff Corps. After the death of his mother when he was two, he was sent home to relatives in England. There he eventually wrote political sketches for the *Westminster Gazette*, as well as short stories that displayed his satirical humor and his fascination with the unusual. When World War I broke out, Munro enlisted at age 43 as a private in the British army. In 1915, he went to France and was killed by a German sniper within a year.

Building Background

Feuding Friends Conduct a quick survey of classmates to determine what kinds of things usually cause quarrels between friends. List on the board things most frequently mentioned, and write the top five in chart form. Then brainstorm ways in which such disagreements can be resolved, writing the best suggestions in the chart.

Things That Cause Quarrels	Ways to Resolve Them

Literary Focus

Irony The word **irony** refers to a contrast between what is expected, or what appears to be, and what really is. You may have noticed irony when someone used a tone of voice to indicate the opposite of what was said. Or maybe you expected one event to occur but something quite surprising happened instead. You even may have noticed irony while watching a sitcom in which you knew more about what was going to happen than the characters did. As you read "The Interlopers," list examples of irony. Don't forget to expect the unexpected!

Writer's Notebook

Here Come the Interlopers Did you know that an *interloper* is someone who intrudes or interferes? Make a web around the word *interloper* listing at least six different people or things that could fit this description. Now preview the art and the first paragraph of this story and predict who the interlopers of the title might be.

Before Reading

Building Background

Discuss with students the concept of a feud. Explain that feuds are long-standing quarrels between groups such as families, clans, and tribes, and that these violent conflicts can begin between individuals and last from one generation to the next.

Literary Focus

Point out that each surprising twist in the story is a clue that the writer is using **irony.** Explain that some of Saki's irony may not be apparent on first reading but will become obvious in hindsight.

Writer's Notebook

To make personal connections with the concept, students can also make a web that names people or things that are interlopers in their lives.

More About Saki

Before devoting most of his time to writing short stories and novels, Saki worked as a journalist in Russia and Paris. Other works include:

- *Reginald* (1904)
- *The Chronicles of Clovis* (1912)
- *The Unbearable Bassington* (1912)
- *The Rise of the Russian Empire* (1900)

SUPPORT MATERIALS OVERVIEW

Unit 1 Resource Book
- Graphic Organizer, p. 97
- Study Guide, p. 98
- Vocabulary, p. 99
- Grammar, p. 100
- Alternate Check Test, p. 101
- Vocabulary Test, p. 102
- Selection Test, pp. 103–104

Building English Proficiency
- Literature Summaries
- Activities, p. 177

Reading, Writing & Grammar SkillBook
- Reading, pp. 74–75
- Grammar, Usage, and Mechanics, pp. 182–183

Technology
- Audiotape 5, Side B
- Personal Journal Software
- Custom Literature Database: For more short stories by Saki, see the database.
- Test Generator Software

During Reading

Selection Objectives

- to explore the theme of facing the consequences of hatred
- to analyze the author's use of irony
- to identify examples of pronoun antecedent agreement

Unit 1 Resource Book
Graphic Organizer, p. 97
Study Guide, p. 98

Theme Link

Even though Ulrich and Georg make peace with each other after years of feuding, they must face the consequences of their hate.

Vocabulary Preview

spur, ridge sticking out from or smaller than the main body of a mountain or mountain range

quarry, animal chased in a hunt; prey

wont, accustomed

plight, condition or situation, usually bad

jest, something said to cause laughter; joke

compact, agreement or contract

lull, period of less noise or violence; brief calm

muster, gather together

Students can add the words and definitions to their Writer's Notebooks.

1 Geographical Note
The Carpathians

The Carpathian Mountains begin in the Czech Republic and extend 930 miles through Slovakia, Poland, Ukraine, and Romania.

2 Literary Focus
Irony

Question What is ironic about the word *beast* in the opening sentence? *(The hunter's prey is a person.)*

THE INTERLOPERS

SAKI

In a forest of mixed growth somewhere on the eastern spurs[1] of the
1 Carpathians,[2] a man stood one winter night watching and listening, as
2 though he waited for some beast of the woods to come within the range of his vision, and, later, of his rifle. But the game for whose presence he kept so keen an outlook was none that figured in the sportsman's calendar as lawful and proper for the chase; Ulrich von Gradwitz[3] patrolled the dark forest in quest of a human enemy.

The forest lands of Gradwitz were of wide extent and well stocked with game; the narrow strip of precipitous woodland that lay on its outskirts was not remarkable for the game it harbored or the shooting it afforded, but it was the most jealously guarded of all its owner's territorial possessions. A famous lawsuit, in the days of his grandfather, had wrested it from the illegal possession of a neighboring family of petty landowners; the dispossessed party had never acquiesced in the judgment of the Courts, and a long series of poaching affrays and similar scandals had embittered the relationships between the families for three generations. The neighbors' feud had grown into a personal one since Ulrich had come to be head of his family; if there was a man in the world whom he detested and wished ill to it was Georg Znaeym,[4] the inheritor of the quarrel and the tireless game snatcher and raider of the disputed border forest.

The feud might, perhaps, have died down or been compromised if the personal ill will of the two men had not stood in the way; as boys they had thirsted for one another's blood, as men each prayed that misfortune might fall on the other, and this wind-scourged winter night Ulrich had banded together his foresters to watch the dark forest, not in quest of four-footed quarry,[5] but to keep a look-

1. spur (spėr), *n.* ridge sticking out from or smaller than the main body of a mountain or mountain range.
2. **Carpathians** (kär pā′thē ənz), mountain chain located in southeast Europe.
3. **Ulrich von Gradwitz** (ül′rik fən gräd′vits)
4. **Georg Znaeym** (gā′ôrg znā′im)
5. quarry (kwôr′ē), *n.* animal chased in a hunt; prey.

SELECTION SUMMARY

The Interlopers

Ulrich von Gradwitz is involved in a heated feud between his family and the family of Georg Znaeym over a strip of land that borders both their properties. One stormy night as Ulrich is out patrolling the forest looking for poachers, he comes face-to-face with Georg. The enemies are about to shoot one another when a huge tree falls on them, pinning them both to the ground and injuring them. They curse and threaten one another, each saying his men are coming soon, and so the two reach a standoff. After a while, Ulrich realizes their mutual plight and becomes sympathetic toward Georg and offers him a drink from his wine flask. Soon, the two men pledge friendship to one another and together they shout for help. Then Ulrich cries out that figures are running toward them. As the figures approach, he sees that, instead of rescuers, they are wolves.

*For summaries in other languages, see the **Building English Proficiency** book.*

Huntsmen on the Edge of Night, an oil by René Magritte, presents the groping, animallike hunters as if they are themselves hunted by some dark force. What details in the painting offer parallels to Georg and Ulrich?

out for the prowling thieves whom he suspected of being afoot from across the land boundary.
3 The roebuck, which usually kept in the sheltered hollows during a storm-wind, were running like driven things tonight, and there was movement and unrest among the creatures that were wont[6] to sleep through the dark hours. Assuredly there was a disturbing element in the forest, and Ulrich could guess the quarter from whence it came.

He strayed away by himself from the watchers whom he had placed in ambush on the crest of the hill, and wandered far down the steep slopes amid the wild tangle of undergrowth, peering through the tree trunks and listening through the whistling and skirling of the wind and the restless beating of the branches for sight or sound of the marauders. If only on this wild night, in this dark, lone spot, he might come across Georg Znaeym, man to man, with none to witness—that was the wish that was uppermost in his thoughts. And as he stepped

6. wont (wunt), *adj.* accustomed.

Art Study

Responses to Caption Questions

Students may suggest that, like Georg and Ulrich, the two figures are powerful and armed, but terrorized and trapped.

René Magritte (1898–1967) was a Belgian painter known mainly for his surrealistic works. A movement in art and literature, surrealism aims to liberate the subconscious mind of the artist, enabling him or her to transcend reality and create images that appear dreamlike.

Question Why might a surrealist painting be more appropriate than a realistic one to illustrate this story? *(Possible response: Many elements described in this story—the dark forest, the whistling wind, the undergrowth, the branches—are dreamlike and suggest a hidden presence.)*

3 Literary Element
Foreshadowing

Questions

- What might roebuck run from besides a poacher? *(a wild animal)*
- What does the running of roebuck suggest to the reader? *(Possible responses: Ulrich's prey is nearby. The running deer are also a warning, foreshadowing the fact that the hunter may be in danger of becoming the hunted.)*

BUILDING ENGLISH PROFICIENCY

Applying Geographical Information

The following activities might help students visualize the story's setting. Students will also consider other locations in the world where rival claims to land possession have resulted in violence.

Activity Ideas

- Have students use an encyclopedia, dictionary, or atlas to locate the Carpathian Mountains (see Geographical Note, page 128.)
- Assign student groups a country affected in some way by the mountains that run through it or that border it. Have the groups briefly research the country's history to learn what role, if any, rival claims to land have played there.
- Encourage students to find out from international news reports where world "hot spots" trace violence to rival claims for land. Allow time for students to share their findings.

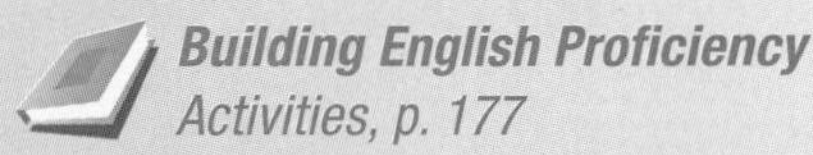

Building English Proficiency Activities, p. 177

4 Reading/Thinking Skills
Predict

Questions

- What are some codes of a "restraining civilization"? *(Possible responses: A person must not kill, lie, steal, and cheat.)*
- Will the men follow the code or their own emotions? *(Possible response: They will probably try to kill each other, but the foreshadowing suggests something unexpected may happen.)*

5 Reading/Thinking Skills
Compare and Contrast

Question How is "Nature's own violence" similar to the men's? How is it different? *(Possible response: Nature's violence is potentially as lethal as the men's. Unlike theirs, Nature's violence is random and not motivated by hatred.)*

6 Literary Focus
Irony

Questions

- Why does Georg laugh? *(Possible response: Ironic events are often perceived as grimly humorous.)*
- What irony does Georg fail to see? *(Possible response: He is a victim of the same "justice" that snares Ulrich.)*

round the trunk of a huge beech he came face to face with the man he sought.

The two enemies stood glaring at one another for a long silent moment. Each had a rifle in his hand, each had hate in his heart and murder uppermost in his mind. The chance had come to give full play to the passions of a lifetime. But a man who has been brought up
4 under the code of a restraining civilization cannot easily nerve himself to shoot down his neighbor in cold blood and without a word spoken, except for an offense against his hearth and honor. And before the moment of hesitation had given way to
5 action, a deed of Nature's own violence overwhelmed them both. A fierce shriek of the storm had been answered by a splitting crash over their heads, and ere they could leap aside a mass of falling beech tree had thundered down on them. Ulrich von Gradwitz found himself stretched on the ground, one arm numb beneath him and the other held almost as helpless in a tight tangle of forked branches, while both legs were pinned beneath the fallen mass. His heavy shooting boots had saved his feet from being crushed to pieces, but if his fractures were not so serious as they might have been, at least it was evident that he could not move from his present position till someone came to release him. The descending twigs had slashed the skin of his face, and he had to wink away some drops of blood from his eyelashes before he could take in a general view of the disaster. At his side, so near that under ordinary circumstances he could almost have touched him, lay Georg Znaeym, alive and struggling, but obviously as helplessly pinioned down as himself. All round them lay a thick-strewn wreckage of splintered branches and broken twigs.

Relief at being alive and exasperation at his captive plight[7] brought a strange medley of pious thank offerings and sharp curses to Ulrich's lips. Georg, who was nearly blinded with the blood which trickled across his eyes, stopped his struggling for a moment to listen,
6 and then gave a short, snarling laugh.

"So you're not killed, as you ought to be, but you're caught, anyway," he cried; "caught fast. Ho, what a jest,[8] Ulrich von Gradwitz snared in his stolen forest. There's real justice for you!"

And he laughed again, mockingly and savagely.

"I'm caught in my own forest land," retorted Ulrich. "When my men come to release us, you will wish, perhaps, that you were in a better plight than caught poaching on a neighbor's land. Shame on you!"

Georg was silent for a moment; then he answered quietly:

"Are you sure that your men will find much to release? I have men, too, in the forest tonight, close behind me, and *they* will be here first and do the releasing. When they drag me out from under these damned branches, it won't need much clumsiness on their part to roll this mass of trunk right over on the top of you. Your men will find you dead under a fallen beech tree. For form's sake I shall send my condolences to your family."

"It is a useful hint," said Ulrich fiercely. "My men had orders to follow in ten minutes' time, seven of which must have gone by already, and when they get me out—I will remember the hint. Only as you will have met your death poaching on my lands, I don't think I can decently send any message of condolence to your family."

"Good," snarled Georg, "good. We'll fight this quarrel out to the death, you and I and our foresters, with no cursed interlopers to come between us. Death and damnation to you, Ulrich von Gradwitz!"

"The same to you, Georg Znaeym, forest thief, game snatcher."

Both men spoke with the bitterness of possible defeat before them, for each knew that it might be long before his men would seek him

7. **plight** (plīt), *n.* condition or situation, usually bad.
8. **jest** (jest), *n.* something said to cause laughter; joke.

MINI-LESSON: LITERARY FOCUS
Irony

A plot develops ironically when the action produces an outcome contrary to the one that the reader was led to expect. In this selection ironic situations occur one after another. Ask students to see how many examples of situational irony they can find in "The Interlopers."

Teach Situational irony occurs when what actually happens is contrary to what is expected or appropriate. Dramatic irony occurs when the reader knows something important that a character in a story or drama does not know and does not expect.

Activity Ideas

- Divide students into small groups to talk about real-life situations they consider ironic.
- Have students compare instances of situational and dramatic irony in "The Rain Came" and "The Interlopers."
- Have students identify the author's purpose for using irony in this story.

out or find him; it was a bare matter of chance which party would arrive first on the scene.

7 Both had now given up the useless struggle to free themselves from the mass of wood that held them down; Ulrich limited his endeavors to an effort to bring his one partially free arm near enough to his outer coat pocket to draw out his wine flask. Even when he had accomplished that operation, it was long before he could manage the unscrewing of the stopper or get any of the liquid down his throat. But what a Heaven-sent draft it seemed! It was an open winter, and little snow had fallen as yet, hence the captives suffered less from the cold than might have been the case at that season of the year; nevertheless, the wine was warming and reviving to the wounded man, and he looked across with something like a throb of pity to where his enemy lay, just keeping the groans of pain and weariness from crossing his lips.

"Could you reach this flask if I threw it over to you?" asked Ulrich suddenly; "there is good wine in it, and one may as well be as comfortable as one can. Let us drink, even if tonight one of us dies."

"No, I can scarcely see anything; there is so much blood caked round my eyes," said Georg, "and in any case I don't drink wine with an enemy."

Ulrich was silent for a few minutes, and lay listening to the weary screeching of the wind. An idea was slowly forming and growing in his brain, an idea that gained strength every time that he looked across at the man who was fighting so grimly against pain and exhaustion. In the pain and languor that Ulrich himself was feeling, the old fierce hatred seemed to be dying down.

8 "Neighbor," he said presently, "do as you please if your men come first. It was a fair compact.[9] But as for me, I've changed my mind. If my men are the first to come, you shall be the first to be helped, as though you were my guest. We have quarreled like devils all our lives over this stupid strip of forest, where the trees can't even stand upright in a breath of wind. Lying here tonight, thinking, I've come to think that we've been rather fools; there are better things in life than getting the better of a boundary dispute. Neighbor, if you will help me to bury the old quarrel I—I will ask you to be my friend."

Georg Znaeym was silent for so long that Ulrich thought, perhaps, he had fainted with the pain of his injuries. Then he spoke slowly and in jerks.

"How the whole region would stare and gabble if we rode into the market-square together. No one living can remember seeing a Znaeym and a von Gradwitz talking to one another in friendship. And what peace there would be among the forester folk if we ended our feud tonight. And if we choose to make peace among our people there is none other to interfere, no interlopers from outside. . . . You would come and keep the Sylvester night[10] beneath my roof, and I would come and feast on some high day[11] at your castle. . . . I would never fire a shot on your land, save when you invited me as a guest; and you should come and shoot with me down in the marshes where the wildfowl are. In all the countryside there are none that could hinder if we willed to make peace. I never thought to have wanted to do other than hate you all my life, but I think I have changed my mind about things too, this last half-hour. And you offered 9

...THERE ARE BETTER THINGS IN LIFE THAN GETTING THE BETTER OF A BOUNDARY DISPUTE.

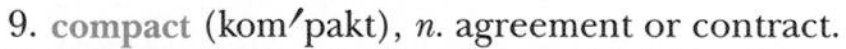

9. compact (kom′pakt), *n.* agreement or contract.
10. **Sylvester night,** New Year's Eve. Festivities honor St. Sylvester.
11. **high day,** any holy day in the Church calendar.

7 Reading/Thinking Skills
Problem-Solving

Ask students to discuss possible solutions for Georg and Ulrich's predicament.

Questions

- How do they react to their dilemma? *(They lie there bickering and threatening each other.)*
- What is ironic about this reaction? *(Possible response: Their best chance for survival is to cooperate until their parties rescue them.)*

8 Literary Element
Dynamic Characters

Question How do both Ulrich and Georg change during the course of the action? *(Both change from violent men driven by blind hatred to reasonable, compassionate neighbors.)*

9 Reader's Response
Making Personal Connections

Pose the generalization that adversity often forms bonds between people, and invite students to share a range of adverse experiences, such as camping trips when the weather was terrible, immigrating to a new country, or a family crisis. Let them debate whether Ulrich and Georg's peace-making is believable or not.

BUILDING ENGLISH PROFICIENCY

Understanding Characters

Let students add to their understanding of the characters by acting out the verbal battle between the main characters.

1. Have students silently reread the conversation on page 130, beginning "So you're not killed" and ending "forest thief, game snatcher."

2. Encourage students to recall the feelings between these two characters. Model the different ways each character speaks, such as *cried, laughed mockingly and savagely, fiercely,* and *snarled.* Invite students to imitate the speaking manner each word suggests.

3. Allow several pairs of students to read and act out the conversation, making it as dramatic as possible.

4. Have students talk about how the characters change. Then let them read parts from page 131 in which the enemies soften toward each other. Remind them to use appropriate tones.

10 Literary Element
Point of View

Questions

- From what point of view is the story told? *(third-person omniscient)*
- Imagine that the story was told from the first-person point of view with Georg as the speaker. How would that have changed the story? *(Possible response: the reader would have been more sympathetic to Georg; by use of third person, the author shows the reader that both characters were equally deserving of their fate.)*

11 Reading/Thinking Skills
Summarize

Question Look back to find the times that "interlopers" are mentioned. *(the title, pages 130 and 131)* Think of all the possible interlopers in the story. Who or what are they? *(Possible responses: Georg and Ulrich; the courts; anyone outside the Znaeym and von Gradwitz lands; the wolves)*

Check Test

1. What was the cause of the feud? *(a lawsuit over land ownership)*
2. How long had the neighbors been feuding? *(three generations)*
3. What happens to Ulrich and Georg just as they meet in the forest? *(A tree falls on them, pinning them together.)*
4. What effect would Georg and Ulrich's friendship have on the forester folk? *(There would be peace among them.)*
5. Why does Ulrich laugh idiotically? *(He sees wolves.)*

Unit 1 Resource Book
Alternate Check Test, p. 101

me your wine flask. . . . Ulrich von Gradwitz, I will be your friend."

10 For a space both men were silent, turning over in their minds the wonderful changes that this dramatic reconciliation would bring about. In the cold, gloomy forest, with the wind tearing in fitful gusts through the naked branches and whistling around the tree trunks, they lay and waited for the help that would now bring release and succor to both parties. And each prayed a private prayer that his men might be the first to arrive, so that he might be the first to show honorable attention to the enemy that had become a friend.

Presently, as the wind dropped for a moment, Ulrich broke silence.

"Let's shout for help," he said; "in this lull[12] our voices may carry a little way."

"They won't carry far through the trees and undergrowth," said Georg, "but we can try. Together, then."

The two raised their voices in a prolonged hunting call.

"Together again," said Ulrich a few minutes later, after listening in vain for an answering halloo.

"I heard something that time, I think," said Ulrich.

"I heard nothing but the pestilential wind," said Georg hoarsely.

There was silence again for some minutes, and then Georg gave a joyful cry.

"I can see figures coming through the wood. They are following in the way I came down the hillside."

Both men raised their voices in as loud a shout as they could muster.[13]

"They hear us! They've stopped. Now they see us. They're running down the hill toward us," cried Ulrich.

"How many of them are there?" asked Georg.

"I can't see distinctly," said Ulrich; "nine or ten."

"Then they are yours," said Georg; "I had only seven out with me."

"They are making all the speed they can, brave lads," said Ulrich gladly.

"Are they your men?" asked Georg. "Are they your men?" he repeated impatiently as Ulrich did not answer.

"No," said Ulrich with a laugh, the idiotic chattering laugh of a man unstrung with hideous fear.

"Who are they?" asked Georg quickly, straining his eyes to see what the other would gladly not have seen.

"Wolves!" 11

12. **lull** (lul), *n.* period of less noise or violence; brief calm.
13. **muster** (mus′tər), *v.* gather together.

MINI-LESSON: GRAMMAR
Pronoun-Antecedent Agreement

Teach The antecedent of a pronoun is the word to which the pronoun refers. As a rule, the pronoun is singular when the antecedent is singular and plural when the antecedent is plural. In both speaking and writing, students may shift number using collective pronouns: *anyone, each, every-body, everyone.* Ask students whether *his* or *their* agrees with the subject pronoun *each* in the following sentence.

"And each prayed a private prayer that (<u>his</u>, their) men might be the first to arrive. . . ."

Activity Ideas

- Have students write sentences using *anyone, each, everybody, everyone.* In these sentences, students can describe the feud in the story or one they have experienced.
- Ask them to check each other's work for proper pronoun-antecedent agreement.

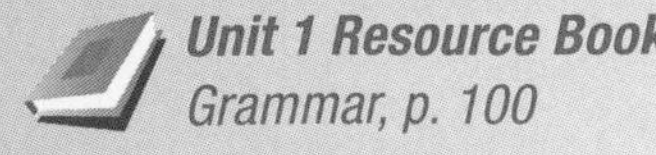
Unit 1 Resource Book
Grammar, p. 100

After Reading

Making Connections

Shaping Your Response

1. Describe your feelings at the end of the story.
2. In your notebook, list three words you would use to describe this story to a friend.
3. Do you think this would have been a better story if the men had been rescued? Why or why not?

Analyzing the Story

4. What information is provided in the **flashback** appearing in the second paragraph of the story?
5. Cite words or phrases from the story that describe the **setting** and convey a **mood** of menace and wildness.
6. Find wording early in the story that **foreshadows** the ending.
7. Identify three different **conflicts** in the story. Which one do you think ultimately proves to be the most important? Explain.

Extending the Ideas

8. Mention some recent international feuds over group boundaries. Find out who the "interlopers" are thought to be in one or two of these disputes.
9. In "The Interlopers," the author exposes petty behavior that causes an enduring feud. What **moral** can you draw from the story that might help people around the world get along better?

Literary Focus: Irony

Irony is a contrast between what appears to be and what actually is. In *verbal irony* the actual meaning of a statement is different from what the statement literally says. *Irony of situation* refers to an occurrence that is contrary to what is expected or intended. *Dramatic irony* refers to a situation in which events or facts not known to a character on stage or in a fictional work are known to the audience.

- What is ironic about the story's title? about the men's encounter of each other in the forest? about the end of the story?

After Reading

MAKING CONNECTIONS

1. Possible responses: shocked, revolted, amused

2. Possible responses: quick-paced, tragic, ironic

3. Possible responses: No, the brutal ending fit the brutal hatred that carried on for so long; yes, the men would have a chance to redeem themselves.

4. The passage reveals that the cause of the feud was an old lawsuit over the ownership of land and the resulting hatred between the land's inheritors.

5. Possible responses: "wind-scourged winter night," "dark forest," "disturbing element in the forest, "driven," and "unrest."

6. Possible responses: "as though he waited for some beast of the woods to come within the range of his vision"; "as men each prayed that misfortune might fall on the other."

7. Possible responses: the original conflict between Ulrich and Georg's grandfathers, the conflict between Ulrich and Georg, and the emotional conflict Ulrich and Georg feel within themselves. The third is most impor-tant, because it fuels the irony. When the story begins, each prays that harm might come to the other; in the end, each prays that he might be first to save the other.

8. Possible response: In Israel, leaders have attempted to resolve conflicts peace-fully, but often smaller radical factions commit terrorist acts and are seen as interlopers in the peace process.

9. Possible responses: Strive for peace within your lifetime, before it is too late. "Love thy neighbor as thyself."

LITERARY FOCUS: IRONY

Possible responses:

- Each man considers the other an interloper on his property. The real interlopers of the title, however, are the storm-driven tree and the wolves.
- The irony of the men's encounter is that they meet as enemies, but they end as friends; they each expect to kill the other and survive, but they are both killed by interlopers in the form of nature.
- The ending is ironic in that when the men finally cooperate and shout for help, they attract wolves, not the expected rescuers.

VOCABULARY STUDY

1. spurs
2. compact
3. quarry
4. wont
5. plight

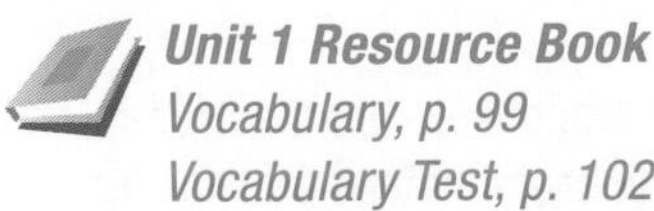

Unit 1 Resource Book
Vocabulary, p. 99
Vocabulary Test, p. 102

WRITING CHOICES

Writer's Notebook Update

Suggest to students that they try to recall an incident in which some force of nature unexpectedly disrupted their lives. Point out that their descriptions can be humorous.

In Lieu of Flowers

Suggest that students write the obituary from the point of view of a family member of either Ulrich or Georg. Remind them that no one knew that the two had become friends before dying.

Surprise! It Wasn't Wolves

Encourage students to consider several possible scenarios for extending the plot by asking several "what if" questions, such as "what if the rescuers are indeed nearby and see the wolves?" or "What if the wolves kill only Ulrich, and Georg then has to explain to ULrich's men what has happened?"

Selection Test

Unit 1 Resource Book, *pp. 103–104*

Vocabulary Study

compact
jest
lull
muster
plight
quarry
spur
wont

Solve the riddles by writing a vocabulary word for each numbered item. If necessary, consult the Glossary at the back of this book.

1. Both cowboys and mountains might have more than one.
2. You might find this in a purse or at a meeting of diplomats.
3. This can refer to prey or to a place where stone is blasted or cut.
4. If you add an apostrophe, this becomes a contraction.
5. This can be a condition or a solemn promise.

Expressing Your Ideas

Writing Choices

Writer's Notebook Update Did you guess that the interlopers would not be human? Did any of the words in your cluster come close to describing the interlopers in the story? Use your web to describe an incident in your life in which an interloper intruded.

In Lieu of Flowers Use your imagination to write an **obituary** for Ulrich von Gradwitz or Georg Znaeym for the local newspaper. Include a nickname, if you think he had one; age; place of residence; date of death; circumstances of the death; list of survivors; and information about the funeral services.

Surprise! It Wasn't Wolves! Some readers would prefer a less violent outcome for the story. Write a **new ending** to the story that maintains the element of surprise but is less violent than the original. Make sure that your ending does not contradict the details provided throughout the story.

Other Options

Tonight's Episode Work with a group to plan a **radio play** of "The Interlopers." Think about how you can best relate the information given in the flashback at the beginning of the story. What music will add to the mood of the story? What sound effects will you use? Present your radio play to the class.

At a Theater Near You Movie posters are advertisements that give the viewer a "sneak preview" of the action and stars of a film. Create a **movie poster** for the film version of "The Interlopers," keeping the tone of the story and giving the viewers just enough information about the story and actors to make them want to buy a ticket.

OTHER OPTIONS

Tonight's Episode

Suggest that the group working on the radio play appoint a director to oversee all aspects of the production. The group will also need at least two actors, a narrator, and a sound crew responsible for music, sound effects, and recording.

At a Theater Near You

Suggest to students that they use computer software to create their posters.

Before Reading

The Boar Hunt

by José Vasconcelos Mexico

José Vasconcelos
1882–1959

Educator, writer, politician, and historian, José Vasconcelos (hō zä′ väs cōn sä′lōs) did much to improve the standard of living in his native land of Mexico. In the decade prior to the revolution of 1910, he graduated from law school and co-founded a group dedicated to the revival of Mexican culture. As Minister of Public Education from 1920 to 1924, he instituted important reforms by opening rural schools, commissioning mural painting, assisting musicians, and inviting other Latin American intellectual leaders to Mexico. His autobiography, *The Mexican Ulysses*, is an excellent study of culture and life in twentieth-century Mexico.

Building Background

To Hunt or Not to Hunt As a class project, conduct a survey to find out how students feel about hunting animals. Use items such as the following, or think of your own. Write each item on the board and tally students' answers. Then make up five rules for hunting.

1. Hunting animals is permissible ____.
   a. always **b.** never **c.** sometimes
2. People can kill animals ____.
   a. for food **b.** for clothing **c.** for sport **d.** for any reason
3. It is ____ that killing certain animals can restore an ecological balance.
   a. true **b.** false **c.** unprovable

Literary Focus

Moral Do you recall childhood fables, such as "The Hare and the Tortoise" or "The Boy Who Cried Wolf"? These stories teach a **moral**, or lesson. For example, the moral of "The Boy Who Cried Wolf" can be stated something like this: "If you try to deceive people, they eventually won't believe you even when you're telling the truth." When you have finished reading "The Boar Hunt," think about the lesson, or moral, it teaches. At what cost does the main character learn this lesson?

Writer's Notebook

Truth or Consequences The theme of this group of stories is "Dealing with Consequences." As you read "The Boar Hunt," jot down words and phrases that seem to suggest what will happen, along with your predictions about these consequences. You might also use the artwork to help make your predictions.

Before Reading

Building Background

Even in communities where hunting is a traditional activity, students may find avid opposition to the practice. Point out that this story, like most good literature, tackles a controversial issue and encourages readers to reevaluate their own positions.

Literary Focus

In addition to thinking about what the main character in the story learns from his experience, ask students to think of examples of how the **moral** can be applied to their own lives.

Writer's Notebook: Truth or Consequences

If students quickly conclude that the boar will hunt the hunter, ask them to jot ideas about other "victims" of a "hunt," such as rain forests threatened by development and children who are exploited by advertising. What might the consequences be?

More About José Vasconcelos

In 1929, Vasconcelos ran for the presidency of Mexico. After defeat by a wide margin, he charged the opposition with fraud and was forced into exile until 1939.

SUPPORT MATERIALS OVERVIEW

Unit 1 Resource Book
- Graphic Organizer, p. 113
- Study Guide, p. 114
- Vocabulary, p. 115
- Grammar, p. 116
- Alternate Check Test, p. 117
- Vocabulary Test, p. 118
- Selection Test, pp. 119–120

Building English Proficiency
- Literature Summaries
- Activities, p. 178
- "The Boar Hunt" in Spanish

Reading, Writing & Grammar SkillBook
- Writing, pp. 117–118
- Grammar, Usage, and Mechanics, pp. 159–160

Technology
- Audiotape 6, Side A
- Personal Journal Software
- Custom Literature Database: For a myth related to this theme, see Diana and Actæon by Thomas Bulfinch on the database.
- Test Generator Software

During Reading

Selection Objectives

- to explore the consequences of man's destruction of nature
- to identify a story's moral
- to identify examples of compound sentences

Unit 1 Resource Book
Graphic Organizer, p. 113
Study Guide, p. 114

Theme Link

Hunters arrogantly slaughter a large number of boars and are forced to deal with the consequences of their actions.

Vocabulary Preview

rejuvenate, make young or vigorous again; renew
lethargy, lack of energy; inactivity
impotent, not having power; helpless
gratifying, satisfying; pleasing
tenaciously, holding fast; stubbornly
sporadic, appearing or happening at intervals in time; occasionally
husbanded, managed carefully; saved
implicit, meant, but not clearly expressed or distinctly stated; implied
infamy, a very bad reputation; public disgrace
ignoble, without honor; disgraceful

Students can add the words and definitions to their Writer's Notebooks.

1 Reader's Response

Making Personal Connections

Would you have fit into this group of friends? Why or why not? *(Possible responses: yes, because of similar interests in hunting and adventure-seeking; no, because of their callous attitude, shown when they killed birds for fun)*

The Boar Hunt

José Vasconcelos

We were four companions, and we went by the names of our respective nationalities: the Colombian, the Peruvian, the Mexican; the fourth, a native of Ecuador, was called Quito[1] for short. Unforeseen chance had joined us together a few years ago on a large sugar plantation on the Peruvian coast. We worked at different occupations during the day and met during the evening in our off time. Not being Englishmen, we did not play cards. Instead, our constant discussions led to disputes. These didn't stop us from wanting to see each other the next night, however, to continue the interrupted debates and support them with new arguments. Nor did the rough sentences of the preceding wrangles indicate a lessening of our affection, of which we assured ourselves reciprocally with the clasping of hands and a look. On Sundays we used to go on hunting parties. We roamed the fertile glens, stalking, generally with poor results, the game of the warm region around the coast, or we entertained ourselves killing birds that flew in the sunlight during the siesta hour.

1 We came to be tireless wanderers and excellent marksmen. Whenever we climbed a hill and gazed at the imposing range of mountains in the interior, its attractiveness stirred us and we wanted to climb it. What attracted us more was the trans-Andean region:[2] fertile plateaus extending on the other side of the range in the direction of the Atlantic toward the immense land of Brazil. It was as if primitive

1. **Ecuador** (ek′wə dôr) . . . **Quito** (kē′tō). Ecuador is located in northwestern South America. Quito is its capital.
2. **trans-Andean region,** the area across—that is, to the east of—the Andes Mountains. The Andes run in a generally north-south direction through the length of South America.

SELECTION SUMMARY

The Boar Hunt

A hunter tells of a trip to the primitive jungles of the trans-Andean region to hunt wild boars. Once in camp, he and his companions, who are from Colombia, Peru, Mexico, and Ecuador, sleep in hammocks that are all tied to a single tree. The next day, after descending the tree, a disturbing sound alarms the men and they quickly return to the hammocks with arms and supplies. Soon a vast herd of wild boars arrives. Suspended safely above their prey, the hunters slaughter boars for hours, but the herd doesn't dwindle. As the hunters watch in terror, the ferocious animals begin to uproot the tree in which the hunters are suspended. Desperate, the narrator leaps to safet in a nearby tree just as the tree falls and the othe three hunters are killed by the boars. The narrator vows never again to hunt for pleasure.

*For summaries in other languages, see the **Building English Proficiency** book.*

nature called us to her breast. The vigor of the fertile, untouched jungles promised to rejuvenate[3] our minds, the same vigor which rejuvenates the strength and the thickness of the trees each year. At times we devised crazy plans. As with all things that are given a lot of thought, these schemes generally materialized. Ultimately nature and events are largely what our imaginations make them out to be. And so we went ahead planning and acting. At the end of the year, with arranged vacations, accumulated money, good rifles, abundant munitions, stone- and mud-proof boots, four hammocks, and a half dozen faithful Indians, our caravan descended the Andean slopes, leading to the endless green ocean.

At last we came upon a village at the edge of
2 the Marañón River.[4] Here we changed our safari. The region we were going to penetrate had no roads. It was unexplored underbrush into which we could enter only by going down the river in a canoe. In time we came to the area where we proposed to carry out the purpose of our journey, the hunting of wild boars.

We had been informed that boars travel in herds of several thousands, occupying a region, eating grass and staying together, exploiting the grazing areas, organized just like an army. They are very easy to kill if one attacks them when
3 they are scattered out satisfying their appetites—an army given over to the delights of victory. When they march about hungry, on the other hand, they are usually vicious. In our search we glided down river between imposing jungles with our provisions and the company of three faithful Indian oarsmen.

One morning we stopped at some huts near the river. Thanks to the information gathered there, we decided to disembark a little farther on in order to spend the night on land and continue the hunt for the boars in the thicket the following day.

Sheltered in a backwater, we came ashore, and after a short exploration found a clearing in which to make camp. We unloaded the provisions and the rifles, tied the boat securely, then with the help of the Indians set up our camp one-half kilometer from the riverbank. In marking the path to the landing, we were careful not to lose ourselves in the thicket. The Indians withdrew toward their huts, promising to return two days later. At dawn we would set out in search of the prey.

Though night had scarcely come and the heat was great, we gathered at the fire to see each other's faces, to look instinctively for protection. We talked a little, confessed to being tired, and decided to go to bed. Each hammock had been tied by one end to a single tree, firm though not very thick in the trunk. Stretching out from this axis in different directions, the hammocks were supported by the other end on other trunks. Each of us carried his rifle, cartridges, and some provisions which couldn't remain exposed on the ground. The sight of the weapons made us consider the place where we were, surrounded by the unknown. A slight feeling of terror made us
laugh, cough, and talk. But fatigue overcame us, 4
that heavy fatigue which compels the soldier to scorn danger, to put down his rifle, and to fall asleep though the most persistent enemy pursues him. We scarcely noticed the supreme grandeur of that remote tropical night.

I don't know whether it was the light of the magnificent dawn or the strange noises which awakened me and made me sit up in my hammock and look carefully at my surroundings. I saw nothing but the awakening of that life which at night falls into the lethargy[5] of the jungle. I called my sleeping companions and, alert and seated in our hanging beds, we dressed ourselves. We were preparing to jump to the ground when we clearly heard a somewhat distant, sudden sound of rustling branches. Since

3. rejuvenate (ri jü′və nāt), *v.* make young or vigorous again; renew.
4. **Marañón** (mā′rā nyôn′) **River,** a river in Peru, flowing north and then east into the Amazon.
5. lethargy (leth′ər jē), *n.* lack of energy; inactivity.

2 Geographical Note
Trans-Andean Peru

The action of "The Boar Hunt" takes place in Northeastern Peru where the Marañón River—one of the Amazon's major tributaries—breaks through the Andean chain and enters the lush lowland jungles. The area remained largely unexplored when this story was written.

3 Literary Element
Personification

Suggest that students find examples in which the boars are personified in military terms. *(page 137—"organized just like an army"; "an army given over to the delights of victory")* More examples can be found on page 139.

Question By consistently comparing them with an army, what human characteristic does the narrator imply that the boars possess? *(Possible responses: discipline, plans to defeat an enemy, strategy, weapons)*

4 Literary Element
Foreshadowing

Question How does the narrator hint that something terrible is going to happen to the hunters? *(Possible response: Before the men fall asleep, they notice being surrounded by the unknown and feel a slight terror.)*

BUILDING ENGLISH PROFICIENCY

ESL
LEP
ELD
SAE
LD

Exploring Key Concepts

Hunting shapes both the plot of this story and the characters in it. Help students prepare a details web, using information from pages 136–137 to consider why the four men considered hunting important. (Sample responses are shown.) Then as students talk about the concept, they can put their personal ideas about the sport in another web. Remind students to refer to the webs in later activities.

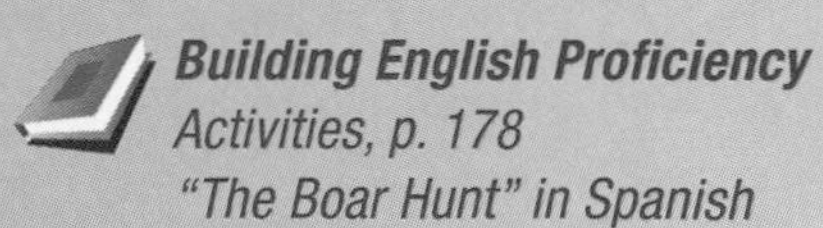
Building English Proficiency
Activities, p. 178
"The Boar Hunt" in Spanish

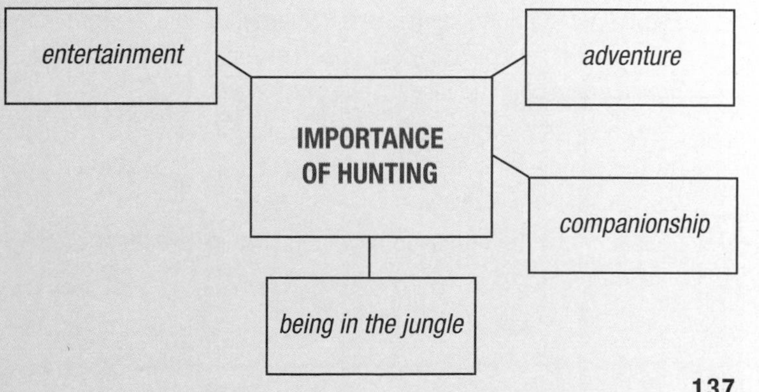

Art Study

Responses to Caption Questions Students may mention similarities such as the herd of peccaries—which are piglike. The hunters and the jungle setting are also similar. Differences may include that the hunters seem more confident in the picture than in the story, and the atmosphere suggests risk, but not terror.

The American painter George Catlin (1796–1872) is known primarily for his vivid portrayals of native North American tribes before their cultures were challenged by European expansion. Catlin also traveled extensively in later years through Central and South America, exhibiting the results in Europe and the United States. Major collections of his work are in the Smithsonian Institution and the American Museum of Natural History.

5 Literary Focus
Moral

Questions What is the author's opinion of this hunt? What details reveal it? *(The author believes this hunt is wrong. Details include that it is so easy to kill the boars, the hunt becomes a slaughter; the hunters regard the animals' suffering as comical; the hunters' happy satisfaction with the purposeless killing.)*

This detail from George Catlin's painting, *A Fight with Peccaries, Rio Trombutas, Brazil,* uses vertical and horizontal lines to contrast the weapons and active thought of human beings with the natural instinct of wild animals. Which details in the painting fit your impressions of the story? Which details seem to depart from the story?

it did not continue, however, we descended confidently, washed our faces with water from our canteens, and slowly prepared and enjoyed breakfast. By about 11:00 in the morning we were armed and bold and preparing to make our way through the jungle.

But then the sound again. Its persistence and proximity in the thicket made us change our minds. An instinct made us take refuge in our hammocks. We cautiously moved our cartridges and rifles into them again, and without consulting each other we agreed on the idea of putting our provisions safely away. We passed them up into the hammocks, and we ourselves finally climbed in. Stretched out face down, comfortably suspended with rifles in hand, we did not have to wait long. Black, agile boars quickly appeared from all directions. We welcomed them with shouts of joy and well-aimed shots. Some fell immediately, giving comical snorts, but many more came out of the jungle. We shot again, spending all the cartridges in the magazine. Then we stopped to reload. Finding ourselves safe in the height of our hammocks, we continued after a pause.

We counted dozens of them. At a glance we made rapid calculations of the magnitude of the destruction, while the boars continued to come out of the jungle in uncountable numbers. Instead of going on their way or fleeing, they seemed confused. All of them emerged from the jungle where it was easy for us to shoot them. Occasionally we had to stop firing because the frequent shooting heated the barrels of our rifles. While they were cooling we were able to joke, celebrating our good fortune. The

MINI-LESSON: GRAMMAR
Compound Sentences

Teach A compound sentence is composed of two or more independent clauses but no subordinate clauses. The clauses are usually linked by a comma and a conjunction, such as *and* or *but.*

We cautiously moved our cartridges and rifles into them again, and without consulting each other we agreed on the idea of putting our provisions safely away.

Spend a few moments identifying the two independent clauses in the example.

Activity Ideas

- Students can find other compound sentences in the selection.
- Then they can divide the compound sentences into independent clauses.
- Have students examine a final draft of their writing and combine some simple sentences into compound sentences. Ask them to evaluate which version of their writing is better.

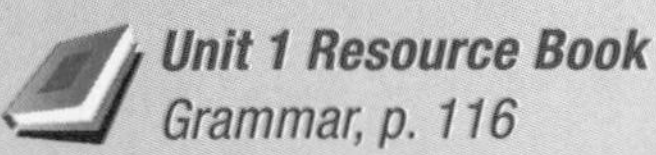

Unit 1 Resource Book
Grammar, p. 116

6 impotent[6] anger of the boars amazed us. They raised their tusks in our direction, uselessly threatening us. We laughed at their snorts, quietly aimed at those who were near, and Bang! a dead boar. We carefully studied the angle of the shoulder blade so that the bullet would cross the heart. The slaughter lasted for hours.

At 4:00 P.M. we noticed an alarming shortage of our ammunition. We had been well supplied and had shot at will. Though the slaughter was gratifying,[7] the boars must have numbered, as we had been informed previously, several thousands, because their hordes didn't diminish. On the contrary, they gathered directly beneath our hammocks in increasing groups. They slashed furiously at the trunk of the tree which held the four points of the hammocks. The marks of the tusks remained on the hard bark. Not without a certain fear we watched them gather compactly, tenaciously,[8] in tight masses against the resisting trunk. We wondered what would happen to a man who fell within their reach. Our shots were now sporadic,[9] well aimed, carefully husbanded.[10] They did not drive away the aggressive beasts, but only redoubled their fury. One of us
7 ironically noted that from being the attackers we had gone on the defensive. We did not laugh very long at the joke. Now we hardly shot at all. We needed to save our cartridges.

The afternoon waned and evening came upon us. After consulting each other, we decided to eat in our hammocks. We applauded ourselves for taking the food up—meat, bread, and bottles of water. Stretching ourselves on our hammocks, we passed things to each other, sharing what we needed. The boars deafened us with their angry snorts.

After eating, we began to feel calm. We lit cigars. Surely the boars would go. Their numbers were great, but they would finally leave peacefully. As we said so, however, we looked with greedy eyes at the few unused cartridges that remained. Our enemies, like enormous angry ants, stirred beneath us, encouraged by the ceasing of our fire. From time to time we carefully aimed and killed one or two of them, driving off the huge group of uselessly enraged boars at the base of the trunk which served as a prop for our hammocks.

Night enveloped us almost without our noticing the change from twilight. Anxiety also overtook us. When would the cursed boars leave? Already there were enough dead to serve as trophies to several dozen hunters. Our feat would be talked about; we had to show ourselves worthy of such fame. Since there was nothing else to do, it was necessary to sleep. Even if we had had enough bullets it would have been impossible to continue the fight in the darkness. It occurred to us to start a fire to drive the herd off with flames, but apart from the fact that we couldn't leave the place in which we were suspended, there were no dry branches in the lush forest. Finally, we slept.

We woke up a little after midnight. The darkness was profound, but the well-known noise made us aware that our enemies were still there. We imagined they must be the last ones which were leaving, however. If a good army needs several hours to break camp and march off, what can be expected of a vile army of boars but disorder and delay? The following morning we would fire upon the stragglers, but this painful thought bothered us: they were in large and apparently active numbers. What were they up to? Why didn't they leave? We thus spent long hours of worry. Dawn finally came, splendid in the sky but noisy in the jungle still enveloped inwardly in shadows. We eagerly waited for the sun to penetrate the foliage in order to survey the appearance of the field of battle of the day before. 8

What we finally saw made us gasp. It terrified

6. impotent (im′pə tənt), *adj.* powerless; helpless.
7. gratifying (grat′ə fī ing), *adj.* satisfying; pleasing.
8. tenaciously (ti nā′shəs lē), *adv.* stubbornly.
9. sporadic (spə rad′ik), *adj.* appearing or happening at intervals in time; occasional.
10. husbanded (huz′bənd əd), *adj.* managed carefully.

6 Reading/Thinking Skills
Make Judgments

Discuss with students what kind of men they think would joke, laugh, and feel gratified while slaughtering more animals than they could ever possibly carry home. *(Possible response: heartless, irresponsible, greedy)*

7 Literary Element
Irony

At this point the characters realize the grim irony of their predicament.

Question Is this an example of dramatic irony or situational irony? *(It is an example of situational irony because what happened is the opposite of what the characters, and readers, expected to happen. Dramatic irony occurs when facts known by the reader are not known by the characters.)*

8 Literary Element
Personification and Metaphor

Discuss with students how the narrator develops the personification of the boars into an extended metaphor: the hunters and the opposing "army of boars" are now encamped on a "field of battle."

BUILDING ENGLISH PROFICIENCY

ESL LEP ELD SAE LD

Exploring Mood

The mood of the men—and the story—shifts abruptly in the paragraph beginning "At 4:00 P.M. we noticed. . . ." Help students to appreciate this change.

Activity Ideas

- Ask students to reread page 138 and the top of page 139. Have them point out phrases that suggest the boars' power, such as "uncountable numbers" and "impotent anger".
- Encourage students to draw a two-panel cartoon titled "Four P.M.: Before and After." Remind them that the hunters' expressions should be clear in both panels.
- Ask students to recall and share comic strips, cartoons, TV programs, or experiences in which "the tables are turned" on a bully or a group of bullies.

9 Reading/Thinking Skills
Compare and Contrast

After students finish the story, direct them to silently reread the sentence beginning "It seemed to us. . . ." and the last paragraph of the story. Discuss whether or not these statements reflect the surviving hunter's philosophy. Encourage students to test their own beliefs against the statements.

Check Test

1. How do the four hunters meet? *(working on a sugar plantation)*
2. Where do they hear of the herds of wild boars? *(in a village at the edge of the river)*
3. How do the hunters react when they first see the boars? *(They shout with joy and shoot them.)*
4. Why do the hunters stop firing occasionally? *(to let the rifle barrels cool off)*
5. What is the last thing the survivor sees before he runs to the river? *(remains of clothing and footwear)*

Unit 1 Resource Book, *Alternate Check Test, p. 117*

us. The boars were painstakingly continuing the work which they had engaged in throughout the entire night. Guided by some extraordinary instinct, with their tusks they were digging out the ground underneath the tree from which our hammocks hung; they gnawed the roots and continued to undermine them like large, industrious rats. Presently the tree was bound to fall and we with it, among the beasts. From that moment we neither thought nor talked. In desperation we used up our last shots, killing more ferocious beasts. Still, the rest renewed their activity. They seemed to be endowed with intelligence. However much we concentrated our fire against them, they did not stop their attack against the tree.

Soon our shots stopped. We emptied our pistols, and then silently listened to the tusks gnawing beneath the soft, wet, pleasant-smelling earth. From time to time the boars pressed against the tree, pushing it and making it creak, eager to smash it quickly. We looked on, hypnotized by their devilish activity. It was impossible to flee because the black monsters covered every inch in sight. 9 It seemed to us that, by a sudden inspiration, they were preparing to take revenge on us for the ruthless nature of man, the unpunished destroyer of animals since the beginning of time. Our imagination, distorted by fear, showed us our fate as an atonement for the unpardonable crimes implicit[11] in the struggle of biological selection. Before my eyes passed the vision of sacred India, where the believer refuses to eat meat in order to prevent the methodical killing of beasts and in order to atone for man's evil, bloody, treacherous slaughter, such as ours, for mere vicious pleasure. I felt that the multitude of boars was raising its accusing voice against me. I now understood the infamy[12] of the hunter, but what was repentance worth if I was going to die with my companions, hopelessly devoured by that horde of brutes with demonlike eyes?

Stirred by terror and without realizing what I was doing, I hung from the upper end of my hammock, I balanced myself in the air, I swung in a long leap, I grasped a branch of a tree facing the one on which the boars were digging. From there I leaped to other branches and to others, reviving in myself habits which the species had forgotten.

The next moment a terrifying sound and unforgettable cries told me of the fall of the tree and the end of my companions. I clung to a trunk, trembling and listening to the chattering of my jaws. Later, the desire to flee gave me back my strength. Leaning out over the foliage, I looked for a path, and I saw the boars in the distance, marching in compressed ranks and holding their insolent snouts in the air. I knew that they were now withdrawing, and I got down from the tree. Horror overwhelmed me as I approached the site of our encampment, but some idea of duty made me return there. Perhaps one of my friends had managed to save himself. I approached hesitantly. Each dead boar made me tremble with fear.

But what I saw next was so frightful that I could not fix it clearly in my mind: remains of clothing—and footwear. There was no doubt; the boars had devoured them. Then I ran toward the river, following the tracks we had made two days before. I fled with great haste, limbs stiff from panic.

Running with long strides, I came upon the boat. With a great effort, I managed to row to the huts. There I went to bed with a high fever which lasted many days.

I will participate in no more hunts. I will contribute, if I have to, to the extermination of harmful beasts. But I will not kill for pleasure. I will not amuse myself with the ignoble[13] pleasure of the hunt.

11. **implicit** (im plis′it), *adj.* meant, but not clearly expressed or distinctly stated; implied.
12. **infamy** (in′fə mē), *n.* a very bad reputation; public disgrace.
13. **ignoble** (ig nō′bəl), *adj.* without honor; disgraceful.

MINI-LESSON: LITERARY FOCUS
Moral

Teach A moral is the teaching that is always concerned with right and wrong and the distinctions between them.

In "The Boar Hunt," the moral is concerned with the distinction between hunting as a sport and the sanctity of animal life.

Activity Ideas

- Challenge students to write continuously for tw minutes on the morality of hunting for sport.
- Open a discussion, inviting students to share several reactions based on their writing. Then take an informal poll to determine which sides of the issue students support.
- Finally, let students reflect on whether or not their opinions were affected by the story.

After Reading

Making Connections

Shaping Your Response

1. By the end of the story, for whom do you feel more compassion—the hunters or the boars? Why?
2. If you were filming this story, what sounds, images, or camera tricks would you use to create a mood of increasing tension?
3. Do you think the outcome of the story is appropriate, or could the author have made his point more effectively another way? Explain.

Analyzing the Story

4. **Personification** is the attributing of human characteristics to nonhuman creatures or objects. Find two instances in which boars are personified; explain what human qualities they seem to have.
5. In what way is the hunters' decision to tie all four hammocks to the same tree significant to the **plot**?
6. Trace the narrator's attitude toward killing animals from the beginning of the story through the very end.
7. This story is set east of the Andes Mountains in Peru. Explain why this **setting** is important to the story.

Extending the Ideas

8. Do you think that cultural settings and conditions such as food supply should determine our **choices** about how we use (and use up) natural resources? Or are there universal rules about conservation that all people should obey? Explain.
9. If you have read "The Interlopers," draw a Venn diagram showing similarities and differences between the men in both stories.

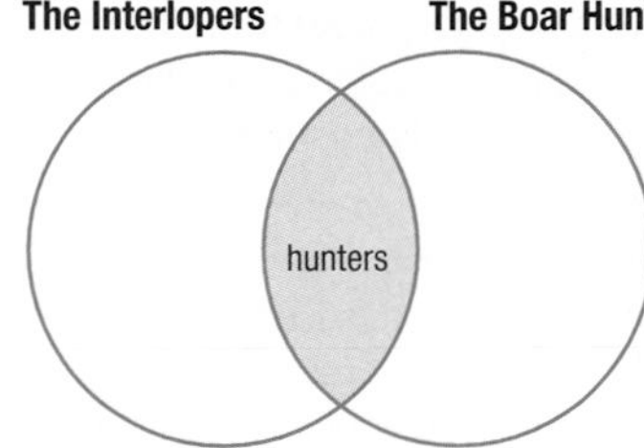

Literary Focus: Moral

A **moral** is a lesson conveyed in a work. In "The Boar Hunt," the narrator learns a lesson after he and his companions become the hunted.

- Explain the moral of "The Boar Hunt."
- Do you think the message of this story would have been conveyed as effectively in a nonfiction article? Explain.

After Reading

MAKING CONNECTIONS

1. Possible responses: the hunters—because it's easier to identify with other humans; the boars—because the hunters are ruthless.

2. Possible responses: close-up shots of the boars' tusks digging into the tree, images of the men shooting wildly at the boars with superimposed shots of more and more boars charging, loud sound effects of rifles shooting and screaming boars.

3. Possible responses: Yes, allowing one hunter to survive and to state the moral was powerful; no, all the hunters should have died and the moral should have been implied.

4. Possible responses: The boars are compared to an army; "they seemed to be endowed with intelligence"; to a persecuted race of people ("I felt the multitude of boars was raising its accusing voice.").

5. Possible response: The hunt begins as an easy slaughter. When the boars become the attackers, they can overwhelm the hunters because they are trapped in the tree.

6. First he kills for pleasure, then sadistically, then out of fear; finally, he vows to never participate in a hunt again.

7. Possible response: In this unexplored wilderness, the hunters underestimate the forces of nature.

8. Possible response: All creatures exploit their environment to survive. Those who manage to balance the need for survival with respect for the environment generally survive longer.

9. Possible responses:

Interlopers	Both	Boar Hunt
enemies, all die, hunting humans, vengeance	men, nature wins, beliefs change	friends, one lives, hunting animals, pleasure

LITERARY FOCUS: MORAL

Possible responses: A responsible hunter respects nature; hunting for pleasure is wrong.

- Possible response: Yes, facts and actual events can be convincing; no, the dramatic fictional account made a stronger impression.

VOCABULARY STUDY

1. b
2. a
3. a
4. b
5. d
6. c
7. d
8. d
9. a
10. c

Unit 1 Resource Book, Vocabulary, p. 115 Vocabulary Test, p. 118

WRITING CHOICES

Writer's Notebook Update

- Students should first establish what they believe is the author's moral.
- Remind students that they can allude to other stories, such as "The Interlopers" to make their points.

Attack of the Killer Broccoli

Some students might prefer to record their advertisements, using tape or video recorders.

What I Think of Your Mink

Ask students if they feel a sense of responsibility to speak out about animal rights. Ask if they have definite opinions on the issue.

Selection Test

Unit 1 Resource Book, pp. 119–120

Vocabulary Study

Number your paper from 1 to 10. Then match each numbered word with the letter of its synonym.

gratifying
husbanded
ignoble
implicit
impotent
infamy
lethargy
rejuvenate
sporadic
tenaciously

1. *impotent* **a.** powerful **b.** helpless **c.** severe **d.** loud
2. *lethargy* **a.** inactivity **b.** denseness **c.** energy **d.** injury
3. *rejuvenate* **a.** renew **b.** impoverish **c.** enlighten **d.** repeat
4. *tenaciously* **a.** flexibly **b.** stubbornly **c.** willfully **d.** reluctantly
5. *husbanded* **a.** wasted **b.** married **c.** cut **d.** managed carefully
6. *implicit* **a.** specific **b.** expressed **c.** implied **d.** obvious
7. *infamy* **a.** sorrow **b.** esteem **c.** fame **d.** disgrace
8. *ignoble* **a.** honorable **b.** fortunate **c.** ignorant **d.** disgraceful
9. *sporadic* **a.** occasional **b.** subsequent **c.** frequent **d.** steady
10. *gratifying* **a.** opposing **b.** envying **c.** satisfying **d.** surprising

Expressing Your Ideas

Writing Choices

Writer's Notebook Update How accurate were your predictions? Go back and see if you can list more clues that point to the outcome. Then write several sentences that complete the following observation: *The fact that the narrator survives makes the ending more (less) effective than if everyone had perished.*

Attack of the Killer Broccoli Imagine that you are a creature or an item in the environment that has been misused by humans. Think of a way to seek revenge. What kind of science fiction movie would this revenge story be? Think of a title for such a movie and write an **advertisement** for it.

What I Think of Your Mink Someone whom you admire is planning to buy a mink coat. This person asks you what you think of the decision. Write a brief **dialogue** in which you express your ideas, including those relating to ecology and to animal rights.

Other Options

You're on the Air Plan a **radio talk program** in your classroom to discuss your class's views of whether animals should be killed for human purposes such as medicine, clothing, and food. One or two students will "host" the program, accept "calls" from listeners, and keep the discussion on track. Other students will "call in" to the program with statements of opinion on the subject. Callers must listen carefully to preceding callers in order to build on previous discussions. Only a host can interrupt a caller.

Drawing a Moral Many cartoons promote greater awareness of ecological problems. Work with a partner to plan and draw a **cartoon** about an ecological issue or moral dilemma presented in "The Boar Hunt."

OTHER OPTIONS

You're on the Air

You might stage this activity by having the host sit at a desk in front of the classroom and have "callers" speak from behind a screen.

Drawing a Moral

Challenge students to convey their ideas in pictures without the help of speech bubbles or captions.

Before Reading

from Red Azalea

by Anchee Min China

Anchee Min
born 1957

Anchee Min (än′shē min) was born in Shanghai, China, during the communist rule of Mao Tse-tung (mä′ō dzu′dùng). During the Cultural Revolution, she become a leader of the Little Red Guards, and was later chosen to star in one of Madame Mao's movies. But her fortunes changed with the death of Chairman Mao, the execution of Madame Mao, and the ensuing political turmoil. In 1983 Min fled to the United States, where she published *Red Azalea* and a novel, *Katherine,* both about the horrors of the revolution. When Min toured China to promote *Red Azalea,* the government ironically touted her as an example of what Chinese women could accomplish.

Building Background

The time line below shows some of the events that preceded and followed the **Cultural Revolution.** Additional information is provided on page 145.

China
Mao Tse-tung

Events Surrounding the Cultural Revolution 1966–1970

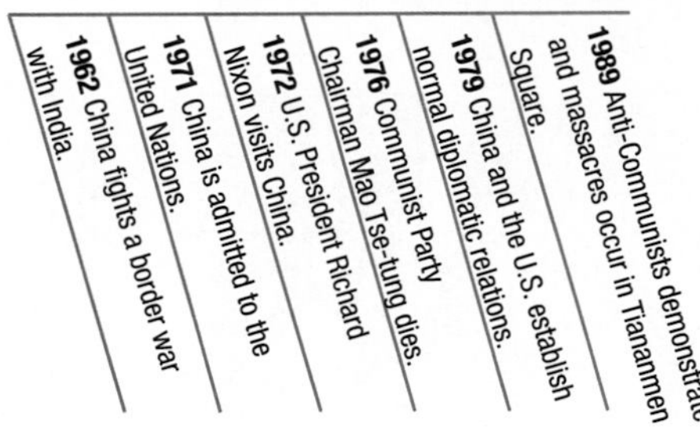
1962 China fights a border war with India.
1971 China is admitted to the United Nations.
1972 U.S. President Richard Nixon visits China.
1976 Communist Party Chairman Mao Tse-tung dies.
1979 China and the U.S. establish normal diplomatic relations.
1989 Anti-Communists demonstrate and massacres occur in Tiananmen Square.

Literary Focus

Conflict The struggle between a character and an opposing force in a story is called **conflict.** A story may have more than one kind of conflict, as you will see in the selection you are about to read.

Writer's Notebook

Pressure Points Growing up is never easy, but growing up in China during the Cultural Revolution presented special challenges. List some of the conflicts and challenges you recall having at age thirteen. Then as you read Anchee Min's autobiography, list the conflicts and challenges she faced as a member of the Little Red Guards.

Before Reading

Building Background

Invite students to share their knowledge of people and events on the time line, and of specific current political events in China. You might bring to class some recent news reports of how Chinese authorities deal with dissidents.

Literary Focus

The **conflicts** in *Red Azalea* involve Anchee Min's moral crisis as she struggles to come to terms with her divided loyalties. Tell students to keep this question in mind as they read: To whom is Anchee Min most loyal—the party, her teacher, her family, or herself?

Writer's Notebook

Suggest that students sort their list into categories, such as conflicts with institutions, family, friends, and themselves.

More about Anchee Min

At 17, Anchee Min was sent to a labor collective where she was later discovered by talent scouts and recruited to work at Shanghai Film Studios. She currently lives in Los Angeles.

SUPPORT MATERIALS OVERVIEW

Unit 1 Resource Book
- Graphic Organizer, p. 105
- Study Guide, p. 106
- Vocabulary, p. 107
- Grammar, p. 108
- Alternate Check Test, p. 109
- Vocabulary Test, p. 110
- Selection Test, pp. 111–112

Building English Proficiency
- Literature Summaries
- Activities, p. 179

Reading, Writing & Grammar SkillBook
- Writing, pp. 107–108
- Grammar, Usage, and Mechanics, pp. 245–246

The World of Work
- International Teacher, p. 5
- Informal Speech, p. 6

Technology
- Audiotape 6, Side B
- Personal Journal Software
- Custom Literature Database: For more autobiographies, see the database.
- Test Generator Software

During Reading

Selection Objectives

- to explore issues of peer pressure and the consequences of disloyalty
- to identify internal and external conflict in a narrative
- to practice the use of verbals

Unit 1 Resource Book
Graphic Organizer, p. 105
Study Guide, p. 106

Theme Link

A student suffers the consequences of betraying her favorite teacher to an oppressive authority.

Vocabulary Preview

proletarian, someone belonging to the proletariat, the lowest class in economic and social status

exploitation, selfish or unfair use

initiative, active part in taking the first steps in any undertaking; lead

insurrection, a rising against established authority; revolt

contort, twist or bend out of shape

Students can add the words and definitions to their Writer's Notebooks.

SELECTION SUMMARY

Red Azalea

Thirteen-year-old Anchee is an exceptional student and model member of the Little Red Guards. One day Chain, the new Communist Party secretary, tells her that she must publicly condemn her favorite teacher, Autumn Leaves, as an American spy. Anchee is shocked and disbelieving. Chain manipulates her and calls her loyalty into question until she finally agrees to write the speech denouncing her teacher. The next day at the public meeting Autumn Leaves is brutally interrogated but denies everything. Chain calls his key witness, Anchee, who reads her damning testimony. Autumn Leaves confronts the girl, calmly urging her to tell the truth, but before the shouting crowd, Anchee hysterically says the teacher poisoned her mind. Later, Anchee bitterly regrets her action, but is never forgiven.

For summaries in other languages, see the ***Building English Proficiency*** *book.*

Red Azalea

Anchee Min

1

During the Cultural Revolution, which began in 1966, Mao Tse-tung, the Chinese Communist leader from 1945 to 1976, authorized radicals in the Communist Party to remove from power any people they believed failed to follow Communist principles. The accused were dismissed from their positions, and the different factions of radicals who replaced them fought for power. Violence often resulted in cities and provinces as a result of these power struggles. Militant student groups called Red Guards were formed, demonstrations that were sometimes violent were held, and universities were closed from 1966 to 1970. At the time this excerpt from Red Azalea *takes place, China was undergoing the turmoil of the Cultural Revolution.* 2

◄ The 1967 propaganda poster entitled *Hail the Defeat of Revisionism in Our China* uses Western perceptions and scale (note the gregarious expressions and muscular proportions) and advertising techniques to sell communism to the Chinese public. Using details from this poster, cite at least five things Maoist China considers important.

Art Study

Responses to Caption Questions
Possible responses: Mao Tse-Tung, literacy, labor, unity, equality of the sexes, conformity, destroying opposition to their beliefs

1 Reading/Thinking Skills
Analogies

At a later point in the reading you might come back to the title and discuss how it fits in the story. Point out to students that red is the international color of the Communist party. An azalea is a flowering shrub cultivated for the variety of its flowers.

Question Why did the author choose this title? *(Possible response: The title might refer to Anchee Min herself: a "beautiful flower" cultivated by the party to be a symbol of communism.)*

2 Literary Element
Setting

Discuss with students the importance of the setting (time period and place) in this selection. Point out that the political events described here are very particular to the historical setting in which they occur, but that parallels can be found in American history, especially during the period of McCarthyism in the early 1950s.

BUILDING ENGLISH PROFICIENCY

Understanding Historical Background

Use visual materials, such as videos and photos in books and magazines, to facilitate discussion about the fervor of the Cultural Revolution and related issues. In class, groups can look for photographs of the Red Guard, students reading at rallies, and other pictures that show the militancy of the movement. The following books are good sources:

Barcata, Louis. China *In the Throes of the Cultural Revolution.* Hart Publishing Co., 1968.

Clayre, Alasdair. *The Heart of the Dragon.* Houghton Mifflin, 1985.

De Lee, Nigel. *Rise of the Asian Superpowers from 1945.* Franklin Watts, 1987.

Library of Nations: *China.* TimeLife Books, 1984.

Peking. TimeLife Books, 1978.

Building English Proficiency
Activities, p. 179

3 Literary Element
Symbolism

Discuss with students the use of symbols as tools to express complex ideas in easily understood terms.

Questions

- What might the "East wind" symbolize? *(Possible response: the ideology of Chinese communism)*
- What might "the fighting drum" symbolize? *(Possible response: the call to violent revolution)*

4 Literary Element
Metaphor

Question What does Anchee mean when she says she was "the opera"? *(Possible response: that she felt grandly larger than life)*

5 Historical Note
The Mao Years

In the documentary *The Mao Years*, former members (now adults) of the Red Guards describe meetings in which a neighbor, teacher, or family member was denounced as an imperialist and "struggled against." Those accused were often beaten or killed. During the five years of the Cultural Revolution, it is estimated that 400,000 people died while being "struggled against."

In school Mao's books were our texts. I was the head of the class on the history of the Communist Party of China. To me, history meant how proletarians[1] won over the reactionaries. Western history was a history of capitalist exploitation.[2] We hung portraits of Marx, Engels, Lenin and Stalin[3] next to Mao in our classrooms. Each morning we bowed to them as well as bowing to Mao, praying for a long, long life for him. My sisters copied my compositions. My compositions were collected slogans. I always began with this: "The East wind is blowing, the fighting drum is beating. Who is afraid in the world today? It is not the people who are afraid of American imperialists.[4] It is the American imperialists who are afraid of the people." Those phrases won me prizes. Space Conqueror[5] looked up to me as if I were a magician. For me, compositions were nothing; it was abacus competitions that were difficult. I wrote compositions for my brother and sisters, but I felt I had not much in common with the children. I felt like an adult. I longed for challenges. I was at the school day and night promoting Communism, making revolution by painting slogans on walls and boards. I led my schoolmates in collecting pennies. We wanted to donate the pennies to the starving children in America. We were proud of what we did. We were sure that we were making red dots on the world's map. We were fighting for the final peace of the planet. Not for a day did I not feel heroic. I was the opera.

I was asked to attend the school's Revolutionary Committee meeting. It was 1970 and I was thirteen years old. I discussed how to carry on the Cultural Revolution at our Long Happiness Elementary School with the committee people, the true revolutionaries. When I raised my hand and said I would like to speak, my face would no longer flush. I knew what I was talking about. Phrases from *People's Daily* and *Red Flag* magazine poured out of my mouth. My speeches were filled with an impassioned and noble spirit. I was honored. In the early seventies my being a head of the Little Red Guards[6] at school brought our family honor. My award certificates were my mother's pride, although she never hung them on the wall. My name was constantly mentioned by the school authority and praised as "Study Mao Thoughts Activist," "Mao's Good Child" and "Student of Excellences." Whenever I would speak through a microphone in the school's broadcasting station, my sisters and brother would be listening in their classrooms and their classmates would look at them with admiration and envy.

The school's new Party secretary, a man named Chain, was a workers' representative from the Shanghai[7] Shipping Factory. He was about fifty years old, extremely thin, like a bamboo stick. He taught me how to hold political meetings. He liked to say, We have to let our little general play a full role in the Cultural Revolution and give full scope to the initiative[8] of the Little Red Guards. He told me not to be afraid of things that I did not understand. You must learn to think like this, he said. If the earth stops spinning, I'll continue to spin.

---

1. **proletarian** (prō′lə ter′ē ən), *n.* someone belonging to the proletariat, the lowest class in economic and social status, including all unskilled laborers.
2. **exploitation** (ek′sploi tā′shən), *n.* selfish or unfair use.
3. **Marx . . . Stalin.** Karl Marx, 1818–1883, was a German political philosopher, writer on economics, and advocate of socialism. Friedrich Engels, 1820–1895, was a German socialist writer. Vladimir Ilyich Lenin, 1870–1924, was a Russian Communist leader, the founder of the Soviet government and its first premier from 1918 to 1924. Joseph Stalin, 1879–1953, was a Soviet political leader and dictator of the Soviet Union from 1929 to 1953.
4. **imperialist,** *n.* someone who favors imperialism, or the policy of extending the rule or authority of one country over other countries and colonies.
5. **Space Conqueror,** one of Anchee Min's siblings.
6. **Little Red Guards,** children in elementary school who formed a younger group of Red Guards.
7. **Shanghai** (shang′hī′), seaport in E. China.
8. **initiative** (i nish′ē ə tiv), *n.* active part in taking the first steps in any undertaking; lead.

MINI-LESSON: LITERARY FOCUS
Conflict

Teach A struggle between opposing forces, characters, or emotions is a conflict. An *internal conflict* is a struggle between opposing emotions, needs, or desires within a single character. An *external conflict* is a struggle between a character and some outside force: another character, the force of nature, or pressure of society.

Activity Idea Discuss with students some examples of conflicts in the plot. Ask students to:

- identify internal and external conflicts
- compare and contrast the conflicts
- evaluate which are universal

6 **QUESTION: Jot down in your notebook any questions you have about the Cultural Revolution.**

It was the first week of November when Secretary Chain called me in. He told me excitedly that the committee had finally dug out a hidden class enemy, an American spy. He said, We are going to have a meeting against her, a rally which two thousand people will be attending. You will be the student representative to speak against her. I asked who it was. Wrinkling his eyebrows, the secretary pronounced a shocking name. It was Autumn Leaves, my teacher. I thought I heard Secretary Chain wrong. But he nodded at me slowly, confirming that I heard him exactly right.

7 I sat down. I actually dropped down on the chair. My legs all of a sudden lost their strength.

Autumn Leaves was a thin, middle-aged lady and was seriously nearsighted. She wore a dark pair of glasses and had a hoarse voice and a short temper. She loved Chinese, mathematics and music. The first day she stepped into the classroom, she asked all the students if any of us could tell what her name Autumn Leaves meant. No one was able to figure it out. Then she explained it. She said that there was a famous poem written in the Tang Dynasty[9] about autumn leaves. It praised the beauty and significance of the falling leaves. It said that when a leaf fell naturally, it symbolized a full life. The touch of the ground meant the transformation of a ripe leaf to fresh mud. It fertilized the seeds through the winter. Its pregnancy came to term with the next spring. She said that we were her spring.

She was an energetic teacher who never seemed to be tired of teaching. Her methods were unique. One moment she raised her arms to shoulder level and stretched them out to the sides, making herself look like a cross when explaining infinity; the next moment she spoke with a strong Hunan[10] accent when explaining where a poet was from. Once she completely lost her voice while trying to explain geometric progression[11] to me. When she finally made me understand, she laughed silently like a mute with her arms dancing in the air. When I thanked her, she said that she was glad that I was serious about learning. She set me up as the example for our class and then the entire grade. When she knew that I wanted to improve my Chinese, she brought me her own books to read. She was this way with all her students. One day when it was raining hard after class, she gave students her raincoat, rain shoes and her umbrella as they went home. She herself went home wet. The next day she had a fever, but she came to class and struggled on, despite her fever. By the time she finished her lecture, she had lost her voice again. There was no way I could picture Autumn Leaves as an American spy. 8

THERE WAS NO WAY I COULD PICTURE AUTUMN LEAVES AS AN AMERICAN SPY.

As if reading my mind, Secretary Chain smiled and asked me if I had ever heard the phrase "Raging flames refine the real gold." I shook my head. He said, It is time for you to test yourself out to see whether you are a real revolutionary or an armchair revolutionary. He recited a Mao quotation: "To have a revolution is not like having a dinner party, not like painting a pretty picture or making embroidery. It is not that easy and relaxing. Revolution is an

9. **Tang** (tāng) **Dynasty,** a Chinese dynasty from A.D. 618 to 907, under which China expanded toward central Asia, Buddhism gained its political influence, printing was invented, and Chinese poetry reached its finest development.
10. **Hunan** (hü nän′), a province in SE central China.
11. **geometric progression,** sequence of numbers in which each number is multiplied by the same factor in order to obtain the following number. 2, 4, 8, 16, and 32 form a geometric progression.

6 Active Reading
Question

Students' questions might include why Mao unleashed the Cultural Revolution and what the policy of the United States was toward China during that period.

7 Reader's Response
Making Personal Connections

Ask students to describe Anchee Min in one sentence. Then explain why this character would or wouldn't be their friend. *(Possible responses: She's a teacher's pet, talented, smart, idealistic, or impressionable. The friendship would depend on whether or not students identified with the character's traits.)*

8 Reading/Thinking Skills
Compare and Contrast

Point out that the teachings of Communism, through Secretary Chain, and those of Autumn Leaves are now both woven into Anchee Min's way of thinking. Do students think the two approaches are contradictory? Put their responses in a Venn diagram.

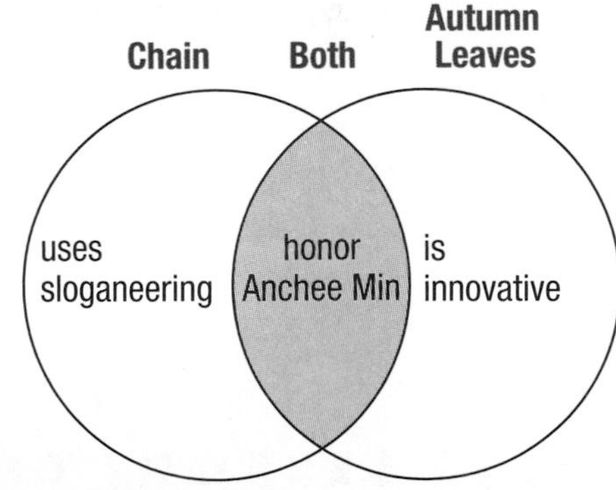

BUILDING ENGLISH PROFICIENCY

ESL
LEP
ELD
SAE
LD

Analyzing Characterization

The narrator's deep admiration for her teacher is central to her conflict—and to students' understanding of the story. Help students consider that characterization.

1. Ask groups of students to talk about reasons that Anchee Min likes and admires her teacher. *(Possible responses: Autumn Leaves's energy, kindness, intelligence, and interest in the students as individuals)* Have students discuss whether or not they agree with her reasons, and why.

2. Extend the discussion by letting students describe teachers they admire. Some students may share their knowledge of why people, groups, or governments might want to discredit or get rid of good teachers.

3. Bring closure by letting students compose a list of qualities that they think a good teacher should have or write a description of an ideal teacher.

9 Reading/Thinking Skills
Discussion

Ask students to discuss how Chain uses the fable to manipulate the narrator. What is his motive? *(Possible response: He is planning violent action against Autumn Leaves, and so he dehumanizes her in the eyes of the narrator by calling her a wolf.)*

10 Reading/Thinking Skills
Evaluate

Ask students to evaluate the tactics Chain uses to confuse the narrator. How does he create a no-win situation for her? *(Possible response: He tells her she is naive and cannot trust her feelings; by doing this he intends to leave her no choice but to trust him.)*

11 Reading/Thinking Skills
Generalization

After reading about Secretary Chain's childhood, open a discussion of what conditions must be present in order for a revolution to occur.

You may wish to mention that the "Liberation" refers to the Communist victory over nationalist forces and General Mao proclaiming China a people's republic.

insurrection[12] in which one class overthrows the other with violent force."

I found my words were blocked by my stiff tongue. I kept saying, Autumn Leaves is my teacher. Secretary Chain suggested that we work on my problem. He lit a cigarette and told me
9 the fable of "A Wolf in Sheep's Skin." He said Autumn Leaves was the wolf. He told me that Autumn Leaves' father was a Chinese American who was still living in America. Autumn Leaves was born and educated in America. Secretary Chain said, The capitalist sent his daughter back to China to educate our children. Don't you see this as problematic?

For the next two hours Secretary Chain convinced me that Autumn Leaves was a secret agent of the imperialists and was using teaching as a weapon to destroy our minds. Secretary Chain asked whether I would tolerate that. Of course not, I said. No one can pull our proletarians back to the old society. Good, said Secretary Chain, tapping my shoulders. He said he knew I would be a sharp spear for the Party. I raised my head and said, Secretary, please tell me what to do. He said, Write a speech. I asked what I should write. He said, Tell the masses how you were mentally poisoned. I said that I did not quite understand the words "mentally poisoned." Secretary Chain
10 said, You are not mature enough to understand that yet. He then asked me to give an opinion on what kind of person I thought Autumn Leaves was. I told him the truth.

Secretary Chain laughed loudly at me. He said that I had already become a victim of the spy who had almost killed me with the skill of the wolf who killed the sheep, leaving no trace of blood. He punched his fist on the table and said loudly, That in itself is wonderful material to be discussed! I felt awkward. He stopped laughing and said, You shouldn't be discouraged by your immaturity.

He made me feel disappointed in myself. Let me help you, he suggested. He asked me the name of the books she loaned me. *An Old Man of Invention,* I began to recall, *The Little Mermaid,* and *Snow White.* He asked for the author's name. I said it was something like Andersen.

Secretary Chain suddenly raised his hand in the air and furrowed his brow. He said, Stop, this is it. Who is Andersen? An old foreign man, I guess, I replied. What were his fairy tales about? About lives of princes, princesses and little people. What does Andersen do now? he asked. I do not know, I replied.

Look how careless you are! Secretary Chain almost yelled at me. He could be a foreign spy! Taking out a little glass vial, Secretary Chain put a few pills into his mouth. He explained that it was the medicine for his liver pain. He said his liver was hurting badly, but he could not tell his doctor about this because he would be hospitalized immediately. He said his pain was getting worse, but he could not afford to waste a second in the hospital. How can I disappoint Chairman Mao, who put his trust in people like us, the working class, the class that was once even lower than the pigs and dogs before Liberation?

His face was turning purple. I suggested that he take a rest. He waved me to go on as he pressed his liver with his hands to endure the pain. He told me that he did not have much schooling. His parents died of hunger when he was five. His brother and little sister were thrown into the sea after they died of cholera.
He was sold to a child dealer for fifteen pounds 11
of rice. He became a child worker in a shipping factory in Shanghai and was beaten often by the owner. After the Liberation he joined the Party and was sent to a workers' night school. He said, I owe our Party a great deal and I haven't worked hard enough to show my appreciation.

I looked at him and was touched. His pain seemed to be increasing. His fingers pressed

12. insurrection (in′sə rek′shən), *n.* a rising against established authority; revolt.

MINI-LESSON: GRAMMAR
Verbals

Teach Types of verbals are: the participle, the gerund, and the infinitive.

A *participle* is a verb form that can be used as an adjective: "He became a child worker in a shipping factory."

A *gerund* is a verb form ending in *-ing* that is used as a noun: "[Autumn Leaves] was using teaching as a weapon to destroy our minds."

An *infinitive* is a verb form, usually preceded by *to*, that can be used as a noun: "To have a revolution is not like having a dinner party. . . ."

Activity Ideas

- Students should identify the verbals in the examples.
- As they read, have them find other examples.
- Then have students create three sentences using an infinitive, a participle, or a gerund. The verbals can be forms of *teach*, *betray*, or *denounce.*

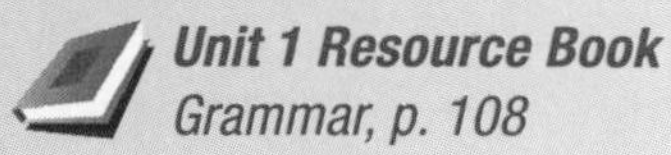
Unit 1 Resource Book
Grammar, p. 108

against his liver harder, but he refused to rest. You know, we found Autumn Leaves' diary and it had a paragraph about you, he said. What . . .
12 what did she say about me? I became nervous. She said that you were one of the very few children who were educable. She put quotation marks around "educable." Can you think of what that means? Without waiting for my reply, Secretary Chain concluded, It was obvious that Autumn Leaves thought that you could be educated into her type, her father's type, the imperialists' type. He pointed out that the purpose of writing this diary was to present it to her American boss as proof of her success as a spy.

My world turned upside down. I felt deeply hurt and used. Secretary Chain asked me whether I was aware of the fact that I was set up as a model by Autumn Leaves to influence the others. Her goal is to make you all *betray* Communism! I felt the guilt and anger. I said to Secretary Chain that I would speak tomorrow. He nodded at me. He said, Our Party trusts you and Mao would be very proud of you.

Pull out the hidden class enemy, the American spy Autumn Leaves! Expose her under the bare sun! the crowd shouted as soon as the meeting started. I was sitting on the stage on one of the risers. Two strong men escorted Autumn Leaves onto the stage facing the crowd of two thousand people, including her students and colleagues. Her arms were twisted behind her. She was almost unrecognizable. Only a few days had passed since I had seen her, but it seemed as though she had aged ten years. Her hair had suddenly turned gray. Her face was colorless. A rectangular board reading "Down with American Spy" hung from her neck. Two men forced her to bow to Mao's portrait three times. One of the men bent her left arm very hard and said, Beg Chairman Mao for forgiveness now! Autumn Leaves refused to say the words. The two men bent her arms up backward. They bent her harder. Autumn Leaves' face contorted[13] in pain and then her mouth moved. She said the words and the men let her loose.

PREDICT: Do you think the narrator will betray Autumn Leaves? Explain. 13

My mouth was terribly dry. It was hard to bear what I saw. The string of the heavy board seemed to cut into Autumn Leaves' skin. I forgot what I was supposed to do—to lead the crowd to shout the slogans—until Secretary Chain came to remind me of my duty.

Long live the great proletarian dictatorship! I shouted, following the slogan menu. I was getting more and more scared when I saw Autumn Leaves struggling with the two men who had been trying to press her head toward the floor while she tried to face the sky. When her eyeglasses fell off, I saw her eyes close tightly.

Secretary Chain shouted at her. The crowd shouted, Confess! Confess! Secretary Chain took the microphone and said that the masses would not have much patience. By acting this way Autumn Leaves was digging her own grave.

Autumn Leaves kept silent. When kicked hard, she said that she had nothing to confess. She said she was innocent. Our Party never accuses anyone who is innocent, said Secretary Chain, and yet the Party would never allow a class enemy to slip away from the net of the proletarian dictatorship. He said now it was time to demonstrate that Autumn Leaves was a criminal. He nodded at me and turned to the crowd. He said, Let's have the victim speak out!

I stood up and felt dizzy. The crowd began clapping their hands. The sunlight was dazzlingly bright and was hurting my eyes. My vision became blurred and I saw a million bees wheeling in front of me sounding like helicopters. As the crowd kept clapping, I moved to the front of the stage. I stopped in front of the

13. **contort** (kən tôrt′), *v.* twist or bend out of shape.

12 Literary Focus
Conflict

Explore with students what internal conflicts must be occurring within Anchee as she asks, "What . . . what did she say about me?" *(Possible response: conflict between her love and faith in her teacher and what Chain and the diary say)*

13 Active Reading
Predict

Most students will probably predict that Anchee Min will betray her teacher. She seems convinced by Chain's arguments, she enjoys her honored position in the Little Red Guards, and she is unlikely to stand up against the angry crowd of two thousand. Some, however, might predict that the girl's love for her teacher will make her stand on the side of truth and personal loyalty.

BUILDING ENGLISH PROFICIENCY

Evaluating an Argument

How valid are Secretary Chain's arguments against Autumn Leaves? Lead a discussion of the charges he makes.

1. Write the following sentence starter on the chalkboard: Autumn Leaves deserves to be denounced because _______.

2. Have students reread the passage beginning "As if reading my mind, . . ." (page 147) to ". . . I do not know, I replied." (page 148). Then ask them to complete the sentence starter in as many ways as they can. *(Possible responses: it's a good test to see if you [Anchee] are a real revolutionary; her father is Chinese American and lives in America; her teaching destroys minds; she lets students read books by foreign authors.)*

3. Have students decide whether each accusation is reasonable, and why.

14 Literary Element
Characterization

Question Characterize Autumn Leaves using one word descriptions. *(Possible responses: courageous, fierce, defiant, and honest)*

15 Literary Element
Characterization

In a short time, the characters have revealed much about themselves. Take this opportunity to discuss whether these characters are stereotypical and "flat," or rounded out. Is Chain merely a puppet of the regime, Autumn Leaves a hapless victim, and Anchee Min a teacher's pet?

The World of Work
International Teacher

For the real-life experiences of a teacher working in an atmosphere of political tension, use—

The World of Work
pp. 5–6

microphone. Taking out the speech I had written last night, I suddenly felt a need to speak with my parents. I had not gone home but slept in the classroom on the table with other Little Red Guards. Five of us wrote the speech. I regretted not having my parents go over the speech with me. I took a deep breath. My fingers were shaking and would not obey in turning the pages.

Don't be afraid, we are all with you, Secretary Chain said in my ear as he came to adjust the height of the microphone. He placed a cup of water in front of me. I took the water and drank it down in one breath. I felt a little better. I began to read.

I read to the crowd that Autumn Leaves was the wolf in sheep's skin. I took out the books she loaned me and showed them to the crowd. As I was delivering my speech, I saw from the corner of my eye that Autumn Leaves had turned her head in my direction. She was murmuring. I became nervous but managed to continue. Comrades,[14] I said, now I understand why Autumn Leaves was so kind to me. She was trying to turn me into an enemy of our country, and a running dog of the imperialists! I read on.

There was some slogan-shouting, during which I glanced secretly at Autumn Leaves. She was breathing hard and was about to fall. I stood, my limbs turning cold. I tried to remove my eyes from Autumn Leaves, but she caught them. I was terrified when I saw her staring at me without her eyeglasses. Her eyes looked like two Ping-Pong balls that almost popped out of her eye sockets.

The crowd shouted, Confess! Confess! Autumn Leaves began to speak slowly to the crowd with her hoarse voice. She said that she would never want to turn any of her students into
14 the country's enemy. She broke into tears. Why would I? she repeated again and again. She was losing her voice. She began to swing her head trying to project her words, but no sound came out. She swung her head again making an effort to let her words out. She said that her father loved this country and that was the reason she came back to teach. Both her father and she believed in education. Spy? What are you talking about? Where did you get this idea? She looked at me.

If the enemy doesn't surrender, let's boil her, fry her and burn her to death! Secretary Chain shouted. The crowd followed, shouting and waving their fists. Secretary Chain signaled for me to go on. But I was trembling too hard to continue. Secretary Chain walked to the microphone from the back of the stage. He took over the microphone. He told the crowd that this was a class enemy's live performance. It had given us an opportunity to learn how deceitful an enemy could be. Can we allow her to go on like this? No! the crowd shouted.

Secretary Chain was ordering Autumn Leaves to shut up and accept the criticism of the revolutionary masses with a correct attitude. Autumn Leaves said that she could not accept any untrue facts. Autumn Leaves said that a young girl such as I should not be used by someone with an evil intention.

You underestimated our Little Red Guard's political awareness, Secretary Chain said with a scornful laugh. Autumn Leaves demanded to speak to me. Secretary Chain told her to go ahead. He said that as a thorough-going dialectical materialist[15] he never underestimated the
role of teachers by negative example. 15

As the crowd quieted down, Autumn Leaves squatted on her heels to seek her glasses on the floor. When she put her glasses back on, she started to question me. I was scared. I did not expect that she would talk to me so seriously. My terror turned into fury. I wanted to get away. I

14. **comrade** (kom′rad), *n.* member of the Communist party.
15. **dialectical** (dī′ə lek′tə kəl) **materialist** (mə tir′ē ə list) a follower of the socialist doctrine that advocates a classless society emerging as the result of a long struggle between economic classes.

MINI-LESSON: VOCABULARY
Negative Connotations

Teach Explain that political rhetoric is often loaded with terms aimed at putting opponents and their ideas in a negative light, such as "running dog of the imperialists."

Challenge students to rephrase this expression to neutralize its negative connotation. *(Possible response: agent of the imperialists)*

Activity Idea Ask students to find examples of negatively charged expressions in the story and in political campaign literature, ads, or articles. Discuss in class how the language can be stated neutrally.

Tsao Yu-tung's painting, *Night Battle,* shows happy and energetic workers laboring into the night to repair a dam. How does this painting, along with the poster on page 144, reinforce the philosophy of Secretary Chain in this story?

said, How dare you put me in such a spot to be questioned like a reactionary? You had used me in the past to serve the imperialists; now you want to use me to get away from the criticism? It would be a shame if I lost to you!

Autumn Leaves called my name and asked if I really believed that she was an enemy of the country. If I did not think so, could I tell her who assigned me to do the speech. She said she wanted the truth. She said Chairman Mao always liked to have children show their honesty. She asked me with the exact same tone she used when she helped me with my homework. Her eyes were demanding me to focus on them. I could not bear looking at her eyes. They had looked at me when the magic of mathematics was explained; they had looked at me when the beautiful Little Mermaid story was told. When I won the first place in the Calculation-with-Abacus Competition, they had looked at me with joy; when I was ill, they had looked at me with sympathy and love. I had not realized the true value of what all this meant to me until I 16
lost it forever that day at the meeting.

I heard people shouting at me. My head felt like a boiling teapot. Autumn Leaves' eyes behind the thick glasses now were like gun barrels shooting at me with fire. Just be honest! her hoarse voice raised to its extreme. I turned to Secretary Chain. He nodded at me as if to say, Are you going to lose to an enemy? He was smiling scornfully. Think about the snake, he said.

Art Study

Responses to Caption Questions
Possible response: Both works are rendered to convey the idea that to find fulfillment one must happily submit without reservation to the party.

Visual Literacy

- What are the values reinforced in this poster? *(Possible responses: gender equality, armed struggle, labor, and industrialization)*
- What mood do the images of electric lights and loudspeakers create? *(Possible responses: excitement, festivity, progress, modernization)*
- Who would you say is the target audience of this poster? *(Possible response: young adults)*

16 Reading/Thinking Skills

Recognize Values

Question What is it that Anchee Min values so much and has lost forever? *(Possible responses: her teacher's love, honesty, compassion, intelligence, sensitivity)*

BUILDING ENGLISH PROFICIENCY

Understanding Causes and Effects

This selection generates many "whys." For example, why does the narrator wish that she could speak to her parents before her speech? Why does Anchee Min agree to denounce Autumn Leaves? Why did Secretary Chain choose Anchee Min? Encourage students to develop and complete a chart, such as the following, that explores the "whys" in this story.

Causes	Effects
Anchee is scared of the Secretary; she needs protection.	Anchee wants to see her parents before her speech.
Anchee is a leader and a respected student. People will believe her.	Secretary Chain chooses Anchee Min to denounce Autumn Leaves.

17 Literary Element
Fable

Point out that fables—tales involving animals, used to teach a moral lesson—are found in cultures worldwide. Chain uses this fable to demonize Autumn Leaves as a snake that must be destroyed. Yet it can be interpreted quite differently within the context of Anchee Min's internal conflict: the girl is the snake who was saved by Autumn Leaves's nurturing and who is about to betray, or "bite," her savior. Challenge students to imagine why this fable would impress Chain. *(Chain was saved by the Party and would never want to be considered a "snake.")*

18 Literary Focus
Conflict

Invite students to identify the main conflict in *Red Azalea* and how it is resolved. *(Possible response: The main conflict is Anchee Min's conflict within herself about whether to betray Autumn Leaves. It is resolved when she does betray the teacher.)*

Check Test

1. What is the age of the narrator? *(thirteen)*
2. Who informs Anchee Min that her teacher is a spy? *(Secretary Chain)*
3. What happens to Autumn Leaves at the party meeting? *(She is publicly humiliated and beaten.)*
4. What is Anchee Min's mother's profession? *(teacher)*
5. What happens to the narrator when she goes home after the meeting? *(Her mother punishes her, making her write a saying by Confucius a thousand times.)*

Unit 1 Resource Book, *Alternate Check Test, p. 109*

Yes, the snake, I remembered. It was a story Mao told in his book. It was about a peasant who found a frozen snake lying in his path on a snowy day. The snake had the most beautiful skin the peasant had ever seen. He felt sorry for her and decided to save her life. He picked up the snake
17 and put her into his jacket to warm her with the heat of his body. Soon the snake woke up and felt hungry. She bit her savior. The peasant died. Our Chairman's point is, Secretary Chain said as he ended the story, to our enemy, we must be absolutely cruel and merciless.

I was never forgiven. Even after twenty-some years. After the Revolution was over. It was after my begging for forgiveness, I heard the familiar hoarse voice say, I am very sorry, I don't remember you. I don't think I ever had you as my student.

It was at that meeting I learned the meaning of the word "betrayal" as well as "punishment."

I MUST FIGHT AGAINST ANYONE WHO DARED TO OPPOSE MAO'S TEACHING.

I turned to look at the wall-size portrait of Mao. It was mounted on the back of the stage. The Chairman's eyes looked like two swinging lanterns. I was reminded of my duty. I must fight against anyone who dared to oppose Mao's teaching. The shouting of the slogans encouraged me.

Show us your standpoint—Secretary Chain passed me the microphone. I did not know why I was crying. I heard myself calling for my parents as I took the microphone. I said Mama, Papa, where are you? The crowd waved their angry fists at me and shouted, Down! Down! Down! I was so scared, scared of losing Secretary Chain's trust, and scared of not being able to denounce[16] Autumn Leaves. Finally, I gathered all my strength and yelled hysterically at Autumn Leaves with tears in my throat: Yes, yes, yes, I do believe that you poisoned me; and I do believe that you are a true enemy! Your dirty tricks will have no more effect on me! If you dare to try them on me again, I'll shut you up! I'll use a needle to stitch your lips together!

Indeed, I was too young then, yet one is never too young to have vanity. When my parents learned about the meeting from Blooming, Coral and Space Conqueror, they were terrified. They talked about disowning me. My mother said, I am a teacher too. How would you like to have my student do the same to me? She shut me out of the house for six hours. She said being my mother made her ashamed.

I wrote what my mother asked of me a thousand times. It was an old teaching passed down since Confucius.[17] It said, Do not treat others how you yourself would not like to be treated. My mother demanded I copy it on rice paper using ink and a brush pen. She said, I want to carve this phrase in your mind. You are not my child if you ever disobey this teaching. 18

16. **denounce** (di nouns′), *v.* condemn publicly.
17. **Confucius** (kən fyü′shəs), 551?–479 B.C., Chinese philosopher and moral teacher.

MINI-LESSON: CRITICAL THINKING
Detecting Bias

Teach Bias is an emotional or ideological prejudice toward one side of an issue or conflict. Ask student what bias is revealed by these statements.

Anchee: We wanted to donate pennies to the starving children in America. *(Americans are selfish and uncaring of the poor.)*

Autumn Leaves: Anchee can be "educated." *(Anchee loves to learn; she will think for herself.)*

Chain: Accept the criticism of the masses with a correct attitude. *(Authority must be obeyed.)*

Activity Idea In order to detect bias students can become familiar with events and figures surrounding the issues. Ask students to:

- research the Cultural Revolution independently
- discuss whether or not they think Anchee Min's representation of events is biased
- discuss if it is possible to find an unbiased account of such emotionally charged events

After Reading

Making Connections

Shaping Your Response

1. Would you recommend that this selection be included in a world literature book? Why or why not?
2. How do you think you would have responded if you had been in Anchee Min's place?
3. Draw a chart like the one below and rate Autumn Leaves as a teacher in each category. Be prepared to explain your ratings.

Quality	Excellent	Average	Poor
dedicated			
energetic			
unselfish			
creative			
inspirational			

Analyzing the Autobiography

4. What do you **infer** are Autumn Leaves's reasons for refusing to beg Chairman Mao for forgiveness?
5. Explain how the **fable** about the peasant and the snake states a **theme** of the story.
6. What **character** traits does Autumn Leaves reveal as she faces her accusers and Anchee Min?
7. Given this **setting**—China during the Cultural Revolution—do you think Anchee Min had a **choice** about whether or not to betray Autumn Leaves? Explain.

Extending the Ideas

8. Although the Cultural Revolution is long over, human rights continues to be an issue in China and in virtually every other country in the world. Cite contemporary examples of people who **choose** to fight for their rights and speak out against human injustice.
9. How does Autumn Leaves compare to your favorite teacher?

Literary Focus: Conflict

Conflict, the struggle between a character and an opposing force, can be *external* (character against character, nature, or society) or *internal* (character torn between opposing emotions involving conscience, duty, desire, etc.).

- What internal and external conflicts are in *Red Azalea?*

After Reading

MAKING CONNECTIONS

1. Possible response: Yes, even though the events in this story are representative of a particular culture, they convey a universal lesson.
2. Possible response: Even though it was wrong, given my age and the pressure from the Secretary, I would have done the same.
3. Possible response: excellent in all categories
4. Possible responses: that she believed she had done nothing wrong; that she would not cave in to fear tactics
5. Possible response: The fable is related to the story's theme of betrayal: Autumn Leaves tries to help Anchee and is "bitten" by her.
6. She is defiant, tough, and righteous.
7. Possible response: She had a choice, but it was a difficult choice. Had she refused, she would have left herself open to similar accusations of betraying Communist ideals.
8. Students might mention school organizations that support human rights, and consult weekly news magazines for contemporary examples of human rights activism.
9. Possible response: They both go beyond what is expected of them.

LITERARY FOCUS: CONFLICT

- Anchee's crisis in choosing between loyalty to the party and to her teacher is *Red Azalea's* main internal conflict.
- The main external conflict is between Secretary Chain and Autumn Leaves. Anchee is caught in the middle of this conflict. Students might also say the main conflict is between a repressive government and freedom of expression.

VOCABULARY STUDY

1. yes
2. no
3. yes
4. yes
5. no

Unit 1 Resource Book,
Vocabulary, p. 107
Vocabulary Test, p. 110

WRITING CHOICES

Writer's Notebook Update

You might draw a large Venn diagram on the chalkboard and have students complete it as a class activity. As a follow up, discuss peer and societal pressure and situations when individuals should resist it.

Compare Notes

Remind students that a comparison includes both similarities and differences. Since many will find it easier to dwell on the differences between the U.S. and China than on similarities, urge students to strike a balance between the two in their writing.

Ask the Author

Students might work in groups or as a class to brainstorm a list of questions. Then they can work individually to group related questions and prioritize them as they would in preparation for an interview.

Selection Test

Unit 1 Resource Book,
pp. 111–112

Vocabulary Study

Use your knowledge of the italicized words to answer *Yes* or *No* to the following questions. Be prepared to explain your answers.

contort
exploitation
initiative
insurrection
proletarian

1. Are people with *initiative* likely to be good leaders?
2. If you *contort* your body, would you be standing straight?
3. Is *insurrection* a synonym for "rebellion"?
4. Does *exploitation* refer to unfair use?
5. Does a *proletarian* belong to the upper classes?

Expressing Your Ideas

Writing Choices

Writer's Notebook Update Now that you have read *Red Azalea*, compare Anchee Min's conflicts and challenges with the ones you described before reading. Make a Venn diagram indicating both common experiences and those unique to you and to Anchee Min.

Compare Notes Develop ideas from your notebook into a **comparison** describing what it was like to be thirteen in the 1990s in the U.S. and in 1970 in China.

Ask the Author Imagine that Anchee Min will be reading this excerpt aloud at your school. In preparation for her presentation, reread the excerpt and write down at least eight **questions** you want to ask the author to clarify the story or to find out more about her family and life in China or her life since she came to the United States.

Autumn Leaves Autumn Leaves explains that her name refers to a poem praising the beauty, significance, and transformation of leaves in the cycle of life. Write your own **poem** that expresses this subject.

Other Options

It's Your Time With a partner, make a **time line**, like that the one on page 143, that lists at least ten important events from the past thirty years in *your* country. Draw your time line on wide butcher paper, illustrate it, and present it to the class.

News Around the World Choose a partner with whom to "co-anchor" a special **news report** on human rights around the world. Gather recent news clips and pictures about human rights demonstrations and violence. Briefly describe each incident, show the location on a map, and display accompanying pictures.

OTHER OPTIONS

It's Your Time

To help students get started:

- discuss various subjects that could be dealt with in a narrowly focused time line, such as events in U.S. space exploration or rock 'n' roll or civil rights.
- suggest they research the "year-in-review" issues of news magazines in the microfilm section of the library.

News Around the World

Other students can support the news reports with a bulletin board display. Students might then work in small teams, focusing on different areas of the world. They should then contribute their findings for an assembly by a team of "designers" who will be responsible for mounting the display around a map of the world.

Before Reading

He-y, Come on Ou-t!

by Shinichi Hoshi Japan

Shinichi Hoshi
born 1926

Many people associate Japanese science fiction exclusively with images of the monster Godzilla or giant attacking ants. But during the 1950s and 1960s, while the Godzilla movies were appearing, talented and serious Japanese science fiction writers were producing stories, and the genre was becoming so popular that there were fan magazines—"fanzines"—and SF clubs. One such writer, Shinichi Hoshi (sin ə shē ô shē), has written over one thousand short stories and uses the genre to explore social and economic issues. In a simple and often humorous style, he portrays the environmental effects resulting from rapid growth and change.

Building Background

It's a Waste *Environmental pollution*, human destruction of the natural environment, is one of the most serious problems facing the world today. Both solid waste (garbage) and hazardous waste (poisonous or polluting substances) threaten health and contaminate the environment. In an effort to enforce conservation, many countries have pollution controls. For example, the U.S. bans DDT and leaded gasoline and stipulates that landfills must be lined with substances that prevent the escape of toxic chemicals into the water supply.

The story you are about to read, although fantasy, presents a very real problem and a dramatic warning about the consequences of irresponsible use of the environment.

Literary Focus

Inference What is the cartoon poking fun at? How can you tell? When you used clues in the cartoon to draw a conclusion, you were making an **inference**. As you read "He-y, Come on Ou-t!" look for clues to help you infer the author's main point.

"There was a whole bunch of people here protesting about something . . . pollution, probably."

Writer's Notebook

What's It All About? Science fiction is set wholly or partly in an unreal world with farfetched events that cannot be explained by current science. Sometimes one or more characters are nonhuman. Judging from the title and the fact that this is a science fiction story, quickwrite your ideas about what "He-y, Come on Ou-t!" might be about.

Before Reading

Building Background

The Japanese are especially attuned to the effects of environmental pollution. Elicit from students what they know about the aftermath of the atomic bombings of Hiroshima and Nagasaki and the lingering health problems caused by radiation poisoning. Another well-documented disaster occurred in the late 1950s in the Japanese fishing village of Minamata, where the dumping of mercury into the ocean resulted in a poisoned food supply. Over 600 villagers died.

Literary Focus

Prompt students to **infer** why people who protest pollution would litter. *(Possible responses: They are insincere; they don't understand the issue, they would rather talk than act.)*

Writer's Notebook

Students are unlikely to infer the story's plot from the title, but to get them started thinking about possibilities, ask:

- Who might be saying "He-y, Come on Ou-t!" and to whom?
- Why do you suppose the title is spelled as it is?

SUPPORT MATERIALS OVERVIEW

Unit 1 Resource Book
- Graphic Organizer, p. 121
- Study Guide, p. 122
- Vocabulary, p. 123
- Grammar, p. 124
- Alternate Check Test, p. 125
- Vocabulary Test, p. 126
- Selection Test, pp. 127–128

Building English Proficiency
- Literature Summaries
- Activities, p. 180

Reading, Writing & Grammar SkillBook
- Reading, pp. 63–64
- Grammar, Usage, and Mechanics, pp. 220–221

Technology
- Audiotape 7, Side A
- Personal Journal Software
- Custom Literature Database: For another view of environmental issues, see "Sell a Country? Why Not Sell the Air?" by Tecumseh on the database.
- Test Generator Software

During Reading

Selection Objectives

- to explore the theme of ecological responsibility
- to infer an author's meaning by examining context clues
- to understand the use of indefinite pronouns

Unit 1 Resource Book
Graphic Organizer, p. 121
Study Guide, p. 122

Theme Link

The villagers' apathy and the greed of the concessionaires begin a cycle that forces them to deal with the consequences of possibly being buried in toxic waste.

Vocabulary Preview

composure, calmness; quietness

contagious, spreading by direct or indirect contact; catching

plausible, appearing true, reasonable, or fair

shrine, a place of worship

throng, a crowd; multitude

Students can add the words and definitions to their Writer's Notebooks.

1 Cultural Note
Shinto Shrines

Shinto, the principal religion of Japan, emphasizes the worship of nature and ancestral spirits at shrines, which are usually built in scenic surroundings associated with particular deities. The shrine described in this story is probably a small roadside oratory, which would not be attended by a priest; nevertheless, it marks a sacred site—one that the villagers are willing to profane.

Question What can you infer from the fact that the hole had been the site of a shrine? *(Possible response: that the hole had at one time been considered sacred space)*

HE—Y, COME ON OU—T!

Shinichi Hoshi

Computer-generated art by David Em titled *Where 3* harnesses the power of technology to create futuristic special effects. What does the passageway in this image have in common with the hole in the village?

The typhoon had passed and the sky was a gorgeous blue. Even a certain village not far from the city had suffered damage. A little distance from the village and near the
1 mountains, a small shrine[1] had been swept away by a landslide.

"I wonder how long that shrine's been here."

"Well, in any case, it must have been here since an awfully long time ago."

"We've got to rebuild it right away."

While the villagers exchanged views, several more of their number came over.

"It sure was wrecked."

"I think it used to be right here."

"No, looks like it was a little more over there."

Just then one of them raised his voice. "Hey what in the world is this hole?"

1. shrine (shrīn), *n.* place of worship.

SELECTION SUMMARY

He-y, Come on Ou-t!

The people of a small village find that an ancient shrine has been swept away by a landslide. A hole in the ground is on the same spot. A man shouts down the hole and hears no echo. Then he drops a pebble in, ignoring an old man's warning that it might bring a curse. The hole appears to be bottomless and soon attracts a crowd. A scientist, after conducting tests, cannot explain the hole's lack of an echo. To save face, he suggests that it be filled in. A concessionaire sees the hole as an opportunity and buys the property. He uses the hole as a toxic waste dump, putting every conceivable type of refuse into it. Soon the government is also dumping waste in it. Everyone is happy until one day a workman up on a high building hears a shout from the sky and a pebble drops on his head.

For summaries in other languages, *see* the ***Building English Proficiency*** *book.*

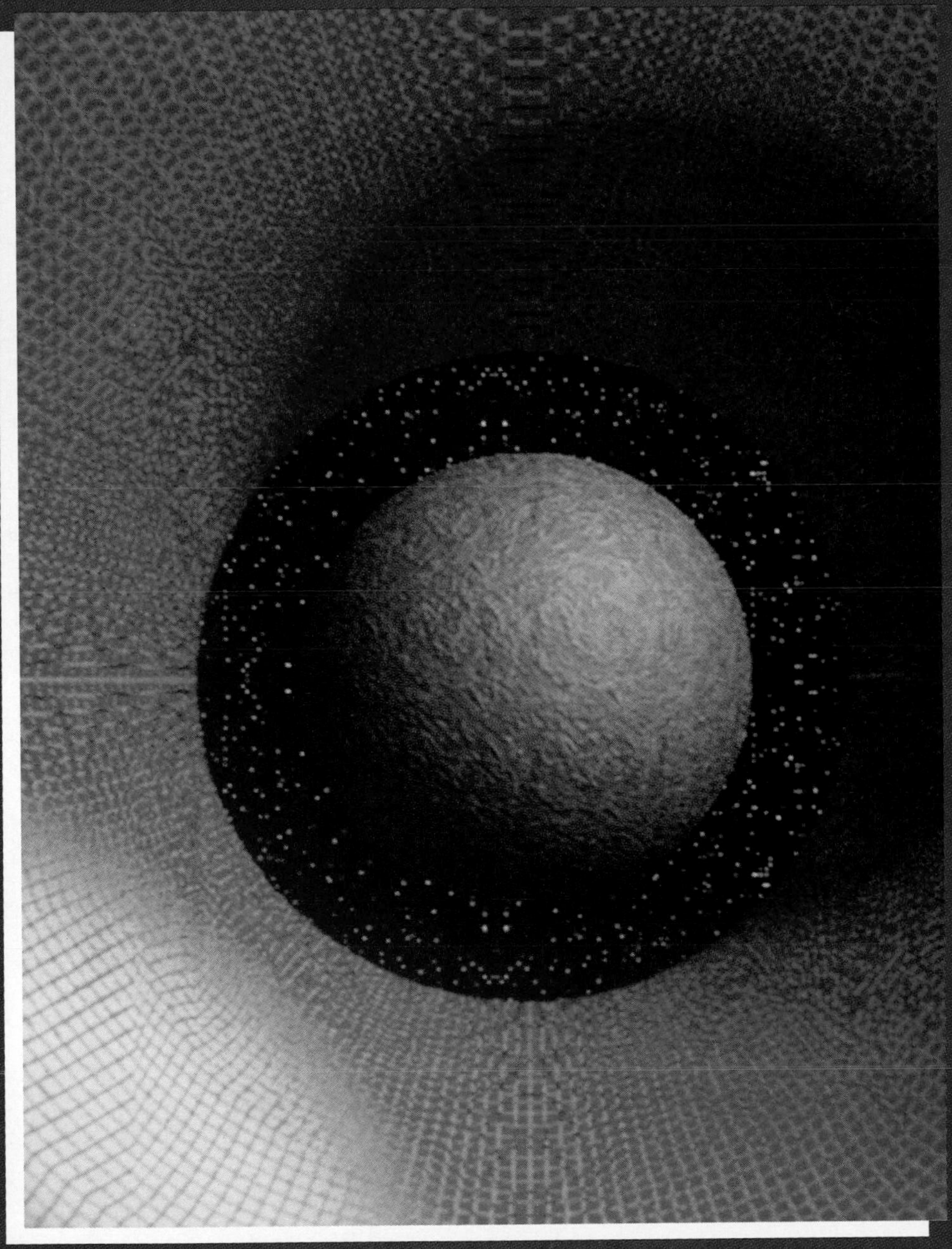

Art Study

Response to Caption Question
Students may suggest that both the image and the hole appear to be gateways to alternate universes.

Visual Literacy Computer-generated art has boomed in recent years along with the development of increasingly sophisticated graphic software programs.

Questions

- Does the planet appear to be earth? *(Possible response: No, it looks like a molten mass, almost like a young planet beginning to cool.)*
- What does the unusual appearance of the stars suggest? *(Possible response: The colors of the stars suggest an alternate universe.)*
- What can be inferred by the large highlight in the lower left corner? *(Possible response: The light source may be from a spaceship in which the viewer is traveling.)*
- How would you define the passageway in this image? *(Possible response: It is a "worm hole" like the ones the* Enterprise *often finds on* StarTrek.*)*

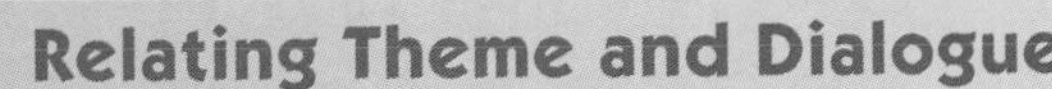

BUILDING ENGLISH PROFICIENCY

Relating Theme and Dialogue

Because this story's opening passage has no dialogue tags, students may need to understand that several people have gathered to view the typhoon's damage.

1. Assign one line of dialogue to each student. Have students read the dialogue several times. Prompt students to guess the number of speakers. *(at least three; enough to give the idea of a group)*

2. When students are comfortable with the dialogue, ask them how the conversation among the villagers demonstrates a sense of community—of people working as a group.

3. Have students discuss when group spirit is a positive force and when it can be a negative force. Urge them to watch for indications as to whether this community has a positive or negative group spirit.

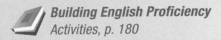

Building English Proficiency
Activities, p. 180

2 Literary Focus
Inference

Discuss with students what they can infer about the author's main point from this statement by the old man. Is there a certain wisdom underlying his superstition? *(Possible response: Yes, he knows that if people do not respect what they do not understand, disasters can occur.)*

3 Literary Focus
Inference

Discuss with students what they can infer about the author's main point from this action by the reporter. Is there wisdom in his action based on what he has witnessed? *(Possible response: Yes, he judges empirically that it is better not to be careless with things about which he knows nothing.)*

4 Literary Element
Dialogue

Point out that the author uses dialogue to advance the plot rather than to develop rounded characters. By exposing the attitudes of the onlookers, the author satirizes the apathy of the public toward important issues. Note how their concern differs from the old man's and the reporter's.

Where they had all gathered there was a hole about a meter in diameter. They peered in, but it was so dark nothing could be seen. However, it gave one the feeling that it was so deep it went clear through to the center of the earth.

There was even one person who said, "I wonder if it's a fox's hole."

"He—y, come on ou—t!" shouted a young man into the hole. There was no echo from the bottom. Next he picked up a pebble and was about to throw it in.

2 "You might bring down a curse on us. Lay off," warned an old man, but the younger one energetically threw the pebble in. As before, however, there was no answering response from the bottom. The villagers cut down some trees, tied them with rope and made a fence which they put around the hole. Then they repaired to the village.

"What do you suppose we ought to do?"

"Shouldn't we build the shrine up just as it was over the hole?"

A day passed with no agreement. The news traveled fast, and a car from the newspaper company rushed over. In no time a scientist came out, and with an all-knowing expression on his face he went over to the hole. Next, a bunch of gawking curiosity seekers showed up; one could also pick out here and there men of shifty glances who appeared to be concessionaires. Concerned that someone might fall into the hole, a policeman from the local substation kept a careful watch.

One newspaper reporter tied a weight to the end of a long cord and lowered it into the hole. A long way down it went. The cord ran out, however, and he tried to pull it out, but it would not come back up. Two or three people helped out, but when they all pulled too hard, the cord parted at the edge of the hole. Another 3 reporter, a camera in hand, who had been watching all of this, quietly untied a stout rope that had been wound around his waist.

The scientist contacted people at his laboratory and had them bring out a high-powered bull horn, with which he was going to check out the echo from the hole's bottom. He tried switching through various sounds, but there was no echo. The scientist was puzzled, but he could not very well give up with everyone watching him so intently. He put the bull horn right up to the hole, turned it to its highest volume, and let it sound continuously for a long time. It was a noise that would have carried several dozen kilometers above ground. But the hole just calmly swallowed up the sound.

In his own mind the scientist was at a loss, but with a look of apparent composure[2] he cut off the sound and, in a manner suggesting that the whole thing had a perfectly plausible[3] explanation, said simply, "Fill it in."

Safer to get rid of something one didn't understand.

The onlookers, disappointed that this was all that was going to happen, prepared to disperse.[4] Just then one of the concessionaires, having broken through the throng[5] and come forward, made a proposal.

"Let me have that hole. I'll fill it in for you."

"We'd be grateful to you for filling it in," replied the mayor of the village, "but we can't 4 very well give you the hole. We have to build a shrine there."

"If it's a shrine you want, I'll build you a fine one later. Shall I make it with an attached meeting hall?"

Before the mayor could answer, the people of the village all shouted out.

"Really? Well, in that case, we ought to have it closer to the village."

"It's just an old hole. We'll give it to you!"

2. **composure** (kəm pō′zhər), *n.* calmness; quietness.
3. **plausible** (plô′zə bəl), *adj.* appearing true, reasonable, or fair.
4. **disperse** (dis pėrs′), *v.* spread in different directions; scatter.
5. **throng** (thrông), *n.* a crowd; multitude.

MINI-LESSON: GRAMMAR
Indefinite Pronouns

Teach Pronouns that do not usually refer to a specific antecedent are called indefinite pronouns. Most indefinite pronouns express the idea of quantity. Remind students to check their writing to make sure these pronouns agree with the verbs.

Activity Ideas

- Ask students to identify the indefinite pronouns in this example from the selection:

  Whatever one wished to discard, the hole accepted it all.

- Have students write several variations of the sentence below by inserting words from the list. Remind students to make sure verbs agree with the indefinite pronouns.

  ____ are worried; ____ knows what to do about the hole.

all	another	any	both
each	everybody	many	most
none	one	several	some

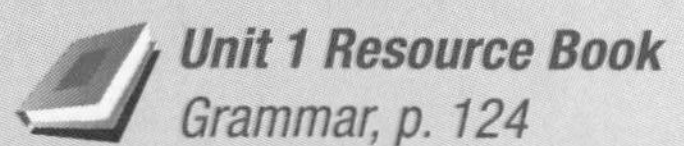

Unit 1 Resource Book
Grammar, p. 124

So it was settled. And the mayor, of course, had no objection.

The concessionaire was true to his promise. It was small, but closer to the village he did build for them a shrine and an attached meeting hall.

About the time the autumn festival was held at the new shrine, the hole-filling company established by the concessionaire hung out its small shingle at a shack near the hole.

The concessionaire had his cohorts[6] mount a loud campaign in the city. "We've got a fabulously deep hole! Scientists say it's at least five thousand meters deep! Perfect for the disposal of such things as waste from nuclear reactors."

Government authorities granted permission. Nuclear power plants fought for contracts. The people of the village were a bit worried
5 about this, but they consented when it was explained that there would be absolutely no above-ground contamination for several thousand years and that they would share in the profits. Into the bargain, very shortly a magnificent road was built from the city to the village.

Trucks rolled in over the road, transporting lead boxes. Above the hole the lids were opened, and the wastes from nuclear reactors tumbled away into the hole.

From the Foreign Ministry and the Defense Agency boxes of unnecessary classified documents were brought for disposal. Officials who came to supervise the disposal held discussions on golf. The lesser functionaries, as they threw in the papers, chatted about pinball.

The hole showed no signs of filling up. It was awfully deep, thought some; or else it might be very spacious at the bottom. Little by little the hole-filling company expanded its business.

Bodies of animals used in contagious[7] disease experiments at the universities were brought out, and to these were added the unclaimed corpses of vagrants.[8] Better than dumping all of its garbage in the ocean, went the thinking in the city, and plans were made for a long pipe to carry it to the hole.

The hole gave peace of mind to the dwellers of the city. They concentrated solely on produc- 6
ing one thing after another. Everyone disliked thinking about the eventual consequences. People wanted only to work for production companies and sales corporations; they had no interest in becoming junk dealers. But, it was thought, these problems too would gradually be resolved by the hole.

Young girls whose betrothals had been arranged discarded old diaries in the hole. There were also those who were inaugurating new love affairs and threw into the hole old photographs of themselves taken with former sweethearts. The police felt comforted as they used the hole to get rid of accumulations of expertly done counterfeit bills. Criminals breathed easier after throwing material evidence into the hole.

Whatever one wished to discard, the hole accepted it all. The hole cleansed the city of its filth; the sea and sky seemed to have become a bit clearer than before.

Aiming at the heavens, new buildings went on being constructed one after the other.

One day, atop the high steel frame of a new building under construction, a workman was taking a break. Above his head he heard a voice shout:

"He—y, come on ou—t!"

But, in the sky to which he lifted his gaze there was nothing at all. A clear blue sky merely spread over all. He thought it must be his imagination. Then, as he resumed his former posi- 7
tion, from the direction where the voice had come, a small pebble skimmed by him and fell on past.

The man, however, was gazing in idle reverie at the city's skyline growing ever more beautiful, and he failed to notice.

---

6. **cohort** (kō′hôrt), *n.* associate or follower.
7. **contagious** (kən tā′jəs), *adj.* spreading by direct or indirect contact; catching.
8. **vagrant** (vā′grənt), *n.* idle wanderer; tramp.

5 Reading/Thinking Skills
Recognize Assumptions

Question What are the assumptions of the people of the village as they consent to the dumping of waste near the village? *(Possible responses: They assume that the government is the expert and that their own fears are unfounded. They also assume they have no moral responsibility to protect future generations from the contamination that is predicted to occur in "several thousand years.")*

6 Reading/Thinking Skills
Make Judgments

Ask students to evaluate the city dweller's dislike of thinking about what was happening around them. Is this typical human behavior? Ask them to predict how this blindness will affect them in the long run.

7 Literary Element
Plot

Pause to allow students to state the connection between this event and the earlier event when the shout and the pebble went into the hole.

Question What will fall out of the sky next? *(everything that was ever dropped into the hole)*

Check Test

1. What happened to the shrine? *(It was swept away by a landslide.)*
2. What did the villagers discover where the shrine had been? *(a bottomless hole)*
3. Who dropped a weight tied to a cord into the hole? *(a newspaper reporter)*
4. What did the concessionaire build over the hole? *(a new shrine)*
5. What happens to the pebble that was tossed down the hole? *(It comes falling out of the sky.)*

Unit 1 Resource Book
Alternate Check Test, p. 125

BUILDING ENGLISH PROFICIENCY

ESL LEP ELD SAE LD

Speculating About the Outcome

At the end of the story, objects that were dumped into the hole begin to reappear. Ask students to consider what will happen next.

1. Have students list items that were dumped into the hole. You might use the graphic organizer shown.

2. Then have students talk about and record what they think will happen as each item falls from the sky and comes through the hole. Extend the discussion to what is thrown away in one day in their school.

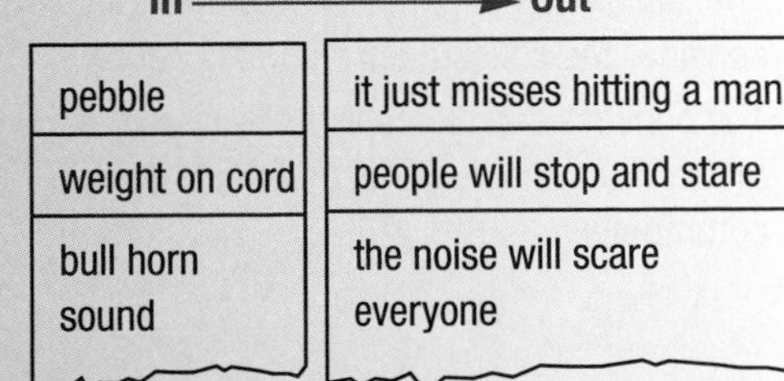

In	Out
pebble	it just misses hitting a man
weight on cord	people will stop and stare
bull horn sound	the noise will scare everyone

After Reading

MAKING CONNECTIONS

1. Possible responses: Closer to fantasy if the actual plot is considered; closer to reality if the potential effect of pollution is considered.

2. Possible response: People throwing garbage down a hole, which lands on people throwing garbage down a hole with a caption reading "What goes around comes around."

3. It could mean that toxic waste comes back to haunt us—that it is recycled in a negative sense.

4. Possible response: Our inability to see our environmental responsibility; the vast problem of pollution; some of its yet unknown effects.

5. The irony is that the hole will do exactly the opposite: It will pour the city's filth on top of it.

6. Possible response: Environmental irresponsibility will bring disaster.

7. Possible responses: *Silkwood*, *C.H.U.D.*, *Godzilla vs. the Smog Monster*.

After Reading

Making Connections

Shaping Your Response

1. Do you think this a realistic story, or is it mostly fantasy? Explain where you would place this story on the spectrum below.

   real ⟷ fantasy

2. Describe a picture and slogan that you would use to make an ecological poster based on this story.
3. What new meaning does this story give to the word *recycle*?

Analyzing the Story

4. What do you think the hole **symbolizes**, or represents?
5. Explain the **irony** in this statement from the story: "The hole cleansed the city of its filth."
6. In your opinion, what is a **theme** of this story.

Extending the Ideas

7. What other stories from books, movies, or TV present similar ecological warnings?

Literary Focus: Inference

When you read stories like "He–y, Come on Ou–t!" you must examine clues, suggestions, or hints, to **infer** the author's meaning. What can you infer about the following people from their actions?

- The scientist cannot explain the hole, yet he says, "Fill it in."
- The concessionaire offers to fill up the hole and build a new shrine.
- The villagers trade the concessionaire the hole for a new shrine.

Vocabulary Study

Word analogy tests require you to understand the relationship between a pair of words and choose another pair of words with the same relationship. Analogies reflect relationships such as these:

- antonyms *(impotent : powerful)*
- synonyms *(beg : implore)*
- part-to-whole *(finger : hand)*
- place-activity *(pool : swim)*

An analogy can be expressed this way: "*Spoke* is to *wheel* as ___ is to ___." To complete this analogy, you would first determine that a spoke is part of a wheel and then decide what other word pair expresses a similar relationship. Study the relationship of each of the following pairs of words in capital letters; then choose another pair that has the same relationship.

LITERARY FOCUS: INFERENCE

Possible responses:

- The scientist, though knowledgeable, doesn't consider the consequences of this action.
- The concessionaire is only interested in making money from the hole, not its effects on his community.
- The villagers also see only the short term benefits they can gain.

You might want to discuss with students the idea that these people are all accomplices in exploiting the hole.

composure
contagious
plausible
shrine
throng

1. COMPOSURE : CALMNESS :: **a.** anger : shout **b.** think : succeed **c.** graduate : study **d.** gratitude : thankfulness
2. PLAUSIBLE : UNBELIEVABLE :: **a.** impossible : doubtful **b.** solemn : serious **c.** lively : dull **d.** agree : wonder
3. INDIVIDUAL : THRONG :: **a.** bird : flock **b.** tree : bush **c.** melody : rhythm **d.** hand : foot
4. SHRINE : PRAY :: **a.** mall : clothes **b.** school : teacher **c.** restaurant : eat **d.** swim : athlete
5. CONTAGIOUS : CATCHING :: **a.** flu : cold **b.** remember : recall **c.** gather : scatter **d.** fish : trout

Expressing Your Ideas

Writing Choices

Writer's Notebook Update Look back at your quickwrite about "He–y, Come on Ou–t!" Did you come close to guessing what the story is about? Now skim the story again, and list five phrases or sentences that would alert a reader to the story plot.

Cutbacks Many people in the wealthier nations choose comfortable lifestyles that consume large amounts of raw materials and energy and produce many wastes. Write a **newspaper editorial** attempting to convince these people that they must choose a lifestyle that is less destructive to the environment.

Front-Page Scandal The construction worker mentioned at the end of the story goes to *The Blab*, which prints the sensationalized story. Write the **story** and **headline** that expose officials who agreed to fill the hole and their attempts to cover up their decision.

Five Years Later In a science fiction **fantasy** of your own, imagine it is five years after the story ends. Describe what the village is like now.

Other Options

Sales Pitch With the help of your classmates, plan an **infomercial** to get viewers to read this story or another story in this book. Remember that your job is to persuade other students to read this story. Present your infomercial to another class.

Comics and Culture With your team rework "He-y, Come on Ou-t!" as a **comic book**, using some of the dialogue from the story. Try to capture the setting and mood in vivid drawings.

Sci-Fi Infomercial With one or two classmates, plan an **infomercial** to tell viewers about the best of science fiction. Explain what makes a work science fiction. Provide examples of outstanding sci-fi television shows, movies, stories, books, and cartoons. Present your infomercial to the class.

OTHER OPTIONS

The infomercial should offer enough hints about the plot, the characters, and the theme to arouse viewers' interest. Actual research about global ecological problems should also be included.

Students should consider how they will announce this advertisement—in the character of an ecological activist, a respected senior newscaster, or another appropriate image.

VOCABULARY STUDY

Analogy

Point out that figuring out analogies is an important thinking skill and a form of questioning on many standardized tests.

1. d
2. c
3. a
4. c
5. b

More Practice

- Toxic waste is to the Earth as ____ is to ____ . *(Possible response: as poison is to our bodies)*
- The Earth is to ecologists as ____ is to ____ . *(Possible response: as a treasure is to its guardians)*
- Environmental activists are to toxic dumpers as ____ is to ____ . *(Possible response: as highway patrol is to speeders)*

Unit 1 Resource Book
Vocabulary, p. 123
Vocabulary Test, p. 126

WRITING CHOICES

Writer's Notebook Update

Some clues to the plot are:

- "Hey, what in the world is this hole?"
- "You might bring down a curse on us. . . ."
- . . . but there was no echo.
- "Let me have that hole. I'll fill it in for you."
- . . . the wastes from nuclear reactors tumbled away into the hole.

Cutbacks

Ask students to research their topic so that their editorial opinion will carry some weight. Suggest that they hunt for articles containing the term "toxic waste" by using the NEXUS system at the public library.

Selection Test

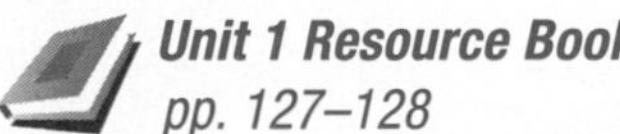

Unit 1 Resource Book,
pp. 127–128

Before Reading

Building Background

Encourage students to talk about what they think each poet means. Students can:

- name or pantomime the feeling of having the top of their heads taken off
- name a situation whey they've understood an important truth
- name some things they glimpsed quickly that left a strong impression

Literary Focus

Sound devices include onomatopoeia, alliteration, and rhyme. Words that sound like their meaning are onomatopoeia. Alliteration is the repetition of consonant sounds at the beginnings of words or within words. In slant rhymes, or half rhymes, the sounds are not exact: *hiss/guess.*

Writer's Notebook

Students may include some of these ideas in the web: emotions, imagination, inspiration, thought-provoking, senses, passion, form, rhythm, rhyme, figurative language.

Connections to **AuthorWorks**

Rita Dove is a featured author in the AuthorWorks CD-ROM series.

Before Reading

Flash Cards by Rita Dove USA
In Memory of Richi by Carmen Tafolla USA
The Rabbit by Edna St. Vincent Millay USA

Building Background

What Is It? Read what three poets have to say about poetry.

"If I feel physically as if the top of my head were taken off, I know that is poetry." *Emily Dickinson*

"Poetry is the art of understanding what it is to be alive." *Archibald MacLeish*

"Poetry is the opening and closing of a door, leaving those who look through to guess about what was seen during a moment." *Carl Sandburg*

What do you think each poet is saying about poetry? Which statement comes closest to *your* view of poetry? Now make up your own statement about poetry.

Literary Focus

Sound Devices Poets use words for their sound effects to convey mood, establish meaning, create music, and unify a work. Even poems with no regular rhyme have **sound devices** such as repeated words and sounds. As you read the following poems aloud, listen for word melodies. Let words and phrases such as *sputtering, hissed, embroidered, tulip trees,* and *high sky* work their magic on you.

Writer's Notebook

Poetry Web Brainstorm with a partner all the things you associate with poetry. Then make a web to show ideas you connect with this word.

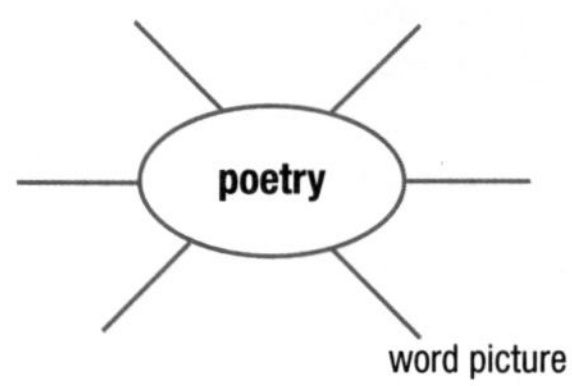

Rita Dove
born 1952

As a child, Rita Dove loved math—"the neatness of fractions, all those pies sliced into ever-diminishing wedges." But drilling with flash cards reminded her of dull routines such as washing dishes and taking out garbage. After mulling over the subject, Dove, who is a self-acknowledged daydreamer, wrote "Flash Cards." Among Dove's many honors are a Pulitzer Prize for poetry and the title of Poet Laureate of the United States, awarded in 1993.

Carmen Tafolla
born 1951

When she was in junior high school, a principal told Carmen Tafolla (tä foi′yä) that she had the "potential to make it all the way to high school" if she'd just quit speaking Spanish. Instead, she kept speaking Spanish and learned English, going on to earn a doctorate degree in bilingual education and gaining a national reputation as a story writer, a memoirist, and a poet. She lives in Texas with her family, three cats, a computer, a houseful of books, and the voices of all the people of her barrio, past and present.

Edna St. Vincent Millay
1892–1950

In November 1920, a slim volume of poems appeared whose bright green cover carried the title *A Few Figs from Thistles.* The author was a young woman named Edna St. Vincent Millay. Young people in the years after World War I, who had lost their idealism, immediately identified with the cynical, defiant spirit of Millay's verse. Millay, who also wrote short stories under the pen name Nancy Boyd, used her poetry to freely express her views of the modern woman, democracy, humanism, and individualism.

More About the Poets

Rita Dove

Dove is the youngest person ever to be named Poet Laureate of the United States; she is also the first African American to hold that post. She won the Pulitzer Prize for *Thomas and Beulah*, published in 1986. Dove has been an English professor since 1981. Other works by the author include:

- *The Yellow House on the Corner,* (1980)
- *Fifth Sunday* (short stories), (1985)
- *Through the Ivory Gate*, (1992)
- *Mother Love,* (1995)

Carmen Tafolla

Tafolla has written several books of poetry as well as a number of books of multicultural literature for children. Other works by the author include: *Curandera,* (Manda Editions).

Edna St. Vincent Millay

A native of Maine, Edna St. Vincent Millay published her first book of poems, *Renascence*, in 1917. She then moved to Greenwich Village in New York City where she lived a bohemian life, writing poetry, working as an actress and playwright, and supporting political and social causes. In 1924 she won the Pulitzer Prize for *The Harp-Weaver.* Other works by the author include:

- *Second April,* (1921)
- *Wine from These Grapes,* (1934)
- *Edna St. Vincent Millay, Selected Poems, The Centenary Edition,* (1992)

SUPPORT MATERIALS OVERVIEW

Unit 1 Resource Book
- Graphic Organizer, p. 129
- Study Guide, p. 130
- Vocabulary, p. 131
- Grammar, p. 132
- Alternate Check Test, p. 133
- Vocabulary Test, p. 134
- Selection Test, pp. 135–136

Building English Proficiency
- Literature Summaries
- Activities, p. 181

Reading, Writing & Grammar SkillBook
- Reading, pp. 47–48
- Grammar, Usage, and Mechanics, pp. 253–254

Technology
- Audiotape 7, Side B
- Personal Journal Software
- Custom Literature Database: For more sonnets, see the database.
- Test Generator Software

During Reading

Selection Objectives

- to explore the theme of dealing with consequences
- to identify and explore sound devices
- to identify and use conjunctions

Unit 1 Resource Book
Graphic Organizer, p. 129
Study Guide, p. 130

Theme Link

The characters of these poems must deal with the consequences of coexisting with others in the world.

Vocabulary Preview

crucial, very important or decisive; critical
dissembled, hidden; disguised
glaze, become smooth, glassy, or glossy
indiscreet, not wise; foolish
kittled, born

Students can add the words and definitions to their Writer's Notebooks.

Art Study

Responses to Caption Question
Possible responses: The speaker can count on education, employment, and a middle class life. The immigrants had to leave the South to find those opportunities.

1 Literary Element
Sonnet Form

Like many contemporary poets, Rita Dove plays variations on the traditional sonnet form. In "Flash Cards," she adapts the strict pentameter, rhyme scheme, and octet/sestet structure to give her poem a colloquial tone. For example, she uses only one exact end rhyme *(pane/rain);* all the others are slant rhymes *(work/dark; Lincoln/ten).*

This panel is from the series *Migration of the Negro,* painted in 1940–41 by Jacob Lawrence. The series of paintings chronicles the movement of Southern African Americans to the urban North to search for greater opportunities, including education. What about "Flash Cards" suggests that the speaker comes from a different social class than the migrants that Lawrence pictures?

1 # Flash Cards

Rita Dove

In math I was the whiz kid, keeper
of oranges and apples. *What you don't understand,*
2 *master,* my father said; the faster
I answered, the faster they came.

I could see one bud on the teacher's geranium,
one clear bee sputtering at the wet pane.
The tulip trees always dragged after heavy rain
so I tucked my head as my boots slapped home.

My father put up his feet after work
and relaxed with a highball and *The Life of Lincoln.*
After supper we drilled and I climbed the dark

before sleep, before a thin voice hissed
numbers as I spun on a wheel. I had to guess.
Ten, I kept saying, *I'm only ten.*

SELECTION SUMMARY

Flash Cards, In Memory of Richi, The Rabbit

The speaker in "Flash Cards" describes being drilled on her math facts so much that, even though she likes math, she has a discomforting dream about numbers. Poet Rita Dove uses onomatopoeia, such as *sputtering* and *hissed,* to add drama to the experience.

"In Memory of Richi" describes the first day of school experience for a new teacher and a first-grade student. The teacher ends the day wanting comfort and "someone's warmth." The child Richi learns for the first time that his Latino heritage and way of speaking are not respected in his school.

The speaker in "The Rabbit" describes a hawk swooping down to seize a rabbit. She expresses anger at the rabbit for refusing to run for cover.

*For summaries in other languages, see the **Building English Proficiency** book.*

In Memory of Richi

Carmen Tafolla

First day
of school
for both of you
—one of you six and glowing copper, running
with eagerness and proud
the other 22, young teacher, eager for this
school.
Your blue eyes warm to his brown coals
as you both chat
and share your missions,
as you ask his name.
He rolls it like a round of wealth
and, deep in Spanish tones, responds 3
"Richi."
You try to imitate, say
"Ritchie."
"No!" he teases, confident,
"It's Ri-chi—just like this."
You notice that each syllable
could rhyme with *see*
and try again.
He pats you on the back.
You go on to your separate tasks—
he to his room, and you to yours.
One day, six hours,
really not a speck of sand
in all this shore of time, and yet,
so crucial,[1]
as you gather papers,
turn to flee the cell
and gain some comfort
in some other place.
Your ray of hope
comes filtering down the hall.
In eagerness for someone's warmth,
you shout and wave,
"Hey, Richi!"
He corrects,
the light and wealth all gone
from his new eyes,
"No.
Ritchie." 4

1. crucial (krü′shəl), *adj.* very important or decisive; critical.

2 Literary Focus
Sound Devices

Rita Dove uses repetition as a sound device. In the first stanza, the vowel sound "a" is repeated several times on accented syllables, in *master, father, faster, answered, faster*. Point out that this is called assonance. She also repeats words: *faster* in the first stanza and *before* in the last stanza.

3 Multicultural Note
Pronunciation

Questions

- How does the poet describe Richi's way of saying his name? *(He "rolls it like a round of wealth" and speaks "deep in Spanish tones.")*
- Why does the teacher have trouble saying Richi's name? *(A native English speaker would be inclined to say Ritchie, short for Richard.)*

4 Reading/Thinking Skills
Figurative Language

Questions

- Look back at the title. About whom do we use the phrase "in memory"? *(about someone who has died)*
- Why would the poet say that Richi has died? Who, then, is Ritchie? *(Possible responses: The English-speaking culture has "killed" the confident Richi who was proud of his heritage. Ritchie, a false identity, remains.)*

BUILDING ENGLISH PROFICIENCY

Making Personal Connections

Most immigrants have stories to tell about their introductions to their new country. Encourage sharing activities such as these.

Activity Ideas

- Students might enjoy sharing the ways in which their names have been mispronounced. Encourage students to tell, if they know, what their names mean in English.
- Students might like to share "first time" experiences—for example, with American foods, customs, or attitudes. You also might encourage American-born students who have traveled abroad to share their first-time experiences in other countries.
- Learning a new language often includes some humorous misunderstandings. Invite volunteers to share such situations.

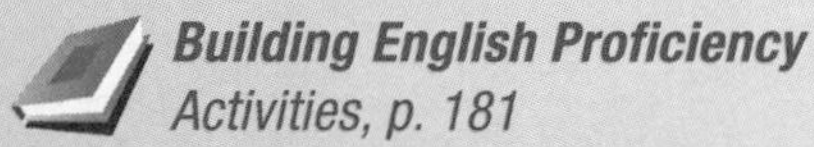
Building English Proficiency
Activities, p. 181

5 Literary Focus
Sound Devices: Repetition

Encourage students to look for repetition of sounds and words in the first stanza.

Questions

- What is an example of alliteration? *(in line 1;* hearing, hawk, high thicket, thatched *in line 4)*
- What are some examples of repeated vowel sounds or syllables? *(In line 3,* dark small rabbits, *and* kittled *and* dissembled.*)*
- What are some examples of rhyme? *(in line 1,* high sky; straw and saw *in lines 4 and 6)*

The poet also uses the repetition of words to create a mood in the last stanza.

6 Reading/Thinking Skills
Recognize Values

Question What seems to be the speaker's greatest concern as revealed in stanza 3? *(Possible response: that she will continue to witness the death agony of the rabbit)*

Open a discussion of whom the rabbit represents. Do students think it is a friend of the poet who she feels is being too passive? Or could it be that the poet is speaking about an aspect of herself that she does not like?

In his 1836 watercolor, *Swainson's Hawk,* John James Audubon combines scientific accuracy with exquisite detail. How do you think Audubon's attitude about the attacking hawk compares with Millay's? ➤

The Rabbit

Edna St. Vincent Millay

5 Hearing the hawk squeal in the high sky
I and the rabbit trembled.
Only the dark small rabbits newly kittled[1] in their neatly dissembled[2]
Hollowed nest in the thicket[3] thatched with straw
Did not respect his cry.
At least, not that I saw.

But I have said to the rabbit with rage and a hundred times, "Hop!
Streak it for the bushes! Why do you sit so still?
You are bigger than a house, I tell you, you are bigger than a hill, you are
a beacon for air-planes!
O indiscreet![4]
6 And the hawk and all my friends are out to kill!
Get under cover!" But the rabbit never stirred; she never will.

And I shall see again and again the large eye blaze
With death, and gently glaze;[5]
The leap into the air I shall see again and again, and the kicking feet;
And the sudden quiet everlasting, and the blade of grass green in the
strange mouth of the interrupted grazer.[6]

---

1. **kittled** (kit′ ld), *adj.* born.
2. **dissembled** (di sem′bəld), *adj.* hidden; disguised.
3. **thicket** (thik′ət), *n.* shrubs, bushes, or small trees growing close together.
4. **indiscreet** (in′dis krēt′), *adj.* not wise; foolish.
5. **glaze** (glāz), *v.* become smooth, glassy, or glossy.
6. **grazer** (grā′zər), *n.* feeder on growing grass.

MINI-LESSON: GRAMMAR
Conjunctions

Teach A conjunction is a word that joins single words or groups of words. A coordinating conjunction joins words, phrases, or clauses that have equal grammatical weight in a sentence. A subordinating conjunction joins two clauses in a way that makes one dependent upon the other.

Look at these lines from "Flash Cards."

After supper we drilled and I climbed the dark before sleep,
before a thin voice hissed
numbers as I spun on a wheel.

In the first line, *and* is a coordinating conjunction. In the second line, the first *before* is used as a preposition, but the second *before* is a subordinating conjunction, as is *as* in the third line.

Activity Idea Students can identify conjunctions and apply what they've learned in writing.

- Have students identify the words, phrases, or clauses joined by the conjunctions above.
- Encourage students to write poems that describe events, using conjunctions in the sentences of the poems.

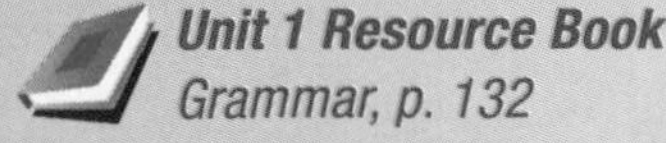

Unit 1 Resource Book
Grammar, p. 132

Collection of The New York Historical Society

Art Study

Responses to Caption Question
Millay views the hawk more from the rabbit's point of view. Since Audubon's interest was in ornithology, he views the hawk scientifically and dispassionately. Audubon's purpose was to portray the bird accurately, whether in flight or on the attack.

John James Audubon, who lived from 1785 to 1851, combined his talents as an artist and naturalist to make a comprehensive record of all the birds in North America. He was born in the West Indies, raised in France, and came to America in 1803, where he worked as a taxidermist, portrait painter, and drawing teacher. *The Birds of America* was published in large folio volumes of hand-colored aquatints during the period from 1827 to 1838.

Check Test

1. In "Flash Cards," who helps the speaker with her math drills? *(her father)*

2. What kind of voice does the speaker hear in her dream? *(a thin, hissing voice)*

3. In "In Memory of Richi," what is the boy's ethnic background? *(Latino)*

4. In "The Rabbit," what does the speaker advise the rabbit to do? *(hop, and streak for the bushes)*

5. In the last line, who or what is the "interrupted grazer"? *(the rabbit)*

Unit 1 Resource Book
Alternate Check Test, p. 133

BUILDING ENGLISH PROFICIENCY

ESL LEP ELD SAE LD

Exploring Poetic Language

Poetic language may challenge some readers.

1. Read this poem aloud several times or play Audiotape 7, side B.

2. Have students work together to give one-sentence prose summaries of each stanza. Write summaries on the chalkboard as students volunteer them.

3. Assign each sentence to a pair or small group of students. Have students write their assigned sentence on a sheet of posterboard and then link poetic words and phrases to it, as shown.

[Get under cover!] → shouted
[indiscreet] → didn't move

I shouted because the rabbit was in danger, but she didn't move.

[hawk and all my friends] → danger

After Reading

MAKING CONNECTIONS

1. Suggest that students identify which concrete images others will be able to identify.

2. Students may relate to the speaker in "Flash Cards" if they remember the feeling of learning math facts, to Richi if they have adjusted to a new culture, or to the speaker in "The Rabbit" in being disturbed by injustice or violence.

3. Possible responses: pressure, prejudice, death.

4. The speaker wants to please the father; he pushes her to do well in school; nevertheless, she feels pressured.

5. Possible responses: *master/faster; pane/rain.* Slant rhymes: *bee/trees; work/dark; hissed/guess.*

6. The teacher has changed from being eager and wanting to go to school to wanting to escape from a "cell" and be comforted. Richi has changed from being confident and eager to feeling devalued and ignored.

7. Just as the rabbit jumps to get away, the hawk grabs it and flies off; the rabbit is kicking its feet and has a blade of grass still in its mouth.

8. All three poems explore the theme of dealing with the consequences of having to coexist with others in the world. Both the speaker in "Flash Cards" and Richi must deal with the pressure of school and growing up in the world. The speaker in "The Rabbit" must deal with trying to understand a death she witnessed.

9. Possible responses: Be understanding of the majority culture's insensitivity. Learn about the new culture so you can find a common ground. Be determined, but not angry.

After Reading

Making Connections

Shaping Your Response

1. Work with a partner to present a still picture, or tableau, that captures a scene or a mood from one of these poems. You might invite classmates to guess what your tableau represents.
2. Which character from the poems do you relate to most? Why?
3. In your notebook, write three words that these poems make you think of.

Analyzing the Poems

4. What **inferences** can you make about the speaker and her father in "Flash Cards"?
5. What **rhymes** or words that sound alike do you find in "Flash Cards"? Before answering, look for words that are repeated or rhymed within lines as well as at the ends of lines.
6. In "In Memory of Richi," how do you think both the teacher and Richi have changed from the beginning of the day to the end?
7. What **image**, or word picture, do you have of the rabbit at the end of Millay's poem?
8. State what you consider the **theme** of two of these poems.

Extending the Ideas

9. In Tafolla's poem, Richi views his name with "new eyes." What advice do you have for students who **choose** to maintain their culture and traditions in American schools?

Literary Focus: Sound Devices

Poets choose and arrange words so that their sounds are pleasing to the ear and appropriate to the meaning. **Sound devices** are elements such as **rhyme, alliteration,** and **onomatopoeia**. As you read poetry, be aware of rhyme (similar word endings such as *right/light* and *rumble/grumble*), alliteration (the repetition of consonant sounds such as *lovely liquid lullaby*), and onomatopoeia (words such as *crack* and *wobble* that suggest the sounds or movements made by objects or activities).

- As someone from the class slowly reads each poem aloud, jot down examples of rhyme, alliteration, and onomatopoeia. Compare your findings to those of your classmates.

LITERARY FOCUS: SOUND DEVICES

For "Flash Cards," students may list *kid, keeper,* and *tulip trees* as alliteration, and *slapped, sputtered,* and *hissed* as onomatopoeia. For "In Memory of Richi," they may list *rolls, round* and *specks, sand* as alliteration. In "The Rabbit," they may list the rhymes *high/sky, straw/saw, still/hill, kill/will.*

Encourage students to discuss how the use of sound devices affects the mood, pace, and energy of each poem.

Vocabulary Study

Choose the letter of the word that is most nearly *opposite* the numbered word.

crucial
dissembled
glaze
indiscreet
kittled

1. *dissembled* **a.** revealed **b.** forgotten **c.** broken **d.** collected
2. *indiscreet* **a.** foolish **b.** quiet **c.** wise **d.** happy
3. *crucial* **a.** necessary **b.** unimportant **c.** lucky **d.** unknown
4. *kittled* **a.** died **b.** born **c.** damaged **d.** remembered
5. *glaze* **a.** become silent **b.** become angry **c.** become bumpy **d.** become angry

Expressing Your Ideas

Writing Choices

Writer's Notebook Compare your poetry web with that of other classmates. Would you add other words and phrases or change the ones you wrote, after reading these poems? Have any of your previous ideas about poetry changed? Use your web to write about your impressions of poetry. You might try to cast your ideas into a poem.

Give Poetry a Good Rap School, parental pressure, violence in nature? The subjects of these poems have found their way into contemporary songs. Working in a small group, recast one of these poems as a **rap**. Feel free to add or change things. Perform your rap for the class.

Start with Art Look at the piece of art at the right. What feelings, event, person, or memory does it bring to mind? Quickly write down your first impressions, while they're still fresh. Let your ideas serve as the beginning of a **poem**. Add some sound devices such as rhyme, alliteration, or onomatopoeia and shape your ideas into a poem.

Other Options

Reader's Theater In a small group, research other poems by Rita Dove, Carmen Tafolla, or Edna St. Vincent Millay. Select several poems to **read aloud** that you think classmates will enjoy. After rehearsing, present your reading to the class.

Show Them a Poem Give a **chalk talk** to the class about poetry—how it differs from prose, how sound devices and images contribute to its effects, and how poets manage to say a lot in a few words. To illustrate your points, write words from the poems in this group or draw pictures to show images.

VOCABULARY STUDY

1. a
2. c
3. b
4. a
5. c

More Practice Encourage students to write a poem using at least three of the vocabulary words. Students should use the words correctly and in a different setting from those of the poems.

Unit 1 Resource Book
Vocabulary, p. 131
Vocabulary Test, p. 134

WRITING CHOICES

Writer's Notebook

Students may want to make a new web about poetry to express any new feelings they have. To write a poem from the items in the web, students may want to try free-writing using the terms they brainstormed.

Give Poetry a Good Rap

Students should feel free to change words or phrases in order to suit the rhythm and nature of the rap. Let the groups practice before performing their raps for the class.

Start with Art

Tell students that the picture may serve as a scaffolding for their poems; that is, it may supply the original idea but the final poem may be something very different.

Selection Test

Unit 1 Resource Book,
pp. 135–136

Transparency Collection
Fine Art Writing Prompt 3

OTHER OPTIONS

Reader's Theater

Students may find poems by Rita Dove and Carmen Tafolla in anthologies of contemporary women poets; Millay may be in older anthologies. You may want to suggest Dove's "Geometry," Tafolla's "La Miss Low," and Millay's "Childhood Is the Kingdom Where Nobody Dies."

Show Them a Poem

Let students know that defining the difference between poetry and prose seems to be a never-ending project for writers and literary critics, though many agree that poetry generally presents an emotional and intellectual experience in highly compact and carefully structured language.

Interdisciplinary Study

Theme Link

These fables, proverbs, and quotations from around the world express the kind of wisdom that people can derive by dealing with the consequences of their actions and assumptions about life.

Curricular Connection: Multicultural

You can use the information in this interdisciplinary study to explore human commonalities that link people of all backgrounds.

Additional Background

- For information about Rumi, see page 118 of this Teacher's Edition.
- Zen is a sect of Buddhism that teaches that enlightenment can be attained through introspection and intuition.
- Jane Austen (1775–1817) is widely regarded as one of the greatest of English novelists. Her novels are admired for their graceful style, satiric wit, and deep moral insights into human nature and customs.
- Dorothy Parker (1893–1967) was an American critic, short-story writer, and poet known for her biting wit.

Unit 1 Resource Book
Study Guide, p. 137

INTERDISCIPLINARY STUDY

Dealing with Consequences

Lessons Through the Ages

Multicultural Connection
Like the selections you have just read, the fable, proverbs, and other works in this Interdisciplinary Study provide truths about people and lessons about life.

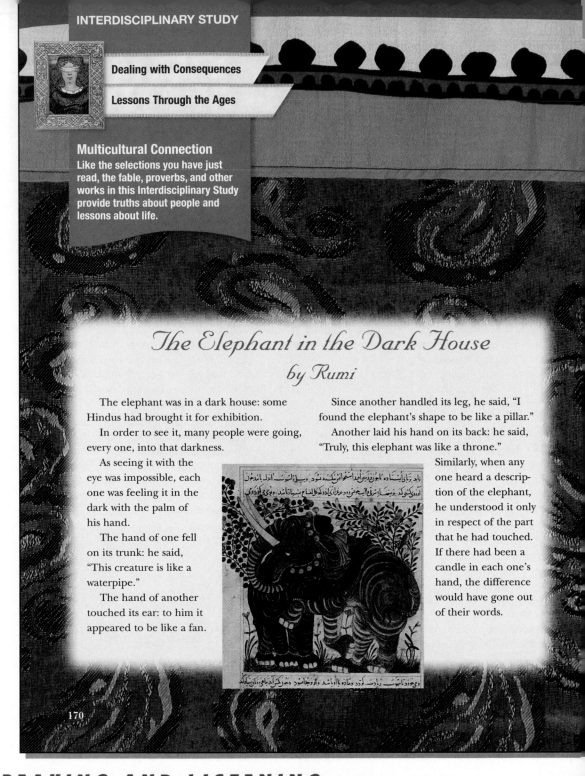

The Elephant in the Dark House

by Rumi

The elephant was in a dark house: some Hindus had brought it for exhibition.

In order to see it, many people were going, every one, into that darkness.

As seeing it with the eye was impossible, each one was feeling it in the dark with the palm of his hand.

The hand of one fell on its trunk: he said, "This creature is like a waterpipe."

The hand of another touched its ear: to him it appeared to be like a fan.

Since another handled its leg, he said, "I found the elephant's shape to be like a pillar."

Another laid his hand on its back: he said, "Truly, this elephant was like a throne."

Similarly, when any one heard a description of the elephant, he understood it only in respect of the part that he had touched. If there had been a candle in each one's hand, the difference would have gone out of their words.

MINI-LESSON: SPEAKING AND LISTENING

Interpretive Reading

Teach Provide the following tips to help students prepare an interesting interpretive reading. of a selection.

- Rehearse your reading as of you were an actor preparing for a role. Read through the piece a few times, first silently then aloud.
- Familiarize yourself with the correct pronunciation of any unusual words.
- Breathe normally and use your ordinary voice. You may raise or lower the pitch of your voice to make the reading more interesting.
- Don't race through the words. If you read a bit slower than you talk in normal conversation, your audience will be able to follow along better. But you can vary your reading rate if the meaning of the piece calls for it.
- Ask a friend to listen as you read and give you feedback.

Activity Idea Have students work in pairs to prepare interpretive readings of the selections on pages 170–171. One person should read while the other acts a coach and provides feedback. Allow enough class time for the readings and for follow-up discussion of the various interpretations.

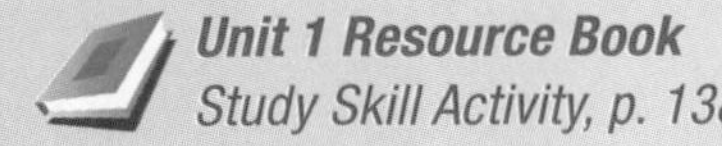

Unit 1 Resource Book
Study Skill Activity, p. 138

TRADITIONAL WISDOM

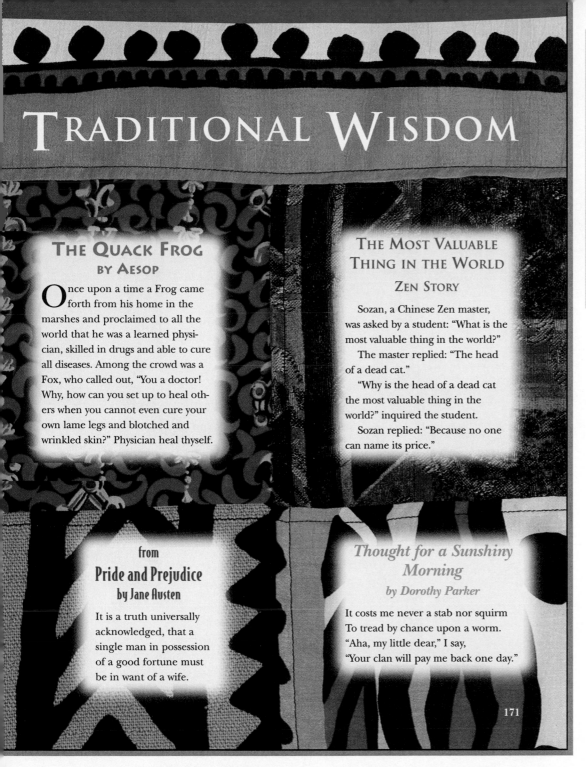

THE QUACK FROG
BY AESOP

Once upon a time a Frog came forth from his home in the marshes and proclaimed to all the world that he was a learned physician, skilled in drugs and able to cure all diseases. Among the crowd was a Fox, who called out, "You a doctor! Why, how can you set up to heal others when you cannot even cure your own lame legs and blotched and wrinkled skin?" Physician heal thyself.

THE MOST VALUABLE THING IN THE WORLD
ZEN STORY

Sozan, a Chinese Zen master, was asked by a student: "What is the most valuable thing in the world?"

The master replied: "The head of a dead cat."

"Why is the head of a dead cat the most valuable thing in the world?" inquired the student.

Sozan replied: "Because no one can name its price."

from Pride and Prejudice
by Jane Austen

It is a truth universally acknowledged, that a single man in possession of a good fortune must be in want of a wife.

Thought for a Sunshiny Morning
by Dorothy Parker

It costs me never a stab nor squirm
To tread by chance upon a worm.
"Aha, my little dear," I say,
"Your clan will pay me back one day."

Art Study

In medieval times, collections of illuminated manuscripts about animals were popular in the Islamic world. These drawings and text, which often combined fact and folklore about different animals, were known as bestiaries. The art on page 170 was done around the thirteenth century, and the text is in Arabic.

Question Using both facts and fiction, what would you write about the elephants pictured?

BUILDING ENGLISH PROFICIENCY

ESL LEP ELD SAE LD

Exploring Key Concepts

Use one or more of the following activities to help students grasp the ideas presented in this feature.

Activity Ideas

- Have each of five groups of students discuss one of the five pieces of "traditional wisdom." Ask a representative from each group to summarize the discussion and offer the group's interpretation of the lesson or piece of advice. Allow the class to consider more than one interpretation.
- Invite students to create artwork, music, or pantomime that reflects any or all of the five pieces of wisdom.
- Have volunteers collaborate on providing a present-day version of any of the five selections. As they compare the results to the original pieces, help them see the element of timelessness in the original stories.

Terms to Know

Talmud (tal′məd), the collection of writings constituting the Jewish civil and religious law

Ashanti (ə shän′tē), former West African kingdom, now part of Ghana

Responding

1. Possible Response Students might say that such "priceless" things as health, happiness, and love are the most valuable. You might suggest that students model their lessons after one of the selections on pages 170–172.

2. Possible Response Most students will probably agree that the truth of Austen's tongue-in-cheek observation is no longer "universally acknowledged." Point out that during Jane Austen's time, it was considered impromper not to be married. Encourage students to use similar wit and irony when writing their truisms.

Research Topics

- The works of Rumi, Jane Austen, or Dorothy Parker
- Proverbs from other nations or cultures

Interdisciplinary Activity Ideas

- Have students work in groups to research and compile an anthology of proverbs, with separate chapters devoted to such topics as growing up, love, marriage, work, coping with life, and death.
- Students can visit a library to find appropriate illustrations in art books to accompany each of the proverbs on page 172.

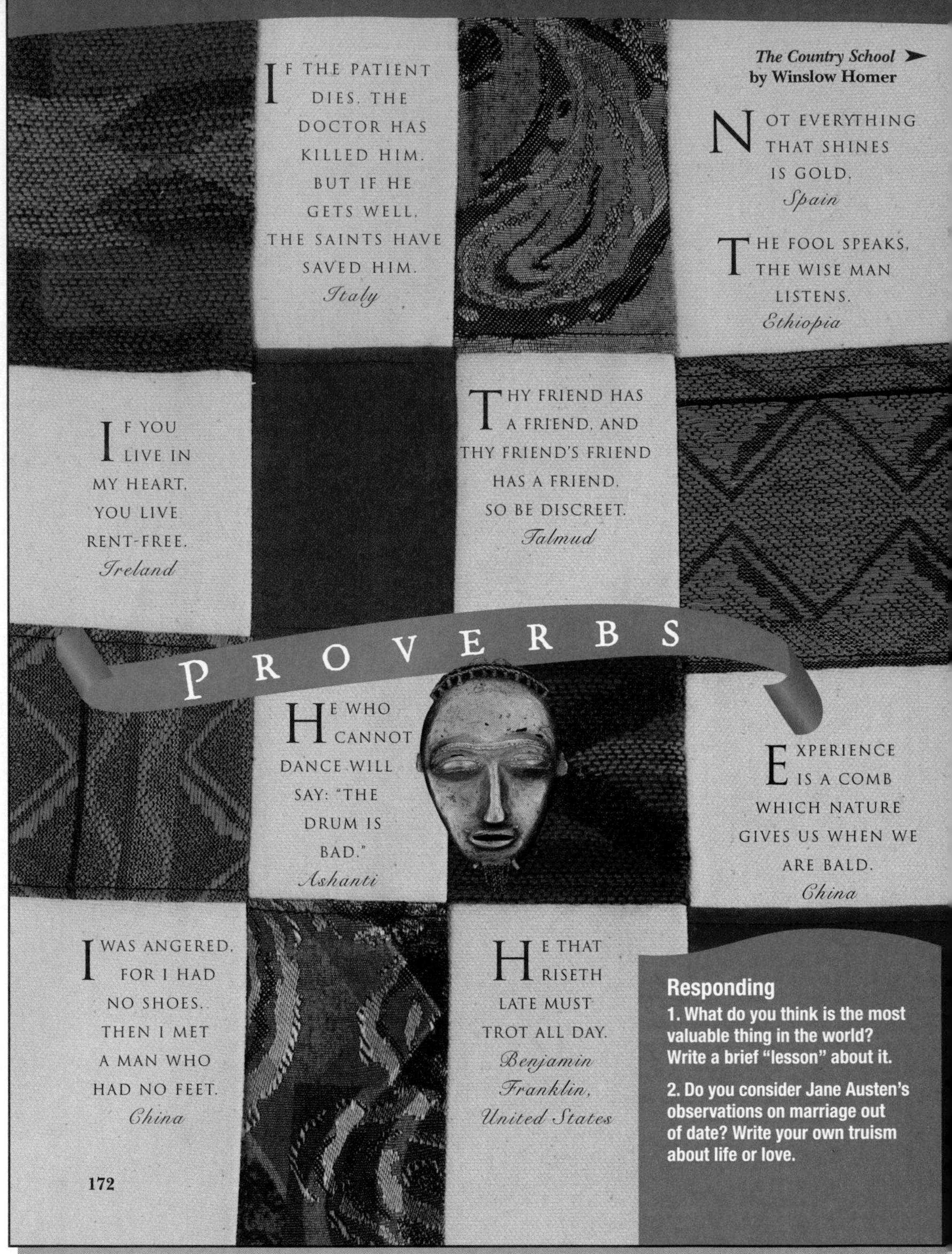

The Country School ➤
by Winslow Homer
IF THE PATIENT DIES, THE DOCTOR HAS KILLED HIM. BUT IF HE GETS WELL, THE SAINTS HAVE SAVED HIM.
Italy
NOT EVERYTHING THAT SHINES IS GOLD.
Spain
THE FOOL SPEAKS, THE WISE MAN LISTENS.
Ethiopia
IF YOU LIVE IN MY HEART, YOU LIVE RENT-FREE.
Ireland
THY FRIEND HAS A FRIEND, AND THY FRIEND'S FRIEND HAS A FRIEND, SO BE DISCREET.
Talmud
PROVERBS
HE WHO CANNOT DANCE WILL SAY: "THE DRUM IS BAD."
Ashanti
EXPERIENCE IS A COMB WHICH NATURE GIVES US WHEN WE ARE BALD.
China
I WAS ANGERED, FOR I HAD NO SHOES. THEN I MET A MAN WHO HAD NO FEET.
China
HE THAT RISETH LATE MUST TROT ALL DAY.
Benjamin Franklin, United States
Responding
1. What do you think is the most valuable thing in the world? Write a brief "lesson" about it.
2. Do you consider Jane Austen's observations on marriage out of date? Write your own truism about life or love.
172

MINI-LESSON: STUDY SKILLS

Create and Use Graphic Organizers

Teach The layout of the proverbs on this page can provide students with a practical lesson in the value of creating and using different kinds of graphic organizers to present information effectively. Explain that different organizations of the same material can often highlight certain aspects and underplay others. For example, the graphic organization of this page isolates each proverb and gives each one equal emphasis, while underplaying the geographical origins. What effect would be achieved by overlaying the proverbs on a world map and visually keying each one to its respective country?

Activity Idea Have students work in teams to create a bulletin board display of the proverbs on page 172. The display should be graphically organized on a map showing the countries of the world. One team might be responsible for reproducing the map on a poster-size sheet of paper, while another makes small flags using stickpins and cutout squares on which the proverbs are inscribed. The flags can then be mounted directly into the appropriate countries on the map. Another team might be charged with finding additional proverbs to represent other nations or cultures.

Art Study

Winslow Homer (1836–1910) was born in Boston and began his career as a freelance illustrator contributing woodcut drawings of Civil War camp life to *Harper's Weekly*. In 1865, within four years of having taught himself to work in oils, he was admitted to full membership in the National Academy of Design. Also a master of watercolor, Homer is probably best known for his naturalistic depictions of New England country life and scenery.

Question What kind of mood does Homer convey in this painting? *(Possible responses: calm, orderly, casual)*

BUILDING ENGLISH PROFICIENCY

Drawing Conclusions

Wisdom on a variety of topics is offered in the proverbs on page 172. Have students focus on the various insights by creating a web such as the one shown. Partners or small groups can discuss the proverbs and find ways of stating them so that they complete this sentence: A wise person ______. Encourage students to compare the conclusions they have drawn while considering the same proverbs.

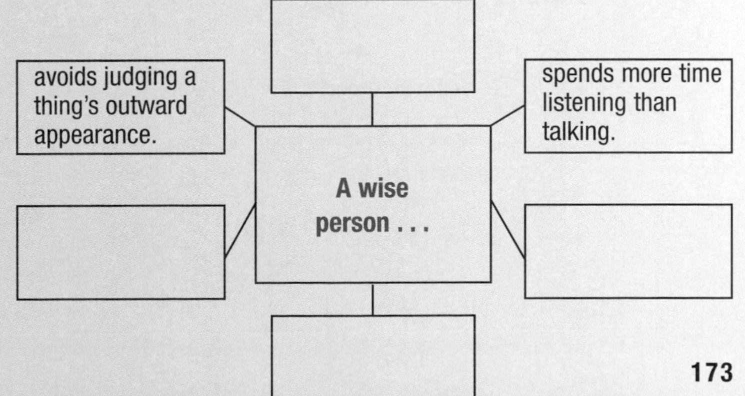

Writing Workshop

WRITER'S BLUEPRINT

Specs

The Specs in the Writer's Blueprint address these writing and thinking skills:

- identifying alternatives
- determining cause and effect
- predicting outcomes
- drawing conclusions
- supporting conclusions
- clarifying pronoun references

These Specs serve as your lesson objectives, and they form the basis for the **Assessment Criteria Specs** for a superior paper, which appear on the final TE page for this lesson. You might want to read them with students when you begin the lesson.

Linking Literature to Writing

An interpretive essay focuses on the literature. Students will be expected to interpret the text, make observations, draw conclusions, and provide evidence for their positions. Have students compare and contrast the different examples of irony found in the literature.

Writing Workshop

Presenting Alternatives

Assignment The main characters in "Red Azalea," "The Boar Hunt," and "The Interlopers" and the villagers in "He—y, Come on Ou—t!" all have something in common. They are faced with dilemmas—difficult choices—that lead to ironic consequences—outcomes that are different from what is expected. Explore these ironic consequences in writing.

WRITER'S BLUEPRINT

Product	An interpretive essay
Purpose	To analyze characters' decisions
Audience	People who have read the stories
Specs	As the writer of a successful essay, you should:

- ❑ Focus on one of the stories listed in "Assignment" above. Begin by explaining the dilemma of the main character (or characters). What difficult choices does he or she face?
- ❑ Go on to explain the decision the character makes and the ironic consequences of that decision. What went wrong with the original plans?
- ❑ Speculate on other alternatives the character could have chosen instead. What other actions might have led to different consequences?
- ❑ Conclude by giving your view of why things went wrong. Consider (1) elements in the character's personality that prevented him or her from making a better choice and (2) circumstances beyond the character's control.
- ❑ Offer evidence from the story to support your analysis, including quotations where appropriate. State cause-effect relationships clearly.
- ❑ Follow the rules of grammar, usage, spelling, and mechanics, including correct pronoun reference.

WRITING WORKSHOP OVERVIEW

Product
Expository writing: An interpretive essay

Prewriting
Chart ironic consequences—Identify alternatives—Analyze the reasons why—Plan your essay
Unit 1 Resource Book
Prewriting Worksheets pp. 139–140

Drafting
As you draft
Transparency Collection
Student Models for Writing Workshop 5, 6

Revising
Ask a partner—Strategy: Clarifying Cause-Effect Relationships
Unit 1 Resource Book
Revising Worksheet p. 141

Editing
Ask a partner—Strategy: Clarifying Pronoun References
Unit 1 Resource Book
Grammar Worksheet p. 142
Grammar Check Test p. 143

Presenting
Role-play
Sketch

Looking Back
Self-evaluate—Reflect—For Your Working Portfolio
Unit 1 Resource Book
Assessment Worksheet p. 144
Transparency Collection
Fine Art Writing Prompt 3

PREWRITING

Chart ironic consequences. Look back at the material on irony on pages 127 and 133. Then in a small group, look at the dilemmas faced by the main characters in "Red Azalea," "The Boar Hunt," "The Interlopers," and "He—y, Come on Ou—t!" Use a chart like the one shown. Then choose the story that you want to interpret in your essay.

The Character's Dilemma	The Ironic Consequences	Supporting Evidence from Story
List the choices facing the character and the decision he or she made.	List the things that went wrong with the character's plans.	List events and quotations that illustrate the dilemma and consequences.

OR . . .
Have each group member take a different story and explain the dilemma and ironic consequences to the rest of the group.

Identify alternatives. On your own, list several instances in the story where the character could have made a different decision and avoided the dilemma. For each instance, complete an If-Then sentence:

If (character) had ______ instead of ________, then _________.

Analyze the reasons why the character did not take these alternatives. List (1) elements of the character's personality and (2) circumstances beyond the character's control that contributed to his or her not taking each alternative. List pieces of evidence—events or quotations from the story—to support your reasons.

Plan your essay. Review your prewriting activities as you make your writing plan. Organize your notes into an outline like the one shown here. Add supporting evidence—events and quotations from the story—for your conclusions.

Introduction	Body	Conclusion
Character's dilemma— difficult choices (+ supporting evidence)	Character's decision Ironic consequences (what went wrong) Alternative choices (+ supporting evidence)	Reasons things went wrong —Character's personality —Circumstances beyond character's control (+ supporting evidence)

STEP 1 PREWRITING

Chart ironic consequences

This activity would work well if small groups of students each discussed a different story and then collectively led a class discussion on that selection. For additional support, see the worksheet referenced below.

Unit 1 Resource Book
Prewriting Worksheet, p. 139

Identify alternatives

Encourage students to read actively by placing themselves in the character's position to consider all the dilemmas confronting him or her. For additional support, see the worksheet referenced below.

Unit 1 Resource Book
Prewriting, p. 140

Analyze the reasons why

Remind students that the purpose of this activity is to determine cause and effect—an important element of their essay.

Plan your essay

Students might visualize their plan as a flowchart where consequences are linked to decisions. Some students may find it easier to create a rough flowchart to show how consequences resulted from decisions made by the character. With this visual guide, students can then create a workable plan for writing.

Connections to **Writer's Notebook**

For selection-related prompts, refer to Writer's Notebook.

Connections to **Writer's Resource**

For additional writing prompts, refer to Writer's Resource.

BUILDING ENGLISH PROFICIENCY

Using Prewriting Helps

Draw attention to some of the prewriting helps on page 175.

- In the "Chart ironic consequences" notes, remind students that irony occurs when one outcome is expected and the opposite occurs. Sometimes another choice would have produced a better outcome; sometimes no choice provides a satisfactory outcome.
- You might try role-playing to help students explore the possibilities of the "Identify alternatives" and "Analyze the reasons why" notes. Encourage a student audience to comment on the outcome of each role-play.

STEP 2 DRAFTING

As you draft

As a class, have students share their ideas for questions and quotations that they might use to begin their papers.

The Student Models

The **transparencies** referenced below are authentic student models. Review them with the students before they draft. These questions will help:

1. How could the writer of model 5 have made the character's dilemma clearer?
2. Notice how much space the writer of model 6 spends summarizing the plot. Does this help the essay or hurt it? Why? Hint: consider the audience listed in the blueprint.
3. Look for unclear pronoun references with *she* in model 5. Tell how you would correct them.

Transparency Collection
Student Models for Writing Workshop 5, 6

STEP 3 REVISING

Ask a partner (Peer assessment)

Model, for students, written comments that are specific and effective as compared to those that are vague and superficial.

Revising Strategy: Clarifying Cause-Effect Relationships

Have students look over the student model and note changes that were made. For additional support, see the mini-lesson at the bottom of this page and the worksheet referenced below.

Unit 1 Resource Book
Revising Worksheet, p. 141

Connections to
Writer's Resource

Refer to the Grammar, Usage, and Mechanics Handbook on Writer's Resource.

STEP 2 DRAFTING

As you draft, follow your writing plan. The following tips may help:

- Begin with a question that asks "What would you expect to happen if . . . ?" and go on to explain the character's dilemma.
- Begin with a quotation from the story and follow with an explanation of how this quotation illustrates the character's dilemma.

OR . . .
Go through the outline orally first, using a tape recorder. Cover each point in the outline. Then listen to the tape and make notes for your writing plan.

STEP 3 REVISING

Ask a partner to comment on your draft before you revise it.

✔ Did I illustrate my explanations with quotations from the literature?

✔ Did I state cause-effect relationships clearly? (See the Beyond Print article on page 179 and the "Revising Strategy" below.)

LITERARY SOURCE
"The typhoon had passed and the sky was a gorgeous blue. Even a certain village not far from the city had suffered damage. A little distance from the village and near the mountains, a small shrine had been swept away by a landslide."
from "He—y, Come on Ou—t!" by Shinichi Hoshi

Revising Strategy

Clarifying Cause-Effect Relationships

Think about cause as *why* something happens and effect as *what* happens. For example, in "He—y, Come on Ou—t!" the typhoon (cause) brings about a landslide (effect). The landslide (cause) sweeps away the shrine (effect).

Look back at your essay to make sure that your cause-effect relationships are clearly expressed. Notice how this student model has been changed, in response to a partner's comment, to clarify why something happened.

Anchee must choose between a teacher whom she truly admires or stay loyal to Chain and the political party, *who think the teacher is a spy*. This teacher was always helpful to all her students and encouraged them to do their very best. Once she worked with Anchee on her geometric progression till she no longer had a voice.

STUDENT MODEL

MINI-LESSON: WRITING STYLE

Clarifying Cause-Effect Relationships

Teach Sometimes one event can cause a chain reaction of effects. A cause creates an effect that creates another effect, and another, and so on. A good example of this is a multicar pile-up on a freeway.

Activity Idea Have newspapers and magazines available for students. Divide the class into groups of two or three and have them find articles that are organized by cause-and-effect relationships. Each group can draw a diagram to illustrate the cause(s) and effect(s) found in the article and share the story and diagram with the rest of the class.

Apply Continuing in small groups, students should then analyze each other's papers for cause-effect relationships.

STEP 4 EDITING

Ask a partner to review your revised draft before you edit. When you edit, look for errors in grammar, usage, spelling, and mechanics. Look over each sentence to make sure your pronouns all have clear antecedents.

Editing Strategy

Clarifying Pronoun References

A pronoun usually takes the place of a noun used earlier—the antecedent of the pronoun. A pronoun must have a clear antecedent.

> *Autumn Leaves* brought *her* books to share with Anchee Min.

The possessive pronoun *her* refers to *Autumn Leaves*, that's clear. But what about this example?

> Anchee Min's parents learned of the betrayal of Autumn Leaves from Blooming, Coral, and Space Conqueror. *They* were terrified.

Who are *They*—Anchee Min's parents or her three siblings? We could clear up this confusion by replacing the pronoun *They* with *Anchee Min's parents*, but that would sound awkward. A better solution would be to move the pronoun closer to its antecedent, as in the example below:

> Anchee Min's parents were terrified when *they* learned of the betrayal of Autumn Leaves from Blooming, Coral, and Space Conqueror.

When you revise, make sure each pronoun has a clear antecedent.

FOR REFERENCE
See the Language and Grammar Handbook at the back of this text for more information on pronoun reference.

STEP 4 EDITING

Ask a partner (Peer assessment)

For visual reinforcement of the editing strategy, have students draw arrows to connect pronouns to antecedents in their peers' essays, using easily erasable pencil.

Editing Strategy: Clarifying Pronoun References

Some students may need a brief review of the definitions of a pronoun and antecedent. Remind students that each pronoun must have a clear antecedent. For additional support, see the mini-lesson at the bottom of this page and the worksheets referenced below.

Unit 1 Resource Book
Grammar Worksheet, p. 142
Grammar Check Test, p. 143

Connections to **Writer's Resource**

Refer to the Grammar, Usage, and Mechanics Handbook on Writer's Resource.

MINI-LESSON: GRAMMAR

Clarifying Pronoun References

Put these sentences on the board and have students tell why any pronoun references are unclear. Then ask students to make suggestions to clarify references. Suggestions are given.

1. As he pulled his car up to the speaker to place his order, it made a loud, hissing noise. (As he pulled his car up to the speaker to place his order, the speaker made a loud, hissing noise.)

2. The coaches told the football team that they would be working out in the weight room. (The coaches announced that the football team would be working out in the weight room.)

3. If students are confused about a new concept, they should ask for help. (Correct)

4. The car was in the middle of the bridge when it began to sway. (The car was in the middle of the bridge when the bridge began to sway.)

Unit 1 Resource Book
Grammar Worksheet, p. 142
Grammar Check Test, p. 143

STEP 5 PRESENTING

Role-play

If students choose to interview their characters on a mock TV talk show, have them work in groups to develop an introduction for the characters and questions for the audience.

Sketch

Encourage students to create a sketch that reveals the emotional state of the character at the crucial moment of decision.

STEP 6 LOOKING BACK

Self-evaluate

The *Assessment Criteria Specs* at the bottom of this page are for a superior paper. You might want to post these in the classroom. Students can then evaluate themselves based on these criteria. For a complete scoring rubric, use the *Assessment Worksheet* referenced below.

Unit 1 Resource Book
Assessment Worksheet, p. 144

Reflect

Encourage students to apply what they have learned about irony to an ironic situation in their own lives. Explain that all writers review their work after a period of time and usually make changes.

To further explore the theme, use the Fine Art Transparency referenced below.

Transparency Collection
Fine Art Writing Prompt 3

STEP 5 PRESENTING

Consider these ideas for presenting your essay.

- Get together in a small group and read each other's papers. Then role-play the characters having a discussion about the alternatives that were proposed. You might want to do this in the format of a TV talk show.
- Make a sketch of the character or characters you dealt with and include it with your essay.

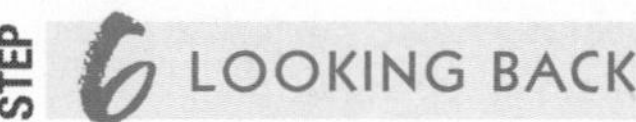

STEP 6 LOOKING BACK

Self-Evaluate. What grade would you give your paper? Look back at the Writer's Blueprint and give your paper a score on each point, from 6 (superior) to 1 (inadequate).

Reflect. Think about what you've learned from writing this essay as you write answers to these questions.

✔ Now that you've explored irony, think of ironic situations you've encountered in your own life. What happened? What made the situations ironic?

✔ Time can make a difference in how you see things that are close to you. Put your final draft away for a few days and read it again, when you're not so close to it. What do you see about it now that you didn't see then?

For Your Working Portfolio Add your essay and reflection responses to your working portfolio.

ASSESSMENT CRITERIA SPECS

6 Superior The writer of a 6 paper impressively meets these criteria:

- Insightfully explains the dilemma the main character faces.
- Argues logically and convincingly about where the character went wrong and what other options he or she could have taken.
- Convincingly explains why things went wrong.
- Shows strong insight into the character by taking into account elements of the character's personality and circumstances beyond the character's control.
- Supports arguments with precise details from the text, including accurate quotes.
- Organizes ideas and structures the paper logically and coherently.
- Makes few, if any, errors in grammar, usage, mechanics, or spelling, including pronoun references.

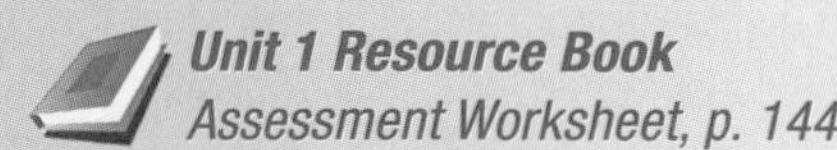

Unit 1 Resource Book
Assessment Worksheet, p. 144

Beyond Print

Analyzing Cause and Effect

A *cause* is any person, thing, or event that produces an effect. It is the reason something happens. An *effect* is the result of an event, idea, or action. It is whatever is produced or made to happen by a cause. The simplest cause-effect relationships are those where one cause has one effect: for example, you turn the ignition key and the car's engine starts.

Cause-effect relationships, however, are usually more complex than those in which a single cause produces a single effect. One type of complex cause-effect relationship occurs when a single cause produces a chain of effects. For example, in Saki's story, "The Interlopers," an old feud leads two men to stalk each other in a forest. They are both injured by a falling tree, leaving them defenseless when attacked by a band of wolves.

Drawing a diagram can help you understand this kind of chain of causation:

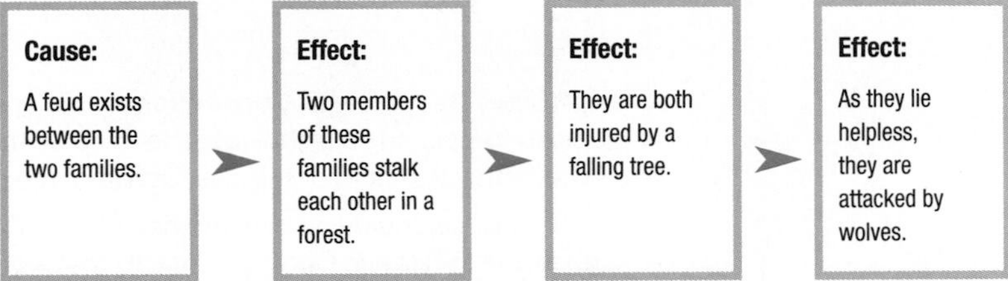

Cause:
A feud exists between the two families.
Effect:
Two members of these families stalk each other in a forest.
Effect:
They are both injured by a falling tree.
Effect:
As they lie helpless, they are attacked by wolves.

Activity Options

1. Diagram the cause-effect relationship that exists in "He—y, Come on Ou—t!"
2. Create a cause-effect diagram in the form of a storyboard illustrating key events in one of the stories in this unit.
3. With a group of students, select a movie that exhibits complex cause-effect relationships, such as *Jurassic Park*, and discuss how they contribute to the film's theme.

Beyond Print

Teaching Objectives

- to understand cause-and-effect relationships
- to analyze complex cause-and-effect relationships in a work of literature or film

Curricular Connection: Study Skills

Recognizing cause-and-effect relationships is essential for comprehending plot development and character motivation; it is also essential in most problem-solving situations.

Introduce

You might introduce your discussion of cause-and-effect relationships by providing a physical demonstration in class of a chain reaction. This might be as simple as a line of toppling dominoes.

Suggest that the simple diagram on this page can be elaborated to show additional causes for the second and third effects: the storm which topples the tree and results in the injuries; and the men's shouting, which attracts the wolves' attention.

Activity Options

Activity 1 Students' diagrams should begin with the typhoon that exposes the hole and initiates the chain of events resulting in the pebble falling from the sky.

Activity 2 You might allow students to work in teams to develop their storyboards.

Activity 3 In *Jurassic Park*, the cause-and-effect relationships help illustrate the theme that tampering with nature can unleash a series of dire consequences.

ANOTHER APPROACH

Construct a Rube Goldberg Contraption

Rube Goldberg (1883–1970) became famous for his zany cartoons depicting laboriously contrived contraptions or schemes intended to bring about a ludicrously simple result. Students might learn much about cause-and-effect relationships by researching some of Goldberg's cartoons and attempting to construct a Rube Goldberg device as a class project. Students may also write a humorous sketch describing a ridiculously complicated chain of events that has a trivial result.

Unit Wrap-Up

MULTICULTURAL CONNECTION

Most students will have had experience in making choices to balance individual needs against those of the larger group. The following questions may facilitate discussion.

Individuality

Can social pressure have a positive effect on an individual? Why?

Possible Response Jing-mei openly rebelled against her mother by screaming and shouting her refusal to play the piano. Rufus cleverly and secretly preserved his individuality by voting for both parties.

Groups

What is the value of tradition in a social or cultural group?

Possible Response Oganda should not have had to sacrifice her life for the rest of the village. However, she was willing to sacrifice the lives of all of the people in the village in order to save her own.

Choices

To what extent are individuals responsible for ensuring that the larger group of which they are a part makes wise choices that affect individual needs and public welfare?

Possible Response Anchee Min should have sought her mother's advice before denouncing her teacher. Villagers should have rebuilt the shrine or conducted scientific studies before using the hole as a dump.

Activities

Activity 1 Students might mention historical, sports, or entertainment figures.

Activity 2 Conform to the group and not earn all As, find other friends, ignore the taunting, or help friends get better grades.

Activity 3 Have students discuss whether reenactments did or did not lead to responsible choices.

Multicultural Connections

Individuality

Part One: Pushing Toward the Top Rufus in "The Voter" walks a thin line between pursuing individual goals and achieving the broader goals of his political machine. Jing-mei in "Two Kinds" rebels against her mother's attempts to impose culturally influenced standards.

■ Compare the ways that Rufus and Jing-mei seek to preserve their individuality while responding to group pressures.

Group

Part Two: Trying to Beat the Odds A character who abandons group interests in favor of personal goals is Oganda in "The Rain Came." Unlike her father, who puts the interests of the larger group over his family bonds, Oganda eventually chooses to escape with her lover, thus forsaking the larger group.

■ Do you think that Oganda has done a good job of balancing individual needs with group obligations? Why or why not?

Choice

Part Three: Dealing with Consequences These selections highlight the need for responsible choices. The price of irresponsible choices can be betrayal, death, or the destruction of the environment.

■ What advice could you give Anchee Min in "Red Azalea" or the village people in "He—y, Come on Ou—t!" that would have led to more informed decisions on their parts?

Activities

1. In a group, brainstorm examples of people in history who managed to maintain their individuality despite strong group pressure.
2. Explain how you would handle this situation: Although you are an honor student, most of your friends get C's. What are some things you could do when they constantly mock you for being a "brain"?
3. Think of situations you have experienced or heard about in which group pressure caused you or someone else to do (or not do) something. (Remember group pressure can be a positive influence.) Then select one of these situations to re-enact.

Independent and Group Projects

Research

Armchair Travelers Form a group and tell your classmates to pack their bags and prepare for adventure in the jungles of Peru, politics in Nigeria, education in China during the Cultural Revolution, or fine dining in France. Review the settings of selections in this unit and have each group member research a different country. Then, with the help of your notes and a world map, take classmates on a culture tour.

Media

Tune In With a small group, choose one of the selections in this unit that would make a good television movie. Create a sixty-second TV commercial that highlights the actors and some dialogue and provides a glimpse of a major scene from the story to pique audience interest. Add sound effects and appropriate music. Now have your classmates tune in as you present your commercial.

Art

In the Mood Work in a group to identify the mood in ten of the selections from this unit. Then research different forms of art—collages, drawings, paintings, sculptures, photographs—to find a piece that captures the mood of each work. To make a mood book, photocopy pictures of the art you find, or create your own artwork, and provide a caption with the title and artist's name. On separate sheets of paper, write a brief explanation of how an artwork captures the mood of each selection. Compile the mood descriptions and art into a book and put it on display for the class or for other grades.

Oral Presentation

Critic's Corner You and your partner are to the world of literary critics what Siskel and Ebert are to the world of movie critics. You voice your opinions of literary works in a weekly thirty-minute television program titled *Meeting the Challenge.* This week's show consists of your critiques of five selections from this unit. Prepare your individual critique for each work and then surprise your partner (and the audience) with your views.

181

UNIT 1 OPTIONS

Research

Encourage students to use reference sources such as the following:

- encyclopedia articles on Peru, Nigeria, China, the Cultural Revolution, and France
- suitable library and online sources, such as recent travel guides and magazine articles

Media

Students may not agree on casting or other aspects of the commercials.

- If a group cannot decide who should play a character such as Jerry in "Through the Tunnel," planning the commercial both ways may help students decide.
- Encourage groups to make every member responsible for some decision(s).

Art

Many libraries have art collections in books and other media, such as CD-ROM. Examples:

- *An Introduction to the Experience of Art* by Rosemary Davidson (New York: Viking, 1994)
- *Techniques of the Great Masters of Art* (Secaucus, NJ: Chartwell Books, 1985)

Oral Presentation

Students may discuss their ideas about the selections and then present the program in class or on videotape.

Connections to **AuthorWorks**

Information for completing this project can be found on the AuthorWorks CD-ROM.

Unit Test

Unit 1 Resource Book,
New Selection, pp. 145–152
Test 1, pp. 153–154
Test 2, pp. 155–160

Part One: On Trial

Planning Unit 2: Making Judgments

Literature	Integrated Language Arts			
	Literary	**Writing/Grammar, Usage and Mechanics**	**Reading, Thinking, Listening, Speaking**	**Vocabulary/Spelling**
Antigone **Part 1** *by Sophocles* Play *(challenging)* p. 191	Protagonist/antagonist Style, flashback Theme, irony Characterization Motivation Foreshadowing Metaphor, plot	Sentence structure Parallel construction Commas	Clarify, summarize Draw conclusions Analyze, question Connect, infer Predict outcomes Compare and contrast	Expand vocabulary using structural analysis Read uncommon, low-frequency words
Part 2 p. 212	Protagonist/antagonist Personality, tone Characterization Metaphor Allusions Suspense, motif Theme	Heroic traits Monologue Persuasive paper Parallel construction	Clarify Draw conclusions Infer, synthesize Predict Recognize cause and effect Question Compare and contrast Predict outcomes Summarize, evaluate Generalize	Expand vocabulary using structural analysis
Twelve Angry Men **Act 1** *by Reginald Rose* Play *(average)* p. 228	Stage directions Symbolism, plot Verbal irony	Verb forms Colloquialisms	Predict outcomes Summarize, infer Recognize assumptions and implications Compare and contrast Visualize Draw conclusions Recognize the use of persuasion Connect	Replace with synonym
Act 2 p. 239	Stage directions Irony	Opinion journal	Relate literature to human concerns Draw conclusions Make personal connections Recognize the use of persuasion Make judgments Analyze, visualize Understand sequence	
Act 3 p. 247	Stage directions Character	Description of most influential evidence and arguments Eight defense questions Opinion paper Ellipses	Draw conclusions Make judgments Visualize Connect	Word association cluster Slang

Meeting Individual Needs

Multi-modal Activities	Mini-Lessons
Analyzing exposition Making cultural connections Expanding vocabulary notebook Exploring the role of the chorus Exploring key ideas Identifying key events Contrasting characters Checking comprehension Exploring parts of speech Analyzing argument	Cause and effect Sentence structure Parallel construction Expand vocabulary using structural analysis Protagonist/antagonist Read uncommon low frequency words Commas
Illustration Summarizing plot events Analyzing key concepts Understanding main characters Understanding motivation Keeping track of sequence Exploring abstract nouns	Parallel construction Protagonist/antagonist Expanding vocabulary using structural analysis
Keeping track of character Exploring adverbs Analyzing argument Keeping track of story details Checking comprehension	Dictionary/glossary Verb forms Colloquialisms Communicate clearly and effectively: pitch, modulation,
Evaluating evidence Exploring idioms Evaluating details	Interpret graphic sources: diagram Listen for information Stage directions
Debate Research Exploring a main idea Analyzing a key passage Relating key statements	Ellipses Slang

Interdisciplinary Studies
Guilty or Innocent?

Format	Content Area	Highlights	Skill
Article: **We the Jurors** *by Barbara Holland*	History	This article gives an overview of justice systems over time.	Use the dictionary
Interview: **Interview with Tamara Camp**	Career	Recent scientific advances provide jurors with evidence to make informed decisions.	Take notes On-line reference sources

Writing Workshop

Mode	Writing Format	Writing Focus	Proofreading Skills
Narrative writing	A scene for a play	Writing realistic dialogue	Writing in script format

Program Support Materials

For Every Selection	For Every Writing Workshop
Unit Resource Book Graphic Organizer Study Guide Vocabulary Worksheet Grammar Worksheet Spelling, Speaking and Listening, or Literary Language Worksheet Alternate Check Test Vocabulary Test Selection Test	**Unit Resource Book** Prewriting Worksheet Revising Strategy Worksheet Editing Strategy Worksheet Presentation Worksheet Writing Rubric **Transparency Collection** Fine Art Transparency Student Writing Model Transparencies

For Every Interdisciplinary Study	Assessment
Unit Resource Book Study Guide Mini-Lesson Skill Worksheet	**Unit Resource Book** TE Check Tests Alternate Check Test (blackline master) Vocabulary Test (blackline master) Selection Test (blackline master) **Test Generator Software** **Assessment Handbook**

Planning Unit 2: Making Judgments

Literature	Integrated Language Arts			
	Literary	Writing/Grammar, Usage and Mechanics	Reading, Thinking, Listening, Speaking	Vocabulary/Spelling
The Flying Doctor *by Moliére* Play *(average)* p. 270	Farce Characterization Dialogue Hyperbole Satire. stereotypes Irony, allusion Pun, dramatic irony Pace	Opening paragraph Review of play Rewrite as a dramatic farce Subordinate and coordinate clauses The tools of the comic play-write	Clarify relationships Evaluate Visualize Make judgments	Related words
The Chameleon *by Anton Chekhov* Short Story *(easy)* p. 283 **The Fox and The Woodcutter** *by Aesop* Poem *(easy)* p, 287 **A Poison Tree** *by William Blake* Poem *(easy)* p. 288	Tone Point of view Dialogue Dialect, irony Personification Fable Connotative language Symbolism	Similarities and differences Consumer complaint Satire Consistent verb tense		Understand poetic usage
Dip in the Pool *by Roald Dahl* Short Story *(average)* p. 292	Plot, setting Simile, metaphor Characterization Point of view Stream of consciousness Suspense, irony Humor	List New ending Explain how story fits the theme Run-on sentences	Compare and contrast Draw conclusions Make judgments Infer	Use context clues for word meaning
The Need to Say It *by Patricia Hampl* Essay *(easy)* p. 305	Narrator	Brief comparison Greeting card Dialogue	Draw conclusions	
Crossroads *by Carlos Solórzano* Play *(average)* p. 310 **Two Bodies** *by Octavio Paz* Poem *(challenging)* p. 317	Foreshadowing Mood	Opinion paragraph Capsule summary Capitalization	Identify author's purpose Recognize main idea Compare and contrast Draw conclusions, infer Relate literature to personal experience Recognize assumptions and implications, connect Evaluate author's point of view Clarify, visualize Summarize	Stage directions

Meeting Individual Needs

Multi-modal Activities	Mini-Lessons
Caricature Comedy skit Locating key facts Exploring plot devices Making career connections Tracking plot events	Subordinate and coordinate clauses Related words Farce The tools of the comic playwrite
Presenting a satiric skit Pop-up storybook Analyzing titles Relating poetry and prose	Analyzing genre Consistent verb tense Understanding poetic usage Tone
Artist's sketch Dialogue Dramatic reading Exploring setting Exploring multiple meanings Recognizing cause and effect Noting characters and details	Run-on sentences Use context clues for word meaning Plot: Conflict Evaluate
Preparing a plan Piece of art Making personal connections	Dialogue
Art talk Presenting the play Exploring stage directions Exploring key statements Making cultural connections Exploring metaphor	Dictionary Foreshadowing Capitalization

Interdisciplinary Studies

Skin Deep

Format	Content Area	Highlights	Skill
Collage: **Crowning Glory**	History	This selection depicts changes in beauty and fashion over time.	Use electronic encyclopedias
Article: **from Mona to Morphing**	Media	This article indicates how various forms of media portray beauty.	

Writing Workshop

Mode	Writing Format	Writing Focus	Proofreading Skills
Expository/descriptive writing	A gallery of stereotypical characters	Using parallel structure	Using adjectives and adverbs correctly

Program Support Materials

For Every Selection	For Every Writing Workshop
Unit Resource Book Graphic Organizer Study Guide Vocabulary Worksheet Grammar Worksheet Spelling, Speaking and Listening, or Literary Language Worksheet Alternate Check Test Vocabulary Test Selection Test	**Unit Resource Book** Prewriting Worksheet Revising Strategy Worksheet Editing Strategy Worksheet Presentation Worksheet Writing Rubric **Transparency Collection** Fine Art Transparency Student Writing Model Transparencies

For Every Interdisciplinary Study	Assessment
Unit Resource Book Study Guide Mini-Lesson Skill Worksheet	**Unit Resource Book** TE Check Tests Alternate Check Test (blackline master) Vocabulary Test (blackline master) Selection Test (blackline master) **Test Generator Software** **Assessment Handbook**

Unit 2 Supplemental Resources

Media and Technology

Part One Selections

Antigone

Videotape Students will enjoy either of two video versions of the play, *Antigone,* 120 minutes, Films for the Humanities & Sciences, 1987, or *Antigone*, 85 minutes, Library Video Company, 1962, which stars Irene Papas.

Community Resources You might invite someone connected with the theater in your community to visit the class and discuss how modern theatrical production compares to that of ancient Athens.

Twelve Angry Men

Videotape Consider showing a dramatization of the deadlocked jury in *Twelve Angry Men*, 95 minutes, Key Video, 1957, starring Henry Fonda.

Home Connection Students might ask a family member who has served on a jury in a criminal trial to visit the classroom and discuss the way in which jury room deliberations are presented in *Twelve Angry Men*.

Part Two Selections

The Flying Doctor

Videotape *Moliere*, 112 minutes, Library Video Company, 1984, stars Anthony Sher. *The Comedy of Manners: Moliere*, 52 minutes, Films for the Humanities & Sciences, contains a production of "The Misanthrope."

Home Connection Molière often used the stock characters of the Italian commedia dell'arte in his comedies. Students might discuss with family members what type of stock characters are featured in modern American forms of popular entertainment, such as television situation comedies, action movies, and video games.

Connections to
Custom Literature Database

For Part One "On Trial"
Selections with Lessons

- *Medea* by Euripedes
- "The Minister's Black Veil" by Nathaniel Hawthorne

Additional theme-related selections can be accessed on the ScottForesman database.

Connections to
Custom Literature Database

For Part Two "Beneath the Surface"
Selections with Lessons

- "The Sentimentality of William Tavener" by Willa Cather
- "The Listeners" by Walter de la Mare

Additional theme-related selections can be accessed on the ScottForesman database.

The Chameleon/The Fox and the Woodcutter/A Poison Tree

Videotape *Anton Chekhov: A Writer's Life*, 37 minutes, Films for the Humanities & Sciences, 1974, gives a profile of the author and his work. *The Birth of Modern Theatre*, 47 minutes, Films for the Humanities & Sciences, features Chekhov and his play, "Uncle Vanya."

Audiotape Boris Karloff reads in *Aesop's Fables*, Caedmon/Harper Audio. Students can hear a selection of Blake's poetry in *Essential Blake*, 58 minutes, Listening Library, 1987.

Home Connection Students might ask family members for examples of what they think are the wisest fables or maxims. The class could collect these examples into a brief anthology and discuss what common features these pieces of advice possess.

Dip in the Pool

Audiotape Students will enjoy listening to the stories of Roald Dahl in *The Roald Dahl Soundbook*, Caedmon/Harper Audio.

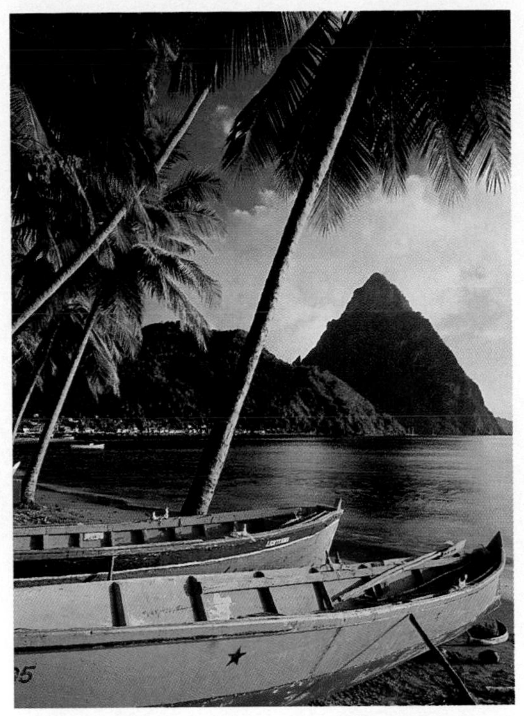

Home Connection For an at-home activity, students might poll family members on what would be their dream vacation and then create a travel brochure drescribing it.

The Need to Say It

Videotape *Daddy Can't Read*, 45 minutes, ABC, is an award-winning drama that takes the stigma away from illiteracy.

Community Resources You might invite a representative from one or more local ethnic cultural centers to visit the class and discuss the type of resources and programs the center offers.

Crossroads/Two Bodies

Videotape In *Octavio Paz, An Uncommon Poet,* 29 minutes, Films for the Humanities & Sciences, the poet talks about politics and poetry.

Videotape Paz is included in *The Simple Acts of Life: The Power of the Word*, 60 minutes, PBS Video, hosted by Bill Moyers.

Home Connection Students might ask family members about dating experiences. Has anyone ever gone on a blind date, and, if so, what was the outcome? Has a family member ever tried using a dating service? Has any ever made a date by placing or answering a newspaper ad?

Connections to
AuthorWorks

Information about the life and times of Anton Chekhov is available on ScottForesman's AuthorWorks CD-ROM.

Connections to
NovelWorks

An audiotape of *Cyrano de Bergerac,* a drama by Edmond Rostand, is one of the many teaching tools included in the ScottForesman NovelWorks kit.

Unit 2

Making Judgments

Art Study

Early Greek mosaics were made with pebbles, not the cubes seen here. They often showed animals and monsters, flowers, and scenes from mythology. By Roman times, it became customary to decorate the floors of houses with mosaics.

Masks, such as those shown in this mosaic, were used in the Greek theater. Because of the way Greek theaters were designed, audience members were seated far from the stage, making the actors' facial expressions impossible to see. Therefore, actors used masks to give their characters stereotyped expressions.

Question How would you describe the expression on each mask? *(Possible responses: The woman looks horrified. The man has an evil laugh.)*

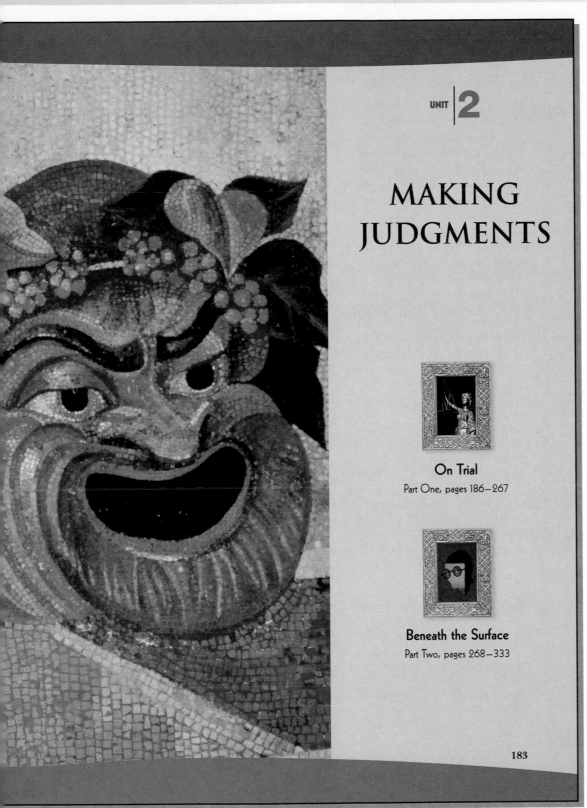

UNIT 2

MAKING JUDGMENTS

183

THEMATIC CONNECTIONS

All aspects of our lives—from daily interactions with others to keeping a society running smoothly—require that we make judgments and act upon them.

Part One
On Trial

Part One features literature that shows the systems of justice in two different times and cultures.

Ideas to Explore

- How can people ensure that justice prevails?
- Why is the jury system in America an important aspect of democracy?

Part Two
Beneath the Surface

The literature in Part Two shows how judgments made in haste can change lives.

Ideas to Explore

- When is it better not to tell everything that's on your mind?
- Why might someone choose to share painful feelings or criticisms with another person?

Art Study

The figure of a woman holding a set of scales has long been a symbol of justice. The face of one man appears to be superimposed on the silhouette of another man's face.

Question Do you think the woman holding scales is a good symbol of justice? Why or why not? (*Possible response: Yes, the idea of weighing the arguments makes sense.)*

Genre Overview: Drama

EXPLORING CONCEPTS

- Reading a play is, in a sense, unnatural, because a play is written to be performed.
- Illustrations, vocabulary definitions, and background information in the margins can support students' reading efforts.
- The cast of characters can help students become oriented to the play before they begin to read.
- Stage directions provide essential information for bringing the play to life, whether on stage or in the reader's mind.

The photograph on page 184 is from *Antigone* and the one on page 185 is from *Twelve Angry Men.*

Question Based on the photographs, which play are you more interested in reading?

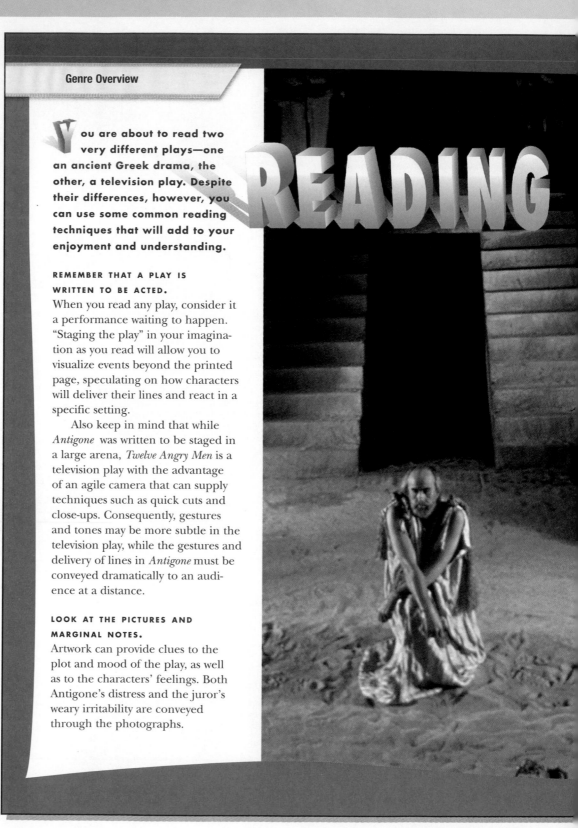

Genre Overview

READING

You are about to read two very different plays—one an ancient Greek drama, the other, a television play. Despite their differences, however, you can use some common reading techniques that will add to your enjoyment and understanding.

REMEMBER THAT A PLAY IS WRITTEN TO BE ACTED.

When you read any play, consider it a performance waiting to happen. "Staging the play" in your imagination as you read will allow you to visualize events beyond the printed page, speculating on how characters will deliver their lines and react in a specific setting.

Also keep in mind that while *Antigone* was written to be staged in a large arena, *Twelve Angry Men* is a television play with the advantage of an agile camera that can supply techniques such as quick cuts and close-ups. Consequently, gestures and tones may be more subtle in the television play, while the gestures and delivery of lines in *Antigone* must be conveyed dramatically to an audience at a distance.

LOOK AT THE PICTURES AND MARGINAL NOTES.

Artwork can provide clues to the plot and mood of the play, as well as to the characters' feelings. Both Antigone's distress and the juror's weary irritability are conveyed through the photographs.

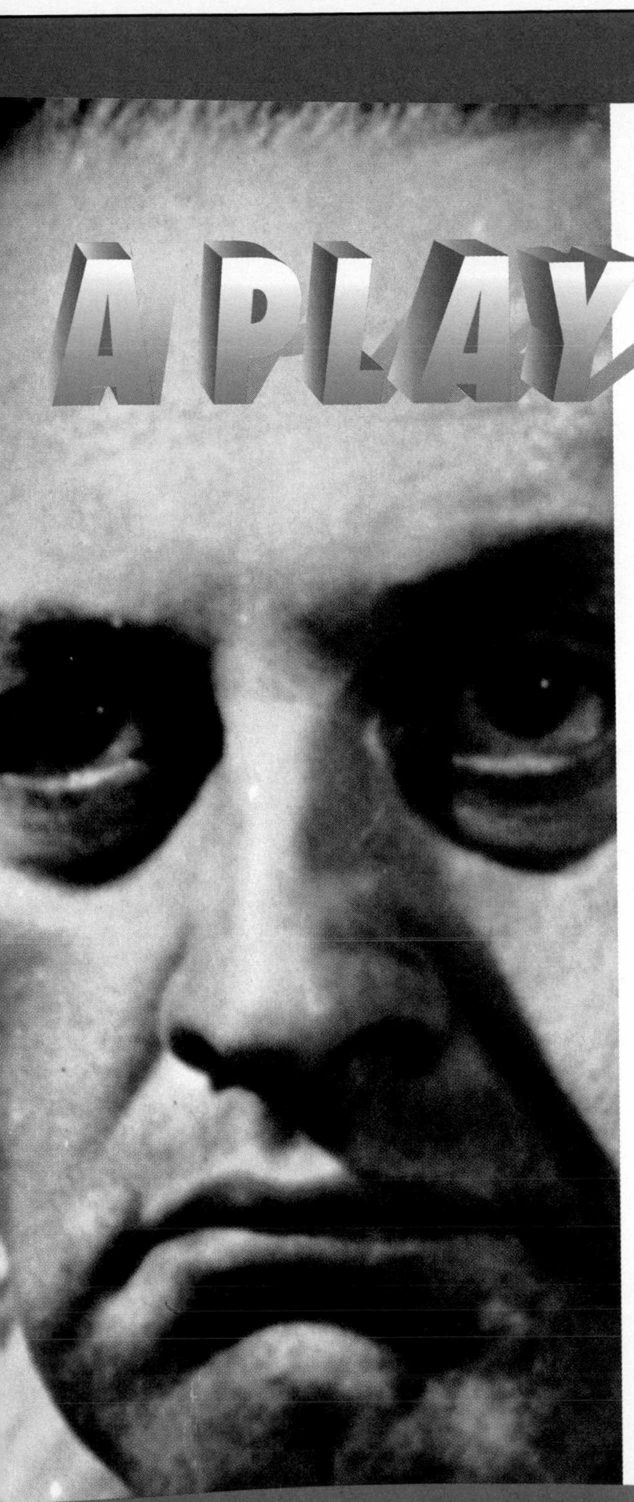

Likewise, notes can provide help on background information and vocabulary. By all means use the notes in a close reading of the text, but don't get bogged down or distracted from understanding the basic story line.

STUDY THE CAST OF CHARACTERS. Examine the cast of characters and refer to it as you read for clarification. This will be particularly important in establishing the family relationships in *Antigone* and in keeping the jurors straight in *Twelve Angry Men.* You might keep track of characters and critical events with a quick notation. For example, you might note each juror's number, along with words such as *loud, flashy, naïve* and *bigot* that the playwright provides to characterize each personality.

PAY ATTENTION TO STAGE DIRECTIONS. These directions indicate how lines are to be delivered (*briskly, flustered, annoyed, amazed*) and provide insights into setting and characters. (Antigone is described in the initial directions as *anxious* and *urgent.*) Note that the hot jury room is "unpleasant-looking" with walls that are "bare, drab, and badly in need of a fresh coat of paint."

Now plunge in and take the play beyond the printed page, visualizing the action, reading aloud and acting out scenes if possible. Move to center stage and enjoy the spirit of drama!

185

MATERIALS OF INTEREST

Books

- *Acting as Reading: The Place of the Reading Process in the Actor's Work* by David Cole (University of Michigan Press, 1992)
- *The Elements of Drama* by J. L. Styan (Cambridge University Press, 1960)

Preview
On Trial

FOR ALL STUDENTS

- What are some events that might lead to a person being on trial?
- What might happen to a person after a trial?

To further explore the theme, use the transparency referred to below.

Transparency Collection
Fine Art Writing Prompt 4

For At-Risk Students

Ask students to discuss fictional television shows they've seen that involved a trial. Then have them compare television shows to newspaper accounts or television coverage of real-life trials. Which is more interesting?

For Students Who Need Challenge

Some famous trials have been made into films, such as *Compulsion,* which chronicled the Loeb-Leopold murder trial. Encourage students to read newspaper accounts and books about a trial that has been filmed and then compare it to the film version.

MULTICULTURAL CONNECTION

Tell students that people of different cultures, social classes, genders, and ages may use different processes for arriving at consensus and may have different standards for how to deal with disagreements.

Ask students to brainstorm some strategies a group of diverse people might use to come to consensus on an issue. *(Possible responses: Give everyone a chance to speak; vote; brainstorm.)*

Part One

On Trial

In *Antigone* and *Twelve Angry Men,* the lives of a young woman in ancient Greece and a contemporary murder suspect are both at the mercy of those who judge them.

Multicultural Connection **Interactions** can become tense when people that have diverse cultural backgrounds or different goals try to arrive at a consensus about important decisions. As you read the following plays, decide in what respects ethnicity, social class, family allegiances, and age influence decision making.

IDEAS THAT WORK

Motivating with Quotes

A way to engage students in the two plays is by providing them with a list of textual lines that express key concepts and themes. Examples:

- "Everybody gets a fair trial. That's the system!"
- "The children . . . of slum backgrounds are potential menaces to society."
- "It takes a great deal of courage to stand alone even if you believe in something very strongly."
- "Better be beaten, if need be, by a man, than let a woman get the better of us."
- "He whom the State appoints must be obeyed . . . be it right—or wrong."

Students write "agree" or "disagree" after each statement. Then, in collaborative learning groups, they share their answers and try to arrive at a consensus. Everyone is actively engaged; discussion is invariably lively; and interest in the plays is high—even before we begin reading!

Lucila O. Dypiangco
Montebello, Californi

About Greek Drama

Greek drama grew out of the religious festivals held in Athens each spring to honor Dionysus (dī′ə nī′səs), god of wine. The earliest festivals consisted of dancing, games, and choral songs led by a conductor. During the sixth century B.C., a poet/leader named Thespis (*thespian* is still a synonym for actor) began to insert spoken lines into the songs, thus introducing the idea of dialogue. As you prepare to read *Antigone*, the following information will help you visualize how Greek drama was originally performed.

The Theater

Performances were held from dawn to dusk in enormous, open-air arenas. A typical arena, such as the theater of Dionysus southwest of the Acropolis, was built into a hillside. This gave the seating area, or *theatron* ("seeing place"), a natural rise so that thousands of spectators had a clear view of the action. At the foot of the seating area was a large circular *orchestra* ("dancing place") where the chorus, in unison or in small groups, sang or chanted and danced—in slow, stately movements.

One or two steps above the orchestra was the platform where the actors performed. Beyond it and facing the audience stood the *skene* (skē′nē), a painted, wooden building behind which the actors could change costumes, and from which they could enter through one of three doors. Our word *scenery* comes from *skene*.

The Actors

Because of the immensity of Greek theaters, the actors—exclusively men—increased their height and impressiveness artificially. Each actor wore a linen, cork, or wood mask painted with a single, exaggerated expression: a sad face for a troubled king, a haggard, worn face for a weary soldier. Each mask had a funnel-shaped mouth opening, like a megaphone, to help project the voice. Elevated boots, padded clothing, and a high headdress could make a six-foot actor appear over seven feet tall. Such items also allowed actors to play more than one role.

The acting style for Greek drama differed from the realistic style of modern drama. The Greek actor could not change facial expressions while on stage, and any gestures or changes in voice had to be noticeable half a hill away. As a result, the Greek acting style was broader and more formal and than ceremonial than contemporary acting.

ABOUT GREEK DRAMA

Teaching Objectives

- to recognize the conventions of Greek Drama
- to understand the Greek concept of tragedy
- to provide background for the play *Antigone*

Introduce

Tell students that this article on Greek drama will aid in their understanding of *Antigone* and also help them visualize how the play would be performed.

Art Study

The mask at the top of page 187 is a detail of a marble relief. The others are terra cotta copies of theatrical masks. The tragic mask on the bottom left side of the page represents King Priam, about 400 B.C.

Follow Up

If possible, display some photographs or paintings that show closeups of open air arenas where Greek drama was originally performed. These images will further help students visualize the placement of characters and chorus members on stage as they read *Antigone*.

The Conventions of Greek Drama

Greek drama differs from modern drama in several other significant ways.

- Unlike most modern audiences, who put a premium on originality, Greek audiences were familiar with the plots and characters of the dramas presented since most plots were derived from myths, legends, or other traditional stories. This familiarity enabled them to focus on the irony of the situations and the poetry of the words.
- The *chorus*, typically a group of twelve to fifteen men, represented either the ideas and feelings of the townspeople or of one of the major characters. The chorus or its leader could have any of the following functions: to recall and interpret past events, to initiate and to comment on the action, or to foretell the future. The role and importance of the chorus varied from play to play; in *Antigone* the chorus represents the elders of the city of Thebes.
- Partly because of the heavy costumes, acts of violence occur offstage and are reported in long, descriptive narratives by a messenger.
- As they were originally written, these ancient plays had no stage directions; those you see in the textbook are supplied by the translator so that you can visualize the action or better understand the motives and emotions of the characters.

The Greek Concept of Tragedy

It is ironic that the joyful Dionysian festivals were the source of the dramatic form we know as tragedy. Borrowing from a story or legend that the Greek audiences knew well, a tragedy shows how a character's proud or willful choices lead to inescapable disaster. Though deeply moralistic, tragedies are more than solemn stories of wrongs being punished. These dramas are complex studies of human beings in conflict with themselves, with society, and with the gods. As an audience, we can appreciate the rightness of the punishment, the sadness of the fall, yet also the nobility of the struggle.

Before Reading

Antigone

by Sophocles Greece

Sophocles
496-406 B.C.

The son of a wealthy armor manufacturer, Sophocles (sof′ə klēz′) studied under the great dramatist Aeschylus (es′kə ləs). His training included play writing, musical composition, and choreography—elements central to Greek drama. His reputedly weak voice led him to abandon acting for writing. In 468 B.C., at the annual Dionysian festival, one of his plays won the play competition. Over his ninety-year life, Sophocles wrote more than 120 tragedies, twenty-four of them winning first prize. He served in the military and is said to have been appointed an official ambassador to several foreign states. Only seven of his plays survive.

Building Background

Imagine the Scene The city Dionysia had begun its festival with an elaborate procession of citizens escorting an image of Dionysus, the "godfather" of theater, to its place of honor in the orchestra. Athenians eagerly await Sophocles' newest tragedy. Will he go home with the skin of the *tragos* (goat), the coveted prize awarded the winner of first place? Eager citizens rise early, for the first tragedy will begin at dawn, followed in the afternoon by a comedy. Some walk to the great amphitheater on the side of the Acropolis; others are carried on the shoulders of slaves. Many carry provisions to throw at an actor whose performance offends. Some remember the time when a dissatisfied audience threw stones, and an actor almost died. But the actors today are Athens's best, and the word in the *agora* (marketplace) is that *Antigone* might win Sophocles another first prize.

Literary Focus

Protagonist/Antagonist The word **protagonist** comes from two Greek words, *protos* and *agoniste*, and means "first actor." Today it refers to the main or chief character in a work of fiction. The protagonist's adversary, or opponent—person, society, or force of nature—is called the **antagonist**. As you read *Antigone*, ask yourself: Who or what is the title character's adversary?

Writer's Notebook

Who's Your Hero? Heroes come in many sizes and guises. Who are some heroes—from literature, movies, and real life? List qualities that make them heroic. Check those qualities that Antigone possesses. You might keep track of your ideas in a chart like this one.

Heroic Qualities	Antigone Possesses

Before Reading

Building Background

To highlight the dramatic qualities of *Antigone,* play a recording—at least of the early scenes. A translation by Dudley Fitts and Robert Fitzgerald (Caedmon TR 320M, 2 LPs, text) will introduce students to text variations from the E. F. Watling translation in their book.

Literary Focus

Introduce the terms **protagonist** and **antagonist** and elicit student examples from movies or TV that fit these terms. Discuss how a protagonist can have both good and bad qualities. Students may differ on who the protagonist of *Antigone* is.

Writer's Notebook

Before beginning to read, students might make a web illustrating qualities of a hero.

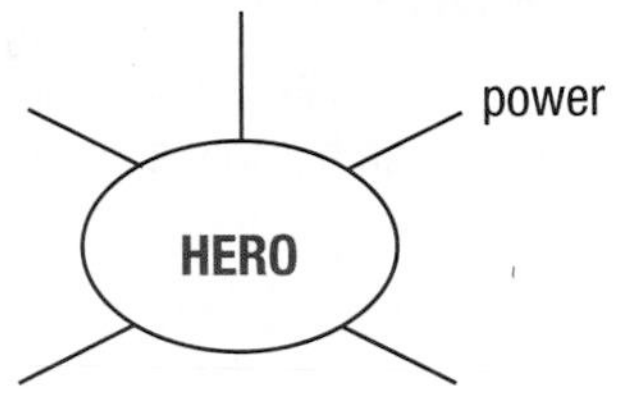

More About Sophocles

The story goes that at ninety, Sophocles was brought to court by his son Iophon for being too senile to manage his affairs. To prove his competence, Sophocles read a choral ode he had just written for *Oedipus at Colonus.*

SUPPORT MATERIALS OVERVIEW

Unit 2 Resource Book
- Graphic Organizers, pp. 1, 9
- Study Guides, pp. 2, 10
- Vocabulary, pp. 3, 11
- Grammar, pp. 4, 12
- Alternate Check Tests, pp. 5, 13
- Vocabulary Tests, pp. 6, 14
- Selection Tests, pp. 7–8, 15–16

Building English Proficiency
- Selection Summaries
- Activities, pp. 182–183
- *Antigone* in Spanish

Reading, Writing & Grammar SkillBook
- Grammar, Usage, and Mechanics, pp. 168–169, 264–267
- Vocabulary Skills, pp. 9–10

Technology
- Personal Journal Software
- Custom Literature Database: For another Greek tragedy, see *Medea* by Euripides on the database.
- Test Generator Software

During Reading

Selection Objectives

- to explore the theme "On Trial"
- to understand the concept of protagonist/antagonist
- to identify parallel construction
- to understand the style and conventions of Greek drama

Unit 2 Resource Book
Graphic Organizer, p. 1
Study Guide, p. 2

Theme Link

Antigone explores the theme "On Trial." Antigone is tried for her transgression and sentenced by Creon. Other characters undergo trials that are metaphoric.

Vocabulary Preview

blasphemy, abuse or contempt for God or sacred things
edict, decree or law proclaimed by a king or other ruler on his sole authority
flagrant, glaringly offensive
flout, treat with contempt
impunity, freedom from injury, punishment, or other bad consequences
onslaught, a vigorous attack
rout, a complete defeat

Students can add the words and definitions to their Writer's Notebooks.

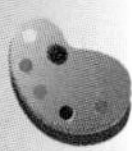

Art Study

Response to Caption Question
Perhaps it depicts the peace, harmony, and bonds of love that will be disrupted by events of the tragedy.

Visual Literacy Most of the pictures that accompany *Antigone* are production photographs. As they read the play, invite students to analyze how a three-dimensional sculpture like this differs from a photograph.

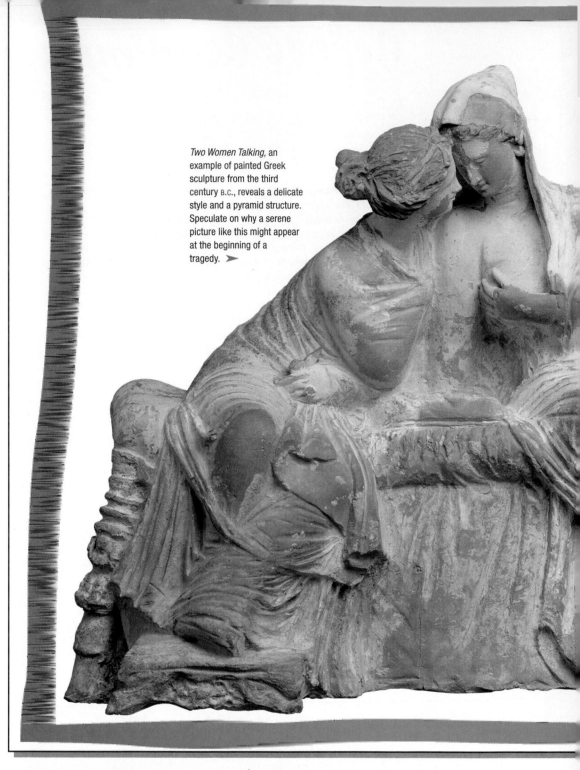

Two Women Talking, an example of painted Greek sculpture from the third century B.C., reveals a delicate style and a pyramid structure. Speculate on why a serene picture like this might appear at the beginning of a tragedy. ➤

SELECTION SUMMARY

Antigone, Part 1

Creon, ruler of Thebes, forbids that the brother of Antigone, Polynices, who has acted against the State, be buried. Antigone turns to her sister Ismene who is unable to help her. A sentry, who reports that the body has been buried, is sent by Creon to unbury it and lie in wait for the culprit. He returns with Antigone, who says that justice requires she act as she did. When Creon condemns Antigone to death, Ismene attempts to share her fate, but Antigone rebuffs her. Antigone's fiancé, Creon's son Haemon, informs his father that public opinion is against him. Creon insults both Haemon and Antigone, and Haemon leaves, declaring that Creon will never see him again. Creon orders that Antigone be left in a cave to die.

*For summaries in other languages, see the **Building English Proficiency** book.*

ANTIGONE

SOPHOCLES

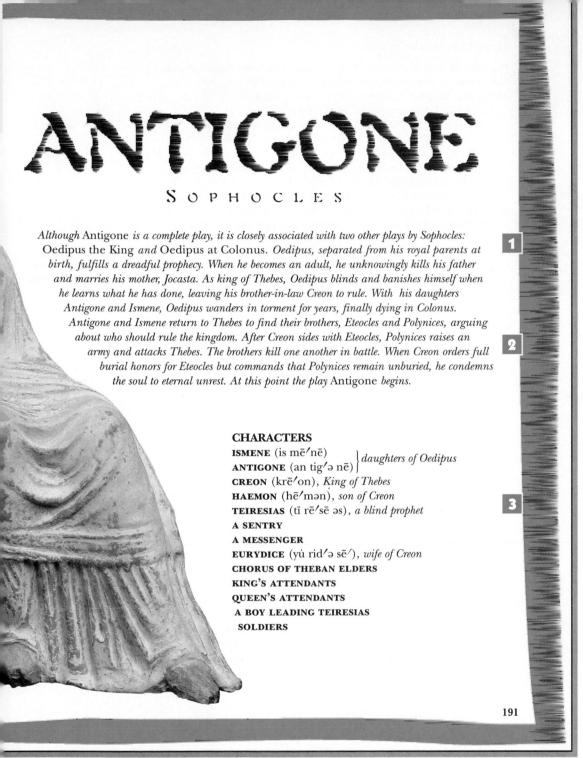

Although Antigone *is a complete play, it is closely associated with two other plays by Sophocles:* 1
Oedipus the King *and* Oedipus at Colonus. *Oedipus, separated from his royal parents at*
birth, fulfills a dreadful prophecy. When he becomes an adult, he unknowingly kills his father
and marries his mother, Jocasta. As king of Thebes, Oedipus blinds and banishes himself when
he learns what he has done, leaving his brother-in-law Creon to rule. With his daughters
Antigone and Ismene, Oedipus wanders in torment for years, finally dying in Colonus.
Antigone and Ismene return to Thebes to find their brothers, Eteocles and Polynices, arguing
about who should rule the kingdom. After Creon sides with Eteocles, Polynices raises an 2
army and attacks Thebes. The brothers kill one another in battle. When Creon orders full
burial honors for Eteocles but commands that Polynices remain unburied, he condemns
the soul to eternal unrest. At this point the play Antigone *begins.*

CHARACTERS

ISMENE (is mē′nē) } *daughters of Oedipus*
ANTIGONE (an tig′ə nē) } *daughters of Oedipus*
CREON (krē′on), *King of Thebes*
HAEMON (hē′mən), *son of Creon*
TEIRESIAS (tī rē′sē əs), *a blind prophet* 3
A SENTRY
A MESSENGER
EURYDICE (yü rid′ə sē′), *wife of Creon*
CHORUS OF THEBAN ELDERS
KING'S ATTENDANTS
QUEEN'S ATTENDANTS
A BOY LEADING TEIRESIAS
SOLDIERS

191

1 Historical Note
The Theban Plays

Sophocles composed these three plays over 36 years. Although *Antigone* was written first (in about 441 B.C.) it records the final events resulting from the curse of Oedipus.

2 Multicultural Note
Mythic Variations

Explain to students that the myths did not exist in a single form, so stories sometimes had variants. A variant of this story is that Polynices and Eteocles made a deal to rule in alternate years and live in exile when they were not ruling. Eteocles ruled the first year, while Polynices went into exile, but after the year expired, Eteocles refused to give up the throne.

3 Multicultural Note
The Wise Blind Man

Other cultural traditions include a figure who is blind but has prophetic vision. Samson in the Hebrew tradition, and Odin in the Norse, are two examples. This play marks the first appearance of Teiresias (also spelled *Tiresias*), the prophet of Apollo, in tragedy.

BUILDING ENGLISH PROFICIENCY

ESL LEP ELD SAE LD

Analyzing Exposition

Use one or more of the following activities to help students grasp the introductory information.

Activity Ideas

- Read aloud the headnote on page 191.
- Have students list the main characters and their actions prior to the play's beginning.
- Students may compare the exposition to a contemporary soap opera. Ask them to predict the play's ending.
- Help students create a character sociogram to depict the family's relationships, as shown to the right.

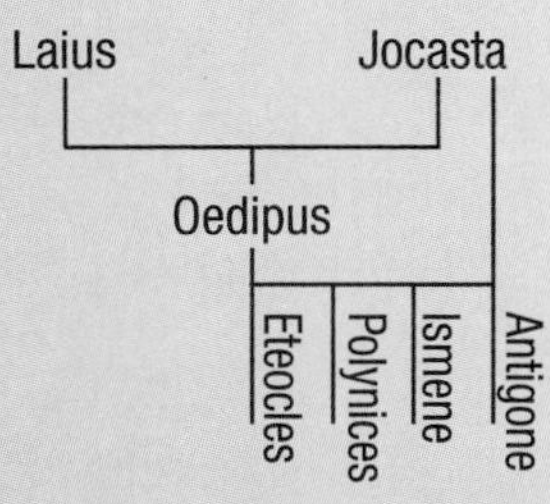

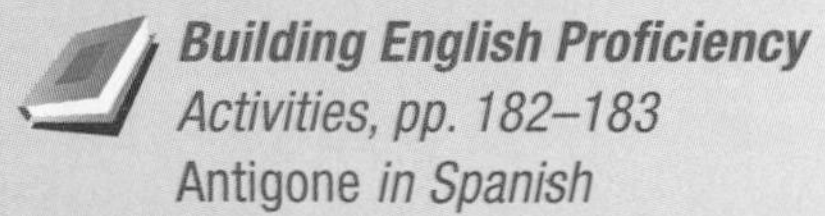

Building English Proficiency
Activities, pp. 182–183
Antigone *in Spanish*

4 Reading/Thinking Skills
Clarify

Possible Response Someone "worthy of your high blood" will be dedicated to family, regardless of the consequences. Antigone presents a clear challenge to Ismene, enlisting her help in burying Polynices.

5 Literary Criticism
Theme

"At every level the *Antigone* focuses on division, charting a myriad of paths by which kinship turns into enmity, union into separation. . . . Thus, Antigone begins as sister to Ismene, niece to Creon, fiancée to Haemon, but the play traces her radical and irrevocable separation from each of these persons. The separation from Ismene is well under way by the middle of the very first scene. . . ."

David H. Porter
Only Connect: Three Studies in Greek Tragedy

Scene: Before the Palace at Thebes.

Enter ISMENE *from the central door of the Palace.* ANTIGONE *follows, anxious and urgent; she closes the door carefully, and comes to join her sister.*

ANTIGONE. O sister! Ismene dear, dear sister Ismene!
You know how heavy the hand of God is upon us;
How we who are left must suffer for our father, Oedipus.
There is no pain, no sorrow, no suffering, no dishonor
We have not shared together, you and I.
And now there is something more. Have you heard this order,
This latest order that the King has proclaimed to the city?
Have you heard how our dearest are being treated like enemies?
ISMENE. I have heard nothing about any of those we love,
Neither good nor evil—not, I mean, since the death
Of our two brothers, both fallen in a day.
The Argive army, I hear, was withdrawn last night.
I know no more to make me sad or glad.
ANTIGONE. I thought you did not. That's why I brought you out here,
Where we shan't be heard, to tell you something alone.
ISMENE. What is it, Antigone? Black news, I can see already.
ANTIGONE. O Ismene, what do you think? Our two dear brothers . . .
Creon has given funeral honors to one,
And not to the other; nothing but shame and ignominy.
Eteocles has been buried, they tell me, in state,
With all honorable observances due to the dead.
But Polynices, just as unhappily fallen—the order
Says he is not to be buried, not to be mourned;
To be left unburied, unwept, a feast of flesh
For keen-eyed carrion birds. The noble Creon!
It is against you and me he has made this order.
Yes, against me. And soon he will be here himself
To make it plain to those that have not heard it,
And to enforce it. This is no idle threat;
The punishment for disobedience is death by stoning.
So now you know. And now is the time to show
Whether or not you are worthy of your high blood. **4**
ISMENE. My poor Antigone, if this is really true,
What more can I do, or undo, to help you?
ANTIGONE. *Will* you help me? Will you do something with me? Will you?
ISMENE. Help you do what, Antigone? What do you mean?
5 **ANTIGONE.** Would you help me lift the body . . . you and me?
ISMENE. You cannot mean . . . to bury him? Against the order?
ANTIGONE. Is he not my brother, and yours, whether you like it
Or not? *I* shall never desert him, never.

12 **Argive army** (är′jīv *or* är′gīv). Polynices's army came from **Argos** (är′gos), a city in southern Greece.

18 **funeral honors.** In Greek mythology, the souls of unburied human beings could not cross the River Styx to the realm of the dead but were compelled to wander forever with no permanent resting place. Burying the dead was a sacred duty for surviving friends and relatives.
19 **ignominy** (ig′nə min′ē), *n.* public shame and disgrace; dishonor.
20 **Eteocles** (i tē′ə klēz).
22 **Polynices** (pol′ə nī′sēz′).

■ What do you think that Antigone expects from someone who is "worthy of your high blood"?

MINI-LESSON: READING/THINKING SKILLS
Cause and Effect

Teach Have a student read aloud lines 17–40, which explain the motivation for Antigone's actions. Help students understand what moves her to act by drawing a cause-effect chart on the board.

Activity Idea As students discover other cause-effect relationships in the play, have them add these to the chart.

Cause	Effect
Creon denies Polynices burial.	Antigone resolves to bury him.

ISMENE. How could you dare, when Creon has expressly forbidden it?
ANTIGONE. He has no right to keep me from my own.
ISMENE. O sister, sister, do you forget how our father
Perished in shame and misery, his awful sin
Self-proved, blinded by his own self-mutilation?
And then his mother, his wife—for she was both—
Destroyed herself in a noose of her own making.
And now our brothers, both in a single day
Fallen in an awful exaction of death for death.
Blood for blood, each slain by the other's hand.
Now we two left; and what will be the end of us,
If we transgress the law and defy our king?
6 O think, Antigone; we are women; it is not for us
To fight against men; our rulers are stronger than we,
And we must obey in this, or in worse than this.
May the dead forgive me, I can do no other
But as I am commanded; to do more is madness.
ANTIGONE. No; then I will not ask you for your help.
Nor would I thank you for it, if you gave it.
Go your own way; I will bury my brother;
And if I die for it, what happiness!
Convicted of reverence—I shall be content
To lie beside a brother whom I love.
We have only a little time to please the living.
But all eternity to love the dead.
There I shall lie for ever. Live, if you will;
7 Live, and defy the holiest laws of heaven.
ISMENE. I do not defy them; but I cannot act
8 Against the State. I am not strong enough.
ANTIGONE. Let that be your excuse, then. I will go
And heap a mound of earth over my brother.
ISMENE. I fear for you, Antigone; I fear—
ANTIGONE. You need not fear for me. Fear for yourself.
ISMENE. At least be secret. Do not breathe a word.
I'll not betray your secret.
ANTIGONE. Publish it
To all the world! Else I shall hate you more.
ISMENE. Your heart burns! Mine is frozen at the thought.
ANTIGONE. I know my duty, where true duty lies.
ISMENE. If you can do it; but you're bound to fail.
ANTIGONE. When I have *tried* and failed, I shall have failed.
ISMENE. No sense in starting on a hopeless task.
ANTIGONE. Oh, I shall hate you if you talk like that!
And *he* will hate you, rightly. Leave me alone
With my own madness. There is no punishment

45 self-mutilation (self′myü′tl ā′shən), *n.* When he realized that he had killed his father and married his mother, Oedipus blinded himself by piercing his eyes with a brooch worn by his wife/mother.

46–7 his mother . . . own making. Jocasta (jō kas′tə), realizing that she was both wife and mother to Oedipus, hanged herself.

52 transgress (trans gres′), *v.* go contrary to; sin against.

■ Which sister do you think makes the wiser decision about burying Polynices?

83 he, Polynices.

6 Multicultural Note
Role of Women

You may wish to encourage students to research the role of women in Greek society at the time of Sophocles to help them understand the magnitude of Antigone's defiance.

7 Literary Criticism
Theme

"The theme of rebellion, the confrontation between two conflicting ideas of politics, which are central to all the modern versions . . . are not the central concern of Sophocles. The apparent familiarity of the ideas to us must not allow us to turn Sophocles into a twentieth-century writer. Like all of his plays the *Antigone* is a celebration at the altar of Dionysus, a presentation of the pattern of . . . [Justice] working through the dance. The *Antigone* is about an insult to death."

Leo Aylen
The Greek Theater

8 Reader's Response
Making Personal Connections

Possible Responses Antigone appears much more defiant than her sister, who confesses she is not strong enough to defy the State. Yet such defiance, even in the light of family allegiance, seems foolhardy.

BUILDING ENGLISH PROFICIENCY

Making Cultural Connections

Antigone's outrage over the judgment passed upon Polynices drives the action of this play. Help students understand Antigone's need to bury Polynices.

Activity Ideas

- Ask students to share beliefs, customs, and ceremonies that modern societies use to show respect for the dead. Offer prompts by mentioning such things as funerals, days of recollection, and special ceremonies for heads of state or military personnel.
- Encourage students to share ways in which the cultures of their heritage demonstrate such regard.
- Urge students to freewrite opinions in their journals, putting themselves in Antigone's place.
- Ask students if they feel that Polynices must be buried. Why or why not?

9 Reading/Thinking Skills
Clarify

Response Antigone vs. Creon or the State

10 Literary Element
Style

Remind students that this work is a translation, and that therefore the style is the style of the translator, not of Sophocles. Discuss some of the choices translators make:

- using archaic or modern language and diction
- adding stage directions or not
- preserving the syntax and word choice of the original language or rendering the text into idiomatic English
- translating poetic passages into poetry or prose

Discuss these issues again, as needed, for example, when students read choruses that use archaic forms and are rendered in English poetry that rhymes.

11 Literary Element
Flashback

Point out that this chorus recounts the events leading to Polynices' and Eteocles' deaths and Creon's rule.

Can rob me of my honorable death.
ISMENE. Go then, if you are determined, to your folly.
But remember that those who love you . . . love you still.
(ISMENE *goes into the Palace.* ANTIGONE *leaves the stage by a side exit.)*

(Enter the CHORUS *of Theban elders.)*
CHORUS. Hail the sun! the brightest of all that ever
Dawned on the City of Seven Gates, City of Thebes!

Hail the golden dawn over Dirce's river
Rising to speed the flight of the white invaders
Homeward in full retreat!

The army of Polynices was gathered against us,
In angry dispute his voice was lifted against us,
Like a ravening bird of prey he swooped around us
With white wings flashing, with flying plumes,
With armed hosts ranked in thousands.

At the threshold of seven gates in a circle of blood
His swords stood round us, his jaws were opened against us;
But before he could taste our blood, or consume us with fire,
He fled, fled with the roar of the dragon behind him
And thunder of war in his ears.

The Father of Heaven abhors the proud tongue's boasting;
He marked the oncoming torrent, the flashing stream
Of their golden harness, the clash of their battle gear;
He heard the invader cry Victory over our ramparts,
And smote him with fire to the ground.

Down to the ground from the crest of his hurricane onslaught
He swung, with the fiery brands of his hate brought low;
Each and all to their doom of destruction appointed
By the god that fighteth for us.

Seven invaders at seven gates seven defenders
Spoiled of their bronze for a tribute to Zeus; save two
Luckless brothers in one fight matched together
And in one death laid low.

Great is the victory, great be the joy
In the city of Thebes, the city of chariots.
Now is the time to fill the temples
With glad thanksgiving for warfare ended;
Shake the ground with the night-long dances,
Bacchus afoot and delight abounding.

9 ■ What does the main conflict in the play appear to be?

90 Dirce's river. Dirce (dėr′sē), the wife of a previous ruler of Thebes, was brutally murdered and her corpse thrown into a stream, thereafter called by her name.

101 the dragon, a metaphor for the army of Thebes. According to legend, Thebes was founded by Cadmus (kad′məs) whose first followers were killed by a dragon. Cadmus slew the dragon and planted its teeth; from the teeth came a race of giants who submitted to Cadmus and re-founded the city.

103–107 The Father of Heaven . . . to the ground. Zeus, who favored the Thebans in the battle, struck down the invading Argive army with thunderbolts.

108 onslaught (ôn′slôt′), *n.* a vigorous attack.

112–113 Seven invaders . . . tribute to Zeus. Polynices and six Argive generals each attacked one of Thebes's seven gates, which were successfully defended by seven Theban heroes. Instead of keeping the armor of the slain Argives, the defenders offered it as a tribute to Zeus.

114–115 Luckless brothers . . . laid low. Antigone's brothers, Eteocles and Polynices, killed each other in single combat, ending the war.

But see, the King comes here,
Creon, the son of Menoeceus,
Whom the gods have appointed for us
In our recent change of fortune,
What matter is it, I wonder,
That has led him to call us together
By his special proclamation?

(The central door is opened, and CREON *enters.)*

CREON. My councillors: now that the gods have brought our city
Safe through a storm of trouble to tranquillity,
I have called you especially out of all my people
To conference together, knowing that you
Were loyal subjects when King Laius reigned,
And when King Oedipus so wisely ruled us,
And again, upon his death, faithfully served
His sons, till they in turn fell—both slayers, both slain,
Both stained with brother-blood, dead in a day—
And I, their next of kin, inherited
The throne and kingdom which I now possess.
No other touchstone can test the heart of a man,
The temper of his mind and spirit, till he be tried
In the practice of authority and rule.
For my part, I have always held the view,
And hold it still, that a king whose lips are sealed
By fear, unwilling to seek advice, is damned.
And no less damned is he who puts a friend
Above his country; I have no good word for him.
As God above is my witness, who sees all,
When I see any danger threatening my people,
Whatever it may be, I shall declare it.
No man who is his country's enemy
Shall call himself my friend. Of this I am sure—
Our country is our life; only when she
Rides safely, have we any friends at all.
Such is my policy for our common weal.

In pursuance of this, I have made a proclamation
Concerning the sons of Oedipus, as follows:
Eteocles, who fell fighting in defense of the city,
Fighting gallantly, is to be honored with burial
And with all the rites due to the noble dead.
The other—you know whom I mean—his brother Polynices,
Who came back from exile intending to burn and destroy
His fatherland and the gods of his fatherland,
To drink the blood of his kin, to make them slaves—

123 Menoeceus (mə nē′sē əs).

12 ■ What background information does the Chorus provide in this speech?

130 tranquillity (trang-kwil′ə tē), *n.* calmness; quiet.

133 King Laius (lā′əs), a former king of Thebes and father of Oedipus.

140 touchstone (tuch′stōn′), *n.* a black stone used to test the purity of gold or silver; hence, any test.

153 she, Thebes.

155 weal (wēl), *n.* well-being; prosperity.

15 ■ Why is Creon willing to bury Eteocles but not Polynices?

12 Reading/Thinking Skills
Summarize

Response It identifies the setting (Thebes) and recounts the attack of the Seven against Thebes, describes how Polynices was killed by and killed his brother, explains that Thebes was victorious, and indicates that Creon, the newly appointed king, is about to make his first special public announcement.

13 Literary Element
Theme

This passage introduces the theme of authority and power that is an essential motif in this play.

14 Literary Focus
Protagonist/Antagonist

Question What does Creon value most highly? *(his country)*

15 Reading/Thinking Skills
Clarify

Response He considers Polynices a traitor who should not be honored.

BUILDING ENGLISH PROFICIENCY

Expanding Vocabulary Notebooks

Suggest that students record unfamiliar terms as they read. Entries for pages 194–195 might include *folly, ravening, consume, appointed, proclamation, tranquillity, temper,* and *pursuance.*

1. Encourage students to begin by using context clues and their own experience to figure out a word's meaning. Model a way to arrive at the meaning of *ravening* in the following sentence: "Like a *ravening* bird of prey he swooped around us. . . ." *(I know a bird of prey attacks and eats its victims.* Swooped *suggests an attack. I think* ravening *must mean "attacking" or "devouring.")*

2. Have students verify their "educated guesses" with a dictionary or thesaurus.

Art Study

This and other photographs of the play appearing in this book are by Jennifer Girard from a production at the Court Theater in Chicago.

Visual Literacy Point out how gestures and body stances are broad and dramatic, in accord with ancient Greek depictions that would appeal to large audiences at great distances.

Question Remind students that although modern theater audiences are positioned closer to the performers than ancient Greek spectators were, live performances still involve broader, more "theatrical" gestures than TV or movie productions, which rely on camera techniques for emphasis, editing, and special effects.

Ask: If you were filming the Sentry's speech (lines 183–194; 202–204; 206–231), what effects could you achieve with the camera? *(Possible responses: cuts from the Sentry himself to the scene he describes; a panning shot to reveal there were no tracks; a flashback to the sentries casting lots)*

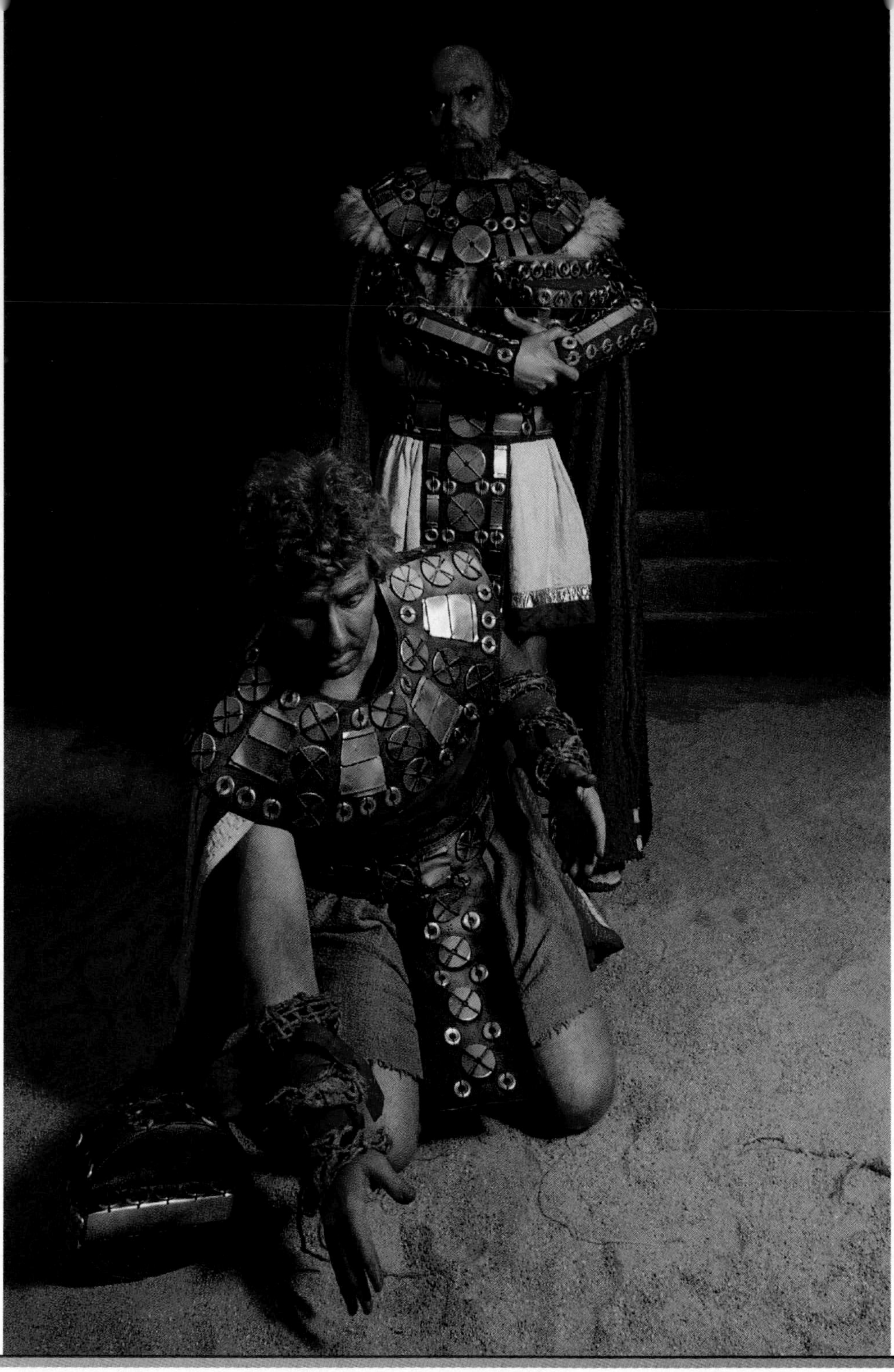

MINI-LESSON: GRAMMAR

Sentence Structure

Teach Point out the Sentry's opening sentences on page 197 (lines 183–194; 202–204):

Ask students to think about what the Sentry is saying and try to connect his meaning with the sentence structure he uses. *(He is anxious about revealing his news and so delays by spinning sentences with interruptions, repetitions, and irrelevancies.)* Lead students to see that the real message is conveyed in lines 202–204.

Activity Idea Have students work in small groups to analyze the Sentry's speech on page 198 (lines 206–231), explaining which phrases and sentence parts are essential to his report and which are nonessential.

He is to have no grave, no burial,
No mourning from anyone; it is forbidden.
He is to be left unburied, left to be eaten
By dogs and vultures, a horror for all to see.
I am determined that never, if I can help it,
Shall evil triumph over good. Alive
Or dead, the faithful servant of his country
Shall be rewarded.

CHORUS. Creon, son of Menoeceus,
You have given your judgment for the friend and for the enemy.
As for those that are dead, so for us who remain,
Your will is law.

CREON. See then that it be kept.

CHORUS. My lord, some younger would be fitter for that task.

CREON. Watchers are already set over the corpse.

CHORUS. What other duty then remains for us?

CREON. Not to connive at any disobedience.

CHORUS. If there were any so mad as to ask for death ——

CREON. Ay, that is the penalty. There is always someone
Ready to be lured to ruin by hope of gain.

(He turns to go. A SENTRY *enters from the side of the stage.* CREON *pauses at the Palace door.)*

SENTRY. My lord: if I am out of breath, it is not from haste.
I have not been running. On the contrary, many a time
I stopped to think and loitered on the way,
Saying to myself "Why hurry to your doom,
Poor fool?" and then I said "Hurry, you fool.
If Creon hears this from another man,
Your head's as good as off." So here I am,
As quick as my unwilling haste could bring me;
In no great hurry, in fact. So now I am here . . .
But I'll tell my story . . . though it may be nothing after all.
And whatever I have to suffer, it can't be more
Than what God wills, so I cling to that for my comfort.

CREON. Good heavens, man, whatever is the matter?

SENTRY. To speak of myself first—I never did it, sir;
Nor saw who did; no one can punish me for that.

CREON. You tell your story with a deal of artful precaution.
It's evidently something strange.

SENTRY. It is.
So strange, it's very difficult to tell.

CREON. Well, out with it, and let's be done with you.

SENTRY. It's this, sir. The corpse . . . someone has just
Buried it and gone. Dry dust over the body
They scattered, in the manner of holy burial.

179 connive (kə nīv′), *v.* cooperate secretly.

186–187 Why hurry . . . poor fool? The sentry worries that what he has to tell Creon will result in his death; killing the messenger who brought bad news was presumably a common practice.

16 Literary Criticism
Central Action

"The *Antigone* is about an insult to death. Death is the focus of life. Any attitude that ignores this is a wrong attitude. The ceremonials with which we surround death are a proper acknowledgment of death's centrality. The action of the *Antigone* is that Creon refuses burial to a corpse. As a result of this insult to death, this affront to fundamental human instinct, he loses everything that gives meaning to his life: the loyalty of his subject citizens, over whom he has just assumed command, the love and the life of his wife, and, above all, his adored son."

Leo Aylen
The Greek Theater

17 Literary Element
Irony

Most of Creon's aphorisms turn out to be ironic. Have students return to this speech after they finish the play, and analyze the irony of these words.

18 Reading/Thinking Skills
Draw Conclusions

Question: What assumption is Creon making here? *(Possible response: that people are disobedient only for gain)*

BUILDING ENGLISH PROFICIENCY

Exploring the Role of the Chorus

A chorus is rarely used in modern drama, so help students understand its function in *Antigone.*

1. The chorus often provides background information. Have students recap what the chorus tells them on page 194, through line 121.

2. The chorus can introduce characters. Ask students to locate the chorus's introduction of Creon on page 195.

3. The chorus comments on what other characters say. Ask students what the chorus is commenting on in lines 172–175 on page 197.

4. To demonstrate that a chorus has more dramatic impact than an individual, have students read lines 172–175 together as a chorus would. Then have a single student read the same lines.

5. Point out that the chorus provides moral insights. Urge students to listen carefully for the comments of the chorus as the play continues.

19 Reading/Thinking Skills
Draw Conclusions

Questions Who does the chorus suspect has buried Polynices? *(the gods)* Why does Creon consider this act blasphemy? *(Polynices has sinned against the gods, burning their temples and desecrating their shrines.)*

20 Reading/Thinking Skills
Clarify

Response Members of rebellious factions in the city. Answers will vary, but most students will identify Antigone.

CREON. What! Who dared to do it?
SENTRY. I don't know, sir.
There was no sign of a pick, no scratch of a shovel;
The ground was hard and dry—no trace of a wheel;
Whoever it was has left no clues behind him.
When the sentry on the first watch showed it us,
We were amazed. The corpse was covered from sight—
Not with a proper grave—just a layer of earth—
As it might be, the act of some pious passer-by.
There were no tracks of an animal either, a dog
Or anything that might have come and mauled the body.
Of course we all started pitching in to each other,
Accusing each other, and might have come to blows,
With no one to stop us; for anyone might have done it,
But it couldn't be proved against him, and all denied it.
We were all ready to take hot iron in hand
And go through fire and swear by God and heaven
We hadn't done it, nor knew of anyone
That could have thought of doing it, much less done it.
Well, we could make nothing of it. Then one of our men
Said something that made all our blood run cold—
Something we could neither refuse to do, nor do,
But at our own risk. What he said was "This
Must be reported to the King; we can't conceal it."
So it was agreed. We drew lots for it, and I,
Such is my luck, was chosen. So here I am,
As much against my will as yours, I'm sure;
A bringer of bad news expects no welcome.
CHORUS. My lord, I fear—I feared it from the first—
That this may prove to be an act of the gods.
CREON. Enough of that! Or I shall lose my patience.
Don't talk like an old fool, old though you be.
Blasphemy, to say the gods could give a thought
To carrion flesh! Held him in high esteem,
I suppose, and buried him like a benefactor—
A man who came to burn their temples down,
Ransack their holy shrines, their land, their laws?
Is that the sort of man you think gods love?
Not they. No. There's a party of malcontents
In the city, rebels against my word and law,
Shakers of heads in secret, impatient of rule;
They are the people, I see it well enough,
Who have bribed their instruments to do this thing.
Money! Money's the curse of man, none greater.
That's what wrecks cities, banishes men from home,

212 pious (pī′əs), *adj.* having or showing reverence for God; righteous.

214 maul (môl), *v.* treat roughly; physically harm.

236 blasphemy (blas′fə mē), *n.* abuse or contempt for God or sacred things.

■ Whom does Creon first suspect has buried Polynices? Whom do you suspect?

246 instrument (in′strə mənt), *n.* thing with or by which something is done; person made use of by another.

MINI-LESSON: GRAMMAR
Parallel Construction

Teach Have a group read the first three stanzas of the chorus on the glory of man (this word refers to both males and females), lines 279–290. Point out the examples of parallel construction: "Through the deeps—through wide-swept valleys"; "birds of the air—Beasts of the field."

Explain that parallel construction in songs is a structural technique in Greek drama and is often maintained by translators. It also appears in the Bible (for example, see page 608 of this book).

Activity Ideas

- Have students find other examples of parallelism in *Antigone.*
- Have students find examples of parallel structure in current song lyrics.

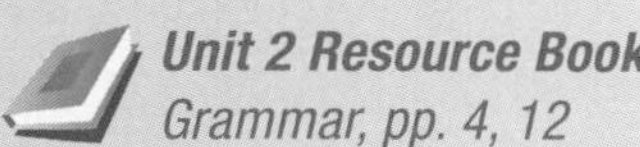

Unit 2 Resource Book
Grammar, pp. 4, 12

Tempts and deludes the most well-meaning soul,
Pointing out the way to infamy and shame.
Well, they shall pay for their success. (*To the* SENTRY.) See to it!
See to it, you! Upon my oath, I swear,
As Zeus is my god above: either you find
The perpetrator of this burial
And bring him here into my sight, or death—
No, not your mere death shall pay the reckoning,
But, for a living lesson against such infamy,
You shall be racked and tortured till you tell
The whole truth of this outrage; so you may learn
To seek your gain where gain is yours to get,
Not try to grasp it everywhere. In wickedness
You'll find more loss than profit.

SENTRY. May I say more?

CREON. No more; each word you say but stings me more.

SENTRY. Stings in your ears, sir, or in your deeper feelings?

CREON. Don't bandy words, fellow, about my feelings.

SENTRY. Though I offend your ears, sir, it is not I
But he that's guilty that offends your soul.

CREON. Oh, born to argue, were you?

SENTRY. Maybe so;
But still not guilty in this business.

CREON. Doubly so, if you have sold your soul for money.

SENTRY. To think that thinking men should think so wrongly!

CREON. Think what you will. But if you fail to find
The doer of this deed, you'll learn one thing:
Ill-gotten gain brings no one any good. *(He goes into the Palace.)*

SENTRY. Well, heaven send they find him. But whether or no,
They'll not find me again, that's sure. Once free,
Who never thought to see another day,
I'll thank my lucky stars, and keep away. *(Exit.)*

CHORUS. Wonders are many on earth, and the greatest of these
Is man, who rides the ocean and takes his way
Through the deeps, through wide-swept valleys of perilous seas
That surge and sway.

He is master of ageless Earth, to his own will bending
The immortal mother of gods by the sweat of his brow,
As year succeeds to year, with toil unending
Of mule and plough.

He is lord of all things living; birds of the air,
Beasts of the field, all creatures of sea and land.
He taketh, cunning to capture and ensnare

254 perpetrator (pėr′pə trā′tər), *n.* one who commits anything bad or foolish.

265 bandy (ban′dē), *v.* exchange.

21 Reader's Response
Challenging the Text

Possible Questions What do you think Creon is trying to accomplish? Do you think this approach will have the result he intends? What can you conclude about Creon's character? How would you have acted if you were Creon? *(Possible responses: He is trying to establish his authority; His plan may backfire and turn people against him; He seems insecure and overwrought; I would not make threats and accusations so quickly, and I would maintain my dignity and calm.)*

22 Historical Note
The Greek Chorus

The practice of performing plays seems to have begun with choral singing and dancing, which evolved into the chorus. It was the function of the chorus, which in *Antigone* represents the townspeople or elders, to serve as a barometer of popular opinion, utter moral proclamations, and provide commentary on events and characters in the play. The chorus interrupted the action at regular intervals to sing and dance in grave, ritualistic ways. As Greek drama evolved, individual persons stepped out of the chorus to act as specific characters.

BUILDING ENGLISH PROFICIENCY

Exploring Key Ideas

Creon's remarks to the Sentry reveal that he has strong opinions about money. Invite exploration of a topic that remains important today. Ask students to provide slang terms for money (*bread, green, bucks)* and explain that a term like *bread* for money indicates that it is considered essential for living.

Activity Ideas

- Work with students to list Creon's reasons for believing money to be "the curse of man."
- Introduce and discuss sayings about money such as "Money makes the world go 'round," "The love of money is the root of all evil," and "Money can't buy happiness."
- Suggest that pairs or small groups of students examine the local newspaper for stories involving money in some way. As they share their stories, keep a tally of whether money is a "curse" or "blessing" in each case.

23 Reading/Thinking Skills
Analyze

Questions What powers do humans possess? what shortcomings? *(Possible responses: Humans are subtle, noble, and resourceful. But they act rashly and eventually die.)*

24 Reading/Thinking Skills
Question

Responses Students might ask the chorus questions such as these: Are you being intentionally ironic? On what basis do you connect a country's laws with divine law? Do you believe that everyone who fails to obey the country's law does so out of pride?

25 Literary Element
Characterization

The Sentry's appearance provides relief from the somber tone and situation. He is exuberant, talkative, relieved, and eager to claim his prize. Whether or not he is comic depends on the production and the audience.

With sleight of hand;

Hunting the savage beast from the upland rocks,
Taming the mountain monarch in his lair,
Teaching the wild horse and the roaming ox
His yoke to bear.

The use of language, the wind-swift motion of brain
He learnt; found out the laws of living together
In cities, building him shelter against the rain
And wintry weather.

23

There is nothing beyond his power. His subtlety
Meeteth all chance, all danger conquereth.
For every ill he hath found its remedy,
Save only death.

O wondrous subtlety of man, that draws
To good or evil ways! Great honor is given
And power to him who upholdeth his country's laws
And the justice of heaven.

But he that, too rashly daring, walks in sin
In solitary pride to his life's end
At door of mine shall never enter in
To call me friend.

(Severally, seeing some persons approach from a distance.)
O gods! A wonder to see!
Surely it cannot be——
It is no other——
Antigone!
Unhappy maid——
Unhappy Oedipus's daughter; it is she they bring.
Can she have rashly disobeyed
The order of our King?

(Enter the SENTRY, *bringing* ANTIGONE *guarded by two more soldiers.)*

25

SENTRY. We've got her. Here's the woman that did the deed.
We found her in the act of burying him. Where's the King?
CHORUS. He is just coming out of the palace now. (*Enter* CREON.)
CREON. What's this? What am I just in time to see?
SENTRY. My lord, an oath's a very dangerous thing.
Second thoughts may prove us liars. Not long since
I swore I wouldn't trust myself again

290 sleight of hand, skill and quickness in moving the hands; tricks of a modern magician.

after 310 severally. Each of the following lines is spoken by a different member of the Chorus.

24

■ What question would you ask the Chorus about this speech?

To face your threats; you gave me a drubbing the first time.
But there's no pleasure like an unexpected pleasure,
Not by a long way. And so I've come again,
Though against my solemn oath. And I've brought this lady,
Who's been caught in the act of setting that grave in order.
And no casting lots for it this time—the prize is mine
And no one else's. So take her; judge and convict her.
I'm free, I hope, and quit of the horrible business.

CREON. How did you find her? Where have you brought her from?

SENTRY. She was burying the man with her own hands, and that's
the truth.

CREON. Are you in your senses? Do you know what you are saying?

SENTRY. I saw her myself, burying the body of the man
Whom you said not to bury. Don't I speak plain?

CREON. How did she come to be seen and taken in the act?

SENTRY. It was this way. After I got back to the place,
With all your threats and curses ringing in my ears,
We swept off all the earth that covered the body,
And left it a sodden naked corpse again;
Then sat up on the hill, on the windward side,
Keeping clear of the stench of him, as far as we could;
All of us keeping each other up to the mark,
With pretty sharp speaking, not to be caught napping this time.
So this went on some hours, till the flaming sun
Was high in the top of the sky, and the heat was blazing.
Suddenly a storm of dust, like a plague from heaven,
Swept over the ground, stripping the trees stark bare,
Filling the sky; you had to shut your eyes
To stand against it. When at last it stopped,
There was the girl, screaming like an angry bird,
When it finds its nest empty and little ones gone.
Just like that she screamed, seeing the body
Naked, crying and cursing the ones that had done it.
Then she picks up the dry earth in her hands,
And pouring out of a fine bronze urn she's brought
She makes her offering three times to the dead.
Soon as we saw it, down we came and caught her.
She wasn't at all frightened. And so we charged her
With what she'd done before, and this. She admitted it,
I'm glad to say—though sorry too, in a way.
It's good to save your own skin, but a pity
To have to see another get into trouble,
Whom you've no grudge against. However, I can't say
I've ever valued anyone else's life
More than my own, and that's the honest truth.

▲ This is an ivory statuette of a tragic actor.

359–360 And pouring . . . to the dead, pouring wine, water, or oil as an offering to the gods.

26 Reading/Thinking Skills
Analyzing

Question Why does the Sentry wish for Antigone's conviction? *(Creon has made it clear that without a conviction the Sentry will be held personally responsible and be tortured to death. There is no evidence that he has anything against Antigone personally.)*

Visual Literacy Point out how the sculptor has used posture and facial expression to dramatize the emotion of fear, as the figure recoils from some horror.

Question What other art can you find that portrays fear through body language and facial expressions?

27 Literary Element
Motivation

Clarify for students that Creon is assuming Antigone was trying to hide her involvement in the burial and avoid capture, which is not the case; she was acting openly according to her conscience with knowledge and acceptance of the consequences.

BUILDING ENGLISH PROFICIENCY

Identifying Key Events

Because the story of Antigone's actions is told secondhand, it may be difficult for students to grasp. To understand the Sentry's tale, have students act out scenes as you read.

1. Have the group perform the soldiers' actions (lines 340–347), note the time passage in line 348, and then use hand motions to illustrate the storm (lines 348–353).
2. Have a student pantomime Antigone's actions (lines 353–360).
3. Let the rest of the group apprehend and accuse Antigone (lines 361–364), noting Antigone's reaction.
4. Ask pairs of students to list the three story details that they consider the most important. Allow pairs to share and explain their choices.

28 Literary Element
Characterization

Point out that Creon has two relationships to Antigone: he is both her uncle and her king.

Question In what capacity is Creon addressing Antigone? Why? *(Possible responses: in his capacity as king; he wants to avoid any appearance of favoritism in dealing with his family, or perhaps he is really disgusted by her loyalty to someone he considers a dangerous traitor.)*

29 Reading/Thinking Skills
Summarize

Response Students may observe that her integrity is more important to her than her life; divine law is more important to her than human law.

30 Reader's Response
Making Personal Connections

Question Do you find anything to admire in Creon's stand? *(Many students will find Creon reprehensible. Some will think that he truly believes he is doing the right thing.)*

CREON (*to* ANTIGONE). Well, what do you say—you, hiding your head there:
Do you admit, or do you deny the deed?
ANTIGONE. I do admit it. I do not deny it.
CREON (*to the* SENTRY). You—you may go. You are discharged from blame.
(*Exit* SENTRY.)
Now tell me, in as few words as you can,
28 Did you know the order forbidding such an act?
ANTIGONE. I knew it, naturally. It was plain enough.
CREON. And yet you dared to contravene it?
ANTIGONE. Yes. 29
That order did not come from God. Justice,
That dwells with the gods below, knows no such law.
I did not think your edicts strong enough
To overrule the unwritten unalterable laws
Of God and heaven, you being only a man.
They are not of yesterday or today, but everlasting
Though where they came from, none of us can tell.
Guilty of their transgression before God
I cannot be, for any man on earth.
I knew that I should have to die, of course,
With or without your order. If it be soon,
So much the better. Living in daily torment
As I do, who would not be glad to die?
This punishment will not be any pain.
Only if I had let my mother's son
Lie there unburied, then I could not have borne it.
This I can bear. Does that seem foolish to you?
Or is it you that are foolish to judge me so?
CHORUS. She shows her father's stubborn spirit: foolish
Not to give way when everything's against her.
CREON. Ah, but you'll see. The over-obstinate spirit
Is soonest broken; as the strongest iron will snap
If over-tempered in the fire to brittleness.
A little halter is enough to break
The wildest horse. Proud thoughts do not sit well
Upon subordinates. This girl's proud spirit
Was first in evidence when she broke the law;
And now, to add insult to her injury,
30 She gloats over her deed. But, as I live,
She shall not flout my orders with impunity.
My sister's child—ay, were she even nearer,
Nearest and dearest, she should not escape
Full punishment—she, and her sister too,

■ What is Antigone's philosophy in lines 377–395?

380 edict (ē′dikt), *n.* degree or law proclaimed by a king or other ruler on his sole authority.

400 over-tempered. The tempering of steel or any other metal involves bringing it to a proper or desired condition of hardness, elasticity, etc., by heating and cooling it.

407 flout (flout), *v.* treat with contempt or scorn.
407 impunity (im pyü′nə tē), *n.* freedom from injury, punishment, or other bad consequences.

MINI-LESSON: VOCABULARY
Expand Vocabulary Using Structural Analysis

Teach Remind students that many words with Greek and/or Latin roots can be analyzed through structural analysis to discover their meanings. Point out the word *contravene* in line 377 on page 202. Explain that if students know that *contra* means "against" and *venire* means "to come" they can figure out that *contravene* means "to set oneself against" someone or something.

Activity Idea Have students use a dictionary with etymological information or their own knowledge to analyze the following words that appear on pages 202 and 203:

transgression
impunity
subordinates
prerogative

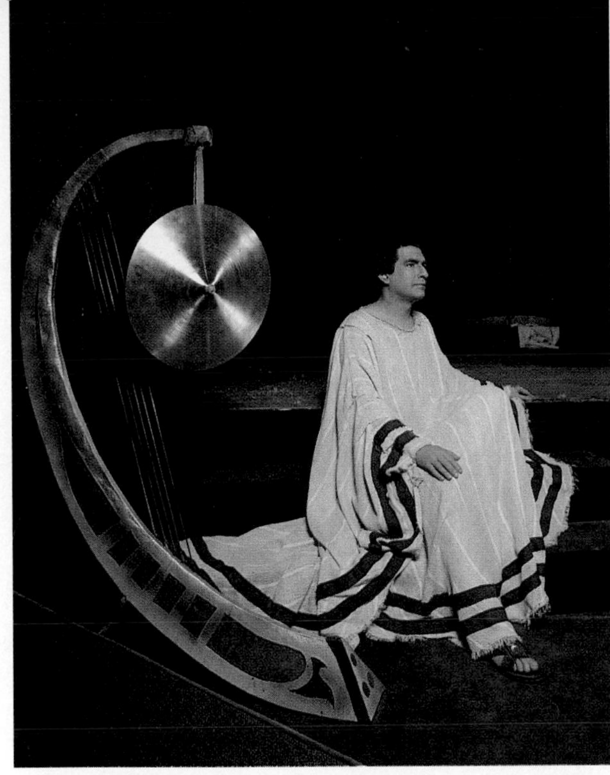

Her partner, doubtless, in this burying.
Let her be fetched! She was in the house just now;
I saw her, hardly in her right mind either.
Often the thoughts of those who plan dark deeds
Betray themselves before the deed is done.
The criminal who being caught still tries
To make a fair excuse, is damned indeed.

ANTIGONE. Now you have caught, will you do more than kill me?

CREON. No, nothing more; that is all I could wish.

ANTIGONE. Why then delay? There is nothing that you can say
That I should wish to hear, as nothing I say
Can weigh with you. I have given my brother burial.
What greater honor could I wish? All these
Would say that what I did was honorable,
But fear locks up their lips. To speak and act
Just as he likes is a king's prerogative.

CREON. You are wrong. None of my subjects thinks as you do.

ANTIGONE. Yes, sir, they do; but dare not tell you so.

CREON. And you are not only alone, but unashamed.

ANTIGONE. There is no shame in honoring my brother.

426 prerogative (pri rog′ə-tiv), *n.* right or privilege that nobody else has.

Visual Literacy Point out the flowing robe worn by a member of the chorus and his noble bearing. Have students visualize how this type of robe would enhance movements of chorus members as they deliver lines.

Question What do you think the gong might be used for? *(Possible responses: to attract the attention of the audience, to supply sound effects, or to punctuate dramatic scenes)*

31 Reading/Thinking Skills
Analyze

Question What does Antigone mean? *(Possible responses: She wonders if Creon will leave her unburied too. She wonders if she will be tortured and stripped of dignity.)*

32 Reading/Thinking Skills
Draw Conclusions

Question To whom does Antigone refer? *(the Theban elders represented by the chorus)*

33 Literary Element
Foreshadowing

This is the first strong hint that Antigone does not stand alone. After completing the play, students can go back and identify lines that foreshadow the turn of public opinion against Creon.

BUILDING ENGLISH PROFICIENCY

ESL
LEP
ELD
SAE
LD

Contrasting Characters

To understand the conflicting views of Antigone and Creon about the burial of Polynices, have students construct a chart that contains statements by both characters to indicate that they have acted rightly. Ask students to read the lines that support their entries. A sample chart is shown.

Antigone's View	Creon's View
• "What greater honor could I wish?" • "Only if I had let my mother's son/ Lie there unburied, then I could not have borne it."	• "She shall not flout my orders with impunity." • ". . . she broke the law."

34 Literary Element
Characterization

Response Probably not—he is too concerned with keeping up the appearance of power to compromise.

35 Literary Focus
Protagonist/Antagonist

Question In what ways are both Creon and Antigone right about honoring the dead? *(Possible responses: Creon feels that burying the dead is honoring the dead. Antigone considers burial a duty to the dead, no matter what they have done.)*

36 Literary Element
Metaphor

Students may find the comparison of gentle, obedient Ismene with a snake to be a sign of paranoia on Creon's part.

37 Reader's Response
Making Personal Connections

Questions Do you feel more sympathy with Ismene or Antigone? Why? *(Possible responses: Ismene, because she is weak and is trying to do the right thing and Antigone rejects her; Antigone, because Ismene does not support her when she needs it most.)*

CREON. Was not his enemy, who died with him, your brother?
ANTIGONE. Yes, both were brothers, both of the same parents.
CREON. You honor one, and so insult the other.
ANTIGONE. He that is dead will not accuse me of that.
CREON. He will, if you honor him no more than the traitor.
ANTIGONE. It was not a slave, but his brother that died with him. **34**
CREON. Attacking his country, while the other defended it.
ANTIGONE. Even so, we have a duty to the dead.
35 **CREON.** Not to give equal honour to good and bad.
ANTIGONE. Who knows? In the country of the dead that may be the law.
CREON. An enemy can't be a friend, even when dead.
ANTIGONE. My way is to share my love, not share my hate.
CREON. Go then, and share your love among the dead.
We'll have no woman's law here, while I live.

(Enter ISMENE *from the Palace.)*

CHORUS. Here comes Ismene, weeping
In sisterly sorrow; a darkened brow,
Flushed face, and the fair cheek marred
With flooding rain.
36 **CREON.** You crawling viper! Lurking in my house
To suck my blood! Two traitors unbeknown
Plotting against my throne. Do you admit
To share in this burying, or deny all knowledge?
ISMENE. I did it—yes—if she will let me say so.
I am as much to blame as she is.
ANTIGONE. No.
That is not just. You would not lend a hand
And I refused your help in what I did.
ISMENE. But I am not ashamed to stand beside you
Now in your hour of trial, Antigone.
ANTIGONE. Whose was the deed, Death and the dead are witness.
I love no friend whose love is only words.
ISMENE. O sister, sister, let me share your death,
Share in the tribute of honor to him that is dead.
ANTIGONE. You shall not die with me. You shall not claim
That which you would not touch. One death is enough.
ISMENE. How can I bear to live, if you must die?
37 **ANTIGONE.** Ask Creon. Is not he the one you care for?
ISMENE. You do yourself no good to taunt me so.
ANTIGONE. Indeed no: even my jests are bitter pains.
ISMENE. But how, O tell me, how can I still help you?
ANTIGONE. Help yourself. I shall not stand in your way.
ISMENE. For pity, Antigone—can I not die with you?

■ Do you think that Creon will eventually reverse his decision to put Antigone to death? Why or why not?

447-448 fair cheek . . . flooding rain. Ismene's face is spoiled by tears.

MINI-LESSON: LITERARY FOCUS
Protagonist/Antagonist

Teach Review the definitions of *protagonist* and *antagonist* under Literary Focus on pages 189 and 225. Initiate a discussion about who is the protagonist of *Antigone* and who or what is the antagonist, offering questions such as the following. Invite students to make a case for either Antigone or Creon as protagonist and to suggest characters or things that could serve as antagonist.

1. Why do you think the play is titled *Antigone* instead of *Creon?*
2. Can a protagonist die midway through a play?
3. Can a protagonist have faults? Can an antagonist have good qualities?

Activity Idea For practice, students might determine a protagonist and antagonist from a story in this book.

ANTIGONE. You chose; life was your choice, when mine was death.
ISMENE. Although I warned you that it would be so.
ANTIGONE. Your way seemed right to some, to others mine.
ISMENE. But now both in the wrong, and both condemned.
ANTIGONE. No, no. You live. My heart was long since dead,
So it was right for me to help the dead.
CREON. I do believe the creatures both are mad;
One lately crazed, the other from her birth.
ISMENE. Is it not likely, sir? The strongest mind
Cannot but break under misfortune's blows.
CREON. Yours did, when you threw in your lot with hers.
ISMENE. How could I wish to live without my sister?
CREON. You have no sister. Count her dead already.
ISMENE. You could not take her—kill your own son's bride?
CREON. Oh, there are other fields for him to plough.
ISMENE. No truer troth was ever made than theirs.
CREON. No son of mine shall wed so vile a creature.
ANTIGONE. O Haemon, can your father spite you so?
CREON. You and your paramour, I hate you both.
CHORUS. Sir, would you take her from your own son's arms?
CREON. Not I, but death shall take her.
CHORUS. Be it so.
Her death, it seems, is certain.
CREON. Certain it is.
No more delay. Take them, and keep them within—
The proper place for women. None so brave
As not to look for some way to escape
When they see life stand face to face with death.
(The women are taken away.)

CHORUS. Happy are they who know not the taste of evil.
From a house that heaven hath shaken
The curse departs not
But falls upon all of the blood,
Like the restless surge of the sea when the dark storm drives
The black sand hurled from the deeps
And the Thracian gales boom down
On the echoing shore.

In life and in death is the house of Labdacus stricken.
Generation to generation,
With no atonement,
It is scourged by the wrath of a god.

And now for the dead dust's sake is the light of promise,
The tree's last root, crushed out

38

■ What other literary couples do you know whose parents oppose their union?

490 paramour (par′ə mùr), *n.* lover.

500–501 The curse . . . upon all of the blood. The curse on Oedipus has passed on to his descendants.
506 the house of Labdacus (lab′də kəs), the ruling family of Thebes. Labdacus, a former king, was the grandfather of Oedipus.
508 atonement (ə tōn′mənt), *n.* a giving of satisfaction for a wrong, loss, or injury.
509 scourge (skėrj), *v.* punish severely.

41

■ What does the Chorus mean by "the tree's last root" in line 511? You may want to refer to the head-note on page 191.

38 Reading/Thinking Skills
Connect

Response Romeo and Juliet; mythic couples such as Pyramus and Thisbe. Students might also offer names of couples from popular literature they have read.

39 Reading/Thinking Skills
Analyzing

Question Do you think Creon really hates Haemon? *(Possible response: No, if he did, he wouldn't care whom Haemon married. He is speaking in anger.)*

40 Literary Element
Characterization

Questions Do you agree that Antigone is likely to try to escape? Why or why not? *(Possible response: Since Antigone knew and accepted her fate even before she committed the act and since she did not try to hide her responsibility for burying Polynices, it is unlikely that she will try to avoid her punishment now.)*

41 Literary Element
Metaphor

Response This refers to the house of Labdacus, of which Antigone and Ismene are the last survivors.

BUILDING ENGLISH PROFICIENCY

Checking Comprehension

The point at which Ismene and Antigone are led away (line 497) provides a good place to check students' comprehension.

1. Assign students to portray Antigone, Ismene, Creon, and the chorus. Then have them read aloud lines 493–497. At the end, have students "freeze," with the soldiers ready to lead Antigone and Ismene out.

2. Invite students to make any comments or ask any questions that they think their characters may have in mind.

3. Encourage students to speak freely, particularly if they are confused or unsure about the charges and counter charges. For example, some may wonder about Ismene's sudden change of heart or Antigone's stubborn refusal of Ismene's offer.

42 Literary Element
Theme

The theme "On Trial" is reinforced here: In this case, it is the gods who pass judgment on mortals and pass sentence condemning them to a life of suffering.

43 Reading/Thinking Skills
Infer

Question What do you infer at this point about the relationship between Creon and Haemon? *(Possible response: Creon expects to be obeyed and Haemon acquiesces.)*

By pride of heart and the sin
Of presumptuous tongue.

For what presumption of man can match thy power,
O Zeus, that art not subject to sleep or time
Or age, living for ever in bright Olympus?
Tomorrow and for all time to come,
As in the past,
This law is immutable:
For mortals greatly to live is greatly to suffer.

Roving ambition helps many a man to good,
And many it falsely lures to light desires,
Till failure trips them unawares, and they fall
On the fire that consumes them. Well was it said,
Evil seems good
To him who is doomed to suffer;

And short is the time before that suffering comes.
But here comes Haemon,
Your youngest son.
Does he come to speak his sorrow
For the doom of his promised bride,
The loss of his marriage hopes?

CREON. We shall know it soon, and need no prophet to tell us.

(*Enter* HAEMON.)
Son, you have heard, I think, our final judgment
On your late betrothed. No angry words, I hope?
Still friends, in spite of everything, my son?

HAEMON. I am your son, sir; by your wise decisions
My life is ruled, and them I shall always obey.
I cannot value any marriage tie
Above your own good guidance.

CREON. Rightly said.
Your father's will should have your heart's first place.
Only for this do fathers pray for sons
Obedient, loyal, ready to strike down
Their fathers' foes, and love their fathers' friends.
To be the father of unprofitable sons
Is to be the father of sorrows, a laughingstock
To all one's enemies. Do not be fooled, my son,
By lust and the wiles of a woman. You'll have bought
Cold comfort if your wife's a worthless one.
No wound strikes deeper than love that is turned to hate.

513 presumptuous (pri-zump′chü əs), *adj.* bold.

519 immutable (i myü′tə-bəl), *adj.* never changing.

525–527 Evil seems good . . . suffering comes. People who convince themselves that the evil they do is good must eventually suffer punishment.

MINI-LESSON: VOCABULARY

Read Uncommon Low-Frequency Words

Teach One of the stylistic techniques used in this translation is archaic verb and pronoun forms. These are found both in the choruses and elsewhere. Point out the pronoun *thy* in line 514 and the verb form *art* in line 515. Draw the chart at the right on the board.

Explain that *art* is an archaic form of *are*, and that the other archaic forms students will find are mostly third-person singular verbs ending in *-eth.*

Second-Person Pronouns	
Nominative	thou
Objective	thee
Possessive	thy

Activity Idea Have students look back at the chorus on pages 199–200 and identify archaic forms found there *(taketh,* line 289; *meeteth,* line 300; *conquereth,* line 300; *hath,* line 301; *upholdeth,* line 305).

This girl's an enemy; away with her,
And let her go and find a mate in Hades.
Once having caught her in a flagrant act—
The one and only traitor in our State—
I cannot make myself a traitor too;
So she must die. Well may she pray to Zeus,
The god of family love. How, if I tolerate
A traitor at home, shall I rule those abroad?
He that is a righteous master of his house
Will be a righteous statesman. To transgress
Or twist the law to one's own pleasure, presume
To order where one should obey, is sinful,
And I will have none of it.
He whom the State appoints must be obeyed
To the smallest matter, be it right—or wrong.
And he that rules his household, without a doubt,
Will make the wisest king, or, for that matter,
The staunchest subject. He will be the man
You can depend on in the storm of war,
The faithfulest comrade in the day of battle.
There is no more deadly peril than disobedience;
States are devoured by it, homes laid in ruins,
Armies defeated, victory turned to rout.
While simple obedience saves the lives of hundreds
Of honest folk. Therefore, I hold to the law,
And will never betray it—least of all for a woman.
Better be beaten, if need be, by a man,
Than let a woman get the better of us.

CHORUS. To me, as far as an old man can tell,
It seems your Majesty has spoken well.

HAEMON. Father, man's wisdom is the gift of heaven,
The greatest gift of all. I neither am
Nor wish to be clever enough to prove you wrong,
Though all men might not think the same as you do.
Nevertheless, I have to be your watchdog,
To know what others say and what they do,
And what they find to praise and what to blame.
Your frown is a sufficient silencer
Of any word that is not for your ears.
But *I* hear whispers spoken in the dark;
On every side I hear voices of pity
For this poor girl, doomed to the cruelest death,
And most unjust, that ever woman suffered
For an honourable action—burying a brother
Who was killed in battle, rather than leave him naked

553 flagrant (flā′grənt), *adj.* glaringly offensive; outrageous.

45 ■ Do you think that Creon's appraisal of Antigone as one who "twist[s] the law to one's own pleasure" is a fair one? Explain.

573 rout (rout), *n.* a complete defeat.

44 Multicultural Note
Burial Rites

Burial rites are important in all cultures—whether by water, underground, or by cremation. Both Egyptians and Vikings buried their dead with pets, servants, and valuables to equip them for the afterlife. You might encourage students to investigate burial customs of other cultures.

45 Reading/Thinking Skills
Evaluate

Response There is no evidence that her act of defiance is selfish or self-serving.

46 Reader's Response
Making Personal Connections

Questions Do you agree about the deadly peril of disobedience? Why or why not? *(Possible response: Students may refer to other sins or failings that they consider more destructive.)*

47 Reading/Thinking Skills
Predict Outcomes

Question How do you think Creon will react to Haemon's speech? *(Possible responses: Since he loves his son, maybe he'll listen. Since he's proud and stubborn, he'll probably reject him.)*

BUILDING ENGLISH PROFICIENCY

Exploring Parts of Speech

Use pages 206–207 to explore differences among parts of speech.

1. List the following sets of words on the board: *presumptuous* (line 513), *presumption* (line 514), *presume* (line 561); *obedient* (line 543), *obey* (line 562); *suffer* (line 526), *suffering* (line 527).
2. Have students identify, or lead them to identify, *presumptuous* and *obedient* as adjectives; *presumption* and *suffering* as nouns; and *presume, obey,* and *suffer* as verbs. Invite comments about what the various forms of the words have in common.
3. Offer the following words from pages 206–207. Ask students to change the word to the part of speech after the colon. (Students may use a dictionary for help.)
   - falsely: adjective (*false)*
   - think: noun (*thought)*
   - disobedience: verb (*disobey)*
   - victory: adjective (*victorious)*
   - clever: adverb (*cleverly)*

Art Study

Recall that when he enters (page 206), Haemon vows he will always obey and be ruled by his father's wise decisions—filial respect that is reflected in his position in this picture. When he exits, however, he leaves in "passionate haste," vowing never to see Creon again.

Visual Literacy Since there were few sets or props in ancient Greek theater, a set of stairs like this could be a valuable staging device.

Question How could you position Haemon and Creon to indicate their relationship?

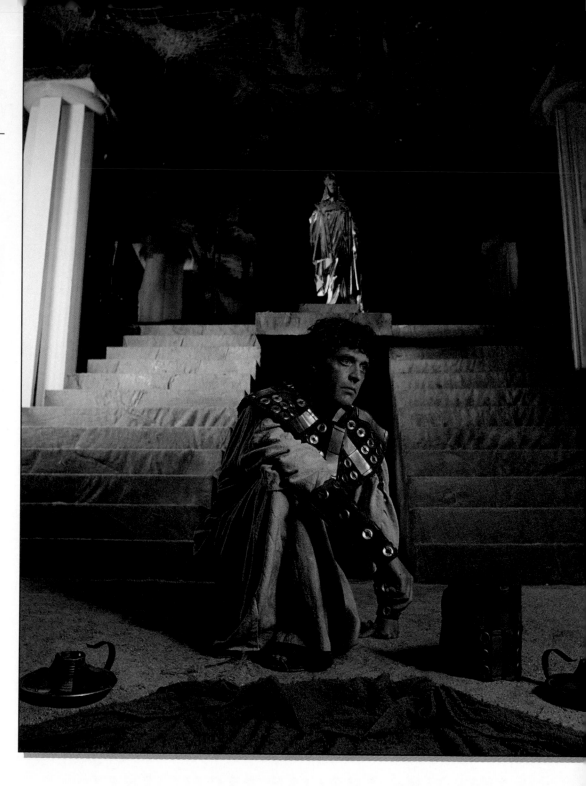

For dogs to maul and carrion birds to peck at.
Has she not rather earned a crown of gold?—
Such is the secret talk about the town.
Father, there is nothing I can prize above
Your happiness and well-being. What greater good
Can any son desire? Can any father
Desire more from his son? Therefore I say,
Let not your first thought be your only thought.
Think if there cannot be some other way.
Surely, to think your own the only wisdom,
And yours the only word, the only will,
Betrays a shallow spirit, an empty heart.
It is no weakness for the wisest man
To learn when he is wrong, know when to yield.
So, on the margin of a flooded river
Trees bending to the torrent live unbroken,
While those that strain against it are snapped off. **49**
A sailor has to tack and slacken sheets
Before the gale, or find himself capsized.
So, father, pause, and put aside your anger.
I think, for what my young opinion's worth,
That, good as it is to have infallible wisdom,
Since this is rarely found, the next best thing
Is to be willing to listen to wise advice.

CHORUS. There is something to be said, my lord, for this point of view,
And for yours as well; there is much to be said on both sides.
CREON. Indeed! Am I to take lessons at my time of life
From a fellow of his age?
HAEMON. No lesson you need be ashamed of.
It isn't a question of age, but of right and wrong.
CREON. Would you call it right to admire an act of disobedience?
HAEMON. Not if the act were also dishonorable.
CREON. And was not this woman's action dishonorable?
HAEMON. The people of Thebes think not.
CREON. The people of Thebes!
Since when do I take my orders from the people of Thebes?
HAEMON. Isn't that rather a childish thing to say?
CREON. No, I am king, and responsible only to myself.
HAEMON. A one-man state? What sort of a state is that?
CREON. Why, does not every state belong to its ruler?
HAEMON. You'd be an excellent king—on a desert island.
CREON. Of course, if you're on the woman's side—
HAEMON. No, no—
Unless you're the woman. It's you I'm fighting for.

■ What questions do you still have about what's happening? Jot them down in your notebook.

617 infallible (in fal′ə bəl), *adj.* free from error.

48 Reading/Thinking Skills
Compare and Contrast

Questions

Compare these lines to lines 143–145.

- Do you consider Creon a wise man? *(Most students won't think he's wise.)*
- Has Creon followed his own advice? Explain. *(Possible response: No, he has refused advice every time it has been offered to him through fear of damaging his authority.)*
- What lines appearing later on this page confirm Creon's unwillingness to reconsider his decision? *(lines 622–623, 629–630, 632, and 634)*

49 Reading/Thinking Skills
Question

Response Students should identify their own points of confusion. *(Possible responses: If Antigone backs off, would Creon forgive her? Could anything happen to change his mind?)*

50 Reading/Thinking Skills
Compare and Contrast

Question How is Haemon's idea of kingship different from Creon's? *(Possible responses: Creon thinks of a king as a tyrant—his will is law. Haemon thinks of a ruler as being responsible to those he rules.)*

BUILDING ENGLISH PROFICIENCY

Analyzing Arguments

To clarify the argument between Creon and Haemon, guide students in an informal debate.

1. Help students identify the arguments with questions such as the following:

- What does Creon say should be a son's first duty to his father? Why?
- How does Creon describe Antigone?
- What duty does Haemon say he has toward his father?
- What support does Haemon give for questioning Creon's decision about Antigone?

2. Conduct a brief debate about duties of parents and children, encouraging each student to share and defend his or her opinion.

3. Students may want to jot down thoughts during the debate to use in answering some of the After Reading questions (page 211).

51 Literary Element
Plot

Explain to students that there is a point in a play at which the conclusion becomes fixed. After students have finished the play, have them consider whether the turning point comes at lines 657–659, at lines 891–901, or elsewhere.

52 Literary Element
Characterization

Response Students may indicate that in other circumstances, Antigone is someone who could enjoy life fully; she does not worship death, but accepts it as her fate.

Check Test

1. Who is Antigone's sister? *(Ismene)*
2. What does Antigone do that angers Creon? *(buries her brother Polynices)*
3. Who supplies commentary on characters and events? *(the chorus)*
4. How did Polynices die? *(He was attacking Thebes when he and Eteocles killed each other.)*
5. What does Haemon want Creon to do? *(change his sentence of death for Antigone)*

Unit 2 Resource Book
Alternate Check Test, p. 5

CREON. What, villain, when every word you speak is against me?
HAEMON. Only because I know you are wrong, wrong.
CREON. Wrong? To respect my own authority?
HAEMON. What sort of respect tramples on all that is holy?
CREON. Despicable coward! No more will than a woman!
HAEMON. I have nothing to be ashamed of.
CREON. Yet you plead her cause.
HAEMON. No, *yours,* and mine, and that of the gods of the dead.
CREON. You'll never marry her this side of death.
HAEMON. Then, if she dies, she does not die alone.
CREON. Is that a threat, you impudent—
HAEMON. Is it a threat
To try to argue against wrong-headedness?
CREON. You'll learn what wrong-headedness is, my friend, to your cost.
HAEMON. O father, I could call you mad, were you not my father.
CREON. Don't toady me, boy; keep that for your lady-love.
HAEMON. You mean to have the last word, then?
CREON. I do.
And what is more, by all the gods in heaven,
I'll make you sorry for your impudence.
(Calling to those within.)
Bring out that she-devil, and let her die
Now, with her bridegroom by to see it done!
HAEMON. That sight I'll never see. Nor from this hour
51 Shall you see me again. Let those that will
Be witness of your wickedness and folly. *(Exit.)*

CHORUS. He is gone, my lord, in very passionate haste.
And who shall say what a young man's wrath may do?
CREON. Let him go! Let him do! Let him rage as never man raged,
He shall not save those women from their doom.
CHORUS. You mean, then, sire, to put them both to death?
CREON. No, not the one whose hand was innocent.
CHORUS. And to what death do you condemn the other?
CREON. I'll have her taken to a desert place
Where no man ever walked, and there walled up
Inside a cave, alive, with food enough
To acquit ourselves of the blood-guiltiness
That else would lie upon our commonwealth.
There she may pray to Death, the god she loves, 52
And ask release from death; or learn at last
What hope there is for those who worship death. *(Exit.)*

This marble relief from the first or second century A.D., is a theater mask that added height to the actor's stature.

667–674 I'll have her taken . . . worship death. If Antigone is provided with enough food to enable her to pray for her life, then whether or not she dies is up to the gods, and Creon and the state are thus blameless.

■ Do you think that Antigone is one of "those who worship death"? Explain.

MINI-LESSON: MECHANICS
Commas

Teach Read line 672 on page 210:

"There she may pray to Death, the god she loves,"

Point out the commas around the final clause. Explain that the clause renames the noun *Death* and is called an appositive. Remind students that an explanation defining a noun is set off by commas. You might provide other examples (Creon, the son of Menoeceus; Haemon, your youngest son)

Activity Ideas

- Have students write five sentences about *Antigone* or the theme, "On Trial," using appositives.
- Have students look in their Writer's Notebook for pieces in which the use of appositives would provide variety and clarity in their work, and make changes as needed.

Part 1

After Reading

Making Connections

Shaping Your Response

1. If you could put a piece of advice or encouragement into a fortune cookie for Antigone, what would you say?
2. If Antigone were alive today, what career do you think she would choose? Why?
3. For whom do you have the most sympathy: Antigone, Ismene, Creon, or Haemon? Explain your reasons.

Analyzing the Play

4. What noble qualities does Antigone reveal? Does she reveal any faults?
5. How would you describe Ismene's **character**?
6. Why do you think Antigone rejects Ismene's offer to help bury Polynices?
7. What opposing ideals do Haemon and Creon reveal through their **interactions**?
8. Do you find the **mood** of the scenes featuring the Sentry humorous? Why or why not?
9. Do you think that Creon exhibits both positive and negative traits? Explain.

Extending the Ideas

10. Why would Antigone's decision to bury Polynices isolate her from both her sister and her city?
11. What modern instances of people who break laws for reasons of personal conscience can you think of? Explain which, if any, of these you think are justified.

Vocabulary Study

On a piece of paper, number from 1-5. Write the word that best completes each sentence. You will not use all the words.

blasphemy
edict
flagrant
flout
impunity
onslaught
rout

1. Antigone is foolish to think she can bury Polynices with ____.
2. Ismene is grieved to think that Antigone would ____ her good advice.
3. The guards catch Antigone in her ____ act of disobedience.
4. After the Argive army flees, Creon claims that the battle ended in a ____.
5. Creon is too proud to tolerate a(n) ____ of curses from Antigone.

LITERARY FOCUS: PROTAGONIST/ANTAGONIST

Remind students that a *protagonist* is the main character in a literary work who is at the center of the action, often in conflict with an external antagonist or with internal forces.

- Ask for a show of hands of students who consider Antigone the protagonist and another show of hands of students who say it's Creon. Then have two groups of representatives present a case for their choice.
- Ask students to offer examples of protagonists on TV and in movies. Can they make any generalizations about media heroes?

After Reading

MAKING CONNECTIONS

1. Possible responses: You will find love beyond the grave; better to die with integrity than live without it.

2. Possible responses: public defender, civil rights advocate, lobbyist.

3. Answers will vary. Students should support their answers with clear reasoning and textual evidence.

4. Answers will vary. Students may identify integrity, responsibility, courage, loyalty, determination. Many students will not find fault with her, but some may cite her stubbornness.

5. Possible responses: gentle, yielding, meek, loving, hesitant, cautious, fearful

6. Possible responses: perhaps to protect her; perhaps to shame her.

7. Possible response: Creon values authority, obedience, and decisiveness; Haemon values public opinion, right-mindedness, and Antigone.

8. Possible response: Yes, he is nervous, repetitive, and has the courage to talk back to Creon.

9. Possible response: Creon is earnest and seeks justice but is stubborn and exercises poor judgment.

10. She severs family bonds and political allegiances.

11. Students may mention people such as Rosa Parks, Gandhi, Thoreau, right-to-life demonstrators, and so forth.

VOCABULARY STUDY

1. impunity
2. flout
3. flagrant
4. rout
5. onslaught

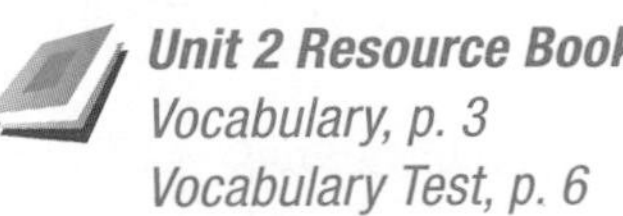
Unit 2 Resource Book
Vocabulary, p. 3
Vocabulary Test, p. 6

Selection Test

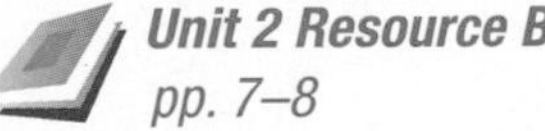
Unit 2 Resource Book
pp. 7–8

During Reading

Theme Link

During the second half of *Antigone,* it is not only the title character who is on trial. Being tested and evaluated are Creon's ideas about authority and Haemon's allegiances both to Antigone and to Creon. Passing judgment on everyone are the gods—the ultimate jury in Greek tragedy.

Vocabulary Preview

blight, disease, or anything that causes destruction or ruin

defilement, destruction of the purity or cleanness of (anything sacred)

expiation, atonement

hapless, unlucky; unfortunate

inexorable, unyielding

insatiable, that cannot be satisfied; greedy

perversity, quality of being contrary and willful

sacrilege, an intentional injury or disrespectful treatment of anything sacred

sovereignty, supreme power

unscathed, not harmed

Students can add the words and definitions to their Writer's Notebooks.

1 Literary Element
Personification

Note that Love is personified as a warrior who attacks victims, disrupts their lives, and drives them mad.

2 Literary Element
Tone

Question How has the chorus's tone changed? *(They seem more openly sympathetic toward Antigone.)*

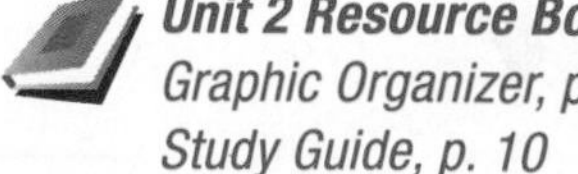

Unit 2 Resource Book
Graphic Organizer, p. 9
Study Guide, p. 10

CHORUS. Where is the equal of Love?
Where is the battle he cannot win,
The power he cannot outmatch?
In the farthest corners of earth, in the midst of the sea,
He is there; he is here
In the bloom of a fair face
Lying in wait;
And the grip of his madness
Spares not god or man,
Marring the righteous man,
Driving his soul into mazes of sin
And strife, dividing a house.
For the light that burns in the eyes of a bride of desire
Is a fire that consumes.
At the side of the great gods
Aphrodite immortal
Works her will upon all.

(The doors are opened and ANTIGONE *enters, guarded.)*
But here is a sight beyond all bearing,
At which my eyes cannot but weep;
Antigone forth faring
To her bridal bower of endless sleep.
ANTIGONE. You see me, countrymen, on my last journey,
Taking my last leave of the light of day;
Going to my rest, where death shall take me
Alive across the silent river.
No wedding day; no marriage music;
Death will be all my bridal dower.
CHORUS. But glory and praise go with you, lady,
To your resting place. You go with your beauty
Unmarred by the hand of consuming sickness,
Untouched by the sword, living and free,
As none other that ever died before you.
ANTIGONE. The daughter of Tantalus, a Phrygian maid,
Was doomed to a piteous death on the rock
Of Sipylus, which embraced and imprisoned her,
Merciless as the ivy; rain and snow
Beat down upon her, mingled with her tears,
As she wasted and died. Such was her story,
And such is the sleep that I shall go to.
CHORUS. She was a goddess of immortal birth,
And we are mortals; the greater the glory,
To share the fate of a god-born maiden,
A living death, but a name undying.

690 Aphrodite (af′rə dī′tē), goddess of love and beauty.

694 faring (fer′ing), ARCHAIC. traveling.

699 silent river, in Greek mythology, one of the rivers that separated the land of the dead from the land of the living.

701 dower (dour), *n.* dowry.

707 the daughter of Tantalus, Niobe (nī′ō bē′), whose children were slain by the gods to punish her for her excessive pride. Overcome with grief, she turned into a stone from which tears continued to flow. The stone was carried by a whirlwind to Mount Sipylus (sip′i ləs) in Phrygia (frij′ē ə), the kingdom of Niobe's father.

SELECTION SUMMARY

Antigone, Part 2

Creon sentences Antigone, as the chorus views her with compassion. The blind prophet Teiresias warns Creon that the gods are displeased and urges him to bury Polynices, but to no avail. Later, however, the king reconsiders and hurries to avert the fate that has been foretold. After performing burial rites for Polynices, he hurries to the cave where Antigone is imprisoned, but finds she has hanged herself. Haemon, who witnesses Antigone's fate, turns on his father and kills himself in grief. On hearing of the misfortunes that have befallen her family, Creon's wife Eurydice commits suicide. Creon goes into self-imposed exile. The chorus speaks of respect for the gods and the conquering of pride in old age.

For summaries in other languages, see the ***Building English Proficiency*** *book.*

Art Study

Visual Literacy Stage designers sometimes use light to set mood.

Questions What is the effect of the light shining on Antigone's face? How might the ancient Greeks have achieved lighting effects? *(Possible responses: She is exposed, intense, and open to death. They may have staged plays at certain times to use natural light to enhance effects.)*

3 Reader's Response
Making Personal Connections

Question Antigone has defied political authority and is suffering the consequences. What contemporary examples can you cite in which individuals defy legal laws which they feel are morally wrong and receive major punishments? *(Possible responses: Answers will vary, but make sure students' examples of civil transgressions are due to a moral commitment rather than mere personal, self-serving goals.)*

BUILDING ENGLISH PROFICIENCY

Summarizing Plot Events

Before students continue reading, have them briefly summarize the plot thus far.

1. Model summarizing, using lines 1–87, as shown. Make clear that only three or four sentences listing the high points are necessary.

- Creon, ruler of Thebes, forbids burial of his nephew Polynices.
- Antigone, sister of Polynices, wants to bury him.
- Antigone is unsuccessful in enlisting the help of her sister Ismene, who is afraid to disobey.
- Antigone vows to bury him herself.

2. Have small groups of students summarize these sections: lines 88–182; lines 183–278; lines 279–444; and lines 445–674. Remind students to recall only the main events.

3. Invite students to share their summaries. You may wish to go back and list characters' feelings where appropriate.

Activity Idea Challenge students to summarize a selection they have read in this book, using no more than three sentences.

4 Literary Element
Tone

Questions These lines echo lines *178–179.*

- What themes are reinforced? *(authority and obedience)*
- Would you agree that Antigone is a victim of her own self-will? *(perhaps so, but her will is based on a legitimate request for a brother's burial)*

5 Reader's Response
Challenging the Text

Question Since she believes that leaving Polynices unburied is a sacrilege, does Antigone have other options? *(Possible responses: She could have gone to Creon first and given her reasons. No, she had no other options—she didn't want his remains attacked by animals.)*

6 Reading/Thinking Skills
Clarify

Possible Response They mention authority and disobedience, and show sympathy to Antigone.

7 Multicultural Note
Afterlife

Antigone believes she will be united with her family in the afterlife—a view of death common to many cultures.

ANTIGONE. Mockery, mockery! By the gods of our fathers,
Must you make me a laughingstock while I yet live?
O lordly sons of my city! O Thebes!
Your valleys of rivers, your chariots and horses!
No friend to weep at my banishment
To a rock-hewn chamber of endless durance,
In a strange cold tomb alone to linger
Lost between life and death for ever.

CHORUS. My child, you have gone your way
To the outermost limit of daring
And have stumbled against Law enthroned.
This is the expiation.
You must make for the sin of your father.

ANTIGONE. My father—the thought that sears my soul—
The unending burden of the house of Labdacus.
Monstrous marriage of mother and son . . .
My father . . . my parents . . . O hideous shame!
Whom now I follow, unwed, curse-ridden,
Doomed to this death by the ill-starred marriage
That marred my brother's life.

CHORUS. An act of homage is good in itself, my daughter;
But authority cannot afford to connive at disobedience.
You are the victim of your own self-will.

ANTIGONE. And must go the way that lies before me.
No funeral hymn; no marriage music;
No sun from this day forth, no light,
No friend to weep at my departing. (*Enter* CREON.)

CREON. Weeping and wailing at the door of death!
There'd be no end of it, if it had force
To buy death off. Away with her at once.
And close her up in her rock-vaulted tomb.
Leave her and let her die, if die she must,
Or live within her dungeon. Though on earth
Her life is ended from this day, her blood
Will not be on our hands.

ANTIGONE. So to my grave,
My bridal bower, my everlasting prison,
I go, to join those many of my kinsmen
Who dwell in the mansions of Persephone,
Last and unhappiest, before my time.
Yet I believe my father will be there
To welcome me, my mother greet me gladly,
And you, my brother, gladly see me come.
Each one of you my hands have laid to rest,
Pouring the due libations on your graves.

718 mockery. Antigone mistakenly thinks that the Chorus, in comparing her to the gods, is making fun of her.

729 expiation (ek′spē ā′shən), *n.* atonement.

■ Describe the role of the Chorus in this scene.

755 Persephone (pėr sef′ə nē), daughter of Zeus and Demeter (di mē′tər); made queen of the lower world (Hades).

761 libation (lī bā′shən), *n.* the wine, water, etc. offered to a god.

MINI-LESSON: USAGE
Parallel Construction

Teach Read the first five lines on page 212:

Where is the equal of Love?
Where is the battle he cannot win,
The power he cannot outmatch?
In the farthest corners of earth, in the midst of the sea,
He is there; he is here. . . .

Recall for students that parallel construction means repeated use of a syntactical structure. Help them see how repeated words and phrases add dramatic impact to these lines.

Activity Idea Have students work in small groups to analyze the parallel construction in another passage from the play. Alternatively, they might examine "The Stone," page 572, to find elements of parallel structure and repetition.

It was by this service to your dear body, Polynices,
I earned the punishment which now I suffer,
Though all good people know it was for your honor.
O but I would not have done the forbidden thing
For any husband or for any son.
For why? I could have had another husband
And by him other sons, if one were lost;
But, father and mother lost, where would I get
Another brother? For thus preferring you,
My brother, Creon condemns me and hales me away,
Never a bride, never a mother, unfriended,
Condemned alive to solitary death.
What law of heaven have I transgressed? What god
Can save me now? What help or hope have I,
In whom devotion is deemed sacrilege?
If this is God's will, I shall learn my lesson
In death; but if my enemies are wrong,
I wish them no worse punishment than mine.

CHORUS. Still the same tempest in the heart
Torments her soul with angry gusts.

CREON. The more cause then have they that guard her
To hasten their work; or they too suffer.

CHORUS. Alas, that word had the sound of death.

CREON. Indeed there is no more to hope for.

ANTIGONE. Gods of our fathers, my city, my home,
Rulers of Thebes! Time stays no longer.
Last daughter of your royal house
Go I, *his* prisoner, because I honored
Those things to which honor truly belongs.

(ANTIGONE *is led away.*)

CHORUS. So, long ago, lay Danae
Entombed within her brazen bower;
Noble and beautiful was she,
On whom there fell the golden shower
Of life from Zeus. There is no tower
So high, no armory so great,
No ship so swift, as is the power
Of man's inexorable fate.

There was the proud Edonian king,
Lycurgus, in rock-prison pent
For arrogantly challenging
God's laws: it was his punishment
Of that swift passion to repent

8 ■ Explain Antigone's argument for defending her brother over a husband or a son.

776 sacrilege (sak′rə lij), *n.* an intentional injury or disrespectful treatment of anyone or anything sacred.

791 Danae (dan′ā ē), a maiden imprisoned in a bronze (brazen) chamber by her father, who feared a prophecy that a child born to Danae would someday kill him. Zeus entered her bronze chamber as a golden rain, and from their union Perseus, who eventually did kill his grandfather, was born.

791–814 So, long ago . . . as upon thee, my child. In these lines, the Chorus compares Antigone's fate to that of three other mortals who had been imprisoned.

798 inexorable (in ek′sər ə bəl), *adj.* relentless, unyielding.

800 Lycurgus (lī kėr′gəs), a Greek king who opposed the worship of Dionysus (dī′ə nī′səs) and was punished by being imprisoned in a cave and driven insane.

8 Reading/Thinking Skills
Clarify

Response Since her mother and father are dead, she will never have another brother. But if she lost one husband, she could marry another, or if she lost a child, bear another.

9 Literary Element
Characterization

Question What does this speech reveal about Antigone? *(Possible response: She is willing to be judged—but only by the God she serves. If God convicts her of impiety, she will accept the judgment.)*

10 Reading/Thinking Skills
Draw Conclusions

Question Why does Antigone call herself "last daughter of your royal house" when her sister Ismene is still living? *(Possible response: Since Ismene refuses to help bury Polynices, she is not worthy of her "high blood" and therefore not truly a member of the royal house.)*

BUILDING ENGLISH PROFICIENCY

ESL LEP ELD SAE LD

Analyzing Key Concepts

The departure of Antigone provides the chance for more discussion about curses and fate.

1. Have students review and share their notes written at the play's beginning. (See page T191.)

2. You may wish to point out that defying the gods and/or Fate is a frequent theme in Greek literature.

3. Ask how the chorus feels about Antigone's claim of a curse. (Some students may recall the idea of a curse from "The Monkey's Paw," page 66.)

4. Encourage students to share their opinions of Antigone's view, supporting their claims with information from the play.

11 Reading/Thinking Skills
Infer

Question Why does Creon call Teiresias "father"? *(It is a sign of respect and probably a mark of his obedience to Teiresias, since obedience seems to be to Creon the fundamental element of the father-son relationship.)*

12 Literary Element
Metaphor

Question What does Teiresias mean by this metaphor? *(Creon is very close to disaster—one misstep will take him over the edge.)*

In slow perception, for that he
Had braved the rule omnipotent
Of Dionysus' sovereignty.

On Phineus' wife the hand of fate
Was heavy, when her children fell
Victims to a stepmother's hate,
And she endured a prison-cell
Where the North Wind stood sentinel
In caverns amid mountains wild.
Thus the grey spinners wove their spell
On her, as upon thee, my child.

(Enter TEIRESIAS, *the blind prophet, led by a boy.)*

TEIRESIAS. Gentlemen of Thebes, we greet you, my companion and I,
Who share one pair of eyes on our journeys together—
For the blind man goes where his leader tells him to.
11 **CREON.** You are welcome, father Teiresias. What's your news?
TEIRESIAS. Ay, news you shall have; and advice, if you can heed it.
CREON. There was never a time when I failed to heed it, father.
TEIRESIAS. And thereby have so far steered a steady course.
CREON. And gladly acknowledge the debt we owe to you.
12 **TEIRESIAS.** Then mark me now; for you stand on a razor's edge.
CREON. Indeed? Grave words from your lips, good priest. Say on.
TEIRESIAS. I will; and show you all that my skill reveals.
At my seat of divination, where I sit
These many years to read the signs of heaven,
An unfamiliar sound came to my ears
Of birds in vicious combat, savage cries
In strange outlandish language, and the whirr
Of flapping wings; from which I well could picture
The gruesome warfare of their deadly talons.
Full of foreboding then I made the test
Of sacrifice upon the altar fire.
There was no answering flame; only rank juice
Oozed from the flesh and dripped among the ashes,
Smoldering and sputtering; the gall vanished in a puff,
And the fat ran down and left the haunches bare.
Thus (through the eyes of my young acolyte,
Who sees for me, that I may see for others)
I read the signs of failure in my quest.
And why? The blight upon us is *your* doing.
The blood that stains our altars and our shrines,
The blood that dogs and vultures have licked up,
It is none other than the blood of Oedipus

806 sovereignty (sov′rən-tē), *n.* supreme power or authority.
807 Phineus' wife. King Phineus (fin′ē əs) imprisoned his former wife and their two sons when he believed false accusations about them made by their stepmother, Idaea (i dē′ə).
813 grey spinners, the three Fates who control the length and nature of human lives.

826 seat of divination, the place where Teiresias sat to listen to the birds, which were believed to foretell (divine) the future.

842 blight (blīt), *n.* disease, or anything that causes destruction or ruin.

Spilled from the veins of his ill-fated son.
Our fires, our sacrifices, and our prayers
The gods abominate. How should the birds
Give any other than ill-omened voices,
Gorged with the dregs of blood that man has shed?
Mark this, my son: all men fall into sin.
But sinning, he is not forever lost
Hapless and helpless, who can make amends
And has not set his face against repentance.
Only a fool is governed by self-will.
 Pay to the dead his due. Wound not the fallen.
It is no glory to kill and kill again.
My words are for your good, as is my will,
And should be acceptable, being for your good.
CREON. You take me for your target, reverend sir,
Like all the rest. I know your art of old,
And how you make me your commodity
To trade and traffic in for your advancement.
Trade as you will; but all the silver of Sardis
And all the gold of India will not buy
A tomb for yonder traitor. No. Let the eagles
Carry his carcass up to the throne of Zeus;
Even that would not be sacrilege enough
To frighten me from my determination
Not to allow this burial. No man's act

853 hapless (hap′lis), *adj.* unlucky; unfortunate.

14 ■ How do you think Creon will respond to Teiresias's plea to forgive Antigone?

864 Sardis (sar′dis), capital of ancient Lydia (present-day Turkey), famous for its wealth and luxury.

Visual Literacy Stage directors use light and shadow to convey meaning.

Question How is shadow used in a meaningful way in this scene with Teiresias? (*Possible responses: Teiresias' eyes are hidden by shadow and this represents his blindness. Shadow also suggests the mystery that surrounds this clairvoyant character.)*

13 Reading/Thinking Skills
Synthesize

Question What is Teiresias' main point? *(If you take my advice, then it's not too late to repent and undo the harm you have set in motion.)*

14 Reading/Thinking Skills
Predict

Response Some students may feel that since it comes from Teiresias, he will listen. Others may think that Creon is so caught up in himself that he can't listen to anyone.

15 Reading/Thinking Skills
Draw Conclusions

Question What motive does Creon ascribe to Teiresias? *(greed)*

BUILDING ENGLISH PROFICIENCY

Understanding Main Characters

The prophet Teiresias is a mysterious figure. Help students understand Teiresias by focusing on information provided in his self-introduction.

1. Have students reread Teiresias' narrative (lines 825–859).

2. Lead students to locate and explain lines that give important information.

3. Ask the following questions:

- What is his seat of divination? (*See sidenote 826.)*
- What happens when Teiresias makes sacrifice upon the altar fire? *(See lines 835–839.)*
- Why is his blindness ironic? *(He sees things that people with sight cannot see.)*
- What does he mean by "Pay to the dead his due"? *(bury Polynices)*

16 Historical Note
Teiresias

Teiresias was said to have lived for seven generations. Because he had experienced life both as a man and as a woman, Zeus called on him to settle a debate with Hera on whether men or women experience more pleasure. Teiresias sided with Zeus, saying women do, and Hera condemned him to blindness to punish him. To make up for the loss of his sight, Zeus gave Teiresias second sight, the gift of prophecy and knowledge of the future.

17 Multicultural Note
Fate and Responsibility

Make sure students understand that fate is not presented here as a force that controls people's destiny. Instead, fate is the consequences of people's actions, for which they must take responsibility. Lead them to understand how this second meaning of fate enriches characterization and the meaning of the play.

Has power enough to pollute the goodness of God.
But great and terrible is the fall, Teiresias,
Of mortal men who seek their own advantage
By uttering evil in the guise of good.
TEIRESIAS. Ah, is there any wisdom in the world?
CREON. Why, what is the meaning of that wide-flung taunt?
TEIRESIAS. What prize outweighs the priceless worth of prudence?
CREON. Ay, what indeed? What mischief matches the lack of it?
TEIRESIAS. And there you speak of your own symptom, sir.
CREON. I am loth to pick a quarrel with you, priest.
TEIRESIAS. You do so, calling my divination false.
CREON. I say all prophets seek their own advantage.
TEIRESIAS. All kings, say I, seek gain unrighteously.
CREON. Do you forget to whom you say it?
TEIRESIAS. No.
16 Our king and benefactor, by my guidance.
CREON. Clever you may be, but not therefore honest.
TEIRESIAS. Must I reveal my yet unspoken mind?
CREON. Reveal all; but expect no gain from it.
TEIRESIAS. Does that still seem to you my motive, then?
CREON. Nor is my will for sale, sir, in your market.
TEIRESIAS. Then hear this. Ere the chariot of the sun
Has rounded once or twice his wheeling way,
You shall have given a son of your own loins
To death, in payment for death—two debts to pay:
One for the life that you have sent to death,
The life you have abominably entombed;
17 One for the dead still lying above ground
Unburied, unhonoured, unblest by the gods below.
You cannot alter this. The gods themselves
Cannot undo it. It follows of necessity
From what you have done. Even now the avenging Furies,
The hunters of Hell that follow and destroy,
Are lying in wait for you, and will have their prey,
When the evil you have worked for others falls on you.
Do I speak this for my gain? The time shall come,
And soon, when your house will be filled with the lamentation
Of men and of women; and every neighbouring city
Will be goaded to fury against you, for upon them
Too the pollution falls when the dogs and vultures
Bring the defilement of blood to their hearths and altars.
I have done. You pricked me, and these shafts of wrath
Will find their mark in your heart. You cannot escape
The sting of their sharpness. Lead me home, my boy.
Let us leave him to vent his anger on younger ears,

880 loth (lōth), *adj.* loath, unwilling.

905–910 The time shall come . . . and altars. This prophecy by Teiresias later comes true when the families of the slain Argive chiefs enlist the aid of the Athenian king, Theseus, to obtain burial rites for their dead. The Athenian army marches against Thebes and conquers it.

910 defilement (di fil′mənt), *n.* destruction of the purity or cleannesss of (anything sacred); desecration.

MINI-LESSON: LITERARY FOCUS
Protagonist/Antagonist

Teach Tell students that in this Greek drama, as in modern plays, the protagonist has a goal and encounters multiple conflicts that interfere with reaching this goal during the rising action.

Activity Idea Have students try analyzing the interaction between Teiresias and Creon in two different ways: Once as they consider Antigone to be the protagonist; once as they consider Creon to be the protagonist. What role does Teiresias have in each case?

Or school his mind and tongue to a milder mood
Than that which now possesses him. Lead on. *(Exit.)*

CHORUS. He has gone, my lord. He has prophesied terrible things.
And for my part, I that was young and now am old
Have never known his prophecies proved false.
CREON. It is true enough; and my heart is torn in two.
It is hard to give way, and hard to stand and abide
The coming of the curse. Both ways are hard.
CHORUS. If you would be advised, my good lord Creon——
CREON. What must I do? Tell me, and I will do it.
CHORUS. Release the woman from her rocky prison.
Set up a tomb for him that lies unburied.
CREON. Is it your wish that I consent to this?
CHORUS. It is, and quickly. The gods do not delay
The stroke of their swift vengeance on the sinner.
CREON. It is hard, but I must do it. Well I know
There is no armor against necessity.
CHORUS. Go. Let your own hand do it, and no other.
CREON. I will go this instant. Slaves there! One and all.
Bring spades and mattocks out on the hill!
My mind is made; 'twas I imprisoned her,
And I will set her free. Now I believe
It is by the laws of heaven that man must live. *(Exit.)*
CHORUS. O Thou whose name is many,
Son of the Thunderer, dear child of his Cadmean bride,
Whose hand is mighty
In Italia,
In the hospitable valley
Of Eleusis,
And in Thebes,
The mother-city of thy worshippers,
Where sweet Ismenus gently watereth
The soil whence sprang the harvest of the dragon's teeth,

Where torches on the crested mountains gleam,
And by the Castalia's stream
The nymph-train in thy dance rejoices,
When from the ivy-tangled glens
Of Nysa and from vine-clad plains
Thou comest to Thebes where the immortal voices
Sing thy glad strains.

Thebes, where thou lovest most to be,
With her, thy mother, the fire-stricken one,

19 ■ If you could ask Tieresias one question on behalf of Antigone, what would it be?

938 Thou whose name is many. The Chorus invokes the god Dionysus, whose native city of Thebes was under his special protection. Bacchus, Iacchus, and God of Wine are three of his many names.
946–947 Ismenus . . . dragon's teeth. The city that Cadmus and the giants founded is near the river Ismenus.
950–952 nymph-train . . . Nysa. When Semele (sem′ə lē), the mother of Dionysus, died, Zeus took his infant son to the nymphs of Nysa (nī′sə), who cared for him during his childhood.
956 thy mother, the fire-stricken one. Zeus had promised Semele that he would grant her one wish. Her wish was to see him in his full splendor as the king of gods and men. Being mortal, she could not endure the sight and was consumed to ashes.

18 Reading/Thinking Skills
Recognize Cause and Effect

Question What has happened? *(Creon, scared by Teiresias' threats, has changed his mind, and is taking advice.)*

19 Reading/Thinking Skills
Question

Possible responses Does Haemon love her? Will Haemon try to rescue her? Will Creon change her sentence?

20 Literary Criticism
Character Analysis

". . . Creon never does surrender his willfulness and his belief that events remain under his control. Even as he prepares to undo his wrong . . . his words express his strong sense of his own will and power. He urgently orders the others to heed his commands to rescue Antigone, emphasizing his own responsibility and control. . . . Creon thus persists in believing that control of action and its consequences lies in his hands."

Rebecca W. Bushnell
Prophesying Tragedy: Sign and Voice in Sophocles' Theban Plays

BUILDING ENGLISH PROFICIENCY

Understanding Motivation

As the play reaches its climax, help students explore Creon's feelings and change of mind.

Activity Ideas

- Have students describe movies, TV programs, or books they know that deal with a character who has an obsessive goal in life. What motivates this character?
- Ask students to scan international or national news stories for hostile political situations between countries and within governments that are the result of revenge.
- Have students review Creon's actions to figure out what he has done that now makes it "hard to give way" (line 921).
- Students may also find it useful to consider when cultural beliefs can influence people's feelings about revenge or forgiveness.

21 Literary Element
Allusions

Response She is abandoned, suffering, crazed.

22 Literary Focus
Protagonist/Antagonist

Question How are the fates of Antigone and Creon alike? *(Possible response: Antigone is alienated and separated from everyone she loves, doomed to a living death in a tomb. Creon, the Messenger says, will suffer a similar fate. He is confined to a living death because he will live without joy, having lost what is most precious to him.)*

23 Literary Element
Suspense

Point out how suspense is created through:

- the Messenger's speech predicting pain for Creon
- mention of a death without identifying the victim
- revelation that Haemon is dead
- repeated questions and interruptions
- misunderstanding about who wielded the weapon that killed him

Sickens for need of thee.
Healer of all her ills;
Come swiftly o'er the high Parnassian hills,
Come o'er the sighing sea.

The stars, whose breath is fire, delight
To dance for thee; the echoing night
Shall with thy praises ring.
Zeus-born, appear! With Thyiads revelling
Come, bountiful
Iacchus, King!

(Enter a MESSENGER, *from the side of the stage.)*

MESSENGER. Hear, men of Cadmus's city, hear and attend,
Men of the house of Amphion, people of Thebes!
What is the life of man? A thing not fixed
For good or evil, fashioned for praise or blame.
Chance raises a man to the heights, chance casts him down,
And none can foretell what will be from what is.
Creon was once an enviable man;
He saved his country from her enemies,
Assumed the sovereign power, and bore it well,
The honoured father of a royal house.
22 Now all is lost; for life without life's joys
Is living death; and such a life is his.
Riches and rank and show of majesty
And state, where no joy is, are empty, vain
And unsubstantial shadows, of no weight
To be compared with happiness of heart.

CHORUS. What is your news? Disaster in the royal house?

MESSENGER. Death; and the guilt of it on living heads.

CHORUS. Who dead? And by what hand?

23 **MESSENGER.** Haemon is dead,
Slain by his own——

CHORUS. His father?

MESSENGER. His own hand.
His father's act it was that drove him to it.

CHORUS. Then all has happened as the prophet said.

MESSENGER. What's next to do, your worships will decide.

(The Palace door opens.)

CHORUS. Here comes the Queen, Eurydice. Poor soul,
It may be she has heard about her son.

(Enter EURYDICE, *attended by women.)*

959 Parnassian hills. Parnassus (pär nas′əs), a mountain in southern Greece, was sacred to Apollo and the nine Muses.

964 Thyiads (thī′yadz), women driven mad by wine and the power of Dionysus. Also called Maenads (mē′nadz).

21 ■ What does Antigone have in common with these gods and goddesses mentioned by the Chorus in lines 938-966?

968 Amphion (am fī′ən), a former king of Thebes.

EURYDICE. My friends, I heard something of what you were saying
As I came to the door. I was on my way to prayer
At the temple of Pallas, and had barely turned the latch
When I caught your talk of some near calamity.
I was sick with fear and reeled in the arms of my women.
But tell me what is the matter; what have you heard?
I am not unacquainted with grief, and I can bear it.
MESSENGER. Madam, it was I that saw it, and will tell you all.
To try to make it any lighter now
Would be to prove myself a liar. Truth
Is always best.
It was thus. I attended your husband,
The King, to the edge of the field where lay the body
Of Polynices, in pitiable state, mauled by the dogs.
We prayed for him to the Goddess of the Roads, and to Pluto,
That they might have mercy upon him. We washed the remains
In holy water, and on a fire of fresh-cut branches
We burned all that was left of him, and raised
Over his ashes a mound of his native earth.
That done, we turned toward the deep rock-chamber
Of the maid that was married with death.
Before we reached it,
One that stood near the accursed place had heard
Loud cries of anguish, and came to tell King Creon.
As he approached, came strange uncertain sounds
Of lamentation, and he cried aloud:
"Unhappy wretch! Is my foreboding true?
Is this the most sorrowful journey that ever I went?
My son's voice greets me. Go, some of you, quickly
Through the passage where the stones are thrown apart,
Into the mouth of the cave, and see if it be
My son, my own son Haemon that I hear.
If not, I am the sport of gods."
We went
And looked, as bidden by our anxious master.
There in the furthest corner of the cave
We saw her hanging by the neck. The rope
Was of the woven linen of her dress.
And, with his arms about her, there stood he
Lamenting his lost bride, his luckless love,
His father's cruelty.
When Creon saw them,
Into the cave he went, moaning piteously.
"O my unhappy boy," he cried again,

24

998 I am not unacquainted with grief. Menoeceus, a son of Creon and Eurydice, had sacrificed himself at the beginning of the war because of a prophecy that Thebes would be saved only if he were killed.

1005 Goddess of the Roads, Hecate (hek′ə tē), a goddess of the underworld who sent apparitions to frighten travelers at night.

This terra cotta statuette of Melpomene (mel pom′ə-nē), the Muse of Tragedy, holding a tragic mask, dates from around 300 B.C.

24 Literary Element
Motif

You might engage students in a discussion of prophecies—a motif that recurs throughout the play.

Question Do prophecies about events and outcomes make characters seem less responsible for their actions? *(Help students see that although outcomes are known, they are nonetheless the result of judgments and actions on the part of characters—that is, they are known but not predetermined.)*

25 Reading/Thinking Skills
Compare and Contrast

Questions How is what Creon does different from what the chorus told him to do (lines 925–926)? Why is this important? *(Possible response: He does the tasks in the opposite order. Antigone [and Haemon] might not have died if Creon had gone to rescue her before burying Polynices.)*

26 Reading/Thinking Skills
Predict Outcomes

Question What do you think will happen? *(Students should take Haemon's statement to Creon in line 646 into account in their answer.)*

BUILDING ENGLISH PROFICIENCY

Keeping Track of Sequence

Help students develop a flow chart to record the succession of events at the play's close.

1. Begin with the events that the messenger relates.
2. Have them note only the main actions.

Polynices is buried.
↓
Antigone is found hanged.
↓
Haemon attacks Creon.
↓
Creon flees.
↓
Haemon kills himself.

27 Literary Element
Theme

When students have finished reading, you may wish to have them go back through the play and examine the lines that refer to madness to understand its role in the play. Have them keep in mind how madness or impairment of critical faculties would affect judgments required in a trial.

28 Reading/Thinking Skills
Summarize

Response The messenger relates the burial of Polynices, the mourning of Antigone who has hanged herself, Haemon's attempt on his father's life, and Haemon's suicide.

29 Literary Element
Characterization

A *foil* is a character whose words, traits, or actions contrast with and thus highlight those of another character.

Question How is the Messenger a foil to Creon? *(Possible response: He becomes more confident, decisive, and insightful as the play advances, while Creon appears to lose his confidence and effectiveness.)*

"What have you done? What madness brings you here
27 To your destruction? Come away, my son,
My son, I do beseech you, come away!"
His son looked at him with one angry stare,
Spat in his face, and then without a word
Drew sword and struck out. But his father fled
Unscathed. Whereon the poor demented boy
Leaned on his sword and thrust it deeply home
In his own side, and while his life ebbed out
Embraced the maid in loose-enfolding arms,
His spurting blood staining her pale cheeks red.
(EURYDICE *goes quickly back into the Palace.*)
Two bodies lie together, wedded in death,
Their bridal sleep a witness to the world
How great calamity can come to man
Through man's perversity.

CHORUS. But what is this?
The Queen has turned and gone without a word.

MESSENGER. Yes. It is strange. The best that I can hope
Is that she would not sorrow for her son
Before us all, but vents her grief in private
Among her women. She is too wise, I think,
To take a false step rashly.

29 **CHORUS.** It may be.
Yet there is danger in unnatural silence
No less than in excess of lamentation.

MESSENGER. I will go in and see, whether in truth
There is some fatal purpose in her grief.
Such silence, as you say, may well be dangerous.
(He goes in.)

(Enter ATTENDANTS *preceding the King.)*

CHORUS. The King comes here.
What the tongue scarce dares to tell
Must now be known
By the burden that proves too well
The guilt, no other man's
But his alone.

(*Enter* CREON *with the body of* HAEMON.)

CREON. The sin, the sin of the erring soul
Drives hard unto death.
Behold the slayer, the slain,
The father, the son.
O the curse of my stubborn will!

1038 unscathed (un skāᴛʜd′), *adj.* not harmed.

28 ■ What events does the Messenger recount in lines 999 to 1042?

1046 perversity (pər vėr′sə tē), *n.* quality of being contrary and willful.

MINI-LESSON: VOCABULARY

Expanding Vocabulary Using Structural Analysis

Teach Explain to students that in English we often avoid using multiple words with the same main root in the same sentence. Ancient Greek writers, however, frequently included a variety of forms based on the same root, and the translator of *Antigone* has preserved this style. Read line 1069—"Son, newly cut off in the newness of youth"—and point out the use of *newly* and *newness.* Explain that analyzing sentences like this is one way to expand word knowledge.

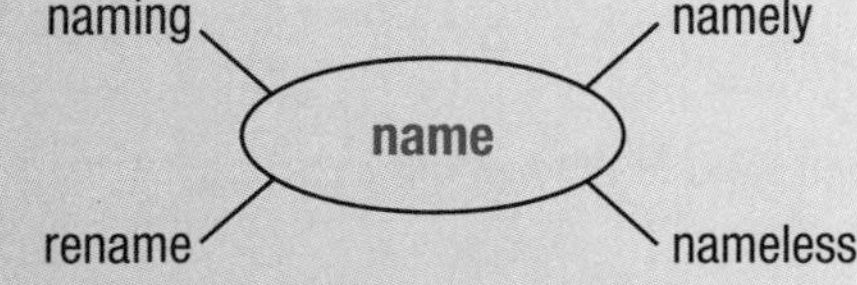

Activity Idea Have students make a word web like the one shown, indicating various words based on the same root. Invite them to use two of these words in a sentence.

Son, newly cut off in the newness of youth,
Dead for my fault, not yours.
CHORUS. Alas, too late you have seen the truth.
CREON. I learn in sorrow. Upon my head
God has delivered this heavy punishment,
Has struck me down in the ways of wickedness,
And trod my gladness under foot.
Such is the bitter affliction of mortal man.

(Enter the MESSENGER *from the Palace.)*
MESSENGER. Sir, you have this and more than this to bear.
Within there's more to know, more to your pain.
CREON. What more? What pain can overtop this pain?
MESSENGER. She is dead—your wife, the mother of him that is dead—
The death wound fresh in her heart. Alas, poor lady!
CREON. Insatiable Death, wilt thou destroy me yet?
What say you, teller of evil?
I am already dead,
And is there more?
Blood upon blood?
More death? My wife?
(The central doors open, revealing the body of EURYDICE.*)*
CHORUS. Look then, and see; nothing is hidden now.
CREON. O second horror!
What fate awaits me now?
My child here in my arms . . . and there, the other . . .
The son . . . the mother . . .

MESSENGER. There at the altar with the whetted knife
She stood, and as the darkness dimmed her eyes
Called on the dead, her elder son and this,
And with her dying breath cursed you, their slayer.
CREON. O horrible . . .
Is there no sword for me
To end this misery?
MESSENGER. Indeed you bear the burden of two deaths.
It was her dying word.
CREON. And her last act?
MESSENGER. Hearing her son was dead, with her own hand
She drove the sharp sword home into her heart.
CREON. There is no man can bear this guilt but I.
It is true, I killed him.
Lead me away, away. I live no longer.
CHORUS. 'Twere best, if anything is best in evil times.
What's soonest done, is best, when all is ill.

30 ■ Do you think that Creon has gained wisdom through this tragedy? Explain.

1082 insatiable (in sā′shə bəl), *adj.* that cannot be satisfied; greedy.

30 Reading/Thinking Skills
Evaluate

Response Creon appears no wiser: he rejects every opportunity to change; even when he finally takes advice he has to do it his way, causing two deaths. He sees his fate as divine punishment rather than the result of bad judgment on his own part.

31 Reader's Response
Making Personal Connections

Question Do you think Creon deserves to be blamed for the death of Haemon? Why? *(Possible responses: He is responsible because by causing Antigone's death, he drives Haemon to despair. Haemon made a choice to commit suicide—no one forced him to do it.)*

BUILDING ENGLISH PROFICIENCY

Exploring Abstract Nouns

As the play draws to its close, speeches are filled with abstract nouns. Help students deepen their understanding of such words.

1. List these abstract nouns from page 222 on the board: *madness, calamity, grief,* and *truth.*

2. Explain that abstract nouns name ideas, feelings, and qualities that cannot be pictured easily. Apply this definition to the words on the board.

3. Have pairs or small groups of students discuss what each abstract noun means and how it applies to a main idea or event in the play.

4. Students can work with other abstract nouns from these pages in the same manner: *life, lamentation, guilt, sin, will, fault, sorrow, wickedness, gladness, evil, misery,* and *happiness.*

32 Reading/Thinking Skills
Generalize

Question What is the function of the chorus here? *(Possible response: The chorus delivers the moral, capsulizes the theme—"pride brought down," and provides closure.)*

Check Test

1. Which of Creon's family members die during this play? *(his son, Haemon; his niece, Antigone; his wife, Eurydice)*

2. With whom does Creon consult after Teiresias leaves? *(the chorus, who represents the elders of Thebes)*

3. How does Antigone die? *(She hangs herself.)*

4. What does Eurydice do as she dies? *(She curses Creon.)*

5. What does the chorus say at the end of the play is the cause of Creon's death? *(his pride)*

Unit 2 Resource Book
Alternate Check Test, p. 13

CREON. Come, my last hour and fairest,
My only happiness . . . come soon.
Let me not see another day.
Away . . . away . . .
CHORUS. The future is not to be known; our present care
Is with the present; the rest is in other hands.
CREON. I ask no more than I have asked.
CHORUS. Ask nothing.
What is to be, no mortal can escape.
CREON. I am nothing. I have no life.
Lead me away . . .
That have killed unwittingly
My son, my wife.
I know not where I should turn,
Where look for help.
My hands have done amiss, my head is bowed
With fate too heavy for me. *(Exit.)*

32
CHORUS. Of happiness the crown
And chiefest part
Is wisdom, and to hold
The gods in awe.
This is the law
That, seeing the stricken heart
Of pride brought down,
We learn when we are old. *(Exit.)*

After Reading

Making Connections

Shaping Your Response

1. If a person like Antigone were in your class, what description might appear beneath her picture in the yearbook?
2. If Antigone and Haemon had married, what kind of marriage do you think they would have had?
3. Use a Venn diagram like the one below to show how the characters of Antigone and Creon are both alike and different.

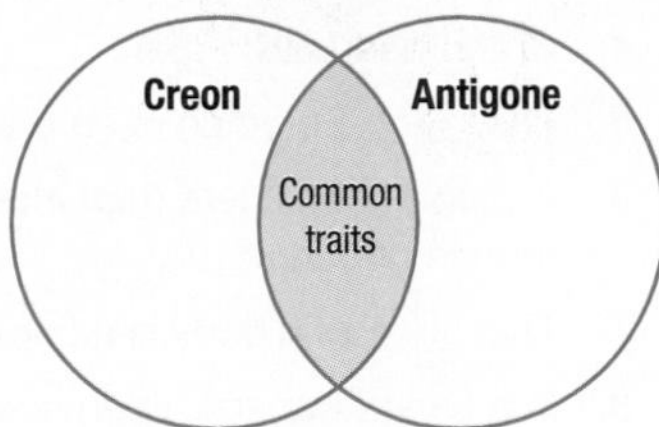

Analyzing the Play

4. In her final appearance, why do you think Antigone makes an **allusion** to the "daughter of Tantalus" (lines 707-713)?
5. How would you describe the **tone** of Creon's remarks during his scene with Antigone?
6. How does the Chorus **personify** Love in its opening ode on page 212?
7. In what way does his accusation of Teiresias serve to **characterize** Creon?
8. At the end of the play, the Chorus states a **theme** of "pride brought down." Explain to which character(s) you think this theme applies.
9. How is Creon's decision to stop and bury Polynices on the way to free Antigone an example of **irony**?
10. Why do you think Eurydice is introduced so late in the play?

Extending the Ideas

11. In *Antigone*, the Chorus is the voice of public opinion, while leaders in today's world rely on polls. Do you think that polls are reliable indicators of public opinion? Why or why not?

Literary Focus: Protagonist/Antagonist

In Greek tragedy, the **protagonist** is the character whose flaws or poor judgment brings about his or her downfall.

- According to this definition, who is the protagonist in this play?
- Do you think that Antigone could have avoided her fate? Why or why not?

After Reading

MAKING CONNECTIONS

1. Possible responses: Seeker of justice; Defier of gods; Strong family ties

2. Possible response: Haemon's gentleness and tact would have balanced Antigone's intensity and impulsiveness.

3. Answers will vary. Some shared qualities: stubbornness, single-mindedness, perseverance, righteousness

4. Both are doomed and imprisoned.

5. Possible responses: unrelenting, cruel, heartless

6. He is an omnipresent warrior who overcomes those he visits and drives them mad.

7. Creon seems paranoid because the charge is groundless.

8. Students will probably say this theme relates to Creon, especially in light of the final line: "We learn when we are old." Antigone's pride is not brought down—she loses no dignity in going to her death.

9. By exercising his judgment instead of following advice, he caused the deaths of Antigone, Haemon, and Eurydice.

10. Possible response: She provides a dramatic conclusion to the family tragedy. With her death, Creon is totally alone.

11. Answers will vary. Students should cite data that support their stands.

LITERARY FOCUS: PROTAGONIST/ANTAGONIST

Before students answer this question, you may wish to direct them to the Mini-Lesson on page 204. Have them look again at the questions.

- Volunteers at the board can list qualities of both Creon and Antigone that would qualify them as protagonists.
- Antigone's fate seems inevitable. Her determination to bury Polynices ennobles her.

VOCABULARY STUDY

1. insatiable
2. perversity
3. unscathed *(Point out, however, that though physically unscathed, Ismene suffers mental anguish.)*
4. expiation
5. hapless
6. sacrilege
7. defilement
8. inexorable
9. blight
10. sovereignty

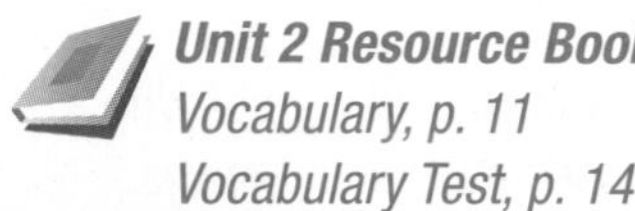

Unit 2 Resource Book
Vocabulary, p. 11
Vocabulary Test, p. 14

WRITING CHOICES

Writer's Notebook Update

Copy the hero chart from page 189 of the pupil book on the board and invite students to add traits from their notebooks. Prompt class discussion about which traits Antigone possesses. Students can use either the class chart or their own chart as the basis for explaining whether or not Antigone is heroic.

Imagine This!

In order to capture the drama and style of a delivered message, students might review the messenger's speech on pages 221–222. Have them note the use of vivid images, direct quotations, and swift narration that lend dramatic impact.

Interactions

Before students write, refer them to techniques for using persuasive devices on page 794. Remind them that whatever pairing they choose to illustrate conflict in the play, they should make a persuasive case for one item in the pair.

Selection Test

Unit 2 Resource Book
pp. 15–16

Vocabulary Study

Number a sheet of paper from 1–10. Using the words listed below, write the word that best completes each sentence.

blight
defilement
expiation
hapless
inexorable
insatiable
perversity
sacrilege
sovereignty
unscathed

1. The gods, with their ____ appetite for revenge, demand that those who disobey them be punished.
2. Creon condemns the ____ of his contrary, willful niece.
3. Although Antigone is punished, Ismene survives the events ____.
4. Creon needs to make ____ for his many sins.
5. The ____ Eurydice is an unfortunate victim of circumstances.
6. Antigone considers it an intentional injury, or ____, for Polynices to remain unburied.
7. The ____ of a body is a crime the Greeks found hateful.
8. In a Greek tragedy, relentless fate moves in a(n) ____ manner.
9. Teiresias accuses Creon of causing the ____ that is spreading.
10. Creon reigns supreme, with absolute ____ over his people.

Expressing Your Ideas

Writing Choices

Writer's Notebook Update Now that you have finished reading the play, examine your chart of heroic traits. Does Antigone have others that you could add to your chart? Explain whether or not you think Antigone is heroic.

Imagine This! Moments before Antigone hangs herself, the god Dionysus saves her. Report this event as a Greek dramatist would: in a **monologue** by a messenger. Be prepared to deliver your monologue in class.

Interactions Working with a partner, find instances in the play that illustrate one of these conflicts: youth vs. age; human law vs. divine law; personal conscience vs. social laws; loyalty to family vs. loyalty to country. Then collaborate on a **persuasive paper** that explores this theme in the play.

Other Options

Characterization in Color Explain whether or not you would use this picture as an **illustration** of Creon at the end of the play.

226 UNIT TWO: MAKING JUDGMENTS

OTHER OPTIONS

Characterization in Color

Have students begin by analyzing the picture and determining what characteristics about the king it portrays. Then they can compare and contrast this characterization with their analysis of Creon's character at the end of the play, and decide if there is a good match.

Before Reading

Twelve Angry Men

by Reginald Rose USA

Reginald Rose
born 1920

Reginald Rose got the idea for *Twelve Angry Men* while serving on the jury of a manslaughter case in New York. The experience left him struck by "the absolute finality of the decision" the jurors had to make. Rose wrote *Twelve Angry Men* in 1954 for television; later he wrote the scripts for both a film and a stage version. He was awarded three Emmys, one for *Twelve Angry Men* and two for the television series *The Defenders,* another work that deals with the American legal system. Rose has said, ". . . my main purpose has always been to project my own view of good and evil—and this is the essence of controversy."

Building Background

Ladies and Gentlemen of the Jury

> *"Murder in the first degree . . . is the most serious charge tried in our criminal courts. . . . One man is dead. The life of another is at stake. If there is a reasonable doubt in your minds as to the guilt of the accused . . . then you must declare him not guilty. If, however, there is no reasonable doubt, then he must be found guilty. Whichever way you decide, the verdict must be unanimous. I urge you to deliberate honestly and thoughtfully."*

If you were a juror listening to these instructions, would you understand your duties? In a small group discuss the meaning of the underlined words. Rewrite the judge's instructions using simpler language. Then present your version of the instructions to the class.

Literary Focus

Stage Directions The written instructions in the script of a play are called **stage directions**. These directions help the reader imagine how the characters look and move as they speak, how the setting looks, and what props appear. In *Twelve Angry Men,* notice the italic typeface used for stage directions and the information these directions convey.

Writer's Notebook

A Change of Heart At different stages, the jurors in *Twelve Angry Men* change their votes in order to reach a unanimous verdict. As you read the play, keep track of the number of jurors voting *guilty* and the number voting *not guilty* as well as the details that cause the jurors to change their votes during their deliberations.

Before Reading

Building Background

Explain that *Twelve Angry Men* is a TV script. Have the film version on hand to use as an introduction or a culminating activity. (RCA VideoDiscs. B/W, 95 minutes. 1957)

Literary Focus

Have students make a chart to record juror information as it is revealed by the **stage directions.**

Juror	Description
Foreman	
Juror Two	
Juror Three	

Writer's Notebook

Alert students to look for details of character interaction that appear to be minor but actually have a large impact on the jurors' final decisions.

More About Reginald Rose

Rose sold his first television script in 1951.

Other works include:

- *The Defender* series
- *Studs Lonigan* (television miniseries) 1979
- *Escape from Sobibor* (television miniseries) 1987

SUPPORT MATERIALS OVERVIEW

Unit 2 Resource Book
- Graphic Organizers, pp. 17, 25, 33
- Study Guides, pp. 18, 26, 34
- Vocabulary, pp. 19, 27, 35
- Grammar, pp. 20, 28, 36
- Alternate Check Tests, pp. 21, 29, 37
- Vocabulary Tests, pp. 22, 30, 38
- Selection Tests, pp. 23–24, 31–32, 39–40

Building English Proficiency
- Selection Summaries
- Activities, pp. 184–186

Reading, Writing & Grammar SkillBook
- Grammar, Usage, and Mechanics, pp. 202–203, 229–230, 243–244, 274–275
- Vocabulary Skills, pp. 9–10

The World of Work
- Judge, p. 7
- Witness Form Report, p. 8

Technology
- Personal Journal Software
- Custom Literature Database: For another selection about a trial, see "A Witch Trial at Mount Holly" by Benjamin Franklin on the database.
- Test Generator Software

During Reading

Selection Objectives

- to explore the theme of being on trial
- to learn about the importance of stage directions in a script of a play
- to learn about colloquialisms

Unit 2 Resource Book
Graphic Organizer, p. 17
Study Guide, p. 18

Theme Link

A man is "On Trial" for his life and a jury of twelve men must decide his guilt or innocence.

Vocabulary Preview

appalled, shocked; dismayed
bickering, petty, noisy quarreling
bigot, intolerant person
intolerant, unwilling to let others do or believe as they want
menace, threat
monopoly, the exclusive possession or control of something
naïve, simple in nature; like a child
rapport, agreement, connection
superficial, concerned with or understanding only what is on the surface; shallow
tempered, softened or moderated

Students can add the words and definitions to their Writer's Notebooks.

1 Reading/Thinking Skills

Predict Outcomes

Question Based on the title, what do you expect to happen in this selection? *(Possible response: a lengthy and heated argument among all the jurors)*

1

Twelve Angry Men

REGINALD ROSE

Twelve Angry Men was produced in 1957 by Henry Fonda and Reginald Rose and directed by Sidney Lumet. The cast includes the following: *Juror 1* (Martin Balsam), *Juror 2* (John Fielder), *Juror 3* (Lee J. Cobb), *Juror 4* (E. G. Marshall), *Juror 5* (Jack Klugman), *Juror 6* (Edward Binns), *Juror 7* (Jack Warden), *Juror 8* (Henry Fonda), *Juror 9* (Joseph Sweeney), *Juror 10* (Ed Begley), *Juror 11* (George Voskovec), *Juror 12* (Robert Webber).

SELECTION SUMMARY

Twelve Angry Men, Act 1

A jury composed of twelve white men has just finished listening to the judge's instructions in a case involving an accusation of first-degree murder. The accused is a nineteen-year-old boy, the member of an unidentified minority. The victim is the boy's father, who was stabbed with a switchknife. The jury takes an initial vote; all jurors except Eight vote *guilty*. As the evidence is reviewed, the personalities of the jurors are revealed. Eight displays a knife identical to the murder weapon, suggests that the boy may have told the truth about having lost his knife, and proposes another vote—this time by secret ballot: if the other jurors are still united in a guilty verdict, he will change his vote.

*For summaries in other languages, see the **Building English Proficiency** book.*

DESCRIPTIONS OF JURORS

FOREMAN (JUROR NUMBER ONE). A small, petty man who is impressed with the authority he has and handles himself quite formally. Not overly bright, but dogged.

JUROR NUMBER TWO A meek, hesitant man who finds it difficult to maintain any opinions of his own. Easily swayed and usually adopts the opinion of the last person to whom he has spoken.

JUROR NUMBER THREE A very strong, very forceful, extremely opinionated man within whom can be detected a streak of sadism. A humorless man who is intolerant[1] of opinions other than his own and accustomed to forcing his wishes and views upon others.

JUROR NUMBER FOUR Seems to be a man of wealth and position. A practiced speaker who presents himself well at all times. Seems to feel a little bit above the rest of the jurors. His only concern is with the facts in this case, and he is appalled[2] at the behavior of the others.

JUROR NUMBER FIVE A naïve,[3] very frightened young man who takes his obligations in this case very seriously, but who finds it difficult to speak up when his elders have the floor.

JUROR NUMBER SIX An honest but dull-witted man who comes upon his decisions slowly and carefully. A man who finds it difficult to create positive opinions, but who must listen to and digest and accept those opinions offered by others which appeal to him most.

JUROR NUMBER SEVEN A loud, flashy, glad-handed salesman type who has more important things to do than to sit on a jury. He is quick to show temper, quick to form opinions on things about which he knows nothing. Is a bully and, of course, a coward.

JUROR NUMBER EIGHT A quiet, thoughtful, gentle man. A man who sees all sides of every question and constantly seeks the truth. A man of strength tempered[4] with compassion. Above all, a man who wants justice to be done and will fight to see that it is.

JUROR NUMBER NINE A mild, gentle old man, long since defeated by life and now merely waiting to die. A man who recognizes himself for what he is and mourns the days when it would have been possible to be courageous without shielding himself behind his many years.

JUROR NUMBER TEN An angry, bitter man. A man who antagonizes almost at sight. A bigot[5] who places no values on any human life save his own. A man who has been nowhere and is going nowhere and knows it deep within him.

JUROR NUMBER ELEVEN A refugee from Europe who had come to this country in 1941. A man who speaks with an accent and who is ashamed, humble, almost subservient to the people around him, but who will honestly seek justice because he has suffered through so much injustice.

JUROR NUMBER TWELVE A slick, bright advertising man who thinks of human beings in terms of percentages, graphs, and polls and has no real understanding of people. A superficial[6] snob, but trying to be a good fellow. 3

ACT ONE

Fade in[7] on a jury box. Twelve men are seated in it, listening intently to the voice of the JUDGE *as he charges them.[8] We do not see the* JUDGE. *He speaks in slow, measured tones and his voice is grave. The camera*

1. **intolerant** (in tol′ər ənt), *adj.* unwilling to let others do or believe as they want.
2. **appalled** (ə pôld′), *adj.* shocked; dismayed.
3. **naïve** (nä ēv′), *adj.* simple in nature; like a child.
4. **tempered** (tem′pərd), *adj.* softened or moderated.
5. **bigot** (big′ət), *n.* intolerant person.
6. **superficial** (sü′pər fish′əl), *adj.* concerned with or understanding only what is on the surface; shallow.
7. **fade in,** term used in television to indicate that the picture or scene is slowly brought into focus. When the camera "fades out," the picture gradually disappears.
8. **he charges them,** he tells them what their duties are as jurors.

This, and the following photos, are stills from the movie *Twelve Angry Men,* which Rose expanded from a one-hour television special to a full-length film.

Visual Literacy Actors convey character through gesture, facial expression, posture, and lines.

Questions

- What conclusions can you draw about the jurors pictured? *(Possible response: They are dressed as if this is a matter for serious reflection; all are paying close attention.)*
- Why do you think the letters in the title are uneven? *(Possible response: They convey the emotions and mismatched personalities of the jurors.)*

2 Literary Focus
Stage Directions

Question Why do you think the jurors have numbers, not names? *(Possible response: They represent universal types.)*

3 Literary Focus
Stage Directions

Questions Based on these descriptions, which jurors do you think will be protagonist and antagonist? *(Possible responses: Eight seems a likely protagonist—thoughtful and just. One, Three, and Seven seem like strong personalities that may influence or antagonize others.)*

BUILDING ENGLISH PROFICIENCY

ESL LEP ELD SAE LD

Keeping Track of Characters

Help students focus on the personality of each juror.

1. Instruct students to fold three sheets of paper into fourths and head each section with a juror's number.
2. After reading the descriptions of jurors, have students jot down two or three qualities or attitudes about each juror to keep in mind as they continue.
3. Encourage students to add to their notes as they read on.

Juror One self-impressed humorless	**Juror Three** opinionated not very bright
Juror Two	**Juror Four**

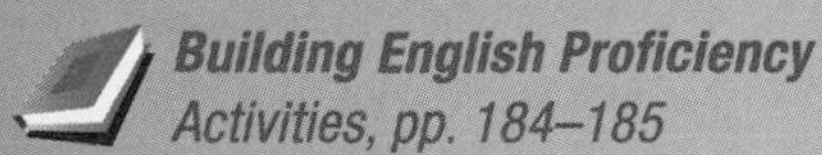
Building English Proficiency Activities, pp. 184–185

4 Reading/Thinking Skills
Summarize

Question Summarize the jury's goal. *(to reach a unanimous verdict)*

5 Literary Focus
Stage Directions

Explain that these stage directions describe the setting where the action takes place and establish the mood of uncertainty and tension.

The World of Work

Judge

For real-life experiences of a judge, use—

The World of Work *pp. 7–8*

6 Literary Element
Symbolism

Question What might the locking of the door symbolize? *(Possible responses: imprisonment. The jurors are confined until they reach a decision.)*

7 Reading/Thinking Skills
Infer

Question What is Three's attitude toward the trial? *(He is trivializing its importance.)*

---

drifts over the faces of the JURYMEN *as the* JUDGE *speaks and we see that most of their heads are turned to camera's left.* SEVEN *looks down at his hands.* THREE *looks off in another direction, the direction in which the defendant would be sitting.* TEN *keeps moving his head back and forth nervously. The* JUDGE *drones on.*

JUDGE. Murder in the first degree—premeditated homicide—is the most serious charge tried in our criminal courts. You've heard a long and complex case, gentlemen, and it is now your duty to sit down to try and separate the facts from the fancy. One man is dead. The life of another is at stake. If there is a reasonable doubt in your minds as to the guilt of the accused . . . then you must declare him not guilty. If, however, there is no reasonable doubt, then he must be found guilty. Whichever way you decide, the verdict must be unanimous. I urge you to deliberate honestly and thoughtfully. You are faced with a
4 grave responsibility. Thank you, gentlemen.

(There is a long pause.)

CLERK *(droning).* The jury will retire.

(And now, slowly, almost hesitantly, the members of the jury begin to rise. Awkwardly, they file out of the jury box and off camera to the left. Camera holds on jury box, then fades out.

Fade in on a large, bare unpleasant-looking room. This is the jury room in the county criminal court of a large Eastern city. It is about 4:00 P.M. The room is furnished with a long conference table and a dozen chairs. The walls are bare, drab, and badly in need of a fresh coat of paint. Along one wall is a row of windows which look
5 *out on the skyline of the city's financial district. High on another wall is an electric clock. A washroom opens off the jury room. In one corner of the room is a water fountain. On the table are pads, pencils, ashtrays. One of the windows is open. Papers blow across the table and onto the floor as the door opens. Lettered on the outside of the door are the words "Jury Room." A uniformed* GUARD *holds the door open. Slowly, almost self-consciously, the twelve* JURORS *file in. The* GUARD *counts them as they enter the door, his lips moving, but no sound coming forth. Four or five of the* JURORS *light cigarettes as they enter the room.* FIVE *lights his pipe, which he smokes constantly throughout the play.* TWO *and* TWELVE *go to the water fountain,* NINE *goes into the washroom, the door of which is lettered "Men." Several of the* JURORS *take seats at the table. Others stand awkwardly around the room. Several look out the windows. These are men who are ill at ease, who do not really know each other to talk to, and who wish they were anywhere but here.* SEVEN, *standing at window, takes out a pack of gum, takes a piece, and offers it around. There are no takers. He mops his brow.)*

SEVEN *(to* SIX*).* Y'know something? It's hot. (SIX *nods.)* You'd think they'd at least air-condition the place. I almost dropped dead in court.

(SEVEN *opens the window a bit wider. The* GUARD *looks them over and checks his count. Then, satisfied, he makes ready to leave.)*

GUARD. Okay, gentlemen. Everybody's here. If there's anything you want, I'm right outside. Just knock.

(He exits, closing the door. Silently they all look at the 6
door. We hear the lock clicking.)

FIVE. I never knew they locked the door.

TEN *(blowing nose).* Sure, they lock the door. What did you think?

FIVE. I don't know. It just never occurred to me.

(Some of the JURORS *are taking off their jackets. Others are sitting down at the table. They still are reluctant to talk to each other.* FOREMAN *is at head of table, tearing slips of paper for ballots. Now we get a close shot of* EIGHT. *He looks out the window. We hear* THREE *talking to* TWO.*)*

THREE. Six days. They should have finished it in 7
two. Talk, talk, talk. Did you ever hear so much talk about nothing?

TWO *(nervously laughing).* Well . . . I guess . . . they're entitled.

THREE. Everybody gets a fair trial. *(He shakes his head.)* That's the system. Well, I suppose you can't say anything against it.

(TWO *looks at him nervously, nods, and goes over to water cooler. Cut*[9] *to shot of* EIGHT *staring out win-*

9. **cut,** switch from one camera to another to show what is happening on another part of the stage.

MINI-LESSON: STUDY SKILLS
Dictionary/Glossary

Teach This play contains some specialized vocabulary that might be termed "legal jargon." Students wishing to know precise meanings should be aware that there are specialized dictionaries of law terms that they can use to find the exact meaning of words and phrases such as the following:

murder in the first degree
premeditated homicide
reasonable doubt
guilt
verdict

Activity Ideas

- Have students find an appropriate dictionary and look up the words listed to the left.
- Have students compare the definitions in the specialized sources with the information they find in standard dictionaries and report their findings to the class.

dow. Cut to table. SEVEN *stands at the table, putting out a cigarette.*)

SEVEN (*to* TEN). How did you like that business about the knife? Did you ever hear a phonier story?

TEN (*wisely*). Well, look, you gotta expect that. You know what you're dealing with.

SEVEN. Yeah, I suppose. What's the matter, you got a cold?

TEN (*blowing*). A lulu. These hot-weather colds can kill you.

(SEVEN *nods sympathetically.*)

FOREMAN (*briskly*). All right, gentlemen. Let's take seats.

8 **SEVEN.** Right. This better be fast, I've got tickets to *The Seven Year Itch*[10] tonight. I must be the only guy in the whole world who hasn't seen it yet. (*He laughs and sits down.*) Okay, your honor, start the show.

(*They all begin to sit down. The* FOREMAN *is seated at the head of the table.* EIGHT *continues to look out the window.*)

FOREMAN (*to* EIGHT). How about sitting down? (EIGHT *doesn't hear him.*) The gentleman at the window.

(EIGHT *turns, startled.*)

FOREMAN. How about sitting down?

EIGHT. Oh, I'm sorry. (*He heads for a seat.*)

9 **TEN** (*to* SIX). It's tough to figure, isn't it? A kid kills his father. Bing! Just like that. Well, it's the element. They let the kids run wild. Maybe it serves 'em right.

FOREMAN. Is everybody here?

TWELVE. The old man's inside.

(*The* FOREMAN *turns to the washroom just as the door opens.* NINE *comes out, embarrassed.*)

FOREMAN. We'd like to get started.

NINE. Forgive me, gentlemen. I didn't mean to keep you waiting.

FOREMAN. It's all right. Find a seat.

(NINE *heads for a seat and sits down. They look at the* FOREMAN *expectantly.*)

FOREMAN. All right. Now, you gentlemen can handle this any way you want to. I mean, I'm not going to make any rules. If we want to discuss it first and then vote, that's one way. Or we can vote right now to see how we stand.

SEVEN. Let's vote now. Who knows, maybe we can all go home.

TEN. Yeah. Let's see who's where.

THREE. Right. Let's vote now.

FOREMAN. Anybody doesn't want to vote? (*He looks around the table. There is no answer.*) Okay, all those voting guilty raise your hands. (*Seven or eight hands go up immediately. Several others go up more slowly. Everyone looks around the table. There are two hands not raised,* NINE'S *hand goes up slowly now as the* FOREMAN *counts.*)

FOREMAN. . . . Nine . . . ten . . . eleven . . . That's eleven for guilty. Okay. Not guilty? (EIGHT'S *hand is raised.*) One. Right. Okay. Eleven to one, guilty. Now we know where we are.

THREE. Somebody's in left field.[11] (*To* EIGHT.) You think he's not guilty?

EIGHT (*quietly*). I don't know.

THREE. I never saw a guiltier man in my life. You sat right in court and heard the same thing I did. The man's a dangerous killer. You could see it.

EIGHT. He's nineteen years old.

THREE. That's old enough. He knifed his own father. Four inches into the chest. An innocent little nineteen-year-old kid. They 10 proved it a dozen different ways. Do you want me to list them?

EIGHT. No.

TEN (*to* EIGHT). Well, do you believe his story?

EIGHT. I don't know whether I believe it or not. Maybe I don't.

SEVEN. So what'd you vote not guilty for?

EIGHT. There were eleven votes for guilty. It's not so easy for me to raise my hand and send a boy off to die without talking about it first.

SEVEN. Who says it's easy for me?

---

10. ***The Seven Year Itch,*** a comedy that opened on Broadway in 1952.

11. **in left field,** SLANG. out of contact with reality; unreasonable or improbable.

8 Reading/Thinking Skills
Recognize Assumptions and Implications

Question What does this speech tell you about Juror Seven? *(He does not take his duty as a juror seriously; he expects a quick decision.)*

9 Multicultural Note
Revealing Bias

Question What can you conclude about Ten from this speech? *(Possible responses: He considers the defendant guilty; he is biased against the minority group of which the defendant is a member.)*

10 Literary Element
Plot

Question What is the conflict that is developing? *(Possible response: Eight wants to give the process of jury deliberation a chance to work, while Three, Seven, and Ten are satisfied with the conclusions they have already drawn on their own and have no interest in carrying out the process.)*

BUILDING ENGLISH PROFICIENCY

ESL LEP ELD SAE LD

Exploring Adverbs

Focus attention on how adverbs guide the stage directions.

1. List on the board the following adverbs from the first two sets of stage directions on page 230: *down, slowly, hesitantly,* and *awkwardly.*

2. Invite volunteers to pantomime an action that illustrates these adverbs.

3. Ask students to locate these adverbs on page 230 and to identify the verb that each adverb modifies. *(*Down *modifies* looks*;* slowly *and* hesitantly *modify* begin*;* awkwardly *modifies* file.*)*

4. Have pairs of students locate other adverbs on pages 230–231 and act out the directions in which they appear.

5. Encourage students to think of other adverbs that could apply to the actions in this scene.

Art Study

Visual Literacy By comparing photographs from earlier and later in the movie, students can see changes of attitude.

Question How have these jurors' attitudes changed since they were in the jury box (p. 228)? *(Possible response: They are no longer focused on the matter at hand and appear bored.)*

11 Reader's Response

Making Personal Connections

As students read the jurors' judgments, encourage them to exercise their own judgment in response.

Question Do you think Eight's point is a valid one? Explain. *(Possible responses: The Constitution guarantees everyone a fair trial; however, this boy doesn't deserve it more because of his background. Society has a special obligation to give the victims of society the full advantage of their rights.)*

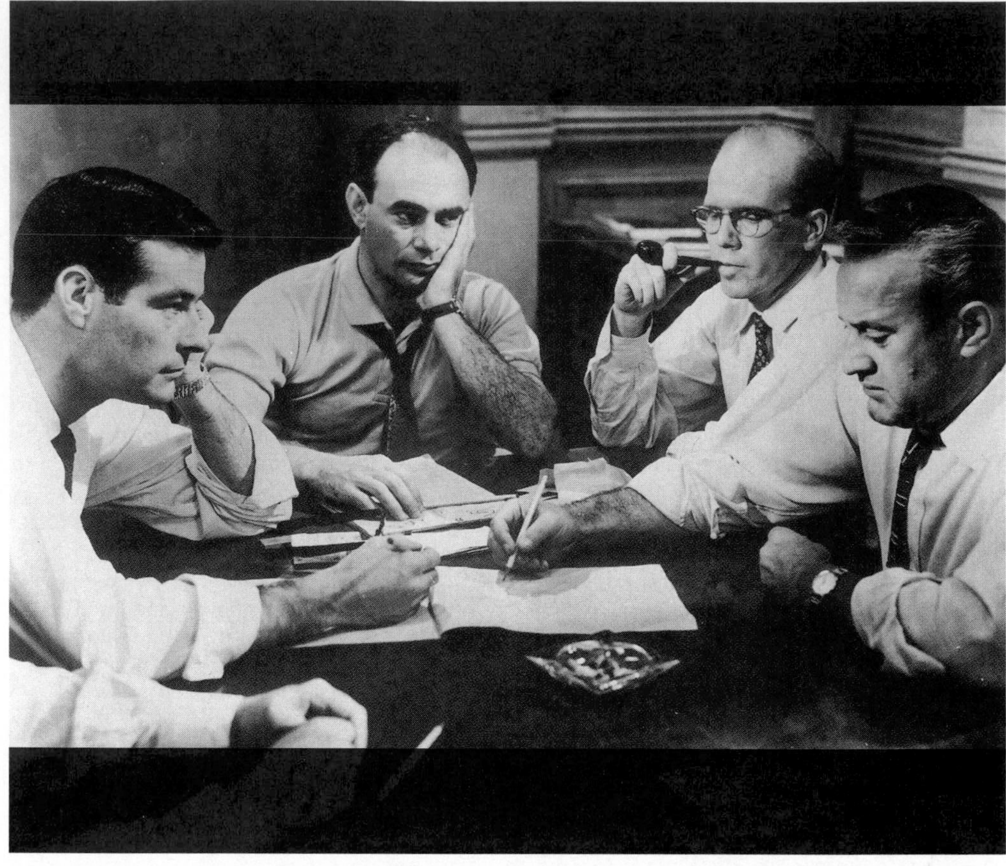

EIGHT. No one.

SEVEN. What, just because I voted fast? I think the guy's guilty. You couldn't change my mind if you talked for a hundred years.

11 **EIGHT.** I don't want to change your mind. I just want to talk for a while. Look, this boy's been kicked around all his life. You know, living in a slum, his mother dead since he was nine. That's not a very good head start. He's a tough, angry kid. You know why slum kids get that way? Because we knock 'em on the head once a day, every day. I think maybe we owe him a few words. That's all.

(He looks around the table. Some of them look back coldly. Some cannot look at him. Only NINE *nods slowly.* TWELVE *doodles steadily.* FOUR *begins to comb his hair.)*

TEN. I don't mind telling you this, mister. We don't owe him a thing. He got a fair trial, didn't he? You know what that trial cost? He's lucky he got it. Look, we're all grownups here. You're not going to tell us that we're supposed to believe him, knowing what he is. I've lived among 'em all my life. You can't believe a word they say. You know that.

NINE *(to* TEN *very slowly).* I don't know that. What a terrible thing for a man to believe! Since

MINI-LESSON: GRAMMAR

Verb Forms

Teach A play's stage directions are written in the present tense. In this play, two different present tense forms are used: simple present tense, and present progressive.

*He **draws** a deep breath and **relaxes.*** (simple present tense, p. 233)

*Some of the jurors **are taking** off their jackets.* (present progressive, p. 230)

Activity Idea Have students use a short story or other work of fiction from their Writer's Notebook as the basis of a scene in a play. They should write one set of stage directions, using appropriate forms of the present tense.

when is dishonesty a group characteristic? You have no monopoly[12] on the truth—

THREE *(interrupting).* All right. It's not Sunday. We don't need a sermon.

NINE. What this man says is very dangerous— (EIGHT *puts his hand on* NINE*'s arm and stops him. Somehow his touch and his gentle expression calm the old man. He draws a deep breath and relaxes.*)

FOUR. I don't see any need for arguing like this. I think we ought to be able to behave like gentlemen.

SEVEN. Right!

FOUR. If we're going to discuss this case, let's discuss the facts.

FOREMAN. I think that's a good point. We have a job to do. Let's do it.

ELEVEN *(with accent).* If you gentlemen don't mind, I'm going to close the window. *(He gets up and does so.) (Apologetically.)* It was blowing on my neck. (TEN *blows his nose fiercely.*)

TWELVE. I may have an idea here. I'm just thinking out loud now, but it seems to me that it's up to us to convince this gentleman— (*Indicating* EIGHT.)—that we're right and he's wrong. Maybe if we each took a minute or two, you know, if we sort of try it on for size—

FOREMAN. That sounds fair enough. Supposing we go once around the table.

SEVEN. Okay, let's start off.

FOREMAN. Right. (*To* TWO.) I guess you're first.

TWO *(timidly).* Oh. Well . . . *(Long pause.)* I just think he's guilty. I thought it was obvious. I mean nobody proved otherwise.

EIGHT *(quietly).* Nobody has to prove otherwise. The burden of proof is on the prosecution.
2 The defendant doesn't have to open his mouth. That's in the Constitution. The Fifth Amendment.[13] You've heard of it.

TWO *(flustered).* Well sure, I've heard of it. I know what it is. I . . . what I meant . . . well, anyway, I think he was guilty.

THREE. Okay, let's get to the facts. Number one,
3 let's take the old man who lived on the second floor right underneath the room where the murder took place. At ten minutes after twelve on the night of the killing he heard loud noises in the upstairs apartment. He said it sounded like a fight. Then he heard the kid say to his father, "I'm gonna kill you." A second later he heard a body falling, and he ran to the door of his apartment, looked out, and saw the kid running down the stairs and out of the house. Then he called the police. They found the father with a knife in his chest.

FOREMAN. And the coroner fixed the time of death at around midnight.

THREE. Right. Now what else do you want?

FOUR. The boy's entire story is flimsy. He claimed he was at the movies. That's a little ridiculous, isn't it? He couldn't even remember what pictures he saw.

THREE. That's right. Did you hear that? (*To* FOUR.) You're absolutely right.

TEN. Look, what about the woman across the street? If her testimony don't prove it, then nothing does.

TWELVE. That's right. She saw the killing, didn't she?

FOREMAN. Let's go in order.

TEN *(loud).* Just a minute. Here's a woman who's lying in bed and can't sleep. It's hot, you know. *(He gets up and begins to walk around, blowing his nose and talking.)* Anyway, she looks out the window, and right across the street she sees the kid stick the knife into his 14
father. She's known the kid all his life. His window is right opposite hers, across the el tracks, and she swore she saw him do it.

EIGHT. Through the windows of a passing elevated train.

TEN. Okay. And they proved in court that you can look through the windows of a passing el

---

12. **monopoly** (mə nop′ə lē), *n.* the exclusive possession or control of something.

13. **The Fifth Amendment,** the amendment to the United States Constitution that guarantees a person on trial for a criminal offense cannot be forced to testify against himself or herself.

12 Reading/Thinking Skills
Compare and Contrast

Playwrights use parallels and contrasts between characters to reveal attitudes and traits.

Question How does the approach of Two differ from that of Eight? *(Possible response: Two reasons from common sense and doesn't account for the special rules that apply in a court of law, while Eight understands those special rules and the idea of "innocent until proven guilty.")*

13 Reader's Response
Making Personal Connections

Question What questions would you ask the old man if you were the defense attorney? *(Answers will vary. Students should suggest questions that examine the validity of the evidence.)*

Question Does the evidence presented on this page convince you that the boy is guilty? Explain. *(Students should justify their responses.)*

14 Reading/Thinking Skills
Visualize

Ask students to try to visualize this scene from a moving el.

BUILDING ENGLISH PROFICIENCY

ESL LEP ELD SAE LD

Analyzing Arguments

Students are likely to respond quickly to the conflict that develops in the jury room. Help them explore opposing theories of Jurors Eight and Ten, expressed on page 232. Write the expression "slum kids" on the board and use it as a springboard for discussion.

Activity Ideas

- Have volunteers paraphrase each juror's opinion.
- Ask for names of stories, movies, and TV programs that have used either opinion in a plot line.
- Encourage students to discuss the kinds of laws and social programs to which each attitude may lead.
- Urge students to offer rebuttals to Ten's statements. Allow them to write in their journals, rather than share them aloud, if they prefer.

15 Literary Focus
Stage Directions

Question Why does Six go to the water fountain? *(Possible response: He's embarrassed and needs a moment to recover.)*

16 Literary Element
Verbal Irony

Question What is Seven's tone of voice when he says, "This is a very fine boy"? *(He is being sarcastic or ironic.)*

17 Reading/Thinking Skills
Draw Conclusions

Encourage students to link the jurors' personal experiences to their views of the trial. Three's experience with his own son is coloring his ideas about the defendant.

18 Reading/Thinking Skills
Recognize the Use of Persuasion

Alert students to techniques jurors use to persuade each other. Four generalizes about people who live in slums and then uses deduction to argue that this generalization applies to the defendant. Five says he lives in a slum and exposes Four's fallacious reasoning.

train at night and see what's happening on the other side. They proved it.

EIGHT. I'd like to ask you something. How come you believed her? She's one of "them," too, isn't she?

(TEN *walks over to* EIGHT.)

TEN. You're a pretty smart fellow, aren't you?

FOREMAN *(rising).* Now take it easy.

(THREE *gets up and goes to* TEN.)

THREE. Come on. Sit down. *(He leads* TEN *back to his seat.)* What're you letting him get you all upset for? Relax.

(TEN *and* THREE *sit down.)*

FOREMAN. Let's calm down now. (*To* FIVE.) It's your turn.

FIVE. I'll pass it.

FOREMAN. That's your privilege. (*To* SIX.) How about you?

SIX *(slowly).* I don't know. I started to be convinced, you know, with the testimony from those people across the hall. Didn't they say something about an argument between the father and the boy around seven o'clock that night? I mean, I can be wrong.

ELEVEN. I think it was eight o'clock. Not seven.

EIGHT. That's right. Eight o'clock. They heard the father hit the boy twice and then saw the boy walk angrily out of the house. What does that prove?

SIX. Well, it doesn't exactly prove anything. It's just part of the picture. I didn't say it proved anything.

FOREMAN. Anything else?

15 **SIX.** No.

(SIX *goes to the water fountain.)*

FOREMAN (*to* SEVEN). All right. How about you?

SEVEN. I don't know, most of it's been said already. We can talk all day about this thing, but I think we're wasting our time. Look at the kid's record. At fifteen he was in reform school. He stole a car. He's been arrested for mugging. He was picked up for knife-fighting. I think they said he stabbed somebody in the arm. This is a very fine boy.

16 **EIGHT.** Ever since he was five years old his father beat him up regularly. He used his fists.

SEVEN. So would I! A kid like that.

THREE. You're right. It's the kids. The way they are—you know? They don't listen. *(Bitter.)* I've got a kid. When he was eight years old he ran away from a fight. I saw him. I was so ashamed, I told him right out, "I'm gonna make a man out of you or I'm gonna bust you up into little pieces trying." When he was fifteen he hit me in the face. He's big, you know. I haven't seen him in three years. Rotten kid! You work your heart out. . . . *(Pause.)* All right. Let's get on with it. *(Looks away embarrassed.)* 17

FOUR. We're missing the point here. This boy—let's say he's a product of a filthy neighborhood and a broken home. We can't help that. We're not here to go into reasons why slums are breeding grounds for criminals. They are. I know it. So do you. The children who come out of slum backgrounds are potential menaces[14] to society.

TEN. You said it there. I don't want any part of them, believe me. 18

(There is a dead silence for a moment, and then FIVE *speaks haltingly.)*

FIVE. I've lived in a slum all my life—

TEN. Oh, now wait a second!

FIVE. I used to play in a backyard that was filled with garbage. Maybe it still smells on me.

FOREMAN. Now let's be reasonable. There's nothing personal—(FIVE *stands up.)*

FIVE. There is something personal!

(Then he catches himself and, seeing everyone looking at him, sits down, fists clenched.)

THREE *(persuasively).* Come on, now. He didn't mean you, feller. Let's not be so sensitive. . . .

(There is a long pause.)

ELEVEN. I can understand this sensitivity.

FOREMAN. Now let's stop the bickering.[15] We're wasting time. (*To* EIGHT.) It's your turn.

EIGHT. All right. I had a peculiar feeling about

14. **menace** (men′is), *n.* threat.
15. **bickering** (bik′ər ing), *n.* petty, noisy quarreling.

MINI-LESSON: USAGE
Colloquialisms

Teach Playwrights may violate certain "rules" of written language in order to make conversation seem realistic. Informal language and slang used by characters are called colloquialisms. For example, Three refers to his son as "Rotten kid" (rather than "poorly behaved child") and says, "I'm gonna bust you up" (rather than "I'll hurt you"). These expressions help establish Three as a tough, violent man.

Activity Ideas

- As they continue to read, have students identify colloquialisms that reveal each juror's character.
- Suggest that students carry their notebooks around for a day and record colloquialisms they overhear. They might want to use some of these when they have occasion to write realistic conversation.

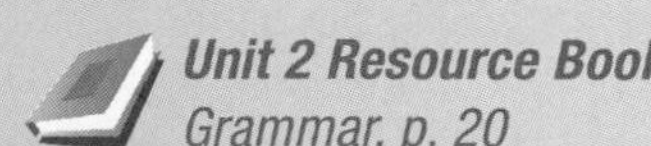

Unit 2 Resource Book
Grammar, p. 20

this trial. Somehow I felt that the defense counsel never really conducted a thorough cross-examination.[16] I mean, he was appointed by the court to defend the boy. He hardly seemed interested. Too many questions were left unasked.

THREE *(annoyed).* What about the ones that were asked? For instance, let's talk about that cute little switch-knife.[17] You know, the one that fine upright kid admitted buying.

9 **EIGHT.** All right. Let's talk about it. Let's get it in here and look at it. I'd like to see it again, Mr. Foreman.

(The FOREMAN *looks at him questioningly and then gets up and goes to the door. During the following dialogue the* FOREMAN *knocks, the* GUARD *comes in, the* FOREMAN *whispers to him, the* GUARD *nods and leaves, locking the door.)*

THREE. We all know what it looks like. I don't see why we have to look at it again. (*To* FOUR.) What do you think? 20

FOUR. The gentleman has a right to see exhibits in evidence.

---

16. **cross-examination,** examination to check a previous examination, especially the questioning of a witness by the lawyer for the opposing side to test the truth of the witness's testimony.
17. **switch-knife,** switchblade knife.

Art Study

Point out the signs of conflict and confrontation in the photograph—Three's raised arm and pointing finger; Eight flanked by Three and Four with all other jurors' attention focused on Three and Eight.

19 Reading/Thinking Skills
Compare and Contrast

Question Contrast Eight's tone with that of Three. *(Possible response: Three is sarcastic, annoyed, and condescending. Eight is frank, straightforward, and serious.)*

20 Historical Note
Playwright Comments

Reginald Rose recalls being rather annoyed when called to serve on a jury of a manslaughter case in New York. "But, strangely, the moment I walked into the courtroom to be empaneled and found myself facing a strange man whose fate was suddenly more or less in my hands, my entire attitude changed. I was hugely impressed with the almost frightening stillness of the courtroom, the impassive, masklike face of the judge, the brisk, purposeful scurrying of the various officials in the room, and the absolute finality of the decision I and my fellow jurors would have to make. . . ."

BUILDING ENGLISH PROFICIENCY

ESL LEP ELD SAE LD

Keeping Track of Story Details

Discussion in the jury room focuses on evidence against the young defendant. To keep track of this evidence, have students begin a web.

1. Write the term *incriminating evidence* on the board. Work with students to compose a definition.
2. Have students identify some things the jurors are considering as evidence, along with the reasons each should be considered.
3. Urge students to add to the web as they continue to read.

INCRIMINATING EVIDENCE
statements, objects used in court to prove a person's guilt

defendant's past record

argument overheard

21 Reading/Thinking Skills
Draw Conclusions

Point out that Four makes a factual error but accepts Eight's correction immediately without argument. He shows the same kind of careful attention to the trial detail that Eight does, although his attitudes differ from Eight's in other ways.

22 Literary Focus
Stage Directions

Questions How does the action described in the stage directions answer Three's assertion? How does the action add dramatic impact? *(Possible responses: It demonstrates unquestionably that there was another knife of the same type available in the neighborhood. The suddenness of the act and the fact it was done by the gentle Eight makes it memorable.)*

THREE *(shrugging)*. Okay with me.

FOUR (*to* EIGHT). This knife is a pretty strong piece of evidence, don't you agree?

EIGHT. I do.

21 **FOUR.** The boy admits going out of his house at eight o'clock after being slapped by his father.

EIGHT. Or punched.

FOUR. Or punched. He went to a neighborhood store and bought a switch-knife. The storekeeper was arrested the following day when he admitted selling it to the boy. It's a very unusual knife. The storekeeper identified it and said it was the only one of its kind he had in stock. Why did the boy get it? *(Sarcastically.)* As a present for a friend of his, he says. Am I right so far?

EIGHT. Right.

THREE. You bet he's right. *(To all.)* Now listen to this man. He knows what he's talking about.

FOUR. Next, the boy claims that on the way home the knife must have fallen through a hole in his coat pocket, that he never saw it again. Now there's a story, gentlemen. You know what actually happened. The boy took the knife home and a few hours later stabbed his father with it and even remembered to wipe off the fingerprints.

(The door opens and the GUARD *walks in with an oddly designed knife with a tag on it.* FOUR *gets up and takes it from him. The* GUARD *exits.)*

FOUR. Everyone connected with the case identified this knife. Now are you trying to tell me that someone picked it up off the street and went up to the boy's house and stabbed his father with it just to be amusing?

EIGHT. No, I'm saying that it's possible that the boy lost the knife and that someone else stabbed his father with a similar knife. It's possible.

(FOUR *flips open the knife and jams it into the table.)*

FOUR. Take a look at that knife. It's a very strange knife. I've never seen one like it before in my life. Neither had the storekeeper who sold it to him.

(EIGHT *reaches casually into his pocket and withdraws an object. No one notices this. He stands up quietly.*)

FOUR. Aren't you trying to make us accept a pretty incredible coincidence?

EIGHT. I'm not trying to make anyone accept it. I'm just saying it's possible.

THREE *(shouting)*. And I'm saying it's not possible. 22

(EIGHT *swiftly flicks open the blade of a switch-knife and jams it into the table next to the first one. They are exactly alike. There are several gasps and everyone stares at the knife. There is a long silence.*)

THREE *(slowly, amazed)*. What are you trying to do?

TEN *(loud)*. Yeah, what is this? Who do you think you are?

FIVE. Look at it! It's the same knife!

FOREMAN. Quiet! Let's be quiet.

(They quiet down.)

FOUR. Where did you get it?

EIGHT. I got it last night in a little junk shop around the corner from the boy's house. It cost two dollars.

THREE. Now listen to me! You pulled a real smart trick here, but you proved absolutely zero. Maybe there are ten knives like that, so what?

EIGHT. Maybe there are.

THREE. The boy lied and you know it.

EIGHT. He may have lied. (*To* TEN.) Do you think he lied?

TEN *(violently)*. Now that's a stupid question. Sure he lied!

EIGHT (*to* FOUR). Do you?

FOUR. You don't have to ask me that. You know my answer. He lied.

EIGHT (*to* FIVE). Do you think he lied?

(FIVE *can't answer immediately. He looks around nervously.*)

FIVE. I . . . I don't know.

SEVEN. Now wait a second. What are you, the guy's lawyer? Listen, there are still eleven of

MINI-LESSON: SPEAKING/LISTENING
Communicate Clearly and Effectively

Teach Unlike genres meant only to be read silently, a play depends on the skilled use of the actors' voices for much of its impact. Stage directions help actors determine the appropriate tone and delivery for their lines.

Activity Idea Students can try out their acting skills by reading the passage that begins at the bottom of page 236, with Eight saying to Five, "Do you think he lied?" Have students volunteer for juror parts and read to the end of the act, using variations in pitch, modulation, volume, and inflection to capture the dynamics of the situation. Remind them to note stage directions in their delivery.

us who think he's guilty. You're alone. What do you think you're gonna accomplish? If you want to be stubborn and hang this jury,[18] he'll be tried again and found guilty, sure as he's born.

EIGHT. You're probably right.

SEVEN. So what are you gonna do about it? We can be here all night.

23 **NINE.** It's only one night. A man may die.

(SEVEN *glares at* NINE *for a long while, but has no answer.* EIGHT *looks closely at* NINE *and we can begin to sense a* rapport[19] *between them. There is a long silence. Then suddenly everyone begins to talk at once.*)

THREE. Well, whose fault is that?

SIX. Do you think maybe if we went over it again? What I mean is—

TEN. Did anyone force him to kill his father? (*To* THREE.) How do you like him? Like someone forced him!

ELEVEN. Perhaps this is not the point.

FIVE. No one forced anyone. But listen—

TWELVE. Look, gentlemen, we can spitball all night here.

TWO. Well, I was going to say—

SEVEN. Just a minute. Some of us've got better things to do than sit around a jury room.

FOUR. I can't understand a word in here. Why do we all have to talk at once?

FOREMAN. He's right. I think we ought to get on with it.

(EIGHT *has been listening to this exchange closely.*)

THREE (*to* EIGHT). Well, what do you say? You're the one holding up the show.

EIGHT (*standing*). I've got a proposition to make.

(*We catch a close shot of* FIVE *looking steadily at him as he talks.* FIVE, *seemingly puzzled, listens closely.*)

EIGHT. I want to call for a vote. I want you eleven men to vote by secret ballot. I'll abstain. If there are still eleven votes for guilty, I won't stand alone. We'll take in a guilty verdict right now. 24

SEVEN. Okay. Let's do it.

FOREMAN. That sounds fair. Is everyone agreed?

(*They all nod their heads.* EIGHT *walks over to the window, looks out for a moment, and then faces them.*)

FOREMAN. Pass these along.

(*The* FOREMAN *passes ballot slips to all of them, and now* EIGHT *watches them tensely as they begin to write. Fade out.*)

18. **hang this jury,** keep this jury from reaching a verdict. A jury that fails to reach a verdict is called a "hung" jury.

19. **rapport** (ra pôr′, ra pôrt′), *n.* agreement; connection.

23 Reading/Thinking Skills
Connect

Question Explain how Nine's change in sympathy might have come about. *(Possible response: Earlier Eight had prevented Nine from being embroiled in an argument with Three and Ten. This may have predisposed Nine to consider Eight's points with an open mind.)*

24 Literary Element
Plot

Eight's "proposition" brings the first act to a suspenseful close. Students may be able to predict that Nine will now vote *not guilty,* making the vote 10–2, both because of the rapport mentioned in the stage direction on page 237 and the fact that this is only the end of first act in a three-act play. If Eight were forced to capitulate now, there would be nothing left to do.

Check Test

1. Who votes "not guilty" on the first ballot? *(Eight)*
2. How does Eight show that the boy might have told the truth about the knife? *(He produces an identical knife.)*
3. From where did the female witness see the murder? *(from her apartment across the street from the boy's, but through the windows of a passing elevated train)*
4. Who is the other witness? *(an old man)*
5. What makes Four doubt that the boy went to the movies? *(The boy couldn't remember what pictures he'd seen.)*

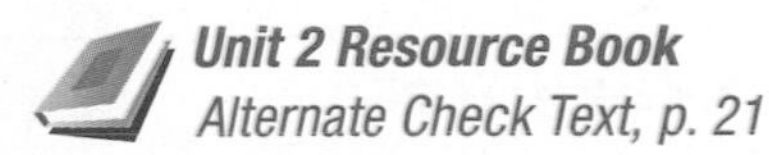
Unit 2 Resource Book
Alternate Check Text, p. 21

BUILDING ENGLISH PROFICIENCY

Checking Comprehension

Let students check their understanding of act one by summarizing.

1. Pair students; have pairs share and discuss the information they have learned. Encourage them to refer to their jurors' notes and detail webs.
2. Have pairs summarize what they have learned about the defendant and the crime.
3. Suggest that partners ask each other at least three questions about information that they consider important.
4. Allow time for pairs to share and discuss information that they did not understand or upon which they disagreed.

After Reading

MAKING CONNECTIONS

1. Students are likely to pick Eight as the preferred boss and Three as the most difficult.

2. Students should use evidence from life to back up their opinions. Someone may note that juries continue to arrive at unanimous verdicts.

3. Students may say there is insufficient information for a judgment now.

4. The oppressively hot weather and a shabby room with a locked door make the general atmosphere uncomfortable and the jurors irritable.

5. Students may identify the protagonist as either Eight or ideals such as Justice or Democracy. They may identify the antagonist(s) as other jurors (Four, Ten, and particularly Three) or attitudes like Prejudice.

6. The testimony on the rarity of the murder weapon supports the prosecution's claim that no one in the vicinity would possess an identical knife. The defense admits the boy had bought a knife but claims he lost it prior to the murder.

7. He proves that another such knife was available in the same neighborhood.

8. Students should support their responses with reasons. Someone may observe that the amendment is a right that many use in testifying.

9. Possible responses: Yes, I have a new appreciation for how important it is. No, I'd be afraid to have that kind of responsibility.

Unit 2 Resource Book
Vocabulary, p. 19
Vocabulary Test, p. 22

Selection Test

Unit 2 Resource Book
pp. 23–24

Act 1

After Reading

Making Connections

Shaping Your Response

1. Conduct a class poll on which juror students would prefer to have as a boss and which they think would be the most difficult boss. Cite character qualities on which you base your decisions.
2. Do you think it's realistic to expect twelve people to agree on any verdict? Why or why not?
3. Based on what you know so far about the trial, would you vote *guilty* or *not guilty?* Why?

Analyzing the Play

4. How does the **setting**—the time of day, the weather, and the room—affect the general atmosphere and the behavior of the jurors?
5. Identify the **protagonist(s)** and the **antagonist(s)** in act 1.
6. How has testimony about the murder weapon figured in the trial, both for the prosecution and the defense?
7. Why might some of the jurors begin to have doubts after Eight takes an identical switchblade knife from his pocket and jams it into the table?

Extending the Ideas

8. If you were a juror, would you assume a defendant was guilty because he or she pleaded the Fifth Amendment on the basis of self-incrimination? Why or why not?
9. Knowing what you know now, would you like to serve on a jury? Why or why not?

Vocabulary Study

appalled
bickering
bigot
intolerant
menace
monopoly
naïve
rapport
superficial
tempered

Replace each italicized item with a synonym from the list.

1. Juror Twelve is a *shallow* snob who is concerned with appearances.
2. Juror Eight is a man of strength *softened* with compassion.
3. The Foreman reminds his fellow jurors to avoid *arguing.*
4. The *simple* young man thinks his elders will laugh at his comments.
5. Since he is a *narrow-minded, intolerant person,* Juror Three is unable to see the good side of people.
6. The audience senses a natural *agreement* between Eight and Nine.
7. Juror Three believes the accused boy is a *threat* to his neighbors.
8. Juror Three has *shocked* the others with his prejudiced comments.
9. Juror Nine tells Ten he has no *total control* of the truth about people in the slums.
10. Some of the jurors grow *impatient* with Three and his strong opinions.

VOCABULARY STUDY

1. superficial
2. tempered
3. bickering
4. naïve
5. bigot
6. rapport
7. menace
8. appalled
9. monopoly
10. intolerant

ACT TWO

Fade in on same scene, no time lapse. EIGHT *stands tensely watching as the* JURORS *write on their ballots. He stays perfectly still as one by one they fold the ballots and pass them along to the* FOREMAN. *The* FOREMAN *takes them, riffles through the folded ballots, counts eleven, and now begins to open them. He reads each one out loud and lays it aside. They watch him quietly, and all we hear is his voice and the sound of* TWO *sucking on a cough drop.*

FOREMAN. Guilty. Guilty. Guilty. Guilty. Guilty. Guilty. Guilty. Guilty. Guilty. *(He pauses at the tenth ballot and then reads it.)* Not Guilty.

(THREE *slams down hard on the table. The* FOREMAN *opens the last ballot.*) Guilty.

TEN *(angry).* How do you like that!

SEVEN. Who was it? I think we have a right to know.

ELEVEN. Excuse me. This was a secret ballot. We agreed on this point, no? If the gentleman wants it to remain secret— 1

THREE *(standing up angrily).* What do you mean? There are no secrets in here! I know who it was. (*He turns to* FIVE.) What's the matter with you? You come in here and you vote

Art Study

Point out to students how the line of the Foreman's wrists and thumbs directs our gaze toward the piece of paper containing the crucial vote. Remind students that the kind of visual subtleties and immediacy (we are looking over the Foreman's shoulder) achieved by the camera would not be possible in a stage production.

Vocabulary Preview

adlib, make up words or music as one goes along; improvise

insignificant, unimportant; trivial

sadist, person displaying cruel tendencies

sheepishly, awkwardly bashful or embarrassed

simulated, fake, pretend

Students can add the words and definitions to their Writer's Notebooks.

1 Reader's Response
Making Personal Connections

Questions

- Do you think the ballot should be revealed? *(Possible responses: No. The person who cast the "not guilty" ballot did it believing the vote would be secret. Yes. In order to convince each other, jurors need to know where everyone stands.)*
- Who do you think cast the "not guilty" ballot? *(Answers will vary. Students may guess Nine.)*

Unit 2 Resource Book
Graphic Organizer, p. 25
Study Guide, p. 26

SELECTION SUMMARY

Twelve Angry Men, Act 2

The Foreman reads the results of the secret ballot, revealing that there is another "not guilty" vote. Eight suggests that the boy's threat to kill his father did not necessarily mean he really intended to, but Three disagrees violently, saying that those words, when screamed, are certainly meant. Jurors examine a diagram of the room and reconsider the male witness's testimony. Nine hypothesizes why the old man might have exaggerated. Eight proposes a simulation of the witness's trip from his bed to the stairs. The re-enactment reveals that the witness could not have seen the boy on the stairs. Three explodes in frustration, accosting Eight and screaming that he wants to kill him, while everyone notes the irony of this threat.

For summaries in other languages, see the ***Building English Proficiency*** *book.*

2 Reading/Thinking Skills
Relate Literature to Human Concerns

Questions

- What does America stand for to Eleven? *(freedom of speech)*
- What do *you* think it stands for? *(Answers might include justice, equality, freedom of speech and religion, democracy, etc.)*

3 Reading/Thinking Skills
Draw Conclusions

Question Why do you suppose Three thought it was Five who had changed his vote? *(Possible response: Like the accused, Five grew up in a slum, according to p. 234. Three wrongly assumed Five would automatically side with someone of his own class.)*

4 Reader's Response
Making Personal Connections

Questions What do you think Nine means? What feelings do you have about the case? *(Possible response: He has an intuition based on Eight's information about the knife that things are less cut and dried than they had seemed. Students should state their personal feelings about the case.)*

guilty and then this slick preacher starts to tear your heart out with stories about a poor little kid who just couldn't help becoming a murderer. So you change your vote. If that isn't the most sickening—

(FIVE *stares at* THREE, *frightened at this outburst.*)

FOREMAN. Now hold it.

THREE. Hold it? We're trying to put a guilty man into the chair where he belongs—and all of a sudden we're paying attention to fairy tales.

FIVE. Now just a minute—

2 **ELEVEN.** Please. I would like to say something here. I have always thought that a man was entitled to have unpopular opinions in this country. This is the reason I came here. I wanted to have the right to disagree. In my own country, I am ashamed to say—

TEN. What do we have to listen to now—the whole history of your country?

SEVEN. Yeah, let's stick to the subject. (*To* FIVE.) I want to ask you what made you change your vote.

(*There is a long pause as* SEVEN *and* FIVE *eye each other angrily.*)

NINE (*quietly*). There's nothing for him to tell you. He didn't change his vote. I did. (*There is a pause.*) Maybe you'd like to know why.

THREE. No, we wouldn't like to know why.

FOREMAN. The man wants to talk.

NINE. Thank you. (*Pointing at* EIGHT.) This gentleman chose to stand alone against us. That's his right. It takes a great deal of courage to stand alone even if you believe in something very strongly. He left the verdict up to us. He gambled for support and I gave it to him. I want to hear more. The vote is ten to two.

TEN. That's fine. If the speech is over, let's go on.

(FOREMAN *gets up, goes to door, knocks, hands* GUARD *the tagged switch-knife and sits down again.*)

3 **THREE** (*to* FIVE). Look buddy, I was a little excited. Well, you know how it is. I . . . I didn't mean to get nasty. Nothing personal.

(FIVE *looks at him.*)

SEVEN (*to* EIGHT). Look, supposing you answer me this. If the kid didn't kill him, who did?

EIGHT. As far as I know, we're supposed to decide whether or not the boy on trial is guilty. We're not concerned with anyone else's motives here.

NINE. Guilty beyond a reasonable doubt. This is an important thing to remember.

THREE (*to* TEN). Everyone's a lawyer. (*To* NINE.) Supposing you explain what your reasonable doubts are.

NINE. This is not easy. So far, it's only a feeling I 4
have. A feeling. Perhaps you don't understand.

TEN. A feeling! What are we gonna do, spend the night talking about your feelings? What about the facts?

THREE. You said a mouthful. (*To* NINE.) Look, the old man heard the kid yell, "I'm gonna kill you." A second later he heard the father's body falling, and he saw the boy running out of the house fifteen seconds after that.

TWELVE. That's right. And let's not forget the woman across the street. She looked into the open window and saw the boy stab his father. She saw it. Now if that's not enough for you . . .

EIGHT. It's not enough for me.

SEVEN. How do you like him? It's like talking into a dead phone.

FOUR. The woman saw the killing through the windows of a moving elevated train. The train had five cars, and she saw it through the windows of the last two. She remembers the most insignificant[1] details.

(*Cut to close shot of* TWELVE, *who doodles a picture of an el train on a scrap of paper.*)

THREE. Well, what have you got to say about that?

EIGHT. I don't know. It doesn't sound right to me.

THREE. Well, supposing you think about it. (*To* TWELVE.) Lend me your pencil.

(TWELVE *gives it to him. He draws a tick-tack-toe*

1. insignificant (in′sig nif′ə kənt), *adj.* unimportant; trivial.

MINI-LESSON: STUDY SKILLS
Interpret Graphic Sources: Diagram

Teach Have students look at the diagram shown in the photograph from the movie *Twelve Angry Men* on page 244. Point out the types of representation used for furniture, stairs, walls, doors, and the el line. Show how measurements are recorded in feet and inches.

Activity Ideas

- Some of the dimensions are not labeled, and part of the diagram is blocked by Henry Fonda's arm. Have students redraw the diagram, filling in missing dimensions and showing what they imagine is blocked from view.
- Have students make up other problems using the diagram and the timing information given in the play. For example: Suppose the witness went to bed, leaving his watch on the bathroom sink when he washed his hands. He wants to get his watch. How long will it take him to get his watch and return to bed?

square on the same sheet of paper on which TWELVE *has drawn the train. He fills in an X, hands the pencil to* TWELVE.)

THREE. Your turn. We might as well pass the time. (TWELVE *takes the pencil.* EIGHT *stands up and snatches the paper away.* THREE *leaps up.*)

THREE. Wait a minute!

EIGHT *(hard).* This isn't a game.

THREE *(angry).* Who do you think you are?

SEVEN *(rising).* All right, let's take it easy.

THREE. I've got a good mind to walk around this table and belt him one!

FOREMAN. Now, please. I don't want any fights in here.

THREE. Did ya see him? The nerve! The absolute nerve!

TEN. All right. Forget it. It don't mean anything.

SIX. How about sitting down.

THREE. This isn't a game. Who does he think he is?

(He lets them sit him down. EIGHT *remains standing, holding the scrap of paper. He looks at it closely now and seems to be suddenly interested in it. Then he throws it back toward* THREE. *It lands in center of table.* THREE *is angered again at this, but* FOUR *puts his hand on his arm.* EIGHT *speaks now and his voice is more intense.)*

EIGHT (*to* FOUR). Take a look at that sketch. How long does it take an elevated train going at top speed to pass a given point?

FOUR. What has that got to do with anything?

EIGHT. How long? Guess.

FOUR. I wouldn't have the slightest idea.

EIGHT (*to* FIVE). What do you think?

5 **FIVE.** About ten or twelve seconds, maybe.

EIGHT. I'd say that was a fair guess. Anyone else?

ELEVEN. I would think about ten seconds, perhaps.

TWO. About ten seconds.

FOUR. All right. Say ten seconds. What are you getting at?

EIGHT. This. An el train passes a given point in ten seconds. That given point is the window of the room in which the killing took place. You can almost reach out of the window of that room and touch the el. Right? *(Several of them nod.)* All right. Now let me ask you this. Did anyone here ever live right next to the el tracks? I have. When your window is open and the train goes by, the noise is almost unbearable. You can't hear yourself think.

TEN. Okay. You can't hear yourself think. Will you get to the point?

EIGHT. The old man heard the boy say, "I'm going to kill you," and one second later he heard a body fall. One second. That's the testimony, right?

TWO. Right.

EIGHT. The woman across the street looked through the windows of the last two cars of the el and saw the body fall. Right? The *last two* cars.

TEN. What are you giving us here?

EIGHT. An el takes ten seconds to pass a given
point or two seconds per car. That el had
been going by the old man's window for at
least six seconds, and maybe more, before
the body fell, according to the woman. The 6
old man would have had to hear the boy say,
"I'm going to kill you," while the front of the
el was roaring past his nose. It's not possible
that he could have heard it.

THREE. What d'ya mean! Sure he could have heard it.

EIGHT. Could he?

THREE. He said the boy yelled it out. That's enough for me.

NINE. I don't think he could have heard it.

TWO. Maybe he didn't hear it. I mean with the el noise—

THREE. What are you people talking about? Are you calling the old man a liar?

FIVE. Well, it stands to reason.

THREE. You're crazy? Why would he lie? What's he got to gain?

NINE. Attention, maybe.

THREE. You keep coming up with these bright sayings. Why don't you send one in to a newspaper? They pay two dollars.

(EIGHT *looks hard at* THREE *and then turns to* NINE.)

5 Reading/Thinking Skills

Recognize the Use of Persuasion

Question Why doesn't Eight make his own estimate? *(His argument will be more convincing if he uses someone else's estimate to prove the point.)*

6 Reader's Response

Making Personal Connections

Questions Are you convinced of Eight's reasoning and conclusion? Why or why not? *(Possible responses: Yes, the math is accurate. No, I've ridden the el and sometimes it stops or slows down, so the timing isn't always consistent and the noise may sometimes lessen or stop.)*

BUILDING ENGLISH PROFICIENCY

Evaluating Evidence

At the end of page 241, lead students to understand that Eight is discrediting a witness's testimony.

Activity Ideas

- Have students read aloud the discussion about time. Ask them to check the mentioned times by the classroom clock.
- Encourage comments from students who have knowledge of a subway's noise and speed.
- Ask students to share any factual data about court trials that they may have learned from newspaper articles or TV news reports.
- Have students consider and discuss reasons that the defendant's lawyer might not have pursued Eight's line of questioning.

7 Reading/Thinking Skills

Draw Conclusions

Question What is Nine's point here? *(Possible response: He, too, has acted to make himself important by convincing himself of something that wasn't quite true.)*

8 Reading/Thinking Skills

Make Judgments

Question What do you think it would take to persuade Three that Eight might be correct? *(Possible responses: seeing it happen in real life. Nothing will convince him—he wants to believe the boy is guilty.)*

9 Reading/Thinking Skills

Draw Conclusions

Question What's the point here? *(Possible responses: Ten makes a grammatical error in his tirade against the boy's ignorance, inadvertently revealing his own ignorance. Eleven, whose native language is not English, offers a grammatical correction which carries an implied condemnation of the sentiment Ten expressed.)*

EIGHT *(softly).* Why might the old man have lied? You have a right to be heard.

7 **NINE.** It's just that I looked at him for a very long time. The seam of his jacket was split under the arm. Did you notice that? He was a very old man with a torn jacket, and he carried two canes. I think I know him better than anyone here. This is a quiet, frightened, insignificant man who has been nothing all his life, who has never had recognition—his name in the newspapers. Nobody knows him after seventy-five years. That's a very sad thing. A man like this needs to be recognized. To be questioned, and listened to, and quoted just once. This is very important.

TWELVE. And you're trying to tell us he lied about a thing like this just so that he could be important?

NINE. No, he wouldn't really lie. But perhaps he'd make himself believe that he heard those words and recognized the boy's face.

8 **THREE** *(loud).* Well, that's the most fantastic story I've every heard. How can you make up a thing like that? What do you know about it?

NINE *(low).* I speak from experience.

(There is a long pause. Then the FOREMAN *clears his throat.)*

FOREMAN (*to* EIGHT). All right. Is there anything else?

(EIGHT *is looking at* NINE. TWO *offers the* FOREMAN *a box of cough drops. The* FOREMAN *pushes it away.*)

TWO *(hesitantly).* Anybody . . . want a cough . . . drop?

FOREMAN *(sharply).* Come on. Let's get on with it.

EIGHT. I'll take one. (TWO almost *gratefully slides him one along the table.*) Thanks. (TWO *nods and* EIGHT *puts the cough drop into his mouth.*) Now. There's something else I'd like to point out here. I think we proved that the old man couldn't have heard the boy say, "I'm going to kill you," but supposing he really did hear it? This phrase. How many times has each of you used it? Probably hundreds. "If you do that once more, Junior, I'm going to murder you." "Come on, Rocky, kill him!" We say it every day. This doesn't mean that we're going to kill someone.

THREE. Wait a minute. The phrase was "I'm going to kill you," and the kid screamed it out at the top of his lungs. Don't try and tell me he didn't mean it. Anybody says a thing like that the way he said it—they mean it.

TEN. And how they mean it!

EIGHT. Well, let me ask you this. Do you really think the boy would shout out a thing like that so the whole neighborhood would hear it? I don't think so. He's much too bright for that.

TEN *(exploding).* Bright! He's a common, ignorant slob. He don't even speak good English! 9

ELEVEN *(slowly).* He *doesn't* even speak good English.

(TEN *stares angrily at* ELEVEN, *and there is silence for a moment. Then* FIVE *looks around the table nervously.*)

FIVE. I'd like to change my vote to not guilty.

(THREE *gets up and walks to the window, furious, but trying to control himself.*)

FOREMAN. Are you sure?

FIVE. Yes. I'm sure.

FOREMAN. The vote is nine to three in favor of guilty.

SEVEN. Well, if that isn't the end. (*To* FIVE.) What are you basing it on? Stories this guy—(*indicating* EIGHT)—made up! He oughta write for *Amazing Detective Monthly.* He'd make a fortune. Listen, the kid had a lawyer, didn't he? Why didn't his lawyer bring up all these points?

FIVE. Lawyers can't think of everything.

SEVEN. Oh, brother! (*To* EIGHT.) You sit in here and pull stories out of thin air. Now we're supposed to believe that the old man didn't get up out of bed, run to the door, and see the kid beat it downstairs fifteen seconds after the killing. He's only saying he did to be important.

FIVE. Did the old man say he ran to the door?

SEVEN. Ran. Walked. What's the difference? He got there.

MINI-LESSON: LISTENING/SPEAKING

Listen for Information

Teach The debate in the bottom half of the first column on page 243 highlights the importance of careful listening in the courtroom.

Activity Idea Have students discuss why listening for information and recall is so important in a trial situation. They should use details from the play to support their reasons. They might then go on to discuss other situations in which understanding and remembering information are particularly important. *(peace negotiations, hostage situations, international agreements, and homework assignments)*

FIVE. I don't remember what he said. But I don't see how he could run.

FOUR. He said he went from his bedroom to the front door. That's enough, isn't it?

EIGHT. Where was his bedroom again?

TEN. Down the hall somewhere. I thought you remembered everything. Don't you remember that?

EIGHT. No. Mr. Foreman, I'd like to take a look at the diagram of the apartment.

SEVEN. Why don't we have them run the trial over just so you can get everything straight?

EIGHT. Mr. Foreman—

FOREMAN *(rising).* I heard you.

(The FOREMAN *gets up, goes to door during following dialogue. He knocks on door,* GUARD *opens it, he whispers to* GUARD, GUARD *nods and closes door.)*

THREE *(to* EIGHT*).* All right. What's this for? How come you're the only one in the room who wants to see exhibits all the time?

FIVE. I want to see this one, too.

THREE. And I want to stop wasting time.

FOUR. If we're going to start wading through all that nonsense about where the body was found . . .

EIGHT. We're not. We're going to find out how a man who's had two strokes in the past three years, and who walks with a pair of canes, could get to his front door in fifteen seconds.

THREE. He said twenty seconds.

TWO. He said fifteen.

THREE. How does he know how long fifteen seconds is? You can't judge that kind of a thing.

NINE. He said fifteen. He was positive about it.

10 **THREE** *(angry).* He's an old man. You saw him. Half the time he was confused. How could he be positive about . . . anything?

(THREE *looks around sheepishly,*[2] *unable to cover up his blunder. The door opens and the* GUARD *walks in, carrying a large pen-and-ink diagram of the apartment. It is a railroad flat.*[3] *A bedroom faces the el tracks. Behind it is a series of rooms off a long hall. In the front bedroom is a diagram of the spot where the body was found. At the back of the apartment we see the entrance into the apartment hall from the building hall. We see a flight of stairs in the building hall. The diagram is clearly labeled and included in the information on it are the dimensions of the various rooms. The* GUARD *gives the diagram to the* FOREMAN.)

GUARD. This what you wanted?

FOREMAN. That's right. Thank you.

(The GUARD *nods and exits.* EIGHT *goes to* FOREMAN *and reaches for it.)*

EIGHT. May I?

(The FOREMAN *nods.* EIGHT *takes the diagram and sets it up on a chair so that all can see it.* EIGHT *looks it over. Several of the* JURORS *get up to see it better.* THREE, TEN, *and* SEVEN, *however, barely bother to look at it.)* 11

SEVEN *(to* TEN*).* Do me a favor. Wake me up when this is over.

EIGHT *(ignoring him).* All right. This is the apartment in which the killing took place. The old man's apartment is directly beneath it and exactly the same. *(Pointing.)* Here are the el tracks. The bedroom. Another bedroom. Living room. Bathroom. Kitchen. And this is the hall. Here's the front door to the apartment. And here are the steps. *(Pointing to front bedroom and then front door.)* Now the old man was in bed in this room. He says he got up, went out into the hall, down the hall to the front door, opened it, and looked out just in time to see the boy racing down the stairs. Am I right?

THREE. That's the story.

EIGHT. Fifteen seconds after he heard the body fall.

ELEVEN. Correct.

EIGHT. His bed was at the window. It's—*(looking closer)*—twelve feet from his bed to the bedroom door. The length of the hall is forty-three feet, six inches. He had to get up out of bed, get his canes, walk twelve feet, open

2. **sheepishly** (shē′pish lē), *adv.* awkwardly bashful or embarrassed.

3. **railroad flat,** long, narrow apartment with rooms joined in a line.

10 Reading/Thinking Skills
Analyzing

Questions

- What is Three's blunder? *(Possible response: In trying to salvage the witness's testimony about seeing the boy running away, Three inadvertently raises doubts about the validity of all his testimony.)*
- What is Three's reaction to his blunder, as indicated in the stage directions? *(He is embarrassed, as indicated by the word* sheepishly.*)*

11 Reading/Thinking Skills
Visualize

Encourage students to imagine that they are directing this play. Ask them how the three jurors who remain seated might express their disinterest. Which jurors would they have get up? How might the actions of these jurors convey their interest? Encourage students to visualize the scene in their minds and then give them an opportunity to explain their choices and perhaps stage the scene in the classroom.

BUILDING ENGLISH PROFICIENCY

Exploring Idioms

Help students increase their knowledge of English idioms. Begin by asking what they should do if you said, "Hold your tongue."

1. Write the following idioms from pages 242–243 on the board: *get on with it; at the top of his lungs; pull out of thin air; beat it;* and *get everything straight.*
2. Invite students who are familiar with any idiom to define it verbally or with an illustration.
3. Suggest that students use context clues to define those that are unfamiliar.
4. Students whose first language is not English might share how they would express each idea in their own language.
5. Have pairs or small groups of students work to define other idioms and use them in original sentences.

Art Study

Visual Literacy Remind students that this movie was shot in black and white.

Questions

- Do you think this movie would be more effective in color, or less so? Explain. *(Possible responses: It's more stark in black and white. The jury room would look dingier and more depressing in black and white. Use of color could add more drama and interest to the movie.)*
- How might a stage director convey information in the diagram to an audience? *(Possible responses: A character could describe it; there could be a large overhead projector screen.)*

12 Reading/Thinking Skills

Recognize Use of Persuasion

Question Why does Eight let the simulated hall be shorter than the real hall and assume that the canes were right beside the bed, when they may not have been? *(Possible response: He is giving every benefit of the doubt against himself, so that if the demonstration takes longer than fifteen seconds, the others will realize that in real life, it might have taken longer still.)*

the bedroom door, walk forty-three feet, and open the front door—all in fifteen seconds. Do you think this possible?

TEN. You know it's possible.

ELEVEN. He can only walk very slowly. They had to help him into the witness chair.

THREE. You make it sound like a long walk. It's not.

(EIGHT *gets up, goes to the end of the room, and takes two chairs. He puts them together to indicate a bed.)*

NINE. For an old man who uses canes, it's a long walk.

THREE (*to* EIGHT). What are you doing?

EIGHT. I want to try this thing. Let's see how long it took him. I'm going to pace off twelve feet—the length of the bedroom. *(He begins to do so.)*

THREE. You're crazy. You can't re-create a thing like that.

ELEVEN. Perhaps if we could see it . . . this is an important point.

THREE *(mad).* It's a ridiculous waste of time.

SIX. Let him do it.

EIGHT. Hand me a chair. *(Someone pushes a chair to him.)* All right. This is the bedroom door. Now how far would you say it is from here to the door of this room?

SIX. I'd say it was twenty feet.

TWO. Just about.

EIGHT. Twenty feet is close enough. All right, from here to the door and back is about forty feet. It's shorter than the length of the hall, wouldn't you say that?

NINE. A few feet maybe.

TEN. Look, this is absolutely insane. What makes 12 you think you can—

EIGHT. Do you mind if I try it? According to you, it'll only take fifteen seconds. We can spare that. *(He walks over to the two chairs now and lies down on them.)* Who's got a watch with a second hand?

TWO. I have.

EIGHT. When you want me to start, stamp your foot. That'll be the body falling. Time me from there. *(He lies down on the chairs.)* Let's say he keeps his canes right at his bedside. Right?

TWO. Right!

EIGHT. Okay. I'm ready.

(They all watch carefully. TWO *stares at his watch, waiting for the second hand to reach sixty. Then, as it does, he stamps his foot loudly.* EIGHT *begins to get up. Slowly he swings his legs over the edges of the chairs, reaches for imaginary canes, and struggles to his feet.* TWO *stares at the watch.* EIGHT *walks as a crippled old man would walk, toward the chair which is serving as the bedroom door. He gets to it and pretends to open it.)*

TEN *(shouting).* Speed it up. He walked twice as fast as that.

(EIGHT, *not having stopped for this outburst, begins to walk the simulated*[4] *forty-foot hallway.)*

4. simulated (sim′yə lāt əd), *adj.* fake; pretend.

MINI-LESSON: LITERARY FOCUS

Stage Directions

Teach While the lines in a play tell *what* each character says, the stage directions tell *how* they deliver their lines and describe what actions accompany this delivery. When delivering lines, it is important to visualize the action described by the stage directions. Ask students to visualize how an elderly man with a cane would get up from a sitting position.

Activity Idea Have students act out the confrontation between Three and Eight that begins at the bottom of column one on page 245. Remind them to use appropriate gestures and tones. You might ask them to "freeze" at certain points, having volunteers offer words that describe their feelings or suggest other ways the lines could be interpreted.

ELEVEN. This is, I think, even more quickly than the old man walked in the courtroom.

EIGHT. If you think I should go faster, I will.

(He speeds up his pace slightly. He reaches the door and turns now, heading back, hobbling as an old man would hobble, bent over his imaginary canes. They watch him tensely. He hobbles back to the chair, which also serves as the front door. He stops there and pretends to unlock the door. Then he pretends to push it open.)

EIGHT *(loud).* Stop.

TWO. Right.

13 **EIGHT.** What's the time?

TWO. Fifteen . . . twenty . . . thirty . . . thirty-one seconds exactly.

ELEVEN. Thirty-one seconds.

(Some of the JURORS *adlib*[5] *their surprise to each other.)*

EIGHT. It's my guess that the old man was trying to get to the door, heard someone racing down the stairs, and assumed that it was the boy.

SIX. I think that's possible.

THREE *(infuriated).* Assumed? Now, listen to me, you people. I've seen all kinds of dishonesty in my day . . . but this little display takes the cake. (*To* FOUR.) Tell him, will you?

(FOUR *sits silently.* THREE *looks at him and then he strides over to* EIGHT.)

THREE. You come in here with your heart bleeding all over the floor about slum kids and injustice and you make up these wild stories, and you've got some soft-hearted old ladies listening to you. Well I'm not. I'm getting real sick of it. *(To all).* What's the matter with you people? This kid is guilty! He's got to burn! We're letting him slip through our fingers here. 14

EIGHT *(calmly).* Our fingers. Are you his executioner?

THREE *(raging).* I'm one of 'em.

EIGHT. Perhaps you'd like to pull the switch.

THREE *(shouting).* For this kid? You bet I'd like to pull the switch!

EIGHT. I'm sorry for you.

THREE *(shouting).* Don't start with me.

EIGHT. What it must feel like to want to pull the switch!

THREE. Shut up!

EIGHT. You're a sadist.[6]

THREE *(louder).* Shut up!

EIGHT *(strong).* You want to see this boy die because you personally want it—not because of the facts.

THREE *(shouting).* Shut up!

(He lunges at EIGHT, *but is caught by two of the* JURORS *and held. He struggles as* EIGHT *watches calmly.)*

THREE *(screaming).* Let me go! I'll kill him. I'll kill him! 15

EIGHT *(softly).* You don't really mean you'll kill me, do you?

(THREE *stops struggling now and stares at* EIGHT. *All the* JURORS *watch in silence as we fade out.)*

---

5. adlib (ad lib′), *v.* make up words or music as one goes along; improvise.
6. sadist (sā′dist, sad′ist), *n.* person displaying cruel tendencies.

13 Reading/Thinking Skills
Understand Sequence

Question Why is the sequence of numbers in Two's line important? *(Possible response: At first, when he reads the number fifteen, it sounds as though the prosecution has been vindicated; but as he adds numbers, it becomes clear the witness could not have been at the stairs at the time he claimed to be.)*

14 Multicultural Note
Slang

Point out that "to burn" is slang for "to be electrocuted in the electric chair." Have students find other examples of Three's use of slang, which establishes his cultural background.

15 Literary Element
Irony

Question Why is this exchange ironic? *(It proves, even to Three, that the words "I'll kill him" may be screamed at someone without a real intention to murder, which Three denied on page 242.)*

Check Test

1. Which jurors change their votes? *(Nine, Five)*
2. Why couldn't the old man have heard the boy shout? *(because of the noise from the passing elevated train)*
3. What exhibit does Eight ask for? *(the room diagram)*
4. Why couldn't the old man have seen the boy running down the stairs fifteen seconds after the murder? *(He couldn't have reached the stairs that quickly.)*
5. What small item does Eight accept from Two? *(a cough drop)*

Unit 2 Resource Book
Alternate Check Test, p. 29

BUILDING ENGLISH PROFICIENCY

Evaluating Details

On page 244, Juror Eleven says, "Perhaps if we could see it . . . This is an important point." Help students realize the importance of acting out the witness's testimony.

1. Have students carefully read and then set up the scene.
2. Invite two or three volunteers to enact the testimony. Suggest that they demonstrate both a 15-second and a 31-second walk.
3. Ask: How important do you think this demonstration will be? Encourage them to share the reasons for their opinion.

After Reading

MAKING CONNECTIONS

1. Ask if any students have changed their vote since the end of act 1.

2. Students may predict Two, Six, and Eleven, all of whom took an interest in the simulation. They should quote lines from the play that substantiate these jurors' changing opinions.

3. Possible responses: the simulation; the final interchange between Eight and Three

4. There are nine guilty votes first. The pause before the Foreman reads the tenth ballot also heightens the suspense.

5. They are based on Nine's personal account of having experienced something similar.

6. There are two ironies: Eleven is not a native speaker of English; Ten is demonstrating his own ignorance as he rants about the defendant's ignorance.

7. Six and Eleven seem convinced; Four is reconsidering; some unidentified jurors are surprised; Two's reaction is not clear. Three is infuriated.

8. Students should support their answers with reasons. Students might want to present opposing views in a debate.

Writer's Notebook Update

Encourage students to include supporting criteria.

VOCABULARY STUDY

1. c **2.** b **3.** a **4.** d **5.** b

Unit 2 Resource Book
Vocabulary, p. 27
Vocabulary Test, p. 30

Selection Test

Unit 2 Resource Book
pp. 31–32

Act 2

After Reading

Making Connections

Shaping Your Response

1. If you were one of the jurors, what would your vote be at the end of this act? Cast your vote with your classmates, showing thumbs up for *guilty* or thumbs down for *not guilty.*
2. Predict who the next juror will be to change his vote. Be prepared to give reasons for this prediction.
3. What do you think are the most important scenes in act 2? Why?

Analyzing the Play

4. How does the playwright create **suspense** as the foreman reads the count at the beginning of act 2?
5. Reread Nine's comments about why the old man may have lied. Are the comments based on fact or on Nine's feelings? Explain.
6. What is **ironic** about Eleven correcting Ten's grammar when he says, "He don't even speak good English!"?
7. What effect does Eight's timed experiment have on the other jurors?

Extending the Ideas

8. Explain whether or not you think that the death penalty should be a sentencing option in a civilized society.

Vocabulary Study

Use your Glossary, if necessary, to answer the following items.

adlib
insignificant
sadist
sheepishly
simulated

1. Three looks around *sheepishly,* which indicates he is ____.
   a. angry **b.** thrifty **c.** embarrassed **d.** energetic
2. *Simulated* means ____.
   a. encouraged **b.** pretend **c.** transmitted **d.** activated
3. Actors who *adlib* lines ____ the words.
   a. make up **b.** enunciate **c.** rehearse **d.** sing
4. Three is called a *sadist* because he is ____.
   a. unhappy **b.** grumpy **c.** vocal **d.** cruel
5. The woman remembers the most *insignificant,* or ____, details.
   a. visual **b.** unimportant **c.** memorable **d.** symbolic

Expressing Your Ideas

Writer's Notebook Update In your notebook, explain whether you think it's good or bad that jurors sometimes change their minds after deliberating.

ACT THREE

Fade in on same scene. No time lapse. THREE *glares angrily at* EIGHT. *He is still held by two* JURORS. *After a long pause, he shakes himself loose and turns away. He walks to the windows. The other* JURORS *stand around the room now, shocked by this display of anger. There is silence. Then the door opens and the* GUARD *enters. He looks around the room.*

GUARD. Is there anything wrong, gentlemen? I heard some noise.

FOREMAN. No. There's nothing wrong. *(He points to the large diagram[1] of the apartment.)* You can take that back. We're finished with it.

(The GUARD *nods and takes the diagram. He looks curiously at some of the* JURORS *and exits. The* JURORS *still are silent. Some of them slowly begin to sit down.* THREE *still stands at the window. He turns around now. The* JURORS *look at him.)*

THREE *(loud).* Well, what are you looking at? 1

(They turn away. He goes back to his seat now. Silently the rest of the JURORS *take their seats.* TWELVE

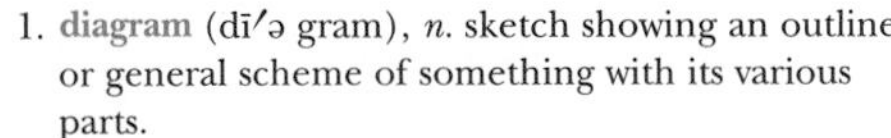

1. diagram (dī′ə gram), *n.* sketch showing an outline or general scheme of something with its various parts.

SELECTION SUMMARY

Twelve Angry Men, Act 3

Jurors take another vote. Six jurors vote for acquittal. Juror Three demonstrates how the boy would have knifed his father, but Five shows the "proper" way to knife someone, using an upward thrust. Seven changes his vote, not out of conviction, but so he can leave sooner. Eight calls for another vote, and all the jurors except Three, Four, and Ten vote for acquittal. After Ten alienates everyone with a speech that displays his bigotry, the jury considers the woman's testimony that she saw the boy commit the murder. Eight notes that she wore glasses but wouldn't have had them on as she tried to sleep, and therefore couldn't have clearly seen the boy. Ten and Four are convinced, and the jury stands 11 to 1 in favor of acquittal. Finally Three capitulates, and the jury votes 12-0 in favor of acquittal.

For summaries in other languages, see the ***Building English Proficiency*** *book.*

During Reading

Art Study

Visual Literacy Discuss the composition of the picture, pointing out that one juror is facing forward, against all the other jurors.

Questions

- Which juror is the focus of attention here? *(Three)*
- How might the positioning of the jurors indicate a general viewpoint? *(Three stands alone.)*

Vocabulary Preview

acquittal, discharge; release
aloft, in the air
bifocals, pair of glasses having two focuses
contort, twist or bend out of shape
despise, feel hatred or scorn for
diagram, sketch showing an outline or general scheme of something with its various parts
intimidate, influence or force by fear
recount, tell in detail
unshakable, undisturbed; not able to be upset

Students can add the words and definitions to their Writer's Notebooks.

1 Reading/Thinking Skills
Draw Conclusions

Question Identify the emotion that Three feels as he says this line. *(Possible responses: anger, frustration, embarrassment)*

Unit 2 Resource Book
Graphic Organizer, p. 33
Study Guide, p. 34

2 Reading/Thinking Skills
Make Judgments

Question Which juror(s) would you say are taking this case personally? Explain your answer. *(Answers will vary. Three has shown the connection between his feelings about his own son and his feeling about the defendant, has attacked Eight verbally, and has taken out his anger on Eight by coming close to assaulting him.)*

3 Reader's Response
Challenging the Text

Expand on this point by asking the following:

- Do you think a hung jury verdict would be an appropriate conclusion for this piece of literature? Why or why not? *(Possible response: No, because it would mean that prejudice, hatred, and bigotry had triumphed over reason and justice.)*
- Why do you think Three makes this proposal? *(Possible response: to save face—he couldn't stand to take in a "not guilty" verdict)*

begins to doodle. TEN *blows his nose, but no one speaks. Then, finally—)*

FOUR. I don't see why we have to behave like children here.

ELEVEN. Nor do I. We have a responsibility. This is a remarkable thing about democracy. That we are . . . what is the word? . . . Ah, notified! That we are notified by mail to come down to this place and decide on the guilt or innocence of a man we have not known before. We have nothing to gain or lose by our verdict. This is one of the reasons why we are strong. We should not make it a personal
2 thing.

(There is a long, awkward pause.)

TWELVE. Well—we're still nowhere. Who's got an idea?

SIX. I think maybe we should try another vote. Mr. Foreman?

FOREMAN. It's all right with me. Anybody doesn't want to vote? *(He looks around the table.)*

SEVEN. All right, let's do it.

THREE. I want an open ballot. Let's call out our votes. I want to know who stands where.

FOREMAN. That sounds fair. Anyone object? *(No one does.)* All right. I'll call off your jury numbers.

(He takes a pencil and paper and makes marks now in one of two columns after each vote.)

FOREMAN. I vote guilty. Number Two?

TWO. Not guilty.

FOREMAN. Number Three?

THREE. Guilty.

FOREMAN. Number Four?

FOUR. Guilty.

FOREMAN. Number Five?

FIVE. Not guilty.

FOREMAN. Number Six?

SIX. Not guilty.

FOREMAN. Number Seven?

SEVEN. Guilty.

FOREMAN. Number Eight?

EIGHT. Not guilty.

FOREMAN. Number Nine?

NINE. Not guilty.

FOREMAN. Number Ten?

TEN. Guilty.

FOREMAN. Number Eleven?

ELEVEN. Not guilty.

FOREMAN. Number Twelve?

TWELVE. Guilty.

FOUR. Six to six.

TEN *(mad).* I'll tell you something. The crime is being committed right in this room.

FOREMAN. The vote is six to six.

THREE. I'm ready to walk into court right now and declare a hung jury. There's no point in 3
this going on anymore.

SEVEN. I go for that, too. Let's take it in to the judge and let the kid take his chances with twelve other guys.

FIVE (*to* SEVEN). You mean you still don't think there's room for reasonable doubt?

SEVEN. No, I don't.

ELEVEN. I beg your pardon. Maybe you don't understand the term "reasonable doubt."

SEVEN *(angry).* What do you mean I don't understand it? Who do you think you are to talk to me like that? *(To all.)* How do you like this guy? He comes over here running for his life, and before he can even take a big breath he's telling us how to run the show. The arrogance of him!

FIVE (*to* SEVEN). Wait a second. Nobody around here's asking where you came from.

SEVEN. I was born right here.

FIVE. Or where your father came from. . . . *(He looks at* SEVEN, *who doesn't answer but looks away.)* Maybe it wouldn't hurt us to take a few tips from people who come running here! Maybe they learned something we don't know. We're not so perfect!

ELEVEN. Please—I am used to this. It's all right. Thank you.

FIVE. It's not all right!

SEVEN. Okay, okay, I apologize. Is that what you want?

FIVE. That's what I want.

FOREMAN. All right. Let's stop the arguing. Who's got something constructive to say?

MINI-LESSON: USAGE
Ellipses

Teach Hesitations are a normal part of conversation. One kind of punctuation that is used to indicate a pause is an ellipses (. . .). When Eleven speaks at the top of page 248, he pauses to find the right word. "That we are . . . What is the word? . . . Ah, notified!" Recall for students that Eleven is an immigrant and his pauses help give a realistic picture of coping with a new language. Ellipses are also used to indicate that words, sentences, or paragraphs have been omitted. (The President said, "We cannot lower taxes . . . without considering the consequences.")

Activity Idea Ask students to find examples of ellipses in newspapers or magazines. Have them bring in what they find and explain to the class why ellipses were used in each case.

TWO *(hesitantly).* Well, something's been bothering me a little . . . this whole business about the stab wound and how it was made, the downward angle of it, you know?

THREE. Don't tell me we're gonna start that. They went over it and over it in court.

TWO. I know they did—but I don't go along with it. The boy is five feet eight inches tall. His father was six two. That's a difference of six inches. It's a very awkward thing to stab *down* into the chest of someone who's half a foot taller than you are.

(THREE *jumps up, holding the knife.)*

THREE. Look, you're not going to be satisfied till you see it again. I'm going to give you a demonstration. Somebody get up.

(He looks around the table. EIGHT *stands up and walks toward him.* THREE *closes the knife and puts it in his pocket. They stand face to face and look at each other for a moment.)*

THREE. Okay. (*To* TWO.) Now watch this. I don't want to have to do it again. (*He crouches down now until he is quite a bit shorter than* EIGHT.) Is that six inches?

TWELVE. That's more than six inches.

4 **THREE.** Okay, let it be more.

(He reaches into his pocket and takes out the knife. He flicks it open, changes its position in his hand, and holds the knife aloft,[2] *ready to stab. He and* EIGHT *look steadily into each other's eyes. Then he stabs downward, hard.)*

TWO *(shouting).* Look out!

(He stops short just as the blade reaches EIGHT*'s chest.* THREE *laughs.)*

SIX. That's not funny.

FIVE. What's the matter with you?

THREE. Now just calm down. Nobody's hurt, are they?

EIGHT *(low).* No. Nobody's hurt.

THREE. All right. There's your angle. Take a look at it. Down and in. That's how I'd stab a taller man in the chest, and that's how it was done. Take a look at it and tell me I'm wrong.

(TWO *doesn't answer.* THREE *looks at him for a moment, then jams the knife into the table, and sits down. They all look at the knife.)*

SIX. Down and in. I guess there's no argument.

(EIGHT *picks the knife out of the table and closes it. He flicks it open and, changing its position in his hand, stabs downward with it.)*

EIGHT (*to* SIX). Did you ever stab a man?

SIX. Of course not.

EIGHT (*to* THREE). Did you?

THREE. All right, let's not be silly.

EIGHT. Did you?

THREE *(loud).* No, I didn't!

EIGHT. Where do you get all your information about how it's done?

THREE. What do you mean? It's just common sense.

EIGHT. Have you ever seen a man stabbed?

THREE *(pauses and looks around the room nervously).* No.

EIGHT. All right. I want to ask you something. The boy was an experienced knife fighter. He was even sent to reform school for knifing someone, isn't that so?

TWELVE. That's right.

EIGHT. Look at this. (EIGHT *closes the knife, flicks it open, and changes the position of the knife so that he can stab overhanded.*) Doesn't it seem like an awkward way to handle a knife?

THREE. What are you asking me for?

(EIGHT *closes the blade and flicks it open, holds it ready to slash underhanded.)*

FIVE. Wait a minute! What's the matter with me? Give me that. *(He reaches out for the knife.)*

EIGHT. Have you ever seen a knife fight?

FIVE. Yes, I have.

EIGHT. In the movies?

FIVE. In my backyard. On my stoop. In the vacant lot across the street. Too many of them. Switch-knives came with the neighborhood where I lived. Funny I didn't think of it before. I guess you try to forget those things. *(Flicking the knife open.)* Anyone who's ever used a switch-knife would never have 5

---

2. aloft (ə lôft′), *adj.* in the air.

4 Reading/Thinking Skills
Visualize

Question What is the impact of this encounter? *(Possible response: Three acts out the hostility he has been directing toward Eight with words. His potential for physical violence and Eight's bravery are clearly revealed.)*

5 Literary Element
Characterization

Have students recall the description of Five on page 229 as someone "who finds it difficult to speak up."

Question What gives him the courage to speak up here? *(Possible response: his firsthand experience viewing knife fights)*

BUILDING ENGLISH PROFICIENCY

Exploring a Main Idea

At the end of page 249, a surprising piece of information comes from mild-mannered Five. Help students realize that Five is using knowledge from his personal life to clarify a point.

1. Have students state Five's objection to the way the knife was used.

2. Ask: Why is Juror Five so sure of his information? Introduce the idiom *street savvy* or *street smarts,* explaining that the phrase refers to knowledge gained through everyday experience rather than from formal education.

3. Invite students to share examples of *street smarts* from movies, TV, reading, or personal experience.

6 Reading/Thinking Skills
Connect

Question How have the Foreman's vote summaries changed as the vote changed? Students might reflect these changes on a chart in their notebooks. *(Responses: Eleven to one, guilty. p. 231; nine to three, guilty. p. 242; six to six. p. 248; nine to three in favor of acquittal. p. 250)*

7 Literary Focus
Stage Directions

Question How would you explain the actions mentioned in the stage directions? *(Possible response: The other jurors are disgusted by Ten's bigotry.)*

stabbed downward. You don't handle a switch-knife that way. You use it underhanded.

EIGHT. Then he couldn't have made the kind of wound which killed his father.

FIVE. No. He couldn't have. Not if he'd ever had any experience with switch-knives.

THREE. I don't believe it.

TEN. Neither do I. You're giving us a lot of mumbo jumbo.

EIGHT (*to* TWELVE). What do you think?

TWELVE *(hesitantly).* Well . . . I don't know.

EIGHT (*to* SEVEN). What about you?

SEVEN. Listen, I'll tell you something. I'm a little sick of this whole thing already. We're getting nowhere fast. Let's break it up and go home. I'm changing my vote to not guilty.

THREE. You're what?

SEVEN. You heard me. I've had enough.

THREE. What do you mean, you've had enough? That's no answer.

ELEVEN *(angry).* I think perhaps you're right. This is not an answer. (*To* SEVEN.) What kind of a man are you? You have sat here and voted guilty with everyone else because there are some theater tickets burning a hole in your pocket. Now you have changed your vote for the same reason. I do not think you have the right to play like this with a man's life. This is an ugly and terrible thing to do.

SEVEN. Now wait a minute . . . you can't talk like that to me.

ELEVEN *(strong).* I can talk like that to you! If you want to vote not guilty, then do it because you are convinced the man is not guilty. If you believe he is guilty, then vote that way. Or don't you have the . . . the . . . guts—the guts to do what you think is right?

SEVEN. Now listen . . .

ELEVEN. Is it guilty or not guilty?

SEVEN *(hesitantly).* I told you. Not . . . guilty.

ELEVEN *(hard).* Why?

SEVEN. I don't have to—

ELEVEN. You have to! Say it! Why?

(They stare at each other for a long while.)

SEVEN *(low).* I . . . don't think . . . he's guilty.

EIGHT *(fast).* I want another vote.

FOREMAN. Okay, there's another vote called for. I guess the quickest way is a show of hands. Anybody object? *(No one does.)* All right. All those voting not guilty, raise your hands.

(TWO, FIVE, SIX, SEVEN, EIGHT, NINE, *and* ELEVEN *raise their hands immediately. Then, slowly,* TWELVE *raises his hand. The* FOREMAN *looks around the table carefully and then he too raises his hand. He looks around the table, counting silently.*)

FOREMAN. Nine. *(The hands go down.)* All those voting guilty.

(THREE, FOUR, *and* TEN *raise their hands.*)

FOREMAN. Three. *(They lower their hands.)* The vote is nine to three in favor of acquittal.[3] 6

TEN. I don't understand you people. How can you believe this kid is innocent? Look, you know how those people lie. I don't have to tell you. They don't know what the truth is. And lemme tell you, they—(FIVE *gets up from table, turns his back to it, and goes to window.*)—don't need any real big reason to kill someone either. You know, they get drunk, and *bang,* someone's lying in the gutter. Nobody's blaming them. That's how they are. You know what I mean? Violent! (NINE *gets up and does the same. He is followed by* ELEVEN.)

TEN. Human life don't mean as much to them as it does to us. Hey, where are you going? Look, these people are drinking and fighting all the time, and if somebody gets killed, 7 so somebody gets killed. They don't care. Oh, sure, there are some good things about them, too. Look, I'm the first to say that. (EIGHT *gets up, and then* TWO *and* SIX *follow him to the window.*)

TEN. I've known a few who were pretty decent, but that's the exception. Most of them, it's like they have no feelings. They can do anything. What's going on here?

(*The* FOREMAN *gets up and goes to the window, followed by* SEVEN *and* TWELVE.)

3. acquittal (ə kwit′l), *n.* discharge; release.

MINI-LESSON: VOCABULARY
Slang

Teach Slang is another technique writers use to distinguish characters. Point out Eleven's uses of slang in the first column on page 250:

- You have sat here and voted guilty with everyone else because there are some theater tickets *burning a hole in your pocket* (that you're impatient to use).
- Or don't you have **. . .** *the guts* to do what you think is right? (the courage)

You may also wish to have students look back on page 245 where Three says of the defendant, "He's got to *burn!"* (be executed in the electric chair)

Activity Idea Have students record other examples of slang that characterize the jurors, using a chart like this one.

Slang expression	Meaning	What it says about the juror

TEN. I'm speaking my piece, and you—Listen to me! They're no good. There's not a one of 'em who's any good. We better watch out. Take it from me. This kid on trial . . .

8 (THREE *sits at table toying with the knife and* FOUR *gets up and starts for the window. All have their backs to* TEN.)

TEN. Well, don't you know about them? Listen to me! What are you doing? I'm trying to tell you something . . . .

(FOUR *stands over him as he trails off. There is a dead silence. Then* FOUR *speaks softly.*)

FOUR. I've had enough. If you open your mouth again, I'm going to split your skull. (FOUR *stands there and looks at him. No one moves or speaks.* TEN *looks at him, then looks down at the table.*)

TEN *(softly).* I'm only trying to tell you. . . .

(*There is a long pause as* FOUR *stares down at* TEN.)

FOUR *(to all).* All right. Sit down, everybody.

(They all move back to their seats. When they are all seated, FOUR *then sits down.)*

FOUR *(quietly).* I still believe the boy is guilty of murder. I'll tell you why. To me, the most damning evidence was given by the woman across the street who claimed she

Art Study

Encourage students to study the facial expressions in this photograph. Discuss the jurors' emotions.

- Who is calm? *(Eight)*
- Who is angry? *(Three)*
- Who is shocked? *(most of the other jurors)*

8 Multicultural Note

Revealing Bias

Ten never reveals who "those people" and "they" are, but they are clearly a social group and class that he looks down upon.

Question Do you think Ten's feelings are caused by fear, a sense of superiority, or something else? Explain. *(There will be a variety of responses. But students should recognize from textual clues that this is an angry, insecure man.)*

BUILDING ENGLISH PROFICIENCY

Analyzing a Key Passage

With the word "I don't understand you people," Ten begins a monologue that helps drive the play to its climax. Examine this passage with students.

1. Have students brainstorm possible groups Ten may be referring to as *them* and *us.* Have them consider factors such as age, race, class, and religion. Ask if perhaps Ten himself is unsure which groups he means by *them* and *us.*

2. Point out that Ten's monologue is interrupted by stage directions. Have students tell what happens at each interruption.

3. Invite students to suggest reasons why the other jurors have moved away from Ten by the end of his speech.

9 Reader's Response
Challenging the Text

Question What if Six had said instead, "The woman who testified couldn't possibly have seen the boy stab his father," rather than build up to his statement with questions? *(Possible response: The buildup adds suspense and drama. His observation is a step-by-step rethinking of the testimony. This seems in keeping with the description of his character on page 229 as "a man who comes upon his decisions slowly and carefully.")*

actually saw the murder committed.

THREE. That's right. As far as I'm concerned, that's the most important testimony.

EIGHT. All right. Let's go over her testimony. What exactly did she say?

FOUR. I believe I can recount[4] it accurately. She said that she went to bed at about eleven o'clock that night. Her bed was next to the open window, and she could look out of the window while lying down and see directly into the window across the street. She tossed and turned for over an hour, unable to fall asleep. Finally she turned toward the window at about twelve-ten and, as she looked out, she saw the boy stab his father. As far as I can see, this is unshakable[5] testimony.

THREE. That's what I mean. That's the whole case.

(FOUR *takes off his eyeglasses and begins to polish them, as they all sit silently watching him.*)

FOUR (*to the* JURY). Frankly, I don't see how you can vote for acquittal. (*To* TWELVE.) What do you think about it?

TWELVE. Well . . . maybe . . . there's so much evidence to sift.

THREE. What do you mean, maybe? He's absolutely right. You can throw out all the other evidence.

FOUR. That was my feeling. (TWO, *polishing his glasses, squints at clock, can't see it.* SIX *watches him closely.*)

TWO. What time is it?

ELEVEN. Ten minutes of six.

TWO. It's late. You don't suppose they'd let us go home and finish it in the morning. I've got a kid with mumps.

FIVE. Not a chance.

SIX (*to* TWO). Pardon me. Can't you see the clock without your glasses?

TWO. Not clearly. Why?

9 **SIX.** Oh, I don't know. Look, this may be a dumb thought, but what do you do when you wake up at night and want to know what time it is?

TWO. What do you mean? I put on my glasses and look at the clock.

SIX. You don't wear them to bed.

TWO. Of course not. No one wears eyeglasses to bed.

TWELVE. What's all this for?

SIX. Well, I was thinking. You know the woman who testified that she saw the killing wears glasses.

THREE. So does my grandmother. So what?

EIGHT. Your grandmother isn't a murder witness.

SIX. Look, stop me if I'm wrong. This woman wouldn't wear her eyeglasses to bed, would she?

FOREMAN. Wait a minute! Did she wear glasses at all? I don't remember.

ELEVEN (*excited*). Of course she did. The woman wore bifocals.[6] I remember this very clearly. They looked quite strong.

NINE. That's right. Bifocals. She never took them off.

FOUR. She did wear glasses. Funny. I never thought of it.

EIGHT. Listen, she wasn't wearing them in bed. That's for sure. She testified that in the midst of her tossing and turning she rolled over and looked casually out the window. The murder was taking place as she looked out, and the lights went out a split second later. She couldn't have had time to put on her glasses. Now maybe she honestly thought she saw the boy kill his father. I say that she saw only a blur.

THREE. How do you know what she saw? Maybe she's farsighted. (*He looks around. No one answers.*)

THREE (*loud*). How does he know all these things? (*There is silence.*)

EIGHT. Does anyone think there still is not a reasonable doubt?

---

4. recount (ri kount′), *v.* tell in detail.
5. unshakable (un shā′kə bl), *adj.* undisturbed; not able to be upset.
6. bifocals (bī fō′kəlz), *n.* pair of glasses having two focuses.

(He looks around the room, then squarely at TEN. TEN *looks down and shakes his head no.)*

THREE *(loud).* I think he's guilty.

EIGHT *(calmly).* Does anyone else?

FOUR *(quietly).* No. I'm convinced.

EIGHT *(to* THREE*).* You're alone.

THREE. I don't care whether I'm alone or not! I have a right.

EIGHT. You have a right.

(There is a pause. They all look at THREE.*)*

THREE. Well, I told you I think the kid's guilty. What else do you want?

EIGHT. Your arguments. *(They all look at* THREE.*)*

THREE. I gave you my arguments.

EIGHT. We're not convinced. We're waiting to hear them again. We have time.

(THREE *runs to* FOUR *and grabs his arm.)*

10 **THREE** *(pleading).* Listen. What's the matter with you? You're the guy. You made all the arguments. You can't turn now. A guilty man's gonna be walking the streets. A murderer. He's got to die! Stay with me.

FOUR. I'm sorry. There's a reasonable doubt in my mind.

EIGHT. We're waiting.

(THREE *turns violently on him.)*

THREE *(shouting).* Well, you're not going to intimidate[7] me! *(They all look at* THREE.*)* I'm entitled to my opinion! *(No one answers him.)* It's gonna be a hung jury! That's it!

EIGHT. There's nothing we can do about that, except hope that some night, maybe in a few months, you'll get some sleep.

FIVE. You're all alone.

NINE. It takes a great deal of courage to stand alone.

(THREE *looks around at all of them for a long time. They sit silently, waiting for him to speak, and all of them despise[8] him for his stubbornness. Then, suddenly, his face contorts[9] as if he is about to cry, and he slams his fist down on the table.)*

THREE *(thundering).* All right!

(THREE *turns his back on them. There is silence for a moment and then the* FOREMAN *goes to the door and knocks on it. It opens. The* GUARD *looks in and sees them all standing. The* GUARD *holds the door for them as they begin slowly to file out.* EIGHT *waits at the door as the others file past him. Finally he and* THREE *are the only ones left.* THREE *turns around and sees that they are alone. Slowly he moves toward the door. Then he stops at the table. He pulls the switch-knife out of the table and walks over to* EIGHT *with it. He holds it in the approved knife-fighter fashion and looks long and hard at* EIGHT, *pointing the knife at his belly.* EIGHT *stares back. Then* THREE *turns the knife around.* EIGHT *takes it by the handle.* THREE *exits.* EIGHT *closes the knife, puts it away, and, taking a last look around the room, exits, closing the door. The camera moves in close on the littered table in the empty room, and we clearly see a slip of crumpled paper on* 11 *which are scribbled the words "Not guilty.")*

(Fade out.)

---

7. **intimidate** (in tim′ə dāt), *v.* influence or force by fear.
8. **despise** (di spīz′) *v.,* feel hatred or scorn for.
9. **contort** (kən tôrt′), *v.* twist or bend out of shape.

10 Reading/Thinking Skills
Draw Conclusions

Question What does Three mean when he says to Four, "You're the guy"? *(Response: He means that Four was the most convincing spokesman among the jurors for the case that the defendant was guilty.)*

11 Reading/Thinking Skills
Make Judgments

Question Why do you think Three changes his vote? *(Response: Some students may think he is bowing to peer pressure. Others may think he now has a "reasonable doubt.")*

Check Test

1. Why does the guard enter the jury room unexpectedly? *(He wants to see what the noise is about.)*
2. Why does Four change his vote? *(He accepts Eight's reasoning that the woman did not have her glasses on in bed.)*
3. How was Five's background useful to the jury's deliberations? *(His knowledge of switch-knife fighting was a key point.)*
4. What do the other jurors do when Ten makes his bigoted speech? *(They turn their backs on him.)*
5. Who is the last juror to change his vote? *(Three)*

Unit 2 Resource Book
Alternate Check Test, p. 37

BUILDING ENGLISH PROFICIENCY

Relating Key Statements

Write the final dialogue of the play on the board: "It takes a great deal of courage to stand alone." Work to connect these words to the play's theme.

1. Ask students to whom Juror Nine is referring in the last line. *(Three)*

2. Have them recall when Nine said these words before, or direct them to page 240. To whom did these words apply at that time? *(Eight)*

3. Ask students if they think that Juror Three is courageous or cowardly for finally agreeing with the others. Make sure they provide support for their opinion.

After Reading

MAKING CONNECTIONS

1. Casting will vary. Students should support their choices with actors who seem suited to specific characters.

2. Questions should be points unanswered by the text.

3. Most students will be convinced by the arguments and simulations and vote *not guilty.*

4. Eleven has a lot at stake in the rights and privileges accorded American citizens, and he does not want to see the American ideals debased.

5. They are disgusted by his blatant bigotry.

6. The jurors realize that it is unlikely that she was wearing her glasses when she reportedly saw the murder.

7. Possible responses: justice vs. prejudice, bigotry, hatred, indifference; Eight vs.Three.

8. Since this is the last barrier to the conflict being resolved, most students will agree that it is the climax.

9. Possible responses: The title emphasizes the emotions involved in what people might think should be a process that relies on reason. Title suggestions should relate to the play and its issues.

10. Most students will think that the conflict resides more in prejudice and personality than in cultural upbringing,but these factors can be related.

11. Possible responses: Blood-spattering tests; DNA testing; fiber testing; etc.

12. The label could apply to any of these groups, and it is probably intended to be purposely vague. Labels dehumanize people by taking away individuality and respect.

Act 3

After Reading

Making Connections

Shaping Your Response

1. If you were casting a remake of the movie version of this play, who would play the jurors? Be prepared to explain your casting choices.

2. In your notebook, write three questions you still have about the facts of the case.

3. If you were a member of the jury, how would you vote at the end of the play? Why?

Analyzing the Play

4. Why do you think Eleven questions Seven so closely after he changes his vote?

5. Explain the behavior of the other jurors when Ten begins to rant and rave about the way "those people" (meaning people like the accused) behave.

6. How is the evidence provided by the woman from beyond the el tracks cast into doubt?

7. What is the main **conflict** of the play?

8. At the end of the play, Five tells Three that he's all alone. Do you consider this the **climax** of the play? Explain.

9. Why do you think these men are referred to as *angry* in the **title**? Can you suggest a better title for the play?

Extending the Ideas

10. Do you think the jurors have difficulty arriving at a consensus because of their differing cultural backgrounds or because of other factors? Explain.

11. If the murder described in *Twelve Angry Men* occurred today, what modern ways of detecting and examining the evidence might be used to prove the guilt or innocence of the boy?

12. Do you think "those people," a label used to describe the accused and people like him, refers to an ethnic, social, or economic group? Why? Explain how labels like this can affect **interactions**.

Literary Focus: Stage Directions

Through his **stage directions** Reginald Rose provides information about the characters and their surroundings. Reread the stage directions on page 230, that begin "And now, slowly, almost hesitantly, . . ."

- What do you learn about the setting?
- What mood do the stage directions relay?
- What can you infer about the characters at this point?

LITERARY FOCUS: STAGE DIRECTIONS

Explain that students are being asked to think about the stage directions on page 230. They may have a difficult time blocking out what they have learned about the setting, mood, and characters in the rest of the play following page 230. Encourage them to reread the passage, and ask them to refer to only to directions on page 230 as they draw their conclusions.

Vocabulary Study

acquittal
aloft
bifocals
contort
despise
diagram
intimidate
recount
unshakable

Use the table of prefixes below to make a word association cluster for two of the vocabulary words in the list. An example cluster for *bifocals* is shown.

Prefix	Meaning	Prefix	Meaning
a-	in, on, to	dia-	through
ac-	to, toward	un-	not
bi-	having two	in-	in, into
con-	with	re-	back
de-	from		

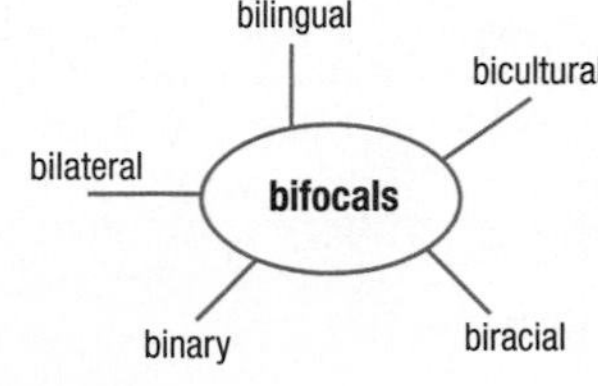

Expressing Your Ideas

Writing Choices

Writer's Notebook Update By the end of the play, all jurors have voted *not guilty* because they have reasonable doubts about facts in the case. Look at the reasons for changing their votes that you listed in your notebook. Describe the evidence and arguments you think were most influential in swaying the jury.

Protect Your Client's Rights The jurors point out that the boy's defense attorney failed to raise pertinent questions during cross-examination of the witnesses. If you were the defense attorney, what would you have asked the old man and the woman based on their testimonies and on what you now know from the jury deliberations? Draw up at least eight **defense questions**.

Two Trials, Two Verdicts Consider who is on trial in *Antigone* and *Twelve Angry Men.* Do you think justice has been served in either play? Using these plays as examples, write an **opinion paper** discussing whether or not you think the jury system is the most effective way to determine guilt or innocence.

Other Options

Sounding Off Critics of the jury system have argued that the number of jurors should be fewer, that jurors should be required to have a certain level of education, or that all cases should be decided by judges alone. Prepare a **debate** on one of the issues raised above, with one group in favor and the other opposed. Gather evidence, present the debate to the class, and let classmates take sides with a show of hands after the debate is presented.

Your Fingerprints Are Showing Jury trials that take place today often present evidence such as DNA patterns and medical reports that rely on the latest technology. Do some **research** on modern methods of analyzing evidence. As a start, you might want to expand the information provided in the interview on page 260. Present your findings to the class.

VOCABULARY STUDY

Students will be able to find words easily in a dictionary. Encourage them to be careful to distinguish these prefixes from other prefixes that are spelled the same (*a*- meaning *not*, for example), as well as portions of root words (e.g., *debtor* begins with *de*, which is not a prefix in this word.)

Unit 2 Resource Book
Vocabulary, p. 35
Vocabulary Test, p. 38

WRITING CHOICES

Writer's Notebook Update

Students will probably focus on the two key witnesses, both of whose testimony is called into question.

Two Trials, Two Verdicts

Encourage students to consider how justice would be achieved without a jury system. Suggest that as they think about a system that uses a single judge, they consider Creon's judgments in *Antigone* as an example of justice in the hands of a single person.

Selection Test

Unit 2 Resource Book
pp. 39–40

Transparency Collection
Fine Art Writing Prompt 4

OTHER OPTIONS

Sounding Off

Before students begin the debate, have them do research to find out the rationale for:

- having twelve jurors
- choosing jurors from the general population without regard to education
- having a jury, not just a judge

They might also refer to the article on pages 256–259.

Your Fingerprints Are Showing

Students may want to consult the following sources as they research:

- court transcripts
- local police detectives
- media coverage of the O. J. Simpson trial dealing with these issues
- laboratories where these kinds of tests are performed
- the attorney general for their state
- criminal lawyers

Interdisciplinary Study

Theme Link

The history of how judgment has been rendered through history puts the concept of a trial into historical context.

Curricular Connection: History

You can use the information in this Interdisciplinary Study to explore with students the history of how a society made laws and judgments based on those laws.

Terms to Know

tribunal, a court of justice

magistrate, a government officer whose job is to administer and enforce the law

gladiator, a person who engages in mortal combat to entertain an audience

nullify, render invalid

Sabbath, Sunday

Unit 2 Resource Book
Study Guide, p. 41

INTERDISCIPLINARY STUDY

On Trial

Guilty or Innocent?

History Connection
Though it may be flawed, today's jury system is far superior to former methods used to determine guilt or innocence—trial by combat, and ordeal by fire, water, or poison.

W T H E

by Barbara Holland

. . . The laws are established, facts discovered, witnesses heard and judgment made. These functions have been separated in our fancier world, but in the early tribunals they were all one. The group called in to consider the matter was made up of witnesses; if no law already applied to the case, they made one that would; they talked it over and decided.

ROMAN GLADIATORS

They were all amateurs. Laws were so simple that ordinary folk could understand them. Now professionals have taken over the courts and, I hear, get well paid for it, but juries are still amateurs called in for the occasion, unattached to the system. The good thing about juries is that they're amateurs. The bad thing about juries is that they're amateurs.

Rome refined the system and separated the law from the facts. A magistrate defined the dispute, cited the law and referred the problem to a citizen judex—a fellow of some standing—who called in a few associates to help. They listened to the speeches, weighed the evidence and pronounced sentence. (Nobody was supervising them, so it helped if one of them was a lawyer, to explain.) This was more orderly than a tribunal. The Romans were passionately fond of order and wrote down all their laws in books.

They were also fond of a good public spectacle, and a convicted criminal could always opt for the arena and entertain the citizens by duking it out with other criminals or prisoners of war. A talented gladiator not only got to live, but he could wind up as a popular sports hero, surrounded by pretty ladies. The Romans loved a winner, regardless of his criminal record.

Meanwhile, the Scandinavians were gathering regularly in tribunals, called Things, dating back further than anyone remembered. Groups of delegates met to represent their districts, and committees of 12 or of multiples of 12 were picked to administer or invent the laws.

In 1976, Cecilia M. Pizzo filed suit in New Orleans to nullify the Louisiana Purchase, claiming that neither Napoleon nor Thomas Jefferson had the authority to make the deal.

In 1972, a Los Angeles judge sentenced a pickpocket to a jail term and ordered that he wear thick woolen mittens in public after he was released.

A Florida law banned unmarried women from parachuting on the Sabbath.

MINI-LESSON: STUDY SKILLS

Use the Dictionary

Teach Point out the countries and peoples named in this article. Explain that it is not always easy to figure out what to call a group of people based on their nationality. A dictionary is a good source to check—some list unusual nationality titles in usage notes.

Activity Idea Have students complete the chart at the right:

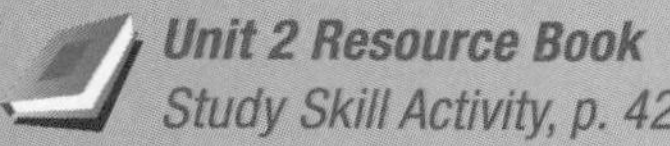

Unit 2 Resource Book
Study Skill Activity, p. 42

Place	People
Rome	
Scandinavia	
Wales	
Africa	
India	
Britain	
Asia	
Germany	
Sweden	

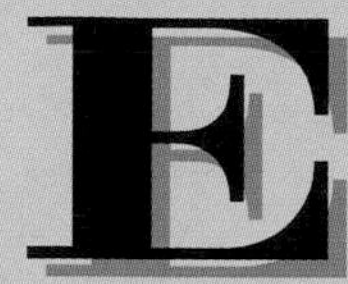

JURORS

Twelve is the solemn number. When Morgan of Glamorgan, Prince of Wales, established trial by jury in A.D. 725, he wrote, "For as Christ and his Twelve Apostles were finally to judge the world, so human tribunals should be composed of the king and twelve wise men." Maybe, though apparently Christ was following an older tradition. The number 12 crops up all over. The zodiac has 12 signs, based on 12 constellations; we divide our days into twice-12 hours, 12 midnight rings in the witching hour. . . .

After Rome fell apart, its former empire went all to sixes and sevens, and its orderly laws decayed into gibberish. In Britain, King Arthur had to set his possibly legendary knights out to ride around righting wrongs and rescuing maidens from sexual harassment, a far from comprehensive judicial system. There were still trials, though, with an ordeal serving as jury.

Great faith has been placed in trial by ordeal, all the way from the Old Testament to the Australian outback. The idea is that something out there "knows" who's guilty and will point to him if given a chance. The chance usually involves fire or water or poison.

Poison was recommended in the Bible and was popular in Africa and Brahmanic India for trials by ordeal. Those who survived at all, though likely to be ill, were considered innocent. The Saxons developed a variation called "corsnaed," a morsel of something that would choke the guilty (perhaps their throats were dry with apprehension). Godwin, Earl of Kent, is said to have choked on his.

Under Saxon law, if you could carry several pounds of glowing red-hot iron in your bare hands for nine steps or walk barefoot over nine red-hot plowshares without getting any blisters, you were not guilty. Similar proof was accepted in Hindu and Scandinavian law. In Britain, Africa and parts of Asia, plunging your arm into boiling water, oil or lead without the usual results proved your innocence.

Water was also knowledgeable stuff. The innocent sank; the guilty floated and could be fished out and dealt with. This was the customary method of identifying witches, who were cross-tied thumb-to-toe before being thrown in. True witches refused to drown and were dried off and burned at the stake. . . .

A WITCH-DUNKING

Folks back then were so primitive that they thought the victim, rather than the law, had been damaged, and bodily harm was redeemed at so much for a finger, so much for an ear, all the way up to murder, which, around the 800s, cost 200 shillings, payable to the deceased's family. (Among the Germans it was payable in sheep.) Thieves paid the value of the stolen object plus a fine; repeat offenders and those who stole from the church paid with a hand or a foot as well.

This would mean that if someone broke your arm while stealing your car, he paid for your arm and your car, and you got to keep

The city fathers of Barre, Vermont, once made it obligatory for everyone to take at least one bath a week—on Saturday night.

In 1978, an accountant named Tom Horsley sued a woman who failed to show up for a date for "breach of oral contract."

In Fairbanks, Alaska, it is illegal to feed alcohol to a moose.

Cats are banned from howling after 9:00 P.M. in Columbus, Georgia.

Additional Background

More familiar to Christ would have been the Old Testament references to the number 12, particularly the twelve tribes of Israel.

Terms to Know

sixes and sevens, in disorder

gibberish, nonsense

outback, remote, rural country

Brahmanic (brä man′ ik), having to do with the sacred power which Hindus believe sustains the universe

breach, violation of a legal obligation

apprehension, fearful anticipation

Hindu, a religion, philosophy, and culture practiced in India, among other places

BUILDING ENGLISH PROFICIENCY

Improving Comprehension

"We the Jurors" contains a great deal of factual detail. A jigsaw activity may help students better comprehend this article.

1. Divide students into groups of 3 to 5 students each.
2. Assign one of the following topics to each group.
   - Law in ancient Rome and Scandinavia
   - Trial by ordeal
   - The rise of the jury system
   - Present-day legal challenges
3. Ask each group to discuss its topic, using information from the article, until they have mastered it.
4. Have each group share or teach the topic in its own way to the other groups.

Terms to Know

capricious, unpredictable and impulsive

incumbent, in office

predecessors, those who came before

perjury, giving false testimony under oath

habeas corpus (ˈhā′bē əs kôr′pəs), a writ or order to release someone from unlawful restraint

blatantly, obviously

domestic, in the home

prosecution, those taking criminal court action against someone on behalf of the state

rowdy, rough and disorderly

bobbed, cut short (said of women's and children's hair)

copiously, a lot

summation, the conclusion of an argument in court

temporary insanity, a short-lived mental disorder that renders someone incapable of telling right from wrong

utopian, impossibly ideal conditions that would only work in a perfect society.

the fine and possibly his foot too. Now he just goes to jail, and you get to pay for his room and board with taxes. Progress has been made.

When William the Conqueror took over England in 1066, he left the Saxon system in place and added some Norman flourishes, like trial by combat. Combat was a judicial entertainment similar to the gladiatorial, in which right was thought to make might—whoever was right would win. The accuser had to do battle with the accused, causing the small and frail to think twice before complaining, but if you were not good at fighting you could hire someone to fight for you. The man with the fiercest hired help won—rather like hiring the most expensive lawyer today.

(Ordeals fell into disuse in the 13th century, but the right to trial by combat stayed on the books until Ashford v. Thornton in 1819.) By Norman times, laws were more complicated, so professionals, called justiciars, were sent around to keep an eye on the courts and the rules of evidence, rather like judges. They knew more about the law and less about what had happened than the jurors did.

THE BENCH BY WILLIAM HOGARTH

We were told in school that jury trials sprang newborn from the Magna Carta, but juries were around before 1215. The Magna Carta just guaranteed them as a right not to be ignored by capricious powers like bad King John, but some kings went right on being capricious anyway. In these enlightened times, we merely torch the neighborhood if we don't like a verdict, but back then, juries got punished if the authorities didn't like it. Since juries were still considered witnesses, a wrong vote was considered perjury. Acquitting unpopular or possibly treasonous people got jurors hauled into the star chamber, where a group of the king's dear friends dealt severely with them. They lost their goods and chattels and went to jail for at least a year; sometimes their wives and children were thrown out of their houses, the houses demolished, the meadows destroyed and even the trees chopped down. . . .

In 1650, under Cromwell, a newly reinstated law called for hanging adulteresses—and scarcely an adulteress was found in the land. In 1670 William Penn was tried for preaching Quaker doctrine, and he couldn't have been guiltier, caught red-handed and far from a first offense. The jurors stubbornly found in his favor and were fined 40 marks apiece for wrongness. Four of them refused to pay and spent a year in prison, until one was brought before the court on habeas corpus, and lo, it was decided that the law couldn't jail jurors for their decisions. We can't put them in jail anymore, but we can select them half to death.

As we limp toward the 21st century, the rural community of nosy neighbors has faded into history, and the problem now is, Who are these jurors? Prince Morgan called them "wise men." Under Edward I, they were to be 12 of the "better and lawful men." (Except for adulteresses, witches and common scolds, legal history doesn't mention women; perhaps they're a recent invention.) It seems to have been so simple then, naming our good, wise, lawful peers. But how do we choose among strangers not necessarily wise but merely registered to vote?

Once the blatantly prejudiced have been sent packing, both sides take up the peremp-

Only two incumbent U.S. Presidents have ever been arrested. None has been tried, convicted, or jailed.

In ancient Persia, judges at trials often sat on cushions upholstered with the skins of their dishonest predecessors in office.

In Minnesota, it was illegal for a woman to dress up and try to impersonate Santa on any city street.

MINI-LESSON: STUDY SKILLS

Take Notes

Teach Point out to students the mentions of places and dates in the selection. Explain that one way to take notes on this spread would be to make a notation for each new place/time listed. Students might include 1066, 13th century, 1215, 1650, 1670, end of 20th century, post-Civil War, the present.

Activity Idea Have students take notes on this spread and create either an outline or time line to show the main developments that the author discusses.

JUDGE LANCE ITO AT THE O.J. SIMPSON TRIAL

tory challenge of turning down jurors for the way they look, dress or comb their hair. A new professional has sprung up among us, the jury-selection consultant. For the O. J. Simpson trial, consultants submitted an 80-page list of 294 questions for prospective jurors, including essay questions like "What do you think is the main cause of domestic violence?" The theory is that we ordinary citizens are such a bunch of sheep that we'll always vote according to our kind, regardless of the evidence. The more narrowly the consultants can identify our kind, the easier it is to predict the vote.

The differing agendas of the prosecution and the defense complicate matters. Prosecution lawyer Jeffrey Toobin says that when he first came to the bar, he was always told to avoid men with beards (too independent) and teachers and social workers (too sympathetic), and aim for "the little old Lutheran lady in pearls, quick to judge and slow to forgive."

For the defense, Clarence Darrow advised not to "take a German; they are bull-headed. Rarely take a Swede; they are stubborn. Always take an Irishman or a Jew; they are the easiest to move to emotional sympathy." . . .

Whatever it may read or watch, the modern jury doesn't know what it was designed to know—its neighbors—and a clever lawyer can sometimes play on it as upon a harp. Such was William Howe of Howe and Hummel, defender of the underworld in rowdy post-Civil War New York. Howe was an enormous, lion-headed man with a wardrobe of costumes for his courtroom performances and a talent for crying copiously over any case, however dull. Once he delivered an hourlong summation, kneeling before the jury. Another time he convinced a jury that his client's trigger finger had accidentally slipped, not once but six times. So many of his clients were forgers that his office accepted only cash, so many were thieves that his office safe contained nothing but a coal scuttle—but murderers were his meat and drink. He personally appeared for more than 650 of them. He virtually invented "temporary insanity." He wept; the jury wept. According to a newspaper account, during his defense of Annie Walden, the "Man-Killing Race-Track Girl," the "sobs of juror nine could have been heard in the corridors, and there was moisture in the eyes of all but one or two of the other jurors."

Howe kept a stable of white-haired mothers, distraught wives and cherubic children available to represent the family of the accused. He once pointed out his own wife and child, who happened to be in the courtroom, as his client's prospective widow and orphan. How would a New York jury know? And how the hometown juries of old would have laughed.

Here and there a voice suggests returning at least minor offenses to neighborhood judicial counsels, as in the old courts of the hundreds, taking the law into our own hands where it began. This may be utopian. We don't want to know our 99 nearest neighbors, let alone be accountable for their behavior. Some of us don't even want to read the papers. We gripe about the results, but we leave civil order to the professionals. It wasn't designed to work that way. . . .

According to an old New Jersey law, anyone slurping soup in a public restaurant was subject to arrest, a fine, and a possible term in jail.

According to an Arkansas law, pay raises were not given to teachers who bobbed their hair.

Responding

1. Conduct a panel discussion on the strengths and weaknesses of the present-day jury system.

2. What do you think of the proposal that neighborhood councils try minor offenses?

Responding

1. You may wish to have students do some more research about the present jury system before they discuss it. Many books and journal articles discuss material that will be helpful to students in forming opinions which they can substantiate with facts.

2. Students may suggest that it is impractical and will make people resent their neighbors.

Research Topics

- The difference between jury trials and bench trials
- Plea bargaining

Interdisciplinary Activity Idea

Laws concerning curfew, parking, pets, garbage, and so on vary from community to community. Students can visit the police department or town council to compile a list of laws and ordinances that would be useful to someone who has just moved to their community.

BUILDING ENGLISH PROFICIENCY

Careers

As they read and discuss this feature, students may express an interest in a career in the field of law. Use one or more of the following activities to expand upon students' interest.

Activity Ideas

- Invite a professional from the law field to speak to students. Provide him or her with some questions ahead of time; afterward, allow time for additional questions.
- Discuss with students any famous trials or law decisions of recent times.
- Invite groups of students to watch and report on any suitable movie that deals with the legal field.

Interdisciplinary Study

Theme Link

Scientific advances help jurors to make informed judgments.

Curricular Connection: Career

You can use the information in this Interdisciplinary Study to explore the importance of scientific facts in determining guilt or innocence.

Terms to Know

forensic, of or used in a court of law

specimen, a sample that will be analyzed and examined

slab, a broad, flat, thick piece of something

probe, a device that is used to monitor an area that is not easily accessible

Responding

1. Have students work in teams. Encourage them to compare the accurancy of each method.

2. Suggest that students relate their explanations, if possible, to a real-life case where DNA is being used as evidence.

INTERDISCIPLINARY STUDY

Career Connection

Recent scientific advances provide jurors with new forms of evidence to help them make informed decisions.

We've come a long way from witch-dunking to DNA! Recent scientific advances provide jurors and others required to determine guilt and innocence with new forms of evidence to help them make informed decisions. Forensic scientist Tamara Camp from the Northern Illinois Police Crime Laboratory describes some of the techniques she uses as a molecular biologist to analyze evidence.

My section of the lab is called forensic biology. We identify stains from body fluids. For example, a specimen of a blood stain found at a crime scene is brought to the lab. This is our unknown, which we call a sample. Since ours is a comparative science, we also collect blood specimens from the victim and from the suspect, and these specimens are called the standards. We compare the sample to the standards and make a probability statement from one of the known persons.

"When we examine blood, we use various methods and look at genetic markers like blood type, DNA, or proteins. To look at proteins, we first take a slab of agar, a jelly-like substance, and embed our blood specimen in it. Then we apply an electric current across the gel, and the protein molecules in the blood will migrate across the agar, with the smaller ones moving faster. We look at the bands of migrated protein to determine whether these patterns match the suspect's specimen. Although the protein type is not as definite for identification as a fingerprint, it is extremely valuable in establishing innocence: if the sample and the suspect's specimen don't match at all, there is no possibility that the suspect could have left the stain.

TAMARA CAMP FORENSIC SCIENTIST

"DNA (deoxyribonucleic acid) typing, the newest crime lab technique, has been widely used only since the 1980s. DNA, called the 'master molecule of life,' can be extracted from body fluids or tissues. One method of typing DNA is to break it into smaller pieces using chemicals. Then it is tagged with a radioactive probe to expose a piece of X-ray film. We study the resulting patterns that resemble a bar code and use them for identification. This is a DNA 'fingerprint.' Another means of DNA identification, called PCR analysis, requires only tiny amounts of a specimen and is quicker, though less definitive."

DNA evidence has been accepted in most courts across the country, although lawyers have argued that the varying probability factors (which can range from 1 in many billion to 1 in 100), are sometimes insufficient to establish guilt. Nonetheless, it is commonly used to settle paternity suits, to protect endangered species of animals, and to identify remains of war veterans. One of DNA's most stunning successes was the identification of a 1994 World Trade Center bomber through his saliva used to lick an envelope.

Responding

1. Research recent uses of technology involving DNA, fingerprinting, polygraph testing, and other methods of detection.

2. Prepare an explanation of DNA testing, complete with graphic aids, that would clarify this process for the average person.

MINI-LESSON: STUDY SKILLS

Online Reference Sources

Teach In addition to print materials, students can use computer online services to find out more about topics that interest them.

Apply If you have an online service available at your school, demonstrate to students how they can initiate a search for technology used in solving crimes.

Activity Idea If an online service is available at your school, encourage several groups of students to pursue information on DNA technology using the computer, while the remaining groups use print materials to find the same information. Have the groups compare their findings.

Reading Mini-Lesson

Chronology and Time Lines

Authors often organize a narrative into chronological, or time, order. In "We the Jurors" (page 256), Barbara Holland tracks the history of the jury system from its earliest times to the present. Introductory phrases such as "After Rome fell apart" and "As we limp toward the 21st century" are one way Holland cues readers to time periods. She indicates when two or more events take place simultaneously with words such as *meanwhile* and *during*. Actual dates within the text also inform readers of time frames and shifts.

Some articles you read may jump around in time or use a literary device known as a flashback to recall events from the past. Sometimes you can make a time line to help clarify the selection's sequence of events.

The Rosemont High School homecoming game was October 15. Our team won, but that's not the whole story. Three days before the big game, the star quarterback, Jamal Rodgers, came down with the flu. By October 13, he was no better. Meanwhile, the rest of the team started practicing with Andy Hicks, the substitute quarterback. The day before the game, Jamal began to feel better. By game day, he was ready to play.

Read the passage to the left. Notice that the first event mentioned in the paragraph is actually the last event in the chronology. The third sentence begins a flashback sequence involving the three days before the game. What introductory words indicate time clues? An abbreviated time line for this passage might look like this:

Oct. 12	Oct. 13	Oct. 14	Oct. 15
Jamal gets flu.	Team practices with Andy Hicks.	Jamal starts feeling better.	Rosemont High wins game.

As you read, pay close attention to the sequence of events. When necessary, fill in time gaps or mentally rearrange events into chronological order in order to understand difficult material.

Activity Options

1. Work with a partner to create a poster-size time line for the events detailed in Barbara Holland's article, "We the Jurors" (page 256).
2. Think of a TV show or movie that uses flashbacks. Discuss with someone who has seen the same feature why you think there were time shifts. Consider also how time shifts were indicated—for example signs of age on a character's face, shifts in the season or setting, camera fadeouts, voice-overs, and so forth.

Reading Mini-Lesson

Teaching Objectives

- to recognize sequence of events
- to take notes in time order
- to recognize words that signal time order

Introduce

Present a simple example of time-order relationships using the words *first, second,* and *third* to introduce the the parts of a sequence. Explain that this is called time order, or chronological order. Have students identify the sequence of events, explaining how the time words helped them. Then have students read the lesson and study the diagram.

Follow Up

After students have studied the time line and related it to the narrative, have them write short narratives about a past event in their own lives, using time-order words.

Activity Options

Activity 1 Refer to the mini-lesson on taking notes, page 258, for another approach to this lesson.

Activity 2 Students may find that mystery shows use this feature most often.

CONTENT AREA READING

Taking Notes from Textbooks

In textbooks where sequence is important, other devices besides time-order words are often used to indicate chronology. Time lines, highlighting, boldface, or subheads may also be used. When you begin a section, check to see how the passage of time is indicated. Then, if you need to take notes that go in chronological order to show a sequence of events, cause-and-effect relationships, or developments, you will know how to identify the sequence times.

Writing Workshop

WRITER'S BLUEPRINT

Specs

The Specs in the Writer's Blueprint address these writing and thinking skills:

- analyzing characters
- describing setting
- applying knowledge
- writing realistic dialogue
- using standard script format

These Specs serve as your lesson objectives, and they form the basis for the **Assessment Criteria Specs** for a superior paper, which appear on the final TE page for this lesson. You might want to read through the Assessment Criteria Specs with students when you begin the lesson.

Linking Literature to Writing

Ask students to generate a list of features common to conflicts they have experienced. Then discuss how those features play out in the conflicts in *Antigone.*

On Trial

Narrative Writing

Writing Workshop

Antigone Updated

Assignment What would the characters from *Antigone* be like if they lived today? How would they react to modern-day problems? Write a scene for a play, set in the present, featuring updated versions of the major characters from *Antigone*. See the Writer's Blueprint for details.

WRITER'S BLUEPRINT

Product	A scene for a play
Purpose	To update *Antigone*
Audience	People who have read or seen a production of *Antigone*
Specs	To write a successful scene, you should:

- ❑ Choose two characters from *Antigone* and update them—turn them into people who have the same personalities but who live now, in the present day. Then choose a modern-day conflict to serve as the basis for your scene.
- ❑ Begin by writing personality profiles of the characters and a description of the setting.
- ❑ Then write the scene itself. Use dialogue that sounds natural—not too formal, but not too informal either. See that your characters behave in ways that are true to the personalities of the original *Antigone* characters.
- ❑ Follow the applicable rules of grammar, usage, spelling, and mechanics. Use the proper form for a play script.

The instructions that follow are designed to lead you to a successful scene.

WRITING WORKSHOP OVERVIEW

Product
Narrative writing: A scene from a play

Prewriting
Revisit Antigone—List modern-day conflicts—Choose your characters and conflict—Visualize the characters—Visualize the setting—Plan
Unit 2 Resource Book
Prewriting Worksheets pp. 43–44

Drafting
Before you write—As you draft
Transparency Collection
Student Models for Writing Workshop 7, 8

Revising
Ask a partner—Strategy: Writing Realistic Dialogue
Unit 2 Resource Book
Revising Worksheet p. 45

Editing
Ask a partner—Strategy: Writing in Script Format
Unit 2 Resource Book
Grammar Worksheet p. 46
Grammar Check Test p. 47

Presenting
Perform
Record

Looking Back
Self-evaluate—Reflect—For Your Working Portfolio
Unit 2 Resource Book
Assessment Worksheet p. 48
Transparency Collection
Fine Art Writing Prompt 4

STEP 1 PREWRITING

Revisit *Antigone*. Your scene will focus on a **protagonist**, a central character who is in conflict with an **antagonist**, a character who opposes the protagonist. With a group, revisit *Antigone* to find pairs of antagonists and protagonists and conflicts in the play. Make notes on what you find and put them into a chart like the one below.

Protagonist–Antagonist	Their Conflict
• Antigone/Ismene	• whether to obey the king's demand to leave their brother unburied

List modern-day conflicts. With your group, list examples of conflicts people might have over issues such as ownership of property, money, legal rights, and family matters.

Choose your characters and conflict. On your own, review your notes and choose the character pair and modern-day conflict you'll use for the focus of your scene.

Visualize the characters. Make notes on the personalities of your protagonist and antagonist. How do they typically behave? See the Literary Source for ideas.

Visualize the setting. Where will your scene take place? Think of the characters and the conflict. Do you see things happening indoors or outdoors? Visualize the setting and make notes on what you see.

Plan your character profiles, setting description, and scene. Follow these steps.

1. Gather together your character notes. These will serve as the basis for the personality profiles you will write for your protagonist and antagonist. See the Literary Source at the right for a good example of a character profile.
2. Gather together your setting notes. These will serve as the basis for the description you will write of your setting. See the Literary Source on page 264 for a good example of the kind of description you should write.
3. Summarize the action. List the key events in your scene and some key lines of dialogue you plan to include when you write your scene.

LITERARY SOURCE

Juror number two. A meek, hesitant man who finds it difficult to maintain any opinions of his own. Easily swayed and usually adopts the opinion of the last person to whom he has spoken.

from *Twelve Angry Men* by Reginald Rose

STEP 1 PREWRITING

Revisit Antigone

Explain the meanings of the prefixes and root words of *protagonist* and *antagonist.*

List modern-day conflicts

Have students skim through current newspapers and magazines to get ideas for their discussions. For more support, see the worksheet referenced below.

Unit 2 Resource Book
Prewriting Worksheet, p. 43

Choose your characters and conflict

Ask students to consider how well a particular conflict would play out using the characters from *Antigone* before making a final decision.

Visualize the characters

You might have the class brainstorm a general list of character traits that can serve as a springboard for their individual notes.

Visualize the setting

Some students may benefit from first sketching the setting.

Plan

Some students may find it easier to follow all the steps in the plan if you lead them through as a group. For more support, see the worksheet referenced below.

Unit 2 Resource Book
Prewriting Worksheet, p. 44

BUILDING ENGLISH PROFICIENCY

ESL LEP ELD SAE LD

Linking Past and Present

Offer students the following suggestions for creating characters who would be believable to today's audiences:

1. Suggest that students think of modern equivalents to the characters' roles. For example, for King Creon, they might choose a governor, a corporate president, or another influential figure—even a teacher!

2. Suggest that students focus on the characters' personalities. For example, Antigone is sure of her beliefs but also impulsive; students might imagine what kinds of modern-day situations someone like that would feel strongly about.

Connections to **Writer's Notebook**

For selection-related prompts, refer to Writer's Notebook.

Connections to **Writer's Resource**

For additional writing prompts, refer to Writer's Resource.

STEP 2 DRAFTING

Before you write

This is an opportunity to clarify any remaining misunderstandings or confusion before students write. Encourage them to ask questions as they review the blueprint and their notes.

As you draft

If students have trouble working out a particular scene, you might offer to improvise through it with them, or have them do so with a classmate.

The Student Models

The **transparencies** referenced below are authentic student models. Review them with the students before they draft. These questions will help:

1. What is the conflict presented in model 7?

2. Is the behavior of the characters in model 8 true to the personalities of the original *Antigone* characters? Explain.

3. Which writer created the more realistic dialogue? Explain.

Transparency Collection
Student Models for Writing Workshop 7, 8

STEP 3 REVISING

Ask a partner (Peer assessment)

Have partners take on different roles in each scene and read through them together. As they read, they should both note problem areas.

STEP 2 DRAFTING

Before you write, reread the Writer's Blueprint and review your notes and writing plan.

As you draft, concentrate on the action rather than matters of correctness, such as spelling and grammar. These ideas might help you as you draft.

- As you profile your protagonist and antagonist, keep in mind that they must behave in ways that are true to the original *Antigone* characters.
- As you describe your setting, be sure to supply enough details for your audience to be able to visualize the scene. See the Literary Source below for an example.

OR . . .
As you draft, narrate portions of your script into a tape recorder. Play the tape back to see if the dialogue flows smoothly and sounds realistic.

LITERARY SOURCE

The room is furnished with a long conference table and a dozen chairs. The walls are bare, drab, and badly in need of a fresh coat of paint. Along one wall is a row of windows which look out on the skyline of the city's financial district. High on another wall is an electric clock. . . .

from *Twelve Angry Men* by Reginald Rose

- As you write the scene, stand up and act out what a character is saying or doing, and then capture what you did in writing.
- As you write dialogue, try to make it as realistic as possible. (See the Revising Strategy in Step 3 of this lesson.)
- Use the standard form for a play script. (See the Editing Strategy in Step 4 of this lesson.)

STEP 3 REVISING

Ask a partner to read your scene and make suggestions before you revise it. Use these questions as a guide.

✔ Have I focused on the conflict between an antagonist and a protagonist?

✔ Are my characters true to the personalities in *Antigone*?

✔ Does my dialogue seem realistic?

MINI-LESSON: WRITING STYLE

Writing Realistic Dialogue

Teach Select an excerpt of dialogue from *Twelve Angry Men* and insert an unrealistic amount of slang. Ask students to listen as you read both versions aloud. Discuss how to choose an appropriate amount of slang to include without going overboard.

Activity Idea Have students work with partners to rewrite a section of dialogue from *Antigone* to be less formal. Tell them to intentionally include too much slang. Then have them switch papers with another pair and revise this new dialogue to be informal, yet realistic.

Apply Tell students to doublecheck the level of informality in their dialogue and revise as needed, using the strategies they just developed.

Revising Strategy

Writing Realistic Dialogue

Realistic dialogue sounds natural when you read it aloud. For example, when real people talk to each other they usually use informal language. Take care, though, that you don't make your dialogue too informal by throwing in too much slang. Notice how the writer of the student model revised dialogue, with the help of a partner's comment.

COMPUTER TIP
When revising, you can define various paragraph styles in the word-processing program to help you indent the dialogue and italicize the directions.

ANNIE. Can ~~ya~~ you believe all that ~~yellin'~~ yelling last night? That landlord's been on Peter's back ever since he moved in~~, ya know? Gimme a break~~. It's the long hair and the ragged clothes, ~~ya know~~ I know it. That landlord is such a bigot~~, ya know?~~. Know what he did?

Too many "ya know"s. Is that how Annie really talks?

STUDENT MODEL

STEP 4 EDITING

Ask a partner to review your revised draft before you edit. Look especially for errors related to script format.

Editing Strategy

Writing in Script Format

When you write in a script format, follow these rules.

- Write the speaker's name in all capitals followed by a period and then the first line of the speech. Indent the remaining lines of the speech by two spaces.
- Always enclose stage directions in parentheses. If you're using a computer, write the stage directions in italics. If you're writing by hand, underline them.

FOR REFERENCE
Look back at *Antigone* if you have any questions about play-script format.

MINI-LESSON: GRAMMAR

Writing in Script Format

Reread with students the section of "The Interlopers" from "Presently, as the wind . . ." to ". . . then George gave a joyful cry". (page 132) Then have students adapt this section into script format. Remind them to follow the rules in the Editing Strategy. Then have students exchange scripts with partners and edit for errors related to script format.

Unit 2 Resource Book
Grammar Worksheet, p. 46
Grammar Check Test, p. 47

Revising Strategy: Writing Realistic Dialogue

Encourage students to train their ears for realistic dialogue by taking notes on brief conversations overheard in a store, at a restaurant, or at a ballgame.

For additional support, see the mini-lesson at the bottom of the preceding page and the worksheet referenced below.

Unit 2 Resource Book
Revising Worksheet, p. 45

Connections to **Writer's Resource**

Refer to the Grammar, Usage, and Mechanics Handbook on Writer's Resource.

STEP 4 EDITING

Ask a partner (Peer assessment)

Suggest that students review each other's drafts twice: first for general problems with grammar, usage, spelling, and mechanics, and second to look specifically at play format.

Editing Strategy: Writing in Script Format

Remind students to use *Antigone* as a model of correct play format while they edit.

For additional support, see the mini-lesson at the bottom of this page and the worksheets referenced below.

Unit 2 Resource Book
Grammar Worksheet, p. 46
Grammar Check Test, p. 47

Connections to **Writer's Resource**

Refer to the Grammar, Usage, and Mechanics Handbook on Writer's Resource.

STEP 5 PRESENTING

Perform

You might suggest that class members nominate each scene for recognition of a particular strength, such as "Best Dialogue," "Best Reading," or "Most Interesting Plot."

Record

Help students gather appropriate props and sound effects materials. Encourage groups to share whenever possible.

STEP 6 LOOKING BACK

Self-evaluate

The *Assessment Criteria Specs* at the bottom of this page are for a superior paper. You might want to post these in the classroom. Students can then evaluate themselves based on these criteria. For a complete scoring rubric, use the *Assessment Worksheet* referenced below.

Unit 2 Resource Book
Assessment Worksheet, p. 48

Reflect

You might suggest that students first brainstorm ideas that come to mind as they react to each question, and then formulate responses based on these ideas.

To further explore the theme, use the Fine Art Transparency referenced below.

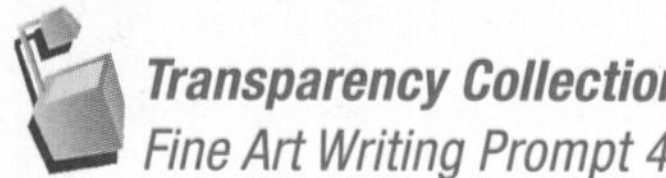

Transparency Collection
Fine Art Writing Prompt 4

STEP 5 PRESENTING

Here are two ideas for presenting your scene.

- In a group, read your scenes to each other with different group members taking the different parts. Choose one scene you all especially liked, rehearse it, and present it to the class.
- Make a videotape or audiotape of your scene, adding the visual or sound effects called for in the script.

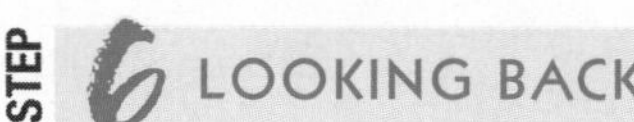

STEP 6 LOOKING BACK

Self-evaluate. What grade would *you* give your paper? Look back at the Writer's Blueprint and give yourself a score for each point, from 6 (superior) down to 1 (inadequate).

Reflect. Think about what you learned from writing your scene as you write in response to these questions.

✔ If you were to write the entire play, how would it end?

✔ How was writing the script for a scene different from other writing assignments you have done? What made it easier or more difficult than writing an essay?

For Your Working Portfolio Add your scene and your reflection responses to your working portfolio.

ASSESSMENT CRITERIA SPECS

Here are the criteria for a superior paper. A full six-level rubric for this paper appears on the Assessment Worksheet referenced below.

6 Superior The writer of a 6 paper impressively meets these criteria:

- Concisely describes the setting and insightfully profiles each character.
- Successfully translates characters and themes from *Antigone* into a modern-day context.
- Constructs a believable and engaging plot with a clearly defined protagonist and antagonist.
- Creates authentic-sounding dialogue that is vivid and reveals character.
- Presents text in correct script format throughout.
- Uses grammar, punctuation, and spelling that is appropriate to the task.

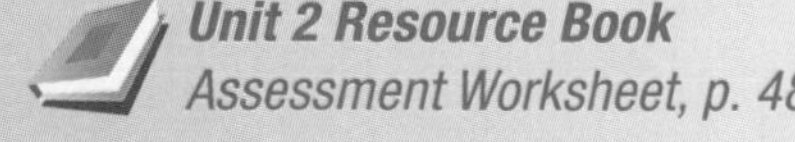

Unit 2 Resource Book
Assessment Worksheet, p. 48

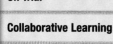

Beyond Print

Weighing the Evidence

Creon is charged with the death of Antigone. If you, the jury, finds him guilty, he will be put to death.

- Divide your class into groups of from six to twelve students.
- Find a space in your classroom or in another area where each group can weigh the evidence, discuss, and try to reach a consensus.
- Jot down ideas about the role that Creon plays in Antigone's death.

Deliberation Tips

Agree on responsibilities. Decide who will serve as a recorder and a spokesperson, and fill other roles as the need arises.

Brainstorm. Collaborate to find as many reasons as possible for Creon's guilt, as well as reasons for his innocence. Work together to put these reasons in order from most persuasive to least persuasive.

Invite discussion. Each group member should express his or her opinions. Group members should encourage everyone to speak, as well as keep discussion going and on track.

Listen carefully and ask questions. Ask for clarification if necessary. Stay with the facts and avoid personal attacks.

Ask for a summary. Have your spokesperson summarize the basic arguments for and against Creon.

Vote. After considering the strongest evidence, cast a secret ballot.

If you have a hung jury, have group members discuss why they voted as they did. Vote again to see if anyone feels differently after deliberation.

Activity Options

1. Discuss how effectively group members worked together. What things did you do well? What things could be improved?
2. Based on your collaboration as a group, discuss what things could be done to make a real jury work together effectively.

Beyond Print

Teaching Objectives

- to reach consensus on a difficult issue
- to present opinions and support them with reasons

Curricular Connection: Speaking/Listening Skills

If possible, provide a recorder for at least one of the groups to tape their discussion.

Introduce

Remind students that although the jury in *Twelve Angry Men* was made up of all white men, juries today are comprised of both men and women of varied races and ethnic backgrounds so that many different viewpoints are represented. Encourage students to form groups as diverse as possible in gender and culture.

Activity Options

Activity 1 Before each group evaluates their effectiveness, have the class decide the criteria for evaluation. Ask students to compare and contrast their "jury" experience with that of the jurors in *Twelve Angry Men.*

Activity 2 Students should bear in mind the differences between debating about a work of fiction in a situation that is free of consequences and deciding a real case in which one or more lives may be at stake.

ANOTHER APPROACH

Written Persuasion

If it seems more appropriate, you may wish to have students work in groups or individually to write a persuasive essay in which they argue for Creon's innocence or guilt.

Students could also write an address in the persona of either the prosecuting attorney or the defense attorney and deliver their work as if it were a closing argument in the case.

Preview

Beneath the Surface

FOR ALL STUDENTS

Have students work in groups to brainstorm a list of myths, folk tales, parables, and proverbs that reflect the importance of looking beneath the surface. Examples: the tricks of Zeus, a wolf in sheep's clothing.

To further explore the theme, use the art transparency referred to below.

Transparency Collection
Fine Art Writing Prompt 5

For At-Risk Students

Some of the selections contain riddles. Explain that a riddle is a question or statement that is worded in such a way that it has a hidden or double meaning.

Have volunteers share familiar riddles with the class.

For Students Who Need Challenge

Have students research and report on the role of the mask in one of the following theatrical or religious traditions.

- Japanese Noh theater
- Ancient Greek theater
- Commedia dell'arte
- Native American shamanism
- African religious ceremonies

MULTICULTURAL CONNECTION

Have students decide on one value that they feel is directly influenced by membership in a particular group. For example: As a member of my family, I feel that eating dinner together each night is important.

Part Two

Beneath the Surface

Do you rely on first impressions, or do you base judgments on second thoughts? The selections you are about to read provide reminders that it's wise to look beneath the surface.

Multicultural Connection **Perspective** involves seeing and interpreting a situation from different cultural viewpoints. As you read the following selections, decide how group values contribute to both the understanding and misunderstanding of what's beneath the surface.

IDEAS THAT WORK

Motivating with Quotes

Reality Bites is the title of a movie made in the mid-1990s. Since this unit shows how people deal with those "bites," stimulate the students' interest by tying their personal experiences to this central theme. Begin by posing these questions:

How many of you believe that knowing the whole truth and facing reality is the best path to follow in life? Why?

After exploring the reasons for the students' answers, write the following quotation on the board:

"Humankind cannot bear very much reality."

T. S. Eliot
Murder in the Cathedral

Then divide the class into groups, asking them to list the ways we avoid facing harsh facts by deceiving ourselves or others.

After the students read the works, discuss Eliot's quotation as applied to the characters in this cluster. How do they mask or evade the truth?

Mary Alice Fite
Columbus, Ohio

Before Reading

The Flying Doctor

by Molière France

Molière
1622–1673

From an early age, John Baptiste Poquelin, who adopted the pen name Molière (mō lyer′), enjoyed attending the theater and watching broad comedies known as farces. He became director of an acting troupe, performed throughout France, and eventually began writing his own satiric comedies. He gained favor at the court of Louis XIV, called the Sun King, and frequently performed his elaborate spectaculars at the king's splendid castle at Versailles. Ironically, Molière suffered a fatal hemorrhage while performing the title role of the hypochondriac in his play, *The Imaginary Invalid;* he finished the performance and died shortly thereafter.

Building Background

Type Casting The rollicking Italian plays popular around the 1500s in Italy and later throughout Europe were known as ***commedia dell'arte*** (kə mā′dē ə del är′tā). Actors (all male) loosely followed a basic script, making up dialogue as they went along. The lively plots often involved love affairs and intrigue and always involved deception. But it was the broadly comic characters that stole the show. These characters included such basic types as Harlequin the clown and Pantaloon the wise old man. The wily servant, whom you are about to encounter in *The Flying Doctor,* was also a popular character type.

Literary Focus

Farce Comedy that involves improbable situations, exaggerated characters, and slapstick action is called **farce**. You can watch this type of comedy in old Marx Brothers or Three Stooges movies. As you read the following play by Molière, look for ways that the writer achieves this broad comedy.

Writer's Notebook

Where's the Plot?

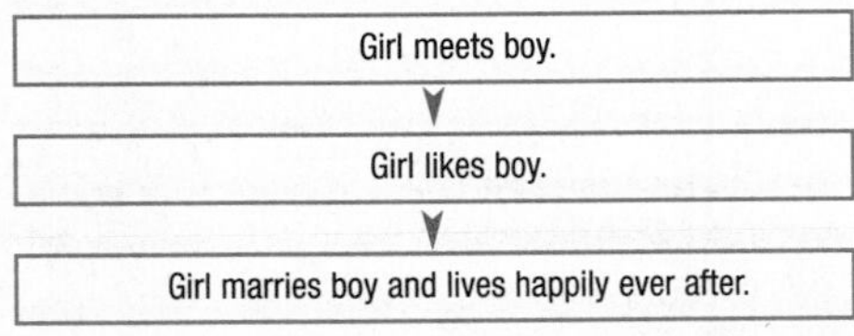
Girl meets boy.
Girl likes boy.
Girl marries boy and lives happily ever after.

A story with this kind of plot wouldn't have much appeal. Audiences cheer love fulfilled, but only after a hard-won battle. Now if the boy's father objected to this match, or if the girl were already engaged, or if there were a serious misunderstanding between them, or an earthquake. . . . In your notebook, suggest a few plot twists to this basic pattern that would make this story outline more exciting.

Before Reading

Building Background

Question What TV programs feature a cast of stereotyped characters in farfetched plots? *(Possible responses: Monty Python's Flying Circus; Saturday Night Live)*

Literary Focus

Point out that the word **farce** comes from the Latin root *farsa,* meaning *stuffed,* and that farces were originally used as comic interludes or "stuffing" between the acts of serious plays.

Writer's Notebook

Suggest that students write about an unlikely, farfetched romantic incident that they have either witnessed, experienced, or heard about in a popular song.

More About Molière

- "Molière remains to this day without rival in the comic exposition of human character." (Benét's *Reader's Encyclopedia)*
- Because Molière's satirical play *Tartuffe* (1664) offended many clergy members, he was denied a Christian funeral and buried at night.

Other works by the author include:

- *The School for Wives,* (1662)
- *Misanthrope,* (1666)
- *The Bourgeois Gentleman,* (1670)

SUPPORT MATERIALS OVERVIEW

Unit 2 Resource Book
- Graphic Organizer, p. 49
- Study Guide, p. 50
- Vocabulary, p. 51
- Grammar, p. 52
- Alternate Check Test, p. 53
- Vocabulary Test, p. 54
- Selection Test, pp. 55–56

Building English Proficiency
- Literature Summaries
- Activities, p. 187

Reading, Writing & Grammar SkillBook
- Vocabulary, pp. 9–10
- Grammar, Usage, and Mechanics, pp. 148–149, 157–160

Technology
- Personal Journal Software
- Custom Literature Database: For another play about a wily servant outsmarting a master, see *Volpone* by Ben Jonson on the database
- Test Generator Software

During Reading

Selection Objectives

- to examine the theme of deception
- to explore the conventions of farce
- to investigate subordinate and coordinate clauses

Unit 2 Resource Book
Graphic Organizer, p. 49
Study Guide, p. 50

Theme Link

The theme "Beneath the Surface" is shown through a lowly servant, Sganarelle, who outwits Gorgibus with a clever disguise.

Vocabulary Preview

device, plan, scheme, or trick
impersonate, pretend to be
attribute, think of as caused by
inimical, unfavorable
aphorism, brief statement expressing a truth
debauchery, corruption

Students can add the words and definitions to their Writer's Notebooks.

Art Study

Responses to Caption Question

- Harlequin's colorful costume suggests a merry nature; his mask suggests trickery and disguise.
- Columbine's coquettish pose and tambourine characterize her as a dancer. Her bonnet and simple dress identify her as a servant.

1 Historical Note
Harlequin/Columbine

Harlequin's name comes from Old French meaning "demon," testifying to this character's devilish pranks. Columbine means "little dove."

The Flying

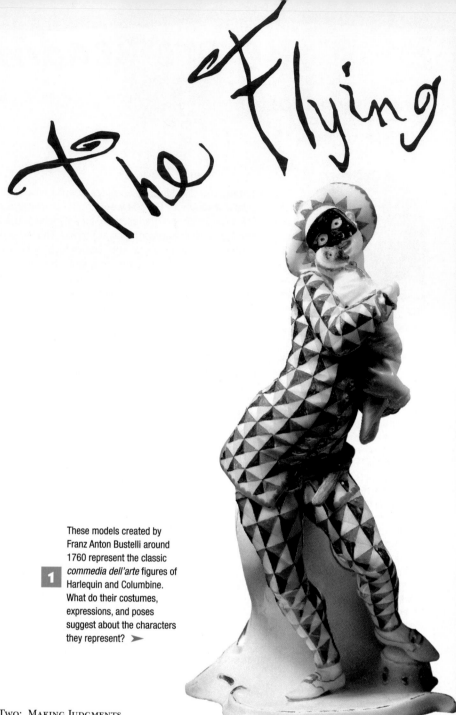

1 These models created by Franz Anton Bustelli around 1760 represent the classic *commedia dell'arte* figures of Harlequin and Columbine. What do their costumes, expressions, and poses suggest about the characters they represent? ➤

SELECTION SUMMARY

The Flying Doctor

Although Valère and Lucile are in love and wish to marry, Lucile's father, Gorgibus, is forcing her to marry the wealthy Villebrequin instead. Lucile's cousin Sabine and Valère involve his servant, Sganarelle, in a scheme to foil Gorgibus' plan. Disguised as a doctor, Sganarelle talks Gorgibus into moving Lucile to the pavilion, where Valère can easily rescue her. When Gorgibus catches him without his doctor's disguise, Sganarelle scrambles to preserve the hoax. By the time Gorgibus finally discovers Sganarelle's deception, Valère has already run off with Lucile and married her. With a little persuasion from Sganarelle, Gorgibus gives his new son-in-law his blessing.

*For summaries in other languages, see the **Building English Proficiency** book.*

Molière

CHARACTERS

GORGIBUS (gôr′jə bəs), *a respectable but simple-minded citizen*
LUCILE *daughter of Gorgibus*
SABINE (sä bēn′), *niece of Gorgibus*
VALÈRE (vä lär′), *young man in love with Lucile*
SGANARELLE (sga′nə rel′), *servant to Valère*
GROS-RENÉ (grō′rə nā), *servant to Gorgibus*
A LAWYER

2

Scene. *A street in a small French town.*

VALÈRE, *a young man, is talking to* SABINE, *a young woman, in front of the house of* GORGIBUS, *her uncle.*

VALÈRE. Sabine, what do you advise me to do?

SABINE. We'll have to work fast. My uncle is determined to make Lucile marry this rich man, Villebrequin, and he's pushed the preparations so far that the marriage would have taken place today if my cousin were not in love with you. But she is—she has told me so—and since my greedy uncle is forcing our hand, we've come up with a device[1] for putting off the wedding. Lucile is pretending to be ill, and the old man, who'll believe almost anything, has sent me for a doctor. If you have a friend we can trust, I'll take him to my uncle and he can suggest that Lucile is not getting nearly enough fresh air. The old boy will then let her live in the pavilion[2] at the end of our garden, and you can meet her secretly, marry her, and leave my uncle to take out his anger on Villebrequin. 3

VALÈRE. But where can I find a doctor who will be sympathetic to me and risk his reputation? Frankly, I can't think of a single one. 4

1. device (di vīs′), *n.* plan, scheme, or trick.
2. **pavilion** (pə vil′yən), *n.* summer house.

2 Multicultural Note
French Pronunciation

Encourage students to read each name out loud according to its phonetic spelling. Point out that some French letters follow their own rules of pronunciation: for example, *é* with this acute accent mark is pronounced like an English "long *a*."

3 Literary Element
Characterization

Question What impression of Gorgibus do you form from Sabine's statements? *(Possible responses: greedy, overbearing, gullible, stubborn, concerned)*

Question Why might Sabine have a biased opinion of Gorgibus? *(Possible response: Sabine is likely to have formed an allegiance to her cousin, who is a young woman like herself.)*

4 Literary Element
Recognize Dramatic Traditions

Up to this point, what elements of the *commedia dell'arte* do you recognize in the play? *(Possible responses: the secret love affair between Valère and Lucile; the farfetched plan to dupe Gorgibus)*

BUILDING ENGLISH PROFICIENCY

Locating Key Facts

Students may find Sabine's opening speech confusing, but it contains information essential to understanding the basic "problem" in the play. Help students grasp this information by asking questions such as the following:

- How are Sabine and Lucile related?
- Who are the lovers?
- Who is trying to keep Valère and Lucile apart?
- Whom does Lucile's father want her to marry? Why?
- Who thought up the scheme to stop the marriage between Lucile and Villebrequin?
- How must a friend of Valère's get involved?
- Why can't Sabine or Valère ask a real doctor for help?

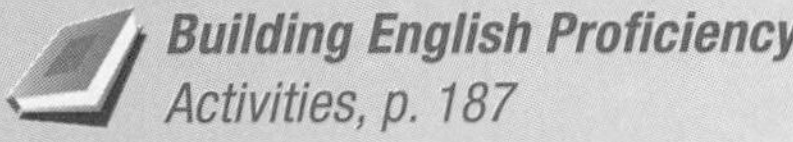
Building English Proficiency
Activities, p. 187

5 Literary Focus
Farce

Farce relies heavily on broad, ridiculous characters to create humor.

Question How do the stage directions identify Sganarelle as a farcical character? *(Just as Valère calls him a "halfwit," Sganarelle wanders onto the stage, concentrating seriously on a yo-yo.)*

6 Literary Element
Dialogue

Point out that a play often relies on dialogue to convey the internal and external conflicts of its characters.

Question Why does Sganarelle shift from self-deprecation to self-confidence in one sentence? *(Possible responses: The temptation of the hundred francs grabs hold. Sganarelle convinces himself that he is indeed as subtle and bright as a doctor.)*

7 Reading/Thinking Skills
Clarify Relationships

Help students form a clear idea of relationships between characters.

Question What does the interaction between Gorgibus and Gros-René reveal about their relationship? *(Gros-René is openly critical of Gorgibus and has keener insight into the situation.)*

SABINE. I was wondering if you could disguise your valet? It'll be easy for him to fool the old man.

VALÈRE. If you knew my valet as I do—He's so dense he'll ruin everything. Still, I can't think of anybody else. I'll try to find him.
5 (SABINE *leaves.*) Where can I start to look for the halfwit? (SGANARELLE *comes in, playing intently with a yo-yo.*) Sganarelle, my dear boy, I'm delighted to see you. I need you for an important assignment. But I don't know what you can do—

SGANARELLE. Don't worry, Master, I can do anything. I can handle any assignment, especially important ones. Give me a difficult job. Ask me to find out what time it is. Or to check on the price of butter at the market. Or to water your horse. You'll soon see what I can do.

VALÈRE. This is more complicated. I want you to impersonate[3] a doctor.

SGANARELLE. A doctor! You know I'll do anything you want, Master, but when it comes to impersonating a doctor, I couldn't do it if I tried—wouldn't know how to start. I think you're making fun of me.

VALÈRE. If you care to try, I'll give you one hundred francs.[4]

SGANARELLE. One hundred whole francs, just for pretending to be a doctor? No, Master, it's impossible. You see I don't have the
6 brains for it. I'm not subtle enough; I'm not even bright. So that's settled. I impersonate a doctor. Where?

VALÈRE. You know Gorgibus? His daughter is lying in there ill—No, it's no use; you'll only confuse matters.

SGANARELLE. I bet I can confuse matters as well as all the doctors in this town put together. Or kill patients as easily. You know the old saying, "After you're dead, the doctor comes." When I take a hand there'll be a new saying: "After the doctor comes, you're dead." Now I think it over, though, it's not that easy to play a doctor. What if something goes wrong?

VALÈRE. What can go wrong? Gorgibus is a simple man, not to say stupid, and you can dazzle him by talking about Hippocrates and Galen.[5] Put on a bold front.

SGANARELLE. In other words, talk about philosophy and mathematics and the like. Leave it to me, Master; if he's a fool, as you say, I think I can swing it. All I need is a doctor's cloak and a few instructions. And also my license to practice, or to put it another way, those hundred francs. (*They go out together.*)

(GORGIBUS *enters with his fat valet,* GROS-RENÉ.)

GORGIBUS. Hurry away and find a doctor. My daughter's sick. Hurry.

GROS-RENÉ. Hell's bells, the trouble is you're trying to marry her off to an old man when she wants a young man; that's the only thing making her sick. Don't you see any connection between the appetite and the illness?

GORGIBUS. I can see that the illness will delay the wedding. Get a move on. 7

GROS-RENÉ. All this running about and my stomach's crying out for a new inner lining of food and now I have to wait for it. I need the doctor for myself as much as for your daughter. I'm in a desperate state. (*He lumbers off.*)

(SABINE *comes in with* SGANARELLE *behind her.*)

SABINE. Uncle, I have good news. I've brought a remarkably skilled doctor with me, a man who has traveled across the world and knows the medical secrets of Asia and Africa. He'll certainly be able to cure Lucile. As luck would have it, somebody pointed him out to me and I knew you'd want to meet him. He's

---

3. impersonate (im pėr′sə nāt), *v.* pretend to be.
4. **one hundred francs** presently worth about $20.
5. **Hippocrates** (hi pok′rə tēz′, 460?-370 B.C.?) . . . **Galen** (gā′lən; A.D. 138-201?), Ancient Greek physicians.

Created in the late 1600s, this painting portrays various actors who appeared at the Théatre Royal in Paris. Molière is at the far left. Judging from the painting, what inferences can you make about the entertainment and characters popular at the time? ➤

MINI-LESSON: GRAMMAR
Independent and Dependent Clauses

Teach Read this sentence from page 271:

> My uncle is determined to make Lucile marry this rich man, Villebrequin, and he's pushed the preparations so far that the marriage would have taken place today. . . .

Point out the coordinating conjunction *and* connecting the two independent clauses, and the subordinating conjunction *that* introducing the dependent clause. Remind students that independent clauses can stand alone and are connected with coordinating conjunctions, while dependent clauses cannot stand alone and are introduced with subordinating conjunctions.

Activity Idea Have students work on the play in small groups, identifying sentences with coordinating and subordinating conjunctions.

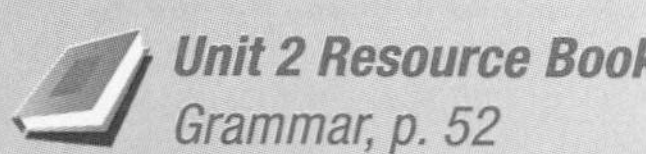

Unit 2 Resource Book
Grammar, p. 52

8 so clever that I wish I were ill myself so that he could cure me.

GORGIBUS. Where is he?

SABINE. Standing right behind me. *(She moves away.)* There he is.

GORGIBUS. Thank you so much for coming, Doctor. I'll take you straight to my daughter, who is unwell. I'm putting all my trust in you.

SGANARELLE. Hippocrates has said—and Galen has confirmed it with many persuasive arguments—that when a girl is not in good health she must be sick. You are right to put your trust in me, for I am the greatest, the most brilliant, the most doctoral physician in the vegetable, mineral, and animal kingdoms.

GORGIBUS. I'm overjoyed to hear it.

SGANARELLE. No ordinary physician am I, no common medico. In my opinion, all others are quacks. I have peculiar talents. I have secrets. *Salamalec* and *shalom aleichem. Nil nisi bonum? Si, Signor. Nein, mein Herr. Para siempre.*[6] But let us begin. *(He takes* GORGIBUS*'s pulse.)* 9

SABINE. He's not the patient. His daughter is. . . . She may be up by now. I'll bring her out. *(She goes into the house and brings* LUCILE *back with her.)*

SGANARELLE. How do you do, Mademoiselle?

6. ***Salamalec . . . siempre,*** words in several languages jumbled together with no meaning.

8 Literary Element

Hyperbole

Explain that *hyperbole*, commonly used for comic effect, is a figure of speech that uses exaggeration to add impact to a statement.

EDITORIAL NOTE The ellipses indicates an omitted passage in which Sganarelle pretends to drink Lucile's urine to diagnose her malady.

9 Historical Note

Molière's Doctors

Molière's grudge against the medical profession was perhaps not unfounded. Most doctors in the seventeenth century were still basing their methods on the misguided hypotheses of Galen, a Greek physician who lived over a thousand years before them. Students in medical school learned Latin and engaged in scholarly debates, but acquired little practical knowledge about curing diseases.

Art Study

Responses to Caption Question

The scene is crowded with energetic characters and masked figures making exaggerated gestures. Audiences probably enjoyed highly physical, boisterous performances, as well as intrigue based on disguises and trickery.

BUILDING ENGLISH PROFICIENCY

Exploring Plot Devices

Masquerade is a common plot device in plays. Use one or more of the following activities as students consider the use of masquerade in this play.

Activity Ideas

- Encourage students to recall situations in TV programs, movies, or books in which a character posed as—or was mistaken for—someone else. Allow them to share details of the problems caused by the masquerade.
- Invite students to offer terms and knowledge a doctor might be expected to know.
- Have students recall Sganarelle's ideas about what kinds of jobs are difficult. If necessary, ask students to read the lines aloud.
- Encourage students to predict some difficulties, problems, or comic situations that Sganarelle is probably going to face.

10 Literary Element
Satire

Explain to students that satire often uses exaggeration to expose and ridicule human follies and vice, as Molière does here with the medical and legal professions.

11 Reading/Thinking Skills
Evaluate

Ask students what they infer about Sganarelle from his ability to respond so quickly in this situation? *(Possible response: Even though he does not know how to write, he is obviously intelligent.)*

12 Reader's Response
Making Personal Connections

Have you ever been in a situation where you had to pretend to be someone else? *(Possible response: Students may have posed on the telephone as someone else.)*

13 Literary Element
Stereotypes

Help students see that this long-winded lawyer's affected speaking style identifies him as a stereotype of his time: a pretentious professional.

So you are sick?

LUCILE. Yes, Doctor.

SGANARELLE. That is a striking sign that you are not well. Do you feel pains in your head, in your kidneys?

LUCILE. Yes, Doctor.

10 **SGANARELLE.** Very good. As one great physician has said in regard to the nature of animal life—well—he said many things. We must attribute[7] this to the interconnections between the humors and the vapors.[8] For example, since melancholy is the natural enemy of joy, and since the bile that spreads through the body makes us turn yellow, and since there is nothing more inimical[9] to good health than sickness, we may conclude with that great man that your daughter is indisposed. Let me write you a prescription.

GORGIBUS. Quick! A table, paper, some ink—

SGANARELLE. Is there anybody here who knows how to write?

11 **GORGIBUS.** Don't you?

SGANARELLE. I have so many things to think of I forget half of them. Now it's obvious to me that your daughter needs fresh air and open prospects.

GORGIBUS. We have a very beautiful garden and a pavilion with some rooms that look out on it. If you agree, I can have her stay there.

SGANARELLE. Let us examine this dwelling. *(They start to go out. The* LAWYER *appears.)*

LAWYER. Monsieur Gorgibus—

GORGIBUS. Your servant, Monsieur.

LAWYER. I hear that your daughter is sick. May I offer my services, as a friend of the family?

GORGIBUS. I have the most scholarly doctor you ever met looking into this.

LAWYER. Really? I wonder if I might be able to meet him, however briefly?

(GORGIBUS *beckons to* SGANARELLE. LUCILE *and* SABINE *have moved offstage.)*

GORGIBUS. Doctor, I would like you to meet one of my dear friends, who is a lawyer and would like the privilege of conversing with you.

SGANARELLE. I wish I could spare the time, Monsieur, but I dare not neglect my patients. Please forgive me. *(He tries to go. The lawyer holds his sleeve.)* 12

13 **LAWYER.** My friend Gorgibus has intimated,[10] Monsieur, that your learning and abilities are formidable, and I am honored to make your acquaintance. I therefore take the liberty of saluting you in your noble work, and trust that it may resolve itself well. Those who excel in any branch of knowledge are worthy of all praise, but particularly those who practice medicine, not only because of its utility, but because it contains within itself other branches of knowledge, all of which render a perfect familiarity with it almost impossible to achieve. As Hippocrates so well observes in his first aphorism,[11] "Life is short, art is long, opportunity fleeting, experiment perilous, judgment difficult: *Vita brevis, ars vero longa, occasio autem praeceps, experimentum periculosum, judicium difficile.*"[12]

SGANARELLE *(confidentially to* GORGIBUS*).* Ficile, bicile, uptus, downtus, inandaboutus, wrigglo, gigolo.[13]

LAWYER. You are not one of those doctors who apply themselves to so-called rational or dogmatic medicine, and I am sure that you conduct your work with unusual success. Experience is the great teacher: *experientia magistra rerum.* The first men who practiced medicine were so esteemed that their daily cures earned them the status of gods on earth. One must not condemn a doctor who does not restore his patients to health, for healing

---

7. **attribute** (ə trib′yüt), *v.* think of as caused by.
8. **the humors and the vapors,** body fluids and gases once considered responsible for health and mood.
9. **inimical** (in im′ə kəl), *adj.* unfavorable.
10. **intimate** (in′tə māt), *v.* hint.
11. **aphorism** (af′ə riz′əm), *n.* brief statement expressing a truth.
12. ***Vita brevis . . . difficile,*** Latin translation of the lawyer's observation, "Life is short . . . judgment difficult."
13. **Ficile . . . gigolo,** nonsense words made to sound like Latin.

MINI-LESSON: VOCABULARY
Related Words

Exploring the relationships between words will help students to gain a deeper understanding of their meanings.

Activity Ideas

- Divide the class into groups. Assign one or more of the following word pairs to each group:
  device, devise
  impersonate, personality
  attribute, contribute
  inimical, enemy
  aphorism, metaphor
- Ask students to look up the definitions of the related words. Then, compare and contrast the words in each pair and brainstorm possible connections. Encourage creative approaches to understanding connections in meaning.

may not be effected by his remedies and wisdom alone. Ovid[14] remarks, "Sometimes the ill is stronger than art and learning combined." Monsieur, I will not detain you longer. I have enjoyed this dialogue and am more impressed than before with your percipience[15] and breadth of knowledge. I take my leave, hoping that I may have the pleasure of conversing with you further at your leisure. I am sure that your time is precious, and . . .

(He goes off, walking backwards, still talking, waving good-bye.)

GORGIBUS. How did he strike you?

SGANARELLE. He's moderately well informed. If I had more time I could engage him in a spirited discussion on some sublime and elevated topic. However, I must go. What is this?

(GORGIBUS *is tucking some money into his hand.*)

GORGIBUS. Believe me, Doctor, I know how much I owe you.

14 **SGANARELLE.** You must be joking, Monsieur Gorgibus. I am no mercenary. *(He takes the money.)* Thank you very much.

(GORGIBUS *goes off, and* SGANARELLE *drops his doctor's cloak and hat at the edge of the stage, just as* VALÈRE *reappears.*)

VALÈRE. Sganarelle, how did it go? I've been worried. I was looking for you. Did you ruin the plan?

SGANARELLE. Marvel of marvels. I played the part so well that Gorgibus thought I knew what I was talking about—and paid me. I looked at his home and told him that his daughter needed air, and he's moved her into the little house at the far end of his garden. You can visit her at your pleasure.

VALÈRE. You've made me very happy, Sganarelle. I'm going to her now. *(He rushes away.)*

SGANARELLE. That Gorgibus is a bigger dimwit than I am to let me get away with a trick like that. Save me—here he comes again. I'll have to talk fast. (GORGIBUS *returns.*)

GORGIBUS. Good morning, Monsieur.

SGANARELLE. Monsieur, you see before you a poor lad in despair. Have you come across a doctor who arrived in town a short while ago and cures people miraculously?

GORGIBUS. Yes, I've met him. He just left my house.

SGANARELLE. I am his brother. We are identical twins and people sometimes take one of us for the other.

GORGIBUS. Heaven help me if I didn't nearly make the same mistake. What is your name? 15

SGANARELLE. Narcissus, Monsieur, at your service. I should explain that once, when I was in his study, I accidentally knocked over two containers perched on the edge of his table. He flew into such a rage that he threw me out and swore he never wanted to see me again. So here I am now, a poor boy without means or connections.

GORGIBUS. Don't worry; I'll put in a good word for you. I'm a friend of his; I promise to bring you together again. As soon as I see him, I'll speak to him about it.

SGANARELLE. I am very much obliged to you, Monsieur.

(He goes out and reappears in the cloak and hat, playing the doctor again and talking to himself.) 16

When patients refuse to follow their doctor's advice and abandon themselves to debauchery[16] and—

GORGIBUS. Doctor, your humble servant. May I ask a favor of you?

SGANARELLE. What can I do for you, Monsieur Gorgibus?

GORGIBUS. I just happened to meet your brother, who is quite distressed—

SGANARELLE. He's a rascal, Monsieur Gorgibus.

GORGIBUS. But he truly regrets that he made you so angry, and—

SGANARELLE. He's a drunkard, Monsieur Gorgibus.

---

14. **Ovid** (43 B.C.-A.D.17), Roman poet.
15. **percipience** (pər sip′ē əns), *n.* shrewdness; ability to perceive.
16. **debauchery** (di bô′chər ē), *n.* corruption.

14 Literary Element
Irony

Question Explain how both Sganarelle's choice of words and his actions are ironic. *(Possible responses: "You must be joking": the joke is actually on Gorgibus; "I am no mercenary": Sganarelle's motivation to impersonate a doctor is purely mercenary.)*

15 Literary Element
Allusion

In Greek mythology, Narcissus, an aloof young hunter, falls in love with his own reflection in a pool of water.

Question Why might Molière have chosen this name for Sganarelle's imaginary twin? *(Possible response: because the twin brother is as unreal as the image that Narcissus saw in the pool)*

16 Reading/Thinking Skills
Visualize

Explain the use of standard costumes and masks to identify stock characters. Tell students that the standard doctor's costume is a long, black professor's cloak; his black felt hat is turned up at the rim.

BUILDING ENGLISH PROFICIENCY

Making Career Connections

Students may better appreciate the humor in Sganerelle's portrayal of a doctor by thinking about careers.

1. In a brief brainstorming session, ask students to name stereotyped characters that appear commonly in TV and movies. (Examples include newspaper or TV reporter, rock star, business executive, chef, fashion model, and librarian.)

- Ask what makes these characters one-dimensional.
- Have students think of people in the media who are portrayed as three-dimensional characters in realistic careers. Ask what prevents these characters from being types.

2. Ask: Do you think contemporary, real-life doctors and lawyers are sometimes viewed as stereotypes? Why or why not?

17 Reading/Thinking Skills
Make Judgments

Question How do Gorgibus' actions contradict his intentions? *(Possible response: His openhearted attempt to mend the quarrel between the "brothers" is compromised by his rude, forceful manner.)*

18 Literary Element
Pun

Question Identify a pun in Sganarelle's comic monologue. What word meanings are being played with here? *(Sganarelle puns on the meaning of* brand *as a "permanent scar" and "a certain type" and* rain *as "precipitation" and "a series of blows.")*

19 Literary Element
Dramatic Irony

Dramatic irony arises from a situation in which the audience knows something that one or more of the characters do not know. Point out to students that the audience sees Sganarelle sneak up right behind the oblivious Gorgibus as he searches for him.

GORGIBUS. But surely, Doctor, you're not going to give the poor boy up?

SGANARELLE. Not another word about him. The impudence of the rogue, seeking you out to intercede for him! I implore you not to mention him to me.

GORGIBUS. In God's name, Doctor, and out of respect for me, too, have pity on him. I'll do anything for you in return. I promised—

SGANARELLE. You plead so insistently that, even though I swore a violent oath never to forgive him—well, I'll shake your hand on it; I forgive him. You can be assured that I am doing myself a great injury and that I would not have consented to this for any other man. Good-bye, Monsieur Gorgibus.

GORGIBUS. Thank you, Doctor, thank you. I'll go off and look for the boy to tell him the glad news.

(He walks off. SGANARELLE *takes off the doctor's cloak and hat.* VALÈRE *appears.)*

VALÈRE. I never thought Sganarelle would do his duty so magnificently. Ah, my dear boy, I don't know how to repay you. I'm so happy I—

SGANARELLE. It's easy for you to talk. Gorgibus just ran into me without my doctor's outfit, and if I hadn't come up with a quick story we'd have been sunk. Here he comes again. Disappear.

(VALÈRE *runs away.* GORGIBUS *returns.)*

GORGIBUS. Narcissus, I've been looking everywhere for you. I spoke to your brother and he forgives you. But to be safe, I want to see the two of you patch up your quarrel in front of me. Wait here in my house, and I'll find him.

SGANARELLE. I don't think you'll find him, Monsieur. Anyhow, I wouldn't dare to wait; I'm terrified of him.

17 **GORGIBUS** *(pushing* SGANARELLE *inside).* Yes, you will stay. I'm locking you in. Don't be afraid of your brother. I promise you that he's not angry now.

(He slams the door and locks it, then goes off to look for the doctor.)

SGANARELLE *(at the upstairs window).* Serves me right; I trapped myself and there's no way out. The weather in my future looks threatening, and if there's a storm I'm afraid I'll feel a rain of blows on my back. Or else they'll brand me across the shoulders with a whip—not exactly the brand of medicine any doctor ever prescribed. Yes, I'm in trouble. But why give up when we've come this far? Let's go the limit. I can still make a bid for freedom and prove that Sganarelle is the king of swindlers. 18

(He holds his nose, closes his eyes, and jumps to the ground, just as GROS-RENÉ *comes back. Then he darts away, picking up the cloak and hat.* GROS-RENÉ *stands staring.)*

GROS-RENÉ. A flying man! What a laugh! I'll wait around and see if there's another one.

(GORGIBUS *reenters with* SGANARELLE *following him in the doctor's outfit.)*

GORGIBUS. Can't find that doctor. Where the devil has he hidden himself? 19

(He turns and SGANARELLE *walks into him.)*

There you are. Now, Doctor, I know you said you forgive your brother, but that's not enough. I won't be satisfied until I see you embrace him. He's waiting here in my house.

SGANARELLE. You are joking. Monsieur Gorgibus. Have I not extended myself enough already? I wish never to see him again.

GORGIBUS. Please, Doctor, for me.

SGANARELLE. I cannot refuse when you ask me like that. Tell him to come down.

(As GORGIBUS *goes into the house,* SGANARELLE *drops the clothes, clambers swiftly up to the window again, and scrambles inside.)*

GORGIBUS *(at the window).* Your brother is waiting for you downstairs, Narcissus. He said he'd do what I asked.

SGANARELLE *(at the window).* Couldn't you please make him come up here? I beg of you—let me see him in private to ask his for-

MINI-LESSON: LITERARY FOCUS
Farce

Teach Point out that slapstick relies on physical humor. The term *slapstick* originated with a literal "slapstick"—a flat wooden instrument used in the *commedia dell'arte*—that made a loud cracking noise to exaggerate physical impact.

Question Identify an example of slapstick in *The Flying Doctor*. *(Possible responses: Sganarelle's jumping from the upstairs window without injuring himself and his many changes in and out of the Doctor's disguise)* Point out that characters performing slapstick often seem indestructible. Their superhuman antics lend an air of magic to the farce.

Activity Idea Students are probably familiar with the use of slapstick from watching TV cartoons like *Ren and Stimpy* or *The Roadrunner*. Divide students into groups and have them draw a simple eight-frame storyboard illustrating slapstick humor.

giveness, because if I go down there he'll show me up and say nasty things to me in front of everybody.

20 **GORGIBUS.** All right. Let me tell him. *(He leaves the window, and* SGANARELLE *leaps out, swiftly puts on his outfit again, and stands waiting for* GORGIBUS *outside the door.)*
Doctor, he's so ashamed of himself he wants to beg your forgiveness in private, upstairs. Here's the key. Please don't refuse me.

SGANARELLE. There is nothing I would not do for you, Monsieur Gorgibus. You will hear how I deal with him.

(He walks into the house and soon appears at the window. GORGIBUS *has his ear cocked at the door below.* SGANARELLE *alternates his voice, playing the characters one at a time.)*

SGANARELLE. So there you are, you scoundrel!
—Brother, listen to me, please. I'm sorry I knocked those containers over—
—You clumsy ox
—It wasn't my fault, I swear it.
—Not your fault, you bumpkin? I'll teach you to destroy my work.
—Brother, no, please—
—I'll teach you to trade on Monsieur Gorgibus's good nature. How dare you ask him to ask me to forgive you!
—Brother, I'm sorry, but—
—Silence, you dog!
—I never wanted to hurt you or—
—Silence, I say—

GROS-RENÉ. What exactly do you think is going on up there?

GORGIBUS. It's the doctor and his brother, Narcissus. They had a little disagreement, but now they're making it up.

GROS-RENÉ. Doctor and his brother? But there's only one man.

SGANARELLE *(at the window).* Yes, you drunkard. I'll thump some good behavior into you. *(Pretends to strike a blow.)* Ah, he's lowering his eyes; he knows what he's done wrong, the jailbird. And now this hypocrite wants to play the good apostle—

GROS-RENÉ. Just for fun, tell him to let his brother appear at the window.

GORGIBUS. I will. *(To* SGANARELLE.*)* Doctor, let me see your brother for a moment.

SGANARELLE. He is not fit to be seen by an honest gentleman like yourself. Besides, I cannot bear to have him next to me.

GORGIBUS. Please don't say no, after all you've done for me.

SGANARELLE. Monsieur Gorgibus, you have such power over me that I must grant whatever you wish. Show yourself, beast!

(He appears at the window as Narcissus.)
Monsieur Gorgibus, I thank you for your kindness.

(He reappears as the doctor.)
Well, Monsieur, did you take a good look at that image of impurity?

GROS-RENÉ. There's only one man there, Monsieur. We can prove it. Tell them to stand by the window together. 21

GORGIBUS. Doctor, I want to see you at the window embracing your brother, and then I'll be satisfied.

SGANARELLE. To any other man in the world I would return a swift and negative answer, but to you, Monsieur Gorgibus, I will yield, although not without much pain to myself. But first I want this knave to beg your pardon for all the trouble he has caused you.

(He comes back as Narcissus.)
Yes, Monsieur Gorgibus, I beg your pardon for having bothered you, and I promise you, brother, in from of Monsieur Gorgibus there, that I'll be so good from now on that you'll never be angry with me again. Please let bygones be bygones.

(He embraces the cloak and hat.)

GORGIBUS. There they are, the two of them together.

GROS-RENÉ. The man's a magician.

(He hides; SGANARELLE *comes out of the house, dressed as the doctor.)*

SGANARELLE. Here is your key, Monsieur. I have left my brother inside because I am ashamed

20 Literary Element
Pace

You might take this opportunity to elicit discussion about the play's comic pace.

- Sganarelle must keep up with an accelerating number of actions within a given time frame.
- The nature of the action—to jump from a window and clamber up to it repeatedly—is improbable and extreme.

21 Literary Focus
Social Context

Question How does the character of Gros-René satirize the class system of master and servant? *(Possible response: Although Gros-René is stereotyped as a fat, lazy servant, he not only proves to be cunning and persistent, but he tells his master what to do, turning the social hierarchy on its head.)*

BUILDING ENGLISH PROFICIENCY

ESL
LEP
ELD
SAE
LD

Tracking Plot Events

As the action in this play rises, events quickly become quite complicated. To help students keep track of the play's action, provide a graphic organizer, such as the one shown, and have them collaborate (perhaps using butcher paper) on completing it.

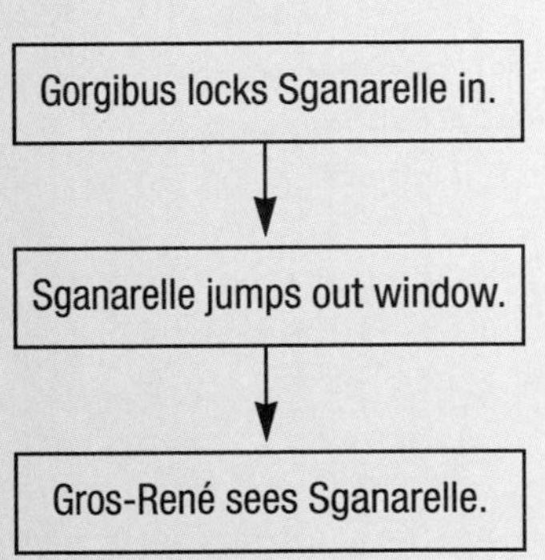
Gorgibus locks Sganarelle in.
Sganarelle jumps out window.
Gros-René sees Sganarelle.

22 Reader's Response
Challenging the Text

Questions

- Why would you expect this play to have a happy ending? *(Possible response: because audiences attending a comedy expect to be amused and don't want to leave on a tragic note)*
- Do you think this ending is realistic? Explain your answer. *(Possible responses: No, it seems unlikely that Gorgibus would accept the deception and disobedience of his daughter so readily. Yes, Gorgibus has already demonstrated his eagerness for reconciliation by encouraging peace between the doctor and his twin.)*

Art Study

Responses to Caption Question
Possible responses: TV: Bart Simpson exemplifies the wily prankster; Movies: Arnold Schwarzenegger typifies the tough warrior who has a heart of gold; Comics: Tank Girl typifies a strong female character that rebels against societal norms.

Check Test

1. Why does Lucile pretend to be ill? *(to delay her wedding to a man she does not want to marry)*
2. What scheme do Sabine and Valère devise? *(to get a fake doctor to convince Gorgibus that Lucile must be moved to the pavilion)*
3. Who is the flying doctor? *(Sganarelle)*
4. Who is Narcissus? *(Sganarelle, pretending to be his own twin brother)*
5. Who exposes Sganarelle's hoax? *(Gros-René)*

Unit 2 Resource Book
Alternate Check Test, p. 53

of him. One does not wish to be seen in his company now that one has some reputation in this town. You may release him whenever you think fit. Good-bye, Monsieur.

(He strides off; then as GORGIBUS *goes into the house he wheels, dropping the cloak and hat, and climbs back through the window.)*

GORGIBUS *(upstairs).* There you are, my boy, you're free. I am pleased that your brother forgave you, although I think he was rather hard on you.

SGANARELLE. Monsieur, I cannot thank you enough. A brother's blessing on you. I will remember you all my life.

(While they are upstairs, GROS-RENÉ *has picked up the cloak and hat, and stands waiting for them. They come out of the door.)*

GROS-RENÉ. Well, where do you think your doctor is now?

GORGIBUS. Gone, of course.

GROS-RENÉ. He's right here, under my arm. And by the way, while this fellow was getting in and out of the cloak, the hat, and the window, Valère ran off with your daughter and married her.

GORGIBUS. I'm ruined! I'll have you strung up, you dog, you knave! Yes, you deserve every name your brother called you— What am I saying?

SGANARELLE. You don't really want to string me up, do you, Monsieur? Please listen for one second. It's true that I was having a game with you while my master was with Mademoiselle Lucile. But in serving him I haven't done you any harm. He's a most suitable partner for her, by rank and by income, by God. Believe me, if you make a row about this you'll only bring more confusion on your head. As for that porker there, let him get lost and take Villebrequin with him. Here come our loving couple.

*(*VALÈRE *enters contritely with* LUCILE. *They kneel to* GORGIBUS.*)*

VALÈRE. We apologize to you.

GORGIBUS. Well, perhaps it's lucky that I was tricked by Sganarelle; he's brought me a fine son-in-law. Let's go out to celebrate the marriage and drink a toast to the health of all the company. 22

(They dance off in couples: VALÈRE *with* LUCILE, GORGIBUS *with* GROS-RENÉ, *and* SGANARELLE *with* SABINE.*)*

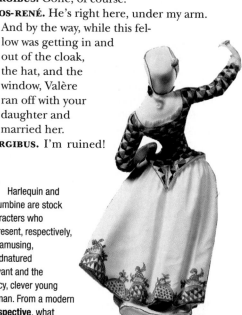

Harlequin and Columbine are stock characters who represent, respectively, the amusing, goodnatured servant and the saucy, clever young woman. From a modern **perspective**, what character types can you identify from comics, TV, or movies? ➤

MINI-LESSON: WRITING STYLE
The Tools of the Comic Playwright

Teach Review with students some of the tools that Molière uses to create humor:

- Satire: pokes fun at human follies
- Hyperbole: exaggerates with words and gestures
- Absurd dialogue: uses puns and nonsensical language
- Pace: accelerates pace to create a chaotic tempo

Activity Idea Provide students with a potentially comic scenario, or have them volunteer suggestions themselves. (For example: Two burly football players decide to join a ballet troupe because they are both interested in the troupe's leading ballerina.) In their Writer's Notebooks, have students write a short dramatic scene using one or more of these elements to create humor. Volunteers can read their scenes to the class.

After Reading

Making Connections

Shaping Your Response

1. Do you think modern audiences are too sophisticated to enjoy Molière's slapstick humor? Why or why not?
2. In your notebook, write three words that describe Sganarelle.
3. Do you consider this a play about love or about something else? Explain.

Analyzing the Play

4. When asked to impersonate a doctor, Sganarelle says, ". . . I don't have the brains for it. I'm not subtle enough; I'm not even bright." Do you agree with his self-appraisal? Explain.
5. How would you **characterize** Gorgibus?
6. What do the following **stage directions** indicate about the Lawyer: *"He goes off, walking backwards, still talking, waving good-bye"?*
7. How does this play illustrate the **theme** "Beneath the Surface"?
8. What aspects of the medical and legal professions does Molière **satirize** in this play?
9. Which characters do you think represent **stereotypes?**

Extending the Ideas

10. Compare *The Flying Doctor* to other works of literature (perhaps ones appearing in this book), movies, or TV programs that satirize human qualities such as greed, hypocrisy, or vanity.

Literary Focus: Farce

A type of comedy that involves broad characters, unlikely situations, and slapstick action is called **farce.** Farce relies heavily on fast pacing, exaggeration, and physical action and often includes mistaken identity and deception. In the hands of Molière, farce is a vehicle for exposing human faults and absurd social customs. Find examples of each of the following in *The Flying Doctor.*

- mistaken identity
- deception
- slapstick action
- broad characters

After Reading

MAKING CONNECTIONS

1. Possible response: No, many television shows and movies rely heavily on slapstick to make modern audiences laugh.

2. Possible responses: witty, clever, dishonest, loyal, athletic

3. Possible response: No, the love story is just a device to set the buffoonery and farce in motion. The play is more about the pretensions of the upper class.

4. Possible response: No, Sganarelle proves through his dodges and dialogue that he is a quite clever master of deceit.

5. Possible response: Gorgibus is absent-minded and headstrong, greedy and generous all at once.

6. Possible response: He is obsequious, long-winded, and ridiculous.

7. Possible response: Molière's theme seems to be that surface appearances can be deceptive: Those who appear to be in charge, like Gorgibus, may be easily manipulated by subordinates. Those who pretend to know everything, like the Lawyer, may be fools. Servants, like Sganarelle, may be the cleverest of all and control the rest.

8. Molière satirizes their tendency to puff themselves up with arcane knowledge and jargon.

9. Possible response: all of them except possibly Sabine. Valère and Lucile represent the lovers who face obstacles; Gorgibus, the overbearing father; Gros-René, the surly servant; Sganarelle, the lovable knave; the Lawyer, the foolish know-it-all.

10. Students might compare the greed of Gorgibus with that of the hunters in "The Boar Hunt."

LITERARY FOCUS: FARCE

- Mistaken identity: Gorgibus thinks Sganarelle has a twin brother named Narcissus; this "twin" is actually Sganarelle without his doctor's disguise.
- Deception: With Sganarelle's help, Lucile deceives her father into believing she is sick so that she can escape and marry Valère.
- Slapstick action: Sganarelle embraces his doctor's cloak and hat as if they were a person.
- Broad characters: Gorgibus is a standard type character who is no deeper or more complex than his surface implies. Sabine is little more than a go-between. Valère and Lucile are stereotypical young lovers.

VOCABULARY STUDY

1. device
2. inimical
3. debauchery
4. attribute
5. impersonate

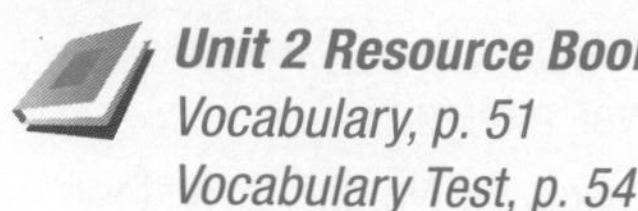

Unit 2 Resource Book
Vocabulary, p. 51
Vocabulary Test, p. 54

WRITING CHOICES

Writer's Notebook Update

Divide students into groups. Have students take turns pretending that they are pitching their "love story" to a team of movie producers (the other students in their group).

Be a Critic

Suggest that students now write an angry letter in response to the review that their partner wrote. Tell them to write in strong disagreement with the review and give reasons for their opinion.

Comic Twist

Have volunteers read their rewritten farces to the class and measure the level of laughs and smiles from the audience. Ask them if they think this would be a helpful tool for a playwright to use when writing a farce.

Selection Test

Unit 2 Resource Book
pp. 55–56

Vocabulary Study

Use context clues to complete each sentence with one of the listed words. Not all the words will be used.

aphorism
attribute
debauchery
device
impersonate
inimical

1. In the farces of Molière, there is often a scheme, or ____, by which to trick a foolish person.
2. Lovers usually overcome ____ circumstances and are eventually united despite unfavorable odds.
3. Molière satirizes ____ in corrupt individuals.
4. Although people often ____ the kind of comedy we call farce to Molière, it existed many centuries before he lived.
5. Do you find it humorous that a lowly servant could ____ a doctor so well?

Expressing Your Ideas

Writing Choices

Writer's Notebook Update Look at the plot twists you suggested. Do you have material for an interesting love story? Maybe, maybe not. Try writing an opening paragraph that would make a reader want to continue. You may have the beginnings of a farce!

Be a Critic Work with a partner, with each of you writing a **review** of the play: one designed to attract an audience, the other designed to keep people away. You might get some ideas of how to sway an audience by reading current film or drama reviews.

Comic Twist In a group, take any story from this book that you think lends itself to comedy and **rewrite** the first page or two as a dramatic farce, complete with stage directions.

Other Choices

Broad Strokes The broadly drawn characters in *The Flying Doctor* lend themselves to artistic expressions. Choose a character to represent in a **caricature,** or exaggerated sketch.

Walk This Way, Sir Review some movies of the Marx brothers, the Three Stooges, or other comedians who are noted for their broad comedy. Make a list of gags that recur throughout such works, such as puns and slapstick like slipping on a banana peel. Work with a small group to put on a **comedy skit** using visual and verbal tricks of comedy.

OTHER OPTIONS

Broad Strokes

Some suggestions for exaggerated features: a stooped back, a large belly, a hooked nose, a mask

Walk This Way, Sir

Students may want to build upon one of the dramatic writing exercises in their Writer's Notebook.

Before Reading

The Chameleon by Anton Chekhov   Russia

The Fox and the Woodcutter by Aesop   Greece

A Poison Tree by William Blake   Great Britain

Building Background

Nothing But the Truth Do you associate truthfulness more with certain professions than with others? Conduct a quick survey to determine which professions classmates associate with truthfulness. How did politicians fare? Are some of the class's opinions based on stereotypical assumptions? Are professionals who are in the public eye more likely to appear dishonest? Are elected officials under more pressure than other professionals to please people? After a discussion, prepare to read about a political figure who acts in his own best interests.

Literary Focus

Tone The **tone** of a selection is the attitude of the writer toward his or her subject. An author communicates a tone, such as awe, anger, fear, humor, and cynicism, through word choice and in the arrangement of ideas, events, and descriptions. As you read "The Chameleon," "The Fox and the Woodcutter," and "A Poison Tree," try to determine each author's attitude toward his subject.

Writer's Notebook

False Fronts Everyone has at some time presented a false front, appearing to be or to feel something that is not authentic. It may have been to save face, to avoid hurting someone's feelings, or to avoid consequences. Think of one such incident and write about the circumstances and your feelings at the time.

Before Reading

Building Background

Encourage students to extend the survey to include the members of their family. Have students compare and contrast the responses of people of different ages, cultural backgrounds, and professions.

Literary Focus

Draw a connection between **tone** in writing to tone of voice in speaking.

- Have students repeat the following sentence using these tones: awe, anger, fear, humor, and cynicism.
  "Didn't she tell you?"
- Invite students to make a list of words to describe various tones.

Words to Indicate Tone	
comic	surprised
peaceful	argumentative
joyous	

Writer's Notebook

Once students recall an incident involving a false front, they should choose a tone that best conveys their feelings.

Connections to **AuthorWorks**

Anton Chekhov and William Blake are featured authors in the AuthorWorks CD-Rom series.

SUPPORT MATERIALS OVERVIEW

Unit 2 Resource Book
- Graphic Organizer, p. 57
- Study Guide, p. 58
- Vocabulary, p. 59
- Grammar, p. 60
- Alternate Check Test, p. 61
- Vocabulary Test, p. 62
- Selection Test, pp. 63–64

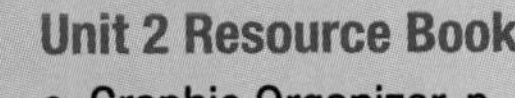

Building English Proficiency
- Literature Summaries
- Activities, p. 188
- "The Chameleon" in Spanish

Reading, Writing & Grammar SkillBook
- Grammar, Usage, and Mechanics, pp. 119–200, 208–209
- Reading, 69

Technology
- Audiotape 8, Side A
- Personal Journal Software
- Custom Literature Database: For another story by Anton Chekhov, see "The Lady with the Dog" on the database.
- Test Generator Software

More About the Poets

Anton Chekhov wrote under many pen names at the start of his literary career, including "My Brother's Brother," "The Man Without Spleen," "Physician Without a Practice," and "Antosha Chekhonte," which was a nickname a schoolteacher had given him. Other works by Chekhov include:

- "The Steppe," (1888)
- *The Sea Gull,* (1896)

Aesop It is also possible that "Aesop" was simply a name like "Mother Goose" that was applied to anonymous didactic stories about animals. This theory is supported by the fact that some of Aesop's fables have been found on Egyptian papyri dating from almost a millennium before his supposed birth.

William Blake is often referred to as a visionary poet. He claimed that as a child he saw angels in a tree and met the prophet Ezekiel in a field. He also insisted that his brother's ghost helped him invent a special etching technique called "illuminated printing." Other works by Blake include:

- *Songs of Innocence,* (1789)
- *The Marriage of Heaven and Hell,* (1793)
- *Songs of Experience,* (1794)

Anton Chekhov

1860–1904

Anton Chekhov grew up in Taganrog, Russia, in the era when czars still ruled the Russian empire. He enrolled in medical school in 1879 and supported his family by writing for magazines and newspapers. Friends and relatives, he observed, "were always condescending toward my writing and constantly advised me in a friendly way not to give up real work [medicine] for scribbling." Nevertheless, he began earning a literary reputation, writing stories and plays about characters caught up in poverty, love, family struggles, and old-world class distinctions. Many of his stories and plays such as *The Cherry Orchard, Uncle Vanya,* and *Three Sisters* have become modern classics.

Aesop

620?–560? B.C.

Although it is not known for certain whether the man Aesop (ē′səp) ever really lived, the most prevalent theory is that he was a slave whose witty stories and tales about animals eventually earned him his freedom. Traveling throughout Greece and Egypt during times of political tyranny, Aesop told fables that barely disguised his political views. His wit and ingenuity usually got him out of tricky situations, but his luck ran out at Delphi when someone planted a gold cup in his bag. After being condemned to death and thrown off a cliff, numerous disasters occurred in Delphi until the citizens made public reparation to Aesop's memory.

William Blake

1757–1827

William Blake received no formal schooling, but "picked up his education as well as he could" by studying Shakespeare, Milton, and the Bible. At fourteen he was apprenticed as an engraver in London and also began writing verse, printing it by himself from engraved copper plates with hand-colored illustrations. Judged by some of his contemporaries to be insane, Blake was recognized as a poetic genius by later generations. His friends, however, appreciated his gifts. As his friend Edward Calvert said, "He was not mad, but perverse and willful; he reasoned correctly from arbitrary, and often false premises."

MINI-LESSON: CRITICAL THINKING

Analyze Genre

Teach Have students analyze the function of genre by drawing a separate genre web for the short story, the fable, and the poem. Ask students to brainstorm what they know about the purpose, the defining characteristics, and some favorite examples of each genre.

Activity Ideas

- Have each student pick a genre to explore in more detail. Ask them to write a short essay about the characteristics and functions of that genre.
- Have students write a short piece that would classify as an example of one of the three focus genres.

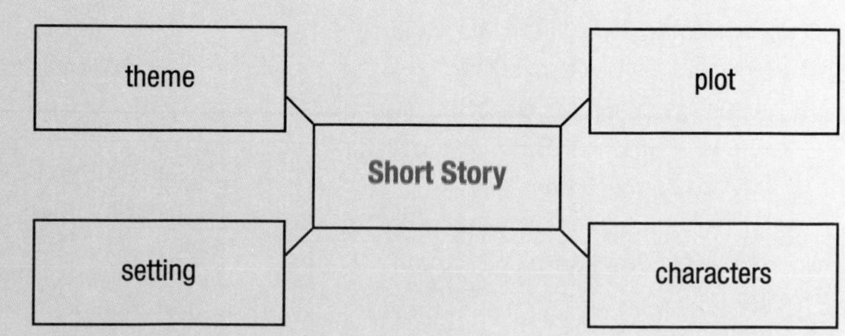

The Chameleon

Anton Chekhov

Across the market square comes Police Inspector Moronoff. He is wearing a new greatcoat and carrying a small package. Behind him strides a ginger-headed constable bearing a sieve filled to the brim with confiscated[1] gooseberries. There is silence all around . . . Not a soul in the square . . . The wide-open doors of the shops and taverns look out dolefully[2] on the world, like hungry jaws; even their beggars have vanished.

"Bite me, would you, you little devil?" Moronoff suddenly hears. "Catch him, lads, catch him! Biting's against the law now! Grab him! Ouch!"

A dog squeals. Moronoff looks round—and sees a dog run out of merchant Spatchkin's woodyard, hopping along on three legs and glancing backwards. A man in a starched calico shirt and unbuttoned waistcoat comes chasing out after it. He runs behind, bends down right over it, and tumbles to the ground catching the dog by the hind legs. There is another squeal and a shout: "Hold him, lads!" Sleepy countenances[3] thrust themselves out of the shop windows and soon a crowd has sprung up from nowhere by the woodyard.

"Looks like trouble, your honor!" says the constable.

Moronoff executes a half-turn to his left and marches towards the throng. He sees the aforementioned man in the unbuttoned shirt is standing at the yard gates and with his right hand raised high in the air is showing the crowd a blood-stained finger. His half-sozzled face seems to be saying "You'll pay for this, you scoundrel!" and his very finger has the air of a victory banner. Moronoff recognizes the man as Grunkin the goldsmith. On the ground in the midst of the crowd, its front legs splayed out and its whole body trembling, sits the actual cause of the commotion; a white borzoi[4] puppy with a pointed muzzle and a yellow patch on its back. 1 The expression in its watering eyes is one of terror and despair.

"What's all this about?" asks Moronoff, cut-

1. confiscated (kon′fə skāt ed), *adj.* seized; taken.
2. dolefully (dōl′fəl lē), *adv.* mournfully.
3. countenance (koun′tə nəns), *n.* expression of the face.
4. **borzoi** (bôr′zoi), *n.* any of a breed of tall, slender, swift dogs with silky hair, developed in Russia; Russian wolfhound.

During Reading

Selection Objectives

- to analyze literary representations of hypocrisy, falsehood, and wrath that illustrate the theme "Beneath the Surface"
- to examine the power of tone as a literary device
- to explore the use of consistent verb tense

Unit 2 Resource Book
Graphic Organizer, p. 57
Study Guide, p. 58

Theme Link

The theme "Beneath the Surface" is shown in three works—about an inspector who bends the law to accommodate his social ambitions, an old man who breaks his word without speaking, and an enemy who steals his own fatal poison. These selections expose the mischief and motivation of dishonest people.

Vocabulary Preview

confiscated, seized; taken
dolefully, mournfully
countenance, expression of the face
compensation, something given to make up for a loss or injury
profound, deeper than what is easily understood
grievance, a cause for complaint
muse, say thoughtfully
ecstatic, feeling great joy
wily, crafty; sly
vixen, a female fox
wrath, a very great anger; rage

Students can add the words and definitions to their Writer's Notebooks.

1 Literary Element
Point of View

Question Ask students to identify the point of view of this story. *(third-person omniscient)*

SELECTION SUMMARIES

The Chameleon, The Fox and the Woodcutter, A Poison Tree

- Inspector Moronoff, who is investigating a dog bite, cannot decide how to proceed. If the dog belongs to a political superior, he must establish its innocence. If the dog is a stray, he must put it down and avenge the accuser's injury. After much vacillation and accusation, the General identifies the dog's powerful owner and turns his back on the bitten man.
- A woodcutter, who promises to help a fox hide from a pursuing hunter, tells the hunter he hasn't seen the fox, but points to her hiding place. The hunter misses the clue, and the fox escapes after reproaching the woodcutter for his hypocrisy.
- The speaker deceitfully nurtures a resentment against his foe until it bears a poisonous apple. His enemy steals the apple, eats it, and dies.

*For summaries in other languages, see the **Building English Proficiency** book. "The Chameleon" in Spanish*

2 Literary Element
Dialogue

Dialogue can reveal important character traits. What clues suggest Grunkin is not as innocent as he claims? *(Possible responses: "minding me own business," the slight cough, and the exaggerations)*

3 Literary Focus
Tone

Explain that the tone of a piece often reflects the author's opinion of his or her subject.

Question What might Moronoff's reaction imply about Chekhov's opinion of the police? *(He may think they are over-zealous show-offs who waste time enforcing trivial laws.)*

4 Active Reading
Clarify

Possible response Someone tells him the dog belongs to General Tartaroff, who is a powerful citizen.

5 Literary Element
Dialect

Point out that the translator conveys Chekhov's use of lower-class Russian dialect as British slang. Provide the meanings of slang terms: *fag* (cigarette), *mug* (face, mouth), *for a lark* (as a joke).

ting through the crowd. "Why are you lot here? What's your finger—? Who shouted just now?"

2 "I was walking along, your honor, minding me own business . . ." Grunkin begins, giving a slight cough, "on my way to see Mitry Mitrich about some firewood—when all of a sudden, for no reason, this little tyke goes for my finger . . . Beg pardon, sir, but I'm a man what's working . . . My work's delicate work. I want compensation[5] for this—after all, I may not be able to lift this finger for a week now . . .There's nothing in the law even that says we have to put up with that from beasts, is there your honor? If we all went round biting, we might as well be dead . . ."

"Hm! All right . . ." says Moronoff sternly, clearing his throat and knitting his brows, "Right . . .Who owns this dog? I shall not let this matter rest. I'll teach you to let dogs run loose! It's time we took a closer look at these people who won't obey regulations! A good fat fine'll teach the blighter[6] what I think of dogs and suchlike vagrant cattle! I'll take him down a peg! Dildin," says the inspector, turning to the constable, "find out who owns this dog, and take 3 a statement! And the dog must be put down. Forthwith! It's probably mad anyway . . . Come on then, who's the owner?"

"Looks like General Tartaroff's!" says a voice from the crowd.

"General Tartaroff's? Hm . . . Dildin, remove my coat for me, will you?. . . Phew it's hot! We must be in for rain . . . What I don't understand, though, is this: how did it manage to bite you?" says Moronoff, turning to Grunkin. "How could it reach up to your finger? A little dog like that, and a hulking great bloke like you! I expect what happened was, you skinned your finger on a nail, then had the bright idea of making some money out of it. I know your lot! You devils don't fool me!"

4

CLARIFY: What do you think causes Moronoff's change in tone?

5 "He shoved a fag in its mug for a lark, your honor, but she weren't having any and went for him . . . He's always stirring up trouble, your honor!"

"Don't lie, Boss-Eye! You couldn't see, so why tell lies? His honor here's a clever gent, he knows who's lying and who's telling the gospel truth . . . And if he thinks I'm lying, then let the justice decide. He's got it all written down there in the law . . . We're all equal now . . . I've got a brother myself who's in the police . . . you may like to know—"

"Stop arguing!"

"No, it's not the General's . . ." the constable observes profoundly.[7] "The General ain't got any like this. His are more setters . . ."

"Are you sure of that?"

"Quite sure, your honor—"

"Well of course I know that, too. The General has dogs that are worth something, thoroughbreds, but this is goodness knows what! It's got no coat, it's nothing to look at—just a load of rubbish . . . Do you seriously think he'd keep a dog like that? Use your brains. You know what'd happen if a dog like that turned up in Petersburg or Moscow? They wouldn't bother looking in the law books, they'd dispatch him—double quick! You've got a grievance,[8] Grunkin, and you mustn't let the matter rest . . . Teach 'em a lesson! It's high time . . ."

"Could be the General's, though . . ." muses[9] the constable aloud. "It ain't written on its

5. compensation (kom′pən sā′shən), *n.* something given to make up for a loss or injury.
6. **blighter** (blīt′er), *n.* rascal.
7. profoundly (prə found′lē), *adv.* going more deeply than what is easily understood.
8. grievance (grē′vəns), *n.* a cause for complaint.
9. muse (myüz), *v.* say thoughtfully.

Boris Kustodiev's political caricature, produced in 1906, satirizes a Russian government official. Find a contemporary political cartoon that uses similar broad strokes to poke fun at a public figure. ➤

MINI-LESSON: GRAMMAR
Consistent Verb Tense

Teach Have students name the verbs in the first paragraph of "The Chameleon." Ask them to identify the tense of each verb. *(comes, is wearing, [is] carrying, strides, is, look, have vanished. All the verbs are present tense, except the last, which is present perfect.)* Explain that once a verb tense has been established, based on the time of the actions being described, every verb should match that tense unless sense requires a shift—as it does at the end of Chekhov's paragraph.

Activity Ideas

Invite students to do one of the following activities:

- Find a short writing sample from your Writer's Notebook that is written in the past tense. Check the verb tenses and correct any inconsistencies.
- Rewrite the writing sample in the present tense, following Chekhov's model.

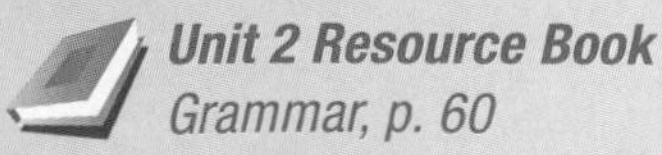

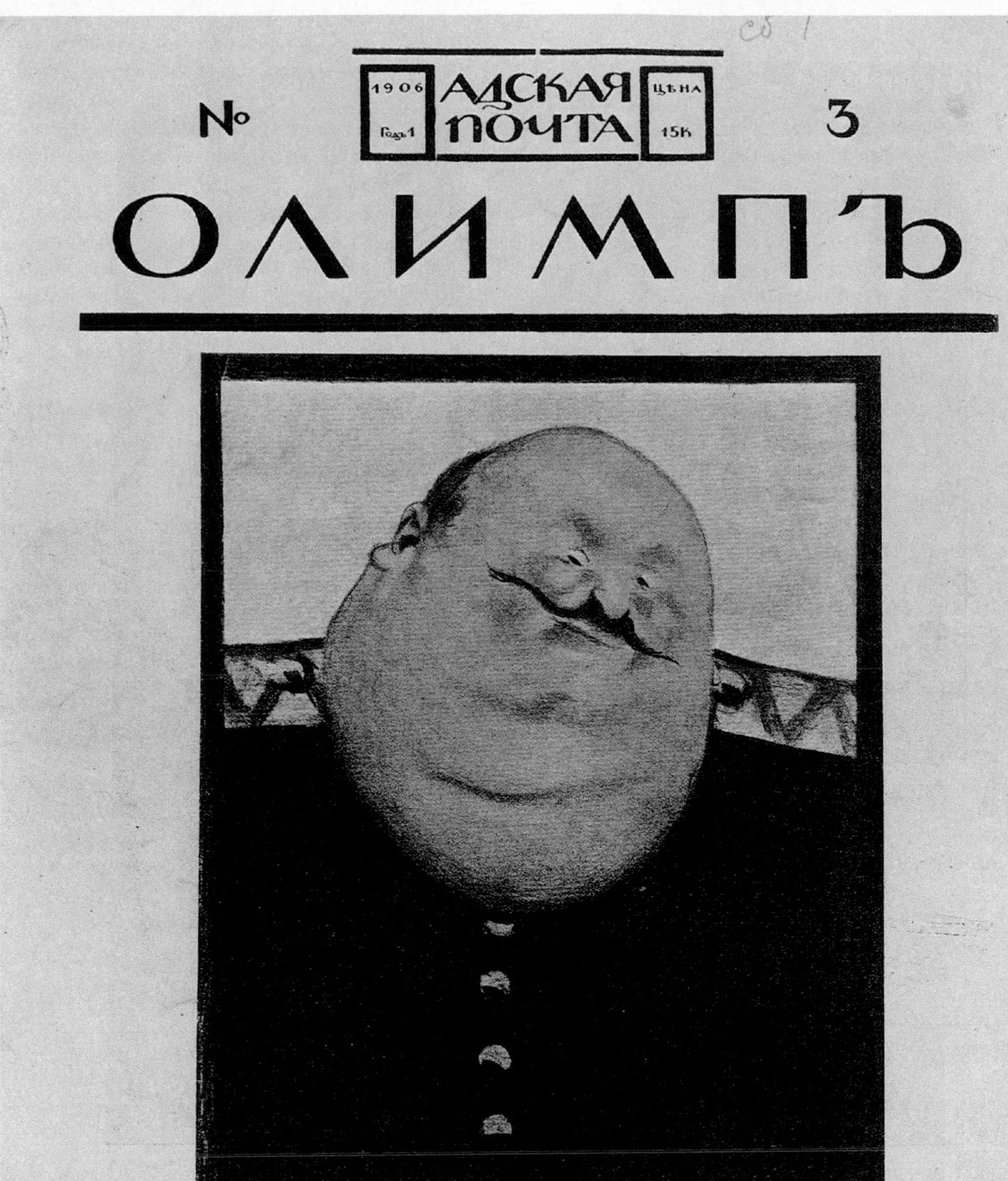

ГРАФЪ ИГНАТЬЕВЪ

The Chameleon 285

Art Study

Response to Caption Question Students can bring in their cartoons and explain the qualities being satirized. Boris Kustodiev was a Russian painter who kept up with changing times—and that was no easy task in turn-of-the-century Russia! As the Bolshevik revolution toppled aristocratic traditions, Kustodiev applied the techniques he had learned in the Old School to the subjects and expressions of the New Russia. Kustodiev helped to create a new visual vocabulary for Russian art that focused on everyday people living colorful, sensual lives. His art still enjoys great popularity in Russia because of the broad appeal of its lively style.

Visual Literacy How does the composition of the caricature add to its biting humor? *(The enormity of the head in relation to the tiny facial features and the way the body fills the frame to overflowing convey the impression that this official is too massive to be contained in any conventional space.)*

Question What aspect of the official is Kustodiev satirizing? Do you think this is an example of biting satire? Why or why not? *(Possible responses: The caricature satirizes the official's gluttony and self-importance. The little, sneering face on the massive, potatolike head suggests that Kustodiev intended his caricature to bite.)*

BUILDING ENGLISH PROFICIENCY

Analyzing Titles

So that students may better understand how Chekhov's main character compares to the chameleon of the story's title, elicit from a student or explain that a chameleon is a small lizard that can change the color of its skin to blend with the surroundings.

Activity Ideas

1. Ask students when it would be advantageous for an animal to change color.

2. Encourage students to brainstorm words that could describe a person who is like a chameleon *(changeable, fickle, inconsistent, two-faced).*

3. Invite students to role-play situations in which a person would have to drastically change his or her personality, appearance, or views.

4. Elicit other animals that are identified by certain characteristics that could be applied to humans *(fox, sheep, snake, bird of prey, weasel).*

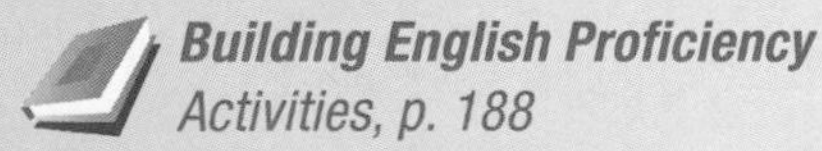
Building English Proficiency
Activities, p. 188

6 Literary Element
Irony

Questions

- Why is the Inspector's choice of the word *delicate* ironic? *(because a moment earlier he called the dog a load of rubbish and threatened to kill it)*
- How does the tirade directed at Grunkin magnify this irony? *(Possible response: because Grunkin is bleeding and could be viewed as delicate himself)*

7 Grammar Skills
Recognize Dialect

Discuss how the author's choice of words places his characters into separate social classes.

- Point to the awkward verb tense used in this passage. Ask students to translate "what come" into conventional English. *(who came)*
- Have students correct the number of "don't go." *(doesn't go)*

8 Active Reading
Evaluate

Possible responses *Some students may answer "yes," because he is careful not to offend his potential political allies. Others may say "no," because he has no backbone or interest in the truth and justice.)*

snout . . . I did see one like that in his yard the other day."

"Course it's the General's!" says a voice from the crowd.

"Hm . . . Help me on with my coat, Dildin old chap . . . There's a bit of a breeze got up . . . It's quite chilly . . . Right, take this dog to the General's and ask them there. Say I found it and am sending it back. And tell them not to let it out on the street in future. It may be worth a lot, and if every swine is going to
6 poke cigarettes up its nose, it won't be for much longer. A dog's a delicate creature . . . And you put your hand down, you oaf! Stop showing your stupid finger off! It was all your own fault!"

"Here comes the General's cook, let's ask him . . . Hey, Prokhor! Come over here a moment, will you? Take a look at this dog . . . One of yours, is it?"

"You must be joking! We've never had none like that!"

"Right, we can stop making enquiries," says Moronoff. "It's a stray! We can cut the chat . . . If everyone says it's a stray, it is a stray . . . So that's that, it must be put down."

7 "No, it's not one of ours," Prokhor continues. "It belongs to the General's brother what come down the other day. Our General don't go much on borzois. His brother does, though—"

"You mean to say his Excellency's brother's arrived? Vladimir Ivanych?"[10] asks Moronoff, his face breaking into an ecstatic[11] smile. "Well blow me down! And I didn't know! Come for a little stay, has he?"

A dog's a delicate creature . . .

"He's on a visit . . ."

"Well I never . . . So he felt like seeing his dear old brother again . . . And fancy me not knowing! So it's his little dog, is it? Jolly good . . . Take him away with you, then . . . He's a good little doggie . . . Pretty quick off the mark, too . . . Took a bite out of this bloke's finger—ha, ha, ha! No need to shiver, little chap! 'Grr-rrr'. . . He's angry, the rascal . . . the little scamp . . ."

8 **EVALUATE: Do you think Moronoff displays the qualities of an effective politician? Explain.**

Prokhor calls the dog over and it follows him out of the woodyard . . .The crowd roars with laughter at Grunkin.

"I'll deal with you later!" Moronoff threatens him, and wrapping his greatcoat tightly round him, resumes his progress across the market square.

10. **Vladimir Ivanych** (vlad′ə mir ē von′ich), a Russian name meaning "Vladimir, son of Ivan."
11. ecstatic (ek stat′ik), *adj.* feeling great joy.

MINI-LESSON: VOCABULARY
Understanding Poetic Usage

Teach Dictionaries commonly apply the usage label *poetic* to any word or meaning that is used chiefly in older poetry (or poetry meant to sound old). Such poetic usage would seem awkward or inappropriate in everyday speech or informal prose.

Apply Have students pick out words in the fable that seem poetic to them. (Possible responses: *spied, fell, pray, bid, leering eye, oaths)*

Activity Ideas

- Have students look up the unfamiliar words in the dictionary to understand their usage and meaning.
- Have students rewrite the fable as prose, using everyday language.

The Fox and the Woodcutter

Aesop

A fox was fleeing. As she fled
A hunter fast behind her sped.
But being wearied, when she spied
9 An old man cutting wood, she cried,
"By all the gods that keep you well,
Hide me among these trees you fell,
And don't reveal the place, I pray."
He swore that he would not betray
The wily[1] vixen;[2] so she hid,
And then the hunter came to bid
The old man tell him if she'd fled,
10 Or if she'd hidden there. He said,
"I did not see her," but he showed
The place the cunning beast was stowed
By pointing at it with his finger.
But still the hunter did not linger.
He put no faith in leering eye,
But trusting in the words, went by.
Escaped from danger for a while
The fox peeked out with coaxing smile.
The old man said to her, "You owe
Me thanks for saving you, you know."
"Most certainly; for I was there
As witness of your expert care.
But now farewell. And don't forget,
The god of oaths will catch you yet
For saving with your voice and lips
11 While slaying with your finger tips."

1. wily (wī′lē), *adj.* crafty; sly.
2. vixen (vik′sən), *n.* a female fox.

9 Literary Element
Personification

Explain that fables commonly personify animals to teach a lesson about human characteristics.

Question What human traits are traditionally associated with the fox? *(Possible responses: cunning, stealth, greed)*

10 Multicultural Note
Fables from India

You might give an example of an influential collection of fables from a non-Western tradition. *The Panchatantra*, passed down in Sanskrit from the 3rd or 4th century A.D., eventually reached Europe where it was translated into many languages.

11 Literary Element
Fable

Question What is the moral of this fable? *(Possible response: A gesture can betray a trust as readily as a word.)*

BUILDING ENGLISH PROFICIENCY

Relating Poetry and Prose

To check students' comprehension, encourage them to use prose to state the main idea and key details of the poems on pages 287 and 288.

1. Have students suggest questions about the poems. *(for example, Why does the fox give a warning to the woodcutter? How does the woodcutter slay the fox "with his fingertips"? What makes the speaker's wrath end or grow, according to the first 4 lines of "A Poison Tree"?)* Invite volunteers to answer the questions.

2. Help students summarize each poem by using cloze paragraphs, as in this example:

In "A Poison Tree," the speaker's _______ grows until it bears an _______, which is eaten by the speaker's _______, causing him to _______.

12 Literary Element
Connotative Language

Discuss the connotations of the words in the title.

- *Poison: evil, corruption, death, pain*
- *Tree: life, growth, branches, fruit*

13 Literary Element
Symbolism

Explain that Blake draws on the symbolism of the Bible. He builds a metaphor on the story of Eve who stole an apple from the Tree of Knowledge and was expelled, with Adam, from the Garden of Eden.

Response to Caption Question
He juxtaposes images of life (a blooming tree) and death (bare branches).

Visual Literacy Tell students that in the original edition of *Songs of Experience,* where this poem first appeared, Blake illustrated his poem with a dark landscape and a barren tree—the foe's dead body stretched out beneath it.

Check Test

1. Who is Grunkin and why is he so upset? *(He is the goldsmith who was just bitten by a dog.)*
2. To whom does the disputed dog belong? *(the General's brother)*
3. In Aesop's fable, how does the hunter respond to the woodcutter's clue? *(He ignores it.)*
4. What does the narrator's enemy in "A Poison Tree" steal? *(an apple)*
5. Why is the narrator happy at the end of the poem? *(His foe is dead.)*

Unit 2 Resource Book
Alternate Check Test, p. 61

This contemporary illustration by Guy Billout hints at death lurking in the shadows of life. How does he highlight these contrasts?

12 A Poison Tree

William Blake

I was angry with my friend:
I told my wrath,[1] my wrath did end.
I was angry with my foe:
I told it not, my wrath did grow.

And I water'd it in fears,
Night & morning with my tears;
And I sunnèd it with smiles,
And with soft deceitful wiles.

13 And it grew both day and night,
Till it bore an apple bright.
And my foe beheld it shine,
And he knew that it was mine,

And into my garden stole,
When the night had veil'd the pole;[2]
In the morning glad I see
My foe outstretch'd beneath the tree.

1. wrath (rath), *n.* very great anger; rage.
2. **night had veil'd the pole**, night had covered one half of the earth, including the North Pole.

MINI-LESSON: LITERARY FOCUS
Tone

Teach Point out that the tone of "A Poison Tree" reflects William Blake's underlying attitude toward the imaginary character he creates to speak this poem. Explain the importance of analyzing the emotional state of the speaker as he reveals his feelings toward his foe.

Question Do you think the speaker feels remorse for what his secret wrath has caused to happen? *(Possible response: No. He probably feels that his enemy's thievery justifies his deadly, hypocritical thoughts.)*

Activity Idea Have students rewrite the story, in verse or prose, imagining that William Blake is speaking directly to his audience about the consequences of repressed wrath.

After Reading

Making Connections

Shaping Your Response

1. Copy the spectrum below into your notebook and mark where you think Inspector Moronoff falls. Be prepared to explain your response.

   trustworthy ←——→ undependable

2. Do you think that Moronoff's name and the picture of him on page 285 provide a good portrayal of his character? Why or why not?
3. In your opinion, which character commits the worst offense — Inspector Moronoff in "The Chameleon," the old man in "The Fox and the Woodcutter," or the speaker in "A Poison Tree"? Explain your thinking.

Analyzing the Selections

4. How do Moronoff's activities with his coat comically reflect his **character?**
5. "The Chameleon" uses **satire**, a way of poking fun at individuals or society to expose weaknesses or evils, to comment on a type of public official. What kind of person do you think the author is satirizing?
6. Why do you think Chekhov chose "The Chameleon" as the **title** of this story?
7. Do you think "The Chameleon," "The Fox and the Woodcutter," and "A Poison Tree" have different **themes** or a common one? Explain.

Extending the Ideas

8. Explain how you can apply themes in "The Fox and the Woodcutter" and "A Poison Tree" to situations in your own life.

Literary Focus: Tone

A selection's **tone** is the author's attitude toward a subject, as revealed through the language of the selection.

- In which of these three selections is the tone humorous? How can you tell?
- In which selection(s) is the tone instructive or moralistic?
- Choose another literary selection in this book and explain whether its tone is humorous, peaceful, angry, or something else.

After Reading

MAKING CONNECTIONS

1. Possible response: Most students will probably place Moronoff closer to the undependable side, although he did make an effort to resolve the crime, which gives him a small degree of trustworthiness.

2. Possible response: Yes; Moronoff is a pun on *moron*, which emphasizes his stupidity. The picture depicts him as a gluttonous oaf.

3. Possible response: Students may answer that, because the speaker in "A Poison Tree" not only causes a death, but even gloats over it, he or she commits the worst offense.

4. Possible response: He keeps taking it off and putting it back on, which parallels the vacillation with his verdict.

5. Possible response: It satirizes social climbers (in this case a police inspector) who sacrifice their integrity to gain the favor of those they consider socially powerful.

6. Possible response: because a chameleon changes its skin color to match its surroundings

7. Possible response: Students may answer that they share a common theme: Beware the hypocritical friend who will smile in your face and stab you in the back to serve his or her interests.

8. Students may apply the themes to shifting loyalties between friends, keeping confidences, and holding grudges.

LITERARY FOCUS: TONE

The tone of "The Chameleon" is humorous. Clues: the roaring laughter of the crowd, the frequent use of irony, the broad characters, the levity of the crime.

- The tone of "The Fox and the Woodcutter" is instructive and moralistic. The tone of "A Poison Tree" is moralistic.
- Possible response: The tone of "The Interlopers" is moralistic and bitter.

VOCABULARY STUDY

Vocabulary words, as used in context, should reflect correct meanings and connotations.

Unit 2 Resource Book
Vocabulary, p. 59
Vocabulary Test, p. 62

WRITING CHOICES

Writer's Notebook Update

Suggest that students use a Story-Comparison Chart to organize their thoughts, noting similarities and differences between their stories and one of the selections they have just read.

My Experiences
Characters Setting Conflict Resolution

Selection Title
Characters Setting Conflict Resolution

Beneath the Surface

Elicit discussion about possible motivations for the advertising industry's dishonesty. *(Possible response: profit)* Ask students to compare this motivation to that of the dishonest characters in the "The Chameleon," "The Fox and the Woodcutter," and "The Poison Tree."

Modernize the Story

Remind students to keep their audience in mind as they write. Effective satire draws its power by giving frustrated audiences a long-awaited opportunity to laugh out loud at an unpopular institution.

Selection Test

Unit 2 Resource Book
pp. 63–64

compensation
confiscated
countenance
dolefully
ecstatic
grievance
muse
profoundly
vixen
wily
wrath

Vocabulary Study

Use eight of the vocabulary words to write about one of the following topics. When you have finished, underline the vocabulary words you have used.

- an account of "The Chameleon" from the dog's point of view
- an opinion article criticizing the special treatment of powerful people
- a brief fable exposing a human weakness

Expressing Your Ideas

Writing Choices

Writer's Notebook Update Reread the notes you wrote about a time when you put on a false front. How does your experience compare with the descriptions mentioned in these three works? Write a paragraph in your notebook explaining the similarities and the differences.

Beneath the Surface Products, like the characters in these selections, can appear to be something they are not. Think about advertisements that suggest unrealistic results—shampoo to make your hair look like a movie star's, gym shoes to improve your basketball game, a diet drink to make you slim and popular. Write a **consumer complaint** letter expressing your dissatisfaction with a product that has not measured up to its promise.

Modernize the Story Work with a partner to modernize "The Chameleon." What type of person, group, or activity in society do you think could be deservedly criticized by using humor? How could you use exaggeration and sarcasm to poke fun at your target? Change or elaborate on the original story to write a **satire** using a modern setting, characters, plot, and language.

Other Options

TV Satire Many television programs are based on satiric skits about political or other newsworthy events. Work with a group to present a satiric **skit** about a political or media figure or event. You might take some cues from the changeable Inspector Moronoff.

Pop-Up Publication Work with a partner to design and illustrate "The Fox and the Woodcutter" or another fable about deceptive appearances as a **pop-up storybook** for children. You may want to review several children's pop-up books to identify an appropriate design for your book. Which character(s) and/or elements of the setting would create the best effect for "popping" off the pages? How can you use the pop-up design to maintain the tone of the fable?

OTHER OPTIONS

TV Satire Improvisation

You might suggest that students start with a loose script that sets the scene and establishes the characters. Observe how an extemporaneous performance can add to a comedic sketch.

Pop-up Publication

- Ask students if they remember reading pop-up books when they were children. How might they improve the design?
- Ask students if they recall fables that they read as children which contain events and lessons that would lend themselves to a visual presentation.

Before Reading

Dip in the Pool

by Roald Dahl   Great Britain

Roald Dahl
1916–1990

Roald Dahl (rü äl däl), noted for stories that blend the horrible and the humorous, said that when an idea for a plot came along, he would "grab it with both hands and hang on to it tight." He scribbled his thoughts with a crayon, a lipstick, whatever was at hand. After serving as a fighter pilot for the Royal Air Force in World War II, Dahl returned to England and started writing short stories in a brick hut in his apple orchard. His stories for children, such as *James and the Giant Peach,* began as bedtime entertainment, and he claimed his ability to "tickle" and "jolt" audiences resulted from his own children's demands to be entertained and shocked.

Building Background

Lively Labels Many of Dahl's titles—*The Magic Finger, The Great Switcheroo, and Twenty-nine Kisses from Roald Dahl*—are as lively as his writing itself. You can analyze the title, "Dip in the Pool," to make some predictions about the story you are about to read. Copy the web below into your notebook. Then with a partner, complete the web by analyzing the words in the title and jotting down associated words, multiple meanings, and story predictions that come to mind.

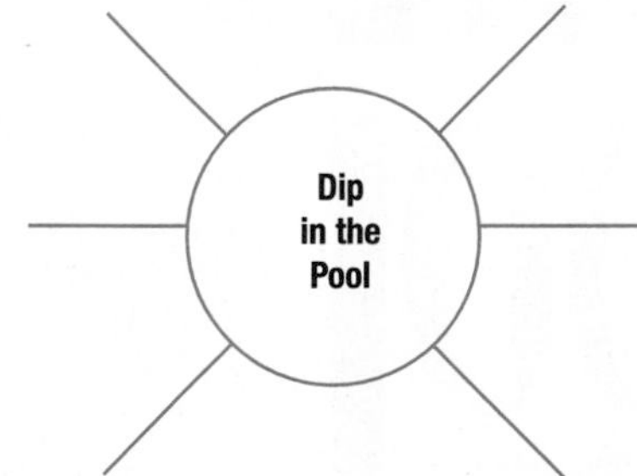

Literary Focus

Plot is a series of related events that present and resolve a conflict. Sometimes a plot is fairly predictable; that is, the author provides clues that a careful reader can use to guess the outcome. An author like Roald Dahl, however, may devise plot twists that catch a reader offguard. Be forewarned!

Writer's Notebook

Creative Solutions Are you a creative problem solver? Can you respond quickly in times of crises? Are you willing to take risks? Have your solutions ever backfired? Think of a time when you were required to think quickly and creatively. In your notebook, write three words that describe how you reacted. Now match wits with Mr. Botibol, a character whose quick thinking may (or may not) earn him a small fortune.

Before Reading

Building Background

After students complete their webs, discuss their associations and story predictions. Some possibilities:

- *dip:* scoop, drop, idiot (slang); *pool:* swimming pool, car pool, game of billiards, a betting/gambling pool
- a person goes swimming; an idiot drowns in a swimming pool; someone steals money from a football pool

Literary Focus

Direct students to read the definition of **plot** in the Glossary of Literary Terms, page 815.

Writer's Notebook

Encourage students to analyze the consequences of their creative solutions. Have time and emotional distance given them a different perspective on the situation?

More About Roald Dahl

- Dahl once listed his favorite recreation as "gaming," which included betting on horse races and playing blackjack.
- In response to criticism of his macabre plots, Dahl has said, "... my nastiness is never gratuitous. It's retribution. Beastly people must be punished."

SUPPORT MATERIALS OVERVIEW

Unit 2 Resource Book
- Graphic Organizer, p. 65
- Study Guide, p. 66
- Vocabulary, p. 67
- Grammar, p. 68
- Alternate Check Test, p. 69
- Vocabulary Test, p. 70
- Selection Test, pp. 71–72

Building English Proficiency
- Literature Summaries
- Activities, p. 189

Reading, Writing & Grammar SkillBook
- Vocabulary, pp. 1–4
- Grammar, Usage, and Mechanics, pp. 142–143

The World of Work
- Meteorologist, p. 9
- Draw a Map, p. 10

Technology
- Audiotape 8, Side A
- Personal Journal Software
- Custom Literature Database: For another story of a man overboard, see "The Book of Jonah" from the Hebrew Bible on the database.
- Test Generator Software

During Reading

Selection Objectives

- to explore the theme that disaster may lurk beneath the surface of a seemingly foolproof plan
- to explore the power and complexity of plot
- to recognize run-on sentences

Unit 2 Resource Book
Graphic Organizer, p. 65
Study Guide, p. 66

Theme Link

The theme "Beneath the Surface" is reflected in Mr. Botibol's careful attention to detail in a plan of deception that goes awry.

Vocabulary Preview

friction, a rubbing of one object against another; a clash
poached, cooked by simmering in a liquid
turbot, a European fish, much valued as food
steward, a person employed on a ship to look after passengers
subside, die down
complacent, self-satisfied
advertent, alert
surreptitiously, secretly
assail, bother, trouble
turbulent, filled with commotion; violent

Students can add the words and definitions to their Writer's Notebooks.

1 Literary Element
Setting

Questions

- What is the setting of this story? *(a luxury cruise ship)*
- What details provide clues about what kind of ship it is? *(the sun deck, the steward service, the main dining room)*

This illustration by Bob Scott shows the huge scale of a luxury liner as it threatens the tiny sails in its path. How do shapes and perspective help establish a mood?

DIP IN THE POOL

Roald Dahl

On the morning of the third day, the sea calmed. Even the most delicate passengers—those who had not been seen around the ship since sailing time—emerged from their cabins and crept up onto the sun deck where the deck steward gave them chairs and tucked rugs around their legs and left them lying in rows, their faces upturned to the pale, almost heatless January sun.

It had been moderately rough the first two days, and this sudden calm and the sense of comfort that it brought created a more genial atmosphere over the whole ship. By the time evening came, the passengers, with twelve hours of good weather behind them, were beginning to feel confident, and at eight o'clock that night the main dining room was filled with people eating and drinking with the assured,
1 complacent[1] air of seasoned sailors.

The meal was not half over when the passengers became aware, by a slight friction[2] between their bodies and the seats of their chairs, that the big ship had actually started rolling again. It was very gentle at first, just a slow, lazy leaning to one side, then to the other, but it was enough to cause a subtle, immediate change of mood over the whole room. A few of

1. complacent (kəm plā′snt), *adj.* self-satisfied.
2. friction (frik′shən), *n.* a rubbing of one object against another; a clash.

SELECTION SUMMARY

Dip in the Pool

Mr. William Botibol is traveling on an ocean liner that has been passing through some bad weather. Every evening some of the ship's passengers place bets based on the number of miles they think the ship will cover that day. After much consultation and calculation, Mr. Botibol bets his entire savings on his conclusion that the ship will be slowed down by more bad weather. Upon waking to a clear sky, Mr. Botibol realizes that he is financially ruined—unless he can somehow interfere with the ship's steady course. Mr. Botibol jumps off the side of the ship so that the time spent rescuing him will improve his chances in the "pool." Unfortunately, the only witness is a senile woman, who assumes that he is taking a swim for his morning exercise. She turns away and Mr. Botibol is left in the middle of the ocean, waving.

*For summaries in other languages, see the **Building English Proficiency** book.*

The World of Work

Meteorologist

For the real-life experiences of a meteorologist who predicts weather, use—

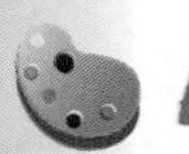

The World of Work
pp. 9–10

Art Study

Responses to Caption Question The perspective establishes tension by placing the viewer as well as the sailboat directly in the ship's path. The sharp angles add to the menacing mood. The extended, white expanse of the ship suggests it could crush anything in its path.

Visual Literacy Artist Bob Scott uses an airbrush to create his highly stylized paintings. The airbrush makes a fine spray of paint that the artist controls with a trigger, which is attached by a hose to an air source. Color is added one section at a time with a masking device called a *frisket.* The style of this painting is influenced by the Art Deco movement, which originated in the 1920s and remained popular until World War II. Art Deco sought to suggest elegance and wealth while incorporating the images of the machine: simple planes and the repetition of symmetrical shapes and lines.

BUILDING ENGLISH PROFICIENCY

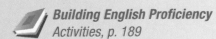

ESL
LEP
ELD
SAE
LD

Exploring Setting

It is unlikely that many students have had firsthand experience with ocean liners. Use one or both of the following activities to help students relate to the story's setting.

Activity Ideas

- Provide pictures of luxury liners in addition to the one on page 293. If possible, include a cross-section view so that students can see the variety of facilities available. (Brochures from a travel agency may be helpful.) Have students comment upon shipboard accommodations and activities.
- Stormy weather causes problems for passengers in this story. Invite students to describe what it is like to travel through storms and experience some form of motion sickness.

Building English Proficiency
Activities, p. 189

2 Literary Element
Simile

Make sure students understand the reference, "as in a car cornering" *(as in a car that is taking a turn at a high speed).* Emphasize the power of *simile* to draw a comparison between familiar and unfamiliar sensations.

3 Literary Element
Metaphor

Questions

- What is the literal meaning of the word *flock*? *(Possible response: a group of birds or sheep that live, feed, and move together)*
- What does the metaphorical context of this word imply about the passengers? *(Possible responses: They don't think for themselves; they gain a sense of comfort and direction from being part of a group.)*

4 Reading/Thinking Skills
Compare and Contrast

Question Compare and contrast the attitudes of the purser and Mr. Botibol in this conversation. *(Possible response: The relaxed purser is unaffected by Mr. Botibol's anxiety. Similarly unaffected by the purser's easy tone, Mr. Botibol nervously pursues his object.)*

the passengers glanced up from their food, hesitating, waiting, almost listening for the next roll, smiling nervously, little secret glimmers of apprehension in their eyes. Some were completely unruffled, some were openly smug, a number of the smug ones making jokes about food and weather in order to torture the few who were beginning to suffer. The movement of the ship then became rapidly more and more violent, and only five or six minutes after the first roll had been noticed, she was swinging heavily from side to side, the passengers bracing
2 themselves in their chairs, leaning against the pull as in a car cornering.

At last the really bad roll came, and Mr. William Botibol, sitting at the purser's[3] table, saw his plate of poached[4] turbot[5] with hollandaise sauce sliding suddenly away from under his fork. There was a flutter of excitement, everybody reaching for plates and wineglasses. Mrs. Renshaw, seated at the purser's right, gave a little scream and clutched that gentleman's arm.

"Going to be a dirty night," the purser said, looking at Mrs. Renshaw. "I think it's blowing up for a very dirty night." There was just the faintest suggestion of relish in the way he said it.

A steward[6] came hurrying up and sprinkled water on the tablecloth between the plates. The excitement subsided.[7] Most of the passengers continued with their meal. A small number, including Mrs. Renshaw, got carefully to their feet and threaded their ways with a kind of concealed haste between the tables and through the doorway.

"Well," the purser said, "there she goes." He
3 glanced around with approval at the remainder of his flock who were sitting quiet, looking complacent, their faces reflecting openly that extraordinary pride that travelers seem to take in being recognized as "good sailors."

When the eating was finished and the coffee had been served, Mr. Botibol, who had been unusually grave and thoughtful since the rolling started, suddenly stood up and carried his cup of coffee around to Mrs. Renshaw's vacant place, next to the purser. He seated himself in her chair, then immediately leaned over and began to whisper urgently in the purser's ear. "Excuse me," he said, "but could you tell me something please?"

The purser, small and fat and red, bent forward to listen. "What's the trouble, Mr. Botibol?"

"What I want to know is this." The man's face was anxious and the purser was watching it. "What I want to know is will the captain already have made his estimate on the day's run—you know, for the auction pool? I mean before it began to get rough like this?"

The purser, who had prepared himself to receive a personal confidence, smiled and leaned back in his seat to relax his full belly. "I should say so—yes," he answered. He didn't bother to whisper his reply, although automatically he lowered his voice, as one does when answering a whisperer.

"About how long ago do you think he did it?"

"Some time this afternoon. He usually does it in the afternoon."

"About what time?"

"Oh, I don't know. Around four o'clock I should guess.

"Now tell me another thing. How does the captain decide which number it shall be? Does he take a lot of trouble over that?"

The purser looked at the anxious frowning face of Mr. Botibol and he smiled, knowing quite well what the man was driving at. "Well, you see, the captain has a little conference with 4

3. **purser** (pėr′sər), *n.* a ship's officer who attends to business matters and is responsible for the welfare of passengers.
4 **poached** (pōchd), *adj.* cooked by simmering in a liquid.
5. **turbot** (tėr′bət, tėr′bō), *n.* a European fish, much valued as food.
6. **steward** (stü′ərd), *n.* a person employed on a ship to look after passangers.
7. **subside** (səb sīd′), *v.* die down.

MINI-LESSON: GRAMMAR
Run-on Sentences

Teach Explain that when two complete sentences are joined by a comma (instead of a *semicolon*, a *period*, or a *conjunction*) the result is a *run-on sentence*. Refer students to the first sentence in the second paragraph on page 292. Explain that if the *and* were omitted after the comma, the result would be a run-on sentence. Explain that a run-on sentence can be corrected in several ways:

- Add a conjunction.
- Add a semicolon.
- Recast into two sentences.

Activity Idea Have students examine and correct the following run-on sentence, using each of the techniques cited above:

The storm was over, Mr. Botibol would lose the pool.

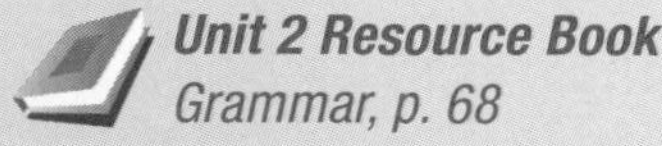
Unit 2 Resource Book
Grammar, p. 68

the navigating officer, and they study the weather and a lot of other things, and then they make their estimate."

Mr. Botibol nodded, pondering this answer for a moment. Then he said, "Do you think the captain knew there was bad weather coming today?"

"I couldn't tell you," the purser replied. He was looking into the small black eyes of the other man, seeing the two single little sparks of excitement dancing in their centers. "I really couldn't tell you, Mr. Botibol. I wouldn't know."

"If this gets any worse it might be worth buying some of the low numbers. What do you think?" The whispering was more urgent, more anxious now.

"Perhaps it will," the purser said. "I doubt the old man allowed for a really rough night. It was pretty calm this afternoon when he made his estimate."

The others at the table had become silent and were trying to hear, watching the purser
5 with that intent, half-cocked, listening look that you can see also at the race track when they are trying to overhear a trainer talking about his chance: the slightly open lips, the upstretched eyebrows, the head forward and cocked a little to one side—that desperately straining, half-hypnotized, listening look that comes to all of them when they are hearing something straight from the horse's mouth.

"Now suppose *you* were allowed to buy a number, which one would *you* choose today?" Mr. Botibol whispered.

"I don't know what the range is yet," the purser patiently answered. "They don't announce the range till the auction starts after dinner. And I'm really not very good at it anyway. I'm only the purser, you know."

At that point Mr. Botibol stood up. "Excuse me, all," he said, and he walked carefully away over the swaying floor between the other tables, and twice he had to catch hold of the back of a chair to steady himself against the ship's roll.

"The sun deck, please," he said to the elevator man.

The wind caught him full in the face as he stepped out onto the open deck. He staggered and grabbed hold of the rail and held on tight with both hands, and he stood there looking out over the darkening sea where the great
waves were welling up high and white horses 6
were riding against the wind with plumes of spray behind them as they went.

"Pretty bad out there, wasn't it, sir?" the elevator man said on the way down. 7

Mr. Botibol was combing his hair back into place with a small red comb. "Do you think we've slackened speed at all on account of the weather?" he asked.

"Oh my word yes, sir. We slacked off considerable since this started. You got to slacken off speed in weather like this or you'll be throwing the passengers all over the ship."

Down in the smoking room people were already gathering for the auction. They were grouping themselves politely around the various tables, the men a little stiff in their dinner jackets, a little pink and overshaved and stiff beside their cool, white-armed women. Mr. Botibol took a chair close to the auctioneer's table. He crossed his legs, folded his arms, and settled himself in his seat with the rather desperate air of a man who has made a tremendous decision and refuses to be frightened.

The pool, he was telling himself, would probably be around seven thousand dollars. That was almost exactly what it had been the last two days with the numbers selling for between three and four hundred apiece. Being a British ship they did it in pounds, but he liked to do his thinking in his own currency. Seven thousand dollars was plenty of money. My goodness yes! And what he would do he would get them to pay him in hundred-dollar bills and he would take it ashore in the inside pocket of his jacket. No problem there. And right away, yes right away, he would buy a Lincoln convert-

5 Reading/Thinking Skills
Visualize

Vivid, sensory images can enable a reader to visualize a scene in detail.

- Ask for volunteers to imitate this facial expression as they imagine it, testing its potential for humor.
- You might elicit discussion about what emotions they associate with placing bets at a race track. *(Possible responses: fear, excitement, nervousness, greediness)*

6 Literary Element
Mood and Metaphor

Questions

- What mood does Dahl create in this description of the sea? *(Possible response: a scary, threatening mood of impending disaster)*
- What does the metaphor comparing the waves to horses make you think about? *(Possible response: that the sea is wild, powerful, and dangerous)*

7 Literary Element
Characterization

Question What does Mr. Botibol's demeanor imply about his character? *(Possible response: He seems meticulous, obsessive, and a little detached from reality.)*

BUILDING ENGLISH PROFICIENCY

Exploring Multiple Meanings

Students may find parts of this story confusing if they aren't aware of the multiple meanings of seemingly simple words. Encourage them to build a web of all the associations they have for each of the following words: *grave, pool, run, range, pounds.* Afterwards, they can add these words (all from pages 294–295) to their vocabulary notebooks. The web at the right shows multiple meanings for *relish.*

Activity Idea Have students share the multiple meanings of these words through pantomime or art.

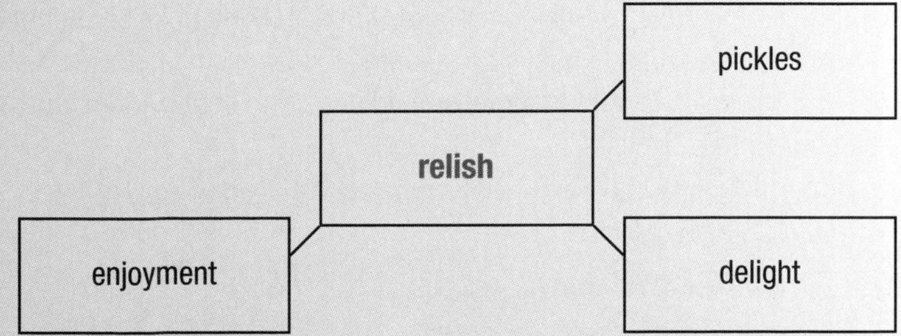

8 Literary Element
Point of View

- Ask students if they have noticed a shift in the story's point of view. *(Possible response: The narrator has moved inside Mr. Botibol's mind to reveal his inner thoughts.)*
- How does this shift affect the reader's attitude toward Mr. Botibol? *(Possible response: The reader suddenly feels a closer identification and sympathy with Mr. Botibol.)*

9 Reading/Thinking Skills
Draw Conclusions

Question If a man's lips are smiling but his eyes are cold, what does that imply about his inner condition? *(He is deceptive, smiling to cover up or hide his intense concentration on other matters.)*

10 Reader's Response
Making Personal Connections

- Ask students if they know any idiomatic expressions to describe Mr. Botibol's strategy. *(Possible responses: "wearing a poker face," "playing possum," or "faking it")*
- Ask students if they have been in an uncomfortable situation in which they had to fake confidence. *(Possible response: encountering an angry dog or a fierce sports opponent)*

ible. He would pick it up on the way from the ship and drive it home just for the pleasure of seeing Ethel's face when she came out the front door and looked at it. Wouldn't that be something, to see Ethel's face when he glided up to the door in a brand-new pale-green Lincoln convertible! Hello Ethel honey, he would say,
8 speaking very casual. I just thought I'd get you a little present. I saw it in the window as I went by, so I thought of you and how you were always wanting one. You like it, honey? he would say. You like the colour? And then he would watch her face.

The auctioneer was standing up behind his table now. "Ladies and gentlemen!" he shouted. "The captain has estimated the day's run, ending midday tomorrow, at five hundred and fifteen miles. As usual we will take the ten numbers on either side of it to make up the range. That makes it five hundred and five to five hundred and twenty-five. And of course for those who think the true figure will be still farther away, there'll be 'low field' and 'high field' sold separately as well. Now, we'll draw the first number out of the hat . . . here we are . . . five hundred and twelve?"

Sit absolutely still and don't look up. It's unlucky to look up.

The room became quiet. The people sat still in their chairs, all eyes watching the auctioneer. There was a certain tension in the air, and as the bids got higher, the tension grew. This wasn't a game or a joke; you could be sure of that by the way one man would look across at another who
9 had raised his bid—smiling perhaps, but only the lips smiling, the eyes bright and absolutely cold.

Number five hundred and twelve was knocked down for one hundred and ten pounds. The next three or four numbers fetched roughly the same amount.

The ship was rolling heavily, and each time she went over, the wooden paneling on the walls creaked as if it were going to split. The passengers held on to the arms of their chairs, concentrating upon the auction.

"Low field!" the auctioneer called out. "The next number is low field."

Mr. Botibol sat up very straight and tense. He would wait, he had decided, until the others had finished bidding, then he would jump in and make the last bid. He had figured that there must be at least five hundred dollars in his account at the bank at home, probably nearer six. That was about two hundred pounds—over two hundred. This ticket wouldn't fetch more than that.

"As you all know," the auctioneer was saying, "low field covers every number *below* the smallest number in the range, in this case every number below five hundred and five. So, if you think this ship is going to cover less than five hundred and five miles in the twenty-four hours ending at noon tomorrow, you better get in and buy this number. So what am I bid?"

It went clear up to one hundred and thirty pounds. Others besides Mr. Botibol seemed to have noticed that the weather was rough. One hundred and forty . . . fifty . . . There it stopped. The auctioneer raised his hammer.

"Going at one hundred and fifty . . ."

"Sixty!" Mr. Botibol called, and every face in the room turned and looked at him.

"Seventy!"

"Eighty!" Mr. Botibol called.

"Ninety!"

"Two hundred!" Mr. Botibol called. He wasn't stopping now—not for anyone.

There was a pause.

"Any advance on two hundred pounds?"

Sit still, he told himself. Sit absolutely still 10

MINI-LESSON: VOCABULARY
Use Context Clues for Word Meaning

Teach Explain to students that when they come across an unfamiliar word, it is possible to guess its meaning by examining its context. Remind them to use on-page footnotes or a dictionary to confirm their guesses about word meanings.

Apply Demonstrate with a word from the selection, such as *complacent*, p. 292.

- Step 1: **What We Know:**
  Its meaning is linked to *assured.*
  "Seasoned sailors feel this way on ships."
- Step 2: **What It Might Mean:**
  Overly confident?
- Step 3: **What We Learned:**
  Refer to footnote 1 on this page to confirm that the word means *self-satisfied.*

and don't look up. It's unlucky to look up. Hold your breath. No one's going to bid you up so long as you hold your breath.

"Going for two hundred pounds . . ." The auctioneer had a pink bald head and there were little beads of sweat sparkling on top of it. "Going . . ." Mr. Botibol held his breath. "Going . . . Gone!" The man banged the hammer on the table. Mr. Botibol wrote out a check and handed it to the auctioneer's assistant, then he settled back in his chair to wait for the finish. He did not want to go to bed before he knew how much there was in the pool.

They added it up after the last number had been sold and it came to twenty-one hundred-odd pounds. That was around six thousand dollars. Ninety per cent to go to the winner, ten per cent to seamen's charities. Ninety per cent of six thousand was five thousand four hundred. Well—that was enough. He could buy the Lincoln convertible and there would be something left over, too. With this gratifying thought he went off, happy and excited, to his cabin.

When Mr. Botibol awoke the next morning he lay quite still for several minutes with his eyes shut, listening for the sound of the gale, waiting for the roll of the ship. There was no sound of any gale and the ship was not rolling. He jumped up and peered out of the porthole. The sea . . . was smooth as glass, the great ship was moving through it fast, obviously making up for time lost during the night. Mr. Botibol turned away and sat slowly down on the edge of his bunk. A fine electricity of fear was beginning to prickle under the skin of his stomach. He hadn't a hope now. One of the higher numbers was certain to win it after this.

11 "Oh my God," he said aloud. "What shall I do?"

What, for example, would Ethel say? It was simply not possible to tell her that he had spent almost all of their two years' savings on a ticket in the ship's pool. Nor was it possible to keep the matter secret. To do that he would have to tell her to stop drawing checks. And what about the monthly installments on the television set and the Encyclopaedia Britannica? Already he 12 could see the anger and contempt in the woman's eyes, the blue becoming gray and the eyes themselves narrowing as they always did when there was anger in them.

"Oh my God. What *shall* I do?"

There was no point in pretending that he had the slightest chance now—not unless the . . . ship started to go backward. They'd have to put her in reverse and go full speed astern and keep right on going if he was to have any chance of winning it now. Well, maybe he should ask the captain to do just that. Offer him ten per cent of the profits. Offer him more if he wanted it. Mr. Botibol started to giggle. Then very suddenly he stopped, his eyes and mouth both opening wide in a kind of shocked surprise. For it was at this moment that the idea 13 came. It hit him hard and quick, and he jumped up from his bed, terribly excited, ran over to the porthole and looked out again. Well, he thought, why not? Why ever not? The sea was calm and he wouldn't have any trouble keeping afloat until they picked him up. He had a vague feeling that someone had done this thing before, but that didn't prevent him from doing it again. The ship would have to stop and lower a boat, and the boat would have to go back maybe half a mile to get him, and then it would have to return to the ship and be hoisted back on board. It would take at least an hour, the whole thing. An hour was about thirty miles. It would knock thirty miles off the day's run. That would do it. "Low field" would be sure to win it then. Just so long as he made certain someone saw him falling over; but that would be simple to arrange. And he'd better wear light clothes, something easy to swim in. Sports clothes, that was it. He would dress as though he were going up to play some deck tennis—just a shirt and a pair of shorts and tennis shoes. And leave his watch behind. What was the time? Nine-fifteen.

11 Literary Focus
Plot

Questions Who is the main character? *(Mr. Botibol)* What conflict is he involved in? *(He is struggling to outwit the other passengers to win the money in the auction pool.)* What might thwart him? *(Possible responses: bad luck, changes in the weather, overconfidence)*

12 Reading/Thinking Skills
Make Judgments

Question How does Mr. Botibol's wife, Ethel, help generate the story's plot? *(Possible responses: His desire to impress her fuels his courage to buy the ticket, and his fear of her goads him into further action.)*

EDITORIAL NOTE The last two sets of ellipses on this page indicate the deletions "Oh Jesus God" and "goddamn," respectively.

13 Literary Element
Stream of Consciousness

The narrator uses interior monologue to reveal Mr. Botibol's chaotic thoughts. Ask: What is his "exciting" idea. *(He will decrease the ship's mileage by jumping overboard, forcing a rescue mission.)*

BUILDING ENGLISH PROFICIENCY

ESL
LEP
ELD
SAE
LD

Recognize Cause and Effect

Focus students' attention on Mr. Botibol's "get rich quick" scheme. Refer them to the second column of page 297 and have them review Mr. Botibol's basic scheme for winning the ship's pool by creating a cause-effect diagram.

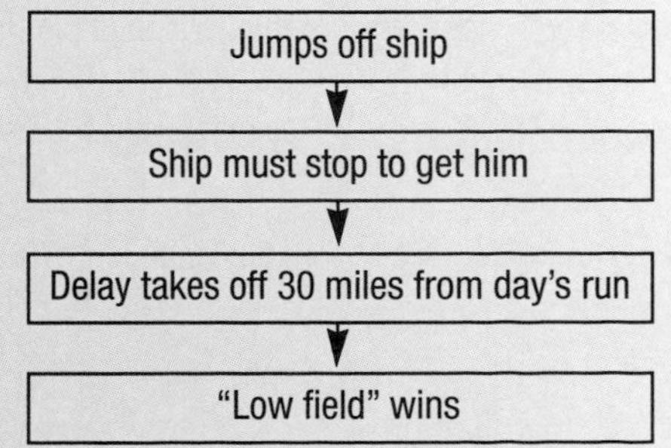
Jumps off ship
Ship must stop to get him
Delay takes off 30 miles from day's run
"Low field" wins

14 Literary Element
Suspense

Question How does the author add suspense to the plot in this passage? *(Possible response: He imposes a time limit that requires Mr. Botibol to move swiftly without much deliberation. The reader wonders if Mr. Botibol will actually jump overboard.)*

15 Literary Element
Irony

Verbal irony often takes the form of understatement, the deliberate downplaying of the importance of something.

- Point out the understatement at the end of this paragraph. *(". . . the thing was a cinch and he could leap overboard with a light heart.")*
- What does the use of irony reveal about Mr. Botibol's state of mind? *(Possible response: He has lost his perspective of reality.)*

16 Literary Focus
Plot

Ask students to note the rising action, or complications, of the plot structure as Mr. Botibol attempts to overcome the obstacles that stand between him and his goal.

14 The sooner the better, then. Do it now and get it over with. Have to do it soon, because the time limit was midday.

Mr. Botibol was both frightened and excited when he stepped out onto the sundeck in his sports clothes. His small body was wide at the hips, tapering upward to extremely narrow sloping shoulders, so that it resembled, in shape at any rate, a bollard.[8] His white skinny legs were covered with black hairs, and he came cautiously out on deck, treading softly in his tennis shoes. Nervously he looked around him. There was only one other person in sight, an elderly woman with very thick ankles and immense buttocks who was leaning over the rail staring at the sea. She was wearing a coat of Persian lamb and the collar was turned up so Mr. Botibol couldn't see her face.

He stood still, examining her carefully from a distance. Yes, he told himself, she would probably do. She would probably give the alarm just as quickly as anyone else. But wait one minute, take your time, William Botibol, take your time. Remember what you told yourself a few minutes ago in the cabin when you were changing? You remember that?

The thought of leaping off a ship into the ocean a thousand miles from the nearest land had made Mr. Botibol—a cautious man at the best of times—unusually advertent.[9] He was by no means satisfied yet that this woman he saw before him was *absolutely certain* to give the alarm when he made his jump. In his opinion there were two possible reasons why she might fail him. Firstly, she might be deaf and blind. It was not very probable, but on the other hand it *might* be so, and why take a chance? All he had to do was check it by talking to her for a moment beforehand. Secondly—and this will demonstrate how suspicious the mind of a man can become when it is working through self-preservation and fear—secondly, it had occurred to him that the woman might herself be the owner of one of the high numbers in the pool and as such would have a sound financial reason for not wishing to stop the ship. Mr. Botibol recalled that people had killed their fellows for far less than six thousand dollars. It was happening every day in the newspapers. So why take a chance on that either? Check on it first. Be sure of your facts. Find out about it by a little polite conversation. Then, provided that the woman appeared also to be a pleasant, kindly human being, the thing was a cinch and he could leap overboard with a light heart. 15

Mr. Botibol advanced casually toward the woman and took up a position beside her, leaning on the rail. "Hullo," he said pleasantly.

She turned and smiled at him, a surprisingly lovely, almost a beautiful smile, although the face itself was very plain. "Hullo," she answered him.

Check, Mr. Botibol told himself, on the first question. She is neither blind nor deaf. "Tell me," he said, coming straight to the point, "what did you think of the auction last night?"

"Auction?" she asked, frowning. "Auction? What auction?"

"You know, that silly old thing they have in the lounge after dinner, selling numbers on the ship's daily run. I just wondered what you thought about it."

She shook her head, and again she smiled, a sweet and pleasant smile that had in it perhaps the trace of an apology. "I'm very lazy," she said. "I always go to bed early. I have my dinner in bed. It's so restful to have dinner in bed."

Mr. Botibol smiled back at her and began to edge away. "Got to go and get my exercise now," he said. "Never miss my exercise in the morning. It was nice seeing you. Very nice seeing you . . ." He retreated about ten paces, and the woman let him go without looking around. 16

Everything was now in order. The sea was

8. **bollard** (bol′ərd), *n.* an upright wooden or metal post.
9. advertent (əd vėrt′nt), *adj.* alert.

MINI-LESSON: LITERARY FOCUS
Plot: Conflict

Teach Explain to students that in this story the plot is generated by both external and internal conflict.

External: Mr. Botibol against his fellow wagerers; Mr. Botibol against nature

Internal: Mr. Botibol's inner struggle involves his greed, desire, and fear.

Activity Ideas

- Have students work in groups to revise the plot, removing the conflicts that threaten Mr. Botibol's goals. *(Possible response: The storm continues through the next day, and/or he decides he is not afraid of his wife.)*
- Have students ask themselves if their revised plot structures would hold a reader's interest as well as the original.

17 calm, he was lightly dressed for swimming, there were almost certainly no man-eating sharks in this part of the Atlantic, and there was this pleasant kindly old woman to give the alarm. It was a question now only of whether the ship would be delayed long enough to swing the balance in his favor. Almost certainly it would. In any event, he could do a little to help in that direction himself. He could make a few difficulties about getting hauled up into the lifeboat. Swim around a bit, back away from them surreptitiously[10] as they tried to come up close to fish him out. Every minute, every second gained would help him win. He began to move forward again to the rail, but now a new fear assailed[11] him. Would he get caught in the propeller? He had heard about that happening to persons falling off the sides of big ships. But then, he wasn't going to fall, he was going to jump, and that was a very different thing. Provided he jumped out far enough he would be sure to clear the propeller.

She looked around quickly and saw sailing past her through the air this small man . . .

Mr. Botibol advanced slowly to a position at the rail about twenty yards away from the woman. She wasn't looking at him now. So much the better. He didn't want her watching him as he jumped off. So long as no one was watching he would be able to say afterward that he had slipped and fallen by accident. He peered over the side of the ship. It was a long, long drop. Come to think of it now,
18 he might easily hurt himself badly if he hit the water flat. Wasn't there someone who once split his stomach open that way, doing a belly flop from the high dive? He must jump straight and land feet first. Go in like a knife. Yes sir. The water seemed cold and deep and gray and it made him shiver to look at it. But it was now or never. Be a man, William Botibol, be a man. All right then . . . now . . . here goes . . .

He climbed up onto the wide wooden toprail, stood there poised, balancing for three terrifying seconds, then he leaped—he leaped up and out as far as he could go and at the same time he shouted *"Help!"*

"Help! Help!" he shouted as he fell. Then he hit the water and went under.

When the first shout for help sounded, the woman who was leaning on the rail started up and gave a little jump of surprise. She looked around quickly and saw sailing past her through the air this small man dressed in white shorts and tennis shoes, spread-eagled and shouting as 19
he went. For a moment she looked as though she weren't quite sure what she ought to do: throw a life belt, run away and give the alarm, or simply turn and yell. She drew back a pace from the rail and swung half around facing up to the bridge, and for this brief moment she remained motionless, tense, undecided. Then almost at once she seemed to relax, and she leaned forward far over the rail, staring at the water where it was turbulent[12] in the ship's wake. Soon a tiny round black head appeared in the foam, an arm was raised about it, once, twice, vigorously waving, and a small faraway voice was heard calling something that was difficult to understand. The woman leaned still farther over the rail, trying to keep the little bobbing black speck in sight, but

10. **surreptitiously** (sėr′əp tish′əs lē), *adv.* secretly.
11. **assail** (ə sāl′), *v.* bother; trouble.
12. **turbulent** (tėr′byə lənt), *adj.* filled with commotion; violent.

17 Literary Element
Characterization

Question Would you consider Mr. Botibol's attitude towards this unique crisis irrational? *(Possible response: Yes—although he is surprisingly focused, he is so attentive to the details that he can't see the absurdity of his plan.)*

18 Reader's Response
Making Personal Connections

Questions

- Can you relate to the contradictory messages that Mr. Botibol is receiving from his confused brain? *(Students might mention similar feelings right before a sports event.)*
- What tone does your inner voice usually take when you are facing a difficult situation? *(Possible response: Students may answer that the tone is chaotic or stern.)*

19 Literary Element
Humor

Question Ask students how the narrator adds humor to this climactic moment. *(Possible response: Mr. Botibol doesn't enter the water "like a knife" as he had planned, but ridiculously "spread-eagled and shouting.")*

BUILDING ENGLISH PROFICIENCY

ESL LEP ELD SAE LD

Noting Characters and Details

Draw students' attention to the large type on pages 299 and 300. Ask why Mr. Botibol needs a key witness *(someone must report "man overboard" to the ship authorities).*

1. Ask students what it means to have a plan backfire.
2. How does Botibol's plan backfire?
3. Why isn't the woman a reliable witness?
4. How does her final description of Botibol as a "nice man" who waves to her further characterize her?

20 Reading/Thinking Skills
Infer

Question What can you infer about the elderly woman from what she says to her companion? Explain how you arrived at this conclusion. *(Possible response: that she is feeble-minded; she is not surprised by the fact that Mr. Botibol jumped overboard but that he did it fully clothed.)*

Check Test

1. What is the setting of this story? *(an ocean liner on the Atlantic Ocean)*
2. What do the passengers bet on in the auction? *(how many miles they think the ship will travel that day)*
3. Is Mr. Botibol's wife traveling with him? *(no)*
4. Why does Mr. Botibol jump overboard? *(to slow the ship so that he will win the auction pool)*
5. What does this woman who witnesses the jump do to help Botibol? *(nothing)*

Unit 2 Resource Book
Alternate Check Test, p. 69

soon, so very soon, it was such a long way away that she couldn't even be sure it was there at all.

A man dived overboard just now, with his clothes on.

After a while another woman came out on deck. This one was bony and angular, and she wore horn-rimmed spectacles. She spotted the first woman and walked over to her, treading the deck in the deliberate, military fashion of all spinsters.

"So *there* you are," she said. The woman with the fat ankles turned and looked at her, but said nothing.

"I've been searching for you," the bony one continued. "Searching all over."

"It's very odd," the woman with the fat ankles said. "A man dived overboard just now, with his clothes on."

"Nonsense!"

"Oh yes. He said he wanted to get some exercise and he dived in and didn't even bother to take his clothes off." 20

"You better come down now," the bony woman said. Her mouth had suddenly become firm, her whole face sharp and alert, and she spoke less kindly than before. "And don't you ever go wandering about on deck alone like this again. You know quite well you're meant to wait for me."

"Yes, Maggie," the woman with the fat ankles answered, and again she smiled, a tender, trusting smile, and she took the hand of the other one and allowed herself to be led away across the deck.

"Such a nice man," she said. "He waved to me."

MINI-LESSON: CRITICAL THINKING
Evaluate

Teach Tell students that Roald Dahl is known for placing unsuspecting, ordinary characters in fantastic (and often dreadful) situations that allow no escape.

Activity Idea Have students consider whether or not "Dip in the Pool" fits into this plot formula. Ask: Is Mr. Botibol an unsuspecting, ordinary person who is placed in a fantastic situation? *(Possible responses: Yes. He is a normal, fastidious, husband who gets into a fantastic bind. No. He is a paranoid, obsessive, unstable person who causes his own downfall.)*

After Reading

Making Connections

Shaping Your Response

1. What do you think is going on in Mr. Botibol's mind at the end of the story? Portray his thoughts and emotions in a cartoonlike drawing.
2. Do you think Mr. Botibol deserves to be rescued? Why or why not?
3. What music or style of music would you choose as the theme song to be played at the end of the story?

Analyzing the Story

4. What contrasting **moods** are in the first three paragraphs? What words establish these moods?
5. Can you find anything in the woman's behavior or appearance before Mr. Botibol jumps that would suggest she will not be a reliable witness? Explain.
6. Choose three words to describe Mr. Botibol's **character** and explain your choices.
7. Explain the **pun(s),** or play on words, in the title.

Extending the Ideas

8. How does this story compare with other stories you have read by Roald Dahl or with other stories having surprise endings?
9. Who do you consider the quicker thinker—Mr. Botibol in "Dip in the Pool" or Inspector Moronoff in "The Chameleon"? You may want to show the characters' similarities and differences in a Venn diagram.

Literary Focus: Plot

The usual pattern of related events in a **plot** is *conflict, climax,* and *resolution,* or *conclusion.*

- Use a chart like the one below to record in your notebook the conflict, climax, and resolution of "Dip in the Pool".

Conflict	
Climax	
Resolution	

- Are you satisfied with the resolution of the story, or can you suggest a more satisfactory conclusion? Explain.

After Reading

MAKING CONNECTIONS

1. Drawings may depict Botibol on an empty ocean, desperately waving his arms. His facial expression or a thought bubble might reflect determination, anxiety, or bewilderment.

2. Possible responses: No, because he jumped. Yes, because though he acted rashly, he doesn't deserve to drown.

3. Some students may suggest a sad, tragic theme because they think he is going to die. Others may suggest an upbeat piece to reflect the absurd ending.

4. Possible moods: Par. 1: peaceful optimism *(calmed, faces upturned);* Par. 2: comfort *(complacent, assured);* Par. 3: tension *(friction, nervously, apprehension)*

5. Some students may note her repetitive speech, self-doubting and apologetic answers, and odd smile. Others may notice nothing strange about her.

6. Botibol is *timid* (fears his wife); *paranoid* (thinks everyone is trying to beat him in the auction); *meticulous* (obsessive about details); *compulsive* and *overconfident* (bets all of his savings).

7. *Pool* refers to the water Botibol jumps into and the betting pool he enters. *Dip* indicates both a little swim and a skimming off of money.

8. Encourage students to think of stories in which foolish or evil characters end up getting the punishment they deserve.

9. Possible responses: Inspector Moronoff, because he changes his mind often and expediently.

Similarities	Differences
seeks to know facts, is impulsive yet cautious, depends on outside opinion.	Moronoff has associates, takes a stand, faces conflict; Botibol is alone, avoids conflict.

LITERARY FOCUS: PLOT

Student plot diagrams will probably include some of the following information.

- Conflict: Mr. Botibol struggles to overcome obstacles preventing him from winning the auction pool. Climax: He jumps overboard. Resolution: His witness fails to sound the alarm; Mr. Botibol is left to his fate in the ocean. (Alternatively, some students may identify the climax as the reader's discovery that the woman is not considered a reliable witness and the resolution as the realization of Mr. Botibol's fate.)
- Most students will think that Mr. Botibol gets exactly what he deserves. Some might imagine him being saved only to lose the pool by the slimmest of margins. Others might prefer that a shark's fin appear on the horizon.

VOCABULARY STUDY

1. surreptitiously
2. steward
3. turbot
4. poached
5. turbulent
6. subside
7. advertent
8. assail
9. friction
10. complacent

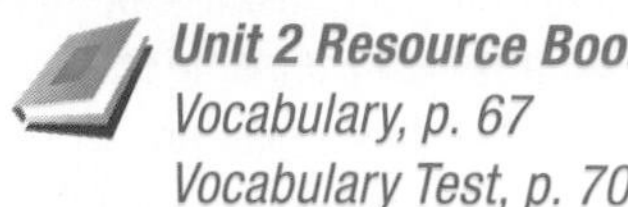

Unit 2 Resource Book
Vocabulary, p. 67
Vocabulary Test, p. 70

WRITING CHOICES

Writer's Notebook Update

Encourage students to compare their lists of creative qualities. Elicit discussion about how creativity can sometimes work against people as it does against Mr. Botibol. Ask students if they ever came up with a solution that was so creative it would not work.

The Next Chapter

Encourage students to share their new endings. Ask them if they think the various endings improve on Dahl's story.

Submerged Thoughts

Remind students to use what they have learned about farce and tone in this unit to help them with their answer.

Selection Test

Unit 2 Resource Book
pp. 71–72

Vocabulary Study

Write the word that best completes each numbered item in the following paragraph.

advertent
assail
complacent
friction
poached
steward
subside
surreptitiously
turbot
turbulent

Come Aboard!

Like Mr. Botibol, you can take the fantasy trip that you have (1) longed for! Welcome aboard the Luxury Liner Tour, where you will get the special attention of a (2), who will take care of your every request. Eat luxury meals, which may include a tasty (3) that has been (4) in a broth. If a (5) storm should arise, be assured that rough waters will soon (6) under the skillful navigation of our captain. All our crew will be (7) to your needs. No troubles will (8) you on this trip. So if you want to escape the irritations and (9) of everyday life, come aboard. You can feel (10) about your choice of LLT for your dream vacation.

Expressing Your Ideas

Writing Choices

Writer's Notebook Update While preparing to read "Dip in the Pool," you assessed yourself as a problem solver. How do you stack up with Mr. Botibol as a quick and creative thinker? Make up a list of six words that you think name qualities a good problem solver should have. Circle qualities that you possess. Underline qualities you think Mr. Botibol possesses.

The Next Chapter Continue the story to show what happens next. Is Mr. Botibol rescued? Does he live on to write a bestseller about winning bets? Is his widow Ethel able to buy the pale-green Lincoln convertible? Use your imagination to write a **new ending** for the story.

Submerged Thoughts Write a brief **explanation** of how this story fits the theme "Beneath the Surface." You may want to pun on the word *surface* as Dahl does on the word *pool* in the story's title.

Other Options

Missing Person Create a news bulletin describing Mr. Botibol and the circumstances surrounding his disappearance. Use details from the story to construct an **artist's sketch** of him to accompany the bulletin.

Talk Your Way Out of This One! Mr. Botibol arrives home, damp and penniless. His wife is waiting at the door for an explanation. Remember that he prides himself on his ability to think quickly and to devise creative solutions to problems. Now work with a partner to write a **dialogue** to deliver to the class.

Stories on Stage Form a group to read other stories by Roald Dahl. Choose one of these stories to perform as a **dramatic reading** for the rest of the class, complete with music, props, and sound effects.

OTHER OPTIONS

Missing Person

Students may want to include the following details:

- What was he wearing when last sighted?
- What are his approximate physical dimensions? *(height, weight, hair)*

Talk Your Way Out of This One!

Remind students that all we know about Ethel is what we can infer from Mr. Botibol's one-sided internal projections. Encourage them to expand on her character.

Stories on Stage

Encourage students to have fun with the farcical elements, playing with the humorous scenes that require physical exaggeration and absurd behavior.

Before Reading

The Need to Say It

By Patricia Hampl USA

Patricia Hampl
born 1946

Of her writing, Patricia Hampl says, "I suppose I write about all the things I intended to leave behind, to grow out of, or deny: being a Midwesterner, a Catholic, a woman." Accordingly her writing expresses a nostalgic and melancholy reflection of events from her youth in Minnesota. Hampl currently is an associate professor of English at the University of Minnesota and a founding member of Loft (for literature and the arts). She gives lectures, presents workshops, and performs readings of her poetry.

Building Background

Things Have Changed in Czechoslovakia The Czech grandmother in "The Need to Say It" would find the country she left 100 years ago vastly changed today. At the end of World War I, Austria-Hungary collapsed, and Czechoslovakia, which was carved from part of it, became a democratic republic. Just before World War II broke out, Germany, Hungary, and Poland claimed various parts of the country. It was freed by Soviet troops by 1945. In 1989, following mass protests, non-Communists took over the government and elected Václav Havel president. On December 31, 1992, Czechoslovakia ceased to exist, and the Czech Republic and Slovakia were formed in its place.

Literary Focus

Narrator A **narrator** is the teller of a story. The two most common narrators are first person and third person. A *first-person narrator,* who is a character within the story, may offer a personal account of his or her experiences, or may focus on what happens to other characters. In this case, the character's opinions will influence the way the story is told. A *third-person narrator* stands anonymously outside the story's action. As you read "The Need to Say It," notice how details are presented and shaped by the narrator.

Writer's Notebook

Joint Efforts Before you read "The Need to Say It," think about a time when you shared your expertise with a family member who needed your help. How did you work together? What task did you accomplish? Would you have been as successful if either of you had tackled the task alone? Would you do things differently now? Note brief answers to these questions in your notebook.

Before Reading

Building Background

Question What would be the challenges of growing up in one culture and then moving to a different culture, with a different language, different customs, and so on? Encourage students who are able to answer from firsthand experience to give specific examples.

Literary Focus

Have students begin a chart to record details they learn about the **narrator** as they read.

Narrator
ten years old imaginative likes cookies and milk

Writer's Notebook

Students might write about non-family members whom they have worked with or assisted in any way.

More About Patricia Hampl

Patricia Hampl has worked as a sales clerk and a telephone operator. Other works by Hampl include:

- *A Romantic Education*, Houghton, (1981)
- *Woman Before an Aquarium*, University of Pittsburgh Press, (1978)

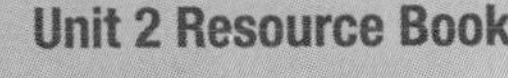

SUPPORT MATERIALS OVERVIEW

Unit 2 Resource Book
- Graphic Organizer, p. 73
- Study Guide, p. 74
- Vocabulary, p. 75
- Grammar, p. 76
- Alternate Check Test, p. 77
- Vocabulary Test, p. 78
- Selection Test, pp. 79–80

Building English Proficiency
- Literature Summaries
- Activities, p. 190

Reading, Writing & Grammar SkillBook
- Grammar, Usage, and Mechanics, pp. 269–270

Technology
- Audiotape 8, Side B
- Personal Journal Software
- Custom Literature Database: For another account of a budding literary life, see *My First Acquaintance with Poets* by William Hazlitt on the database.
- Test Generator Software

During Reading

Selection Objectives

- to explore the theme "Beneath the Surface"
- to identify the type of narrator used
- to review the punctuation of quotations

Unit 2 Resource Book
Graphic Organizer, p. 73
Study Guide, p. 74

Theme Link

The theme "Beneath the Surface" is reflected as the narrator writes letters for her grandmother. She realizes that her judgment about what constitutes a good personal letter differs from her grandmother's ideas.

Vocabulary Preview

garrulity, wordiness
loathsome, disgusting
motif, distinctive figure or pattern in a design, painting, etc.
reticence, tendency to be silent or say little
taint, stain or spot

Students can add the words and definitions to their Writer's Notebooks.

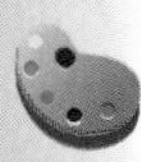

Art Study

Response to Caption Question They both extend themselves into their letters: the girl in the painting, literally; the narrator in the story, figuratively.

Question What other details in the picture reinforce the girl's absorption in her writing? *(Response: Leaning her hand on her forehead closes in the range of her vision and focuses her view on the paper; her intertwined legs suggest she is "wrapped up" in her work.)*

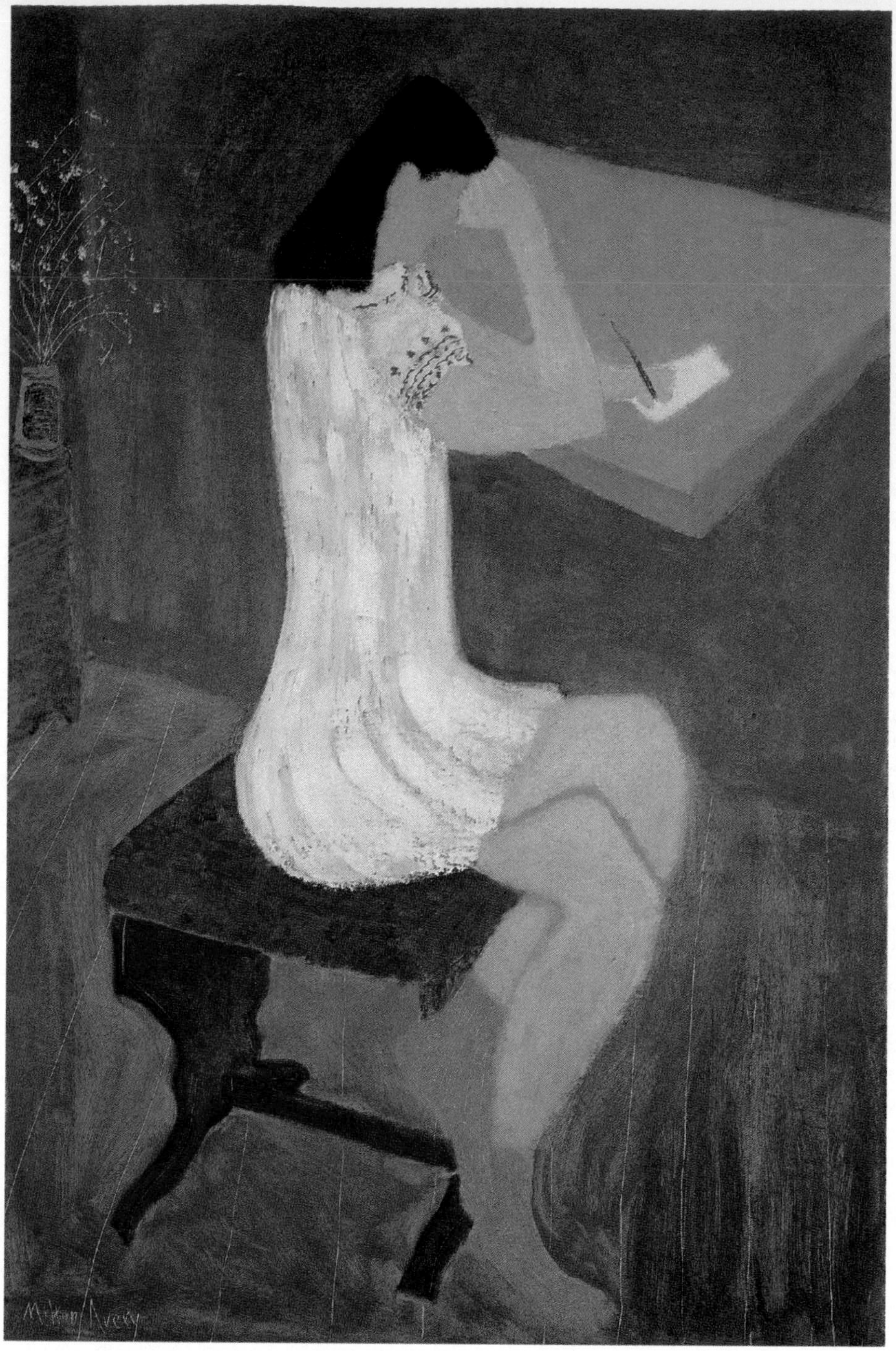

SELECTION SUMMARY

The Need to Say It

The ten-year-old narrator has a grandmother who was born and raised in Czechoslovakia but now lives next door in Minnesota. Her grandmother does not write English, and asks the narrator to write a letter for her to her sister in California in exchange for cookies and milk. The narrator is not impressed with the stationery or with her grandmother's terse letter-writing style, both of which she criticizes at length. Soon, the narrator begins padding the letters with her own anecdotes, and then takes over her grandmother's letter writing entirely, writing in the persona of her grandmother, and unconcerned about this deceit. The narrator agrees to teach her grandmother to write the word *love* to give her complete control of the sign-off, but she forgets to explain about the comma, so that the words *Love Teresa* look like a command.

*For summaries in other languages, see the **Building English Proficiency** book.*

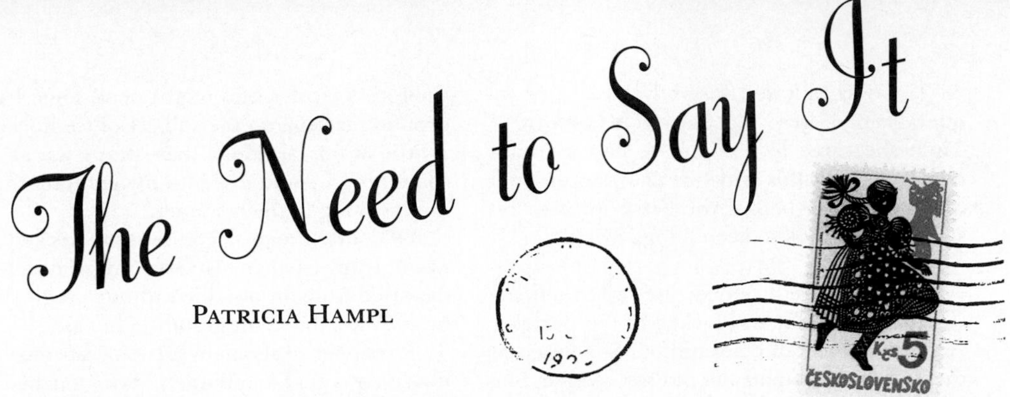

The Need to Say It

PATRICIA HAMPL

1 My Czech[1] grandmother hated to see me with a book. She snatched it away if I sat still too long (dead to her), absorbed in my reading. "Bad for you," she would say, holding the loathsome[2] thing behind her back, furious at my enchantment.

She kept her distance from the printed word of English, but she lavished attention on her lodge newspaper which came once a month, written in the quaint nineteenth-century Czech she and her generation had brought to America before the turn of the century. Like wedding cake saved from the feast, this language, over the years, had become a fossil, still recognizable but no longer something to be put in the mouth.

Did she read English? I'm not sure. I do know that she couldn't—or didn't—write it. That's where I came in.

My first commissioned work was to write letters for her. "You write for me, honey?" she would say, holding out a ballpoint she had been given at a grocery store promotion, clicking it like a castanet. My fee was cookies and milk, payable before, during, and after completion of the project.

I settled down at her kitchen table while she rooted around the drawer where she kept coupons and playing cards and bank calendars. Eventually she located a piece of stationery and a mismatched envelope. She laid the small, pastel sheet before me, smoothing it out; a floral motif[3] was clotted across the top of the page and bled down one side. The paper was so insubstantial even ballpoint ink seeped through 2
to the other side. "That's okay," she would say. "We only need one side."

True. In life she was a gifted gossip, unfurling an extended riff of chatter from a bare motif of rumor. But her writing style displayed a brevity[4] that made Hemingway's prose[5] look like nattering garrulity.[6] She dictated her letters as if 3
she were paying by the word.

"Dear Sister," she began, followed by a little time-buying cough and throat-clearing. "We are all well here." Pause. "And hope you are well too." Longer pause, the steamy broth of inspiration heating up on her side of the table. Then, in a lurch, "Winter is hard so I don't get out much."

◄ In Milton Avery's 1941 oil titled *Girl Writing*, the writing paper seems like an extension of the girl herself. What does the writer in the painting have in common with the girl in the story?

1. **Czech** (chek), *adj.* of or having to do with what was formerly Czechoslovakia, its people, or language.
2. loathsome (lōᴛʜ′səm), *adj.* disgusting.
3. motif (mō tēf′), *n.* a distinctive figure or pattern in a design, painting, etc.
4. **brevity** (brev′ə tē), *n.* shortness in speech or writing; conciseness.
5. **Hemingway's prose**. Ernest Hemingway (1899–1961) was a novelist and short story writer noted for his lean, condensed style.
6. garrulity (gə rü′lə tē), *n.* wordiness.

1 Reading/Thinking Skills
Draw Conclusions

Question Why might the grandmother feel this way? *(Possible responses: She might be jealous because she cannot read English; she might really think that books are not of much value; she might be envious of her granddaughter's enjoyment.)*

2 Literary Focus
Narrator

Narrators reveal themselves through their choice of details.

Question How is the narrator critical of her grandmother? *(She focuses on details that make her grandmother seem to have poor taste and be cheap—the mismatched envelope; the small piece of insubstantial paper; the "clotted" design.)*

3 Reader's Response
Challenging the Text

Questions

- How does the narrator show disdain for her grandmother's writing style? *(by comparisons to Hemingway and telegrams, by her "time-buying cough," by word choice, such as* lurch.*)*
- Do you think her feelings are appropriate? Explain. *(Probably not—she does not account for her grandmother's displacement from her native culture or show any sympathy.)*

BUILDING ENGLISH PROFICIENCY

ESL LEP ELD SAE LD

Making Personal Connections

Students gaining English proficiency might use one or more of the following activities to help them identify with the author and the task of writing her grandmother's letters.

Activity Ideas

- Invite students to share ways in which they may be helping relatives and friends learn or use the English language. Ask: What challenges do they—or you—face?
- Invite students to share some of their own frustrations with English. Ask: Do you ever feel as the grandmother does? How?
- What is it like to take dictation? Tape a brief paragraph; then play it for a group of volunteers, who attempt to write what they hear. Play the tape again as students check their work—and have them comment on the difficulty of taking dictation.

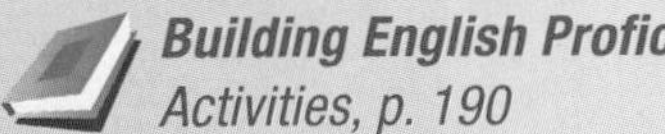

Building English Proficiency
Activities, p. 190

4 Literary Focus
Narrator

Narrators reveal themselves through what they say and do in a story.

Question What does this passage reveal about the narrator's attitude toward her grandmother? *(Possible response: She thinks she can take over her life through letters.)*

5 Reader's Response
Making Personal Connections

Question Do you think the narrator has a good relationship with her grandmother? Why or why not? *(Possible responses: Yes, they are close and see each other daily. They communicate well, and do things for one another. No, the young girl doesn't show proper respect for her grandmother.)*

Check Test

1. What one thing did the grandmother enjoy reading? *(her lodge newspaper)*
2. What did the narrator get in exchange for writing letters? *(cookies and milk)*
3. What was the grandmother's name? *(Teresa)*
4. What word did the narrator teach her grandmother to write? *(love)*
5. How old was the narrator at the time the story took place? *(ten)*

Unit 2 Resource Book
Alternate Check Test, p.77

This was followed instantly by an unconquerable fit of envy: "Not like you in California." Then she came to a complete halt, perhaps demoralized by this evidence that you can't put much on paper before you betray your secret self, try as you will to keep things civil.

She sat, she brooded, she stared out the window. She was locked in the perverse reticence[7] of composition. She gazed at me, but I understood she did not see me. She was looking for her next thought. "Read what I wrote," she would finally say, having lost not only what she was looking for but what she already had pinned down. I went over the little trail of sentences that led to her dead end.

More silence, then a sigh. She gave up the ghost. "Put 'God bless you,'" she said. She reached across to see the lean rectangle of words on the paper. "Now leave some space," she said, "and put 'Love.'" I handed over the paper for her to sign.

She always asked if her signature looked nice. She wrote her one word—Teresa—with a flourish. For her, writing was painting, a visual art, not declarative but sensuous.

She sent her lean documents regularly to her only remaining sister who lived in Los Angeles, a place she had not visited. They had last seen each other as children in their village in Bohemia.[8] But she never mentioned that or anything from that world. There was no taint[9] of reminiscence in her prose.

Even at ten I was appalled by the minimalism of these letters. They enraged me. "Is that all you have to say?" I would ask her, a nasty edge to my voice.

It wasn't long before I began padding the text. Without telling her, I added an anecdote[10] my father had told at dinner the night before, or I conducted this unknown reader through the heavy plot of my brother's attempt to make first string on the St. Thomas hockey team. I allowed myself a descriptive aria on the beauty of Minnesota winters (for the benefit of my California reader who might need some background material on the subject of ice hockey). A little of this, a little of that—there was always something I could toss into my grandmother's meager soup to thicken it up.

Of course the protagonist of the hockey tale was not "my brother." He was "my grandson." I departed from my own life without a regret and breezily inhabited my grandmother's.

I complained about my hip joint, I bemoaned the rising cost of hamburger, I even touched on the loneliness of old age, and hinted at the inattention of my son's wife (that is, my own mother, who was next door, oblivious to treachery).[11]

In time, my grandmother gave in to the inevitable. Without ever discussing it, we understood that when she came looking for me, clicking her ballpoint, I was to write the letter, and her job was to keep the cookies coming. I abandoned her skimpy floral stationery, which badly cramped my style, and thumped down on the table a stack of ruled 8 ½ by 11.

"Just say something interesting," she would say. And I was off to the races.

I took over her life in prose. Somewhere along the line, though, she decided to take full possession of her sign-off. She asked me to show her how to write "Love" so she could add it to "Teresa" in her own hand. She practiced the new word many times on scratch paper before she allowed herself to commit it to the bottom of a letter.

But when she finally took the leap, I realized I had forgotten to tell her about the comma. On a single slanting line she had written: *Love Teresa.* The words didn't look like a closure, but a command.

7. reticence (ret′ə sens), *n.* tendency to be silent or say little.
8. **Bohemia** (bō hē′mē ə), *n.* former country in central Europe, now a region of the Czech Republic.
9. taint (tānt), *n.* a stain or spot.
10. **anecdote** (an′ik dōt), *n.* a short account of some interesting incident or single event.
11. **treachery** (trech′ər ē), *n.* deceit.

MINI-LESSON: GRAMMAR
Dialogue

Teach Write the following sentence on the board to elicit discussion about the rules for punctuating quotations.

"Just say something interesting," she would say.

- Ask: How can you tell which are the grandmother's actual words?
- Review that a direct quotation usually begins with a capital letter, is enclosed in quotation marks, and is set off from the rest of the sentence by a punctuation mark.

Activity Idea Have students write a brief dialogue in which the narrator explains to a friend how she embellishes her grandmother's letters. Remind them to punctuate quotations correctly.

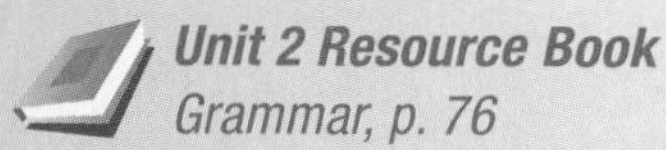

Unit 2 Resource Book
Grammar, p. 76

After Reading

Making Connections

Shaping Your Response

1. Would you like to have this grandmother or the narrator in your family circle? Explain.
2. In your opinion, was the narrator lying by writing her grandmother's letters? Why or why not?
3. Who do you think benefited most from these letter-writing sessions, grandmother or granddaughter? Explain.

Analyzing the Essay

4. To whom do you think the **title** "The Need to Say It" refers? Why?
5. What might the author have meant by saying "you can't put much on paper before you betray your secret self"?
6. Do you think the grandmother and granddaughter have any **character traits** in common? Explain.

Extending the Ideas

7. Think of people you know or have read about who have left their native countries for various reasons. Why might they not talk about their homelands?
8. The narrator says, "I departed from my own life without regret and breezily inhabited my grandmother's." What professions might enable someone to "inhabit" another person's life? Explain.

Literary Focus: Narrator

A story's **narrator** is often the most important character. It can be helpful to know directly what this character is thinking, feeling, and so on.

- Why do you think Patricia Hampl made the granddaughter the narrator when the focus of the story seems to be on the grandmother?
- How might the grandmother describe herself and her granddaughter if *she* were telling the story?

After Reading

MAKING CONNECTIONS

1. Students should give details about character traits to substantiate their judgments.

2. Possible responses: No, her grandmother gave tacit approval to what she was doing, so it wasn't wrong. No, her grandmother could not write the kind of letters she wanted to, and her granddaughter could. Yes, because the narrator did it for bad motives—not to help her grandmother, but because she didn't like her grandmother's way of doing things.

3. Some students may think that neither really benefited since it was a relationship based on deception. Others may see a mutual respect and affection between the two and a relationship in which both benefited.

4. Possible responses: to the narrator who feels compelled to take over her grandmother's letters; to the grandmother, who speaks through the young girl.

5. Possible response: It might be an ironical statement, reflecting on what the narrator unintentionally reveals about herself in this story.

6. Possible response: They are both determined and perhaps domineering. Just as the grandmother controls the narrator's reading, the narrator controls her grandmother's writing.

7. Possible responses: The memories are too painful. There are not appropriate words in their new language to describe their old life. Nobody shows any interest.

8. Possible response: Actors pretend to be other people in their roles; psychiatrists, in some respects, "get inside" their the minds of their patients.

LITERARY FOCUS: NARRATOR

- Possible responses: This third-person narration allows the grandmother to be vividly characterized through the eyes of an imaginative ten-year-old.
- Possible responses: If the grandmother were narrator, the focus might shift to her granddaughter; the grandmother wouldn't describe herself as vividly as her granddaughter does, nor would she be able to recount details that were fabricated in the letters.

VOCABULARY STUDY

1. d
2. b
3. c
4. d
5. a

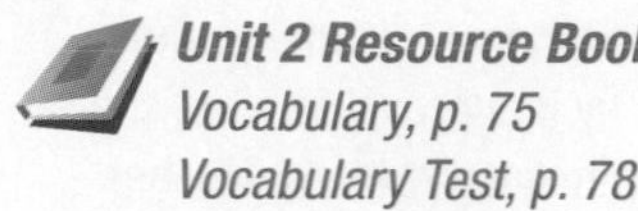

Unit 2 Resource Book
Vocabulary, p. 75
Vocabulary Test, p. 78

WRITING CHOICES

Thinking of You

Provide an assortment of "thinking of you" greeting cards with poems inside. Have students vote on which style seems to fit what the grandmother would like and which seem appropriate to the narrator's aesthetic. Tell them to try to use the narrator's judgment in deciding what to write in the card.

Selection Test

Unit 2 Resource Book
pp. 79–80

Vocabulary Study

On your paper, write the letter of the best definition for each word.

garrulity
loathsome
motif
reticence
taint

1. *loathsome* a. harmless b. favorite c. frightening d. disgusting

2. *motif* a. cause b. design c. memory d. book

3. *garrulity* a. shyness b. shortness c. wordiness d. vulgarity

4. *taint* a. memory b. belief c. lie d. stain

5. *reticence* a. silence b. gleam c. rumor d. laughter

Expressing Your Ideas

Writing Choices

Writer's Notebook Update Now that you've read "The Need to Say It," reread your notes about a time when you teamed up with someone to accomplish a task. Write a brief comparison of your situation and the one described in the story. How are the two situations alike? How are they different?

Thinking of You Imagine you are the granddaughter in "The Need to Say It." You've done such a good job "padding the text" in your grandmother's letters that now she wants you to write a **greeting card** sentiment to her sister. Write a "Thinking of You" poem for the grandmother to send.

Other Options

Take Action You may know people in your community who are unable to read and write in English. Does anyone help them interpret the written symbols of our language? Think about starting a literacy service with one or more partners. As a group, investigate the needs of illiterate people in your area and prepare a **plan** for how you might help these people on a regular basis. Think of a name for your organization, and create advertisements and posters to advertise your services.

The Art of Lettering The narrator of "The Need to Say It" describes her grandmother's handwriting as "painting, a visual art, not declarative but sensuous." Use the grandmother's name—Teresa, your own name, or a name of your choice to create a piece of **art**. You might consider using calligraphy or a computer program.

OTHER OPTIONS

Take Action

If such a service already exists, students could consider becoming volunteers in it. They could also consider helping people who are not illiterate, but who speak a native language other than English, for example, by becoming peer tutors to ESL students in their own school.

The Art of Lettering

Students might enjoy making a greeting card using stylized lettering.

Before Reading

Crossroads by Carlos Solórzano Mexico
Two Bodies by Octavio Paz Mexico

Carlos Solórzano
born 1922

Carlos Solórzano (sō lôr zä′nō) describes the characters in his drama as people locked in a struggle to attain liberty. After receiving degrees in architecture and literature, he studied drama in Paris. A professor at the National University of Mexico, he also directed its theater.

Octavio Paz
born 1914

Octavio Paz (ok tä′vē ō päz) has observed that "a poem is a shell that echoes the music of the world." At nineteen, he published his first book of poetry, earning a reputation as one of Mexico's most gifted writers. As a young man, he served in the diplomatic corps in France and Japan. Later, he was appointed Mexico's ambassador in India. He won the Nobel Prize in 1990 "for impassioned writings with wide horizons."

Building Background

Imagine the Scene On the first day back to school, you discover that your high school is really wired—computer network wired, that is. From the English writing lab, you can log on to the great communications highway and chat with people across the country. Soon you're discussing politics with someone in Washington, D. C., basketball with a fellow fan in Phoenix, and personal problems with juliet75@aol.com, who lives in Denver and whose online warmth and sympathetic understanding make her your favorite correspondent. When your parents announce that the family is going to Colorado, you alert juliet75@aol.com and arrange to meet her in the lobby of your hotel. You arrive early, looking eagerly for a girl with a white flower on her dress. When juliet75@aol.com finally shows up, you are amazed.

Brainstorm with classmates possible outcomes of this scenario. Then prepare to read about a similar experience.

Literary Focus

Foreshadowing Just as a teacher might alert you to what to expect on a test, an author may provide hints of what will eventually happen in a story. Such clues are called **foreshadowing**. You may find examples of foreshadowing in movies as well: a significant cough may foreshadow a character's death; a special glance between characters may clue viewers into their later collaboration or romance. As you read *Crossroads*, be alert to examples of foreshadowing.

Writer's Notebook

Common Ground Consider how differing **perspectives** due to heritage, culture, age, experience, religion, values, or social class might affect a romantic relationship. Which of these factors do you think is most important for a couple to have in common? Rank them in order of importance.

Before Reading

Building Background

Ask students to describe a time when their expectations were not met or their hopes were dashed.

Literary Focus

Point out the value of rereading a selection to confirm examples of **foreshadowing**. On second reading, readers are more alerted to clues and more conscious of the writer's craft.

Writer's Notebook

You may wish to have students interview multicultural couples and get their perspectives to provide a basis for their speculation.

More About Carlos Solórzano and Octavio Paz

Solórzano's works have been translated into English, French, Russian, Italian, Hungarian, Polish, and German. Other works include:

- *The Hands of God*, Hiram College, (1968)

Paz calls himself a political "disillusioned leftist." Other works by Paz include:

- *Early Poems: 1935–1955*, New Directions, (1973)
- *The Collected Poems, 1957–1987 Bilingual Edition*, New Editions, (1987)

SUPPORT MATERIALS OVERVIEW

Unit 2 Resource Book
- Graphic Organizer, p. 81
- Study Guide, p. 82
- Vocabulary, p. 83
- Grammar, p. 84
- Alternate Check Test, p. 85
- Vocabulary Test, p. 86
- Selection Test, pp. 87–88

Building English Proficiency
- Literature Summaries
- Activities, p. 191

Reading, Writing & Grammar SkillBook
- Vocabulary, pp. 7–8
- Grammar, Usage, and Mechanics, pp. 259–260

Technology
- Audiotape 8, Side B
- Personal Journal Software
- Custom Literature Database: For another account of unrequited love, see "The Kiss" by Anton Chekhov on the database.
- Test Generator Software

During Reading

Selection Objectives

- to explore the theme of making judgments based on outward appearances
- to recognize foreshadowing
- to understand conventions for capitalizing geographical areas but not directions

Unit 2 Resource Book
Graphic Organizer, p. 81
Study Guide, p. 82

Theme Link

These selections explore changing or deceptive relationships.

Vocabulary Preview

dejectedly, sadly
entreatingly, in a begging or praying manner
forcefully, powerfully
indifferently, in a manner that shows little interest
imperturbably, calmly

Students can add the words and definitions to their Writer's Notebooks.

Responses to Caption Question The man is standing alone; he has his back to the viewer; he is dwarfed by the train; his posture looks resigned.

Visual Literacy The mood of a painting results from many things. Have students comment on how each of the following factors contributes to the mood of the work:

- color
- point of view
- scale

Crossroads
A Sad Vaudeville[1]

CARLOS SOLÓRZANO

CHARACTERS
FLAGMAN
TRAIN
MAN
WOMAN

Setting. Stage empty, dark. At one end, a semaphore[2] that alternately flashes a green light and a red one. In the center, hanging from the ceiling, a big clock whose hands show five o'clock sharp.

The characters will move mechanically, like characters in the silent movies. The MAN *in fast motion; the* WOMAN, *in slow motion. As the curtain rises, the* FLAGMAN *is at the end of the stage, opposite the semaphore, with a lighted lantern in his hand. He is standing very stiffly and indifferently.[3]*

FLAGMAN *(staring into space, in an impersonal voice).* The trains from the North travel toward the South, the trains from the North travel toward the South, the trains from the North travel toward the South. *(He repeats the refrain[4] several times while the* TRAIN *crosses the back of the stage. The* TRAIN *will be formed by three men dressed in gray. As they pass by, they each mechanically perform a pantomime with one arm extended,*

1. **vaudeville** (vôd′vil), *n.* a theatrical entertainment featuring a variety of acts, such as songs, dances, acrobatic feats, and trained animals.
2. **semaphore** (sem′ə fôr), *n.* an upright structure with movable arms or an arrangement of colored lights, lanterns, flags, etc., used in railroad signaling.
3. **indifferently,** (in dif′ər ənt lē), *adv.* in a manner that shows little interest.
4. **refrain** (ri frān′), *n.* phrase or verse recurring regularly.

SELECTION SUMMARY

Crossroads: A Sad Vaudeville, Two Bodies

Crossroads begins with a Flagman reciting a litany about the directions of the trains. The Man arrives on a train, searching for a Woman with whom he has fallen in love. The Man describes the Woman to the Flagman, who claims not to have seen her. The Woman arrives but denies her identity. It is revealed that the Woman has deceived the Man about her age in an attempt to win his love. Now that they are meeting in person, she is afraid. When she shows him her face, she sees in his reaction that there can be no romance between them, so she leaves. The Man, who does not realize that the Woman and his fantasy love are the same person, despairs, while the indifferent Flagman continues his litany.

In "Two Bodies," Paz writes about the different relationships two bodies can have in the night.

For summaries in other languages, see the ***Building English Proficiency*** *book.*

This contemporary illustration by Robert Gantt Steele contrasts a simple figure of a man with the complex lattice work of a train station and the powerful engineering of a moving train. How does the artist create an aura of loneliness, insignificance, and alienation about the figure?

the hand on the shoulder of the man in front, and the other arm making a circular motion, synchronized with the rhythm of the FLAGMAN*'s words.)*

1 The trains from the North travel toward the South *(etc.)*.

(Loud train whistle. The MAN *who comes at the end of the* TRAIN *breaks free of it by making a movement as though he were jumping off. The* TRAIN *disappears on the right.)*

MAN *(carrying a small valise. He glances around the place, then looks at the clock, which he compares with his watch. He is young, serene of face, approximately twenty-five years old. He addresses the* FLAGMAN). Good afternoon. *(As a reply, he receives the latter's refrain.)* Is this the place this ticket indicates? *(He places it in front of the* FLAGMAN*'s eyes. The* FLAGMAN *nods.)* A train stops here, just about now, doesn't it?

FLAGMAN *(without looking at him)*. Trains never stop here.

MAN. Are you the flagman?

FLAGMAN. They call me by many names.

MAN. Then, perhaps you've seen a woman around here.

FLAGMAN. I've seen no one.

MAN *(approaching him)*. Do you know? The woman I'm looking for is . . .

FLAGMAN *(interrupting)*. They all look alike.

MAN. Oh, no! She's different. She's the woman that I've been waiting for for many years. She'll be wearing a white flower on her dress. Or is it yellow? *(He searches nervously in his pockets and takes out a paper that he reads.)* No, it's white . . . that's what she says in her letter. *(The* FLAGMAN *takes a few steps, feeling ill at ease.)* Pardon me for telling you all this, but now you'll be able to understand how important it is for me to find this woman, because . . .

FLAGMAN *(interrupting again)*. What woman?

MAN. The one that I'm looking for.

FLAGMAN. I don't know what woman you're looking for.

MAN. The one that I've just told you about.

FLAGMAN. Ah. . . .

MAN. Perhaps she has passed by and you didn't see her. *(The* FLAGMAN *shrugs his shoulders.)* Well, I guess that I have to tell you everything to see if you can remember. She's tall, slender, with black hair and big blue eyes. She's wearing a white flower on her dress. . . . *(Anxiously.)* Hasn't she been around here?

FLAGMAN. I can't know if someone I don't know has been around.

MAN. Excuse me. I know that I'm nervous but I have the impression that we aren't speaking the same language, that is, that you aren't answering my questions. . . .

FLAGMAN. That's not my job.

MAN. Nevertheless, I believe that a flagman ought to know how to answer questions. *(Transition.)* She wrote to me that she'd be here at five, at the railroad crossing of . . . 2
(He reads the ticket.) I'll never know how to pronounce this name, but I know that it's here. We chose this point because it's halfway between our homes. Even for this kind of date, a romantic one, one must be fair. *(The* FLAGMAN *looks at him without understanding.)* Yes, romantic. *(With ingenuous[5] pride.)* Maybe I'll bore you, but I must tell you that one day I saw an ad in a magazine. It was hers. How well written that ad was! She 3
said that she needed a young man like me, to establish relations with so as not to live so alone. *(Pause.)* I wrote to her and she answered me. Then I sent her my photo and she sent me hers. You can't imagine what a beauty!

FLAGMAN *(who has not heard most of the account)*. Is she selling something?

---

5. **ingenuous** (in jen′yü əs), *adj.* simple and natural.

1 Reading/Thinking Skills
Identify Author's Purpose

Question What is the significance of the Flagman's droning litany and the Man emerging from being part of the Train? *(Possible response: The distinctions between human beings and mechanical devices are not clear-cut, indicating humanity's alienation.)*

2 Reading/Thinking Skills
Recognize Main Idea

Question Why do you think the characters and the station in the play are unnamed? *(Possible responses: It is another sign of alienation—the man can describe the woman he loves, but he doesn't even know her name; it makes the play express a universal problem instead of a particular situation.)*

3 Literary Element
Foreshadowing

Question Do you think the Woman will accomplish what she set out to do when she wrote the ad? Why or why not? *(Possible response: Students may note the problems of communication that have arisen already in the play and the use of the word* sad *in the subtitle, and suspect that in this hostile atmosphere, romance is not likely to flourish.)*

BUILDING ENGLISH PROFICIENCY

Exploring Stage Directions

In a very real sense, the characters in this play are just "going through the motions." The unusual stage directions will be easier for students to grasp if they "go through the motions" themselves.

1. Ask students to recall any science fiction movies or TV programs that feature robots. Students also may have seen silent movies or performances by mimes. Encourage volunteers to perform actions as a robot or silent film actor.

2. Have students keep these examples in mind as they try moving in the ways suggested by the stage directions—mechanically fast, mechanically slow, stiffly.

3. Let a group of students also attempt to synchronize the "train's" motions with the Flagman's lines.

4. Have volunteers perform dialogue and movements. Discuss students' impressions about this place and these people.

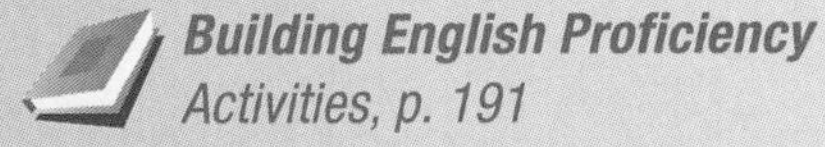

Building English Proficiency
Activities, p. 191

4 Reading/Thinking Skills

Compare and Contrast

Question How do the Man's and the Flagman's interpretations of the Woman's motives differ? *(Possible responses: The Man believes the Woman's story that she is shy. The Flagman thinks that she is trying to project an image.)*

5 Reading/Thinking Skills

Draw Conclusions

Question What does the Flagman mean? *(He may mean that people who have seen each other don't necessarily know each other well.)*

6 Literary Focus

Foreshadowing

Question What is the Flagman suggesting? *(Possible response: It doesn't matter whether they are discussing a man or a woman—if the person isn't coming, the gender is immaterial.)*

MAN *(surprised).* Who?

FLAGMAN. The woman who placed the ad.

MAN. No, for heaven's sake! She placed that ad because she said that she was shy, and she thought it might help and . . .

4 FLAGMAN. Everyone sells something.

MAN *(impatiently).* You just don't understand me.

FLAGMAN. It's possible. . . .

MAN. Well, I mean . . . understand how excited I am on coming to meet someone whom I don't know but who . . .

FLAGMAN. How's that?

MAN *(upset).* That is, I know her well, but I haven't seen her.

FLAGMAN. That's very common.

5 MAN. Do you think so?

FLAGMAN. The contrary's also common.

MAN. I don't understand.

FLAGMAN. It isn't necessary.

MAN. But you only speak nonsense! I should warn you that although I've an inclination toward romantic things, I'm a man who isn't pleased by jokes in bad taste. *(The* FLAGMAN *shrugs his shoulders again.)* Besides, this delay upsets me as does this dark place with that clock that doesn't run. It seems like a timeless place.

(Suddenly a loud train whistle is heard. The semaphore comes to life flashing the green light. The flagman again adopts his rigid posture, staring into space, he repeats his refrain.)

FLAGMAN *(loudly).* The trains from the South travel toward the North. The trains from the South travel toward the North. The trains from the South travel toward the North *(etc.).*

(The TRAIN *passes across the back of the stage, from right to left.)*

MAN *(shouting).* There, on that train! . . . She should be on it. *(He rushes to meet the* TRAIN *which passes by without stopping, almost knocking him down. The* MAN *remains at stage center, his arms at his sides. Disillusioned.)* She wasn't on it.

FLAGMAN. It's only natural.

MAN. What do you mean?

FLAGMAN. He's never coming. . . .

MAN. Who?

FLAGMAN. The man we're waiting for.

MAN. But it's a question of a woman.

FLAGMAN. It's the same. 6

MAN. How is a man going to be the same as a woman?

FLAGMAN. He isn't the same, but in a certain way he is.

MAN. You change your mind quickly.

FLAGMAN. I don't know.

MAN *(furiously).* Then, what is it that you do know?

FLAGMAN *(indifferently).* Where they're going.

MAN. The trains?

FLAGMAN. They all go to the same place.

MAN. What do you mean?

FLAGMAN. They come and go, but they end by meeting one another. . . .

MAN. That would be impossible.

FLAGMAN. But it's true. The impossible is always true.

MAN *(as if these last words brought him back to reality, he abandons his furious attitude and calms down).* You're right in what you say. *(Hesitating.)* For example, my meeting with that woman seems impossible and it's the only certain thing of my whole existence. *(Suddenly, with an unexpected tone of anguish.)* But it's five ten. *(He looks at his watch.)* And she isn't coming. *(He takes the arm of the* FLAGMAN *who remains indifferent.)* Help me, do all that is possible to remember! I'm sure that if you want to, you can tell me if you saw her or not. . . .

FLAGMAN. One can't know by just seeing a person whether it was the one who placed an ad in the newspaper.

MAN *(once again containing his ill humor).* But I already described what she's like to you! . . .

FLAGMAN *(imperturbably).*[6] I'm sorry. I forgot. . . .

(Meanwhile a WOMAN *dressed in black has come in behind the* MAN. *She is tall and slim. Her face is cov-*

6. imperturbably (im′pər tėr′bə blē), *adv.* calmly.

MINI-LESSON: STUDY SKILLS

Dictionary

Teach Read the stage directions at the bottom of the first column on page 312. Point out that the word *disillusioned* stands alone, so readers have no sentence context clues to help determine its meaning. Students should recognize when they need to use a dictionary to determine precise meaning.

Activity Idea Identify the following words for students and have them determine whether there is sufficient context to determine meaning, or whether they need to consult a dictionary. To determine a meaning, or to confirm a meaning they think is correct, have them look up the word and record the definition.

- p. 311—synchronized (col. 1, top)
- p. 311—transition (col. 2, middle)
- p. 312—inclination (col. 1, middle)
- p. 313—habitual (col. 1), bottom

Georgia O'Keeffe's 1932 oil painting, *White Trumpet Flower*, reveals rich textures and delicate details embedded in a plain flower. Do you consider this an appropriate flower to represent the woman in *Crossroads* or would you suggest another kind of flower?

7 *ered by a heavy veil. She walks softly with a pantomime motion. On her dress she wears a very large white flower. On seeing her the* FLAGMAN *raises his lantern and examines her. The* MAN, *blinded by the light, covers his eyes. On seeing herself discovered, the* WOMAN *tears the white flower violently from her dress. She puts it in her purse and turns her back, remaining motionless.)*

MAN *(still covering his eyes).* Ooh! You're going to blind me with that lantern.

FLAGMAN *(returning to his habitual stiffness).* I beg your pardon. . . .

MAN *(to the* FLAGMAN*).* Someone has come in, right?

FLAGMAN. It's not important.

MAN *(recovering from the glare, he notices the presence of the* WOMAN *and runs toward her. He stops suddenly).* Ah . . . *(Timidly.)* I beg you to. . . .

WOMAN *(her back turned).* Yes?

MAN *(embarrassed).* I thought that you . . . were someone . . .

WOMAN. Yes . . .

MAN *(with determination).* Someone I'm looking for. *(She does not move. Pause.)* Will you permit me to see you from the front?

WOMAN. From the front?

MAN *(upset).* Yes . . . it's absolutely necessary that I see you . . . 8

WOMAN *(without turning).* But . . . why? *(She begins to turn slowly.)*

Art Study

Responses to Caption Question
Possible responses: The flower is appropriate because it is beautiful, fragile, and sensuous—all the traits that the Woman wants the Man to identify with her. The flower is not appropriate because it is too large and showy and probably wouldn't fit in a purse. A white rose just coming out of bud would be better.

7 Reading/Thinking Skills
Infer

Question What do you think is the significance of the veil? *(Possible responses: It is another sign of alienation; the Woman is hiding something—maybe she is deformed or old.)*

8 Reading/Thinking Skills
Relate Literature to Personal Experience

Questions

- What various ways do we have of recognizing someone we know? *(Possible responses: face, voice, posture, walk, clothes, writing style, gesture, attitudes, beliefs, values, etc.)*
- What is the Man depending on for recognition? *(Possible response: the Woman's face)*

BUILDING ENGLISH PROFICIENCY

Exploring Key Statements

Draw students' attention to this statement by the flagman on page 312: "The impossible is always true." The statement seems contradictory, but it is key to understanding the play—and it will turn out to be true.

Have students construct a t-chart of events and thoughts from real life that seem to prove the statement.

What Seems Impossible	How It Is True
that people could fly	airplanes, rockets

9 **Reading/Thinking Skills**

Draw Conclusions

Question Why is the Man confused? (*Possible response: There is only one woman present and she seems to resemble the Woman's photo, but she is veiled and not wearing the flower that is meant to be a signal, and she gives cryptic answers to his requests.)*

10 **Reading/Thinking Skills**

Recognize Assumptions and Implications

The Man rejects the Woman's suggestion that the one he is looking for is afraid of revealing herself on the grounds that it is absurd, despite the evidence around him that life is absurd.

11 **Literary Element**

Mood

Question What role do you think the Flagman has in establishing the mood? *(Possible response: Every time a character has recourse to him, his answers remind us that the world is absurd, that people are inhuman, and that we cannot count on our expectations being met. His dialogue is the prime means of establishing a mood of futility.)*

MAN. Well . . . in order to . . . *(On seeing that her face is covered, he backs away.)* You aren't wearing anything on your dress . . . and nevertheless . . .

9

WOMAN *(trembling)*. And nevertheless?

MAN. You have the same stature and build. . . .

WOMAN *(with a jesting*[7] *tone)*. Really?

MAN *(with distrust)*. Could you tell me how you got here? I didn't see a train.

WOMAN *(interrupting, stammering)*. I arrived . . . ahead of time . . . and I waited.

MAN. Ahead of what time?

WOMAN. We all wait for a time. Aren't you waiting for it?

MAN *(sadly)*. Yes.

WOMAN. I believe that there is but one moment to recognize one another, to extend our hands. One mustn't let it pass by.

MAN. What do you mean by that? Who are you?

WOMAN. Now I'm the woman I've always wanted to be.

MAN *(timidly)*. Will you let me see your face?

WOMAN *(frightened)*. Why?

MAN. I need to find that one face, the special one, the different one.

WOMAN *(moving away)*. I am sorry. I can't.

MAN *(following her with a tortured motion)*. Excuse me. I'm stupid, I know. For a moment I thought that you could be she. But it's absurd. If it were so, you'd come straight to me, for we have called one another from afar.

WOMAN *(trembling)*. Perhaps she's more afraid of finding the one she seeks than of letting him pass by without stopping.

10

MAN. No, that would also be absurd. *(Transition.)* In any case, I beg your pardon. *(He moves away and sits down on his small suitcase, his back to the* WOMAN.*)* I'll wait here.

(In the meantime, while the MAN *is not looking at her, the* WOMAN *has raised her veil with long slow movements. When she uncovers her face, it is obvious that she is old. Her forehead is furrowed by deep wrinkles. She is like the mask of old age. This face contrasts obviously with her body, still slender, ageless.)*

WOMAN *(to the* FLAGMAN *who stares at her)*. You saw me from the beginning, didn't you? Why didn't you tell him?

FLAGMAN *(indifferently)*. Whom?

WOMAN *(pointing to the* MAN*)*. Him, the only one. 11

FLAGMAN. I'd forgotten him.

WOMAN *(in a surge of anguish)*. Shall I tell him that I'm that woman he's waiting for? Will he recognize in this old face the unsatisfied longing still in this body of mine? How can I tell him that I need him even more than when I was young, as young as I am in that touched-up photo that he's looking at?

(In the meantime, the MAN *studies the photograph with fascination. The* WOMAN *covers her face again with the veil and goes up to the* MAN.*)*

WOMAN. Is she very late?

MAN *(his back turned)*. Of course. . . .

WOMAN. It would hurt you a great deal if she wouldn't come!

MAN *(turning forcefully)*.[8] She has to come.

WOMAN. Nevertheless, you must realize that perhaps she's afraid to reveal herself, that maybe she's waiting for you to discover her.

MAN. I don't understand.

WOMAN *(very close to the* MAN*)*. I have a friend . . . who always lived alone, thinking nevertheless that the best thing for her was to get together with someone. *(She pauses. The* MAN *listens to her, interested.)* She was ugly, very ugly, perhaps that was why she dreamed of a man instead of looking for him. She liked to have her pictures taken. She had the photographs touched up, so that the picture turned out to be hers, but at the same time it was someone else's. She used to write to young men, sending them her photograph. She called them close to her house, with loving words. . . . When they arrived, she'd wait behind the windows; she wouldn't let herself be seen . . . .

MAN. Why are you telling me all this?

WOMAN *(without hearing)*. She'd see them. She knew that they were there on account of her.

7. **jesting** (jest′ing), *adj.* joking; making fun of.
8. **forcefully** (fôrs′fəl lē), *adv.* powerfully.

MINI-LESSON: LITERARY FOCUS

Foreshadowing

Teach Read the Woman's long speech at the bottom of the second column on page 314. Why is the Woman telling the Man about this other woman? Help students realize that the woman is talking about herself, and that this speech foreshadows the way the relationship of the Man and the Woman will end—with waiting and disillusionment.

Activity Ideas

- After students have finished the selection, have them work in groups to find examples of foreshadowing in this work.
- Have students return to an earlier selection, for example, *Antigone* or *Twelve Angry Men*, and identify examples of foreshadowing.

Each day, a different one. She accumulated many memories, the faces, the bodies of those strong men who had waited for her.

MAN. How absurd! I think. . . .

WOMAN. You're also strong and young.

MAN *(confused)*. Yes, but . . .

WOMAN. And today she's one day older than yesterday.

MAN *(after allowing a pause)*. Really I don't see what relation all this can have to . . .

WOMAN *(drawing near and placing her hand on the MAN's head)*. Perhaps you'll understand now. Close your eyes. *(She passes her hand over the eyes of the MAN in a loving manner.)* Have you never felt fear?

MAN. Fear? Of what?

WOMAN. Of living, of being . . . as if all your life you'd been waiting for something that never comes?

MAN. No. . . . *(He opens his eyes.)*

12 **WOMAN.** Tell me the truth. Close your eyes, those eyes that are separating us now. Have you been afraid?

(The MAN closes his eyes.)

MAN *(hesitatingly)*. Well, a little. . . .

WOMAN *(with an absent voice)*. A suffering . . . in solitude . . .

MAN. Yes, at times. . . . *(He takes the WOMAN's hand.)*

WOMAN. Above all when you begin to fall asleep. The solitude of your body, a body alone, that inevitably ages.

MAN. Yes, but . . .

WOMAN. The solitude of the heart that tries hard every night to prolong its cry against silence.

MAN. I've felt something like that . . . but . . . not so clearly . . . not so pointedly.

13 **WOMAN.** It's that . . . perhaps you were waiting for that voice, the one of someone invented by you, to your measure. . . .

MAN. Yes . . . I think that's it.

WOMAN. Would you be able to recognize that voice with your eyes open?

MAN. I'm sure that I could. . . .

WOMAN. Even if it were a voice invented many years before, in the dark inmost recesses of time?

MAN. It wouldn't matter. I'd know how to recognize it.

WOMAN. Then, is that what you're waiting for?

MAN. Yes, I'm here for her sake, looking for her.

WOMAN. She's waiting for you also. *(The WOMAN raises the veil little by little until she leaves her withered face in the open.)* She'll be only a memory for you, if you don't allow yourself to be overcome by time. Time is her worst enemy. Will you fight it?

(They are seated very close to one another.)

MAN. Yes.

WOMAN. All right. . . . Open your eyes.

(The MAN opens his eyes slowly and is surprised to find himself held by the WOMAN's two hands. He stands up with a brusque[9] movement.)

MAN *(bewildered)*. Excuse me, I'm confused . . .

WOMAN *(entreatingly)*.[10] Oh, no! . . . Don't tell me that . . .

MAN. It was a stupidity of mine . . .

WOMAN *(imploringly)*. But you said . . .

MAN. It's ridiculous! For a moment I thought that you were she. Understand me. It was a wild dream . . .

WOMAN *(grieved)*. Yes, yes . . .

MAN. I don't know how I could . . .

WOMAN *(calming herself)*. I understand you. A wild dream and nothing more . . .

MAN. You're really very kind to pardon me. . . . *(Looking at his watch, astonished.)* It's five thirty! . . . *(Pause.)*

WOMAN *(sadly)*. Yes. . . . Now I believe that she won't come.

MAN. How would that be possible?

WOMAN. It's better that way.

MAN. Who are you to tell me that?

WOMAN. No one. *(She opens her purse.)* Do you want this white flower? 14

9. **brusque** (brusk), *adj.* abrupt in manner or speech.
10. entreatingly (en trēt′ing lē), *adv.* in a begging or praying manner.

12 Reading/Thinking Skills
Analyze

Question How are the Man's eyes separating him and the Woman? *(Possible responses: He does not recognize her because he is trusting his eyes to see the face in the photo and the flower; his view of her face will separate them ultimately.)*

13 Reader's Response
Making Personal Connections

Questions

- Have you ever invented an imaginary person to fall in love with? *(Students may answer yes or no depending on their experience and willingness to be candid. They may prefer to write in their journals.)*
- Why is this a satisfying and unsatisfying experience? *(Possible response: It is satisfying to have someone who responds to what you want and need, but unsatisfying to love something/someone that can never be real.)*

14 Reading/Thinking Skills
Draw Conclusions

Question What does the Woman mean by saying she is "No one"? *(Possible response: She means that she will never have any significance in his life—she is no one to him.)*

BUILDING ENGLISH PROFICIENCY

Making Cultural Connections

Solórzano exposes a belief deeply rooted in Western romance—the idea that everyone has a "perfect" romantic match. Focus students' attention on this idea with one or more of the following activities.

Activity Ideas

- Invite small groups to list names of movies, TV programs, songs, and books based upon the idea of the existence of a "special someone." Have students share their lists and then rate each entry on its believability.
- Have students examine ads and comment on the messages they convey about romance and relationships.
- Invite volunteers to share beliefs from their native cultures about the qualities that a romantic ideal should have and the standards needed to ensure a good relationship.

15 Reading/Thinking Skills
Connect

Question What earlier lines in the play does this speech recall? *(the Woman's story about "a friend," which was actually about herself)*

16 Reading/Thinking Skills
Recognize Main Idea

The Flagman may mean that the Man is not really looking for reality (the Woman), but for an idealization that does not exist. The futility of this endeavor provides one theme in this play.

17 Reading/Thinking Skills
Evaluate Author's Point of View

Questions What is the significance of the play ending just as it began? Do you agree with this philosophy? *(Possible responses: The use of the same inane litany shows the fundamental absurdity of life. It indicates that nothing has been accomplished or changed by the action of the play. We have come full circle and ended where we started. Yes, sometimes you get nowhere in life. No, there is always hope that things will change and improve.)*

MAN *(snatching it from her).* Where did you get it? Why are you giving it to me?

WOMAN. I picked it up . . . in passing . . .

MAN *(with great excitement).* But then, she has been here. Perhaps she has gotten lost or mistaken the place. Or perhaps, while I was here talking with you, she has passed by without stopping.

WOMAN *(covering her face).* I already told you that there is but a moment to recognize oneself, to close one's eyes . . .

MAN. But now . . . what can I do in order to . . . find her?

WOMAN. Wait . . . as everyone does . . . Wait . . . *(She takes the flower again.)*

15 MAN. But, what about you?

WOMAN. I'll continue searching, calling them, seeing them pass by. When you're old, you'll understand. *(The train whistle is heard. The* WOMAN *moves away from the* MAN, *with sorrowful movements.)* Good-bye, good-bye . . .

MAN *(to himself).* Who can this woman be who speaks to me as if she knew me? *(He runs toward her. He checks himself.)* Good-bye . . .

(The semaphore flashes the green light. The FLAGMAN *becomes stiff in order to repeat his refrain.)*

FLAGMAN. The trains from the North travel toward the South, the trains from the North travel toward the South, the trains from the North travel toward the South, the trains from the North travel toward the South *(etc.).*

(The TRAIN *crosses the back of the stage. The* WOMAN *waves the flower sadly and with long movements approaches the* TRAIN. *She gets on it. The* FLAGMAN *repeats his refrain while the* TRAIN *leaves dragging the* WOMAN, *who goes off with writhing and anguished pantomime movements.)*

MAN *(with a certain sadness, to the* FLAGMAN *who remains indifferent).* There was something in her that . . . anyhow, I believe it's better that that woman has left.

FLAGMAN. Which one, sir?

MAN. That one, the one who had picked up a white flower . . .

FLAGMAN. I didn't notice that. . . .

MAN. No? *(He looks at the* FLAGMAN *dejectedly.)*[11] But, really, haven't you seen the other one?

FLAGMAN. What other one?

MAN. The one that I'm looking for.

FLAGMAN. I don't know who it can be. . . .

MAN. One who is wearing a white flower, but who isn't the one that you saw a moment ago. 16

FLAGMAN *(harshly).* I saw the one that you aren't looking for, and the one you're looking for I didn't see!

MAN *(irritated).* Can't you be useful for anything? What the devil are you good for?

(Loud train whistle.)

FLAGMAN. What did you say?

MAN *(shouting).* What the devil are you good for!

(Green light of the semaphore. The TRAIN *crosses the back of the stage very slowly.)*

FLAGMAN *(in a distant voice).* The trains from the North travel toward the South, the trains from the North travel toward the South, the trains from the North travel toward the South, the trains from the North travel toward the South *(etc.).* 17

(The MAN *covers his head with his hands, desperate. The* FLAGMAN *repeats his refrain while the* TRAIN *passes by slowly. Before it leaves the stage, the curtain falls gently.)*

CURTAIN

---

11. dejectedly (di jek′tid lē), *adv.* sadly.

MINI-LESSON: GRAMMAR

Capitalization

Teach Have students look at the Flagman's final speech. Point out that the capital letters beginning the words *North* and *South* let you know that they are regions, not directions. Directions and compass points are not capitalized, but regions are.

Activity Idea Ask students to write down the phrases you are about to dictate, applying the rules of capitalization above.

- the Eastern Hemisphere
- the Near East
- Go west ten miles
- Southeast Asia
- the West Coast
- eastern Kansas
- the Midwest

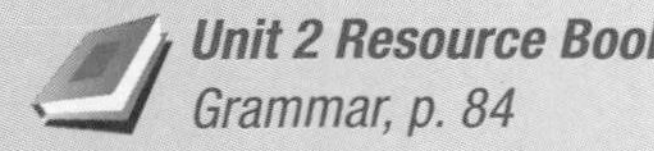
Unit 2 Resource Book
Grammar, p. 84

Two Bodies

Octavio Paz

18 Two bodies face to face
are at times two waves
and night is an ocean.

19 Two bodies face to face
are at times two stones
and night a desert.

Two bodies face to face
are at times two roots
laced into night.

Two bodies face to face
are at times two knives
and night strikes sparks.

20 Two bodies face to face
are two stars falling
in an empty sky.

Starry Night by Vincent Van Gogh conveys an agitated quality through writhing lines and bold brushwork. Do you think this painting echoes the emotional state of the two bodies in the poem, or would you suggest a different piece of art?

18 Reading/Thinking Skills
Clarify

The phrase "at times" suggests that the narrator believes that relationships change.

19 Reading/Thinking Skills
Visualize

Encourage students to form a mental image for each stanza in order to better understand the metaphors.

20 Reading/Thinking Skills
Summarize

Question Choose a word to describe the relationships evoked by each of the last three stanzas. *(Possible responses: Stanza 3—united in love; Stanza 4—fighting; Stanza 5—alienated and alone.)*

Art Study

Response to Caption Question

Most students may agree that Van Gogh's bold, twisting brushwork conveys the fluid dynamics of the relationship described in the poem.

Check Test

1. What color flower does the Woman agree to wear so the man can identify her? *(white)*

2. Why are the Man and the Woman meeting at this particular train station? *(It is halfway between their homes.)*

3. What does the Woman's veil conceal? *(her wrinkled face)*

4. How does the Man first learn about the Woman? *(in an ad)*

5. At what time of day is "Two Bodies" set? *(at night)*

Unit 2 Resource Book
Alternate Check Test, p. 85

BUILDING ENGLISH PROFICIENCY

Exploring Metaphor

"Two Bodies" is a chain of metaphors. To help students access these metaphors, begin by discussing figurative language in an everyday setting.

1. Write the following words on the board: *anger, nervousness, surprise,* and *grief.* Have students talk about what it feels like to experience each emotion.

2. Show how some of these responses could be turned into metaphors. *(Nervousness is shaking hands of ice; Surprise is a flash of feathery light; Melted lead sizzles behind my angry eyes.)*

3. Elicit student responses about what two people in a relationship could have in common with waves, stones, roots, knives, and stars.

After Reading

MAKING CONNECTIONS

1. Possible responses: I would tell the Man to deal with reality, not his fantasies. I would tell the Woman to be honest and not conceal the truth.

2. In answering, students should refer to their own experiences or knowledge of life.

3. Possible response: No, he is in love with an idea, not a real person, and she has a long-term pattern of deception which she would not find easy to break.

4. Possible response: It is an impersonal location for a romantic meeting, not conducive to intimacy.

5. Possible response: He might be a modern prophet because he seems to know what will happen and is able to see through appearances.

6. Possible response: to increase the sense of alienation and dehumanization; to lend a sense of universality.

7. Students may say that the cycle of train arrivals and departures gives a sense of an eternal present in which nothing can change and no relationships can develop. This projects the sense of alienation that the playwright is seeking to convey.

8. Possible response: No relationship is what you expect or what it seems to be.

9. In providing answers, students may note that, unlike *Crossroads,* many stories about mismatched couples lend themselves to comedy—for example, TV sitcoms about odd couples. Comments on the success or failure of the partnerships should be based on the works mentioned.

After Reading

Making Connections

Shaping Your Response

1. What advice would you give the Man and the Woman about seeking future relationships?
2. The Woman says, "I believe that there is but one moment to recognize one another, to extend our hands. One mustn't let it pass by." Do you agree? Explain.
3. Do you think that this couple could be happy together? Why or why not?

Analyzing the Selections

4. Why might Solórzano have chosen a train station for the **setting** of the play?
5. Who or what might the Flagman **symbolize,** or represent?
6. Why do you think the characters are identified only as the Man, the Woman, and the Flagman?
7. How and why does the playwright emphasize the idea of time?
8. What similarities in **theme** can you find between *Crossroads* and "Two Bodies"?

Extending the Ideas

9. What other stories, movies, or TV episodes can you think of in which two people of widely differing ages teamed up? Were these successful partnerships? Explain.

Literary Focus: Foreshadowing

Foreshadowing is a literary technique by which authors hint or imply what will happen. Foreshadowing can appear in dialogue, in gestures, and in a setting or a situation. For example, the train that goes nowhere might foreshadow the futile relationship between the Man and the Woman. How does each of the following foreshadow the conclusion of *Crossroads?*

- "One can't know by just seeing a person whether it was the one who placed an ad in the newspaper."
- The Woman's act of tearing off the flower
- The observation: "Perhaps she's more afraid of finding the one she seeks than of letting him pass by without stopping."

LITERARY FOCUS: FORESHADOWING

- The Man is unwilling to recognize the Woman as the one with whom he has been corresponding and fallen in love.
- She is afraid to acknowledge that she is the woman he is expecting; by this act, she severs herself from emotional ties.
- Just as she distanced herself from commitment and emotional involvement as a young woman, she is afraid of a relationship now.

Vocabulary Study

Stage directions often contain adverbs that indicate how the actors should deliver their lines. Match each word with the letter of its meaning. Then deliver the following sentence in five different ways, using each of the numbered adverbs as your cue: "May I help you?"

dejectedly
entreatingly
forcefully
imperturbably
indifferently

1. indifferently	**a.** powerfully
2. imperturbably	**b.** neutrally
3. entreatingly	**c.** calmly
4. dejectedly	**d.** in a begging manner
5. forcefully	**e.** sadly

Expressing Your Ideas

Writing Choices

Writer's Notebook Update Which of these factors do you feel contributed to the miscommunication between the Man and the Woman in *Crossroads*: heritage, culture, age, experience, religion, values, social class. Write a paragraph expressing your opinions on the subject.

It Might Have Been Both the title *Crossroads* and the title of Robert Frost's poem "The Road Not Taken" suggest that the choices we make affect our lives forever. Write a **capsule** summary of what might have happened had the Woman revealed her identity.

> **Looking for Love**
>
> Tall, red-haired computer programmer,
> extremely funny, attractive, fit.
> Looking for energetic, nonsmoking female athlete
> to share life's adventures.
>
> **P.O. Box 3359**

Write an ad for the Personal column of your local newspaper, itemizing what you're like and what you're looking for in an ideal mate.

Other Options

Look Again Examine the picture. What do you see? Look again. Now prepare a brief **art talk** explaining how this picture relates to the theme, "Beneath the Surface." Invite classmates to write captions for the picture.

Stage It! This brief play can be staged in your classroom. Props such as the flower and the semaphore can be easily made, or, like the 3-person train, enacted. Decide whether or not music would enhance your **presentation**, rehearse your parts, and entertain your classmates.

VOCABULARY STUDY

1. b
2. c
3. d
4. e
5. a

Unit 2 Resource Book
Vocabulary, p. 83
Vocabulary Test, p. 86

WRITING CHOICES

Looking for Love

Encourage students to alter the format of the standard "personal ad" in order to better express their individuality. For example, they might write a poem.

Selection Test

Unit 2 Resource Book
pp. 87–88

Transparency Collection
Fine Art Writing Prompt 5

OTHER OPTIONS

Stage It!

Make sure students understand all the vocabulary in the stage directions before they begin. Remind them that since the stage is bare and the props few, they should invest their actions and words with special significance. Encourage them to try to create blocking that shows the relationships between the characters, and that places the actors in positions in which they can be easily seen and heard by the audience.

Interdisciplinary Study

Theme Link

The proverb "Beauty is only skin deep" warns us to be careful when judging an individual's value, because surface appearances can be deceptive. Besides, fashion is fickle, and what is considered beautiful today might be absurd and ugly tomorrow.

Curricular Connection: History

You can use the information in this Interdisciplinary Study to demonstrate that although fashions and defining characteristics may have changed throughout history, human beings have always been deceived by appearances and perpetually seduced by an elusive ideal of beauty.

Terms to Know

Masai (mä sī′), a member of a tribe in Kenya and parts of Tanzania, known for hunting and raising cattle.

coiffure (kwä fyůr′), hairstyle

Historical Note

Point out that fashions in hair are usually set by influential members of society, which have included royal courts and privileged socialites, and film stars, professional athletes, and models in today's world.

Unit 2 Resource Book
Study Guide, p. 89

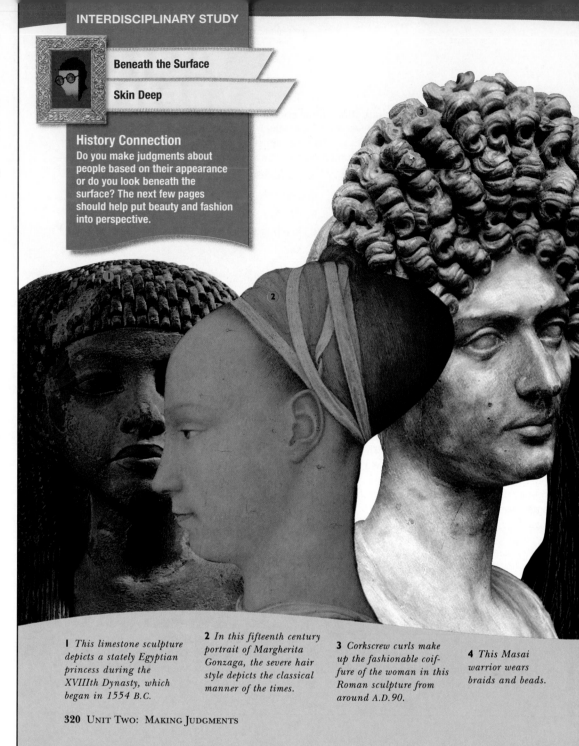

INTERDISCIPLINARY STUDY

Beneath the Surface

Skin Deep

History Connection

Do you make judgments about people based on their appearance or do you look beneath the surface? The next few pages should help put beauty and fashion into perspective.

1 *This limestone sculpture depicts a stately Egyptian princess during the XVIIIth Dynasty, which began in 1554 B.C.*

2 *In this fifteenth century portrait of Margherita Gonzaga, the severe hair style depicts the classical manner of the times.*

3 *Corkscrew curls make up the fashionable coiffure of the woman in this Roman sculpture from around A.D. 90.*

4 *This Masai warrior wears braids and beads.*

MINI-LESSON: STUDY SKILLS

Use Electronic Encyclopedias

Teach Students can access an electronic encyclopedia, such as *Grolier's Multimedia Encyclopedia* or Funk & Wagnall's *Infopedia,* by either inserting a CD-ROM disc or using the Internet. A helpful feature of these programs is the word search function, which will search through the entire body of information and inform the user which articles contain a chosen word.

Apply Explain that students might narrow their topic before they perform the word search. For example, instead of searching for "hair" they might search for "wig" or "baldness." Some programs will narrow the topic for them: when they enter "hair," the screen will display the articles that contain that word—Angora cat, counterculture, tomahawk, and so on.

Activity Idea Suggest that students choose an article of interest from the Interdisciplinary Study. Have them pick five words to use in a word search that would provide more information on the article's topic.

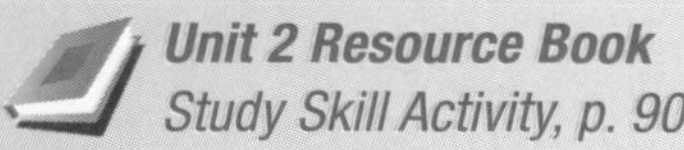

Unit 2 Resource Book
Study Skill Activity, p. 90

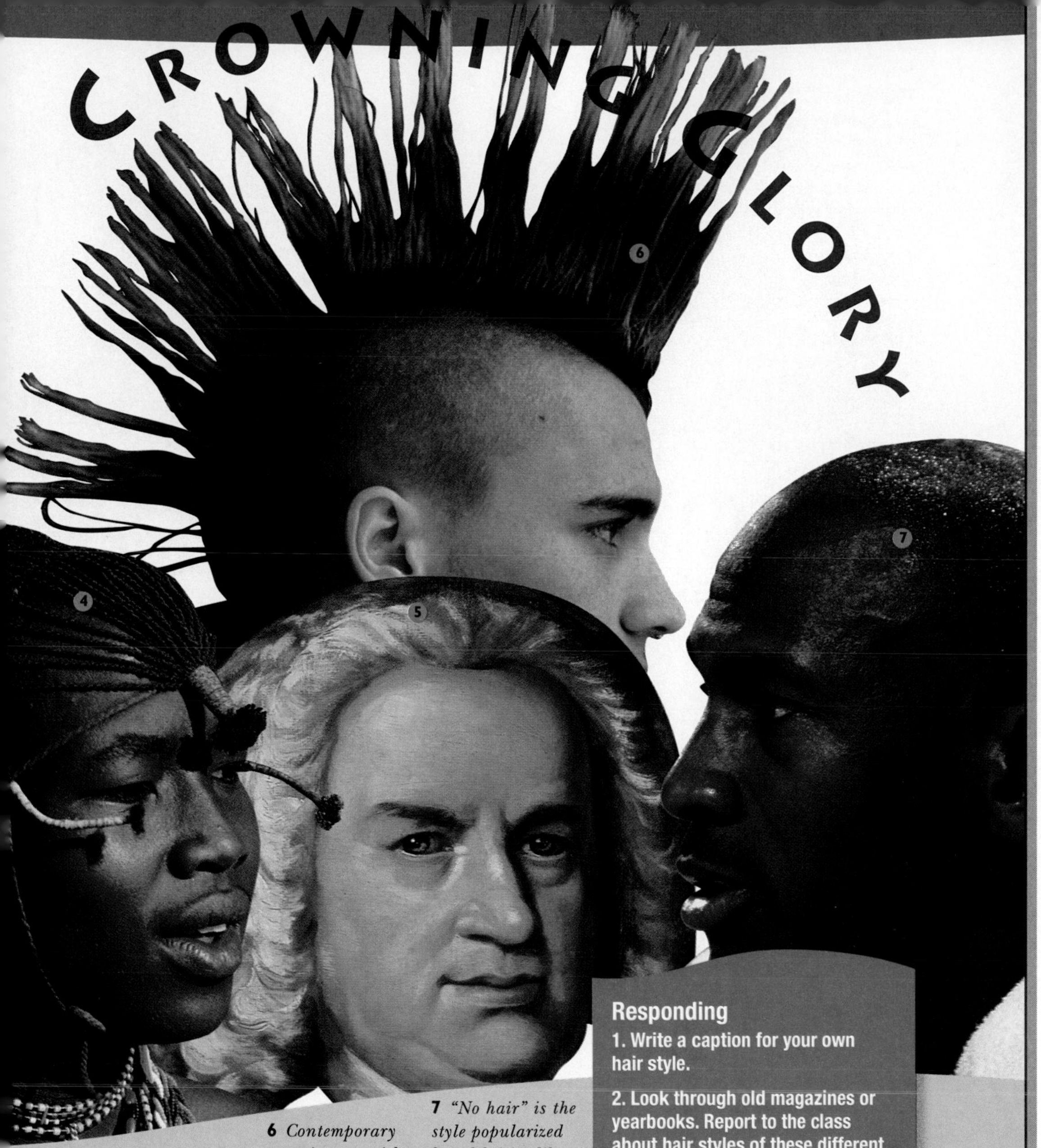

CROWNING GLORY

5 *Fashionable men of the eighteenth century, like German composer Johann Sebastian Bach (1685-1750), wore powdered wigs.*

6 *Contemporary experiments with hair styles achieve a spiked effect.*

7 *"No hair" is the style popularized by celebrities like Michael Jordan.*

Responding

1. Write a caption for your own hair style.
2. Look through old magazines or yearbooks. Report to the class about hair styles of these different periods.
3. With a partner, debate the pros and cons of having rules about hair styles in schools or places of work.

Visual Literacy Historians and anthropologists often depend on a civilization's artwork to provide information about its cultural patterns.

Question Why might some of these portraits and sculptures give a biased impression about the historical era? *(Possible Response: because only the privileged classes could afford to commission a portrait or bust.)*

Responding

1. Possible Responses Responses should include the name of the hairstyle and a description of its cultural context.

2. Possible Responses Students should try to connect fashion trends to cultural and historical events and movements.

3. Possible Responses Suggest that students use supporting examples from their own experiences or the experiences of family members.

BUILDING ENGLISH PROFICIENCY

Responding to Information

The information in this feature is presented in the pictures and their captions. Encourage students to use their dialogue journals as they examine both. For example, on the left side of the chart, they could note specific details about a particular hair style; on the right side, they could express an opinion about it, jot down a question for further consideration, and so on. Afterward, invite volunteers to share their comments.

Fact/Detail	My Response
That Egyptian style involved a lot of braiding.	Was it a wig?
Powdered wigs—c. 200 years ago.	Bach's wig looks so uncomfortable!

Interdisciplinary Study

Theme Link

Art and the media often present images that are too perfect to be replicated by common people. Portraits and photography of real people can cover up physical flaws. People who are praised for their physical beauty are often thought of as having no other qualities that deserve admiration

Curricular Connection: Media

You can use the information in this Interdisciplinary Study to explore how art and the media not only reflect a society's standard of beauty, but also play a large part in shaping it.

Art Study

The *Mona Lisa*, also known as *La Gioconda,* is a portrait of a Florentine noblewoman painted by the Italian artist Leonardo Da Vinci between 1503 and 1505. Her enigmatic half-smile has made the portrait famous throughout the centuries.

Terms to Know

damasked, patterned
dun, dull gray-brown
belied, misrepresented

INTERDISCIPLINARY STUDY

Media Connection

The *Mona Lisa*, long considered a standard of beauty, may now have competition from computer enhanced images such as the one pictured on the opposite page. In a sonnet, Shakespeare mocks the idealized qualities of beauty and instead praises his real, flesh-and-blood lover.

FROM MONA

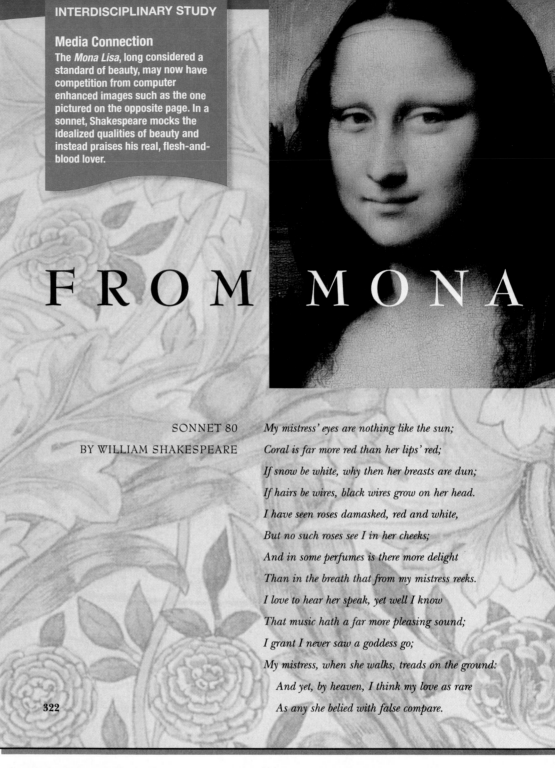

SONNET 80
BY WILLIAM SHAKESPEARE

My mistress' eyes are nothing like the sun;
Coral is far more red than her lips' red;
If snow be white, why then her breasts are dun;
If hairs be wires, black wires grow on her head.
I have seen roses damasked, red and white,
But no such roses see I in her cheeks;
And in some perfumes is there more delight
Than in the breath that from my mistress reeks.
I love to hear her speak, yet well I know
That music hath a far more pleasing sound;
I grant I never saw a goddess go;
My mistress, when she walks, treads on the ground:
And yet, by heaven, I think my love as rare
As any she belied with false compare.

322

MINI-LESSON: VISUAL LITERACY

Use of Shadow

Teach Point out that Leonardo da Vinci was a master at using light and shadow to create a three-dimensional effect in his paintings. He created an astonishing natural look by using soft lighting and soft edges that blur into shadow.

Apply Explain that the shadow used in modeling is part of the perceived surface of an object. The pattern of an object's surface shadow changes according to its orientation towards the source of light. In a painting, shaded areas seem to recede and lighter areas seem to come forward.

Activity Idea Have students work in pairs. They can either stand beneath a strong light source or use a flashlight to observe how different angles of light affect the shadows on each other's face.

AMERICA'S CHANGING FACE

It began as an experiment. *Time* magazine's design staff combined computerized images of fourteen models from seven different ethnic groups. They played with percentages, mixed, matched, and morphed until they created the face of a woman whose features were 35% Southern European, 17.5% Middle Eastern, 17.5% African, 15% Anglo-Saxon, 7.5% Asian, and 7.5% Hispanic. The resulting multiethnic image was so beautiful that several staff members claimed to have fallen in love on sight.

Have the norms for beauty changed? In past centuries beautiful woman were often portrayed as pale and sedentary. Today, they often appear in art and the media as active people with a wide range of skin tones.

The woman in the magazine picture is fictional, it's true. But so are many models we see in magazines. They start out as real people, of course. Yet after imaging specialists finish slimming their hips, filling in wrinkles and pores, lightening shadows, and erasing blemishes, the models attain a state of impossible perfection. They are no longer people, but idealized images that reflect our values and dreams.

So next time you see an image of your ideal, ask yourself what qualities he or she embodies. And remember, if someone looks too good to be true—he or she probably is.

TO MORPHING

SPECIAL ISSUE
TIME
Take a good look at this woman. She was created by a computer from a mix of several races. What you see is a remarkable preview of . . .
THE NEW FACE OF AMERICA
How Immigrants Are Shaping the World's First Multicultural Society

Responding

1. Explain how the *Mona Lisa* fits—or does not fit—your concept of beauty.
2. Does the computer-enhanced woman on the cover of *Time* (special issue, Fall 1993) meet your standards of beauty? Do you think standards of beauty have changed in the past generation to fit our changing society? Why or why not?
3. Do you think the lover addressed in Shakespeare's sonnet should be flattered or insulted? Explain.

Art Study

Time magazine created this image on a computer by using software that was developed from equipment used in Hollywood to simulate metamorphosis on film and video. Students might be familiar with these effects from viewing Michael Jackson's "Black or White" video and movies such as *Terminator 2*.

Responding

1. Possible Response Students might answer that they are conditioned to believe the *Mona Lisa* is beautiful because it is a famous icon.

2. Possible Response Students' opinions of the computer-enhanced image will vary.

3. Possible Response Responses should reflect an ability to recognize the direct, unpretentious expression of admiration behind the ironic conceits.

Interdisciplinary Activity Ideas

- Each student can create a collage of "beautiful" people, using pictures from magazines.
- Each student can make a list of who they think are the five most beautiful people and write a brief explanation of their choices.

BUILDING ENGLISH PROFICIENCY

Exploring Key Concepts

Both "Sonnet 80" and "America's Changing Face" deal with the basic question of "What makes a person attractive?" Use the following activity to help students explore that question.

1. Divide the class into groups of 3 to 5 students each; give each group five pieces of tagboard, each piece measuring 4" x 12".
2. Explain that groups should find and write five characteristics of an attractive person. Answers should not be gender specific but may relate to standards of physical beauty (such as sparkling eyes or clean hair) as well as to personality traits (such as having a sense of humor or being a good listener).
3. Have each group arrange its answers in order, from what they think is the most important to the least important reason.
4. Invite groups to examine and comment upon the others' responses.

Writing Workshop

WRITER'S BLUEPRINT

Specs

The Specs in the Writer's Blueprint address these writing and thinking skills:

- recognizing stereotypes
- describing
- classifying
- using parallel structure
- using adjectives and adverbs

These Specs serve as your lesson objectives, and they form the basis for the **Assessment Criteria Specs** for a superior paper, which appear on the final TE page for this lesson. You might want to read through the Assessment Criteria Specs with students when you begin the lesson.

Linking Literature to Writing

Encourage students to become *active* readers by questioning the assumptions behind each stereotype presented in the literature.

Writing Workshop

Exploring Stereotypes

Assignment The crooked politician, the lonely spinster, the scheming servant—these stereotypical characters show up in the selections in this part of the unit. These and other stereotypical characters also show up in scores of other stories in literature and the mass media. Now explore stereotypical characters in pictures and words.

WRITER'S BLUEPRINT

Product	A gallery of stereotypical characters
Purpose	To explore stereotypes from literature and the mass media
Audience	People who want to become more knowledgeable about what they read and watch
Specs	As the creator of a successful gallery of characters, you should:

- ❑ Make notes on stereotypical characters—the oversimplified, conventional types of characters who seem to show up again and again in literature and the mass media.
- ❑ Choose four distinctly different stereotypical characters for your gallery and make visuals—drawings or collages—to represent them.
- ❑ Write a description to accompany each of your four visuals. What does this character typically look like? How does this character typically feel and behave? Include likes and dislikes, how this character relates to others, and examples of this character from literature and the mass media.
- ❑ Use parallel structure to help knit each description together.
- ❑ Follow the rules of grammar, usage, spelling, and mechanics. Avoid confusing adjectives with adverbs.

WRITING WORKSHOP OVERVIEW

Product
Expository/Descriptive writing: A gallery of stereotypical characters

Prewriting
Review the literature—Brainstorm a list—Make webs—Try a quickwrite—Create your visuals—Plan your descriptions—Ask a partner
Unit 2 Resource Book
Prewriting Worksheets pp. 91–92

Drafting
Before you draft—As you draft
Transparency Collection
Student Models for Writing Workshop 9, 10

Revising
Ask a partner—Strategy: Using Parallel Structure
Unit 2 Resource Book
Revising Worksheet p. 93

Editing
Ask a partner—Strategy: Using Adjectives and Adverbs Correctly
Unit 2 Resource Book
Grammar Worksheet p. 94
Grammar Check Test p. 95

Presenting
Read Aloud
Display

Looking Back
Self-evaluate—Reflect—For Your Working Portfolio
Unit 2 Resource Book
Assessment Worksheet p. 96
Transparency Collection
Fine Art Writing Prompt 5

PREWRITING

Review the literature. Create a chart listing stereotypical characters from the selections in this part of the unit. State the stereotype each character represents in the center column. In the last column, note descriptive details from the literature that help define each stereotype.

Character	Stereotype Character Represents	Descriptive Details
the woman in *Crossroads*	the lonely spinster	hides her age; afraid of finding the right man; fearful of revealing herself; lives alone

LITERARY SOURCE
WOMAN (*very close to the MAN*): I have a friend . . . who always lived alone, thinking nevertheless that the best thing for her was to get together with someone. (*She pauses. The MAN listens to her, interested.*) She was ugly, very ugly, perhaps that was why she dreamed of a man instead of looking for him.
from *Crossroads* by Carlos Solórzano

Brainstorm a list of stereotypical characters. In a group or with a partner, brainstorm a list of stereotypical characters from literature and the mass media and add them to your chart.

Remember, you're not looking for one particular character, like, say, Batman. You're looking for a character type, such as The Superhero. Other examples: the prim librarian, the sensitive poet, the alienated adolescent, the perky cheerleader.

Compile a nice long list to give yourself plenty of options to choose from.

Make webs for the four character types you choose. List descriptive details radiating out from the center.

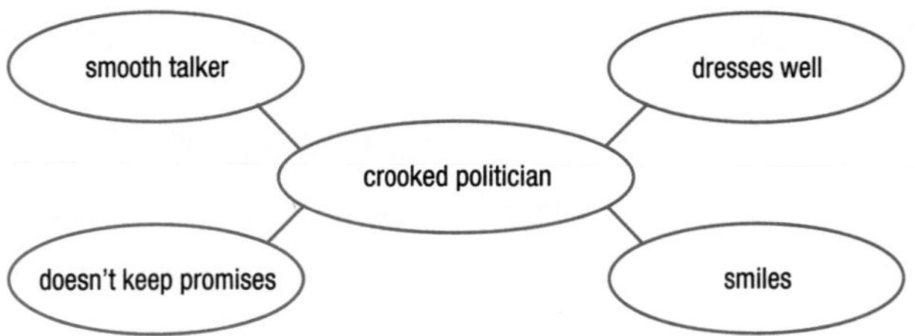

STEP 1 PREWRITING

Review the literature

You might generate the first two columns of the chart as a class before having students complete the third column independently.

Brainstorm a list

Provide students with magazines and TV listings to scan for stereotypical images and characters. For additional support, see the worksheet referenced below.

Unit 2 Resource Book
Prewritng Worksheet, p. 91

Make webs

Remind students to include many facets of a person's character—style, clothes, leisure activities, work habits, and the like.

BUILDING ENGLISH PROFICIENCY

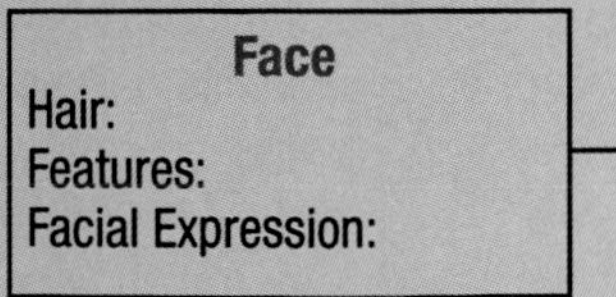

Responding to Visual Cues

Offer students the following suggestions for creating stereotypes.

1. Have students find visual images in books, magazines, and videos.
2. Ask students to complete this chart for each character.

Face	Body	Clothing
Hair: Features: Facial Expression:	Posture/Gestures: Figure (fat, thin?): Unusual Features:	Colors: Style: Typical Features:

Try a quickwrite

Keep students moving by timing the quickwrite and breaking it up into segments for each stereotypical figure.

Create your visuals

Students may use some of the images they found in the magazines. Suggest students use ideas they find in the movies, newspapers, or on television.

Plan your descriptions

Some students may want to include a narrative device, such as a fictional account of a meeting with this character, that gives a more defined purpose to their descriptions. See the worksheet referenced below for support.

Unit 2 Resource Book
Prewriting Worksheet, p. 92

Ask a partner (Peer assessment)

Encourage students to listen one time through for general impressions and then take specific notes during a second reading.

Connections to
Writer's Notebook

For selection-related prompts, refer to Writer's Notebook.

Connections to
Writer's Resource

For additional writing prompts, refer to Writer's Resource.

OR . . .
Working in a group, have each group member portray a character type, using typical words, gestures, and expressions, while other group members try to guess which character type is being portrayed.

Try a quickwrite. Write for two minutes or so about each of the character types you've chosen. Include details about the character's appearance and behavior. Use your webs for inspiration. If you find that you don't have enough to write about, do some more thinking or select other character types.

Create your visuals. Make one to illustrate each of your four character types. You might draw a picture that includes descriptive details from your web, or make a collage from newspaper and magazine clippings consisting of words and images that all in some way suggest the appearance or personality of your character type.

Plan your descriptions. First, read the character descriptions from *Twelve Angry Men* on page 229. They're good models. Your descriptions should be as specific as those. Then look back at your prewriting activities as you make your writing plan. You might organize your notes for each character type into categories like these:

Character type

- How character typically looks—clothes, facial features, gestures
- How character typically behaves—temperament, mannerisms
- How character typically feels
- Character's likes and dislikes
- How character relates to other people
- Examples of this character type from literature and the mass media (Batman and Wonder Woman as examples of The Superhero, etc.)

Ask a partner to review your plan.

✔ Have I chosen four distinctly different stereotypical characters to write about?

✔ Have I followed the Specs in the Writer's Blueprint?

Use any helpful comments from your partner to revise your plan.

MINI-LESSON: WRITING STYLE

Using Parallel Structure

Teach Use parallel structure to keep your sentences from sounding awkward and unbalanced.

Activity Idea Have students suggest ways to rewrite these sentences to make them parallel in structure. Suggested answers are in parentheses.

1. The cat was lying in the sun, purring loudly, and it stretched. (stretching)

2. First we ate dinner, then went to the movie, deciding finally to get coffee and dessert. (and finally stopped for coffee and dessert)

3. After the hike, the girls were tired, dirty, and wanting to eat. (and hungry)

4. The cars in the parking lot were hit by flying debris, dented by large hailstones, and lightning struck them. (struck by lightning)

Apply Have students review a peer's paper to look for errors in parallel structure.

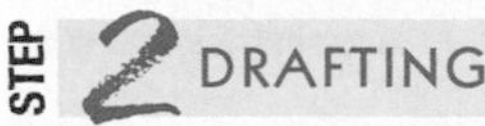

STEP 2 DRAFTING

Before you write, look back at your prewriting materials and writing plan and reread the last three points in the Writer's Blueprint.

As you draft, concentrate on getting the ideas from your writing plan on paper. Try these drafting tips to help you get started.

- Keep your sketches or collages in front of you as you write.
- When describing how characters look, start at the toes and work up or vice-versa.
- Mention specific examples from literature and the mass media to help define each character type.
- Use parallel structure to help knit each description together. See the Revising Strategy in Step 3 of this lesson.

Notice how this writer used a famous pair of characters to help define one of his character types. (He'll correct technical mistakes later on, at the editing stage.)

> The sidekick is almost always shorter than the hero. This is to emphasize his inferioruty to the hero. A typical example is Robin and Batman. The sidekick must be good humored and never resent being continusly upstaged by the hero.

STUDENT MODEL

STEP 3 REVISING

Ask a partner to comment on your draft before you revise it. Use this checklist as a guide.

✔ Have I followed the Specs in the Writer's Blueprint?

✔ Does each written description belong with the corresponding sketch or collage?

✔ Did I use parallel structure to help knit each description together?

STEP 2 DRAFTING

As you draft

Encourage students to see this part of the writing process as a time to generate a lot of ideas. It is easier to pare down a paper later, during revising, than to limit and overcorrect early in the process.

The Student Models

The **transparencies** referenced below are authentic student models. Review them with the students before they draft. These questions will help:

1. For the Moronoff entry, the writer of model 9 never gave a label to this character, such as the lonely spinster or the scheming servant. What label would you give to this character?

2. The writer of model 10 didn't include any examples of the characters. What are some examples of the lonely spinster and the sidekick from literature and mass media that you know?

3. How did the writer of model 9 use parallel structure in the next-to-last sentence of the first entry?

Transparency Collection
Student Models for Writing Workshop 9, 10

STEP 3 REVISING

Ask a partner (Peer assessment)

Encourage students to respond to what they like about the piece, as well as what needs revising.

BUILDING ENGLISH PROFICIENCY

Planning a Revising Strategy

Students can use the following plan to make partner comments more effective.

1. Have students show partners their visuals before sharing the written work. Partners can describe visuals aloud, adding their own reactions to the stereotype (*not* to the artwork). Students might take notes on partners' comments to help in their revisions.

2. When partners are shown the written work, they might comment on discrepancies between the written and visual work. These comments might help students give their writing a sharper focus.

Revising Strategy: Using Parallel Structure

Have students look over the revising strategy instructions and ask them to explain why this stylistic principle is called *parallel structure.* You might want to have a volunteer read the definition of *parallel* from a dictionary. For additional support, see the mini-lesson at the bottom of page 326 and the worksheet referenced below.

Unit 2 Resource Book
Revising Worksheet, p. 93

Connections to
Writer's Resource

Refer to the Grammar, Usage, and Mechanics Handbook on Writer's Resource.

STEP 4 EDITING

Ask a partner (Peer assessment)

Remind students to use the proofreading symbols that appear on the inside back cover of the text.

Revising Strategy

Using Parallel Structure

Parallel structure is the use of phrases or sentences that are similar, or parallel, in meaning and structure in order to knit together coordinate ideas.

Not parallel The crooked politician is always *smiling, shaking* hands, and *asked* everyone for large contributions. (The sentence suddenly switches from *-ing* words to an *-ed* word. The sentence sounds rough and clumsy.)

Revised to be parallel The crooked politician is always smiling, shaking hands, and asking everyone for large contributions. (Now, with everything in the *-ing* form, the sentence sounds smooth and graceful.)

The revised student model below shows another kind of parallel structure. Here, the writer has knitted the two parts of a sentence more firmly together by beginning each one with the same word.

STUDENT MODEL

She is the definition of wild. If you see her in the halls at school and all of her clothes match you KNOW there is a problem, and ~~when~~ if her hair is the same color for more than 3 months, there must be something wrong (or a small money shortage).

Reread your descriptions to see if you can help knit ideas together with parallel structure.

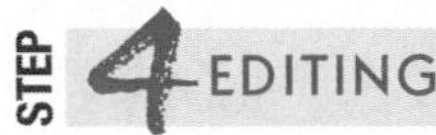

Ask a partner to review your revised draft before you edit. When you edit, look for errors in grammar, usage, spelling, and mechanics. Look over each sentence to make sure you avoid confusing adjectives with adverbs.

MINI-LESSON: GRAMMAR

Using Adjectives and Adverbs Correctly

Write these sentences on the board and have students determine whether the underlined word is used correctly. Have students make suggestions to correct errors.

1. We got this milk a week ago. Does it smell <u>badly</u> to you? (Should be the adjective *bad* because it follows linking verb *smell.*)

2. Perform yoga exercises <u>slow</u>. (Should be the adverb *slowly* because it modifies the action verb *perform.*)

3. The car alarm sounded <u>loud</u> and <u>irritating</u>. (These are adjectives used correctly to modify noun *alarm.*)

4. We finished <u>last</u>. (This adverb is used correctly to modify verb *finished.*)

5. The time passed so <u>quick</u> that we were amazed. (Should be the adverb *quickly* because it modifies the action verb *passed.*)

Unit 2 Resource Book
Grammar Worksheet, p. 94
Grammar Check Test, p. 95

Editing Strategy

Using Adjectives and Adverbs Correctly

Don't confuse adjectives and adverbs in your writing. Words like *good*, *bad*, *real*, and *strong* are adjectives that modify nouns or pronouns, not verbs. Words like *well*, *badly,* and *really* are adverbs. Use them to modify verbs, adjectives, or other adverbs.

Don't write:	She drives *real* good.
Write:	She drives *really* well.
Don't write:	Her car is rusting *bad*.
Write:	Her car is rusting *badly*.

Take care to avoid confusing adjectives and adverbs in your writing.

FOR REFERENCE
See the Language and Grammar Handbook at the back of this text for more information on using adjectives and adverbs correctly.

STEP 5 PRESENTING

Consider these ideas for presenting your work.

- Read your descriptions aloud in a small group, but don't tell which description goes with which visual. Let the group try to match the two.
- Display a class gallery of stereotypical characters. Give guided tours to students and teachers.

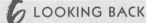

STEP 6 LOOKING BACK

Self-Evaluate. What grade would *you* give your paper? Look back at the Writer's Blueprint and give your paper a score on each item, from 6 (superior) to 1 (inadequate).

Reflect. Think about what you've learned from this assignment as you write answers to these questions.

✔ Why do you think the mass media rely so heavily on stereotypes?

✔ Which part of this assignment did you find most enjoyable, the visual part or the writing part? Why?

For Your Working Portfolio Add your gallery and reflection responses to your working portfolio.

ASSESSMENT CRITERIA SPECS

Here are the criteria for a superior paper. A full six-level rubric for this paper appears on the *Assessment Worksheet* referenced below.

6 Superior The writer of a 6 paper impressively meets these criteria:

- Creates striking visuals to represent four distinctly different stereotypical characters who will be immediately recognizable to people who read literature and watch and listen to mass media.
- Writes insightful descriptions of each character type which, together with the accompanying visuals, present vivid and accurate portrayals of familiar stereotypical characters.
- Uses parallel structure to knit the elements of each description into an effective whole.
- Makes few, if any, mistakes in punctuation, grammar, and spelling, and avoids confusing adjectives and adverbs.

Unit 2 Resource Book
Assessment Worksheet, p. 96

Editing Strategy: Using Adjectives and Adverbs Correctly

For additional support, see the mini-lesson at the bottom of page 328 and the worksheets referenced below.

Unit 2 Resource Book
Grammar Worksheet, p. 94
Grammar Check Test, p. 95

Connections to **Writer's Resource**

Refer to the Grammar, Usage, and Mechanics Handbook on Writer's Resource.

STEP 5 PRESENTING

Read Aloud

Discuss with students how the visual imagery interacts with the imagery of the texts.

Display

You might consider mounting the display in the library or multimedia room.

STEP 6 LOOKING BACK

Self-evaluate

The *Assessment Criteria Specs* at the bottom of this page are for a superior paper. You might want to post these in the classroom. Students can then evaluate themselves based on these criteria. For a complete scoring rubric, use the *Assessment Worksheet* referenced below.

Unit 2 Resource Book
Assessment Worksheet, p. 96

Reflect

Consider holding a class discussions on stereotypes. To further explore the theme, use the Fine Art Transparency referenced below.

Transparency Collection
Fine Art Writing Prompt 5

Beyond Print

Teaching Objectives

- to explore skills that make works of art more accessible to a viewer
- to give students confidence in the value of their personal reactions to a work of art

Curricular Connection: Visual Literacy

You can use the information in this article to give students a chance to discuss their relationship with the world of visual art. You might ask students if they have artwork or posters on their walls at home. Encourage students to approach the article with these art works in mind.

Introduce

The *Mona Lisa* is probably the most famous work of art in the world. Ask students to name other works of art which have become cultural icons, such as *American Gothic* by Grant Wood and *Starry Night* by Vincent Van Gogh.

Beyond Print

Looking at Images

What do the varied artworks represented in this book—paintings, sculpture, collages, photographs, signs, film stills, and posters—have in common? They are all forms of communication. What can you do to understand what these artists are trying to say? Try these approaches.

1. **Determine the artist's purpose.** As you look at works of art, try to figure out what the artist was trying to convey or accomplish. Some works are created for everyday use—pottery or quilts, for example. Others serve as tributes, such as stamps or commemorative coins. Many are purely decorative, such as figurines. Art can be promotional or commercial, such as ads, posters, or shop signs. Photographs may create a mood, state an opinion, or capture a special effect.
2. **Remember that every artist has a point of view.** In analyzing a piece of art, consider the artist who produced it and the times in which the artist lived. How might culture shape the artist's attitudes? Is the artist depicting a culture or a social class to which he or she does not belong? Does the artist espouse a special idea or philosophy? From whose vantage point are subjects seen? Is there a *we-they* attitude? Are details such as clothing, facial features, and lifestyles portrayed accurately? Is the tone respectful? cynical? humorous?
3. **Note details that lead to the big picture.** Try to detect patterns in shapes, colors, lines, and textures. Is there a focal point that draws your attention? Do things such as facial expressions, shadows, surroundings, and print provide clues to what's going on? If you're still stumped about a work of art, put it aside for a while; then look at it "fresh" and try to get an overall impression. Ask yourself if it reminds you of anything that you've experienced, seen, or felt.
4. **Be an active viewer.** Not everybody loves the *Mona Lisa!* Viewing art is a personal experience, and individuals will react differently to a piece of art, depending on personal tastes, experiences, and familiarity with various types of artwork. In fact, the feelings you had about a work of art last year may be very different from those you have today about the same work. If you view art actively, knowledgeably, and with an open mind, you can enjoy a most enriching experience.

ANOTHER APPROACH

From the Artist's Perspective

Suggest that students choose an artwork that they have completed in an art class or at home and submit it to the process of analysis outlined above. How do their powers of appreciation change when they are approaching a work of their own creation?

Activity Options

1. The picture on this page is of Pocahontas, daughter of an Indian chief of Virginia, who aided the Jamestown colonists on several occasions.
   - What do you think the artist is trying to communicate?
   - Explain whether or not this seems to be an authentic portrayal of a Native American woman. On what do you base your opinion?
   - What can you infer about the artist's cultural background and perspective?
2. With a small group, view a work of art in this book, applying the four approaches mentioned on the opposite page. Don't be afraid to have different opinions. Then present your analyses to the class in the form of an Art Critic's Choice panel.

Ætatis suæ 21. A. 1616.
Matoaks als Rebecka daughter to the mighty Prince
Powhatan Emperour of Attanoughkomouck als Virginia
converted and baptized in the Christian faith, and
Wife to the wor.ll Mr Tho: Rolff.

Activity Options

Activity 1 Have students create a chart with the following headings to help them answer the questions.

What We Know from Viewing the Art
Pocahontas was a Native American, but she is pictured in English clothing.

What We Know from Historical Accounts
Pocahontas married a tobacco planter and visited the court of England.

What We Can Infer
This is not a portrayal of the normal Native American woman in the colonies, but a portrayal of an exception.

Activity 2 Remind students that their own cultures and personal experiences will influence how they view different works of art.

BUILDING ENGLISH PROFICIENCY

Making Personal Connections

Students may not think of themselves as qualified to interpret art. Assure them that they can offer valid interpretations.

1. Ask them either (1) to find a piece of artwork or a photograph that they like in a source of their own choosing (including magazine advertisements or movie posters) or (2) to create a piece of artwork that pleases them.

2. Have students assemble in small groups to display their visuals and explain what they think their choices are trying to say. Invite members of each group to ask questions and add comments to clarify meaning.

3. Bring groups together for a sharing of responses.

4. Have the class choose four pieces from among the visuals submitted that it thinks best exemplify each of the four approaches on page 330.

Unit Wrap-Up

MULTICULTURAL CONNECTION

Students may be disturbed by the bias against different cultures and women that is explored in Parts One and Two of Unit 2. The following ideas and questions may facilitate discussion.

Interaction

- People of various cultures may have different styles of interaction.
- People from the same culture but of different genders may have different approaches in problem-solving situations.

Possible Response Antigone would interact most effectively with Juror Eight, because he is constantly seeking the truth.

Possible Response There are many open-minded people who can separate evaluating their own experience with individuals from making a judgment about an entire group or culture.

Perspective

- Everyone has a perspective, whether or not it is acknowledged.
- Perspective is not a bad thing—but people must guide the building of their perspectives.

Possible Response It might depend on the role the profession has in that culture's way of life. No, I think that poets are of more value to society than athletes. Yes, if people are willing to pay to see athletes, then athletes should get the money.

Activities

Activity 1 Inform students that it would be wise to ask their interviewee to tell a little about his or her experience first, so that no inappropriate questions are asked.

Activity 2 The musical work could be presented in a school; the clothing could be on display in a store; and the TV program could be viewed in the electronics department at a department store.

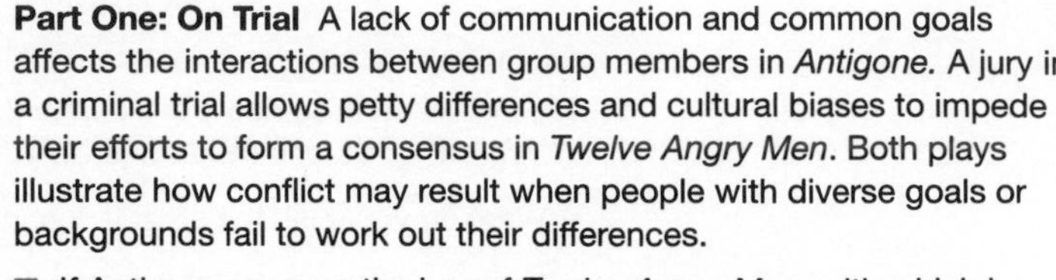

Multicultural Connections

Interaction

Part One: On Trial A lack of communication and common goals affects the interactions between group members in *Antigone.* A jury in a criminal trial allows petty differences and cultural biases to impede their efforts to form a consensus in *Twelve Angry Men*. Both plays illustrate how conflict may result when people with diverse goals or backgrounds fail to work out their differences.

■ If Antigone were on the jury of *Twelve Angry Men,* with which jury member do you think she would interact most effectively? Why?

■ Prospective jury members are screened in an attempt to ensure that people with cultural biases do not serve. Do you think it is possible to find twelve jury members who will be fair and unbiased in reaching a verdict? Why or why not?

Perspective

Part Two: Beneath the Surface Perspective is the vantage point from which you view and react to the world. Your culture has a profound influence on how you view others and life in general.

■ Doctors, lawyers, and politicians are objects of satire in some of these works. Why do you think that particular professions are accorded more respect in some cultures than in others? Do you think it's fair that a professional athlete earns a considerably higher salary in the U.S. than, say, a professional poet? Explain.

Activities

Work in small groups on the following activities.

1. Interview people who have recently immigrated to the U.S. Ask them what things they consider important in life, what they would do if they won the lottery, what their favorite food is, who their favorite celebrity is, and what they found hardest to adjust to in this new country. Then present the cultural insights you gain in a TV-type documentary titled *Perspective.*
2. Plan a skit that shows how several people with different cultural values might react differently to a musical work, an article of clothing, or a TV program.

Independent and Group Projects

Writing

Evaluating a Character The selections in this unit include characters who have one thing in common—they each make judgments about a situation and react to the best of their ability under the circumstances. Write a character study of one of the characters in this unit. Evaluate that character's personality, actions, and ability to make valid judgments.

Mass Media

On the Air You and two classmates—taking the roles of interviewer, interviewee, and commentator—are presenting a segment of a weekly news program titled *Making Judgments.* Prepare a report to be performed live for the class or videotaped. This report will consist of (1) an introduction of the interviewee; (2) an interview with one of the following: Antigone, the young man acquitted in *Twelve Angry Men,* or the Man or Woman in *Crossroads;* (3) a wrap-up after the interview in which the commentator makes his or her own personal judgments about the character.

Research

Famous Trials Find out about a noted trial in history—for example, that of Socrates, Joan of Arc, Catherine of Aragon, Galileo, Alfred Dreyfus, Lizzie Borden, John Scopes, the Chicago Seven, or O. J. Simpson. Prepare a legal lesson for classmates, complete with pictures, facts, and an analysis of evidence. Or, if you prefer, work with a group to perform a reenactment of high points of the trial.

Art

Eye Foolers The selections in the second half of this unit examine deceptive appearances. Find or draw a picture that conveys an idea of deception. You might consider art dealing with optical illusions, such as the works of M. C. Escher, computer art, or photographs that portray false or misleading impressions.

UNIT 2 OPTIONS

Writing

Encourage students to use the following elements to create their character studies:

- what the character says
- what the character does
- what others say about the character
- how the character interacts with others

Mass Media

Students may not agree on the character it would be best to interview.

- Have students write down the pros and cons of interviewing each character.
- Encourage groups to allow all members to share in the decision making.

Research

If you feel that some trials may be too sensitive to explore, you may wish to set guidelines that limit the kinds of trials that students study.

Art

Because many works of deceptive art are *trompe l'oeil,* you may wish to introduce this term to help students in their research.

Unit Test

Unit 2 Resource Book
New Selection, pp. 97–104
Test 1, pp. 105–106
Test 2, pp. 107–112

Part One: Arthurian Legends

Planning Unit 3: Answering the Call

Literature	Integrated Language Arts			
	Literary	**Writing/Grammar, Usage and Mechanics**	**Reading, Thinking, Listening, Speaking**	**Vocabulary/Spelling**
The Coronation of Arthur *by Sir Thomas Malory* Legend *(average)* p. 340 **from The Hollow Hills** *by Mary Stewart* Historical Fiction *(average)* p. 344	Style Characterization	Paragraph Interior monologue Special issue Understanding the origins and development of the English language Semicolon	Cause and effect Sequence Characterization Compare and contrast Draw conclusions	Synonyms
Youth and Chivalry from A Distant Mirror *by Barbara Tuchman* Nonfiction *(average)* p. 350	Sensory details	Archeological finds List survival skills How-to steps Analyzing grammatical structures	Analyze Make judgments Cause and effect Draw conclusions	
The Tale of Sir Launcelot du Lake *by Sir Thomas Malory* Legend *(average)* p. 358 **from The Once and Future King** *by T. H. White* Historical Fiction *(average)* p. 365	Allusion, plot Style, character Conflict Characterization	Opinion—Does Chivalry exist? Opinion essay—status of women Brief narrative Understand the origins and development of the English language Singular and plural nouns Sentence punctuation	Infer Make judgments	
The Death of King Arthur *by Sir Thomas Malory* Legend *(average)* p. 371 **from Idylls of the King** *by Alfred, Lord Tennyson* Poem *(challenging)* *p. 378*	Denotation and connotation Allusion, sensory details Archetype, tone, poetry	Comparison Obituary Last letter Capitalization of titles	Infer, compare and contrast Make judgments, predict Make analogies	Synonyms

Meeting Individual Needs

Multi-modal Activities	Mini-Lessons
Creating a board game Creating a drawing or a model Dramatic reading Building background Exploring key events Visualizing the setting	Understanding the origins and development of the English language Reflecting on style Semicolon
Composing a song Castle tour Checking comprehension Recognizing the use of persuasion Analyzing grammatical structures	Sensory detail Analyzing grammatical structures
Modernizing the story-screenplay Media resource list Trivia quiz Sequencing story events Building vocabulary Exploring infinitives Linking past and present Exploring tone	Understanding the origins and development of the English language Singular and plural nouns Sentence punctuation Allusions
Coat of arms New knight Exploring leadership Exploring key events Recognizing cause and effect Analyzing mood	Connotation/denotation Capitalization of titles Etymology Storytelling

Interdisciplinary Studies
Arthurian Legends

Format	Content Area	Highlights	Skill
Article: **Knights in Many Guises**	Multicultural	This selection of pictures depicts various forms of knights.	Draw conclusions/evaluate art
Article: **Chivalry Updated**	Multicultural	These pages provide various descriptions of behaviors that may be considered knightly.	Create and use graphic organizers

Writing Workshop

Mode	Writing Format	Writing Focus	Proofreading Skills
Persuasive writing	A proposal for a quest game	Being clear and concise	Capitalizing proper nouns and proper adjectives

Program Support Materials

For Every Selection	For Every Writing Workshop
Unit Resource Book Graphic Organizer Study Guide Vocabulary Worksheet Grammar Worksheet Spelling, Speaking and Listening, or Literary Language Worksheet Alternate Check Test Vocabulary Test Selection Test	**Unit Resource Book** Prewriting Worksheet Revising Strategy Worksheet Editing Strategy Worksheet Presentation Worksheet Writing Rubric **Transparency Collection** Fine Art Transparency Student Writing Model Transparencies

For Every Interdisciplinary Study	Assessment
Unit Resource Book Study Guide Mini-Lesson Skill Worksheet	**Unit Resource Book** TE Check Tests Alternate Check Test (blackline master) Vocabulary Test (blackline master) Selection Test (blackline master) **Test Generator Software** **Assessment Handbook**

Part Two: Main Kinds of Heroes

Planning Unit 3: Answering the Call

Literature	Integrated Language Arts			
	Literary	Writing/Grammar, Usage and Mechanics	Reading, Thinking, Listening, Speaking	Vocabulary/Spelling
And of Clay Are We Created *by Isabel Allende* Short Story *(average)* p. 396	Point of view Connotation Foreshadowing Characterization Symbol, metaphor Archetype	Web of heroic qualities Letter Editorial Commas in introductory clauses	Identify alternatives Literal and figurative language Draw conclusions	Replace with synonym Use dictionaries for word meaning
A Soldier of Urbina *by Jorge Luis Borges* Poem *(challenging)* p. 409 **Lineage** *by Margaret Walker* Poem *(average)* p. 411 **The Gift** *by Li-Young Lee* Poem *(average)* p. 411 **Turning Pro** *by Ishmael Reed* Poem *(easy)* p. 412	Metaphor Allusion Theme Rhythm Imagery Mood	Discuss metaphors Poem Interview Use standard sentence punctuation	Understand sequence	Word webs
The Secret Room *by Corrie ten Boom* Autobiography *(average)* p. 417	Idioms, dialogue Style Characterization Metaphor, plot Humor	Opening paragraph for an encyclopedia article News clip Book jacket Proper punctuation of dates	Identify alternatives Draw conclusions Infer Generalize Make judgments Main Idea	Word pairs Use context clues for word meaning
The Street of the Cañon *by Josefina Niggli* Short Story *(average)* p. 429	Imagery Irony Plot	Speculate on romance Letter to Miss Manners Gossip column Punctuation of adjectives in series	Infer Classify Synthesize	Expand vocabulary using structural analysis

Meeting Individual Needs

Multi-modal Activities	Mini-Lessons
Develop teen rescue/relief plan Photographs/video Press conference Making personal connections Sequence Story events Exploring dramatic tension Point of view	Commas in introductory clauses Interview Use dictionaries for word meaning Recognize cause and effect
Lyrics Creating a greeting card Reading aloud Expanding vocabulary notebooks	Metaphor Using standard sentence punctuation
Proposal Drawing a diagram Annotated bibliography Understanding mood Organizing information Relating verb tenses	Idioms Proper punctuation of dates Use context clues for word meaning Use problem-solving skills
Art talk Research Sequencing story events Inventing scenes	Punctuation of adjectives in series Expand vocabulary using structural analysis

Interdisciplinary Studies
Heroes Around the World

Format	Content Area	Highlights	Skill
Interview: **Modern Heroes** *by Michael Dorris*	Multicultural	This interview consists of a discussion on contemporary heroes.	
Collage: **Mapping Out Heroes**	History	These pictures identify a few legendary heroes.	Interpreting atlases
Article: **Press Power** *by Emilia Askari*	Career	This article discusses the media's power to create or destroy heroes.	Interpreting the news

Writing Workshop

Mode	Writing Format	Writing Focus	Proofreading Skills
Expository writing	An interpretive essay	Making smooth transitions	Correcting stringy sentences

Program Support Materials

For Every Selection

Unit Resource Book
Graphic Organizer
Study Guide
Vocabulary Worksheet
Grammar Worksheet
Spelling, Speaking and Listening, or Literary Language Worksheet
Alternate Check Test
Vocabulary Test
Selection Test

For Every Writing Workshop

Unit Resource Book
Prewriting Worksheet
Revising Strategy Worksheet
Editing Strategy Worksheet
Presentation Worksheet
Writing Rubric
Transparency Collection
Fine Art Transparency
Student Writing Model Transparencies

For Every Interdisciplinary Study

Unit Resource Book
Study Guide
Mini-Lesson Skill Worksheet

Assessment

Unit Resource Book
TE Check Tests
Alternate Check Test (blackline master)
Vocabulary Test (blackline master)
Selection Test (blackline ma
Test Generator Software
Assessment Handbook

Media and Technology

Part One Selections

The Coronation of Arthur

Audiotape *King Arthur Soundbook,* Caedmon/Harper Audio, is read by Ian Richardson from the version written by Howard Pyle. Students may enjoy Twain's story of Camelot in *Connecticut Yankee in King Arthur's Court,* Durkin-Hayes, 1993.

Videotape A wealth of material is presented in the three-video set, *Le Morte D'Arthur, The Making of the King*, and *The World of Sir Thomas Mallory*, 50 minutes each, Library Video Company. Also consider *Ancient Mysteries Series: Camelot,* 50 minutes, A&E/Library Video Company, 1996, and *Knights of the Round Table*, 117 minutes, starring Robert Taylor and Ava Gardner, Library Video Company, 1953.

Community Resources If your community holds a Renaissance Fair, students who have attended or participated might describe or bring photos of costumes, food, musicians, and various events such as archery contests and jousting.

from The Hollow Hills

Audiotape *The Hollow Hills,* 180 minutes, is available from Dove Audio, 1990.

Community Resources Students might use the resources of their local library to research places in Britain associated with Arthur, particularly Glastonbury, where some say the Isle of Avalon really existed. Ancient Welsh legends tell of a British general who fought in the area of Glastonbury around A.D. 500. Glastonbury is southwest of London in the county of Somerset.

Youth and Chivalry

Audiotape Students may enjoy an unabridged reading of *A Distant Mirror*, Recorded Books, 1984.

Videotape Students may enjoy Bill Moyer's interview with the author in *Barbara Tuchman: A World of Ideas,* 30 minutes, PBS Video.

Home Connection Barbara Tuchman writes of the kinds of children's playthings common in medieval times. Students might ask older relatives what kinds of toys, books, and games they had as children. What were their favorites? Were the toys made at home or purchased? How many toys did they have? If these relatives have kept favorite childhood books or playthings, they might be asked to bring them to class for display.

The Tale of Sir Launcelot du Lake

Community Resources Malory includes no details on what the four queens who met Sir Launcelot were wearing. Some students might like to use the resources of their local library to research what men and women wore in the Middle Ages—from about 400 to 1400.

from The Once and Future King

Audiotape *The Book of Merlyn and King Arthur* and *Merlyn's Animal Council,* from T. H. White and read by Christopher Plummer, are available from Caedmon/Harper Audio.

Home Connections Since fighting seems to be an integral part of human nature, students might discuss with family members some basic reasons for warfare, whether on neighborhood streets or between nations. Why did the knights fight? Do people fight for any of the same reasons today? Greed, hate, self-defense, and desire for domination might be among the reasons mentioned.

The Death of King Arthur

Videotape *Victorian Poetry*, 28 minutes, Films for the Humanities & Sciences, includes the work of Tennyson and others.

Community Resources Queen Gwynevere takes refuge in the Tower of London. Some

Connections to
Custom Literature Database

For Part One "Arthurian Legends" Selections with Lessons

- "Of Sir Galahad and Sir Percival and the Quest of the Holy Grail" from *The Boy's King Arthur* by Sidney Lanier
- "The Defence of Guenevere" by William Morris

Additional theme-related selections can be accessed on the ScottForesman database.

Advice of Merlyn

Christopher Plummer reads from the works of T. H. White on *The Book of Merlyn and King Arthur* and *Merlyn's Animal Council.*

students might like to research the history of that famous London site, once a fortification, later a prison (where Henry VIII had two of his wives beheaded), and now a tourist attraction. Guidebooks and travel brochures will be helpful resources.

Part Two Selections

And of Clay Are We Created

Videotape Students will enjoy a video portrait of the author in *Isabel Allende*, 56 minutes, Films for the Humanities & Sciences, 1994. Also consider showing *House of the Spirits,* 109 minutes, Live Home Video, 1993, based on Allende's novel.

Community Resources You might invite a local newspaper photographer or reporter to speak about memorable events that person has covered. Students might ask which event left the deepest impression, and why, whether the person has had any funny experiences while covering a story, and how one would prepare for seeking a job as news reporter or photographer.

A Soldier of Urbina, Lineage, the Gift, Turning Pro

Videotape *The Inner World of Jorge Luis Borges*, 28 minutes, Films for the Humanities & Sciences, explores Borges' haunts in Buenos Aires as he talks about his life and work.

Audiotape Hear the author reading her work in *Margaret Walker Reads*, 57 minutes, American Audio Prose Library.

Videotape *Li-Young Lee*, 30 minutes, Instructional Video, features Lee as he discusses his poetry and his life. In *Voices of Memory: The Power of the Word*, 60 minutes, PBS Video, hosted by Bill Moyers, Lee and his poetry are featured.

Audiotape Volume IV of *Selected Shorts*, 150 minutes, American Audio Prose Library, is devoted to stories and poems about baseball.

Home Connection Students might ask older family members to name heroes in the family, either people whose deeds went unnoticed by the world at large, or people who may have served in a war, taken part in a rescue, or come through a difficult ordeal bravely. Students might then do a little more investigation of that family member.

The Secret Room

Audiotape *Anne Frank: Diary of a Young Girl,* Spoken Arts, is read by Julie Harris.

Videotape The film, *Hiding Place,* 2 hours 25 minutes, Bridgestone Productions, 1975, is based on the life of Corrie Ten Boom. Consider the Wonderworks program, *Miracle at Moreaux*, 60 minutes, PBS Video, based on a true incident about a nun in Nazi Germany. *The Diary of Anne Frank,* 170 minutes, Media Basics, stars Shelley Winters in a version faithful to the original diary.

Community Resources There may be people in your community who survived the Holocaust or who have experienced persecution in other countries more recently. If so, ask them to speak to the class about their experiences, including ideas they may have on how such tragedies can be avoided.

The Street of the Cañon

Home Connection The mysterious stranger is a familiar character in the literature of the world. Students might like to discuss with friends and family radio programs, movies, books, and television programs that involve someone (almost always a man) who arrives in a community, performs some remarkable deed (either evil or good), and then disappears.

Connections to
Custom Literature Database

For Part Two "Many Kinds of Heroes" Selections with Lessons

- *Don Quixote* by Miguel de Cervantes
- *Babur-nama* by Babur

Additional theme-based selections can be accessed on the ScottForesman database.

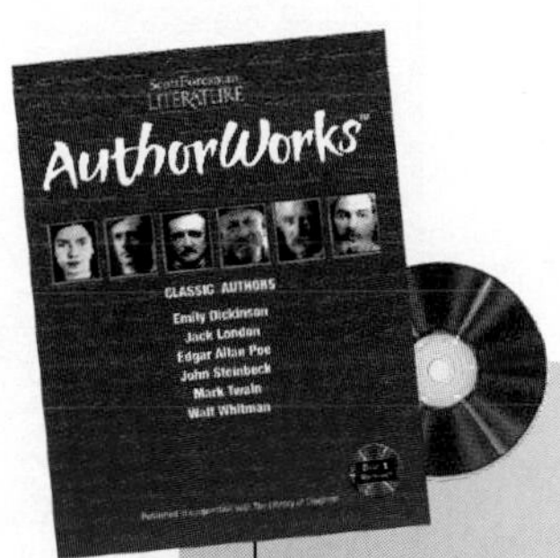

Connections to
AuthorWorks

Information about the life and times of Isabel Allende is available on ScottForesman's AuthorWorks CD-ROM.

Unit 3

Answering the Call

Art Study

La Belle Dame Sans Merci (The Beautiful Lady Without Pity—French), pages 334–335, was painted by Sir Frank Dicksee. It shows a fairy-lady bewitching the knight who has fallen totally into her power. This concept has also been expressed poetically by John Keats and Alain Chartier, and artistically by Walter Crane.

Question What is the relationship between the lady and the knight? How can you tell? *(Possible response: The lady has the knight in her power. The way she leans over him, the way he gazes up at her, and his stiff posture with arms outstretched show this.)*

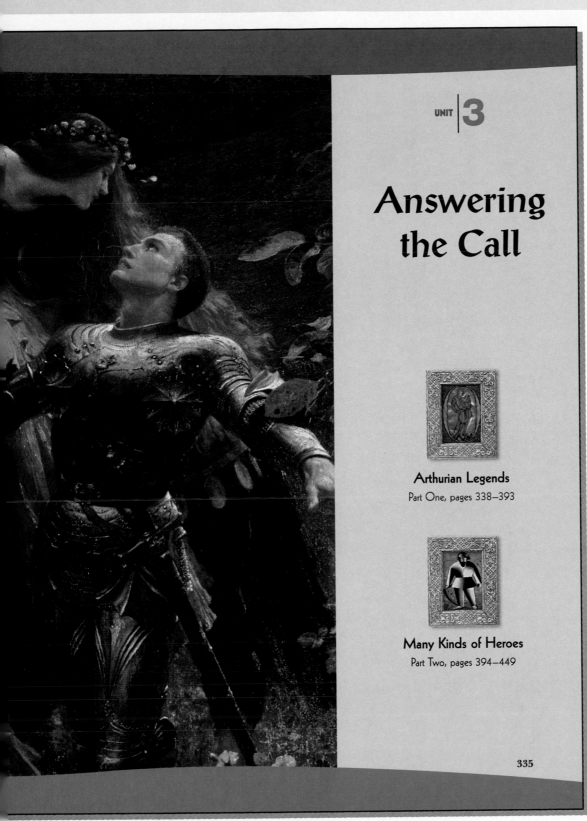

UNIT 3

Answering the Call

Arthurian Legends

Many Kinds of Heroes

335

THEMATIC CONNECTIONS

Answering the call to heroism used to be straightforward—heroes were knights and knights were the heroes. More recently, we find heroes in many unexpected places. This unit explores all kinds of heroes who answered the call.

Part One

Arthurian Legends

Part One features literature that shows men who answered the call to become knights and seek justice.

Ideas to Explore

- Is there any equivalent of a knight in society today?
- How are Arthurian legends retold today?

Part Two

Many Kinds of Heroes

The literature in Part Two deals with the concept of the hero in a variety of cultures, times, and conditions.

Ideas to Explore

- How many ways are there to "answer the call"?
- Do societies differ in their ideas of what is heroic?

The Gawain initial represents Sir Gawain—one of the greatest of King Arthur's knights. *The Mower* was created by the Russian painter Kasimir Melevich.

Genre Overview: Arthurian Legend

 Art Study

Morgan Le Fay is a painting by Anthony Frederick Augustus Sandys, an English painter who lived from 1829 to 1904. Sandys's illustrations are powerful and dramatic with strong contrasts of light and shade. According to Arthurian legends, Morgan Le Fay was an evil sorceress who used magic to fly and transform herself into other shapes.

Question Do you think the artist has done a good job of portraying his subject's traits? *(Students may may comment that even though Morgan Le Fay seems to be casting a spell, her expression looks more pained than evil.)*

EXPLORING CONCEPTS

- Legends are a form of historical fiction that celebrates folk and/or national heroes.
- Legends often have more than one version because they were orally retold for generations.
- Legends include extraordinary and magical events.
- Good and evil are clearly distinguished.
- The action is episodic.

Genre Overview

Morgan le Fay
by Frederick Sandys

Reading Arthurian Legends

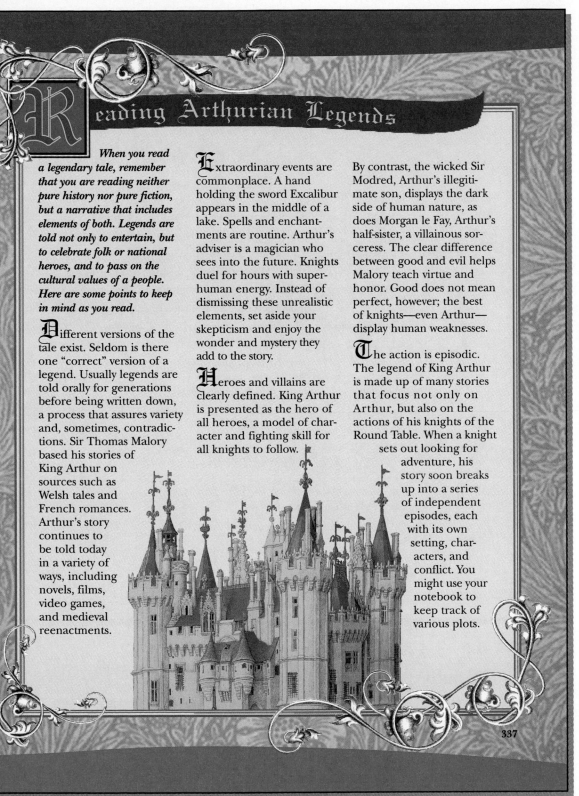

When you read a legendary tale, remember that you are reading neither pure history nor pure fiction, but a narrative that includes elements of both. Legends are told not only to entertain, but to celebrate folk or national heroes, and to pass on the cultural values of a people. Here are some points to keep in mind as you read.

Different versions of the tale exist. Seldom is there one "correct" version of a legend. Usually legends are told orally for generations before being written down, a process that assures variety and, sometimes, contradictions. Sir Thomas Malory based his stories of King Arthur on sources such as Welsh tales and French romances. Arthur's story continues to be told today in a variety of ways, including novels, films, video games, and medieval reenactments.

Extraordinary events are commonplace. A hand holding the sword Excalibur appears in the middle of a lake. Spells and enchantments are routine. Arthur's adviser is a magician who sees into the future. Knights duel for hours with superhuman energy. Instead of dismissing these unrealistic elements, set aside your skepticism and enjoy the wonder and mystery they add to the story.

Heroes and villains are clearly defined. King Arthur is presented as the hero of all heroes, a model of character and fighting skill for all knights to follow. By contrast, the wicked Sir Modred, Arthur's illegitimate son, displays the dark side of human nature, as does Morgan le Fay, Arthur's half-sister, a villainous sorceress. The clear difference between good and evil helps Malory teach virtue and honor. Good does not mean perfect, however; the best of knights—even Arthur—display human weaknesses.

The action is episodic. The legend of King Arthur is made up of many stories that focus not only on Arthur, but also on the actions of his knights of the Round Table. When a knight sets out looking for adventure, his story soon breaks up into a series of independent episodes, each with its own setting, characters, and conflict. You might use your notebook to keep track of various plots.

337

MATERIALS OF INTEREST

Books

- *Sir Thomas Malory: Tales of King Arthur* edited and abridged by Michael Senior (Schocken Books, 1981)
- *The Once and Future King* by T. H. White (G. P. Putnam's Sons, 1958)
- *Tales of King Arthur* by James Riordan (Rand McNally & Company, 1982)

Multimedia

The King Arthur Soundbook read by Ian Richardson (Caedmon audio cassettes SBC 118, 240 minutes, 46 seconds, 1975)

Connections to **Custom Literature Database**

For more selections by Sir Thomas Malory, see "Arthur Marries Gwynevere" and Le Morte d'Arthur, Book 21, Chapters 5–7

Preview

Arthurian Legends

FOR ALL STUDENTS

- How were the ideals of the society expressed in the stories of the knights of King Arthur?
- Do you tend to follow individual or group codes?

To further explore the theme, use the transparency referred to below.

Transparency Collection
Fine Art Writing Prompt 6

For At-Risk Students

Ask students to

- Discuss modern stories of good and evil that they know. *(Students may mention Star Wars.)*
- Discuss games that focus on the struggle between good and evil, such as Dungeons and Dragons™.

For Students Who Need Challenge

Encourage students to find and examine parodies of Arthurian legend, such as *Monty Python and the Holy Grail.*

For Visual Students

Students may enjoy finding more art that was created to illustrate Arthurian legend, bringing their favorite piece to class, and explaining why they find it appealing.

MULTICULTURAL CONNECTION

Encourage students to discuss groups that they are part of or know about that embody the same codes that medieval knights followed.

Part One

Arthurian Legends

The stories of chivalry that originated during the twelfth century featured noble knight-heroes and tales of high adventure, excitement, and triumph of good over evil.

Multicultural Connection The concept of **Group** for medieval knights involved the collective development of codes, rules for behavior that they were expected to follow. In Arthurian legends, these group codes uphold loyalty, bravery, honesty, and courtesy. As you read, decide how the characters in these selections follow or depart from these codes of honor.

IDEAS THAT WORK

Hero Worship

In Joseph Campbell's book *The Hero with a Thousand Faces*, the hero follows a standard path: separation–initiation–return. My students write about a moment in their lives to illustrate this heroic path. The stage they especially enjoy is the return. There they have to describe in rich detail how as heroes they have to struggle with fabulous forces and return with a boon.

I encourage discussion with Nathaniel Hawthorne's journal entry: "A hero cannot be a hero unless in an heroic world." What is a heroic world? Does today's world qualify?

I have students compare and contrast the traits of Prometheus with comic-book action heroes.

As a prelude to creative writing assignments, I introduce the word *prosopopoeia,* which is "the impersonation of an absent or imaginary speaker." I encourage students to write as if the marble block or King Arthur's sword were telling the legend.

Jacinto Jesus Cardona
San Antonio, Texas

Before Reading

The Coronation of Arthur by Sir Thomas Malory Great Britain

from The Hollow Hills by Mary Stewart Great Britain

Sir Thomas Malory
1408–1471

The charges that led to Sir Thomas Malory's imprisonment may have been trumped up by political enemies. During this long imprisonment, Malory wrote *Le Morte d'Arthur*, a reworking of the Arthurian legend. After his death, this work was published by William Caxton on the newly invented printing press.

Mary Stewart
born 1916

For most of her career, Florence Elinor, whose pen name is Mary Stewart, specialized in romantic thrillers. But in 1970, Stewart published *The Crystal Cave,* her first work of historical fiction. Giving a new twist to Arthurian material, Stewart placed her story in fifth-century Britain and told events from Merlin's viewpoint.

Building Background

Larger Than Life! Almost every nation has a legendary hero—brave, noble, larger than life! (You will become acquainted with some of these heroes in the Interdisciplinary Study that begins on page 382.) Great Britain had Arthur, whose exploits continue to fascinate people today. Working in small groups, list on the blackboard things that you associate with Arthur and his times. You might use a chart such as the one below, or make up your own categories.

Medieval Life	The Round Table	Ideals of Chivalry	Weapons and Armor	Knights

Literary Focus

Style includes choices such as the following:

- *Types of words* (Are they plain or fancy?)
- *Purpose of the work* (Is it to inform, amuse, argue, describe?)
- *Tone* (Is it humorous, serious, angry, and so forth?)
- *Mood* (Is it mysterious, peaceful, nostalgic, and so forth?)
- *Use of figurative language* (Is the work purely literal? somewhat figurative? highly figurative?)
- *Sound devices* (Are the sounds and rhythms of words important?)

You will notice that the two selections you are about to read treat the same subject matter in very different styles.

Writer's Notebook

That's Great! William Shakespeare observed: "Some are born great, some achieve greatness, and some have greatness thrust upon them." Do you agree with this observation? By which of these ways would *you* rather gain greatness? Jot down your thoughts before you read. Then, as you read, decide how Arthur achieves greatness.

Before Reading

Building Background

You may wish to suggest some other categories for consideration

- roles of men and women
- kingship
- feudalism

Literary Focus

Students can develop a chart with the headings **Style Elements** and **Examples.** They can note on the chart examples of style as they read.

Writer's Notebook

Explain to students that in the play *Twelfth Night,* the phrase "some have greatness thrust upon them" was spoken in jest to trick a gullible character.

More About Sir Thomas Malory and Mary Stewart

While Malory set his Arthurian tales in the Middle Ages in about the twelfth century, Mary Stewart set hers in the fifth century, much closer to the time that the "real" Arthur would have lived. Other works by Stewart include

- *The Moon Spinners,* (1959)
- *The Hollow Hills,* (1973)

SUPPORT MATERIALS OVERVIEW

Unit 3 Resource Book

- Graphic Organizer, p. 1
- Study Guide, p. 2
- Vocabulary, p. 3
- Grammar, p. 4
- Alternate Check Test, p. 5
- Vocabulary Test, p. 6
- Selection Test, pp. 7–8

Building English Proficiency

- Literature Summaries
- Activities, p. 192

Reading, Writing & Grammar SkillBook

- Reading, pp. 41–42
- Grammar, Usage, and Mechanics, pp. 267–268

Technology

- Audiotape 9, Side A
- Personal Journal Software
- Custom Literature Database: For more of Malory's account of the Arthurian legend, see the database.
- Test Generator Software

During Reading

Selection Objectives

- to explore the theme of answering the call
- to explore the use of style
- to identify and use semicolons

Unit 3 Resource Book
Graphic Organizer, p. 1
Study Guide, p. 2

Theme Link

Arthur answers the call of destiny in these two versions of the legend of his kingship.

Vocabulary Preview

balefully, destructively or threateningly
bestow, give (something) as a gift
duly, rightly; suitably
ignoble, not of noble birth or position; humble
jeopardy, risk; danger
precedence, higher position or rank; great importance
prerogative, right or privilege that nobody else has
rite, solemn ceremony
rune, inscription or letter
tumultuous, very noisy or disorderly

Students can add the words and definitions to their Writer's Notebooks.

1 Historical Note
Arthur's Family History

In other versions, Margause, Elaine, and Morgana le Fay (note spelling differences) are Igraine's daughters by her deceased husband, the Duke of Tintagel.

Response to Caption Question
Arthur's attire symbolizes his position as "first knight of the realm." The setting foreshadows the tragic end of his vision.

THE CORONATION OF ARTHUR

SIR THOMAS MALORY

The marriage of King Uther and Igraine was celebrated joyously, and then, at the king's request, Igraine's sisters were also married: Margawse, who later bore Sir Gawain, to King Lot of Lowthean and
1 Orkney; Elayne, to King Nentres of Garlot. Igraine's daughter Morgan le Fay, was put to school in a nunnery; in after years she was to become a witch, and to be married to King Uryens of Gore,

In this 1903 painting titled *King Arthur,* Charles Ernest Butler captures the drama and solemnity of Arthur's crowning. Speculate on why Arthur is pictured in armor rather than regal robes and why the setting is dark and ominous. ➤

340

SELECTION SUMMARY

The Coronation of Arthur, The Hollow Hills

The Coronation of Arthur In "The Coronation of Arthur," an episode from Malory's *Le Morte D'Arthur,* King Uther and Queen Igraine marry and bring forth a son, Arthur. The magician Merlin arranges for the infant to be secretly taken to be raised by Sir Ector. Uther dies after declaring that Arthur will be the rightful successor to the throne. In the years that follow, the nobles vie for the crown. Yet it is only Arthur, as a young man, who can draw out a magical sword from an anvil, proving that he is the true King of Britain. Both commoners and nobles swear him their allegiance.

The Hollow Hills Mary Stewart's "The Hollow Hills" is a modern novelist's account of Arthur drawing the sword from the stone. In this scene, Merlin, the narrator, presides over the ceremony and uses the old sword of a Roman ruler of ancient Britain.

*For summaries in other languages, see the **Building English Proficiency** book.*

and give birth to Sir Uwayne of the Fair Hands.[1]

A few months later it was seen that Igraine was with child. . . .

2 Sometime later Merlin appeared before the king. "Sire," he said, "you know that you must provide for the upbringing of your child?"

"I will do as you advise," the king replied.

"That is good," said Merlin. . . . "Your child is destined for glory, and I want him brought to me for his baptism. I shall then give him into the care of foster parents who can be trusted not to reveal his identity before the proper time. Sir Ector would be suitable: he is extremely loyal, owns good estates, and his wife has just borne him a child. She could give her child into the care of another woman, and herself look after yours."

Sir Ector was summoned, and gladly agreed to the king's request, who then rewarded him handsomely. When the child was born he was at once wrapped in a gold cloth and taken by two knights and two ladies to Merlin, who stood waiting at the rear entrance to the castle in his beggar's disguise. 3 Merlin took the child to a priest, who baptized him with the name of Arthur, and thence to Sir Ector, whose wife fed him at her breast.

Two years later King Uther fell sick, and his enemies once more overran his kingdom, inflicting heavy losses on

1. **Margawse . . . Sir Uwayne of the Fair Hands.** The royal relatives and descendants are named here because they figure later in the tales of King Arthur. Sir Gawain, for example, becomes one of the most celebrated knights at the Round Table.

NOTABLE NAMES IN THE ARTHURIAN WORLD 4

UTHER PENDRAGON King of Britain and father of Arthur. He gives his son to Merlin for secret upbringing and dies two years later.

IGRAINE wife of Uther Pendragon; mother of Arthur.

MERLIN prophet and magician. He arranges for Arthur to be raised by Sir Ector and serves as Arthur's adviser during childhood and the early years of Arthur's reign.

GWYNEVERE Arthur's queen. The Round Table is her dowry. She later falls in love with Sir Launcelot. Many writers spell her name Guinevere.

CAMELOT where Arthur holds his court.

EXCALIBUR Arthur's magical sword.

LADY OF THE LAKE a supernatural being who gives Excalibur to Arthur. She is one of the queens who carry the mortally wounded Arthur to Avalon where he may be healed.

MORGAN LE FAY a sorceress who often plots against Arthur. She is Arthur's half-sister.

SIR LAUNCELOT the bravest of Arthur's knights. His love for Queen Gwynevere eventually destroys the fellowship of the Round Table. His name is often rendered as Sir Launcelot du Lake or Sir Lancelot.

SIR KAY the son of Sir Ector. He and Arthur are reared as brothers. When Arthur becomes king, the churlish Kay is appointed Royal Seneschal and becomes a knight.

SIR GAWAIN nephew of Arthur and knight of the Round Table. His strength—like that of the sun—grows each morning and then wanes during the afternoon.

SIR MODRED a knight of the Round Table, often identified as Arthur's nephew or illegitimate son. He tries to usurp the throne during Arthur's absence abroad. Arthur slays Modred but receives a fatal wound. Some writers spell the name Mordred.

SIR BEDIVERE surviving companion of Arthur who returns Excalibur to the Lady of the Lake at the dying king's request.

2 Reading/Thinking Skills
Cause and Effect

Foreseeing that Uther Pendragon will die soon, Merlin directs the king to provide for his child. Engage students in a discussion of what the possible effects of the king's death would be. They may speculate that Uther's knights and barons and the Saxons—without a strong king to guide them—will fight among themselves and bring great unrest to the land. Also, because Uther's heir is a baby, Uther's enemies will try to kill the baby once Uther is dead. Without Arthur to unite Britain, the glory of the country would be at stake.

3 Historical Note
Rites and Customs

Baptism was an important rite to Merlin not only because he is Christian, but also because baptismal records were a source for documenting lineage.

Students may be unfamiliar with the term *wet nurse*—a woman hired to nurse the baby of another woman. This practice was not uncommon in Europe in earlier times.

4 Reader's Response
Making Personal Connections

Let students talk about who their favorite Arthurian character is and which name they'd pick for themselves.

BUILDING ENGLISH PROFICIENCY

Building Background

Use one or more of the following activities to help students focus on Arthurian legend and lore.

Activity Ideas

- Draw an outline of a knight or display a picture of Arthur. Ask students to suggest the most important qualities that a knight possesses. When they respond, prompt them to give examples or use gestures to demonstrate the meanings. *(Possible responses: honor, loyalty, humility, strength, and courage)*
- Invite students to share heroic legends and legendary figures from their native cultures. As they do, point out likenesses and differences to Arthurian legend.
- Students may enjoy watching and responding to one or more of the many movies based on the Arthurian legend. Include both animated and realistic versions.

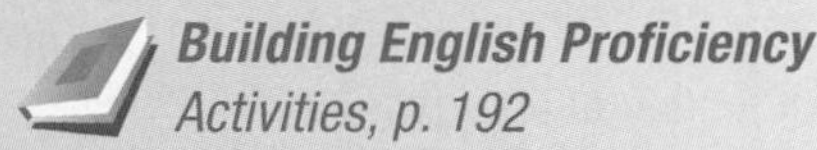
Building English Proficiency
Activities, p. 192

5 Reading/Thinking Skills
Sequence

Question How did events after Uther's death fit with the wishes he expressed? *(Possible response: The barons ignored his wishes that his son Arthur be his heir and fought among themselves for the kingship.)*

6 Multicultural Note
Roman Catholicism

Malory's retelling of the Arthur story places it in the context of the Roman Catholic culture of medieval Europe. Clerics, such as the Archbishop, and rites such as the Mass prepare the reader for the culminating quest of Arthur's knights—the search for the Holy Grail which in the Christian tradition is the cup that Jesus Christ used at the Last Supper and therefore, exceedingly precious. On page 343 are references to three feast days: Candlemas, a feast that falls on February 2 and commemorates the purification of the Virgin Mary (Jesus' mother); Easter, the feast celebrating Jesus' rising from the dead; and Pentecost, the feast that celebrates the coming of the Holy Spirit.

him as they advanced. Merlin prophesied that they could be checked only by the presence of the king himself on the battlefield, and suggested that he should be conveyed there on a horse litter. King Uther's army met the invader on the plain at St. Albans, and the king duly[2] appeared on the horse litter. Inspired by his presence, and by the lively leadership of Sir Brastius and Sir Jordanus, his army quickly defeated the enemy and the battle finished in a rout. The king returned to London to celebrate the victory.

But his sickness grew worse, and after he had lain speechless for three days and three nights Merlin summoned the nobles to attend the king in his chamber on the following morning. "By the grace of God," he said, "I hope to make him speak."

In the morning, when all the nobles were assembled, Merlin addressed the king: "Sire, is it your will that Arthur shall succeed to the throne, together with all its prerogatives?"[3]

The king stirred in his bed, and then spoke so that all could hear: "I bestow[4] on Arthur God's blessing and my own, and Arthur shall succeed to the throne on pain of forfeiting my blessing." Then King Uther gave up the ghost. He was buried and mourned the next day, as befitted his rank, by Igraine and the nobility of Britain.

5 During the years that followed the death of King Uther, while Arthur was still a child, the ambitious barons fought one another for the throne, and the
6 whole of Britain stood in jeopardy.[5] Finally the day came when the Archbishop of Canterbury,[6] on the advice of Merlin, summoned the nobility to London for Christmas morning. In his message the Archbishop promised that the true succession to the British throne would be miraculously revealed. Many of the nobles purified themselves during their journey, in the hope that it would be to them that the succession would fall.

The Archbishop held his service in the city's greatest church (St. Paul's), and when matins[7] were done the congregation filed out to the yard. They were confronted by a marble block into which had been thrust a beautiful sword. The block was four feet square, and the sword passed through a steel anvil which had been struck in the stone, and which projected a foot from it. The anvil had been inscribed with letters of gold:

WHOSO PULLETH OUTE THIS SWERD OF THIS STONE AND ANVYLD IS RIGHTWYS KYNGE BORNE OF ALL BRYTAYGNE.[8]

The congregation was awed by this miraculous sight, but the Archbishop forbade anyone to touch the sword before mass had been heard. After mass, many of the nobles tried to pull the sword out of the stone, but none was able to, so a watch of ten knights was set over the sword, and a tournament proclaimed for New Year's Day, to provide men of noble blood with the opportunity of proving their right to the succession.

Sir Ector, who had been living on an estate near London, rode to the tournament with Arthur and his own son Sir Kay, who had been recently knighted. When they arrived at the tournament, Sir Kay found to his annoyance that his sword was missing from its sheath, so he begged Arthur to ride back and fetch it from their lodging. 7

Arthur found the door of the lodging locked and bolted, the landlord and his wife having left for the tournament. In order not to disappoint his brother, he rode on to St. Paul's, determined to get for him the sword which was lodged in the stone. The yard was empty, the guard also having

2. **duly** (dü′lē), *adv.* rightly; suitably.
3. **prerogative** (pri rog′ə tiv), *n.* right or privilege that nobody else has.
4. **bestow** (bi stō′), *v.* give (something) as a gift.
5. **jeopardy** (jep′ər dē), *n.* risk; danger.
6. **Archbishop of Canterbury**, an official who now serves as head of the Church of England at Canterbury Cathedral.
7. **matins** (mat′nz), *n.* morning prayers.
8. **WHOSO . . . BRYTAYGNE.** "Whoever pulls this sword out of this stone and anvil is rightwise king born of all Britain."

MINI-LESSON: GRAMMAR
Origins and Development of the English Language

Display the anvil's inscription on the overhead projector or board and let students read it aloud. Then note the paraphrase of the inscription on the bottom of page 342.

Activity Ideas

- Ask students to identify language differences between the original inscription and the paraphrase. Examples are
  1. spelling differences (*swerd* and *sword*)
  2. differences in verb and pronoun forms (*whoso* and *whoever; pulleth* and *pulls*)
  3. different syntax, or pattern of words in the sentence (*pulleth oute* and *pulls this sword out*)
- Have students imagine that they are script writers for new movie versions of the Arthurian legend and Robin Hood's adventures. Let them discuss the type of language they would use in the dialogue. Would the actors use modern American English, modern British English, or English from an older period? Then have them write dialogue for a brief scene.

slipped off to see the tournament, so Arthur strode up to the sword, and, without troubling to read the inscription, tugged it free. He then rode straight back to Sir Kay and presented him with it.

Sir Kay recognized the sword, and taking it to Sir Ector, said, "Father, the succession falls to me, for I have here the sword that was lodged in the stone." But Sir Ector insisted that they should all ride to the churchyard, and once there bound Sir Kay by oath to tell how
7 he had come by the sword. Sir Kay then admitted that Arthur had given it to him. Sir Ector turned to Arthur and said, "Was the sword not guarded?"

"It was not," Arthur replied.

"Would you please thrust it into the stone again?" said Sir Ector. Arthur did so, and first Sir Ector and then Sir Kay tried to remove it, but both were unable to. Then Arthur, for the second time, pulled it out. Sir Ector and Sir Kay both knelt before him.

"Why," said Arthur, "do you both kneel before me?"

"My lord," Sir Ector replied, "there is only one man living who can draw the sword from the stone, and he is the true-born King of Britain." Sir Ector then told Arthur the story of his birth and upbringing.

"My dear father," said Arthur, "for so I shall
8 always think of you—if, as you say, I am to be king, please know that any request you have to make is already granted."

Sir Ector asked that Sir Kay should be made Royal Seneschal,[9] and Arthur declared that while they both lived it should be so. Then the three of them visited the Archbishop and told him what had taken place.

> . . . THERE IS ONLY ONE MAN LIVING WHO CAN DRAW THE SWORD FROM THE STONE . . .

All those dukes and barons with ambitions to rule were present at the tournament on New Year's Day. But when all of them had failed, and Arthur alone had succeeded in drawing the sword from the stone, they protested against one so young, and of ignoble[10] blood, succeeding to the throne.

The secret of Arthur's birth was known only to a few of the nobles surviving from the days of King Uther. The Archbishop urged them to make Arthur's cause their own; but their support proved ineffective. The tournament was repeated at Candlemas and at Easter, and with the same outcome as before.

Finally at Pentecost,[11] when once more Arthur alone had been able to remove the sword, the commoners arose with a tumultuous[12] cry and demanded that Arthur should at once be made king. The nobles, knowing in their hearts that the commoners were right, all knelt before Arthur and begged forgiveness for having delayed his succession for so long. Arthur forgave them, and then, offering his sword at the high altar, was dubbed first
knight of the realm. The coronation took place 9
a few days later, when Arthur swore to rule justly, and the nobles swore him their allegiance.

King Arthur's first task was to re-establish those nobles who had been robbed of their lands during the troubled years since the reign of King Uther. Next, to establish peace and order in the counties near London. . . .

9. **Royal Seneschal,** the steward (or manager) in charge of the royal household.
10. ignoble (ig nō′bəl), *adj.* not of noble birth or position; humble.
11. **Candlemas . . . Pentecost,** two church festivals.
12. tumultuous (tü mul′chü əs), *adj.* very noisy or disorderly.

7 Reading/Thinking Skills
Inference

Point out that Arthur and Kay, who we infer to be nearly the same age, are considered brothers. The boys spent years training to become knights, first serving as pages (from approximately age seven into the teens), and then as squires. A squire's chief function was to serve his master. Kay has recently become a knight, and it is likely that Arthur is a squire.

8 Literary Element
Characterization

Question What can you conclude about Arthur's character? *(Possible responses: He is humble, unassuming, loyal, generous.)*

9 Literary Focus
Style

Elicit from students key details that Malory chooses to relate in the brief description of the coronation: the acclaim of the commoners, the sincerity and allegiance of the nobles, Arthur's generous forgiveness.

Question Tone is revealed by the author's word choice and arrangement of ideas, events, and descriptions. What tone is conveyed by the language and details of this paragraph? *(Possible responses: a noble tone; a simple yet elegant tone; a chivalrous tone)*

BUILDING ENGLISH PROFICIENCY

Exploring Key Events

Arthur's removal of the sword Excalibur from its rock is one of the most famous scenes of the Arthur cycle. Help students become familiar with it by acting it out.

1. Read through the scene together; then assign roles or allow students to volunteer to render the event in their own words.

2. Encourage students to fashion some classroom materials into a sword in a stone (a yardstick and a box, perhaps).

3. Provide a list of words necessary to the plot. A sample list is shown.

4. Conclude by having students discuss how this event ensured loyalty to Arthur.

Word List	
sword	stone
king	crown
allegiance	birth
noble	

10 Reading/Thinking Skills
Compare and Contrast

Questions

- What two roles are being contrasted here? *(Merlin's role and that of a priest)*
- What elements are compared and/or contrasted? *(church rites and this ceremony—which students cannot yet identify; those inside the chapel and those outside; the light and the gloom; God and "the driving god")*

11 Reading/Thinking Skills
Draw Conclusions

Question What do you think is the significance of Cador's and Lot's presence, position in the chapel, and exchanged look? *(Possible response: They may be powerful nobles, each of whom wishes the throne for himself and therefore dislikes the other.)*

THE HOLLOW HILLS

MARY STEWART

As you read, keep in mind that Merlin is the narrator.

The place was small, the throng of men great. But the awe of the occasion prevailed; orders were given, but subdued; soft commands which might have come from priests in ritual rather than warriors recently in battle. There were no rites[1] to follow, but somehow men kept their places; kings and nobles and kings' guards within the chapel, the press of lesser men outside in the silent clearing and overflowing into the gloom of the forest
10 itself. There, they still had lights; the clearing was ringed with light and sound where the horses waited and men stood with torches ready; but forward under the open sky men came lightless and weaponless, as beseemed them in the presence of God and their King. And still, this one night of all the great nights, there was no priest present; the only intermediary was myself, who had been used by the driving god for thirty years, and brought at last to this place.

At length all were assembled, according to order and precedence.[2] It was as if they had divided by arrangement, or more likely by instinct. Outside, crowding the steps, waited the little men from the hills; they do not willingly come under a roof. Inside the chapel, to my right, stood Lot, King of Lothian, with his group of friends and followers; to the left Cador, and those who went with him. There were a hundred others, perhaps more, crowded into that small and echoing space, but these two, the white Boar
of Cornwall, and the red Leopard of Lothian,[3] 11
seemed to face one another balefully[4] from either side of the altar, with Ector four-square and watchful at the door between them. Then Ector, with Cei[5] behind him, brought Arthur forward, and after that I saw no one but the boy.

The chapel swam with color and the glint of

1. rite (rīt), *n.* solemn ceremony.
2. precedence (pres′ə dəns), *n.* higher position or rank; great importance.
3. **white Boar . . . Lothian.** Two kings, Cador of Cornwall and Lot of Lothian, use the symbols of a white boar and a red leopard, respectively, on their flags or emblems.
4. balefully (bāl′fə lē), *adv.* destructively or threateningly.
5. **Cei** (kā), variant spelling of *Kay,* Ector's son.

MINI-LESSON: LITERARY FOCUS
Style

Have students imagine that they are in a writer's workshop with Malory and Stewart and have been asked to respond to their writing. Let students do so by choosing an author and responding to the following:

1. This is the way I felt after reading your story about Arthur. ____

2. It seems to me that your purpose is to ____. I think so because ____.

3. What I noticed most about your writing was ____. Some examples of this are ____.

4. If I decided to experiment with elements of your style, I would imitate the way you ____.

Remind students to refer to page 339 for a list of style choices.

◄ *May*, from *Book of Hours* (c. 1416), is a calendar picture of a seasonal landscape. What inferences can you draw about nobility, architecture, courtship, and entertainment of the time from this picture?

Art Study

Responses to Caption Questions
Nobility: They enjoyed music, riding, ornate clothing, believed in astrology, and kept pet dogs. Architecture: It was ornate and reached skywards with many turrets and pointed roofs. Courtship: These young people seem to enjoy courting as a group, though some are engaged (or about to be) in one-to-one conversation. Entertainment: Music and a ride in the fresh air seem to provide entertainment.

This is the calendar picture for May, and these young people are going Maying, a traditional festivity. The musicians play a trombone, flutes, and a *buisine* (the long pipe with a wide end). The ladies have decorated their hair and wimple with wild rose. The palace in the back is the Palais de la Cité in Paris. The man in front on the gray horse may be the duke.

BUILDING ENGLISH PROFICIENCY

Visualizing the Setting

Help students understand how Stewart uses setting to increase the drama. Begin visualizing the setting by noting that the episode begins with the words "*the place*" and ask students to identify it. Suggest that they draw the scene, individually or as partners, as volunteers expand on the description of the setting. Make sure key details, described below, are present in their drawings.

chapel: *kings and nobles and king's guards within the chapel* (p. 344)

altar: *the stone of the altar* (p. 346)

lamps: *flames from nine lamps, flaring and then dying* (p. 346)

flames: *flames running along the blade of the sword* (p. 346)

Students may need these points clarified about the setting:

- The passage beginning "Arthur came slowly forward." (page 346), at first describes what is actually happening in the chapel. Later, other places are mentioned but they refer to Merlin's memories of Arthur's life.
- The references to fire and light are often imagery describing the reflection of the flames from the lamps.

12 Literary Focus
Style

Questions

- What elements of style do you notice in Stewart's writing? Look back at the list of style choices on page 339. *(Possible responses: figurative language, dramatic, serious tone, suspenseful mood, rich description)*
- What figures of speech are used in this paragraph? *(simile: "sword . . . as a jewel . . ."; personification: "runes danced" and "emeralds burned"; metaphor: "chapel was a dark globe")*

13 Reading/Thinking Skills
Draw Conclusions

Question What is the importance of Cador's and Lot's speeches? *(Possible response: They are, in effect, renouncing or withdrawing their previous claims to the throne and accepting Arthur's claim. This is important because they appear to be the two most powerful nobles.)*

Check Test

1. In Malory's version, who chose Sir Ector to raise Arthur? *(Merlin)*
2. According to Malory, where was the tournament held? *(in London)*
3. What was Arthur's first task as king in Malory's version? *(to re-establish nobles who were displaced during the unrest)*
4. In "The Hollow Hills," who called for someone to take up the sword? *(Merlin)*
5. How did the sword feel when Arthur touched it? *(cool)*

Unit 3 Resource Book
Alternate Check Test, p. 5

jewels and gold. The air smelled cold and fragrant, of pines and water and scented smoke. The rustle and murmuring of the throng filled the air and sounded like the rustle of flames licking through a pile of fuel, taking hold. . . .

Flames from the nine lamps, flaring and then dying; flames licking up the stone of the altar; flames running along the blade of the sword until it glowed white hot. I stretched my hands out over it, palms flat. The fire licked my robe, blazing white from sleeve and finger, but where it touched, it did not even singe. It was the ice-cold fire, the fire called by a word out of the dark, with the searing heat at its heart, where the sword lay. [12] The sword lay in its flames as a jewel lies embedded in white wool. *Whoso taketh this sword. . . .*[6] The runes[7] danced along the metal: the emeralds burned. The chapel was a dark globe with a center of fire. The blaze from the altar threw my shadow upwards, gigantic, into the vaulted roof. I heard my own voice, ringing hollow from the vault like a voice in a dream.

"Take up the sword, he who dares."

[13] Movement, and men's voices, full of dread. Then Cador: "That is the sword. I would know it anywhere. I saw it in his hand, full of light.[8] It is his, God witness it. I would not touch it if Merlin himself bade me."

There were cries of, "Nor I, nor I," and then, "Let the King take it up, let the High King show us Macsen's[9] sword."

Then finally, alone, Lot's voice, gruffly: "Yes. Let him take it. I have seen, by God's death, I have seen. If it is his indeed, then God is with him, and it is not for me."

Arthur came slowly forward. Behind him the place was dim, the crowd shrunk back into darkness, the shuffle and murmur of their presence no more than the breeze in the forest trees outside. Here between us, the white light blazed and the blade shivered. The darkness flashed and sparkled, a crystal cave of vision, crowded and whirling with bright images.[10] A white stag, collared with gold. A shooting star, dragon-shaped, and trailing fire. A king, restless and desirous, with a dragon of red gold shimmering on the wall behind him. A woman, white-robed and queenly, and behind her in the shadows a sword standing in an altar like a cross. A circle of vast linked stones standing on a windy plain with a king's grave at its center. A child, handed into my arms on a winter night. A grail, shrouded in mouldering cloth, hidden in a dark vault. A young king, crowned.

He looked at me through the pulse and flash of vision. For him, they were flames only, flames which might burn, or not; that was for me. He waited, not doubtful, nor blindly trusting; waiting only.

"Come," I said gently. "It is yours."

He put his hand through the white blaze of fire and the hilt slid cool into the grip for which, a hundred and a hundred years before, it had been made.

6. **Whoso . . . sword.** The words "Whoso taketh [takes] this sword from under this stone is rightwise King born of all Britain" appear in their entirety earlier in Stewart's novel.
7. **rune** (rün), *n.* inscription or letter.
8. **I saw . . . light.** Cador had seen Arthur with the same sword earlier, when it was found in a cavern.
9. **Macsen's.** *Macsen* is the British name for the Roman ruler Magnus Maximus, who lived in the fourth century in Britain. Mary Stewart has introduced the idea that the sword once belonged to another ruler of Great Britain, a new twist on the Arthurian legend.
10. **bright images.** Merlin proceeds to identify images of a stag, a shooting star, and other omens and scenes from Arthur's life up to this point.

MINI-LESSON: GRAMMAR
Semicolons

"For him, they were flames only, flames which might burn, or not; that was for me." (page 346)

Display the sentence and point out the semicolon. Explain that semicolons have several usages in English.

- to separate main clauses that contain commas in a compound sentence
- to separate items in a series when the items contain commas
- to separate main clauses when the conjunction *(and, but, for, or, yet)* has been omitted
- to separate main clauses connected by adverbs such as *however, nevertheless,* and *for example*

Activity Idea Have students locate other sentences containing semicolons in Stewart's work and identify the usage that they demonstrate.

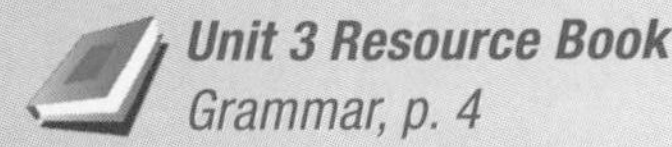
Unit 3 Resource Book
Grammar, p. 4

After Reading

Making Connections

Shaping Your Response

1. What were your feelings toward Arthur as you read these selections?
2. Do you think Arthur is fortunate to have such an acquaintance as Merlin? Why or why not?
3. Which of these narratives would you prefer portraying in art? Why?

Analyzing the Legends

4. What does Malory imply is the cause of unrest in Britain during Arthur's childhood?
5. What details **foreshadow** that Arthur may encounter opposition during his rule?
6. List three personal qualities that you think **characterize** Arthur.
7. What differences do you find in **setting** and **tone** in Stewart's and Malory's accounts?
8. What details in Malory's account does Stewart change or add to in order to heighten dramatic effect?

Extending the Ideas

9. Compare Arthur to other heroes that you know of, such as Odysseus, Hercules, and other legendary figures. Do these heroes seem more concerned with individual goals or with the welfare of the **groups** they lead?
10. What public "tests" do politicians undergo today to prove their ability to lead?

Literary Focus: Style

Reread the description of **style** that appears before the Malory selection, as well as the two passages below. Then comment on the difference in styles, referring to things such as imagery, mood, and repetition.

- "The yard was empty, the guard also having slipped off to see the tournament, so Arthur strode up to the sword and, without troubling to read the inscription, tugged it free." *Malory*
- "He put his hand through the white blaze of fire and the hilt slid cool into the grip for which, a hundred and a hundred years before, it had been made." *Stewart*

LITERARY FOCUS: STYLE

Point out that readers can analyze style by looking into the work and finding specific features such as imagery and sound devices. They can also look to their own reactions to determine the mood, tone, and purpose of the work.

After Reading

MAKING CONNECTIONS

1. Possible responses: admiration, increased interest in him

2. From reading these accounts, students will probably answer yes because Merlin prevents Arthur from being killed and helps to make sure he attains his rightful position. Others who have read more about Merlin may offer another view.

3. Students who prefer Mallory's version can share details of the scenes they would choose to depict; those who prefer Stewart can speculate how they would render her rich visual imagery.

4. the lack of a strong leader to unify the nobles who warred among themselves for the right to wear the crown

5. the recurrent unrest among the nobles; Merlin's insistence that Uther formally name his successor before the assembled nobles; the unwillingness of the nobles to grant Arthur the title even after he alone could pull the sword from the stone

6. Possible responses: loyalty, courage, trust, generosity

7. Malory depicts a society in which power rests in the people, and an ordered system is recognized, if not always adhered to. Stewart presents an older and wilder society, full of mystery, symbolism, magic, and portent, and in which the power of God is manifest.

8. the sword's origin, the trial to achieve the sword, the opposition to Arthur's coronation

9. Answers will vary depending on the hero and culture students choose.

10. Possible responses: straw polls, debates, primaries, interviews by the press, elections

VOCABULARY STUDY

1. h
2. d
3. c
4. g
5. f
6. b
7. i
8. e
9. a
10. j

More Practice Students can use the vocabulary words in a brief written or oral summary of the coronation. The account should be given in the voice of a commoner.

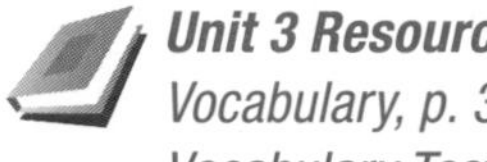

Unit 3 Resource Book
Vocabulary, p. 3
Vocabulary Test, p. 6

WRITING CHOICES

Writer's Notebook Update

Point out that people may become great for more than one reason. Ask students to brainstorm other possible causes of greatness, for example, being in the right place at the right time.

Second Best

Remind students that as a knight and a noble, Kay was bound to be loyal to his country. At the same time, he was like a brother to Arthur, and would have the usual jealousies and rivalries that exist between siblings.

Extra! Extra!

Inform students how they can access desktop publishing software so that they can design and print copies of their newspaper.

Selection Test

Unit 3 Resource Book
pp. 7–8

Vocabulary Study

Match the numbered word with the letter of its correct synonym.

balefully
bestow
duly
ignoble
jeopardy
precedence
prerogative
rite
rune
tumultuous

1. balefully	**a.** noisy or disorderly
2. bestow	**b.** rightly
3. ignoble	**c.** humble
4. jeopardy	**d.** give
5. precedence	**e.** unique privilege
6. duly	**f.** higher rank
7. rite	**g.** danger
8. prerogative	**h.** destructively
9. tumultuous	**i.** solemn ceremony
10. rune	**j.** inscription

Expressing Your Ideas

Writing Choices

Writer's Notebook Update Review the quotation by Shakespeare about greatness. Then write a paragraph applying this quotation to Arthur.

Second Best What do you think were Sir Kay's thoughts and feelings at discovering Arthur's true identity? Write Sir Kay's reactions in the form of an **interior monologue**—one of those uncensored dialogues people have with themselves.

Extra! Extra! As editor of the *Camelot Chronicle*, you and your staff are to publish a **special issue** about the new king. It might include items such as the following: a news story on Arthur's early life and how he became king, comic strips, an interview with Arthur focusing on his plans for the future, political cartoons, an editorial about the future of Britain under King Arthur, advertisements for products of the time.

Other Options

Name of the Game Working in a group of three or four, create a **board game** based on the legends of King Arthur's time. The game should have a definite goal (attaining the crown, perhaps), penalties, and rewards.

Draw Your Sword Do some research on ancient weapons to discover what a medieval sword looked like. Combine these details with your imagination to create a **drawing** or a **model** of the sword in the stone. Alternatively, you might research weaponry of war or honor in different cultures and create artwork based on your findings.

A Dramatic Moment Mary Stewart's account lends itself to a **dramatic reading**. A narrator can prepare a reading of the account, up to the paragraph beginning, "Arthur came slowly forward." The remainder can be acted, with music. Special effects can be achieved by lighting, colored cloth, and simple props.

OTHER OPTIONS

Name of the Game

Students may enjoy creating game pieces representing medieval symbols and weapons. Pieces might also represent people in various levels of feudal society—from kings to serfs.

Draw Your Sword

Remind students who choose to draw not to forget the anvil. Students who choose to do research may be interested in studying Japanese or Chinese sword making.

Before Reading

Youth and Chivalry from A Distant Mirror

by Barbara Tuchman USA

Barbara Tuchman
1912–1989

Best-selling historian Barbara Tuchman found stories worth telling, researched available information, visited the sites, and then wove historical accounts into exciting narratives. For *A Distant Mirror: The Calamitous Fourteenth Century,* from which the following excerpt is taken, she crossed the same mountains traveled by Crusaders more than six centuries earlier. Her lively narration, thorough research, ability to tie the past to the present, and keen eye for details earned her two Pulitzer prizes.

Building Background

How Does a Culture Sound? What are the sounds of your typical day? alarm clocks buzzing? water running? trains rumbling? car radio playing? locker doors slamming? How do these compare with the sounds heard in the 1300s? According to historian Johan Huizinga: "One sound rose ceaselessly above the noises of busy life and lifted all things unto a sphere of order and serenity: the sound of bells. . . . They were known by their names: big Jacqueline, or the bell Roland. Every one knew the difference in meaning of the various ways of ringing." Why might bells have been important to the people of the Middle Ages? How would bells have suggested order and serenity?

Literary Focus

Sensory Details Writers use **sensory details,** or words that appeal to the senses, to create images and feelings in their readers. Such words help readers see, hear, feel, smell, and taste the world the writer portrays. For example, Barbara Tuchman describes a mother "delousing her child's hair with his head in her lap" and a book of advice on "not spitting or picking teeth with a knife." Make a chart like the one below, and list examples of appropriate details that you find in this historical account.

Sight	Sound	Touch	Smell	Taste

Writer's Notebook

Were They Really Like That? In the following excerpt from *A Distant Mirror*, Tuchman presents a picture of everyday life over six centuries ago. Imagine that a team of archaeologists unearths your house six hundred years from now. Make a list of five items they might find that would give them a clue to life today. List five other items that might confuse or puzzle them.

Before Reading

Building Background

Ask students to share their ideas of chivalry. Mention that chivalry was the code of conduct that a knight was to follow. A knight was to be courageous and skilled in war and horsemanship, hence the origin of the word which is from the French *cheval*, or horse. He would also be pure, faithful in love, and filled with religious zeal.

Literary Focus

As an exercise, students can quickly write as many **sensory details** as they can about something in their classroom setting. Let them share their details.

Writer's Notebook

As students make their choices, they might want to consider the effects that the passage of six hundred years will have on the objects they choose.

More About Barbara Tuchman

Tuchman's book, *A Distant Mirror,* follows the life of Enguerrand de Coucy VII, a nobleman and knight from France who is related to the French and the English royal families. Tuchman has also written *The Zimmerman Telegram,* (1966)

SUPPORT MATERIALS OVERVIEW

Unit 3 Resource Book
- Graphic Organizer, p. 9
- Study Guide, p. 10
- Vocabulary, p. 11
- Grammar, p. 12
- Alternate Check Test, p. 13
- Vocabulary Test, p. 14
- Selection Test, pp. 15–16

Building English Proficiency
- Literature Summaries
- Activities, p. 193

Reading, Writing & Grammar SkillBook
- Vocabulary, pp. 3–4
- Reading, pp. 36–37
- Writing, pp. 107–108
- Grammar, Usage, and Mechanics, pp. 250–252

Technology
- Audiotape 9, Side B
- Personal Journal Software
- Custom Literature Database: For more readings on British history, see the Magna Carta and works by Bede on the database.
- Test Generator Software

During Reading

Selection Objectives

- to analyze grammatical structures
- to identify sensory details
- to explore the theme of answering the call

Unit 3 Resource Book
Graphic Organizer, p. 9
Study Guide, p. 10

Theme Link

Tuchman's work details life in the medieval period in which Malory set his rendering of Arthurian Legends.

Vocabulary Preview

advocate, support
aloof, unsympathetic, reserved
atrophy, waste away
capricious, changeable
conjecture, guess; admit without sufficient evidence
degrading, dishonorable
eradicable, that can be gotten rid of or destroyed
ribald, offensive in speech; obscene
rudiment, part to be learned first; beginning
ruse, scheme or device to mislead others; trick

Students can add the words and definitions to their Writer's Notebooks.

1 Reading/Thinking Skills
Analyze

Question What kinds of evidence do you think Tuchman will need to provide to support this claim? *(Possible responses: Examples in art and literature in which children should appear but don't; dismissive comments about children. Students may observe that it is difficult to establish a lack of interest, since much goes on at any time period that is not recorded.)*

During the 1400s, a Flemish artist illuminated this manuscript page showing a tournament at Arthur's court. What does this scene illustrate about society and the life of the nobility in the time of Arthur's legendary reign? ➤

Youth and Chivalry

BARBARA TUCHMAN

1 Of all the characteristics in which the medieval age differs from the modern, none is so striking as the comparative absence of interest in children. Emotion in relation to them rarely appears in art or literature or documentary evidence. The Christ child is of course repeatedly pictured, usually in his mother's arms, but prior to the mid-14th century he is generally held stiffly, away from her body, by a mother who is aloof[1] even when nursing. Or else the holy infant lies alone on the ground, swaddled or sometimes quite naked and uncovered, while an unsmiling mother gazes at him abstractedly. Her separateness from the child was meant to indicate his divinity. If the ordinary mother felt a warmer, more intimate emotion, it found small expression in medieval art because the attitudes of motherhood were preempted[2] by the Virgin Mary.

In literature the chief role of children was to die, usually drowned, smothered, or abandoned in a forest on the orders of some king fearing prophecy or mad husband testing a wife's endurance. Women appear rarely as mothers. They are flirts, bawds, and deceiving wives in the popular tales, saints and martyrs in the drama, unattainable objects of passionate and illicit love in the romances. Occasionally motherhood may break through, as when an English preacher, to point a moral in a sermon, tells how a mother "that hath a childe in wynter when the childes hondes ben cold, the modur taketh hym a stree

1. **aloof** (ə lüf′), *adj.* unsympathetic; reserved.
2. **preempt** (prē empt′), *v.* take over beforehand.

SELECTION SUMMARY

Youth and Chivalry

From her research, Tuchman concludes that the striking difference between the medieval age and the modern age is the lack of interest in children on the part of the medievals. She shows that art, writing, and other documents do not provide evidence of emotional attachment between parents and children. Tuchman advances the theory that high infant mortality might have led to the suppression of parental feelings. Tuchman maintains that child-rearing was not treated in books of advice though many other subjects were. She concludes that "on the whole, babies and young children appear to have been left to survive or die without great concern in the first five or six years." After a brief discussion of toys and childish behavior, Tuchman discusses medieval education of boys and girls.

*For summaries in other languages, see the **Building English Proficiency** book.*

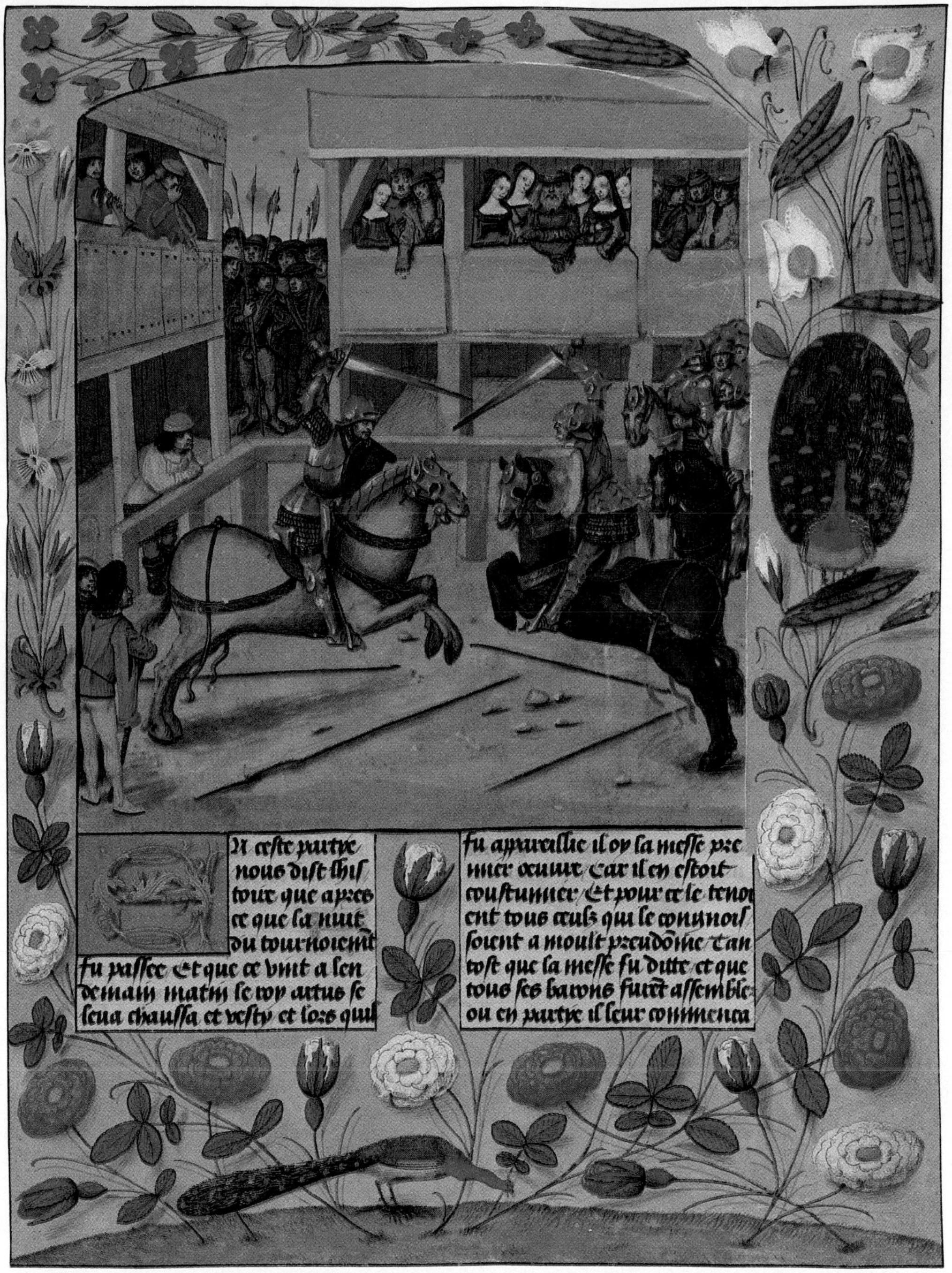

Art Study

Responses to Caption Questions
Society—There was a strict division in society, as shown by the king and queen and their court in the boxes, and the common folk standing outside the stadium. The class of knights is clearly differentiated from the rest of society by their attire and activity. The nobles' clothing seems to be more colorful and more differentiated than that of the commoners'. Life of the nobility—Both ladies and men of the nobility enjoyed watching formal games in which skills of warriors were displayed.

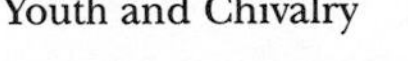

BUILDING ENGLISH PROFICIENCY

ESL LEP ELD SAE LD

Checking Comprehension

With the wealth of detail that Tuchman provides, students may find it difficult to keep track of information. Suggest that they choose details from the reading that stand out for them about child-rearing or the education of youth. As they talk about what impressed them, create a details web to capture their ideas.

Afterward, students might enjoy using the data to create a comparison-contrast chart showing the differences in education between boys and girls in the age of Arthur.

Education of children of nobility

girls	boys
medical training	*riding horses*
Latin language	*hawking*
music	*skills needed in war*

Building English Proficiency
Activities, p. 193

2 Historical Note
Infant Mortality

In the fourteenth century, the bubonic plague wiped out about a third of the population of Europe and Asia.

You may wish to have students read Ben Jonson's poems, written in the early seventeenth century, on the early deaths of his two children. The poems are titled, "On My First Son" and "On My First Daughter," and are available on the Custom Literature Database. Ask students to consider whether they think parental feelings changed markedly from the fourteenth to the seventeenth centuries.

3 Active Reading
Clarify

Possible response She is making the point that circumstances in the environment may force both humans and animals to behave in an unnatural or abnormal way.

4 Reading/Thinking Skills
Make Judgments

Question Which of Philip of Novara's attitudes and advice would your parents agree with? Why? *(Possible responses: They might agree with his belief in a strict upbringing and his attitude that parents and children can form tender, loving relationships. Students may debate what is meant by "severity" and "a strict upbringing.")*

[straw] or a rusche and byddeth him warme itt, not for love of the stree to hete it . . . but for to hete the childes honds."[3] An occasional illustration or carving in stone shows parents teaching a child to walk, a peasant mother combing or delousing her child's hair with his head in her lap, a more elegant mother of the 14th century knitting a child's garment on four needles, an acknowledgment from a saint's life of the "beauty of infancy," and from the 12th century *Ancren Riwle*[4] a description of a peasant mother playing hide-and-seek with her child and who, when he cries for her, "leapeth forth lightly with outspread arms and embraceth and kisseth him and wipeth his eyes." These are isolated mentions which leave the empty spaces between more noticeable.

Medieval illustrations show people in every other human activity—making love and dying, sleeping and eating, in bed and in the bath, praying, hunting, dancing, plowing, in games and in combat, trading, traveling, reading and writing—yet so rarely with children as to raise the question: Why not?

Maternal love, like sex, is generally considered too innate[5] to be eradicable,[6] but perhaps under certain unfavorable conditions it may
2 atrophy.[7] Owing to the high infant mortality of the times, estimated at one or two in three, the investment of love in a young child may have been so unrewarding that by some ruse[8] of nature, as when overcrowded rodents in captivity will not breed, it was suppressed. Perhaps also the frequent childbearing put less value on the product. A child was born and died and another took its place.

3 **CLARIFY: What point is the author making with the comparison to rodents?**

Well-off noble and bourgeois families bore more children than the poor because they married young and because, as a result of employing wet-nurses, the period of infertility was short. They also raised more, often as many as six to ten reaching adulthood. Guillaume de Coucy,[9] grandfather of Enguerrand VII, raised five sons and five daughters; his son Raoul raised four of each. Nine out of the twelve children of Edward III[10] and Queen Philippa of England reached maturity. The average woman of twenty, it has been estimated, could expect about twelve years of childbearing, with live births spaced out—owing to stillbirths, abortions, and nursing—at fairly long intervals of about thirty months. At this rate, the average of births per family was about five, of whom half survived.

Like everything else, childhood escapes a flat generalization. Love and lullabies and cradle-rocking did exist. God in his grace, wrote Philip of Novara in the 13th century, gave children three gifts: to love and recognize the person who nurses him at her breast; to
show "joy and love" to those who play with him; 4
to inspire love and tenderness in those who rear him, of which the last is the most important, for "without this, they will be so dirty and annoying in infancy and so naughty and

3. **"that hath a childe . . . the childes honds,"** that has a child in winter when the child's hands be cold, the mother takes him a straw or a rush [grasslike plant] and bids him warm it, not for love of the straw to heat it . . . but to heat the child's hands.
4. ***Ancren Riwle,*** a book of devotional advice, probably written for nuns.
5. **innate** (i nāt′), *adj.* natural, inborn.
6. **eradicable** (i rad′ə kə bəl), *adj.* that can be gotten rid of or destroyed.
7. **atrophy** (at′rə fē), *v.* waste away.
8. **ruse** (rüz), *n.* scheme or device to mislead others; trick.
9. **Guillaume de Coucy** (gē yōm′ də kü sē′) . . . **Enguerrand** (eng′yə rän) **VII.** In her narrative, *A Distant Mirror,* Tuchman details the life of de Coucy, "the most skilled and experienced of all the knights of France."
10. **Edward III**, king of England who lived from 1312-1377 and reigned for fifty years.

MINI-LESSON: LITERARY FOCUS
Sensory Details

Teach Read aloud the first full paragraph on page 353 which begins, "Books of advice. . . ." Tell students that the list Tuchman includes is full of sensory details, images, and facts that appeal to our senses of sight, touch, taste, smell, and hearing. Have volunteers identify an example from this paragraph that applies to each sense.

Activity Idea Using the sensory details from Tuchman's research, students can write a paragraph of historical fiction. Prompt them to imagine a character who is a youth of medieval times who encounters an adventure. Challenge students to use at least three sensory details from the passage.

capricious[11] that it is hardly worth nurturing them through childhood." Philip advocated,[12] however, a strict upbringing, for "few children perish from excess of severity but many from being permitted too much."

5 Books of advice on child-rearing were rare. There were books—that is, bound manuscripts—of etiquette, housewifery, deportment, home remedies, even phrase books of foreign vocabularies. A reader could find advice on washing hands and cleaning nails before a banquet, on eating fennel and anise in case of bad breath, on not spitting or picking teeth with a knife, not wiping hands on sleeves, or nose and eyes on the tablecloth. A woman could learn how to make ink, poison for rats, sand for hourglasses; how to make hippocras or spiced wine, the favorite medieval drink; how to care for pet birds in cages and get them to breed: how to obtain character references for servants and make sure they extinguished their bed candles with fingers or breath, "not with their shirts"; how to grow peas and graft roses; how to rid the house of flies; how to remove grease stains with chicken feathers steeped in hot water; how to keep a husband happy by ensuring him a smokeless fire in winter and a bed free of fleas in summer. A young married woman would be advised on fasting and alms-giving and saying prayers at the sound of the matins bell "before going to sleep again," and on walking with dignity and modesty in public, not "in ribald[13] wise with roving eyes and neck stretched forth like a stag in flight, looking this way and that like unto a runaway horse." She could find books on estate management for times when her husband was away at war, with advice on making budgets and withstanding sieges and on tenure and feudal law so that her husband's rights would not be invaded.

6 **EVALUATE: Do you think that a medieval housewife had more or less power than her modern counterpart?**

But she would find few books for mothers with advice on breast-feeding, swaddling, bathing, weaning, solid-feeding, and other complexities of infant care, although these might seem to have been of more moment for survival of the race than breeding birds in cages or even keeping husbands comfortable. When breast-feeding was mentioned, it was generally advocated—by one 13th century encyclopedist, Bartholomew of England in his *Book on the Nature of Things*—for its emotional value. In the process the mother "loves her own child most tenderly, embraces and kisses it, nurses and cares for it most solicitously." A physician of the same period, Aldobrandino of Siena, who practiced in France, advised frequent cleaning and changing and two baths a day, weaning on porridge made of bread with honey and milk, ample playtime and unforced teaching at school, with time for sleep and diversion. But how widely his humane teaching was known or followed it is impossible to say. 7

On the whole, babies and young children appear to have been left to survive or die without great concern in the first five or six years. What psychological effect this may have had on character, and possibly on history, can only be conjectured.[14] Possibly the relative emotional blankness of a medieval infancy may account for the casual attitude toward life and suffering of the medieval man. 8

Children did, however, have toys: dolls and doll carriages harnessed to mice, wooden knights and weapons, little animals of baked clay, windmills, balls, battledores and shuttlecocks,[15] stilts and seesaws and merry-go-rounds. Little boys were like little boys of any time, "living without thought or care," according to

11. **capricious** (kə prish′əs), *adj.* changeable.
12. **advocate** (ad′və kāt), *v.* support.
13. **ribald** (rib′əld), *adj.* offensive in speech; obscene.
14. **conjecture** (kən jek′chər), *v.* guess; admit without sufficient evidence.
15. **battledores and shuttlecocks.** A battledore is a small racquet used to hit a shuttlecock (a cork with feathers) back and forth in badminton or similar games.

5 Literary Focus
Sensory Details

After reading Tuchman's account of housewife's duties with its many sensory details, students can brainstorm a list of a modern homemaker's duties. They can then put the list in the form of a Venn diagram with the headings **Medieval, Both, Modern.**

6 Active Reading
Evaluate

Possible response Students may observe that the housewife's duties listed here are those of a member of the privileged class. In caring for a household, the wife was also caring for the family's wealth. In that way, her role may have been regarded with more respect than a housewife's role today.

7 Reading/Thinking Skills
Cause and Effect

In the fourteenth century, before books were printed, information was copied by hand, making books extremely expensive and fairly rare.

Question Then, to whom or what would medieval mothers go for information and advice on child-rearing? *(Possible responses: Midwives, servants, older women in the family, and clergy were used as authorities.)*

8 Reading/Thinking Skills
Draw Conclusions

Question In Malory's account of Arthur's upbringing, the infant Arthur is taken from his parents to be raised by Sir Ector. From what you know about medieval child-rearing practices, would that have been considered a good or poor act of parenting? *(Possible responses: Since Arthur's life may have been in danger, it was a good act; a person who was trusted by the parents probably was considered as good as the parents themselves.)*

BUILDING ENGLISH PROFICIENCY

Recognizing the Use of Persuasion

Point out that Tuchman takes a stand in her writing. Challenge students to state the author's opinions in their own words. Some responses might be

- Medieval parents did not act loving toward their children.
- When a child died, adults did not feel as sorry as we do now because so many children died.
- People in medieval times showed no interest in children.

Follow by letting students state their own opinions about child-rearing. The opinions can be developed into informal persuasive speeches or panel discussions.

9 Historical Note
Medieval Terms

patron saint, a saint considered to be the special guide of a person, a place, or an institution

page, a boy who serves a knight as an apprentice

squire, the next step toward knighthood after being a page

to hawk, to hunt small prey using specially trained hawks

quintain, a target for the practice of tilting, a medieval contest in which two mounted knights rode at each other, each trying to use a long pole called a lance to unseat the other

heraldry, the study of coats of arms and genealogies

elocution, public speaking

10 Active Reading
Connect

Possible response Students should give examples of differences in physical, religious, and intellectual training.

Check Test

1. Which child is shown repeatedly in medieval art? *(the Christ child)*
2. Why did the rich have more children than the poor? *(They married younger and used wet nurses.)*
3. Who wrote *Book on the Nature of Things*? *(Bartholomew of England)*
4. At what age were children recognized and treated as adults? *(seven)*
5. Why were women often better educated than men? *(in order to be prepared for religious life)*

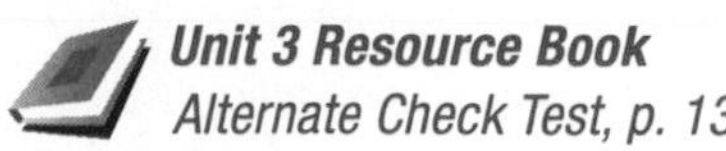

Unit 3 Resource Book
Alternate Check Test, p. 13

Bartholomew of England, "loving only to play, fearing no danger more than being beaten with a rod, always hungry and hence disposed to infirmities from being overfed, wanting everything they see, quick to laughter and as quick to tears, resisting their mothers' efforts to wash and comb them, and no sooner clean but dirty again." Girls were better behaved, according to Bartholomew, and dearer to their mothers. If children survived to age seven, their recognized life began, more or less as miniature adults. Childhood was already over. The childishness noticeable in medieval behavior, with its marked inability to restrain any kind of impulse, may have been simply due to the fact that so large a proportion of active society was actually very young in years. About half the population, it has been estimated, was under twenty-one, and about one third under fourteen.

A boy of noble family was left for his first seven years in the charge of women, who schooled him in manners and to some
9 extent in letters. Significantly, St. Anne, the patron saint of mothers, is usually portrayed teaching her child, the Virgin Mary, how to read from a book. From age eight to fourteen the noble's son was sent as a page to the castle of a neighboring lord, in the same way that boys of lower orders went at seven or eight to another family as apprentices or servants. Personal service was not considered degrading:[16] a page or even a squire as a grown man assisted his lord to bathe and dress, took care of his clothes, waited on him at table while sharing noble status. In return for free labor, the lord provided a free school for the sons of his peers. The boy would learn to ride, to fight, and to hawk, the three chief physical elements of noble life, to play chess and backgammon, to sing and dance, play an instrument, and compose, and other romantic skills. The castle's private chaplain or a local abbey would supply his religious education, and teach him the rudiments[17] of reading and writing and possibly some elements of the grammar-school curriculum that non-noble boys studied.

At fourteen or fifteen, when he became a squire, the training for combat intensified. He learned to pierce the swinging dummy of the quintain with a lance, wield the sword and a variety of other murderous weapons, and know the rules of heraldry and jousting. As squire he led his lord's war-horse to battle and held it when the fighting was on foot. He assisted the seneschal in the business of the castle, kept the keys, acted as confidential courier, carried the purse and valuables on a journey. Book learning had little place in this program, although a young noble, depending on his bent, could make some acquaintance of geometry, law, elocution, and, in a few cases, Latin.

Women of noble estate were frequently more accomplished in Latin and other school learning than the men, for though girls did not leave home at seven like boys, their education was encouraged by the Church so that they might be better instructed in the faith and more fitted for the religious life in a nunnery, should their parents wish to dedicate them, with suitable endowment, to the Church. Besides reading and writing in French and Latin, they were taught music, astronomy, and some medicine and first aid. . . .

CONNECT: How does your education compare with that of a young male or female noble? 10

16. **degrading** (di grā′ding), *adj.* dishonorable.
17. **rudiment** (rü′də mənt), *n.* part to be learned first; beginning.

MINI-LESSON: GRAMMAR
Analyzing Grammatical Structures

Teach Diagramming sentences can be a useful tool for many students. You might begin by demonstrating diagrams for simple sentences consisting of a subject, predicate, direct object (or subject complement), and modifiers. For example:

Like everything else, childhood escapes a flat generalization.

childhood | escapes | generalization
Like everything else; a; flat

Activity Idea Have students practice diagramming these sentences from the selection:

- Women appear rarely as mothers.
- Books of advice on child-rearing were rare.
- A boy of noble family was left for his first seven years in the charge of women.

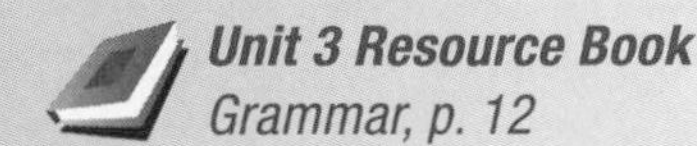

Unit 3 Resource Book
Grammar, p. 12

After Reading

Making Connections

Shaping Your Response

1. What are the advantages and disadvantages you can see in growing up in the 1300s?
2. Do you think the term *chivalry* had more meaning for males than for females? Why or why not?
3. What words would you use to describe a medieval boy's education? a medieval girl's?

Analyzing the Selection

4. What **allusions** does Tuchman make to other historical people or documents to support her observations?
5. What examples can you find of male-female **stereotypes** in this account?
6. What **images** of medieval life in this account do you find memorable?

Extending the Ideas

7. Study the description of a medieval wife's duties in the seventh paragraph that begins, "Books of advice. . . ." Do you think it was harder to be a housewife then or now? Explain.
8. Do you agree with Philip of Novara that "few children perish from excess of severity but many from being permitted too much"? Why or why not?
9. Describe how your education differs from that of your fourteenth-century male or female counterpart. Explain which kind of education you consider more practical.

Literary Focus: Sensory Details

Tuchman's use of **sensory details** makes her historical account lively and memorable. Look at the chart you filled out as you read. In a paragraph, explain what these details reveal about life in the Middle Ages.

Vocabulary Study

advocate
aloof
atrophy
capricious
conjecture
degrading
eradicable
ribald
rudiment
ruse

Number a paper from 1 to 10. Then complete each sentence with one of the listed words.

1. Even pure knights enjoyed offensive, ____ tales.
2. Since divorce was forbidden, medieval marriages were not ____.
3. Did the church ____ chastity until marriage?
4. Youths learned each basic ____ of reading and writing.
5. Mothers were reserved and ____ toward children because many died before their teens.

LITERARY FOCUS: SENSORY DETAILS

Students who are having trouble getting started may be assisted by this exercise. Encourage students to imagine that Tuchman's essay included no sensory detail whatsoever. Ask them to consider and discuss what would be lost. Then have them return to the assigned topic.

After Reading

MAKING CONNECTIONS

1. Students may cite the lack of health care and technological advances as a disadvantage; some may be attracted by the adventurous aspects of medieval life; others may disagree with some of Tuchman's interpretations.

2. The code of conduct probably had more meaning for males since it prescribed behavior of knights; however, since chivalry idealized women, the code implied conduct for them also.

3. Possible responses: boys—physical, military, not academic; girls—academic and artistic.

4. *Ancren Riwle;* Philip of Novara, *Book on the Nature of Things* by Bartholomew of England

5. Possible responses: Philip of Novara describing children as dirty, naughty, and annoying; girls described as being better behaved than boys. Students should support their opinions with details from the text.

6. Students should refer to sensory details such as a squire leading his lord's warhorse to battle, and a bed free of fleas.

7. Students should describe what, in their view, are the duties of a homemaker now, and use that description as the basis of comparison.

8. Possible responses: Severity is good to an extent, but may have led to child abuse. Permitting children to develop their individual talents is more important.

9. In their answers, students should refer to the courses they are taking and compare them with the descriptions in Tuchman's article.

VOCABULARY STUDY

1. ribald
2. eradicable
3. advocate
4. rudiment
5. aloof
6. atrophy
7. ruse
8. degrading
9. capricious
10. conjecture

Unit 3 Resource Book
Vocabulary, p. 11
Vocabulary Test, p. 14

WRITING CHOICES

Survival Skills

If students have older siblings or friends who have gone to college or moved away from home, they might want to interview them to see what skills they have found to be the most important.

Selection Test

Unit 3 Resource Book
pp. 15–16

6. A knight's skill might ____ from lack of use in peace time.
7. One ____ knights might employ to enter an enemy castle was dressing as a monk.
8. Knights considered association with lowly peasants ____.
9. Children were as mischievous and ____ then as they are today.
10. What would you ____ about the status of women from this account?

Expressing Your Ideas

Writing Choices

Writer's Notebook Update Look again at the first list of five items archaeologists might find in your house. Write conclusions they could draw from them about life around the year 2000. Then write about the second list of items and the erroneous (and perhaps humorous) conclusions that might result. Use sensory details and some vocabulary words to enliven your writing.

Survival Skills What skills do you consider essential for a person your age in today's society? For example, do you consider changing a tire important? changing a baby? fixing a meal? fixing a VCR? speaking a second language? **List** ten skills, present them to classmates, and be prepared to defend your choices.

Home Improvement How-to books are just as popular today as during the medieval period. Think of a problem that might occur in any modern household—a clogged sink, a broken window—and write a list of **how-to steps** explaining how to fix it. Since your reader will be totally dependent on your directions, choose precise words for each of the steps in the process.

Other Options

A Little Knight Music In the Middle Ages, troubadours composed songs about knights' heroic adventures. Compose your own **song** about medieval life or knighthood. Present your song, accompanied by a guitar or recorder if possible, to classmates.

Castles in the Air Working in small groups, research a medieval castle—its architectural features, maintenance, inhabitants, and any other areas of interest. Make a model, draw, or use photographs of the castle to take the class on a **castle tour**. Show how the castle reflects medieval life.

356 UNIT THREE: ANSWERING THE CALL

OTHER OPTIONS

A Little Knight Music

Students may enjoy looking at a book of troubadour's lyrics. *Lyrics of the Troubadours and Trouveres,* (1973) by Frederick Goldin includes both original texts and translations of lyrics from the eleventh to the thirteenth centuries, as well as a song written by Richard the Lion-Hearted when he was in captivity.

Before Reading

The Tale of Sir Launcelot du Lake by Sir Thomas Malory Great Britain
from The Once and Future King by T. H. White Great Britain

T. H. White
1906–1964

Perhaps his career as a teacher gave Terence Hanbury White his rare gift for writing books that appeal to both adults and children. Born in Bombay, India, White grew up in England. At thirty, he resigned his teaching position to research filmmaking, falconry, and Arthurian lore. His most celebrated work, *The Once and Future King,* became the basis for the musical *Camelot,* which has enjoyed tremendous success since it first appeared in 1960. The excerpt from his book that appears here shows how White plays on Malory's original, viewing things from a twentieth-century perspective.

Building Background

A Very Good Knight When things were a bit slow in the castle, a knight who began "feeling weary of his life at the court," set out for adventure, as Launcelot does in the account you are about to read. Such quests gave knights an opportunity to practice the chivalric code, which was based on certain rules and customs. In compliance with this code, knights pledged:

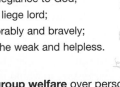

- supreme allegiance to God;
- loyalty to a liege lord;
- to act honorably and bravely;
- to protect the weak and helpless.

Note how this code values **group welfare** over personal goals. Although knights generally upheld this code, they sometimes abandoned fair play and loyalty in pursuit of their own interests. Sir Launcelot (whose pursuit of Queen Gwynevere is a betrayal of King Arthur) is a fascinating and complex character because he displays both idealized qualities and human weaknesses.

Literary Focus

Allusion An **allusion** is a reference to a real, mythical, or literary event, thing, person, or place. An allusion to "thirty pieces of silver" brings to mind both the biblical character Judas and his act of betrayal. Authors employ allusions because they are economical ways to reinforce meaning or emotion. T. H. White's use of contemporary allusions to describe medieval life helps enliven his writing and establish a playful tone.

Writer's Notebook

A Man of Honor For many readers, Launcelot represents the ideal knight. Make a web of characteristics you associate with a "knight in shining armor" and be prepared to explain each trait. As you read the following excerpts, add other qualities that Launcelot exhibits.

Before Reading

Building Background

Have students brainstorm legends, stories from the American West, books or movies that involve a quest or journey.

Literary Focus

For students who are not familiar with this **allusion,** refer them to The Gospel of Matthew, "The Death of Jesus" on the Custom Literature Database.

Writer's Notebook

Start the discussion by playing the following songs. Invite student reaction.

- "C'est Moi"—Lancelot's introduction of himself in the musical *Camelot*
- "My White Knight"—Marian's description of her ideal man from *The Music Man*

More About T. H. White

"The best thing for being sad . . . is to learn something. That is the only thing that never fails," White wrote in *The Once and Future King.* Learning was a true mission for White who mastered such skills as archery, oil painting, reading medieval Latin shorthand, and flying an airplane.

Other books by White include

- *Mistress Masham's Repose,* (1946)
- *The Master: An Adventure Story,* (1957)

SUPPORT MATERIALS OVERVIEW

Unit 3 Resource Book
- Graphic Organizer, p. 17
- Study Guide, p. 18
- Vocabulary, p. 19
- Grammar, p. 20
- Alternate Check Test, p. 21
- Vocabulary Test, p. 22
- Selection Test, pp. 23–24

Building English Proficiency
- Literature Summaries
- Activities, p. 194

Reading, Writing & Grammar SkillBook
- Vocabulary, pp. 7–8
- Reading, pp. 76–78
- Grammar, Usage, and Mechanics, pp. 173–174

Technology
- Audiotapes 9, Side B, and 10, Side A
- Personal Journal Software
- Custom Literature Database: For more about heroes, see works by Malory and Howard Pyle on the database.
- Test Generator Software

During Reading

Selection Objectives

- to explore the theme of Arthurian legend
- to recognize and understand literary allusions
- to identify singular and plural nouns

Unit 3 Resource Book
Graphic Organizer, p. 17
Study Guide, p. 18

Theme Link

Malory and White reveal how Launcelot answered the call to become the best knight in Camelot.

Vocabulary Preview

impale, pierce through with something pointed
melée, confused fight
prowess, bravery; skill
shillelagh, club used in fights
unfledged, inexperienced

Students can add the words and definitions to their Writer's Notebooks.

1 Historical Note
The Round Table

The Round Table is said by Malory to have been a wedding present from Gwynevere's father to Arthur. It was the table at which the full company of the king's knights were to sit—one hundred and fifty in all. Because it was round, no knight seated at it could have precedence over another, for it had no head and no foot.

EDITORIAL NOTE Variant spellings for *Lancelot* are used.

THE TALE OF SIR LAUNCELOT DU LAKE

SIR THOMAS MALORY

1 When King Arthur returned from Rome he settled his court at Camelot, and there gathered about him his knights of the Round Table, who diverted[1] themselves with jousting and tournaments. Of all his knights one was supreme, both in prowess[2] at arms and in nobility of bearing, and this was Sir Launcelot, who was also the favorite of Queen Gwynevere, to whom he had sworn oaths of fidelity.

One day Sir Launcelot, feeling weary of his life at the court, and of only playing at arms, decided to set forth in search of adventure. He asked his nephew Sir Lyonel to accompany him, and when both were suitably armed and mounted, they rode off together through the forest.

At noon they started across a plain, but the intensity of the sun made Sir Launcelot feel sleepy, so Sir Lyonel suggested that they should rest beneath the shade of an apple tree that grew by a hedge not far from the road. They dismounted, tethered their horses, and settled down.

"Not for seven years have I felt so sleepy," said Sir Launcelot, and with that fell fast asleep, while Sir Lyonel watched over him.

Soon three knights came galloping past, and Sir Lyonel noticed that they were being pursued by a fourth knight, who was one of the most powerful he had yet seen. The pursuing knight overtook each of the others in turn, and as he did so, knocked each off his horse with a thrust of his spear. When all three lay stunned he dismounted, bound them securely to their horses with the reins, and led them away.

Without waking Sir Launcelot, Sir Lyonel mounted his horse and rode after the knight, and as soon as he had drawn close enough, shouted his challenge. The knight turned about and they charged at each other, with the result that Sir Lyonel was likewise flung from his horse, bound, and led away a prisoner.

The victorious knight, whose name was Sir Tarquine, led his prisoners to his castle, and there threw them on the ground, stripped them naked, and beat them with thorn twigs. After that he locked them in the dungeon where many other prisoners, who had received like treatment, were complaining dismally.

Meanwhile, Sir Ector de Marys,[3] who liked to accompany Sir Launcelot on his adventures, and finding him gone, decided to ride after him. Before long he came upon a forester.

"My good fellow, if you know the forest hereabouts, could you tell me in which direction I am most likely to meet with adventure?"

1. **divert** (də vėrt′), *v.* amuse; entertain.
2. prowess (prou′is), *n.* bravery; skill.
3. **Sir Ector de Marys,** Sir Launcelot's half-brother.

SELECTION SUMMARY

The Tale of Sir Launcelot du Lake, from The Once and Future King

In Malory's account, Sir Launcelot, praised as the supreme knight of the Round Table, seeks adventure. His companion, Lyonel is captured by opposing knights and imprisoned in the castle of Sir Tarquine along with other knights of the Round Table. In the attempt to defeat Tarquine, Sir Ector de Marys also is imprisoned. At the same time, four queens, including Morgan le Fay, have taken Launcelot to their castle as a prisoner. He escapes with the help of the daughter of King Bagdemagus, and then fights for her father in a tournament. He goes on to defeat Tarquine and free the prisoners.

White's account relates the same adventures in the tone of a modern, somewhat amused observer.

For summaries in other languages, see the ***Building English Proficiency*** *book.*

"Sir, I can tell you: Less than a mile from here stands a well-moated castle. On the left of the entrance you will find a ford where you can water your horse, and across from the ford a large tree from which hang shields of many famous knights. Below the shields hangs a caldron, of copper and brass: strike it three times with your spear, and then surely you will meet with adventure—such, indeed, that if you sur-
2 vive it, you will prove yourself the foremost knight in these parts for many years."

"May God reward you!" Sir Ector replied.

The castle was exactly as the forester had described it, and among the shields Sir Ector recognized several as belonging to knights of the Round Table. After watering his horse, he knocked on the caldron and Sir Tarquine, whose castle it was, appeared.

They jousted, and at the first encounter Sir Ector sent his opponent's horse spinning twice about before he could recover.

"That was a fine stroke; now let us try again," said Sir Tarquine.

This time Sir Tarquine caught Sir Ector just below the right arm and, having impaled[4] him
3 on his spear, lifted him clean out of the saddle, and rode with him into the castle, where he threw him on the ground.

"Sir," said Sir Tarquine, "you have fought better than any knight I have encountered in the last twelve years; therefore, if you wish, I will demand no more of you than your parole[5] as my prisoner."

"Sir, that I will never give."

"Then I am sorry for you," said Sir Tarquine, and with that he stripped and beat him and locked him in the dungeon with the other prisoners. There Sir Ector saw Sir Lyonel.

"Alas, Sir Lyonel, we are in a sorry plight. But tell me, what has happened to Sir Launcelot? For he surely is the one knight who could save us."

"I left him sleeping beneath an apple tree, and what has befallen him since I do not know," Sir Lyonel replied; and then all the unhappy prisoners once more bewailed their lot.

While Sir Launcelot still slept beneath the apple tree, four queens started across the plain. They were riding white mules and accompanied by four knights who held above them, at the tips
of their spears, a green silk canopy, to protect 4
them from the sun. The party was startled by the neighing of Sir Launcelot's horse and, changing direction, rode up to the apple tree, where they discovered the sleeping knight. And as each of the queens gazed at the handsome Sir Launcelot, so each wanted him for her own.

"Let us not quarrel," said Morgan le Fay.[6] "Instead, I will cast a spell over him so that he remains asleep while we take him to my castle and make him our prisoner. We can then oblige him to choose one of us for his paramour."[7]

Sir Launcelot was laid on his shield and borne by two of the knights to the Castle Charyot, which was Morgan le Fay's stronghold. He awoke to find himself in a cold cell, where a young noblewoman was serving him supper.

"What cheer?" she asked.

"My lady, I hardly know, except that I must have been brought here by means of an enchantment."

"Sir, if you are the knight you appear to be, you will learn your fate at dawn tomorrow." And with that the young noblewoman left him. Sir Launcelot spent an uncomfortable night but at dawn the four queens presented themselves and Morgan le Fay spoke to him:

"Sir Launcelot, I know that Queen Gwynevere loves you, and you her. But now you are my prisoner, and you will have to choose: either to take one of us for your paramour, or to die miserably in this cell—just as you please.

---

4. **impale** (im pāl′), *v.* pierce through with something pointed.
5. **parole** (pə rōl′), *n.* word [*French*]; here, word of honor not to escape.
6. **Morgan le Fay,** a sorceress, half-sister of King Arthur.
7. **paramour** (par′ə mür), *n.* lover.

2 Reading/Thinking Skills
Infer

Question What can you infer from Sir Ector's statement about his opinion of this adventure? *(Possible response: The defender of the castle is a great warrior, perhaps one that no one can defeat.)*

3 Literary Element
Plot

Question What effect does this event—Sir Ector's defeat at the hands of Sir Tarquine—have on the plot? *(Possible response: By showing that Tarquine can defeat a great knight like Ector, Malory increases tension; now the reader knows that Launcelot is the only hope.)*

4 Historical Note
The Color Green

In European culture, green is sometimes associated with evil and temptation. In *Sir Gawain and the Green Knight,* Gawain is tested by a Green Knight and tempted by the green kirtle of the Green Knight's wife. Students may be familiar with the witch called "The Lady of the Green Kirtle" in C. S. Lewis's Narnia book, *The Silver Chair.*

For stories about sir Gawain, see the Custom Literature Database.

BUILDING ENGLISH PROFICIENCY

ESL LEP ELD SAE LD

Sequencing Story Events

Often the introduction of characters and action seems to "interrupt" the main story line. Help students create a flowchart tracking the different paths the characters take during the sequence of events in this Arthurian tale. You may wish to point out that the events are a series of adventures, but that in Malory's account, "adventure" might mean "knightly service."

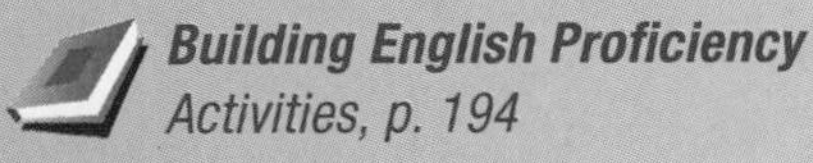

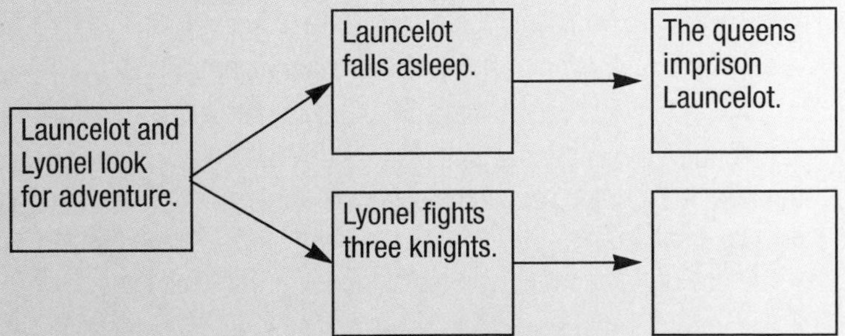

5 Literary Element
Style

Point out to students that Malory's account holds to conventions of the Arthurian legend. Magic is one such element. It is used for good by Merlin and for evil by others. Justice being settled by a fight is also typical. The accuser and accused each chose a champion, and the two champions fought. The person whose champion won was assumed to be in the right.

6 Reading/Thinking Skills
Make Judgments

Have students discuss Launcelot's conflict in attempting to fulfill the chivalric code. He is bound to be loyal to his fellow knights of the Round Table, yet he is also bound to help a lady who needs him. Which, in students' opinions, is the proper course of action?

7 Literary Element
Character

Questions

- Why does Launcelot disguise himself for the battle? *(to avoid recognition by his fellow knights whom he must oppose)*
- What do you think this says about the character of Launcelot? *(Some students may feel this is a clever solution; others may say he is deceitful.)*

Now I will tell you who we are: I am Morgan le Fay, Queen of Gore; my companions are the Queens of North Galys, of Estelonde, and of the Outer Isles. So make your choice."

5 "A hard choice! Understand that I choose none of you, lewd sorceresses that you are; rather will I die in this cell. But were I free, I would take pleasure in proving it against any who would champion you that Queen Gwynevere is the finest lady of this land."

"So, you refuse us?" asked Morgan le Fay.

"On my life, I do," Sir Launcelot said finally, and so the queens departed.

Sometime later, the young noblewoman who had served Sir Launcelot's supper reappeared.

"What news?" she asked.

"It is the end," Sir Launcelot replied.

6 "Sir Launcelot, I know that you have refused the four queens, and that they wish to kill you out of spite. But if you will be ruled by me, I can save you. I ask that you will champion my father at a tournament next Tuesday, when he has to combat the King of North Galys, and three knights of the Round Table, who last Tuesday defeated him ignominiously."[8]

"My lady, pray tell me, what is your father's name?"

"King Bagdemagus."

"Excellent, my lady, I know him for a good king and a true knight, so I shall be happy to serve him."

"May God reward you! And tomorrow at dawn I will release you, and direct you to an abbey which is ten miles from here, and where the good monks will care for you while I fetch my father."

"I am at your service, my lady."

As promised, the young noblewoman released Sir Launcelot at dawn. When she had led him through the twelve doors to the castle entrance, she gave him his horse and armor, and directions for finding the abbey.

"God bless you, my lady; and when the time comes I promise I shall not fail you."

Sir Launcelot rode through the forest in search of the abbey, but at dusk had still failed to find it, and coming upon a red silk pavilion, apparently unoccupied, decided to rest there overnight, and continue his search in the morning. . . .

As soon as it was daylight, Sir Launcelot armed, mounted, and rode away in search of the abbey, which he found in less than two hours. King Bagdemagus' daughter was waiting for him, and as soon as she heard his horse's footsteps in the yard, ran to the window, and, seeing that it was Sir Launcelot, herself ordered the servants to stable his horse. She then led him to her chamber, disarmed him, and gave him a long gown to wear, welcoming him warmly as she did so.

King Bagdemagus' castle was twelve miles away, and his daughter sent for him as soon as she had settled Sir Launcelot. The king arrived with his retinue[9] and embraced Sir Launcelot, who then described his recent enchantment, and the great obligation he was under to his daughter for releasing him.

"Sir, you will fight for me on Tuesday next?"

"Sire, I shall not fail you; but please tell me the names of the three Round Table knights whom I shall be fighting."

"Sir Modred, Sir Madore de la Porte, and Sir Gahalantyne. I must admit that last Tuesday they defeated me and my knights completely."

"Sire, I hear that the tournament is to be fought within three miles of the abbey. Could you send me three of your most trustworthy knights, clad in plain armor, and with no device,[10] and a fourth suit of armor which I 7
myself shall wear? We will take up our position just outside the tournament field and watch while you and the King of North Galys enter into combat with your followers; and then, as soon as you are in difficulties, we will come to

8. **ignominiously** (ig′nə min′ē əs lē), *v.* shamefully.
9. **retinue** (ret′n ü), *n.* followers, including friends, companions, and servants.
10. **device** (di vīs′), *n.* heraldic emblem of identification.

MINI-LESSON: GRAMMAR
Origins and Development of the English Language

Display the following sentences from page 360.

"My lady, pray tell me, what is your father's name?"

"I know him for a good king and a true knight."

Point out that the underlined expressions are not commonly heard in modern English, though some people still respond "God bless you" to a sneeze. Explain that:

- the use of the word pray in the sentence given is obsolete
- the phrase in the second sentence is no longer considered idiomatic—we use a different construction

Activity Idea Have students look through the selection and the earlier selection by Malory for other examples of usage that would not be heard today and paraphrase them in contemporary English.

This was a popular railway poster in 1924 by Maurice Greiffenhagen. Note how the curves of the horse's neck, the knight's helmet, and the archway unify the images of travel and adventure. Do you think the commercial purpose of this poster makes it any less effective as a work of art? Why or why not?

your rescue, and show your opponents what kind of knights you command."

This was arranged on Sunday, and on the following Tuesday Sir Launcelot and the three knights of King Bagdemagus waited in a copse,[11] not far from the pavilion which had been erected for the lords and ladies who were to judge the tournament and award the prizes.

The King of North Galys was the first on the field, with a company of ninescore[12] knights; he was followed by King Bagdemagus with fourscore[13] knights, and then by the three knights of the Round Table, who remained apart from both companies. At the first encounter King Bagdemagus lost twelve knights, all killed, and the King of North Galys six.

With that, Sir Launcelot galloped onto the field, and with his first spear unhorsed five of the King of North Galys' knights, breaking the backs of four of them. With his next spear he 8

11. **copse** (kops), *n.* clump of trees.
12. **ninescore** (nīn′skôr′), *n.* nine times twenty, or 180.
13. **fourscore** (fôr′skôr′), *n.* four times twenty, or 80.

Art Study

Response to Caption Questions
Some students may feel that a piece of artwork has a life of its own, apart from the artist's purpose, and may be a highly effective work of art. Allow students to react to the color, subject, and composition of the work, as apart from its purpose. Some students may point out that "commercial" does not necessarily imply "aesthetically diminished." They may point out that fine art is sometimes used to advertise showings at museums, thus acquiring a commercial purpose.

8 Historical Note
Unhorsed

Students may not be familiar with the verb *horse* meaning "to provide with a horse," of which this word is the antonym.

BUILDING ENGLISH PROFICIENCY

Building Vocabulary

Students acquiring English may find the language on pages 360–361, particularly the dialogue, hard to follow. Let them work together in pairs or small groups to "translate" the conversations into contemporary English.

1. Assign 10–15 lines to a pair or small group.
2. Have individuals first read aloud the whole passage while the group comments on the general meaning.
3. Encourage them to look up words with which they are unfamiliar.
4. As groups share their "translations," invite other students to suggest phrasing that would make the translations smoother.

9 Literary Element
Conflict

Students will recognize the conflict as one person against another. Let them go further by discussing how Malory establishes Launcelot as a legendary hero. Also let them decide what makes Tarquine a worthy opponent.

You may wish to note here that a miscreant is someone whose beliefs are in error—a heretic or wicked person. There is a definite heroes-and-villains theme in Arthurian legend, and most of those killed by the knights of the Round Table deserve to die by the standards of the day.

charged the king, and wounded him deeply in the thigh.

"That was a shrewd blow," commented Sir Madore, and galloped onto the field to challenge Sir Launcelot. But he too was tumbled from his horse, and with such violence that his shoulder was broken.

Sir Modred was the next to challenge Sir Launcelot, and he was sent spinning over his horse's tail. He landed head first, his helmet became buried in the soil, and he nearly broke his neck, and for a long time lay stunned.

> MY LADY, I AM RIDING IN SEARCH OF ADVENTURE . . .

Finally Sir Gahalantyne tried; at the first encounter both he and Sir Launcelot broke their spears, so both drew their swords and hacked vehemently at each other. But Sir Launcelot, with mounting wrath, soon struck his opponent a blow on the helmet which brought the blood streaming from eyes, ears, and mouth. Sir Gahalantyne slumped forward in the saddle, his horse panicked, and he was thrown to the ground, useless for further combat.

Sir Launcelot took another spear, and unhorsed sixteen more of the King of North Galys' knights, and with his next, unhorsed another twelve; and in each case with such violence that none of the knights ever fully recovered. The King of North Galys was forced to admit defeat, and the prize was awarded to King Bagdemagus.

That night Sir Launcelot was entertained as the guest of honor by King Bagdemagus and his daughter at their castle, and before leaving was loaded with gifts.

"My lady, please, if ever again you should need my services, remember that I shall not fail you."

The next day Sir Launcelot rode once more through the forest, and by chance came to the apple tree where he had previously slept. This time he met a young noblewoman riding a white palfrey.

"My lady, I am riding in search of adventure; pray tell me if you know of any I might find hereabouts."

"Sir, there are adventures hereabouts if you believe that you are equal to them; but please tell me, what is your name?"

"Sir Launcelot du Lake."

"Very well, Sir Launcelot, you appear to be a sturdy enough knight, so I will tell you. Not far away stands the castle of Sir Tarquine, a knight who in fair combat has overcome more than sixty opponents whom he now holds prisoner. Many are from the court of King Arthur, and if you can rescue them, I will then ask you to deliver me and my companions from a knight who distresses us daily, either by robbery or by other kinds of outrage." 9

"My lady, please first lead me to Sir Tarquine, then I will most happily challenge this miscreant knight of yours."

When they arrived at the castle, Sir Launcelot watered his horse at the ford, and then beat the caldron until the bottom fell out. However, none came to answer the challenge, so they waited by the castle gate for half an hour or so. Then Sir Tarquine appeared, riding toward the castle with a wounded prisoner slung over his horse, whom Sir Launcelot recognized as Sir Gaheris, Sir Gawain's brother and a knight of the Round Table.

"Good knight," said Sir Launcelot, "it is known to me that you have put to shame many of the knights of the Round Table. Pray allow your prisoner, who I see is wounded, to recover, while I vindicate the honor of the knights whom you have defeated."

MINI-LESSON: GRAMMAR

Singular and Plural Nouns

Read the following sentence from page 363 to students and display it on the board or overhead projector:

> "I know that among Sir Tarquine's prisoners are two of my brethren, Sir Lyonel and Sir Ector, also your own brother, Sir Gawain."

Point out that brethren is a plural form of brother, standard in Middle English, but now chiefly used in a religious sense.

Activity Idea Have students make a list of nouns with unusual plural forms (not ending in *-s*). Remind them to make the verbs agree when using these plural forms as subjects of sentences.

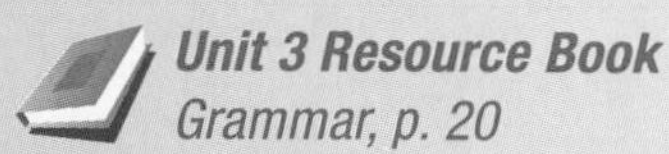

"I defy you, and all your fellowship of the Round Table," Sir Tarquine replied.

"You boast!" said Sir Launcelot.

At the first charge the backs of the horses were broken and both knights stunned. But they soon recovered and set to with their swords, and both struck so lustily[14] that neither shield nor armor could resist, and within two hours they were cutting each other's flesh, from which the blood flowed liberally. Finally they paused for a moment, resting on their shields.

"Worthy knight," said Sir Tarquine, "pray hold your hand for a while, and if you will, answer my question."

"Sir, speak on."

"You are the most powerful knight I have fought yet, but I fear you may be the one whom in the whole world I most hate. If you are not, for the love of you I will release all my prisoners and swear eternal friendship."

"What is the name of the knight you hate above all others?"

"Sir Launcelot du Lake; for it was he who slew my brother, Sir Carados of the Dolorous Tower, and it is because of him that I have killed a hundred knights, and maimed as many more, apart from the sixty-four I still hold prisoner. And so, if you are Sir Launcelot, speak up, for we must then fight to the death."

"Sir, I see now that I might go in peace and good fellowship, or otherwise fight to the death; but being the knight I am, I must tell you: I am Sir Launcelot du Lake, son of King Ban of
10 Benwick, of Arthur's court, and a knight of the Round Table. So defend yourself!"

"Ah! this is most welcome."

Now the two knights hurled themselves at each other like two wild bulls; swords and shields clashed together, and often their swords drove into the flesh. Then sometimes one, sometimes the other, would stagger and fall, only to recover immediately and resume the contest. At last, however, Sir Tarquine grew faint, and unwittingly lowered his shield, Sir Launcelot was swift to follow up his advantage, and dragging the other down to his knees, unlaced his helmet and beheaded him.

Sir Launcelot then strode over to the young noblewoman: "My lady, now I am at your service, but first I must find a horse."

Then the wounded Sir Gaheris spoke up: "Sir, please take my horse. Today you have overcome the most formidable knight, excepting only yourself, and by so doing have saved us all. But before leaving, please tell me your name."

"Sir Launcelot du Lake. Today I have fought to vindicate the honor of the knights of the Round Table, and I know that among Sir Tarquine's prisoners are two of my brethren, Sir Lyonel and Sir Ector, also your own brother, Sir Gawain. According to the shields there are also: Sir Brandiles, Sir Galyhuddis, Sir Kay, Sir Alydukis, Sir Marhaus, and many others. Please release the prisoners and ask them to help themselves to the castle treasure. Give them all my greetings and say I will see them at the next Pentecost. And please request Sir Ector and Sir Lyonel to go straight to the court and await me there."

When Sir Launcelot had ridden away with the young noblewoman, Sir Gaheris entered the castle, and finding the porter[15] in the hall, threw him on the ground and took the castle keys. He then released the prisoners, who, seeing his wounds, thanked him for their deliverance.

"Do not thank me for this work, but Sir Launcelot. He sends his greetings to you all, and asks you to help yourselves to the castle treasure. He has ridden away on another quest, but said that he will see you at the next Pentecost." . . . 11

Sir Launcelot returned to Camelot two days before the feast of Pentecost, and at the court was acclaimed by many of the knights he had met on his adventures.

14. **lustily** (lust′ə lē), *v.* vigorously.
15. **porter** (pôr′tər), *n.* gatekeeper.

10 Literary Element
Style

Ask students to recall the elements of Malory's prose they may have noted in his account of Arthur's birth and coronation. *(His style has little imagery and is episodic; its simplicity imparts a tone of stately importance to the events he relates.)* Call their attention to the simile "like two wild bulls" and discuss how the style is different. *(Realistic dialogue, hyperbole, and vivid details add dramatic tension missing from the earlier account.)*

11 Literary Focus
Allusion

Have students notice the allusion to "the next Pentecost." This refers to the yearly renewal of the Round Table oath and to the gathering associated with the ceremony. Pentecost is primarily an important religious holy day.

BUILDING ENGLISH PROFICIENCY

Exploring Infinitives

Reading pages 362–363 gives students the opportunity to discuss the adventures and explore the infinitive construction.

1. Read aloud the following sentence from page 362 and identify the infinitive: "That was a shrewd blow," commented Sir Marador, and galloped onto the field *to challenge* Sir Launcelot.

2. Explain that *to challenge* is an action typical of knightly adventures. Ask students to talk about when they have challenged someone. Mention that the infinitive is easily recognizable because it is composed of a verb and the word *to,* and that it is the base form of a verb.

3. Ask them to find other infinitive phrases on pages 362–363. These include: *to admit, to deliver* (p. 362); *to recover, to vindicate, to help* (p. 363). Let them practice using these verbs as infinitives or in other forms, for example, *to help, helped, has helped.*

4. Explain or act out the meanings of the words and ask students to talk about which knights performed the actions.

12 Historical Note
Defeat

Several different fates met knights who were defeated in battle in Arthurian legend. Sometimes they were killed, as Tarquine was. Sometimes they yielded and were taken as prisoners. At other times, they gave their word to be someone else's prisoner; for example, Launcelot might send knights he defeated to Camelot to kneel to Queen Gwynevere and do her bidding. They gave their word *(parole)*, and he released them, trusting them to follow his instructions.

12 Sir Gaheris described to the court the terrible battle Sir Launcelot had fought with Sir Tarquine, and how sixty-four prisoners had been freed as a result of his victory.

Sir Kay related how Sir Launcelot had twice saved his life, and then exchanged armor with him, so that he should ride unchallenged.

Sir Gawtere, Sir Gylmere, and Sir Raynolde described how he had defeated them at the bridge, and forced them to yield as prisoners of Sir Kay; and they were overjoyed to discover that it had been Sir Launcelot nevertheless.

> . . . Sir Launcelot became the most famous knight at King Arthur's court.

Sir Modred, Sir Mador, and Sir Gahalantyne described his tremendous feats in the battle against the King of North Galys; and Sir Launcelot himself described his enchantment by the four queens, and his rescue at the hands of the daughter of King Bagdemagus. . . .

And thus it was, at this time that Sir Launcelot became the most famous knight at King Arthur's court.

MINI-LESSON: GRAMMAR

Sentence Punctuation

Display the next to last sentence on page 364 on the board or overhead projector. Point out the ellipses at the end of the sentence. Explain that ellipses have two main functions.

- They can show a pause in dialogue.
- They can show that a section of text has been deleted.

Discuss other ways that breaks in a text are shown, for example, a line of asterisks or a large space in the text.

Activity Idea Ask students to think of reasons that parts might be deleted from the text. *(to provide the reader with the most pertinent information; to remove text that might be considered difficult; to make the text agree with an author's or editor's view)* Have students discuss what questions these deletions might bring up for the reader. *(Possible response: The reader may want to see an original source to understand the text fully.)*

THE ONCE AND FUTURE KING

T. H. WHITE

When the fair damsel came in with the next meal, she showed signs of wanting to talk to him. Lancelot[1] noticed that she was a bold creature, who was probably fond of getting her own way.

"You said you might be able to help me?"

The girl looked suspiciously at him and said: "I can help you if you are who you are supposed to be. Are you really Sir Lancelot?"

"I am afraid I am."

"I will help you," she said, "if you will help me."

Then she burst into tears.

While the damsel is weeping, which she did 13 in a charming and determined way, we had better explain about the tournaments which used to take place in Gramarye[2] in the early days. A real tournament was distinct from a joust. In a joust the knights tilted or fenced with each other singly, for a prize. But a tournament was more like a free fight. A body of knights would pick sides, so that there were twenty or thirty on either side, and then they would rush together harum-scarum. These mass battles were considered to be important—for instance, once you had paid your green fee for the tournament, you were admitted on the same ticket to fight in the jousts—but if you had only paid the jousting fee, you were not allowed to fight in the tourney. People were liable to be dangerously injured in the mêlées.[3] They were not bad things altogether, provided they were properly controlled. Unfortunately, in the early days, they were seldom controlled at all.

Merry England in Pendragon's time was a little like Poor Ould Ireland in O'Connell's.[4] There were factions. The knights of one county, or the inhabitants of one district, or the retainers[5] of one nobleman, might get themselves into a state in which they felt a hatred for the faction which lived next door. This hatred would 14 become a feud, and then the king or leader of the one place would challenge the leader of the other one to a tourney—and both factions would go to the meeting with full intent to do each other mischief. It was the same in the days of Papist and Protestant, or Stuart and

1. **Lancelot**, modern spelling of Launcelot.
2. **Gramarye** (gram′ər ē), a term White uses for the geographical area of England in which the events take place.
3. **mêlée** (mā′lā), *n.* confused fight.
4. **Pendragon's time . . . O'Connell's.** Pendragon is Uther Pendragon, Arthur's father. "Poor, Ould Ireland" in the time of Daniel O'Connell (1775-1847), Irish leader known as the "Liberator," was wracked by battles for the freedom of Ireland from Great Britain.
5. **retainer** (ri tā′nər), *n.* attendant who serves a person of rank.

13 Literary Element
Style

Point out to students the contrast between the way the narrator is presented here and in the other selections of Arthurian legend they have read. This narrator has a very different relationship with the reader—he is explicit about the fact that he is telling a story, and comes out of the story frame, as an actor would while speaking an *aside,* to explain historical and cultural details for the contemporary reader. He also provides more modern parallels to help the reader comprehend. Have students comment on the way this technique affects the story's tone.

14 Literary Focus
Allusion

Question In what tone of voice would you read these lines? Why? *(sarcastic, ironic; White's allusion to merry England is immediately contradicted by his description of feuding.)*

Students may be interested to learn that, according to the *Oxford English Dictionary, merry* in the term *Merry England* originally meant "pleasant, delightful in aspect or condition" and was used as early as the fourteenth century. Later, it was understood to mean "joyous."

BUILDING ENGLISH PROFICIENCY

Linking Past and Present

Use one or more of the following activities to help students relate some of the elements of White's story.

Activity Ideas

- Invite students to visualize and make comments about White's description of a tournament. Also refer to Malory's account on pages 361–362. Ask: What sporting event does a tournament remind you of? How is it similar to or different from a modern professional sporting event?
- White describes the England of that era as filled with factional strife. Encourage students to relate that situation to current events or to the history of their various homelands.

Art Study

Responses to Caption Questions
Possible responses: Lancelot's swoon, or fainting, may be a sign of his devotion, purity of intention, or exhaustion from his amazing feats.

15 Literary Element
Characterization

Question How do these actions characterize Sir Lancelot? *(Possible response: He is honorable and generous—he prevents the noblewoman from having to request his help by offering it. He is somewhat funny since he is so careful to do what is expected of a knight.)*

16 Literary Element
Style

Question How is White's purpose different from Malory's? *(Possible response: Malory is chronicling Arthurian legend in English, paying attention to detail. White is amusing the reader by making the characters human and less heroic than we'd expect them to be.)*

This battle scene from *Le Roman de Lancelot du Lac*, completed in the early 1300s, depicts Lancelot fighting for King Bagdemagus, as the queen and her ladies look on. After defeating all challengers, Lancelot allegedly faints when he sees the queen. What does his behavior indicate about chivalry in general and Lancelot in particular? ➤

Orangeman,[6] who would meet together with shillelaghs[7] in their hands and murder in their hearts.

"Why are you crying?" asked Sir Lancelot.

"Oh dear," sobbed the damsel. "That horrid King of Northgalis has challenged my father to a tournament next Tuesday, and he has got three knights of King Arthur's on his side, and my poor father is bound to lose. I am afraid he will get hurt."

"I see. And what is your father's name?"

"He is King Bagdemagus."

15 Sir Lancelot got up and kissed her politely on the forehead. He saw at once what he was expected to do.

"Very well," he said. "If you can rescue me out of this prison, I will fight in the faction of King Bagdemagus next Tuesday."

"Oh, thank you," said the maiden, wringing out her handkerchief. "Now I must go, I am afraid, or they will miss me downstairs."

Naturally she was not going to help the magic Queen of Northgalis to keep Lancelot in prison—when it was the King of

6. **Papist . . . Orangemen,** references to religious disputes and wars in British history between Roman Catholics (sometimes called Papists) and Protestants. The royal Stuart family included James II, who reigned 1685-1688 and had Catholic sympathies. He was forcibly replaced by the Dutch Protestant, William of Orange, whose reign lasted 1689-1702.
7. **shillelagh** (shə lā′lē), *n.* a club used in fights.

MINI-LESSON: LITERARY FOCUS

Allusions

Read the following sentence from pages 365–366:

"It was the same in the days of Papist and Protestant, or Stuart and Orangeman, who would meet together with shillelaghs in their hands and murder in their hearts."

Explain that this is an allusion—a reference to a real, mythical, or literary event, thing, person, or place outside the context of the story being told. Point out that in this case, the introductory words of the sentence make it clear that White is using an allusion. Other signals include quotation marks, and references to proper nouns that are outside the story context.

Activity Idea Divide students into small groups. Give each group a copy of White's book *The Once and Future King*, and assign each group one of the four sections of the book. Have each group find 5–10 allusions and write an explanation of each allusion they identify.

16

Northgalis himself who was going to fight her father. . . .

There is no need to give a long description of the tourney. Malory gives it. Lancelot picked three knights who were recommended by the young damsel to go with him, and he arranged that all four of them should bear the vergescu. This was the white shield carried by unfledged[8] knights, and Lancelot insisted on this arrangement because he knew that three of his own brethren of the Round Table were going to fight on the other side. He did not want them to recognize him, because it might cause ill-feeling at court. On the other hand, he felt that it was his duty to fight against them because of the promise which he had given to the damsel. The King of Northgalis, who was the leader of the opposite side, had one hundred and sixty knights in his faction, and King Bagdemagus only had eighty. Lancelot went for the first knight of the Round Table, and put his shoulder out of joint. He went for the second one so hard that the unlucky fellow was carried over his horse's tail and buried his helm[9] several inches in the ground. He hit the third knight on the head so hard that his nose bled, and his horse ran away with him. By the time he had broken the thigh of the King of Northgalis, everybody could see that to all intents and purposes[10] the tournament was over.

8. **unfledged** (un flejd′), *adj.* inexperienced.
9. **helm** (helm), *n.* helmet. [*Old English*]
10. **to all intents and purposes,** in almost every way.

Check Test

1. What kind of tree did Launcelot sleep under? *(apple)*

2. Why did Tarquine hate Launcelot? *(Launcelot had killed Tarquine's brother.)*

3. How was a joust different from a tournament? *(A joust was a contest between two knights for a prize. A tournament was a free fight.)*

4. How many knights did the King of Northgalis have? *(160)*

5. Which knights did Lancelot fight with? *(the three knights from the Round Table and the King)*

Unit 3 Resource Book
Alternate Check Test, p. 21

BUILDING ENGLISH PROFICIENCY

Exploring Tone

To help students understand that White's tone is light and tongue-in-cheek, have them act out the events on pp. 366–367.

1. Ask students to pay particular attention to words and phrases that tell *how* characters do things. For example, the girl's handkerchief is so sodden from crying that she must "wring it out."

2. Let them act, leading them, if necessary, to present exaggerated portrayals.

3. Students may enjoy listening to a recording of "C'est Moi" and "Then You May Take Me to the Fair" from the musical *Camelot.* These songs express the same tone as White's passage.

After Reading

MAKING CONNECTIONS

1. Students should explain what qualities of Launcelot the actor would portray well and on what information they are basing the character.

2. Possible responses: Chivalry today is seen when people are fair, good sports, and tolerant instead of violent. Or, a code of honor generally isn't followed as shown by prevalent cheating on tests.

3. Possible responses: He saves his comrades, fulfills his duty, and fights for a lady in distress.

4. Possible responses: The descriptions of the warrior's serious wounds and the beheading of Tarquine are violent; the image of the four queens riding on white mules under a green canopy is romantic.

5. While she seems helpless and weak, her determination suggests that Lancelot, the supposed strong one, will do whatever she wants.

6. She couldn't have cried enough to soak a handkerchief that much.

7. Possible examples: Malory's serious, dramatic tone is shown in Launcelot's speeches, such as ". . . I will most happily challenge this miscreant knight. . . ." White is humorous and ironic when describing the damsel as a "bold creature" rather than modest.

8. Students may think that a damsel is younger and that "my lady" is more formal and respectful.

9. Possible responses: sporting events, particularly boxing matches, fencing, and football; because people enjoy contests of physical strength

10. Possible responses: Launcelot's love for Gwynevere came at the expense of the welfare of the group; through his chivalric deeds, he put the welfare of the group first.

After Reading

Making Connections

Shaping Your Response

1. If you were a Hollywood director, what actor would you cast as Launcelot? Why?
2. Do you think that some aspects of chivalry displayed by Launcelot are still alive today? Explain.

Analyzing the Legends

3. In Malory's account, how does Launcelot display the codes of chivalry?
4. What evidence do you find to indicate that chivalry is both romantic and barbaric?
5. What is **ironic** about White's description of the damsel weeping in a "determined way"?
6. In what way is White's **image** of the damsel "wringing out her handkerchief" an example of **hyperbole,** or exaggeration?
7. What is the difference in **tone** between these two selections? Find passages that indicate each tone.
8. The daughter of King Bagdemagus is referred to as "my lady" in Malory's account, while White refers to her as a "damsel." What different associations do these terms have for you?

Extending the Ideas

9. What kinds of contests today are similar to the jousts and tournaments both authors describe? Why do you think such contests still exist?
10. Based on what you have learned about Launcelot, would you say that he pursued individual glory or the welfare of the **group**? Explain.

Literary Focus: Allusion

White uses the term "green fee," an **allusion** to a fee paid in order to play golf.

- What similarities do you think he is implying exist between a golf game and a medieval tournament?
- If someone called you a Launcelot, what do you think he or she would mean by this allusion?
- Why do you think White compares feuding medieval knights to battling factions from later centuries?

LITERARY FOCUS: ALLUSION

Possible responses:

- Golf is a leisure activity that can be expensive. White may be suggesting that just as nobles competed in tournaments, wealthier people today play golf.
- A Launcelot might be idealistic, athletic, willing to help others, and attractive to women.
- Perhaps White is suggesting that chivalry was an ideal that actual medieval life did not meet, and that centuries later nations are still struggling to meet that ideal.

Vocabulary Study

Write the letter of the most appropriate answer for each numbered item.

impale
mêlée
prowess
shillelagh
unfledged

1. When Launcelot was an *unfledged* knight, he had ____.
   a. fought many battles **b.** fought few battles
   c. just become married **d.** become injured
2. What could one use to *impale* a knight?
   a. a horse **b.** a coin **c.** a chess game **d.** a pointed object
3. A *mêlée* is a ____.
   a. small weapon **b.** sweet dessert **c.** confused fight **d.** sword
4. A knight who displayed his *prowess* would show his ____.
   a. beloved **b.** shield **c.** horse **d.** skill
5. Bagdemagus's *shillelagh* probably resembled a ____.
   a. baseball bat **b.** gremlin **c.** violin **d.** small animal

Expressing Your Ideas

Writing Choices

Writer's Notebook Update Now that you have read the selections, review your web about a knight. Would you add any other words? Which qualities do you consider important today? Write several sentences illustrating the observation: "Chivalry exists (does not exist) today."

Fair Maidens and Feminists Consider how women are portrayed in the selections about the Middle Ages that you have read so far. Do you think the status of females has changed in the past six centuries? Write an **opinion essay** that explains the steps women have taken forward or backward.

My Excellent Adventure Although you may not have encountered dragons or dungeons, you too have had adventures worthy of a knight. Write a brief **narrative** about a quest or battle in your life and your noble efforts to emerge victorious. Include an allusion to Arthur's time. Adopt a humorous tone if you wish.

Other Options

Lance and the Lakers Choose one episode from Launcelot's story and retell it in a modern setting. Suppose, for example, that King Bagdemagus were the owner of a professional basketball team. How would Lance Lott be able to assist (or foil) him? Write a brief **screenplay** to videotape and present in class.

Looking for Something? Think about the Quest theme in movies, books, TV programs, and video games. Work with a group to present a **media resource list** of titles illustrating this theme. Accompany your list with a brief description of what each title is about.

Multicultural Quest Quiz What was the object of the quest in *Indiana Jones and the Last Crusade?* Who were the samurai? What was the Sumerian hero Gilgamesh seeking? Work with a group to make up a **trivia quiz** of quests and pursuits from around the world, both factual and fictional. Challenge your classmates to answer the quiz.

VOCABULARY STUDY

1. b
2. d
3. c
4. d
5. a

Unit 3 Resource Book
Vocabulary, p. 19
Vocabulary Test, p. 21

WRITING CHOICES

Fair Maidens and Feminists

If students do not mention it, point out that they have not read any selection by a medieval woman. Suggest that they may want to find and read at least one such source before they draw conclusions about the status of women at that time.

My Excellent Adventure

Prompt students to portray themselves as being complex, like Launcelot. As they characterize themselves in the adventure, suggest that they show their amazing strengths, and at least one unfortunate weakness.

Selection Test

Unit 3 Resource Book
pp. 23–24

OTHER OPTIONS

Lance and the Lakers

Students can begin by thinking about who can be considered a "knight in shining armor" today. What is the modern equivalent of a king? a tournament? Encourage students to make the dialogue of their screenplay fit the setting and characters.

Multicultural Quest Quiz

Folklore collections from other countries can be used to find out about

- Sundiata, King of Mali, returning to claim his kingdom
- Odysseus trying to get home from the Trojan War
- Moses leading the Hebrew people out of Egypt

Before Reading

Building Background

For more information about Middle English, see "Introduction" pages 17–18 of *Sir Thomas Malory: Tales of King Arthur* edited and abridged by Michael Senior, Schocken, 1981.

Literary Focus

As an exercise, ask students to imagine that someone's address is 10 Cambridge Street, and then say the address, substituting the following for "Street": road, lane, square, avenue, boulevard. Ask them to explain **connotations** of the various versions.

Writer's Notebook

Point out to students that our culture emphasizes the counterpoint of good guy-bad guy, from the understanding of God and the Devil to the game of cops and robbers. Explain that not all cultures have pairs like these.

More About Alfred, Lord Tennyson

Before Tennyson had turned thirteen, he had written poetry in the styles of Alexander Pope, Sir Walter Scott, and John Milton. Other works by Tennyson include *The Poems of Tennyson*, ed. Christopher Ricks, London, 1969.

Before Reading

The Death of King Arthur by Sir Thomas Malory Great Britain

from Idylls of the King by Alfred, Lord Tennyson Great Britain

Alfred, Lord Tennyson
1809–1893

Just as another boy might train to be an athlete or singer, the young Tennyson focused on becoming a poet, writing an epic poem of six thousand lines by the age of twelve. More than any other poet of the nineteenth century, he became the voice of the Victorian Age, representing its hopes as well as its concerns about the conflict between emerging scientific principles and religion. In 1850 he became England's poet laureate. A man of dignity, courage, and devotion to duty, it seems appropriate that Tennyson chose to explore Arthurian tales in his own poetic narrative, *Idylls of the King.*

Building Background

Malory and Middle English Sir Thomas Malory wrote *Le Morte d'Arthur* in Middle English. The following passage describes — in Malory's original language — a scene you will encounter in the next selection. Try reading this passage aloud and translating it. Then compare it to the translation that appears at the bottom of column 1 on page 376.

THAN SIR BEDWERE . . . BOUNDE THE GYRDYLL ABOUTE THE HYLTIS, AND THREW THE SWERDE AS FARRE INTO THE WATIR AS HE MYGHT. AND THERE CAM AN ARME AND AN HONDE ABOVE THE WATIR, AND TOKE HIT AND CLEYGHT HIT, AND SHOKE HIT THRYSE AND BRAUNDYSSHED, AND THAN VANYSSHED WITH THE SWERDE INTO THE WATIR.

Literary Focus

Denotation and Connotation If you look up the word *car* in a dictionary, you will find it described something like this: "a four-wheeled passenger vehicle driven by an internal combustion engine." Yet this word may suggest other things to you: *freedom, expense, independence, power, speed, being sixteen.* The dictionary definition of a word is its **denotation.** The associations and added meanings are its **connotations.** Be on the lookout in the following selections for words such as *chains, dawn, king, flag,* and *sword,* which are rich in connotations.

Writer's Notebook

Batman Needs the Joker In the selection by Malory that you are about to read, you will meet a classic villain, Sir Modred, King Arthur's illegitimate son and rival. Before starting to read, jot down the names of hero/villain pairs from literature, TV, video games, and movies. Think about why so many stories have such pairs.

SUPPORT MATERIALS OVERVIEW

Unit 3 Resource Book
- Graphic Organizer, p. 25
- Study Guide, p. 26
- Vocabulary, p. 27
- Grammar, p. 28
- Alternate Check Test, p. 29
- Vocabulary Test, p. 30
- Selection Test, pp. 31–32

Building English Proficiency
- Literature Summaries
- Activities, p. 195

Reading, Writing & Grammar SkillBook
- Vocabulary, pp. 5–6
- Grammar, Usage, and Mechanics, pp. 259–260

The World of Work
- Marine Recruiter, p. 11
- Project Plan, p. 12

Technology
- Audiotape 10, Sides A and B
- Personal Journal Software
- Custom Literature Database: For more poems by Tennyson, see the database.
- Test Generator Software

The Death of King Arthur

Sir Thomas Malory

The beginning of the end of Arthur's reign comes with the discovery by knights of the Round Table of the love between Launcelot and Gwynevere. Arthur feels forced by law to burn his wife at the stake. Launcelot saves Gwynevere at the last moment, but in the process kills two brothers of Gawain, Arthur's favorite nephew. Arthur leads an attack on Launcelot in France, but Launcelot seriously wounds Gawain. While Arthur is away in France, Modred, Arthur's mean-spirited illegitimate son, seizes the throne. Arthur hastens back to England.

During the absence of King Arthur from Britain, Sir Modred, already vested with sovereign powers, had decided to usurp[1] the throne. Accordingly, he had false letters written—announcing the death of King Arthur in battle—and delivered to himself. Then, calling a parliament, he ordered the letters to be read and persuaded the nobility to elect him king. The coronation took place at Canterbury and was celebrated with a fifteen-day feast. 1

Sir Modred then settled in Camelot and made overtures to Queen Gwynevere to marry him. The queen seemingly acquiesced, but as soon as she had won his confidence, begged leave to make a journey to London in order to prepare her trousseau. Sir Modred consented, and the queen rode straight to the Tower[2] which, with the aid of her loyal nobles, she manned and provisioned for her defense.

Sir Modred, outraged, at once marched against her, and laid siege to the Tower, but despite his large army, siege engines,[3] and guns, was unable to effect a breach. He then tried to entice[4] the queen from the Tower, first by guile[5] and then by threats, but she would listen to neither. Finally the Archbishop of Canterbury came forward to protest:

"Sir Modred, do you not fear God's displeasure?. . . If you do not

1. usurp (yü zėrp′), *v.* seize by force.
2. **Tower,** Tower of London, a stronghold of several buildings located on the banks of the Thames River.
3. **siege engines,** mechanical equipment such as catapults.
4. entice (en tīs′), *v.* tempt; lure.
5. guile (gīl), *n.* sly trick; cunning.

During Reading

Selection Objectives

- to explore Arthurian legend
- to understand connotation and denotation
- to capitalize titles when they appear as part of proper nouns

Unit 3 Resource Book
Graphic Organizer, p. 25
Study Guide, p. 26

Theme Link

When Arthur discovers he is dying, he leaves England to answer a new call, leaving his name immortalized in legend.

Vocabulary Preview

carnage, slaughter of a great number of people
dauntless, brave
ensue, follow
entice, tempt; lure
guile, sly trick; cunning
usurp, seize by force

Students can add the words and definitions to their Writer's Notebooks.

1 Reading/Thinking Skills
Infer

Question

- What do you infer is the basis of Modred's power? *(Possible responses: force, intimidation)*
- How is this similar to or different from Arthur's rule? *(Possible responses: Arthur's right to rule derived from his lineage, and Modred used his birthright as part of his ruse to take the throne; Arthur strove to rule by developing just laws and holding up the ideals of the Round Table; Modred chose to defy ideals in favor of force.)*

SELECTION SUMMARY

The Death of King Arthur, Idylls of the King

The mean-spirited Sir Modred, Arthur's bastard son, seizes the throne. Battles and the tragic deaths of many knights ensue. Finally, in a great battle, Arthur's troops are slaughtered. Only four men are left—Modred, Arthur, Sir Bedivere, and Sir Lucas. Arthur, feeling that it is his responsibility to prevent more evil, kills Modred, but receives a death wound from him. Arthur orders Sir Bedivere to throw Excalibur into the lake and a hand rises from beneath the water to grasp it. Finally, Arthur is borne away on a barge. His tomb at Glastonbury is inscribed: "Here lies Arthur, the once and future king."

In a scene from *Idylls of the King,* Tennyson shows Arthur and Bedivere talking just before the dying king departs on the barge for the mythical island of Avalon, here spelled Avilion.

*For summaries in other languages, see the **Building English Proficiency** book.*

2 Reading/Thinking Skills
Compare and Contrast

At this point you may wish to discuss the inferences made about Modred's rule and compare them with the reasons Malory gives.

3 Reading/Thinking Skills
Make Judgments

Question Do you agree with Gawain that the blame is his? Why or why not? *(Possible responses: Some students may agree; others may say that if Launcelot and Gwynevere had not done anything blameworthy in the first place, there would have been no reason to burn the queen, so the guilt is theirs. Others may say that the fact that there was so much support for Modred indicates that there was fundamental unrest that would have surfaced sooner or later.)*

4 Literary Element
Characterization

Question What traits do Arthur and Gawain exhibit through this moving dialogue? *(Possible responses: They are heroic, compassionate, respectful, generous of spirit, and forgiving.)*

revoke your evil deeds I shall curse you with bell, book, and candle."[6]

"Fie on you! Do your worst!" Sir Modred replied.

"Sir Modred, I warn you take heed! Or the wrath of the Lord will descend upon you."

"Away, false priest, or I shall behead you!"

The Archbishop withdrew, and after excommunicating[7] Sir Modred, abandoned his office and fled to Glastonbury.[8] There he took up his abode as a simple hermit, and by fasting and
2 prayer sought divine intercession in the troubled affairs of his country.

Sir Modred tried to assassinate the Archbishop, but was too late. He continued to assail[9] the queen with entreaties and threats, both of which failed, and then the news reached him that King Arthur was returning with his army from France in order to seek revenge.

Sir Modred now appealed to the barony to support him, and it has to be told that they came forward in large numbers to do so. Why? it will be asked. Was not King Arthur, the noblest sovereign Christendom had seen, now leading his armies in a righteous cause? The answer lies in the people of Britain, who, then as now, were fickle. Those who so readily transferred their allegiance to Sir Modred did so with the excuse that whereas King Arthur's reign had led them into war and strife, Sir Modred promised them peace and festivity.

Hence it was with an army of a hundred thousand that Sir Modred marched to Dover[10] to battle against his own father, and to withhold from him his rightful crown.

As King Arthur with his fleet drew into the harbor, Sir Modred and his army launched forth in every available craft, and a bloody battle ensued[11] in the ships and on the beach. If King Arthur's army were the smaller, their courage was the higher, confident as they were of the righteousness of their cause. Without stint they battled through the burning ships, the screaming wounded, and the corpses floating on the blood-stained waters. Once ashore they put Sir Modred's entire army to flight.

The battle over, King Arthur began a search for his casualties, and on peering into one of the ships found Sir Gawain, mortally wounded. Sir Gawain fainted when King Arthur lifted him in his arms; and when he came to, the king spoke:

"Alas! dear nephew, that you lie here thus, mortally wounded! What joy is now left to me on this earth? You must know it was you and Sir Launcelot I loved above all others, and it seems that I have lost you both."

"My good uncle, it was my pride and my stub- 3
bornness that brought all this about, for had I not urged you to war with Sir Launcelot your subjects would not now be in revolt. Alas, that Sir Launcelot is not here, for he would soon drive them out! And it is at Sir Launcelot's hands that I suffer my own death: the wound which he dealt me has reopened. I would not wish it otherwise, because is he not the greatest and gentlest of knights?

"I know that by noon I shall be dead, and I repent bitterly that I may not be reconciled to Sir Launcelot; therefore I pray you, good uncle,
give me pen, paper, and ink so that I may write 4
to him."

A priest was summoned and Sir Gawain confessed;[12] then a clerk brought ink, pen, and

6. **curse you with bell, book and candle,** expulsion from the Catholic Church. After pronouncing sentence, the officiating cleric closes his book, quenches the candle by throwing it to the ground, and tolls the bell as for one who has died.
7. **excommunicating** (ek′skə myü′nə kā′ting), *n.* severing from membership in the church.
8. **Glastonbury,** a town in present-day Somerset and the site of an ancient abbey thought in legends to be the burial place of King Arthur.
9. **assail** (ə sāl′), *v.* attack with hostile words, arguments, or abuse.
10. **Dover,** port city on the south coast of England, across from France.
11. **ensue** (en sü′), *v.* follow.
12. **confess** (kən fes′), *v.* make a confession to a priest.

MINI-LESSON: GRAMMAR
Capitalization of Titles

Display the following sentences from page 371 on the board or the overhead projector:

"Sir Modred then settled in Camelot and made overtures to Queen Gwynevere to marry him. The queen seemingly acquiesced, but as soon as she had won his confidence, begged leave to make a journey to London in order to prepare her trousseau."

Ask students to find a word that appears capitalized in one place, but lower case in another. Explain that titles, such as *queen* are capitalized when they are part of a proper noun—the name of a particular person, place, or thing, but not when they are used as common nouns to name a general class of people, places, or things.

Activity Idea As an exercise, students can proofread their own writing for correct capitalization of titles. Have them check their Writer's Notebooks and other assignments done during the unit on the Arthurian legend in which they used words in titles and as common nouns.

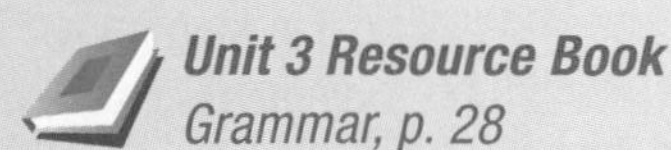

Unit 3 Resource Book
Grammar, p. 28

What details in *Le Morte D'Arthur*, painted in 1861 by James Archer, suggest hope? Who do you think the figures in the background might be?

paper, and Sir Gawain wrote to Sir Launcelot as follows:

"Sir Launcelot, flower of the knighthood: I, Sir Gawain, son of King Lot of Orkney and of King Arthur's sister, send you my greetings!

"I am about to die; the cause of my death is the wound I received from you outside the city of Benwick; and I would make it known that my death was of my own seeking, that I was moved by the spirit of revenge and spite to provoke you
5 to battle.

"Therefore, Sir Launcelot, I beseech you to visit my tomb and offer what prayers you will on my behalf; and for myself, I am content to die at the hands of the noblest knight living.

"One more request: that you hasten with your armies across the sea and give succor[13] to our noble king. Sir Modred, his bastard son, has usurped the throne and now holds against him with an army of a hundred thousand. He would have won the queen, too, but she fled to the Tower of London and there charged her loyal
supporters with her defense. 6

"Today is the tenth of May, and at noon I shall give up the ghost; this letter is written partly with my blood. This morning we fought our way ashore, against the armies of Sir Modred, and that is how my wound came to be

13. **succor** (suk′ər), *n.* assistance.

Art Study

Responses to Caption Questions
Hope is suggested by the soft colors on the horizon, the peaceful mood, the angel who appears on the right holding the grail, and the tender care the queens are lavishing on Arthur. The figures may be Merlin and Nimue.

5 Reading/Thinking Skills
Predict

Questions

- Do you think Launcelot will come? Why? *(Possible responses: No, he has no reason to trust Gawain. Yes, Gawain gives too many reasons for him not to come.)*
- Which of Gawain's reasons do you think would be most persuasive to Launcelot? *(Possible responses: Gwynevere being in danger; Arthur's being in danger; the danger to the society of the Round Table)*

6 Literary Element
Allusion

Students may be interested to know that Sir Gawain alludes to noon because an enchantment had been cast on him when he was a youth. This spell causes his strength to increase for three hours each morning, reaching a peak at noon, and then decreasing. Arthur understands the allusion to mean that Gawaine will be doubly weakened at noon, and die.

BUILDING ENGLISH PROFICIENCY

Exploring Leadership

Write the word *king* on the board. Invite students to suggest other terms and titles for this position. Encourage students to mention words from other languages and other eras. Prompt them with questions such as:

- What rulers do you know of?
- What are their titles?
- In your opinion, what would make you follow a leader, and what would turn you away from one?

In the discussion, encourage students to use Arthur and his ideals as examples.

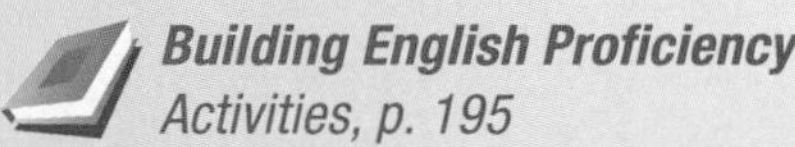

Building English Proficiency
Activities, p. 195

7 Literary Element
Allusion

Extreme Unction is the sacrament in which a priest anoints and prays for someone in danger of death. It is believed that this ritual will either help the person through the dying process or give them strength to live.

8 Literary Element
Sensory Details

Invite students to visualize or even draw this vivid dream. Point out that Malory's audience would assume that any dream mentioned in a romance would be a prophetic one. Discuss what the dream prophesies. *(Arthur's death and the destruction of the Round Table)*

9 Reader's Response
Challenging the Text

Question Would you have signed the treaty if you had been Arthur? Why or why not? *(Possible responses: No, I would never have given Modred rights to the throne. Yes, because when Launcelot came, he could help defeat Modred, and, if Modred was dead, he couldn't inherit the kingdom.)*

reopened. We won the day, but my lord King Arthur needs you, and I too, that on my tomb you may bestow your blessing."

Sir Gawain fainted when he had finished, and the king wept. When he came to he was given
7 extreme unction, and died, as he had anticipated, at the hour of noon. The king buried him in the chapel at Dover Castle, and there many came to see him, and all noticed the wound on his head which he had received from Sir Launcelot.

Then the news reached Arthur that Sir Modred offered him battle on the field at Baron Down.[14] Arthur hastened there with his army, they fought, and Sir Modred fled once more, this time to Canterbury.

When King Arthur had begun the search for his wounded and dead, many volunteers from all parts of the country came to fight under his flag, convinced now of the rightness of his cause. Arthur marched westward, and Sir Modred once more offered him battle. It was assigned for the Monday following Trinity Sunday,[15] on Salisbury Down.

Sir Modred levied fresh troops from East Anglia and the places about London, and fresh volunteers came forward to help Arthur. Then, on the night of Trinity Sunday, Arthur was vouchsafed[16] a strange dream:

He was appareled in gold cloth and seated in a chair which stood on a pivoted scaffold. Below him, many fathoms deep, was a dark well, and in the water swam serpents, dragons, and wild beasts. Suddenly the scaffold tilted and Arthur was flung into the water, where all the creatures struggled toward him and began tearing him limb from limb.

8 Arthur cried out in his sleep and his squires hastened to waken him. Later, as he lay between waking and sleeping, he thought he saw Sir Gawain, and with him a host of beautiful noblewomen. Arthur spoke:

Alas for this fateful day!

"My sister's son! I thought you had died; but now I see you live, and I thank the lord Jesu! I pray you, tell me, who are these ladies?"

"My lord, these are the ladies I championed in righteous quarrels when I was on earth. Our lord God has vouchsafed that we visit you and plead with you not to give battle to Sir Modred tomorrow, for if you do, not only will you yourself be killed, but all your noble followers too. We beg you to be warned, and to make a treaty with Sir Modred, calling a truce for a month, and granting him whatever terms he may demand. In a month Sir Launcelot will be here, and he will defeat Sir Modred."

Thereupon Sir Gawain and the ladies vanished, and King Arthur once more summoned his squires and his counselors and told them his vision. Sir Lucas and Sir Bedivere were commissioned to make a treaty with Sir Modred. They were to be accompanied by two bishops and to grant, within reason, whatever terms he demanded.

The ambassadors found Sir Modred in command of an army of a hundred thousand and unwilling to listen to overtures of peace. However, the ambassadors eventually prevailed on him, and in return for the truce granted him suzerainty of Cornwall and Kent,[17] and succession to the British throne when King Arthur
died. The treaty was to be signed by King Arthur 9
and Sir Modred the next day. They were to meet

14. **Down**, an expanse of rolling, grassy land. Though Baron Down no longer appears on maps, Salisbury Down, or Plain, is famous as the site of Stonehenge.
15. **Trinity Sunday,** feast day honoring the Holy Trinity, observed the eighth Sunday after Easter.
16. **vouchsafe** (vouch sāf′), *v.* grant.
17. **suzerainty** (sü zə ran′tē) **of Cornwall and Kent,** dominion or power over two southern counties of England.

MINI-LESSON: LITERARY FOCUS
Connotation/Denotation

Point out to students that besides having at least one dictionary definition, or denotation, many words have strong positive or negative associations, or connotations.

Activity Idea Ask students to work with a partner as they decide which of the words in each pair that follows has a positive connotation, which has a negative connotation, and which, if any, have mixed connotations. They may wish to put their responses in webs and add other words that show the positive or negative connotations.

- gold-money
- serpent-snake
- visionary-dreamer
- industrious-ambitious

between the two armies, and each was to be accompanied by no more than fourteen knights.

Both King Arthur and Sir Modred suspected the other of treachery, and gave orders for their armies to attack at the sight of a naked sword. When they met at the appointed place the treaty was signed and both drank a glass of wine.

Then, by chance, one of the soldiers was bitten in the foot by an adder which had lain concealed in the brush. The soldier unthinkingly drew his sword to kill it, and at once, as the sword flashed in the light, the alarums were given, trumpets sounded, and both armies galloped into the attack.

"Alas for this fateful day!" exclaimed King Arthur, as both he and Sir Modred hastily mounted and galloped back to their armies. There followed one of those rare and heartless battles in which both armies fought until they were destroyed. King Arthur, with his customary valor, led squadron after squadron of cavalry into the attack, and Sir Modred encountered him unflinchingly. As the number of dead and wounded mounted on both sides, the active combatants continued dauntless[18] until nightfall, when four men alone survived.

King Arthur wept with dismay to see his beloved followers fallen; then, struggling toward him, unhorsed and badly wounded, he saw Sir Lucas the Butler and his brother, Sir Bedivere.

"Alas!" said the king, "that the day should come when I see all my noble knights destroyed! I would prefer that I myself had fallen. But what has become of the traitor Sir Modred, whose evil ambition was responsible
10 for this carnage?"[19]

Looking about him King Arthur then noticed Sir Modred leaning with his sword on a heap of the dead.

"Sir Lucas, I pray you give me my spear, for I have seen Sir Modred."

"Sire, I entreat you, remember your vision—how Sir Gawain appeared with a heaven-sent message to dissuade you from fighting Sir Modred. Allow this fateful day to pass; it is ours, for we three hold the field, while the enemy is broken."

"My lords, I care nothing for my life now! And while Sir Modred is at large I must kill him: there may not be another chance."

"God speed you, then!" said Sir Bedivere.

When Sir Modred saw King Arthur advance with his spear, he rushed to meet him with drawn sword. Arthur caught Sir Modred below the shield and drove his spear through his body; Sir Modred, knowing that the wound was mortal, thrust himself up to the handle of the spear, and then, brandishing his sword in both hands, struck Arthur on the side of the helmet, cutting through it and into the skull beneath; then he crashed to the ground, gruesome and dead.

King Arthur fainted many times as Sir Lucas and Sir Bedivere struggled with him to a small chapel nearby, where they managed to ease his wounds a little. When Arthur came to, he thought he heard cries coming from the battlefield.

"Sir Lucas, I pray you, find out who cries on the battlefield," he said.

Wounded as he was, Sir Lucas hobbled painfully to the field, and there in the moonlight saw the camp followers stealing gold and jewels from the dead, and murdering the wounded. He returned to the king and reported to him what he had seen, and then added:

"My lord, it surely would be better to move you to the nearest town?"

"My wounds forbid it. But alas for the good Sir Launcelot! How sadly I have missed him today! And now I must die—as Sir Gawain warned me I would—repenting our quarrel with my last breath."

18. dauntless (dônt′lis), *adj.* brave.
19. carnage (kär′nij), *n.* slaughter of a great number of people.

10 Literary Focus

Denotation and Connotation

Question What impact does the word *carnage* have compared to the word *casualties? (Possible responses:* Carnage *evokes thoughts of blood and horrifying wounds, while* casualties *suggests names on a list.)*

Literary Criticism

". . . [Modred's] pedigree is a vital part of the tragedy of King Arthur. It is why Sir Thomas Mallory called his very long book the *Death of Arthur.* Although nine-tenths of the story seems to be about knights jousting and quests for the holy grail and things of that sort, the narrative is a whole and it deals with the reasons why the young man came to grief at the end. It is the tragedy . . . of sin coming home to roost. That is why we have to take note of the parentage of Arthur's son Modred, and to remember, when the time comes, that the king had slept with his own sister. He did not know he was doing so, and perhaps it may have been due to her, but it seems, in tragedy, that innocence is not enough."

T. H. White
The Once and Future King

BUILDING ENGLISH PROFICIENCY

Exploring Key Events

Dreams were of great importance during the Middle Ages, for they were believed to be unveilings of the future. Work with students to explore Arthur's dream on page 374.

1. Let pairs of students draw the scene depicted in Arthur's first dream on page 374. Talk about the pivoted scaffold, the dark well, and the wild beasts so that they understand the literal meaning.

2. Let students identify what they think each item in the dream symbolizes. Here you may want to help students understand that the pivoted scaffold symbolizes the action into which Arthur is forced by the "chance event" of the soldier who unwittingly started the war by drawing his sword to kill an adder (page 375).

3. List responses on the chalkboard. Ask students what they think the dream predicts, and why.

4. Continue reading, having students tell when an event or action seems to fit the symbols in Arthur's dream. Note these opposite the appropriate symbol on the chalkboard.

11 Literary Element
Archetype

Spectacle is a common element in the medieval romance. Sometimes the spectacle is created with beautiful images, other times it is painted with gruesome details, such as Sir Lucas's wound bursting open. Invite students to recall other instances of the spectacle of war.

12 Reading/Thinking Skills
Make Analogies

Question What other betrayals in literature or history does this betrayal bring to mind? *(Possible responses: Peter's betrayal of Jesus; Launcelot's and Gwynevere's betrayal of Arthur)*

13 Multicultural Note
Perspective

Point out that these black hoods are probably a sign of mourning. Explain that not all cultures use black as a color of mourning; in fact, some cultures use white.

Sir Lucas and Sir Bedivere made one further attempt to lift the king. He fainted as they did so.

11 Then Sir Lucas fainted as part of his intestines broke through a wound in the stomach. When the king came to, he saw Sir Lucas lying dead with foam at his mouth.

"Sweet Jesu, give him succor!" he said. "This noble knight has died trying to save my life—alas that this was so!"

Sir Bedivere wept for his brother.

"Sir Bedivere, weep no more," said King Arthur, "for you can save neither your brother nor me; and I would ask you to take my sword Excalibur to the shore of the lake and throw it in the water. Then return to me and tell me what you have seen."

"My lord, as you command, it shall be done."

Sir Bedivere took the sword, but when he came to the water's edge, it appeared so beautiful that he could not bring himself to throw it in, so instead he hid it by a tree, and then returned to the king.

"Sir Bedivere, what did you see?"

"My lord, I saw nothing but the wind upon the waves."

"Then you did not obey me; I pray you, go swiftly again, and this time fulfill my command."

Sir Bedivere went and returned again, but this time too he had failed to fulfill the king's command.

"Sir Bedivere, what did you see?"

"My lord, nothing but the lapping of the waves."

12 "Sir Bedivere, twice you have betrayed me! And for the sake only of my sword: it is unworthy of you! Now I pray you, do as I command, for I have not long to live."

This time Sir Bedivere wrapped the girdle[20] around the sheath and hurled it as far as he could into the water. A hand appeared from below the surface, took the sword, waved it thrice, and disappeared again. Sir Bedivere returned to the king and told him what he had seen.

"Sir Bedivere, I pray you now help me hence, or I fear it will be too late."

Sir Bedivere carried the king to the water's edge, and there found a barge in which sat many beautiful ladies with their queen. All were wearing black hoods, and when they saw the 13
king, they raised their voices in a piteous lament.

"I pray you, set me in the barge," said the king.

Sir Bedivere did so, and one of the ladies laid the king's head in her lap; then the queen spoke to him:

"My dear brother, you have stayed too long: I fear that the wound on your head is already cold."

Thereupon they rowed away from the land and Sir Bedivere wept to see them go.

"My lord King Arthur, you have deserted me! I am alone now, and among enemies."

"Sir Bedivere, take what comfort you may, for my time is passed, and now I must be taken to Avalon for my wound to be healed. If you hear of me no more, I beg you pray for my soul."

The barge slowly crossed the water and out of sight while the ladies wept. Sir Bedivere walked alone into the forest and there remained for the night.

In the morning he saw beyond the trees of a copse a small hermitage. He entered and found a hermit kneeling down by a fresh tomb. The hermit was weeping as he prayed, and then Sir Bedivere recognized him as the Archbishop of Canterbury, who had been banished by Sir Modred.

"Father, I pray you, tell me, whose tomb is this?"

"My son, I do not know. At midnight the body was brought here by a company of ladies. We buried it, they lit a hundred candles for the

20. **girdle** (gėr′dl), *n.* a band encircling the waist.

MINI-LESSON: STUDY SKILLS
Etymology

Point out to students that the word *succor* is used several times in this selection, and is defined on page 373. Explain that there are a lot of different ways of assisting another person. Also point out the word *barge* and tell students that it might be interesting to find out exactly what kind of sailing vessel Malory had in mind.

If students want to know more about the precise meaning of *succor*, they can consult a dictionary with etymologies, like *The American Heritage Dictionary of English Language.* Here, they can learn that *succor* comes from the Latin *sub-* meaning "under" and *currere,* meaning "to run." Ask students to visualize someone running under something to support it and keep it from harm.

Activity Idea Encourage students to look up other words that they think may have interesting backgrounds, or for which they would like to know more precise meanings. Possible choices include *fulfill, girdle, sheath, liege.*

14 service, and rewarded me with a thousand bezants."[21]

"Father, King Arthur lies buried in this tomb."

Sir Bedivere fainted when he had spoken, and when he came to he begged the Archbishop to allow him to remain at the hermitage and end his days in fasting and prayer.

"Father, I wish only to be near to my true liege."

"My son, you are welcome; and do I not recognize you as Sir Bedivere the Bold, brother to Sir Lucas the Butler?"

Thus the Archbishop and Sir Bedivere remained at the hermitage, wearing the habits of hermits and devoting themselves to the tomb with fasting and prayers of contrition.

15 Such was the death of King Arthur as written down by Sir Bedivere. By some it is told that there were three queens on the barge: Queen Morgan le Fay, the Queen of North Galys, and the Queen of the Waste Lands; and others include the name of Nyneve, the Lady of the Lake who had served King Arthur well in the past, and had married the good knight Sir Pelleas.

A hand appeared from below the surface, took the sword, waved it thrice, and disappeared again.

In many parts of Britain it is believed that King Arthur did not die and that he will return to us and win fresh glory and the Holy Cross of our Lord Jesu Christ; but for myself I do not believe this, and would leave him buried peacefully in his tomb at Glastonbury, where the Archbishop of Canterbury and Sir Bedivere humbled themselves, and with prayers and fasting honored his memory. And inscribed on his tomb, men say, is this legend:

HIC IACET ARTHURUS, REX QUONDAM REXQUE FUTURUS.[22]

21. **bezant** (bez′ənt), *n.* gold coin.

22. **HIC . . . FUTURUS**, "Here lies Arthur, the once and future king." [*Latin*]

14 Multicultural Note
Perspective

Many cultures have seasons or practices of fasting and prayer. In the Christian tradition there is the season of Lent; in the Hebrew tradition, Yom Kippur; in the Muslim tradition, Ramadan.

15 Literary Element
Tone

Open a discussion of the change in the narrator's tone. Information is presented not as fact, but as what is "told" by "some." This continues into the last paragraph where the narrator states his personal views. Have students think about how this compares with the tone of the narration in earlier Malory passages. *(Possible response: Earlier his tone is simple and unemotional; at other times it is dramatic; here it is personal.)*

The World of Work
Marine Recruiter

For a look at real-life issues of military service from the point of view of a marine recruiter, use—

The World of Work
pp. 11–12

BUILDING ENGLISH PROFICIENCY

Recognizing Cause and Effect

Have students imagine that Arthur and his court have one chance to meet again in Avalon. There they all sit in a circle, both women and men, and discuss why the Round Table and Camelot came to an end.

Suggest that students—taking the parts of the king, Merlin, ladies, knights, archbishop, and other characters—sit in circles and discuss the causes of the end of the Round Table. To prepare, have students:

- talk about their character informally with a partner
- refer to the text for specific speeches, events, and descriptions
- make brief notes about their character

As a result of their discussion, each "Round Table" should come to agreement on three reasons that Arthur's reign ended in destruction.

16 Literary Element
Poetry

Point out to students that an idyll is a poem, sometimes narrative and epic in scope. Tennyson spent sixty years writing his idylls recounting the Arthurian legends. The poet uses blank verse, the form in which some of the greatest poetry, such as the tragedies of Shakespeare and the epics of Milton, is written.

Question What could be inferred about Tennyson's reasons for using blank verse? *(Possible response: He wanted to express a tone of epic importance to the legend of Arthur.)*

17 Literary Focus
Denotation and Connotation

Question Read line 26, substituting *eat* for *nourish*. Which has more appropriate connotations? (Nourish *suggests a deeper sense of feeding both mind and body.*)

Prompt students to choose several words that evoke interesting associations for them, and then substitute other words to observe the effect.

16

Idylls of the King

Alfred, Lord Tennyson

Then loudly cried the bold Sir Bedivere:
"Ah! my Lord Arthur, whither shall I go?
Where shall I hide my forehead and my eyes?
For now I see the true old times are dead,
When every morning brought a noble chance,
And every chance brought out a noble knight.
Such times have been not since the light that led
The holy Elders with the gift of myrrh.[1]
But now the whole Round Table is dissolved
Which was an image of the mighty world,
And I, the last, go forth companionless,
And the days darken round me, and the years,
Among new men, strange faces, other minds."
And slowly answer'd Arthur from the barge:
"The old order changeth, yielding place to new,
And God fulfills himself in many ways,
Lest one good custom should corrupt the world.
Comfort thyself: what comfort is in me?
I have lived my life, and that which I have done
May He within himself make pure! but thou,
If thou shouldst never see my face again,
Pray for my soul. More things are wrought by prayer
Than this world dreams of. Wherefore, let thy voice
Rise like a fountain for me night and day.
17 For what are men better than sheep or goats
That nourish a blind life within the brain,
If, knowing God, they lift not hands of prayer
Both for themselves and those who call them friend?
For so the whole round earth is every way
Bound by gold chains about the feet of God.
But now farewell. I am going a long way
With these thou seest—if indeed I go—
For all my mind is clouded with a doubt—
To the island-valley of Avilion;
Where falls not hail, or rain, or any snow,
Nor ever wind blows loudly; but it lies
Deep-meadow'd, happy, fair with orchard lawns
And bowery hollows crown'd with summer sea,
Where I will heal me of my grievous wound."
So said he, and the barge with oar and sail
Moved from the brink, like some full-breasted swan
That, fluting a wild carol ere her death,
Ruffles her pure cold plume, and takes the flood

MINI-LESSON: SPEAKING AND LISTENING
Storytelling

Suggest that students choose a favorite heroic tale or legend to tell the class. You may wish to provide them with more of Malory's stories, Howard Pyle's stories about King Arthur and Robin Hood, or other selections which can be found on the Custom Literature Database. To prepare, students can

- read the selection to become thoroughly familiar with it
- decide how they will tell it—possibly by delivering a straightforward rendition of the plot, by making the story dramatic and suspenseful, or by giving it a modern twist
- practice before they present their stories

With swarthy webs. Long stood Sir Bedivere
Revolving many memories, till the hull
Look'd one black dot against the verge of dawn,
And on the mere[2] the wailing died away.

1. **holy Elders with the gift of myrrh**, the wise men in the Gospel of Matthew who follow the star to Bethlehem to offer the infant Jesus gifts of gold, frankincense, and myrrh (a fragrant gum resin from the myrrh shrub used for making incense, perfume, and medicine).
2. **mere** (mir), *n.* lake or pond.

Note the geometric patterns and lines in this detail by Aubrey Beardsley from a 1909 edition of *Le Morte d'Arthur.* Where do the dominant lines direct your eyes? What does this direction suggest?

Art Study

Responses to Caption Questions
Bedivere's raised arm and the uplifted sword direct the viewer's eyes up and out of the picture. This suggests that we turn our thoughts and attention to God.

Check Test

1. What did Modred want Gwynevere to do? *(marry him)*

2. Why did Gawain write to Launcelot? *(to take responsibility for the war between Arthur and Launcelot, to ask Launcelot to pray for him, and to ask him to return and fight with Arthur against Modred)*

3. Who were the four men left after the final battle? *(Modred, Arthur, Bedivere, and Lucas)*

4. What did Arthur ask Bedivere to throw in the lake? *(Excalibur)*

5. What does Arthur say makes men different from sheep and goats? *(They can pray for themselves and for others.)*

Unit 3 Resource Book
Alternate Check Test, p. 29

BUILDING ENGLISH PROFICIENCY

Analyzing Mood

Help students understand how Tennyson creates the somber mood of this poem.

1. Read the poem once.

2. Then ask students to say, in one or a few words, what is going on. *(Possible responses: saying good-by, dying, leaving, remembering)*

3. Let students identify parts that are difficult or interesting, and discuss them.

4. Assign one or two sentences to pairs or small groups, who then rewrite the sentence(s) as prose and read them to the class.

5. Have them jot down words and phrases that have a feeling of sadness and finality. Students can then share circled words.

After Reading

MAKING CONNECTIONS

1. Possible responses: Evidence of Arthur's triumph is that his deeds survive in legend; tragic events in his life were the losses of his wife's love and his friendship with Launcelot, and the destruction of the Round Table.

2. Possible responses: Some students may think that Launcelot becomes king; some that civil war continues for many years with no king.

3. Possible responses: honorable, justice-seeking, romantic, violent

4. Arthur's dream of falling in the well may foreshadow his death, the destruction of his ideals, or both. The second dream foreshadows his death at Modred's hand.

5. He feels that it is his responsibility to put an end to Modred's evil, no matter what the personal cost.

6. Possible responses: the description of Lucas's death, the large numbers killed in the battle, and the fight between Modred and Arthur

7. It could be literally true if Arthur returns from Avilion to rule again, or figuratively true if his ideals come to be valued enough that they again form the basis of government.

8. By referring to myrrh, Bedivere draws a parallel between Jesus and Arthur.

9. In a general sense, change is always occurring and the old always gives way to the new. Arthur speaks of worldly power giving way to spriritual ideals, and students may not agree that this specific idea applies today.

10. Possible responses: many political and entertainment figures; students may comment that like Arthur, Gwynevere, and Lancelot, these people are complex, having many positive and negative qualities.

After Reading

Making Connections

Shaping Your Response

1. Do you think Arthur's life was a triumph or a tragedy? Why?
2. Who do you think will be Arthur's successor as king? Why?
3. In your notebook, write down at least three words that describe your impressions of Arthurian times.

Analyzing the Selections

4. In Malory's account, how do Arthur's two dreams **foreshadow** the future?
5. Why do you think Arthur chooses to engage in personal combat with Modred?
6. What **images** in Malory's account emphasize the grimness and savagery of the last battle?
7. Explain how the label, "the once and future king," which seems to be a contradiction, or **paradox,** can be true.
8. What is the purpose of the **allusion** Bedivere makes in Tennyson's poem?

Extending the Ideas

9. Arthur observes, "The old order changeth, yielding place to new." Do you think these words apply as much today as they did in Arthur's era? Why or why not?
10. What modern celebrities can you think of whose character or actions have brought about their own downfalls?

Literary Focus: Connotation and Denotation

chains
dawn
king
flag
sword

Write two of these words in separate circles, leaving room to write the dictionary definition, or **denotation,** of each word. After writing the definition, draw spokes radiating from each circle. On the spokes, write the **connotations,** or associations, that you have for each word. You may want to read the article on Connotation and Denotation on page 492 before you do this activity.

LITERARY FOCUS: CONNOTATION AND DENOTATION

Denotations:

chains, series of metal or other links joined together
dawn, beginning of day
king, male ruler of a nation
flag, emblem signal, standard
sword, weapon with a long, sharp blade fixed in a handle

Possible connotations:

chains, armor
dawn, light over a castle
king, Arthur, glimmering
flag, America, battle standard
sword, might, blood

Vocabulary Study

Write a synonym from the list to replace each italicized word in the sentences below. You will not use all the words.

carnage
dauntless
ensue
entice
guile
usurp

1. A true knight remained *brave* in the face of extraordinary obstacles.
2. No one could *lure* a knight away from his noble mission.
3. After a glorious victory, a celebration would *follow.*
4. Even victorious knights would regret the *slaughter* caused by battles.
5. Sir Modred did not observe the code of chivalry when he tried to *seize* the crown.

Expressing Your Ideas

Writing Choices

Writer's Notebook Update Write a comparison between Arthur and Modred and one of the hero/villain pairs you noted in your notebook. Explain what you think would be lost if the heroes had no foils, or opposites. You might use some of the vocabulary words in your comparison.

The Once and Future King Write an **obituary** for King Arthur that contains descriptions, quotations, or testimonials to him from the selections you have read. You might accompany the obituary with a sketch.

Last Letter Imagine that Arthur, like Gawain, had time to write one letter before he died. To whom do you think he would write? Gwynevere? Launcelot? his subjects? Would he be forgiving? accusing? consoling? encouraging? Choose a recipient; then write Arthur's last **letter.**

Other Options

Put on a Coat The medieval knight, along with warriors of other cultures, represented his skills, heritage, and allegiance on his personal heraldic shield, or **coat of arms**. Design a coat of arms for one of the characters you have just read about, or for yourself, which reflects family background, interests, culture, personality traits, and accomplishments. Accompany your coat of arms with a motto.

Knightworthy Create a **new knight** for King Arthur's Round Table. This could be someone noteworthy, real or fictional, from any era. Describe in words or draw that person's physical characteristics, clothing, and armor, as well as character traits that make him or her "knightworthy."

VOCABULARY STUDY

1. dauntless
2. entice
3. ensue
4. carnage
5. usurp

Unit 3 Resource Book
Vocabulary, p. 27
Vocabulary Test, p. 30

WRITING CHOICES

Writer's Notebook Update, The Once and Future King

In both activities, students' work will be enhanced by further knowledge of Arthurian legend. Encourage students to read more about Arthur in selections by Malory, White, and Stewart. Or provide them with various stories by Howard Pyle, such as "The Winning of a Sword," from *The Story of King Arthur and His Knights*—available on the Custom Literature Database.

Last Letter

After students have completed this assignment, you may wish to show them how this idea was handled at the end of *The Once and Future King.*

Selection Test

Unit 3 Resource Book
pp. 31–32

Transparency Collection
Fine Art Writing Prompt 6

OTHER OPTIONS

Put on a Coat

Remind students about the kings who used a boar and a leopard to represent themselves in Mary Stewart's retelling of the legend. Point out that in Native American culture it is also customary for people to have a special connection with an animal, and encourage them to view some illustrations showing totem poles. Invite students to study the way different cultures create symbolic identification. They may also wish to look at some books on heraldry.

Knightworthy

Encourage students to imagine that a knight from another culture has come to England. This idea was used in the movie *Robin Hood: Prince of Thieves* in which a Muslim returns from the Crusades with Robin. This will allow for interesting interactions as the ideals of two cultures meet and mix or come into conflict.

Interdisciplinary Study

Theme Link

Because Arthurian Legends are focused on knighthood, we can use them as a basis of comparison to knighthood in other societies, times, and cultures.

Curricular Connection: Multicultural

You can use the information in this Interdisciplinary Study to explore with students the various manifestations that knighthood has taken through the ages, as well as some contemporary ideas about knighthood.

Terms to Know

samurai ('sam′u ri), members of an elite class of feudal Japanese aristocrats who were trained in fighting, and are characteristically pictured with a samurai sword

jousting, a combat between two knights using lances while on horseback

Unit 3 Resource Book
Study Guide, p. 33

INTERDISCIPLINARY STUDY

Arthurian Legends

Knights in Many Guises

Knights

Multicultural Connection

Knighthood has existed in many ages and cultures. The code of chivalry—with some adaptations—still exists today. Look for traces of Arthur in the world around you.

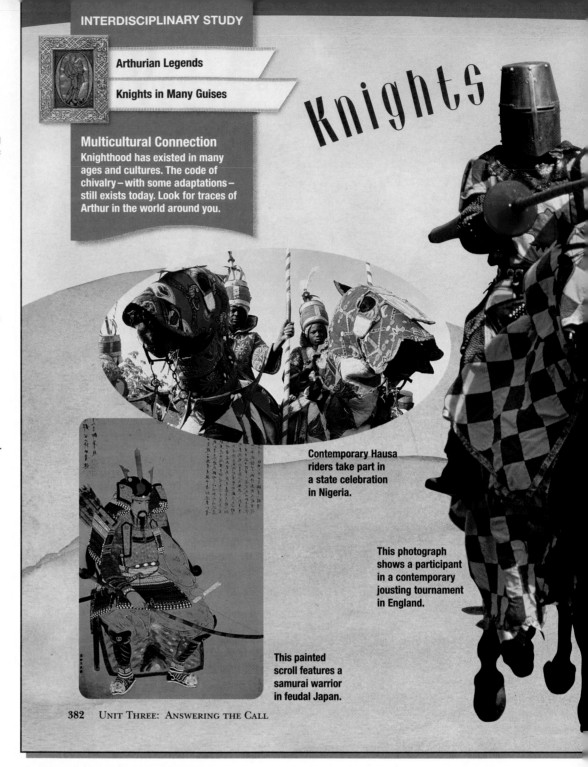

Contemporary Hausa riders take part in a state celebration in Nigeria.

This photograph shows a participant in a contemporary jousting tournament in England.

This painted scroll features a samurai warrior in feudal Japan.

MINI-LESSON: VISUAL LITERACY

Draw Conclusions/Evaluate Art

Teach The illustrations and art included on pages 382–383 are an important feature of this Interdisciplinary Study. Explain to students that in addition to making these pages look attractive, they also provide information. By paying attention to the illustrations, students can learn more about a subject than is included in the brief captions.

Activity Idea Students can practice evaluating art by studying the images on this spread of the Interdisciplinary Study.

- Divide the class into six groups.
- Assign one image to each group.
- Have each group list things that they learned by studying their image.
- You can help each group by posing questions for them to consider:

  What does the knight's outfit and action tell you about a knight's duties?

  What does the way the knight is depicted tell you about a knight's role in society?

Unit 3 Resource Book
Study Skill Activity, p. 34

in Many Guises

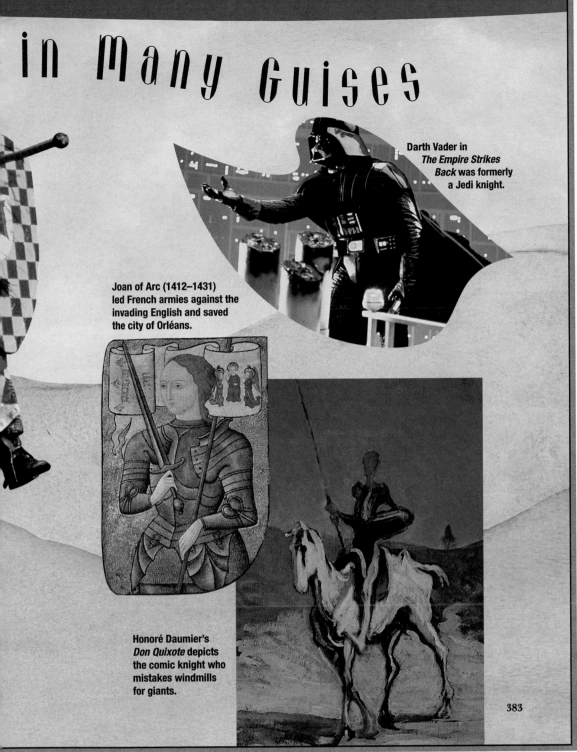

Darth Vader in *The Empire Strikes Back* was formerly a Jedi knight.

Joan of Arc (1412–1431) led French armies against the invading English and saved the city of Orléans.

Honoré Daumier's *Don Quixote* depicts the comic knight who mistakes windmills for giants.

383

Additional Background

Darth Vader The *Star Wars* movies include *Star Wars, The Empire Strikes Back,* and *The Return of the Jedi.*

Joan of Arc Joan of Arc's story has been retold several times. Students may enjoy reading Shaw's play *Saint Joan.*

Don Quixote Students may enjoy reading Cervantes' novel, which parodies the codes of chivalry.

BUILDING ENGLISH PROFICIENCY

Responding to Visual Cues

Use one or more of the following activities to help students grasp the information in this pictorial.

Activity Ideas

- Have students explore the images and captions, left to right. Allow time for students to use their dialogue journals to respond to the images and information.
- Ask groups of students to choose one of the items depicted. Have them improvise a skit in which they reveal something (factual or fictional) about the life and values of the knight depicted.
- Ask students to imagine that this pictorial will be expanded. Call on volunteers to name other examples of "knights" from history or popular culture (as in the case of Batman, who is called the "Dark Knight") that they would add to the display.

Terms to Know

pulchritude (pul′krə tüd), extraordinary physical beauty

gaiety, showiness or bright color

mail, flexible armor made of small metal rings

casque (kask), a helmet, especially the one-piece kind with no visor, worn in the sixteenth century

green, a grassy field, used as the site of a tournament

Additional Background

Many areas of the United States sponsor Renaissance fairs as well as jousting tournaments. Travel guides can provide more information.

Interdisciplinary Activity Idea

Ask students to imagine that a modern political, sports, or entertainment figure is the hero or heroine of a legend that they are relating to their grandchildren. Encourage them to do research to write a short tale that mixes fact and fiction. Remind them to describe the codes of conduct that a hero would follow in today's world.

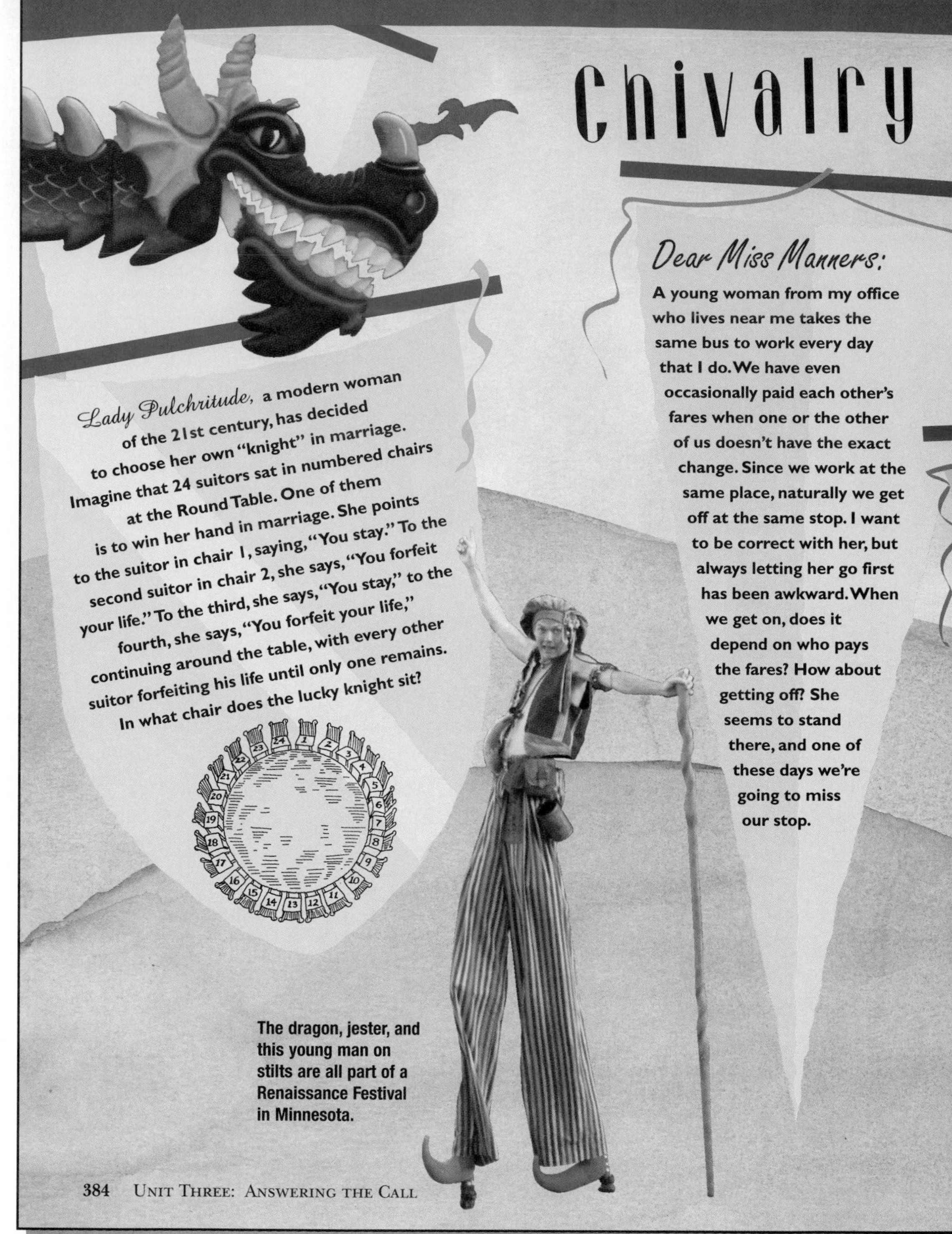

Chivalry
Lady Pulchritude, a modern woman of the 21st century, has decided to choose her own "knight" in marriage. Imagine that 24 suitors sat in numbered chairs at the Round Table. One of them is to win her hand in marriage. She points to the suitor in chair 1, saying, "You stay." To the second suitor in chair 2, she says, "You forfeit your life." To the third, she says, "You stay," to the fourth, she says, "You forfeit your life," continuing around the table, with every other suitor forfeiting his life until only one remains. In what chair does the lucky knight sit?
1
2
3
4
5
6
7
8
9
10
11
12
13
14
15
16
17
18
19
20
21
22
23
24
Dear Miss Manners:
A young woman from my office who lives near me takes the same bus to work every day that I do. We have even occasionally paid each other's fares when one or the other of us doesn't have the exact change. Since we work at the same place, naturally we get off at the same stop. I want to be correct with her, but always letting her go first has been awkward. When we get on, does it depend on who pays the fares? How about getting off? She seems to stand there, and one of these days we're going to miss our stop.

The dragon, jester, and this young man on stilts are all part of a Renaissance Festival in Minnesota.

MINI-LESSON: STUDY SKILLS

Create and Use Graphic Organizers

Teach A useful strategy for solving brainteasers is to construct a graphic organizer to better see the information. The organizer can then be marked to show how the information is being manipulated.

Activity Idea Have students use a graphic organizer as they try to solve the brainteaser on page 384. Many students will copy the picture on the page, simplify it, and then cross out numbers as the suitors are eliminated. However, another method would be to copy the numbers 1–24, and cross out all the even numbers.

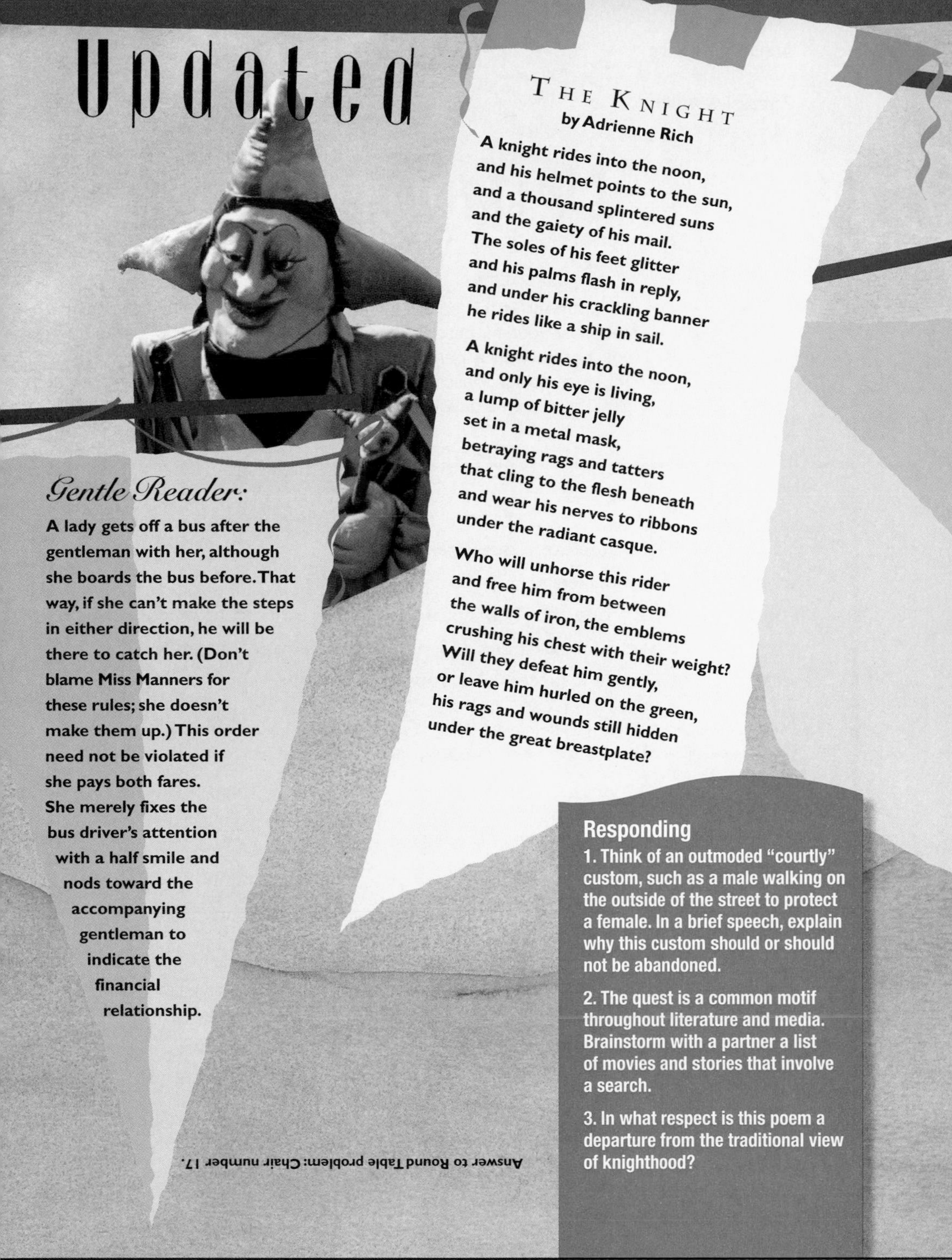

Updated

The Knight
by Adrienne Rich

A knight rides into the noon,
and his helmet points to the sun,
and a thousand splintered suns
and the gaiety of his mail.
The soles of his feet glitter
and his palms flash in reply,
and under his crackling banner
he rides like a ship in sail.

A knight rides into the noon,
and only his eye is living,
a lump of bitter jelly
set in a metal mask,
betraying rags and tatters
that cling to the flesh beneath
and wear his nerves to ribbons
under the radiant casque.

Who will unhorse this rider
and free him from between
the walls of iron, the emblems
crushing his chest with their weight?
Will they defeat him gently,
or leave him hurled on the green,
his rags and wounds still hidden
under the great breastplate?

Gentle Reader:

A lady gets off a bus after the gentleman with her, although she boards the bus before. That way, if she can't make the steps in either direction, he will be there to catch her. (Don't blame Miss Manners for these rules; she doesn't make them up.) This order need not be violated if she pays both fares. She merely fixes the bus driver's attention with a half smile and nods toward the accompanying gentleman to indicate the financial relationship.

Answer to Round Table problem: Chair number 17.

Responding

1. Think of an outmoded "courtly" custom, such as a male walking on the outside of the street to protect a female. In a brief speech, explain why this custom should or should not be abandoned.

2. The quest is a common motif throughout literature and media. Brainstorm with a partner a list of movies and stories that involve a search.

3. In what respect is this poem a departure from the traditional view of knighthood?

Responding

1. Possible Response Suppposedly the man walks on the street side so that if a passing car sends a spray of water or debris over the curb, he, rather than the woman, will be splashed. Students may say that the man's clothing is just as valuable as the women's. Another custom is opening a car door for a female passenger. Students may say that now that women drive, they should hold the door open for any passenger, male or female.

2. Possible Response Students may include a wide variety of sources, such as *The Wizard of Oz, Star Wars* movies, *The Incredible Journey, Labyrinth,* etc.

3. Possible Response In the second stanza, his suffering and the dehumanization of his attire are emphasized rather than his courage and endurance. In the third stanza, it is suggested that losing would free him of the prison of his armor and be a blessing, rather than a humiliating event, as it is usually portrayed.

BUILDING ENGLISH PROFICIENCY

ESL LEP ELD SAE LD

Making Cultural Connections

Help students make a personal connection to the feature and prepare for Responding Activity, 1.

1. Remind students that many customs vary, not only across centuries but also across cultures.

2. Using the chart shown, invite students to name different customs relating to matters of courtship, offering assistance, showing respect for parents, expressing thanks, and so on. Whenever possible, have students identify the culture or country of origin for each custom.

Cultural Customs

Culture/Country	Courtship	Offering Assistance	Showing Respect for Parents	Expressing Thanks

Writing Workshop

WRITER'S BLUEPRINT

Specs

The Specs in the Writer's Blueprint address these writing and thinking skills:

- defining terms
- setting goals
- overcoming obstacles
- using connotations
- using visuals to reinforce text
- persuading
- capitalizing proper nouns and proper adjectives

These Specs serve as your lesson objectives, and they form the basis for the **Assessment Criteria Specs** for a superior paper, which appear on the final TE page for this lesson. You might want to read through the Assessment Criteria Specs with students when you begin the lesson.

Linking Literature to Writing

As you review the literature selections, discuss with students why the archetypal quest story translates so well into video games and adventure board games.

Writing Workshop

A Quest Game

Assignment In this part of the unit you read tales of a far-off time when people set out in quest of freedom, kingship, and victory in battle. Now collaborate with a partner or group to design a quest of your own. Together, design, describe, and explain an original board game or video game based on a quest.

WRITER'S BLUEPRINT

Product	A proposal for a quest game
Audience	Game makers
Purpose	As a group, to (1) propose an idea for a board or video game based on a quest and (2) persuade a game maker to buy it
Specs	To create a successful proposal, your group should:

- ❑ Make a cover sheet listing the title of your quest game and names of team members. Begin by giving an overview of the world in which your game unfolds—the time period and place, real or imagined.
- ❑ Go on to explain the other key elements:
  —the goal of the quest on which your game is based
  —the characters, good and evil
  —the obstacles characters face and the tools to help overcome them
  Use colorful language with rich connotations.
- ❑ Include strategic illustrations such as drawings, diagrams, and maps to help explain the game.
- ❑ Conclude by giving your audience five convincing reasons why they should buy your idea and market your game. What makes it unique and appealing? Be specific.
- ❑ Follow the rules of grammar, usage, spelling, and mechanics. Take care to correctly capitalize proper nouns and proper adjectives.

WRITING WORKSHOP OVERVIEW

Product
Persuasive writing: A proposal for a quest game

Prewriting
Brainstorm key elements—Discuss key elements—Brainstorm persuasive reasons—Make a game plan–Ask another group
Unit 3 Resource Book
Prewriting Worksheets pp. 35–36

Drafting
Before you write—As you write
Transparency Collection
Student Models for Writing Workshop 11, 12

Revising
Ask another group—Strategy: Being Clear and Concise
Unit 3 Resource Book
Revising Worksheet p. 37

Editing
Work with another group—Strategy: Capitalizing Proper Nouns and Proper Adjectives
Unit 3 Resource Book
Grammar Worksheet p. 38
Grammar Check Test p. 39

Presenting
Presentation—Advertisement—Box—Play—Submit

Looking Back
Self-evaluate—Reflect—For Your Working Portfolio
Unit 3 Resource Book
Assessment Worksheet p. 40
Transparency Collection
Fine Art Writing Prompt 6

STEP 1 PREWRITING

Brainstorm key elements of the world in which your game takes place. You'll want the names of people, places, and things to be vivid, so try to think of words and phrases that have strong **connotations** of dread, help, wealth, and power, as in the Literary Source below at the right. Categorize your ideas under headings like those in the Key Elements chart.

Key Elements

Time and Place	Goals of a Quest	Forces for Good	Forces for Evil	Perilous Obstacles	Helps
Medieval England	justice, gold, kingship	Lancelot, Arthur, Lady of the Lake	Sir Modred, Morgan Le Fay	dragons, serpents, deep wells	swords, armor, horses, boats

Discuss key elements. By now your game should be taking shape in your mind. Get together and discuss your key elements. As you discuss, make preliminary sketches of the game board or, if it's a video game, sketches of some of the screens.

Brainstorm persuasive reasons for why a game maker should buy your idea. Have each group member list as many reasons as possible. Then share your lists and rate each reason on a scale of 10 (highly persuasive) down to 1 (not persuasive at all). Choose your top five reasons and arrange them in order of importance.

Make a game plan. Organize your notes and sketches based on the Specs in the Writer's Blueprint. Make notes on these categories:

- Title
- Team members
- Overview of world —time —place
- Goal
- Characters
- Obstacles
- Five good reasons the game maker should buy your idea (from least to most important)
- Illustrations (maps, sketches of characters, drawings of video game screens, diagrams of rooms, etc.)

LITERARY SOURCE
"He was appareled in *gold cloth* and seated in a chair which stood on a *pivoted scaffold*. Below him, *many fathoms deep*, was a *dark well*, and in the water swam *serpents*, *dragons*, and *wild beasts*."
from *The Death of King Arthur* by Sir Thomas Malory

STEP 1 PREWRITING

Brainstorm key elements

Students can find myriad resources and information about interactive games on the Internet. Many game publishers have web sites that young people can visit. For additional support, see the worksheet referenced below.

Discuss key elements

Encourage students to consider a variety of ideas and approaches to each decision. For additional support, see the worksheet referenced below.

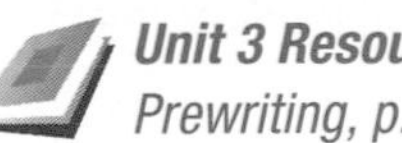

Unit 3 Resource Book
Prewriting, p. 35

Brainstorm persuasive reasons

Set a time limit for brainstorming sessions. Encourage students within groups to each write down the ideas generated. If only one person is recording the ideas, some may not get recorded. Students can compare lists and create a master list, possibly eliminating some reasons as they go. For additional support, see the worksheet referenced below.

Unit 3 Resource Book
Prewriting, p, 36

Make a game plan

Students must practice their organizational skills in order for collaboration to be effective. Ask students to take time in planning the division of tasks.

BUILDING ENGLISH PROFICIENCY

Using Prewriting Helps

Draw attention to some of the prewriting helps provided on page 387.

- In the "Literary Source" notes, point out the vivid imagery in Mallory's description. Encourage students to think about the "look" of their game as well as its "play."
- For the "Brainstorm persuasive reasons" activity, encourage students also to brainstorm all possible objections to their game—and then to come up with answers to the objections. (Role-playing can be of help here.)

Ask another group (Peer assessment)

Encourage students to view this peer review as their first opportunity to try out their "sales pitch."

Connections to **Writer's Notebook**

For selection-related prompts, refer to Writer's Notebook.

Connections to **Writer's Resource**

For additional writing prompts, refer to Writer's Resource.

STEP 2 DRAFTING

The Student Models

The **transparencies** referenced below are authentic student models. Review them with the students before they draft. These questions will help:

1. Did you find five convincing reasons to buy the idea presented in model 11? Make suggestions to the writer to strengthen the conclusion.

2. What are the key elements in model 12?

Transparency Collection
Student Model Transparencies 11, 12

STEP 3 REVISING

Ask another group (Peer assessment)

Students may want to discuss exactly what makes a game engaging before they begin critiquing the proposals. Encourage students to give specific feedback based on specific criteria.

Ask another group to examine your game plan and comment on it.

✔ Are we on the right track? Does our plan look like it could be turned into a game that would be fun to play?

✔ Are we following the Specs in the Writer's Blueprint?

Consider their comments as you finalize your game plan, but if they suggest going off in a direction that doesn't work for you, stick with your own ideas. Remember, this is *your* game.

STEP 2 DRAFTING

Before you write, divide up the work among the members of the group. Be sure someone's in charge of each part of your game plan.

As you write, use your game plan and the Writer's Blueprint as guides. As you work, remember, this is just a draft. Things are bound to change, so don't try to get everything perfect the first time through. Here are some drafting ideas.

- Keep it simple. Since this is a proposal that involves a good deal of explanation, break up your copy into separate pieces. Don't produce long paragraphs. That way you're more likely to keep things clear and concise.
- Cooperate. Communicate. Make sure everyone knows what everyone else is doing. If you make a major change, such as adding a new character or changing one of the rules, make sure your other group members know about it—and approve.
- When you write up your reasons for why game makers should buy your ideas, present them in order of importance.

COMPUTER TIP
If your word processing program has a built-in thesaurus, use it as you revise to help make your language richer and more precise.

STEP 3 REVISING

Ask another group to look over your game and comment before you revise it.

✔ Are we explaining a game, as we should be? Or are we just telling a story instead?

✔ Are our reasons persuasive? Could we find better reasons?

✔ Are our explanations clear and concise?

MINI-LESSON: WRITING STYLE

Being Clear and Concise

Activity Idea Have students bring to class the description of or the directions for their favorite game. Using these as examples, discuss how well the writers succeeded in making their meanings clear. Have students make suggestions to clarify or shorten the examples.

Apply Encourage students to reread their drafts to check for clarity and conciseness, and make changes, using the examples as guides.

Revising Strategy

Being Clear and Concise

When explaining a concept as complex as a game, do your readers a favor and make your explanations as brief and uncomplicated as you can.

complicated	First, at the bottom of the mountain, there's a warrior that Ipi meets named Morg. He has a red spear. Another warrior is halfway up. He has a spear too. He has to face Amba at the top, who carries a yellow spear. He is also a warrior.
concise	Moving up the mountain, Ipi must confront three different spear-carrying warriors.

STUDENT MODEL

Notice how the lengthy, choppy first passage has been pared down to one simple sentence that still contains the important information and clears up the confusion about whom the pronoun "he" refers to. When you revise:

- Simplify the complicated.
- Clarify the confusing.
- Compress the lengthy.

Revising Strategy: Being Clear and Concise

Have volunteers make up wordy sentences and other volunteers revise to make them concise. This could be done orally, as a class or in small groups.

For additional support, see the mini-lesson at the bottom of page 388 and the worksheet referenced below.

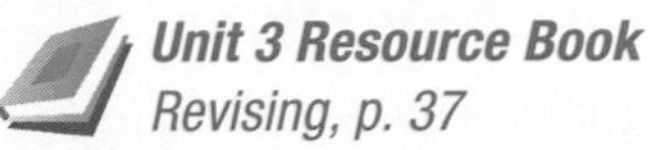

Unit 3 Resource Book
Revising, p. 37

Connections to **Writer's Resource**

For additional writing prompts, refer to Writer's Resource.

BUILDING ENGLISH PROFICIENCY

ESL LEP ELD SAE LD

Clarifying Explanations

Use one or both of the following activities to help students clarify their explanations.

Activity Ideas

- Suggest that students prepare one sentence to explain their ideas to someone who is not familiar with it.
- Suggest that students visualize a formula for their explanations, as shown.

Character:
Character's goal:
Character's enemy/enemies:
Where character is/must go:

STEP 4 EDITING

Work with another group (Peer assessment)

Rather than working independently, group members should discuss their responses together.

Editing Strategy: Capitalizing Proper Nouns and Proper Adjectives

Students might have fun explaining how these rules apply to their fictitious names and places. For additional support, see the mini-lesson at the bottom of this page and the worksheets referenced below.

Unit 3 Resource Book
Grammar Worksheet, p. 38
Grammar Check Test, p. 39

Connections to **Writer's Resource**

For additional writing prompts, refer to Writer's Resource.

Work with another group to review and comment on your revised draft before you edit. Pay special attention to errors with capitalizing proper nouns and proper adjectives.

Editing Strategy

FOR REFERENCE
For more rules on capitalization, see the Language and Grammar Handbook at the back of this text.

Capitalizing Proper Nouns and Proper Adjectives

Your game probably will have lots of names for particular people, places, and things. Follow these rules for capitalizing proper nouns and proper adjectives:

- Capitalize words that name a particular person, place, or thing. Capitalize only the important words in a noun of two or more words:

the Lady of the Lake **Excalibur** **the Isle of Avalon**

- Capitalize proper adjectives—but not the nouns they modify:

the English king **Arthurian legends** **a Christian church**

Notice how this writer fixed mistakes with proper nouns and proper adjectives.

This quest takes place in the 1990s, but it has medieval characters in it. Somehow King Arthur's Sword (s), excalibur (E), has been hidden (i.e., lost) in a modern shopping mall. Your job is to find the sword and get it back safely to King Arthur's Court (c). You will have some assistance from sir (S) Lancelot, King Arthur's most trusted and courageous knight.

MINI-LESSON: GRAMMAR

Capitalizing Proper Nouns and Proper Adjectives

Remind students that a proper noun names a particular person, place, or thing, and proper adjectives are formed from proper nouns. Write these phrases on the board and have students make any needed corrections to proper nouns and proper adjectives. Corrections are in parentheses.

1. gulf of tonkin (Gulf of Tonkin)
2. Brazilian Coffee (coffee)
3. the Girl scouts of America (Scouts)
4. the American Flag (flag)
5. the West side of the river (west)
6. Logan elementary school (Elementary School)
7. east Indian cuisine (East)
8. Sunset boulevard (Boulevard)
9. Statue Of Liberty (of)
10. the Bolivian Economy (economy)

Unit 3 Resource Book
Grammar Worksheet, p. 38
Grammar Check Test, p. 39

STEP 5 PRESENTING

Here are some ideas for presenting your finished proposal.

- Assemble your proposal and present it to another group. Rehearse your presentation first. Remember, your goal is to be persuasive. Ask your audience how well you did.
- Create an advertisement for your game.
- Design a box for your game.
- Try it out. If you've made a board game, try playing it with friends.
- Do you really think you have a good idea for your game? Do you think you've created a truly effective proposal? Then find the address of a company that makes games and submit your proposal.

STEP 6 LOOKING BACK

Self-evaluate. How well do you think your finished product meets the Specs in the Writer's Blueprint? Rate yourself on each item in the blueprint, from 6 (superior) to 1 (inadequate).

Reflect. What was it like working on a project where success depends on how well you work as a group? Write your reactions to these questions:

✔ What were some of the advantages of working in a group?

✔ What were some of the problems that cropped up?

✔ How did you go about trying to solve them and how successful were you?

✔ What advice would you have for other groups who collaborate on other projects?

For Your Working Portfolio Add your finished product and reflection responses to your working portfolio. If you created a board game, you could take photos of the board and any game pieces you created and put them in your portfolio along with your drawings and writing.

ASSESSMENT CRITERIA SPECS

6 Superior The writer of a 6 paper impressively meets these criteria:

- Vividly describes the world in which the game unfolds, creating an intriguing environment that offers the kinds of goals and obstacles that draw players into a game.
- Thoroughly defines the key elements of the game, including goals, characters, obstacles, and tools.
- Uses colorful language with rich connotations to name and describe these elements.
- Includes strategic illustrations that both give vital information and help create a vivid picture of the world in which the game takes place.
- Concludes by giving specific, convincing reasons that would appeal to a professional in the field of game-making.
- Makes few, if any, errors in grammar, usage, spelling, and mechanics, including correctly capitalizing proper nouns and proper adjectives.

Unit 3 Resource Book
Assessment Worksheet, p. 40

STEP 5 PRESENTING

Presentation

Before students present their proposals you might sneak in an interdisciplinary math lesson by asking students to price their product according to estimated production costs and market demand.

Advertisement, Box

Encourage groups to be creative about packaging and advertising. This is a great opportunity for visual and creative students to exhibit their talents.

Play

You might arrange a game day on which students all try out their games.

Submit

Help interested students find addresses where they could submit proposals.

STEP 6 LOOKING BACK

Self-evaluate

The *Assessment Criteria Specs* at the bottom of this page are for a superior paper. You might want to post these in the classroom. Students can then evaluate themselves based on these criteria. For a complete scoring rubric, use the *Assessment Worksheet* referenced below.

Unit 3 Resource Book
Assessment Worksheet, p. 40

Reflect

These writing activities could serve as a springboard to class discussion on collaboration and ways to enhance cooperative learning in the future.

To further explore the theme, use the Fine Art Transparency referenced below.

Transparency Collection
Fine Art Transparency 6

Beyond Print

Teaching Objectives

- to evaluate a painting using context, composition, and a critical view
- to identify the subject, setting, mood, and interest focus of a painting

Curricular Connection: Visual Literacy

You can use the material in this article to give students practice in becoming more familiar with strategies for interpreting a painting.

Introduce

Point out that just as there are strategies to use in analyzing and evaluating literature, there are also skills and strategies that can be used to gain understanding of works of art. Have students read the article and try to analyze the painting on page 393.

Beyond Print

Looking at Paintings

St. George and the Dragon by Paolo Uccello depicts a legendary knight, St. George, in the process of rescuing a lady in distress from a horrible monster. At first glance, the painting appears to be a traditional portrayal of a knight in combat: the white steed; the armored hero; the helpless lady; the ferocious enemy. But look more closely. Is the damsel in serious distress? What is she holding? Does the knight look like a muscular champion of good? Does the dragon seem at all frightening? When analyzing this or any piece of art, keep three C's in mind.

Context

Determine the meaning. What is the subject? Does the picture tell a story? Is the artist painting a contemporary scene, or going back or ahead in time to find a subject? What details help establish meaning? How does the artist feel about this subject? In this painting, for example, the leashed dragon and the unnaturally elongated lance suggest the painter's ironic intent.

Composition

Look at the focal point, colors, and shapes. How and where does the artist attract your attention? How do colors and shapes affect the meaning and mood of the work? Note how Uccello draws your eyes to the dragon by using the long shaft of the lance and the downward spiral of the leash. How do the colors Uccello selects influence your feelings about this painting? Shapes add interest and balance to this work. Note, for example, that the outline of the cave almost swallows the dragon. If the cave were turned upside-down, it would be the same shape as the sky.

Critical View

Decide whether the artist achieved his or her objective and whether or not you like the painting. After analyzing a painting and deciding that an artist has accomplished his or her objective, you still may not like the work. Or you might enjoy viewing a piece of art that you think is not very successful. The important thing is that you have analyzed its con-

ANOTHER APPROACH

What's Your Perspective of Uccello's Perpective?

Inform students that the artist Paolo Uccello is widely considered the father of perspective. Explain that perspective is the technique artists use to represent three-dimensional objects and space relationships on a two-dimensional surface such as a canvas. Have students examine the painting carefully to find evidence of Uccello's use of perspective. These questions may facilliitate a discussion.

- Do you think that Uccello took his subject matter seriously or was he just decorating a canvas? Why?
- Do the knight and his horse seem much closer to the dragon than the lance would indicate? Do you think Uccello makes effective use of space? Why?

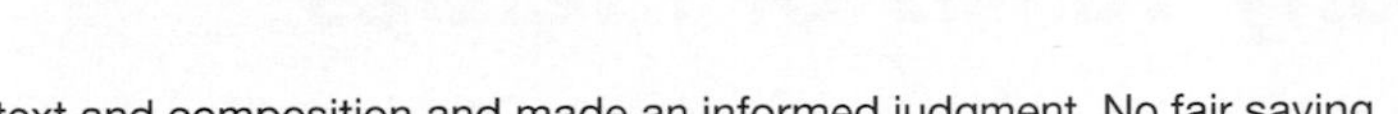

text and composition and made an informed judgment. No fair saying, I like (don't like) it, but I don't know why!

Activity Options

1. Paint the same story from another viewpoint—for example, the dragon's, the woman's, the horse's, or an aerial view. Use shapes, colors, and details to let a reader know your tone and meaning.
2. Analyze another work of art in this book, using the three C's.

Activity Options

Activity 1 Students may tend to avoid using the lady's point of view because her expression and gesture are not very clear.

Activity 2 Remind students that these are strategies for paintings and encourage them to choose a painting to analyze. Afterwards, have students look at a different art medium, and discuss what the strategies for analyzing it might be.

BUILDING ENGLISH PROFICIENCY

Making Personal Connections

Use one or both of the following activities to help students grasp the three "C's" in this feature.

Activity Ideas

- As students look closely at *St. George and the Dragon,* ask them to freewrite and jot down other notes in their journals. (Encourage responses in first languages other than English.) If possible, let them take a break and come back to the painting again, adding to their notes. Then have students circle comments that seem to relate to each of the three C's.
- As students consider any work of art, invite them to imagine themselves as the artist. Ask: If you had created this work of art and were offering it to a museum or art dealer, could you sell it? How would you explain its colors and shapes? What would you say about its meaning and why you created it?

Preview

Many Kinds of Heroes

FOR ALL STUDENTS

Many families have their own private set of myths and legends, involving relatives that have achieved feats of heroism. Have students write a brief narrative about a legendary family figure.

To further explore the theme, use the Fine Art Transparency referred to below.

Transparency Collection
Fine Art Transparency 7

For At-Risk Students

Ask students to

- choose a favorite superhero from comic books, television, or the movies
- draw a picture of this hero and include a caption that identifies and defines the characteristics that make him or her a hero

For Students Who Need Challenge

According to Joseph Campbell in *Hero With a Thousand Faces*, a hero passes through three stages: separation, initiation, and return. Have students write an essay explaining how either Rolf Carlé or Corrie ten Boom exemplifies this journey.

MULTICULTURAL CONNECTION

Let students explore the concept of individuality. Suggest that they

- make an outline of a human being to represent themselves and in it write words that describe their individuality
- draw a similar image for each of several characters in the selections
- answer the question in the second paragraph on page 394 by making a list of the group standards that characters faced

Part Two

Many Kinds of Heroes

What's happened to our heroes? you might ask. Gone are the noble knights of old. In their place, are the little heroes, the antiheroes, the people who cope rather than conquer. As you read the following selections, decide where each character falls on a broad hero spectrum.

Multicultural Connection **Individuality** allows us to redefine heroism in specific cultural settings. As you read the following selections, determine how individuals respond heroically to their circumstances and their surroundings. Have these characters accepted or rejected group standards in their heroic efforts?

Literature

Interdisciplinary Study **Heroes Around the World**

Reading Mini-Lesson

Writing Workshop **Expository Writing**

Beyond Print Technology

IDEAS THAT WORK

Listening to Living Voices

A wide vista is open to students when they leave Arthurian heroes and move to the present. Students should hear the power of living voices and in them find the heroic.

I'd ask students to write briefly about heroes and to share with partners for an antiheroic perspective, or create a student value line about heroes and fold the line, creating a dialogue of opposites.

With the poems, I'd utilize a jigsaw approach, providing expert groups with epic characteristics of heroes for measuring the heroic quality of the group's poem and drawing conclusions. Students could create a heroic model based on the group's poem.

While reading the short stories, divergent thinkers may find new ways of seeing heroes and new heroes may materialize in the readings.

Carlton Jordan
Parsippany, New Jersey

Before Reading

And of Clay Are We Created

by Isabel Allende Chile

Isabel Allende
born 1942

A major Chilean writer now living in the United States, Isabel Allende (ä yen′dā) says that many factors helped her become a writer: "The storytelling of my mother, the books I read, the love of words, this desire that I've always had to communicate." Allende, formerly a journalist, combines these influences with personal experiences—such as the assassination in 1973 of her uncle, Chilean President Salvador Allende—to realistically portray violence, inequality, poverty, and illiteracy. "Those things appear constantly. . . . We cannot control everything in our reality." Allende's words proved prophetic with the death in 1992 of her daughter Paula, a victim of a hospital mishap.

Building Background

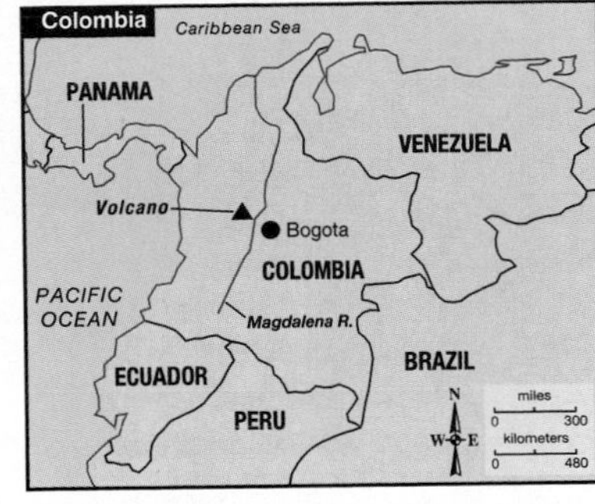

Fiction Based on Fact In November 1985, a volcanic flow of mud and lava buried the town of Armero, Colombia, killing more than 20,000. National attention was focused on attempts to rescue thirteen-year-old Omairo Sánchez, who was mired neck-deep in mud. Rescuers unsuccessfully tried to free the girl's legs, which were caught way below the surface in the death grip of her aunt. After sixty hours, the girl died of heart failure. The story you are about to read is based on this incident.

Literary Focus

Point of View Just as a photographer directs a camera to capture selected images and impressions, a writer of fiction chooses a narrator who determines what the reader will learn. The relationship between the narrator of a story and the story he or she relates is called the **point of view**.

Writer's Notebook

Who Are the Heroes? Many people who *make* the news are considered heroes—firefighters, athletes, the person-on-the-street who responds in times of crisis. But how about those who *record* news—photographers and reporters, who sometimes endanger their lives in order to bring news to the public? Before you read, jot down a definition of heroism that could apply to many kinds of people.

Before Reading

Building Background

Lead students in a discussion of the role of television journalists in covering dramatic events such as natural disasters and wars. Have students speculate on the effects of such events on the reporters.

Literary Focus

Have students compare the role of the narrator in a story with that of a television reporter. Is the television reporter more like an omniscient (all-knowing) narrator, or more like a narrator who is also a character in the story? For definitions of omniscient and other types of narrative **points of view,** see page 43.

Writer's Notebook

Open a discussion about qualities that a hero must possess. Point out that epic heroes were held up as embodiments of all the social and personal qualities that the particular culture valued. Most had great courage and strength. Their origins could be common, royal, or half-supernatural, but all had to perform a great deed that was of national significance.

Connections to **AuthorWorks**

Isabel Allende is a featured author in the AuthorWorks CD-ROM series.

SUPPORT MATERIALS OVERVIEW

Unit 3 Resource Book
- Graphic Organizer, p. 41
- Study Guide, p. 42
- Vocabulary, p. 43
- Grammar, p. 44
- Alternate Check Test, p. 45
- Vocabulary Test, p. 46
- Selection Test, pp. 47–48

Building English Proficiency
- Literature Summaries
- Activities, p. 196

Reading, Writing & Grammar SkillBook
- Writing, pp. 126–127
- Grammar, Usage, and Mechanics, pp. 261–266

Technology
- Personal Journal Software
- Custom Literature Database: For a news article about a disaster, see "The Story of an Eye-Witness" by Jack London on the database.
- Test Generator Software

During Reading

Selection Objectives

- to explore different aspects of the theme of heroism
- to understand the use of point of view in fiction
- to use commas with introductory clauses and phrases

Unit 3 Resource Book
Graphic Organizer, p. 41
Study Guide, p. 42

Theme Link

Rolf Carlé and Azucena are examples of different kinds of heroes—those who bravely endure suffering.

Vocabulary Preview

cataclysm, any violent change or upheaval
viscous, thick, like heavy syrup; sticky
devastation, waste, destruction
quagmire, soft, muddy ground
pandemonium, wild disorder
impotence, helplessness
futile, not successful, useless
visceral, arising from instinct or strong feelings, not intellectual or rational
candid, frank and sincere
tribulation, great trouble; severe trial

Students can add words and definitions to their Writer's Notebook.

1 Literary Element
Connotation

Volunteers can explain why Lily is a "First Communion" name and what associations come to mind. (*Possible responses: Associations are white, purity, innocence; when Roman Catholic children take their First Communion, they consume bread, and sometimes wine, consecrated as the body and blood of Jesus. Girls typically wear a white dress and veil.)*

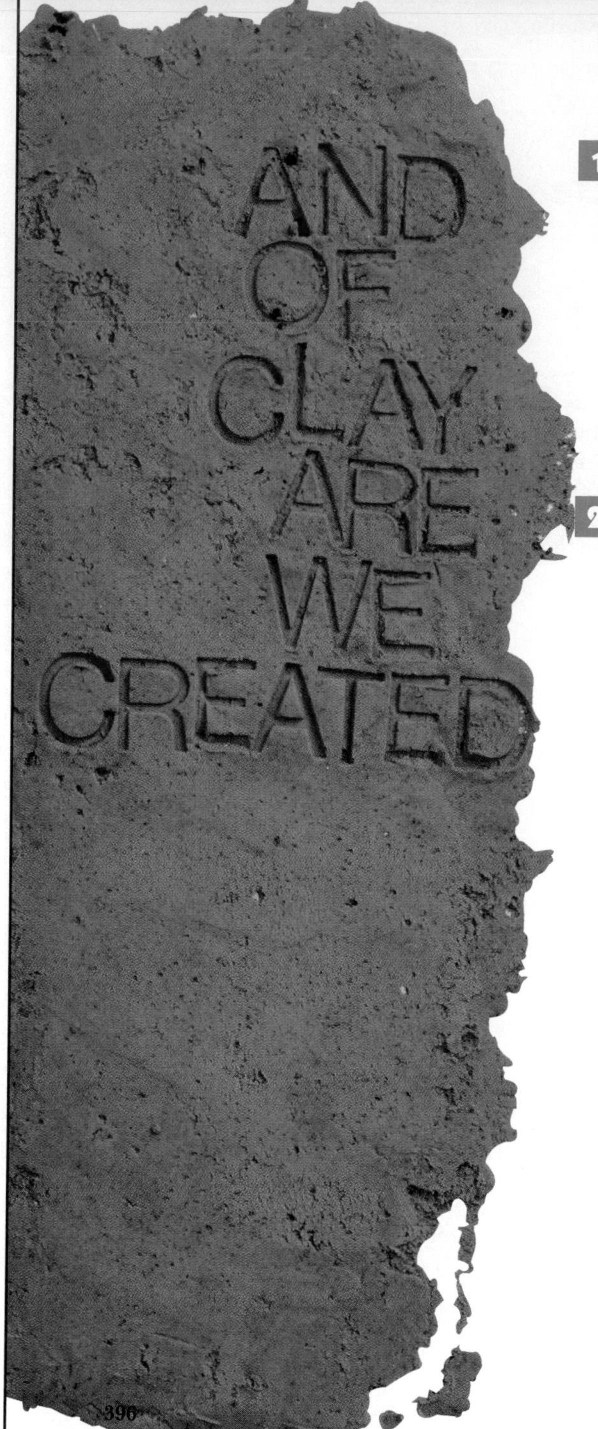

1 They discovered the girl's head protruding from the mudpit, eyes wide open, calling soundlessly. She had a First Communion name, Azucena. Lily. In that vast cemetery where the odor of death was already attracting vultures from far away, and where the weeping of orphans and wails of the injured filled the air, the little girl obstinately clinging to life became the symbol of the tragedy. The television cameras transmitted so often the unbearable image of the head budding like a black squash from the clay that there was no one who did not recognize her and know her name. And every time we saw her on the screen, right behind her was Rolf Carlé, who had gone there on assignment,
2 never suspecting that he would find a fragment of his past, lost thirty years before.

First a subterranean sob rocked the cotton fields, curling them like waves of foam. Geologists had set up their seismographs weeks before and knew that the mountain had awakened again. For some time they had predicted that the heat of the eruption could detach the eternal ice from the slopes of the volcano, but no one heeded their warnings; they sounded like the tales of frightened old women. The towns in the valley went about their daily life, deaf to the moaning of the earth, until that fateful Wednesday night in November when a prolonged roar announced the end of the world, and walls of snow broke loose, rolling in an avalanche of clay, stones, and water that descended on the villages and buried them beneath unfathomable meters of telluric vomit. As soon as the survivors emerged from the paralysis of that first awful terror, they could see that houses, plazas, churches, white cotton plantations, dark coffee forests, cattle pastures—all had disappeared. Much later, after soldiers and volunteers had arrived to rescue the living and try to assess the magnitude of the cataclysm,[1] it was calculated that beneath the mud lay more

1. cataclysm (kat′ə kliz′əm), *n.* any violent change or upheaval.

SELECTION SUMMARY

And of Clay Are We Created

A volcanic eruption in Colombia buries villages under a landslide. When photojournalist Rolf Carlé arrives at the scene he finds a teenage girl, named Azucena, or Lily, who has been buried nearly to her shoulders in the sticky quagmire. His attempts to free her fail, and he appeals for a pump. Although the media come with more reporters and equipment, the pump never comes. The four-day ordeal is viewed on TV by millions.

As Rolf Carlé and Azucena wait, he comforts her, but he is gradually drawn into terrifying memories of his childhood in war-torn Austria. Azucena finally dies, and Rolf Carlé returns home, able now to confront his past.

*For summaries in other languages, see the **Building English Proficiency** book.*

Max Ernst used vivid oil paints to create *Two Cardinal Points* in 1950. What qualities of nature are suggested in the deep layers of earth and the brilliant colors? Explain whether or not you associate these qualities with a volcano.

2 Literary Element
Foreshadowing

Remind students that foreshadowing is a hint given to the reader of what is to come. Point out that this foreshadowing is particularly interesting after the ghastly description that preceded it. Acknowledge that they probably have questions about Rolf, and let students share them.

Responses to Caption Question
Students may suggest its depth, variety, and beauty. A volcano may bring to mind darkness and destruction, not brilliance.

Max Ernst was co-founder of dadaism, an art movement that appeared during and after World War I. As a reaction to the war's horror and meaninglessness, dadaism emphasized chance, the irrational, and unregulated imagination.

Visual Literacy Artists can use texture, or showing in art what would appeal to the sense of touch, to suggest the solidity of an image.

Question What objects in the painting especially show texture? (*the two lowest layers of earth and the sixth from the bottom*)

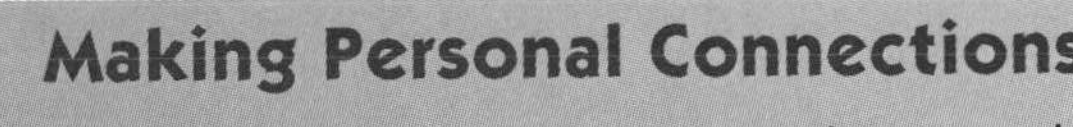

Making Personal Connections

Students born in other countries may have experienced disasters such as the one in this story. If appropriate, invite volunteers to share their experiences and feelings, either orally or in writing.

Students also may want to discuss the narrator's assumption that Rolf Carlé's childhood wounds will heal and he will "return from his nightmares" (page 404). You may wish to ask questions such as these:

- Do you agree with the saying "Time heals all wounds"? Can memories as vivid as Rolf's fade? Why or why not?
- Is the narrator too optimistic about Rolf's ability to deal with his memories and Azucena's death? Why or why not?

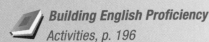

Activities, p. 196

3 Literary Focus
Point of View

Questions

- Who is telling the story? *(a woman who lives with Rolf Carlé)*
- From which point of view is this story told? How can you tell? *(from the first-person point of view; narrator uses the pronoun "I")*

Remind students that they should not assume that Allende is speaking as herself, even though she uses "I." In the first-person point of view, the persona or mask created by the author is the narrator.

4 Geographical Note
The Colombian Andes

Colombia is dominated by three Andean mountain ranges that cross the country like spines whose "bones" soar to over 16,000 feet. The ability to mount large-scale disaster relief efforts is hampered by the need to bring supplies via mountain roads.

5 Active Reading
Clarify

Possible responses The camera lens serves as a barrier or filter to lessen the effects of horrifying events. In the same way, some people may watch violent or tragic events on TV and not be affected.

than twenty thousand human beings and an indefinite number of animals putrefying in a viscous[2] soup. Forests and rivers had also been swept away, and there was nothing to be seen but an immense desert of mire.

3 When the station called before dawn, Rolf Carlé and I were together. I crawled out of bed, dazed with sleep, and went to prepare coffee while he hurriedly dressed. He stuffed his gear in the green canvas backpack he always carried, and we said good-bye, as we had so many times before. I had no presentiments. I sat in the kitchen, sipping my coffee and planning the long hours without him, sure that he would be back the next day.

He was one of the first to reach the scene, because while other reporters were fighting their way to the edges of that morass in jeeps, bicycles, or on foot, each getting there however he could, Rolf Carlé had the advantage of
4 the television helicopter, which flew him over the avalanche. We watched on our screens the footage captured by his assistant's camera, in which he was up to his knees in muck, a microphone in his hand, in the midst of a bedlam of lost children, wounded survivors, corpses, and devastation.[3] The story came to us in his calm voice. For years he had been a familiar figure in newscasts, reporting live at the scene of battles and catastrophes with awesome tenacity. Nothing could stop him, and I was always amazed at his equanimity in the face of danger and suffering; it seemed as if nothing could shake his fortitude or deter his curiosity. Fear seemed never to touch him, although he had confessed to me that he was not a courageous man, far from it. I believe that the lens of the camera had a strange effect on him; it was as if it transported him to a different time from which he could watch events without actually participating in them. When I knew him better, I came to realize that this fictive distance seemed to protect him from his own emotions.

CLARIFY: How does the camera serve to protect Rolf Carlé? 5

Rolf Carlé was in on the story of Azucena from the beginning. He filmed the volunteers who discovered her, and the first persons who tried to reach her; his camera zoomed in on the girl, her dark face, her large desolate eyes, the plastered-down tangle of her hair. The mud was like quicksand around her, and anyone attempting to reach her was in danger of sinking. They threw a rope to her that she made no effort to grasp until they shouted to her to catch it; then she pulled a hand from the mire and tried to move, but immediately sank a little deeper. Rolf threw down his knapsack and the rest of his equipment and waded into the quagmire,[4] commenting for his assistant's microphone that it was cold and that one could begin to smell the stench of corpses.

"What's your name?" he asked the girl, and she told him her flower name. "Don't move, Azucena," Rolf Carlé directed, and kept talking to her, without a thought for what he was saying, just to distract her, while slowly he worked his way forward in mud up to his waist. The air around him seemed as murky as the mud.

It was impossible to reach her from the approach he was attempting, so he retreated and circled around where there seemed to be firmer footing. When finally he was close enough, he took the rope and tied it beneath her arms, so they could pull her out. He smiled at her with that smile that crinkles his eyes and makes him look like a little boy; he told her that everything was fine, that he was here with her now, that soon they would have her out. He signaled the others to pull, but as soon as the cord tensed, the girl screamed. They tried again, and her shoulders and arms appeared, but they

2. **viscous** (vĭs′kəs), *adj.* thick, like heavy syrup; sticky.
3. **devastation** (dĕv′ə stā′shən), *n.* waste; destruction.
4. **quagmire** (kwăg′mīr′), *n.* soft, muddy ground.

MINI-LESSON: GRAMMAR
Commas in Introductory Clauses

Point out the introductory clauses in these sentences from the second paragraph on page 398:

When the station called before dawn, Rolf Carlé and I were together.

When I knew him better, I came to realize that this fictive distance seemed to protect him from his own emotions.

Question What punctuation follows an introductory clause? (*a comma*)

Activity Ideas

For practice students can

- identify other sentences in the passage that have introductory clauses
- write a paragraph that uses introductory clauses to help explain when and how a disaster occurred
- check their own writing for the use of commas after introductory clauses

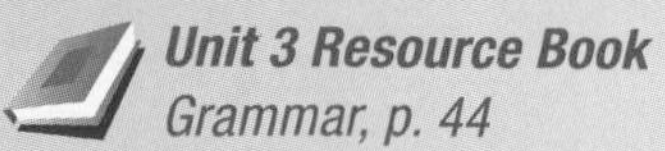

Unit 3 Resource Book
Grammar, p. 44

could move her no farther; she was trapped. Someone suggested that her legs might be caught in the collapsed walls of her house, but she said it was not just rubble, that she was also held by the bodies of her brothers and sisters clinging to her legs.

6 "Don't worry, we'll get you out of here," Rolf promised. Despite the quality of the transmission, I could hear his voice break, and I loved him more than ever. Azucena looked at him, but said nothing.

During those first hours Rolf Carlé exhausted all the resources of his ingenuity to rescue her. He struggled with poles and ropes, but every tug was an intolerable torture for the imprisoned girl. It occurred to him to use one of the poles as a lever but got no result and had to abandon the idea. He talked a couple of soldiers into working with him for a while, but they had to leave because so many other victims were calling for help. The girl could not move, she barely could breathe, but she did not seem desperate, as if an ancestral resignation allowed her to accept her fate. The reporter, on the other hand, was determined to snatch her from death. Someone brought him a tire, which he placed beneath her arms like a life buoy, and then laid a plank near the hole to hold his weight and allow him to stay closer to her. As it was impossible to remove the rubble blindly, he tried once or twice to dive toward her feet, but emerged frustrated, covered with mud, and spitting gravel. He concluded that he would have to have a pump to drain the water, and radioed a request for one, but received in return a message that there was no available transport and it could not be sent until the next morning.

"We can't wait that long!" Rolf Carlé shouted, but in the pandemonium[5] no one stopped to commiserate. Many more hours would go by before he accepted that time had stagnated and reality had been irreparably distorted.

A military doctor came to examine the girl, and observed that her heart was functioning well and that if she did not get too cold she could survive the night.

"Hang on, Azucena, we'll have the pump tomorrow," Rolf Carlé tried to console her.

"Don't leave me alone," she begged.

"No, of course I won't leave you."

Someone brought him coffee, and he helped the girl drink it, sip by sip. The warm liquid revived her and she began telling him about her small life, about her family and her school, about how things were in that little bit of world before the volcano had erupted. She was thirteen, and she had never been outside her village. Rolf Carlé, buoyed by a premature optimism, was convinced that everything would end well: the pump would arrive, they would drain the water, move the rubble, and Azucena would be transported by helicopter to a hospital where she would recover rapidly and where he could visit her and bring her gifts. He thought, *She's already too old for dolls, and I don't know what would please her; maybe a dress. I don't know much about women,* he concluded, amused, reflecting that although he had known many women in his lifetime, none had taught him these details. To pass the hours he began to tell Azucena about his travels and adventures as a newshound, and when he exhausted his memory, he called upon imagination, inventing things he thought might entertain her. From time to time she dozed, but he kept talking in the darkness, to assure her that he was still there and to overcome the menace of uncertainty. 7

EVALUATE: Do you think that Rolf Carlé's optimism is justified? Why or why not? 8

That was a long night.

Many miles away, I watched Rolf Carlé and the girl on a television screen. I could not bear

5. pandemonium (pan′də mō′nē əm), *n.* wild disorder.

6 Literary Element
Characterization

Question Is Rolf Carlé behaving as usual? Why or why not? *(No, he usually does not get involved personally. Now he is emotional and desperately wants to free the girl.)*

7 Literary Focus
Point of View

Note that here the narrator reveals Rolf Carlé's actual thoughts, as if she were omniscient. Students may infer that, after the ordeal was over, Rolf Carlé told the narrator what he had been thinking.

A narrator's attitude toward his or her subject is capable of variation; it can range from one of apparent indifference to one of extreme conviction and feeling.

Question What is this narrator's attitude toward her subject? *(Possible response: one of empathy, deep concern, intimacy)*

8 Active Reading
Evaluate

Possible responses Many students, perhaps influenced by the happy endings often found in TV rescue dramas, may assume that help will come. Some students may recognize cues such as the author's use of the phrase "premature optimism" or the likelihood of the plot being extended.

BUILDING ENGLISH PROFICIENCY

Sequencing Story Events

As the story progresses, students may have difficulty in moving between subplots and flashbacks, so encourage them to map the sequence of the story's events.

1. Explain that the first paragraph opens "in the middle" of the story's events: as in a news story, the author "grabs" the reader's attention with one tragic event that symbolizes a disaster.
2. Let them begin mapping at the second paragraph, where the story's real "start" begins.
3. Urge them to be alert for the story's opening event as they map.

Volcano erupts and buries a valley.
↓
Rolf Carlé flies to the scene.
↓
Rolf Carlé films the rescuers finding Azucena.
↓
[ ]
↓
[ ]

9 Literary Focus
Point of View

Question The first-person narrator tells the story as she watches the events on TV. Do you think it would have been more or less dramatic if she had been on the scene, giving an eyewitness account? Why? *(Possible responses: Both would have been dramatic. To focus on Rolf Carlé's change and development, Allende puts the narrator at a physical distance, yet still able to see and hear everything.)*

10 Literary Element
Symbol

Question What does the lens symbolize? *(Possible response: Rolf Carlé's emotional separation from pain and suffering)*

the wait at home, so I went to National Television, where I often spent entire nights with Rolf editing programs. There, I was near his world, and I could at least get a feeling of what he lived through during those three decisive days. I called all the important people in the city, senators, commanders of the armed forces, the North American ambassador, and the president of National Petroleum, begging them for a pump to remove the silt, but obtained only vague promises. I began to ask for urgent help on radio and television, to see if there wasn't
9 *someone* who could help us. Between calls I would run to the newsroom to monitor the satellite transmissions that periodically brought new details of the catastrophe. While reporters selected scenes with most impact for the news report, I searched for footage that featured Azucena's mudpit. The screen reduced the disaster to a single plane and accentuated the tremendous distance that separated me from Rolf Carlé; nonetheless, I was there with him. The child's every suffering hurt me as it did him; I felt his frustration, his impotence.[6] Faced with the impossibility of communicating with him, the fantastic idea came to me that if I tried, I could reach him by force of mind and in that way give him encouragement. I concentrated until I was dizzy—a frenzied[7] and futile[8] activity. At times I would be overcome with compassion and burst out crying; at other times, I was so drained I felt as if I were staring through a telescope at the light of a star dead for a million years.

I watched that hell on the first morning broadcast, cadavers of people and animals awash in the current of new rivers formed overnight from the melted snow. Above the mud rose the tops of trees and the bell towers of a church where several people had taken refuge and were patiently awaiting rescue teams. Hundreds of soldiers and volunteers from the Civil Defense were clawing through rubble searching for survivors, while long rows of ragged specters awaited their turn for a cup of hot broth. Radio networks announced that their phones were jammed with calls from families offering shelter to orphaned children. Drinking water was in scarce supply, along with gasoline and food. Doctors, resigned to amputating arms and legs without anesthesia, pled that at least they be sent serum and painkillers and antibiotics; most of the roads, however, were impassable, and worse were the bureaucratic[9] obstacles that stood in the way. To top it all, the clay contaminated by decomposing bodies threatened the living with an outbreak of epidemics.

Azucena was shivering inside the tire that held her above the surface. Immobility and tension had greatly weakened her, but she was conscious and could still be heard when a microphone was held out to her. Her tone was humble, as if apologizing for all the fuss. Rolf Carlé had a growth of beard, and dark circles beneath his eyes; he looked near exhaustion. Even from that enormous distance I could sense the quality of his weariness, so different from the fatigue of other adventures. He had completely forgotten the camera; he could not look 10
at the girl through a lens any longer. The pictures we were receiving were not his assistant's

He had completely forgotten the camera; he could not look at the girl through a lens any longer.

6. **impotence** (im′pə təns), *n.* helplessness.
7. **frenzied** (fren′zēd), *adj.* greatly excited; frantic.
8. **futile** (fyü′tl), *adj.* not successful; useless.
9. **bureaucratic** (byůr′ə krat′ik), *adj.* marked by an excessive insistence on rigid routine that causes delays in getting things done.

MINI-LESSON: SPEAKING AND LISTENING
Interview

Teach Explain to students that news reporters often interview people at the scene of an important event. A good interviewer must

- determine the main topics for the interview
- organize a series of questions to develop the topics
- ask questions clearly and listen to the answers, which in turn may suggest further questions

To remind students of the importance of interview skills, ask them to name situations when they would conduct an interview, or be interviewed. *(Possible responses: conduct an interview for a research paper or news article; be interviewed for a job or college admission)*

Activity Idea Have pairs of students practice interviewing skills by doing the following:

- One student gives a topic that he or she would like to be interviewed about.
- The other student conducts the interview.
- The students then switch roles.

but those of other reporters who had appropriated Azucena, bestowing on her the pathetic responsibility of embodying the horror of what had happened in that place. With the first light Rolf tried again to dislodge the obstacles that held the girl in her tomb, but he had only his hands to work with; he did not dare use a tool for fear of injuring her. He fed Azucena a cup of the cornmeal mush and bananas the Army was distributing, but she immediately vomited it up. A doctor stated that she had a fever, but added that there was little he could do: antibiotics were being reserved for cases of gangrene. A priest also passed by and blessed her, hanging a medal of the Virgin around her neck. By evening a gentle, persistent drizzle began to fall.

11 "The sky is weeping," Azucena murmured, and she, too, began to cry.

"Don't be afraid," Rolf begged. "You have to keep your strength up and be calm. Everything will be fine. I'm with you, and I'll get you out somehow."

12 Reporters returned to photograph Azucena and ask her the same questions, which she no longer tried to answer. In the meanwhile, more television and movie teams arrived with spools of cable, tapes, film, videos, precision lenses, recorders, sound consoles, lights, reflecting screens, auxiliary motors, cartons of supplies, electricians, sound technicians, and cameramen: Azucena's face was beamed to millions of screens around the world. And all the while Rolf Carlé kept pleading for a pump. The improved technical facilities bore results, and National Television began receiving sharper pictures and clearer sound; the distance seemed suddenly compressed, and I had the horrible sensation that Azucena and Rolf were by my side, separated from me by impenetrable glass. I was able to follow events hour by hour; I knew everything my love did to wrest the girl from her prison and help her endure her suffering; I overheard fragments of what they said to one another and could guess the rest; I was present when she taught Rolf to pray, and when he distracted her with the stories I had told him in a thousand and one nights beneath the white mosquito netting of our bed. 13

CONNECT: Do you think the public is entitled to watch personal suffering such as Azucena's? Why or why not?

When darkness came on the second day, Rolf tried to sing Azucena to sleep with old Austrian folk songs he had learned from his mother, but she was far beyond sleep. They spent most of the night talking, each in a stupor of exhaustion and hunger, and shaking with cold. That night, imperceptibly, the unyielding floodgates that had contained Rolf Carlé's past for so many years began to open, and the torrent of all that had lain hidden in the deepest and most secret layers of memory poured out, leveling before it the obstacles that had blocked his consciousness for so long. He could not tell it all to Azucena; she perhaps did not know there was a world beyond the sea or time previous to her own; she was not capable of imagining Europe in the years of the war. So he could not tell her of defeat, nor of the afternoon the Russians had led them to the concentration camp to bury prisoners dead from starvation. Why should he describe to her how the naked bodies piled like a mountain of firewood resembled fragile china? How could he tell this dying child about ovens and gallows? Nor did he mention the night that he had seen his mother naked, shod in stiletto-heeled red boots, sobbing with humiliation. There was much he did not tell, but in those hours he relived for the first time all the things his mind had tried to erase. Azucena had surrendered her fear to him and so, without wishing it, had obliged Rolf to confront his own. There, beside that hellhole of mud, it was impossible for Rolf to flee from himself any longer, and the visceral[10] terror he had

10. **visceral** (vis′ər əl), *adj.* arising from instinct or strong feelings; not intellectual or rational.

11 Literary Element
Metaphor

Questions

- What metaphor does Azucena use here? *(She compares the falling rain to weeping.)*
- What mood does this metaphor help create? *(Possible responses: sadness, hopelessness)*

12 Reading/Thinking Skills
Identify Alternatives

The media deploys a sophisticated array of technology at the scene of this tragedy, yet no one can bring a simple pump that might free Azucena.

Question If you were involved with Azucena's plight, what would you do to try to help? *(Possible responses: Since the media can reach the site by helicopter, they could arrange to take a pump, medical supplies, or other things with them.)*

13 Active Reading
Connect

Possible responses Some students may say that people have a right to be informed, or suggest that people need to experience suffering so they can be motivated to help. Other students may suggest that the media sensationalizes suffering too much, and that it is unhealthy for people to take such an interest in it.

BUILDING ENGLISH PROFICIENCY

Exploring Dramatic Tension

Explain the word *tension* by holding up a rubber band and showing it as below while describing the tension:

limp—*no tension*
stretched out—*some tension*
pulled to the breaking point—*a lot of tension*

Help students understand that in a story there is emotional tension, and that one by one, certain events increase tension. Propose that pairs of students draw four boxes to represent TV screens. In them, they can draw the four most dramatic, tension-filled moments of the events on pages 400-401. Remind students to show increasing tension.

14 Reading/Thinking Skills
Literal and Figurative Language

Question In what way does Rolf Carlé, like Azucena, find himself "trapped in a pit without escape?" *(Possible response: Now that he has let himself feel Azucena's fears, he can't escape his own fears caused by terrors of his childhood.)*

15 Literary Element
Archetype

Rolf Carlé now feels himself to be trapped and buried like Azucena. The experience of death, burial, and rebirth, found in many myths, can suggest a deep change in personality.

Question In what ways do you think this experience will change Rolf Carlé? *(Possible responses: Rolf Carlé will not seek danger by day and have to conquer frightful dreams at night; he may be more loving and understanding of others; instead of distancing himself from people, he may get involved and help them.)*

16 Active Reading
Clarify

Rolf Carlé is trapped by terrors from his childhood that he can't forget. The feeling is so strong that he feels he has become Azucena.

lived as a boy suddenly invaded him. He reverted to the years when he was the age of Azucena, and younger, and, like her, found him-
14 self trapped in a pit without escape, buried in life, his head barely above ground; he saw before his eyes the boots and legs of his father, who had removed his belt and was whipping it in the air with the never-forgotten hiss of a viper coiled to strike. Sorrow flooded through him, intact and precise, as if it had lain always in his mind, waiting. He was once again in the armoire where his father locked him to punish him for imagined misbehavior, there where for eternal hours he had crouched with his eyes closed, not to see the darkness, with his hands over his ears, to shut out the beating of his heart, trembling, huddled like a cornered animal. Wandering in the mist of his memories he found his sister Katharina, a sweet, retarded child who spent her life hiding, with the hope that her father would forget the disgrace of her having been born. With Katharina, Rolf crawled beneath the dining room table, and with her hid there under the long white tablecloth, two children forever embraced, alert to footsteps and voices. Katharina's scent melded with his own sweat, with aromas of cooking, garlic, soup, freshly baked bread, and the unexpected odor of putrescent clay. His sister's hand in his, her frightened breathing, her silk hair against his cheek, the candid[11] gaze of her eyes. Katharina . . . Katharina materialized before him, floating on the air like a flag, clothed in the white tablecloth, now a winding sheet, and at last he could weep for her death and for the guilt of having abandoned her. He understood then that all his exploits as a reporter, the feats that had won him such recognition and fame, were merely an attempt to keep his most ancient fears at bay, a stratagem for taking refuge behind a lens to test whether reality was more tolerable from that perspective. He took excessive risks as an exercise of courage, training by day to conquer the monsters that tormented him by night. But he had come face to face with the moment of truth; he could not continue to escape his past. He *was* Azucena; he 15
was buried in the clayey mud; his terror was not the distant emotion of an almost forgotten childhood, it was a claw sunk in his throat. In the flush of his tears he saw his mother, dressed in black and clutching her imitation-crocodile pocketbook to her bosom, just as he had last seen her on the dock when she had come to put him on the boat to South America. She had not come to dry his tears, but to tell him to pick up a shovel: the war was over and now they must bury the dead.

CLARIFY: Why do you think Rolf Carlé finally felt that "he *was* Azucena"? 16

"Don't cry. I don't hurt anymore. I'm fine," Azucena said when dawn came.

"I'm not crying for you," Rolf Carlé smiled. "I'm crying for myself. I hurt all over."

The third day in the valley of the cataclysm began with a pale light filtering through storm clouds. The President of the Republic visited the area in his tailored safari jacket to confirm that this was the worst catastrophe of the century; the country was in mourning; sister nations had offered aid; he had ordered a state of siege; the Armed Forces would be merciless, anyone caught stealing or committing other offenses would be shot on sight. He added that it was impossible to remove all the corpses or count the thousands who had disappeared; the entire valley would be declared holy ground, and bishops would come to celebrate a solemn mass for the souls of the victims. He went to the Army field tents to offer relief in the form of vague promises to crowds of the rescued, then to the improvised hospital to offer a word of encouragement to doctors and

11. **candid** (kan′did), *adj.* frank and sincere.

MINI-LESSON: VOCABULARY
Use Dictionaries for Word Meaning

Teach Explain that a dictionary provides a definition that often includes synonyms. Remind students to look for the synonyms because they are easy to understand and remember.

Activity Idea Divide the class into groups. Give each group five words from the vocabulary words for this selection. Group members work together to

- list one or more synonyms for each of their words
- check the dictionary for additional synonyms
- use a synonym of each vocabulary word in a written sentence
- exchange sentence sets with other groups
- substitute the original vocabulary words for the synonyms in sentences from the other group

Word List	
cataclysm	viscous
devastation	quagmire
pandemonium	impotence
futile	visceral
candid	tribulation

This 1990 print done with pen, brush, and ink by Rocío Maldonado is titled *La Mano*, or *The Hand.* What is your immediate response to this image? Explain whether or not you think it would be effective as a poster publicizing a national disaster.

nurses worn down from so many hours of tribulations.[12] Then he asked to be taken to see Azucena, the little girl the whole world had seen. He waved to her with a limp statesman's hand, and microphones recorded his emotional voice and paternal tone as he told her that her courage had served as an example to the nation. Rolf Carlé interrupted to ask for a pump, and the President assured him that he personally would attend to the matter. I caught a glimpse of Rolf for a few seconds kneeling beside the mudpit. On the evening news broadcast, he was still in the same position; and I, glued to the screen like a fortune-teller to her crystal ball, could tell that something fundamental had changed in him. I knew somehow that during the night his defenses had crumbled and he had given in to grief; finally he was vulnerable. The girl had touched a part of him that he him-

12. **tribulation** (trib′yə lā′shən), *n.* great trouble; severe trial.

Art Study

Responses to Caption Question Because of the context of the selection, students will probably interpret the hand in the picture as a plea for help. Many students will suggest that this simple but striking image would be effective as a poster for disaster relief.

Rocio Maldonado's paintings and drawings often reflect images from Mexico's religion and popular culture, as well as reflecting women's concerns. She has been recognized as one of Mexico's most important contemporary artists.

Visual Literacy Composition is the choice and placement of objects in a work of art.

Question Why do you think the painting has only one object—a hand? *(Possible response: to focus the reader's attention on this one object, without any background to distract)*

Question What do you think is suggested by the placement and arrangement of the hand? *(Possible response: Most students will suggest that the hand shows a reaching up and out for help. Some students may suggest that it shows the solid reality of human flesh.)*

BUILDING ENGLISH PROFICIENCY

Point of View

Discuss with students that the story is written from the first-person point of view in which the narrator speaks using "I." Model examples of sentences with "I" and ask students to state others.

Clarify that the narrator is Rolf Carlé's friend, who remains in the city and watches the events on TV. Tell students to imagine that another character was the narrator. Then have partners briefly retell the events of the story to one another, using the first-person point of view, but as if the narrator were Rolf Carlé, Azucena, or a rescuer on the scene.

If students have created sequence charts (page 399), they can refer to them as they narrate.

17 Reading/Thinking Skills
Draw Conclusions

Question Who do you think acted as a hero in this story? *(Possible responses: Azucena for her courage in facing death; Rolf Carlé for his courage in facing his own terror; the narrator for supporting Rolf Carlé as he changes)*

Check Test

1. What is Azucena's problem? *(She is trapped in clay soil and rubble following a volcanic eruption.)*
2. How does Rolf Carlé get to the scene of the disaster? *(by helicopter)*
3. What prevents Azucena from sinking into the clay? *(a tire beneath her arms that serves as a life buoy)*
4. Who is aware of Azucena's plight? *(the reporter, other workers on the scene, millions of TV viewers)*
5. What does Rolf Carlé pray for? *(that Azucena would have a quick death)*

Unit 3 Resource Book
Alternate Check Test, p. 45

self had no access to, a part he had never shared with me. Rolf had wanted to console her, but it was Azucena who had given him consolation.

I recognized the precise moment at which Rolf gave up the fight and surrendered to the torture of watching the girl die. I was with them, three days and two nights, spying on them from the other side of life. I was there when she told him that in all her thirteen years no boy had ever loved her and that it was a pity to leave this world without knowing love. Rolf assured her that he loved her more than he could ever love anyone, more than he loved his mother, more than his sister, more than all the women who had slept in his arms, more than he loved me, his life companion, who would have given anything to be trapped in that well in her place, who would have exchanged her life for Azucena's, and I watched as he leaned down to kiss her poor forehead, consumed by a sweet, sad emotion he could not name. I felt how in that instant both were saved from despair, how they were freed from the clay, how they rose above the vultures and helicopters, how together they flew above the vast swamp of corruption and laments. How, finally, they were able to accept death. Rolf Carlé prayed in silence that she would die quickly, because such pain cannot be borne.
17

By then I had obtained a pump and was in touch with a general who had agreed to ship it the next morning on a military cargo plane. But on the night of that third day, beneath the unblinking focus of quartz lamps and the lens of a hundred cameras, Azucena gave up, her eyes locked with those of the friend who had sustained her to the end. Rolf Carlé removed the life buoy, closed her eyelids, held her to his chest for a few moments, and then let her go. She sank slowly, a flower in the mud.

The girl had touched a part of him that he himself had no access to. . .

You are back with me, but you are not the same man. I often accompany you to the station and we watch the videos of Azucena again; you study them intently, looking for something you could have done to save her, something you did not think of in time. Or maybe you study them to see yourself as if in a mirror, naked. Your cameras lie forgotten in a closet; you do not write or sing; you sit long hours before the window, staring at the mountains. Beside you, I wait for you to complete the voyage into yourself, for the old wounds to heal. I know that when you return from your nightmares, we shall again walk hand in hand, as before.

MINI-LESSON: READING/THINKING SKILLS
Recognizing Cause and Effect

Teach Remind students that the plot of a story is often driven by a chain of events or series of causes and effects. In this selection, Azucena's ordeal was caused by a volcanic eruption. Because she was trapped, she was weakened and exposed to the elements, which in turn caused her death.

Activity Idea Pairs of students can draw a cause and effect chart for a character of their choice. A sample is shown for the character of Rolf Carlé. Encourage students to put in the chart causes and effects that advanced the plot.

Rolf Carlé	
Cause	**Effect**
He is a photo journalist.	He is sent to cover a disaster.
He gets emotionally involved.	He throws down his equipment.

After Reading

Making Connections

Shaping Your Response

1. In your opinion, does this story, based on an actual incident, seem stranger than fiction? Explain.
2. Do you think that this story should be included in a world literature anthology? Why or why not?
3. Do you think that all heroes, like Rolf Carlé, must forget their **individual** needs in trying to help someone else? Why or why not?

Analyzing the Story

4. Explain the **irony** in the narrator's observations of the "improved technical facilities" that ensure worldwide coverage of Azucena's tragedy.
5. Find five memorable **images** in this story and explain why they appeal to you.
6. How do you think this story reflects the **theme** "Many Kinds of Heroes"?
7. What is the significance of the fact that Rolf "could not look at the girl through a lens any longer"?
8. Explain this **paradox:** Rolf Carlé and Azucena "were freed from the clay" only after they were able to accept death.
9. What do you think the **title** means?

Extending the Ideas

10. With a group, brainstorm stories, movies, or news accounts in which a disaster provides an opportunity for greater self-awareness. Why do you think a disaster might lead to self-knowledge?

Literary Focus: Point of View

This story is told by a *first-person* narrator—a character who presents events from a personal **point of view**, drawing readers directly into the action.

- Who is the narrator of this story?
- Speculate on why this narrator is able to supply more information about Rolf than he himself can.
- How does the narrator's focus shift in the final paragraph?

After Reading

MAKING CONNECTIONS

1. Possible responses: It's hard to believe that Azucena would not have been rescued; or, it's believable, based on natural disasters and the disaster victims seen on TV.

2. Many students will feel that the story should be included because of its fine writing and its setting in a Latin American culture. Some students may find the story too gruesome.

3. Students will recognize that heroism involves sacrificing one's comfort or safety to help others.

4. The media is able to bring many people and their advanced technology to the scene by helicopter, but no one can bring a simple pump that might save Azucena's life.

5. Examples are the girl's head protruding from the clay, the President waving weakly to the dying girl, Rolf Carlé's haggard appearance, the weeping sky, Rolf Carlé and his sister under the table, Rolf Carlé and Azucena "soaring" after her death.

6. Possible responses: Rolf Carlé and Azucena both show heroic qualities such as courage and bravery in doing a great deed. They may discuss whether Rolf Carlé's internal terror was greater than the external terrors around him.

7. It shows that he has lost his sense of detachment as a reporter, and that he, as a person suffering great internal torment, identified with her.

8. The acceptance of her death seemed to free them from the confinement of the struggle against it.

9. In a way, Rolf and Azucena were "created" or reborn through their struggle with the clay quagmire.

10. Students should recognize that people learn more about their strengths, weaknesses, and values, as they respond to crises.

LITERARY FOCUS: POINT OF VIEW

Responses

- She is the woman companion of Rolf Carlé who was with him when he left for the disaster.
- The narrator witnessed the change in him and may have greater insight into human nature.
- The narrator shifts to the present tense and focuses on what has changed in Rolf Carlé.

VOCABULARY STUDY

1. devastation, cataclysm
2. pandemonium, visceral
3. quagmire, viscous
4. impotence, tribulation
5. futile, candid

More Practice Have students write a paragraph about a natural disaster they have seen on TV, or an imagined one. Students should use at least five of the vocabulary words in their paragraph.

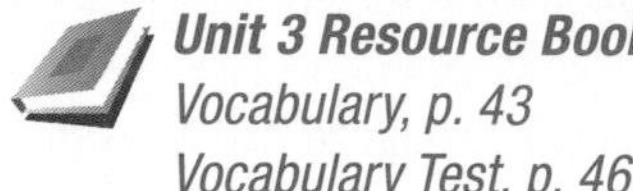

Unit 3 Resource Book
Vocabulary, p. 43
Vocabulary Test, p. 46

WRITING CHOICES

Writer's Notebook Update

Suggest that students consider that heroic qualities can involve both how one responds to a crisis and the attitudes or values that impel someone to help others. Also have students consider that heroes cannot always overcome obstacles, and that the way Azucena faces the inevitable might also be heroic.

The Write to Know

Ask volunteers to do a telephone interview with a member of the local press to find out the policies of the local newspapers on professional and moral responsibilities of the media.

Selection Test

Unit 3 Resource Book
pp. 47–48

Vocabulary Study

candid
cataclysm
devastation
futile
impotence
pandemonium
quagmire
tribulation
visceral
viscous

Replace each italicized word in the sentences below with a synonym from the list.

1. The terrible *destruction* from the *upheaval* was clear to rescuers.
2. Wild *disorder* broke out when people followed their *instinctive* tendencies toward self-preservation.
3. The girl could not be removed from the *swamp* of *sticky* clay.
4. Rolf's *helplessness* in rescuing the girl was a terrible *trial* in his life.
5. Knowing that her dream of being rescued was *useless*, Azucena was *frank* about facing death.

Expressing Your Ideas

Writing Choices

Writer's Notebook Update Which characters in the story fit the definition of *hero* that you wrote in your notebook? If necessary, change or adjust your definition of heroism based on this story. Then make a web of heroic qualities.

Hero of the Year Imagine that *Time* magazine is accepting nominations for an annual Hero of the Year award. Write a **letter** to the nominating committee, identifying someone you think should be honored as Hero of the Year. Refer to the web of heroic qualities that you made in your notebook.

The Write to Know There's a fine line between the individual's right to privacy and the public's right to know. Do you think that in its effort to report the news, the media sometimes crosses the boundaries of good taste into sensationalism? Express your ideas on the subject in an **editorial.**

Other Options

Disaster Team Natural disasters, such as hurricanes, tornadoes, and earthquakes, occur every year. If a community near you were struck by such a catastrophe, would you be able to offer rescue or relief services to the survivors? With your group, develop a **teen rescue/relief plan** to help a community whose citizens are displaced, injured, or emotionally upset from the disastrous events.

Private Eye Using a camera or a video-camera, focus on details from a scene that you want the viewer to see, and capture the mood, impression, and feelings of the moment. Share your **photographs** or **video** with the class.

Political Fallout As president of the Republic, your administration is being criticized for not heeding the geologists' warnings and thus preventing the death of 20,000 citizens. Hold a **press conference** in which you answer reporters' questions and explain your plans for a new law that will ensure timely evacuations of areas threatened by future natural disasters.

OTHER OPTIONS

Disaster Team

For more information about an international agency and its emergency relief work, see The World of Work, pp. 3–4.

Before Reading

A Soldier of Urbina by Jorge Luis Borges Argentina
Lineage by Margaret Walker USA
The Gift by Li-Young Lee USA
Turning Pro by Ishmael Reed USA

Building Background

Echoes of Admiration

> By law of Nature, no man can admire, for no man can understand, that of which he has no echo in himself.
>
> *Francis Thompson*

What do you think Thompson means? To prove or disprove his observation, think of the characteristics of someone you admire. Then compare those characteristics to those you possess.

Literary Focus

Metaphor

Reprinted with special permission of North America Syndicate.

- What two things are being compared in this cartoon?
- What do these two things have in common?

An implied comparison between two essentially unlike things is called a **metaphor.** A comparison between life and an elevator (or a roller coaster) implies that both have their ups and downs, highs and lows.

Writer's Notebook

A Hero Is a Tower The poems you are about to read capture special qualities of unsung heroes through metaphors. For example, there is a father whose hands are "two measures of tenderness." Think of someone you consider heroic and describe a quality of that person (gentleness, wisdom, stubbornness, strength, etc.) in terms of a metaphor.

Before Reading

Building Background

These points may clarify the meaning of this passage for students:

- A quality of another person echoes, or corresponds to, something in oneself.
- This resonance allows one to understand the other's qualities.
- The understanding can lead to admiration.

Literary Focus

Mention that when writing about nonphysical subjects, such as emotions or attitudes, it is often necessary to compare them to concrete or physical figures. Let students create other **metaphors** for life, such as:

- Life is *(but an empty dream).*
- Life is *(a road we walk on once).*

Writer's Notebook

To help students construct metaphors, you can have them fill out a chart in which they identify heroic qualities and what they compare them to.

Heroic quality	Compared to
quiet strength	a great tree standing against a storm
gentle strength; tenderness	a mother elephant with baby
unstoppable power	Superman, freight train

SUPPORT MATERIALS OVERVIEW

Unit 3 Resource Book
- Graphic Organizer, p. 49
- Study Guide, p. 50
- Vocabulary, p. 51
- Grammar, p. 52
- Alternate Check Test, p. 53
- Vocabulary Test, p. 54
- Selection Test, pp. 55–56

Building English Proficiency
- Literature Summaries
- Activities, p. 197
- "The Soldier of Urbina" in Spanish

Reading, Writing & Grammar SkillBook
- Reading, pp. 51–52
- Grammar, Usage, and Mechanics, pp. 267–270

Technology
- Audiotapes 10, Side B, and 11, Side A
- Personal Journal Software
- Custom Literature Database: For related works, see "Childe Roland to the Dark Tower Came" by Browning, *Don Quixote* by Cervantes, and "Ode to Niagara" by Heredia.
- Test Generator Software

More About the Poets

Margaret Walker

When she won the Yale Younger Poets Series Award in 1942, Margaret Walker became, according to Richard K. Barksdale, "the first Black woman in American literary history to be so honored in a prestigious national competition." She has also written *For My People*, (1942).

Jorge Luis Borges

Anthony Kerrigan describes Borges' writing as " . . . a species of international literary metaphor. He knowledgeably makes a transfer of inherited meanings from Spanish and English, French and German. . . . " Among Borges's works is *In Praise of Darkness*, (1974).

Ishmael Reed

His first novel, *The Free-Lance Pallbearers*, (1967), satirized aspects of both white and black culture, leading to criticism. He later responded that "The mainstream aspiration for Afro-Americans is for more freedom—and not slavery—including freedom of artistic expression."

Jorge Luis Borges
1899–1986

Born in Buenos Aires, Argentina, Jorge Luis Borges (hôr′hā lwēs bôr′hās) had written a short story in Spanish by the time he was six and at nine had read the works of authors such as Dickens, Twain, Poe, and Cervantes. From 1919 to 1921, Borges was in Spain, where his first poems were published. Borges also wrote short stories, essays, and movie scenarios. By the time he was thirty, his eyesight was seriously impaired, a degenerative condition he referred to as a "slow, summer twilight."

Margaret Walker
born 1915

As a child, Margaret Walker listened to her grandmother's bedtime stories about slavery, vowing to preserve those tales in writing. She kept her promise by writing poetry and novels that have validated the folk roots of African American life. Walker believes, however, that "writers should not write exclusively for black or white audiences, but most inclusively." She adds, "All humanity must be involved in both the writing and in the reading" of the human condition.

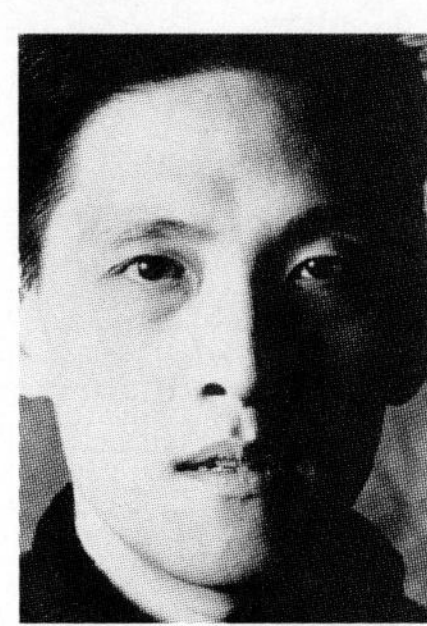

Li-Young Lee
born 1957

Much of Li-Young Lee's poetry describes his father, who had been Chairman Mao's personal physician until the senior Lee and his wife fled China's political turmoil. Li-Young Lee was born in Indonesia shortly before his father's two-year imprisonment during a period of anti-Chinese sentiment. The family escaped to Hong Kong, where Lee's father became a distinguished evangelical preacher, and later fled to the United States. Lee's relaxed style of writing blends images pertaining to cultural politics and personal longings.

Ishmael Reed
born 1938

Novelist, poet, essayist, and critic, Ishmael Reed uses the language and beliefs of folk culture in unusual ways to satirize America's cultural arrogance and racism. Reed's poetic techniques include striking images as well as phonetic spellings and unconventional capitalization. In the introduction to his book, *Writin' Is Fightin'*, Reed compares the life of a boxer who spars with opponents to that of a black male who is confronted by a hostile society.

A Soldier of Urbina

Jorge Luis Borges

Feeling himself unfitted for the strain
Of battles like the last he fought at sea,
This soldier, doomed to sordid[1] usury,[2]
Wandered unknown throughout his own harsh Spain.

To blot out or to mitigate[3] the pain
Of all reality, he hid in dream;
1 A magic past was opened up to him
Through Roland and the tales of Ancient Britain.

At sunset he would contemplate[4] the vast
Plain with its copper light lingering on;
He felt himself defeated, poor, alone,

Ignorant of what music he was master;
2 Already, in the still depths of some dream,
Don Quixote and Sancho were alive in him.

A Soldier of Urbina refers to the Spanish writer Miguel de Cervantes (ser vän′tēz), the author of the novel, *Don Quixote.* Cervantes, who was wounded in battle, sold into slavery, and jailed for debt, finally took up a literary career. The adventures of Don Quixote and his sidekick, Sancho Panza, satirize medieval romances of chivalry such as the story of Roland.

1. sordid (sôr′did), *adj.* filthy, contemptible.
2. usury (yü′zhər ē), *n.* the lending of money at an unusually high or unlawful rate of interest.
3. **mitigate** (mit′ə gāt), *v.* make less harsh.
4. contemplate (kon′təm plāt). *v.* gaze at; think about.

During Reading

Selection Objectives

- to identify various heroic qualities
- to identify and construct metaphors
- to apply standard sentence punctuation rules

Unit 3 Resource Book
Graphic Organizer, p. 49
Study Guide, p. 50

Theme Link

Heroism is painted in many shades in these poems—as an escape and a discovery. It is shown in the tender act of a father and when a person believes in himself despite the odds.

Vocabulary Preview

sordid, filthy, contemptible
usury, lending of money at an unusually high or unlawful rate of interest
contemplate, gaze at, think about
lineage, descent in a direct line from a common ancestor
shard, a broken piece
scribe, writer, author

Students can add the words and definitions to their Writer's Notebooks.

1 Literary Element
Allusion

Point out that Roland, celebrated in a poem about 1100 A.D., had been killed because, out of chivalric pride, he had refused to call for reinforcements. The Arthurian legends from ancient Britain were a source of allegory and romance.

2 Literary Element
Theme

Lead students in a discussion of whether Cervantes hides among old heroes or discovers the hero within himself.

SELECTION SUMMARY

Lineage, The Soldier of Urbina, Turning Pro, The Gift

Varied aspects of heroism can be seen in the four poems. "The Soldier of Urbina" suggests how the author Miguel Cervantes may have moved from outward failure to an inward power of heroic imagination. "Lineage" conveys a simple yet powerful picture of the speaker's ancestors, whose heroism was expressed in working the land, physical strength, and pure spirit. "The Gift" uses language rich in metaphor to show how a father can transmit heroic virtues to his son in an act of healing. Finally, "Turning Pro" depicts an aging baseball pitcher who perseveres and triumphs despite his physical shortcomings.

*For summaries in other languages, see the **Building English Proficiency** book.*

You may wish to explain that a sharecropper is a person who farms land for the owner in return for part of the crops. Whether the sharecropper was black or white, the connotation is that of poverty.

Responses to Caption Questions The word *sharecropper*, connoting an anonymous, lowly occupation, stands in sharp contrast to the strength, dignity, and individuality of the woman in the portrait.

Elizabeth Catlett's work has often focused on the dignity of African Americans suffering under an unjust system. One critic has said that *Sharecropper* portrays a woman "whose features look as if they had been sculpted by a lifetime of hard work."

Visual Literacy The dignity of the sharecropper is shown in the composition or arrangement of parts of the picture, especially the hat and white hair framing the face. It is also shown in the balance of the green and brown colors.

Question What elements in the picture do you think especially show the woman's strength or dignity? (*Possible responses: simple clothes, her wise gaze forward, the sculpted lines of the face*)

MINI-LESSON: LITERARY FOCUS

Metaphor

Teach Remind students that they use metaphors frequently. Some common ones are "time is money" and "on the road to success." A metaphor, the comparison between two unrelated nouns, is one of the most important poetic elements.

Activity Ideas

- Pairs of students can identify metaphors in "The Gift." Their findings can be organized in a chart as shown.

Metaphor	Actual quality or object
a well of dark water; a prayer	the father's voice
two measures of tenderness	the father's hands

- Students can use the following prompts to create metaphors about themselves. Then they can choose one metaphor and build it into a complete poem.

In my past I was a ____.
In the mirror I am a ____.
In my dreams I am a ____.
In my fears I am a ____.
In my car I am a ____.

Lineage

Margaret Walker

My grandmothers were strong.
They followed plows and bent to toil.
They moved through fields sowing seed.
They touched earth and grain grew.
They were full of sturdiness and singing.
My grandmothers were strong.

My grandmothers are full of memories
Smelling of soap and onions and wet clay
With veins rolling roughly over quick hands
They have many clean words to say.
My grandmothers were strong.
Why am I not as they?

3

4

lineage (lin′ē ij), *n.* descent in a direct line from a common ancestor.

In her woodcut, Elizabeth Catlett uses lines and planes to create an extraordinary image of dignity, pain, and endurance. Why might the artist have chosen to title this work, so obviously a portrait of an **individual**, simply *Sharecropper?* What title might you have given it?

The Gift

5

Li-Young Lee

To pull the metal splinter from my palm
my father recited a story in a low voice.
I watched his lovely face and not the blade.
Before the story ended, he'd removed
the iron sliver I thought I'd die from.

I can't remember the tale,
but hear his voice still, a well
of dark water, a prayer.
And I recall his hands,
two measures of tenderness
he laid against my face,
the flames of discipline
he raised above my head.

Had you entered that afternoon
you would have thought you saw a man
planting something in a boy's palm,
a silver tear, a tiny flame.
Had you followed that boy
you would have arrived here,
where I bend over my wife's right hand.

Look how I shave her thumbnail down
so carefully she feels no pain.
Watch as I lift the splinter out.
I was seven when my father
took my hand like this,

and I did not hold that shard[1]
between my fingers and think,
Metal that will bury me,
christen it Little Assassin,
Ore Going Deep for My Heart.
And I did not lift up my wound and cry,
Death visited here!
I did what a child does
when he's given something to keep.
I kissed my father.

1. shard (shärd), *n.* broken piece.

3 Literary Element
Rhythm

When read aloud, "Lineage" has the steady, strong rhythm of a chant.

Question Why might the author have chosen this kind of rhythm? *(Possible responses: to fit the simplicity of the subject, to echo the rhythms of work)*

4 Reader's Response
Making Personal Connections

Question Do you look to your forebears for models of strength, or to fictitious characters? *(Students should mention what strengths relatives, friends, characters in fiction, or celebrities have shown.)*

5 Literary Focus
Metaphor

Challenge students to explain how the title "The Gift" may be a metaphor. Remind students that metaphors compare two unlike things that have something in common. No connecting words such as *like* or *as* are used. In the discussion, let students reread the third verse which shows that the father's actions were so powerful that they influenced the boy throughout life.

BUILDING ENGLISH PROFICIENCY

Expanding Upon Poetic Ideas

Encourage students to increase their understanding and enjoyment of "The Gift" on page 411.

Activity Ideas

- In "The Gift," the speaker recalls a childhood injury. Invite students to recall a childhood injury they thought they'd "die from." Prompt them to share how it seemed at the time and how they view it now.
- Reread with students the first two verses and ask why the father told a story. *(to take the boy's attention away from the pain of removing the sliver)*
- Let students react to the father's gentleness. How would they have reacted if they were in the father's place? Why?
- Students might be ready to write a few lines to expand upon their own memories.

Building English Proficiency
Activities, p. 197
"The Soldier of Urbina" in Spanish

6 Literary Element
Imagery

Question After reading this poem, what visual or physical details stand out for you? *(Possible responses: the shortstop could be your son; faking you out, name lit up the scoreboard; fans carried you on their shoulders)*

7 Reading/Thinking Skills
Understand Sequence

Question What are the three main stages that the player in this poem goes through? *(criticized for no longer playing well enough; wins with a shut-out in a key game; sent to the major leagues as a result)*

8 Literary Element
Mood

Question What mood do these images and events help create? *(Possible responses: triumph, glory)*

Turning Pro

Ishmael Reed

There are just so many years
you can play amateur baseball
without turning pro
All of a sudden you realize
you're ten years older than
everybody in the dugout
6 and that the shortstop could
be your son

7

The front office complains
about your slowness in making
the line-up
They send down memos about
your faulty bunts and point out
how the runners are always faking
you out
"His ability to steal bases
has faded" they say
They say they can't convince
the accountant that there's such
a thing as "old Time's Sake"
But just as the scribes[1] were
beginning to write you
off
as a has-been on his last leg
You pulled out that fateful
shut-out
and the whistles went off
and the fireworks scorched a
747
8 And your name lit up the scoreboard
and the fans carried you on their
shoulders right out of the stadium
and into the majors

1. **scribe** (skrīb), *n.* writer; author.

Baseball Machine, a painted polychrome wood sculpture by Leo Jensen, is a construction that can be played as a game by laying it flat, spinning the bats, and making the ball bounce. Do you think that the playful purpose of this work makes it any less effective as a work of art? Why or why not? ➤

MINI-LESSON: GRAMMAR
Using Standard Sentence Punctuation

Ask students to scan the four poems on pages 409–412 and observe the punctuation. Let them point out examples of lines with punctuation as it would be in prose sentences and lines that do not follow prose punctuation. *(The first verse of "Lineage" is punctuated like prose; most of the other poems are not.)* Ask them to explain circumstances under which the following sentence punctuation would be used: period, comma, semicolon.

Question Why do you think some kinds of poetry do not use standard sentence punctuation? (*Possible responses: because not all poems use complete sentences; because poetry conveys images and meanings in a different way from prose sentences)*

Activity Idea Students can practice using standard sentence punctuation as they paraphrase one of the four poems in a brief paragraph.

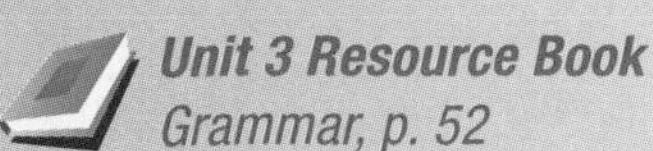
Unit 3 Resource Book
Grammar, p. 52

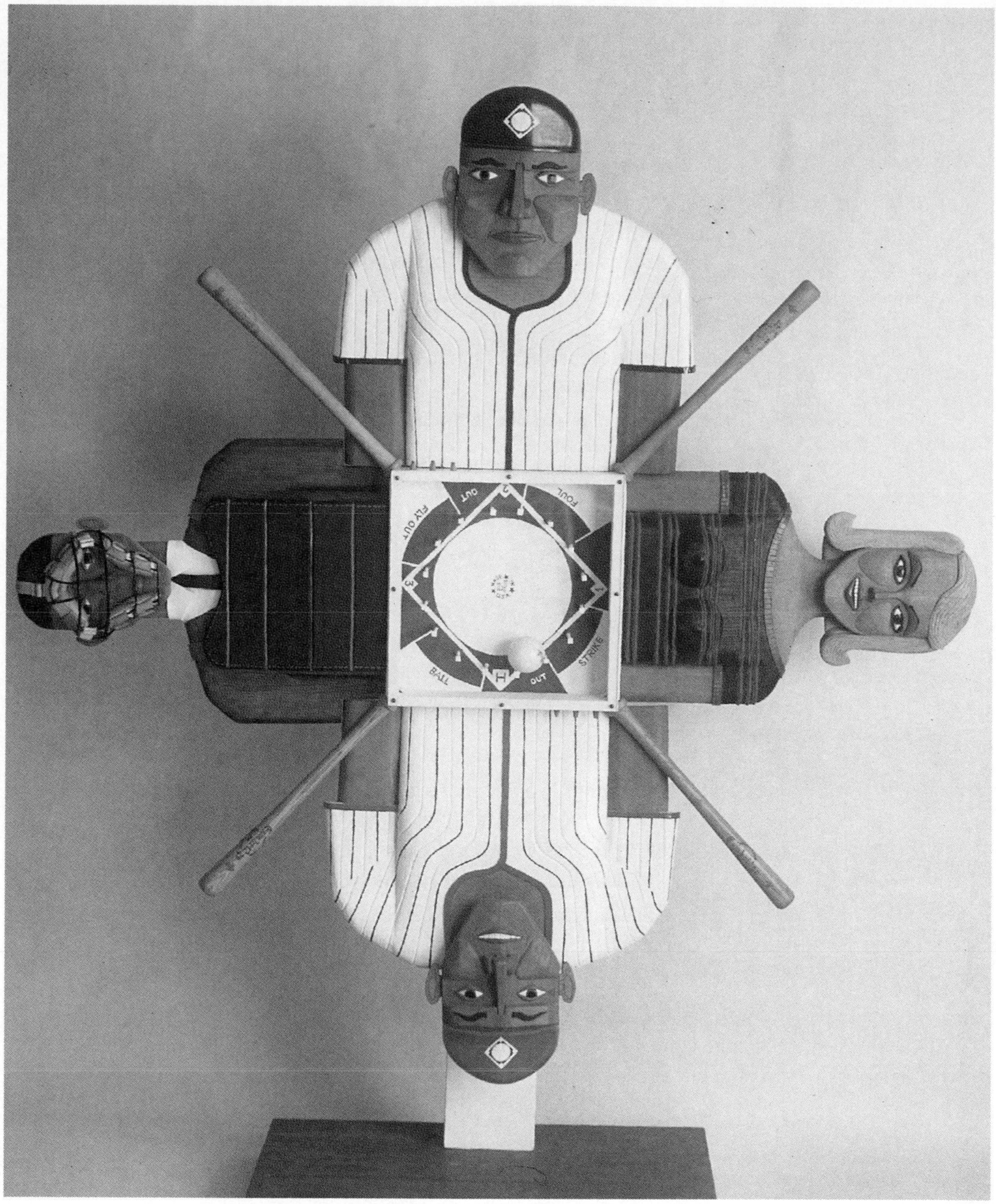

Art Study

Responses to Caption Questions Most students will probably say that the playful aspect of the art work adds to rather than detracts from its effectiveness. Some students may have trouble identifying this non-traditional work with conventional art.

Leo Jensen has done award-winning work in a variety of media including bronze sculpture, wood carving, acrylic, and watercolor.

Visual Literacy Symmetry is the arrangement of corresponding elements so that they mirror one another.

Question What elements in *Baseball Machine* particularly show symmetry? *(Possible responses: the bodies and heads of the four players, the crossed bats, the diamond)*

Check Test

1. In "A Soldier of Urbina," who is the person being described? (*the writer Miguel de Cervantes, author of* Don Quixote)

2. How is the speaker in "Lineage" probably related to the persons described in the poem? (*She is their descendant, if not literally their granddaughter.*)

3. How does the speaker in "The Gift" repeat what had happened to him in his childhood? (*He removes a splinter from his wife's hand in the same way his father had removed a shard of metal from his.*)

4. How old was the speaker when his father removed the splinter? (*seven*)

5. What problem does the player in "Turning Pro" face? (*He is getting older, slowing down, not playing so well.*)

Unit 3 Resource Book
Alternate Check Test, p. 53

BUILDING ENGLISH PROFICIENCY

ESL LEP ELD SAE LD

Expanding Vocabulary Notebooks

The combination of baseball jargon in "Turning Pro" as well as more ordinary slang may challenge students. Ask volunteers to use, explain, and demonstrate terms such as *bunt, fake out, steal bases, has-been, line-up,* and others. Encourage them to make a T-chart in their notebooks as shown.

turning pro	moving from the amateur sports leagues to professional
front office	the sports team's managers

Continue the discussion by asking volunteers to find hints about the positions played by the subject of the poem. (They may infer that the subject of the poem is a pitcher from the lines "You pulled out that fateful / shut-out," but the poet may be referring to any older player playing any position.) Also invite students to draw a baseball diamond on the board and explain the game to others.

After Reading

MAKING CONNECTIONS

1. Responses should be supported by reasons why a person is admirable or heroic and examples from the poems.

2. You may wish to prompt students by asking them to visualize their impressions of one of the poems.

3. For their symbols students can show a key image, such as a plow for "Lineage," a metal shard and a flame for "The Gift," and a baseball for "Turning Pro."

4. Possible responses: sowing seed, grain grew, sturdiness and singing

5. Possible responses: soap—regard for cleanliness; onions—harvesting food and nourishing others; wet clay—hard-to-work soil; veins—blood, life, strength.

6. Possible responses: in pain emotionally, a dreamer, imaginative, on the verge of creating something great

7. Possible responses: that perseverance can make up for physical problems, that heroic performance is possible at any age

8. At the end the mood changes from one of fright to a mood of loving calmness.

9. Possible responses: that physical labor and a simple life are better than her life; that her grandmothers faced their lives more courageously than she faces hers

10. Examples cited by students should have identifiable heroic characteristics such as the accomplishment of a great deed, helping others, or standing by one's beliefs. Students may say that there are both positive and negative aspects of heroism in American culture.

After Reading

Making Connections

Shaping Your Response

1. Which poem most closely reflects your idea of a person to be admired? Why?
2. Work with a partner or group to capture a moment from one of these poems in a "freeze frame" tableau for classmates to identify.
3. Design a symbol for one of the poems. Explain your choice.

Analyzing the Poems

4. Cite examples of **alliteration,** repeated consonant sounds, in "Lineage."
5. Explain what each of the following indicates about the grandmothers in "Lineage": soap, onions, wet clay, veins.
6. How would you **characterize** Cervantes, the Soldier of Urbina, as described in this poem?
7. State a **moral** that you think is illustrated in "Turning Pro."
8. Describe how the **mood** shifts in the final stanza of "The Gift."

Extending the Ideas

9. What response might be given to the question in line 12 of "Lineage"?
10. Make a mental list of Americans who have achieved heroic status throughout history, such as media celebrities, cowboys, legendary figures, sports "greats," and news headliners. Then try to arrive at some generalizations about what heroism means in American culture.

Literary Focus: Metaphor

A **metaphor** is a figure of speech involving an implied comparison between two different things. Refer to "The Gift" to answer the following questions:

- What is the "silver tear" in line 17?
- In what way is the metal sliver comparable to a "Little Assassin"?

LITERARY FOCUS

Possible responses

- The silver tear may be the shard that had been removed from the boy's hand; it may also be the father's tenderness and love that the speaker keeps forever.
- It has a dagger-like shape; to the boy it was so painful that he said "I thought I'd die."

Vocabulary Study

contemplate
lineage
scribe
shard
sordid
usury

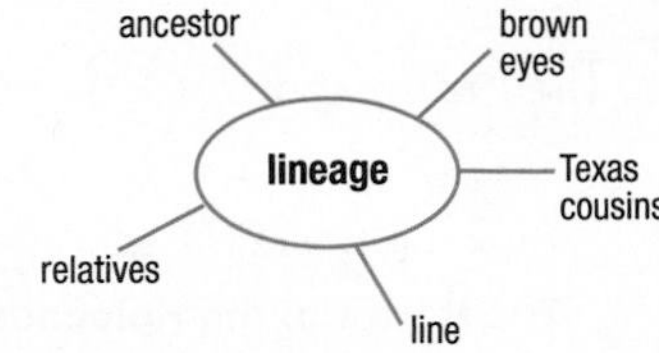

Study the web for *lineage,* thinking about the relationship of the words on the branches to *lineage*. Then make a web to illustrate the meanings and associations you have for one of the listed words.

Expressing Your Ideas

Writing Choices

Writer's Notebook Update Look again at the metaphor you created. Exchange metaphors with a classmate and try to explain what character trait you think is being emphasized in his or her work. Discuss anything that doesn't seem clear and revise accordingly.

Celebratory Poetry Write a **poem** to celebrate the life of someone special—a family member, acquaintance, or public figure. You might get ideas from your notebook or from the word web that you made in the Vocabulary Study.

One More Question As Margaret Walker grew up, she asked her grandmother many questions about the bedtime stories she told. The information Walker gathered during these discussions helped her write "Lineage." **Interview** someone who can shed light on you and your culture. Write down your questions beforehand. Then summarize the information you gather in an oral report to the class.

Other Options

Lyrics Heroic In a small group, analyze a song or rap about a hero (or an antihero). Or you may write **lyrics** describing a hero and create your own song or rap. In either case, be prepared to explain or perform your song for the class with your teacher's approval.

Hallmark Heroes Had enough of this hero business? Create a **greeting card** honoring someone for being just plain ordinary, for doing everyday things. Your card might be humorous, or a sincere tribute to the "common person." You might deliver the card in person to give that nonhero a lift.

Speaking Up To enjoy poetry, try reading it aloud. Choose one of the poems in this group to **read aloud** to the class. You might use special effects or have a classmate pantomime as you read the words.

VOCABULARY STUDY

Related words should usually be aspects, parts, or examples of the vocabulary word as shown in the sample web.

Unit 3 Resource Book
Vocabulary, p. 51
Vocabulary Test, p. 54

WRITING CHOICES

Writer's Notebook Update

Students can create additional metaphors to describe other aspects of the character being portrayed.

One More Question

This activity is an excellent opportunity to explore multicultural perspectives and find out what other people and cultures value.

Selection Test

Unit 3 Resource Book
pp. 55–56

OTHER OPTIONS

Lyrics Heroic

Students can discuss whether the person portrayed in the song or rap is really a hero, and the values implied by the celebration of that person.

Before Reading

Building Background

Connect this eye-witness account with others about the Holocaust, such as *The Diary of Anne Frank* or the movie *Schindler's List.*

Question What are other examples of rescuing people from oppression? *(Possible responses: the Underground Railroad in pre-Civil War America; the student movement in China in 1989)*

Literary Focus

Point out that **idioms** often illustrate how the same word is used differently, as in these examples: *make up my face, make up after a fight, make up a story.* Ask students to think of idioms with *run,* such as *stockings run, a run on a bank, run an ad in a newspaper.*

Writer's Notebook

Students might begin by expanding the time line on page 416 and adding events relating to the Holocaust.

More About Corrie ten Boom

In 1944, the Nazis arrested the ten Boom family. Corrie's father and brother died in prison. Because of a clerical error, Corrie was released from the concentration camp at Ravensbrück. The next day, all women in the camp were executed.

Before Reading

The Secret Room

by Corrie ten Boom The Netherlands

Corrie ten Boom
1892–1983

When German armies occupied Holland and started exterminating Jews, "my own family and my friends and I did all that we could do to save Jewish lives until we were betrayed and arrested. . . . From that moment forward, everything in our lives was changed." Thus spoke Corrie ten Boom, whose father died in prison and whose sister Betsie died in a German concentration camp. After a clerical error caused Corrie ten Boom to be released from the same concentration camp, she returned to her home, regained her health, and after the war established a home for victims of Nazi purges. Ten Boom's autobiography, *The Hiding Place,* records her experiences.

Building Background

The Horror of the Holocaust During the **Third Reich** (Germany from 1933 to 1945), the Nazi dictator Adolf Hitler took away the citizenship of Jewish people. The Nazis burned Jewish books, destroyed their synagogues, and looted and burned their stores. Jews were methodically persecuted, enslaved, and exterminated. By the end of World War II, an estimated six million European Jews had died.

1936	Germany reoccupies the Rhineland.
1938	Germany invades Austria and Czechoslovakia.
1939	Germany invades Poland. World War II begins.
1940	Germany invades Denmark, Norway, Belgium, the Netherlands, Luxembourg, and France. Italy invades Greece and British Somaliland.
1941	Germany invades Yugoslavia, Greece.
1942	Germany beseiges Stalingrad.
1943	Italy surrenders to the Allies.
1945	Germany surrenders to the Allies.

Literary Focus

Idioms "Hold your tongue!" "Hit the hay." These are **idioms** whose meanings cannot be understood from the ordinary meaning of the words in them. Idioms can often "throw dust in a person's eyes," or mislead someone who is unfamiliar with them. "Take the bull by the horns"—that is, attack the problem fearlessly—as you read "The Secret Room" by watching for idioms and using context to determine their meanings.

Writer's Notebook

What Else Do You Know? Brainstorm with a small group other information you know about the Holocaust and conditions in Nazi Germany. Then quickwrite several sentences to summarize this information.

SUPPORT MATERIALS OVERVIEW

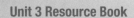

Unit 3 Resource Book
- Graphic Organizer, p. 57
- Study Guide, p. 58
- Vocabulary, p. 59
- Grammar, p. 60
- Alternate Check Test, p. 61
- Vocabulary Test, p. 62
- Selection Test, pp. 63–64

Building English Proficiency
- Literature Summaries
- Activities, p. 198

Reading, Writing & Grammar SkillBook
- Reading, pp. 32–35
- Writing, pp. 121–122
- Grammar, Usage, and Mechanics, pp. 270–271

The World of Work
- Builder, p.13
- Write a Progress Report, p. 14

Technology
- Audiotape 11, Side A
- Personal Journal Software
- Custom Literature Database: For poems about heroic women during wartime, see "Barbara Frietchie" and " The Female Patriots" on the the database.
- Test Generator Software

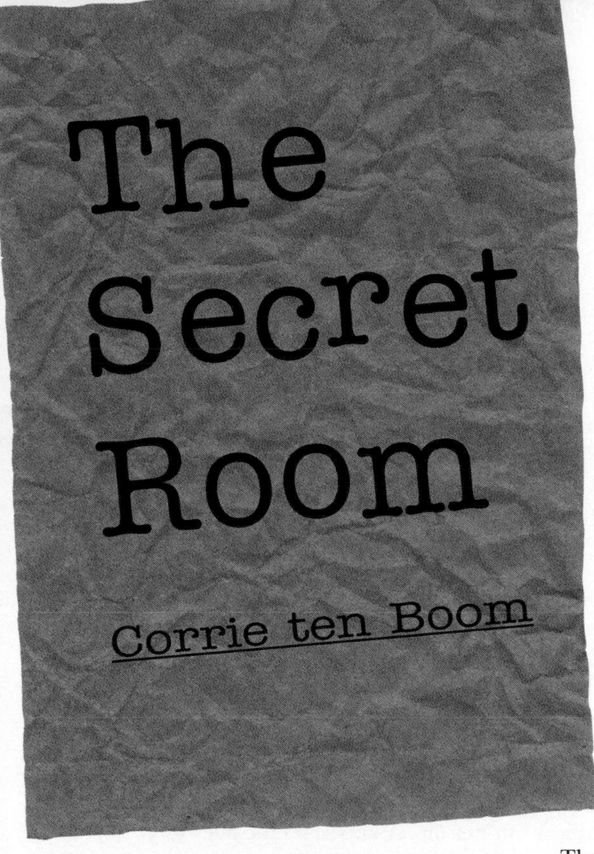

The Secret Room

Corrie ten Boom

When Nazi armies invaded Corrie ten Boom's homeland in 1940, she and her fellow citizens observed many dreadful changes. Living in the Dutch city of Haarlem (här′ləm) *with her sister, Betsie, and elderly father, she tried to maintain the appearance of an ordinary life, working as a watchmaker at the Beje* (bā′yā), *their combined home and shop. But as the following excerpt makes clear, there was also an unseen side to her life.*

Other family members introduced in ten Boom's story are Peter, her nephew; Willem (vil′əm), *her minister brother (who ran a home for the aged at Hilversum that he used as an escape route for fleeing Jews); Tine and Kik, Willem's wife and son; and Nollie, Peter's mother and another sister of Corrie's.*

It was Sunday, May 10, 1942, exactly two years after the fall of Holland. The sunny spring skies, the flowers in the lamppost boxes, did not at all reflect the city's mood. German soldiers wandered aimlessly through the streets, some looking as if they had not yet recovered from a hard Saturday night.

Each month the occupation seemed to grow harsher, restrictions more numerous. The latest heartache for Dutchmen was an edict[1] making it a crime to sing the "Wilhelmus,"[2] our national anthem.

Father, Betsie, and I were on our way to the Dutch Reformed church in Velsen,[3] a small town not far from Haarlem, where Peter had won the post of organist in competition against forty older and more experienced musicians. The organ at Velsen was one of the finest in the country; though the train seemed slower each time, we went frequently.

Peter was already playing, invisible in the tall organ loft, when we squeezed into the crowded pew. That was one thing the occupation had done for Holland: churches were packed.

After hymns and prayers came the sermon, a good one today, I thought. The closing prayers were said. And then, electrically, the whole church sat at attention. Without preamble,

1. edict (ē′dikt), *n.* decree or law.
2. **"Wilhelmus"** (vil′helm əs).
3. **Velsen** (vel′zən). Other Netherlands locations mentioned in the selection are Rotterdam, Amsterdam, Utrecht (yü′trəkt), and Aerdenhout (er′dən hout′).

During Reading

Selection Objectives

- to explore heroism in acts of resistance to oppression
- to recognize the use of idioms
- to punctuate dates correctly

Unit 3 Resource Book
Graphic Organizer, p. 57
Study Guide, p. 58

Theme Link

The theme "Many Kinds of Heroes" is shown in the ways that ordinary people can resist evil and do good despite great personal risk.

Vocabulary Preview

edict, decree or law
furtive, done quickly and with stealth, secret
tentative, hesitating
dilemma, difficult choice
aplomb, assurance, poise
uncanny, strange and mysterious
pungent, sharply affecting the organs of taste and smell
liaison, connection between military units, branches of a service, etc., to secure proper cooperation
haphazard, not planned; random
daunt, overcome with fear, frighten

Students can add the words and definitions to their Writer's Notebooks.

SELECTION SUMMARY

The Secret Room

Corrie ten Boom and her family live in Holland during the Nazi occupation of World War II. Because of their religious faith and humanitarian feeling, they help Jewish refugees who are fleeing from Nazi police. Their efforts involve them in increasingly risky activities such as hiding refugees, helping them flee to the countryside, and scheming to obtain precious ration cards.

Eventually Corrie is led to meet the Dutch underground, which sends an expert architect and workers to construct a secret room in the ten Boom's building.

For summaries in other languages, see the ***Building English Proficiency*** *book.*

1 Historical Note
Netherlands in World War II

To quell resistance to their rule, the Germans did not allow signs of Dutch patriotism, such as singing the anthem. The Netherlands (Holland) had been neutral during World War I. When World War II began, the country again declared neutrality. The Germans invaded, however, and quickly overran the country despite resistance that included the flooding of dikes. The German occupation resulted in the deaths of some 240,000 victims, many of them Jews.

2 Reader's Response
Making Personal Connections

Question If you were Peter, would you have played the anthem or found some other way to defy the Nazis? *(Possible responses: A few students may say they would avoid all risk. Many other students may feel the gesture, while courageous, was not worth the risk, and that it would have been better to do something that tangibly hurt the Nazis or helped the Dutch. Other students may suggest that the act was inspiring and helped preserve the spirit of resistance.)*

every stop pulled out to full volume, Peter was playing the "Wilhelmus"!

Father, at eighty-two, was the first one on his feet. Now everyone was standing. From somewhere in back of us a voice sang out the words. Another joined in, and another. Then we were all singing together, the full voice of
1 Holland singing her forbidden anthem. We sang at the top of our lungs, sang our oneness, our hope, our love for Queen and country. On this anniversary of defeat it seemed almost for a moment that we were victors.

Afterward we waited for Peter at the small side door of the church. It was a long time before he was free to come away with us, so many people wanted to embrace him, to shake his hand and thump his back. Clearly he was enormously pleased with himself.

But now that the moment had passed I was, as usual, angry with him. The Gestapo[4] was certain to hear about it, perhaps already had: their eyes and ears were everywhere. For what had Peter risked so much? Not for people's lives but for a gesture. For a moment's meaningless defiance.

At Bos en Hoven Straat,[5] however, Peter was a hero as one by one his family made us describe again what had happened. The only members of the household who felt as I did were the two Jewish women staying at Nollie's. One of these was an elderly Austrian lady whom Willem had sent into hiding here.

The other woman was a young, blonde, blue-eyed Dutch Jew with flawless false identity papers supplied by the Dutch national underground itself. The papers were so good and Annaliese looked so unlike the Nazi stereotype of a Jew that she went freely in and out of the house, shopping and helping out at the school, giving herself out to be a friend of the family whose husband had died in the bombing of Rotterdam.

I spent an anxious afternoon, tensing at the sound of every motor, for only the police, Germans, and NSBers[6] had automobiles nowadays. But the time came to go home to the Beje and still nothing had happened.

I worried two more days, then decided either Peter had not been reported or that the Gestapo had more important things to occupy them. It was Wednesday morning just as Father and I were unlocking our workbenches that Peter's little sister Cocky burst into the shop.

"Opa! Tante Corrie![7] They came for Peter! They took him away!"

"Who? Where?"

But she didn't know and it was three days before the family learned that he had been taken 2
to the federal prison in Amsterdam.

> We sang at the top of our lungs, sang our oneness, our hope, our love. . .

It was 7:55 in the evening, just a few minutes before the new curfew hour of 8:00. Peter had been in prison for two weeks. Father and Betsie and I were seated around the dining-room table, Father replacing watches in their pockets and Betsie doing needlework, our big, black, slightly Persian cat curled contentedly in her lap. A knock on the alley door made me glance in the window mirror. There in the bright spring twilight stood a woman. She carried a small suitcase and—odd for the time of year—wore a fur coat, gloves, and a heavy veil.

I ran down and opened the door. "Can I come in?" she asked. Her voice was high-pitched in fear.

"Of course." I stepped back. The woman looked over her shoulder before moving into the little hallway.

---

4. **Gestapo** (gə stä′pō), an official organization of secret police in Nazi Germany, known for its brutality.
5. **Straat** (strät), street.
6. **NSBers.** The letters stand for the Dutch name of the National Socialist Movement. The members of this Dutch political party collaborated with the Nazis.
7. **Opa!** (ō′pä), **Tante** (tän′tə) **Corrie!** Grandfather, Auntie Corrie.

MINI-LESSON: LITERARY FOCUS
Idioms

Teach Some idioms can add color and flavor to language. Saying "Their eyes and ears were everywhere" paints a more vivid picture than just saying "They were watching and listening to everything." Other idioms, such as "pay a visit," are simply everyday conversation and don't particularly add to the quality of the language.

Activity Idea Have students suggest examples of idioms from other selections in this book and put the idioms in a chart like the one shown.

Point out that while good writers use idioms in informal writing, they avoid slang, which is not a standard part of the language. Some students may wish to make a similar chart with slang expressions and their meanings.

Students can also discuss how each idiom might confuse people who are learning English.

Idiom	Meaning
do it if it killed him, p. 13	determined to do it
secondhand piano, p. 23	used piano
Roof's spirits fell, p. 40	Roof was disappointed

"My name is Kleermaker. I'm a Jew."

"How do you do?" I reached out to take her bag, but she held on to it. "Won't you come upstairs?"

Father and Betsie stood up as we entered the dining room. "Mrs. Kleermaker, my father and my sister."

3 "I was about to make some tea!" cried Betsie. "You're just in time to join us!"

Father drew out a chair from the table and Mrs. Kleermaker sat down, still gripping the suitcase. The "tea" consisted of old leaves which had been crushed and reused so often they did little more than color the water. But Mrs. Kleermaker accepted it gratefully, plunging into the story of how her husband had been arrested some months before, her son gone into hiding. Yesterday the S.D.—the political police who worked under the Gestapo—had ordered her to close the family clothing store. She was afraid now to go back to the apartment above it. She had heard that we had befriended a man on this street. . . .

"In this household," Father said, "God's people are always welcome."

"We have four empty beds upstairs," said Betsie. "Your problem will be choosing which one to sleep in!"

Just two nights later the same scene was repeated. The time was again just before 8:00 on another bright May evening. Again there was a furtive[8] knock at the side door. This time an elderly couple was standing outside.

"Come in!"

It was the same story: the same tight-clutched possessions, the same fearful glance and tentative[9] tread. The story of neighbors arrested, the 4
fear that tomorrow their turn would come.

That night after prayer time the six of us faced our dilemma.[10] "This location is too dangerous," I told our three guests. "We're half a block from the main police headquarters. And 5
yet I don't know where else to suggest."

Clearly it was time to visit Willem again. So the next day I repeated the difficult trip to Hilversum. "Willem," I said, "we have three Jews staying right at the Beje. Can you get places for them in the country?"

Willem pressed his fingers to his eyes and I noticed suddenly how much white was in his beard. "It's getting harder," he said. "Harder

8. furtive (fėr′tiv), *adj.* done quickly and with stealth; secret.
9. tentative (ten′tə tiv), *adj.* hesitating.
10. dilemma (də lem′ə), *n.* difficult choice.

◄ This building, called the Beje, contained the ten Boom family home, the watch shop, and eventually the secret room.

3 Literary Element
Dialogue

Question What does the dialogue between the ten Booms and Mrs. Kleermaker suggest about the family's attitude toward strangers? *(Possible responses: good-heartedness, tolerance, friendliness)*

4 Literary Element
Style

Point out to students that this statement is not a complete sentence grammatically. Mention that short, pithy sentences, which are sometimes grammatically incomplete, are a feature of a colloquial, informal writing. Frequent contractions are used also.

You may wish to ask students to restate the lines as a grammatical sentence, compare the two versions in context, and comment on the effect on the reader.

5 Reading/Thinking Skills
Identify Alternatives

Question What possible solutions might you suggest for the ten Boom's dilemma? *(Possible responses: find another place to send refugees; create a hiding place inside the house; move to a location farther from the police)*

BUILDING ENGLISH PROFICIENCY

ESL LEP ELD SAE LD

Understanding Mood

Ask students to name titles of songs that give them a patriotic feeling. You may wish to play recordings of patriotic anthems of the United States or other countries. Discuss the feelings that arise when singing them. *(Possible responses: memories of home, good times, patriotism, pride in one's country)*

Have a volunteer read the scene on page 418 describing the singing of the "Wilhelmus." Ask students to visualize the moment and tell their reactions.

Activity Ideas

- Ask how hearing the "Wilhelmus" sets the mood for what follows. *(It creates the tense expectation that there will be retaliation.)*
- If appropriate, invite volunteers to share experiences or knowledge about people in other countries who have had to flee government oppression.
- Groups of students may benefit greatly from watching and reporting on movies about World War II and/or the Nazi occupation such as *Schindler's List* or *The Diary of Anne Frank.*

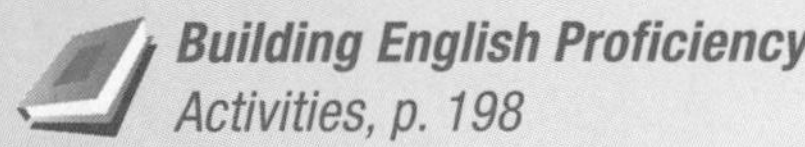

Building English Proficiency
Activities, p. 198

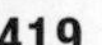

6 **Literary Element**

Characterization

Question What does mentioning that Willem is a clergyman add to his characterization? *(Possible response: Since clergy people aren't normally thieves, it shows that he opposes the current authority; it may also show that he is unusually bold and resourceful.)*

7 **Reading/Thinking Skills**

Predict

Question Imagine that Fred supports the persecution of the Jews. What events would occur next in the plot? *(Possible responses: He would report Corrie to the authorities; she would be put in prison; people she was hiding would go to concentration camps.)*

8 **Historical Note**

Ration Cards

Explain that *ration* means to restrict the consumption of a commodity, food, etc. Open a discussion of why rationing would be practiced during wartime. Invite volunteers to share anecdotes they may have heard about rationing during World War II, when food, clothing, and gasoline were rationed.

every month. They're feeling the food shortage now even on the farms. I still have addresses, yes, a few. But they won't take anyone without a ration card."

"Without a ration card! But Jews aren't issued ration cards!"

"I know." Willem turned to stare out the window. For the first time I wondered how he and Tine were feeding the elderly men and women in their care.

"I know," he repeated. "And ration cards can't be counterfeited. They're changed too often and they're too easy to spot. Identity cards are different. I know several printers who do them. Of course you need a photographer."

A photographer? Printers? What was Willem talking about? "Willem, if people need ration cards and there aren't any counterfeit ones, what do they do?"

Willem turned slowly from the window. He seemed to have forgotten me and my particular problem. "Ration cards?" He gestured vaguely. "You steal them."

6 I stared at this Dutch Reformed clergyman. "Then, Willem, could you steal . . . I mean . . . could you get three stolen cards?"

"No, Corrie! I'm watched! Don't you understand that? Every move I make is watched!"

He put an arm around my shoulder and went on more kindly. "Even if I can continue working for a while, it will be far better for you to develop your own sources. The less connection with me—the less connection with anyone else—the better."

Joggling home on the crowded train, I turned Willem's words over and over in my mind. "Your own sources." That sounded so—so professional. How was I going to find a source of stolen ration cards? Who in the world did I know? . . .

And at that moment a name appeared in my mind.

Fred Koornstra.

Fred was the man who used to read the electric meter at the Beje. The Koornstras had a retarded daughter, now a grown woman, who attended the "church" I had been conducting for the feebleminded for some twenty years. And now Fred had a new job working for the Food Office. Wasn't it in the department where ration books were issued?

That evening after supper I bumped over the brick streets to the Koornstra house. The tires on my faithful old bicycle had finally given out and I joined the hundreds clattering about town on metal wheel rims. Each bump reminded me jarringly of my fifty years.

Fred, a bald man with a military bearing, came to the door and stared at me blankly when I said I wanted to talk to him about the Sunday service. He invited me in, closed the door, and said, "Now Corrie, what is it you really came to see me about?"

("Lord," I prayed silently, "if it is not safe to confide in Fred, stop this conversation now before it is too late.") "I must first tell you that we've had some unexpected company at the Beje. First it was a single woman, then a couple, when I got back this afternoon, another couple." I paused for just an instant. "They are 7
Jews."

Fred's expression did not change.

"We can provide safe places for these people but they must provide something too. Ration 8
cards."

Fred's eyes smiled. "So. Now I know why you came here."

"Fred, is there any way you can give out extra cards? More than you report?"

"None at all, Corrie. Those cards have to be accounted for a dozen ways. They're checked and double-checked."

The hope that had begun to mount in me tumbled. But Fred was frowning.

"Unless—" he began.

"Unless?"

"Unless there should be a holdup. The Food Office in Utrecht was robbed last month—but the men were caught."

MINI-LESSON: GRAMMAR

Proper Punctuation of Dates

Point out that when a date has two or more parts, the parts are separated by commas:

It was Sunday, May 10, 1942, exactly two years after the fall of Holland.

The Allies began the liberation of Europe on D-Day, June 6, 1944.

Show the parts of the date: the name of the day, the month and calendar number of the day, and the year.

Activity Idea

Have students find five more dates that were important in World War II. Ask them to write one sentence explaining the significance of each date. Remind them to punctuate the dates correctly.

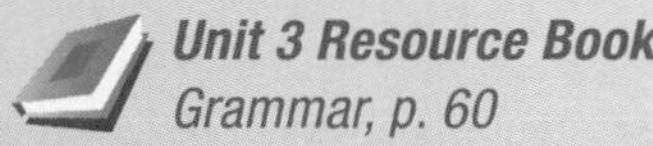

Unit 3 Resource Book
Grammar, p. 60

He was silent a while. "If it happened at noon," he said slowly, "when just the record clerk and I are there . . . and if they found us tied and gagged . . ." He snapped his fingers. "And I know just the man who might do it! Do you remember the—"

9 "Don't!" I said, remembering Willem's warning. "Don't tell me who. And don't tell me how. Just get the cards if you possibly can."

Fred stared at me a moment. "How many do you need?"

I opened my mouth to say, "Five." But the number that unexpectedly and astonishingly came out instead was, "One hundred."

When Fred opened the door to me just a week later, I gasped at the sight of him. Both eyes were a greenish purple, his lower lip cut and swollen.

"My friend took very naturally to the part," was all he would say.

But he had the cards. On the table in a brown envelope were one hundred passports to
10 safety. Fred had already torn the "continuing coupon" from each one. This final coupon was presented at the Food Office the last day of each month in exchange for the next month's card. With these coupons Fred could "legally" continue to issue us one hundred cards.

We agreed that it would be risky for me to keep coming to his house each month. What if he were to come to the Beje instead, dressed in his old meterman uniform?

The meter in the Beje was in the back hall at the foot of the stairs. When I got home that afternoon I pried up the tread of the bottom step, as Peter had done higher to hide a radio, and found a hollow space inside. Peter would be proud of me, I thought as I worked—and was flooded by a wave of lonesomeness for that brave and cocksure boy. The hinge was hidden deep in the wood, the ancient riser undisturbed. I was ridiculously pleased with it.

We had our first test of the system on July 1. Fred was to come in through the shop as he always had, carrying the cards beneath his shirt. He would come at 5:30, when Betsie would have the back hall free of callers. To my horror at 5:25 the shop door opened and in stepped a policeman.

He was a tall man with close-cropped 11
orange-red hair whom I knew by name—Rolf van Vliet—but little else. Rolf had brought in a watch that needed cleaning, and he seemed in a mood to talk. My throat had gone dry, but Father chatted cheerfully as he took off the back of Rolf's watch and examined it. What were we going to do? There was no way to warn Fred Koornstra. Promptly at 5:30 the door of the shop opened and in he walked, dressed in his blue workclothes. It seemed to me that his chest was too thick by a foot at least.

With magnificent aplomb[11] Fred nodded to Father, the policeman, and me. "Good evening." Courteous but a little bored.

He strode through the door at the rear of the shop and shut it behind him. My ears strained to hear him lift the secret lid. There! Surely Rolf must have heard it too.

The door behind us opened again. So great was Fred's control that he had not ducked out the alleyway exit, but came strolling back through the shop.

"Good evening," he said again.

"Evening."

He reached the street door and was gone. We had got away with it this time, but somehow, some way, we were going to have to work out a warning system.

For meanwhile, in the weeks since Mrs. Kleermaker's unexpected visit, a great deal had happened at the Beje. Supplied with ration cards, Mrs. Kleermaker and the elderly couple and the next arrivals and the next had found homes in safer locations. But still the hunted people kept coming, and the needs were often more complicated than ration cards and addresses. If a Jewish woman became pregnant,

11. aplomb (ə plom′), *n.* assurance; poise.

9 Reading/Thinking Skills
Infer

Question Why does Corrie not want to know the name of the person who may help to steal the cards? *(Possible response: If she doesn't know it, she can't implicate him if she is caught.)*

10 Literary Element
Metaphor

Have students note what Corrie calls the ration cards. *(passports to safety)*

11 Literary Element
Plot

Question How does the scene in the shop with Fred and the policeman contribute to the plot of the narrative? *(It reinforces the sense of danger in the reader's mind; it builds suspense and reaches a minor climax.)*

BUILDING ENGLISH PROFICIENCY

ESL LEP ELD SAE LD

Organizing Information

Carrie ten Boom becomes involved with the Dutch underground because of her individual efforts to help persecuted Jews. To help students understand how she does become a part of the movement, have them draw two-panel cartoons.

- The first panel of each cartoon shows a problem and the second panel, the solution. Pairs of students or individuals choose one problem-solution to depict. Some problem-solution pairs are needing a source of stolen ration cards—asking Fred Koornstra; getting cards from Fred—finding a place to hide them.
- Later the whole group can review the cartoons and put them in order to show how these events led Corrie to the underground.

12 Reading/Thinking Skills
Generalize

Question What two personal resources does Corrie have that she believes will help her? *(an extensive social network and her religious faith)*

13 Reading/Thinking Skills
Make Judgments

Question How does having many odd spaces and being a great distance from the street help defeat searchers? Base your judgment on the diagram of the ten Boom's building. *(Possible responses: The many odd spaces might serve as hiding spaces; they also make it harder for searchers to notice walls that don't match up. The distance from the street gives people more time to hide when searchers arrive.)*

The World of Work
Builder

For the real-life experiences of a home builder, use—

The World of Work
pp. 13–14

where could she go to have her baby? If a Jew in hiding died, how could he be buried?

"Develop your own sources," Willem had said. And from the moment Fred Koornstra's name had popped into my mind, an uncanny[12] realization had been growing in me. We were friends with half of Haarlem! We knew nurses in the maternity hospital. We knew clerks in the Records Office. We knew someone in every business and service in the city.

We didn't know, of course, the political views of all these people. But—and here I felt a strange leaping of my heart—God did! I knew I was not clever or subtle or sophisticated; if the Beje was becoming a meeting place for need
12 and supply, it was through some strategy far higher than mine.

A few nights after Fred's first "meterman" visit the alley bell rang long after curfew. I sped downstairs, expecting another sad and stammering refugee. Betsie and I had already made up beds for four new overnight guests that evening: a Jewish woman and her three small children.

But to my surprise, close against the wall of the dark alley, stood Kik. "Get your bicycle," he ordered with his usual young abruptness. "And put on a sweater. I have some people I want you to meet."

"Now? After curfew?" But I knew it was useless to ask questions. Kik's bicycle was tireless too, the wheel rims swathed in cloth. He

12. uncanny (un kan′ē), *adj.* strange and mysterious.

The rooms of the building offered many odd spaces, and there was a great distance between the street and the hiding place. 13

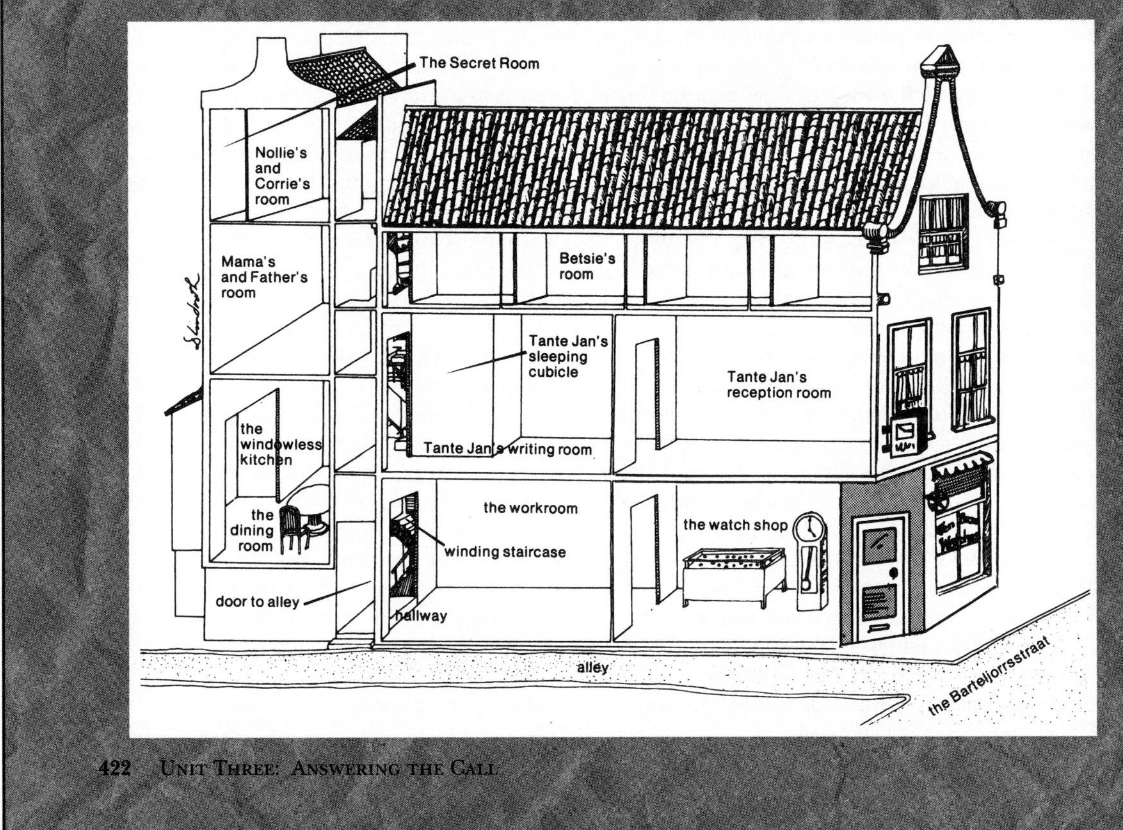

MINI-LESSON: VOCABULARY
Use Context Clues for Word Meaning

Display this phrase:

"After two years, rich, black, pungent Dutch coffee"

Lead students to recall their own experience of coffee to guess that *pungent* probably means having a powerful flavor that sharply hits the senses of taste and smell. The context of the sentence and knowing that rationing of food was part of the story help provide clues for the meaning of the word *pungent*. Descriptions and sentence structure can also provide context clues to word meaning.

Activity Ideas

- Have students identify context clues in the selection that can help them determine the meaning of the following words: *edict, furtive, dilemma, daunt, tentative.*
- Have students write sentences that include context clues that might help readers guess the meaning of the following words from this selection: *aplomb, uncanny, pungent, liaison, haphazard.*

wrapped mine also to keep down the clatter, and soon we were pedaling through the blacked-out streets of Haarlem at a speed that would have scared me even in daylight.

"Put a hand on my shoulder," Kik whispered. "I know the way."

We crossed dark side streets, crested bridges, wheeled round invisible corners. At last we crossed a broad canal and I knew we had reached the fashionable suburb of Aerdenhout.

We turned into a driveway beneath shadowy trees. To my astonishment Kik picked up my bicycle and carried both his and mine up the front steps. A serving girl with starched white apron and ruffled cap opened the door. The entrance hall was jammed with bicycles.

Then I saw him. One eye smiling at me, the other at the door, his vast stomach hastening ahead of him. Pickwick![13]

He led Kik and me into the drawing room where, sipping coffee and chatting in small groups, was the most distinguished-looking group of men and women I had ever seen. But all my attention, that first moment, was on the inexpressibly fragrant aroma in that room. Surely, was it possible, they were drinking real coffee?

Pickwick drew me a cup from the silver urn on the sideboard. It was coffee. After two years, rich, black, pungent[14] Dutch coffee. He poured himself a cup too, dropping in his usual five lumps of sugar as though rationing had never been invented. Another starched and ruffled maid was passing a tray heaped high with cakes.

Gobbling and gulping I trailed about the room after Pickwick, shaking the hands of the people he singled out. They were strange introductions for no names were mentioned, only, occasionally, an address, and "Ask for Mrs. Smit." When I had met my fourth Smit, Kik explained with a grin, "It's the only last name in the underground."

So this was really and truly the underground! But—where were these people from? I had never laid eyes on any of them. A second later I realized with a shiver down my spine that I was meeting the national group.

Their chief work, I gleaned from bits of conversation, was liaison[15] with England and the Free Dutch forces fighting elsewhere on the continent. They also maintained the underground route through which downed Allied plane crews reached the North Sea coast. 14

But they were instantly sympathetic with my efforts to help Haarlem's Jews. I blushed to my hair roots to hear Pickwick describe me as "the head of an operation here in this city." A hollow space under the stairs and some haphazard[16] friendships were not an operation. The others here were obviously competent, disciplined, and professional.

But they greeted me with grave courtesy, murmuring what they had to offer as we shook hands. False identity papers. The use of a car with official government plates. Signature forgery.

In a far corner of the room Pickwick introduced me to a frail-appearing little man with a wispy goatee. "Our host informs me," the little man began formally, "that your headquarters building lacks a secret room. This is a danger for all, those you are helping as well as yourselves and those who work with you. With your permission I will pay you a visit in the coming week. . . ." 15

Years later I learned that he was one of the most famous architects in Europe. I knew him only as Mr. Smit.

Just before Kik and I started our dash back to the Beje, Pickwick slipped an arm through mine. "My dear, I have good news. I

13. **Pickwick** (pik′wik). The author recognizes one of her wealthy Dutch customers who looks like Pickwick, the title character in a novel by Charles Dickens.
14. **pungent** (pun′jənt), *adj.* sharply affecting the organs of taste and smell.
15. **liaison** (lē′ā zon′), *n.* connection between military units, branches of a service, etc., to secure proper cooperation.
16. **haphazard** (hap′haz′ərd), *adj.* not planned; random.

14 Historical Note
The European Underground in World War II

The activities of the ten Booms and their friends were directed mainly toward helping Jews escape the Nazi police agencies. The underground that Corrie now meets had a broader purpose of striking back against the Nazis and helping the Allies liberate Europe. By early 1943 the Nazis had been defeated in North Africa and more or less halted in Russia, but the D-Day landings were long months away.

15 Literary Focus
Idioms

Point out to students that one element of a writer's style is word choice or diction. Remind students that good writers write colloquially whenever possible—as if they were conversing. Mention that ten Boom follows this rule by using idioms, such as "pay you a visit" (page 423), "churches were packed" (page 417), and others.

Question What effect does ten Boom's use of idioms have on the reader? *(Possible response: The story is easier to read, believable, and dramatic.)*

BUILDING ENGLISH PROFICIENCY

Relating Verb Tenses

You can use Carrie ten Boom's memories to review the difference between the past and past perfect tenses. First, ask the students to informally relate the events on pages 422 as if they were Corrie, being sure to use the words *growing, popped, beds.*

1. Explain that most of the verbs in this passage are in the simple past tense; model some examples. Then point out that when verb phrases begin with *had,* they express events that took place before the main action of the story. Such phrases are in the past perfect tense.

2. On the chalkboard, write these verb phrases from page 422:
- had been growing
- had popped
- had (already) made up

3. Have students retell the events, using correct verb forms. Model sentences for them when needed. You may wish to have students find these verb phrases in context on page 423.

16 Literary Element
Humor

Question How does the author use humor in her narrative here? (*She shows her father failing to understand about the "Smits."*)

Question What purpose do you think is served by injecting humor into a serious situation? *(Possible response: It provides comic relief—a chance for the reader to relax for a moment; it provides a contrast between the grave purpose of "Smit's" visit and the ordinary context in which these events take place.)*

17 Reading/Thinking Skills
Generalization

Question Based on Mr. "Smit's" remarks, what characteristics would you say a good secret room should have? *(Possible responses: out-of-the-way location, no obvious entrance, place where two floors or walls don't quite meet)*

understand that Peter is about to be released." . . .

So he was, three days later, thinner, paler, and not a whit daunted[17] by his two months in a concrete cell. Nollie, Tine, and Betsie used up a month's sugar ration baking cakes for his welcome-home party.

> As long as the sign was in place, it was safe to enter.

And one morning soon afterward the first customer in the shop was a small thin-bearded man named Smit. Father took his jeweler's glass from his eye. If there was one thing he loved better than making a new acquaintance, it was discovering a link with an old one.

16 "Smit," he said eagerly. "I know several Smits in Amsterdam. Are you by any chance related to the family who—"

"Father," I interrupted, "this is the man I told you about. He's come to, ah, inspect the house."

"A building inspector? Then you must be the Smit with offices in the Grote Hout Straat. I wonder that I haven't—"

"Father!" I pleaded, "he's not a building inspector, and his name is not Smit."

"Not Smit?"

Together Mr. Smit and I attempted to explain, but Father simply could not understand a person's being called by a name not his own. As I led Mr. Smit into the back hall we heard him musing to himself, "I once knew a Smit on Koning Straat. . . ."

Mr. Smit examined and approved the hiding place for ration cards beneath the bottom step. He also pronounced acceptable the warning system we had worked out. This was a triangle-shaped wooden sign advertising "Alpina Watches" which I had placed in the dining-room window. As long as the sign was in place, it was safe to enter.

But when I showed him a cubbyhole behind the corner cupboard in the dining room, he shook his head. Some ancient redesigning of the house had left a crawl space in that corner and we'd been secreting jewelry, silver coins, and other valuables there since the start of the occupation. Not only the rabbi had brought us his library but other Jewish families had brought their treasures to the Beje for safekeeping. The space was large enough that we had believed a person could crawl in there if necessary, but Mr. Smit dismissed it without a second glance.

"First place they'd look. Don't bother to change it though. It's only silver. We're interested in saving people, not things."

He started up the narrow corkscrew stairs, and as he mounted so did his spirits. He paused in delight at the odd-placed landings, pounded on the crooked walls, and laughed aloud as the floor levels of the two old houses continued out of phase.

"What an impossibility!" he said in an awe-struck voice. "What an improbable, unbelievable, unpredictable impossibility! Miss ten Boom, if all houses were constructed like this one, you would see before you a less worried man."

At last, at the very top of the stairs, he entered my room and gave a little cry of delight. "This is it!" he exclaimed.

"You want your hiding place as high as possible," he went on eagerly. "Gives you the best chance to reach it while the search is on below." He leaned out the window, craning his thin neck, the little faun's beard pointing this way 17
and that.

"But . . . this is my bedroom. . . ."

Mr. Smit paid no attention. He was already measuring. He moved the heavy, wobbly old wardrobe away from the wall with surprising ease and pulled my bed into the center of the room. "This is where the false wall will go!" Excitedly he drew out a pencil and drew a line

17. daunt (dônt), *v.* overcome with fear; frighten.

MINI-LESSON: READING/THINKING SKILLS
Use Problem-Solving Skills

Teach Ask students to list the problems that the ten Booms and other members of the underground had to solve in this selection. Next, ask students to identify skills that they used in solving each problem. For example, getting the ration cards involved skills of communication, judgment about other people, and acting (faking a convincing robbery).

Activity Idea Present this scenario: Your town is occupied by a foreign military government. A group of sixteen-year-olds has been accused of blowing up a military jeep. The youths are in jail and no one has been allowed to see them. The townspeople are beginning to commit more violent acts. The mayor fears that soon a citizen may be killed by the occupation forces.

Have student volunteers form groups who represent the occupation forces and the citizens. They focus on the following:

- The occupation forces group must develop a way to restore and keep order.
- The citizens must find a way to help the jailed youths.

As groups develop solutions, the scenario will expand until a resolution or disaster occurs.

along the floor thirty inches from the back wall. He stood up and gazed at it moodily.

"That's as big as I dare," he said. "It will take a cot mattress, though. Oh, yes. Easily!"

I tried again to protest, but Mr. Smit had forgotten I existed. Over the next few days he and his workmen were in and out of our house constantly. They never knocked. At each visit each man carried in something. Tools in a folded newspaper. A few bricks in a briefcase. "Wood!" he exclaimed when I ventured to wonder if a wooden wall would not be easier to build. "Wood sounds hollow. Hear it in a minute. No, no. Brick's the only thing for false walls."

After the wall was up, the plasterer came, then the carpenter, finally the painter. Six days after he had begun, Mr. Smit called Father, Betsie, and me to see.

18 We stood in the doorway and gaped. The smell of fresh paint was everywhere. But surely nothing in this room was newly painted! All four walls had that streaked and grimy look that old rooms got in coal-burning Haarlem. The ancient molding ran unbroken around the ceiling, chipped and peeling here and there, obviously undisturbed for a hundred and fifty years. Old water stains streaked the back wall, a wall that even I, who had lived half a century in this room, could scarcely believe was not the original, but set back a precious two-and-a-half feet from the true wall of the building.

Built-in bookshelves ran along this false wall, old, sagging shelves whose blistered wood bore the same water stains as the wall behind them. Down in the far lefthand corner, beneath the bottom shelf, a sliding panel, two feet high and two wide, opened into the secret room.

Mr. Smit stooped and silently pulled this panel up. On hands and knees Betsie and I crawled into the narrow room behind it. Once inside we could stand up, sit or even stretch out one at a time on the single mattress. A concealed vent, cunningly let into the real wall, allowed air to enter from outside.

"Keep a water jug there," said Mr. Smit, crawling in behind us. "Change the water once a week. Hardtack and vitamins keep indefinitely. Anytime there is anyone in the house whose presence is unofficial, all possessions except the clothes actually on his back must be stored in here."

Dropping to our knees again, we crawled single file out into my bedroom. "Move back into this room," he told me. "Everything exactly as before."

With his fist he struck the wall above the bookshelves.

"The Gestapo could search for a year," he said. "They'll never find this one."

18 Reading/Thinking Skills
Main Idea

Question What is the main idea of this paragraph? *(The hidden room was concealed by making the walls appear to be absolutely unchanged.)*

Check Test

1. How old is Corrie's father? *(eighty-two)*
2. Why does Corrie need to get more ration cards? *(Jews cannot be resettled in the countryside without them.)*
3. What warning system does Corrie set up in the watch shop? *(When an "Alpina Watches" sign is in the dining room window, it is safe to enter.)*
4. In whose bedroom is the secret room? *(in Corrie's)*
5. What kind of heat do people in Haarlem use? *(They burn coal.)*

Unit 3 Resource Book
Alternate Check Test, p. 61

After Reading

MAKING CONNECTIONS

1. Students' questions may relate to facts such as the number of Jews she hid, or later events, such as how their activities were discovered.

2. Possible responses: when Corrie asks Fred to help her; when she feels her faith supporting her; when Fred enters the shop with the stolen ration cards and the policeman is there; when Corrie meets the underground; when the architect is delighted with finding a spot for a secret room

3. Possible responses: Corrie ten Boom is heroic because she risks her life to help victims of oppression, because of her resourcefulness, and her ability to live on beyond the tragic deaths of her family.

4. Responses should reflect that the song is a national anthem that reflects their identity and traditions as a people; by forbidding the song, the German occupation was obliterating their Dutch identity.

5. It helps establish the setting and atmosphere of danger and resistance in occupied Holland.

6. Character traits include courage, tenacity, resourcefulness, faith, and good judgment.

7. Possible responses: Food is scarce and must be rationed; there is little activity in the city at night due to the curfew.

8 Students might point out efforts of groups such as Amnesty International or the United Nations refugee agencies.

9. Common characteristics include courage, steadfastness, and faith. Ten Boom probably emphasizes resourcefulness and judgment more, while Arthur and Lancelot emphasize nobility and personal honor.

After Reading

Making Connections

Shaping Your Response

1. In your notebook, write three questions you would like to ask Corrie ten Boom.
2. What do you think are the most important moments in the selection? Why?
3. Does Corrie ten Boom measure up to your idea of a hero? Why or why not?

Analyzing the Autobiography

4. Why do you think Peter's playing the "Wilhelmus" arouses such intense feelings in the audience?
5. How does this episode in the church help set the **mood** for what follows in this narrative?
6. What **character** traits does ten Boom have that make her valuable in the underground movement?
7. Make two **inferences** about wartime living conditions based on ten Boom's autobiographical account.

Extending the Ideas

8. After the war, Corrie ten Boom set up a home in the Netherlands for other victims of Nazi atrocities. How do her efforts compare with current efforts to protect victims of war around the world?
9. In a Venn diagram, compare ten Boom with Arthur or Launcelot as heroes, noting common and differing heroic qualities.

Literary Focus: Idiom

An **idiom** is a phrase or an expression whose meaning cannot be understood from the ordinary meaning of the words in it. For example, when Corrie ten Boom says of the Gestapo, "their eyes and ears were everywhere," she is speaking figuratively, not literally. What does she mean? Use a chart like the one below to record two other idioms and their meanings. Then illustrate the literal meaning of one of the idioms.

Idiom	Meaning

LITERARY FOCUS: IDIOM

Possible responses

Idiom	Meaning
ducked out, p. 421	left quietly or sneakily
laid eyes on, p. 423	saw
started our dash, p. 423	began to run
pay you a visit, p. 423	visit you

Vocabulary Study

Tell whether the following word pairs are synonyms, antonyms, or neither by writing *S, A,* or *N* on your paper.

aplomb
daunt
dilemma
edict
furtive
haphazard
liaison
pungent
tentative
uncanny

1. furtive: secret
2. aplomb: vegetable
3. uncanny: ordinary
4. pungent: sharp
5. liaison: connection to secure cooperation
6. haphazard: planned
7. daunt: frighten
8. tentative: confident
9. edict: memory
10. dilemma: difficult choice

Expressing Your Ideas

Writing Choices

Writer's Notebook Update Use the quickwrite you did before reading "The Secret Room," along with ideas in ten Boom's account, as the basis for a paragraph that might launch an encyclopedia article.

Underground Tipster Your name is "Smit," and you have been asked to write a **news clip** for all of the other Smits in the underground to help them provide a haven for Jews. Write down concise tips that you think would be helpful, and provide a title for the news clip.

An Inspiring Flap "The Secret Room" is an excerpt from Corrie ten Boom's autobiography, *The Hiding Place*. If you were publishing the book, what would you want readers to know at a glance about ten Boom and her experiences during the German occupation? Write a paragraph for the inside flap of the **book jacket**.

Other Options

Preservation Society The Haarlem preservation society is concerned with the preservation of historical landmarks and memorials. Prepare a **proposal**, supported with historical facts, asking the Haarlem city council to designate buildings and sites as either landmarks or memorials to those who risked their lives to aid Jews during the German occupation.

The Architect in You Working with a partner, take a critical look at the buildings in which you both live. Which building do you think is more conducive to containing a secret room? Where would be the best location for a secret room in that building? Using the diagram of the Beje (page 422) as a model, draw a **diagram**.

Making Referrals Compile a list of resources about the Holocaust—books, movies, magazines, and personal interviews. Prepare an **annotated bibliography** of eight sources.

VOCABULARY STUDY

1. s
2. n
3. a
4. s
5. s
6. a
7. s
8. a
9. n
10. s

Unit 3 Resource Book
Vocabulary, p. 59
Vocabulary Test, p.62

WRITING CHOICES

Writer's Notebook Update

Remind students that the first paragraph of an encyclopedia article typically includes a general statement or definition of the topic.

An Inspiring Flap

Have students look at book jackets and generalize about how writers of jacket copy try to interest book buyers. Have students incorporate some of the generalizations in their jacket copy.

Selection Test

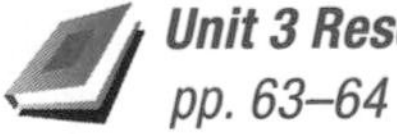

Unit 3 Resource Book
pp. 63–64

OTHER OPTIONS

The Architect in You

Students who have access to computer-aided design (CAD) programs may wish to experiment by creating other buildings with secret rooms.

Making Referrals

Have students examine an annotated bibliography and generalize about the kind of information presented about each book or other source. Have students apply their generalizations to their bibliographies.

Before Reading

Building Background

Point out that cultural differences exist within groups that speak the same language. Then ask students to consider the effect of geography on social life. If villages are in separate valleys with mountains in between, is it more likely that each village will develop a distinct culture? How might lack of frequent contact contribute to hostility toward "outsiders" from other villages?

Literary Focus

Help students distinguish between **imagery** and its opposite—abstraction and explanation. Challenge them to create images for the following:

- Gonzalez is daring.
- activities of the night

Writer's Notebook

Question Why might a bold suitor choose an unconventional gift as a romantic expression? *(Possible responses: to intrigue someone, to show individuality)*

More About Josefina Niggli

Niggli's first novel, *Mexican Village*, is set in Hidalgo, the home village of the mysterious stranger in "The Street of the Cañon." She has also written *Step Down, Elder Brother,* (1947).

Before Reading

The Street of the Cañon

by Josefina Niggli Mexico

Josefina Niggli
born 1910

Born in Monterrey, Mexico, in the year of the great Mexican revolution, Josefina Niggli (nig′lē) moved to Texas in order to escape political turmoil. There, as a teenager, she began to write. Her spirited characters lead lives complicated by conflicts involving love, pride, deceit, and tradition. In addition to stories, poems, and plays, Niggli has written scripts for radio and film. Probably best known for her novel, *Mexican Village,* a classic portrait of small-town life and customs, Niggli explores the human comedy against a tapestry of rural Mexican life.

Building Background

Niggli Country The area south of Laredo, Texas, during the 1920s was composed of small Mexican villages located in valleys separated by low mountains. Petty feuds could isolate one village from another. The town of Hidalgo, named after a rebel priest who helped bring about Mexico's War of Independence against Spain, undoubtedly fought feuds, held festivals, and cherished traditions similar to those represented in "The Street of the Cañon."

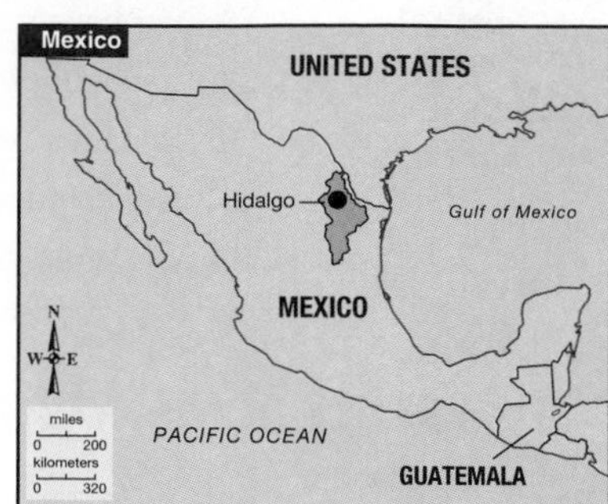

Literary Focus

Imagery The use of concrete details that appeal to the five senses is called **imagery.** In "The Street of the Cañon," you are invited to share a banquet, to enjoy the scent of spring breezes, and to spy on young lovers who dance to violins. Let imagery work its magic on you as you step into the story.

Writer's Notebook

Romancing the Cheese We generally think of flowers, candy, or jewelry as romantic expressions. In this story, however, a young man courts a girl with an unlikely item. Before reading this story, write down an unusual but romantic gift you have received or have heard about and the circumstances that made it romantic.

SUPPORT MATERIALS OVERVIEW

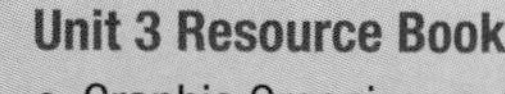

Unit 3 Resource Book
- Graphic Organizer, p. 65
- Study Guide, p. 66
- Vocabulary, p. 67
- Grammar, p. 68
- Alternate Check Test, p. 69
- Vocabulary Test, p. 70
- Selection Test, pp. 71–72

Building English Proficiency
- Literature Summaries
- Activities, p. 199

Reading, Writing & Grammar SkillBook
- Vocabulary, pp. 9–10
- Reading, pp. 43–44
- Writing, pp. 105–106
- Grammar, Usage, and Mechanics, pp. 224–225, 261–264

Technology
- Audiotape 11, Side B
- Personal Journal Software
- Custom Literature Database: For a characterization of a mysterious gaucho, see "A Portrait of Facundo" on the database.
- Test Generator Software

The Street of the Cañon

Josefina Niggli

1 It was May, the flowering thorn was sweet in the air, and the village of San Juan Iglesias[1] in the Valley of the Three Marys was celebrating. The long, dark streets were empty because all of the people, from the lowest-paid cowboy to the mayor, were helping Don Roméo Calderón[2] celebrate his daughter's eighteenth birthday.

On the other side of the town, where the Cañon Road led across the mountains to the Sabinas Valley, a tall, slender man, a package clutched tightly against his side, slipped from shadow to shadow. Once a dog barked, and the man's black suit merged into the blackness of a wall. But no voice called out, and after a moment he slid into the narrow, dirt-packed street again.

The moonlight touched his shoulder and spilled across his narrow hips. He was young, no more than twenty-five, and his black curly head was bare. He walked swiftly along, heading always for the distant sound of guitar and flute. If he met anyone now, who could say from which direction he had come? He might be a trader from Monterrey or a buyer of cow's milk from farther north in the Valley of the Three Marys. Who would guess that an Hidalgo[3] man dared to walk alone in the moonlit streets of San Juan Iglesias?

Carefully adjusting his flat package so that it was not too prominent, he squared his shoulders and walked jauntily[4] across the street to the laughter-filled house. Little boys packed in the doorway made way for him, smiling and nodding to him. The long, narrow room with the orchestra at one end was filled with whirling dancers. Rigid-backed chaperones were gossiping together, seated in their straight chairs against the plaster walls. Over the scene was the yellow glow of kerosene lanterns, and the air was hot with the too sweet perfume of gardenias, tuberoses, and the pungent scent of close-packed humanity.

The man in the doorway, while trying to appear at ease, was carefully examining every smiling face. If just one person recognized him, the room would turn on him like a den of

1. **San Juan Iglesias,** (sän hwän ē gle′sē äs).
2. **Don Roméo Calderón,** (dōn rō me′ō käl də rōn′).
3. **Hidalgo,** (ē däl′gō).
4. jauntily (jôn′tə lē), *adv.* in an easy and lively way.

During Reading

Selection Objectives

- to appreciate that the enemy of a hero regards him or her as a villain
- to practice using the dictionary to learn word meanings
- to apply correct punctuation to adjectives in a series

Unit 3 Resource Book
Graphic Organizer, p. 65
Study Guide, p. 66

Theme Link

The theme of "Many Kinds of Heroes" is shown in the actions of a bold romantic who woos a young woman in an enemy village.

Vocabulary Preview

jauntily, in an easy and lively way
officious, too ready to offer services; meddlesome
audaciously, courageously taking risks; daringly
imperiously, haughtily or arrogantly
disdain, scorn
blandly, in a smoothly agreeable, polite manner
apprehension, fear
propriety, proper behavior

Students can add the words and definitions to their Writer's Notebooks.

1 Literary Focus
Imagery

Question Imagine that you are making a movie of this story. What images in the beginning of the story are written so vividly that you would want to film them? *(Possible responses: dark streets, man moving from shadow to shadow, faint music and lighted house in the distance)*

SELECTION SUMMARY

The Street of the Cañon

A stranger comes to San Juan Iglesias, carrying a package. He enters the home of Don Romeo Calderón who is hosting his daughter Sarita's eighteenth birthday party. After leaving his package on a table with other gifts, the stranger charms a chaperone into permitting him to dance with Sarita. She tells him of the bitter rivalry between Hidalgo people and those of San Juan. She also tells of her fear of Pepe Gonzalez, a Hidalgo man who made a daring attempt to steal the bones of a famous historian from a grave in San Juan and remove them to his town. Just as the stranger's gift—a cheese known only to be made in Hidalgo—is discovered on the feast table, he quickly asks Sarita for another meeting and vanishes. She realizes that she has been dancing with Pepe Gonzalez.

*For summaries in other languages, see the **Building English Proficiency** book.*

2 Multicultural Note
Greetings

The generous and courteous greeting of strangers is an important custom in traditional Hispanic culture. Invite students from different cultural backgrounds to explain how guests are greeted and treated in their culture.

3 Historical Note
Accidental Cheese?

Cheese was probably discovered by accident when people began to carry milk in pouches made from animal stomachs. The bacteria in the milk and digestive juices from the stomach formed a curd in the milk, making a crude cheese. Organized cheese making dates back at least to 2,000 B.C.

4 Literary Element
Irony

Open a discussion of double meanings in the Hidalgo man's dialogue. Even his simple compliments may have double meanings. For example, if we suspect that the stranger wants to marry Don Romeo's daughter, what is the underlying meaning of his wish that "the earth always be fertile beneath her feet"? *(He would take her to Hidalgo, and it would be his own land that would be fertile.)* Encourage students to look for other ironic statements.

snarling mountain cats, but so far all the laughter-dancing eyes were friendly.

Suddenly a plump, officious[5] little man, his round cheeks glistening with perspiration, pushed his way through the crowd. His voice, many times too large for his
2 small body, boomed at the man in the doorway, "Welcome, stranger, welcome to our house." Thrusting his arm through the stranger's, and almost dislodging the package, he started to lead the way through the maze of dancers. "Come and drink a toast to my daughter—to my beautiful Sarita.[6] She is eighteen this night."

In the square patio the gentle breeze ruffled the pink and white oleander bushes. A long table set up on sawhorses held loaves of flaky-crusted French bread, stacks of thin, delicate tortillas,[7] plates of barbecued beef, and long red
3 rolls of spicy sausages. But most of all there were cheeses, for the Three Marys was a cheese-eating valley. There were yellow cheese and white cheese and curded cheese from cow's milk. There was even a flat white cake of goat cheese from distant Linares,[8] a delicacy too expensive for any but feast days.

To set off this feast were bottles of beer floating in ice-filled tin tubs, and another table was covered with bottles of mescal, of tequila, of maguey wine.

Don Roméo Calderón thrust a glass of tequila into the stranger's hand. "Drink, friend, to the prettiest girl in San Juan. As pretty as my fine fighting cocks, she is. On her wedding day she takes to her man, and by the Blessed Ribs may she find him soon, the best fighter in my flock. Drink deep, friend. Even the rivers flow with wine."

The Hidalgo man laughed and raised his
4 glass high. "May the earth be always fertile beneath her feet."

Someone called to Don Roméo that more guests were arriving, and with a final delighted pat on the stranger's shoulder, the little man scurried away. As the young fellow smiled after his retreating host, his eyes caught and held another pair of eyes—laughing black eyes set in a young girl's face. The last time he had seen that face it had been white and tense with rage, and the lips clenched tight to prevent an outgushing stream of angry words. That had been in February, and she had worn a white lace shawl over her hair. Now it was May, and a gardenia was a splash of white in the glossy, dark braids. The moonlight had mottled his face that February night, and he knew that she did not recognize him. He grinned impudently[9] back at her, and her eyes widened, then slid sideways to one of the chaperones. The fan in her small hand snapped shut. She tapped its parchment tip against her mouth and slipped away to join the dancing couples in the front room. The gestures of a fan translate into a coded language on the frontier. The stranger raised one eyebrow as he interpreted the signal.

But he did not move toward her at once. Instead, he inched slowly back against the table. No one was behind him, and his hands quickly unfastened the package he had been guarding so long. Then he nonchalantly walked into the front room.

The girl was sitting close to a chaperone. As he came up to her, he swerved slightly toward the bushy-browed old lady.

"Your servant, señora. I kiss your hands and feet."

The chaperone stared at him in astonishment. Such fine manners were not common to the town of San Juan Iglesias.

"Eh, you're a stranger," she said. "I thought so."

"But a stranger no longer, señora, now that I have met you." He bent over her, so close she

5. **officious** (ə fish′əs), *adj.* too ready to offer services.
6. **Sarita,** (sä rē′tä).
7. **tortilla** (tôr tē′yə), *n.* thin, flat, round cake made of corn meal.
8. **Linares,** (lē nä′res).
9. **impudently** (im′pyə dənt lē), *adv.* rudely.

MINI-LESSON: LITERARY FOCUS
Imagery

Teach Ask students why writers often use vivid imagery in their work. Review the major reasons, such as drawing the reader into the story, creating mood, establishing or fleshing out setting, and helping to introduce the characters.

Activity Idea Have students review examples of imagery in the selection and then use a chart, like the one shown, to analyze their effects on the plot, mood, suspense, characters and other narrative elements.

Students can review imagery in other reading selections from the point of view of the author's purpose.

Image	Author's Purpose
flowering thorn sweet in air	sets mood; establishes time and place
moon shining on young man	adds to mood; introduces character
gardenias, tuberoses, pungent scent of close-packed humanity	establishes setting

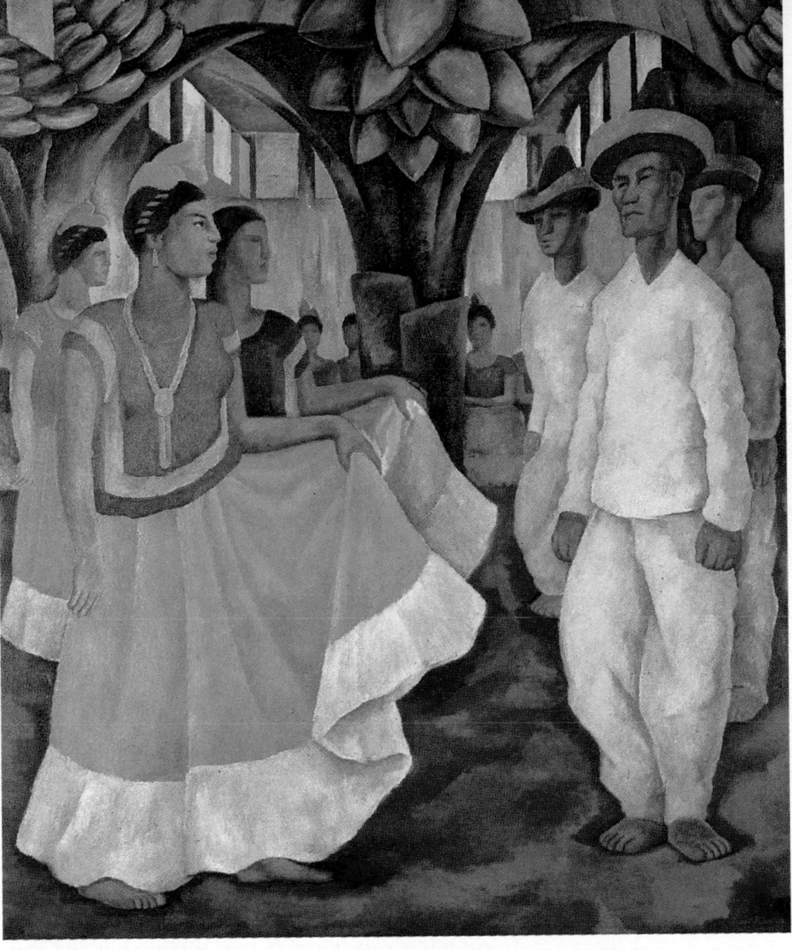

This oil painting titled *Fiesta Tehuanas*, or *Dance in Tehuantepec*, illustrates some of Diego Rivera's trademarks—bold color, simple forms, and architectural harmony. Mention several things in this story that the painting captures and several other things it does not portray.

could smell the faint fragrance of talcum on his freshly shaven cheek. "Will you dance the *parada* with me?"

This request startled her eyes into popping open beneath the heavy brows. "So, my young rooster, would you flirt with me, and I old enough to be your grandmother?"

5 "Can you show me a prettier woman to flirt with in the Valley of the Three Marys?" he asked audaciously.[10]

She grinned at him and turned toward the girl at her side. This young fool wants to meet you, my child."

The girl blushed to the roots of her hair and shyly lowered her white lids. The old woman laughed aloud.

"Go out and dance, the two of you. A man clever enough to pat the sheep has a right to play with the lamb."

The next moment they had joined the circle of dancers, and Sarita was trying to control her laughter.

10. audaciously (ô dā′shəs lē), *adv.* courageously taking risks; daringly.

Art Study

Responses to Caption Questions Possible responses: Story elements captured are the dance, the atmosphere of gaiety and tradition; not captured are the central characters, the cheeses and other foods, the underlying conflict.

Diego Rivera studied in Paris, absorbing the new art movements of neoimpressionism and cubism. When he returned to Mexico in the 1920s, he painted realistic murals to tell the story of a struggling people. His work was a foundation of the Mexican school of muralism.

Visual Literacy Repetition and symmetry can be used to create a feeling of reliable patterns and harmony.

Question What elements in the painting show repetition and which show symmetry? *(Possible responses: repetition—the rows of dancers and their similar costumes; symmetry—the pairing of the dancers, arches, pennants and fruits on the ceiling)*

5 Reading/Thinking Skills
Infer

Question Why does the stranger flatter the chaperone before asking Sarita to dance? *(Possible response: By cleverly winning over the chaperone, he impresses both her and Sarita.)*

BUILDING ENGLISH PROFICIENCY

ESL LEP ELD SAE LD

Sequencing Story Events

Invite students to discuss coming of age and courtship rituals that the story brings to mind. Let them share events that they have attended that are similar to the eighteenth birthday party. Some students may have been chaperoned in a formal sense; others may have been chaperoned informally.

Question What are the events in the courtship of Sarita and Pepe Gonzalez beginning with their meeting in February?

Students can respond by using a sequence-of-events map that "flows backward" to the couple's meeting in February. Have them continue mapping the sequence of events forward as the couple's eyes meet.

The Hidalgo man sees Sarita.
↓
Sarita joins the dancers . . .
↓
[ ]

Students may want to discuss in greater detail, or even act out, the silent interaction between the Hidalgo man and Sarita.

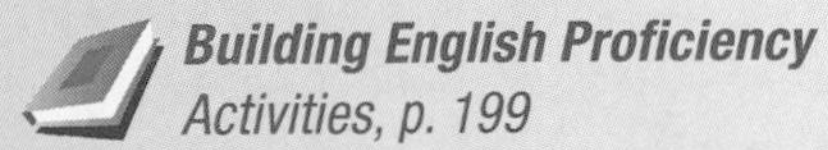

Building English Proficiency *Activities, p. 199*

6 Literary Element
Plot

Question How does the incident involving the song "Virgencita" advance the plot? *(Possible responses: It shows that Sarita does not suspect the stranger of being from Hidalgo so she freely tells him her views of people from Hidalgo.)*

7 Multicultural Note
Relics

Many cultures revere the bones of the dead. In Hispanic and other Roman Catholic cultures, the bones of the saints, called relics, are believed to have supernatural powers. Stealing anyone's bones is viewed as a desecration and insult. Thus the stealing of Don Rómolo Balderas's bones is viewed as a serious matter by the people of San Juan Iglesias.

8 Reader's Response
Making Personal Connections

After reading about the attempt to steal the bones, students may be reminded of pranks rival groups or schools play on one another. Discuss how such acts keep feuds alive and what the consequences of pranks may be.

"She is the worst dragon in San Juan. And how easily you won her!"

"What is a dragon," he asked imperiously,[11] "when I longed to dance with you?"

"Ay," she retorted, "you have a quick tongue. I think you are a dangerous man."

In answer he drew her closer to him and turned her toward the orchestra. As he reached the chief violinist, he called out, "Play the *Virgencita,*[12] 'The Shy Young Maiden.'"

The violinist's mouth opened in soundless surprise. The girl in his arms said sharply, "You heard him, the *Borachita,*[13] 'The Little Drunken Girl.'"

With a relieved grin the violinist tapped his music stand with his bow, and the music swung into the sad farewell of a man to his sweetheart:

Farewell, my little drunken one.
I must go to the capital
To serve the master
Who makes me weep for my return.

The stranger frowned down at her. "Is this a joke, señorita?" he asked coldly.

"No," she whispered, looking about her quickly to see if the incident had been observed.
6 "But the *Virgencita* is the favorite song of Hidalgo, a village on the other side of the mountains in the next valley. The people of Hidalgo and San Juan Iglesias do not speak."

"That is a stupid thing," said the man from Hidalgo as he swung her around in a large turn. "Is not music free as air? Why should one town own the rights to a song?"

The girl shuddered slightly. "Those people from Hidalgo—they are wicked monsters. Can you guess what they did not six months since?"

The man started to point out that the space of time from February to May was three months, but he thought it better not to appear too wise. "Did these Hidalgo monsters frighten you, señorita? If they did, I personally will kill them all."

She moved closer against him and tilted her face until her mouth was close to his ear. "They
attempted to steal the bones of Don Rómolo 7
Balderas."[14]

"Is it possible?" He made his eyes grow round and his lips purse up in disdain.[15] "Surely not that! Why, all the world knows that Don Rómolo Balderas was the greatest historian in the entire republic.[16] Every school child reads his books. Wise men from Quintana Roo to the Río Bravo[17] bow their heads in admiration to his name. What a wicked thing to do!" He hoped his virtuous tone was not too virtuous for plausibility, but she did not seem to notice.

"It is true! In the night they came. Three devils!"

"Young devils, I hope."

"Young or old, who cares? They were devils. The blacksmith surprised them even as they were opening the grave. He raised such a shout that all of San Juan rushed to his aid, for they
were fighting, I can tell you. Especially one of 8
them—their leader."

"And who was he?"

"You have heard of him doubtless. A proper wild one named Pepe Gonzalez."[18]

"And what happened to them?"

"They had horses and got away, but one, I think, was hurt."

The Hidalgo man twisted his mouth, remembering how Rubén the candymaker had ridden across the whitewashed line high on the cañon trail that marked the division between the Three Marys' and the Sabinas' sides of the mountains and then had fallen in a faint from

11. **imperiously** (im pir′ē əs lē), *adv.* in a haughty or arrogant manner.
12. ***Virgencita,*** (vēr hen sē′tä).
13. ***Borachita,*** (bō rä chē′tä).
14. **Don Rómolo Balderas,** (dōn rō′mō lō bäl de′ras).
15. **disdain** (dis dān′), *n.* scorn.
16. **the entire republic,** Mexico.
17. **Quintana Roo to the Río Bravo,** from the Yucatan peninsula in southeast Mexico north to the Rio Grande.
18. **Pepe Gonzalez,** (pe′pā gōn sä′les).

MINI-LESSON: GRAMMAR
Punctuation of Adjectives in Series

Point out that adjectives are often used in series to describe different aspects of a person, place, or thing. Commas are used to separate the adjectives or adjective phrases. For example:

Suddenly a plump, officious little man, his round cheeks glistening with perspiration, pushed his way through the crowd.

Plump and *officious* are two different adjectives describing the man, so they are separated by a comma.

Activity Ideas

- Have students look for other sentences in the selection that have two or more adjectives.
- Let them explain why the punctuation is used in each case.
- Then they can write a paragraph that describes a party they have recently attended. Paragraphs must include adjectives in a series.

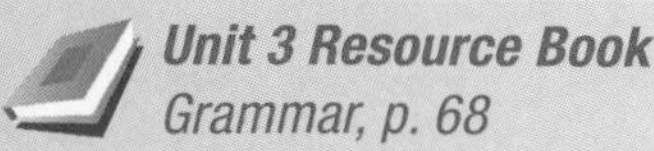
Unit 3 Resource Book
Grammar, p. 68

his saddle because his left arm was broken. There was no candy in Hidalgo for six weeks, and the entire Sabinas Valley resented that broken arm as fiercely as did Rubén.

The stranger tightened his arm in reflexed anger about Sarita's waist as she said, "All the world knows that the men of Hidalgo are sons of the mountain witches."

"But even devils are shy of disturbing the honored dead," he said gravely.

"'Don Rómolo was born in our village,' Hidalgo says. 'His bones belong to us.' Well, anyone in the valley can tell you he died in San Juan Iglesias, and here his bones will stay! Is that not proper? Is that not right?"

To keep from answering, he guided her through an intricate dance pattern that led them past the patio door. Over her head he could see two men and a woman staring with amazement at the open package on the table.

His eyes on the patio, he asked blandly,[19]
9 "You say the leader was one Pepe Gonzalez? The name seems to have a familiar sound."

"But naturally. He has a talent." She tossed her head and stepped away from him as the music stopped. It was a dance of two *paradas*. He slipped his hand through her arm and guided her into place in the large oval of parading couples. Twice around the room and the orchestra would play again.

"A talent?" he prompted.

"For doing the impossible. When all the world says a thing cannot be done, he does it to prove the world wrong. Why, he climbed to the top of the Prow, and not even the long-vanished Joaquín Castillo had ever climbed that mountain before. And this same Pepe caught a mountain lion with nothing to aid him but a rope and his two bare hands."

"He doesn't sound such a bad friend," protested the stranger, slipping his arm around her waist as the music began to play the merry song of the soap bubbles:

Pretty bubbles of a thousand colors
That ride on the wind
And break as swiftly
As a lover's heart.

The events in the patio were claiming his attention. Little by little he edged her closer to the door. The group at the table had considerably enlarged. There was a low murmur of excitement from the crowd.

"What happened?" asked Sarita, attracted by the noise.

"There seems to be something wrong at the table," he answered, while trying to peer over the heads of the people in front of him. Realizing that this might be the last moment of peace he would have that evening, he bent toward her.

"If I come back on Sunday, will you walk 10
around the plaza with me?"

She was startled into exclaiming, "Ay, no!"

"Please. Just once around."

"And you think I'd walk more than once with you, señor, even if you were no stranger? In San Juan Iglesias, to walk around the plaza with a girl means a wedding."

"Ha, and you think that is common to San Juan alone? Even the devils of Hidalgo respect that law." He added hastily at her puzzled upward glance. "And so they do in all the villages." To cover his lapse he said softly, "I don't even know your name."

A mischievous grin crinkled the corners of her eyes. "Nor do I know yours, señor. Strangers do not often walk the streets of San Juan."

Before he could answer, the chattering in the patio swelled to louder proportions. Don Roméo's voice lay on top, like thick cream on milk. "I tell you it is a jewel of a cheese. Such flavor, such texture, such whiteness. It is a jewel of a cheese."

---

19. **blandly** (bland′lē), *adv.* in a smoothly agreeable, polite manner.

9 Reading/Thinking Skills
Infer

Question What do you think is the identity of the young man? What clues in the story support your statement? (*Possible responses: He is probably Pepe Gonzalez. The young man was identified earlier as being from Hidalgo. Now he is revealed as already knowing the details of the stealing of the bones. Pepe Gonzalez is described as "having a talent to do the impossible," and this audacity is evident in the young man.)*

10 Reading/Thinking Skills
Classify

Question Do you think the stranger is "romantic" in a modern sense in your culture? Classify what is romantic about the stranger and what is romantic behavior today. Then, define "romantic."

To classify romantic behavior, students might make a chart similar to this sample.

Romantic now	Romantic in "The Street of the Cañon"
walk on the beach in the moonlight cuddling in front of a fireplace	courting a girl in a rival town sophisticated manners

BUILDING ENGLISH PROFICIENCY

Inventing Scenes

After the story has been read, students can plot out the scene that might follow the ending. To prepare, students can do the following:

- Identify the key events of the story, such as the encounter of Sarita and Pepe Gonzalez during the stealing of the bones, Pepe Gonzalez's entrance to town, his attending the party, his dance with Sarita, the discovery of the cheese from Hidalgo, and Pepe Gonzalez's disappearance.
- Working in groups, let students invent another series of events using a sequence chart for their notes. The first event of the new scene can be Pepe Gonzalez's disappearance.

Pepe Gonzalez disappears.
↓
↓
↓
↓

11 Literary Focus
Imagery

Point out how the vivid imagery in the description of Tío Daniel heightens the tension. Let students identify the senses appealed to in this passage.

12 Reading/Thinking Skills
Synthesize

Question What do you think is Pepe Gonzalez's purpose in coming to Don Romeo's house? Base your responses on Pepe Gonzalez's actions and existence of the rivalry. *(Possible responses: He sincerely loves Sarita and wants her for his wife; he only wants to win Sarita to insult the town; he will try to lure her away as another strike against the town.)*

Check Test

1. How old is Sarita? *(eighteen)*
2. In what month did the stranger first see Sarita? *(February)*
3. Who is the first person the stranger asks for a dance? *(the chaperone)*
4. What injury did the candymaker incur when he rode with the Hidalgo men to steal the bones? *(He broke his left arm.)*
5. Where is the stranger when his gift of cheese is found to be from Hidalgo? *(He has disappeared.)*

Unit 3 Resource Book
Alternate Check Test, p. 69

"What has happened?" Sarita asked of a woman at her elbow.

"A fine goat's cheese appeared as if by magic on the table. No one knows where it came from."

"Probably an extra one from Linares," snorted a fat, bald man on the right.

"Linares never made such a cheese as this," said the woman decisively.

"Silence!" roared Don Roméo. "Old Tío[20] Daniel would speak a word to us."

A great hand of silence closed down over the mouths of the people. The girl was standing on tiptoe trying vainly to see what was happening. She was hardly aware of the stranger's whispering voice, although she remembered the words that he said. "Sunday night—once around the plaza."

She did not realize that he had moved away, leaving a gap that was quickly filled by the blacksmith.

11 Old Tío Daniel's voice was a shrill squeak, and his thin, stringy neck jutted forth from his body like a turtle's from its shell. "This is no cheese from Linares," he said with authority, his mouth sucking in over his toothless gums between his sentences. "Years ago, when the great Don Rómolo Balderas was still alive, we had such cheese as this—ay, in those days we had it. But after he died and was buried in our own sainted ground, as was right and proper. . . ."

"Yes, yes," murmured voices in the crowd. He glared at the interruption. As soon as there was silence again, he continued:

"After he died, we had it no more. Shall I tell you why?"

"Tell us, Tío Daniel," said the voices humbly.

"Because it is made in Hidalgo!"

The sound of a waterfall, the sound of a wind in a narrow cañon, and the sound of an angry crowd are much the same. There were no distinct words, but the sound was enough.

"Are you certain, Tío?" boomed Don Roméo.

"As certain as I am that a donkey has long ears. The people of Hidalgo have been famous for generations for making cheese like this—especially that wicked one, that owner of a cheese factory, Timotéo Gonzalez, father to Pepe, the wild one, whom we have good cause to remember."

"We do, we do," came the sigh of assurance.

"But on the whole northern frontier there are no vats like his to produce so fine a product. Ask the people of Chihuahua, of Sonora. Ask the man on the bridge at Laredo, or the man in his boat at Tampico, '*Hola,* friend, who makes the finest goat cheese?'

"And the answer will always be the same, 'Don Timotéo of Hidalgo.'"

It was the blacksmith who asked the great question. "Then where did that cheese come from, and we haters of Hidalgo these ten long years?"

No voice said, "The stranger," but with one fluid movement every head in the patio turned toward the girl in the doorway. She also turned, her eyes wide with something that she realized to her own amazement was more apprehension[21] than anger.

But the stranger was not in the room. When the angry, muttering men pushed through to the street, the stranger was not on the plaza. He was not anywhere in sight. A few of the more religious crossed themselves for fear that the Devil had walked in their midst. "Who was he?" one voice asked another. But Sarita, who was meekly listening to a lecture from Don Roméo on the propriety[22] of dancing with strangers, did not have to ask. She had a strong suspicion that
she had danced that night within the circling 12
arm of Pepe Gonzalez.

20. **Tío** (tē′ō), Spanish for uncle.
21. **apprehension** (ap′ri hen′shən), *n.* fear.
22. **propriety** (prə prī′ə tē), *n.* proper behavior.

MINI-LESSON: VOCABULARY
Expand Vocabulary Using Structural Analysis

Explain that sentence structure can sometimes help students determine the meaning of an unknown word. For example:

He made his eyes grow round and his lips purse up in *disdain.*

Also explain that the sentence has a compound predicate *(made his eyes grow round and [made] his lips purse up in disdain).* This structure tells you that the actions of his eyes and lips are probably parallel in meaning, and this helps you guess that *disdain* means scorn.

Activity Ideas

- Have students look for other sentences in the selection that contain unfamiliar words.
- Referring to elements such as subject, predicate, clauses, and so on, students should describe the structure of the sentence.
- Have students determine what parts of the sentence are related to the unknown word.
- Students can determine whether these parts provide clues to the meaning.

After Reading

Making Connections

Shaping Your Response

1. What do you think are the chances of survival for this budding romance? Why?
2. If you could give some advice to Sarita, what would you say?
3. Do you agree that love can make people do bold and crazy things? Explain.

Analyzing the Story

4. How do Sarita's **individual** goals conflict with the expectations of her family and community? Do you think that there is a way to reconcile the two sets of goals? Why or why not?
5. Sarita's chaperone says, "A man clever enough to pat the sheep has a right to play with the lamb." What does she mean by this **proverb?**
6. Sarita observes that Pepe Gonzalez has "a talent for the impossible." How does this detail help **characterize** him?

Extending the Ideas

7. What in the story supports the following critical evaluation of one of Niggli's **themes**: "Tradition is seen as an immensely important aspect of . . . life, and social customs are emphasized as key elements in day-to-day activities"?
8. Would the fathers you know welcome a total stranger into their houses on such an occasion? Why or why not?
9. What modern conflicts can you think of within or between groups, schools, towns, states, or countries? Do you think the reasons for these conflicts are legitimate or silly? Explain.

Literary Focus: Imagery

In "The Street of the Cañon," Niggli uses **images** that appeal to the five senses. Find an image that appeals to each sense and write it beside the appropriate label in a chart such as the one below.

Sense	Example
Sight	
Smell	
Hearing	
Taste	
Touch	

LITERARY FOCUS: IMAGERY

Possible responses

Sense	Example
Sight	yellow glow of kerosene lanterns
Smell	too sweet perfume of gardenias
Hearing	voice was a shrill squeak
Taste	long red rolls of spicy sausages
Touch	tapped its parchment tip against her mouth

After Reading

MAKING CONNECTIONS

1. Possible responses: The romance is unlikely to survive because of the hatred between the two towns; the young man is clever and charming enough to overcome even this obstacle; he might spirit Sarita away.

2. Possible responses: Be careful because your suitor is dangerous and hates your people; follow your heart.

3. Possible responses: Love is a strong emotion and often leads people into conflict with tradition; romantic daring is a staple of literature, the movies, and TV.

4. Possible responses: Sarita seems interested in exploring her own romantic feelings; her family and town probably want her to marry a local man; their union could be a way to bring peace or incite greater conflict.

5. The older woman is the sheep who must protect Sarita, the lamb. By showing good manners to the chaperone, the stranger is permitted to be social with Sarita.

6. It confirms what the reader already knows about his boldness—trying to steal the bones, and being present at the party. It creates suspense about what the character will do next.

7. Much of the action in the story depends on traditional customs (the birthday party, treatment of the dead) and standards of behavior (courting).

8. Possible response: Many American families do not have such a custom and would consider a stranger to be a "party-crasher."

9. Possible responses: foreign conflicts (Bosnia, Northern Ireland) and local ones (such as between gangs); there are often complex social, emotional, economic reasons for such conflicts.

VOCABULARY STUDY

Words chosen by students will vary. Some words will fit more naturally with a particular scene (apprehension—the dog; propriety—the argument with parents.) Words should be used correctly in context.

Unit 3 Resource Book
Vocabulary, p. 67
Vocabulary Test, p. 70

WRITING CHOICES

Writer's Notebook Update

Students should conclude that it is not so much the object itself but intentions, feelings, and context that make it romantic.

Dear Miss Manners

A volunteer can review standard letter form and present it to the class.

Selection Test

Unit 3 Resource Book
pp. 71–72

Transparency Collection
Fine Art Writing Prompt 7

Vocabulary Study

apprehension
audaciously
blandly
disdain
imperiously
jauntily
officious
propriety

Use at least four vocabulary words to describe one of the following scenes.

- You encounter a large, fierce-looking, unleashed dog on the sidewalk.
- You are chaperoning ten fifth-graders, who refuse to go to sleep, at a slumber party.
- You and a parent are expressing different opinions on whether or not you should go to a particular event.

Expressing Your Ideas

Writing Choices

Writer's Notebook Update In a paragraph, compare your idea of a romantic gift to Pepe's choice in "The Street of the Cañon." Speculate on what in general makes a "romantic" gift romantic.

Dear Miss Manners Write a **letter** to Miss Manners, the etiquette expert, in which you defend or criticize the concept of chaperones in today's society. You might want to use humor to describe a specific incident that happened to you or to someone you know.

Eavesdropping At the end of the story, Sarita is "meekly listening" to a lecture from her father "on the propriety of dancing with strangers." You are close enough to hear what Don Roméo is saying. Report the conversation in a **gossip column**.

Other Options

Wall Art and Life In the twentieth century, several Mexican artists became world famous for their murals—pictures painted on walls. With a group, research one of the following artists: Diego Rivera, José Clemente Orozco, or David Alfaro Siqueiros. Present information and examples of the artist's work to the class in an **art talk.** You might refer to the Beyond Print article titled "Looking at Paintings," page 392, for tips in discussing art.

Dress Rehearsal As a group, do some **research** on the kinds of clothes dancers at a party in a Mexican village in the early 1900s might have worn, the music that could have been played, and the dance steps that might have been performed. Demonstrate your findings for classmates.

OTHER OPTIONS

Wall Art and Life

Students might want to look in reference works under the topic "Mexican muralism," and explore social conditions to which these artists were responding.

Many Kinds of Heroes

Heroes Around the World

Multicultural Connection
Compare the real-life heroes that Michael Dorris mentions with the larger-than -life fictional heroes on pages 438-439. Who would you say are legendary heroes in your country?

by Michael Dorris

In the following interview, Michael Dorris, a writer of French, Modoc Indian, and Irish ancestry, discusses contemporary heroes. One such hero is Rosa Parks, an activist who triggered the civil rights movement in the U.S. when she refused to give up her bus seat to a white passenger in 1955. Another personal hero was Dorris's adopted son Adam who was born with fetal alcohol syndrome, an affliction passed to a newborn by a drinking mother.

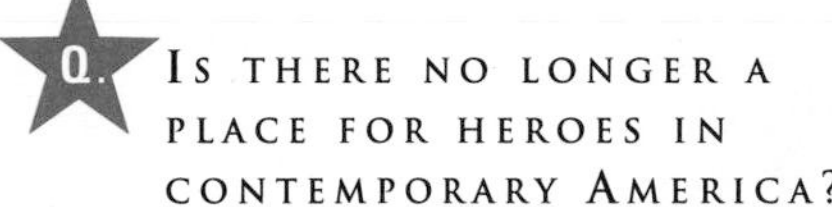

Q. IS THERE NO LONGER A PLACE FOR HEROES IN CONTEMPORARY AMERICA?

A. It's not that we have no heroes anymore. The problem is that we just don't recognize the heroes we have. We make the Terminator a hero or Barney a hero, and we barely react when Rosa Parks gets beaten up in her own home. What a horrible thing, what a truly horrible thing!

Q. WHO WOULD BE SOME OF YOUR OTHER CANDIDATES FOR HEROES IN AMERICA TODAY?

A. Well, I think Jimmy Carter is a real hero in this society. I happened to be on the podium with him at the American Booksellers Association convention in California a couple of years ago, and he was introduced as the only person who has ever used the American presidency as a steppingstone to greatness. He came across as genuinely wise and articulate and positive.

Being positive, I think is part of being a hero—maybe the hardest part, because if you're a hero you're smart enough to know all the reasons why you *should* be discouraged. Social life, after all, is simply a collective illusion, a shared set of boundaries and possibilities. If we all believe something to be true, in an odd way it is true. Maybe a hero is the person who inspires a collective belief in our best dream of ourselves as a people.

Our late son was such a hero. Without ever being aware of it or knowing what it meant, the example of his life and his inherent charisma forced those who encountered him to ask questions. His small, brave story, told in *The Broken Cord,* changed a lot of lives and saved a lot of lives.

He evoked a heartbreaking sense of what he might have been but for the insult he suffered before birth. Even when he was unconscious in the hospital before he died, he made a profound impact on the doctors. There was something about his very presence that reminded them of why they were in medicine.

I think there are a whole lot of heroes, and most of them are people that we know personally. They're our parents or our children or our brothers and sisters who are going through adversity. We don't have to reach out to Abraham Lincoln to be inspired; we can find heroism in ordinary people and in the daily, undramatic crises of faith and hope that we encounter and struggle through against the odds.

Interdisciplinary Study

Theme Link

The heroes of legend and myth do have their counterparts in contemporary society, but heroism is often defined by the members of a group or family, who hold up individuals among them as models.

Curricular Connection: Multicultural

Discuss Dorris's statement that a hero represents the "best dream of ourselves as a people." Challenge students to describe a hero for the United States in the twenty-first century. Volunteers might use the description to create a monument or statue of the "dream hero."

Additional Background

Michael Dorris is married to another well-known writer, Louise Erdrich. He adopted his late son, Adam, and two other children before he was married. In *The Broken Cord* Dorris describes Adam's struggle against the effects of Fetal Alcohol Syndrome, which were physical and mental abnormalities and behavioral problems.

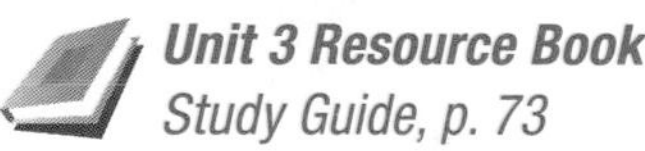

Unit 3 Resource Book
Study Guide, p. 73

BUILDING ENGLISH PROFICIENCY

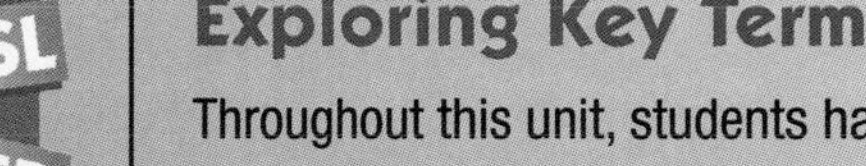

Exploring Key Terms

Throughout this unit, students have been challenged to define (and redefine) their understanding of the word *heroism.* To help students grasp this feature, and to prepare them for "Responding" on page 439, work with them to create a semantic web arising from the word. Students should begin with the definitions suggested by Michael Dorris and then can add others of their own.

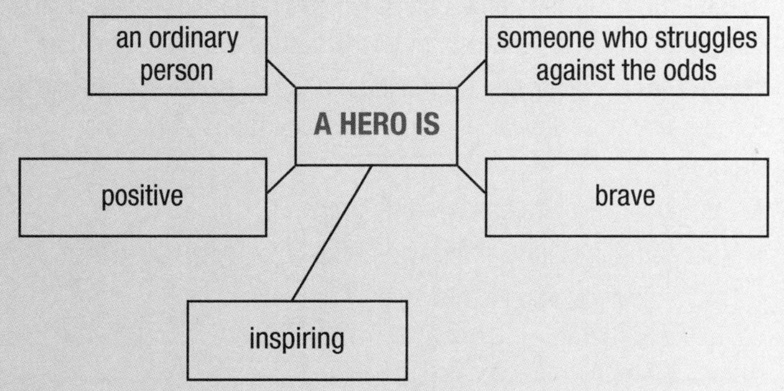

Terms to Know

Quetzalcoatl (ket säl′kô ät′ əl), the feather serpent god, Ancient Mesoamerican deity of self-sacrifice, wisdom, and science. As Ehetacl, god of the wind. Taught the Aztecs agriculture, metal works, the arts, and the calendar.

Maui (mow′ē), Polynesia's great trickster hero, master of devices, who gave humans the gift of fire. He slowed the motion of the sun to give his mother time to cook her meals.

Gilgamesh (gil′gə mesh′), hero of the Mesopotamian Epic of Gilgamesh, a long Akkadian poem about man's search for immortality, composed about 2000 B.C.

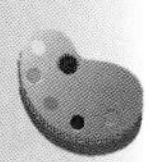

Art Study

Explain that when a work of art represents a mythical person or scene, it will often utilize a set of recognizable, traditional images or symbols. The study of these images is called iconography.

According to the epic of Gilgamesh, the hero faced many tests, often against animals, in his quest for the plant, Never Grow Old, that would bring him immortality.

Question What are the icons in this 8th-century Assyrian relief of Gilgamesh? *(the branch in his hand that represents the plant Never Grow Old, the elixir of immortality, and the lion in his arms that represents one of the lions that he fought)*

MAPPING

MEXICO

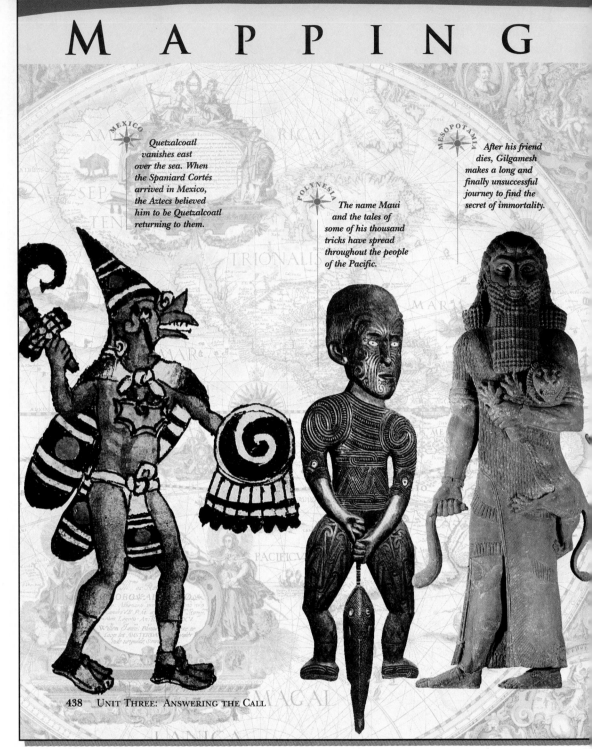

Quetzalcoatl vanishes east over the sea. When the Spaniard Cortés arrived in Mexico, the Aztecs believed him to be Quetzalcoatl returning to them.

POLYNESIA

The name Maui and the tales of some of his thousand tricks have spread throughout the people of the Pacific.

MESOPOTAMIA

After his friend dies, Gilgamesh makes a long and finally unsuccessful journey to find the secret of immortality.

MINI-LESSON: STUDY SKILLS

Interpret Atlases

Teach Some of the heroes on these two pages represent civilizations that no longer exist, at least not in their ancient geographical form.

Activity Idea Have students use an atlas to locate the international borders that now define the geographic locations of these ancient empires.

- The Persian Empire has become Iran.
- Mesopotamia is known today as Iraq.
- The Aztec civilization is now a part of Mexico.
- Scandinavia was divided into Denmark, Sweden, Holland, Finland, and Iceland.
- The subcontinent of India was divided into Pakistan, Bangladesh, and India.

Volunteers can consult historical resources and then show the original borders of the above civilizations by marking their outlines on a modern atlas.

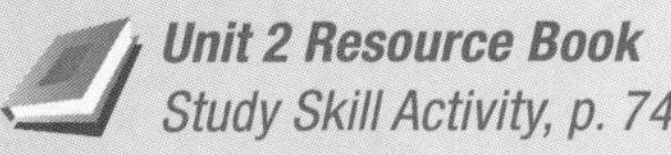

Unit 2 Resource Book
Study Skill Activity, p. 74

OUT HEROES

Brynhild is chief of the Valkyries, "the choosers of the slain," who guide dead warriors to the afterworld.

SCANDINAVIA

Sita and her husband Rama represent the ideals of married life in Indian tradition.

INDIA

Rustem mistakenly kills his son, Sohrab, in combat.

PERSIA

Responding

1. What does Dorris mean when he says: "Maybe a hero is the person who inspires a collective belief in our best dream of ourselves as a people?" Do you agree with his statement? Explain.

2. Make up your own definition of heroism.

3. With a partner, research in greater depth a hero who appears on this map.

439

Responding

1. Possible Responses Dorris might mean that a hero embodies the qualities that are important to a nation and that by recognizing a hero, we as a people agree on what we want our nation to represent. Some students may feel that it would be difficult for different groups to accept a single hero. Others may feel that everyone can be inspired by heroes who show courage, conviction, and strength.

2. Possible Responses Students' responses may reflect the qualities of heroes in the unit selections, of those on pages 438–439, and of people they know who have inspired them.

3. Possible Responses Suggest that students use their findings to decide who in modern times could be compared to the hero they research.

Interdisciplinary Activity Idea

Students can create a heroes map. Divide students into groups to research the legends and heroes mentioned on pages 438–439 and those of cultural regions such as Russia, Ireland, Alaska, China, and Japan. Place a world map on a bulletin board in the classroom, and have students pin the names of each hero onto its proper geographical location.

BUILDING ENGLISH PROFICIENCY

Responding to Visual Images

Open a discussion of the images on the page. Encourage students to share prior knowledge about the heroes shown, telling

- additional stories or facts
- names of weapons, animals, dress items
- settings in which the heroes dwelled
- meanings of symbols, emblems, and markings

Extend the discussion by pointing out that people recognize national heroes such as these by their clothing or symbols. In contrast, Dorris suggests that heroes can be the ordinary people we see every day.

Activity Idea Discuss which clothing and symbols would be appropriate for a national or even planetary hero. After students suggest details, they can draw or make a collage to represent the image.

Interdisciplinary Study

Theme Link

By granting TV time or newspaper space to certain people, journalists may influence people's ideas of what is heroic.

Curricular Connection: Career

You can use Askari's comments to explore the ethical responsibilities faced by modern journalists.

Term to Know

run amok (ə muk′), also spelled *amuck*, behave wildly; run about in a murderous frenzy

Responding

Possible Responses Encourage students to give examples of persons from many walks of life—politics, business, monarchies, civil rights, sports, entertainment, clerical, and so on. Students may discuss whether companies exploit or create heroes by paying them to be spokespersons for their products.

Interdisciplinary Activity Idea

Students can research the topic of yellow journalism. They might analyze a tabloid publication to examine the ways that the press can distort and fabricate the truth.

INTERDISCIPLINARY STUDY

Career Connection

A journalist reminds us of the power of the media to create or destroy heroes.

Currently living in the Detroit area and writing freelance on environmental issues, Emilia Askari has covered a variety of beats for newspapers in Miami, Los Angeles, and Detroit. Her work has made her aware of the power of the press to create heroes, as she explains in the following interview.

PRESS POWER

Emilia Askari, journalist

Journalists create heroes—and antiheroes. They don't sit around scratching their heads and wondering, 'Who are we going to make a hero today?' But simply because we do our jobs—and ask questions and tell the stories—heroes are created in the process. Some people who achieve heroic status are common folks who have heroism thrust upon them; others work hard to acquire a heroic image—or have a public relations image maker to help things along.

"There is an element of luck as to who is made a hero. In the cycle of news, Monday is a slow day, since most of the news involves government, which is closed over the weekend. Someone who saves a child from a burning building has greater chances of making the news on Monday than on Thursday.

"Usually a single newspaper article doesn't create a hero, but it can happen. In fact, it once happened because of an article that I wrote in Los Angeles. One day an elderly woman barged into the newsroom and said, 'I have an important story that I must tell!' I took her aside and listened to her fantastic tale: her tawdry life as a young beauty, and the description of her daughter, who decided to turn her own life around and escape the crime-ridden neighborhood. The girl earned a GED (General Educational Development) and was now about to graduate from medical school and become a surgeon. After verifying the woman's story, I wrote an article about her that appeared on the front page.

The daughter received offers to make a TV movie of her life. The article probably had a greater impact in Los Angeles, being so close to Hollywood, than it would have had in Detroit.

"Hero-making can happen in reverse, sometimes to a whole class of people—especially when people of color or the poor are stereotyped. This happened with the 1995 Oklahoma City bombing in which a federal office was bombed and many people were killed. Police and the media originally described the incident as a Middle East-type terrorist attack. On the basis of that label, anyone from an Arab country became suspect. One man was even detained at the airport simply because of his nationality. Upon investigation, however, Middle Easterners were cleared from any involvement in the crime."

Ms. Askari concludes, "I really enjoy my job and I'm proud of my work. I try to do a public service—gathering, sorting, and conveying information—and try to provide a balance to public officials who have power and might run amuck if the media did not keep the public informed."

Responding

With a group, brainstorm examples of hero-making or hero-bashing in the media. Do you feel that advertising helps shape our concepts of heroism? Explain.

MINI-LESSON: LISTENING SKILLS

Interpreting the News

Teach Discuss Emilia Askari's statement that "someone who saves a child from a burning building has greater chances of making the news on Monday than on Thursday."

Explain that most television news programs are commercial ventures that fund their operations through the sale of advertisements. Not only must these enterprises cover the news, but they must also make their program interesting enough to attract and maintain a wide audience. Encourage students to examine the commercial pressure that influences the selection of news items to be broadcast on any given day.

Activity Idea Have students listen to the evening news every night for a week. Encourage them to classify and graph the percentages of items that receive press coverage within the week. Finally, evaluate whether students agree with the emphasis placed on various types of stories.

Reading Mini-Lesson

Classifying

Whenever you create files on a computer, arrange your CDs in some order, use subject dividers in a notebook, or put your socks into a special drawer, you are using classification to make your personal life a bit more orderly. Libraries, supermarkets, and the Yellow Pages of the phone directory use methods of classifying for easy public access.

In addition, classifying is a basic thinking skill that good readers use to group new ideas into more familiar categories or to break large categories into smaller groups. Likewise, classification is a tool for mentally storing knowledge (for example, famous Texans, mystery writers, state capitals).

Much of the information on heroes in the Interdisciplinary Study on pages 437–440 lends itself to classification. The map displays heroes according to different geographic areas. In his interview, Michael Dorris mentions personal heroes, historical heroes, and media heroes.

Use the following headings, along with headings of your own, to make a chart in which you classify the heroes listed at the left. (You may need to review information in the Interdisciplinary Study.) Note that one hero may fit into several categories. Think of other heroes to add to the chart.

Terminator
Rosa Parks
Abraham Lincoln
Quetzalcoatl
Brynhild
Sita
a favorite teacher
Jimmy Carter
King Arthur
Indiana Jones
Michael Dorris's son Adam

Geographical	Historical	Media	Personal	Legendary

Activity Options

1. Using categories such as Adventure, Comedy, Romance, Drama, Fantasy, Westerns, and Sports, work with a group to classify your favorite films, TV shows, video games, or books. List the results on a chart and present it to the class.
2. Create a list of survey questions to classify the people in your class. For example, you could create categories and subcategories such as pet owners (owners of cats, dogs, or unusual pets), musicians, team members, or movie buffs.

Reading Mini-Lesson

Teaching Objectives

- to explain the steps involved in classification
- to recognize practical uses for classifying
- to classify the subjects within "Heroes Around the World"

Introduce

Ask students what methods they use to classify their notebooks, clothes, or CDs. Students can suggest classification systems they use frequently, such as those in the library, in telephone books, and in supermarkets.

Follow Up

Have students analyze information on the chart and note to which category students added the most names.

Activity Options

Activity 1 Discuss how classification can lead to misinformation when items don't fit a single category.

Activity 2 Let students analyze the data from the point of view of an advertiser.

CONTENT AREA READING

Classification as a Tool for Comparison

One of the benefits of classifying while reading is that similarities and differences between categories are easier to see.

- A quick glance at the chart will show which heroes fall into the same categories, as well as which heroes fall into more than one category.
- It is very helpful to see which subjects or characteristics show up in more than one category, because an analysis of similarities might reveal cross-cultural influences.

Writing Workshop

WRITER'S BLUEPRINT

Specs

The Specs in the Writer's Blueprint address these writing and thinking skills:

- defining
- analyzing
- comparing and contrasting
- making judgments
- making transitions
- avoiding stringy sentences

These Specs serve as your lesson objectives, and they form the basis for the **Assessment Criteria Specs** for a superior paper, which appear on the final TE page for this lesson. You might want to read through the Assessment Criteria Specs with students when you begin the lesson.

Linking Literature to Writing

Go over the literature in this part of the unit with students and have them pick out potential heroes. List these heroes on the board and have students discuss why they made the choices they did.

Writing Workshop

What Makes a Hero?

Assignment You have read about many kinds of heroes. Now write an essay in which you express your own thoughts about heroism.

WRITER'S BLUEPRINT

Product	An interpretive essay
Purpose	To explore the concept of heroism
Audience	Your teacher, classmates, and friends
Specs	As the writer of a successful essay, you should:

- ❑ Decide on your own definition of a hero, including the four traits that you feel are most important to a hero. Then choose the two characters from the selections who come closest to living up to your definition.
- ❑ Begin your paper by giving your own definition of a hero, keeping in mind that readers may not see a hero in the same way that you do.
- ❑ Go on to analyze how well your two characters live up to your definition of a hero, citing specific details from the stories in support of your analysis.
- ❑ Structure your paper in one of two ways:
  —deal with each trait from your definition, one at a time, and measure the characters against it, or
  —deal with each character, one at a time, and measure her or him against the traits in your definition.
- ❑ Conclude by telling which character comes closer to being your idea of a hero and why.
- ❑ Make smooth transitions between thoughts.
- ❑ Follow the rules of grammar, usage, spelling, and mechanics. Avoid stringy sentences.

WRITING WORKSHOP OVERVIEW

Product
Expository writing: An interpretive essay

Prewriting
Discuss heroic traits—Rate the characters—Chart heroic traits—Plan your essay
Unit 3 Resource Book
Prewriting Worksheets pp. 75–76

Drafting
Before your draft—As you draft
Transparency Collection
Student Models for Writing Workshop 13, 14

Revising
Ask a partner—Strategy: Making Smooth Transitions
Unit 3 Resource Book
Revising Worksheet p. 77

Editing
Ask a partner—Strategy: Correcting Stringy Sentences
Unit 3 Resource Book
Grammar Worksheet p. 78
Grammar Check Test p. 79

Presenting
Debate
Poster

Looking Back
Self-evaluate—Reflect—For Your Working Portfolio
Unit 3 Resource Book
Assessment Worksheet p. 80
Transparency Collection
Fine Art Writing Prompt 7

STEP 1 PREWRITING

Discuss heroic traits. With a partner, discuss real or fictional people you think of as heroic. What do they do and think, outwardly and inwardly, that makes them heroic? List character traits that come to mind as you discuss what makes someone heroic.

Then, on your own, decide on four traits that you feel are most important for a true hero to possess. Here are some suggestions for heroic traits:

> courageous, remains calm in the face of danger, determined, has great patience, helpful, honest, slow to anger, respects the law, has great physical strength, does not wish to harm others, merciful, speedy, athletic, decisive, loving, quick-witted, clever, shy and quiet, friendly, never gives up, aggressive, generous, impulsive, respects the rights of others, is a loner, is a leader, feels superior and shows it, unconventional, charismatic, secretive

OR . . .
Try a quickwrite before you discuss. Write for five minutes or so about what comes to mind when you think of heroes. Use your quickwrite when you discuss heroic traits with a partner.

Rate the characters in the stories in this part of the unit on a scale of 1–10, with 10 being most heroic and 1 least heroic. Then choose the two characters who received your highest rating.

Chart heroic traits. Measure each character against your four traits, using a chart like the one that follows. Find specific examples of things the characters say and do that demonstrate these traits.

Character	#1 Courageous	#2______	#3______	#4______
Peter from "The Secret Room"	Peter plays "Wilhelmus" in church, knowing the anthem is forbidden and he could be imprisoned. This is inner courage–inner strength, not physical.			

LITERARY SOURCE
". . . Peter was playing the 'Wilhelmus'! . . . Then we were all singing together, the full voice of Holland singing her forbidden anthem. We sang at the top of our lungs, sang our oneness, our hope. . . ."
from "The Secret Room" by Corrie ten Boom

STEP 1 PREWRITING

Discuss heroic traits

Students might rank order their list of heroic traits from most important to least important. For more support, see the worksheet referenced below.

Unit 3 Resource Book
Prewriting Worksheet, p. 75

Rate the characters

Have students defend their characters before their small group as if they were recommending the characters for an award.

Chart heroic traits

Discuss with students the ways in which character can be revealed through action and dialogue. For more support, see the worksheet referenced below.

Unit 3 Resource Book
Prewriting Worksheet, p. 76

BUILDING ENGLISH PROFICIENCY

ESL LEP ELD SAE LD

Exploring a Topic

Students can use the following activity to help them determine a hero's traits.

1. Invite students to visualize a real (for example, historical) or fictional (for example, cinematic) hero.

2. Encourage students to imagine that person in a dangerous situation and to describe that situation to a partner.

3. Students can work alone to identify the traits that the hero might display in that situation.

4. After students share their list with partners, the partners might suggest additional traits implied by the situation.

Plan your essay

Encourage students to consider the *Or . . .* option. Discuss the pros and cons of the two approaches. Be sure students see that one approach emphasizes the characters while the other emphasizes the traits.

Connections to **Writer's Notebook**

For selection-related prompts, refer to Writer's Notebook.

Connections to **Writer's Resource**

For additional writing prompts, refer to Writer's Resource.

STEP 2 DRAFTING

As you draft

Before students begin drafting, briefly preview the revising focus: smooth transitions.

The Student Models

The **transparencies** referenced below are authentic student models. Review them with the students before they draft. These questions will help:

1. Which kind of structure did the writer of model 13 use ? (See point 4 in the blueprint.)

2. What four traits does the wriiter of model 14 choose? Does the writer deal with each of those traits in the essay?

3. Look over both models for smooth transitions between sentences and paragraphs. Which model does a better job of making transitions?

Transparency Collection
Student Models for Writing Workshop 13, 14

STEP 3 REVISING

Ask a partner (Peer assessment)

Have peer editors mark the transitions they find in their partner's paper, and mark any places where they feel transitions are needed.

Plan your essay. Create a plan like the one shown, pulling together the information you've gathered up to now.

Introduction
- Your definition of a hero
- Transition to Body (See the Revising Strategy in Step 3 of this lesson.)

Body
- Character #1
  - Trait one and detail from the story
  - Trait two and detail from the story

  and so on
- Transition to Character #2
- Character #2 (same as above)
- Transition to Conclusion

Conclusion
- Which character is more of a hero
- Reasons why

OR . . .
Organize the body of your essay around the four traits and discuss them one at a time. Show how your two characters exemplify each trait.

STEP 2 DRAFTING

Before you write, review your discussion notes, chart, and writing plan. Then reread the Writer's Blueprint.

As you draft, concentrate on getting the ideas from your writing plan down on paper. Here are some drafting tips.

- As you move from idea to idea, knit them together with smooth transitions. See the Revising Strategy in Step 3 of this lesson.
- Be sure that your examples are specific and true to what happens in the story.

STEP 3 REVISING

Ask a partner for comments on your draft before you revise it.

✔ Have I explained my definition of a hero in detail?

✔ Have I used specific details from the literature to show how well my two characters live up to my definition of a hero?

✔ Have I made smooth transitions between paragraphs?

COMPUTER TIP
Use the Cut and Paste functions of your word processor to rearrange the paragraphs in your essay to find the best order.

MINI-LESSON: WRITING STYLE

Making Smooth Transitions

Teach Tell students that writers use transitions not only to connect ideas, but to show how they are connected.

Activity Idea Read the sentences below and have students tell which of the six ways from the chart each transition exemplifies. Then have students suggest different transitional words that would change the meaning slightly.

Instead, he chose to take the noble route.

Most importantly, she never forgot her original goals.

Similarly, neither character began life with noble beginnings.

It follows then, that you can fairly accurately predict her reactions to such behavior.

Despite all these contradictions, the two still managed to understand each other.

Apply Encourage students to look for the places in the outline or essay where one idea leads to another and determine if transitional phrases would help the reader make the connection.

Revising Strategy

Making Smooth Transitions

Use transitional sentences to connect the paragraphs within an essay. In the same way, use transitional phrases, like those below, to connect sentences within a paragraph.

To signal a new idea:	first, next
To compare (show similarities):	in the same way, similarly
To contrast (show differences):	on the other hand, in spite of
To conclude or summarize:	as a result, in conclusion
To add information:	furthermore, for instance
To clarify:	in other words, put another way

Notice how a transitional sentence has been added in the student model to connect the paragraphs.

Carlé is an extremely strong character. He is always able to get the best scoops on the news. Furthermore, he is courageous, risking his life to get the story in even very dangerous places. His bravery and skill as a journalist have made him famous.

In spite of his fame as a reporter, Rolf Carlé is still very level-headed. He didn't mind being in the public eye and being disheveled in front of the world as he tried to save a 13-year-old girl. He was willing to put his personal comfort aside to help her any way he could.

Ask a partner to review your revised draft before you edit. When you edit, look for errors in grammar, usage, spelling, and mechanics. Be on the lookout for stringy sentences.

REVISING STRATEGY: Making Smooth Transitions

Read aloud the student model without and then with revisions. Have students analyze and discuss the effects of the changes. For additional support, see the mini-lesson at the bottom of page 444 and the worksheet referenced below.

Unit 3 Resource Book
Revising Worksheet, p. 77

Connections to Writer's Resource

Refer to the Grammar, Usage, and Mechanics Handbook on Writer's Resource.

STEP 4 EDITING

Ask a partner (Peer assessment)

As students edit, encourage them to pay careful attention to sentences that are long and wordy.

MINI-LESSON: GRAMMAR

Correcting Stringy Sentences

Encourage students to be creative as they construct several possible ways of editing the stringy sentences that follow. Have groups put their revisions on the board or pieces of posterboard to show the entire class. Each group should choose a representative to explain how they made their revisions.

Laurie had to help her family out and she learned about the importance of hard work early and she never forgot the lessons learned on the job even years later.

Peter played music in church and he played well and we always enjoyed singing the hymns as he played and he played the national anthem of Holland, "Wilhelmus," and we were so overcome with pride that we began to sing.

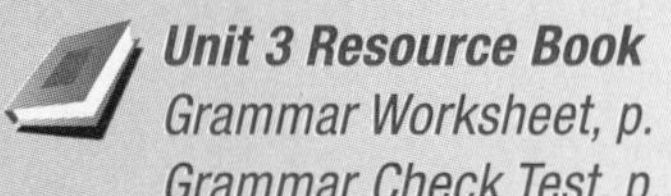

Unit 3 Resource Book
Grammar Worksheet, p. 78
Grammar Check Test, p. 79

Editing Strategy: Correcting Stringy Sentences

Have students read the uncorrected sentence aloud and comment on the way it sounds.

For additional support, see the mini-lesson at the bottom of page 445 and the worksheets referenced below.

Unit 3 Resource Book
Grammar Worksheet, p. 78
Grammar Check Test, p. 79

Connections to **Writer's Resource**

Refer to the Grammar, Usage, and Mechanics Handbook on Writer's Resource.

STEP 5 PRESENTING

Debate

Have students review the rules for a debate.

Poster

Supply old magazines and newspapers for students to use.

STEP 6 LOOKING BACK

Self-evaluate

The *Assessment Criteria Specs* at the bottom of this page are for a superior paper. You might want to post these in the classroom. Students can then evaluate themselves based on these criteria. For a complete scoring rubric, use the *Assessment Worksheet* referenced below.

Unit 3 Resource Book
Assessment Worksheet, p. 80

Reflect

Students may want to address their response to this real-life hero in the form of a letter of appreciation.

To further explore the theme, use the Fine Art Transparency referenced below.

Transparency Collection
Fine Art Writing Prompt 7

Editing Strategy

FOR REFERENCE
You'll find more tips on revising stringy sentences in the Language and Grammar Handbook at the back of this text.

Correcting Stringy Sentences

In a stringy sentence, several independent clauses are strung together with one *and* after another. Correct stringy sentences by breaking them into individual sentences or turning independent clauses into subordinate clauses or phrases.

Stringy Sentence: Corrie ten Boom wanted to help Jews but she knew it was dangerous *and* she planned to have a secret room to hide them *and* she went looking for an architect in the underground to design and build the hiding place.

Corrected: Even though she knew it was dangerous, Corrie ten Boom wanted to help Jews. She planned to have a secret room to hide them. To find someone to build her hiding place, she went looking for an architect in the underground.

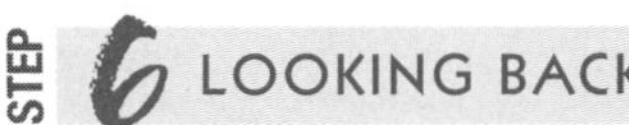

STEP 5 PRESENTING

- Use your essays as the basis for a class debate on the question: What makes a true hero?
- Get together with a partner or a small group and design a poster that illustrates the traits that a true hero should have.

STEP 6 LOOKING BACK

Self-evaluate. Look back at the Writer's Blueprint and give yourself a score for each item, from 6 (superior) to 1 (inadequate).

Reflect. Reflect on the following questions in writing:

✔ Who would be a real-life person who lives up to my definition of a hero? Why?

✔ How am I doing as a writer in terms of being technically correct? How would I rate my spelling, grammar, usage, and mechanics skills?

For Your Working Portfolio Add your finished paper and your reflection responses to your working portfolio.

ASSESSMENT CRITERIA SPECS

Here are the criteria for a superior paper. A full six-level rubric for this paper appears on the *Assessment Worksheet* referenced below.

6 Superior The writer of a 6 paper impressively meets these criteria:

- With confidence, authority, and sophistication, presents a clear definition of a hero in terms of four primary character traits.
- Thoroughly analyzes the extent to which two literary characters embody this definition.
- Offers significant evidence for these analyses by citing relevant examples from the text.
- Presents ideas within a structure that logically ties all the information together, making smooth transitions between thoughts.
- Makes it clear which character comes closer to living up to this definition and why.
- Rarely makes errors in grammar, usage, spelling, and punctuation. Avoids stringy sentences.

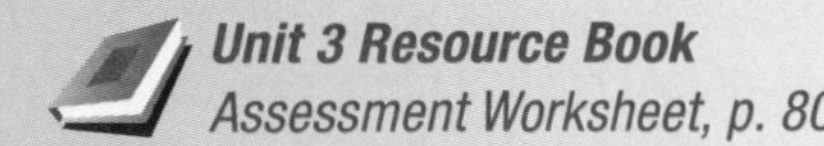

Unit 3 Resource Book
Assessment Worksheet, p. 80

Beyond Print

Multimedia Presentations

Welcome to the Information Age! Among the many wonders of modern technology—computers, VCRs, CD-ROMs, and programs such as HyperCard—is the power to transform traditional speeches into exciting media events. Any time you use a combination of media to communicate to an audience, you are making a multimedia presentation. This includes speech, posters, slides, video, projected images, graphs, computers, recordings, or even skits.

A great tool in producing any multimedia presentation is the computer. Hooking the computer to a projection unit allows you to use the program during an oral presentation, much like a slide projector but with animation, special effects, sound, and video. You can even create an interactive program in which viewers manipulate the type and order of information they receive by merely clicking a button.

The key to successful multimedia presentations is organization. Each piece of media you add makes the presentation more complex, so spend time thinking and practicing. Don't create posters or computer screens that are "busy" or unclear.

Here are some hints for using multimedia in oral presentations.

- Use pictures and music that will supplement the information, not distract the audience.
- Use large type (for readability) and important heads (for emphasis) in projections. Present additional details orally.
- Apply writing skills to ensure concise, clear, and correctly spelled text.
- Plan, organize, and practice presenting your material.
- Project your voice so that everyone can hear.

Activity Option

Prepare a multimedia presentation based on a selection, an author, or a theme related to the selections in the group titled Many Kinds of Heroes. Start by preparing a speech and adding a simple graphic, such as a poster, graph, transparency, or computer image, and music.

Beyond Print

Teaching Objectives

- to explain the concept of a multimedia presentation
- to describe the technology that is often incorporated into multimedia presentations
- to suggest ways to improve a multimedia presentation

Curricular Connection: Technology Skills

You can use the material in this article to inspire students to use technology in their speeches and oral presentations.

Introduce

Ask students to relate their impressions of multimedia presentations: for example, a presentation booth at a museum, a laser light show at a musical performance, a teacher's use of an overhead projector, or an amateur film video they made, wrote, and directed.

Activity Option

Remind students to think about how they can use visual and audio support as an integral part of their presentation, rather than an afterthought thrown in for special effects.

ANOTHER APPROACH

Multimedia in the Arts

Explain that the use of multimedia formats has become common among dance companies, theaters, opera houses, popular musicians, and performance artists. Ask students to describe the use of multimedia in a performance capacity: for example, performances by David Copperfield, magician; or Laurie Anderson, performance artist.

Involve students in a discussion about the parts of multimedia presentations that make the most impact on them. Discuss the impact of sound tracks and sound effects, color, action, and graphics. Suggest that they use the information from the discussion when choosing visual and audio aids for their next presentation.

Unit Wrap-Up

MULTICULTURAL CONNECTION

Group

- Heroes are interesting because they face dilemmas and dramatic inner conflicts in trying to live up to codes and ideals. Have students recall that helping King Bagdemagus's daughter required Arthur to fight his own knights. Students may cite instances of their experiences of group codes being contradictory.
- Note that the characters who can attain such perfection are more often the figures of fantasy and legend, not of realistic fiction.

Possible Responses

- Survival in battle usually depends on the troops acting with unquestioned obedience to a leader; any individual dissension could cause confusion which in turn could allow the enemy a fatal advantage.
- Students may differ on whether it was individual matters, such as Lancelot's affair with Gwynevere, and the treachery of his sister and her son Modred, who eventually killed Arthur, that caused the fall of the Round Table, or whether groups were dissatisfied with the ideals of Arthur.

Individuality

- Heroism is as much a product of circumstances as a testimony to character.
- Individuals often call upon hitherto unknown reserves of strength and courage when they are faced with danger.

Possible Responses

- Their intimate contact with someone else's problems gives them a different perspective on their own lives.
- Corrie ten Boom discovers a courageous, resourceful, conspiratorial side to herself that she has never known. Rolf Carlé faces his past and begins a healing process that will make him stronger him stronger.

Multicultural Connections

Group

Part One: Arthurian Legends For medieval knights, the concept of *group* was determined by the codes and rules for behavior embodied in chivalry. Although the ideal knight was to act on behalf of his king, his country, and his lady, knights sometimes pursued their own interests rather than those of the group.

■ In what respects is it necessary for any group engaged in battle, including modern-day military bodies, to pursue group interests rather than individual goals?

■ To what degree was the end of the Arthurian era caused by group differences and dissent?

Individuality

Part Two: Many Kinds of Heroes All heroes—not just knights—must subordinate individual goals in pursuing the common good. Ironically, however, characters like Rolf Carlé and Corrie ten Boom arrive at individual self-knowledge in their efforts to meet the needs of others.

■ How can people learn to know themselves through their helping of others?

■ Compare the ways that Corrie ten Boom and Rolf Carlé emerge as stronger individuals through their acts of unselfishness.

Activities

1. Stage a debate on the following topic: "Modern heroes are (are not) individuals. Instead, they are generic types created by the media."
2. With a group, brainstorm what qualities seem to characterize the modern hero. Explain whether or not the modern hero seems more independent than his or her Arthurian counterparts.

Activities

Activity 1 Divide the class into opposing teams. Have students on each team research heroes from the past and present to support their arguments.

Activity 2 Encourage students to include heroes from other countries and cultures in their definition of the modern hero.

Independent and Group Projects

Writing

The Making of a Legend This unit includes legendary Arthurian heroes and heroes who aren't legends—that is, not until now! Rewrite as a legend a scene from one of the selections, adding a few extraordinary events, a touch of magic, and a villain. Make your hero a superhero in the Arthurian tradition!

Comics

Heroes in the Comics Your first encounter with fictitious heroes may have been with the superheroes portrayed in the comics and cartoons, such as Superman, Wonder Woman, and the Ninja Turtles. Using ideas from these sources and your imagination, make up a comic strip about an episode in the life of your own hero.

Film

Batman and Beyond As well-known movie critics, you and a partner have been selected to compile the prestigious catalog of *Famous Folks in Flicks.* Scan your memory banks, enlist the help of a movie buff, and look up titles in a reference book such as *Halliwell's Film Guide* to find movies that focus on heroes past or present. Select ten movies to endorse in a movie guide. Write a brief review of each.

Research

Big Shots Who are the people who have gained fame over the past fifty years? Choose an area and a focus (for example, Top Female Athletes of the 1970s, Leading Actors in Recent Soaps). With a group, research back issues of magazines for photographs and descriptions of people that fit your category. Then present your information in a slide show, video, or scrapbook.

Entertainment

Heroes You Should Know Create a trivia game of past and present heroes, including some from this unit. Begin by making lists of names. Then categorize them into different groups, such as Politics, Sports, Media, Explorers, Inventors, and so forth. Create trivia cards on which you summarize information that identifies each hero. You can play this as a card game or a board game with markers.

UNIT 3 OPTIONS

Writing

Legends were originally handed down by word of mouth, leaving room for much exaggeration and distortion of truth. Have students work in pairs to rewrite each other's scenes, exaggerating the hero's achievements and characteristics.

Comics

The combination of written words and images is a powerful format for expression.

- Have students cover the captions in their comic strips. Does the meaning still come across?
- Have students consider the captions separately from the drawings. How does the absence of visual support change the mood of their narrative?
- For more about the art form of comic books, rendered in comic book form, see *Understanding Comics, The Invisible Art* by Scott McCloud, (1993).

Film

Encourage students to take a poll of family members and friends to compile a list of movies that portray heroic characters from which to choose their "top ten."

Unit Test

Unit 3 Resource Book
New Selection pp. 81–88
Test 1, pp. 89–90
Test 2, pp. 91–96

Research

There are several ways to use magazines and periodicals for this project.

- Students can browse through a volume of bound magazines, such as *Time*, glancing at covers to see whose achievements warranted press attention.
- Encourage students to draw conclusions from their research. They can evaluate whether the heroes have remained on a pedestal or fallen, or whether the famous people have qualities that would be appreciated today or not.

Entertainment

Students might bring in trivia and educational board games from home to use as models for the project.

Glossary of Vocabulary Words

a hat	o hot	ü rule			
ā age	ō open	ch child		a in about
ä far	ô order, all	ng long		e in taken
e let	oi oil	sh she	ə	i in pencil
ē equal	ou out	th thin		o in lemon
ė term	u cup	ᴛʜ then		u in circus
i it	ů put	zh measure		
ī ice				

A

abscess (ab′ses), *n.* pus resulting from infected tissues of the body.

abyss (ə bis′), *n.* bottomless or very great depth.

acquittal (ə kwit′l), *n.* discharge; release.

adlib (ad lib′), *v.* make up words or music as one goes along; improvise.

advertent (əd vėrt′nt), *adj.* alert.

advocate (ad′və kāt), *v.* support.

albeit (ôl bē′it), *conj.* even though; although.

aloft (ə lôft′), *adj.* in the air.

aloof (ə lüf′), *adj.* unsympathetic; reserved.

amulet (am′yə lit), *n.* a small object worn as a magic charm against evil, disease, or bad luck.

anguish (ang′gwish) *n.* severe physical pain or mental suffering.

antimacassar (an′ti mə kas′ər), *n.* a small covering to protect the back or arms of a chair, sofa, etc., against soiling.

aperture (ap′ər chər), *n.* an opening; hole.

aphorism (af′ə riz′əm), *n.* brief statement expressing a truth.

aplomb (ə plom′), *n.* assurance; poise.

appalled (ə pôld′), *adj.* shocked; dismayed.

apprehension (ap′ri hen′shən), *n.* fear.

arable (ar′ə bəl), *adj.* suitable for producing crops which require plowing and tillage.

arpeggio (är pej′ē ō), *n.* the sounding of the individual notes of a chord.

assail (ə sāl′), *v.* bother; trouble.

atrophy (at′rə fē), *v.* waste away.

attribute (ə trib′yüt), *v.* think of as caused by.

audaciously (ô dā′shəs lē), *adv.* courageously taking risks; daringly.

audible (ô′də bəl), *adj.* that can be heard; loud enough to be heard.

austere (ô stir′), *adj.* stern in manner or appearance.

avaricious (av′ə rish′əs), *adj.* greedy for wealth.

B

balefully (bāl′fə lē), *adv.* destructively or threateningly.

barbaric (bär bar′ik), *adj.* not civilized; coarse.

belligerent (bə lij′ər ənt), *adj.* fond of fights.

bequeath (bi kwēᴛʜ′), *v.* give or leave (money or property) by a will.

bereaved (bi rēvd′), *adj.* deprived ruthlessly; robbed.

beseeching (bē sēch′ing), *adj.* asking earnestly; begging.

bestow (bi stō′), *v.* give (something) as a gift.

betoken (bi tō′kən), *v.* indicate.

bickering (bik′ər ing), *n.* petty, noisy quarreling.

bicultural (bī kul′chər əl), *adj.* having distinct cultures existing side by side.

bifocals (bī fō′kəlz), *n.* pair of glasses having two focuses.

bigot (big′ət), *n.* intolerant person.

bilaterally (bī lat′ər əl ē), *adv.* on two sides.

bilingual (bī ling′gwəl), *adj.* able to speak another language as well or almost as well as one's own.

blandly (bland′lē), *adv.* in a smoothly agreeable, polite manner.

blasphemy (blas′fə mē), *n.* abuse or contempt for God or sacred things.

blight (blīt), *n.* disease, or anything that causes destruction or ruin.

bootless (büt′lis), *adj.* in vain; useless.

brazenly (brā′zn lē), *adv.* boldly.

brooding (brü′ding), *adj.* worried.

C

calabash (kal′ə bash), *n.* a gourdlike fruit whose dried shell is used to make bottles, bowls, drums, pipes, and rattles.

candid (kan′did), *adj.* frank and sincere.

capricious (kə prish′əs), *adj.* changeable.

carnage (kär′nij), *n.* slaughter of a great number of people.

cascade (ka skād′), *v.* fall or pour.

castellated (kas′tl ā′tid), *adj.* built like a castle with turrets and battlements.

cataclysm (kat′ə kliz′əm), *n.* any violent change or upheaval.

censure, (sen′shər), *v.* express disapproval of; blame.

chateau or **château** (sha tō′), *n.* a large country house.

chauvinist (shō′və nist), *n.* person excessively enthusiastic about his or her sex, race, or group.

chronic (kron′ik), *adj.* never stopping.

commodious (kə mō′dē əs), *adj.* having plenty of room.

communal (kə myü′nl), *adj.* owned jointly by all.

compact (kom′pakt), *n.* 1 agreement or contract. 2 a small case containing face powder or rouge.

compensation (kom′pən sā′shən), *n.* something given to make up for a loss or injury.

complacent (kəm plā′snt), *adj.* self-satisfied.

composure (kəm pō′zhər), *n.* calmness; quietness.

comprehensible (kom′pri hen′sə bəl), *adj.* able to be understood.

confiscated (kon′fə skāt əd), *adj.* seized; taken.

conjecture (kən jek′chər), *v.* guess; admit without sufficient evidence.

conniving (kə nī′ving), *adj.* giving aid to wrongdoing by not telling of it or by helping it secretly.

consort (kən sôrt′), *v.* accompany.

contagious (kən tā′jəs), *adj.* spreading by direct or indirect contact; catching.

contemplate (kon′təm plāt). *v.* gaze at; think about.

contort (kən tôrt′), *v.* twist or bend out of shape.

contrition (kən trish′ən), *n.* guilt.

convivial (kən viv′ē əl), *adj.* sociable.

countenance (koun′tə nəns), *n.* face.

crag (krag), *n.* steep, rugged rock or cliff rising above others.

cropped (kropt), *adj.* cut short; clipped.

crucial (krü′shəl), *adj.* very important or decisive;

cubicle (kyü′bə kəl), *n.* a very small room or compartment.

D

daunt (dônt), *v.* overcome with fear; frighten.

dauntless (dônt′lis), *adj.* brave.

dawdle (dô′dl), *v.* waste time; loiter.

debauchery (di bô′chər ē), *n.* corruption.

decorum (di kôr′əm), *n.* proper behavior; good taste in conduct, speech, or dress.

defilement (di fīl′mənt), *n.* destruction of the purity or cleannesss of (anything sacred); desecration.

deflect (di flekt′), *v.* bend or turn aside.

degrading (di grā′ding), *adj.* dishonorable.

dejectedly (di jek′tid lē), *adv.* sadly.

demeanor (di mē′nər), *n.* behavior; manner.

denizen (den′ə zən), *n.* inhabitant or occupant of a place or region.

deploy (di ploi′), *v.* spread out in a planned or strategic position.

despise (di spīz′), *v.* feel hatred or scorn for.

despot (des′pət), *n.* ruler having unlimited power.

devastate (dev′ə stāt′), *v.* make desolate; destroy.

devastation (dev′ə stā′shən), *n.* waste; destruction.

device (di vīs′), *n.* plan, scheme, or trick.

diagram (dī′ə gram), *n.* sketch showing an outline or general scheme of something with its various parts.

dilemma (də lem′ə), *n.* difficult choice.

disconsolate (dis kon′sə lit), *adj.* without hope; unhappy.

discord (dis′kôrd), *n.* disagreement of opinions and aims; dissension.

discordant (dis kôrd′nt), *adj.* not in harmony.

discourse (dis kôrs′), *v.* talk, converse.

disdain (dis dān′), *n.* scorn.

disparage (dis par′ij), *v.* belittle; discredit.

dispel (dis pel′), *v.* drive away.

disperse (dis pėrs′), *v.* go off in different directions.

dissembled (di sem′bəld), *adj.* hidden; disguised.

distortion (dis tôr′shən), *n.* twisting out of shape.

distraction (dis trak′shən), *n.* disturbance of thought.

diverge (də vėrj′), *v.* move or lie in different directions from the same point.

doggedly (dô′gid lē), *adv.* not giving up; stubbornly.

dolefully (dōl′fəl lē), *adv.* mournfully.

droll (drōl), *adj.* odd and amusing.

dubious (dü′bē əs), *adj.* filled with or being in doubt; uncertain.

duly (dü′lē), *adv.* rightly; suitably.

E

ecstatic (ek stat′ik), *adj.* feeling great joy.

edict (ē′dikt), *n.* degree or law proclaimed by a king or other ruler on his sole authority.

elapse (i laps′), *v.* slip away; pass.

elixir (i lik′sər), *n.* medicine with special curing powers.

emanate (em′ə nāt′), *v.* come forth; spread out.

embark (em bärk′), *v.* set out.

embellishment (em bel′ish mənt), *n.* decoration; adornment.

ember (em′bər), *n.* ashes in which there is still some fire.

en masse (en mas′), in a group; all together. *[French]*

enhance (en hans′), *v.* add to; heighten.

ensue (en sü′), *v.* follow.

entice (en tīs′), *v.* tempt; lure.

entranced (en transd′), *adj.* delighted; charmed.

entreatingly (en trēt′ing lē), *adv.* in a begging or praying manner.

eradicable (i rad′ə kə bəl), *adj.* that can be gotten rid of or destroyed.

essence (es′ns), *n.* that which makes a thing what it is; important feature or features.

euphemism (yü′fə miz′əm), *n.* use of a mild or indirect expression instead of a harsh, direct one.

expiation (ek′spē ā′shən), *n.* atonement.

exploitation (ek′sploi tā′shən), *n.* selfish or unfair use.

F

falsetto (fôl set′ō), *n.* an artifically high-pitched voice, especially in a man.

fawn (fôn), *v.* try to get favor or notice by slavish acts.

fiasco (fē as′kō), *n.* a complete or ridiculous failure; humiliating breakdown.

flagrant (flā′grənt), *adj.* glaringly offensive; outrageous.

flout (flout), *v.* treat with contempt or scorn.

fluently (flü′ənt lē), *adv.* speaking or writing easily and rapidly.

forcefully (fôrs′fəl lē), *adv.* powerfully.

frenzied (fren′zēd), *adj.* greatly excited; frantic.

friction (frik′shən), *n.* a rubbing of one object against another; a clash.

frigid (frij′id), *adj.* cold in feeling or manner.

funereal (fyü nir′ē əl), *adj.* gloomy.

furtive (fėr′tiv), *adj.* done quickly and with stealth to avoid being noticed; sly.

futile (fyü′tl), *adj.* not successful; useless.

G

galvanized (gal′və nīzd), *adj.* covered with a thin coating of zinc to prevent rust.

garrulity (gə rü′lə tē), *n.* wordiness.

glaze (glāz), *v.* become smooth, glassy, or glossy.

gratifying (grat′ə fī ing), *adj.* satisfying; pleasing.

grievance (grē′vəns), *n.* a cause for complaint.

grievous (grē′vəs), *adj.* causing great pain or suffering.

grimace (grə mās′, grim′is), *n.* a twisting of the face; ugly or funny smile.

guile (gīl), *n.* sly trick; cunning.

H

haphazard (hap′haz′ərd), *adj.* not planned; random.

hapless (hap′lis), *adj.* unlucky; unfortunate.

heed (hēd), *n.* careful attention.

homage (hom′ij), *n.* dutiful respect.

husbanded (huz′bənd əd), *adj.* managed carefully; saved.

hypocrisy (hi pok′rə sē), *n.* pretense.

I

ignoble (ig nō′bəl), *adj.* not of noble birth or position; without honor; humble.

imminent (im′ə nənt), *adj.* about to occur.

impale (im pāl′), *v.* pierce through with something pointed.

impel (im pel′), *v.* cause to move forward.

imperceptible (im′pər sep′tə bəl), *adj.* gradual.

imperiously (im pir′ē əs lē), *adv.* haughtily or arrogantly.

impersonate (im pėr′sə nāt), *v.* pretend to be.

imperturbably (im′pər tėr′bə blē), *adv.* calmly.

impiety (im pī′ə tē), *n.* lack of respect.

implicit (im plis′it), *adj.* meant, but not clearly expressed or distinctly stated; implied.

impotence (im′pə təns), *n.* helplessness.

impotent (im′pə tənt), *adj.* powerless; helpless.

improvise (im′prə vīz), *v.* make up on the spur of the moment.

impunity (im pyü′nə tē), *n.* freedom from injury, punishment, or other bad consequences.

incandescent (in′kən des′nt), *adj.* shining brightly; brilliant.

incredulous (in krej′ə ləs), *adj.* doubting; skeptical.

incur (in kər′), *v.* bring on oneself.

indifferently, (in dif′ər ənt lē), *adv.* in a manner that shows little interest.

indiscreet (in′dis krēt′), *adj.* not wise; foolish.

inexorable (in ek′sər ə bəl), *adj.* relentless, unyielding.

infamy (in′fə mē), *n.* a very bad reputation; public disgrace.

inimical (in im′ə kəl), *adj.* unfavorable.

initiative (i nish′ē ə tiv), *n.* active part in taking the first steps in any undertaking; lead.

insatiable (in sā′shə bəl), *adj.* that cannot be satisfied; greedy.

inscrutable (in skrü′tə bəl), *adj.* so mysterious or obscure that one cannot make out its meaning.

insidious (in sid′ē əs), *adj.* working secretly or subtly.

insignificant (in′sig nif′ə kənt), *adj.* unimportant; trivial.

insurrection (in′sə rek′shən), *n.* a rising against established authority; revolt.

inter (in tėr′), *v.* bury.

interminable (in tėr′mə nə bəl), *adj.* seemingly endless.

intimidate (in tim′ə dāt), *v.* 1 frighten. 2 influence or force by fear.

intolerant (in tol′ər ənt), *adj.* unwilling to let others do or believe as they want.

irrefutable (i ref′yə tə bəl), *adj.* undeniable.

irreproachable (ir′i prō′chə bəl), *adj.* free from blame; faultless.

J

jauntily (jôn′tē lē), *adv.* in an easy and lively way.

jeopardy (jep′ər dē), *n.* risk; danger.

jest (jest), *n.* something said to cause laughter; joke.

K

kittled (kit′ld), *adj.* born.

L

labyrinth (lab′ə rinth′), *n.* a confusing, complicated passage or arrangement.

legacy (leg′ə sē), *n.* something handed down in a will.

lethargy (leth′ər jē), *n.* lack of energy; inactivity.

liaison (lē′ā zon′), *n.* connection between military units, branches of a service, etc., to secure proper cooperation.

lineage (lin′ē ij), *n.* descent in a direct line from a common ancestor.

listlessly (list′lis lē), *adv.* seemingly too tired to care about anything.

loathsome (lōᴛʜ′səm), *adj.* disgusting.

loiter (loi′tər), *v.* linger idly or aimlessly.

lull (lul), *n.* period of less noise or violence; brief calm.

luminous (lü′mə nəs) *adj.* full of light; shining.

lustrous (lus′trəs), *adj.* shining; glossy.

M

malicious (mə lish′əs), *adj.* showing ill will; spiteful.

maligned (mä līnd′), *adj.* spoken against; slandered.

marrow (mar′ō), *n.* the inmost or essential part.

meager (mē′gər), *adj.* scanty.

meet (mēt), *adj.* fitting; appropriate.

mêlée (mā′lā), *n.* confused fight.

menace (men′is), *n.* threat.

mesmerizing (mez′mə rī′zing), *adj.* hypnotic.

meticulous (mə tik′yə ləs), *adj.* extremely or excessively careful about small details.

mettle (met′l), *n.* spirit, courage.

millet (mil′it), *n.* a cereal grass cultivated as a food grain.

mimic (mim′ik), *v.* make fun of by imitating.

minutely (mī nüt′lē), *adv.* in a small way or detailed manner.

misconstrue (mis′kən strü′), *v.* misunderstand; misinterpret.

monopoly (mə nop′ə lē), *n.* the exclusive possession or control of something.

motif (mō tēf′), *n.* a distinctive figure or pattern in a design, painting, etc.

muse (myüz), *v.* say thoughtfully.

muster (mus′tər), *v.* gather together.

mute (myüt), *adj.* silent.

mutilated (myü′tl āt′əd), *adj.* cut, torn, or broken off a limb or other important part of; maimed.

myriad (mir′ē əd), *n.* a great number.

N

naïve (nä ēv′), *adj.* simple in nature; like a child.

naught (nôt), *n.* nothing.

nonentity (non en′tə tē), *n.* a person or thing of little or no importance.

O

odious (ō′dē əs), *adj.* hateful; offensive.

officious (ə fish′əs), *adj.* too ready to offer services.

onslaught (ôn′slôt′), *n.* a vigorous attack.

oppressive (ə pres′iv), *adj.* hard to bear.

P

pandemonium (pan′də mō′nē əm), *n.* wild disorder.

passé (pa sā′), *adj.* old, stale. *[French]*

peevishness (pē′vish nəs), *n.* irritability; crossness.

perfunctorily (pər fungk′tər ə lē), *adv.* mechanically; indifferently.

peril (per′əl), *n.* danger.

perilous (per′ə ləs), *adj.* dangerous.

permeated (pėr′mē āt əd), *adj.* spread throughout; filled with.

peruse (pə rüz′), *v.* read, especially thoroughly and carefully.

perversity (pər vėr′sə tē), *n.* quality of being contrary and willful.

pigment (pig′mənt), *n.* natural substance that colors skin tissue.

piqued (pēkd), *adj.* aroused; stirred up.

plausible (plô′zə bəl), *adj.* appearing true, reasonable, or fair.

plight (plīt), *n.* 1 condition or situation, usually bad. 2 a solemn promise or pledge.

pluck (pluk), *v.* pull or tug.

poached (pōchd), *adj.* cooked by simmering in a liquid.

poppy (pop′ē), *n.* a bright red.

portent (pôr′tent), *n.* sign.

precarious (pri ker′ē əs), *adj.* not safe or secure; uncertain.

precedence (pres′ə dəns), *n.* higher position or rank; great importance.

preoccupation (prē ok′yə pā′shən), *n.* thing that absorbs or engrosses.

prerogative (pri rog′ə tiv), *n.* right or privilege that nobody else has.

presage (pri sāj′), *v.* predict.

pressurized (presh′ə rīzd′), *adj.* having the atmospheric pressure inside (the cabin of an aircraft) kept at a normal level in spite of the altitude.

presumptuous (pri zump′chü əs), *adj.* acting without permission or right; bold.

pretext (prē′tekst), *n.* a false reason concealing the real reason; misleading excuse.

primal (prī′məl), *adj.* fundamental.

prodigious (prə dij′əs), *adj.* very great; huge.

prodigy (prod′ə jē), *n.* person endowed with amazing brilliance or talent, especially a remarkably talented child.

profoundly (prə found′lē), *adv.* going more deeply than what is easily understood.

proletarian (prō′lə ter′ē ən), *n.* someone belonging to the proletariat, the lowest class in economic and social status, including all unskilled laborers.

promontory (prom′ən tôr′ē), *n.* high point of land extending from the coast.

propriety (prə prī′ə tē), *n.* proper behavior.

prosaic (prō zā′ik), *adj.* ordinary; not exciting.

prostrate (pros′trāt), *adj.* lying flat with face downward.

proverbial (prə vėr′bē əl), *adj.* relating to proverbs; commonly spoken of.

proviso (prə vī′zō), *n.* any provision or stipulation.

prowess (prou′is), *n.* bravery; skill.

puissant (pyü′ə sənt), *adj.* powerful.

pungent (pun′jənt), *adj.* sharply affecting the organs of taste and smell.

Q

quagmire (kwag′mīr′), *n.* soft, muddy ground.

quarry (kwôr′ē), *n.* 1 animal chased in a hunt; prey. 2 place where stone, slate, etc., is dug, cut, or blasted out for use in building.

R

rampant (ram′pənt), *adj.* growing without any limits.

rapport (ra pôr′, ra pôrt′), *n.* agreement; connection.

rebuke (ri byük′), *v.* express disapproval of.

recount (ri kount′), *v.* tell in detail.

redundant (ri dun′dənt), *adj.* not needed; extra.

refracted (ri frak′təd), *adj.* bent (a ray of light, waves, etc.) from a straight course.

rejuvenate (ri jü′və nāt), *v.* make young or vigorous again; renew.

rent (rent), *n.* tear; torn place.

reprimand (rep′rə mand), *v.* criticize.

reproach (ri prōch′), *n.* blame or disapproval.

resplendent (ri splen′dənt), *adj.* very bright; splendid.

retaliation (ri tal′ē ā′shən), *n.* paying back wrong.

reticence (ret′ə sens), *n.* tendency to be silent or say little.

revelry (rev′əl rē), *n.* boisterous merrymaking or festivity.

reverberate (ri vėr′bər āt′), *v.* echo back.

reverie (rev′ər ē), *n.* dreamy thoughts, especially of pleasant things.

ribald (rib′əld), *adj.* offensive in speech; obscene.

rite (rīt), *n.* solemn ceremony.

ritualist (rich′ü ə list), *n.* person who practices or advocates observance of the form or system of rites, or ceremonies.

rock crystal, a colorless, transparent variety of quartz, often used for jewelry, ornaments, etc.

rook (rük), *n.* a bird that resembles the crow.

rout (rout), *n.* a complete defeat.

rubicund (rü′bə kund), *adj.* reddish; ruddy.

rudiment (rü′də mənt), *n.* part to be learned first; beginning.

rummage (rum′ij), *v.* search in a disorderly way.

rune (rün), *n.* inscription or letter.

ruse (rüz), *n.* scheme or device to mislead others; trick.

S

sacrilege (sak′rə lij), *n.* an intentional injury or disrespectful treatment of anyone or anything sacred.

sadist (sā′dist, sad′ist), *n.* person displaying cruel tendencies.

sagacious (sə gā′shəs), *adj.* wise in a keen, practical way; shrewd.

scribe (skrīb), *n.* writer; author.

scrutinize (skrüt′n īz), *v.* examine closely.

serenity (sə ren′ə tē), *n.* quiet; calmness.

servile (sėr′vəl), *adj.* like that of a slave.

sexton (sek′stən), *n.* person who takes care of a church building.

shard (shärd), *n.* broken piece.

sheepishly (shē′pish lē), *adv.* awkwardly bashful or embarrassed.

sheer (shir), *adj.* unmixed with anything else; complete.

shillelagh (shə lā′lē), *n.* a club used in fights.

shoal (shōl), *n.* a large number.

shrewd (shrüd), *adj.* clever; keen.

shrine (shrīn), *n.* place of worship.

simulated (sim′yə lāt əd), *adj.* fake; pretend.

skeptical (skep′tə kəl), *adj.* doubtful.

sordid (sôr′did), *adj.* filthy, contemptible.

soulful (sōl′fəl), *adj.* full of feeling; deeply emotional or passionate.

sovereignty (sov′rən tē), *n.* supreme power or authority.

spinster (spin′stər), *n.* an unmarried woman, especially an older woman.

sporadic (spə rad′ik), *adj.* appearing or happening at intervals in time; occasional.

spur (spėr), *n.* 1 ridge sticking out from or smaller than the main body of a mountain or mountain range. 2 a spiked instrument worn on a rider's heel for urging a horse on.

staidness (stād′nes), *n.* the condition of having a settled, quiet character.

statistic (stə tis′tik), *n.* a numerical fact about people, the weather, business conditions, etc., in order to show their significance.

steward (stü′ərd), *n.* a person employed on a ship to look after passangers.

stifle (stī′fəl), *v.* keep back; stop.

subdued (səb düd′), *adj.* suppressed; toned down.

subside (səb sīd′), *v.* die down.

subversive (səb vėr′siv), *adj.* tending to overthrow; causing ruin.

superficial (sü′pər fish′əl), *adj.* concerned with or understanding only what is on the surface; shallow.

supplication (sup′lə kā′shən), *n.* a humble and earnest prayer.

surplice (sėr′plis), *n.* a broad-sleeved, white gown or vestment worn by members of the clergy and choir singers.

surreptitiously (sėr′əp tish′əs lē), *adv.* secretly, deceptively.

T

taciturn (tas′ə tėrn′), *adj.* silent.

taint (tānt), *n.* a stain or spot.

talisman (tal′is mən, tal′iz mən), *n.* stone, ring, etc., engraved with figures or characters supposed to have magic power; charm.

tantamount (tan′tə mount), *adj.* equal; equivalent.

tempered (tem′pərd), *adj.* softened or moderated.

tenaciously (ti nā′shəs lē), *adv.* stubbornly.

tentative (ten′tə tiv), *adj.* hesitating.

tepid (tep′id), *adj.* lukewarm.

theology (thē ol′ə jē), *n.* study of religion and religious beliefs.

throng (thrông), *n.* a crowd; multitude.

translucent (tran slü′snt), *adj.* letting light through without being transparent.

traumatized (trô′mə tīzd), *adj.* undergoing great shock.

tribulation (trib′yə lā′shən), *n.* great trouble; severe trial.

tumultuous (tü mul′chü əs), *adj.* very noisy or disorderly.

turbot (tėr′bət, tėr′bō), *n.* a European fish, much valued as food.

turbulent (tėr′byə lənt), *adj.* filled with commotion; violent.

U

ulterior (ul tir′ē ər), *adj.* beyond what is seen or expressed; hidden.

unassailable (un ə sāl′ə bəl), *adj.* not able to be attacked (with violent blows, hostile words, arguments, or abuse).

uncanny (un kan′ē), *adj.* something that is strange and mysterious.

unequivocally (un′i kwiv′ə kəl ē), *adv.* clearly.

unfledged (un flejd′), *adj.* inexperienced.

unmolested (un mə lest′əd), *adj.* undisturbed.

unscathed (un skāᴛʜd′), *adj.* not harmed.

unshakable (un shā′kə bl), *adj.* undisturbed; not able to be upset.

usurp (yü zėrp′), *v.* seize by force.

usury (yü′zhər ē), *n.* the lending of money at an unusually high or unlawful rate of interest.

V

virile (vir′əl), *adj.* vigorous; forceful.

visceral (vis′ər əl), *adj.* arising from instinct or strong feelings; not intellectual or rational.

viscous (vis′kəs), *adj.* thick like heavy syrup; sticky.

vixen (vik′sən), *n.* a female fox.

vociferousness (vō sif′ər əs nəs), *n.* noisiness; shouting.

W

waft (waft), *n.* breath or puff of air, wind, scent, etc.

waveringly (wā′vər ing lē), *adv.* unsteadily.

wily (wī′lē), *adj.* crafty; sly.

wisteria (wi ster′ē ə), *n.* a climbing shrub of the pea family with large drooping clusters of purple, blue, or white flowers.

wistful (wist′fəl), *adj.* longing; yearning.

wizened (wiz′nd), *adj.* dried up; withered.

wont (wunt), *adj.* accustomed.

wrath (rath), *n.* very great anger; rage.

Z

zeal (zēl), *n.* eager desire or effort; earnest enthusiasm.

Glossary of Literary Terms

Words in small capital letters within entries refer to other entries in the Glossary of Literary Terms.

A

alliteration (ə lit′ə rā′shən), the REPETITION of consonant sounds at the beginnings of words or within words, particularly in accented syllables. It can be used to reinforce meaning, unify thought, or create a musical effect. "The setting sun silhouettes a sailboat" is an example of alliteration.

allusion (ə lü′zhən), a brief reference to a person, event, or place, real or fictitious, or to a work of art. A writer who describes a shortage or something that is missing with the words "The cupboard is bare" is alluding to the nursery rhyme "Old Mother Hubbard."

analogy (ə nal′ə jē), a literal comparison made between two items, situations, or ideas that are somewhat alike but unlike in most respects. Frequently an unfamiliar or complex object or idea will be compared to a familiar or simpler one in order to explain the first.

antagonist (an tag′ə nist), a character in a story or play who opposes the chief character, or PROTAGONIST.

assonance (as′n əns), the REPETITION of similar vowel sounds followed by different consonant sounds in stressed syllables or words. It is sometimes used instead of RHYME. *Made* and *played* are examples of rhyme; *made* and *pale* are examples of assonance.

autobiography, story of all or part of a person's life written by the person who lived it. *Kaffir Boy* (page 456) is an autobiography.

B

ballad, a NARRATIVE passed on in the oral tradition. It often makes use of REPETITION and DIALOGUE.

biography, an account of a person's life written by someone else.

blank verse, unrhymed verse written in IAMBIC PENTAMETER—that is, ten-syllable lines with five unstressed syllables alternating with five stressed syllables. The following blank-verse lines are spoken by Julius Caesar. Note that the stressed syllables are marked ′ and the unstressed syllables are marked ˘.

> Have I in conquest stretched mine arm so far,
> To be afeard to tell graybeards the truth?

See also page 675.

C

characterization, the methods authors use to acquaint a reader with their characters. We may learn about characters through their DIALOGUE and actions, or through what others say about them.

climax, the decisive point in a story or play when the central problem of the PLOT must be resolved in one way or another. Not every story or play has a dramatic climax. Sometimes a character may simply resolve a problem in his or her mind. At times there is no resolution of the plot; the climax then comes when a character realizes that a resolution is impossible.

comedy, a play written primarily to amuse the audience. In addition to arousing laughter, comic writing often appeals to the intellect.

conflict, struggle between two opposing forces. The four basic kinds of conflict are: (1) a person against another person; (2) a person against nature; (3) a person against society; and (4) two elements within a person struggling for mastery. More than one kind of conflict can be present in a work. In *Red Azalea,* page 145, Anchee Min experiences several kinds of conflict: struggling within herself, with Secretary Chain, and with the principles of the Cultural Revolution.

connotation, the emotional associations surrounding a word or phrase, as opposed to its literal meaning or DENOTATION. Some connotations are fairly universal, others quite personal.

See also page 492.

consonance (kon′sə nəns), the repetition of similar or identical consonant sounds that are preceded by different vowel sounds. The *m* sound is repeated in the following lines.

The moan of doves in immemorial elms,
And murmuring of innumerable bees.
Alfred, Lord Tennyson

couplet, a pair of rhyming lines with the same METER.

D

denotation, the strict, literal meaning of a word.

See also CONNOTATION.

dialect, a form of speech that is characteristic of a particular region or class, differing from the standard language in pronunciation, vocabulary, and grammatical form. The mother in "Two Kinds" (page 19) speaks in dialect.

dialogue, conversation between two or more people in a literary work. Dialogue can help develop the CHARACTERIZATION of those speaking and those spoken about, create MOOD, advance PLOT, and develop THEME.

diction, writers' choices of words, determined by their subject, audience, and desired effect. Diction may be casual or formal, simple or complex, old-fashioned or modern.

dimeter (dim′ə tər), line of VERSE having two metrical feet.

drama, a literary genre in verse or prose, written to be acted, that tells a story through the speech and actions of the characters; a play. *Julius Caesar* (page 679) is an example of drama.

See also pages 184–185.

E

end rhyme, the rhyming of words at the ends of lines of POETRY.

See also INTERNAL RHYME *and* RHYME.

essay, a brief prose composition that presents a personal viewpoint. "Woman from America" (page 632) is an essay that expresses the views of Bessie Head.

exposition, the beginning of a work of FICTION, particularly a play, in which the author sets the atmosphere and TONE, explains the SETTING, introduces the characters, and provides the reader with any other information needed to understand the PLOT.

extended metaphor, a figure of speech that compares two things throughout an entire work or a great part of it. It is more common in poetry than in prose.

See also METAPHOR.

F

fable, a brief TALE, in which the characters often are animals, told to point out a MORAL truth. "The Fox and the Woodcutter" (page 287) is one of many fables by Aesop.

falling action, the RESOLUTION of a dramatic PLOT, which takes place after the CLIMAX.

fantasy/science fiction. Both fantasy and science fiction are literary works set wholly or partly in an unreal world. Often, at least one character is unlike a human being. Frequently the PLOT concerns events that cannot be explained by current science. For example, Poe's classic story, "The Masque of the Red Death (page 95)," is a fantasy.

farce, comedy that involves improbable situations, exaggerated characters, and slapstick action. Farce relies on fast pacing, exaggeration, and physical action, and often includes mistaken identity and deception. *The Flying Doctor* by Molière (page 270) is a farce.

fiction, a type of literature drawn from the imagination of the author, that tells about imaginary people and events. NOVELS, SHORT STORIES, and many plays are fiction.

figurative language, language used in a nonliteral way to express a suitable relationship between essentially unlike things. SIMILE and METAPHOR are both examples of figurative language.

flashback, interruption of a NARRATIVE to show events that happened before that particular point in time.

folk literature, a type of literature that has been passed orally from generation to generation and written down only after centuries. The authors of folk literature, such as epics, LEGENDS, and the like, are unknown.

foot, in VERSE, a group of syllables usually consisting of one accented syllable and all unaccented syllables associated with it, as in the following lines by Robert Herrick. (Note that each foot is shown within slanted lines.)

Then be/not coy,/but use/your time,/
And, while/ye may,/go marry;/

foreshadowing, a hint given to the reader of what is to come.

free verse, a type of POETRY that differs from conventional VERSE in being free from a fixed pattern of METER and RHYME, but that uses RHYTHM and other devices.

G

genre (zhän rə), a form or type of literary work. For example, the NOVEL, SHORT STORY, DRAMA, and poem are all genres.

H

haiku (hī′kü), a brief poem of three lines that often consist of five syllables, seven syllables, and five syllables, respectively. Haiku often describe scenes in nature. Haiku poems appear on page 616.

hero, the central character in a NOVEL, SHORT STORY, DRAMA, or other work of FICTION. When the central character is a female, she is often called a heroine. The term *hero,* however, can be used to refer to both males and females.

historical fiction, fiction set in a time other than that in which it is written. The excerpt from *The Once and Future King* (page 365) is historical fiction based on Arthurian LEGEND.

hyperbole (hī pėr′bə lē), a figure of speech involving great exaggeration. The effect may be satiric or comic.

I

iambic pentameter, a line consisting of five two-syllable metrical feet—that is, five unstressed syllables alternating with five stressed syllables.

See also BLANK VERSE.

idiom, an expression whose meaning cannot be understood from the ordinary meaning of the words in it. For example, to "hold your tongue" or to "be all ears" are idioms.

imagery, sensory details that provide vividness in a literary work and tend to arouse emotions or feelings in a reader.

inference, a reasonable conclusion about the behavior of a character or the meaning of an event drawn from the limited information presented by the author.

internal rhyme, rhyming words or accented syllables within a line which may or may not have a rhyme at the end of the line as well.

inversion, reversal of the usual order of the parts of a sentence, primarily for emphasis or to achieve a certain RHYTHM or RHYME. Inversion is sometimes called *anastrophe* (ə nas′trə fē). The following line from *Julius Caesar* illustrates inversion:

Go you down that way towards the Capitol.

irony, the term used to describe a contrast between what is expected, or what appears to be, and what really is. In *verbal irony,* the actual meaning of a statement is different from (often the opposite of) what the statement literally says. *Irony of situation* refers to an occurrence that is contrary to what is expected. *Dramatic irony* refers to a situation in which events or facts not known to a character on stage or in a fictional work are known to the audience or reader.

L

legend, a story handed down from the past, often associated with some period in the history of a people. A legend differs from a MYTH in having some historical truth and often less of the supernatural. Malory's *Le Morte d'Arthur* and other Arthurian TALES are based on legends of King Arthur and the Knights of the Round Table.

See also page 337.

light verse, short poems written chiefly to amuse or entertain. "One Perfect Rose" (page 503) is an example of light verse.

lyric, a poem, usually short, that expresses some basic emotion or state of mind. A lyric usually creates a single impression and is highly personal. It may be rhymed or unrhymed. "If You'll Only Go to Sleep" (page 562) is a lyric.

M

metaphor (met′ə fôr), a figure of speech that involves an implied comparison between two different things. "His eyes are dark pools" is a metaphor.

meter, the pattern of stressed and unstressed syllables in POETRY.

mood, the overall atmosphere or prevailing feeling within a work of art. Words such as *peaceful, gloomy, mysterious,* and *expectant* can be used to describe mood.

moral, the lesson or teaching in a FABLE or story.

motivation, the process of presenting a convincing cause for the actions of a character in a dramatic or fictional work in order to justify those actions. Motivation usually involves a combination of external events and the character's personality traits. The mother's actions in "Tuesday Siesta" (page 510) are motivated by her love for her son and her desire to see him properly buried.

mystery, a work of fiction that contains a puzzling problem or an event not explained until the end, so as to keep the reader in suspense.

myth, a traditional story connected with the religion or beliefs of a people, usually attempting to account for something in nature. In ancient Greek myths, for example, lightning was depicted as thunderbolts cast down from Mount Olympus by the god Zeus. A myth has less historical background than a LEGEND.

N

narrative, a story or an account of an event or a series of events. A narrative may be true or fictional.

narrator, the teller of a story. The narrator may be a character in the story or someone outside the story.

See also POINT OF VIEW.

nonfiction, literature about real people and events, rather than imaginary ones. Nonfiction includes history, AUTOBIOGRAPHY, BIOGRAPHY, ESSAY, and article.

See also pages 452–453.

novel, a long work of NARRATIVE prose FICTION dealing with characters, situations, and settings that imitate those of real life. A novelette is a short novel. A similar type of work, the novella, is longer than a short story but not as long as a novel.

O

onomatopoeia (on′ə mä′tə pē′ə), a word or words used in such a way that the sound imitates the sound of the thing described. Words such as *crack, gurgle,* and *swoosh* are onomatopoetic. The following lines from "Willliam and Helen" by Sir Walter Scott illustrate onomatopoeia:

> Tramp! tramp! along the land they rode,
> Splash! Splash! along the sea.

P

parable, a brief fictional work that concretely illustrates an abstract idea or teaches some lesson or truth. It differs from a FABLE in that the characters in it are generally people rather than animals. "How Much Land Does a Man Need?" (page 775) can be considered a parable.

paradox, a statement, person, or situation that seems at first to be self-contradictory but that has a valid meaning. In *Antigone,* Teiresias, the blind seer, is a paradox.

pentameter (pen tam′ə tər), a metrical line of five feet.

See also IAMBIC PENTAMETER.

persona (pėr sō′nə), the mask or voice of the author or the author's creation in a particular work.

See also NARRATOR *and* POINT OF VIEW.

personification (pėr son′ə fə kā′shən), the representation of abstractions, ideas, or inanimate objects as living things or as human beings by endowing them with human qualities. In "Sunday Morning" (page 598) , the sun is described as "naked" and the sea as a "green monster." Personification is one kind of FIGURATIVE LANGUAGE.

play *See* DRAMA.

plot, a series of happenings in a literary work. The word is used to refer to the action as it is organized around a CONFLICT and builds through complication to a CLIMAX followed by the RESOLUTION. A plot diagram appears on page 65.

poetry, a literary GENRE that creates an emotional response by the imaginative use of words patterned to produce a desired effect through RHYTHM, sound, and meaning. Poetry may be rhymed or unrhymed. Among the many forms of poetry are the LYRIC, SONNET, and BALLAD. Most of the selections in Unit 5 are poems.

point of view, the relation between the teller of the story and the characters in it. The teller, or NARRATOR, may be a character in the story, in which case it is told from the *first-person* point of view. A writer who describes, in the *third person,* the thoughts and actions of any or all of the characters as the need arises is said to use the *omniscient* (om nish′ənt) point of view. A writer who, in the third person, follows along with one character and tends to view events from that character's perspective is said to use a *limited omniscient* point of view. An author who describes only what can be seen, like a newspaper reporter, is said to use the *dramatic* point of view.

See also NARRATOR *and* PERSONA.

prologue, section that precedes the main body of a work and serves as an introduction.

protagonist (prō tag′ə nist), the leading character in a literary work.

proverb, a brief, traditional saying that contains popular wisdom. An Ashanti proverb states, "No one tests the depth of a river with both feet."

psalm, (säm, sälm), a song or poem in praise of God. The term is most often applied to the hymns in the Book of Psalms of the Bible.

pun, a play on words; a humorous use of a word where it can have different meanings, or of two or more words with the same or nearly the same sound but different meanings. In the opening scene of *Julius Caesar,* a cobbler puns on words such as *sole* and *soul.*

Q

quatrain (kwôt′rān), verse STANZA of four lines. This stanza may take many forms, according to line lengths and rhyme patterns.

R

realism, a way of representing life that emphasizes ordinary people in everyday experiences.

repetition, a poetic device in which a sound, word, or phrase is repeated for emphasis or effect.

resolution (rez′ə lü′shən), the part of a PLOT following the CLIMAX in which the complications of the plot are resolved or settled.

rhyme, exact repetition of sounds in at least the final accented syllables of two or more words. For example, William Blake wrote in "A Poison Tree" (page 288):

> I was angry with my *friend;*/I told my wrath, my wrath did *end.*

rhyme scheme, any pattern of rhyme in a STANZA.

rhythm (riᴛʜ′əm), the arrangement of stressed and unstressed sounds in speech and writing. Rhythm in poetry may be regular or irregular.

rising action, the part of a dramatic plot that leads up to the CLIMAX. In rising action, the complication caused by the CONFLICT of opposing forces is developed.

romance, a long NARRATIVE in poetry or prose that originated in the medieval period. Its main elements are adventure, love, and magic. There are elements of the romance in the LEGENDS of Arthur.

romanticism, a way of representing life that, unlike REALISM, tends to portray the uncommon. The material selected often deals with extraordinary people in unusual SETTINGS having unusual experiences. In romantic literature there often is a stress on past times and an emphasis on nature.

S

satire, a technique in writing that employs wit to ridicule a subject, usually some social institution or human weakness, with the purpose of pointing out problems in society or inspiring reform. In "The Censors" (page 30), Luisa Valenzuela satirizes both government censorship and people who succumb to it.

scansion (skan′shən), the marking off of lines of poetry into feet.
See also RHYTHM.

science fiction *See* FANTASY.

setting, the time (both time of day or season and period in history) and place in which the action of a NARRATIVE occurs. The setting may be suggested through DIALOGUE and action, or it may be described by the narrator or one of the other characters. Setting contributes strongly to the MOOD or atmosphere and plausibility of a work. For example, the heat and poverty of the setting of "Tuesday Siesta" (page 510) contribute to a mood of oppressiveness and futility.

short story, a prose NARRATIVE that is shorter than a novel and that generally describes just one event or a tightly constructed series of events. Although brief, a short story must have a beginning, a middle, and an end.
See also pages 2–3.

simile (sim′ə lē), a figure of speech involving a comparison using a word such as *like* or *as:* "Her hair looked like spun gold."

slant rhyme, rhyme in which the vowel sounds are not quite identical, as in these lines: Gather friends and gather *foods*. Count your blessings, share your *goods*.

soliloquy (sə lil′ə kwē), a dramatic convention that allows a CHARACTER alone on stage to speak his or her thoughts aloud. If someone else is on stage but cannot hear the character's words, the speech becomes an *aside.*

sonnet, a LYRIC poem with a traditional form of fourteen IAMBIC PENTAMETER lines and one of a variety of RHYME SCHEMES.

sound devices, the choice and arrangement of words to please the ear and suit meaning. RHYME, RHYTHM, ASSONANCE, ONOMATOPOEIA, and ALLITERATION are examples of sound devices.

speaker, the imaginary voice a poet chooses to "tell" a poem. This "I," who presents information in the first person, is not necessarily the poet.

speech, a literary composition written to be given as a public talk. A speech may be formal or informal in style, and the topic usually depends on the intended audience. The Nobel speeches of Albert Camus and Elie Wiesel appear on pages 525–529.

stage directions, directions given by the author of a play to indicate the action, costumes, SETTING, arrangement of the stage, and other instructions to the actors and director of the DRAMA. Stage directions are usually written in italics. For example, in *Twelve Angry Men* (page 228), we are introduced to the jury room, which is *a large, bare, unpleasant-looking room* full of men *who are ill at ease.*

stanza, a group of lines that are set off and form a division in a poem.

stereotype (ster′ē ə tīp′), a conventional character, PLOT, or SETTING that possesses little or no individuality or complexity. Inspector Moronoff in "The Chameleon" (page 283) is a stereotype of a politician who acts according to his own best interests.

style, the distinctive handling of language by an author. It is part of an author's special way of choosing words, shaping sentences, and expressing thoughts.

suspense, the methods an author uses to maintain readers' interest, and the resulting MOOD of anxious uncertainty in many interesting stories. In her excerpt from *An American Childhood* (page 475), Annie Dillard builds suspense as she describes a chase.

symbol, a person, place, event, or object that has meaning in itself but also suggests other meanings as well. The flag, for example, is a symbol for patriotism.

T

tale, a spoken or written NARRATIVE, usually less complicated than a SHORT STORY.

theme, an underlying meaning of a literary work. A single work may have several themes. A theme may be directly stated but more often is implied.

tone, an author's attitude toward the subject of his or her literary work and toward the reader.

tragedy, dramatic or narrative writing in which the main character suffers disaster after a serious and significant struggle but faces his or her downfall in such a way as to attain heroic stature. The play *Julius Caesar* is considered a tragedy because of the fate that befalls the overly ambitious Caesar.

trimeter (trim′ə tər), line of VERSE having three metrical feet.

V

verse, in its most general sense, a synonym for poetry. Verse also may be used to refer to poetry carefully composed as to RHYTHM and RHYME SCHEME, but of inferior literary value.

Language and Grammar Handbook

Skill-building worksheets can be found in the *Reading, Writing and Grammar SkillBook,* referenced in the blue tabs throughout this handbook.

Are you sometimes confused when your teacher returns papers with comments such as, "Incorrect subject-verb agreement," or "Unclear antecedent for your pronoun"? This Handbook will help you respond to such comments as you edit your writing and also provide answers to questions that arise about language during peer- and self-evaluation.

The Handbook is alphabetically arranged with each entry explaining a term or concept. For example, if you can't remember when to use *accept* and *except,* look up the entry **accept, except** and you'll find an explanation of the meaning of each word and a sentence (many from selections in this book) using each word.

accept, except The similarity in sound causes these words to be confused. *Accept* means "to take or receive; consent to receive; say yes to." It is always a verb. *Except* is most commonly used as a preposition meaning "but."

- ◆ It is with a profound sense of humility that I accept the honor you have chosen to bestow upon me.
  from "Nobel Acceptance Speech" by Elie Wiesel
- ◆ Everyone broke into a nervous laugh, except me.
  from *Kaffir Boy* by Mark Mathabane

p. 210

active and passive voice A verb is said to be in the active voice when its subject is the doer of the action, and in the passive voice when its subject is the receiver of the action. A passive verb is a form of the verb *be* plus the past participle of the verb: *is* written, *had been* written, *will be* written, and so on.

ACTIVE: The teacher prepared the class for the exam.
PASSIVE: The class was prepared for the exam by the teacher.

Active verbs are more natural, direct, and forceful than passive verbs. Passive verbs are useful and effective, however, when the doer of the action is unknown, unimportant, or obvious, or when special emphasis is wanted for the receiver of the action:

- ◆ My name was constantly mentioned by the school authority. . . .
  from *Red Azalea* by Anchee Min
- ◆ The power of his eyes was considerably enhanced by their position. . . .
  from "An Astrologer's Day" by R. K. Narayan

p. 224

adjective Adjectives are modifiers that describe nouns and pronouns and make their meaning more exact. Adjectives tell *what kind, which one,* or *how many.*

What kind:	*white* rose	*fast* car	*tall* building
Which one:	*this* book	*that* movie	*those* shirts
How many:	*three* days	*few* customers	*many* runners

See also **comparative forms of adjectives and adverbs.**

p. 226

adverb Adverbs modify verbs, adjectives, or other adverbs. They tell *how, when,* or *where* about verbs.

How:	carefully	rapidly	bravely
When:	later	now	yesterday
Where:	there	near	outside

See also **comparative forms of adjectives and adverbs.**

affect, effect *Affect* is a verb. It is most frequently used to mean "to influence." *Effect* is mainly used as a noun meaning "result" or "consequence."

◆ The weather always affects my allergies.

◆ Your dirty tricks will have no more effect on me!
from *Red Azalea* by Anchee Min

In formal English, *effect* is also used as a verb meaning "to bring about or make happen."

◆ Sir Modred . . . laid siege to the Tower, but despite his large army, siege engines, and guns, was unable to effect a breach.
from "The Death of King Arthur" by Sir Thomas Malory

agreement

p. 212
p. 218
p. 222

1. subject-verb agreement When the subject and verb of a sentence are both singular or both plural, they agree in number. This is called subject-verb agreement. Usually, singular verbs in the present tense end in *s.* Plural verbs do not have the *s* ending.

Michael drives. (singular subject; singular verb)
Kate and Michael drive. (plural subject; plural verb)

p. 191 Pronouns generally follow the same rule. However, *I* and *you* always take plural verbs.

	Singular	Plural
1st person	I drive	we drive
2nd person	you drive	you drive
3rd person	he/she/it drives	they drive

Changes also occur with the verb *to be* in both the present and past tense.

Present Tense		Past Tense	
I am	we are	I was	we were
you are	you are	you were	you were
he/she/it is	they are	he/she/it was	they were

p. 214 **a. Most compound subjects joined by *and* or *both . . . and* are plural and are followed by plural verbs.**

- A sofa and a chair were in front of the fireplace.

b. A compound subject joined by *or, either . . . or,* or *neither . . . nor* is followed by a verb that agrees in number with the closer subject.

- Neither Maria nor her relatives live there anymore.
- Neither her relatives nor Maria lives there anymore.

Problems arise when it isn't obvious what the subject is. The following rules should help you with some of the most troublesome situations.

c. Phrases or clauses coming between the subject and the verb do not affect the subject-verb agreement.

- A variety of trades and occupations was represented all along its way. . . .
  from "An Astrologer's Day" by R. K. Narayan

- . . . the freedom, maybe even the life, of both sender and receiver is in jeopardy.
  from "Nobel Acceptance Speech" by Albert Camus

d. Singular verbs are used with singular indefinite pronouns—*each, every, either, neither, anyone, anybody, one, everyone, everybody, someone, somebody, nobody, no one.*

- Neither of us was hungry.
  from "Rain Music" by Longhang Nguyen

e. Plural indefinite pronouns take plural verbs. They are *both, few, many,* and *several.*

◆ Both of these authors write science fiction.

p. 220

f. The indefinite pronouns *all, any, most, none,* and *some* can be either singular or plural depending on their meaning in a sentence.

Singular	Plural
All of the journey *was* exciting.	*All* of the travelers *were* hungry.
Most of the voyage *was* calm.	*Most* of the inns *were* full.
None of the menu *was* in English.	*None* of the chairs *were* empty.

g. The verb agrees with the subject regardless of the number of the predicate complement (after a form of a linking verb).

◆ The greatest problem was the mosquitoes.

◆ Mosquitoes were the biggest problem.

h. Unusual word order does not affect agreement; the verb generally agrees with the subject, whether the subject follows or precedes it.

◆ . . . and there flows a ruddier light through the blood-colored panes . . . .
from "The Masque of the Red Death" by Edgar Allan Poe

In informal English, you may often hear sentences like "There's a book and some paper for you on my desk." *There's* is a contraction for "There is." Technically, since the subject is a *book and some paper,* the verb should be plural and the sentence should begin, "There are. . . ." Since this may sound strange, you may want to revise the sentence to something like "A book and some paper are on my desk." Be especially careful of sentences beginning with *There;* be sure the verb agrees with the subject.

◆ There are no secrets in here!
from *Twelve* Angry Men by Reginald Rose

◆ There was a flutter of excitement, everybody reaching for plates. . . .
from "Dip in the Pool" by Roald Dahl

2. Pronoun-antecedent agreement An *antecedent* is a word, clause, or phrase to which a pronoun refers. The pronoun agrees with its antecedent in person, number, and gender.

◆ The girl took off her shoes. Then she went to the washroom to put the bouquet of flowers in some water.
from "Tuesday Siesta" by Gabriel García Márquez

a. Singular pronouns are generally used to refer to the indefinite pronouns *one, anyone, each, either, neither, everybody, everyone, somebody, someone, nobody,* and *no one.*

◆ Neither (a) of the women could practice her (p) tennis.

◆ Everybody (a) brought his (p) ticket to the gate.

The second sentence poses problems. It is clearly plural in meaning, and *everybody* may not refer to men only. To avoid the latter problem, you could write "Everybody brought his or her ticket to the gate." This solution is clumsy and wordy, though. Sometimes it is best to revise:

◆ The students brought their tickets to the gate.

This sentence is now clear and nonsexist.

among, between *Among* implies more than two persons, places, or things. *Between* usually refers to two, followed either by a plural or by two expressions joined by *and*—not by *or.*

◆ All these years . . . she thought she understood them. But now she discovered that she was a stranger among them.
from "The Rain Came" by Grace Ogot

◆ Between semesters, James hiked fifty miles.
◆ Sam couldn't decide between the fish sandwich and the pasta.

See also **between you and me.**

apostrophe (') An apostrophe is used in possessive words, both singular and plural, and in contractions. It is also used to form the plurals of letters and numbers.

Jeffrey's jacket	A's and B's	won't
women's basketball	6's and 7's	wasn't

It may be used to indicate places in words in which certain sounds or letters are omitted.

◆ "Where are we going, Gran'ma?" I said. . . .
from *Kaffir Boy* by Mark Mathabane

p. 167

appositive An *appositive* is a word or word group that follows another word or word group and identifies or explains it more fully. It is usually set off by commas or dashes.

◆ The latest heartache for Dutchmen was an edict making it a crime to sing the "Wilhelmus," our national anthem.
from "The Secret Room" by Corrie ten Boom

◆ The library staffed two assistants—Rachel and Ben.

If, however, the appositive is used to specify a particular person or thing, it is not set off.

- ◆ Moronoff recognizes the man as Grunkin the goldsmith.
  from "The Chameleon" by Anton Chekhov

awkward writing A general term (abbreviated *awk*) sometimes used in theme correcting to indicate such faults as inappropriate word choice, unnecessary repetition, clumsy phrasing, confusing word order, or any other weakness or expression that makes reading difficult and obscures meaning.

Many writers have found that reading their first drafts aloud helps them detect clumsy or unclear phrasing in their work. Once identified, awkward construction can almost always be improved by rethinking and rewording.

B

bad, badly In formal English and in writing, *bad* (the adjective) is used to modify a noun or pronoun and is used after a linking verb. *Badly* (the adverb) modifies a verb.

- ◆ She felt bad about hurting his feelings. (Adjective used with linking verb *felt*)
- ◆ The game was played badly. (Adverb modifying a verb)

HINT: To check yourself, realize that you would never say "between we." You would say "between us," *us* being the objective form of the pronoun *we.*

between you and me After **prepositions** such as *between,* use the objective form of the personal pronouns: *between you and **me,** between you and **her,** between you and **him,** between you and **us,** between you and **them.***

- ◆ The misunderstanding is between you and her.
- ◆ Was the agreement between you and them?
- ◆ Here between us, the white light blazed and the blade shivered.
  from *The Hollow Hills* by Mary Stewart

borrow, lend To *borrow* means to "get something from someone else with the understanding that it will be returned." To *lend* means to "let another have or use something temporarily."

- ◆ I borrowed a pen from Dad; he borrowed my calculator.
- ◆ Carlos offered to lend me his video.

Borrow is often followed by *from*—never by *off* or *off of.*

bring, take To *bring* means to "carry something toward." To *take* means to "carry something away."

- ◆ "Bring him back two weeks from today."
  from *Kaffir Boy* by Mark Mathabane
- ◆ I rubbed the old silk against my skin, then wrapped them in tissue and decided to take them home with me.
  from "Two Kinds" by Amy Tan

C

capitalization

p. 256

1. Capitalize all proper nouns and adjectives.

Proper Nouns	Proper Adjectives
Canada	Canadian
China	Chinese
Victoria	Victorian

p. 259

2. Capitalize people's names and titles.

General Powell	Bishop Clark
Justice Ginsburg	Dr. Fernandez
Ms. Sarah Stoner	Grandma
Uncle Jack	Senator Hanrahan

3. Capitalize the names of ethnic groups, languages, religions, revered persons, deities, religious bodies, buildings, and writings. Also capitalize any adjectives made from these names.

Indo-European	Buddha
German	Catholicism
Islam	Allah
Grace Lutheran Church	the Bible

NOTE: Do not capitalize directions of the compass or adjectives that indicate direction: Front Street runs north and south. The weather map showed showers in the northwest.

4. Capitalize geographical names (except for articles and prepositions) and any adjectives made from these names.

Australia	the Red Arrow Highway
Gila River	Danish pastry
Straits of Mackinac	Spanish rice
the Rockies	Southern accent
Arctic Circle	Gettysburg
Tampa Bay	Zion National Park

NOTE: Earth, sun, and moon are not capitalized unless used with the names of other planets: Is Venus closer to the Sun than Saturn? The earth revolves around the sun.

5. Capitalize the names of structures, organizations, and bodies in the universe.

the Capitol	the House of Representatives
Carnegie Hall	the United Way
the Eiffel Tower	Neptune
the Cubs	the Milky Way

6. Capitalize the names of historical events, times, and documents.

the Hundred Years' War	the Elizabethan Period
the Treaty of Versailles	the Emancipation Proclamation

NOTE: Do not capitalize the names of the seasons.

7. Capitalize the names of months, days, holidays, and time abbreviations.

February	Sunday
Thanksgiving	A.M. P.M.

NOTE: Some modern poets do not begin each line with a capital letter.

8. Capitalize the first letters in sentences, lines of poetry, and direct quotations.

◆ If thou shouldst never see my face again,
Pray for my soul. More things are wrought by prayer
Than this world dreams of.

from *Idylls of the King* by Alfred, Lord Tennyson

◆ The announcer said, "It will be cloudy and windy."

9. Capitalize certain parts of letters and outlines.

Dear Mrs. Moore,   Sincerely yours,

I. Early types of automobiles
- A. Gasoline powered
  1. Haynes
  2. Ford
  3. Other makes
- B. Steam powered
- C. Electric cars

10. Capitalize the first, last, and all other important words in titles. *See also* **italics.**

book	Dickens's *Great Expectations*
newspaper	story in the *Washington Post*
play and movie	starred in *Showboat*
television series	liked *Murphy Brown*
short story	read "The Monkey's Paw"
music (long)	saw *The Pirates of Penzance*
music (short)	sang "Swing Low, Sweet Chariot"
work of art	Winslow Homer's *Breezing Up*
magazine	*Seventeen* magazine

p. 148

clause A clause is a group of words that has a subject and a verb. A clause is independent when it can stand alone and make sense. A dependent clause has a subject and a verb, but when it stands alone it is incomplete, and the reader is left wondering about the meaning.

Independent Clause	Dependent Clause
s v	s v
Bailey White wrote *Mama Makes Up Her Mind*.	Since Bailey White wrote *Mama Makes Up Her Mind*.

p. 267

colon (:) A colon is often used to explain or clarify what has preceded it.

- That was one thing the occupation had done for Holland: churches were packed.
  from "The Secret Room" by Corrie ten Boom

A colon is also used after phrases that introduce a list or quotation.

- When he prepared for his hike, he packed the following items: a map, extra batteries, and a flashlight.
- One old man said: "Our son is a good man. . . ."
  from "The Voter" by Chinua Achebe

p. 261
p. 265

comma (,) Commas are used to show a pause or separation between words and word groups in sentences, to avoid confusion in sentences, to separate items in addresses, in dialogue, and in figures.

1. Use commas between items in a series. Words, phrases, and clauses in a series are separated by commas.

- He knows that they examine, sniff, feel, and read between the lines of each and every letter. . . .
  from "The Censors" by Luisa Valenzuela

NOTE: If the items in a series are all separated by a word like *and,* no comma is necessary: Rain and wind and sleet all hampered the rescue.

2. Use a comma after certain introductory words and groups of words such as clauses and prepositional phrases of five words or more.

- When my mother began dropping hints that I would soon be going to school, I vowed never to go. . . .
  from *Kaffir Boy* by Mark Mathabane

- During the absence of King Arthur from Britain, Sir Modred had decided to usurp the throne.
  from "The Death of King Arthur" by Sir Thomas Malory

3. Use a comma to set off nouns of direct address. The name or title by which persons (or animals) are addressed is called a noun of direct address.

- "Did you give him anything for it, Father?" inquired Mrs. White. . . .
  from "The Monkey's Paw" by W. W. Jacobs

- Sire, is it your will that Arthur shall succeed to the throne. . . ?
  from "The Coronation of Arthur" by Sir Thomas Malory

4. Use commas to set off interrupting elements and appositives. Any phrase or clause that interrupts the flow of a sentence is often set off by commas. Parenthetical expressions like *of course, after all, to be sure, on the other hand, I suppose,* and *as you know;* and words like *yes, no, oh,* and *well* are all set off by commas.

◆ The average woman of twenty, it has been estimated, could expect about twelve years of childbearing. . . .
from "Youth and Chivalry" by Barbara Tuchman

◆ The reporter, on the other hand, was determined to snatch her from death.
from "And of Clay Are We Created" by Isabel Allende

5. Use a comma before a coordinating conjunction *(and, but, for, or, nor, yet, so)* in a compound sentence.

◆ Both men spoke with the bitterness of possible defeat before them, for each knew that it might be long before his men would seek him out or find him. . . .
from "The Interlopers" by Saki

◆ She was exhausted, but the path was still winding.
from "The Rain Came" by Grace Ogot

◆ The girl was twelve years old, and it was the first time she'd ever been on a train.
from "Tuesday Siesta" by Gabriel García Márquez

6. Use a comma after a dependent clause that begins a sentence. Do not use a comma before a dependent clause that follows the independent clause.

◆ Though night had scarcely come and the heat was great, we gathered at the fire to see each other's faces. . . .
from "The Boar Hunt" by José Vasconcelos

◆ Occasionally we had to stop firing because the frequent shooting heated the barrels of our rifles.
from "The Boar Hunt" by José Vasconcelos

7. Use a comma to separate items in an address. The number and street are considered one item. The state and Zip Code are also considered one item. Use a comma after the Zip Code if it is within a sentence.

Diane Wong
5341 Palm Dr.
Messa, AZ 85210

Todd's address is 721 N. Buckeye, Columbus, OH 73215, but don't have his phone number.

8. Use a comma to separate numerals greater than three digits.

900,321 4,500

9. Use commas in punctuating dialogue. *See* **dialogue.**

Comma splice *See* **run-on sentence.**

p. 230

comparative forms of adjectives and adverbs To show a greater degree of the quality or characteristic named by an adjective or adverb, *-er* or *-est* is added to the word, or *more* or *most* is put before it.

Positive: Ron is quiet.

Comparative: Ron is quieter than Allen.

Superlative: Ron is the quietest person in the class.

More and *most* are generally used with longer adjectives and adverbs, and with all adverbs ending in *-ly.*

Positive: The movie was peculiar.

Comparative: The second movie was more peculiar than the first.

Superlative: The movie was the most peculiar one I have ever seen.

◆ Jan is more likely than Pat to enter the marathon.

The *comparative* forms are usually used in comparing two things or people, and the *superlative* in comparing more than two.

◆ Kim is the fastest runner on the team.
◆ Sarita is the taller of the two sisters.

Writers sometimes have trouble phrasing comparisons so that a reader can see immediately what things are being compared.

Faulty: The seats in the auditorium are better than the theater. [Seats are being compared to a theater.]

Corrected: The seats in the auditorium are better than those in the theater. *See also* **modifiers.**

p. 253

conjunction A conjunction is a word that links one part of a sentence to another. It can join words, phrases, or entire sentences.

dash (—) A dash is used to indicate a sudden break or change of thought.

◆ By the time the last man had spoken it was possible—without great loss of dignity—to pick up the things from the floor.
from "The Voter" by Chinua Achebe

dialogue Dialogue is often used to enliven many types of writing. Notice the paragraphing and punctuation of the following passage.

◆ "Tell me," he said, coming straight to the point, "what did you think of the auction last night?"

"Auction?" she asked, frowning. "Auction? What auction?"
from "Dip in the Pool" by Roald Dahl

See also **quotation marks.**

direct address *See* **comma 3.**

E

ellipsis (. . .) An ellipsis is used to indicate that words (or sentences or paragraphs) have been omitted. An ellipsis consists of three dots, but if the omitted portion would have completed the sentence, a fourth dot is added for the period.

> Next, to establish peace and order in the counties near London. . . .
> from "The Coronation of Arthur" by Sir Thomas Malory

exclamation point (!) An exclamation mark is used at the end of an exclamatory sentence—one that shows excitement or strong emotion. Exclamation points can also be used with strong interjections.

F

fragment *See* **sentence fragment.**

G

gerund A verb form usually ending in *-ing* that is used as a noun. In the sentence following, *going* is the object of the preposition *by.*

p. 242

- It was unexplored underbrush into which we could enter only by going down the river in a canoe.
  from "The Boar Hunt" by José Vasconcelos

A gerund used as the object of a preposition should be related to the subject. Otherwise the phrase will dangle.

Dangling: After driving one block, the tire was flat.
Corrected: After driving one block, she noticed the tire was flat.

good, well *Good* is used as an adjective to modify a noun or pronoun. Do not use it to modify a verb. *Well* is usually used as an adverb to modify a verb.

- Her teacher commented that she had written a good paper.
- Kathleen behaved well when, some months later, her fiancé was reported missing, presumed killed.
  from "The Demon Lover" by Elizabeth Bowen
- "Dear Sister," she began, followed by a little time-buying cough and throat clearing. "We are all well here."
  from "The Need to Say It" by Patricia Hampl

HINT: When you are referring to health, use *well* if the meaning is "not ill."

If the meaning is "pleasant" or "in good spirits," use *good:*

◆ I feel really good today!

hopefully This is often used to mean "it is hoped," or "I hope," as in the sentence, "Hopefully she will be able to console herself." However, in formal writing, avoid this usage and write the sentence as follows:

◆ They hoped she would, in a year or two, console herself. . . .
from "The Demon Lover" by Elizabeth Bowen

however Words like *however, moreover, nevertheless,* and *consequently,* (known as conjunctive adverbs) require special punctuation. If the word comes within a clause, it is generally set off by commas.

◆ The man, however, was gazing in idle reverie at the city's skyline growing ever more beautiful. . . .
from "He—y, Come on Ou—t!" by Shinichi Hoshi

If the conjunctive adverb separates two independent clauses, a semicolon is used preceding the word.

◆ I like sports; however, I seldom have time to be on a team.

p. 244

infinitive An infinitive is the simple form of the verb, usually preceded by *to.* Infinitives are used as nouns, adjectives, or adverbs. In the following passage, each infinitive acts as an adjective.

◆ A time to weep, and a time to laugh: a time to mourn, and a time to dance. . . .
from Ecclesiastes

p. 255

interjection An interjection is a word or phrase used to express strong emotion.

Ouch! Stay off my foot.
Yes! I was accepted.
Oh, no, the show is sold out!

NOTE: In handwritten or non-computer writing, use underlining to indicate italics.

italics Italic type is used to indicate titles of whole works such as books, magazines, newspapers, plays, films, and so on. It is also used to indicate foreign words and phrases.

◆ ". . . there's still a table by the bay window, if *madame* and *monsieur* would like to enjoy the view."
from "The Other Wife" by Colette

NOTE: In formal English, the correct way to respond to a question such as, "Who's there?" is "It is I." This sounds too formal in some situations, however. While it is not correct to say, "It's them," "It's him," "It's us," or "It's her," "It's me" is generally accepted as standard usage.

its, it's *Its* is the possessive form of the personal pronoun *it; it's* is the contraction meaning "it is."

- He brought the lamp close and tilted it at the money . . . to make sure he had not mistaken its value.
  from "The Voter" by Chinua Achebe
- Juan knows there won't be a problem with the letter's contents, that it's irreproachable, harmless.
  from "The Censors" by Luisa Valenzuela

lay, lie This verb pair presents problems because, in addition to the similarity between the words, the past tense of *lie* is *lay.* The verb *to lay,* means "to put or place something somewhere."

Present	Past	Past Participle
lay	laid	(has) laid

The principal parts of the verb to *lie,* which means "to rest," "to be at rest," or "in a reclining position," are the following.

Present	Past	Past Participle
lie	lay	(has) lain

Notice how the verbs are used in the following sentences.

- "Our cattle lie dying in the fields," they reported. "Soon it will be our children and then ourselves." (The cattle are in a reclining position.)
  from "The Rain Came" by Grace Ogot
- "I will lay down my life, if necessary, and the life of my household, to save this tribe from the hands of the enemy." (I will put down my life.)
  from "The Rain Came" by Grace Ogot
- America was where all my mother's hopes lay. (Where all my mother's hopes rested.)
  from "Two Kinds" by Amy Tan
- But his sickness grew worse, and after he had lain speechless for three days and three nights Merlin summoned the nobles. . . . (He had been in a reclining position.)
  from "The Coronation of Arthur" by Sir Thomas Malory

NOTE: *Lied* refers only to not telling the truth: Many people thought he *lied* on the witness stand.

lead, led The present tense of this verb rhymes with *seed;* the past tense (and past participle) is spelled *led* and rhymes with *red.*

- I forgot what I was supposed to do—to lead the crowd to shout the slogans—until Secretary Chain came to remind me of my duty.
  from *Red Azalea* by Anchee Min

◆ I led my schoolmates in collecting pennies. We wanted to donate the pennies to the starving children in America.
from *Red Azalea* by Anchee Min

Hint: Remember that *lose* often means the opposite of *gain.* Each word has just four letters.

lose, loose *Lose* (to lose one's way, to lose a watch) is a verb; *loose* (to come loose, loose-fitting) is an adjective.

◆ As Oganda opened the gate a child, a young child, broke loose from the crowd and ran toward her.
from "The Rain Came" by Grace Ogot

◆ In marking the path to the landing, we were careful not to lose ourselves in the thicket.
from "The Boar Hunt" by José Vasconcelos

M

p. 232
p. 236

modifier A modifier is a word or group of words that restrict, limit, or make more exact the meaning of other words. The modifiers of nouns and pronouns are usually adjectives, participles, adjective phrases, and adjective clauses. The modifiers of verbs, adjectives, and adverbs are adverbs, adverb phrases, and adverb clauses. In the following examples, the italicized words modify the words that directly follow them in boldface type.

◆ The *seventh* ***apartment*** was *closely* ***shrouded*** in *black velvet* ***tapestries***. . . .
from "The Masque of the Red Death" by Edgar Allan Poe

HINT: When trying to decide which pronoun to use, remember that you would not say "Myself is going to the game." You would say *I*.

myself (and himself, herself, and so on) Be careful not to use *myself* and the other reflexive and intensive pronouns when you simply need to use the personal pronoun *I* or its objective form *me.*

Incorrect: John and myself are going to the game.
Correct: John and I are going to the game.

Incorrect: Chidi told Laura and myself a funny story.
Correct: Chidi told Laura and me a funny story.

N

none, no one When *none* tells how many, a plural verb is generally used, unless the idea of "not a single one" is to be emphasized, as in the following example.

◆ . . . Oganda fought desperately to find another exit. . . .
But there was none.
from "The Rain Came" by Grace Ogot

No one is singular and is often used for emphasis.

◆ For some time they had predicted that the heat of the eruption could detach the eternal ice from the slopes of the volcano, but no one heeded their warnings.
from "And of Clay Are We Created" by Isabel Allende

See also **agreement 1f.**

p. 169
p. 173

noun A noun is a word that names a person, place, thing, or idea. Most nouns are made plural by adding *-s* or *-es* to the singular. When you are unsure about a plural form, check a dictionary.

P

p. 165

parallel construction Items in a sentence that are of equal importance should be expressed in parallel (or similar) forms. These can take the form of noun phrases, verb phrases, infinitive phrases, and prepositional phrases.

◆ We sang at the top of our lungs, sang our oneness, our hope, our love for Queen and country.
from "The Secret Room" by Corrie ten Boom

◆ The boy would learn to ride, to fight, and to hawk . . . to play chess and backgammon, to sing and dance, play an instrument, and compose. . . .
from "Youth and Chivalry" by Barbara Tuchman

parentheses ( ) Parentheses are used to enclose words that interrupt or add explanation to a sentence. They are also used to enclose references to page numbers, chapters, or dates. Punctuation marks that belong to the sentence come after the parentheses, not before.

◆ I allowed myself a descriptive aria on the beauty of Minnesota winters (for the benefit of my California reader who might need some background material on the subject of ice hockey).
from "The Need to Say It" by Patricia Hampl

◆ Langston Hughes (1902–1967) was part of the Harlem Renaissance.

p. 240

participle A participle is a verb form used in forming various tenses of verbs. The present participle ends in *-ing:* growing. The past participle usually ends in *-ed, -t, -d, -en,* or *-n:* scared, kept, said, risen, blown.

I am thinking. We were running. Leaves have blown away.

Participles are also used as adjectives, modifying nouns and pronouns.

◆ The purser looked at the anxious frowning face of Mr. Botibol and he smiled. . . .
from "Dip in the Pool" by Roald Dahl

p. 175
p. 177

possessive case The possessive case is formed in various ways. For singular nouns and indefinite pronouns, add an apostrophe and *s.*

my sister's car   someone's shoe   everybody's grade

For plural nouns ending in an *s,* add only an apostrophe.

the doctors' offices   the babies' pool   the churches' members

However, if the plural is irregular and does not end in *s,* add an apostrophe and then an *s.*

NOTE: Apostrophes are not used with personal pronouns to show possession.

◆ . . . even when a suspicion of a smile flickered across the other women's faces . . . I thought that a rare distinction lit up my mother's face.
from "My Father Writes to My Mother" by Assia Djebar

p. 250

prepositions Prepositions are words such as *about, between, during, from, of, over, until,* and *with* that show the relationship between a noun or pronoun and some other word in a sentence.

p. 250

prepositional phrase Prepositional phrases are groups of words that begin with a preposition and end with a noun or pronoun. These phrases act as modifiers and create vivid pictures for the reader. Notice the three prepositional phrases in the following sentence.

◆ This woman from America married a man of our village and left her country to come and live with him here.
from "Woman from America" by Bessie Head

p. 179
p. 181
p. 193

pronoun Subject pronouns are used as subjects of sentences. Object pronouns can be used as direct objects, indirect objects, or objects of prepositions.

When a pronoun is used as the subject of a sentence, the pronoun is in the nominative case and is called a subject pronoun: *He* and *I* met at the movies.

p. 183

Subject Pronouns			
Singular	I	you	he, she, it
Plural	we	you	they

HINT: When you are uncertain about whether to use a subject pronoun or an object pronoun in a sentence, take out the first pronoun to test the sentence. (You wouldn't say "The coach asked *he* to arrive early.")

When a pronoun is used as an object, the pronoun is in the objective case and is called an object pronoun: The coach asked *me* and *him* to arrive early.

Object Pronouns			
Singular	me	you	him, her, it
Plural	us	you	them

See also **agreement 2** *for pronoun-antecedent agreement.*

Q

p. 269

quotation marks (" ") Quotation marks enclose a speaker's exact words. They are also used to enclose some titles. When you use someone's exact words in your writing, use the following rules:

1. Enclose all quoted words within quotation marks.

◆ Anchee Min wrote, "I stood up and felt dizzy."

2. The first word of a direct quotation begins with a capital letter. When a quotation is broken into two parts, use two sets of quotation marks. Use one capital letter if the quote is one sentence. Use two capital letters if it is two sentences.

◆ "You'd better close the window," the woman said. "Your hair will get full of soot."
from "Tuesday Siesta" by Gabriel García Márquez

3. Use a comma between the words that introduce the speaker and the words that are quoted. Place the end punctuation or the comma that ends the quotation inside the quotation marks. Put question marks and exclamation points inside the quotation marks only if they are a part of the quotation. Begin a new paragraph each time the speaker changes.

◆ "Come along," she said, frowning slightly. "What's your name, dear?"
"I don't know," I said finally.
from "By Any Other Name" by Santha Rama Rau

When a quoted passage is made up of more than one paragraph, opening quotation marks are put at the beginning of each paragraph, but closing marks are put only at the end of the last paragraph. *See also* **dialogue.**

R

raise, rise Use *raise* to mean "lift"; use *rise* to mean "get up."

Present	Past	Past Participle	Present Participle
raise	raised	had raised	is raising
rise	rose	had risen	is rising

◆ Then he sank trembling into a chair as the old woman, with burning eyes, walked to the window and raised the blind.
from "The Monkey's Paw" by W. W. Jacobs

◆ I rose obediently and started to walk toward my sister.
from "By Any Other Name" by Santha Rama Rau

reflexive pronouns Reflexive pronouns reflect the action of the verb back to the subject. An intensive pronoun adds emphasis to the noun or pronoun just named.

- ◆ That woman must be talking to herself. [reflexive]
- ◆ Merlin prophesied that they could be checked only by the presence of the king himself on the battlefield. . . . [intensive]
  from "The Coronation of Arthur" by Sir Thomas Malory

p. 142

run-on sentence A run-on sentence occurs when there is only a comma (known as a comma splice) or no punctuation between two independent clauses. Separate the clauses into two complete sentences, join them with a semicolon, or join them with a comma and a coordinating conjunction.

Run-on: The man bought his groceries then he went to the party.
Run-on: The man bought his groceries, then he went to the party.
Correct: The man bought his groceries. Then he went to the party.
Correct: The man bought his groceries; then he went to the party.
Correct: The man bought his groceries, and then he went to the party.

Sometimes, in narrative writing, authors choose to use run-ons for effect, such as in the following passage.

- ◆ She sat, she brooded, she stared out the window.
  from "The Need to Say It" by Patricia Hampl

See also **stringy sentences.**

p. 267

semicolon (;) Use this punctuation mark to separate the two parts of a compound sentence when they are not joined by a comma and a conjunction.

- ◆ In the day he made his speeches; at night his stalwarts conducted their whispering campaign.
  from "The Voter" by Chinua Achebe

sentence fragment A fragment often occurs when one sentence is finished, but another thought occurs to the writer. That thought is written and punctuated as a complete sentence, even though it may be missing a subject, verb, or both.

Fragment: I love reading mysteries. *Especially on cold evenings.*
Correct: I love reading mysteries, especially on cold evenings.

As with run-ons, fragments are sometimes used by writers for effect.

- ◆ I was never forgiven. Even after twenty-some years. After the Revolution was over.
  from *Red Azalea* by Anchee Min

sit, set Use *sit* to mean "to sit down"; use *set* to mean "to put something somewhere."

Present	Past	Past Participle	Present Participle
sit	sat	had sat	is sitting
set	set	had set	is setting

- ◆ Who is that sitting next to Diego?
- ◆ Laura set the sandwiches on the counter.

stringy sentences A stringy sentence is one in which several independent clauses are strung together with *and.* Since all the ideas seem to be treated equally, a reader may have difficulty seeing how they are related. Correct a stringy sentence by breaking it into individual sentences or changing some of the independent clauses into subordinate clauses or phrases.

Stringy sentence: I went to the library to find a book about Henry VIII for my research paper and then I met Martin and he wanted me to help him find a newspaper article on microfilm and when the library closed I still didn't have my book and my paper was overdue.

Corrected: When I went to the library to find a book about Henry VIII for my research paper, I met Martin. He wanted me to help him find a newspaper article on microfilm. Consequently, when the library closed, I still didn't have my book, and my paper was overdue.

Corrected: I met Martin when I went to the library to find a book about Henry VIII for my research paper. Since Martin wanted me to help him find a newspaper article on microfilm, the library closed before I could get my book. As a result, my paper was overdue.

T

their, there, they're *Their* is a possessive, *there* is an introductory word or adverb of place, and *they're* is the contraction for "they are."

HINT: Remember that *there* has the word *here* in it; these two words are related in that they can both be indicators of place.

◆ The blinding midday heat had forced the people into their huts.
from "The Rain Came" by Grace Ogot

◆ There were sharp pains, and sudden dizziness, and then profuse bleeding. . . .
from "The Masque of the Red Death" by Edgar Allan Poe

◆ Those cards have to be accounted for in a dozen ways. They're checked and double-checked.
from "The Secret Room" by Corrie ten Boom

to, too, two *To* is a preposition that means "toward, in that direction" or is used in the infinitive form of the verb, as in "to follow" or "to run." *Too* means "also" or "more than enough." *Two* means "more than one."

◆ To take two tests in one day is too much.

V

p. 195
p. 199
p. 201
p. 203
p. 205

verb A verb is a word that tells about an action or a state of being. The form or tense of the verb tells whether the action occurred in the past, is occurring in the present, or will occur in the future.

verb shifts in tense Use the same tense to show two or more actions that occur at the same time.

Incorrect: Marla arrives *(present)* early and parked *(past)* her bike.
Correct: Marla arrived *(past)* early and parked *(past)* her bike.

When the verb in the main clause is in the present tense, the verb in the subordinate clause is in whatever tense expresses the meaning intended.

◆ Jeremy *thinks* that the popcorn *was* too salty.
◆ Anna *believes* that she *passed* the test.

W

p. 189

who, whom *Who* is used as a subject; *whom* is used as a direct object or the object of a preposition.

◆ Auntie Lindo's daughter, Waverly, who was about my age, was standing farther down the wall about five feet away.
from "Two Kinds" by Amy Tan

◆ Danielle couldn't decide whom she would ask for a ride.
◆ Give the leftovers to whomever you wish.

who's, whose *Who's* is a contraction meaning "who is." *Whose* is a possessive.

- Who's the fellow in the straw hat?
- Whose gym bag is in my locker?

would of This expression is often used mistakenly because it sounds like *would've,* the contraction for *would have.* In formal writing, write out *would have,* and you won't be confused.

NOTE: In sentences beginning with the phrase "If (I) had" or when referring to a wish in the past, use the verb *had*—not *would have had.*

- I would have called, but Dad was on the phone.

Incorrect: If I would have had more time, I could make my paper better.

Correct: If I had more time, I could make my paper better.

Correct: If I had had more time, I could have made my paper better.

your, you're *Your* is the possessive form of the personal pronoun *you; you're* is a contraction meaning "you are."

- The woman added, "We hear you and your friends laughing every Saturday night. . . ."
  from "Living Well. Living Good." by Maya Angelou
- You're too small to have them.
  from "By Any Other Name" by Santha Rama Rau

Index of Skills and Strategies

Literary Genres, Terms, and Techniques

Writing Forms, Modes, and Processes

Reading/Thinking Strategies

Vocabulary and Study Skills

Grammar, Usage, Mechanics, and Spelling

Speaking, Listening, and Viewing

Interdisciplinary Connections

Multicultural Awareness and Appreciation

Media and Technology

Index of Fine Art and Artists

Index of Authors and Titles

Acknowledgments

continued from iv

118 From *Innumeracy* by John Allen Paulos. Copyright © 1988 by John Allen Paulos. Reprinted by permission of Hill and Wang, a division of Farrar, Straus & Giroux, Inc.

136 "The Boar Hunt" by José Vasconcelos, trans. by Paul Waldorf from *The Muse in Mexico: A Mid-Century Miscellany,* Supplement to the Texas Quarterly, Vol. II. Reprinted by permission of University of Texas Press.

145 From *Red Azalea* by Anchee Min. Copyright © 1994 by Anchee Min. Reprinted by permission of Pantheon Books, a division of Random House, Inc.

156 "He—y, Come on Ou—t!" by Shinichi Hoshi, translated by Stanleigh H. Jones, Jr. Reprinted by permission of the author.

164 "Flash Cards" from *Grace Notes* by Rita Dove. Copyright © 1989 by Rita Dove. Reprinted by permission of W. W. Norton & Company, Inc.

165 "In Memory of Richi" from *Sonnets to Human Beings and Other Selected Works* by Carmen Tafolla. Copyright © 1992 by Carmen Tafolla. Reprinted by permission of the author.

166 "The Rabbit" by Edna St. Vincent Millay from *Collected Poems.* Copyright 1939, © 1967 by Edna St. Vincent Millay and Norma Millay Ellis. Reprinted by permission of Elizabeth Barnett, Literary Executor.

170 "The Elephant in the Dark House" from *Rumi, Poet and Mystic* translated by Reynold A. Nicholson. Reprinted by permission of George, Allen and Unwin, an imprint of HarperCollins Publishers Limited.

171 "Thought For a Sunshiny Morning" by Dorothy Parker from *The Portable Dorothy Parker* by Dorothy Parker. Introduction by Brendan Gill. Copyright 1928, renewed © 1956 by Dorothy Parker. Reprinted by permission of Viking Penguin, a division of Penguin Books USA Inc.

191 *Antigone* from *The Theban Plays* by Sophocles, translated by E. F. Watling. Copyright 1947 E. F. Watling. Reprinted by permission of Penguin Books Ltd.

228 *Twelve Angry Men* by Reginald Rose. Copyright © 1956, renewed 1984 Reginald Rose. Reprinted by permission of International Creative Management, Inc.

256 "We the Jurors" from "Do You Swear That You Will Well and Truly Try . . .?" by Barbara Holland, *Smithsonian,* March 1995, Vol. 25, #12. Reprinted by permission of the author.

270 Adapted from *The Flying Doctor* from *One-Act Comedies of Moliére,* translated by Albert Bermel. Copyright © 1962, 1963, 1964, 1975 by Albert Bermel. Reprinted by permission of Applause Theatre Books, 211 W. 71st St., New York, NY 10023.

283 "The Chameleon" from *Chekhov: The Early Stories, 1883–1888* translated by Patrick Miles and Harvey Pitcher. Copyright © 1982 by Patrick Miles and Harvey Pitcher. Reprinted by permission of John Murray Publishers, Ltd.

287 "The Fox and the Woodcutter" from *Aesop's Fables,* trans. by Dennison B. Hull. Copyright © 1960 The University of Chicago Press. Reprinted by permission of The University of Chicago Press.

292 Adapted from "Dip in the Pool" by Roald Dahl from *Someone Like You* by Roald Dahl. Copyright 1948 by Roald Dahl. Reprinted by permission of the author and the Watkins/Loomis Agency.

305 From "The Need To Say It" by Patricia Hampl. Copyright © 1991 by Patricia Hampl. Originally published in *The Writer on Her Work* edited by Janet Sternberg. Published by W. W. Norton. Reprinted by permission of Rhoda Weyr Agency, NY.

310 This work originally appeared as *Crossroads* by Carlos Solórzano in *Selected Latin American One-Act Plays,* Francesca Colecchia and Julio Matas, eds. and trans. Published in 1973 by the University of Pittsburgh Press. Reprinted by permission of the Publisher.

317 "Two Bodies" from *Selected Poems* by Octavio Paz. Copyright © 1973 by Octavio Paz and Muriel Rukeyser. Reprinted by permission of New Directions Publishing Corp.

340, 371 From *Le Morte d'Arthur* by Sir Thomas Malory, translated by Keith Baines. Translation copyright © 1962 by Keith Baines, renewed © 1990 by Francesca Evans. Introduction © 1962 by Robert Graves, renewed © 1990 by Beryl Graves. Reprinted by permission of Dutton Signet, a division of Penguin Books USA Inc.

344 From *The Hollow Hills* by Mary Stewart. Copyright © 1977 by Mary Stewart. Reprinted by permission of William Morrow & Company, Inc. and Hodder & Stoughton Ltd.

350 "Youth and Chivalry" from *A Distant Mirror* by Barbara Tuchman. Copyright © 1978 by Barbara W. Tuchman. Reprinted by permission of Alfred A. Knopf, Inc.

358 From *Le Morte d'Arthur* by Sir Thomas Malory, translated by Keith Baines. Translation copyright © 1962 by Keith Baines, renewed © 1990 by Francesca Evans. Introduction © 1962 by Robert Graves, renewed © 1990 by Beryl Graves. Reprinted by permission of Dutton Signet, a division of Penguin Books USA Inc. Abridged.

365 From *The Once and Future King* by T. H. White. Reprinted by permission of David Higham Associates.

384–385 "Bus Chivalry" from *Miss Manners' Guide to Excruciatingly Correct Behavior* by Judith Martin. Copyright © 1979, 1980, 1981, 1982 by United Features Syndicates, Inc. Reprinted by permission of Scribner, a Division of Simon & Schuster Inc.

384 From *Math for Smarty Pants* by Marilyn Burns. Copyright © 1982 by Yolla Bolly Press. Reprinted by permission of Little, Brown and Company.

385 "The Knight" from *Collected Early Poems: 1950–1970* by Adrienne Rich. Copyright © 1993 by Adrienne Rich. Copyright © 1967, 1963, 1962, 1961, 1960, 1959, 1958, 1957, 1956, 1955, 1954, 1953, 1952, 1951 by Adrienne Rich. Copyright © 1984, 1975, 1971, 1969, 1966 by W. W. Norton & Company, Inc. Reprinted by permission of W. W. Norton & Company, Inc.

396 "And of Clay Are We Created" from *The Stories of Eva Luna* by Isabel Allende, translated from the Spanish by Margaret Sayers Peden. Copyright © 1989 by Isabel Allende. English translation copyright © 1991 by Macmillan Publishing Company. Reprinted by permission of Scribner, an imprint of Simon & Schuster, Inc.

409 "A Soldier of Urbina" from *Jorge Luis Borges Selected Poems* 1923–1967 by Jorge Luis Borges. Copyright © 1968, 1969, 1970, 1971, 1972 by Jorge Luis Borges, Emece Editores, S. A. and Normal Thomas Di Giovanni. Reprinted by permission of Delacorte Press/Seymour Lawrence, a division of Bantam Doubleday Dell Publishing Group, Inc.

411 "Lineage" from *This is My Century: New and Collected Poems* by Margaret Walker Alexander. Reprinted by permission of The University of Georgia Press.

411 "The Gift" from *Rose* by Li-Young Lee. Copyright © 1986 by Li-Young Lee. Reprinted by permission of BOA Editions, Ltd., 92 Park Ave., Brockport, NY 14420.

412 "Turning Pro" from *New and Collected Poems* by Ishmael Reed. Copyright © 1988 by Ishmael Reed. Reprinted by permission of Ellis J. Freedman.

417 "The Secret Room" from *The Hiding Place* by Corrie ten Boom with John and Elizabeth Sherrill. Copyright © 1971 by Corrie ten Boom and John and Elizabeth Sherrill. Reprinted by permission of Chosen Books.

429 "The Street of the Cañon" from *Mexican Village* by Josefina Niggli. Copyright 1945 by The University of North Carolina Press. Reprinted by permission of the publisher.

437 From "Heroic Possibilities" by Michael Dorris, *Teaching Tolerance,* Spring 1995, Vol. 4, No. 1, pp. 13–14. Copyright © 1995 Southern Poverty Law Center. Reprinted by permission of Teaching Tolerance.

456 Adapted from *Kaffir Boy* by Mark Mathabane. Copyright © 1986 by Mark Mathabane. Reprinted by permission of Simon & Schuster, Inc.

469 "Living Well. Living Good." from *Wouldn't Take Nothing For My Journey Now* by Maya Angelou. Copyright © 1993 by Maya Angelou. Reprinted by permission of Random House Inc.

475 Excerpt from *An American Childhood* by Annie Dillard. Copyright © 1987 by Annie Dillard. Reprinted with permission of HarperCollins Publishers, Inc.

481 "By Any Other Name" from *Gifts of Passage* by Santha Rama Rau. Originally appeared in *The New Yorker.* Copyright 1951 by Vasanthi Rama Rau Bowers. Copyright renewed. Reprinted by permission of HarperCollins Publishers, Inc.

488 "The Naming of Cats" from *Old Possum's Book of Practical Cats.* Copyright 1939 by T. S. Eliot and renewed © 1967 by Esme Valerie Eliot. Reprinted by permission of Harcourt Brace & Company and Faber and Faber Limited, London.

489 Illustration from *Old Possum's Book of Practical Cats* by T. S. Eliot. Illustration copyright © 1982 by Edward Gorey. Reprinted by permission of Harcourt Brace & Company.

503 "One Perfect Rose" by Dorothy Parker from *The Portable Dorothy Parker* by Dorothy Parker. Introduction by Brendan Gill. Copyright 1929 renewed © 1957 by Dorothy Parker. Reprinted by permission of Viking Penguin, a division of Penguin Books USA Inc.

504 "Daybreak in Alabama" from *Selected Poems* by Langston Hughes. Copyright 1948 by Alfred A. Knopf, Inc. and renewed © 1976 by the Executors of the Estate of Langston Hughes. Reprinted by permission of the publisher.

506 "The Flying Cat" from *Hugging the Jukebox* by Naomi Shihab Nye. Copyright © 1982 Naomi Shihab Nye. Reprinted by permission of the author.

510 "Tuesday Siesta" from *No One Writes to the Colonel* by Gabriel García Márquez. Copyright © 1968 in the English translation by Harper & Row, Publishers, Inc. Reprinted by permission of HarperCollins Publishers, Inc.

518 "A Preacher Ought to Be Good-Looking" from *The Pillow Book of Sei Shōnagon,* trans. by Ivan Morris. Copyright © 1967 by Columbia University Press. Reprinted with permission of the publisher.

518 "Elegant Things" from *The Pillow Book of Sei Shōnagon,* trans. by Ivan Morris. Copyright © 1967 by Columbia University Press. Reprinted with permission of the publisher.

518 "Things That Give A Good Feeling" from *The Pillow Book of Sei Shōnagon,* trans. by Ivan Morris. Copyright © 1967 by Columbia University Press. Reprinted with permission of the publisher.

518 "Things That Have Lost Their Power" from *The Pillow Book of Sei Shōnagon,* trans. by Ivan Morris. Copyright © 1967 by Columbia University Press. Reprinted with permission of the publisher.

520 "Porsche" from *Mama Makes up Her Mind: and Other Dangers of Southern Living* by Bailey White, pp. 19–21. Copyright © 1993 by Bailey White. Reprinted by permission of Addison-Wesley Publishing Company, Inc.

536 Lyrics from "Mercedes Benz" by Janis Joplin, Michael McClure and Bobby Neuwirth. Copyright © 1970 Strong Arm Music. Reprinted by permission. All Rights Reserved.

553 "A New Dress" by Ruth Dallas from *Collected Poems.* Copyright © 1987 by John McIndoe Publishers. Reprinted by permission of the University of Otago Press, New Zealand.

554 "Those Winter Sundays" from *Angle of Ascent: New and Selected Poems* by Robert Hayden. Copyright © 1966 by Robert Hayden. Reprinted by permission of Liveright Publishing Corporation.

556 "Tía Chucha" from *The Concrete River* by Luis Rodriguez. Copyright © 1991 by Luis J. Rodriguez. Reprinted by permission of Curbstone Press.

561 "Girls Can We Educate We Dads?" from *When I Dance.* Copyright © 1991, 1988 by James Berry. Reprinted by permission of Harcourt Brace & Company and Penguin Books Ltd.

562 "If You'll Only Go To Sleep" from *The Collected Poems of Gabriela Mistral* by Doris Dana. Copyright © 1961, 1964, 1970, 1971 by Doris Dana. Reprinted by arrangement with Doris Dana, c/o Joan Daves Agency as agent for the proprietor.

563 "Mi prima Agueda" from *Poesias Completas Y El Minutero* by Ramón López Velarde, edited by Antonio Castro Leal, 3/E, 1963. Reprinted by permission of Editorial Porrua S. A., Mexico.

564 From "My Cousin Agatha" (orig.: "Mi prima Agueda") by Ramón López Velarde from *The Yellow Canary Whose Eye Is So Black,* edited and translated by Cheli Durán. Copyright © 1977 by Cheli Durán Ryan. Reprinted by permission of Simon & Schuster Books for Young Readers, an imprint of Simon & Schuster Children's Publishing Division.

564 "My Cousin Agueda" by Ramón López Velarde from *Spanish-American Literature in Translation,* translated by Willis Knapp Jones. Copyright © 1963 by Frederick Ungar Publishing Company, Inc. Reprinted by permission of the publisher.

570 "First Frost" from *Antiworlds and the Fifth Ace: Poetry* by Andrei Voznesensky, edited by Patricia Blake and Max Hayward. Copyright © 1966, 1967 by Basic Books, Inc. Copyright © 1963 by Encounter Ltd. Copyright renewed. Reprinted by permission of Basic Books, a division of HarperCollins Publishers, Inc.

571 "For Anne Gregory" by W. B. Yeats from *The Poems of W. B. Yeats: A New Edition,* edited by Richard J. Finneran. Copyright 1933 by Macmillan Publishing Company, renewed © 1961 by Bertha Georgia Yeats. Reprinted by permission of Simon & Schuster, Inc.

571 "The Fist" from *Collected Poems 1948–1984* by Derek Walcott. Copyright © 1986 by Derek Walcott. Reprinted by permission of Farrar, Straus & Giroux, Inc.

572 "The Stone" from *Collected Poems* by W. W. Gibson. Reprinted by permission of Mr. Michael Gibson and Macmillan General Books, London.

579 "The Other" by Judith Ortiz Cofer from *Reaching for the Mainland* appearing in *Triple Crown,* 1987. Reprinted by permission of Bilingual Press/Editorial Bilingüe, Arizona State University, Tempe, AZ.

580 "To Julia de Burgos" by Julia de Burgos, translated by Maria Arrillaga, 1971. Reprinted by permission of Maria Consuelo Saez Burgos.

583 "We Are Many" from *Five Decades: Poems 1925–1970* by Pablo Neruda, translated by Ben Belitt. Copyright © 1961, 1969, 1972, 1974 by Ben Belitt. Reprinted by permission of Grove/Atlantic, Inc.

586 Abridgement of "Reading a Family Portrait" by Caroline Sloat. Copyright © 1982 by Caroline Sloat. Reprinted by permission of the author

598 "Sunday Morning" by Oscar Peñaranda. Copyright © 1969 by Oscar Peñaranda. Reprinted by permission of the author.

605 "Ceremony" by Leslie Marmon Silko. Copyright © 1981 by Leslie Marmon Silko. Reprinted by permission of Wylie, Aitken & Stone, Inc.

606 "A Story" from *The Collected Poems* 1931–1987 by Czeslaw Milosz. Translated by Renata Gorczynski and Robert Pinsky. Copyright © 1988 by Czeslaw Milosz Royalties, Inc. First published by The Ecco Press in 1988. Reprinted by permission of The Ecco Press.

607 "The Road Not Taken" by Robert Frost from *The Poetry of Robert Frost* edited by Edward Connery Lathem. Published in 1969 by Henry Holt and Co., Inc. Reprinted by permission of Henry Holt and Co., Inc.

608 *The Holy Bible.* Cleveland: The World Publishing Co.

614 "This is a Photograph of Me" from *The Circle Game* by Margaret Atwood, House of Anansi Press, Toronto, 1978. Reprinted with the permission of Stoddart Publishing Co., Limited, Don Mills, Ontario, Canada.

615 "Water Picture" from *The Complete Poems to Solve* by May Swenson. Copyright © 1966 by May Swenson. Copyright © 1993 by The Literary Estate of May Swenson. Originally appeared in *The New Yorker.* Reprinted by permission of Simon & Schuster Books for Young Readers, an imprint of Simon & Schuster Children's Publishing Division.

616 "On a Bare Branch," "Clouds Now and Then" and "Spring" by Matsuo Bashō from *The Penguin Book of Japanese Verse* translated by Geoffrey Bownas and Anthony Thwaite. Copyright © 1964 Geoffrey Bownas and Anthony Thwaite. Reprinted by permission of Penguin Books Ltd., England.

616 "Spring Rain," "Mosquito Buzz" and "Sudden Shower" by Yosa Buson from *The Penguin Book of Japanese Verse* translated by Geoffrey Bownas and Anthony Thwaite. Copyright © 1964 Geoffrey Bownas and Anthony Thwaite. Reprinted by permission of Penguin Books Ltd., England.

620 From "The Cerebral Snapshot" from *Sunrise with Seamonsters* by Paul Theroux. Copyright © 1985 by Cape Cod Scriveners. All rights reserved. Reprinted by permission of Houghton Mifflin Co.

632 "The Woman from America" by Bessie Head. Reprinted by permission of John Johnson Ltd.

637 Adapted from "Rain Music" by Longhang Nguyen. Copyright © 1992 by Longhang Nguyen. Reprinted by permission of the author.

644 "My Father Writes to My Mother" by Assia Djebar. Reprinted by permission of Quartet Books Ltd.

652 "For the White Poets Who Would Be Indian" from *Bone Dance: New and Selected Poems 1965–1993* by Wendy Rose. Copyright © 1994 by Wendy Rose. Reprinted by permission of Malki Museum Press.

652 "Legal Alien" by Pat Mora from *Chants,* 1985. Reprinted by permission of Arte Publico Press, University of Houston.

653 "I am not with those who left their land . . ." by Anna Akhmatova, translated by Peter Norman from *The Akhmatova Journals: Volume One 1938–1941* by Lydia Chukovskaya. Copyright © 1994 by Lydia Chukovskaya. Reprinted by permission of Farrar, Straus & Giroux, Inc.

654 "Jerusalem" from *The Selected Poetry of Yehuda Amichai* by Yehuda Amichai. Edited and translated by Chana Bloch and Stephen Mitchell. English translation copyright © 1986 by Chana Bloch and Stephen Mitchell. Reprinted by permission of HarperCollins Publishers, Inc.

656 "Dos Patrias" and "Two Countries" by José Martí from *José Martí: Major Poems.* Translated by Elinor Randall, edited by Philip S. Foner. Copyright © 1982 by Holmes & Meier Publishers, Inc. Reprinted by permission of the publisher, Holmes & Meier, New York.

659 "It's Hard to Smile" from "Koreans Have a Reason Not to Smile" by Connie Kang, *The New York Times,* September 8, 1990. Copyright © 1990 by The New York Times Company. Reprinted by permission.

764 "Caesar's Commentaries on the Gallic Wars" from *Shrinklits* by Maurice Sagoff. All rights reserved. Reprinted by permission of Workman Publishing Company, Inc.

766 "The Balek Scales" from *18 Stories* by Heinrich Böll, trans. by Leila Vennewitz. Copyright © 1966 by Heinrich Böll. Reprinted by arrangement with Verlag Kiepenheuer & Witsch, c/o Joan Daves Agency as agent for the proprietor and by permission of Leila Vennewitz.

775 "How Much Land Does a Man Need?" from *Twenty-three Tales* by Leo Tolstoy, translated by Louise and Aylmer Maude, 1906. Reprinted by permission of Oxford University Press, Oxford.

788 John Tebbel and Sarah Miles Watts, *The Press and the Presidency.* New York: Oxford University Press, 1985, pp. 535–36, 541.

Acknowledgments

Illustration

Unless otherwise acknowledged, all photographs are the property of Scott, Foresman and Company. Page abbreviations are as follows: (t)top, (c)center, (b)bottom, (l)left, (r)right, (INS)inset.

Cover (detail) and Frontispiece *The Afterglow in Egypt* by William Holman Hunt, 1834. Southampton City Art Gallery.

ix Scala/Art Resource

xi Bridgeman/Art Resource

xiii Tsing-Fang Chen, *Human Achievement,* Lucia Gallery, New York City/Superstock, Inc.

xvii Boris Kustodiev, *The Fair*, 1908/Scala/Art Resource

xviii Jean-Leon Gerome, *Death of Caesar*, 1859, The Walters Art Gallery, Baltimore

xxiv Photo Reunion des Musées Nationaux

xxxii–1 Antonio Ruiz, *The Bicycle Race*, 1938. Philadelphia Museum of Art; Purchased by Nebinger Fund.

1, 4, 50, 56, 62 (icon) Normand Cousineau/SIS

1, 64, 114, 119, 125 (icon) Husain Haqqash, *Akbar Hunting a Tiger Near Gwalior*, From the Akbar-Nama, By Courtesy of the Board of Trustees of the Victoria and Albert Museum, London/Bridgeman Art Library, London/Superstock, Inc.

1, 126, 170, 174, 179 (icon) Wheel of Fortune tarot card, The Pierpont Morgan Library/Art Resource

2 Private Collection. Photo: Jeffrey Ploskonka

3(t) From the collection of Nancy Berliner

3(b) Stuart Handler Family Collection, Evanston, Illinois/Photo: P.P.O.W.

5 Jill Krementz

10–11 Stuart Handler Family Collection, Evanston, Illinois/Photo: P.P.O.W.

17(l) Photo by Robert Foothorap

17(r) Sidney Harris

18–19 © Service photographique, Ville de Nice, © 1995 Succession H. Matisse, Paris/Artists Rights Society (ARS), New York

25 From the collection of Nancy Berliner

29(t) Layle Silbert

29(b) Drawing by Lorenz; ©1977 New Yorker Magazine, Inc.

31 Collection Nelly and Guido Di Tella, Buenos Aires/Museum of Modern Art, Oxford

35 Don Hamerman

37 Collection IWALEWA-Haus-INV.Nr. 14106

43 Corbis-Bettmann Archive

44 Tate Gallery, London/Art Resource

50(l) Scala/Art Resource

50(r) Cynthia Johnson/Time-Warner, Inc.

51(tl) Steve Schapiro/Gamma-Liaison

51(tr) Suolang Loubu/Xinhua/Gamma-Liaison

51(br) Copyright British Museum

53 Copyright British Museum

63 Everett Collection, Inc.

65 Granger Collection, New York

68 National Portrait Gallery, London/Superstock, Inc.

77 Culver Pictures Inc.

78 Aarhus Kunstmuseum

86 AP/Wide World

88 British Library, MS OR 5259 fols 56v-57r

93 Reprinted with permission of Four Winds Press, an imprint of Macmillan Publishing Company from *Calendar Art* written and illustrated by Leonard Everett Fisher. ©1987 Leonard Everett Fisher.

94 Poems, Manuscripts Dept/Lilly Library, Indiana University, Bloomington, IN.

96 Giraudon/Art Resource

105 Courtesy of Herbert Cole/Photo by unknown photographer

110 Private Collection. Photo: Jeffrey Ploskonka

114 Photofest

115(t) Superstock, Inc.

115(br) Superstock, Inc.

115(bl) UPI/Corbis-Bettmann

127 Viking Press

129 Bridgeman/Art Resource

135 AP/Wide World

138 Neg. No. 323730 Painting by George Catlin, Courtesy Department Library Services, American Museum of Natural History

143(l) Emily Da

143(r) UPI/Corbis-Bettmann

144 From *Prop Art: Over 1000 Contemporary Political Posters* by Gary Yanker. Darien House, New York, distributed by New York Graphic Society, 1972. Copyright ©1972 by Gary Yanker.

151 Huhsien County, People's Republic of China

155(t) Courtesy of Sinchosha Publishing Co., Tokyo

155(b) Doug Wright, "Editorial Cartoons," (1973)

157 Courtesy of David Em

163(t) Fred Viebahn/Vintage Books

163(b) Courtesy Carmen Tafolla

163(b) Courtesy, Vassar College

164 Jacob Lawrence, *In the North the Negro had better educational facilities. Panel 58 from THE MIGRATION SERIES.* (1940–41; text and title revised by the artist, 1993.) Tempera on gesso on composition board, 12 x 18 (30.5 x 45.7 cm). The Museum of Modern Art, New York. Gift of Mrs. David M. Levy. Photograph © The Museum of Modern Art, New York.

167 Collection of The New-York Historical Society

169 Private Collection/Bridgeman Art Collection, London/Superstock, Inc.

170 The Pierpont Morgan Library/Art Resource/M500f.13

170 (icon) The Pierpont Morgan Library/Art Resource

172 National Museum of African Art, Eliot Elisofon Photographic Archives, Smithsonian Institution

173 The Saint Louis Art Museum/Superstock, Inc.

180 Collection IWALEWA-Haus-INV.Nr. 14106

181(t) Private Collection. Photo: Jeffrey Ploskonka
181(c) From the collection of Nancy Berliner

181(b) Collection Nelly and Guido Di Tella, Buenos Aires/Museum of Modern Art, Oxford

182–183 Scala/Art Resource

183, 186, 256, 262, 267 (icon) Bob Daemmrich/Image Works

184 Jennifer Girard

185 Museum of Modern Art/Film Stills Archive

187(tl) Alinari/Art Resource

187(tr), (br) Copyright British Museum

187(bl) Staatliche Museen, Berlin, Antikensammlung

188 Superstock, Inc.

189 Corbis-Bettmann Archive

190–191 Copyright British Museum

196, 203, 208, 213, 217, 224 Jennifer Girard

196, 228, 232, 235, 239, 244, 247, 251 Museum of Modern Art, Film Stills Archive

201 Bulloz

210 Copyright British Museum

221 Staatliche Museen, Berlin, Antikensammlung

226 Georges Rouault, *The Old King*, (detail), 1916-36. The Carnegie Museum of Art, Pittsburgh; Patrons Art Fund, 40.1

227 AP/Wide World

256 Scala/Art Resource

256–257 Palazzo Della Ragione, Padua/Mauro Magliani/Superstock, Inc.

258 Copyright British Museum

259 Lester Sloan/Gamma-Liaison

260 Courtesy Tamara Camp

270–271 The Metropolitan Museum of Art, The Lesley and Emma Sheafer Collection, Bequest of Emma A. Sheafer, 1973 (1974.356.524-525)

273 Giraudon/Art Resource

278 The Metropolitan Museum of Art, The Lesley and Emma Sheafer Collection, Bequest of Emma A. Sheafer, 1973 (1974.356.524-525)

282(t) Corbis-Bettmann Archive

282(c) Corbis-Bettmann Archive

282(b) National Portrait Gallery, London

285 *Adskaya Pochta*, 1906, No. 3

288 Guy Billout/Stock Illustration Source, Inc.

293 Bob Scott/Koralik Associates

303 Rhett J. Arens

304 The Phillips Collection, Washington, D.C.

309 UPI/Corbis-Bettmann

310 Robert Gantt Steele

320(l) Erich Lessing/Art Resource

320(c) Erich Lessing/Art Resource

320(r) Alinari/Art Resource

320–321(b) Andrea Booner/Tony Stone Images

321(t) Alistair Spooner/Gamma-Liaison

321(bc) Vienna Society for the Friends of Music/E. T. Archive, London/Superstock, Inc.

321(br) Focus on Sports, Inc.

322 Musée du Louvre/Superstock, Inc.

323 ©1993 Time, Inc., Reprinted by permission.

331 National Portrait Gallery, Washington, D. C., Smithsonian Institution

332 Museum of Modern Art, Film Stills Archive

333 Jennifer Girard

334–335 Bridgeman/Art Resource

335, 338, 382, 386, 392 (icon) Pierpont Morgan Library/Art Resource

335, 394, 437, 442, 447 (icon) Kasimir Malevich, *The Mower*, Russian State Museum, St.Petersburg /A.Burkatousky/Superstock, Inc.

336 Bridgeman/Art Resource

337 Giraudon/Art Resource

339 Courtesy William Morrow, photo by Mark Gerson

340 Courtesy of Sotheby's

345 Giraudon/Art Resource

349 © Randi Hendrix

351 The Bodleian Library, Oxford

356 Y Swyddfa Gymreig/Welsh Office

357 AP/Wide World

361 Bridgeman/Art Resource

366–367 The Pierpont Morgan Library/Art Resource

370 National Portrait Gallery, London

373 Bridgeman/Art Resource

381 E. Hugo

382(tl) National Museum of African Art, Eliot Elisofon Photographic Archives, Smithsonian Institution (GHSA89(6335)

382(bl) Skinsness

382-383(c) Pete Dancs/Tony Stone Images

382(icon) Pierpont Morgan Library/Art Resource

383(t) Photofest

383(bl) Giraudon/Art Resource

383(br) Superstock, Inc.

384(t) K. Marine

384(b) K. Marine

385 K. Marine

393 Bridgeman/Art Resource

395 AP/Wide World

397 The Menil Collection, Houston, Gift of Philippa and Heiner Friedrich. Photo by Paul Hester, Houston

403 The Metropolitan Museum of Art, Hilson Fund, Inc. Gift, 1990 (1990.188)

407 Reprinted with special permission of North America Syndicate

408(t) Organization of American States

408(tc) University of Georgia Press

408(bc) B. O. A. Editions, Ltd., photo by Arthur Furst

408(b) ©1990 Jay Blakesberg

410 The Evans Tibbs Collection

413 Courtesy of Leo Jensen

416 Courtesy Archives of The Billy Graham Center, Wheaton, IL

419 Courtesy Archives of The Billy Graham Center, Wheaton, IL

422 Courtesy Archives of The Billy Graham Center, Wheaton, IL

428 Gary V. Fields

431 Private Collection. Courtesy of Sotheby's, New York

437(icon) Kasimir Malevich, *The Mower,* Russian State Museum, St.Petersburg/A.Burkatousky/ Superstock, Inc.

438(l) Granger Collection, New York

438(c) Hamburg Museum

438(r) Giraudon/Art Resource

438–439(background) British Library

439(l) Granger Collection, New York

439(c) Culver Pictures Inc.

439(r) Ancient Art & Architecture Collection/Ronald Sheridan Photo-Library

440 Courtesy Emilia Askari

448 Bridgeman/Art Resource

449 The Evans Tibbs Collection

450–451 Tsing-Fang Chen, *Human Achievement*, (detail) Lucia Gallery, New York City/Superstock, Inc.

452 From *An American Childhood* by Annie Dillard. Copyright ©1987 by Annie Dillard, All rights reserved. Harper & Row Publishers, Inc., New York

453 From *Kaffir Boy* by Mark Mathabane. Copyright ©1986 by Mark Mathabane. Macmillan Publishers, New York

455(l) Gail Mathabane

455(r) South Light/ Gamma Liaison

456 David Turnley/Black Star

463 David Turnley/Black Star

468(l) AP/Wide World Photos

468(r) United States Bureau of Labor Statistics

469 Howard University Gallery of Art, Washington, D.C.

474 Rollie McKenna

475 Corbis-Bettmann Archive

480(l) UPI/Corbis-Bettmann

480(r) British Library

483 Superstock, Inc.

489 From *Old Possum's Book of Practical Cats* by T. S. Eliot. Drawings by Edward Gorey, Harcourt Brace Jovanovich Publishers. Copyright 1939 by T. S. Eliot. Copyright renewed ©1967 by Esme Valerie Eliot. Illustrations copyright ©1982 by Edward Gorey.

502(t) Viking Press

502(c) UPI/Corbis-Bettmann

502(b) Michael Nye

505 Art and Artifacts Division, Schomberg Center for Research in Black Culture, The New York Public Library, Astor, Lenox and Tilden Foundations

506 Oleg Tselkov, *With Cat*, 1993, oil on canvas, 51" x 38", Courtesy of The Sloane Gallery/ Contemporary Russian Art, Denver, Colorado

509 AP/Wide World **510** El pequeño cementerio de Culebra, by María de Mater O'Neill. ©1990 María de Mater O'Neill. Oils crayons, oils on linen. 64" x 94". Photograph by John Betancourt. Collection of Iliana Fonts.

517 Spencer Jarnigan

518 Copyright British Museum

521 The Sculpture Park at Le Monciel, Jouy-en Josas, France

524(t) Ricki Rosen

524(b) Hulton Deutsch Collection Ltd.

527 Roger-Viollet

532-533(t) David LeBon/Tony Stone Images

532(b) Superstock, Inc.

533(t) Superstock, Inc.

533(c) Superstock, Inc.

533-534(b) Keith Bernstein/FSP/Gamma Liaison

534(t) Courtesy, General Motors Corporation

534-535 E. Hugo

535(b) Martyn Goddard/Tony Stone Images

536 John Turner/Tony Stone Images

544 David Turnley/Black Star

545 Tsing-Fang Chen, *Human Achievement*, (detail) Lucia Gallery, New York City/Superstock, Inc.

546-547 Boris Kustodiev, *The Fair*, (detail), 1908/Scala/Art Resource

547, 550, 586, 590, 593, 596, 619, 624, 628 (icon) Superstock, Inc.

548–549 AP/Wide World

551 Drawing by Stan Hunt; ©1987 The New Yorker Magazine, Inc.

552(t) Courtesy of University of Otago Press

554-555 Collection Leontine D. Scott

559 Drawing by Lorenz; ©1995 The New Yorker Magazine, Inc.

560(t) Courtesy Harcourt Brace & Company

560(c) Organization of American States

562 Galerie Garces Velasquez, Bogata

565 Jeanette Ortiz Osorio

569(t) AP/Wide World

569(tc) National Portrait Gallery, London

569(bc) Evan Richman/Reuters/Corbis-Bettmann

570 Burt Glinn/Magnum Photos

573 Franz Altschuler

577 Christie's, London/Superstock, Inc./©1995 Artists Rights Society(ARS), New York/SPADEM, Paris

578(t) Courtesy of Arte Publico Press

578(b) AP/Wide World

581 Reproduced by authorization of the Instituto Nacional de Bellas Artes y Literatura, Mexico City

582 Superstock, Inc.

587 Gift of Maxim Karolik for the M. and M. Karolik Collection of American Paintings, 1815–1865. Courtesy, Museum of Fine Arts, Boston

588(t) Kobal Collection

588(c) Everett Collection, Inc.

588(bl) Kobal Collection

588(br) Everett Collection, Inc.

589(tl) Photofest

589(tr) Everett Collection, Inc.

589(b) Photofest

597(t) Courtesy of Oscar Peñaranda

597(b) Trustees of Amherst College

599 Ansel Adams, *Silverton Colorado*, c. 1951. Photograph by Ansel Adams, Copyright ©1993 by the Trustees of the Ansel Adams Publishing Trust. All Rights Reserved.

603(c) UPI/Corbis-Bettmann

603(t) ©1981 Linda Fry Poverman

603(b) Dartmouth College

604 Jerry Jacka

609 Roloff Beny

613(t) Laurence Acland

613(tc) UPI/Corbis-Bettmann

613(bc) Collection Kimiko and John Powers. Photo: Fogg Art Museum, Harvard University

614-615 Robert Amft

616 Chishaku-in temple, Kyoto/I.S.E.I., Tokyo, Japan

619 Courtesy, Wade Patton

620-621 Mitch Reardon/Tony Stone Images

622(tl) Howard Sochurek/Stock Market

622(tr) The Harold E. Edgerton 1992 Trust, courtesy of Palm Press, Inc.

622(c) North American Philips corporation

629 André Kertész, American, 1894–1985, *Shadows of the Eiffel Tower* (view looking down from tower to people underneath), silver gelatin print, 1929. 16.5 x 21.9 cm, Julien Levy Collection, Special Photography Acquisition Fund, 1979.77, photograph ©1994 The Art Institute of Chicago. All Rights Reserved.

631 Courtesy Heineman Publishers, Oxford, England. Photo: Michael Uaha

633 Christine Kristen

636 Courtesy of Longhang Nguyen

639 Superstock, Inc.

643 Courtesy of Quartet Books Limited

644 Isabel Cutler/Gamma Liaison

651(t) Courtesy of Arte Público Press

651(tc) Pat Wolk

651(c) RIA-Novosti/Sovfoto

651(bc) Layle Silbert

651(b) Corbis-Bettmann Archive

653 Scala/Art Resource

654-655 Esais Baitel/Gamma Liaison

659(all) AP/Wide World

660(all) AP/Wide World

661(t) Farnood/Sipa Press

661(b) Ricardo Beliel/GLMR/Gamma Liaison

662(t) Michael Dwyer/Stock Boston

662(b) Leong Ka Tai/Material World

670(t) Reproduced by authorization of the Instituto Nacional de Bellas Artes y Literatura, Mexico City

670(b) Jeanette Ortiz Osorio

671 Roloff Beny

672–673 Jean-Leon Gerome, *Death of Caesar,* 1859 (detail), The Walters Art Gallery, Baltimore

673, 676, 787, 791, 797(icon) Christie's, London/Superstock, Inc.

674–675 Museum of Modern Art, Film Stills Archive

677 National Portrait Gallery, London

681 Courtesy of Sotheby's

687 Museum of Modern Art, Film Stills Archive

733 Drawing by Robert Mankoff; ©1987 The New Yorker Magazine, Inc.

734(t) Copyright British Museum

735 Scale drawing by Irwin Smith from *Shakespeare's Globe Playhouse: A Modern Reconstruction in Text and Scale Drawings* by Irwin Smith. Charles Scribner's Sons, New York, 1956. Hand colored by Cheryl Kucharzak

737 Photofest

747 Christie's, London/Superstock, Inc.

756 Ancient Art & Architecture Collection/Ronald Sheridan Photo-Library

765 McGraw Hill

767 Collection John P. Axelrod. Photo: Marisa del Ray Gallery

774 Granger Collection, New York

775 Tass/Sovfoto

780 Novosti/Sovfoto

787 Pete Souza/The White House

788 Pete Souza/The White House

789 Courtesy Diego Muñoz

Custom Literature Database

The *ScottForesman Custom Literature Database* is a collection of over 1400 literary selections. Over 200 titles in the database have lessons to support students as they read. Eight indices—Title, Author, Genre, Subject, Nationality, Literary Themes, Anthology Correlations, and Lessons for Selected Titles—help you navigate through the database, allowing you to search for, view, and print the exact selection you want. The Anthology Correlations index lets you identify titles in the database correlated to *ScottForesman Literature and Integrated Studies.*

Address to the Apostles from Bible, Matthew, 10:5–42*

African Proverbs

"Aladdin, or The Wonderful Lamp" from *A Thousand and One Nights*

"Ali Baba and the Forty Thieves" from *A Thousand and One Nights*

Anglo-Saxon Riddles

Apocalyptic Utterances from Bible, Matthew 24:4–25:46

Articles of Confederation

Babylonian Law from *The Hammurabi Code*

Battle of Brunanburh, The

"Battle of Otterbourne, The"

Bhagavad Gita

Bible, Acts of the Apostles

Bible, Corinthians 1:13

Bible, Genesis 1–3

Bible, John

Bible, Luke 10:25–37*

Bible, Mark

Bible, Psalm 1

Bible, Psalm 8

Bible, Psalm 23 in Six Translations

Bible, Psalm 24

Bible, Psalm 91

Bible, Psalm 100*

Bible, Psalm 137

Bible, Ruth*

"Birth of Hatshepsut, The"

Birth of Jesus, The from Bible, Matthew 1:18–4:17

"Bonnie George Campbell"

"Bonny Barbara Allan"

Book of Jonah, The from The Hebrew Bible

"Brahman, the Tiger and the Six Judges, The"*

Brown v. *Board of Education of Topeka**

"Caedmon's Hymn"

Chinese Exclusion Act*

Civil Rights Act of 1964*

"Clementine"

Code of Manu, The

Constitution of the Confederate States of America, The

Constitution of the United States

Death of Jesus, The from Bible, Matthew 26:14–28:20

"Deep River"

"Demon Lover, The"

"Descent of Ishtar into the Underworld, The"

Dred Scott v. *Sandford*

"Egyptian Love Song"

"Emergence Song"

"Enchanted Horse, The" from *A Thousand and One Nights*

Everyman

"Experiences of a Chinese Immigrant" from *The Independent**

"Follow the Drinking Gourd"*

"Get Up and Bar the Door"

Gibbons v. *Ogden*

"Go Down, Moses"*

Hammurabi Code, The

"How Thoutii Took the Town of Joppa"

"Joshua Fit de Battle ob Jericho"

Kingdom of Heaven Parables from Bible, Matthew 13:1–52

Laws, The from Bible, Exodus 19:1–23:33

"Little Old Sod Shanty on the Claim, The"

"Lord Randal"

Magna Carta

Marbury v. *Madison*

"May Colvin"*

Mayflower Compact, The

NAACP v. *Alabama*

"Old Chisholm Trail, The"

On Humility and Forgiveness from Bible, Matthew 18:1–35

Parables from Bible, Luke*

"Pat Works on the Railway"

"Peasant and the Workman, The"

Plessy v. *Ferguson*

Preamble to the Constitution of the Knights of Labor

Prince Shotuku's Constitution

Resolution of the Stamp Act Congress

"Scheherazade" from *A Thousand and One Nights*

"Seafarer, The"

Second Shepherd's Play, The

Seneca Falls Declaration of Sentiments and Resolutions, The

Sermon on the Mount from Bible, Matthew 5:1–7:27

"Seven Voyages of Sindbad the Sailor, The" from *A Thousand and One Nights**

"Shenandoah"

"Shipwrecked Sailor, The"

*Sir Gawain and the Green Knight**

"Sir Patrick Spens"*

Song of Creation

"Story of Rhampsinites, The"

"Story of the Fisherman, The" from *A Thousand and One Nights*

"Sumer is icumen in"

Sura LXXV—The Resurrection from *The Koran*

Sura LXXVI—Man from *The Koran*

"Swing Low, Sweet Chariot"

"Three Ravens, The"

Treaty of Peace with Great Britain

Trustees of Dartmouth College v. *Woodward*

"Twa Corbies, The"

Virginia Bill of Rights

Vishnu Purana

Volstead Act, The

"Wanderer, The"

"Western Wind"

"Wife of Usher's Well, The"

Adams, Henry

Education of Henry Adams, The, Chapter XXV, "The Dynamo and the Virgin"

"Prayer to the Virgin of Chartres"

Addison, Joseph

"Artifices in Tragedy" from *The Spectator*

"Party Patches" from *The Spectator*

"Sir Roger at Church" from *The Spectator*

"Westminster Abbey" from *The Spectator*

"Will Wimble" from *The Spectator**

"Wit: True, False, and Mixed"

Aelfric, Abbot

"Colloquy on the Occupations, A"

Aesop

"Crow and the Pitcher, The"

"Fox and the Crow, The"

"Fox and the Grapes, The"

---

*This selection includes background information, a study guide, and comprehension and critical thinking questions in a lesson on the disc.

Custom Literature Database

"Hound and the Hare, The"

"Mice and the Weasels, The"

"North Wind and the Sun, The"

Alcaeus
"Drinking Song"
"Summer"
"Winter"

Alcott, Louisa May
"Amy's Valley of Humiliation" from *Little Women**
Hospital Sketches
"Old-Fashioned Thanksgiving, An"*
"Onawandah, Fourth Spinning Wheel Story"

Alighieri, Dante
Divine Comedy, The, " The Inferno," Canto I
Divine Comedy, The, "The Inferno," Canto III
Divine Comedy, The, "The Inferno," Canto XXXIV

Alline, Henry
"The Conduct of Most Sailors"

Anacreon
"Beauty"
"Combat, The"
"Cup, The"
"Love"

Andersen, Hans Christian
"Emperor's New Clothes, The"*
"Little Mermaid, The"
"Red Shoes, The"
"Snow Queen, The"
"Steadfast Tin Soldier, The"
"Swineherd, The"
"Thumbelina"
'Tinder-Box, The"
'gly Duckling, The"*

lerson, Sherwood
covery of a Father"*
n Day"

mous
dent, The
d to me a kingdom is"
s a Lady Sweet and Kind"

Anthony, Susan B.
On Woman's Right to Suffrage*
"Political Economy of Women"

Antin, Mary
"Immigrant Goes to School, An" from *The Promised Land**

Aristotle
Poetics, The

Arnold, Matthew
"Isolation, To Marguerite"
"Last Word, The"
"Requiescat"
"Scholar-Gipsy, The"
"Self-Dependence"
"Thyrsis"

Aspinwall, Alicia
"Upsidedownians, The"

Aulnoy, Comtesse d'
"White Cat, The"
"Yellow Dwarf, The"

Aupaumut, Hendrick
A Short Narration of My Last Journey to the Western Contry

Babur
*Babur-nama**

Bacon, Francis
"Of Studies"
"Of Truth"

Bambara, Toni Cade
"Blues Ain't No Mockin Bird"*
"Happy Birthday"*

Barbour, Ralph Henry
"Brewster's Debut"

Beach, Lewis
Clod, The*

Bede
Ecclesiastical History of the English People, The, Book II, Chapters 9–13*
Ecclesiastical History of the English People, The, Book IV, Chapter 24

Behn, Aphra
"Lady's Looking Glass, The"
"Love in Fantastic Triumph Sat from Abdelazar"
Oroonoko

Bellamy, Edward
*Looking Back**

Belloc, Hilaire
"Lion, The"
"Yak, The"

Benét, Stephen Vincent
"By the Waters of Babylon"

Benet, William Rose
"Skater of Ghost Lake, The"

Bennet, John
"Fritz the Master Fiddler"

Bierce, Ambrose
"Occurrence at Owl Creek Bridge, An"

Blackwell, Alice Stone
Indifference of Women, The*

Blake, William
"And did those feet" from *Milton*
"Chimney Sweeper, The" from *Songs of Experience*
"Chimney Sweeper, The," from *Songs of Innocence*
"Divine Image, The" from *Songs of Innocence*
"Holy Thursday" from *Songs of Experience*
"Holy Thursday" from *Songs of Innocence*
"Human Abstract, The" from *Songs of Experience*
"Infant Joy"
"Infant Sorrow"
Introduction ("Hear the voice of the Bard") from *Songs of Experience*
Introduction ("Piping down the valleys") from *Songs of Innocence*
"Lamb, The" from *Songs of Innocence*
"Nurse's Song" from *Songs of Experience*
"Poison Tree, A"
"Proverbs of Hell" from *The Marriage of Heaven and Hell*
"Sick Rose, The"
Song ("How sweet I roamed")
"Tyger, The" from *Songs of Experience*

Bleecker, Ann Eliza
"On the Immensity of Creation"

Boas, Franz
"Raven's Adventures"
"Sedna, Mistress of the Underworld"

Boswell, James
Life of Samuel Johnson, LL.D, The
London Journal, 1762–1763

Bradstreet, Anne
"Contemplations"
"Prologue, The"
"To My Dear and Loving Husband"
"Upon the Burning of Our House, July 10th, 1666"

Brontë, Emily
"No coward soul is mine"
"Remembrance"
Song ("The linnet in the rocky dells")

Brooke, Rupert
"Peace"*

Brooks, Gwendolyn
"Pete at the Zoo"

Brothers Grimm
"Bremen Town Musicians, The"*
"Elves and the Shoemaker, The"
"Fisherman and His Wife, The"
"Frog Prince, The"
"Gallant Tailor, The"
"Hansel and Grethel"
"Juniper Tree, The"
"Rapunzel"
"Rumpelstiltskin"*
"Sleeping Beauty, The"
"Snow-white"
"Twelve Dancing Princesses, The"

Brown, Dee
"Katlian and the Iron People"*

Brown, John
Last Speech

Browning, Elizabeth Barrett
Sonnet 1 ("I thought once how Theocritus had sung") from *Sonnets from the Portuguese*
Sonnet 14 ("If thou must love me, let it be for naught") from *Sonnets from the Portuguese*
Sonnet 26 ("I lived with visions for my company") from *Sonnets from the Portuguese*

Sonnet 28 ("My letters! all dead paper, mute and white!") from *Sonnets from the Portuguese*

Sonnet 43 ("How do I love thee?") *from Sonnets from the Portuguese*

Browning, Robert

"Andrea del Sarto"*

"Caliban Upon Setebos"

"Childe Roland to the Dark Tower Came"

"Fra Lippo Lippi"

"Home Thoughts, From Abroad"

"How They Brought the Good News from Ghent to Aix"*

"Love Among the Ruins"

"Meeting at Night"*

"Parting at Morning"

"Pied Piper of Hamelin, The"

"Porphyria's Lover"

"Prospice"

"Rabbi Ben Ezra"

"Soliloquy of the Spanish Cloister"

"Summum Bonum"

"Year's at the spring, The"

Bryan, William Jennings

Cross of Gold, The

Bryant, William Cullen

"Thanatopsis"

"To a Waterfowl"

"To the Fringed Gentian"

"Waiting by the Gate"

Bulfinch, Thomas

"Adventures of Aeneas, The"

"Adventures of Ulysses"

"Apollo and Daphne"

"Apollo and Hyacinthus"

"Atalanta"

"Bacchus and Ariadne"

"Bellerophon, Pegasus, and the Chimaera"

"Cadmus"

"Castor and Pollux"

"Centaurs, The"

"Cupid and Psyche"*

"Daedalus"*

"Death of Baldur, The"

"Diana and Actæon"

"Echo and Narcissus"

"Golden Fleece, The"*

"Hercules"

"Hero and Leander"

"Medea and Jason"

"Meleager"

"Midas"

"Minerva"

"Myrmidons, The"

"Niobe"

"Of the Joys of Valhalla"

"Orpheus and Eurydice"

"Perseus and Medusa"

"Phaeton"*

"Prometheus and Pandora"*

"Proserpine"

"Pygmalion"

"Pyramus and Thisbe"

"Sphinx, The"

"Theseus"

"Trojan War, The"

"Venus and Adonis"

Bunyan, John

Pilgrim's Progress, The

Burnett, Frances Hodgson

"Editha's Burglar"

Burney, Fanny

Diary, The

Burns, Robert

"Ae Fond Kiss"

"Auld Lang Syne"

"Cotter's Saturday Night, The"

"Highland Mary"

"John Anderson My Jo"

"Man's a Man for A' That, A"

"My Heart's in the Highlands"*

"My Jean"

"O, wert thou in the cauld blast"

"Red, Red Rose, A"

"Sweet Afton"

"Tam o' Shanter"

"To a Louse"*

Byron, Lord (George Gordon)

Childe Harold's Pilgrimage, Canto IV, Stanzas CLXXVIII–CLXXXIV

Don Juan, Canto I, Stanzas 1, 6–10, 13, 15, 17–20, 23–27, 32, 33, 37–41, 44, 45, 47–50, 54, 55, 60–62, 69–72, 75–79, 86, 87, 90–92

Don Juan, Canto III, Stanzas 1–16

"On This Day I Complete My Thirty-Sixth Year"*

"She walks in beauty"

"So we'll go no more a-roving"

"Sonnet on Chillon"

"Stanzas for Music"

"When We Two Parted"

"Written After Swimming from Sestos to Abydos"

Cabeza de Vaca, Alavar Nunez

Relation of Alvar Nunuez Cabeza de Vaca, Chapter VII

Cain, Reverend Richard H.

Address of the State Convention to the White Inhabitants of South Carolina

Calhoun, John Caldwell

Slavery

Campion, Thomas

"Cherry-Ripe"

"Man of Life Upright, The"

"My Sweetest Lesbia"

"Now Winter Nights Enlarge"

"Rose-cheeked Laura"

"When to her lute Corinna sings"

Carlyle, Thomas

*French Revolution, The**

"Midas" from *Past and Present*

Carroll, Lewis (Charles Lutwidge Dodgson)

Alice's Adventures in Wonderland

"Crocodile, The" from *Alice's Adventures in Wonderland*

"Father William" from *Alice's Adventures in Wonderland*

"Jabberwocky" from *Through the Looking Glass*

"Mad Carpenter's Song, The"*

"Mock Turtle Song, The" from *Alice's Adventures in Wonderland*

"Walrus and the Carpenter, The" from *Alice's Adventures in Wonderland*

Cather, Willa

"Sculptor's Funeral, The"*

"Sentimentality of William Tavener, The"*

Cervantes, Miguel de

*Don Quixote**

Chaucer, Geoffrey

"Clerk's Prologue, The" from *The Canterbury Tales*

"Clerk's Tale, The" from *The Canterbury Tales*

"General Prologue, The" from *The Canterbury Tales*

"Nun's Priest's Tale, The" from *The Canterbury Tales*

"Pardoner's Tale, The" from *The Canterbury Tales*

"Prologue to the Nun's Priest's Tale, The," from *The Canterbury Tales*

"Wife of Bath's Prologue, The" from *The Canterbury Tales*

"Wife of Bath's Tale, The" from *The Canterbury Tales**

Chekhov, Anton

"Bet, The"

"Bishop, The"

*Boor, The**

Cherry Orchard, The, Act One

Cherry Orchard, The, Act Two

Cherry Orchard, The, Act Three

Cherry Orchard, The, Act Four

"Darling, The"

"Day in the Country, A"

"Kiss, The"

"Lady with the Dog, The"

"Misery"

"Upheaval, An"*

Chesterfield, Lord (Philip Stanhope)

Letters to his Son

Chesterton, G. K.

"Two Taverns, The"

Chief Joseph

I Will Fight No More Forever

Child, Lydia Maria

Letter to Colonel P. H. Anderson

---

*This selection includes background information, a study guide, and comprehension and critical thinking questions in a lesson on the disc.

Custom Literature Database

Chopin, Kate
"Pair of Silk Stockings, A"*

Christie, Agatha
"Third-Floor Flat, The"*

Churchill, Winston
Blood, Sweat, and Tears
Dunkirk
Iron Curtain Has Descended, An*
Their Finest Hour

Clay, Henry
On the Compromise of 1850

Clough, Arthur Hugh
"Epi-Strauss-um"
"Latest Decalogue, The"
"Say not the struggle nought availeth"

Cobb, Frank I. and Walter Lippmann
Interpretation of President Wilson's Fourteen Points

Coleridge, Samuel Taylor
Biographia Literaria
"Christabel"
"Eolian Harp, The"
"Frost at Midnight"
"Kubla Khan"
"Rime of the Ancient Mariner, The"
"This Lime-Tree Bower My Prison"

Colum, Padraic
"Aegir's Feast: How Thor Triumphed"
"Baldur's Doom"
"Building of the Wall, The"
"Children of Loki, The"
"Dwarf's Hoard, and the Curse That It Brought"
How Brock Brought Judgement on Loki"
…w Freya Gained Her Necklace …d How Her Loved One Was Lost …Her"
… Thor and Loki Be-Fooled …m the Giant"
…nd Her Apples: How Loki Put …ds in Danger"
"Odin Goes to Mimir's Well; His Sacrifice for Wisdom"
"Sif's Golden Hair: How Loki Wrought Mischief in Asgard"
"Sigurd's Youth" from *The Children of Odin*
"Thor and Loki in the Giants' City"
"Twilight of the Gods, The"
"Valkyrie, The"

Conrad, Joseph
Secret Sharer, The
*Youth**

Crane, Stephen
"Bride Comes to Yellow Sky, The"
"Do not weep, maiden, for war is kind"
"Episode of War, An"
"I met a seer"
"Man saw a ball of gold in the sky, A"
"Mystery of Heroism, A"
"Open Boat, The"*
Red Badge of Courage, The
"Think as I Think"

Crevecoeur, Michel-Guillaume Jean de
Letters from an American Farmer

Curtin, Jeremiah, and Hewitt, J. N. B.
"Woman Who Fell from the Sky, The"

Curtis, Natalie
"Creation"
"Deathless One and the Wind, The"
"Morning Star and the Evening Star, The"
"Origin of Corn and Pemmican, The"
"Stories of Wak-Chung-Kaka, the Foolish One"
"Story of Gomoidema Pokoma-Kiaka, The"
"Story of the First Mother, The"
"Story of Wakiash and the First Totem-Pole, The"*
"Vision of the Earth-Maker, A"*

Davis, Jefferson
Inaugural Address of Jefferson Davis
Last Message to the People of the Confederacy
Message to Congress

Davis, Richard H.
"Midsummer Pirates"

de la Mare, Walter
"All But Blind"
"All That's Past"
"Cake and Sack"
"Dwelling Place, The"
"Flight, The"
"Listeners, The"*
"Nobody Knows"
"Silver"
"Song of the Mad Prince, The"
"Tartary"
"Up and Down"

De Quincey, Thomas
"On the Knocking at the Gate in *Macbeth*"
"Poetry of Pope, The"

Defoe, Daniel
Essay Upon Projects, An
Journal of the Plague Year, A

Dekker, Thomas
"Lullaby"

Delgado, Reverend Father Fray Carlos
Report Made By Reverend Father Fray Carlos Delgado

Dickens, Charles
David Copperfield
"Signalman, The"*

Dickinson, Emily
"Alter! When the Hills do"
"Apparently with no surprise"
"Because I could not stop for death"
"Bustle in a House, The"
" 'Faith' Is a fine invention"
" 'Hope' is the thing with feathers"
"I felt a Funeral, in my Brain"
"I heard a Fly buzz – when I died"
"I like to see it lap the Miles"
"I taste a liquor never brewed"
"I Years had been from Home"
"I'll tell you how the Sun rose"
"If you were coming in the Fall"
"Morns are meeker than they were, The"
"Much Madness is divinest Sense"
"Narrow Fellow in the grass, A"*
"Of all the Souls that stand create"
"Some keep the Sabbath going to Church"
"Success is counted sweetest"*
"Surgeons must be very careful"
"There's a certain Slant of light"
"This is my letter to the World"
"To make a prairie it takes a clover"
"Triumph – may be of several kinds"*

Dixon, Roland B.
"Creation, The"
"Theft of Fire, The"

Donne, John
"Bait, The"
"Ecstacy, The"
"Flea, The"
"Indifferent, The"
Meditation 17 from *Devotions*
"On His Mistress"
Song ("Go and catch a falling star")
Sonnet 4 ("At the round earth's imagined corners, blow") from *Holy Sonnets**
Sonnet 6 ("This is my play's last scene; here heavens appoint") from *Holy Sonnets*
Sonnet 10 ("Death, be not proud, though some have called thee") from *Holy Sonnets**
Sonnet 14 ("Batter my heart, three-personed God; for You") from *Holy Sonnets*
"Sun Rising, The"
"Valediction: Forbidding Mourning, A"
"Woman's Constancy"

Dorsey, George and Kroeber, Alfred L.
"Star Husband, The"

Douglass, Frederick
*Life and Times of Frederick Douglass, The**
Meaning of July Fourth for the Negro, The*
Narrative of the Life of Frederick Douglass, The
Oration in Memory of Abraham Lincoln

Dowson, Ernest
"Cynara"
"They are not long"

Doyle, Sir Arthur Conan
"Adventure of the Blue Carbuncle, The"*
*Hound of the Baskervilles, The**
"Man with the Twisted Lip, The"*
"Musgrave Ritual, The"
"Redheaded League, The"
"Silver Blaze"

Dryden, John
Absalom and Achitophel
Essay of Dramatic Poesy, An
"I Feed a Flame Within"
Mac Flecknoe
Preface to *Fables Ancient and Modern, The*
"Song for St. Cecilia's Day, A"
"Song Sung by Venus in Honor of Britannia"
"To the Memory of Mr. Oldham"

DuBois, W. E. B.
Behold the Land
Crisis, The
"Of the Meaning of Progress" from *The Souls of Black Folk*
"Of the Sorrow Songs" from *The Souls of Black Folk*

Dunbar, Paul Laurence
"Booker T. Washington"*
"Douglass"*
"Keep A-Pluggin' Away"*
"Life's Tragedy"*
"Love's Apotheosis"*
"We Wear the Mask"

Duncan, Sara Jeannette
Saunterings

Eastman, Charles
*From the Deep Woods to Civilization**

Edwards, Jonathan
Personal Narrative
"Sarah Pierrepont"
"Sinners in the Hands of an Angry God"

Eisenhower, Dwight
Atoms for Peace

Eliot, George
"Lifted Veil, The"*

Elizabeth I
"When I was fair and young"

Emerson, Ralph Waldo
"American Scholar, The"
"Brahma"
"Concord Hymn"
"Days"
"Each and All"
"Experience"
"Fable"
Journals
"Maxims"
"Nature"
"Rhodora, The"
"Self-Reliance"
"Snowstorm, The"

Emmett, Daniel
"Dixie"*

Euripides
*Medea**

Fitzgerald, Edward
Rubáiyát of Omar Khayyám, The

Forster, E. M.
"Celestial Omnibus, The"

Franklin, Benjamin
Autobiography of Benjamin Frankin, The, Franklin's Childhood
Autobiography of Benjamin Franklin, The, Seeking Moral Perfection
"Dialogue Between Franklin and the Gout"
"Edict by the King of Prussia, An"
"Ephemera, The"
Letter of November 21, 1783
"Receipt to Make a New England Funeral Elegy, A"
Speech at the Constitutional Convention
"Way to Wealth, The"
"Whistle, The"
"Witch Trial at Mount Holly, A"*

Freeman, Mary E. Wilkins
"New England Nun, A"*

Freneau, Philip
"Indian Burying-Ground, The"
"On the Memorable Victory"
"To a Caty-Did"
"Wild Honeysuckle, The"

Frost, Robert
"Death of the Hired Man, The"*
"It Bids Pretty Fair"
"Oven Bird, The"
"Pasture, The"
"Road Not Taken, The"
"Runaway, The"
"Time to Talk, A"
"Wood-Pile, The"

Fuller, Margaret
"Woman in the Nineteenth Century"

Garrison, William Lloyd
"Liberator, The"
On the Death of John Brown

Gascoigne, George
"Lullaby of a Lover"

Gilbert, W. S.
"Aesthete, The"
"Englishman, The" from *H. M. S. Pinafore*
"Let the Punishment Fit the Crime" from *The Mikado*
"Policeman's Lot, The"
"They'll None of 'Em Be Missed"

Gissing, George
"Scrupulous Father, The"*

Goddard, Pliny Earle
"Creation, The"

Goldsmith, Oliver
She Stoops to Conquer, Act One
She Stoops to Conquer, Act Two
She Stoops to Conquer, Act Three
She Stoops to Conquer, Act Four
She Stoops To Conquer, Act Five

Gray, Thomas
"Bard, The"
"Elegy Written in a Country Churchyard"*
"Ode on a Distant Prospect of Eton College"
"Sonnet on the Death of Richard West"

Gregory, Lady Augusta
"Boy Deeds of Cuchulain"
*Spreading the News**

Greville, Fulke, Lord Brooke
"Chorus Sacerdotum"
"Of His Cynthia"
"You Little Stars"

Haines, Alice Calhoun
"Tenderhearted Dragon, A"

Hale, Edward Everett
"Man Without a Country, The"*

Hale, Lucretia P.
"Mrs. Peterkin's Tea-party"
"Peterkins Celebrate the Fourth of July, The"

Hancock, H. Irving
"Rip Van WInkle Man-O'-War, The"

Hardy, Thomas
"Afterwards"
"Ah, are you digging on my grave?"
"Beeny Cliff"
"Channel Firing"
"Convergence of the Twain, The"
"Darkling Thrush, The"
"Epitaph on a Pessimist"
"Hap"*
"In Tenebris"
"In Time of 'The Breaking of Nations' "*
"Man He Killed, The"
"Neutral Tones"
*Our Exploits at West Poley**
"Three Strangers, The"
"Walk, The"
"When I Set Out for Lyonesse"
"Withered Arm, The"

Harper, Ellen Watkins
Colored People in America, The
On the Twenty-Fourth Anniversary of the American Anti-Slavery Society

Harris, Joel Chandler
"Creature with No Claws, The"
"Wonderful Tar-Baby Story, The"

---

*This selection includes background information, a study guide, and comprehension and critical thinking questions in a lesson on the disc.

larte, Bret
Baby Sylvester"
Brown of Calaveras"
lliad of Sandy Bar, The"
Luck of Roaring Camp, The"
Miggles"
Outcasts of Poker Flat, The"*
Plain Language from Truthful James"
Tennessee's Partner"

lawthorne, Nathaniel
'Birthmark, The"
'Dr. Heidegger's Experiment"
"Drowne's Wooden Image"
"Golden Touch, The"*
"Maypole of Merry Mount, The"
"Minister's Black Veil, The"*
"My Kinsman, Major Molineaux"
Notebooks, The
"Rappacinni's Daughter"
"Young Goodman Brown"*

Hayford, J. E. Casely
"As in a Glass Darkly" from *Ethiopia Unbound*
"Black Man's Burden, The" from *Ethiopia Unbound*
"Gold Coast Native Institutions"
"Saving the Wind" from *Ethiopia Unbound*

Hayne, Paul Hamilton
"Aspects of the Pines"

Hazlitt, William
"Macbeth"
My First Acquaintance with Poets
"On Going a Journey"

Heine, Heinrich
"Loreley, The"*

lenley, William Ernest
'nvictus"

ry, Patrick
ech in the Virginia Convention, rch 23, 1775

t, George
he"

eet"

"*

"Love (III)"
"Man"
"Pulley, The"
"Redemption"
"Virtue"*

Heredia y Heredia, Jose Maria
"Ode to Niagara"

Herrick, Robert
"Argument of His Book, The" from *Hesperides*
"Corinna's Going A-Maying"
"Ode for Ben Jonson, An"
"To the Virgins, to Make Much of Time"
"Upon Julia's Clothes"

Hobbes, Thomas
Leviathan, Part I, Chapters 13–15

Holmes, Oliver Wendell
"Ballad of the Oysterman, The"
"Chambered Nautilus, The"
"Last Leaf, The"
"My Last Walk with the Schoolmistress"
"Old Ironsides"

Hoover, Herbert
Philosophy of Rugged Individualism, The

Hopkins, Gerard Manley
"Carrion Comfort"*
"Felix Randal"
"God's Grandeur"
"Habit of Perfection, The"
"No worst, there is none"*
"Pied Beauty"
"Spring and Fall"
"Thou Art Indeed Just, Lord"
"Windhover, The"

Horace
"Ad Leuconeon"
"Death of Cleopatra, The"
"Golden Mean, The"
"Ship of State, The"

Housman, A. E.
"Loveliest of trees, the cherry now"
"Night is freezing fast, The"
"Oh, when I was in love with you"
"On moonlit heath and lonesome bark"
"To an Athlete Dying Young"
"White in the moon the long road lies"

Howard, Henry, Earl of Surrey
"Alas, So All Things Now Do Hold Their Peace"
"Love, that doth reign and live within in my thought"
"Lover's Vow, A"

Howe, Julia Ward
"Battle Hymn of the Republic, The"*

Howells, William Dean
"Christmas Every Day"*
"Editha"

Hudson, W. H.
Idle Days in Patagonia, The, Chapter XII*

Hughes, Rupert
"Latest News About the Three Wishes, The"

Hunt, James Henry Leigh
"Abou Ben Adhem and the Angel"

Huxley, Thomas Henry
"Method of Scientific Investigation, The"

Irving, Washington
"Early Life in Manhattan" from *A History of New York*
"Legend of Sleepy Hollow, The"*
"Rip Van Winkle"
Tour on the Prairies, A

Jackson, Andrew
Second Inaugural Address

Jacobs, Harriet Ann
Incidents in the Life of a Slave Girl, Chapter I*

Jacobs, Joseph
"Dick Whittington and His Cat"*
"Jack and the Beanstalk"
"Jack the Giant-Killer"

Jacobs, W. W.
*Monkey's Paw, The**

James, Henry
"Four Meetings"
"Middle Years, The"
"Real Thing, The"

James, William
"On a Certain Blindness in Human Beings"

Jefferson, Thomas
Declaration of Independence, The
Jefferson's First Inaugural Address
Virginia Statute of Religious Liberty

Jewett, Sarah Orne
"Courting of Sister Wisby, The"
"Hiltons' Holiday, The"
"Miss Tempy's Watchers"
"Native of Winby, A"*
"White Heron, A"

Johnson, Andrew
Johnson's Proclamation of Amnesty

Johnson, James Weldon
Autobiography of an Ex-Colored Man, The, Chapters 1–2*
Autobiography of an Ex-Colored Man, The, Chapters 3–4*

Johnson, Lyndon
Speech at Johns Hopkins University

Johnson, Pauline
"Corn Husker, The"
"Silhouette"

Johnson, Samuel
Dictionary of the English Language
*Life of Milton, The**
London
"On Choosing Friends" from *the Rambler* No. 160
"On Fiction" from *the Rambler* No. 4
"On Forgiveness" from *the Rambler* No. 185
"On Self-Indulgence" from *the Rambler* No. 155
"On Spring" from *the Rambler* No. 5
"On the Death of Dr. Robert Levet"
"On the Tyranny of Parents" from *the Rambler* No. 148
Preface to Shakespeare, The

Jonson, Ben
"Elegy, An"
"Ode to Himself, An"
"On My First Daughter"
"On My First Son"
"Song: To Celia"
"Still to Be Neat"

"To Cynthia"
"To John Donne"
"To John Donne"
"To the Memory of My Beloved, the Author Mr. William Shakespeare"
"To the Reader"
"Triumph of Charis, The"
Volpone, Act One
Volpone, Act Two
Volpone, Act Three
Volpone, Act Four
Volpone, Act Five

Keats, John
"Bright star, would I were steadfast as thou art"
"Eve of St. Agnes, The"*
Letter to George and Thomas Keats, December 21–27, 1817
Letter to George and Georgiana Keats, February 14–May 3, 1819
"Lines on the Mermaid Tavern"
"Ode on a Grecian Urn"*
"Ode on Melancholy"
"On First Looking into Chapman's Homer"
"This Living Hand"
"To Autumn"
"To Benjamin Bailey"
"When I Have Fears"

Kennedy, John F.
John F. Kennedy's Inaugural Address*
Kennedy's Speech at American University

Kipling, Rudyard
"Ballad of East and West, The"
"Butterfly That Stamped, The"
"Danny Deever"
"Elephant's Child, The"*
"Envoi"
"How the Camel Got His Hump"
"How the First Letter Was Written"*
"Kaa's Hunting"
"King's Ankus, The"
"Man Who Was, The"
"Man Who Would Be King, The"
"Mary Postgate"*
"Miracle of Purun Bhagat, The"
"Miss Youghal's Sais"
"Mowgli's Brothers"
"Red Dog"
"Seal Lullaby"
"Story of Muhammad Din, The"
"Tiger! Tiger!"

Knight, Sarah Kemble
*Journal of Madam Knight, The**

La Fontaine, Jean de
"Acorn and the Pumpkin, The"
"Boy and the Schoolmaster, The"
"Nothing Too Much"

La Salle, Robert de
Relation of the Discoveries and Voyages of Cavelier de La Salle

Lamb, Charles
"Christ's Hospital"
"Dissertation upon Roast Pig, A"*
"Dream Children"
"Old China"
"Old Familiar Faces, The"
"Sanity of True Genius"
"Superannuated Man, The"
"Two Races of Men, The"

Lanier, Sidney
"Marshes of Glynn, The"
"Of King Arthur" from *The Boy's King Arthur*
"Of Sir Galahad and Sir Percival and the Quest of the Holy Grail" from *The Boy's King Arthur**
"Of Sir Gareth of Orkney" from *The Boy's King Arthur*
"Of Sir Tristam" from *The Boy's King Arthur*
"On the Death of Arthur" from *The Boy's King Arthur*
"Song of the Chattahoochee"
"Story of a Proverb, The"

Lanyer, Amelia
"Eve's Apology In Defense of Women" from *Salve Deus Rex Judaeorum*

Lardner, Ring
"Alibi Ike"
"Champion"
"Haircut"
"Love Nest, The"

Laughlin, Gail
Conditions of Wage-Earning Women

Lear, Edward
"Jumblies, The"
"Owl and the Pussy-Cat, The"

Lee, Robert E.
Lee's Farewell to His Army
Letter to His Son
Letter to P. G. T. Beauregard

Letts, Winifred M.
"Pomona in London"

Li Po
"Ancient Airs"
"Drinking Alone By Midnight"
"Thoughts While Studying at Hanlin Academy Sent to My Colleagues at the Chi-hsien Academy"
"Written in Behalf of My Wife"

Lincoln, Abraham
Emancipation Proclamation, The
Farewell Address at Springfield, Illinois
First Inaugural Address
Gettysburg Address
House Divided, A
Letter to Horace Greeley
Letter to Mrs. Bixby
Lincoln's Last Public Address
Lincoln's Plan of Reconstruction
Second Inaugural Address*
War to Preserve the Union, A

Lincoln, Abraham, and Douglas, Stephen A. Lincoln-Douglas
Lincoln–Douglas Debates, The

Locke, John
Second Treatise on Government, The

London, Jack
Cruise of the Dazzler, The
"In a Far Country"*
"Story of an Eye-Witness, The"*
"To Build a Fire"
"War"*
"Where the Trail Forks"

Longfellow, Henry Wadsworth
"Arsenal at Springfield, The"
"Children's Hour, The"
"Cross of Snow, The"
"Day Is Done, The"
"Divina Commedia Sonnets One and Two"
"Evening Star, The"
"Mezzo Cammin"
"Nature"
"Paul Revere's Ride"
"Psalm of Life, A"*
"Rainy Day, The"
"Ropewalk, The"
"Skeleton in Armor, The"*
"Snow-Flakes"
"Song of Hiawatha, The"*
"Sound of the Sea, The"
"Tide Rises, the Tide Falls, The"
"Village Blacksmith, The"*
"Wreck of Hesperus, The"*

Lovelace, Richard
"To Althea, from Prison"
"To Lucasta, Going to the Wars"

Lowell, James Russell
"Auspex"*
"Courtin', The"
"First Snowfall, The"
"Ode Recited at the Harvard Commemoration"
"She Came and Went"
"Stanzas on Freedom"
"To the Dandelion"

Lyly, John
"Apelles' Song"

MacArthur, Douglas
Address to the Corps of Cadets, West Point
Old Soldiers Never Die

Macaulay, Thomas Babington
History of England, "The London Coffee Houses"
History of England, Vol 1, Chapter III, "The Condition of England in 1685"

Macdonald, George
"Little Daylight"

---

*This selection includes background information, a study guide, and comprehension and critical thinking questions in a lesson on the disc.

Custom Literature Database

Major, Charles
"Big Bear, The"

Malory, Sir Thomas
"Arthur Marries Gwynevere"
Morte d'Arthur, Le, Book 21, Chapters 5–7

Marlowe, Christopher
"Passionate Shepherd to His Love, The"*
Tragical History of Doctor Faustus, The, Act One
Tragical History of Doctor Faustus, The, Act Two
Tragical History of Doctor Faustus, The, Act Three
Tragical History of Doctor Faustus, The, Act Four
Tragical History of Doctor Faustus, The, Act Five

Marshall, George C.
Marshal Plan, The

Marvell, Andrew
"Bermudas"
"Dialogue Between the Soul and Body, A"
"Garden, The"
"Picture of Little T. C. in a Prospect of Flowers, The"

Masefield, John
"Cargoes"*
"Sea-Fever"*

Masters, Edgar Lee
"Cooney Potter"
"Dow Kritt"
"Hortense Robbins"
"Mrs. Kessler"
"Samuel Gardner"

Mather, Cotton
*Wonders of the Invisible World, The**

Maupassant, Guy de
"Boule de Suif" (Ball of Fat)
"Devil, The"
"Diamond Necklace, The"
"Horla, The"
"Piece of String, The"*
"Two Friends"*

McCrae, John
"In Flanders Fields"*

McNeil, Everett
"King of the Golden Woods, The"

Melville, Herman
"Art"
"Bartleby the Scrivener"
"Maldive Shark, The"
"Portent, The"
"Shiloh"

Meredith, George
"Lucifer in Starlight"

Mill, John Stuart
Autobiography of John Stuart Mill, The
On Liberty
"Black Hero of the Ranges, The"*

Milton, John
"Il Penseroso"
"L'Allegro"
"Lycidas"
"On Shakespeare"
"On the Late Massacre in Piedmont"
Paradise Lost, Book VI
Paradise Lost, Book IX*
Paradise Lost, Book XII
"When I consider how my light is spent"

Monroe, James
Monroe Doctrine, The

Montagu, Lady Mary Wortley
"Answer to a Love-Letter in Verse, An"
"Lady's Resolve, The"
"On The Death of Mrs. Bowes"

Moore, Milcah Martha
"Female Patriots, The"

Moore, Thomas
"Harp that once through Tara's halls, The"
"Minstrel Boy, The"

More, Hannah
"Slavery, a Poem"

Morris, William
"Apology, An" from *The Earthly Paradise*
"Defence of Guenevere, The"*
"Haystack in the Floods, The"
"Love Is Enough"

Morton, Sarah Wentworth
"African Chief, The"

Nashe, Thomas
"Autumn"
"Litany in Time of Plague, A"

Nesbit, E.
"Beautiful As the Day"
"Jungle, The"
"Plush Usurper, The"*
"Pride of Perks, The" from *The Railway Children**

Newman, John Henry Cardinal
"Lead, Kindly Light"

Nightingale, Florence
Cassandra

Northup, Solomon
"Christmas on the Plantation" from *Twelve Years a Slave*
"Picking Cotton" from *Twelve Years a Slave*

O. Henry (William Sidney Porter)
"After Twenty Years"
"Cop and the Anthem, The"*
"Furnished Room, The"
"Hearts and Hands"*
"Man Higher Up, The"*
"Ransom of Red Chief, The"*
"Retrieved Reformation, A"*
"Unfinished Story, An"

Owen, Wilfred
"Anthem for Doomed Youth"*
"Strange Meeting"

Ozaki, Yei Theodora
"Momotaro, or the Story of the Son of a Peach"
"Story of Urashima Taro, the Fisher Lad, The"*
"Tongue-Cut Sparrow, The"

Paine, Thomas
American Crisis, The
Common Sense

Palou, Francisco
Life of Junípero Serra

Parris, Robert
"Refusal to Pay Taxes, A" from *The Liberator*

Peacock, Thomas Love
"War Song of Dinas Vawr, The"

Pepys, Samuel
Diary, The

Perrault, Charles
"Bluebeard"
"Cinderella"
"Little Red Ridinghood"
"Puss in Boots"

Plato
Apology
Crito
Phaedo

Po Chu-i
"After Passing the Examination"
"Chu Ch'en Village"*
"Escorting Candidates to the Examination Hall"
"Golden Bells"*
"In Early Summer Lodging in a Temple to Enjoy the Moonlight"
"Old Man with the Broken Arm, The"
"On Board Ship: Reading Yu Chen's Poems"
"Prisoner, The"
"Remembering Golden Bells"*
"Watching the Reapers"

Poe, Edgar Allan
"Annabel Lee"
"Bells, The"
"Cask of Amontillado, The"
"Eldorado"
"Fall of the House of Usher, The"*
"Hop-Frog"
"Israfel"
"Ligeia"
"Masque of the Red Death, The"
"Oval Portrait, The"
"Philosophy of Composition, The"
Poetic Principle, The
"Purloined Letter, The"*
"Tell-Tale Heart, The"
"To Helen"*
"Ulalume"
"William Wilson"

Pope, Alexander
"Eloisa to Abelard"
"Epistle to Dr. Arbuthnot"
"Epistle to Miss Blount"
"Essay on Criticism, An"
Essay on Man, An
"Rape of the Lock, The"

Pyle, Howard
"Enchanted Island, The"
"Epilogue" from *The Merry Adventures of Robin Hood*
"Good Gifts and a Fool's Folly"*
"King Richard Cometh to Sherwood Forest" from *The Merry Adventures of Robin Hood*
"King Stork"
"Prologue" from *The Merry Adventures of Robin Hood*
"Robin Hood and Allan a Dale" from *The Merry Adventures of Robin Hood*
"Robin Hood and Guy of Gisbourne" from *The Merry Adventures of Robin Hood*
"Robin Hood Seeketh the Curtal Friar" from *The Merry Adventures of Robin Hood*
"Robin Hood Turns Butcher" from *The Merry Adventures of Robin Hood*
"Shooting-Match at Nottingham Town, The" from *The Merry Adventures of Robin Hood*
"Story of Sir Gawaine, The" from *The Story of King Arthur and His Knights*
"Winning of a Queen, The" from *The Story of King Arthur and His Knights*
"Winning of a Sword, The" from *The Story of King Arthur and His Knights*
"Winning of Kinghood, The" from *The Story of King Arthur and His Knights*

Quintero, Serafin and Joaquin Alvarez
*Sunny Morning, A**

Raleigh, Sir Walter
"Even Such Is Time"
"Nature, that washed her hands in milk"
"Nymph's Reply to the Shepherd, The"
"Sir Walter Raleigh to His Son"
"To Queen Elizabeth"
"What Is Our Life"

Rand, Silas
"Bird Whose Wings Made the Wind, The"
"Glooscap"

Ransome, Arthur
"Baba Yaga"
"Fire-bird, the Horse of Power and the Princess Vasilissa, The"
"Fool of the World and the Flying Ship, The"

Richards, Laura E.
"Chop-Chin and the Golden Dragon"

Riley, James Whitcomb
"When the frost is on the punkin"

Robinson, Edward Arlington
"Luke Havergal"
"Miniver Cheevy"*
"Mr. Flood's Party"

Roosevelt, Franklin Delano
First Inaugural Address
Four Freedoms Speech
Japanese Relocation Order*

Roosevelt, Franklin Delano and Churchill, Winston S.
Atlantic Charter, The

Roosevelt, Theodore
Roosevelt Corollary to the Monroe Doctrine, The

Rossetti, Christina
"Birthday, A"*
"Goblin Market"
"Sleeping at last"
Song ("When I am dead, my dearest")
"Up-Hill"

Rossetti, Dante Gabriel
"Blessed Damozel, The"
"Eden Bower"
"Sestina (after Dante)"
"Silent Noon"
"Woodspurge, The"

Ruskin, John
Modern Painters
Praeterita

Ryan, Abram Joseph
"Conquered Banner, The"

Sa'di
"Old Man, The" from *Tales from the Gulistan*
"Padshah and the Hermit, The" from *Tales from the Gulistan*
"Padshah and the Slave, The" from *Tales from the Gulistan*
"Solitary Dervish, The" from *Tales from the Gulistan*
"Son of a Rich Man and The Dervish Boy, The" from *Tales from the Gulistan*
"Thief and the Pious Man, The" from *Tales from the Gulistan*

Saki (H. H. Munro)
"Esme"
"Laura"
"Mrs. Packletide's Tiger"
"Sredni Vashtar"
"Tobermory"

Sandburg, Carl
"Chicago"*
"Fog"

Sappho
"Bride, A"*
"Forgotten"
"Garlands"
"Hesperus the Bringer"
"Hymn to Aphrodite"*
"Love's Distraction"
"Ode to Anactoria"

Sarmiento, Domingo Faustino
"Portrait of Facundo, A" from *Life in the Argentine Republic in the Days of the Tyrants*

Sassoon, Siegfried
"Glory of Women"
"Rear Guard, The"
"They"

Scott, Sir Walter
"My Native Land"
"Proud Maisie"*
"Soldier, Rest! Thy Warfare O'er"

Service, Robert W.
"Shooting of Dan McGrew, The"

Seward, William H.
Irrepressible Conflict, An

Shakespeare, William
"All the world's a stage" from *As You Like It**
"Blow, blow thou winter wind!" from *As You Like It*
"Fear no more the heat o' the sun" from *Cymbeline*
Hamlet, Prince of Denmark, Act One
Hamlet, Prince of Denmark, Act Two
Hamlet, Prince of Denmark, Act Three
Hamlet, Prince of Denmark, Act Four
Hamlet, Prince of Denmark, Act Five
King Lear, Act One
King Lear, Act Two
King Lear, Act Three
King Lear, Act Four
King Lear, Act Five
Midsummer Night's Dream, A, Act One
Midsummer Night's Dream, A, Act Two
Midsummer Night's Dream, A, Act Three
Midsummer Night's Dream, A, Act Four
Midsummer Night's Dream, A, Act Five
Much Ado About Nothing, Act One
Much Ado About Nothing, Act Two
Much Ado About Nothing, Act Three
Much Ado About Nothing, Act Four

*This selection includes background information, a study guide, and comprehension and critical thinking questions in a lesson on the disc.

g, Act Five

m *Twelfth*

of Venice, Act One

of Venice, Act Two

or of Venice, Act Three

oor of Venice, Act Four

Moor of Venice, Act Five

ore" from *Much Ado Nothing*

1 ("From fairest creatures we re increase")

et 3 ("Look in thy glass, and tell he face thou viewest")

onnet 8 ("Music to hear, why hear'st thou music sadly?")

Sonnet 12 ("When I do count the clock that tells the time")

Sonnet 15 ("When I consider every-thing that grows")

Sonnet 18 ("Shall I compare thee to a summer's day?")

Sonnet 22 ("My glass shall not per-suade me I am old")

Sonnet 23 ("As an unperfect actor on the stage")

Sonnet 27 ("Weary with toil, I haste me to my bed")

Sonnet 29 ("When, in disgrace with fortune and men's eyes")

Sonnet 30 ("When to the sessions of sweet silent thought")*

Sonnet 33 ("Full many a glorious morning have I seen")

Sonnet 46 ("Mine eye and heart are at mortal war")

Sonnet 47 ("Betwixt mine eye and heart a league is took")

Sonnet 49 ("Against that time, if ever that time come")

Sonnet 51 ("Thus can my love excuse the slow offense")

Sonnet 54 ("O, how much more doth beauty beauteous seem")

Sonnet 55 ("Not marble nor the gilded monuments")*

Sonnet 56 ("Sweet love, renew thy force!")

Sonnet 62 ("Sin of self-love posses-seth all mine eye")

Sonnet 64 ("When I have seen by Time's fell hand defaced")

Sonnet 65 ("Since brass, nor stone, nor earth, nor boundless sea")

Sonnet 71 ("No longer mourn for me when I am dead")

Sonnet 73 ("That time of year though mayst in me behold")

Sonnet 76 ("Why is my verse so bar-ren of new pride?")

Sonnet 80 ("O, how faint when I of you do write")

Sonnet 87 ("Farewell! Thou art too dear for my possessing")

Sonnet 92 ("But do thy worst to steal thyself away")

Sonnet 93 ("So shall I live, supposing thou art true")

Sonnet 94 ("They that have power to hurt and will do none")

Sonnet 97 ("How like a winter hath my absence been")

Sonnet 98 ("From you have I been absent in the spring")

Sonnet 104 ("To me, fair friend, you never can be old")

Sonnet 106 ("When in the chronicle of wasted time")

Sonnet 107 ("Not mine own fears nor the prophetic soul")

Sonnet 109 ("O, never say that I was false of heart")

Sonnet 110 ("Alas, 'tis true, I have gone here and there")

Sonnet 113 ("Since I left you, mine eye is in my mind")

Sonnet 115 ("Those lines that I before have writ do lie")

Sonnet 116 ("Let me not to the mar-riage of true minds")

Sonnet 120 ("That you were once unkind befriends me now")

Sonnet 128 ("How oft, when thou, my music, music play'st")

Sonnet 129 ("Th' expense of spirit in a waste of shame")

Sonnet 132 ("Thine eyes I love, and they, as pitying me")

Sonnet 138 ("When my love swears that she is made of truth")

Sonnet 140 ("Be wise as thou art cruel")

Sonnet 144 ("Two loves I have, of comfort and despair")

Sonnet 146 ("Poor soul, the center of my sinful earth")

Sonnet 147 ("My love is as a fever, longing still")

Taming of the Shrew, The, Act One

Taming of the Shrew, The, Act Two

Taming of the Shrew, The, Act Three

Taming of the Shrew, The, Act Four

Taming of the Shrew, The, Act Five

Tempest, The, Act One

Tempest, The, Act Two

Tempest, The, Act Three

Tempest, The, Act Four

Tempest, The, Act Five

"Under the Greenwood Tree" from *As You Like It*

"Who Is Silvia?" from *Two Gentlemen of Verona*

"Winter" from *Love's Labour's Lost*

Shaw, Bernard

Epilogue from *Pygmalion*

Shelley, Mary

Frankenstein

Shelley, Percy Bysshe

"Cloud, The"

Defence of Poetry, A

"Dirge, A"

"England in 1819"

"Hymn of Pan"

"Lines: 'When the lamp is shattered' "

"Song to the Men of England"

"To a Skylark"*

"To Jane: The Invitation"

"To—" ("Music, When Soft Voices Die")

"To Wordsworth"

Sheridan, Richard Brinsley

School for Scandal, The, Act One

School for Scandal, The, Act Two

School for Scandal, The, Act Three

School for Scandal, The, Act Four

School for Scandal, The, Act Five

Sidney, Sir Philip

"My true love hath my heart" from *The Arcadia*

"Oft Have I Mused"

Sonnet 31 ("With how sad steps, Oh Moon, thou climb'st the skies") from *Astrophel and Stella*

Sonnet 39 ("Come sleep! O sleep the certain knot of peace") from *Astrophel and Stella*

Sonnet 41 ("Having this day my horse, my hand, my lance") from *Astrophel and Stella*

"Thou Blind Man's Mark"

Skinner, Alanson, and Slaterlee, John V.

"Manabozho"

Smith, John

Description of New England, A

Generall Historie of Virginia, New England, and the Summer Isles, The

Sophocles

Antigone

Electra

Oedipus at Colonus

Oedipus the King

Southey, Robert

"Cataract of Lodore, The"

"Old Man's Comforts, The"*

" 'You are old, Father William' "*

Spenser, Edmund

"Epithalamion"

Faerie Queene, The, from Canto I

Sonnet 1 ("Happy ye leaves when as those lilly hands") from *Amoretti*

Sonnet 26 ("Sweet is the rose, but grows upon a briar") from *Amoretti*

Sonnet 30 ("My love is like to ice, and I to fire") from *Amoretti*

Sonnet 34 ("Like a ship, that through the ocean wide") from *Amoretti*

Sonnet 54 ("Of this worlds theatre in which we stay") from *Amoretti*

Sonnet 67 ("Lyke as a huntsman after weary chase") from *Amoretti*

Sonnet 75 ("One day I wrote her name upon the strand") from *Amoretti*

Sonnet 79 ("Men call you fayre, and you doe credit it") from *Amoretti*

Stansbury, Joseph

"Ode for the Year 1776"

Custom Literature Database

Wheatley, Phillis
Letter to Rev. Occum
"To His Excellency General Washington"
"To S. M., A Young African Painter on Seeing His Works"
"To the Right Honourable William, Earl of Dartmouth"

Whitman, Walt
"A Child's Amaze"
"As Toilsome I Wander'd Virginia's Woods"
"Beat! Beat! Drums!"*
"Beautiful Women"
"Bivouac on a Mountain Side"
"Cavalry Crossing a Ford"
"Crossing Brooklyn Ferry"*
"For You O Democracy"*
"I saw in Louisiana a live-oak growing"
"Joy, Shipmate, Joy!"
"Noiseless patient spider, A"
"On the Beach at Night"
"On the Beach at Night Alone"
"Passage to India"
"Sight in Camp in the Daybreak Gray and Dim, A"
"Song of Myself," 1,16,17,24
"Song of Myself," 3
"Sparkles from the Wheel"
"We Two Boys Together Clinging"
"When I heard the learn'd astronomer"
"When Lilacs Last in the Dooryard Bloomed"*

Whittier, John Greenleaf
"Barbara Frietchie"*
"Hampton Beach"
"Ichabod"
"Kansas Emigrants, The"
"Telling the Bees"

Wiesel, Elie
Acceptance Speech for the Nobel Peace Prize

Wilde, Oscar
"Ballad of Reading Gaol, The"*
"Birthday of the Infanta, The"
"Canterville Ghost, The"
"De Profundis"
"Few Maxims for the Instruction of the Over-Educated, A"
"Grave of Shelley, The"
"Happy Prince, The"
Importance of Being Earnest, The, Act One*
Importance of Being Earnest, The, Act Two
Importance of Being Earnest, The, Act Three
"Phrases and Philosophies for the Use of the Young"
"Prison Reform" from the *Daily Chronicle*
"Symphony in Yellow"

Wilson, Woodrow
First Inaugural Address
Peace Without Victory

Wordsworth, William
"Composed upon Westminster Bridge"*
"Elegiac Stanzas"
"Expostualtion and Reply"
"I travelled among unknown men"
"I Wandered Lonely as a Cloud"
"It is a beauteous evening, calm and free"*
"Lines Written in Early Spring"
"London, 1802"
"Lucy Gray"
"Michael"
"Nuns fret not at their convent's narrow room"
"Ode: Intimations of Immortality from Recollections of Early Childhood"*
Preface to *Lyrical Ballads*
Prelude, The, Book 1
"Resolution and Independence"
"She Dwelt Among the Untrodden Ways"
"slumber did my spirit seal, A"
"Solitary Reaper, The"
"Strange fits of passion have I known"
"Three Years She Grew"
"To a Skylark"

Wyatt, Sir Thomas
"Divers Doth Use"
"He is not dead that sometime hath a fall"
"My lute awake!"
"They Flee from Me"
"Varium et Mutabile"
"Whoso List to Hunt"

Zimmermann, Arthur
Zimmerman Note, The

---

*This selection includes background information, a study guide, and comprehension and critical thinking questions in a lesson on the disc.

Steele, Sir Richard
"Alexander Selkirk"
"Country Manners" from *The Spectator*
"Spectator Club, The" from *The Spectator*

Stevens, Wallace
"Anecdote of the Jar"*

Stevenson, Robert Louis
"El Dorado"
"Lantern-Bearers, The"*
"Lodging for the Night, A"
"Requiem"
"Sire de Maletroit's Door, The"
"Thrawn Janet"

Stockton, Annis Boudinot
"Exemptore Ode in a Sleepless Night by a Lady Attending on Her Husband in a Long and Painful Illness, An"

Stockton, Frank
"Castle of Bim, The"*
"Floating Prince, The"
"How the Aristocrats Sailed Away"
"Lady, or the Tiger?, The"*

Stowe, Harriet Beecher
"Ghost in the Mill, The"*
"Slave Warehouse, The" from *Uncle Tom's Cabin*

Suckling, Sir John
"Constant Lover, The"
"Out Upon It!"
Song ("Why so pale and wan, fond lover?")

Swift, Jonathan
"Description of a City Shower, A"*
"Satirical Elegy on the Death of a Late Famous General, A"
"Voyage to Brobdingnag, A" of *Gulliver's Travels**
"Voyage to Lilliput, A" from Chapter 1 of *Gulliver's Travels*
"Voyage to Lilliput, A" from Chapter 3 of *Gulliver's Travels*

Swinburne, Algernon Charles
"Garden of Proserpine, The"
"When the Hounds of Spring Are on Winter's Traces" from *Choruses from Atalanta in Calydon*

T'ao Ch'ien
"In the Quiet of the Morning"
"Peach-Blossom Fountain, The"
"Reading the Book of Hills and Seas"
"Returning to the Fields"
"Substance, Shadow, and Spirit"

Taylor, Edward
"Huswifery"
"Upon a Spider Catching a Fly"
"Upon What Base?"

Tecumseh
Sell a Country! Why Not Sell the Air?*

Tennyson, Alfred Lord
"Break, Break, Break"
"Charge of the Light Brigade, The"*
"Eagle, The"
"Flower in the crannied wall"
"In Memoriam" 1, 2, 7, 11, 27, 28, 34, 50, 54, 55, 56, 67, 88, 95, 106,115, 119, 121, 130*
"Kraken, The"
"Lady Clare"*
"Locksley Hall"
"Lotos-Eaters, The"
"Merlin and the Gleam"*
"Morte D'Arthur"
"Now Sleeps the Crimson Petal"
"Song of the Brook, The"
"Splendor Falls, The"
"Tears, Idle Tears"
"Tithonus"

Thayer, Ernest L.
"Casey at the Bat"*

Thomas, Edward
"Adlestrop"
"Cat May Look at a King, A"*
"Cherry Trees, The"
"Look Before You Leap"
"Never Look a Gift Horse in the Mouth"
"Owl, The"
"Rain"
"Tears"

Thompson, Francis
"Hound of Heaven, The"

Thomson, James
"Rule, Britannia!"

Thoreau, Henry David
Civil Disobedience
Walden

Thucydides
Funeral Speech of Pericles
Melian Dialogue, The

Timrod, Henry
"Charleston"
"Ethnogenesis"

Truman, Harry S.
Truman Doctrine, The*

Truth, Sojourner
Ain't I a Woman?

Tu Fu
"Farewell of an Old Man"
"Meandering River, Two Poems"
"Night Thoughts Aboard a Boat"
"Random Pleasures: Nine Quatrains"
"Recruiting Officer of Shih-hao"

Turell, Jane Colman
"Lines On Childbirth"

Twain, Mark
Adventures of Huckleberry Finn, The
"Baker's Bluejay Yarn"
"Californian's Tale, The"
"Cat and the Pain Killer, The" from *The Adventures of Tom Sawyer*
"Cecil Rhodes and the Shark"
"Celebrated Jumping Frog of Calaveras County, The"
"'Cub' Pilot's Experience, A" from *Life on the Mississippi**
"'Cub' Wants to be a Pilot" from *Life on the Mississippi**
"Diary of Adam and Eve, The"
"Dog's Tale, A"
"Great French Duel, The"
"Invalid's Story, The"
"Legend of the Capitoline Venus"
"Man That Corrupted Hadleyburg, The"
"Punch, Brothers, Punch"*
"Story of the Bad Little Boy, The"
"Story of the Good Little Boy, The"
"Story Without an End, A"
"Tom and the Loose Tooth" from *The Adventures of Tom Sawyer**

Tzu, Lao
Tao Te Ching

Vallejo, Mariano Guadalupe
Recuerdos historicos y personales

Vargas, Don Diego de
Letter on the Reconquest of New Mexico

Vaughan, Henry
"Retreat, The"

Vega, Luis Lazo de
History of the Miraculous Apparition of the Virgin of Guadalupe in 1531

Villeneuve, Madame de
"Beauty and the Beast"*

Virgil
Aeneid, The, from Book Two*

Walker, David
"Walker's Appeal"

Walters, Joseph J.
"Guanya Pau, A Story of an African Princess"

Wang Wei
"Enjoying Coolness"
"Red Peonies"
"Seeing Someone Off"
"Suffering from the Heat"
"To Subprefect Chang"

Washington, Booker T.
American Standard, The*
Atlanta Exposition Address
"My Struggle for an Education" from *Up from Salvery**
Up from Slavery

Washington, George
Farewell Address to the People of the United States*
Washington's First Inaugural Address

Wharton, Edith
"Afterward"*
"Angel at the Grave"
"Other Two, The"

*This selection includes background information, a study guide, and comprehension and critical thinking questions in a lesson on the disc.